KEY TO WORLD MAP PAGES

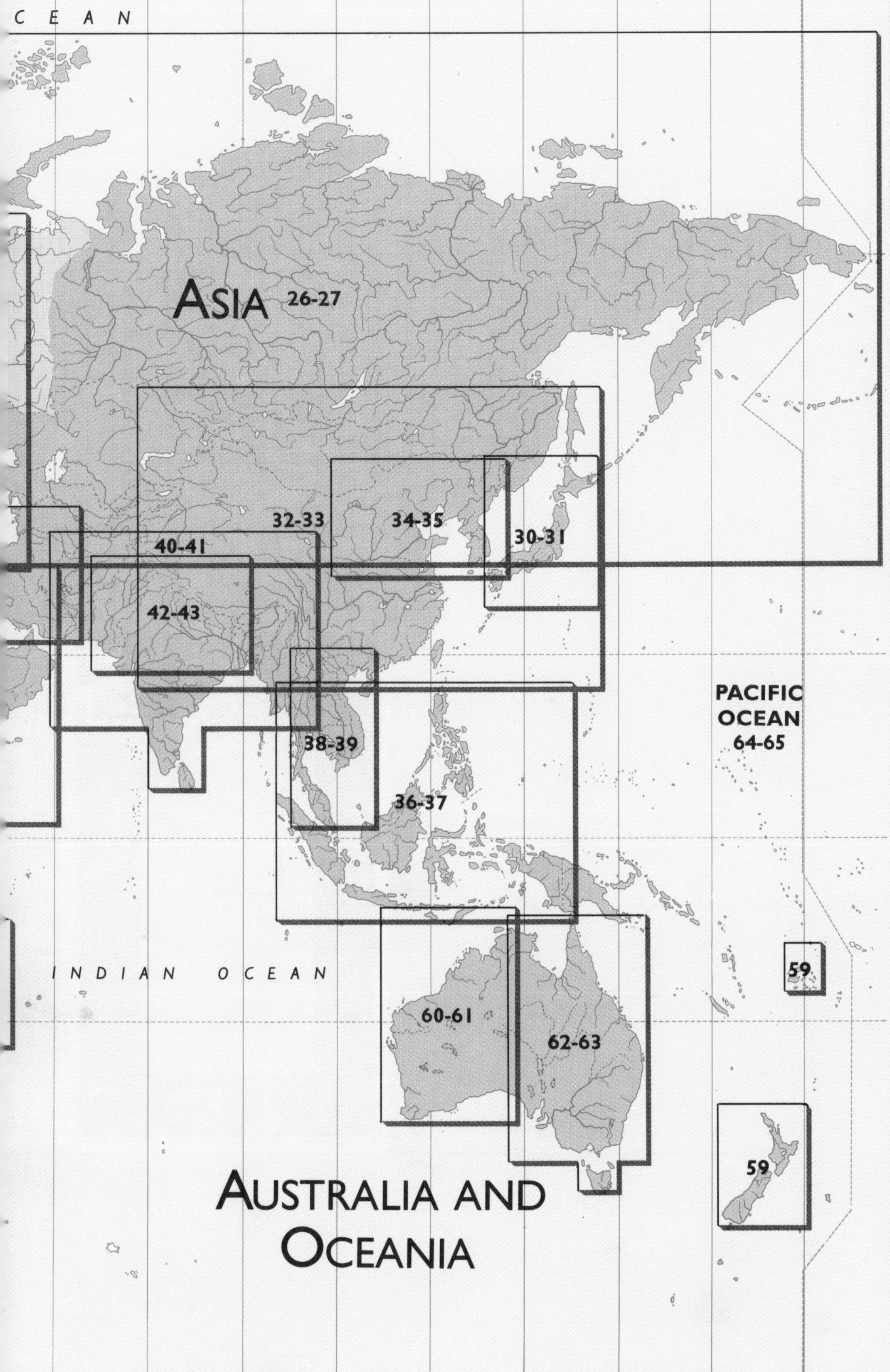

ASIA 26-27

32-33

34-35

30-31

40-41

42-43

38-39

36-37

PACIFIC OCEAN 64-65

INDIAN OCEAN

60-61

62-63

59

59

AUSTRALIA AND OCEANIA

WORLD ATLAS

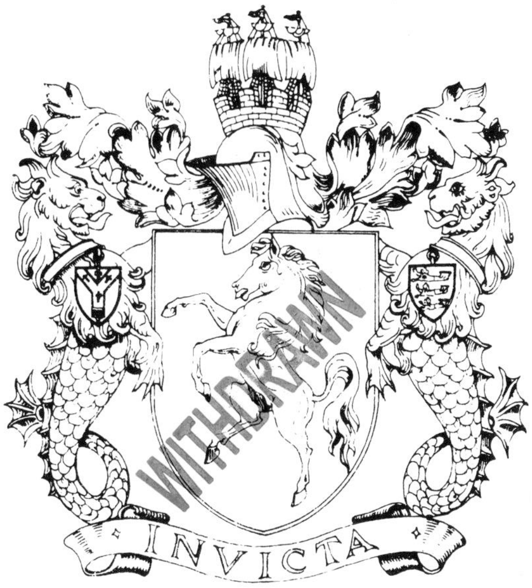

The World in Focus
Cartography by Philip's

Picture Acknowledgements
Page 14
Science Photo Library/NOAA

Illustrations
Stefan Chabluk

CONSULTANTS
Philip's are grateful to the following people for acting as specialist
geography consultants on 'The World in Focus' front section:

Professor D. Brunsden, Kings College, University of London, UK
Dr C. Clarke, Oxford University, UK
Dr I. S. Evans, Durham University, UK
Professor P. Haggett, University of Bristol, UK
Professor K. McLachlan, University of London, UK
Professor M. Monmonier, Syracuse University, New York, USA
Professor M-L. Hsu, University of Minnesota, Minnesota, USA
Professor M. J. Tooley, University of St Andrews, UK
Dr T. Unwin, Royal Holloway, University of London, UK

Published in Great Britain in 1999
by George Philip Limited,
a division of Octopus Publishing Group Limited,
2–4 Heron Quays, London E14 4JP

Cartography by Philip's

ISBN 0–540–07708–9

A CIP catalogue record for this book is available from the British Library.

Printed in China

Details of other Philip's titles and services can be found on our website at: www.philips-maps.co.uk

Philip's is proud to announce that its World Atlases
are now published in association with The Royal
Geographical Society (with The Institute of British
Geographers).

The Society was founded in 1830 and given a
Royal Charter in 1859 for 'the advancement of
geographical science'. It holds historical collections
of national and international importance, many of
which relate to the Society's association with and
support for scientific exploration and research
from the 19th century onwards. It was pivotal

in establishing geography as a teaching and research
discipline in British universities close to the turn of
the century, and has played a key role in geographical
and environmental education ever since.

Today the Society is a leading world centre for
geographical learning – supporting education, teaching,
research and expeditions, and promoting public
understanding of the subject.

The Society welcomes those interested in geography
as members. For further information, please visit the
website at: www.rgs.org

PHILIP'S

WORLD ATLAS

NINTH EDITION

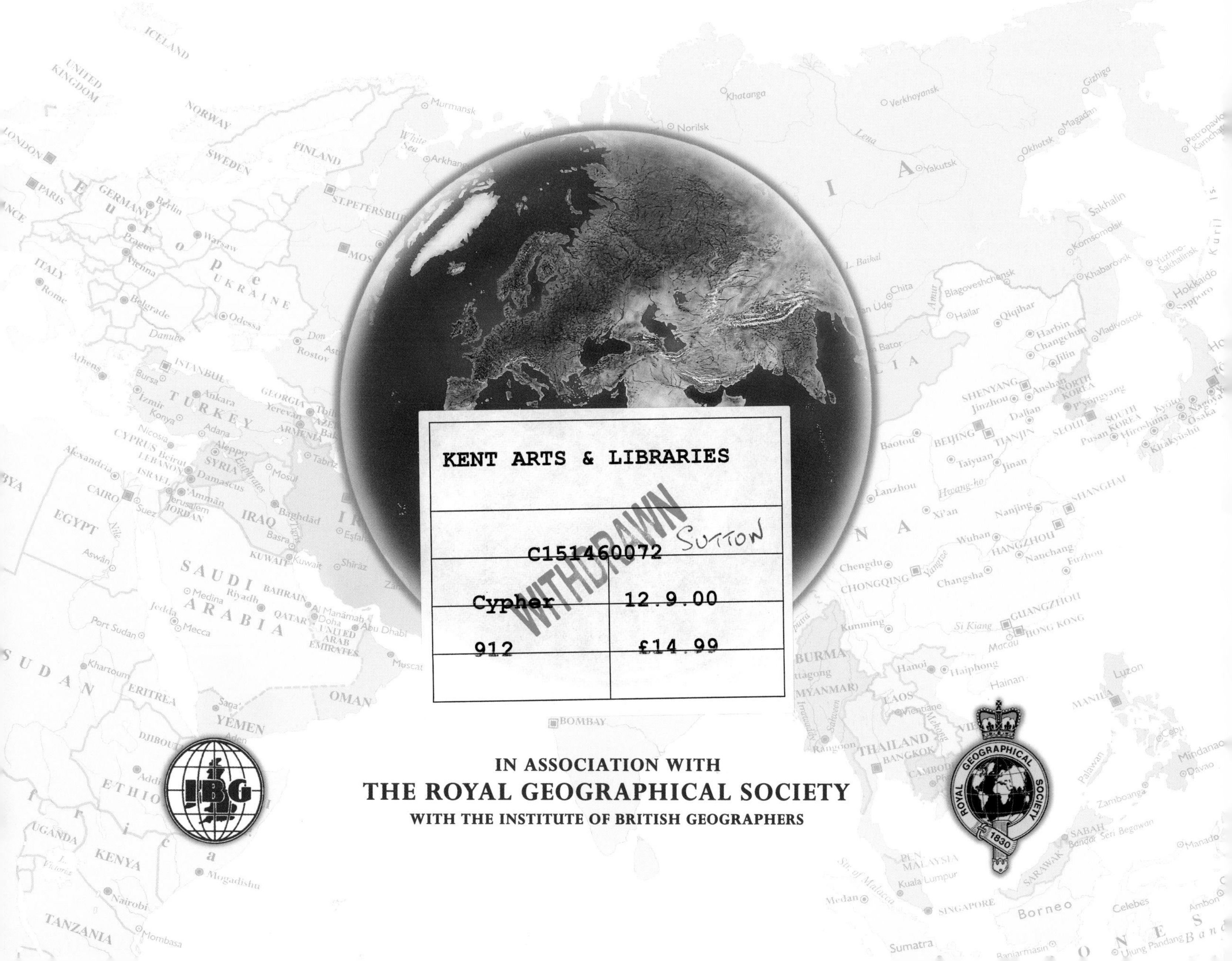

IN ASSOCIATION WITH
THE ROYAL GEOGRAPHICAL SOCIETY
WITH THE INSTITUTE OF BRITISH GEOGRAPHERS

Contents

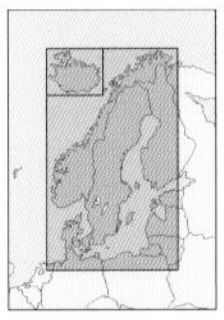

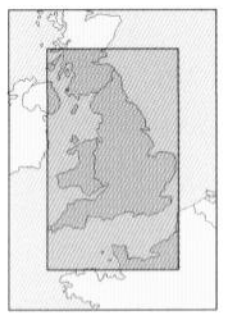

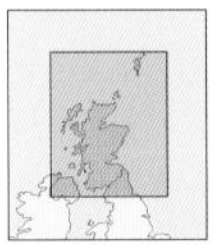

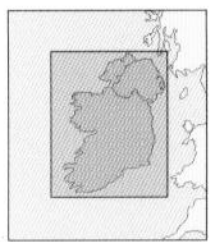

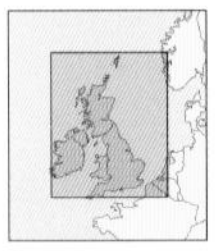

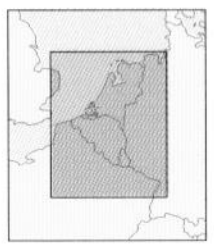

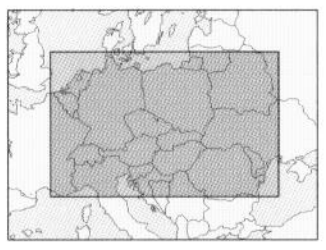

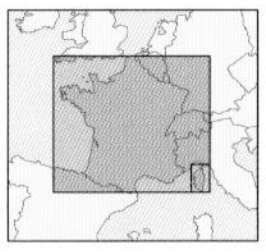

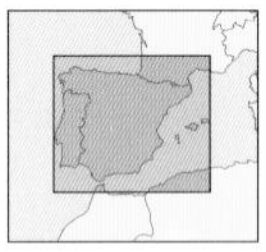

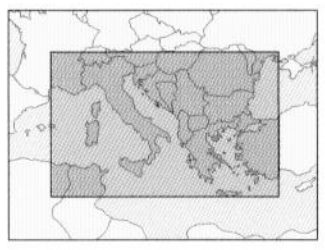

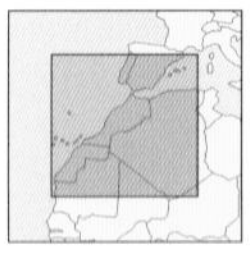

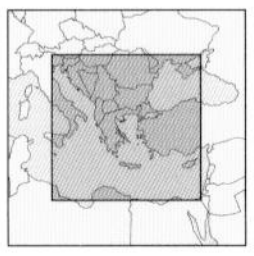

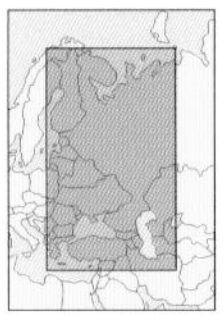

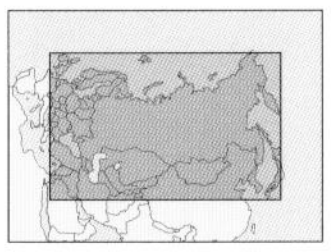

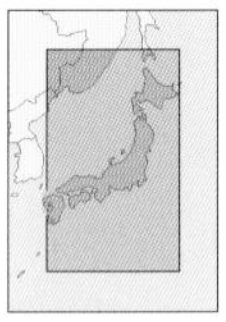

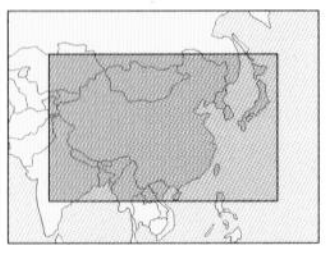

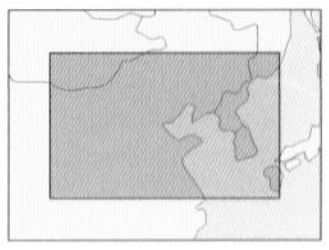

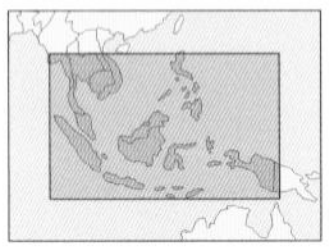

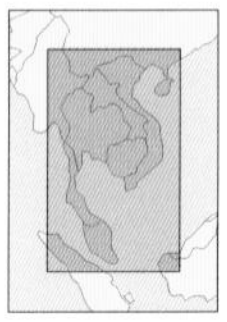

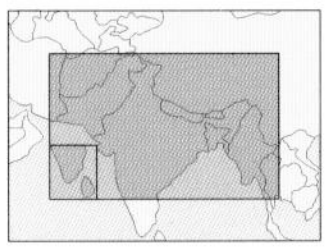

v

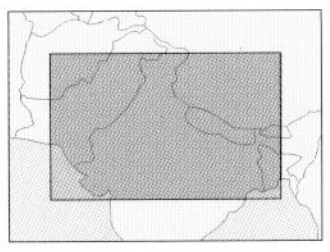

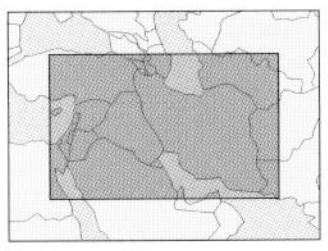

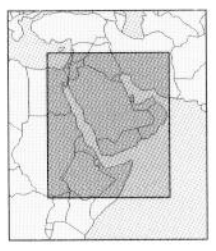

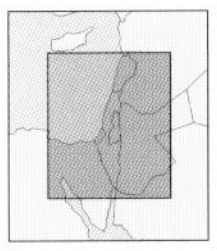

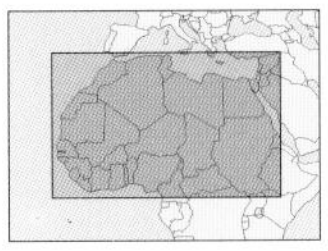

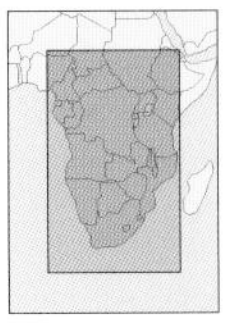

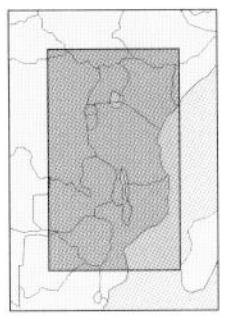

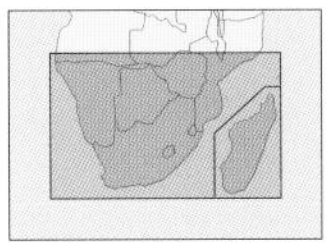

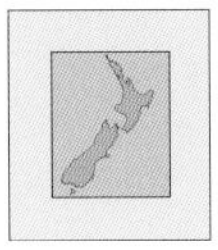

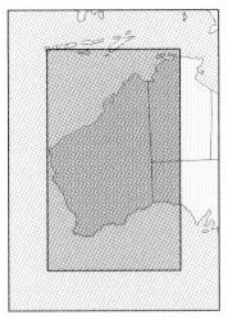

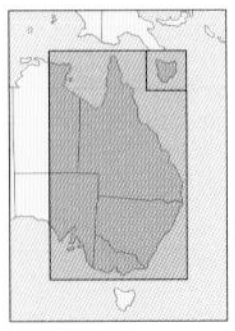

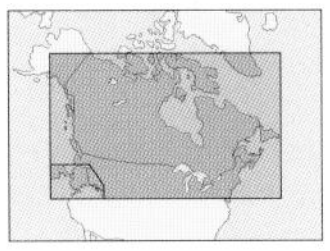

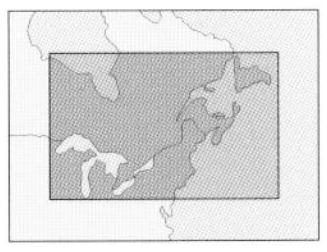

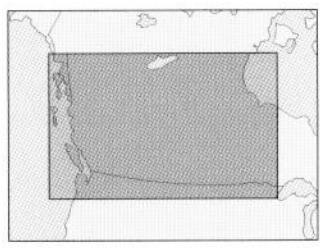

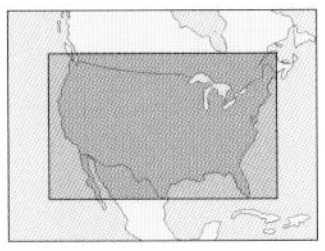

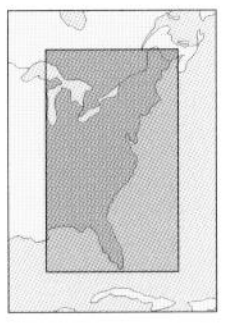

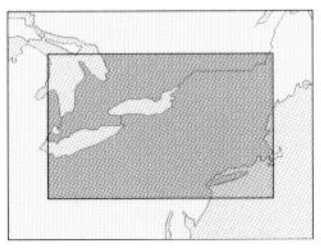

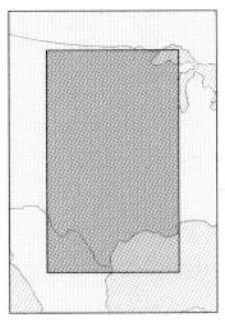

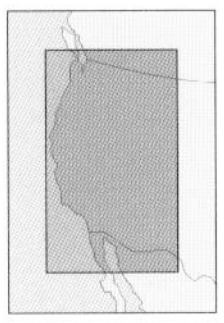

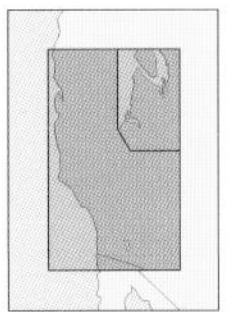

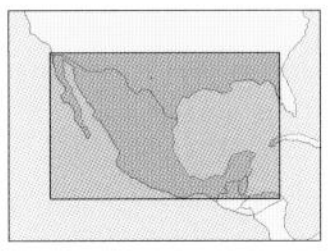

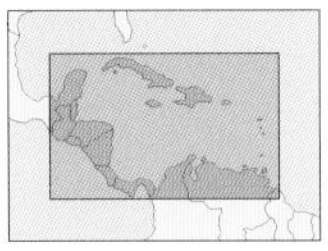

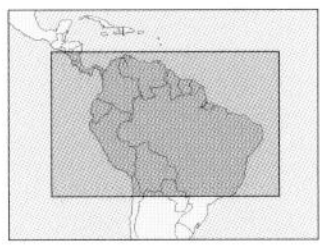

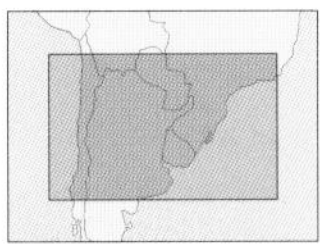

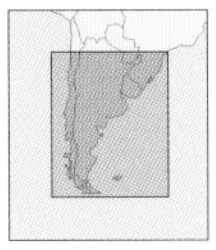

World Statistics: Countries

This alphabetical list includes all the countries and territories of the world. If a territory is not completely independent, then the country it is associated with is named. The area figures give the total area of land, inland water and ice. The population figures are 1998 estimates. The annual income is the Gross National Product per capita in US dollars. The figures are the latest available, usually 1997.

Country/Territory	Area km² Thousands	Area miles² Thousands	Population Thousands	Capital	Annual Income US $
Adélie Land (France)	432	167	0.03	–	–
Afghanistan	652	252	24,792	Kabul	600
Albania	28.8	11.1	3,331	Tirana	750
Algeria	2,382	920	30,481	Algiers	1,490
American Samoa (US)	0.20	0.08	62	Pago Pago	2,600
Andorra	0.45	0.17	75	Andorra La Vella	16,200
Angola	1,247	481	11,200	Luanda	340
Anguilla (UK)	0.1	0.04	11	The Valley	6,800
Antigua & Barbuda	0.44	0.17	64	St John's	7,330
Argentina	2,767	1,068	36,265	Buenos Aires	8,750
Armenia	29.8	11.5	3,422	Yerevan	530
Aruba (Netherlands)	0.19	0.07	69	Oranjestad	15,890
Ascension Is. (UK)	0.09	0.03	1.5	Georgetown	–
Australia	7,687	2,968	18,613	Canberra	20,540
Austria	83.9	32.4	8,134	Vienna	27,980
Azerbaijan	86.6	33.4	7,856	Baku	510
Azores (Portugal)	2.2	0.87	238	Ponta Delgada	–
Bahamas	13.9	5.4	280	Nassau	11,940
Bahrain	0.68	0.26	616	Manama	7,840
Bangladesh	144	56	125,000	Dhaka	270
Barbados	0.43	0.17	259	Bridgetown	6,560
Belarus	207.6	80.1	10,409	Minsk	2,150
Belgium	30.5	11.8	10,175	Brussels	26,420
Belize	23	8.9	230	Belmopan	2,700
Benin	113	43	6,101	Porto-Novo	380
Bermuda (UK)	0.05	0.02	62	Hamilton	31,870
Bhutan	47	18.1	1,908	Thimphu	390
Bolivia	1,099	424	7,826	La Paz/Sucre	950
Bosnia-Herzegovina	51	20	3,366	Sarajevo	300
Botswana	582	225	1,448	Gaborone	4,381
Brazil	8,512	3,286	170,000	Brasília	4,720
British Indian Ocean Terr. (UK)	0.08	0.03	0	–	–
Brunei	5.8	2.2	315	Bandar Seri Begawan	15,800
Bulgaria	111	43	8,240	Sofia	1,140
Burkina Faso	274	106	11,266	Ouagadougou	240
Burma (= Myanmar)	677	261	47,305	Rangoon	1,790
Burundi	27.8	10.7	5,531	Bujumbura	180
Cambodia	181	70	11,340	Phnom Penh	300
Cameroon	475	184	15,029	Yaoundé	650
Canada	9,976	3,852	30,675	Ottawa	19,290
Canary Is. (Spain)	7.3	2.8	1,494	Las Palmas/Santa Cruz	–
Cape Verde Is.	4	1.6	399	Praia	1,010
Cayman Is. (UK)	0.26	0.10	35	George Town	20,000
Central African Republic	623	241	3,376	Bangui	320
Chad	1,284	496	7,360	Ndjaména	240
Chatham Is. (NZ)	0.96	0.37	0.05	Waitangi	–
Chile	757	292	14,788	Santiago	5,020
China	9,597	3,705	1,236,915	Beijing	860
Christmas Is. (Australia)	0.14	0.05	2	The Settlement	–
Cocos (Keeling) Is. (Australia)	0.01	0.005	1	West Island	–
Colombia	1,139	440	38,581	Bogotá	2,280
Comoros	2.2	0.86	545	Moroni	450
Congo	342	132	2,658	Brazzaville	660
Congo (= Zaïre)	2,345	905	49,001	Kinshasa	110
Cook Is. (NZ)	0.24	0.09	20	Avarua	900
Costa Rica	51.1	19.7	3,605	San José	2,640
Croatia	56.5	21.8	4,672	Zagreb	4,610
Cuba	111	43	11,051	Havana	1,300
Cyprus	9.3	3.6	749	Nicosia	13,420
Czech Republic	78.9	30.4	10,286	Prague	5,200
Denmark	43.1	16.6	5,334	Copenhagen	32,500
Djibouti	23.2	9	650	Djibouti	850
Dominica	0.75	0.29	78	Roseau	3,090
Dominican Republic	48.7	18.8	7,999	Santo Domingo	1,670
Ecuador	284	109	12,337	Quito	1,590
Egypt	1,001	387	66,050	Cairo	1,180
El Salvador	21	8.1	5,752	San Salvador	1,810
Equatorial Guinea	28.1	10.8	454	Malabo	530
Eritrea	94	36	3,842	Asmara	570
Estonia	44.7	17.3	1,421	Tallinn	3,330
Ethiopia	1,128	436	58,390	Addis Ababa	110
Falkland Is. (UK)	12.2	4.7	2	Stanley	–
Faroe Is. (Denmark)	1.4	0.54	41	Tórshavn	23,660
Fiji	18.3	7.1	802	Suva	2,470
Finland	338	131	5,149	Helsinki	24,080
France	552	213	58,805	Paris	26,050
French Guiana (France)	90	34.7	162	Cayenne	10,580
French Polynesia (France)	4	1.5	237	Papeete	7,500
Gabon	268	103	1,208	Libreville	4,230
Gambia, The	11.3	4.4	1,292	Banjul	320
Georgia	69.7	26.9	5,109	Tbilisi	840
Germany	357	138	82,079	Berlin/Bonn	28,260
Ghana	239	92	18,497	Accra	370
Gibraltar (UK)	0.007	0.003	29	Gibraltar Town	5,000
Greece	132	51	10,662	Athens	12,010
Greenland (Denmark)	2,176	840	59	Nuuk (Godthåb)	15,500
Grenada	0.34	0.13	96	St George's	2,880
Guadeloupe (France)	1.7	0.66	416	Basse-Terre	9,200
Guam (US)	0.55	0.21	149	Agana	6,000
Guatemala	109	42	12,008	Guatemala City	1,500
Guinea	246	95	7,477	Conakry	570
Guinea-Bissau	36.1	13.9	1,206	Bissau	240
Guyana	215	83	820	Georgetown	690
Haiti	27.8	10.7	6,781	Port-au-Prince	330
Honduras	112	43	5,862	Tegucigalpa	700
Hong Kong (China)	1.1	0.40	6,707	–	22,990
Hungary	93	35.9	10,208	Budapest	4,430
Iceland	103	40	271	Reykjavik	26,580
India	3,288	1,269	984,000	New Delhi	390
Indonesia	1,905	735	212,942	Jakarta	1,110
Iran	1,648	636	64,411	Tehran	4,700
Iraq	438	169	21,722	Baghdad	2,000
Ireland	70.3	27.1	3,619	Dublin	18,280
Israel	27	10.3	5,644	Jerusalem	15,810
Italy	301	116	56,783	Rome	20,120
Ivory Coast (Côte d'Ivoire)	322	125	15,446	Yamoussoukro	690
Jamaica	11	4.2	2,635	Kingston	1,560
Jan Mayen Is. (Norway)	0.38	0.15	1	–	–
Japan	378	146	125,932	Tokyo	37,850
Johnston Is. (US)	0.002	0.0009	1	–	–
Jordan	89.2	34.4	4,435	Amman	1,570
Kazakstan	2,717	1,049	16,847	Astana	1,340
Kenya	580	224	28,337	Nairobi	330
Kerguelen Is. (France)	7.2	2.8	0.7	–	–
Kermadec Is. (NZ)	0.03	0.01	0.1	–	–
Kiribati	0.72	0.28	85	Tarawa	920
Korea, North	121	47	21,234	Pyŏngyang	1,000
Korea, South	99	38.2	46,417	Seoul	10,550
Kuwait	17.8	6.9	1,913	Kuwait City	17,390
Kyrgyzstan	198.5	76.6	4,522	Bishkek	440
Laos	237	91	5,261	Vientiane	400
Latvia	65	25	2,385	Riga	2,430
Lebanon	10.4	4	3,506	Beirut	3,350
Lesotho	30.4	11.7	2,090	Maseru	670
Liberia	111	43	2,772	Monrovia	770
Libya	1,760	679	4,875	Tripoli	6,510
Liechtenstein	0.16	0.06	32	Vaduz	33,000
Lithuania	65.2	25.2	3,600	Vilnius	2,230
Luxembourg	2.6	1	425	Luxembourg	45,360
Macau (China)	0.02	0.006	429	Macau	7,500
Macedonia	25.7	9.9	2,009	Skopje	1,090
Madagascar	587	227	14,463	Antananarivo	250
Madeira (Portugal)	0.81	0.31	253	Funchal	–
Malawi	118	46	9,840	Lilongwe	220
Malaysia	330	127	20,993	Kuala Lumpur	4,680
Maldives	0.30	0.12	290	Malé	1,080
Mali	1,240	479	10,109	Bamako	260
Malta	0.32	0.12	379	Valletta	12,000
Marshall Is.	0.18	0.07	63	Dalap-Uliga-Darrit	1,890
Martinique (France)	1.1	0.42	407	Fort-de-France	10,000
Mauritania	1,030	412	2,511	Nouakchott	450
Mauritius	2.0	0.72	1,168	Port Louis	3,800
Mayotte (France)	0.37	0.14	141	Mamoundzou	1,430
Mexico	1,958	756	98,553	Mexico City	3,680
Micronesia, Fed. States of	0.70	0.27	127	Palikir	2,070
Midway Is. (US)	0.005	0.002	2	–	–
Moldova	33.7	13	4,458	Chişinău	540
Monaco	0.002	0.0001	32	Monaco	25,000
Mongolia	1,567	605	2,579	Ulan Bator	390
Montserrat (UK)	0.10	0.04	12	Plymouth	4,500
Morocco	447	172	29,114	Rabat	1,250
Mozambique	802	309	18,641	Maputo	90
Namibia	825	318	1,622	Windhoek	2,220
Nauru	0.02	0.008	12	Yaren District	10,000
Nepal	141	54	23,698	Katmandu	210
Netherlands	41.5	16	15,731	Amsterdam/The Hague	25,820
Netherlands Antilles (Neths)	0.99	0.38	210	Willemstad	10,400
New Caledonia (France)	18.6	7.2	192	Nouméa	8,000
New Zealand	269	104	3,625	Wellington	16,480
Nicaragua	130	50	4,583	Managua	410
Niger	1,267	489	9,672	Niamey	200
Nigeria	924	357	110,532	Abuja	260
Niue (NZ)	0.26	0.10	2	Alofi	–
Norfolk Is. (Australia)	0.03	0.01	2	Kingston	–
Northern Mariana Is. (US)	0.48	0.18	50	Saipan	11,500
Norway	324	125	4,420	Oslo	36,090
Oman	212	82	2,364	Muscat	4,950
Pakistan	796	307	135,135	Islamabad	490
Palau	0.46	0.18	18	Koror	5,000
Panama	77.1	29.8	2,736	Panama City	3,080
Papua New Guinea	463	179	4,600	Port Moresby	940
Paraguay	407	157	5,291	Asunción	2,010
Peru	1,285	496	26,111	Lima	2,460
Philippines	300	116	77,736	Manila	1,220
Pitcairn Is. (UK)	0.03	0.01	0.05	Adamstown	–
Poland	313	121	38,607	Warsaw	3,590
Portugal	92.4	35.7	9,928	Lisbon	10,450
Puerto Rico (US)	9	3.5	3,860	San Juan	7,800
Qatar	11	4.2	697	Doha	11,600
Queen Maud Land (Norway)	2,800	1,081	0	–	–
Réunion (France)	2.5	0.97	705	Saint-Denis	4,500
Romania	238	92	22,396	Bucharest	1,420
Russia	17,075	6,592	146,861	Moscow	2,740
Rwanda	26.3	10.2	7,956	Kigali	210
St Helena (UK)	0.12	0.05	7	Jamestown	–
St Kitts & Nevis	0.36	0.14	42	Basseterre	5,870
St Lucia	0.62	0.24	150	Castries	3,500
St Pierre & Miquelon (France)	0.24	0.09	7	Saint Pierre	–
St Vincent & Grenadines	0.39	0.15	120	Kingstown	2,370
San Marino	0.06	0.02	25	San Marino	20,000
São Tomé & Príncipe	0.96	0.37	150	São Tomé	330
Saudi Arabia	2,150	830	20,786	Riyadh	6,790
Senegal	197	76	9,723	Dakar	550
Seychelles	0.46	0.18	79	Victoria	6,850
Sierra Leone	71.7	27.7	5,080	Freetown	200
Singapore	0.62	0.24	3,490	Singapore	32,940
Slovak Republic	49	18.9	5,393	Bratislava	3,700
Slovenia	20.3	7.8	1,972	Ljubljana	9,680
Solomon Is.	28.9	11.2	441	Honiara	900
Somalia	638	246	6,842	Mogadishu	500
South Africa	1,220	471	42,835	C. Town/Pretoria/Bloem.	3,400
South Georgia (UK)	3.8	1.4	0.05	–	–
Spain	505	195	39,134	Madrid	14,510
Sri Lanka	65.6	25.3	18,934	Colombo	800
Sudan	2,506	967	33,551	Khartoum	800
Surinam	163	63	427	Paramaribo	1,000
Svalbard (Norway)	62.9	24.3	4	Longyearbyen	–
Swaziland	17.4	6.7	966	Mbabane	1,210
Sweden	450	174	8,887	Stockholm	26,220
Switzerland	41.3	15.9	7,260	Bern	44,220
Syria	185	71	16,673	Damascus	1,150
Taiwan	36	13.9	21,908	Taipei	12,400
Tajikistan	143.1	55.2	6,020	Dushanbe	330
Tanzania	945	365	30,609	Dodoma	210
Thailand	513	198	60,037	Bangkok	2,800
Togo	56.8	21.9	4,906	Lomé	330
Tokelau (NZ)	0.01	0.005	2	Nukunonu	–
Tonga	0.75	0.29	107	Nuku'alofa	1,790
Trinidad & Tobago	5.1	2	1,117	Port of Spain	4,230
Tristan da Cunha (UK)	0.11	0.04	0.33	Edinburgh	–
Tunisia	164	63	9,380	Tunis	2,090
Turkey	779	301	64,568	Ankara	3,130
Turkmenistan	488.1	188.5	4,298	Ashkhabad	630
Turks & Caicos Is. (UK)	0.43	0.17	16	Cockburn Town	5,000
Tuvalu	0.03	0.01	10	Fongafale	600
Uganda	236	91	22,167	Kampala	320
Ukraine	603.7	233.1	50,125	Kiev	1,040
United Arab Emirates	83.6	32.3	2,303	Abu Dhabi	17,360
United Kingdom	243.3	94	58,970	London	20,710
United States of America	9,373	3,619	270,290	Washington, DC	28,740
Uruguay	177	68	3,285	Montevideo	6,020
Uzbekistan	447.4	172.7	23,784	Tashkent	1,010
Vanuatu	12.2	4.7	185	Port-Vila	1,290
Vatican City	0.0004	0.0002	1	–	–
Venezuela	912	352	22,803	Caracas	3,450
Vietnam	332	127	76,236	Hanoi	320
Virgin Is. (UK)	0.15	0.06	13	Road Town	–
Virgin Is. (US)	0.34	0.13	118	Charlotte Amalie	12,000
Wake Is.	0.008	0.003	0.3	–	–
Wallis & Futuna Is. (France)	0.20	0.08	15	Mata-Utu	–
Western Sahara	266	103	280	El Aaiún	300
Western Samoa	2.8	1.1	224	Apia	1,170
Yemen	528	204	16,388	Sana	270
Yugoslavia	102.3	39.5	10,500	Belgrade	2,000
Zambia	753	291	9,461	Lusaka	380
Zimbabwe	391	151	11,044	Harare	750

World Statistics: Physical Dimensions

Each topic list is divided into continents and within a continent the items are listed in order of size. The bottom part of many of the lists is selective in order to give examples from as many different countries as possible. The order of the continents is the same as in the atlas, beginning with Europe and ending with South America. The figures are rounded as appropriate.

World, Continents, Oceans

	km²	miles²	%
The World	509,450,000	196,672,000	–
Land	149,450,000	57,688,000	29.3
Water	360,000,000	138,984,000	70.7
Asia	44,500,000	17,177,000	29.8
Africa	30,302,000	11,697,000	20.3
North America	24,241,000	9,357,000	16.2
South America	17,793,000	6,868,000	11.9
Antarctica	14,100,000	5,443,000	9.4
Europe	9,957,000	3,843,000	6.7
Australia & Oceania	8,557,000	3,303,000	5.7
Pacific Ocean	179,679,000	69,356,000	49.9
Atlantic Ocean	92,373,000	35,657,000	25.7
Indian Ocean	73,917,000	28,532,000	20.5
Arctic Ocean	14,090,000	5,439,000	3.9

Ocean Depths

	m	ft
Atlantic Ocean		
Puerto Rico (Milwaukee) Deep	9,220	30,249
Cayman Trench	7,680	25,197
Gulf of Mexico	5,203	17,070
Mediterranean Sea	5,121	16,801
Black Sea	2,211	7,254
North Sea	660	2,165
Indian Ocean	m	ft
Java Trench	7,450	24,442
Red Sea	2,635	8,454
Pacific Ocean	m	ft
Mariana Trench	11,022	36,161
Tonga Trench	10,882	35,702
Japan Trench	10,554	34,626
Kuril Trench	10,542	34,587
Arctic Ocean	m	ft
Molloy Deep	5,608	18,399

Mountains

		m	ft
Europe			
Elbrus	*Russia*	5,642	18,510
Mont Blanc	*France/Italy*	4,807	15,771
Monte Rosa	*Italy/Switzerland*	4,634	15,203
Dom	*Switzerland*	4,545	14,911
Liskamm	*Switzerland*	4,527	14,852
Weisshorn	*Switzerland*	4,505	14,780
Taschorn	*Switzerland*	4,490	14,730
Matterhorn/Cervino	*Italy/Switzerland*	4,478	14,691
Mont Maudit	*France/Italy*	4,465	14,649
Dent Blanche	*Switzerland*	4,356	14,291
Nadelhorn	*Switzerland*	4,327	14,196
Grandes Jorasses	*France/Italy*	4,208	13,806
Jungfrau	*Switzerland*	4,158	13,642
Grossglockner	*Austria*	3,797	12,457
Mulhacén	*Spain*	3,478	11,411
Zugspitze	*Germany*	2,962	9,718
Olympus	*Greece*	2,917	9,570
Triglav	*Slovenia*	2,863	9,393
Gerlachovka	*Slovak Republic*	2,655	8,711
Galdhöpiggen	*Norway*	2,468	8,100
Kebnekaise	*Sweden*	2,117	6,946
Ben Nevis	*UK*	1,343	4,406
Asia		m	ft
Everest	*China/Nepal*	8,848	29,029
K2 (Godwin Austen)	*China/Kashmir*	8,611	28,251
Kanchenjunga	*India/Nepal*	8,598	28,208
Lhotse	*China/Nepal*	8,516	27,939
Makalu	*China/Nepal*	8,481	27,824
Cho Oyu	*China/Nepal*	8,201	26,906
Dhaulagiri	*Nepal*	8,172	26,811
Manaslu	*Nepal*	8,156	26,758
Nanga Parbat	*Kashmir*	8,126	26,660
Annapurna	*Nepal*	8,078	26,502
Gasherbrum	*China/Kashmir*	8,068	26,469
Broad Peak	*China/Kashmir*	8,051	26,414
Xixabangma	*China*	8,012	26,286
Kangbachen	*India/Nepal*	7,902	25,925
Trivor	*Pakistan*	7,720	25,328
Pik Kommunizma	*Tajikistan*	7,495	24,590
Demavend	*Iran*	5,604	18,386
Ararat	*Turkey*	5,165	16,945
Gunong Kinabalu	*Malaysia (Borneo)*	4,101	13,455
Fuji-San	*Japan*	3,776	12,388
Africa		m	ft
Kilimanjaro	*Tanzania*	5,895	19,340
Mt Kenya	*Kenya*	5,199	17,057
Ruwenzori (Margherita)	*Ug./Congo (Z.)*	5,109	16,762
Ras Dashan	*Ethiopia*	4,620	15,157
Meru	*Tanzania*	4,565	14,977
Karisimbi	*Rwanda/Congo (Zaïre)*	4,507	14,787
Mt Elgon	*Kenya/Uganda*	4,321	14,176
Batu	*Ethiopia*	4,307	14,130
Toubkal	*Morocco*	4,165	13,665
Mt Cameroon	*Cameroon*	4,070	13,353
Oceania		m	ft
Puncak Jaya	*Indonesia*	5,029	16,499
Puncak Trikora	*Indonesia*	4,750	15,584
Puncak Mandala	*Indonesia*	4,702	15,427
Mt Wilhelm	*Papua New Guinea*	4,508	14,790
Mauna Kea	*USA (Hawaii)*	4,205	13,796
Mauna Loa	*USA (Hawaii)*	4,170	13,681
Mt Cook (Aoraki)	*New Zealand*	3,753	12,313
Mt Kosciuszko	*Australia*	2,237	7,339
North America		m	ft
Mt McKinley (Denali)	*USA (Alaska)*	6,194	20,321
Mt Logan	*Canada*	5,959	19,551
Citlaltepetl	*Mexico*	5,700	18,701
Mt St Elias	*USA/Canada*	5,489	18,008
Popocatepetl	*Mexico*	5,452	17,887
Mt Foraker	*USA (Alaska)*	5,304	17,401
Ixtaccihuatl	*Mexico*	5,286	17,342
Lucania	*Canada*	5,227	17,149
Mt Steele	*Canada*	5,073	16,644
Mt Bona	*USA (Alaska)*	5,005	16,420
Mt Whitney	*USA*	4,418	14,495
Tajumulco	*Guatemala*	4,220	13,845
Chirripó Grande	*Costa Rica*	3,837	12,589
Pico Duarte	*Dominican Rep.*	3,175	10,417
South America		m	ft
Aconcagua	*Argentina*	6,960	22,834
Bonete	*Argentina*	6,872	22,546
Ojos del Salado	*Argentina/Chile*	6,863	22,516
Pissis	*Argentina*	6,779	22,241
Mercedario	*Argentina/Chile*	6,770	22,211
Huascaran	*Peru*	6,768	22,204
Llullaillaco	*Argentina/Chile*	6,723	22,057
Nudo de Cachi	*Argentina*	6,720	22,047
Yerupaja	*Peru*	6,632	21,758
Sajama	*Bolivia*	6,542	21,463
Chimborazo	*Ecuador*	6,267	20,561
Pico Colon	*Colombia*	5,800	19,029
Pico Bolivar	*Venezuela*	5,007	16,427
Antarctica		m	ft
Vinson Massif		4,897	16,066
Mt Kirkpatrick		4,528	14,855

Rivers

		km	miles
Europe			
Volga	*Caspian Sea*	3,700	2,300
Danube	*Black Sea*	2,850	1,770
Ural	*Caspian Sea*	2,535	1,575
Dnepr (Dnipro)	*Black Sea*	2,285	1,420
Kama	*Volga*	2,030	1,260
Don	*Black Sea*	1,990	1,240
Petchora	*Arctic Ocean*	1,790	1,110
Oka	*Volga*	1,480	920
Dnister (Dniester)	*Black Sea*	1,400	870
Vyatka	*Kama*	1,370	850
Rhine	*North Sea*	1,320	820
N. Dvina	*Arctic Ocean*	1,290	800
Elbe	*North Sea*	1,145	710
Asia		km	miles
Yangtze	*Pacific Ocean*	6,380	3,960
Yenisey–Angara	*Arctic Ocean*	5,550	3,445
Huang He	*Pacific Ocean*	5,464	3,395
Ob–Irtysh	*Arctic Ocean*	5,410	3,360
Mekong	*Pacific Ocean*	4,500	2,795
Amur	*Pacific Ocean*	4,400	2,730
Lena	*Arctic Ocean*	4,400	2,730
Irtysh	*Ob*	4,250	2,640
Yenisey	*Arctic Ocean*	4,090	2,540
Ob	*Arctic Ocean*	3,680	2,285
Indus	*Indian Ocean*	3,100	1,925
Brahmaputra	*Indian Ocean*	2,900	1,800
Syrdarya	*Aral Sea*	2,860	1,775
Salween	*Indian Ocean*	2,800	1,740
Euphrates	*Indian Ocean*	2,700	1,675
Amudarya	*Aral Sea*	2,540	1,575
Africa		km	miles
Nile	*Mediterranean*	6,670	4,140
Congo	*Atlantic Ocean*	4,670	2,900
Niger	*Atlantic Ocean*	4,180	2,595
Zambezi	*Indian Ocean*	3,540	2,200
Oubangi/Uele	*Congo (Zaïre)*	2,250	1,400
Kasai	*Congo (Zaïre)*	1,950	1,210
Shaballe	*Indian Ocean*	1,930	1,200
Orange	*Atlantic Ocean*	1,860	1,155
Cubango	*Okavango Swamps*	1,800	1,120
Limpopo	*Indian Ocean*	1,600	995
Senegal	*Atlantic Ocean*	1,600	995
Australia		km	miles
Murray–Darling	*Indian Ocean*	3,750	2,330
Darling	*Murray*	3,070	1,905
Murray	*Indian Ocean*	2,575	1,600
Murrumbidgee	*Murray*	1,690	1,050
North America		km	miles
Mississippi–Missouri	*Gulf of Mexico*	6,020	3,740
Mackenzie	*Arctic Ocean*	4,240	2,630
Mississippi	*Gulf of Mexico*	3,780	2,350
Missouri	*Mississippi*	3,780	2,350
Yukon	*Pacific Ocean*	3,185	1,980
Rio Grande	*Gulf of Mexico*	3,030	1,880
Arkansas	*Mississippi*	2,340	1,450
Colorado	*Pacific Ocean*	2,330	1,445
Red	*Mississippi*	2,040	1,270
Columbia	*Pacific Ocean*	1,950	1,210
Saskatchewan	*Lake Winnipeg*	1,940	1,205
South America		km	miles
Amazon	*Atlantic Ocean*	6,450	4,010
Paraná–Plate	*Atlantic Ocean*	4,500	2,800
Purus	*Amazon*	3,350	2,080
Madeira	*Amazon*	3,200	1,990
São Francisco	*Atlantic Ocean*	2,900	1,800
Paraná	*Plate*	2,800	1,740
Tocantins	*Atlantic Ocean*	2,750	1,710
Paraguay	*Paraná*	2,550	1,580
Orinoco	*Atlantic Ocean*	2,500	1,550
Pilcomayo	*Paraná*	2,500	1,550
Araguaia	*Tocantins*	2,250	1,400

Lakes

		km²	miles²
Europe			
Lake Ladoga	*Russia*	17,700	6,800
Lake Onega	*Russia*	9,700	3,700
Saimaa system	*Finland*	8,000	3,100
Vänern	*Sweden*	5,500	2,100
Asia		km²	miles²
Caspian Sea	*Asia*	371,800	143,550
Lake Baykal	*Russia*	30,500	11,780
Aral Sea	*Kazakstan/Uzbekistan*	28,687	11,086
Tonlé Sap	*Cambodia*	20,000	7,700
Lake Balqash	*Kazakstan*	18,500	7,100
Africa		km²	miles²
Lake Victoria	*East Africa*	68,000	26,000
Lake Tanganyika	*Central Africa*	33,000	13,000
Lake Malawi/Nyasa	*East Africa*	29,600	11,430
Lake Chad	*Central Africa*	25,000	9,700
Lake Turkana	*Ethiopia/Kenya*	8,500	3,300
Lake Volta	*Ghana*	8,500	3,300
Australia		km²	miles²
Lake Eyre	*Australia*	8,900	3,400
Lake Torrens	*Australia*	5,800	2,200
Lake Gairdner	*Australia*	4,800	1,900
North America		km²	miles²
Lake Superior	*Canada/USA*	82,350	31,800
Lake Huron	*Canada/USA*	59,600	23,010
Lake Michigan	*USA*	58,000	22,400
Great Bear Lake	*Canada*	31,800	12,280
Great Slave Lake	*Canada*	28,500	11,000
Lake Erie	*Canada/USA*	25,700	9,900
Lake Winnipeg	*Canada*	24,400	9,400
Lake Ontario	*Canada/USA*	19,500	7,500
Lake Nicaragua	*Nicaragua*	8,200	3,200
South America		km²	miles²
Lake Titicaca	*Bolivia/Peru*	8,300	3,200
Lake Poopo	*Peru*	2,800	1,100

Islands

		km²	miles²
Europe			
Great Britain	*UK*	229,880	88,700
Iceland	*Atlantic Ocean*	103,000	39,800
Ireland	*Ireland/UK*	84,400	32,600
Novaya Zemlya (N.)	*Russia*	48,200	18,600
Sicily	*Italy*	25,500	9,800
Corsica	*France*	8,700	3,400
Asia		km²	miles²
Borneo	*Southeast Asia*	744,360	287,400
Sumatra	*Indonesia*	473,600	182,860
Honshu	*Japan*	230,500	88,980
Sulawesi (Celebes)	*Indonesia*	189,000	73,000
Java	*Indonesia*	126,700	48,900
Luzon	*Philippines*	104,700	40,400
Hokkaido	*Japan*	78,400	30,300
Africa		km²	miles²
Madagascar	*Indian Ocean*	587,040	226,660
Socotra	*Indian Ocean*	3,600	1,400
Réunion	*Indian Ocean*	2,500	965
Oceania		km²	miles²
New Guinea	*Indonesia/Papua NG*	821,030	317,000
New Zealand (S.)	*Pacific Ocean*	150,500	58,100
New Zealand (N.)	*Pacific Ocean*	114,700	44,300
Tasmania	*Australia*	67,800	26,200
Hawaii	*Pacific Ocean*	10,450	4,000
North America		km²	miles²
Greenland	*Atlantic Ocean*	2,175,600	839,800
Baffin Is.	*Canada*	508,000	196,100
Victoria Is.	*Canada*	212,200	81,900
Ellesmere Is.	*Canada*	212,000	81,800
Cuba	*Caribbean Sea*	110,860	42,800
Hispaniola	*Dominican Rep./Haiti*	76,200	29,400
Jamaica	*Caribbean Sea*	11,400	4,400
Puerto Rico	*Atlantic Ocean*	8,900	3,400
South America		km²	miles²
Tierra del Fuego	*Argentina/Chile*	47,000	18,100
Falkland Is. (E.)	*Atlantic Ocean*	6,800	2,600

Philip's World Maps

The reference maps which form the main body of this atlas have been prepared in accordance with the highest standards of international cartography to provide an accurate and detailed representation of the Earth. The scales and projections used have been carefully chosen to give balanced coverage of the world, while emphasizing the most densely populated and economically significant regions. A hallmark of Philip's mapping is the use of hill shading and relief colouring to create a graphic impression of landforms: this makes the maps exceptionally easy to read. However, knowledge of the key features employed in the construction and presentation of the maps will enable the reader to derive the fullest benefit from the atlas.

Map sequence

The atlas covers the Earth continent by continent: first Europe; then its land neighbour Asia (mapped north before south, in a clockwise sequence), then Africa, Australia and Oceania, North America and South America. This is the classic arrangement adopted by most cartographers since the 16th century. For each continent, there are maps at a variety of scales. First, physical relief and political maps of the whole continent; then a series of larger-scale maps of the regions within the continent, each followed, where required, by still larger-scale maps of the most important or densely populated areas. The governing principle is that by turning the pages of the atlas, the reader moves steadily from north to south through each continent, with each map overlapping its neighbours. A key map showing this sequence, and the area covered by each map, can be found on the endpapers of the atlas.

Map presentation

With very few exceptions (e.g. for the Arctic and Antarctica), the maps are drawn with north at the top, regardless of whether they are presented upright or sideways on the page. In the borders will be found the map title; a locator diagram showing the area covered and the page numbers for maps of adjacent areas; the scale; the projection used; the degrees of latitude and longitude; and the letters and figures used in the index for locating place names and geographical features. Physical relief maps also have a height reference panel identifying the colours used for each layer of contouring.

Map symbols

Each map contains a vast amount of detail which can only be conveyed clearly and accurately by the use of symbols. Points and circles of varying sizes locate and identify the relative importance of towns and cities; different styles of type are employed for administrative, geographical and regional place names. A variety of pictorial symbols denote features such as glaciers and marshes, as well

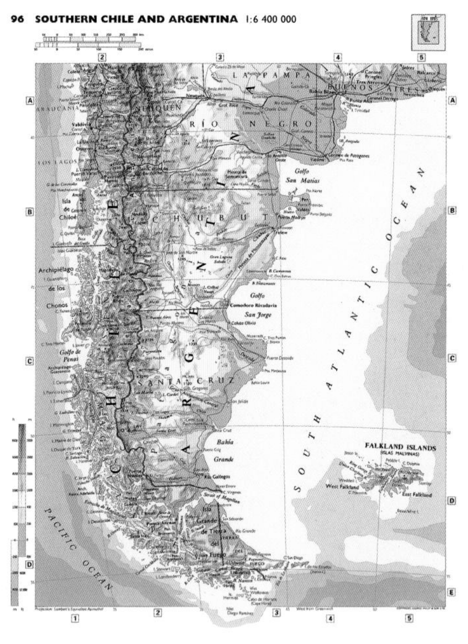

as man-made structures including roads, railways, airports and canals. International borders are shown by red lines. Where neighbouring countries are in dispute, for example in the Middle East, the maps show the *de facto* boundary between nations, regardless of the legal or historical situation. The symbols are explained on the first page of the World Maps section of the atlas.

Map scales

The scale of each map is given in the numerical form known as the 'representative fraction'. The first figure is always one, signifying one unit of distance on the map; the second figure, usually in millions, is the number by which the map unit must be multiplied to give the equivalent distance on the Earth's surface. Calculations can easily be made in centimetres and kilometres, by dividing the Earth units figure by 100 000 (i.e. deleting the last five 0s). Thus 1:1 000 000 means 1 cm = 10 km. The calculation for inches and miles is more laborious, but 1 000 000 divided by 63 360 (the number of inches in a mile) shows that the ratio 1:1 000 000 means approximately 1 inch = 16 miles. The table below provides distance equivalents for scales down to 1:50 000 000.

LARGE SCALE		
1:1 000 000	1 cm = 10 km	1 inch = 16 miles
1:2 500 000	1 cm = 25 km	1 inch = 39.5 miles
1:5 000 000	1 cm = 50 km	1 inch = 79 miles
1:6 000 000	1 cm = 60 km	1 inch = 95 miles
1:8 000 000	1 cm = 80 km	1 inch = 126 miles
1:10 000 000	1 cm = 100 km	1 inch = 158 miles
1:15 000 000	1 cm = 150 km	1 inch = 237 miles
1:20 000 000	1 cm = 200 km	1 inch = 316 miles
1:50 000 000	1 cm = 500 km	1 inch = 790 miles
SMALL SCALE		

Measuring distances

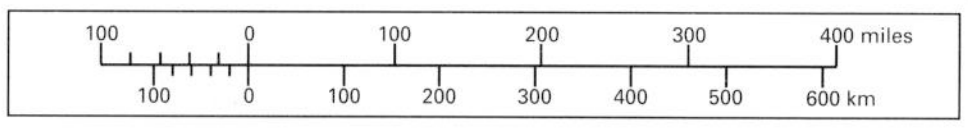

Although each map is accompanied by a scale bar, distances cannot always be measured with confidence because of the distortions involved in portraying the curved surface of the Earth on a flat page. As a general rule, the larger the map scale (i.e. the lower the number of Earth units in the representative fraction), the more accurate and reliable will be the distance measured. On small-scale maps such as those of the world and of entire continents, measurement may only be accurate along the 'standard parallels', or central axes, and should not be attempted without considering the map projection.

Latitude and longitude

Accurate positioning of individual points on the Earth's surface is made possible by reference to the geometrical system of latitude and longitude. Latitude *parallels* are drawn west–east around the Earth and numbered by degrees north and south of the Equator, which is designated 0° of latitude. Longitude *meridians* are drawn north–south and numbered by degrees east and west of the *prime meridian*, 0° of longitude, which passes through Greenwich in England. By referring to these co-ordinates and their subdivisions of minutes ($\frac{1}{60}$th of a degree) and seconds ($\frac{1}{60}$th of a minute), any place on Earth can be located to within a few hundred metres. Latitude and longitude are indicated by blue lines on the maps; they are straight or curved according to the projection employed. Reference to these lines is the easiest way of determining the relative positions of places on different maps, and for plotting compass directions.

Name forms

For ease of reference, both English and local name forms appear in the atlas. Oceans, seas and countries are shown in English throughout the atlas; country names may be abbreviated to their commonly accepted form (e.g. Germany, not The Federal Republic of Germany). Conventional English forms are also used for place names on the smaller-scale maps of the continents. However, local name forms are used on all large-scale and regional maps, with the English form given in brackets only for important cities – the large-scale map of Russia and Central Asia thus shows Moskva (Moscow). For countries which do not use a Roman script, place names have been transcribed according to the systems adopted by the British and US Geographic Names Authorities. For China, the Pin Yin system has been used, with some more widely known forms appearing in brackets, as with Beijing (Peking). Both English and local names appear in the index, the English form being cross-referenced to the local form.

The
WORLD IN
FOCUS

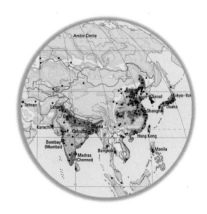

Planet Earth

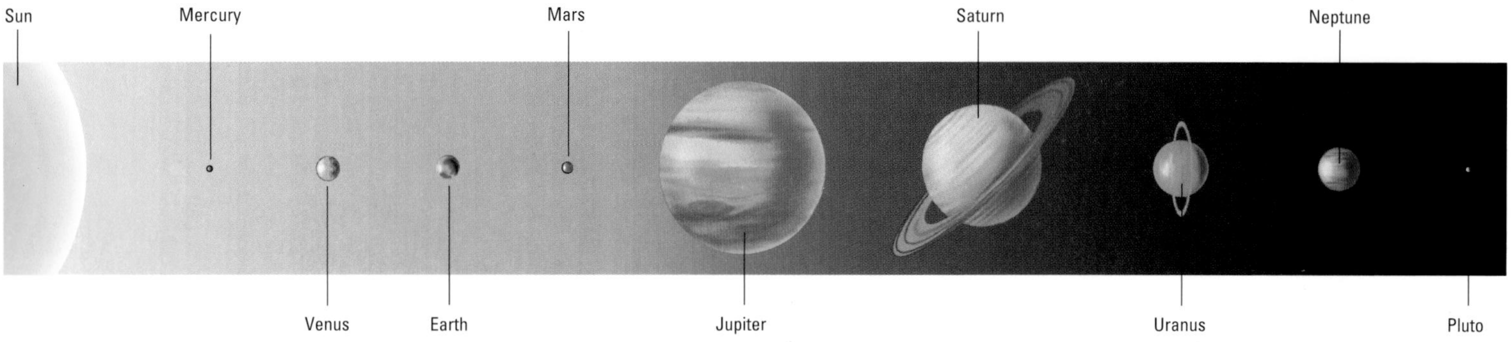

Sun — Mercury — Mars — Saturn — Neptune

Venus — Earth — Jupiter — Uranus — Pluto

The Solar System

A minute part of one of the billions of galaxies (collections of stars) that comprises the Universe, the Solar System lies some 27,000 light-years from the centre of our own galaxy, the 'Milky Way'. Thought to be over 4,700 million years old, it consists of a central sun with nine planets and their moons revolving around it, attracted by its gravitational pull. The planets orbit the Sun in the same direction – anti-clockwise when viewed from the Northern Heavens – and almost in the same plane. Their orbital paths, however, vary enormously.

The Sun's diameter is 109 times that of Earth, and the temperature at its core – caused by continuous thermonuclear fusions of hydrogen into helium – is estimated to be 15 million degrees Celsius. It is the Solar System's only source of light and heat.

Profile of the Planets

	Mean distance from Sun (million km)	Mass (Earth = 1)	Period of orbit (Earth years)	Period of rotation (Earth days)	Equatorial diameter (km)	Number of known satellites
Mercury	57.9	0.055	0.24 years	58.67	4,878	0
Venus	108.2	0.815	0.62 years	243.00	12,104	0
Earth	149.6	1.0	1.00 years	1.00	12,756	1
Mars	227.9	0.107	1.88 years	1.03	6,787	2
Jupiter	778.3	317.8	11.86 years	0.41	142,800	16
Saturn	1,427	95.2	29.46 years	0.43	120,000	20
Uranus	2,871	14.5	84.01 years	0.75	51,118	15
Neptune	4,497	17.1	164.80 years	0.80	49,528	8
Pluto	5,914	0.002	248.50 years	6.39	2,320	1

All planetary orbits are elliptical in form, but only Pluto and Mercury follow paths that deviate noticeably from a circular one. Near perihelion – its closest approach to the Sun – Pluto actually passes inside the orbit of Neptune, an event that last occurred in 1983. Pluto did not regain its station as outermost planet until February 1999.

The Seasons

Seasons occur because the Earth's axis is tilted at a constant angle of 23½°. When the northern hemisphere is tilted to a maximum extent towards the Sun, on 21 June, the Sun is overhead at the Tropic of Cancer (latitude 23½° North). This is midsummer, or the summer solstice, in the northern hemisphere.

On 22 or 23 September, the Sun is overhead at the Equator, and day and night are of equal length throughout the world. This is the autumn equinox in the northern hemisphere. On 21 or 22 December, the Sun is overhead at the Tropic of Capricorn (23½° South), the winter solstice in the northern hemisphere. The overhead Sun then tracks north until, on 21 March, it is overhead at the Equator. This is the spring (vernal) equinox in the northern hemisphere.

In the southern hemisphere, the seasons are the reverse of those in the north.

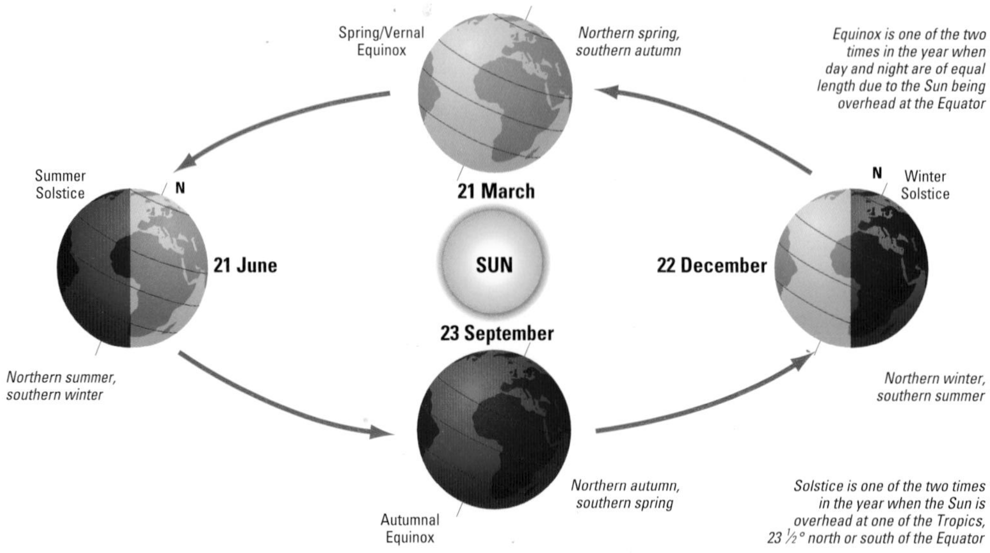

Day and Night

The Sun appears to rise in the east, reach its highest point at noon, and then set in the west, to be followed by night. In reality, it is not the Sun that is moving but the Earth rotating from west to east. The moment when the Sun's upper limb first appears above the horizon is termed sunrise; the moment when the Sun's upper limb disappears below the horizon is sunset.

At the summer solstice in the northern hemisphere (21 June), the Arctic has total daylight and the Antarctic total darkness. The opposite occurs at the winter solstice (21 or 22 December). At the Equator, the length of day and night are almost equal all year.

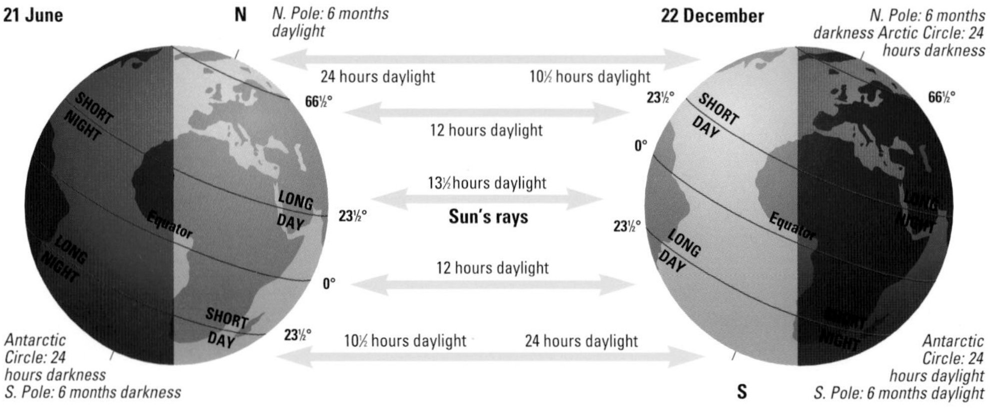

Time

Year: The time taken by the Earth to revolve around the Sun, or 365.24 days.

Leap Year: A calendar year of 366 days, 29 February being the additional day. It offsets the difference between the calendar and the solar year.

Month: The approximate time taken by the Moon to revolve around the Earth. The 12 months of the year in fact vary from 28 (29 in a Leap Year) to 31 days.

Week: An artificial period of 7 days, not based on astronomical time.

Day: The time taken by the Earth to complete one rotation on its axis.

Hour: 24 hours make one day. Usually the day is divided into hours AM (ante meridiem or before noon) and PM (post meridiem or after noon), although most timetables now use the 24-hour system, from midnight to midnight.

Sunrise

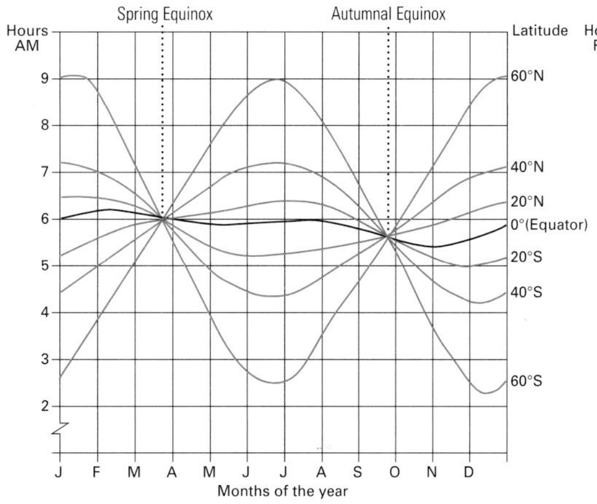

Hours AM — *Latitude* — graph with Spring Equinox and Autumnal Equinox marked; latitudes 60°N, 40°N, 20°N, 0°(Equator), 20°S, 40°S, 60°S; Months of the year (J F M A M J J A S O N D)

Sunset

Hours PM — *Latitude* — graph with Spring Equinox and Autumnal Equinox marked; latitudes 60°S, 40°S, 20°S, 0°(Equator), 20°N, 40°N, 60°N; Months of the year (J F M A M J J A S O N D)

The Moon

The Moon rotates more slowly than the Earth, making one complete turn on its axis in just over 27 days. Since this corresponds to its period of revolution around the Earth, the Moon always presents the same hemisphere or face to us, and we never see 'the dark side'. The interval between one full Moon and the next (and between new Moons) is about 29½ days – a lunar month. The apparent changes in the shape of the Moon are caused by its changing position in relation to the Earth; like the planets, it produces no light of its own and shines only by reflecting the rays of the Sun.

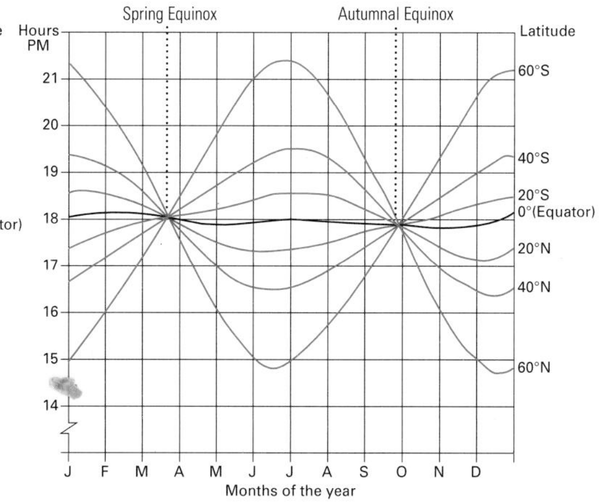

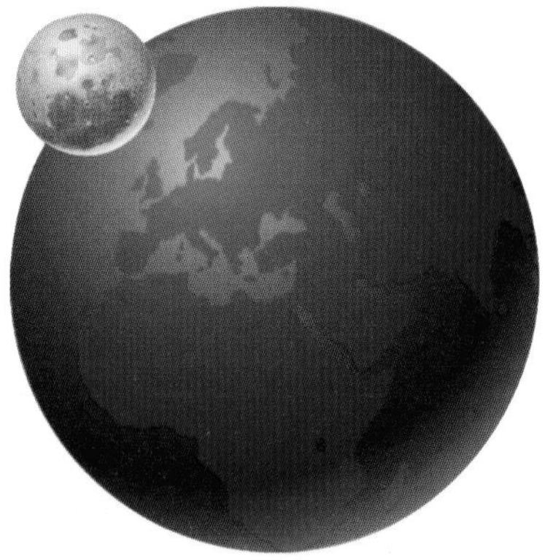

Phases of the Moon

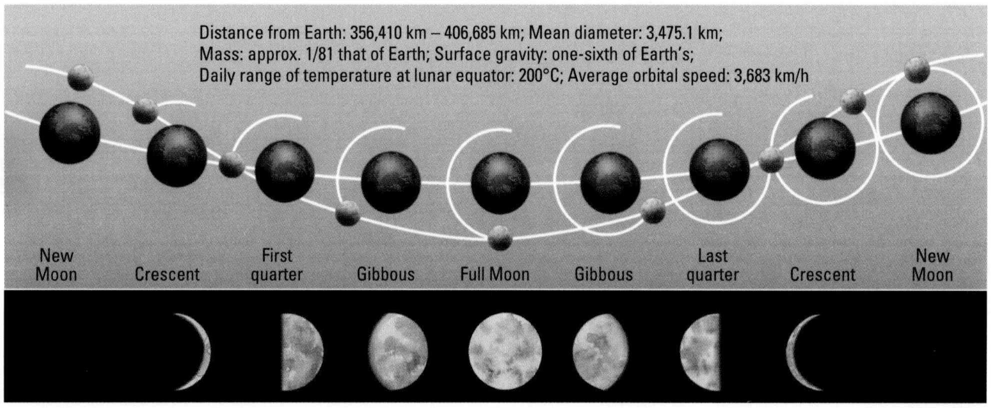

Distance from Earth: 356,410 km – 406,685 km; Mean diameter: 3,475.1 km; Mass: approx. 1/81 that of Earth; Surface gravity: one-sixth of Earth's; Daily range of temperature at lunar equator: 200°C; Average orbital speed: 3,683 km/h

New Moon — Crescent — First quarter — Gibbous — Full Moon — Gibbous — Last quarter — Crescent — New Moon

Eclipses

When the Moon passes between the Sun and the Earth it causes a partial eclipse of the Sun (1) if the Earth passes through the Moon's outer shadow (P), or a total eclipse (2) if the inner cone shadow crosses the Earth's surface. In a lunar eclipse, the Earth's shadow crosses the Moon and, again, provides either a partial or total eclipse.

Eclipses of the Sun and the Moon do not occur every month because of the 5° difference between the plane of the Moon's orbit and the plane in which the Earth moves. In the 1990s only 14 lunar eclipses are possible, for example, seven partial and seven total; each is visible only from certain, and variable, parts of the world. The same period witnesses 13 solar eclipses – six partial (or annular) and seven total.

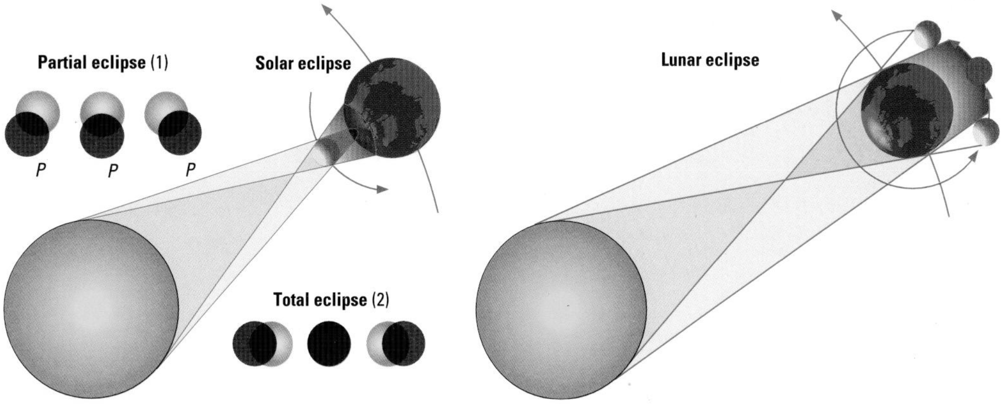

Partial eclipse (1) — P P P — Solar eclipse — Total eclipse (2) — Lunar eclipse

Tides

The daily rise and fall of the ocean's tides are the result of the gravitational pull of the Moon and that of the Sun, though the effect of the latter is only 46.6% as strong as that of the Moon. This effect is greatest on the hemisphere facing the Moon and causes a tidal 'bulge'. When the Sun, Earth and Moon are in line, tide-raising forces are at a maximum and Spring tides occur: high tide reaches the highest values, and low tide falls to low levels. When lunar and solar forces are least coincidental with the Sun and Moon at an angle (near the Moon's first and third quarters), Neap tides occur, which have a small tidal range.

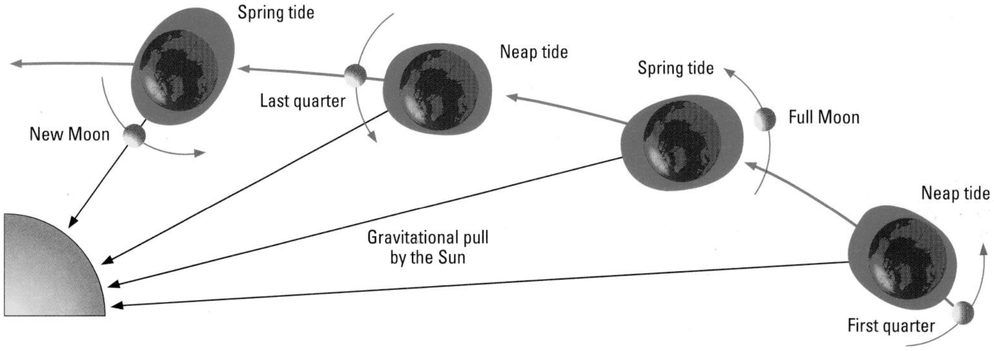

Spring tide — Neap tide — Spring tide — Last quarter — Full Moon — New Moon — Gravitational pull by the Sun — Neap tide — First quarter

Restless Earth

The Earth's Structure

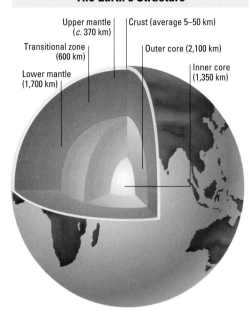

Upper mantle (c. 370 km)
Crust (average 5–50 km)
Transitional zone (600 km)
Outer core (2,100 km)
Lower mantle (1,700 km)
Inner core (1,350 km)

Continental Drift

About 200 million years ago the original Pangaea landmass began to split into two continental groups, which further separated over time to produce the present-day configuration.

180 million years ago

135 million years ago

Present day

— Trench
— Rift
▨ New ocean floor
— Zones of slippage

Notable Earthquakes Since 1900

Year	Location	Richter Scale	Deaths
1906	San Francisco, USA	8.3	503
1906	Valparaiso, Chile	8.6	22,000
1908	Messina, Italy	7.5	83,000
1915	Avezzano, Italy	7.5	30,000
1920	Gansu (Kansu), China	8.6	180,000
1923	Yokohama, Japan	8.3	143,000
1927	Nan Shan, China	8.3	200,000
1932	Gansu (Kansu), China	7.6	70,000
1933	Sanriku, Japan	8.9	2,990
1934	Bihar, India/Nepal	8.4	10,700
1935	Quetta, India (now Pakistan)	7.5	60,000
1939	Chillan, Chile	8.3	28,000
1939	Erzincan, Turkey	7.9	30,000
1960	Agadir, Morocco	5.8	12,000
1962	Khorasan, Iran	7.1	12,230
1968	N.E. Iran	7.4	12,000
1970	N. Peru	7.7	66,794
1972	Managua, Nicaragua	6.2	5,000
1974	N. Pakistan	6.3	5,200
1976	Guatemala	7.5	22,778
1976	Tangshan, China	8.2	255,000
1978	Tabas, Iran	7.7	25,000
1980	El Asnam, Algeria	7.3	20,000
1980	S. Italy	7.2	4,800
1985	Mexico City, Mexico	8.1	4,200
1988	N.W. Armenia	6.8	55,000
1990	N. Iran	7.7	36,000
1993	Maharashtra, India	6.4	30,000
1994	Los Angeles, USA	6.6	51
1995	Kobe, Japan	7.2	5,000
1995	Sakhalin Is., Russia	7.5	2,000
1997	N.E. Iran	7.1	2,500
1998	Takhar, Afghanistan	6.1	4,200
1998	Rostaq, Afghanistan	7.0	5,000

The highest magnitude recorded on the Richter scale is 8.9 in Japan on 2 March 1933 which killed 2,990 people.

Earthquakes

Earthquake magnitude is usually rated according to either the Richter or the Modified Mercalli scale, both devised by seismologists in the 1930s. The Richter scale measures absolute earthquake power with mathematical precision: each step upwards represents a tenfold increase in shockwave amplitude. Theoretically, there is no upper limit, but the largest earthquakes measured have been rated at between 8.8 and 8.9. The 12–point Mercalli scale, based on observed effects, is often more meaningful, ranging from I (earthquakes noticed only by seismographs) to XII (total destruction); intermediate points include V (people awakened at night; unstable objects overturned), VII (collapse of ordinary buildings; chimneys and monuments fall) and IX (conspicuous cracks in ground; serious damage to reservoirs).

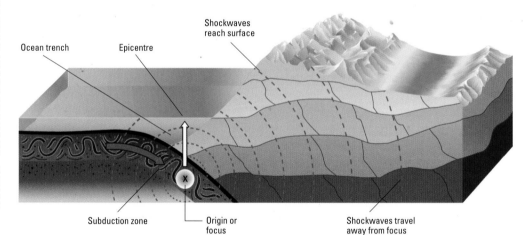

Ocean trench
Epicentre
Shockwaves reach surface
Subduction zone
Origin or focus
Shockwaves travel away from focus

Structure and Earthquakes

▨ Mobile land areas
▨ Submarine zones of mobile land areas
▨ Stable land platforms
▨ Submarine extensions of stable land platforms
▨ Mid-oceanic volcanic ridges
▨ Oceanic platforms

1976⊙ Principal earthquakes and dates

Earthquakes are a series of rapid vibrations originating from the slipping or faulting of parts of the Earth's crust when stresses within build up to breaking point. They usually happen at depths varying from 8 km to 30 km. Severe earthquakes cause extensive damage when they take place in populated areas, destroying structures and severing communications. Most initial loss of life occurs due to secondary causes such as falling masonry, fires and flooding.

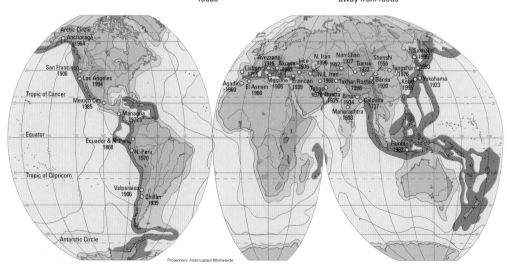

Projection: Interrupted Mollweide

Plate Tectonics

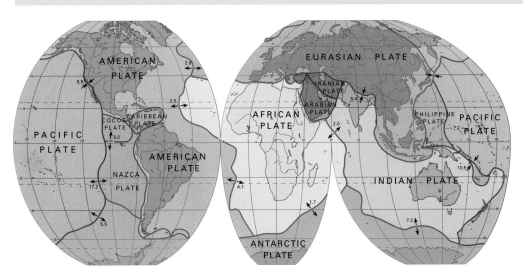

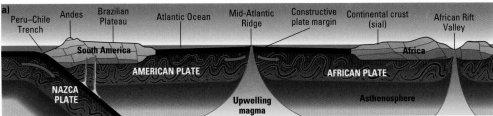

a) Peru–Chile Trench · Andes · Brazilian Plateau · Atlantic Ocean · Mid-Atlantic Ridge · Constructive plate margin · Continental crust (sial) · African Rift Valley · South America · Africa · AMERICAN PLATE · AFRICAN PLATE · NAZCA PLATE · Upwelling magma · Asthenosphere

The drifting of the continents is a feature that is unique to Planet Earth. The complementary, almost jigsaw-puzzle fit of the coastlines on each side of the Atlantic Ocean inspired Alfred Wegener's theory of continental drift in 1915. The theory suggested that the ancient super-continent, which Wegener named Pangaea, incorporated all of the Earth's landmasses and gradually split up to form today's continents.

The original debate about continental drift was a prelude to a more radical idea: plate tectonics. The basic theory is that the Earth's crust is made up of a series of rigid plates which float on a soft layer of the mantle and are moved about by continental convection currents within the Earth's interior. These plates diverge and converge along margins marked by seismic activity. Plates diverge from mid-ocean ridges where molten lava pushes upwards and forces the plates apart at rates of up to 40 mm [1.6 in] a year.

The three diagrams, left, give some examples of plate boundaries from around the world. Diagram (a) shows sea-floor spreading at the Mid-Atlantic Ridge as the American and African plates slowly diverge. The same thing is happening in (b) where sea-floor spreading at the Mid-Indian Ocean Ridge is forcing the Indian plate to collide into the Eurasian plate. In (c) oceanic crust (sima) is being subducted beneath lighter continental crust (sial).

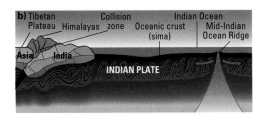

b) Tibetan Plateau · Himalayas · Collision zone · Oceanic crust (sima) · Indian Ocean · Mid-Indian Ocean Ridge · Asia · India · INDIAN PLATE

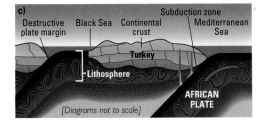

c) Destructive plate margin · Black Sea · Continental crust · Subduction zone · Mediterranean Sea · Turkey · Lithosphere · AFRICAN PLATE · [Diagrams not to scale]

Volcanoes

Volcanoes occur when hot liquefied rock beneath the Earth's crust is pushed up by pressure to the surface as molten lava. Some volcanoes erupt in an explosive way, throwing out rocks and ash, whilst others are effusive and lava flows out of the vent. There are volcanoes which are both, such as Mount Fuji. An accumulation of lava and cinders creates cones of variable size and shape. As a result of many eruptions over centuries, Mount Etna in Sicily has a circumference of more than 120 km [75 miles].

Climatologists believe that volcanic ash, if ejected high into the atmosphere, can influence temperature and weather for several years afterwards. The 1991 eruption of Mount Pinatubo in the Philippines ejected more than 20 million tonnes of dust and ash 32 km [20 miles] into the atmosphere and is believed to have accelerated ozone depletion over a large part of the globe.

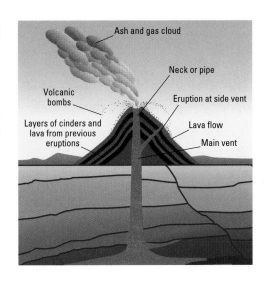

Ash and gas cloud · Neck or pipe · Volcanic bombs · Eruption at side vent · Layers of cinders and lava from previous eruptions · Lava flow · Main vent

Distribution of Volcanoes

Volcanoes today may be the subject of considerable scientific study but they remain both dramatic and unpredictable: in 1991 Mount Pinatubo, 100 km [62 miles] north of the Philippines capital Manila, suddenly burst into life after lying dormant for more than six centuries. Most of the world's active volcanoes occur in a belt around the Pacific Ocean, on the edge of the Pacific plate, called the 'ring of fire'. Indonesia has the greatest concentration with 90 volcanoes, 12 of which are active. The most famous, Krakatoa, erupted in 1883 with such force that the resulting tidal wave killed 36,000 people and tremors were felt as far away as Australia.

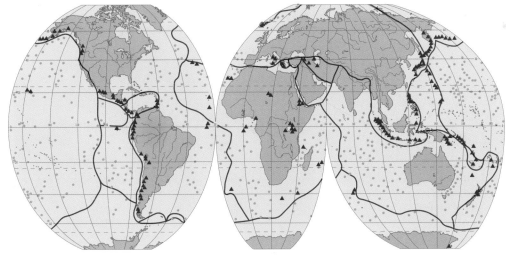

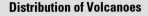

- Submarine volcanoes
▲ Land volcanoes active since 1700
—— Boundaries of tectonic plates

Landforms

The Rock Cycle

James Hutton first proposed the rock cycle in the late 1700s after he observed the slow but steady effects of erosion.

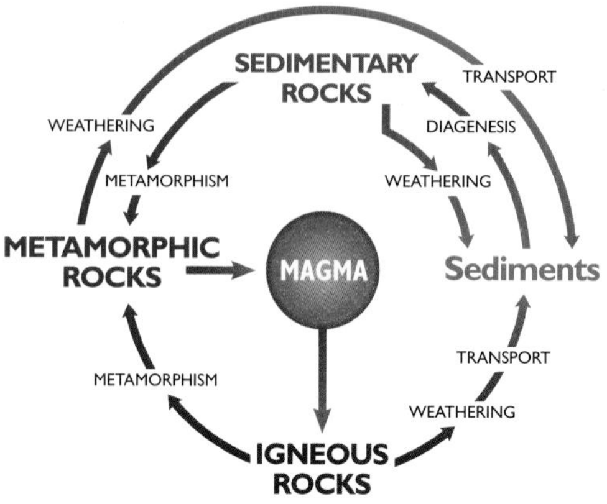

Above and below the surface of the oceans, the features of the Earth's crust are constantly changing. The phenomenal forces generated by convection currents in the molten core of our planet carry the vast segments or 'plates' of the crust across the globe in an endless cycle of creation and destruction. A continent may travel little more than 25 mm [1 in] per year, yet in the vast span of geological time this process throws up giant mountain ranges and creates new land.

Destruction of the landscape, however, begins as soon as it is formed. Wind, water, ice and sea, the main agents of erosion, mount a constant assault that even the most resistant rocks cannot withstand. Mountain peaks may dwindle by as little as a few millimetres each year, but if they are not uplifted by further movements of the crust they will eventually be reduced to rubble and transported away.

Water is the most powerful agent of erosion – it has been estimated that 100 billion tonnes of sediment are washed into the oceans every year. Three Asian rivers account for 20% of this total, the Huang He, in China, and the Brahmaputra and Ganges in Bangladesh.

Rivers and glaciers, like the sea itself, generate much of their effect through abrasion – pounding the land with the debris they carry with them. But as well as destroying they also create new landforms, many of them spectacular: vast deltas like those of the Mississippi and the Nile, or the deep fjords cut by glaciers in British Columbia, Norway and New Zealand.

Geologists once considered that landscapes evolved from 'young', newly uplifted mountainous areas, through a 'mature' hilly stage, to an 'old age' stage when the land was reduced to an almost flat plain, or peneplain. This theory, called the 'cycle of erosion', fell into disuse when it became evident that so many factors, including the effects of plate tectonics and climatic change, constantly interrupt the cycle, which takes no account of the highly complex interactions that shape the surface of our planet.

Mountain Building

Mountains are formed when pressures on the Earth's crust caused by continental drift become so intense that the surface buckles or cracks. This happens where oceanic crust is subducted by continental crust or, more dramatically, where two tectonic plates collide: the Rockies, Andes, Alps, Urals and Himalayas resulted from such impacts. These are all known as fold mountains because they were formed by the compression of the rocks, forcing the surface to bend and fold like a crumpled rug. The Himalayas are formed from the folded former sediments of the Tethys Sea which was trapped in the collision zone between the Indian and Eurasian plates.

The other main mountain-building process occurs when the crust fractures to create faults, allowing rock to be forced upwards in large blocks; or when the pressure of magma within the crust forces the surface to bulge into a dome, or erupts to form a volcano. Large mountain ranges may reveal a combination of those features; the Alps, for example, have been compressed so violently that the folds are fragmented by numerous faults and intrusions of molten igneous rock.

Over millions of years, even the greatest mountain ranges can be reduced by the agents of erosion (most notably rivers) to a low rugged landscape known as a peneplain.

Types of faults: Faults occur where the crust is being stretched or compressed so violently that the rock strata break in a horizontal or vertical movement. They are classified by the direction in which the blocks of rock have moved. A normal fault results when a vertical movement causes the surface to break apart; compression causes a reverse fault. Horizontal movement causes shearing, known as a strike-slip fault. When the rock breaks in two places, the central block may be pushed up in a horst fault, or sink (creating a rift valley) in a graben fault.

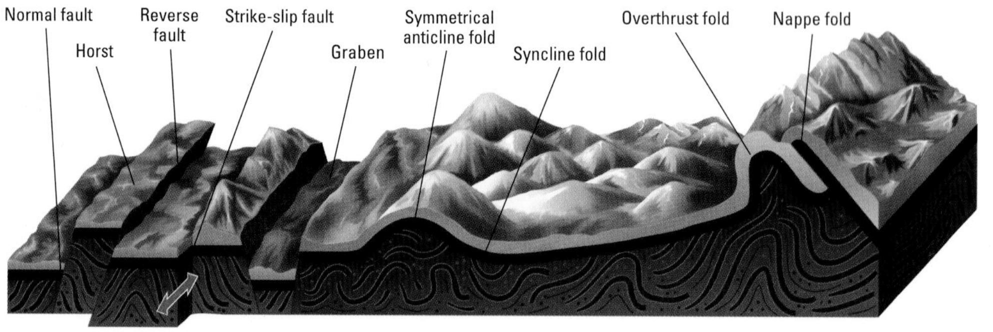

Types of fold: Folds occur when rock strata are squeezed and compressed. They are common therefore at destructive plate margins and where plates have collided, forcing the rocks to buckle into mountain ranges. Geographers give different names to the degrees of fold that result from continuing pressure on the rock. A simple fold may be symmetric, with even slopes on either side, but as the pressure builds up, one slope becomes steeper and the fold becomes asymmetric. Later, the ridge or 'anticline' at the top of the fold may slide over the lower ground or 'syncline' to form a recumbent fold. Eventually, the rock strata may break under the pressure to form an overthrust and finally a nappe fold.

Continental Glaciation

Ice sheets were at their greatest extent about 200,000 years ago. The maximum advance of the last Ice Age was about 18,000 years ago, when ice covered virtually all of Canada and reached as far south as the Bristol Channel in Britain.

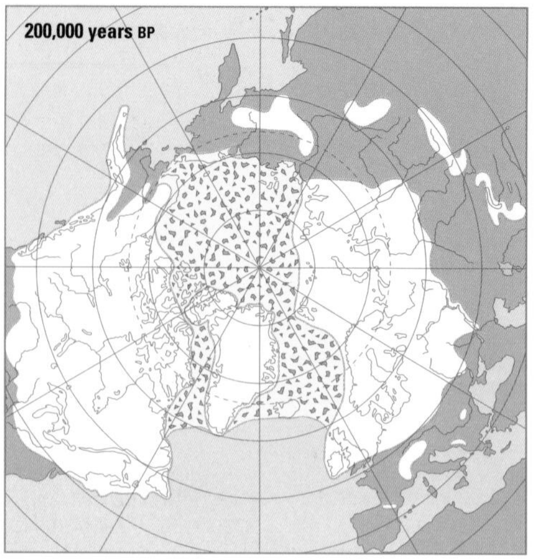

200,000 years BP

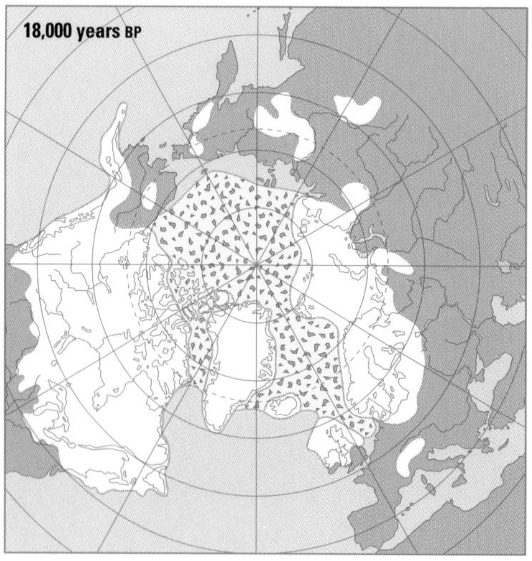

18,000 years BP

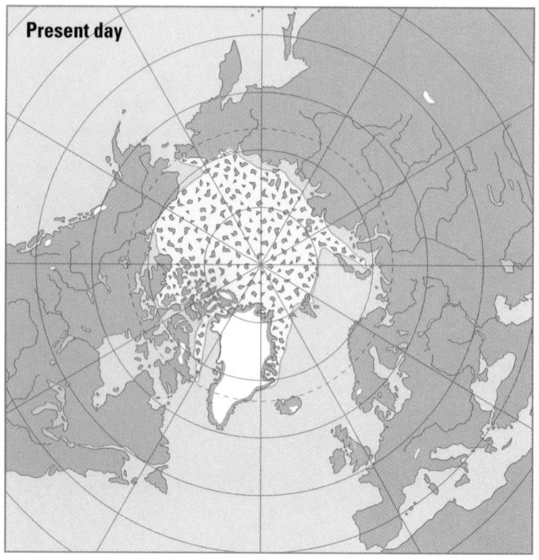

Present day

Natural Landforms

A stylized diagram to show a selection of landforms found in the mid-latitudes.

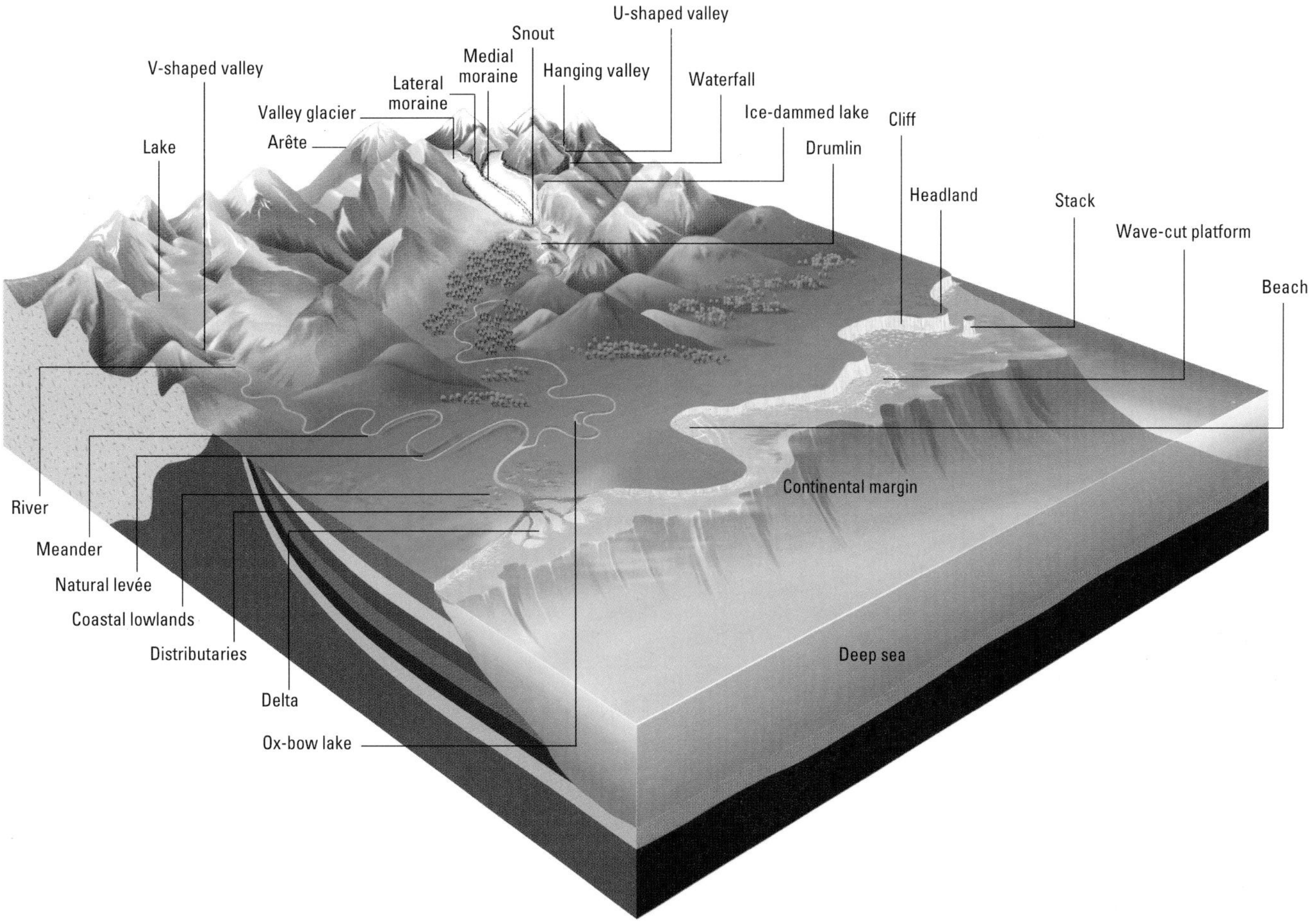

Desert Landscapes

The popular image that deserts are all huge expanses of sand is wrong. Despite harsh conditions, deserts contain some of the most varied and interesting landscapes in the world. They are also one of the most extensive environments – the hot and cold deserts together cover almost 40% of the Earth's surface.

The three types of hot desert are known by their Arabic names: sand desert, called *erg*, covers only about one-fifth of the world's desert; the rest is divided between *hammada* (areas of bare rock) and *reg* (broad plains covered by loose gravel or pebbles).

In areas of *erg*, such as the Namib Desert, the shape of the dunes reflects the character of local winds. Where winds are constant in direction, crescent-shaped *barchan* dunes form. In areas of bare rock, wind-blown sand is a major agent of erosion. The erosion is mainly confined to within 2 m [6.5 ft] of the surface, producing characteristic, mushroom-shaped rocks.

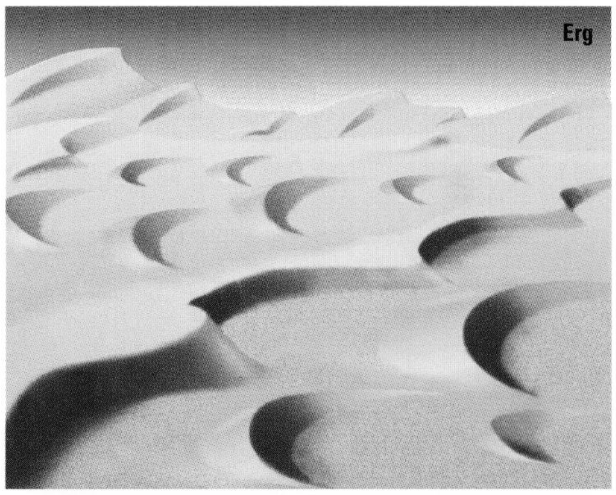
Erg

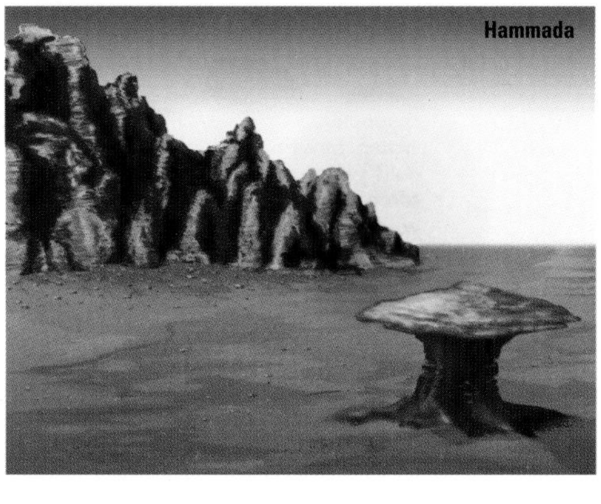
Hammada

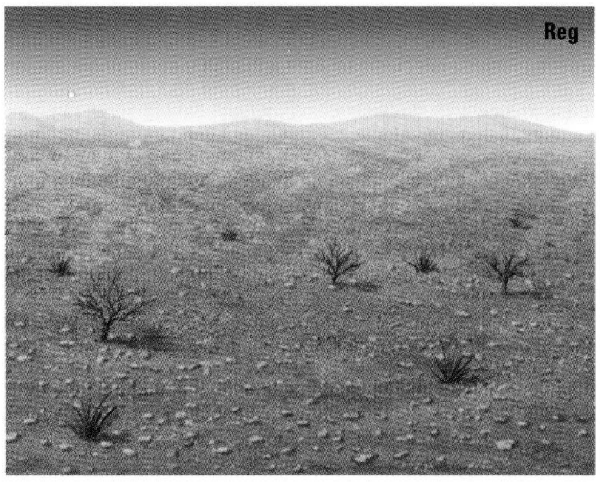
Reg

Surface Processes

Catastrophic changes to natural landforms are periodically caused by such phenomena as avalanches, landslides and volcanic eruptions, but most of the processes that shape the Earth's surface operate extremely slowly in human terms. One estimate, based on a study in the United States, suggested that 1 m [3 ft] of land was removed from the entire surface of the country, on average, every 29,500 years. However, the time-scale varies from 1,300 years to 154,200 years depending on the terrain and climate.

In hot, dry climates, mechanical weathering, a result of rapid temperature changes, causes the outer layers of rock to peel away, while in cold mountainous regions, boulders are prised apart when water freezes in cracks in rocks. Chemical weathering, at its greatest in warm, humid regions, is responsible for hollowing out limestone caves and decomposing granites.

The erosion of soil and rock is greatest on sloping land and the steeper the slope, the greater the tendency for mass wasting – the movement of soil and rock downhill under the influence of gravity. The mechanisms of mass wasting (ranging from very slow to very rapid) vary with the type of material, but the presence of water as a lubricant is usually an important factor.

Running water is the world's leading agent of erosion and transportation. The energy of a river depends on several factors, including its velocity and volume, and its erosive power is at its peak when it is in full flood. Sea waves also exert tremendous erosive power during storms when they hurl pebbles against the shore, undercutting cliffs and hollowing out caves.

Glacier ice forms in mountain hollows and spills out to form valley glaciers, which transport rocks shattered by frost action. As glaciers move, rocks embedded into the ice erode steep-sided, U-shaped valleys. Evidence of glaciation in mountain regions includes cirques, knife-edged ridges, or arêtes, and pyramidal peaks.

Oceans

The Great Oceans

Relative sizes of the world's oceans

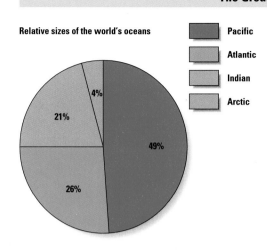

- Pacific
- Atlantic
- Indian
- Arctic

4%
21%
49%
26%

In a strict geographical sense there are only three true oceans – the Atlantic, Indian and Pacific. The legendary 'Seven Seas' would require these to be divided at the Equator and the addition of the Arctic Ocean – which accounts for less than 4% of the total sea area. The International Hydrographic Bureau does not recognize the Antarctic Ocean (even less the 'Southern Ocean') as a separate entity.

The Earth is a watery planet: more than 70% of its surface – over 360,000,000 sq km [140,000,000 sq miles] – is covered by the oceans and seas. The mighty Pacific alone accounts for nearly 36% of the total, and 49% of the sea area. Gravity holds in around 1,400 million cu. km [320 million cu. miles] of water, of which over 97% is saline.

The vast underwater world starts in the shallows of the seaside and plunges to depths of more than 11,000 m [36,000 ft]. The continental shelf, part of the landmass, drops gently to around 200 m [650 ft]; here the seabed falls away suddenly at an angle of 3° to 6° – the continental slope. The third stage, called the continental rise, is more gradual with gradients varying from 1 in 100 to 1 in 700. At an average depth of 5,000 m [16,500 ft] there begins the aptly-named abyssal plain – massive submarine depths where sunlight fails to penetrate and few creatures can survive.

From these plains rise volcanoes which, taken from base to top, rival and even surpass the tallest continental mountains in height. Mount Kea, on Hawaii, reaches a total of 10,203 m [33,400 ft], some 1,355 m [4,500 ft] more than Mount Everest, though scarcely 40% is visible above sea level.

In addition, there are underwater mountain chains up to 1,000 km [600 miles] across, whose peaks sometimes appear above sea level as islands such as Iceland and Tristan da Cunha.

The Ocean Depths

Average and maximum depths of the world's great oceans, in metres

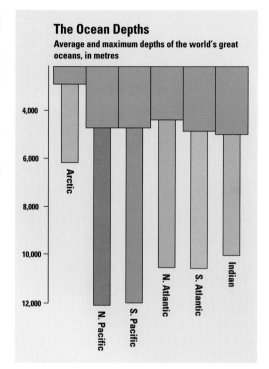

Ocean Currents

January temperatures and ocean currents

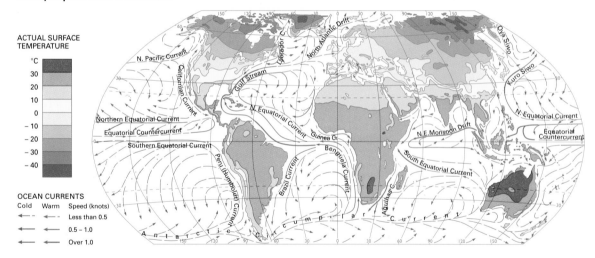

ACTUAL SURFACE TEMPERATURE

°C
30
20
10
0
- 10
- 20
- 30
- 40

OCEAN CURRENTS
Cold   Warm   Speed (knots)
←- -   ←-   Less than 0.5
←—   ←—   0.5 – 1.0
←——   ←——   Over 1.0

July temperatures and ocean currents

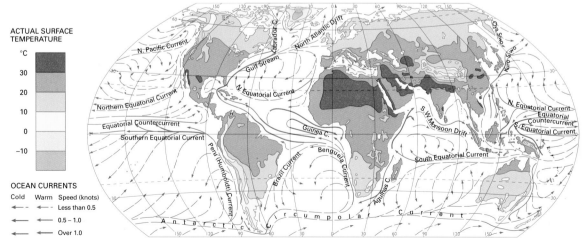

ACTUAL SURFACE TEMPERATURE

°C
30
20
10
0
–10

OCEAN CURRENTS
Cold   Warm   Speed (knots)
←- -   ←-   Less than 0.5
←—   ←—   0.5 – 1.0
←——   ←——   Over 1.0

Moving immense quantities of energy as well as billions of tonnes of water every hour, the ocean currents are a vital part of the great heat engine that drives the Earth's climate. They themselves are produced by a twofold mechanism. At the surface, winds push huge masses of water before them; in the deep ocean, below an abrupt temperature gradient that separates the churning surface waters from the still depths, density variations cause slow vertical movements.

The pattern of circulation of the great surface currents is determined by the displacement known as the Coriolis effect. As the Earth turns beneath a moving object – whether it is a tennis ball or a vast mass of water – it appears to be deflected to one side. The deflection is most obvious near the Equator, where the Earth's surface is spinning eastwards at 1,700 km/h [1,050 mph]; currents moving polewards are curved clockwise in the northern hemisphere and anti-clockwise in the southern.

The result is a system of spinning circles known as gyres. The Coriolis effect piles up water on the left of each gyre, creating a narrow, fast-moving stream that is matched by a slower, broader returning current on the right. North and south of the Equator, the fastest currents are located in the west and in the east respectively. In each case, warm water moves from the Equator and cold water returns to it. Cold currents often bring an upwelling of nutrients with them, supporting the world's most economically important fisheries.

Depending on the prevailing winds, some currents on or near the Equator may reverse their direction in the course of the year – a seasonal variation on which Asian monsoon rains depend, and whose occasional failure can bring disaster to millions.

World Fishing Areas

Main commercial fishing areas (numbered FAO regions)

Catch by top marine fishing areas, thousand tonnes (1992)

1. Pacific, NW	[61]	24,199	29.3%
2. Pacific, SE	[87]	13,899	16.8%
3. Atlantic, NE	[27]	11,073	13.4%
4. Pacific, WC	[71]	7,710	9.3%
5. Indian, W	[51]	3,747	4.5%
6. Indian, E	[57]	3,262	4.0%
7. Atlantic, EC	[34]	3,259	3.9%
8. Pacific, NE	[67]	3,149	3.8%

 Principal fishing areas

Leading fishing nations

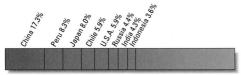

China 17.3% Peru 8.3% Japan 8.0% Chile 5.9% U.S.A. 5.9% Russia 4.4% India 4.3% Indonesia 3.6%

World total (1993): 101,417,500 tonnes
(Marine catch 83.1% Inland catch 16.9%)

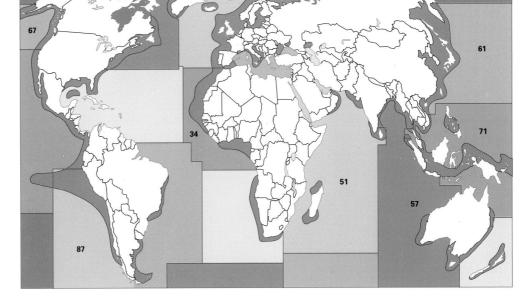

Marine Pollution

Sources of marine oil pollution (latest available year)

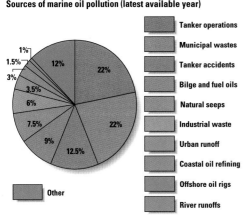

1%, 1.5%, 3%, 3.5%, 6%, 7.5%, 9%, 12.5%, 22%, 22%, 12%

- Tanker operations
- Municipal wastes
- Tanker accidents
- Bilge and fuel oils
- Natural seeps
- Industrial waste
- Urban runoff
- Coastal oil refining
- Offshore oil rigs
- River runoffs

 Other

Oil Spills

Major oil spills from tankers and combined carriers

Year	Vessel	Location	Spill (barrels)**	Cause
1979	Atlantic Empress	West Indies	1,890,000	collision
1983	Castillo De Bellver	South Africa	1,760,000	fire
1978	Amoco Cadiz	France	1,628,000	grounding
1991	Haven	Italy	1,029,000	explosion
1988	Odyssey	Canada	1,000,000	fire
1967	Torrey Canyon	UK	909,000	grounding
1972	Sea Star	Gulf of Oman	902,250	collision
1977	Hawaiian Patriot	Hawaiian Is.	742,500	fire
1979	Independenta	Turkey	696,350	collision
1993	Braer	UK	625,000	grounding
1996	Sea Empress	UK	515,000	grounding

Other sources of major oil spills

1983	Nowruz oilfield	The Gulf	4,250,000†	war
1979	Ixtoc 1 oilwell	Gulf of Mexico	4,200,000	blow-out
1991	Kuwait	The Gulf	2,500,000†	war

** 1 barrel = 0.136 tonnes/159 lit./35 Imperial gal./42 US gal. † estimated

River Pollution

Sources of river pollution, USA (latest available year)

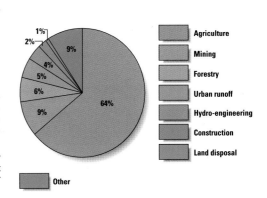

1%, 2%, 9%, 4%, 5%, 6%, 9%, 64%

- Agriculture
- Mining
- Forestry
- Urban runoff
- Hydro-engineering
- Construction
- Land disposal

Other

Water Pollution

- Severely polluted sea areas and lakes
- Polluted sea areas and lakes
- Areas of frequent oil pollution by shipping
- ◤ Major oil tanker spills
- ▲ Major oil rig blow-outs
- ▼ Offshore dumpsites for industrial and municipal waste
- — Severely polluted rivers and estuaries

The most notorious tanker spillage of the 1980s occurred when the *Exxon Valdez* ran aground in Prince William Sound, Alaska, in 1989, spilling 267,000 barrels of crude oil close to shore in a sensitive ecological area. This rates as the world's 28th worst spill in terms of volume.

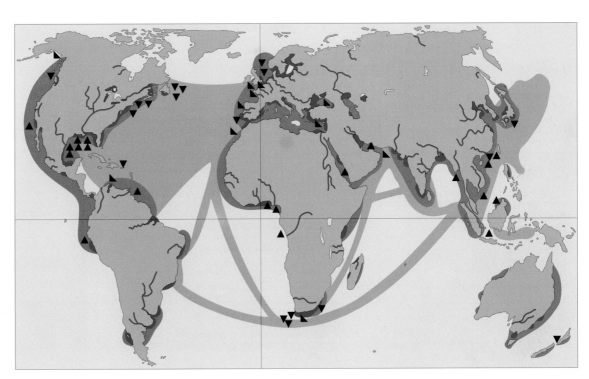

Climate

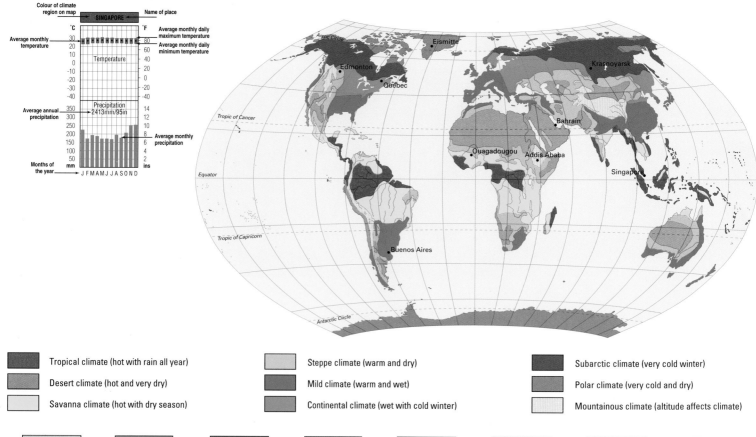

- ■ Tropical climate (hot with rain all year)
- ■ Desert climate (hot and very dry)
- ■ Savanna climate (hot with dry season)
- ■ Steppe climate (warm and dry)
- ■ Mild climate (warm and wet)
- ■ Continental climate (wet with cold winter)
- ■ Subarctic climate (very cold winter)
- ■ Polar climate (very cold and dry)
- ■ Mountainous climate (altitude affects climate)

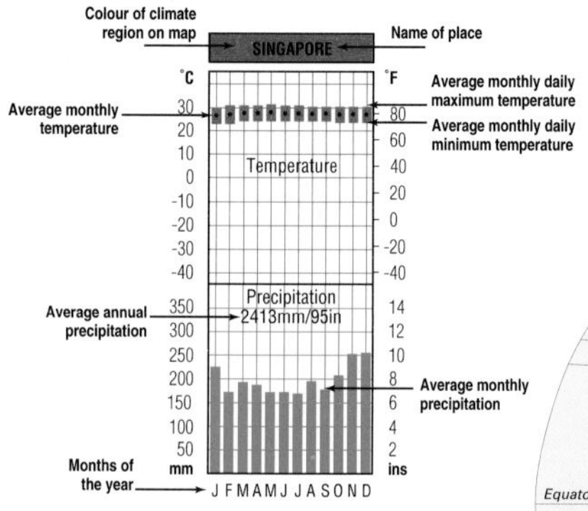

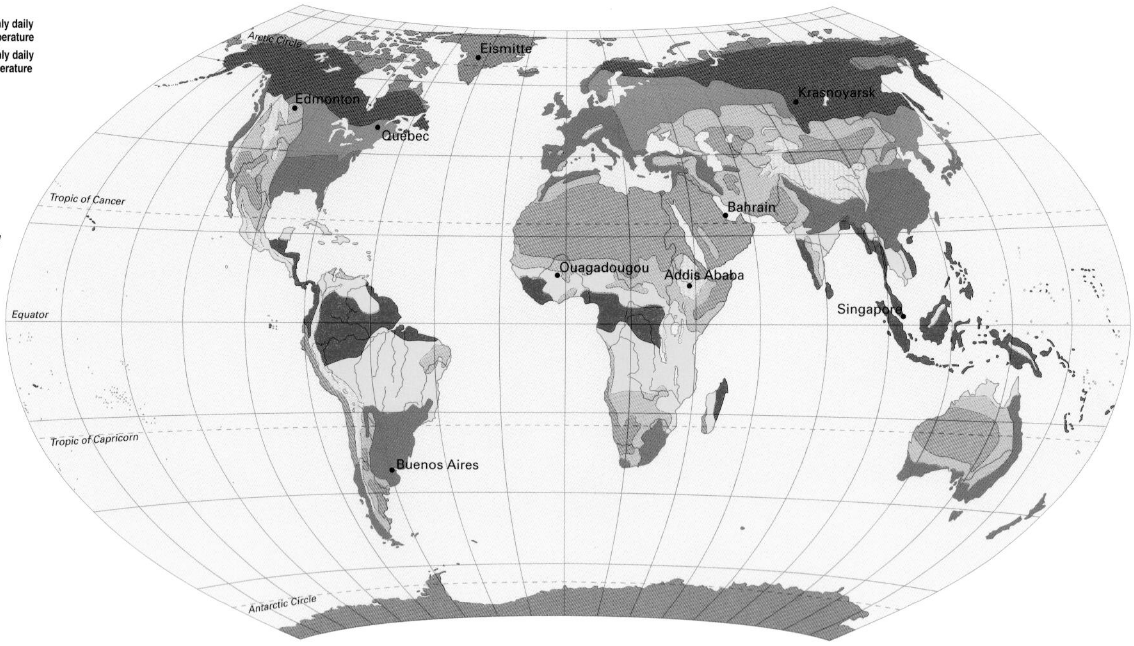

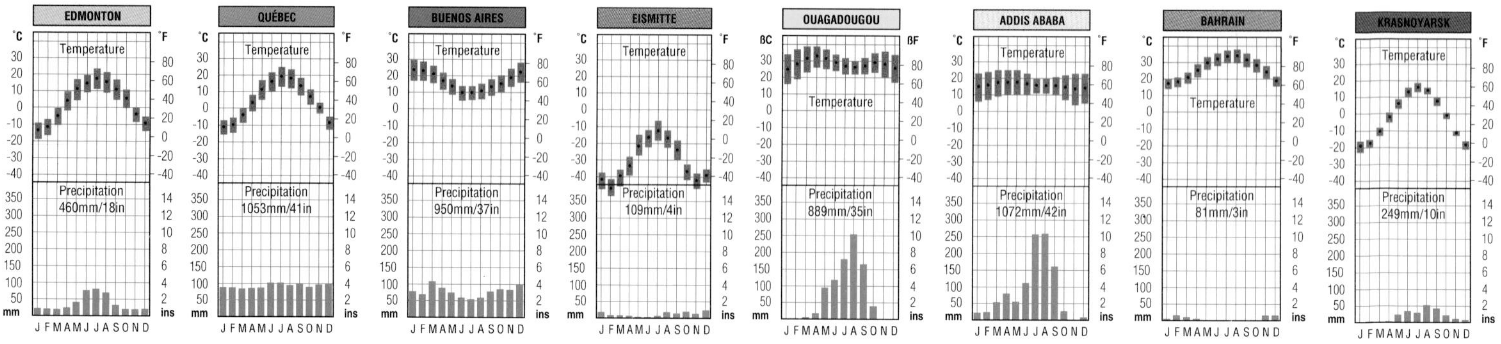

Climate Records

Temperature
Highest recorded shade temperature: Al Aziziyah, Libya, 58°C [136.4°F], 13 September 1922.

Highest mean annual temperature: Dallol, Ethiopia, 34.4°C [94°F], 1960–66.

Longest heatwave: Marble Bar, W. Australia, 162 days over 38°C [100°F], 23 October 1923 to 7 April 1924.

Lowest recorded temperature (outside poles): Verkhoyansk, Siberia, –68°C [–90°F], 6 February 1933.

Lowest mean annual temperature: Plateau Station, Antarctica, –56.6°C [–72.0°F]

Pressure
Longest drought: Calama, N. Chile, no recorded rainfall in 400 years to 1971.

Wettest place (12 months): Cherrapunji, Meghalaya, N. E. India, 26,470 mm [1,040 in], August 1860 to August 1861. Cherrapunji also holds the record for the most rainfall in one month: 2,930 mm [115 in], July 1861.

Wettest place (average): Mawsynram, India, mean annual rainfall 11,873 mm [467.4 in].

Wettest place (24 hours): Cilaos, Réunion, Indian Ocean, 1,870 mm [73.6 in], 15–16 March 1952.

Heaviest hailstones: Gopalganj, Bangladesh, up to 1.02 kg [2.25 lb], 14 April 1986 (killed 92 people).

Heaviest snowfall (continuous): Bessans, Savoie, France, 1,730 mm [68 in] in 19 hours, 5–6 April 1969.

Heaviest snowfall (season/year): Paradise Ranger Station, Mt Rainier, Washington, USA, 31,102 mm [1,224.5 in], 19 February 1971 to 18 February 1972.

Pressure and winds
Highest barometric pressure: Agata, Siberia (at 262 m [862 ft] altitude), 1,083.8 mb, 31 December 1968.

Lowest barometric pressure: Typhoon Tip, Guam, Pacific Ocean, 870 mb, 12 October 1979.

Highest recorded wind speed: Mt Washington, New Hampshire, USA, 371 km/h [231 mph], 12 April 1934. This is three times as strong as hurricane force on the Beaufort Scale.

Windiest place: Commonwealth Bay, Antarctica, where gales frequently reach over 320 km/h [200 mph].

Climate

Climate is weather in the long term: the seasonal pattern of hot and cold, wet and dry, averaged over time (usually 30 years). At the simplest level, it is caused by the uneven heating of the Earth. Surplus heat at the Equator passes towards the poles, levelling out the energy differential. Its passage is marked by a ceaseless churning of the atmosphere and the oceans, further agitated by the Earth's diurnal spin and the motion it imparts to moving air and water. The heat's means of transport – by winds and ocean currents, by the continual evaporation and recondensation of water molecules – is the weather itself. There are four basic types of climate, each of which can be further subdivided: tropical, desert (dry), temperate and polar.

Composition of Dry Air

Nitrogen	78.09%	Sulphur dioxide	trace
Oxygen	20.95%	Nitrogen oxide	trace
Argon	0.93%	Methane	trace
Water vapour	0.2–4.0%	Dust	trace
Carbon dioxide	0.03%	Helium	trace
Ozone	0.00006%	Neon	trace

El Niño

In a normal year, south-easterly trade winds drive surface waters westwards off the coast of South America, drawing cold, nutrient-rich water up from below. In an El Niño year (which occurs every 2–7 years), warm water from the west Pacific suppresses up-welling in the east, depriving the region of nutrients. The water is warmed by as much as 7°C [12°F], disturbing the tropical atmospheric circulation. During an intense El Niño, the south-east trade winds change direction and become equatorial westerlies, re-sulting in climatic extremes in many regions of the world, such as drought in parts of Australia and India, and heavy rainfall in south-eastern USA. An intense El Niño occurred in 1997–8, with resultant freak weather conditions across the entire Pacific region.

Normal year

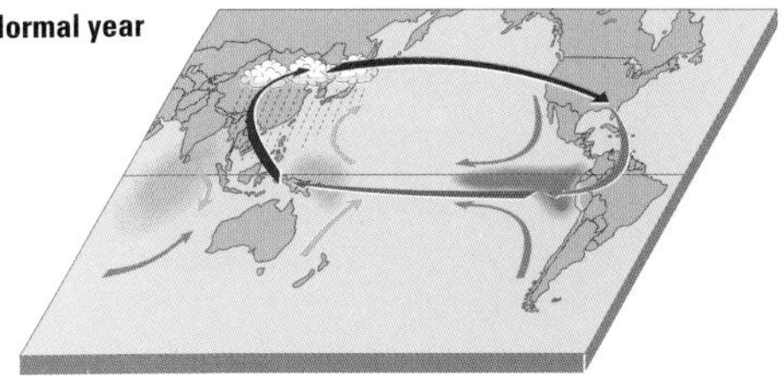

El Niño event

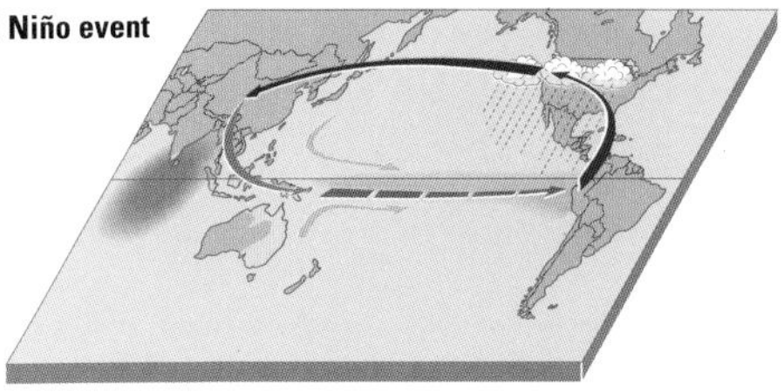

Beaufort Wind Scale

Named after the 19th-century British naval officer who devised it, the Beaufort Scale assesses wind speed according to its effects. It was originally designed as an aid for sailors, but has since been adapted for use on the land.

Scale	Wind speed km/h	mph	Effect
0	0–1	0–1	**Calm** Smoke rises vertically
1	1–5	1–3	**Light air** Wind direction shown only by smoke drift
2	6–11	4–7	**Light breeze** Wind felt on face; leaves rustle; vanes moved by wind
3	12–19	8–12	**Gentle breeze** Leaves and small twigs in constant motion; wind extends small flag
4	20–28	13–18	**Moderate** Raises dust and loose paper; small branches move
5	29–38	19–24	**Fresh** Small trees in leaf sway; wavelets on inland waters
6	39–49	25–31	**Strong** Large branches move; difficult to use umbrellas
7	50–61	32–38	**Near gale** Whole trees in motion; difficult to walk against wind
8	62–74	39–46	**Gale** Twigs break from trees; walking very difficult
9	75–88	47–54	**Strong gale** Slight structural damage
10	89–102	55–63	**Storm** Trees uprooted; serious structural damage
11	103–117	64–72	**Violent storm** Widespread damage
12	118+	73+	**Hurricane**

Conversions
°C = (°F − 32) × 5/9; °F = (°C × 9/5) + 32; 0°C = 32°F
1 in = 25.4 mm; 1 mm = 0.0394 in; 100 mm = 3.94 in

Temperature

Average temperature in January

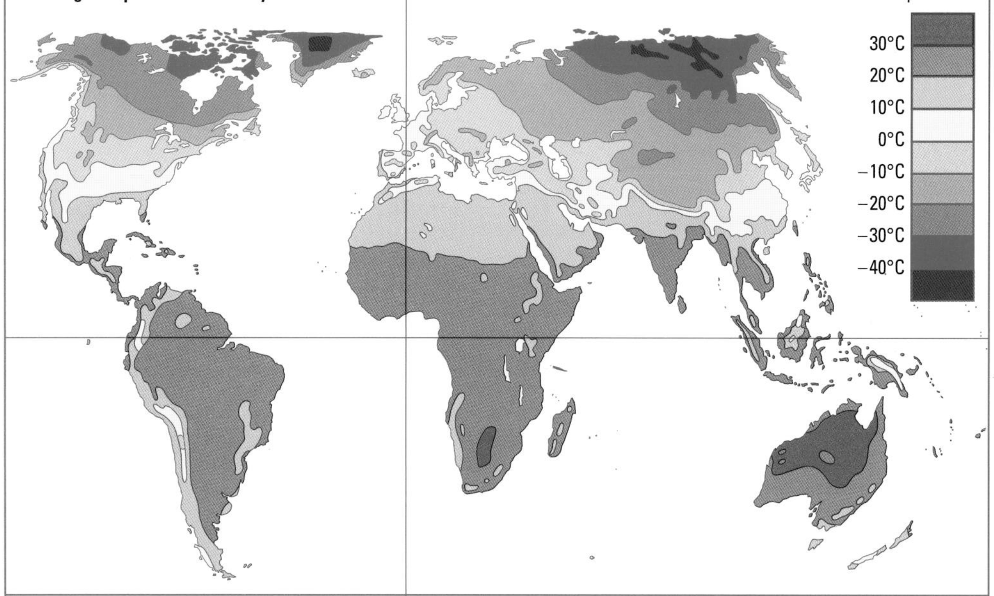

Temperature
30°C
20°C
10°C
0°C
−10°C
−20°C
−30°C
−40°C

Average temperature in July

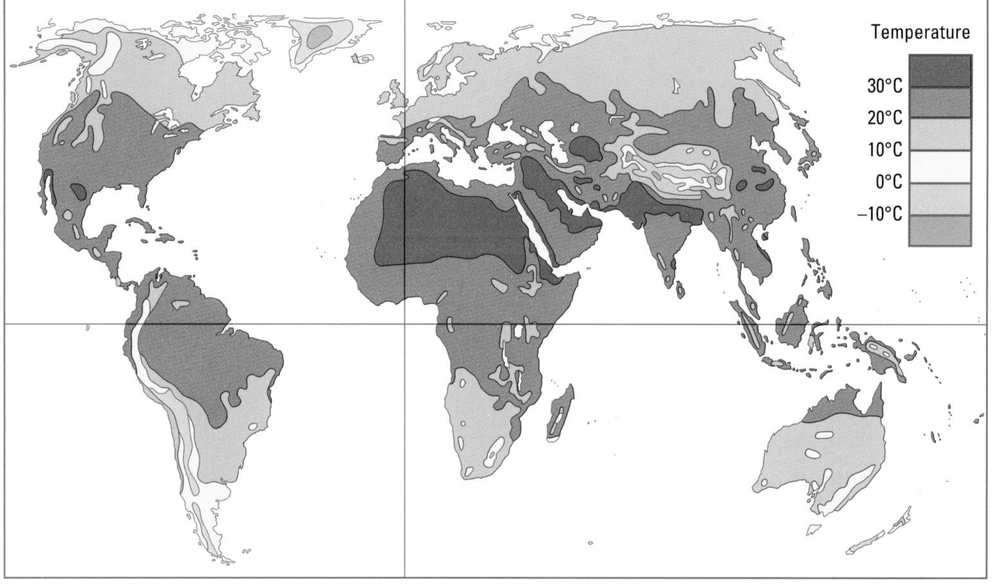

Temperature
30°C
20°C
10°C
0°C
−10°C

Precipitation

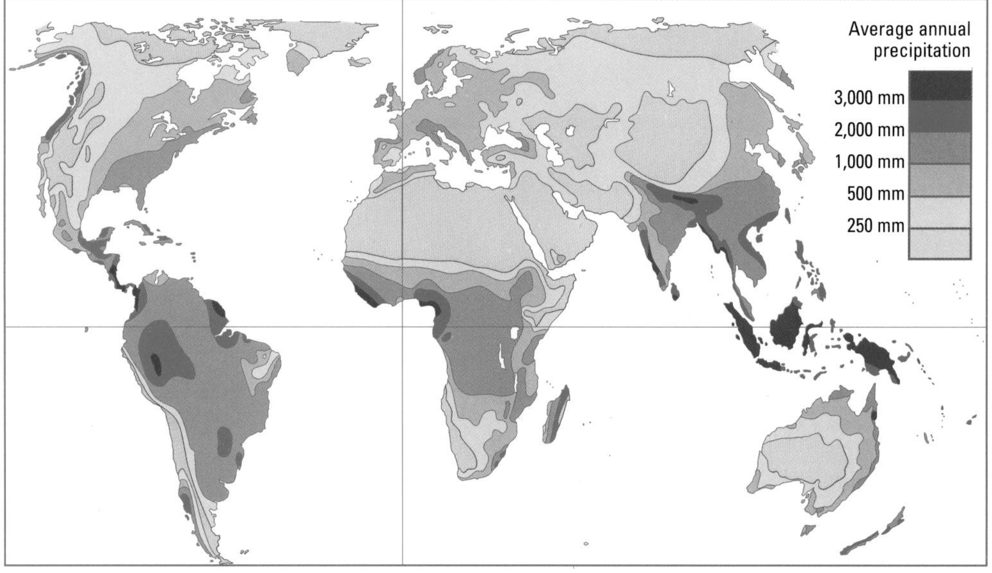

Average annual precipitation
3,000 mm
2,000 mm
1,000 mm
500 mm
250 mm

Water and Vegetation

The Hydrological Cycle

The world's water balance is regulated by the constant recycling of water between the oceans, atmosphere and land. The movement of water between these three reservoirs is known as the hydrological cycle. The oceans play a vital role in the hydrological cycle: 74% of the total precipitation falls over the oceans and 84% of the total evaporation comes from the oceans.

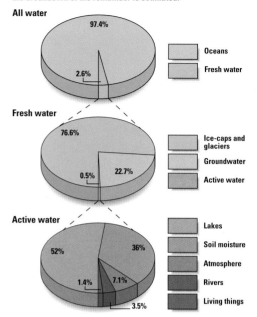

Water Distribution

The distribution of planetary water, by percentage. Oceans and ice-caps together account for more than 99% of the total; the breakdown of the remainder is estimated.

All water
- 97.4% Oceans
- 2.6% Fresh water

Fresh water
- 76.6% Ice-caps and glaciers
- 22.7% Groundwater
- 0.5% Active water

Active water
- 52% Lakes
- 36% Soil moisture
- 7.1% Atmosphere
- 3.5% Rivers
- 1.4% Living things

Water Utilization

	Domestic	Industrial	Agriculture

The percentage breakdown of water usage by sector, selected countries (1996)

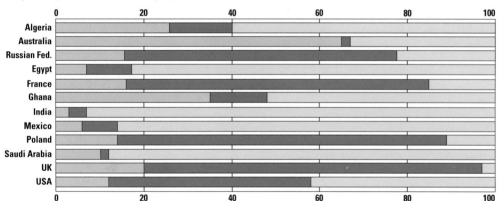

Countries: Algeria, Australia, Russian Fed., Egypt, France, Ghana, India, Mexico, Poland, Saudi Arabia, UK, USA

Water Usage

Almost all the world's water is 3,000 million years old, and all of it cycles endlessly through the hydrosphere, though at different rates. Water vapour circulates over days, even hours, deep ocean water circulates over millennia, and ice-cap water remains solid for millions of years.

Fresh water is essential to all terrestrial life. Humans cannot survive more than a few days without it, and even the hardiest desert plants and animals could not exist without some water. Agriculture requires huge quantities of fresh water: without large-scale irrigation most of the world's people would starve. In the USA, agriculture uses 42% and industry 45% of all water withdrawals.

The United States is one of the heaviest users of water in the world. According to the latest figures the average American uses 380 litres a day and the average household uses 415,000 litres a year. This is two to four times more than in Western Europe.

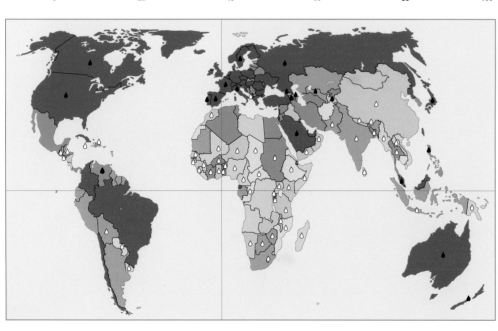

Water Supply

Percentage of total population with access to safe drinking water (1995)

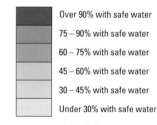

- Over 90% with safe water
- 75 – 90% with safe water
- 60 – 75% with safe water
- 45 – 60% with safe water
- 30 – 45% with safe water
- Under 30% with safe water

- △ Under 80 litres per person per day domestic water consumption
- ▲ Over 320 litres per person per day domestic water consumption

NB: 80 litres of water a day is considered necessary for a reasonable quality of life.

Least well-provided countries

Paraguay	8%	Central Afr. Rep. 18%
Afghanistan	10%	Bhutan 21%
Cambodia	13%	Congo (D. Rep.) 25%

Natural Vegetation

Regional variation in vegetation

	Tundra and mountain vegetation
	Needleleaf evergreen forest
	Mixed needleleaf evergreen & broadleaf deciduous trees
	Broadleaf deciduous woodland
	Mid-latitude grassland
	Evergreen broadleaf and deciduous trees & shrubs
	Semi-desert scrub
	Desert
	Tropical grassland (savanna)
	Tropical broadleaf rainforest and monsoon forest
	Subtropical broadleaf and needleleaf forest

The map shows the natural 'climax vegetation' of regions, as dictated by climate and topography. In most cases, however, agricultural activity has drastically altered the vegetation pattern. Western Europe, for example, lost most of its broadleaf forest many centuries ago, while irrigation has turned some natural semi-desert into productive land.

Land Use by Continent

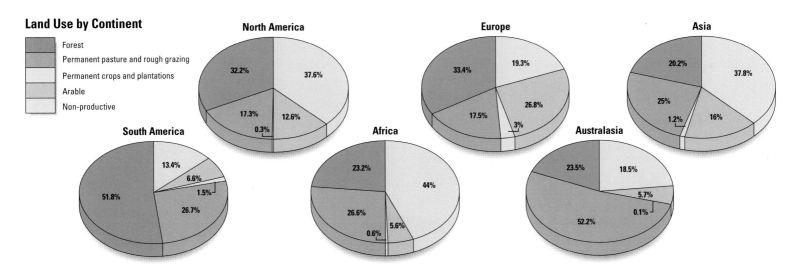

	Forest
	Permanent pasture and rough grazing
	Permanent crops and plantations
	Arable
	Non-productive

North America
37.6%, 32.2%, 17.3%, 0.3%, 12.6%

Europe
19.3%, 33.4%, 26.8%, 17.5%, 3%

Asia
37.8%, 20.2%, 25%, 1.2%, 16%

South America
13.4%, 6.6%, 1.5%, 51.8%, 26.7%

Africa
44%, 23.2%, 26.6%, 0.6%, 5.6%

Australasia
18.5%, 23.5%, 5.7%, 0.1%, 52.2%

Forestry: Production

	Forest and woodland (million hectares)	Annual production (1996, million cubic metres)	
		Fuelwood and charcoal	Industrial roundwood*
World	*3,987.9*	*1,864.8*	*1,489.5*
S. America	829.3	193.0	129.9
N. & C. America	709.8	155.4	600.4
Africa	684.6	519.9	67.9
Asia	131.8	905.2	280.2
Europe	157.3	82.4	369.7
Australasia	157.2	8.7	41.5

Paper and Board

Top producers (1996)**		Top exporters (1996)**	
USA	85,173	Canada	13,393
China	30,253	USA	9,113
Japan	30,014	Finland	8,529
Canada	18,414	Sweden	7,483
Germany	14,733	Germany	6,319

* roundwood is timber as it is felled
** in thousand tonnes

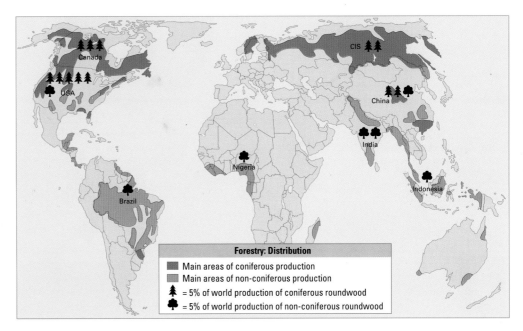

Forestry: Distribution

- Main areas of coniferous production
- Main areas of non-coniferous production
- 🌲 = 5% of world production of coniferous roundwood
- ♣ = 5% of world production of non-coniferous roundwood

Environment

Humans have always had a dramatic effect on their environment, at least since the development of agriculture almost 10,000 years ago. Generally, the Earth has accepted human interference without obvious ill effects: the complex systems that regulate the global environment have been able to absorb substantial damage while maintaining a stable and comfortable home for the planet's trillions of lifeforms. But advancing human technology and the rapidly-expanding populations it supports are now threatening to overwhelm the Earth's ability to compensate.

Industrial wastes, acid rainfall, desertification and large-scale deforestation all combine to create environmental change at a rate far faster than the great slow cycles of planetary evolution can accommodate. As a result of overcultivation, overgrazing and overcutting of groundcover for firewood, desertification is affecting as much as 60% of the world's croplands. In addition, with fire and chain-saws, humans are destroying more forest in a day than their ancestors could

have done in a century, upsetting the balance between plant and animal, carbon dioxide and oxygen, on which all life ultimately depends.

The fossil fuels that power industrial civilization have pumped enough carbon dioxide and other so-called greenhouse gases into the atmosphere to make climatic change a near-certainty. As a result of the combination of these factors, the Earth's average temperature has risen by approximately 0.5°C [1°F] since the beginning of the 20th century, and it is still rising.

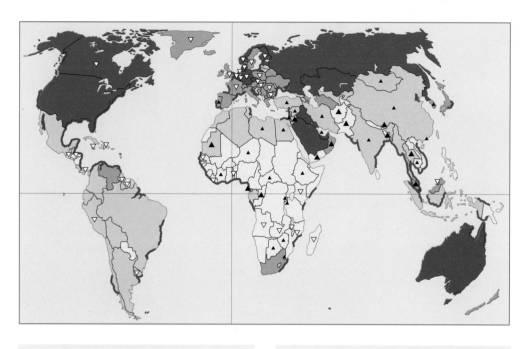

Global Warming

Carbon dioxide emissions in tonnes per person per year (1995)

- Over 10 tonnes of CO_2
- 5 – 10 tonnes of CO_2
- 1 – 5 tonnes of CO_2
- Under 1 tonne of CO_2

Changes in CO_2 emissions 1980–90

- ▲ Over 100% increase in emissions
- ▲ 50–100% increase in emissions
- ▽ Reduction in emissions
- — Coastal areas in danger of flooding from rising sea levels caused by global warming

High atmospheric concentrations of heat-absorbing gases, especially carbon dioxide, appear to be causing a steady rise in average temperatures worldwide – up to 1.5°C [3°F] by the year 2020, according to some estimates. Global warming is likely to bring with it a rise in sea levels that may flood some of the Earth's most densely populated coastal areas.

Greenhouse Power

Relative contributions to the Greenhouse Effect by the major heat-absorbing gases in the atmosphere.

The chart combines greenhouse potency and volume. Carbon dioxide has a greenhouse potential of only 1, but its concentration of 350 parts per million makes it predominate. CFC 12, with 25,000 times the absorption capacity of CO_2, is present only as 0.00044 ppm.

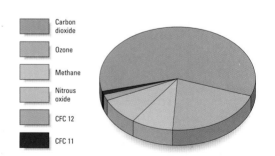

- Carbon dioxide
- Ozone
- Methane
- Nitrous oxide
- CFC 12
- CFC 11

Ozone Layer

The ozone 'hole' over the northern hemisphere on 12 March 1995.

The colours represent Dobson Units (DU). The ozone 'hole' is seen as the dark blue and purple patch in the centre, where ozone values are around 120 DU or lower. Normal levels are around 280 DU. The ozone 'hole' over Antarctica is much larger.

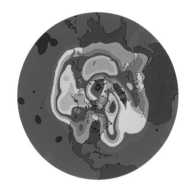

Carbon Dioxide

Carbon dioxide released in millions of tonnes (1992)

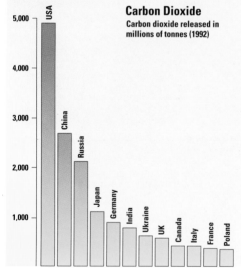

The Greenhouse Effect

Carbon dioxide is increased by burning fossil fuels and cutting forests

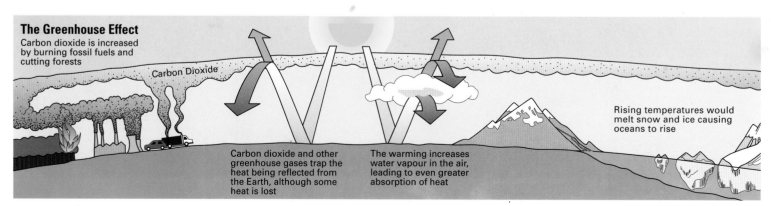

Carbon Dioxide

Carbon dioxide and other greenhouse gases trap the heat being reflected from the Earth, although some heat is lost

The warming increases water vapour in the air, leading to even greater absorption of heat

Rising temperatures would melt snow and ice causing oceans to rise

Desertification

- Existing deserts
- Areas with a high risk of desertification
- Areas with a moderate risk of desertification
- Former areas of rainforest
- Existing rainforest

Forest Clearance

Thousands of hectares of forest cleared annually, tropical countries surveyed 1981–85 and 1987–90. Loss as a percentage of remaining stocks is shown in figures on each column.

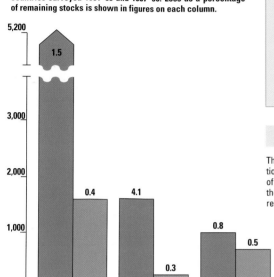

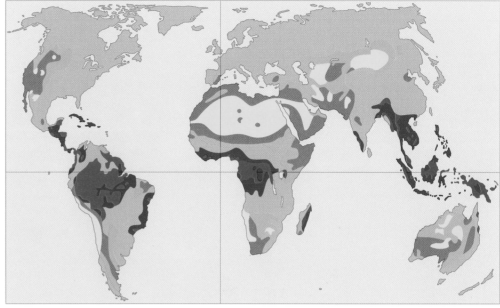

Deforestation

The Earth's remaining forests are under attack from three directions: expanding agriculture, logging, and growing consumption of fuelwood, often in combination. Sometimes deforestation is the direct result of government policy, as in the efforts made to resettle the urban poor in some parts of Brazil; just as often, it comes about despite state attempts at conservation. Loggers, licensed or unlicensed, blaze a trail into virgin forest, often destroying twice as many trees as they harvest. Landless farmers follow, burning away most of what remains to plant their crops, completing the destruction.

- 1987–90
- 1981–85

Brazil — 1.5 / 0.4
India — 4.1 / 0.3
Indonesia — 0.8 / 0.5
Burma — 2.1 / 0.3
Thailand — 2.5 / 2.4
Vietnam — 2.0 / 0.7
Philippines — 1.5 / 1.0
Costa Rica — 7.6 / 4.0
Cameroon — 0.6 / 0.4

Ozone Depletion

The ozone layer, 25–30 km [15–18 miles] above sea level, acts as a barrier to most of the Sun's harmful ultra-violet radiation, protecting us from the ionizing radiation that can cause skin cancer and cataracts. In recent years, however, two holes in the ozone layer have been observed during winter: one over the Arctic and the other, the size of the USA, over Antarctica. By 1996, ozone had been reduced to around a half of its 1970 amount. The ozone (O_3) is broken down by chlorine released into the atmosphere as CFCs (chlorofluorocarbons) – chemicals used in refrigerators, packaging and aerosols.

Air Pollution

Sulphur dioxide is the main pollutant associated with industrial cities. According to the World Health Organization, at least 600 million people live in urban areas where sulphur dioxide concentrations regularly reach damaging levels. One of the world's most dangerously polluted urban areas is Mexico City, due to a combination of its enclosed valley location, 3 million cars and 60,000 factories. In May 1998, this lethal cocktail was added to by nearby forest fires and the resultant air pollution led to over 20% of the population (3 million people) complaining of respiratory problems.

Acid Rain

Killing trees, poisoning lakes and rivers and eating away buildings, acid rain is mostly produced by sulphur dioxide emissions from industry and volcanic eruptions. By the mid 1990s, acid rain had sterilized 4,000 or more of Sweden's lakes and left 45% of Switzerland's alpine conifers dead or dying, while the monuments of Greece were dissolving in Athens' smog. Prevailing wind patterns mean that the acids often fall many hundred kilometres from where the original pollutants were discharged. In parts of Europe acid deposition has slightly decreased, following reductions in emissions, but not by enough.

World Pollution

Acid rain and sources of acidic emissions (latest available year)

Acid rain is caused by high levels of sulphur and nitrogen in the atmosphere. They combine with water vapour and oxygen to form acids (H_2SO_4 and HNO_3) which fall as precipitation.

- Regions where sulphur and nitrogen oxides are released in high concentrations, mainly from fossil fuel combustion
- Major cities with high levels of air pollution (including nitrogen and sulphur emissions)

Areas of heavy acid deposition

pH numbers indicate acidity, decreasing from a neutral 7. Normal rain, slightly acid from dissolved carbon dioxide, never exceeds a pH of 5.6.

- pH less than 4.0 (most acidic)
- pH 4.0 to 4.5
- pH 4.5 to 5.0
- Areas where acid rain is a potential problem

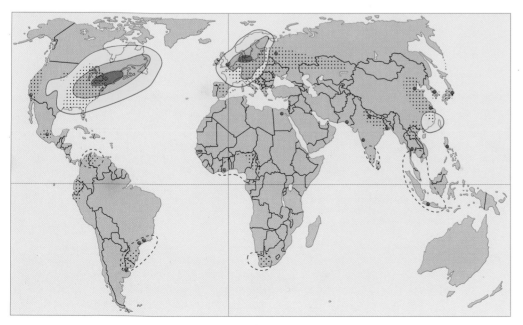

Population

Demographic Profiles

Developed nations such as the UK have populations evenly spread across the age groups and, usually, a growing proportion of elderly people. The great majority of the people in developing nations, however, are in the younger age groups, about to enter their most fertile years. In time, these population profiles should resemble the world profile (even Kenya has made recent progress with reducing its birth rate), but the transition will come about only after a few more generations of rapid population growth.

World

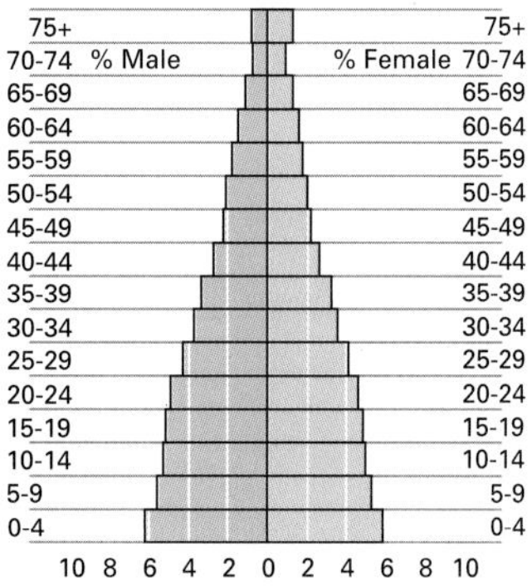

UK   **Kenya**

India   **Saudi Arabia**

USA   **China**

Most Populous Nations [in millions (1998 estimates)]

1. China	1,237	9. Bangladesh	125	17. Iran	64
2. India	984	10. Nigeria	111	18. Thailand	60
3. USA	270	11. Mexico	99	19. France	59
4. Indonesia	213	12. Germany	82	20. UK	59
5. Brazil	170	13. Philippines	78	21. Ethiopia	58
6. Russia	147	14. Vietnam	76	22. Italy	57
7. Pakistan	135	15. Egypt	66	23. Ukraine	50
8. Japan	126	16. Turkey	65	24. Congo (=Zaïre)	49

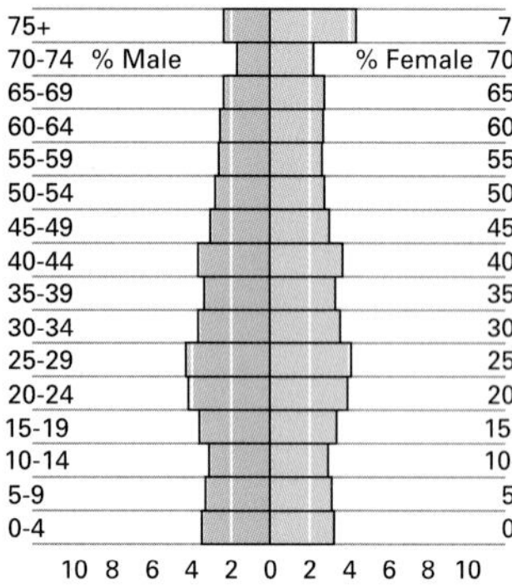

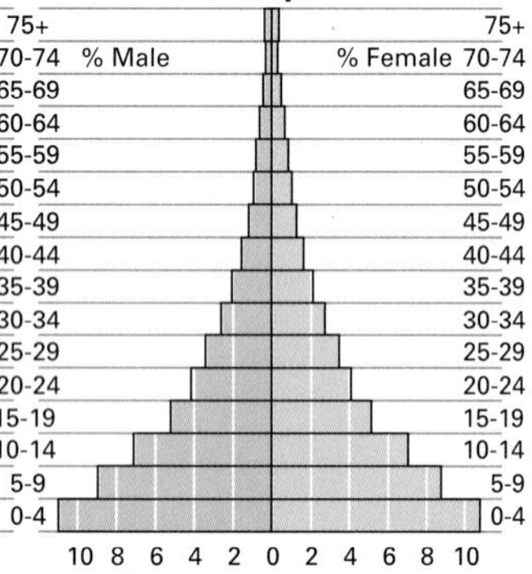

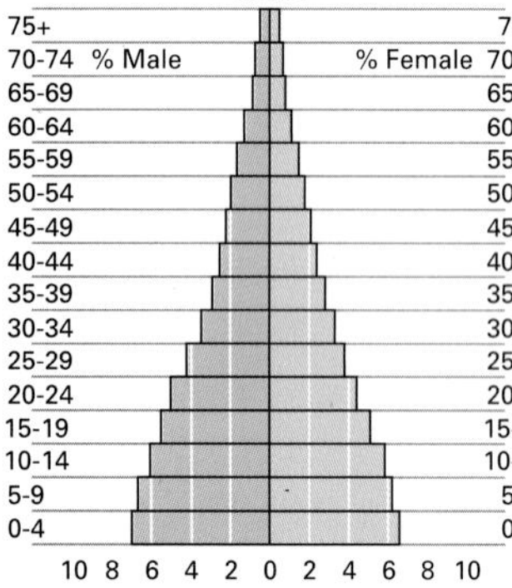

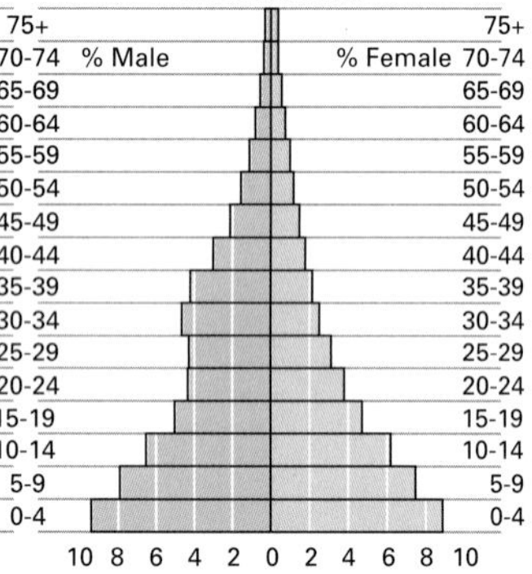

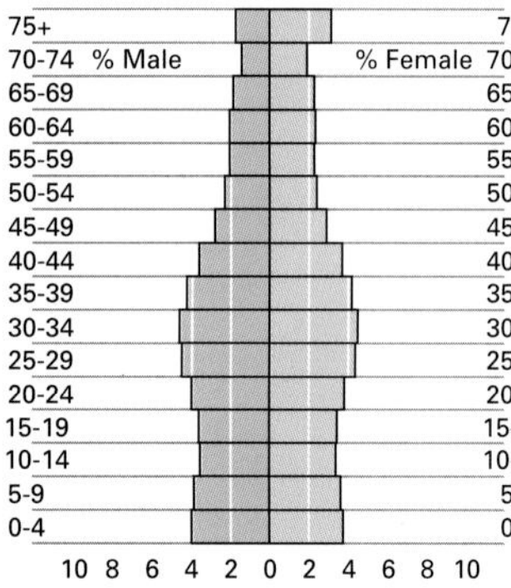

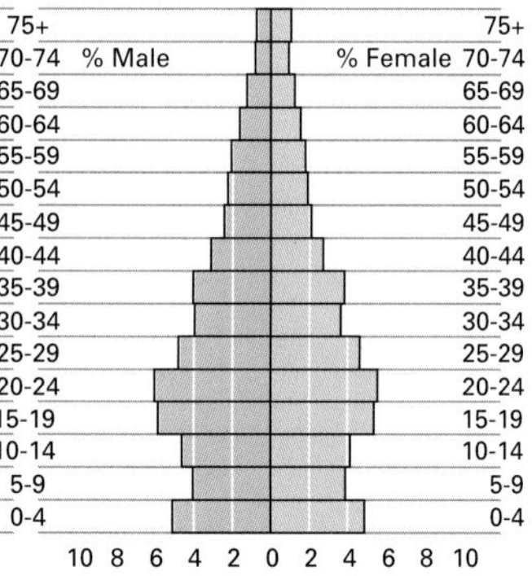

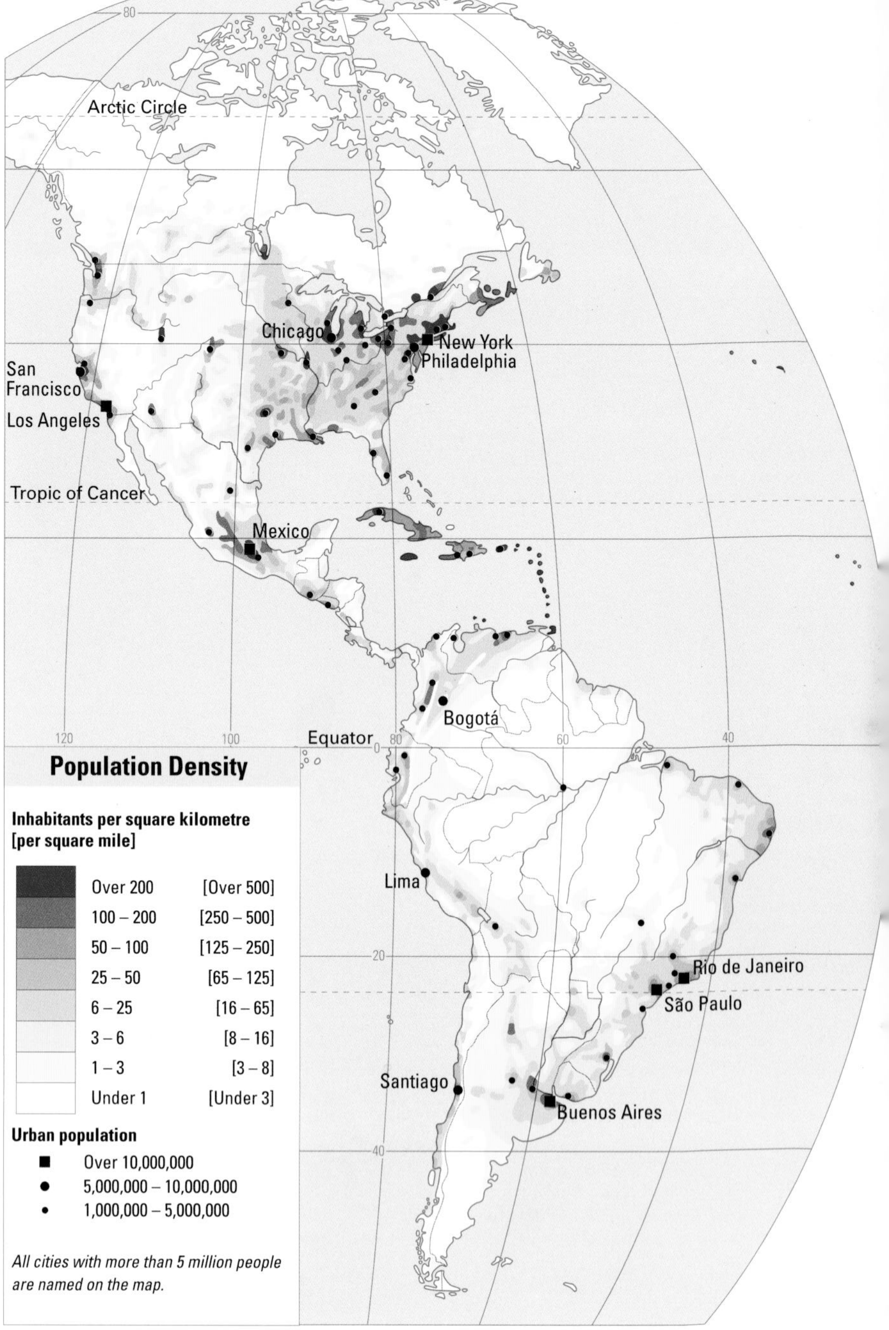

Population Density

Inhabitants per square kilometre [per square mile]

	Over 200	[Over 500]
	100 – 200	[250 – 500]
	50 – 100	[125 – 250]
	25 – 50	[65 – 125]
	6 – 25	[16 – 65]
	3 – 6	[8 – 16]
	1 – 3	[3 – 8]
	Under 1	[Under 3]

Urban population

■   Over 10,000,000
●   5,000,000 – 10,000,000
•   1,000,000 – 5,000,000

All cities with more than 5 million people are named on the map.

Continental Comparisons

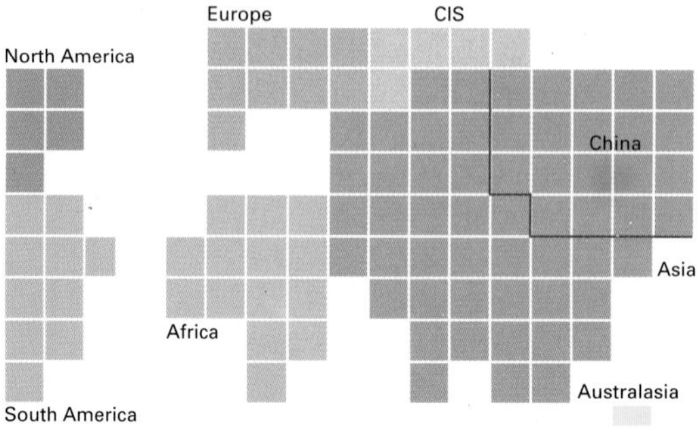

Each square in the diagram above represents 1% of the total world population (1995).

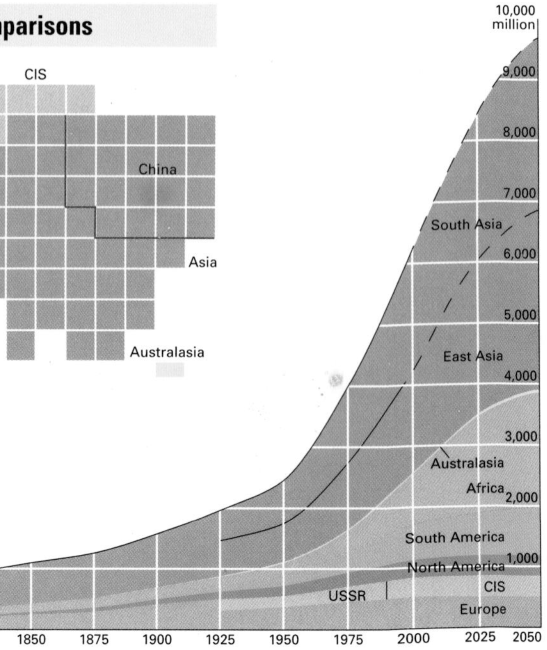

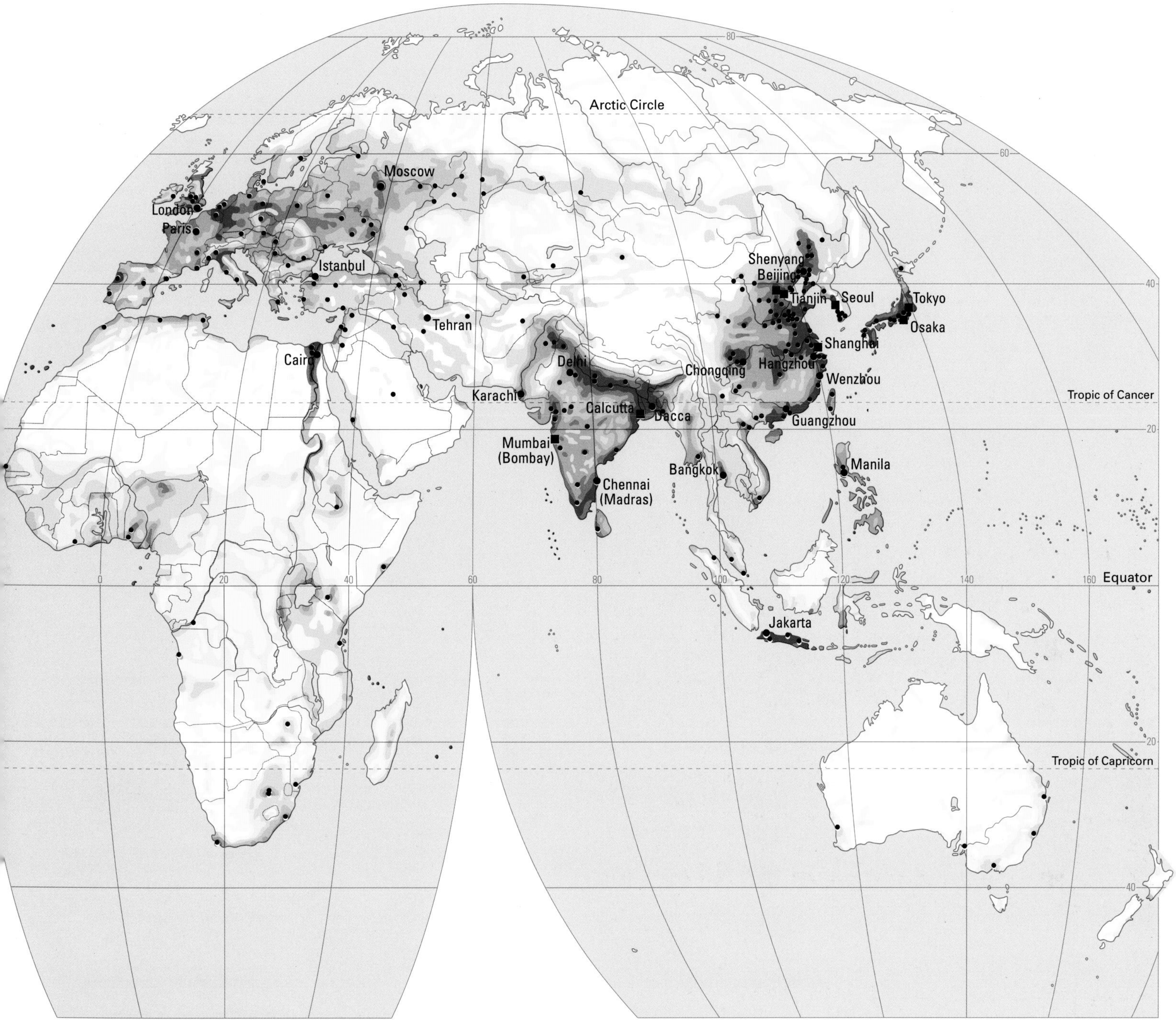

Arctic Circle

London
Paris

Moscow

Istanbul

Shenyang
Beijing

Tehran

Tianjin Seoul

Tokyo

Cairo

Delhi

Shanghai

Osaka

Karachi

Chongqing

Hangzhou

Wenzhou

Calcutta

Dacca

Tropic of Cancer

Mumbai
(Bombay)

Guangzhou

Chennai
(Madras)

Bangkok

Manila

Equator

Jakarta

Tropic of Capricorn

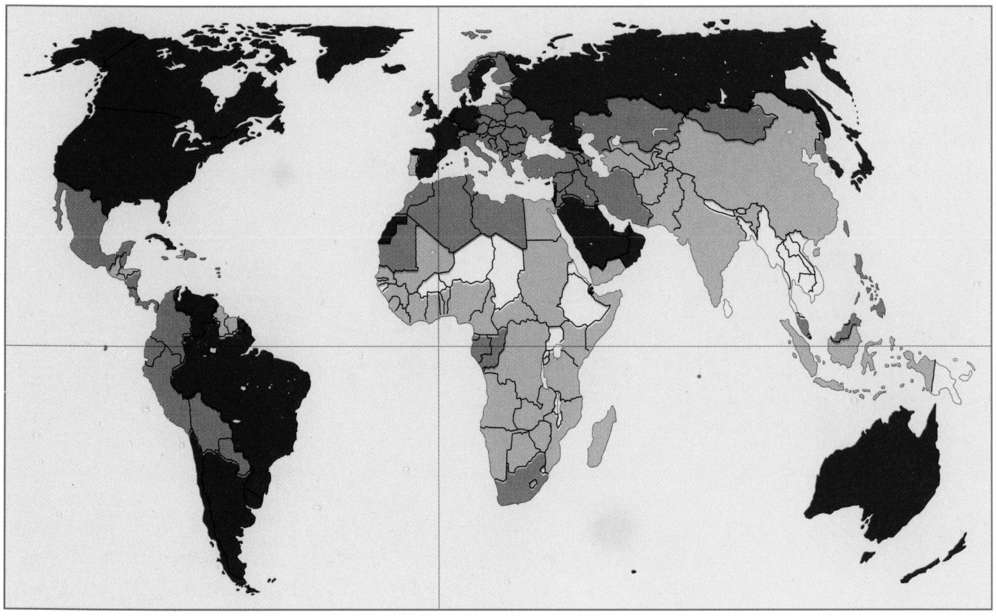

Urban Population

Percentage of total population living in towns and cities (1997)

Over 75%

50 – 75%

25 – 50%

10 – 25%

Under 10%

Most urbanized		Least urbanized	
Singapore	100%	Rwanda	6%
Belgium	97%	Bhutan	8%
Israel	91%	Burundi	8%
Uruguay	91%	Nepal	11%
Netherlands	89%	Swaziland	12%

[UK 89%]

The Human Family

Predominant Languages

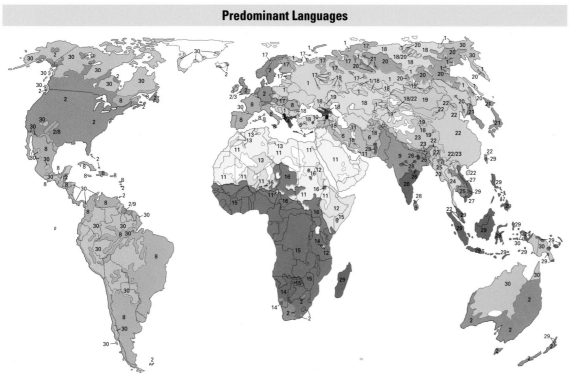

Languages of the World

Language can be classified by ancestry and structure. For example, the Romance and Germanic groups are both derived from an Indo-European language believed to have been spoken 5,000 years ago.

Mother tongues (in millions)
Chinese 1,069 (Mandarin 864), English 443, Hindi 352, Spanish 341, Russian 293, Arabic 197, Bengali 184, Portuguese 173, Malay-Indonesian 142, Japanese 125, French 121, German 118, Urdu 92, Punjabi 84, Korean 71.

Official languages (% of total population)
English 27%, Chinese 19%, Hindi 13.5%, Spanish 5.4%, Russian 5.2%, French 4.2%, Arabic 3.3%, Portuguese 3%, Malay 3%, Bengali 2.9%, Japanese 2.3%.

INDO-EUROPEAN FAMILY

1. Balto-Slavic group (incl. Russian, Ukrainian)
2. Germanic group (incl. English, German)
3. Celtic group
4. Greek
5. Albanian
6. Iranian group
7. Armenian
8. Romance group (incl. Spanish, Portuguese, French, Italian)
9. Indo-Aryan group (incl. Hindi, Bengali, Urdu, Punjabi, Marathi)
10. CAUCASIAN FAMILY

AFRO-ASIATIC FAMILY

11. Semitic group (incl. Arabic)
12. Kushitic group
13. Berber group

14. KHOISAN FAMILY

15. NIGER-CONGO FAMILY

16. NILO-SAHARAN FAMILY

17. URALIC FAMILY

ALTAIC FAMILY

18. Turkic group
19. Mongolian group
20. Tungus-Manchu group
21. Japanese and Korean

SINO-TIBETAN FAMILY

22. Sinitic (Chinese) languages
23. Tibetic-Burmic languages

24. TAI FAMILY

AUSTRO-ASIATIC FAMILY

25. Mon-Khmer group
26. Munda group
27. Vietnamese

28. DRAVIDIAN FAMILY (incl. Telugu, Tamil)

29. AUSTRONESIAN FAMILY (incl. Malay-Indonesian)

30. OTHER LANGUAGES

Predominant Religions

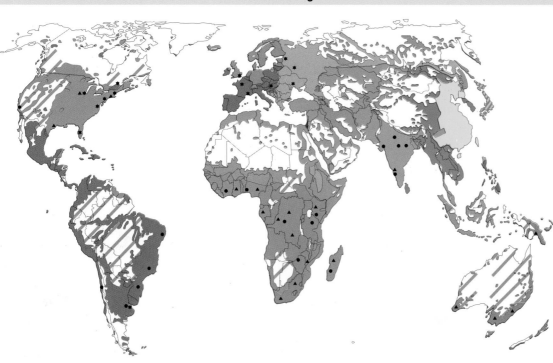

Religious Adherents

Religious adherents in millions:

Christian	1,669	Hindu	663
Roman Catholic	952	Buddhist	312
Protestant	337	Chinese Folk	172
Orthodox	162	Tribal	92
Anglican	70	Jewish	18
Other Christian	148	Sikhs	17
Muslim	966		
Sunni	841		
Shia	125		

- Roman Catholicism
- Orthodox and other Eastern Churches
- Protestantism
- Sunni Islam
- Shia Islam
- Buddhism
- Hinduism
- Confucianism
- Judaism
- Shintoism
- Tribal Religions

18

CARTOGRAPHY BY PHILIP'S. COPYRIGHT GEORGE PHILIP LTD

United Nations

Created in 1945 to promote peace and co-operation and based in New York, the United Nations is the world's largest international organization, with 185 members and an annual budget of US $2.6 billion (1996–97). Each member of the General Assembly has one vote, while the permanent members of the 15-nation Security Council – USA, Russia, China, UK and France – hold a veto. The Secretariat is the UN's principal administrative arm. The 54 members of the Economic and Social Council are responsible for economic, social, cultural, educational, health and related matters. The UN has 16 specialized agencies – based in Canada, France, Switzerland and Italy, as well as the USA – which help members in fields such as education (UNESCO), agriculture (FAO), medicine (WHO) and finance (IFC). By the end of 1994, all the original 11 trust territories of the Trusteeship Council had become independent.

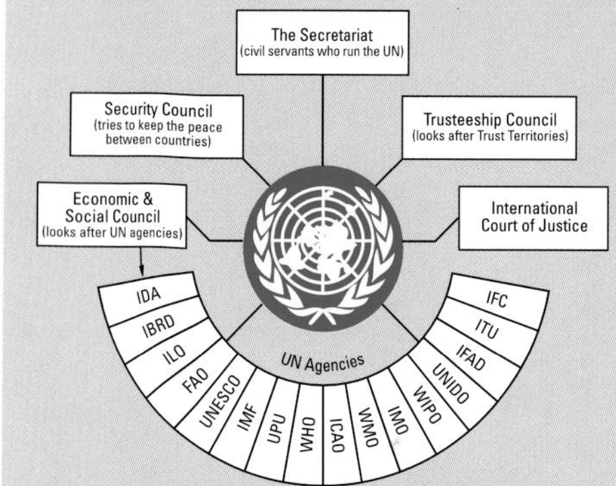

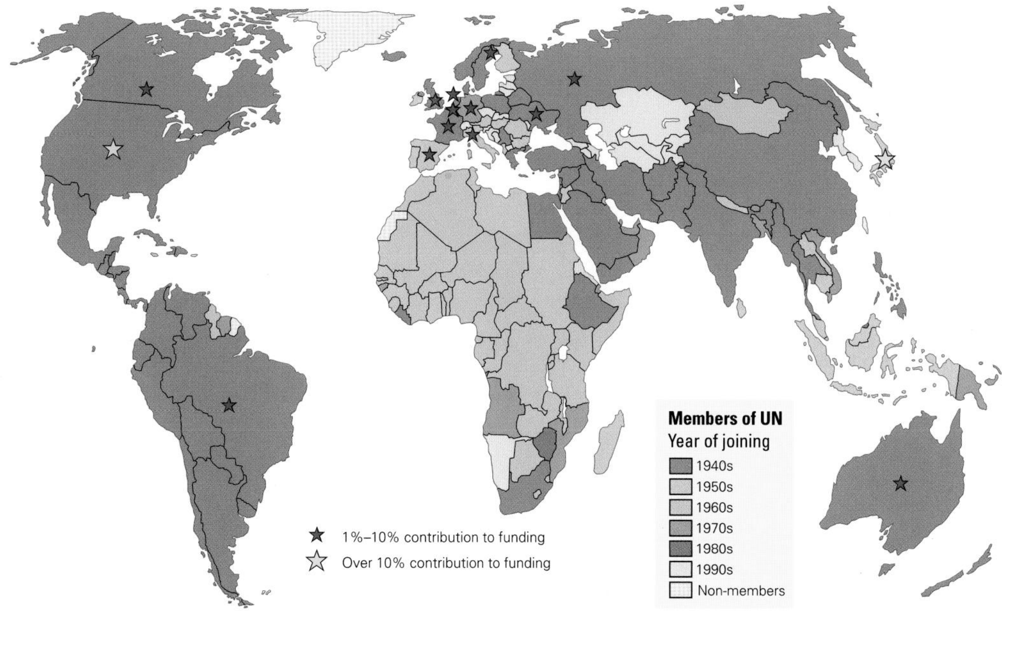

Members of UN
Year of joining
- 1940s
- 1950s
- 1960s
- 1970s
- 1980s
- 1990s
- Non-members

★ 1%–10% contribution to funding
☆ Over 10% contribution to funding

MEMBERSHIP OF THE UN In 1945 there were 51 members; by December 1994 membership had increased to 185 following the admission of Palau. There are 7 independent states which are not members of the UN – Kiribati, Nauru, Switzerland, Taiwan, Tonga, Tuvalu and the Vatican City. All the successor states of the former USSR had joined by the end of 1992. The official languages of the UN are Chinese, English, French, Russian, Spanish and Arabic.

FUNDING The UN budget for 1996–97 was US $2.6 billion. Contributions are assessed by the members' ability to pay, with the maximum 25% of the total, the minimum 0.01%. Contributions for 1996 were: USA 25.0%, Japan 15.4%, Germany 9.0%, France 6.4%, UK 5.3%, Italy 5.2%, Russia 4.5%, Canada 3.1%, Spain 2.4%, Brazil 1.6%, Netherlands 1.6%, Australia 1.5%, Sweden 1.2%, Ukraine 1.1%, Belgium 1.0%.

International Organizations

EU European Union (evolved from the European Community in 1993). The 15 members – Austria, Belgium, Denmark, Finland, France, Germany, Greece, Ireland, Italy, Luxembourg, Netherlands, Portugal, Spain, Sweden and the UK – aim to integrate economies, co-ordinate social developments and bring about political union. These members of what is now the world's biggest market share agricultural and industrial policies and tariffs on trade. The original body, the European Coal and Steel Community (ECSC), was created in 1951 following the signing of the Treaty of Paris.
EFTA European Free Trade Association (formed in 1960). Portugal left the original 'Seven' in 1989 to join what was then the EC, followed by Austria, Finland and Sweden in 1995. Only 4 members remain: Norway, Iceland, Switzerland and Liechtenstein.
ACP African-Caribbean-Pacific (formed in 1963). Members have economic ties with the EU.
NATO North Atlantic Treaty Organization (formed in 1949). It continues after 1991 despite the winding up of the Warsaw Pact. The Czech Republic, Hungary and Poland were the latest members to join in 1999.
OAS Organization of American States (formed in 1948). It aims to promote social and economic co-operation between developed countries of North America and developing nations of Latin America.
ASEAN Association of South-east Asian Nations (formed in 1967). Burma and Laos joined in 1997.
OAU Organization of African Unity (formed in 1963). Its 53 members represent over 94% of Africa's population. Arabic, French, Portuguese and English are recognized as working languages.
LAIA Latin American Integration Association (1980). Its aim is to promote freer regional trade.
OECD Organization for Economic Co-operation and Development (formed in 1961). It comprises the 29 major Western free-market economies. Poland, Hungary and South Korea joined in 1996. 'G8' is its 'inner group' comprising Canada, France, Germany, Italy, Japan, Russia, the UK and the USA.
COMMONWEALTH The Commonwealth of Nations evolved from the British Empire; it comprises 16 Queen's realms, 32 republics and 5 indigenous monarchies, giving a total of 53.
OPEC Organization of Petroleum Exporting Countries (formed in 1960). It controls about three-quarters of the world's oil supply. Gabon left the organization in 1996.

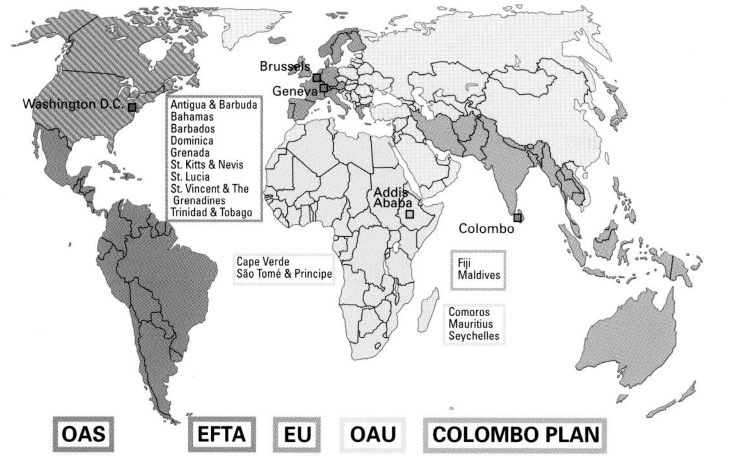

| OAS | EFTA | EU | OAU | COLOMBO PLAN |

ARAB LEAGUE (formed in 1945). The League's aim is to promote economic, social, political and military co-operation. There are 21 member nations.
COLOMBO PLAN (formed in 1951). Its 26 members aim to promote economic and social development in Asia and the Pacific.

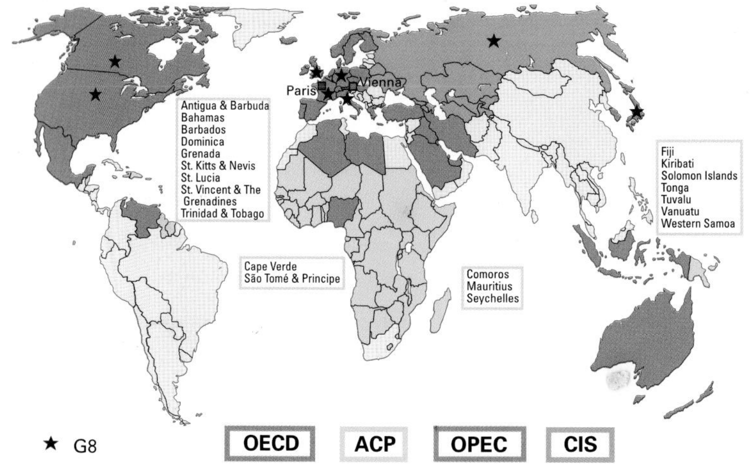

★ G8

| OECD | ACP | OPEC | CIS |

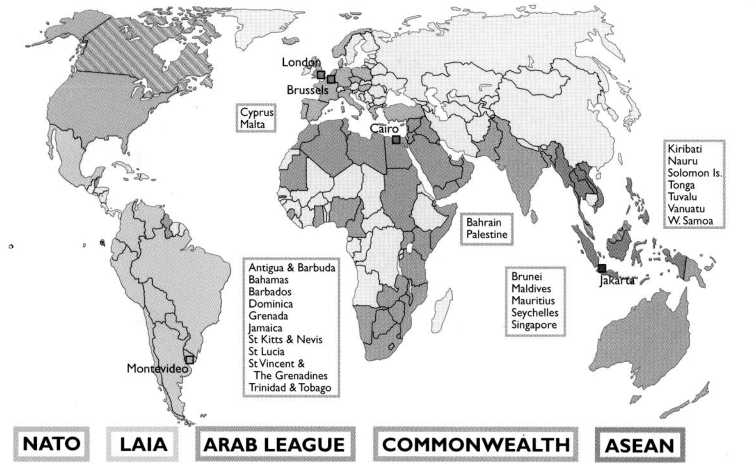

| NATO | LAIA | ARAB LEAGUE | COMMONWEALTH | ASEAN |

Wealth

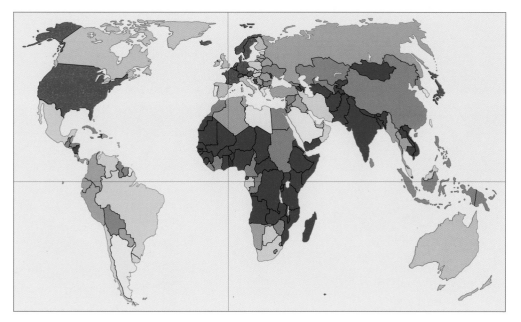

Levels of Income

Gross National Product per capita: the value of total production divided by the population (1997)

- Over 400% of world average
- 200 – 400% of world average
- 100 – 200% of world average

[World average wealth per person US $6,316]

- 50 – 100% of world average
- 25 – 50% of world average
- 10 – 25% of world average
- Under 10% of world average

GNP per capita growth rate (%), selected countries, 1985–94

Thailand	8.2	Brazil	−0.4
Chile	6.9	Zimbabwe	−0.6
Japan	3.2	USA	−1.3
Germany	1.9	UK	−1.4
Australia	1.2	Armenia	−12.9

Wealth Creation

The Gross National Product (GNP) of the world's largest economies, US $ million (1997)

1.	USA	7,690,100	23.	Turkey	199,500
2.	Japan	4,772,300	24.	Denmark	171,400
3.	Germany	2,319,300	25.	Thailand	169,600
4.	France	1,526,400	26.	Hong Kong	164,400
5.	UK	1,220,200	27.	Norway	158,900
6.	Italy	1,155,400	28.	Poland	138,900
7.	China	1,055,400	29.	South Africa	130,200
8.	Brazil	773,400	30.	Saudi Arabia	128,900
9.	Canada	583,900	31.	Greece	126,200
10.	Spain	570,100	32.	Finland	123,800
11.	South Korea	485,200	33.	Portugal	103,900
12.	Russia	403,500	34.	Singapore	101,800
13.	Netherlands	402,700	35.	Malaysia	98,200
14.	Australia	380,000	36.	Philippines	89,300
15.	India	373,900	37.	Israel	87,600
16.	Mexico	348,600	38.	Colombia	86,800
17.	Switzerland	313,500	39.	Venezuela	78,700
18.	Argentina	305,700	40.	Chile	73,300
19.	Belgium	268,400	41.	Egypt	71,200
20.	Sweden	232,000	42.	Pakistan	67,200
21.	Austria	225,900	43.	Ireland	66,400
22.	Indonesia	221,900	44.	Peru	60,800

The Wealth Gap

The world's richest and poorest countries, by Gross National Product per capita in US $ (1997)

1.	Luxembourg	45,360	1.	Mozambique	90
2.	Switzerland	44,220	2.	Ethiopia	110
3.	Japan	37,850	3.	Congo (D. Rep.)	110
4.	Norway	36,090	4.	Burundi	180
5.	Liechtenstein	33,000	5.	Sierra Leone	200
6.	Singapore	32,940	6.	Niger	200
7.	Denmark	32,500	7.	Rwanda	210
8.	Bermuda	31,870	8.	Tanzania	210
9.	USA	28,740	9.	Nepal	210
10.	Germany	28,260	10.	Malawi	220
11.	Austria	27,980	11.	Chad	240
12.	Iceland	26,580	12.	Madagascar	250
13.	Belgium	26,420	13.	Mali	260
14.	Sweden	26,220	14.	Yemen	270
15.	France	26,050	15.	Cambodia	300
16.	Netherlands	25,820	16.	Bosnia-Herzegovina	300
17.	Monaco	25,000	17.	Gambia, The	320
18.	Hong Kong	22,990	18.	Haiti	330
19.	Finland	20,580	19.	Kenya	330
20.	UK	18,700	20.	Angola	340

GNP per capita is calculated by dividing a country's Gross National Product by its total population.

Continental Shares

Shares of population and of wealth (GNP) by continent

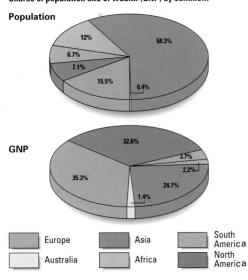

Population

58.3% · 12% · 6.7% · 7.1% · 15.5% · 0.4%

GNP

32.6% · 3.7% · 2.2% · 24.7% · 1.4% · 35.3%

- Europe
- Asia
- South America
- Australia
- Africa
- North America

Inflation

Average annual rate of inflation (1990–96)

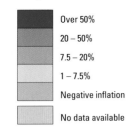

- Over 50%
- 20 – 50%
- 7.5 – 20%
- 1 – 7.5%
- Negative inflation
- No data available

Highest average inflation

Congo (D. Rep.)	2747%
Georgia	2279%
Angola	1103%
Turkmenistan	1074%
Armenia	897%

Lowest average inflation

Oman	−3.0%
Bahrain	−0.5%
Brunei	−0.0%
Saudi Araba	1.0%
Japan	1.0%

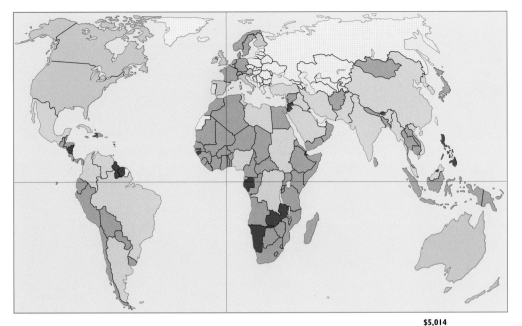

International Aid

Aid provided or received, divided by the total population, in US $ (1995)

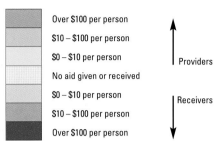

- Over $100 per person
- $10 – $100 per person
- $0 – $10 per person
- No aid given or received — **Providers**
- $0 – $10 per person — **Receivers**
- $10 – $100 per person
- Over $100 per person

Top 5 providers per capita (1994)		Top 5 receivers per capita (1994)	
France	$279	São Tomé & P.	$378
Denmark	$260	Cape Verde	$314
Norway	$247	Djibouti	$235
Sweden	$201	Surinam	$198
Germany	$166	Mauritania	$153

Debt and Aid

International debtors and the aid they receive (1996)

Although aid grants make a vital contribution to many of the world's poorer countries, they are usually dwarfed by the burden of debt that the developing economies are expected to repay. In 1992, they had to pay US $160,000 million in debt service charges alone – more than two and a half times the amount of Official Development Assistance (ODA) the developing countries were receiving, and US $60,000 million more than total private flows of aid in the same year. In 1990, the debts of Mozambique, one of the world's poorest countries, were estimated to be 75 times its entire earnings from exports.

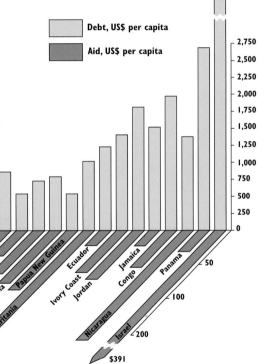

- Debt, US$ per capita
- Aid, US$ per capita

Distribution of Spending

Percentage share of household spending, selected countries

- Food
- Clothing
- Energy & Housing
- Medicine & Education
- Transport
- Other

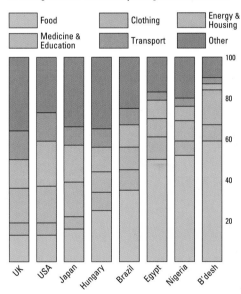

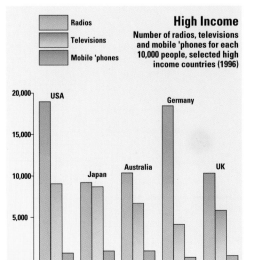

High Income

- Radios
- Televisions
- Mobile 'phones

Number of radios, televisions and mobile 'phones for each 10,000 people, selected high income countries (1996)

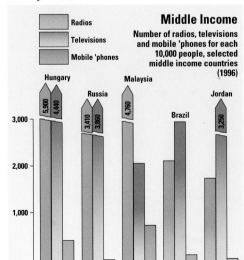

Middle Income

- Radios
- Televisions
- Mobile 'phones

Number of radios, televisions and mobile 'phones for each 10,000 people, selected middle income countries (1996)

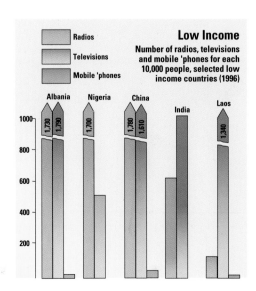

Low Income

- Radios
- Televisions
- Mobile 'phones

Number of radios, televisions and mobile 'phones for each 10,000 people, selected low income countries (1996)

Quality of Life

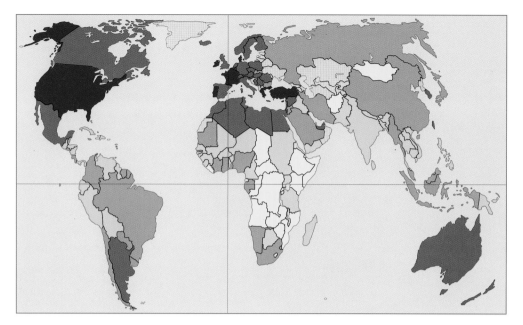

Daily Food Consumption

Average daily food intake in calories per person (1995)

	Over 3,500 calories per person
	3,000 – 3,500 calories per person
	2,500 – 3,000 calories per person
	2,000 – 2,500 calories per person
	Under 2,000 calories per person
	No available data

Top 5 countries		Bottom 5 countries	
Cyprus	3,708 cal.	Congo (D.Rep.)	1,879 cal.
Denmark	3,704 cal.	Djibouti	1,831 cal.
Portugal	3,639 cal.	Togo	1,754 cal.
Ireland	3,638 cal.	Burundi	1,749 cal.
USA	3,603 cal.	Mozambique	1,678 cal.

[UK 3,149 calories]

Hospital Capacity

Hospital beds available for each 1,000 people (1996)

Highest capacity		Lowest capacity	
Switzerland	20.8	Benin	0.2
Japan	16.2	Nepal	0.2
Tajikistan	16.0	Afghanistan	0.3
Norway	13.5	Bangladesh	0.3
Belarus	12.4	Ethiopia	0.3
Kazakstan	12.2	Mali	0.4
Moldova	12.2	Burkina Faso	0.5
Ukraine	12.2	Niger	0.5
Latvia	11.9	Guinea	0.6
Russia	11.8	India	0.6

[UK 4.9] [USA 4.2]

Although the ratio of people to hospital beds gives a good approximation of a country's health provision, it is not an absolute indicator. Raw numbers may mask inefficiency and other weaknesses: the high availability of beds in Kazakstan, for example, has not prevented infant mortality rates over three times as high as in the United Kingdom and the United States.

Life Expectancy

Years of life expectancy at birth, selected countries (1997)

The chart shows combined data for both sexes. On average, women live longer than men worldwide, even in developing countries with high maternal mortality rates. Overall, life expectancy is steadily rising, though the difference between rich and poor nations remains dramatic.

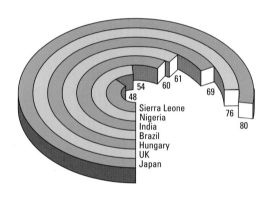

Sierra Leone 48
Nigeria 54
India 60
Brazil 61
Hungary 69
UK 76
Japan 80

Causes of Death

Causes of death for selected countries by % (1992–94)

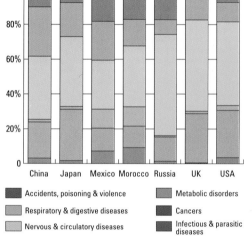

China, Japan, Mexico, Morocco, Russia, UK, USA

Accidents, poisoning & violence	Metabolic disorders
Respiratory & digestive diseases	Cancers
Nervous & circulatory diseases	Infectious & parasitic diseases

Child Mortality

Number of babies who will die under the age of one, per 1,000 births (average 1990–95)

	Over 150 deaths per 1,000 births
	100 – 150 deaths per 1,000 births
	50 – 100 deaths per 1,000 births
	20 – 50 deaths per 1,000 births
	10 – 20 deaths per 1,000 births
	Under 10 deaths per 1,000 births

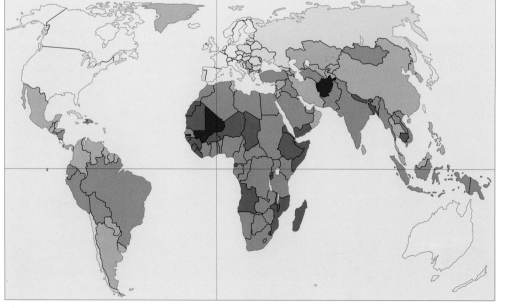

Highest child mortality		Lowest child mortality	
Afghanistan	162	Hong Kong	6
Mali	159	Denmark	6
Sierra Leone	143	Japan	6
Guinea-Bissau	140	Iceland	5
Malawi	138	Finland	5

[UK 8 deaths]

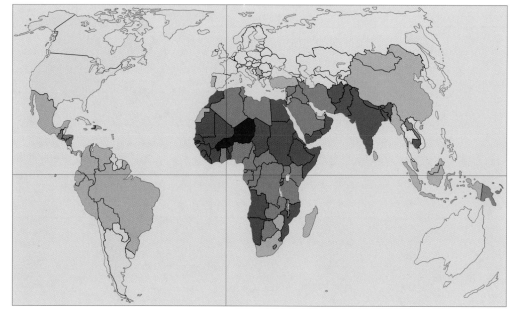

Illiteracy

Percentage of the total population unable to read or write (latest available year)

- Over 75% of population illiterate
- 50 – 75% of population illiterate
- 25 – 50% of population illiterate
- 10 – 25% of population illiterate
- Under 10% of population illiterate

Educational expenditure per person (latest available year)

Top 5 countries		Bottom 5 countries	
Sweden	$997	Chad	$2
Qatar	$989	Bangladesh	$3
Canada	$983	Ethiopia	$3
Norway	$971	Nepal	$4
Switzerland	$796	Somalia	$4

Fertility and Education

Fertility rates compared with female education, selected countries (1992–95)

- Percentage of females aged 12–17 in secondary education
- Fertility rate: average number of children borne per woman

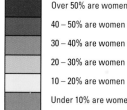

Living Standards

At first sight, most international contrasts in living standards are swamped by differences in wealth. The rich not only have more money, they have more of everything, including years of life. Those with only a little money are obliged to spend most of it on food and clothing, the basic maintenance costs of their existence; air travel and tourism are unlikely to feature on their expenditure lists. However, poverty and wealth are both relative: slum dwellers living on social security payments in an affluent industrial country have far more resources at their disposal than an average African peasant, but feel their own poverty nonetheless. A middle-class Indian lawyer cannot command a fraction of the earnings of a counterpart living in New York, London or Rome; nevertheless, he rightly sees himself as prosperous.

The rich not only live longer, on average, than the poor, they also die from different causes. Infectious and parasitic diseases, all but eliminated in the developed world, remain a scourge in the developing nations. On the other hand, more than two-thirds of the populations of OECD nations eventually succumb to cancer or circulatory disease.

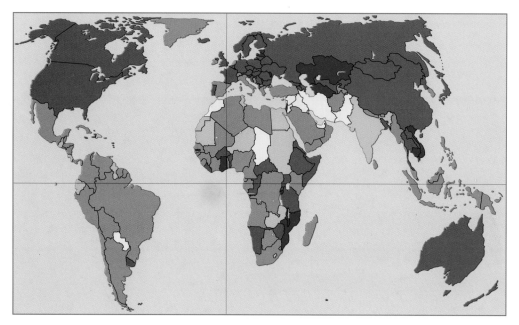

Women in the Workforce

Women in paid employment as a percentage of the total workforce (latest available year)

- Over 50% are women
- 40 – 50% are women
- 30 – 40% are women
- 20 – 30% are women
- 10 – 20% are women
- Under 10% are women

Most women in the workforce		Fewest women in the workforce	
Cambodia	56%	Saudi Arabia	4%
Kazakstan	54%	Oman	6%
Burundi	53%	Afghanistan	8%
Mozambique	53%	Algeria	9%
Turkmenistan	52%	Libya	9%

[USA 45] [UK 44]

Energy

Production

[Each square represents 1% of world energy production]

North America   Europe   CIS

Middle East   Japan

Africa   Asia

South America   Australasia

Consumption

[Each square represents 1% of world energy consumption]

North America   Europe   CIS

Middle East

Africa   Asia

Japan

South America   Australasia

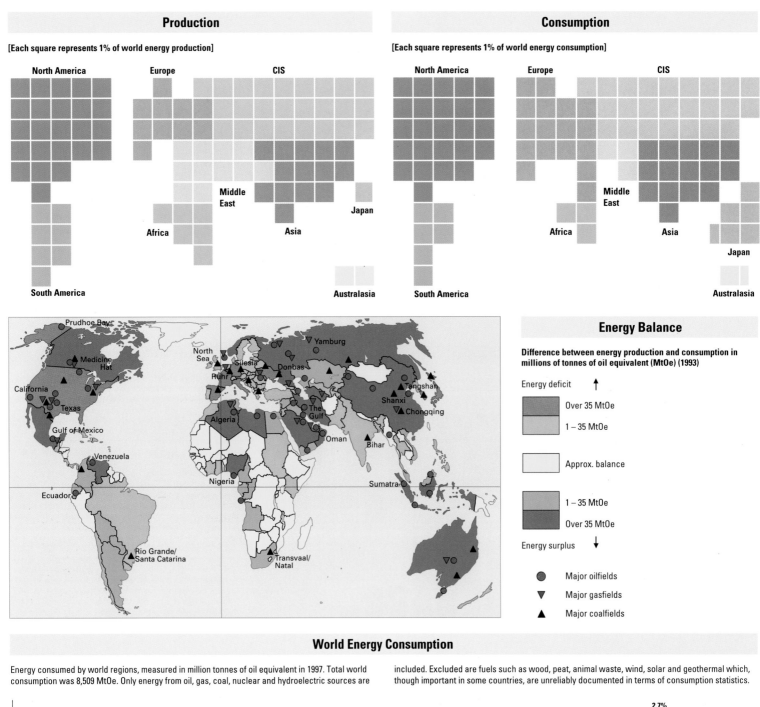

Energy Balance

Difference between energy production and consumption in millions of tonnes of oil equivalent (MtOe) (1993)

Energy deficit ↑

Over 35 MtOe

1 – 35 MtOe

Approx. balance

1 – 35 MtOe

Over 35 MtOe

Energy surplus ↓

● Major oilfields

▼ Major gasfields

▲ Major coalfields

Map labels: Prudhoe Bay, Medicine Hat, California, Texas, Gulf of Mexico, Venezuela, Ecuador, Rio Grande/Santa Catarina, North Sea, Ruhr, Silesia, Algeria, Nigeria, Transvaal/Natal, Yamburg, Donbas, The Gulf, Oman, Shanxi, Tangshan, Chongqing, Bihar, Sumatra

World Energy Consumption

Energy consumed by world regions, measured in million tonnes of oil equivalent in 1997. Total world consumption was 8,509 MtOe. Only energy from oil, gas, coal, nuclear and hydroelectric sources are included. Excluded are fuels such as wood, peat, animal waste, wind, solar and geothermal which, though important in some countries, are unreliably documented in terms of consumption statistics.

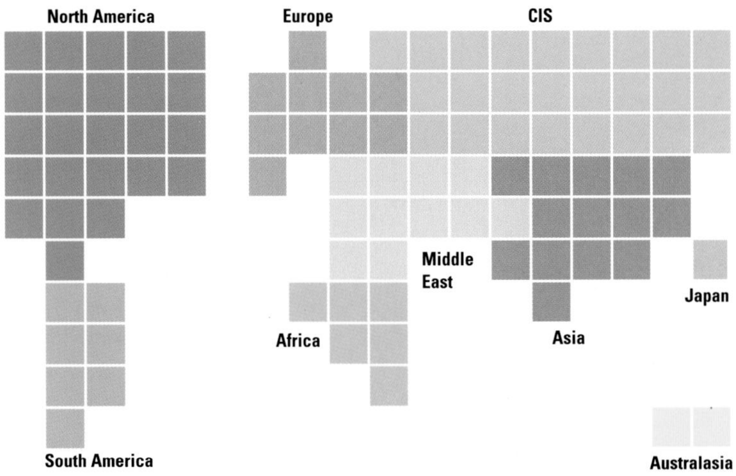

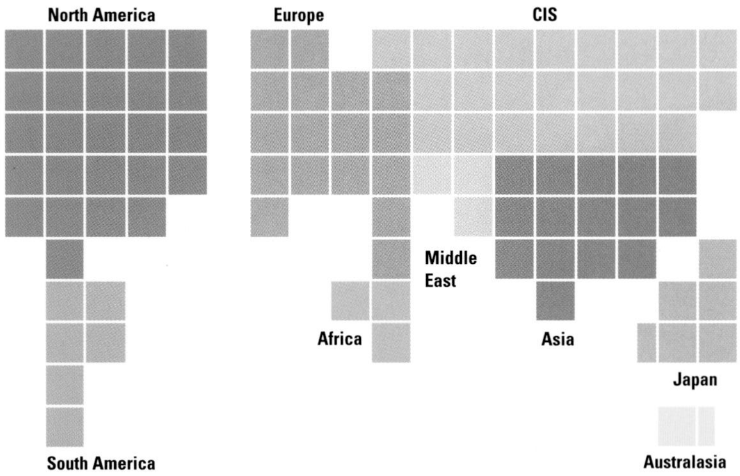

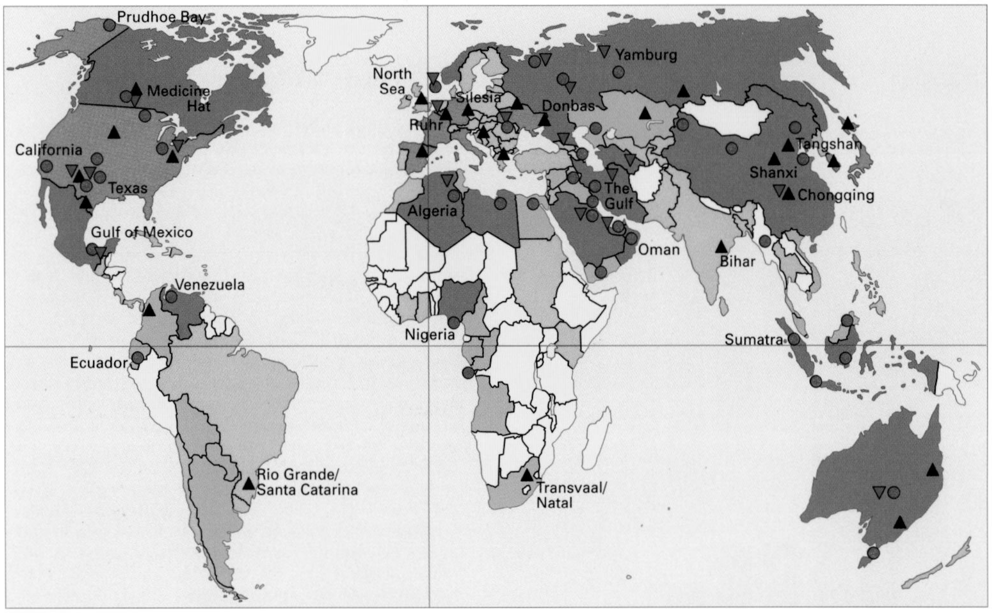

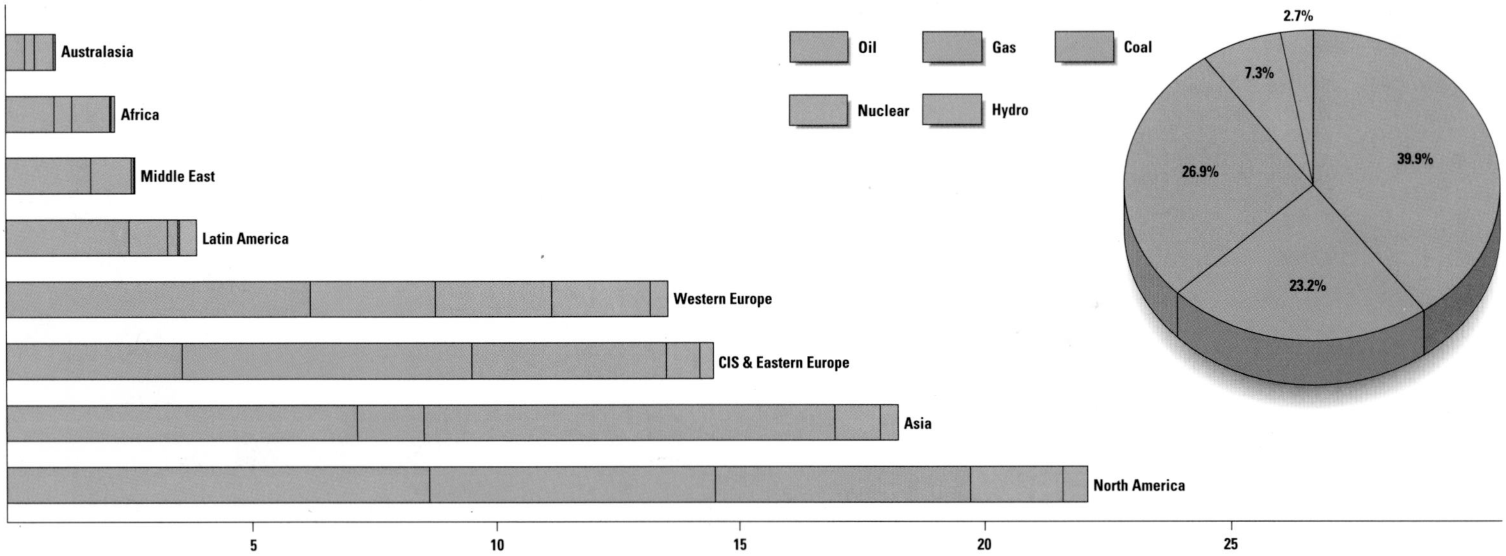

Oil   Gas   Coal

Nuclear   Hydro

Bar chart regions: Australasia, Africa, Middle East, Latin America, Western Europe, CIS & Eastern Europe, Asia, North America

Pie chart: 2.7%, 7.3%, 39.9%, 26.9%, 23.2%

Energy

Energy is used to keep us warm or cool, fuel our industries and our transport systems, and even feed us; high-intensity agriculture, with its use of fertilizers, pesticides and machinery, is heavily energy-dependent. Although we live in a high-energy society, there are vast discrepancies between rich and poor; for example, a North American consumes 13 times as much energy as a Chinese person. But even developing nations have more power at their disposal than was imaginable a century ago.

The distribution of energy supplies, most importantly fossil fuels (coal, oil and natural gas), is very uneven. In addition, the diagrams and map opposite show that the largest producers of energy are not necessarily the largest consumers. The movement of energy supplies around the world is therefore an important component of international trade. In 1995, total world movements in oil amounted to 1,815 million tonnes.

As the finite reserves of fossil fuels are depleted, renewable energy sources, such as solar, hydro-thermal, wind, tidal and biomass, will become increasingly important around the world.

Nuclear Power

Percentage of electricity generated by nuclear power stations, leading nations (1995)

1. Lithuania..............85%	11. Spain....................33%
2. France.................77%	12. Finland.................30%
3. Belgium...............56%	13. Germany.............29%
4. Slovak Rep. 49%	14. Japan..................29%
5. Sweden...............48%	15. UK.......................27%
6. Bulgaria..............41%	16. Ukraine...............27%
7. Hungary..............41%	17. Czech Rep. 22%
8. Switzerland.........39%	18. Canada...............19%
9. Slovenia..............38%	19. USA.....................18%
10. South Korea........33%	20. Russia.................12%

Although the 1980s were a bad time for the nuclear power industry (major projects ran over budget, and fears of long-term environmental damage were heavily reinforced by the 1986 disaster at Chernobyl), the industry picked up in the early 1990s. However, whilst the number of reactors is still increasing, orders for new plants have shrunk. This is partly due to the increasingly difficult task of disposing of nuclear waste.

Hydroelectricity

Percentage of electricity generated by hydroelectric power stations, leading nations (1995)

1. Paraguay...........99.9%	11. Rwanda.............97.6%
2. Congo (Zaïre)....99.7%	12. Malawi..............97.6%
3. Bhutan...............99.6%	13. Cameroon..........96.9%
4. Zambia...............99.5%	14. Nepal................96.7%
5. Norway.............99.4%	15. Laos..................95.3%
6. Ghana...............99.3%	16. Albania..............95.2%
7. Congo...............99.3%	17. Iceland..............94.0%
8. Uganda.............99.1%	18. Brazil 92.2%
9. Burundi............98.3%	19. Honduras..........87.6%
10. Uruguay...........98.0%	20. Tanzania...........87.1%

Countries heavily reliant on hydroelectricity are usually small and non-industrial: a high proportion of hydroelectric power more often reflects a modest energy budget than vast hydroelectric resources. The USA, for instance, produces only 9% of power requirements from hydroelectricity; yet that 9% amounts to more than three times the hydropower generated by all of Africa.

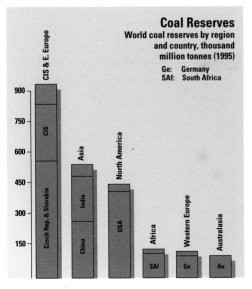

Fuel Exports

Fuels as a percentage of total value of exports (1990–94)

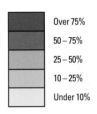

- Over 75%
- 50 – 75%
- 25 – 50%
- 10 – 25%
- Under 10%

Conversion Rates

1 barrel = 0.136 tonnes or 159 litres or 35 Imperial gallons or 42 US gallons

1 tonne = 7.33 barrels or 1,185 litres or 256 Imperial gallons or 261 US gallons

1 tonne oil = 1.5 tonnes hard coal or 3.0 tonnes lignite or 12,000 kWh

1 Imperial gallon = 1.201 US gallons or 4.546 litres or 277.4 cubic inches

Measurements

For historical reasons, oil is traded in 'barrels'. The weight and volume equivalents (shown right) are all based on average-density 'Arabian light' crude oil.

The energy equivalents given for a tonne of oil are also somewhat imprecise: oil and coal of different qualities will have varying energy contents, a fact usually reflected in their price on world markets.

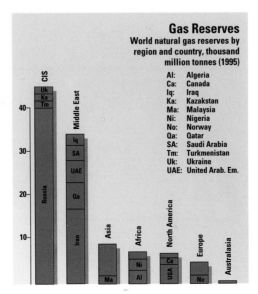

Coal Reserves

World coal reserves by region and country, thousand million tonnes (1995)

Ge: Germany
SAf: South Africa

Gas Reserves

World natural gas reserves by region and country, thousand million tonnes (1995)

Al: Algeria
Ca: Canada
Iq: Iraq
Ka: Kazakstan
Ma: Malaysia
Ni: Nigeria
No: Norway
Qa: Qatar
SA: Saudi Arabia
Tm: Turkmenistan
Uk: Ukraine
UAE: United Arab. Em.

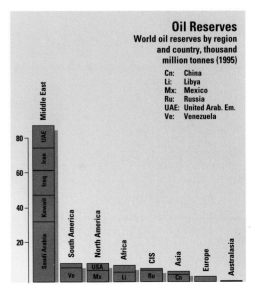

Oil Reserves

World oil reserves by region and country, thousand million tonnes (1995)

Cn: China
Li: Libya
Mx: Mexico
Ru: Russia
UAE: United Arab. Em.
Ve: Venezuela

Production

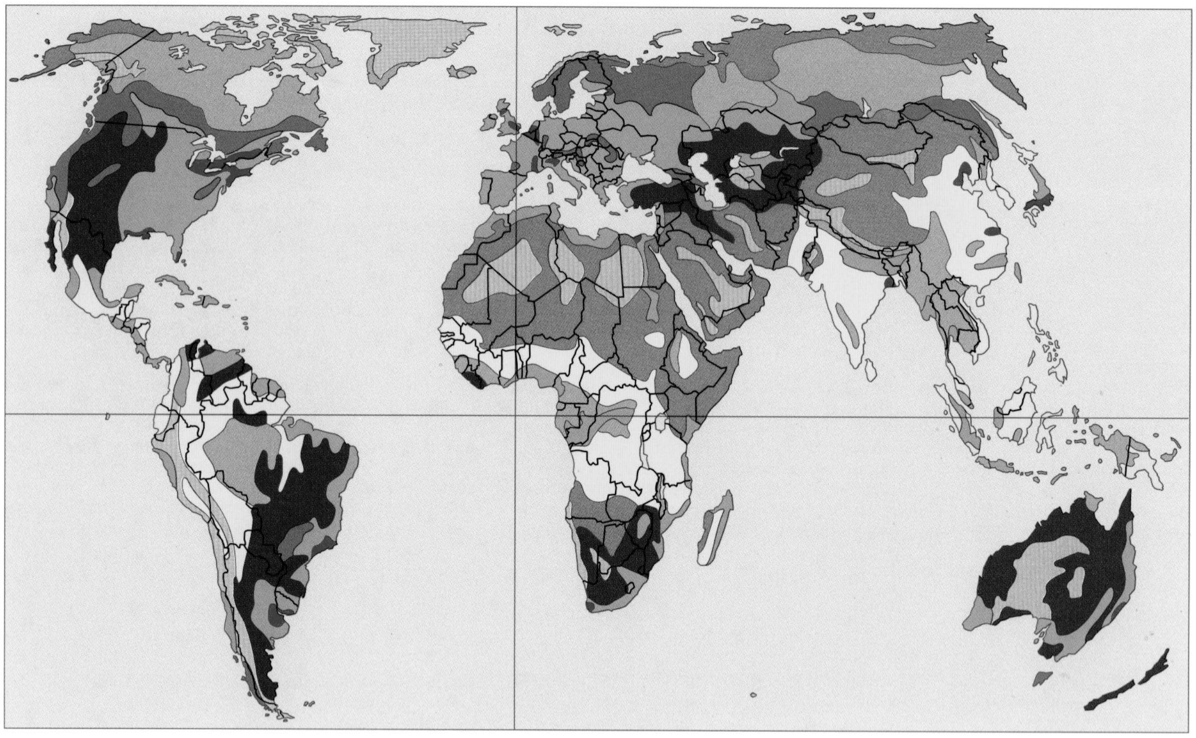

Agriculture

Predominant type of farming or land use.

- Nomadic herding
- Hunting, fishing and gathering
- Subsistence agriculture
- Commercial ranching
- Commercial livestock and grain farming
- Urban areas
- Forestry
- Unproductive land

The development of agriculture has transformed human existence more than any other. The whole business of farming is constantly developing: due mainly to the new varieties of rice and wheat, world grain production has increased by over 70% since 1965. New machinery and modern agricultural techniques enable relatively few farmers to produce enough food for the world's 6 billion or so people.

Staple Crops

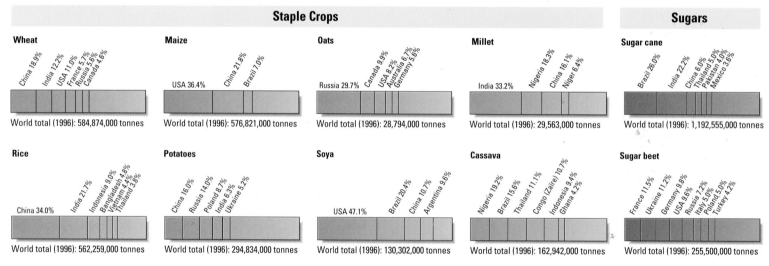

Wheat

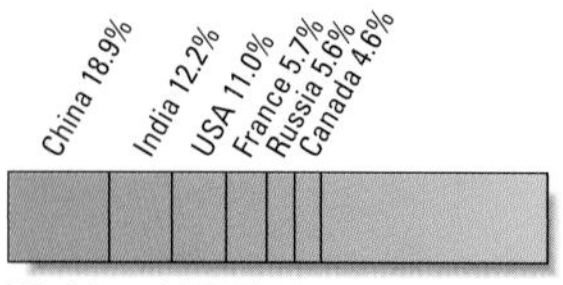

China 18.9% India 12.2% USA 11.0% France 5.7% Russia 5.6% Canada 4.6%

World total (1996): 584,874,000 tonnes

Maize

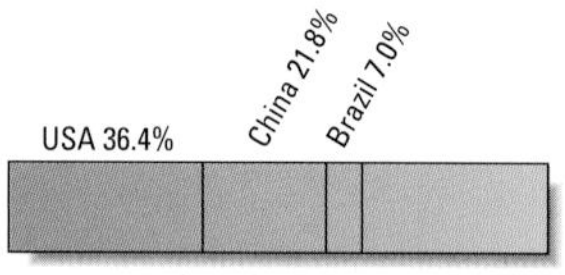

USA 36.4% China 21.8% Brazil 7.0%

World total (1996): 576,821,000 tonnes

Oats

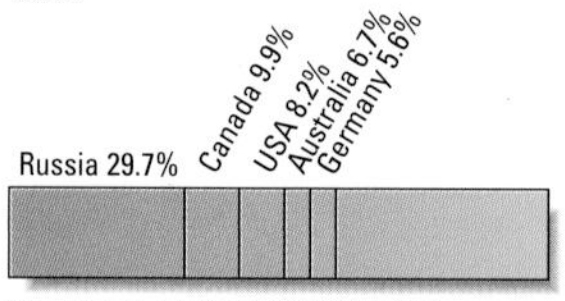

Russia 29.7% Canada 9.9% USA 8.2% Australia 6.7% Germany 5.6%

World total (1996): 28,794,000 tonnes

Millet

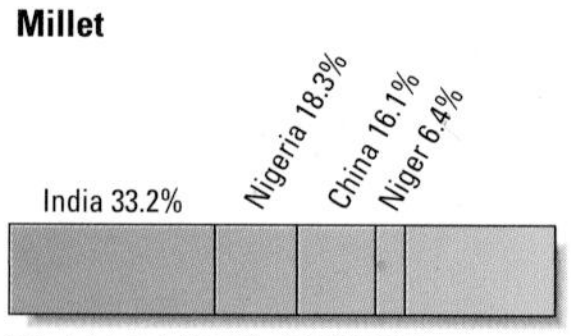

India 33.2% Nigeria 18.3% China 16.1% Niger 6.4%

World total (1996): 29,563,000 tonnes

Rice

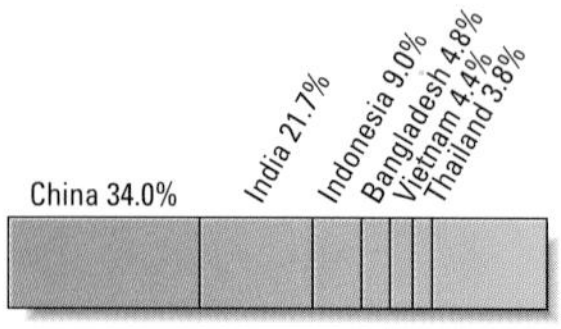

China 34.0% India 21.7% Indonesia 9.0% Bangladesh 4.8% Vietnam 4.4% Thailand 3.8%

World total (1996): 562,259,000 tonnes

Potatoes

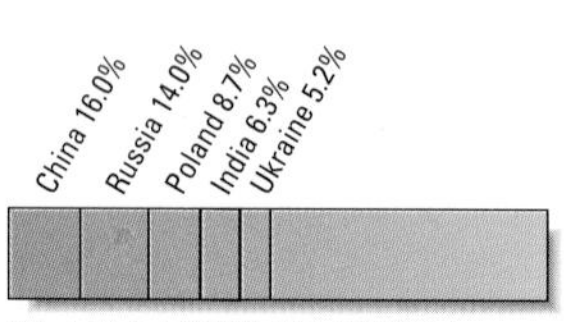

China 16.0% Russia 14.0% Poland 8.7% India 6.3% Ukraine 5.2%

World total (1996): 294,834,000 tonnes

Soya

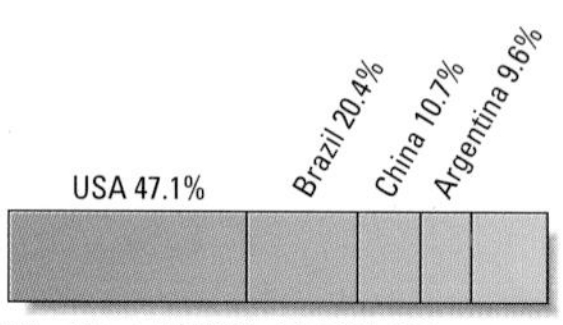

USA 47.1% Brazil 20.4% China 10.7% Argentina 9.6%

World total (1996): 130,302,000 tonnes

Cassava

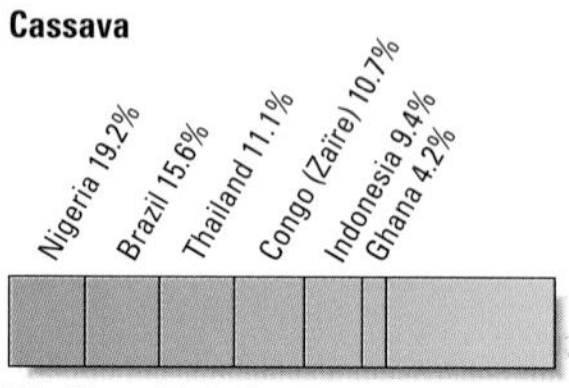

Nigeria 19.2% Brazil 15.6% Thailand 11.1% Congo (Zaire) 10.7% Indonesia 9.4% Ghana 4.2%

World total (1996): 162,942,000 tonnes

Sugars

Sugar cane

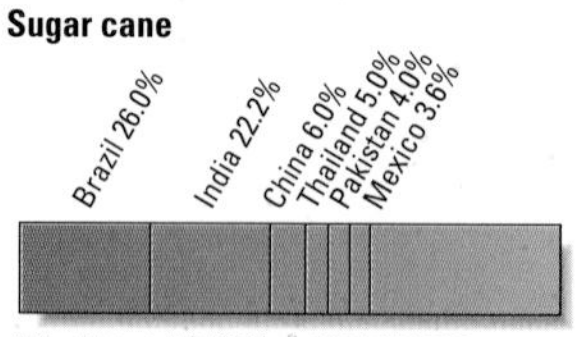

Brazil 26.0% India 22.2% China 6.0% Thailand 5.0% Pakistan 4.0% Mexico 3.6%

World total (1996): 1,192,555,000 tonnes

Sugar beet

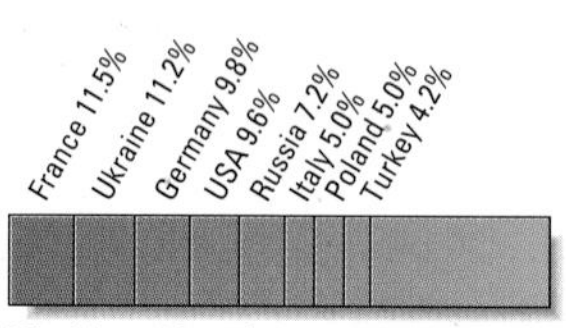

France 11.5% Ukraine 11.2% Germany 9.8% USA 9.6% Russia 7.2% Italy 5.0% Poland 5.0% Turkey 4.2%

World total (1996): 255,500,000 tonnes

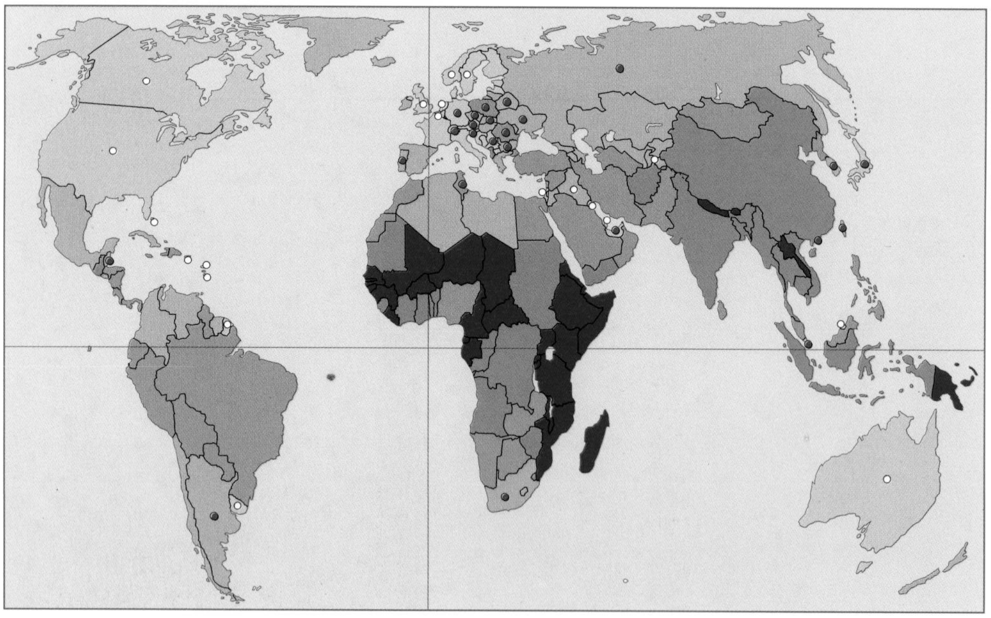

Balance of Employment

Percentage of total workforce employed in agriculture, including forestry and fishing (1990–92)

- Over 75% in agriculture
- 50 – 75% in agriculture
- 25 – 50% in agriculture
- 10 – 25% in agriculture
- Under 10% in agriculture

Employment in industry and services

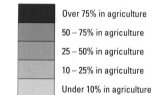

- Over a third of total workforce employed in manufacturing
- Over two-thirds of total workforce employed in service industries (work in offices, shops, tourism, transport, construction and government)

Mineral Production

*Figures for aluminium are for refined metal; all other figures refer to ore production.

Copper
Chile 26.9% | USA 19.9% | Canada 7.8% | Indonesia 5.1% | Australia 4.8% | China 4.7% | Poland 4.6% | Zambia 3.7%

World total (1995): 9,311,000 tonnes*

Iron
China 15.0% | Brazil 11.9% | Australia 9.0% | Russia 4.3% | India 3.9% | USA

World total (1995): 1,020,000 tonnes*

Chromium
S. Africa 35.9% | Kazakstan 20.2% | India 9.1% | Turkey 7.9% | Finland 5.8% | Zimbabwe 5.2%

World total (1994): 10,000,000 tonnes*

Gold
S. Africa 22.9% | USA 14.5% | Australia 11.2% | Canada 6.6% | Russia 6.2% | China 6.0%

World total (1995): 2,275 tonnes*

Uranium
Canada 31.9% | Australia 11.3% | Niger 8.8% | USA 7.2% | Russia 6.4% | Uzbekistan 6.1% | S. Africa 5.0% | Kazakstan 4.9%

World total (1995): 32,976 tonnes*

Lead
Australia 18.4% | USA 14.3% | Peru 8.5% | China 7.7% | Mexico 5.9%

World total (1995): 2,751,000 tonnes*

Tin
China 27.7% | Indonesia 23.6% | Peru 11.4% | Brazil 9.9% | Bolivia 7.4% | Russia 4.6%

World total (1995): 195,000 tonnes*

Manganese
S. Africa 17.3% | China 16.9% | Ukraine 15.0% | Australia 14.0% | Brazil 12.8% | Gabon 9.6%

World total (1994): 7,000,000 tonnes*

Silver
Mexico 18.1% | Peru 13.8% | USA 10.5% | Canada 9.0% | Chile 7.5% | Australia 6.7%

World total (1995): 13,800 tonnes*

Aluminium
USA 28.9% | Canada 9.9% | China 8.2% | Australia 5.9% | Brazil 5.7%

World total (1995): 22,706,000 tonnes*

Mercury
Spain 52.8% | China 19.4% | Algeria 10.3% | Kyrgyzstan 6.0% | Finland 3.2%

World total (1995): 2,837 tonnes*

Zinc
Canada 16.5% | Australia 13.9% | China 11.3% | Peru 10.2% | USA 8.9% | Mexico 5.0%

World total (1995): 6,728,000 tonnes*

Nickel
Russia 24.8% | Canada 18.7% | New Caledonia 13.8% | Australia 10.2% | Indonesia 9.0%

World total (1995): 967,000 tonnes*

Diamonds
Australia 37.8% | Congo (Zaire) 18.5% | Botswana 15.6% | Russia 11.6% | South Africa 8.4%

World total (1995): 107,900,000 carats

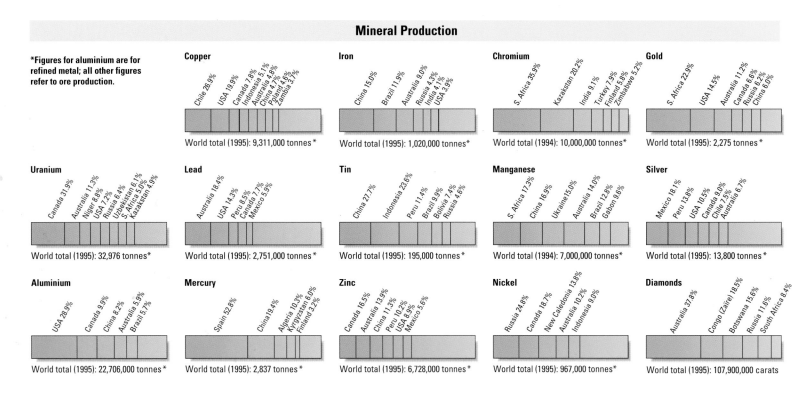

Mineral Distribution

The map shows the richest sources of the most important minerals. Major mineral locations are named.

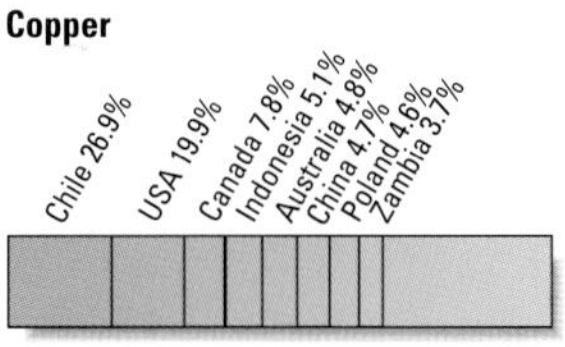

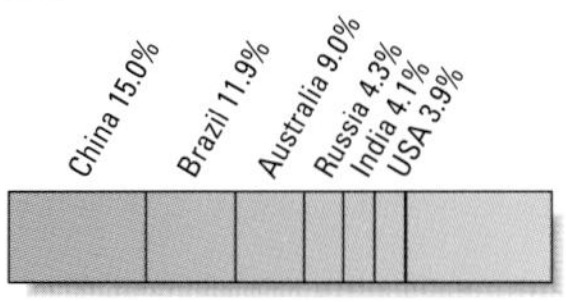

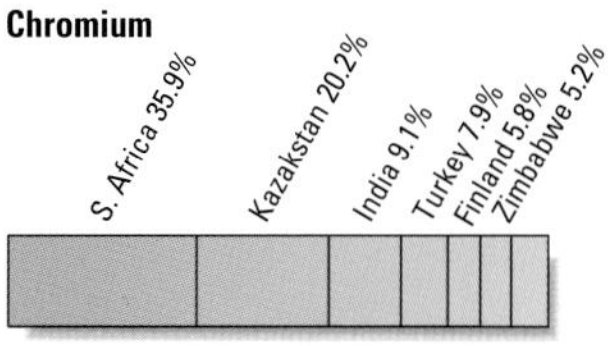

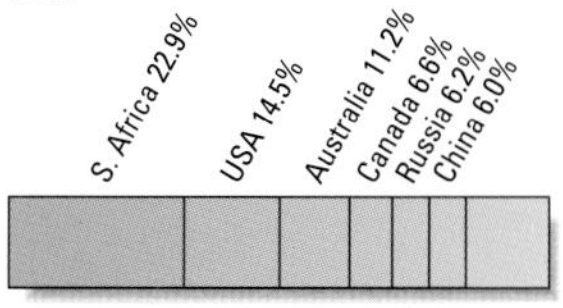

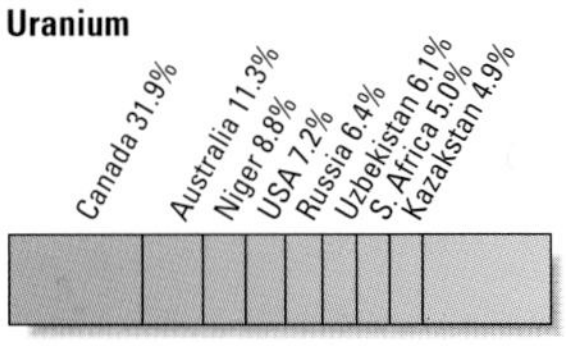

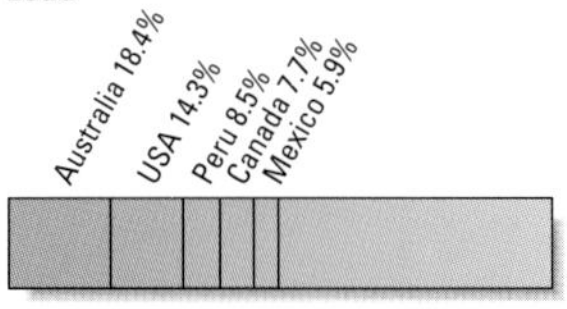

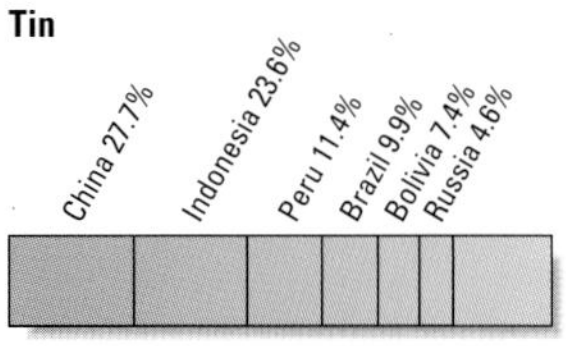

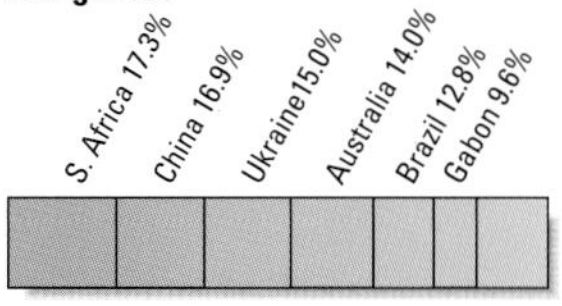

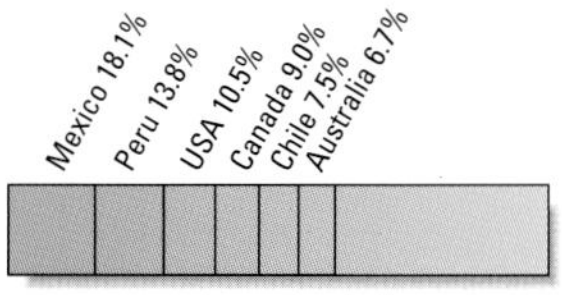

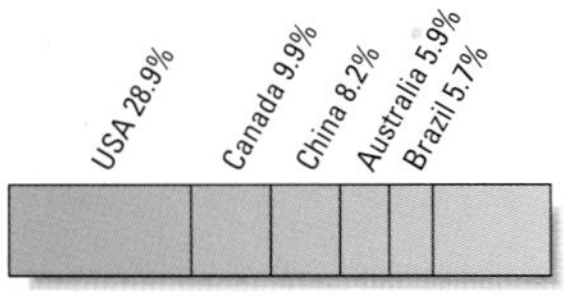

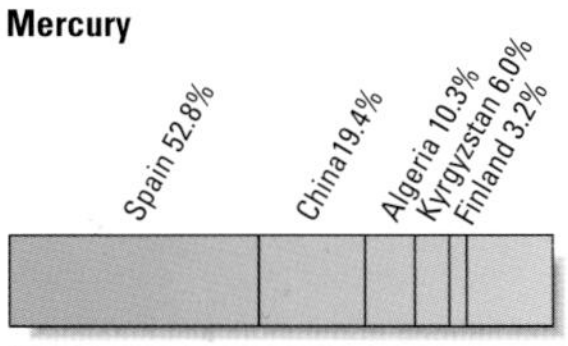

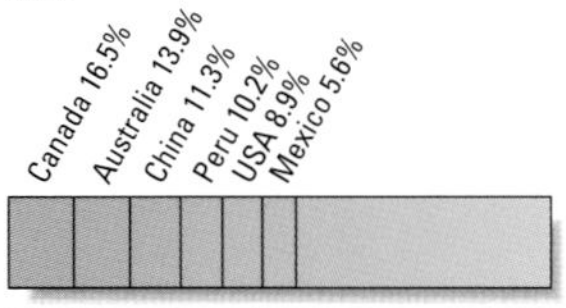

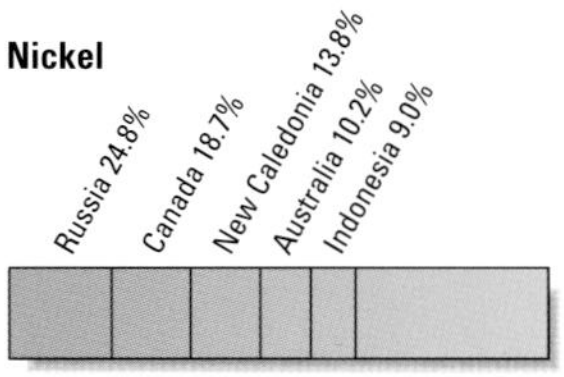

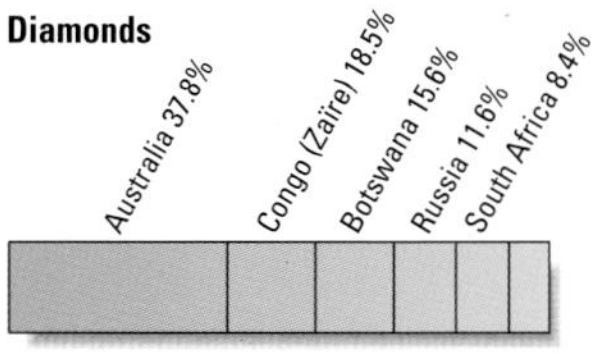

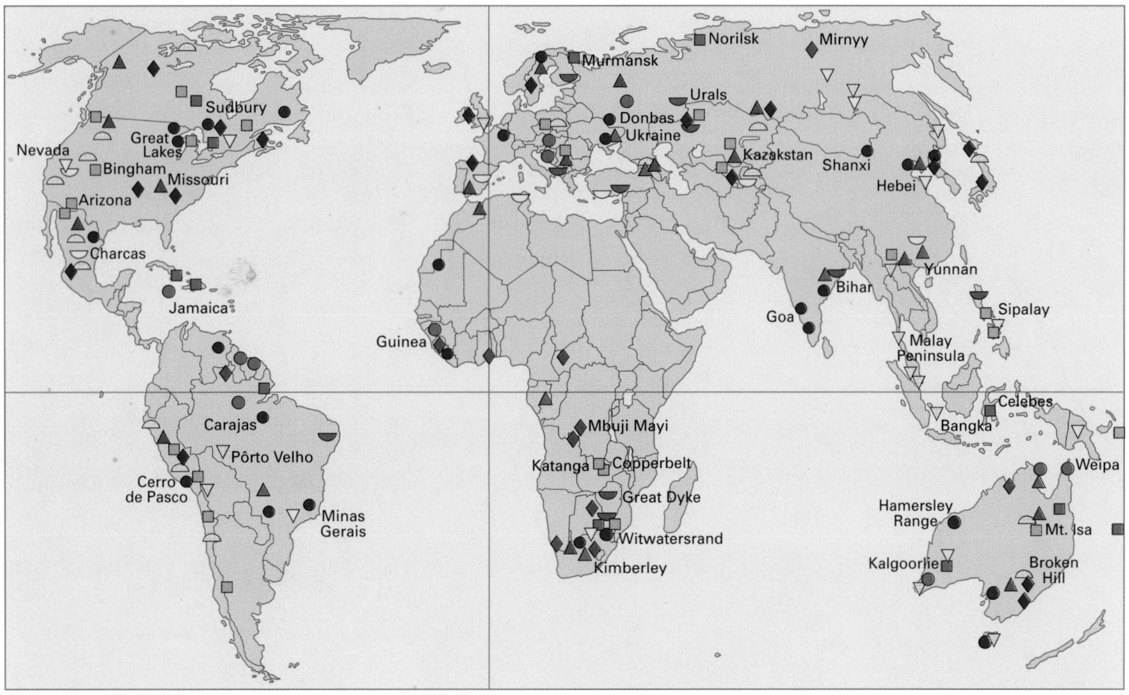

Light metals
- ● Bauxite

Base metals
- ■ Copper
- ▲ Lead
- ▽ Mercury
- ▽ Tin
- ◆ Zinc

Iron and ferro-alloys
- ● Iron
- ◣ Chrome
- ▲ Manganese
- ■ Nickel

Precious metals
- ▽ Gold
- ◠ Silver

Precious stones
- ◆ Diamonds

The map does not show undersea deposits, most of which are considered inaccessible.

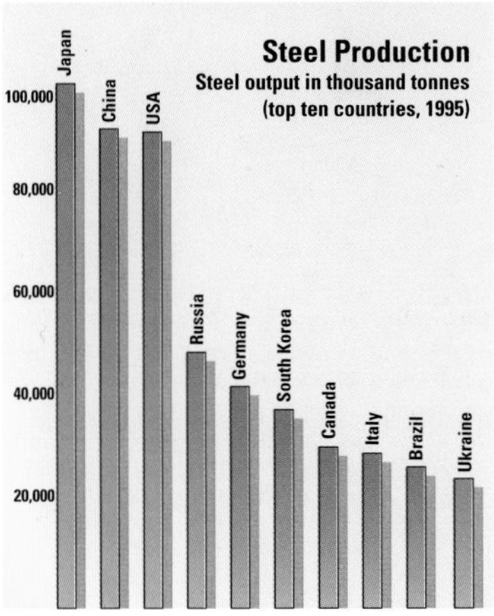

Steel Production
Steel output in thousand tonnes (top ten countries, 1995)

Japan, China, USA, Russia, Germany, South Korea, Canada, Italy, Brazil, Ukraine

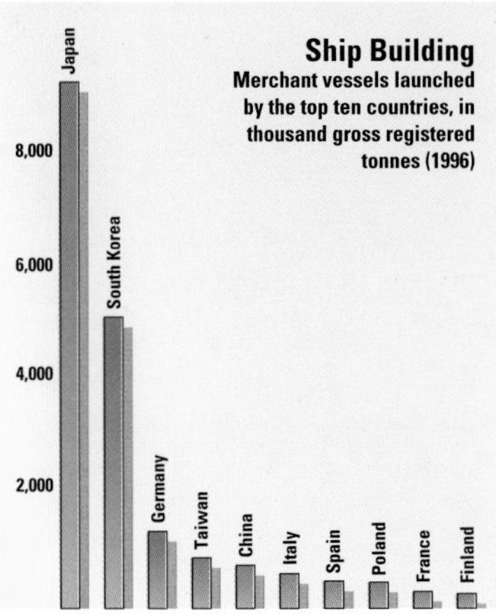

Ship Building
Merchant vessels launched by the top ten countries, in thousand gross registered tonnes (1996)

Japan, South Korea, Germany, Taiwan, China, Italy, Spain, Poland, France, Finland

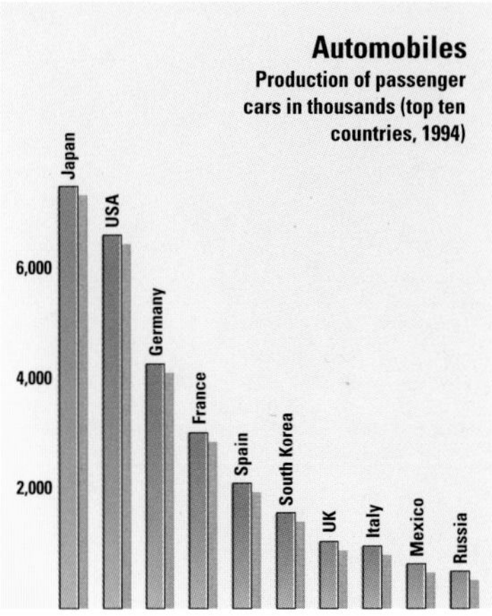

Automobiles
Production of passenger cars in thousands (top ten countries, 1994)

Japan, USA, Germany, France, Spain, South Korea, UK, Italy, Mexico, Russia

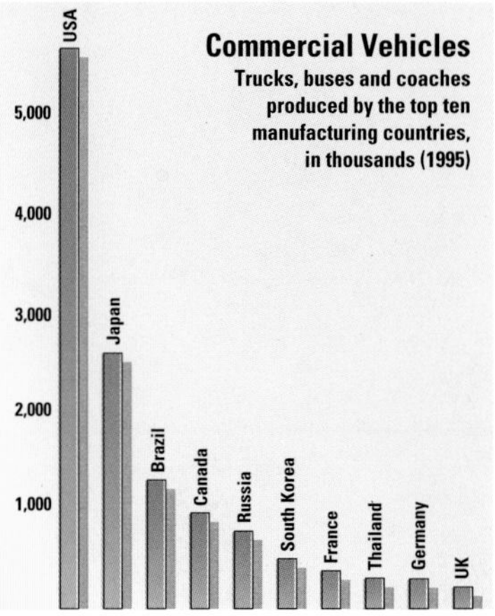

Commercial Vehicles
Trucks, buses and coaches produced by the top ten manufacturing countries, in thousands (1995)

USA, Japan, Brazil, Canada, Russia, South Korea, France, Thailand, Germany, UK

Trade

Share of World Trade

Percentage share of total world exports by value (1996)

Over 10% of world trade

5 – 10% of world trade

1 – 5% of world trade

0.5 – 1% of world trade

0.1 – 0.5% of world trade

Under 0.1% of world trade

International trade is dominated by a handful of powerful maritime nations. The members of 'G8', the inner circle of OECD (see page 19), and the top seven countries listed in the diagram below, account for more than half the total. The majority of nations – including all but four in Africa – contribute less than one quarter of 1% to the worldwide total of exports; the EU countries account for 40%, the Pacific Rim nations over 35%.

The Main Trading Nations

The imports and exports of the top ten trading nations as a percentage of world trade (1994). Each country's trade in manufactured goods is shown in dark blue.

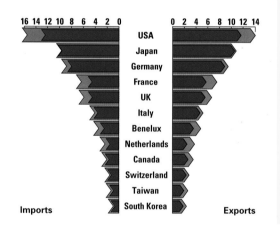

16 14 12 10 8 6 4 2 0   0 2 4 6 8 10 12 14

USA
Japan
Germany
France
UK
Italy
Benelux
Netherlands
Canada
Switzerland
Taiwan
South Korea

Imports   Exports

Patterns of Trade

Thriving international trade is the outward sign of a healthy world economy, the obvious indicator that some countries have goods to sell and others the means to buy them. Global exports expanded to an estimated US $3.92 trillion in 1994, an increase due partly to economic recovery in industrial nations but also to export-led growth strategies in many developing nations and lowered regional trade barriers. International trade remains dominated, however, by the rich, industrialized countries of the Organization for Economic Development: between them, OECD members account for almost 75% of world imports and exports in most years. However, continued rapid economic growth in some developing countries is altering global trade patterns. The 'tiger economies' of South-east Asia are particularly vibrant, averaging more than 8% growth between 1992 and 1994. The size of the largest trading economies means that imports and exports usually represent only a small percentage of their total wealth. In export-concious Japan, for example, trade in goods and services amounts to less than 18% of GDP. In poorer countries, trade – often in a single commodity – may amount to 50% of GDP.

Traded Products

Top ten manufactures traded, by value in billions of US $ (latest available year)

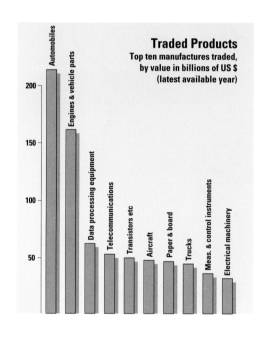

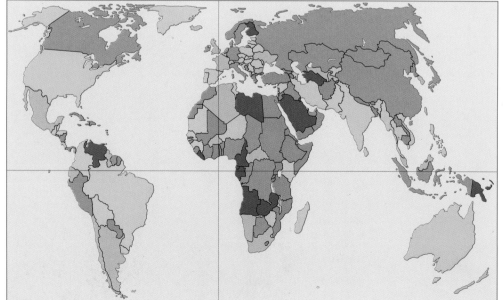

Balance of Trade

Value of exports in proportion to the value of imports (1995)

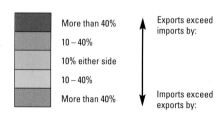

More than 40%

10 – 40%

10% either side

10 – 40%

More than 40%

Exports exceed imports by:

Imports exceed exports by:

The total world trade balance should amount to zero, since exports must equal imports on a global scale. In practice, at least $100 billion in exports go unrecorded, leaving the world with an apparent deficit and many countries in a better position than public accounting reveals. However, a favourable trade balance is not necessarily a sign of prosperity: many poorer countries must maintain a high surplus in order to service debts, and do so by restricting imports below the levels needed to sustain successful economies.

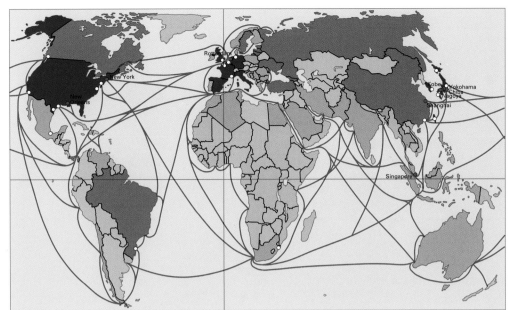

Freight unloaded in millions of tonnes (latest available year)

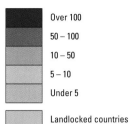

- Over 100
- 50 – 100
- 10 – 50
- 5 – 10
- Under 5
- Landlocked countries

Major seaports

- ● Over 100 million tonnes per year
- ○ 50–100 million tonnes per year
- ── Major shipping routes

Cargoes

Type of seaborne freight

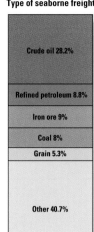

- Crude oil 28.2%
- Refined petroleum 8.8%
- Iron ore 9%
- Coal 8%
- Grain 5.3%
- Other 40.7%

Merchant Fleets

Merchant fleets in thousand gross tonnage (1994). A large number of vessels are registered in Liberia and Panama but they are not part of the national fleet.

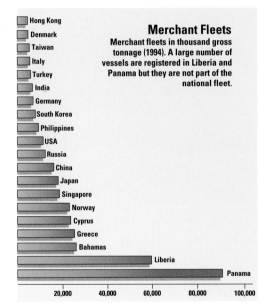

Hong Kong, Denmark, Taiwan, Italy, Turkey, India, Germany, South Korea, Philippines, USA, Russia, China, Japan, Singapore, Norway, Cyprus, Greece, Bahamas, Liberia, Panama

20,000 40,000 60,000 80,000 100,000

The Great Ports

Total Cargo Traffic (1995) '000 tonnes

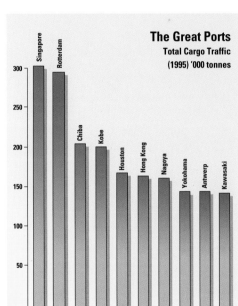

Singapore, Rotterdam, Chiba, Kobe, Houston, Hong Kong, Nagoya, Yokohama, Antwerp, Kawasaki

World Shipping

World merchant fleet by type of vessel and deadweight tonnage (latest available year)

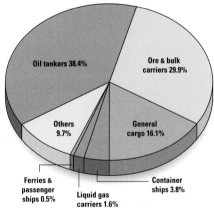

- Oil tankers 38.4%
- Ore & bulk carriers 29.9%
- General cargo 16.1%
- Others 9.7%
- Container ships 3.8%
- Liquid gas carriers 1.6%
- Ferries & passenger ships 0.5%

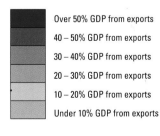

Dependence on Trade

Value of exports as a percentage of Gross Domestic Product (1997)

- Over 50% GDP from exports
- 40 – 50% GDP from exports
- 30 – 40% GDP from exports
- 20 – 30% GDP from exports
- 10 – 20% GDP from exports
- Under 10% GDP from exports

- ○ Most dependent on industrial exports (over 75% of total exports)
- ● Most dependent on fuel exports (over 75% of total exports)
- ● Most dependent on mineral and metal exports (over 75% of total exports)

Travel and Tourism

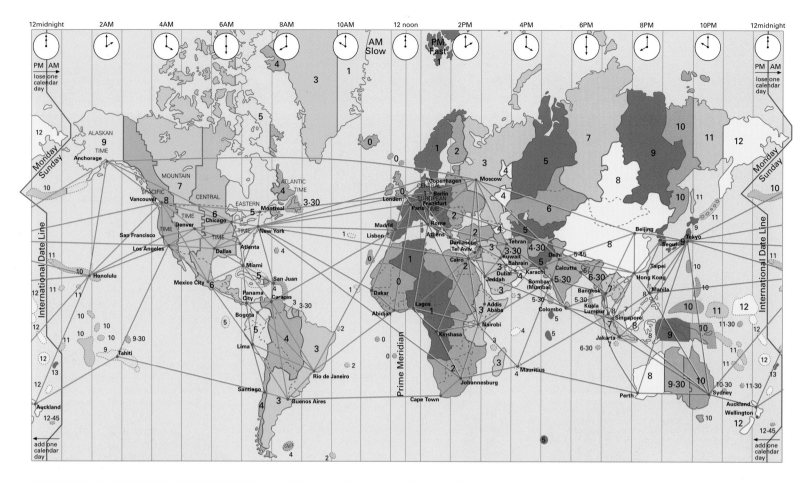

Time Zones

Zones using GMT	Zones fast of GMT	Certain time zones are affected by the incidence of 'summer time' in countries where it is adopted.	
Zones slow of GMT	Half-hour zones		
- - - International boundaries	Time zone boundaries	Actual Solar Time, when it is noon at Greenwich, is shown along the top of the map.	
10 Hours slow or fast of GMT	International Date Line		
	Selected air routes		

The world is divided into 24 time zones, each centred on meridians at 15° intervals, which is the longitudinal distance the sun travels every hour. The meridian running through Greenwich, London, passes through the middle of the first zone.

Rail and Road: The Leading Nations

Total rail network ('000 km) (1995)	Passenger km per head per year	Total road network ('000 km)	Vehicle km per head per year	Number of vehicles per km of roads
1. USA 235.7	Japan 2,017	USA 6,277.9	USA....................12,505	Hong Kong 284
2. Russia 87.4	Belarus.............1,880	India 2,962.5	Luxembourg 7,989	Taiwan 211
3. India 62.7	Russia 1,826	Brazil 1,824.4	Kuwait 7,251	Singapore 152
4. China.................54.6	Switzerland 1,769	Japan 1,130.9	France 7,142	Kuwait................140
5. Germany............41.7	Ukraine.............1,456	China 1,041.1	Sweden 6,991	Brunei..................96
6. Australia 35.8	Austria.............1,168	Russia 884.0	Germany 6,806	Italy 91
7. Argentina 34.2	France 1,011	Canada 849.4	Denmark 6,764	Israel 87
8. France...............31.9	Netherlands 994	France 811.6	Austria.................6,518	Thailand 73
9. Mexico..............26.5	Latvia................918	Australia 810.3	Netherlands 5,984	Ukraine.................73
10. South Africa 26.3	Denmark 884	Germany 636.3	UK 5,738	UK 67
11. Poland..............24.9	Slovak Rep. 862	Romania............461.9	Canada 5,493	Netherlands 66
12. Ukraine 22.6	Romania 851	Turkey 388.1	Italy.....................4,852	Germany 62

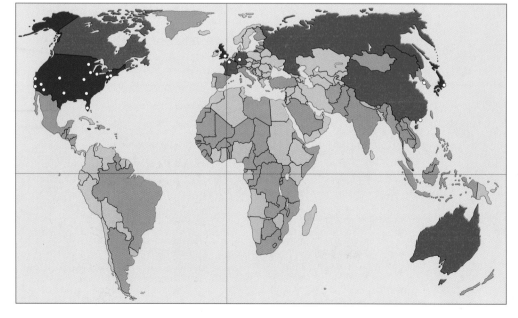

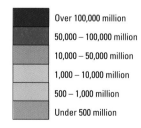

Air Travel

Passenger kilometres (the number of passengers – international and domestic – multiplied by the distance flown by each passenger from the airport of origin) (1996)

	Over 100,000 million
	50,000 – 100,000 million
	10,000 – 50,000 million
	1,000 – 10,000 million
	500 – 1,000 million
	Under 500 million

○ Major airports (handling over 25 million passengers in 1995)

World's busiest airports (total passengers)		World's busiest airports (international passengers)	
1. Chicago	(O'Hare)	1. London	(Heathrow)
2. Atlanta	(Hatsfield)	2. London	(Gatwick)
3. Dallas	(Dallas/Ft Worth)	3. Frankfurt	(International)
4. Los Angeles	(Intern'l)	4. New York	(Kennedy)
5. London	(Heathrow)	5. Paris	(De Gaulle)

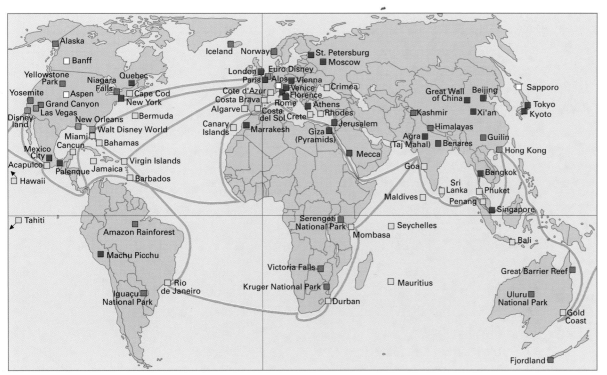

Destinations

- ■ Cultural and historical centres
- □ Coastal resorts
- □ Ski resorts
- ▨ Centres of entertainment
- ■ Places of pilgrimage
- ▨ Places of great natural beauty
- — Popular holiday cruise routes

Visitors to the USA

Overseas travellers to the USA, thousands (1997 estimates)

1.	Canada	13,900
2.	Mexico	12,370
3.	Japan	4,640
4.	UK	3,350
5.	Germany	1,990
6.	France	1,030
7.	Taiwan	885
8.	Venezuela	860
9.	South Korea	800
10.	Brazil	785

In 1996, the USA earned the most from tourism, with receipts of more than US $75 billion.

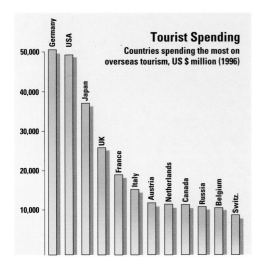

Tourist Spending

Countries spending the most on overseas tourism, US $ million (1996)

Importance of Tourism

		Arrivals from abroad (1996)	% of world total (1996)
1.	France	66,800,000	10.2%
2.	USA	49,038,000	7.5%
3.	Spain	43,403,000	6.6%
4.	Italy	34,087,000	5.2%
5.	UK	25,960,000	3.9%
6.	China	23,770,000	3.6%
7.	Poland	19,514,000	3.0%
8.	Mexico	18,667,000	2.9%
9.	Canada	17,610,000	2.7%
10.	Czech Republic	17,400,000	2.7%
11.	Hungary	17,248,000	2.6%
12.	Austria	16,642,000	2.5%

In 1996, there was a 4.6% rise, to 593 million, in the total number of people travelling abroad. Small economies in attractive areas are often completely dominated by tourism: in some West Indian islands, for example, tourist spending provides over 90% of total income.

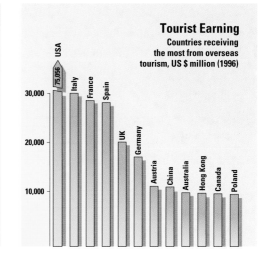

Tourist Earning

Countries receiving the most from overseas tourism, US $ million (1996)

Tourism

Tourism receipts as a percentage of Gross National Product (1994)

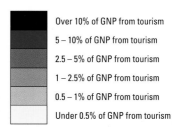

- ■ Over 10% of GNP from tourism
- ▨ 5 – 10% of GNP from tourism
- ▨ 2.5 – 5% of GNP from tourism
- ▨ 1 – 2.5% of GNP from tourism
- ▨ 0.5 – 1% of GNP from tourism
- □ Under 0.5% of GNP from tourism

Countries spending the most on promoting tourism, millions of US $ (1996)

Australia	88
Spain	79
UK	79
France	73
Singapore	54

Fastest growing tourist destinations, % change in receipts (1994–5)

South Korea	49%
Czech Republic	27%
India	21%
Russia	19%
Philippines	18%

The World In Focus: Index

WORLD MAPS

SETTLEMENTS

■ **PARIS**　　■ **Berne**　　◉ Livorno　　◎ Brugge　　⊙ Algeciras　　○ *Frejus*　　○ *Oberammergau*　　○ *Thira*

Settlement symbols and type styles vary according to the scale of each map and indicate the importance of towns on the map rather than specific population figures

∴　Ruins or Archæological Sites　　　　　　ᵛ　Wells in Desert

ADMINISTRATION

——————　International Boundaries

– – – –　International Boundaries (Undefined or Disputed)

·············　Internal Boundaries

National Parks

Country Names
NICARAGUA

Administrative Area Names

KENT

CALABRIA

International boundaries show the *de facto* situation where there are rival claims to territory

COMMUNICATIONS

——————　Principal Roads

———　Other Roads

┼╌╌┼　Road Tunnels

⤙　Passes

⊕　Airfields

———　Principal Railways

– – –　Railways Under Construction

———　Other Railways

┼╌╌┼　Railway Tunnels

·············　Principal Canals

PHYSICAL FEATURES

～～～　Perennial Streams

– –＿　Intermittent Streams

◯　Perennial Lakes

⬯　Intermittent Lakes

Swamps and Marshes

Permanent Ice and Glaciers

▲ 8848　Elevations in metres

▼ 8500　Sea Depths in metres

1134　Height of Lake Surface Above Sea Level in metres

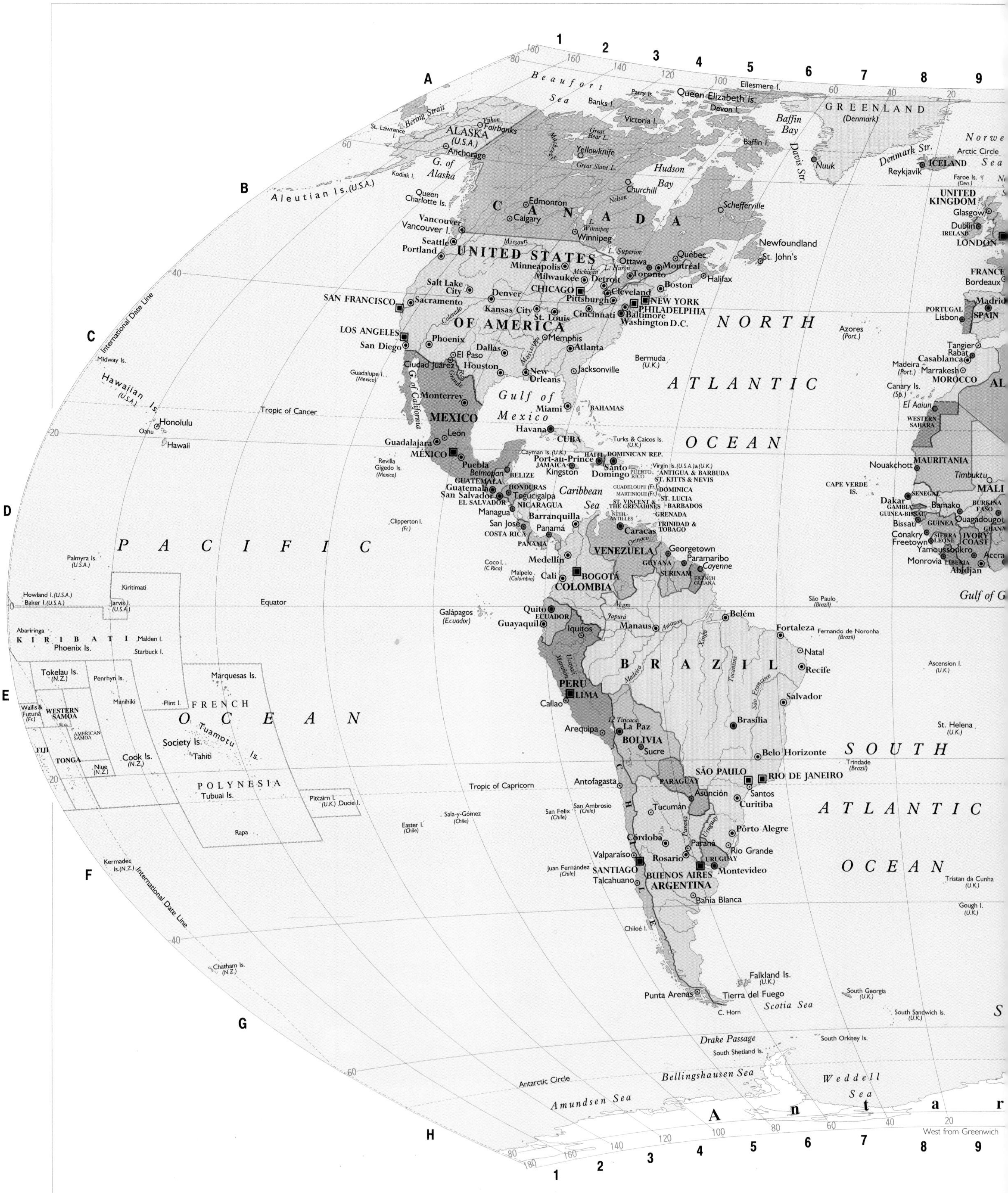

A

Beaufort Sea

Queen Elizabeth Is.
Ellesmere I.
GREENLAND
(Denmark)

Banks I.
Parry Is.
Devon I.
Norwe

Victoria I.
Baffin
Bay
Arctic Circle

St. Lawrence I.
Bering Strait
Yukon
Fairbanks
ALASKA
(U.S.A.)
Anchorage
Great
Bear L.
Mackenzie
Great Slave L.
Yellowknife
Baffin I.
Davis Str.
Denmark Str.
Nuuk
ICELAND
Reykjavik
Faroe Is.
(Den.)
Sea

B

Aleutian Is. (U.S.A.)
Kodiak I.
G. of
Alaska
Queen
Charlotte Is.
Hudson
Bay
Churchill
Nelson
Scheffervlle
UNITED
KINGDOM
Glasgow
Dublin
IRELAND
LONDON

Vancouver
Vancouver I.
Seattle
Portland
CANADA
Edmonton
Calgary
Winnipeg
Winnipeg
L. Superior
Ottawa
Québec
St. John's
Newfoundland
FRANCE
Bordeaux

Salt Lake
City
UNITED STATES
Minneapolis
Milwaukee
L. Michigan
L. Huron
Detroit
Toronto
Montréal
Boston
Halifax
PORTUGAL
Lisbon
Madrid
SPAIN

SAN FRANCISCO
Sacramento
Denver
CHICAGO
Pittsburgh
Cleveland
NEW YORK
PHILADELPHIA
Baltimore
Washington D.C.
NORTH
Azores
(Port.)

C

LOS ANGELES
San Diego
Phoenix
Kansas City
St. Louis
Cincinnati
OF AMERICA
Dallas
Memphis
Atlanta
Bermuda
(U.K.)
ATLANTIC
Tangier
Casablanca
Rabat
MOROCCO
AL

El Paso
Ciudad Juárez
Houston
New
Orleans
Jacksonville
Madeira
(Port.)
Marrakesh
Canary Is.
(Sp.)
El Aaiun
WESTERN
SAHARA

Guadalupe I.
(Mexico)
Colorado
G. of California
Monterrey
Gulf of
Mexico
Miami
BAHAMAS
OCEAN

Tropic of Cancer

Hawaiian Is.
(U.S.A.)
Honolulu
Oahu
Hawaii
MEXICO
León
Havana
CUBA
Turks & Caicos Is.
(U.K.)
MAURITANIA
Nouakchott
Timbuktu

Guadalajara
MÉXICO
Puebla
Belmopan
BELIZE
Port-au-Prince
HAITI
JAMAICA
Kingston
DOMINICAN REP.
Santo
Domingo
PUERTO
RICO
Virgin Is. (U.S.A.)&(U.K.)
ANTIGUA & BARBUDA
ST. KITTS & NEVIS
CAPE VERDE
IS.
Dakar
SENEGAL
MALI

Revilla
Gigedo Is.
(Mexico)
GUATEMALA
HONDURAS
Tegucigalpa
San Salvador
EL SALVADOR
NICARAGUA
Managua
GUADELOUPE (Fr.)
DOMINICA
MARTINIQUE (Fr.)
ST. LUCIA
ST. VINCENT &
THE GRENADINES
BARBADOS
GUINEA-BISSAU
GAMBIA
BURKINA
FASO
Bamako
Ouagadougou

D

Clipperton I.
(Fr.)
San José
COSTA RICA
Panamá
Barranquilla
Caribbean
Sea
GRENADA
TRINIDAD &
TOBAGO
NTH.
ANTILLES
Bissau
Conakry
SIERRA
LEONE
IVORY
COAST
Yamoussoukro

PACIFIC
PANAMA
Medellín
Caracas
VENEZUELA
Georgetown
Paramaribo
GUYANA
SURINAM
FRENCH
GUIANA
Cayenne
Freetown
Monrovia
LIBERIA
Accra
Abidjan

Palmyra I.
(U.S.A.)
Coco I.
(C.Rica)
Cali
Malpelo I.
(Colombia)
BOGOTÁ
COLOMBIA
São Paulo
(Brazil)
Gulf of G

Howland I. (U.S.A.)
Baker I. (U.S.A.)
Kiritimati
Equator
Galápagos
(Ecuador)
Quito
ECUADOR
Guayaquil
Iquitos
Napo
Manaus
Amazon
Belém
Fortaleza
Fernando de Noronha
(Brazil)

Abariringa
KIRIBATI
Malden I.
Jarvis I.
(U.S.A.)
Phoenix Is.
Starbuck I.
Japurá
Madeira
Natal
Ascension I.
(U.K.)

E

Tokelau Is.
(N.Z.)
Penrhyn Is.
Manihiki
Marquesas Is.
Flint I.
FRENCH
PERU
LIMA
Callao
BRAZIL
Xingu
Tocantins
São Francisco
Recife
Salvador

Wallis &
Futuna
(Fr.)
WESTERN
SAMOA
AMERICAN
SAMOA
OCEAN
Tuamotu
Society Is.
Tahiti
Arequipa
L. Titicaca
La Paz
BOLIVIA
Sucre
Madeira
St. Helena
(U.K.)
SOUTH

FIJI
TONGA
Niue
(N.Z.)
Cook Is.
(N.Z.)
POLYNESIA
Tubuai Is.
Tropic of Capricorn
Antofagasta
PARAGUAY
Asunción
Curitiba
Santos
SÃO PAULO
RIO DE JANEIRO
Belo Horizonte
Brasília
Trindade
(Brazil)
ATLANTIC

Kermadec
Is. (N.Z.)
Chatham Is.
(N.Z.)
Easter I.
(Chile)
Sala-y-Gómez
(Chile)
San Ambrosio
(Chile)
San Felix
(Chile)
Tucumán
Paraná
Pôrto Alegre
Rio Grande
Córdoba
Paraná
Pitcairn I.
(U.K.)
Ducie I.
Rapa
URUGUAY
Montevideo
Tristan da Cunha
(U.K.)
OCEAN

F

International Date Line
Juan Fernández
(Chile)
Valparaíso
SANTIAGO
Talcahuano
Rosario
BUENOS AIRES
ARGENTINA
Bahía Blanca
Gough I.
(U.K.)

Chiloé I.

Falkland Is.
(U.K.)
South Georgia
(U.K.)

G

Punta Arenas
Tierra del Fuego
C. Horn
Scotia Sea
South Sandwich Is.
(U.K.)
S

Drake Passage
South Orkney Is.
South Shetland Is.
Bellingshausen Sea
Weddell
Sea

Antarctic Circle
Amundsen Sea
Antar

H
West from Greenwich

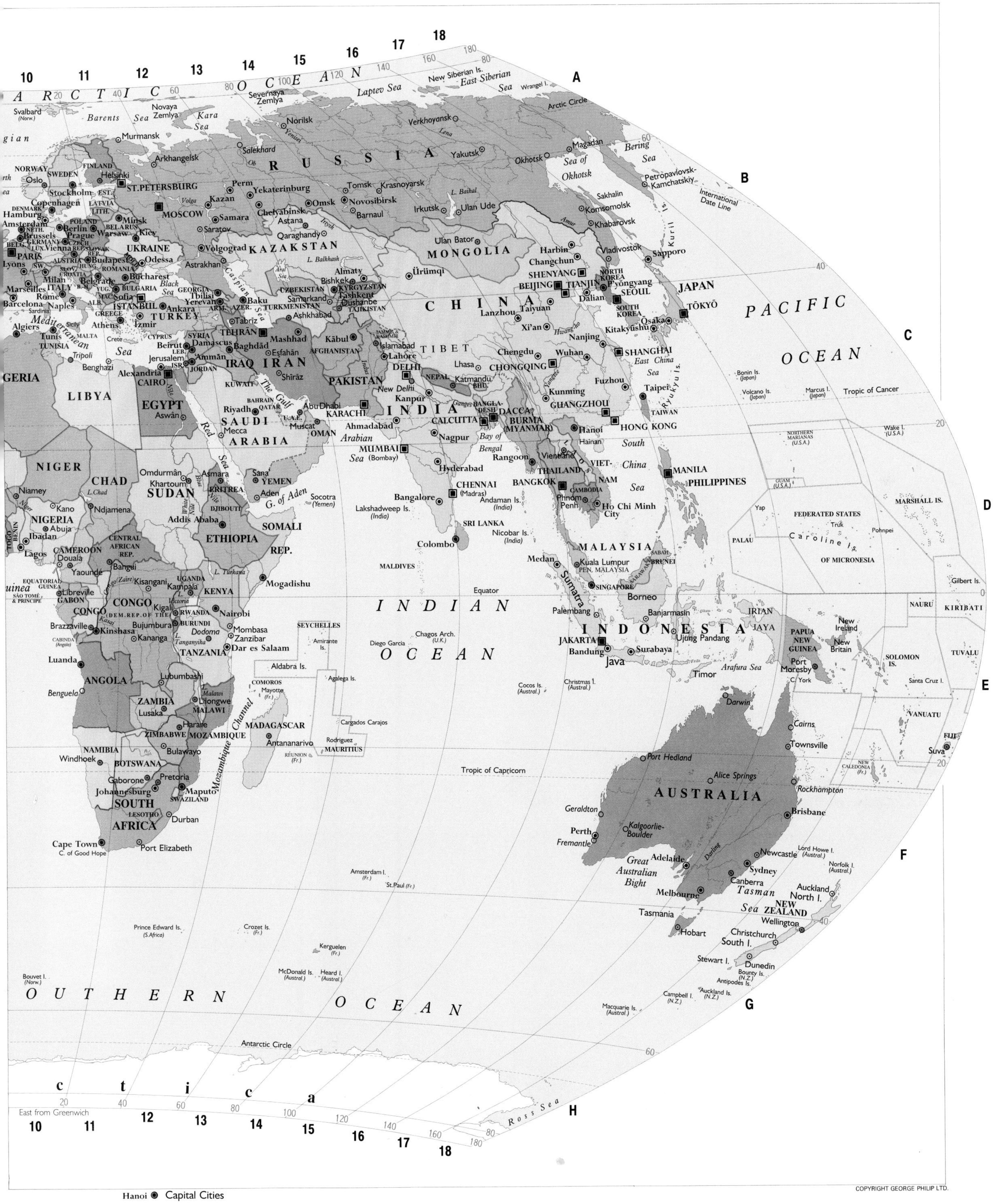

1:80 000 000

A

B

C

D

E

F

G

H

10 11 12 13 14 15 16 17 18

ARCTIC OCEAN

20 40 60 80 100 120 140 160 180

Svalbard
(Norw.)
Barents Sea
Novaya Zemlya
Kara Sea
Severnaya Zemlya
Norilsk
Yenisey
Salekhard
Laptev Sea
New Siberian Is.
East Siberian Sea
Wrangel I.
Arctic Circle

NORWAY
SWEDEN
FINLAND
Murmansk
Arkhangelsk
Ob
RUSSIA
Verkhoyansk
Lena
Yakutsk
Okhotsk
Magadan
Sea of Okhotsk
Bering Sea
International Date Line

Oslo
Helsinki
ST.PETERSBURG
EST.
Perm
Yekaterinburg
Tomsk Krasnoyarsk
L. Baikal
Irkutsk
Petropavlovsk-Kamchatskiy
60

Stockholm
DENMARK
Copenhagen
Hamburg
Amsterdam
NETH.
Brussels
BELG.
Berlin
POLAND
Prague
LUX.
Warsaw
CZECH REP.
PARIS
GERMANY
SLOVAK
Vienna
AUSTRIA
Budapest
HUNG.
MOSCOW
Volga
Kazan
Chelyabinsk
Omsk
Novosibirsk
Barnaul
Ulan Ude
Sapporo
Sakhalin
Komsomolsk
Khabarovsk
Amur
Kuril

Lyons
SWITZ.
Milan
Belgrade
CROATIA
ROMANIA
Bucharest
Samara
Saratov
Astana
Qaraghandy
Ulan Bator
MONGOLIA
Harbin
Changchun
Vladivostok
40

Marseilles
ITALY
YUG.
Sofia
BULGARIA
UKRAINE
Kiev
Odessa
Volgograd
KAZAKSTAN
Aral Sea
Almaty
Bishkek
Ürümqi
SHENYANG
NORTH KOREA
Pyongyang
SEOUL
JAPAN
TŌKYŌ

Barcelona
Rome
Naples
ALB.
MAC.
GREECE
ISTANBUL
Ankara
GEORGIA
Tbilisi
Yerevan
ARM.
AZER.
Baku
L. Balkhash
Tashkent
UZBEKISTAN
Samarkand
Bishkek
KYRGYZSTAN
CHINA
BEIJING
TIANJIN
Dalian
SOUTH KOREA
Osaka
Kitakyūshū

Algiers
TUNISIA
MALTA
Sardinia
Sicily
Athens
Izmir
TURKEY
CYPRUS
Beirut
SYRIA
Damascus
Mashhad
Tehran
TURKMENISTAN
Ashkhabad
TAJIKISTAN
Dushanbe
Kābul
AFGHANISTAN
Lanzhou
Taiyuan
Xi'an
Huang He
Nanjing
SHANGHAI
PACIFIC OCEAN

GERIA
LIBYA
Tripoli
Benghazi
Mediterranean Sea
Crete
Jerusalem
LEB.
ISRAEL
JORDAN
Amman
Baghdad
IRAQ
IRAN
Esfahān
Shīrāz
Islamabad
Lahore
PAKISTAN
Lhasa
TIBET
New Delhi
DELHI
NEPAL
Katmandu
BHT.
Chengdu
CHONGQING
Wuhan
East China Sea
Fuzhou
HONG KONG
GUANGZHOU
Taipei
TAIWAN
Ryukyus
Bonin Is.
(Japan)
Volcano Is.
(Japan)
Marcus I.
(Japan)
Tropic of Cancer
20

Alexandria
CAIRO
EGYPT
Aswân
Red Sea
SAUDI ARABIA
KUWAIT
The Gulf
BAHRAIN
QATAR
Riyadh
Abu Dhabi
U.A.E.
Muscat
OMAN
KARACHI
Ahmadabad
INDIA
Kanpur
BANGLA-DESH
DACCA
CALCUTTA
BURMA
MYANMAR
Kunming
Hainan
Hanoi
South China Sea
Wake I.
(U.S.A.)
NORTHERN MARIANAS
(U.S.A.)

NIGER
CHAD
Omdurmân
Khartoum
SUDAN
Asmara
ERITREA
Sana
YEMEN
Aden
Mecca
Arabian Sea
MUMBAI
(Bombay)
Nagpur
Hyderabad
Bay of Bengal
Rangoon
VIET-NAM
THAILAND
BANGKOK
CAMBODIA
MANILA
PHILIPPINES
GUAM
(U.S.A.)
MARSHALL IS.

Niamey
NIGERIA
Kano
Ndjamena
L. Chad
CENTRAL AFRICAN REP.
DJIBOUTI
Addis Ababa
ETHIOPIA
SOMALI REP.
Bangalore
CHENNAI
(Madras)
Andaman Is.
(India)
Phnom Penh
Ho Chi Minh City
Yap
FEDERATED STATES
Truk
Pohnpei
Caroline Is.
OF MICRONESIA
PALAU
Gilbert Is.

Abuja
Ibadan
Lagos
BENIN
CAMEROON
Douala
Yaoundé
EQUATORIAL GUINEA
SÃO TOMÉ & PRÍNCIPE
Kisangani
UGANDA
Kampala
KENYA
L. Turkana
Mogadishu
Colombo
SRI LANKA
Nicobar Is.
(India)
MALDIVES
Lakshadweep Is.
(India)
MALAYSIA
Kuala Lumpur
PEN. MALAYSIA
SABAH
BRUNEI
NAURU
KIRIBATI

Libreville
GABON
Brazzaville
CONGO
DEM. REP. OF THE CONGO
Kinshasa
CABINDA
(Angola)
RWANDA
Kigali
BURUNDI
Bujumbura
Zaire
Kananga
Dodoma
Nairobi
Mombasa
Zanzibar
Tanganyika
TANZANIA
Dar es Salaam
SEYCHELLES
Amirante Is.
Diego Garcia
Chagos Arch.
(U.K.)
Equator
INDIAN OCEAN
SINGAPORE
Palembang
Sumatra
Banjarmasin
Borneo
Ujung Pandang
IRIAN JAYA
INDONESIA
PAPUA NEW GUINEA
Port Moresby
C. York
New Ireland
New Britain
SOLOMON IS.
Santa Cruz I.
TUVALU

Luanda
Benguela
ANGOLA
Lubumbashi
Kasai
Victoria
Lusaka
ZAMBIA
MALAWI
Lilongwe
Malawi
COMOROS
Mayotte
(Fr.)
Aldabra Is.
Agalega Is.
(Fr.)
MADAGASCAR
Antananarivo
Cargados Carajos
Rodriguez
(Fr.)
MAURITIUS
RÉUNION
(Fr.)
OCEAN
JAKARTA
Bandung
Java
Surabaya
Timor
Arafura Sea
Darwin
Cocos Is.
(Austral.)
Christmas I.
(Austral.)
VANUATU
NEW CALEDONIA
(Fr.)
FIJI
Suva
20

NAMIBIA
Windhoek
BOTSWANA
Gaborone
Harare
ZIMBABWE
MOZAMBIQUE
Bulawayo
Mozambique Channel
Tropic of Capricorn
Amsterdam I.
(Fr.)
St.Paul (Fr.)
Port Hedland
Alice Springs
AUSTRALIA
Geraldton
Rockhampton
Brisbane
Cairns
Townsville
Lord Howe I.
(Austral.)

Johannesburg
Pretoria
Maputo
SWAZILAND
SOUTH AFRICA
LESOTHO
Durban
Cape Town
C. of Good Hope
Port Elizabeth
Kalgoorlie-Boulder
Perth
Fremantle
Great Australian Bight
Adelaide
Melbourne
Darling
Newcastle
Sydney
Canberra
Norfolk I.
(Austral.)
Auckland
North I.
NEW ZEALAND
Tasman Sea
Wellington
40

SOUTHERN OCEAN
Prince Edward Is.
(S.Africa)
Crozet Is.
(Fr.)
Kerguelen
(Fr.)
McDonald Is.
(Austral.)
Heard I.
(Austral.)
Macquarie Is.
(Austral.)
Campbell I.
(N.Z.)
Auckland Is.
(N.Z.)
Tasmania
Hobart
Christchurch
South I.
Stewart I.
Dunedin
Bounty I.
(N.Z.)
Antipodes Is.
(N.Z.)
Ross Sea

Bouvet I.
(Norw.)

Antarctic Circle

East from Greenwich
20 40 60 80 100 120 140 160 180

10 11 12 13 14 15 16 17 18

Hanoi ● Capital Cities

COPYRIGHT GEORGE PHILIP LTD.

100 0 200 400 600 800 1000 1200 1400 km
100 0 200 400 600 800 1000 miles

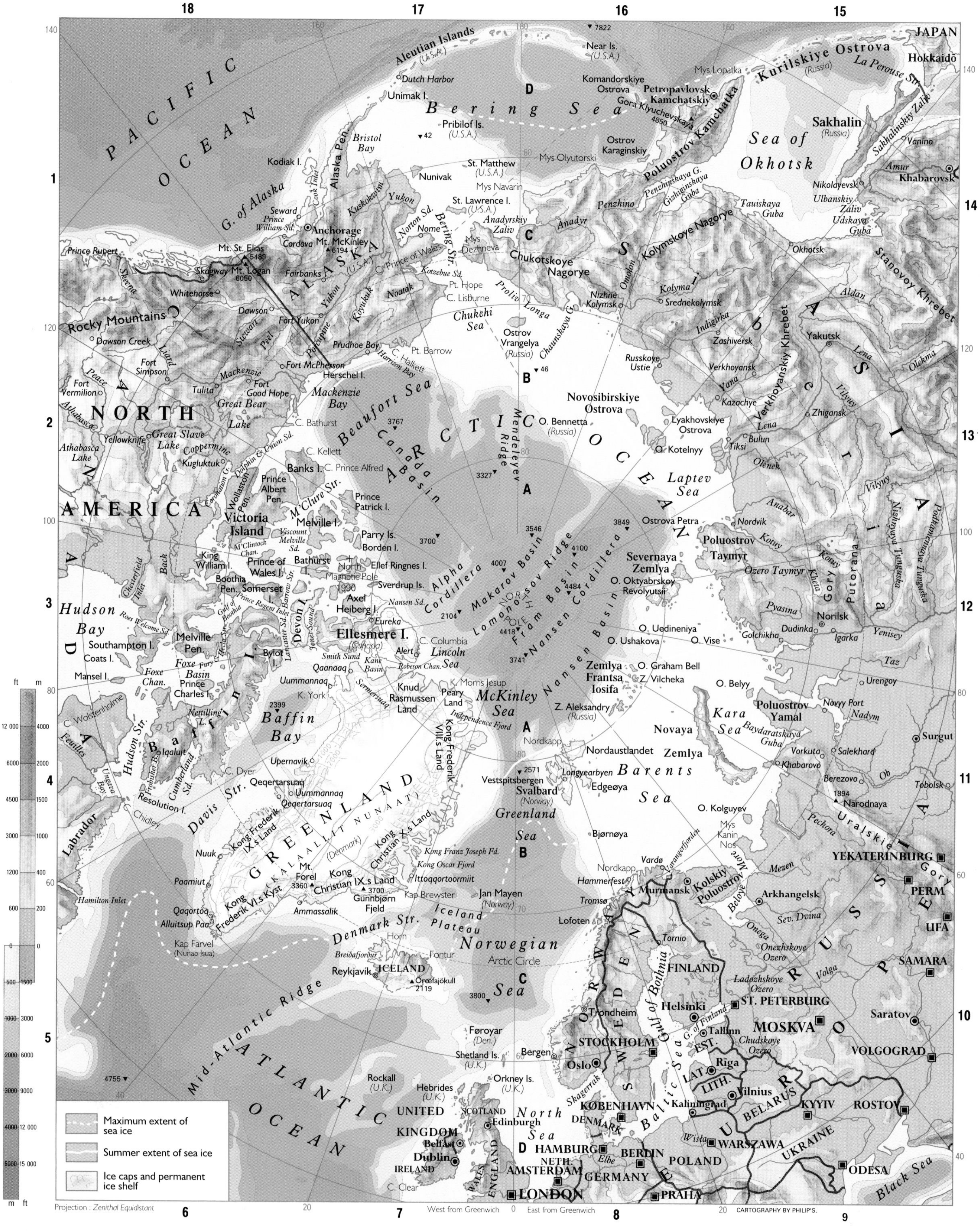

18   17   16   15

JAPAN

PACIFIC OCEAN

Aleutian Islands (U.S.A.)
Near Is. (U.S.A.)
▼7822
Hokkaidō
Kurilskiye Ostrova (Russia)
La Perouse Str.

Dutch Harbor
Komandorskiye Ostrova
Petropavlovsk-Kamchatskiy
Gora Klyuchevskaya 4850
Sea of Okhotsk
Sakhalin (Russia)
Sakhalinskiy Zaliv
Vanino

Unimak I.
Bering Sea
D
Poluostrov Kamchatka
Nikolayevsk
Ulbanskiy Guba
Amur
Khabarovsk

Pribilof Is. (U.S.A.)
Bristol Bay
▼42
St. Matthew (U.S.A.)
Mys Olyutorski
Penzhino
Penzhinskaya G.
Gizhiginskaya Guba
Tauiskaya Guba
Udskaya Guba

Kodiak I.
G. of Alaska
Nunivak
St. Lawrence I. (U.S.A.)
Mys Navarin
Anadyr
Okhotsk

1
Seward
Prince William Sd.
Anchorage
Cook Inlet
Kuskokwim
Nome
Bering Str.
Anadyrskiy Zaliv
Kolymskoye Nagorye
14

Prince Rupert
Mt. St. Elias 5489
Cordova Mt. McKinley 6194
ALASKA (U.S.A.)
C. Prince of Wales
Mys Dezhneva
Chukotskoye Nagorye
Stanovoy Khrebet

Skagway Mt. Logan 6050
Fairbanks
Norton Sd.
Pt. Hope
Prolив Longa
Nizhne Kolymsk
Kolyma
Srednekolymsk
Indigirka
Zashiversk
Yakutsk

Whitehorse
Dawson
Fort Yukon
Yukon
Kotzebue Sd.
C. Lisburne
Chukchi Sea
Ostrov Vrangelya (Russia)
Verkhoyansk
Lena
Olekma

ROCKY MOUNTAINS
Stewart
Fort McPherson
Prudhoe Bay
Pt. Barrow
Chaunskaya G.
▼46
Verkhoyanskiy Khrebet
Aldan

Dawson Creek
Liard
Mackenzie
Herschel I.
Harrison Bay
Russkoye Ustie
Yana
Kazachye
Zhigansk
120

Fort Simpson
Great Bear Lake
C. Bathurst
Mackenzie Bay
Beaufort Sea
▼3767
ARCTIC
Mendeleyev Ridge
O. Bennetta (Russia)
Novosibirskiye Ostrova
Lyakhovskiye Ostrova
Bulun

2
Fort Vermilion
Peace
NORTH
Coppermine
C. Kellett
Canada Basin
Lena
Tiksi
Olenek

Athabasca
Yellowknife
Great Slave Lake
Kugluktuk
Banks I.
C. Prince Alfred
▼3327
OCEAN
Laptev Sea
Kotelnyy
13

Athabasca Lake
CANADA
AMERICA
Dolphin & Union Sd.
Coronation G.
Prince Albert Pen.
Prince Patrick I.
A
▼3546
▼3849
Ostrova Petra
Nordvik
Anabar

Victoria Island
Melville I.
M'Clure Str.
Borden I.
▼3700
4007
Lomonosov Ridge
4100
Poluostrov Taymyr
Ozero Taymyr
Khatanga

King William I.
Viscount Melville Sd.
Parry Is.
Alpha Cordillera
Makarov Basin
4484
Severnaya Zemlya
Gory Putorana
100

100
Prince of Wales I.
Bathurst
Ellef Ringnes I.
Nansen Sd.
NORTH POLE
4418
Nansen Cordillera
O. Oktyabrskoy Revolyutsii
Pyasina
Norilsk

Boothia Pen.
Somerset
Magnetic Pole 1990
Sverdrup Is.
2104
Fram Basin
Nansen Basin
▼3741
O. Uedineniya
O. Vise
Golchikha
Igarka
Dudinka

3
Hudson Bay
Rees Welcome Sd.
Back
Axel Heiberg I.
Eureka
Nansen Sd.
O. Ushakova
Zemlya Frantsa Iosifa
Yenisey
12

Southampton I.
Melville Pen.
Devon I.
Ellesmere I. (Sisimiut)
Alert
Lincoln Sea
C. Columbia
O. Graham Bell
Z. Vilcheka
O. Belyy
Urengoy

Coats I.
Foxe Basin
Boothia
Gulf of Boothia
Prince Regent Inlet
Lancaster Sound
Bylot I.
Smith Sund
Robeson Chan.
Zemlya Aleksandry (Russia)
Kara Sea
Taz

Mansel I.
Foxe Chan.
Prince Charles I.
Jones Sound
Uummannaq
Kane Basin
K. Morris Jesup
Peary Land
McKinley Sea
Novaya Zemlya
Poluostrov Yamal
Novyy Port
Nadym
80

80
ft m
C. Wolstenholme
▼2399
Nettling L.
Baffin I.
K. York
Knud Rasmussen Land
Independence Fjord
Nordkapp
Baydaratskaya Guba
Vorkuta
Khabarovo
Salekhard
Surgut

12 000 4000
Cumberland Sd.
Baffin Bay
Sermersuaq
Kong Frederik VIII.s Land
Zemlya
Nordaustlandet
Barents Sea
O. Kolguyev
Berezovo
Tobolsk
11

6000 2000
4
Iqaluit
Frobisher Bay
Davis Str.
Upernavik
Qeqertarsuaq
Greenland
Sea
▼2571
Vestspitsbergen
Longyearbyen
Edgeøya
Svalbard (Norway)
▼1894
Narodnaya
Uralskie Gory

4500 1500
Resolution I.
C. Dyer
Qeqertarsuaq
Uummannaq
GREENLAND (KALAALLIT NUNAAT)
Nordkapp
Bjørnøya
Mys Kanin Nos
Pechora
Ural'skie Gory

3000 1000
Ungava Bay
Feuilles
C. Chidley
Nuuk
Kong Frederik IX.s Land
Kong Christian X.s Land
(Denmark)
Kong Franz Joseph Fd.
Vardø
Hammerfest
More
Mezen
YEKATERINBURG
Gory
60

1200 400
Labrador
Hamilton Inlet
Paamiut
Kong Oscar Fjord
Ittoqqortoormiit
Kong Christian IX.s Land
▼3700
Kap Brewster
Jan Mayen (Norway)
Tromsø
Murmansk
Kolskiy Poluostrov
Belove
Arkhangelsk
Sev. Dvina
PERM
UFA

600 200
Qaqortoq
Kong Frederik VI.s Kyst
Mt. Forel 3360
Gunnbjørn Fjeld
Iceland Plateau
Lofoten
Nordkapp
Onega
Onezhskoye Ozero
SAMARA

0
5
Alluitsup Paa
Ammassalik
Denmark Str.
Horn
Norwegian Sea
Arctic Circle
Ladozhskoye Ozero
St. Peterburg
Saratov

500 1500
Kap Farvel (Nunap Isua)
Breiðafjörður
▼4755
Fontur
FINLAND
Tornio
Helsinki
MOSKVA

1000 3000
Mid-Atlantic Ridge
Reykjavík
ICELAND
Öræfajökull 2119
▼3800
C
SWEDEN
Gulf of Bothnia
Trondheim
Chudskoye Ozero
EST.
Tallinn
VOLGOGRAD
10

2000 6000
Føroyar (Den.)
STOCKHOLM
G. of Finland
Riga
LAT.
ROSTOV

3000 9000
ATLANTIC
Shetland Is. (U.K.)
Bergen
Oslo
Baltic Sea
LITH.
Vilnius
Kaliningrad
BELARUS
KYYIV

4000 12 000
Rockall (U.K.)
Hebrides (U.K.)
Orkney Is. (U.K.)
Skagerrak
KØBENHAVN
DENMARK
WARSZAWA
UKRAINE
ODESA

5000 15 000
OCEAN
UNITED KINGDOM
SCOTLAND
North Sea
Edinburgh
Belfast
Dublin
IRELAND
C. Clear
WALES
ENGLAND
D
HAMBURG
NETH.
AMSTERDAM
LONDON
GERMANY
BERLIN
POLAND
PRAHA
Black Sea
40

m ft

Maximum extent of sea ice
Summer extent of sea ice
Ice caps and permanent ice shelf

1:33 000 000 **ANTARCTICA**

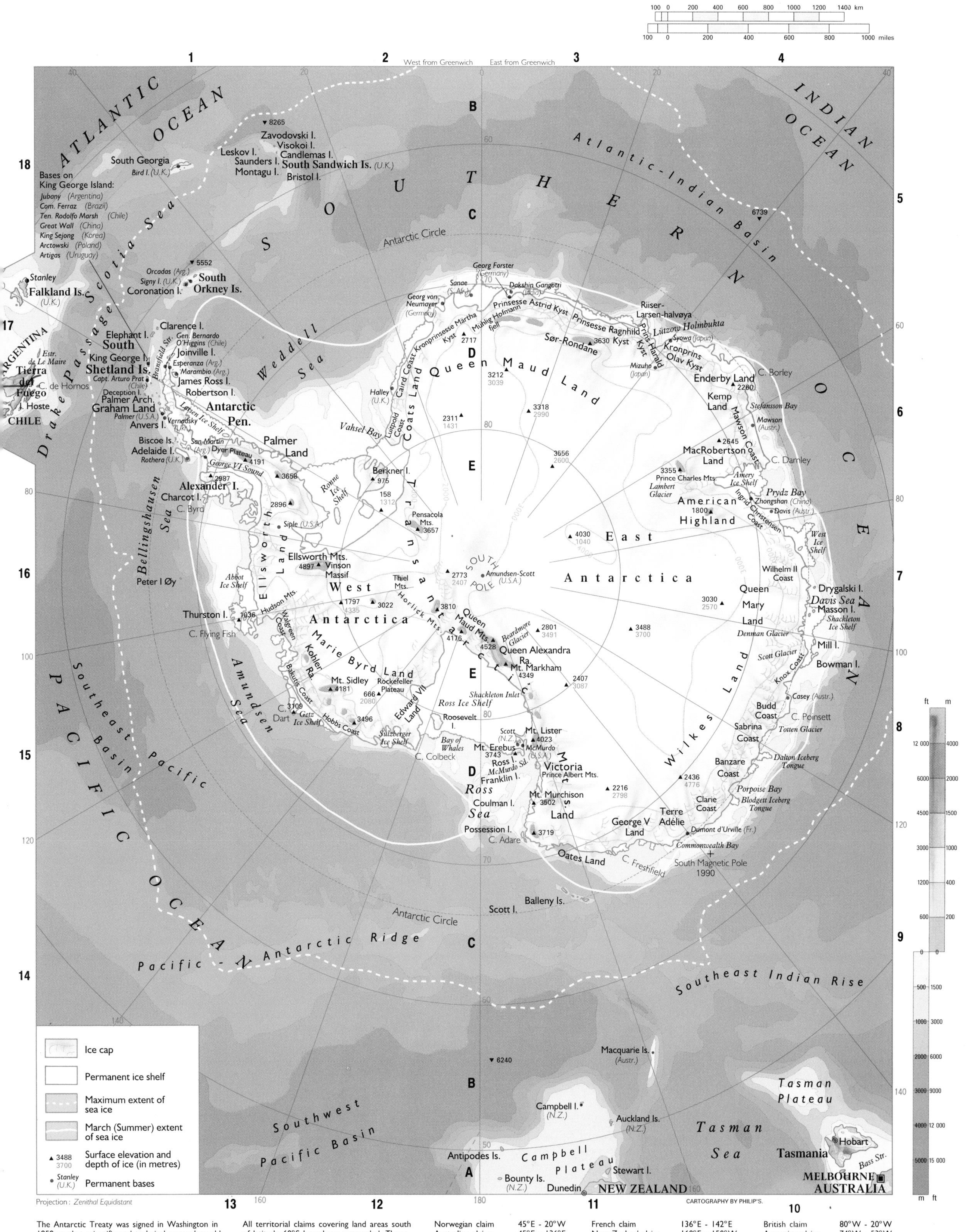

100 0 200 400 600 800 1000 1200 1400 km
100 0 200 400 600 800 1000 miles

ATLANTIC OCEAN

West from Greenwich   East from Greenwich

SOUTHERN

Atlantic–Indian Basin

INDIAN OCEAN

▼8265
Zavodovski I.
Leskov I.   Visokoi I.
Saunders I.   Candlemas I.
Montagu I.   **South Sandwich Is.** (U.K.)
Bristol I.

South Georgia
Bird I. (U.K.)

Bases on
King George Island:
Jubany   (Argentina)
Com. Ferraz   (Brazil)
Ten. Rodolfo Marsh   (Chile)
Great Wall   (China)
King Sejong   (Korea)
Arctowski   (Poland)
Artigas   (Uruguay)

Antarctic Circle

▼6739

Stanley
Falkland Is.
(U.K.)

Orcadas (Arg.) ▼5552
Signy I. (U.K.)   **South
Coronation I.   Orkney Is.**

Scotia Sea

Weddell Sea

Georg Forster
(Germany)
Sanae (S. Afr.)   Dakshin Gangotri (India)
Georg von
Neumayer   Prinsesse Astrid Kyst   Prinsesse Ragnhild Kyst
(Germany)   Kronprinsesse Martha   Mühlig Hofmann   Riiser-
Kyst   fjell   Sør-Rondane   Larsen-halvøya
▲2717   ▲3630 Kyst   Syowa (Japan)
Kronprins
Mizuho   Olav Kyst
(Japan)   **Enderby Land** C. Borley
▲2260

Kemp
Land
Stefansson Bay

Queen Maud Land
▲3212   Mawson
3039   ▲3318   (Austr.)
2990   MacRobertson
▲2311   ▲2645   Land
1431   ▲3355   C. Damley
▲3656   Prince Charles Mts   Amery
2600   Lambert   Ice Shelf   Prydz Bay
Glacier   Zhongshan (China)
American   1800   Ingrid Christensen   Davis (Austr.)
Highland   ▲   Coast   West
▲4030   Ice Shelf
1040

ARGENTINA
Estr.
de Le Maire   Elephant I.
Tierra   Clarence I.   **East
del   Gen. Bernardo   Antarctica**
Fuego   O'Higgins (Chile)   SOUTH
J. Hoste   **South   Joinville I.   POLE   Queen
CHILE   Shetland Is.   Esperanza (Arg.)   Amundsen-Scott   Mary
C. de Homos   Marambio (Arg.)   ▲2773   (U.S.A.)   Land
King George I.   James Ross I.   2407   ▲3030
Capt. Arturo Prat   Robertson I.   2570
(Chile)   Wilhelm II
Deception I.   Coast
Palmer Arch.
Graham Land   ▲3488   Drygalski I.
Palmer (U.S.A.)   3700   Davis Sea
Anvers I.   Vernadsky   Masson I.
(U.K.)   Queen   Shackleton
Biscoe Is.   San Martin   Maud Mts   Mill I.   Ice Shelf
**Palmer   (Arg.)   ▲4176   Scott Glacier
Adelaide I.   Dyer Plateau   Land**   Beardmore   Knox Coast   Bowman I.
Rothera (U.K.)   ▲4191   Queen Alexandra   ▲2801
Alexander I.   ▲3658   Ra.   3491
▲2987   Transantarctic   Mt. Markham   Budd
Charcot I.   ▲2896   Berkner I.   Mts   ▲4349   Casey (Austr.)   Coast
C. Byrd   Ronne   975   ▲2407   C. Poinsett
Ice   158   Shackleton Inlet   3087   Sabrina   Totten Glacier
Siple (U.S.A.)   Shelf   1312   Coast
Pensacola   Ross Ice Shelf   Dalton Iceberg
Mts   Edward VII   Banzare   Tongue
Ellsworth Mts   ▲3657   Land   Coast
4897   Vinson   Roosevelt   Porpoise Bay
**West   Massif   I.   Scott (N.Z.)   Mt. Lister   Clarie   Blodgett Iceberg
Antarctica   Thiel   ▲4023   Coast   Tongue
Mts   Bay of   McMurdo (U.S.A.)   ▲2436
▲1797   ▲3022   Whales   Mt. Erebus   **Victoria   4776   Terre
4335   ▲3810   3743   Prince Albert Mts   George V   Adélie
Hudson Mts   C. Colbeck   Ross   Franklin I.   Land**   Land   Dumont d'Urville (Fr.)
Thurston I.   ▲1936   McMurdo Sd.   Mt. Murchison   Commonwealth Bay
Marie Byrd Land   Ross   ▲3502   South Magnetic Pole
C. Flying Fish   Mt. Sidley   Sea   1990
Peter I Øy   ▲4181   Rockefeller   Coulman I.   Oates Land
Kohler   Plateau   ▲2216   C. Freshfield
Ra.   666   2798
Bellingshausen   Dart   2080   Possession I.   ▲3719
Sea   ▲3709   Getz   C. Adare
Ice Shelf   Hobbs Coast   ▲3496
Abbot   Salzberger
Ice Shelf   Ice Shelf

PACIFIC OCEAN

Southeast
Pacific
Basin

Amundsen
Sea

Pacific–Antarctic Ridge

Antarctic Circle

Scott I.

Balleny Is.

Southeast Indian Rise

Tasman
Plateau

Southwest
Pacific Basin

▼6240

Macquarie Is.
(Austr.)

Campbell I.
(N.Z.)

Auckland Is.
(N.Z.)

Tasman
Sea

Hobart
Tasmania

MELBOURNE
AUSTRALIA

Antipodes Is.   Campbell
Bounty Is.   Plateau
(N.Z.)   Stewart I.
Dunedin   **NEW ZEALAND**
(N.Z.)

Wilkes Land

ft   m
12 000   4000
9000   3000
6000   2000
4500   1500
3000   1000
1200   400
600   200
0   0
500   1500
1000   3000
2000   6000
3000   9000
4000   12 000
5000   15 000
m   ft

Ice cap
Permanent ice shelf
Maximum extent of sea ice
March (Summer) extent of sea ice
▲3488 Surface elevation and depth of ice (in metres)
3700
● Stanley Permanent bases
(U.K.)

Projection: Zenithal Equidistant

CARTOGRAPHY BY PHILIP'S.

The Antarctic Treaty was signed in Washington in 1959 so that scientific and technical research could continue unhampered by international politics.

All territorial claims covering land areas south of latitude 60°S have been suspended. Those claims were:

Norwegian claim   45°E – 20°W
Australian claims   45°E – 136°E
142°E – 160°E

French claim   136°E – 142°E
New Zealand claim   160°E – 150°W
Chilean claim   90°W – 53°W

British claim   80°W – 20°W
Argentine claim   74°W – 53°W

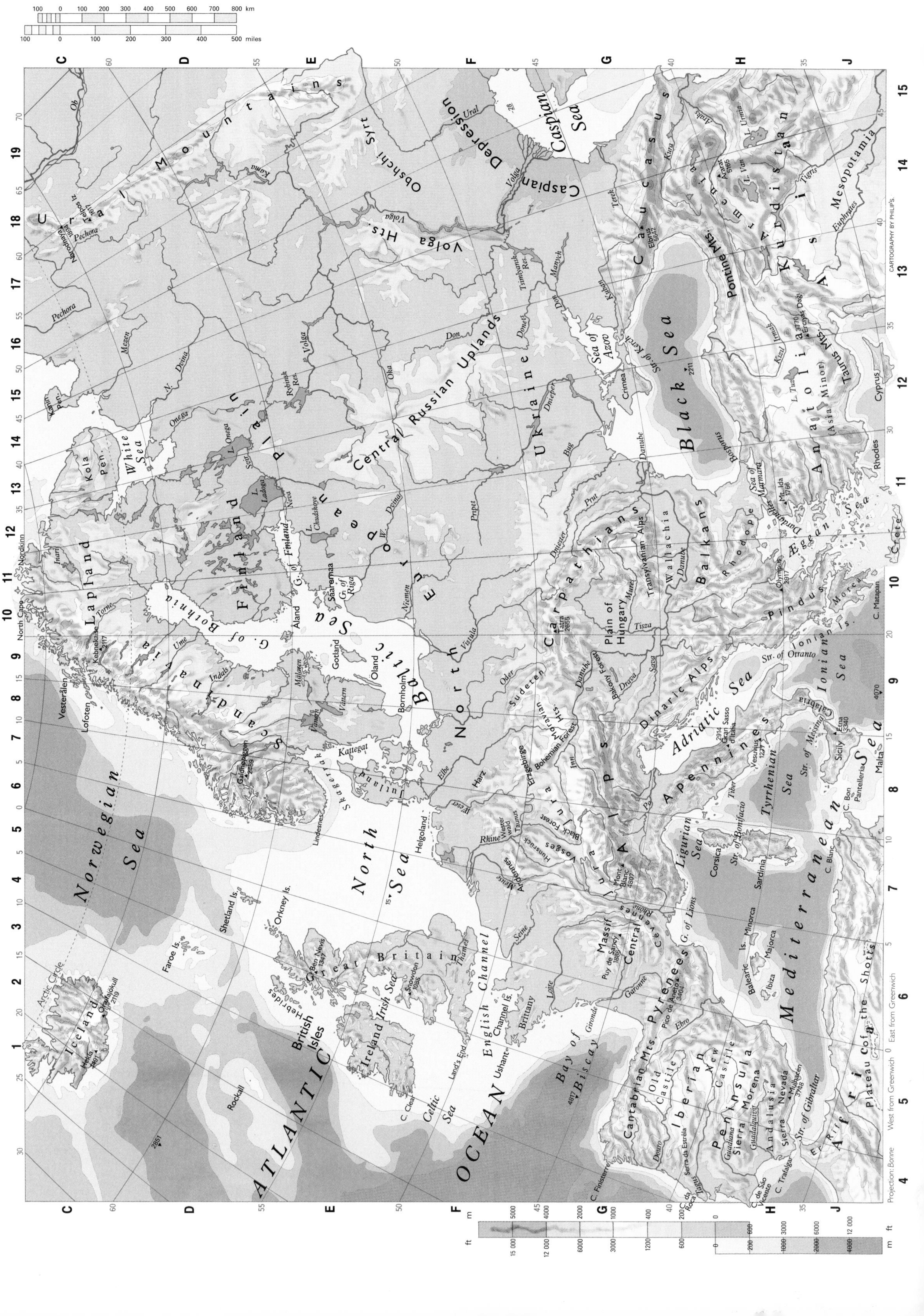

Scale:
100 0 100 200 300 400 500 600 700 800 km
100 0 100 200 300 400 500 miles

CARTOGRAPHY BY PHILIP'S

Projection Bonne

West from Greenwich 0 East from Greenwich

Seas and oceans
ATLANTIC OCEAN
Norwegian Sea
North Sea
Mediterranean Sea
Black Sea
Caspian Sea
White Sea
Baltic Sea
Adriatic Sea
Tyrrhenian Sea
Ionian Sea
Ligurian Sea
Aegean Sea
Sea of Azov
Sea of Marmara
Irish Sea
Celtic Sea
Kattegat
Skagerrak
G. of Finland
G. of Bothnia
G. of Riga
Bay of Biscay
G. of Lions
English Channel
Strait of Gibraltar
Str. of Messina
Str. of Bonifacio
Str. of Otranto

Land features
Ural Mountains
Caspian Depression
Obshchi Syrt
Volga Hts.
Central Russian Uplands
Scandinavia
Lapland
Finland
Ukraine
Carpathians
Caucasus
Pontine Mts.
Armenia
Kurdistan
Mesopotamia
Anatolia (Asia Minor)
Taurus Mts.
Balkans
Pindus
Dinaric Alps
Transylvanian Alps
Wallachia
Plain of Hungary
Bohemian Forest
Sudeten
Erzgebirge
Harz
Alps
Apennines
Pyrenees
Massif Central
Cévennes
Vosges
Ardennes
Jura
Black Forest
Cantabrian Mts.
Old Castile
New Castile
Iberian Peninsula
Sierra Morena
Sierra Nevada
Andalusia
Plateau of the Shotts
Africa

Mont Blanc 4807
Matterhorn
Mt. Elbruz 5642
Ararat 5165
Etna 3340
Olympus 2917
Vesuvius
Snowdon 1085
Ben Nevis 1347
Galdhøpiggen 2469
Kebnekaise 2117
Hvannadalshnúkur 2119
Hekla

Rivers and lakes
Volga
Ural
Don
Donets
Dnieper
Dniester
Prut
Danube
Tisza
Drava
Sava
Oder
Elbe
Weser
Rhine
Seine
Loire
Garonne
Ebro
Duero
Tagus
Guadiana
Guadalquivir
Po
Tiber
Rhône
Thames
Vistula
Niemen
Oka
Kama
Pechora
Mezen
N. Dvina
Ob
Euphrates
Tigris
Kura
Terek
L. Ladoga
L. Onega
L. Chudskoye
Rybinsk Res.
Tsimlyansk Res.

Islands and places
Iceland
British Isles
Great Britain
Ireland
Hebrides
Shetland Is.
Orkney Is.
Faroe Is.
Rockall
Channel Is.
Ushant
Land's End
C. Clear
Jutland
Gotland
Öland
Bornholm
Åland
Saaremaa
Vesterålen
Lofoten
North Cape
Kola Pen.
Kanin Pen.
Novaya Zemlya
Corsica
Sardinia
Sicily
Malta
Crete
Rhodes
Cyprus
Balearic Is.
Ibiza
Majorca
Minorca
Morea
C. Matapan
Crimea
C. St. Vincent
C. Trafalgar
C. Finisterre
C. Bon
Pantelleria
Calabria

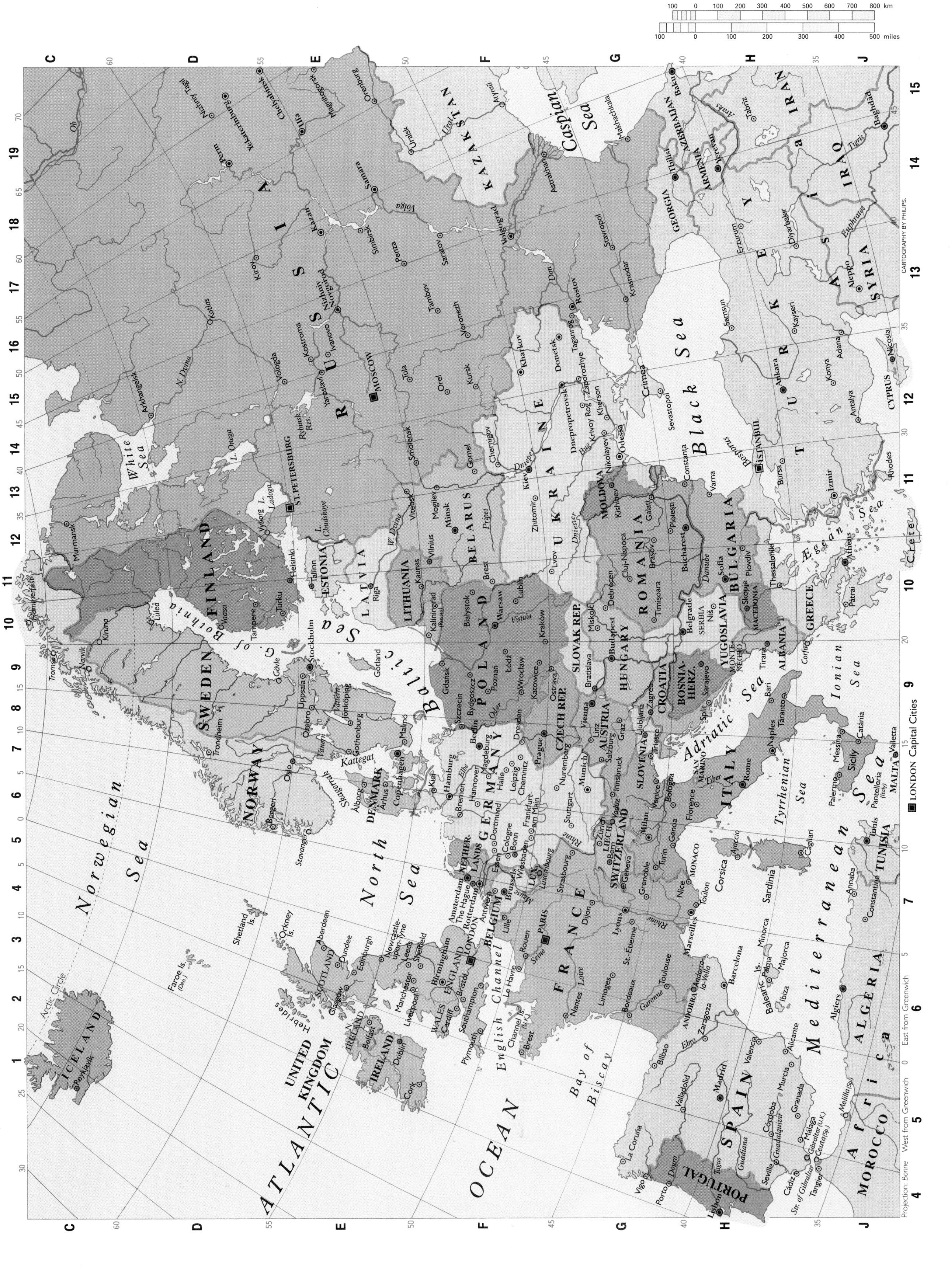

100   0   100 200 300 400 500 600 700 800 km
100   0   100   200   300   400   500 miles

C   60   D   55   E   50   F   45   G   40   H   35   J

19   18   17   16   15   14   13   12

Ob
Nizhny Tagil
Chelyabinsk
Orenburg
Ufa
Magnitogorsk

KAZAKHSTAN

Ural'sk
Aktyubinsk

Caspian
Sea

AZERBAIJAN
Baku
IRAN
Tabriz

Perm

Kama

Kazan

Samara

Saratov

Penza
Tambov

Voronezh

Kirov

Kostroma

Vologda
N. Dvina

L. Onega

White
Sea

Murmansk

Arkhangelsk

R   U   S   S   I   A

MOSCOW

Yaroslavl'
Rybinsk
Nizhny Novgorod
Ivanovo

Tula
Orel
Kursk

Kharkov
Donetsk

UKRAINE

Dnepropetrovsk
Zaporozhye
Krivoy Rog
Nikolayev
Kherson
Odessa

Rostov
Taganrog
Krasnodar
Stavropol
Astrakhan

GEORGIA
Tbilisi
ARMENIA
Yerevan

Erzurum
Kayseri

T   U   R   K   E   Y

Ankara
Konya
Antalya

Adana
Aleppo
SYRIA

Erevan

IRAQ
Baghdad
Mosul
Tigris
Euphrates
Diyarbakir

St. PETERSBURG
L. Ladoga
Vyborg
L. Chudskoye
Smolensk
Mogilev
Minsk
BELARUS
W. Dvina
Pskov
Velikiye Luki

Chernigov
Kiev
Zhitomir
Gomel
Pripet
Brest
Lvov
Ternopol

MOLDOVA
Kishinev
Dniester
Galati
Ploiesti
Bucharest
Constanta
Varna
BULGARIA
Sofia
Plovdiv

ROMANIA
Cluj-Napoca
Brasov
Timisoara
Debrecen
Miskolc
Budapest
HUNGARY

Black   Sea

Sevastopol
Crimea

Bosporus
ISTANBUL
Bursa
Izmir
Aegean
Sea
Rhodes

Thessaloniki
MACEDONIA
Skopje
Nis
SERBIA
Belgrade
YUGOSLAVIA
MONTE-
NEGRO
Tirana
ALBANIA
Corfu

GREECE
Athens
Patrai
Ionian
Sea

CYPRUS
Nicosia

Crete

70   65   60   55   50   45   40   35

FINLAND

Helsinki
Tampere
Turku
Vaasa

Tornio
Oulu

Kemijärvi

Kiruna

G. of Bothnia

ESTONIA
Tallinn
LATVIA
Riga

LITHUANIA
Kaunas
Vilnius
Kaliningrad

Baltic   Sea

Gdansk
Szczecin
Bydgoszcz
Poznan
POLAND
Warsaw
Lublin
Lodz
Wroclaw
Krakow
Katowice
Vistula
Oder
Bialystok

SLOVAK REP.
Bratislava
CZECH REP.
Prague
Ostrava
Brno

AUSTRIA
Vienna
Linz
Graz
SLOVENIA
Ljubljana
Zagreb
CROATIA
BOSNIA-
HERZ.
Sarajevo
Split
Trieste
Venice
Adriatic
Sea
Bari
Taranto
San
MARINO
Florence
Bologna
Naples

SWEDEN

Stockholm
Uppsala
Örebro
Gothenburg
Norrköping
Jönköping
Malmö
Gotland
Öland

Göteborg

Östersund

Sundsvall

Luleå

NORWAY

Oslo
Bergen
Trondheim
Stavanger
Narvik
Tromsø

Kattegat

DENMARK
Copenhagen
Aalborg
Aarhus
Kiel
Odense
Elbe
Hamburg
Bremen
Hannover
Magdeburg
Berlin
Leipzig
Dresden
Halle
GERMANY
Cologne
Essen
Dortmund
Frankfurt
Nuremberg
Munich
Stuttgart
Main
Chemnitz

Rhine
NETHER-
LANDS
Amsterdam
The Hague
Rotterdam
Antwerp
BELGIUM
Brussels
LUX.
Luxembourg

Strasbourg
Basle
Zürich
Bern
SWITZERLAND
Geneva
Liechtenstein
Innsbruck
Salzburg

Lille

PARIS
Le Havre
Rouen
Seine
Dijon
Nantes
Loire
Limoges
Bordeaux
Garonne
Toulouse
St. Étienne
Lyons
Grenoble
Nice
Toulon
Marseilles
Rhône
MONACO
Turin
Milan
Genoa
Corsica

FRANCE

ITALY
Rome
Tiber

Tyrrhenian
Sea
Sardinia
Cagliari
Palermo
Messina
Sicily
Catania
Pantelleria
(Italy)
MALTA
Valletta

■ LONDON Capital Cities

Norwegian
Sea

Shetland Is.
Orkney Is.
Aberdeen
Dundee
Edinburgh
SCOTLAND
Glasgow
UNITED
KINGDOM
Newcastle-
upon-Tyne
Leeds
Sheffield
Manchester
Liverpool
ENGLAND
Birmingham
Cardiff
WALES
Bristol
Southampton
Plymouth
LONDON
English Channel
Brest
Hebrides

Faroe Is.
(Den.)

IRELAND
Dublin
Belfast
N. IRELAND
Cork

ICELAND
Reykjavik

Arctic Circle

ATLANTIC

OCEAN

North
Sea

Bay
of
Biscay

SPAIN
Madrid
Valladolid
Bilbao
Zaragoza
Barcelona
Valencia
Murcia
Alicante
Córdoba
Sevilla
Granada
Málaga
Cádiz
Guadalquivir
Ebro
La Coruña
Vigo
Balearic Is.
Minorca
Majorca
Ibiza
ANDORRA
Andorra-
la-Vella

PORTUGAL
Lisbon
Porto
Douro
Tagus
Guadiana

Mediterranean   Sea

Gibraltar (UK)
Ceuta (Sp.)
Tangier
Str. of Gibraltar
Melilla
(Sp.)

MOROCCO
A f r i c a
ALGERIA
Algiers
Oran
Constantine
Annaba
TUNISIA
Tunis

Africa

Projection: Bonne   West from Greenwich   0   East from Greenwich

CARTOGRAPHY BY PHILIPS.

1   2   3   4   5   6   7   8   9   10

SCANDINAVIA 1:5 000 000

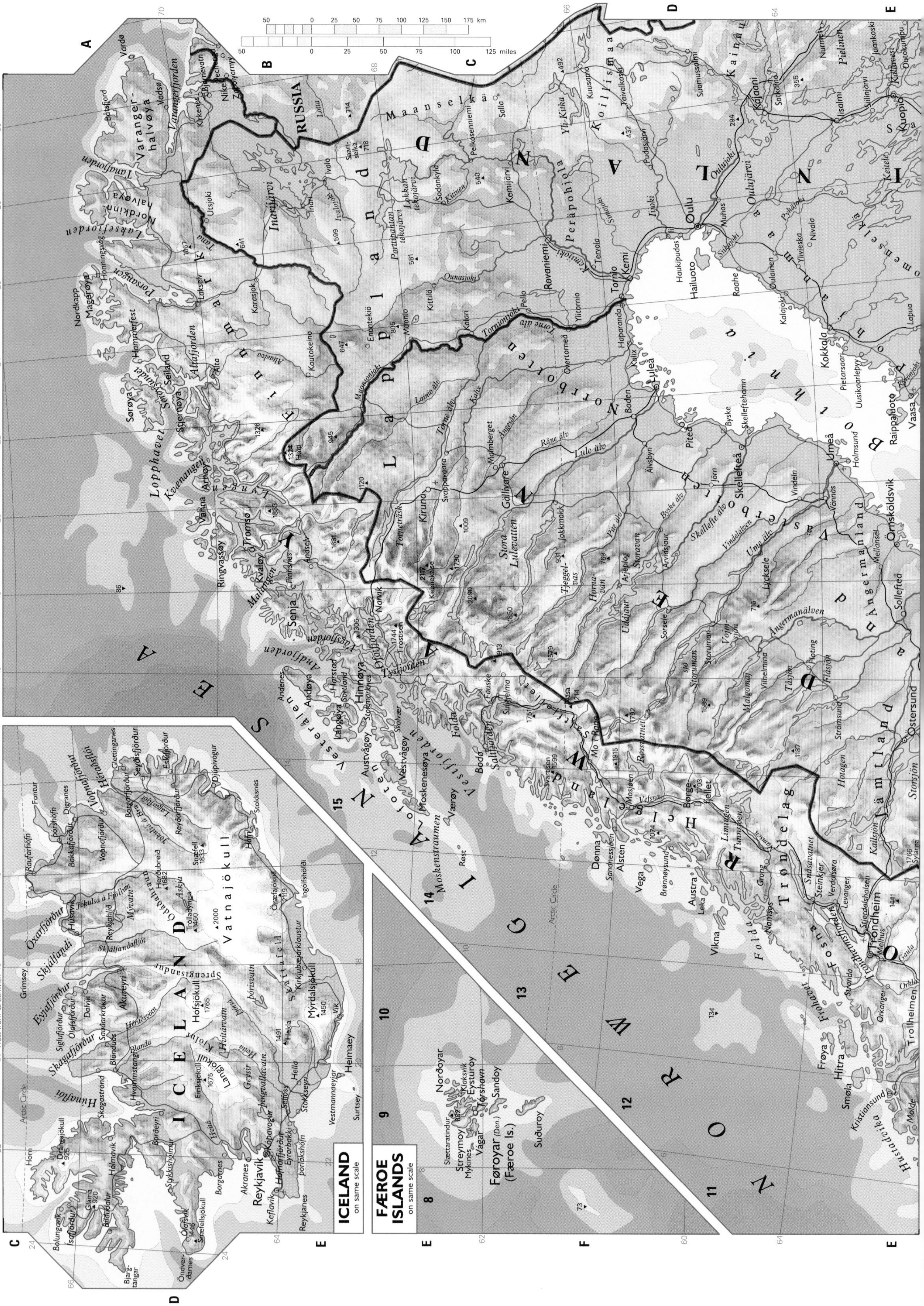

ICELAND
on same scale

FÆROE
ISLANDS
on same scale

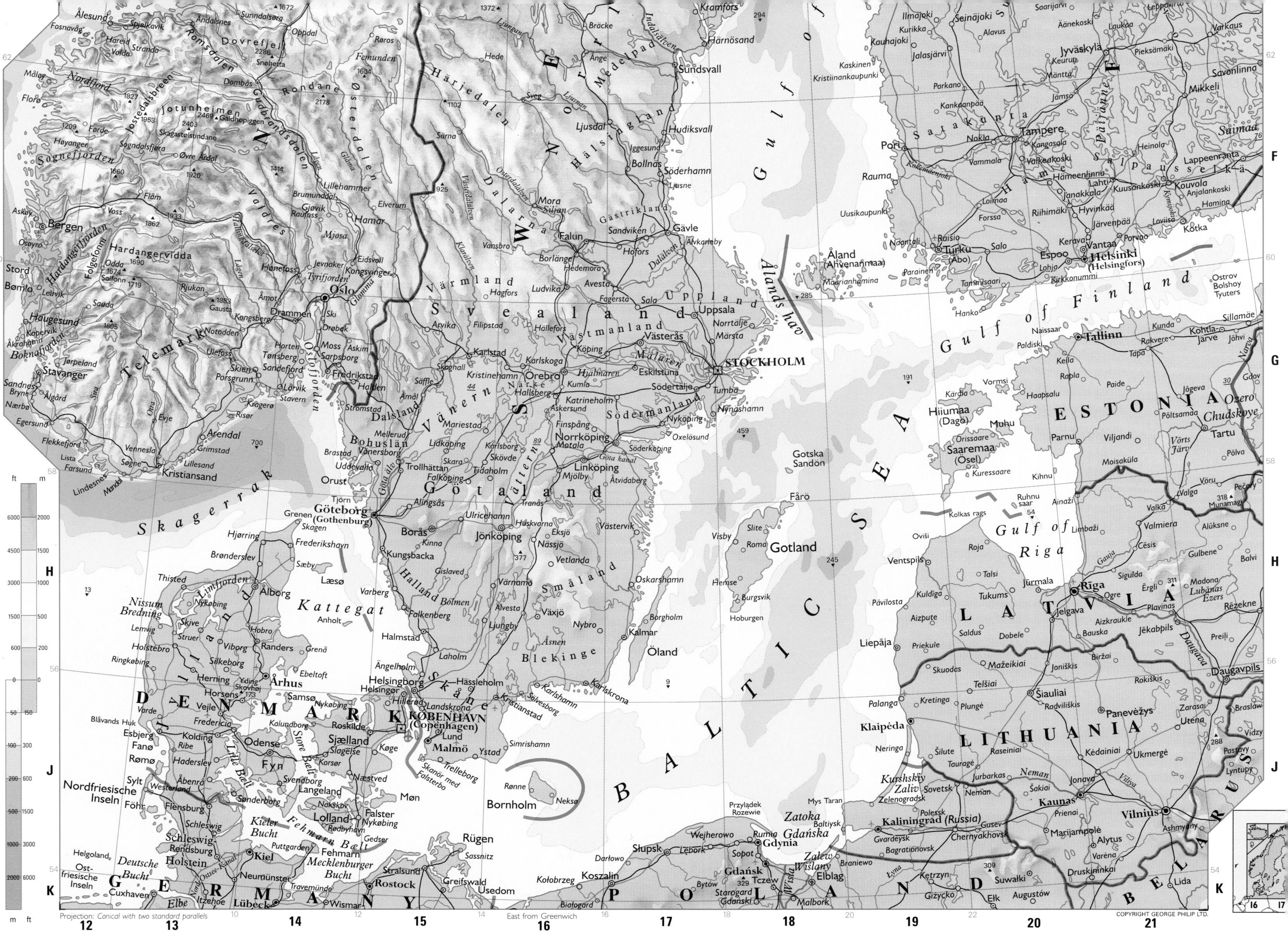

BALTIC SEA
Gulf of Finland
Gulf of Riga
Ålands hav
Skagerrak
Kattegat
ESTONIA
LATVIA
LITHUANIA
DENMARK
POLAND
GERMANY
BELARUS
STOCKHOLM
Oslo
Helsinki (Helsingfors)
Tallinn
Riga
Vilnius
KØBENHAVN (Copenhagen)
Göteborg (Gothenburg)
Malmö
Kaliningrad (Russia)
Gdańsk
Gdynia
Klaipėda
Kaunas
Tartu
Turku (Åbo)
Tampere
Bergen
Stavanger
Kristiansand
Uppsala
Västerås
Örebro
Norrköping
Linköping
Jönköping
Gotland
Öland
Bornholm
Saaremaa (Ösel)
Hiiumaa (Dagö)
Åland (Ahvenanmaa)
Svealand
Götaland
Norrland
Dalarna
Värmland
Småland
Skåne
Jylland
Sjælland
Fyn
Telemark
Vänern
Vättern
Mälaren
Rügen
Rostock
Lübeck
Kiel
Flensburg
Århus
Odense
Ålborg
Sundsvall
Gävle
Kalmar
Karlskrona
Visby
Liepāja
Ventspils
Pärnu
Šiauliai
Daugavpils
Jelgava
Projection: Conical with two standard parallels
East from Greenwich
COPYRIGHT GEORGE PHILIP LTD.

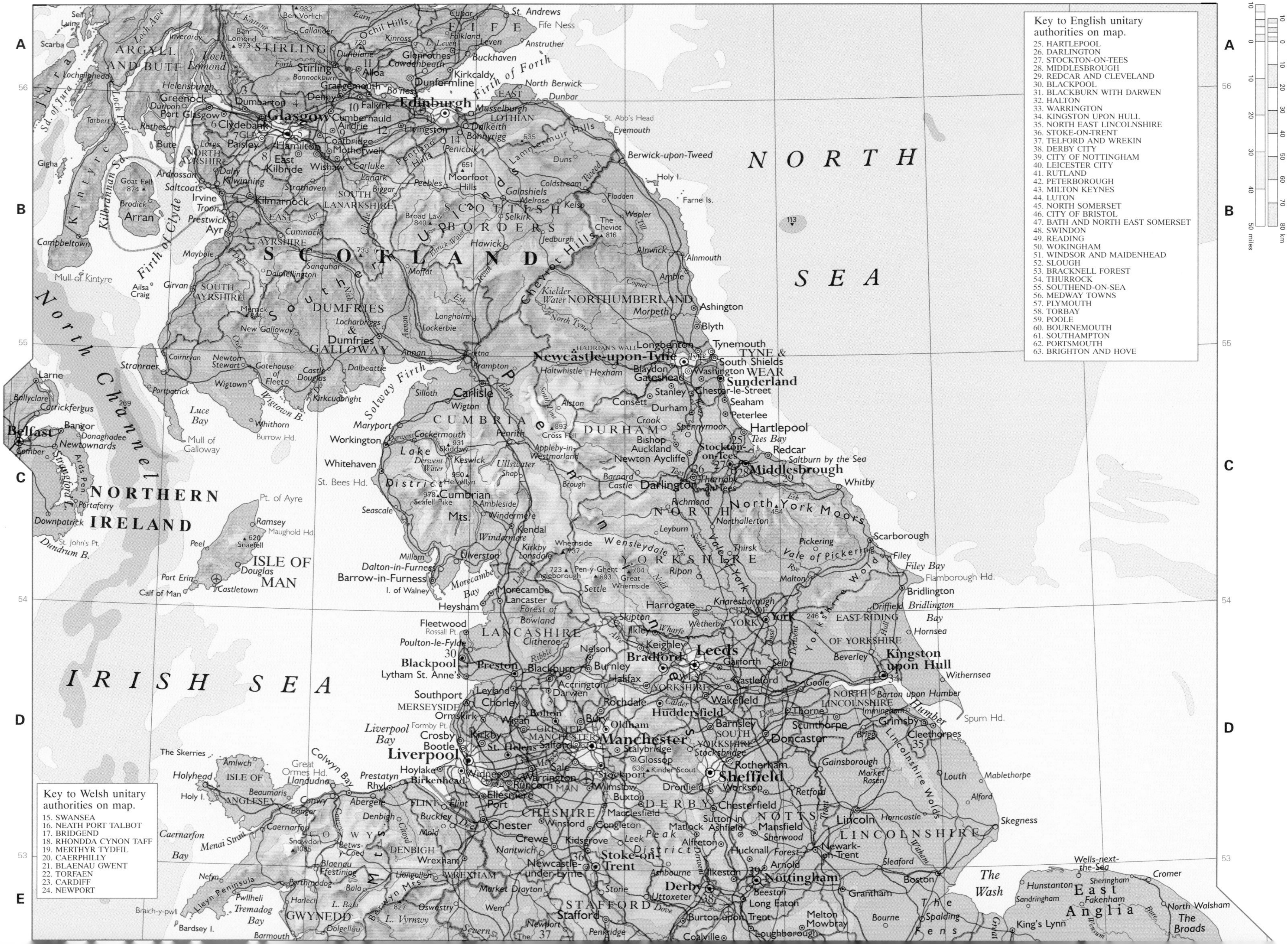
10 0 10 20 30 40 50 60 70 80 km
10 0 10 20 30 40 50 miles
Key to English unitary authorities on map.
25. HARTLEPOOL
26. DARLINGTON
27. STOCKTON-ON-TEES
28. MIDDLESBROUGH
29. REDCAR AND CLEVELAND
30. BLACKPOOL
31. BLACKBURN WITH DARWEN
32. HALTON
33. WARRINGTON
34. KINGSTON UPON HULL
35. NORTH EAST LINCOLNSHIRE
36. STOKE-ON-TRENT
37. TELFORD AND WREKIN
38. DERBY CITY
39. CITY OF NOTTINGHAM
40. LEICESTER CITY
41. RUTLAND
42. PETERBOROUGH
43. MILTON KEYNES
44. LUTON
45. NORTH SOMERSET
46. CITY OF BRISTOL
47. BATH AND NORTH EAST SOMERSET
48. SWINDON
49. READING
50. WOKINGHAM
51. WINDSOR AND MAIDENHEAD
52. SLOUGH
53. BRACKNELL FOREST
54. THURROCK
55. SOUTHEND-ON-SEA
56. MEDWAY TOWNS
57. PLYMOUTH
58. TORBAY
59. POOLE
60. BOURNEMOUTH
61. SOUTHAMPTON
62. PORTSMOUTH
63. BRIGHTON AND HOVE
Key to Welsh unitary authorities on map.
15. SWANSEA
16. NEATH PORT TALBOT
17. BRIDGEND
18. RHONDDA CYNON TAFF
19. MERTHYR TYDFIL
20. CAERPHILLY
21. BLAENAU GWENT
22. TORFAEN
23. CARDIFF
24. NEWPORT
NORTH SEA
IRISH SEA
North Channel
SCOTLAND
NORTHERN IRELAND
ISLE OF MAN
NORTHUMBERLAND
DURHAM
CUMBRIA
NORTH YORKSHIRE
LANCASHIRE
LINCOLNSHIRE
East Anglia
The Wash

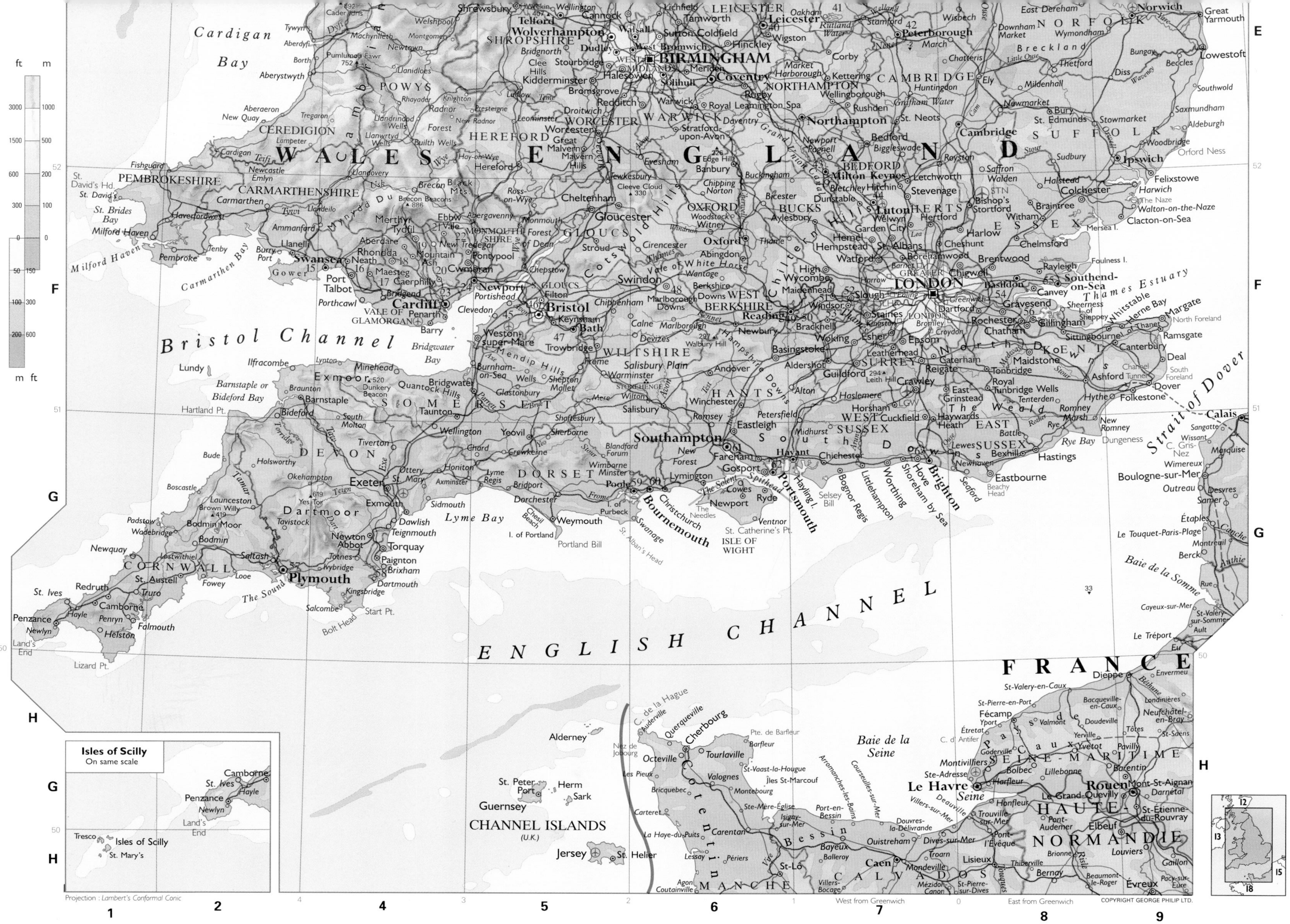

II

E F G H

9 8 7 6 5 4 3 2 1

Great Yarmouth
Lowestoft
Norwich
Beccles
Bungay
Southwold
Aldeburgh
Orford Ness
NORFOLK
Diss
Saxmundham
Harleston
Wymondham
East Dereham
Downham Market
Thetford
Breckland
Bury St. Edmunds
Stowmarket
Woodbridge
Felixstowe
Harwich
Walton-on-the-Naze
Clacton-on-Sea
SUFFOLK
Newmarket
Sudbury
Holstead
Braintree
Witham
Maldon
The Naze
Mersea I.
Foulness I.
ENGLAND
Cambridge
Saffron Walden
Bishop's Stortford
Harlow
Chelmsford
Brentwood
Rayleigh
Canvey Island
Southend-on-Sea
Thames Estuary
Sheerness
Sheppey
Whitstable Bay
Herne Bay
Margate
North Foreland
Ramsgate
ESSEX
HERTS
Chesham
Hatfield
Hertford
Hemel Hempstead
Watford
Enfield
GREATER LONDON
LONDON
Dartford
Gravesend
Rochester
Chatham
Gillingham
Maidstone
Sittingbourne
Canterbury
Deal
South Foreland
Dover
Folkestone
Ashford Tunnel
Strait of Dover
Calais
Marquise
C. Gris-Nez
Wissant
Boulogne-sur-Mer
FRANCE

ENGLISH CHANNEL

BIRMINGHAM
Coventry
Leicester
Northampton
Milton Keynes
Luton
Bedford
WALES
SHROPSHIRE
HEREFORD
WORCESTER
Bristol
Bath
Cardiff
Swansea
DEVON
CORNWALL
DORSET
SOMERSET
Plymouth
Exeter
Torquay
Bournemouth
Southampton
Portsmouth
ISLE OF WIGHT
Brighton
Hove
Worthing
Eastbourne
Hastings
SUSSEX
SURREY
HANTS

CHANNEL ISLANDS (U.K.)
Alderney
Guernsey
St. Peter Port
Herm
Sark
Jersey
St. Helier

FRANCE
Dieppe
Le Havre
Rouen
HAUTE-NORMANDIE
SEINE-MARITIME
Caen
Cherbourg
Cotentin
CALVADOS
MANCHE
Baie de la Seine
NORMANDIE
Évreux

Cardigan Bay
Bristol Channel
Lyme Bay

East from Greenwich | West from Greenwich

Isles of Scilly
On same scale
Tresco
Isles of Scilly
St. Mary's

ft m
3000
1500
600
300
0
1000
500
200
100
0
m ft
-50 150
-100 300
-200 600

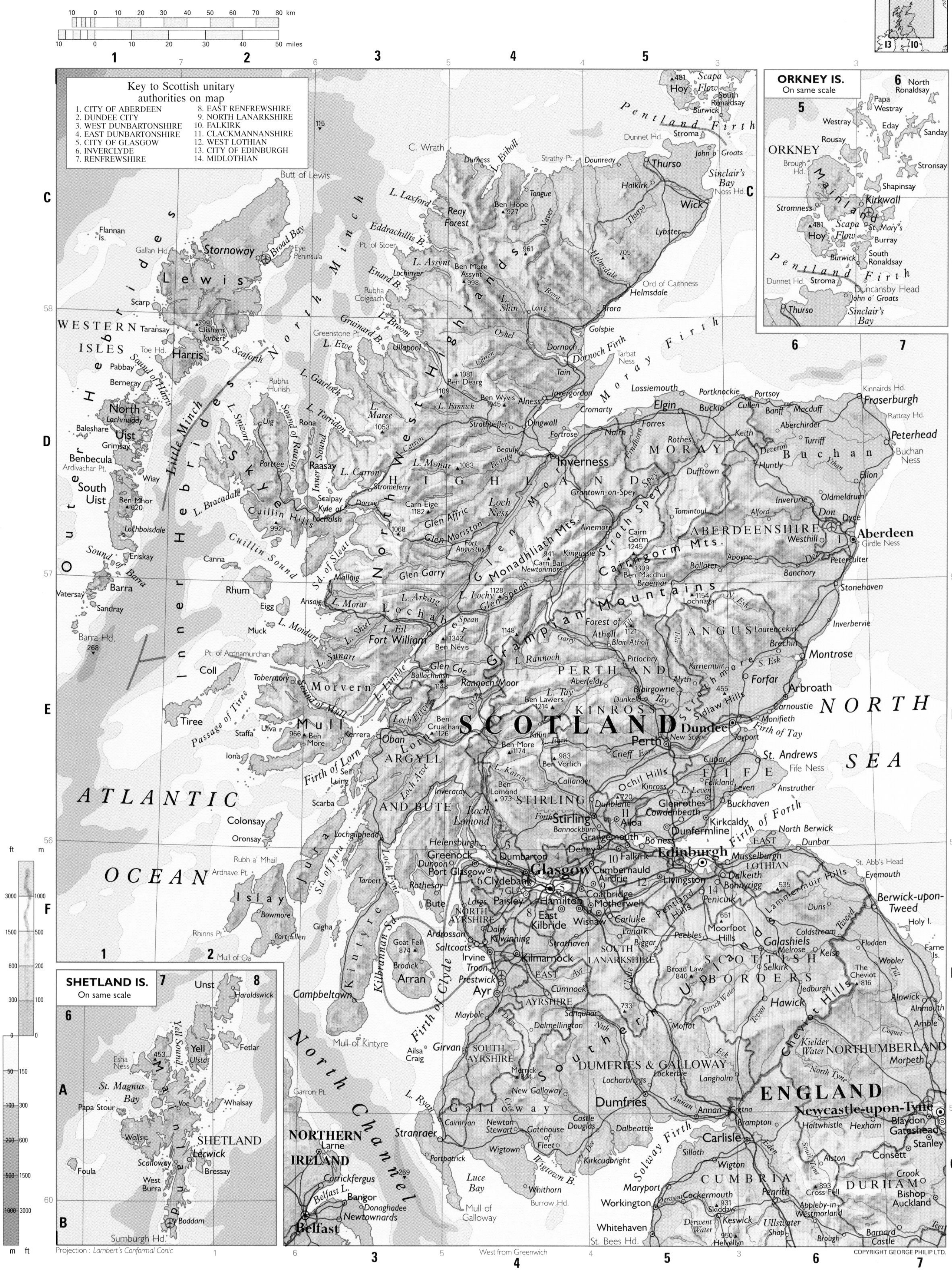

Key to Scottish unitary authorities on map

1. CITY OF ABERDEEN
2. DUNDEE CITY
3. WEST DUNBARTONSHIRE
4. EAST DUNBARTONSHIRE
5. CITY OF GLASGOW
6. INVERCLYDE
7. RENFREWSHIRE
8. EAST RENFREWSHIRE
9. NORTH LANARKSHIRE
10. FALKIRK
11. CLACKMANNANSHIRE
12. WEST LOTHIAN
13. CITY OF EDINBURGH
14. MIDLOTHIAN

ORKNEY IS.
On same scale

SHETLAND IS.
On same scale

Projection : Lambert's Conformal Conic

West from Greenwich

COPYRIGHT GEORGE PHILIP LTD.

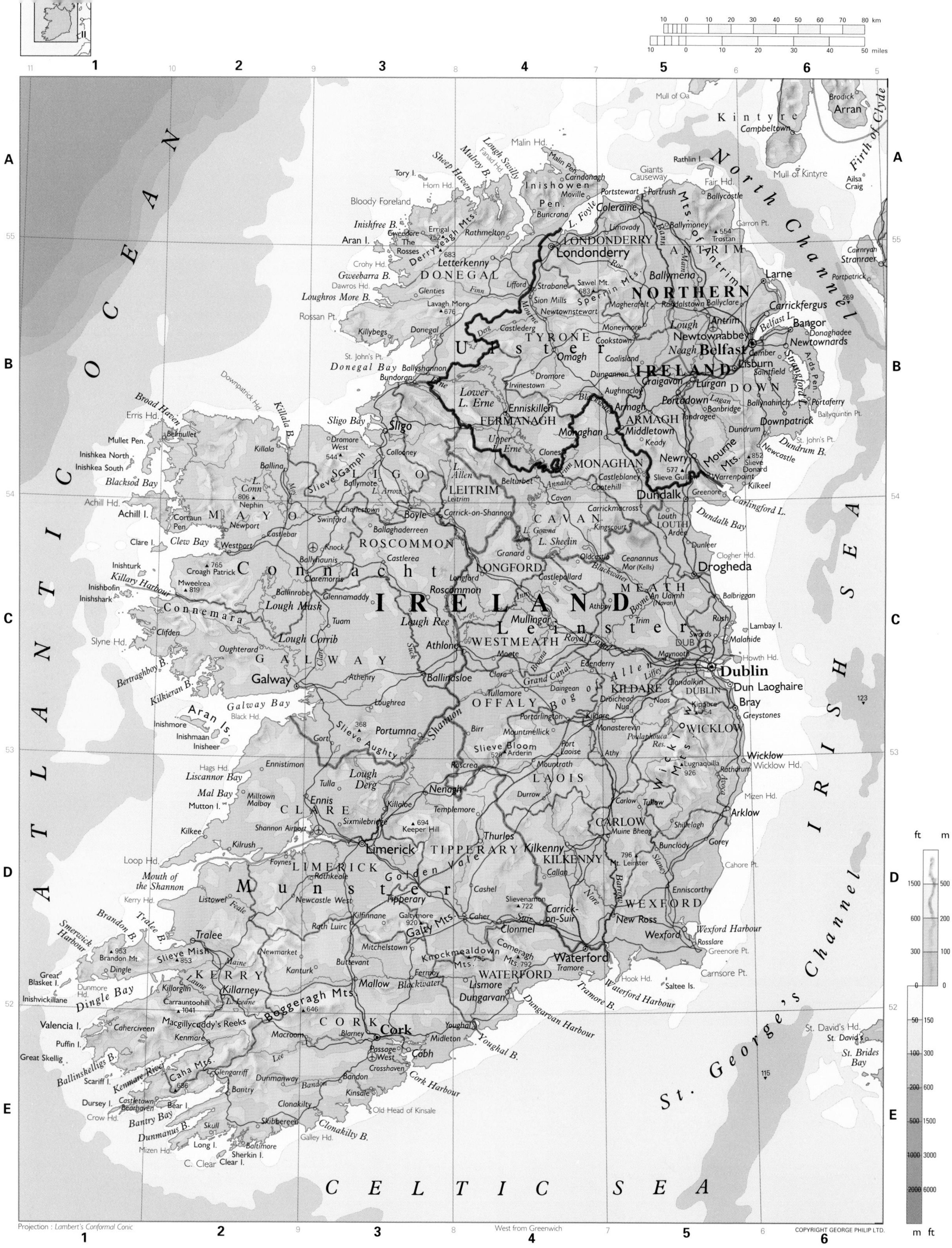

0 10 20 30 40 50 60 70 80 km
0 10 20 30 40 50 miles
1 2 3 4 5 6
A B C D E
ATLANTIC OCEAN
CELTIC SEA
IRISH SEA
North Channel
St. George's Channel
IRELAND
NORTHERN IRELAND
Ulster
Connacht
Leinster
Munster
Kintyre
Campbeltown
Mull of Oa
Brodick
Arran
Firth of Clyde
Rathlin I.
Mull of Kintyre
Ailsa Craig
Cairnryan
Stranraer
Portpatrick
Malin Hd.
Lough Swilly
Fanad Hd.
Mulroy B.
Sheep Haven
Tory I.
Horn Hd.
Bloody Foreland
Inishowen Pen.
Malin Pen.
Carndonagh
Moville
Buncrana
Giants Causeway
Portstewart
Portrush
Coleraine
Fair Hd.
Ballycastle
Garron Pt.
Ballymoney
Trostan
Limavady
L. Foyle
LONDONDERRY
Londonderry
ANTRIM
Mts. of Antrim
Inishfree B.
Gweedore
Errigal
Derryveagh Mts.
Rathmelton
Aran I.
The Rosses
Letterkenny
Crohy Hd.
Gweebarra B.
Dawros Hd.
DONEGAL
Glenties
Lifford
Strabane
Sawel Mt.
Sperrin Mts.
Ballymena
Larne
NORTHERN
Loughros More B.
Lavagh More
Sion Mills
Newtownstewart
Magherafelt
Randalstown
Ballyclare
Carrickfergus
Rossan Pt.
Killybegs
Donegal
Castlederg
TYRONE
Moneymore
Lough Neagh
Antrim
Newtownabbey
Belfast L.
Bangor
Donaghadee
Newtownards
Cookstown
Omagh
Coalisland
Belfast
Comber
St. John's Pt.
Donegal Bay
Ballyshannon
Bundoran
Dungannon
Lisburn
Saintfield
Ards Pen.
Strangford L.
Dromore
Irvinestown
Aughnacloy
Craigavon
Lurgan
DOWN
Portaferry
Ballyquintin Pt.
Lower L. Erne
Enniskillen
FERMANAGH
Blackwater
Armagh
ARMAGH
Portadown
Tandragee
Banbridge
Ballynahinch
Downpatrick
Middletown
Monaghan
Dundrum
St. John's Pt.
Dundrum B.
Upper L. Erne
Clones
Keady
Newcastle
MONAGHAN
Newry
Mourne Mts.
Slieve Donard
Slieve Gullion
Warrenpoint
Kilkeel
Castleblaney
Cootehill
Greenore
Carlingford L.
Dundalk
Dundalk Bay
Broad Haven
Erris Hd.
Downpatrick Hd.
Killala B.
Belmullet
Sligo Bay
Sligo
Dromore West
Mullet Pen.
Inishkea North
Inishkea South
Killala
Ballina
Slieve Gamph
SLIGO
Collooney
Ballymote
L. Arrow
L. Allen
LEITRIM
Leitrim
Belturbet
Annalee
Cavan
Carrickmacross
L. Conn
Nephin
Blacksod Bay
Achill Hd.
Achill I.
Corraun Pen
MAYO
Newport
Charlestown
Swinford
Boyle
Ballaghaderreen
Carrick-on-Shannon
CAVAN
Louth
LOUTH
Ardee
Kingscourt
Clare I.
Clew Bay
Westport
Castlebar
Knock
Ballyhaunis
ROSCOMMON
Castlerea
L. Gowna
L. Sheelin
Granard
LONGFORD
Oldcastle
Ceanannus Mor (Kells)
Dunleer
Clogher Hd.
Drogheda
Inishturk
Croagh Patrick
Killary Harbour
Mweelrea
Inishbofin
Inishshark
Claremorris
Longford
Roscommon
Castlepollard
MEATH
Ballinrobe
Glennamaddy
Lough Mask
Tuam
Lough Ree
Athboy
Boyne
An Uaimh (Navan)
Balbriggan
Connemara
Slyne Hd.
Clifden
Lough Corrib
Athlone
Mullingar
Trim
Rush
Lambay I.
WESTMEATH
Royal Canal
Swords
DUB
Malahide
Oughterard
GALWAY
Clare
Suck
Moate
Maynooth
Howth Hd.
Bertraghboy B.
Galway
Athenry
Ballinasloe
Clara
Brosna
Edenderry
Grand Canal
Bog of Allen
Liffey
KILDARE
Clondalkin
Dublin
DUBLIN
Dun Laoghaire
Kilkieran B.
Tullamore
OFFALY
Daingean
Naas
Droichead Nua
Kippure
Bray
Aran Is.
Galway Bay
Black Hd.
Loughrea
Greystones
Inishmore
Inishmaan
Inisheer
Portumna
Slieve Aughty
Shannon
Birr
Portarlington
Kildare
Monasterevin
Poulaphouca Res.
WICKLOW
Gort
Mountmellick
Slieve Bloom
Arderin
Port Laoise
Athy
Wicklow Mts.
Wicklow
Wicklow Hd.
Hags Hd.
Ennistimon
Liscannor Bay
Lough Derg
Roscrea
Mountrath
LAOIS
Lugnaquilla
Rathdrum
Avoca
Mal Bay
Milltown Malbay
Tulla
Nenagh
Durrow
Mizen Hd.
Mutton I.
Ennis
CLARE
Killaloe
Templemore
Carlow
Tullow
Arklow
Shannon Airport
Sixmilebridge
Keeper Hill
Thurles
CARLOW
Shillelagh
Kilkee
Kilrush
Limerick
Muine Bheag
Bunclody
Gorey
Loop Hd.
Foynes
LIMERICK
TIPPERARY
Kilkenny
KILKENNY
Mt. Leinster
Rathkeale
Golden Vale
Callan
Barrow
Slaney
Cahore Pt.
Mouth of the Shannon
Cashel
Enniscorthy
Kerry Hd.
Listowel
Feale
Newcastle West
Tipperary
Slievenamon
Nore
WEXFORD
Brandon B.
Tralee B.
Kilfinnane
Galtymore
Galty Mts.
Caher
Carrick-on-Suir
New Ross
Wexford Harbour
Smerwick Harbour
Tralee
Rath Luirc
Clonmel
Suir
Wexford
Rosslare
Greenore Pt.
Brandon Mt.
Slieve Mish
Maine
Newmarket
Mitchelstown
Knockmealdown Mts.
Comeragh Mts.
Waterford
Tramore
Carnsore Pt.
Great Blasket I.
Dingle
KERRY
Kanturk
Buttevant
Fermoy
WATERFORD
Hook Hd.
Saltee Is.
Dunmore Hd.
Inishvickillane
Dingle Bay
Killorglin
Laune
Killarney
L. Leane
Mallow
Blackwater
Lismore
Dungarvan
Tramore B.
Waterford Harbour
Carrauntoohill
Boggeragh Mts
Dungarvan Harbour
Valencia I.
Cahirciveen
Macgillycuddy's Reeks
CORK
Blarney
Cork
Youghal
Midleton
Youghal B.
Puffin I.
Kenmare
Macroom
Passage West
Cobh
St. David's Hd.
St. David's
St. Brides Bay
Great Skellig
Ballinskelligs B.
Kenmare River
Caha Mts.
Glengarriff
Lee
Dunmanway
Bandon
Crosshaven
Cork Harbour
Scariff I.
Bantry
Kinsale
Dursey I.
Castletown Bearhaven
Bear I.
Clonakilty
Crow Hd.
Bantry Bay
Old Head of Kinsale
Dunmanus B.
Skull
Skibbereen
Clonakilty B.
Mizen Hd.
Long I.
Baltimore
Sherkin I.
Galley Hd.
C. Clear
Clear I.
ft m
1500 500
600 200
300 100
0 0
50 150
100 300
200 600
500 1500
1000 3000
2000 6000
m ft
Projection : Lambert's Conformal Conic
West from Greenwich
COPYRIGHT GEORGE PHILIP LTD.

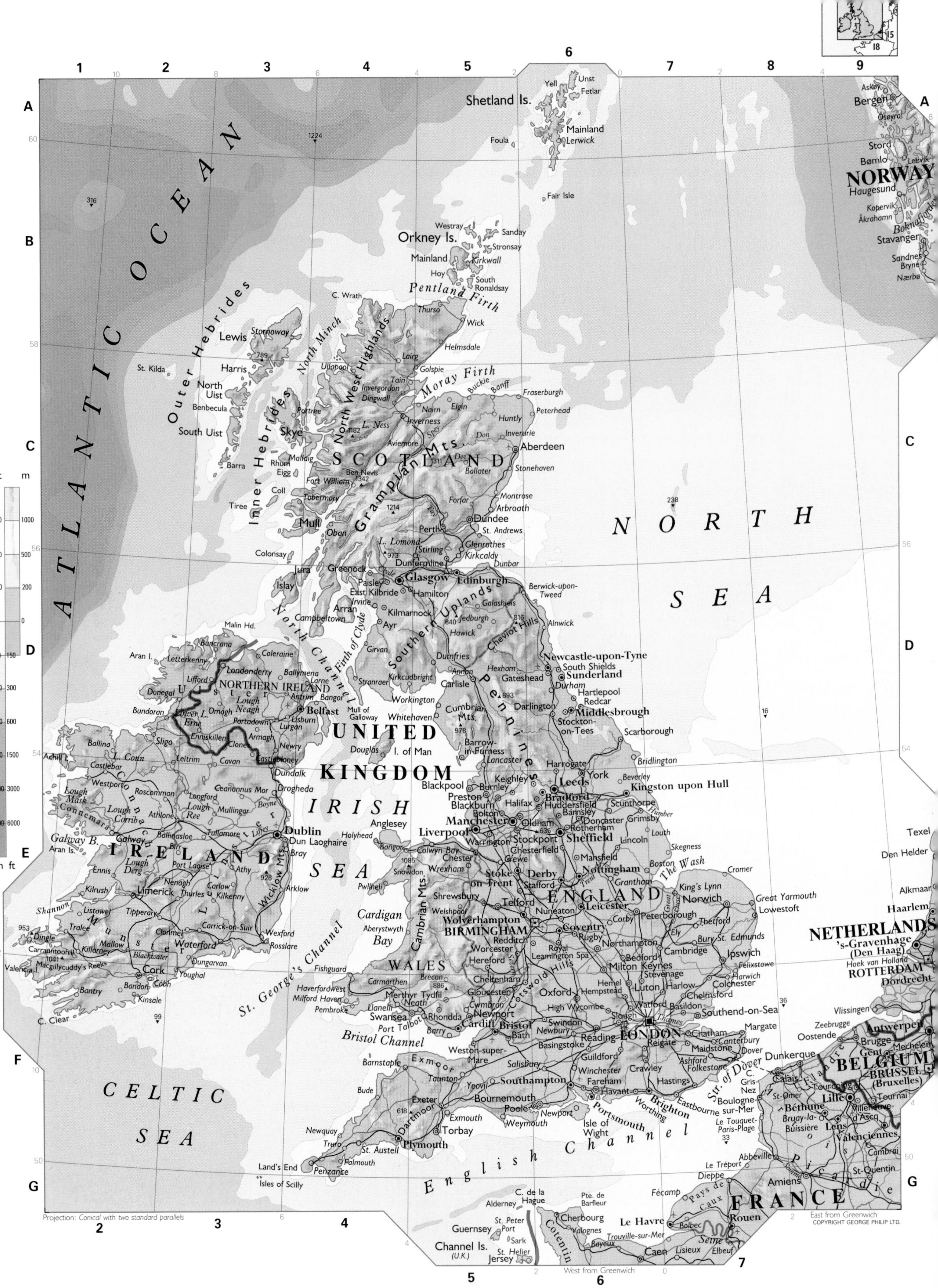

ATLANTIC OCEAN
NORTH SEA
CELTIC SEA
IRISH SEA
English Channel
UNITED KINGDOM
SCOTLAND
NORTHERN IRELAND
ENGLAND
WALES
IRELAND
NORWAY
NETHERLANDS
BELGIUM
FRANCE
Shetland Is.
Yell
Unst
Fetlar
Mainland
Lerwick
Foula
Fair Isle
Orkney Is.
Westray
Sanday
Stronsay
Kirkwall
Hoy
South Ronaldsay
Pentland Firth
C. Wrath
Thurso
Wick
Helmsdale
Outer Hebrides
Lewis
Stornoway
Harris
St. Kilda
North Uist
Benbecula
South Uist
Barra
North Minch
North West Highlands
Ullapool
Lairg
Golspie
Tain
Invergordon
Dingwall
Moray Firth
Buckie
Banff
Fraserburgh
Peterhead
Elgin
Nairn
Inverness
L. Ness
Spey
Huntly
Inverurie
Aberdeen
Stonehaven
Inner Hebrides
Portree
Skye
Mallaig
Aviemore
Grampian Mts.
Ballater
Dee
Rhum
Eigg
Ben Nevis
Fort William
Coll
Tiree
Tobermory
Mull
Oban
Forfar
Montrose
Arbroath
Dundee
Perth
St. Andrews
Tay
L. Lomond
Stirling
Glenrothes
Kirkcaldy
Dunfermline
Dunbar
Colonsay
Jura
Islay
Greenock
Paisley
Glasgow
Edinburgh
East Kilbride
Hamilton
Irvine
Arran
Campbeltown
Kilmarnock
Ayr
Southern Uplands
Galashiels
Jedburgh
Hawick
Cheviot Hills
Berwick-upon-Tweed
Alnwick
North Channel
Firth of Clyde
Girvan
Dumfries
Annan
Stranraer
Kirkcudbright
Mull of Galloway
Malin Hd.
Buncrana
Coleraine
Aran I.
Letterkenny
Londonderry
Ballymena
Larne
Lifford
Donegal
Lough Neagh
Antrim
Bangor
Belfast
Omagh
Lower L. Erne
Portadown
Lisburn
Lurgan
Enniskillen
Armagh
Newry
Clones
Bundoran
Sligo
Ballina
Achill I.
Castlebar
L. Conn
Westport
Leitrim
Cavan
Castleblaney
Dundalk
Drogheda
Ceanannus Mor
Boyne
Roscommon
Longford
Lough Mask
Lough Corrib
Connemara
Athlone
Lough Ree
Mullingar
Galway
Galway B.
Aran Is.
Ballinasloe
Tullamore
Liffey
Dublin
Dun Laoghaire
Bray
Birr
Port Laoise
Athy
Ennis
Lough Derg
Kilrush
Nenagh
Limerick
Thurles
Carlow
Kilkenny
Wicklow Mts.
Arklow
Shannon
Listowel
Tipperary
Tralee
Clonmel
Carrick-on-Suir
Wexford
Rosslare
Dingle
Carrantoohill
Killarney
Mallow
Blackwater
Waterford
Valencia I.
Macgillycuddy's Reeks
Cork
Cobh
Dungarvan
Youghal
Bandon
Bantry
Kinsale
C. Clear
Newcastle-upon-Tyne
South Shields
Sunderland
Hexham
Gateshead
Durham
Hartlepool
Redcar
Middlesbrough
Carlisle
Pennines
Darlington
Stockton-on-Tees
Workington
Whitehaven
Cumbrian Mts.
Scarborough
Barrow-in-Furness
I. of Man
Douglas
Lancaster
Harrogate
Bridlington
York
Beverley
Kingston upon Hull
Keighley
Leeds
Blackpool
Burnley
Preston
Blackburn
Bradford
Halifax
Huddersfield
Bolton
Barnsley
Scunthorpe
Grimsby
Humber
Manchester
Oldham
Doncaster
Rotherham
Liverpool
Stockport
Sheffield
Warrington
Chesterfield
Lincoln
Louth
Anglesey
Holyhead
Bangor
Colwyn Bay
Chester
Crewe
Mansfield
Skegness
Snowdon
Wrexham
Stoke on Trent
Derby
Nottingham
Boston
The Wash
Cromer
Pwllheli
Stafford
Trent
Grantham
King's Lynn
Norwich
Great Yarmouth
Lowestoft
Shrewsbury
Telford
Leicester
Welshpool
Cambrian Mts.
Cardigan Bay
Wolverhampton
Nuneaton
Corby
Peterborough
Thetford
BIRMINGHAM
Coventry
Ely
Bury St. Edmunds
Aberystwyth
Redditch
Rugby
Northampton
Worcester
Royal Leamington Spa
Bedford
Cambridge
Ipswich
Hereford
Milton Keynes
Felixstowe
Stevenage
Harwich
Fishguard
Brecon
Cheltenham
Hemel Hempstead
Luton
Harlow
Colchester
Carmarthen
Gloucester
Oxford
Chelmsford
Haverfordwest
Milford Haven
Pembroke
Merthyr Tydfil
Neath
Llanelli
Swansea
Cwmbran
Newport
High Wycombe
Watford
Basildon
Southend-on-Sea
Rhondda
Port Talbot
Cardiff
Bristol
Swindon
Slough
Thames
Barry
Bath
Newbury
Reading
LONDON
Chatham
Margate
Canterbury
Maidstone
Dover
Bristol Channel
Basingstoke
Guildford
Reigate
Weston-super-Mare
Salisbury
Winchester
Crawley
Ashford
Folkestone
Barnstaple
Exmoor
Taunton
Yeovil
Southampton
Fareham
Havant
Hastings
Bude
Exeter
Bournemouth
Poole
Weymouth
Newport
Isle of Wight
Portsmouth
Worthing
Brighton
Eastbourne
Dartmoor
Exmouth
Torbay
Newquay
Truro
St. Austell
Plymouth
Falmouth
Land's End
Penzance
Isles of Scilly
St. George's Channel
Str. of Dover
Alderney
C. de la Hague
Pte. de Barfleur
Guernsey
St. Peter Port
Sark
Channel Is. (U.K.)
St. Helier
Jersey
Cherbourg
Valognes
Cotentin
Bayeux
Caen
Lisieux
Trouville-sur-Mer
Le Havre
Bolbec
Fécamp
Pays de Caux
Rouen
Elbeuf
Seine
Dieppe
Le Tréport
Abbeville
Somme
Amiens
Picardie
St-Quentin
Cambrai
Le Touquet-Paris-Plage
Boulogne-sur-Mer
C. Gris-Nez
Calais
Dunkerque
St-Omer
Béthune
Bruay-la-Buissière
Lens
Lille
Villeneuve-d'Ascq
Valenciennes
Tourcoing
Tournai
Flandre
Oostende
Zeebrugge
Brugge
Gent
Antwerpen
Mechelen
BRUSSEL (Bruxelles)
Vlissingen
Dordrecht
ROTTERDAM
Hoek van Holland
's-Gravenhage (Den Haag)
Haarlem
Alkmaar
Den Helder
Texel
Askøy
Bergen
Osøyro
Stord
Bømlo
Leirvik
Haugesund
Kopervik
Åkrahamn
Boknafjorden
Stavanger
Sandnes
Bryne
Nærbø
1224
316
789
1182
1342
1214
973
840
816
893
978
636
1085
926
886
618
953
1041
238
16
36
33
99
ft m
3000 1000
1500 500
600 200
0 0
50 150
100 300
200 600
500 1500
1000 3000
2000 6000
m ft
Projection: Conical with two standard parallels
West from Greenwich
East from Greenwich
COPYRIGHT GEORGE PHILIP LTD.

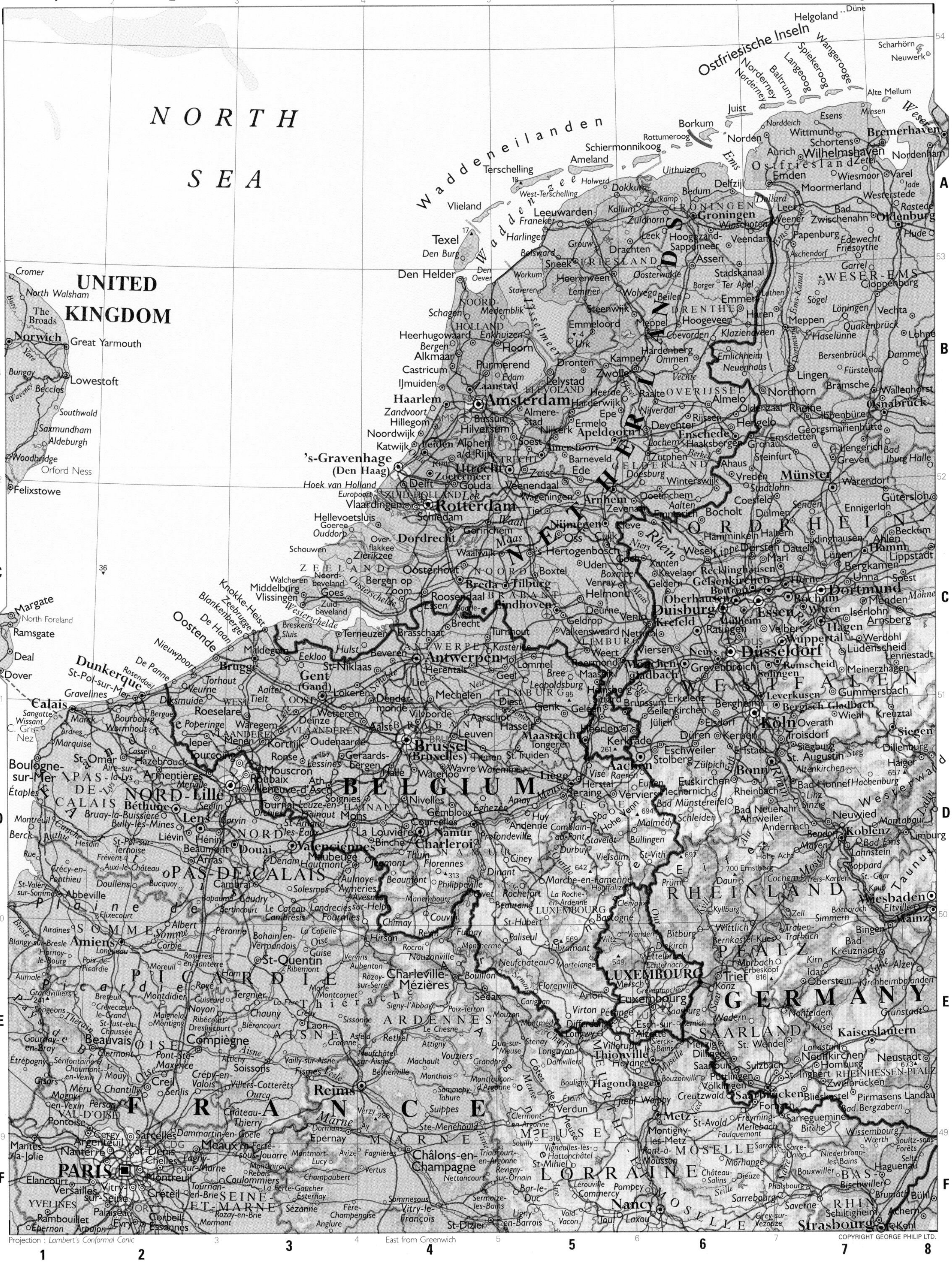

10 0 10 20 30 40 50 60 70 80 90 km
10 0 10 20 30 40 50 60 miles

NORTH SEA

UNITED KINGDOM

Cromer
North Walsham
The Broads
Norwich Great Yarmouth
Bungay Lowestoft
Beccles
Southwold
Saxmundham
Aldeburgh
Woodbridge Orford Ness
Felixstowe

Margate
North Foreland
Ramsgate
Deal
Dover
Calais
Sangatte
Wissant
C. Gris Nez
Boulogne-sur-Mer
Étaples
Le Touquet
Berck
Rue
Montreuil

NETHERLANDS

Helgoland Düne
Ostfriesische Inseln
Scharhörn Neuwerk
Wangerooge
Spiekeroog
Langeoog
Baltrum
Norderney
Juist Borkum
Waddeneilanden
Schiermonnikoog
Ameland
Terschelling
West-Terschelling
Vlieland
Texel
Den Burg
Den Helder

Bremerhaven
Nordenham
Wesermünde
Wilhelmshaven Varel
Emden Oldenburg
Leer
Groningen Winschoten

Leeuwarden
Franeker Harlingen
Sneek
Heerenveen
Assen
Emmen

Haarlem
Amsterdam
's-Gravenhage (Den Haag)
Delft
Rotterdam
Dordrecht
Vlaardingen
Schiedam

Utrecht
Arnhem
Nijmegen
Apeldoorn
Deventer
Enschede
Zwolle
Almelo

's-Hertogenbosch
Eindhoven
Tilburg
Breda
Roosendaal

Münster
Osnabrück
Dortmund
Essen Bochum
Duisburg
Krefeld
Düsseldorf
Wuppertal
Köln
Bonn
Aachen

ZEELAND
Middelburg
Vlissingen
Goes

BELGIUM
Brussel (Bruxelles)
Antwerpen
Gent (Gand)
Brugge
Oostende
Mechelen
Leuven
Namur
Charleroi
Mons
Liège
Verviers

LUXEMBOURG
Luxembourg
Diekirch
Arlon

GERMANY
Koblenz
Wiesbaden
Mainz
Trier
Saarbrücken
Kaiserslautern

FRANCE
Lille
Dunkerque
Roubaix
Valenciennes
Douai
Lens
Béthune
Arras
Cambrai
Amiens
Abbeville
St-Quentin
Reims
Châlons-en-Champagne
Laon
Soissons
Compiègne
Beauvais
Charleville-Mézières
Sedan
Verdun
Metz
Nancy
Strasbourg
PARIS
Versailles

Projection: Lambert's Conformal Conic
East from Greenwich

COPYRIGHT GEORGE PHILIP LTD.

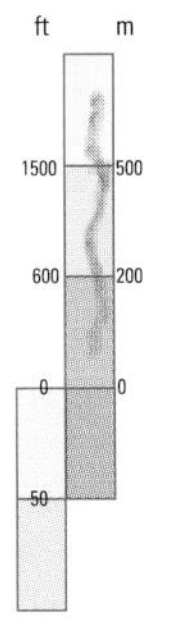

Underlined towns give their name to the administrative area in which they stand.

ft m
1500
600
0
m ft

MIDDLE EUROPE 1:5 000 000

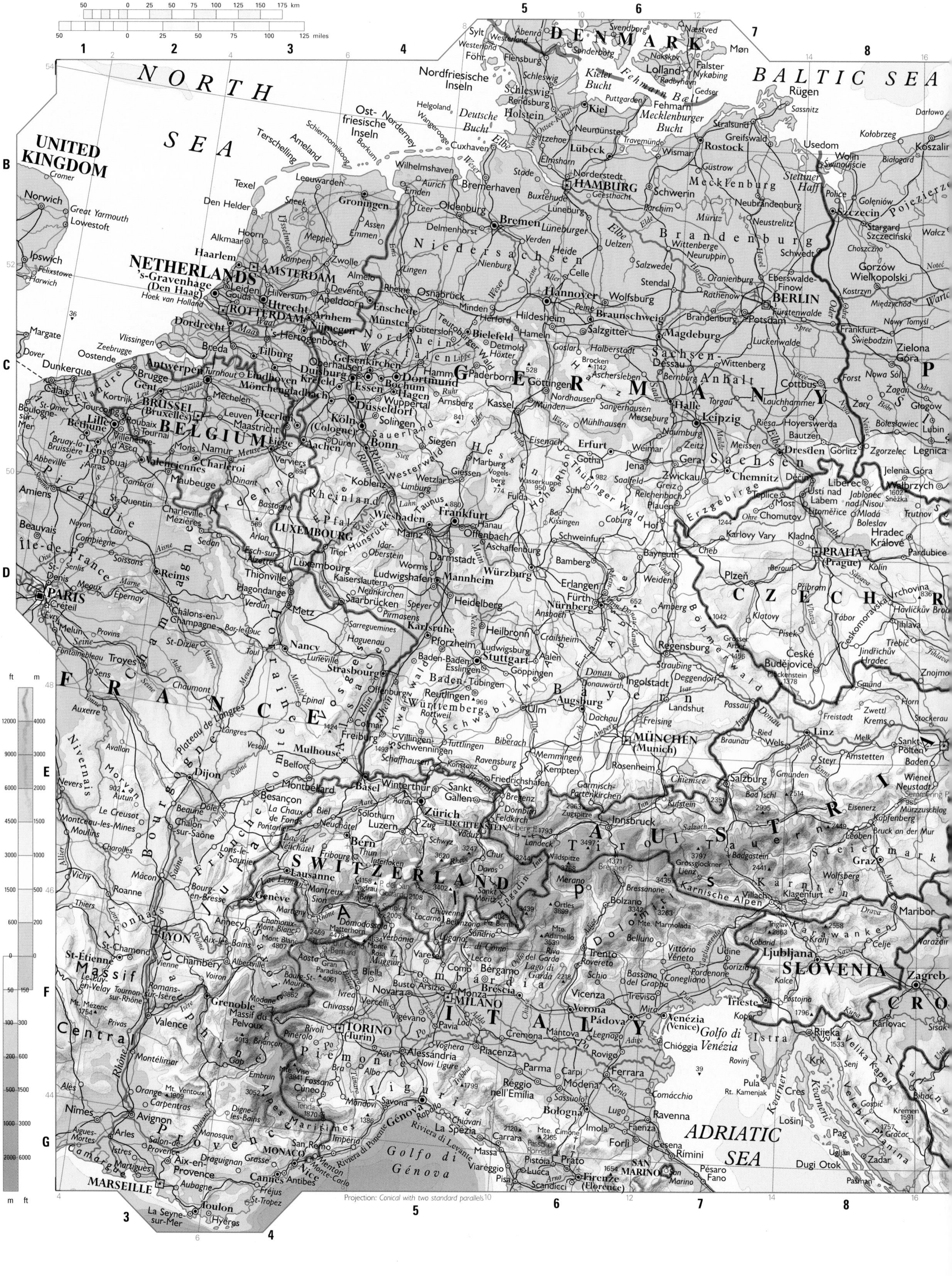

0 25 50 75 100 125 150 175 km
0 25 50 75 100 125 miles
NORTH SEA
BALTIC SEA
UNITED KINGDOM
DENMARK
NETHERLANDS
BELGIUM
LUXEMBOURG
GERMANY
FRANCE
SWITZERLAND
LIECHTENSTEIN
AUSTRIA
CZECH R.
SLOVENIA
ITALY
MONACO
SAN MARINO
ADRIATIC SEA
Golfo di Génova
Golfo di Venézia
AMSTERDAM
's-Gravenhage (Den Haag)
ROTTERDAM
BRUSSEL (Bruxelles)
PARIS
BERLIN
HAMBURG
MÜNCHEN (Munich)
PRAHA (Prague)
LYON
MARSEILLE
MILANO
TORINO (Turin)
Frankfurt
Köln (Cologne)
Zürich
Bern
Genève
Venézia (Venice)
Ljubljana
Zagreb
Firenze (Florence)
Génova
Bologna
Strasbourg
Stuttgart
Nürnberg
Leipzig
Dresden
Hannover
Bremen
Projection: Conical with two standard parallels

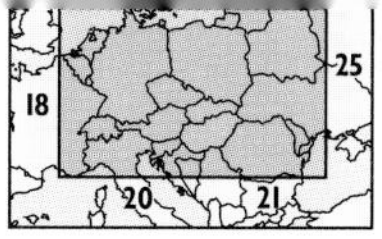

LITHUANIA
BELARUS
POLAND
UKRAINE
SLOVAK REP.
HUNGARY
ROMANIA
MOLDOVA
BOSNIA-HERZEGOVINA
YUGOSLAVIA
BULGARIA
C.Z.E.CH REP.
CROATIA

Vilnius · Kaliningrad (Russia) · Gdynia · Gdańsk · Elbląg · Olsztyn · Suwałki · Hrodna · MINSK · Mahilyow · Krychaw · Cherykaw · Babruysk · Homyel · Dobrush

Szczecinek · Słupsk · Lębork · Sopot · Bytów · Chojnice · Świecie · Grudziądz · Brodnica · Toruń · Bydgoszcz · Piła · Inowrocław · Gniezno · Poznań · Września · Śrem · Kościan · Leszno · Ostrów Wielkopolski · Kalisz · Konin · Turek · Koło · Kutno · Łódź · Pabianice

WARSZAWA (Warsaw) · Legionowo · Pruszków · Otwock · Siedlce · Mińsk Mazowiecki · Żyrardów · Skierniewice · Grójec · Radom · Puławy · Lublin · Chełm · Zamość

Białystok · Łomża · Ostrołęka · Ciechanów · Mława · Płock · Włocławek · Pułtusk · Ostrów Mazowiecka · Bielsk Podlaski · Hajnówka · Biała Podlaska · Brest · Malaryta · Pinsk · Stolin

Wrocław · Świdnica · Oława · Dzierżoniów · Kłodzko · Nysa · Opole · Częstochowa · Kielce · Tarnobrzeg · Rzeszów · Przemyśl · Lviv (Lvov)

Katowice · Gliwice · Zabrze · Bytom · Sosnowiec · Chorzów · Tychy · Kraków · Oświęcim · Bielsko-Biała · Tarnów · Nowy Sącz · Krosno · Sanok

Ostrava · Frýdek-Místek · Havířov · Karviná · Cieszyn · Żilina · Martin · Trenčín · Nitra · Bratislava · WIEN (Vienna) · Košice · Prešov · Humenné · Uzhhorod · Mukacheve · Berehove · Khust

Olomouc · Přerov · Prostějov · Vyškov · Brno · Zlín

Ivano-Frankivsk · Chernivtsi · Kolomyya · Ternopil · Khmelnytskyy · Vinnytsya · Lutsk · Rivne · Dubno · Zhytomyr · KYYIV (Kiev) · Bila Tserkva · Uman

Kovel · Lyuboml · Novovolynsk · Volodymyr-Volynskyy · Chervonohrad · Korosten · Novohrad-Volynskyy · Fastiv · Vasylkiv

BUDAPEST · Miskolc · Eger · Nyíregyháza · Debrecen · Szolnok · Kecskemét · Szeged · Pécs · Kaposvár · Szombathely · Zalaegerszeg · Nagykanizsa · Győr · Tatabánya · Veszprém · Székesfehérvár

Oradea · Satu Mare · Baia Mare · Cluj-Napoca · Turda · Târgu Mureş · Reghin · Bistrița · Alba-Iulia · Deva · Hunedoara · Arad · Timişoara · Reşiţa · Caransebeş · Lugoj

Braşov · Sibiu · Făgăraş · Piatra Neamţ · Bacău · Roman · Iaşi · Vaslui · Bârlad · Focşani · Galaţi · Brăila · Buzău · Ploieşti · Târgovişte · Piteşti · Râmnicu Vâlcea · Târgu-Jiu · Craiova · Drobeta-Turnu-Severin · Slatina · BUCUREŞTI (Bucharest) · Constanţa · Călăraşi · Slobozia · Mangalia

Chişinău · Tiraspol · Tighina · Bălţi · Orhei · Cahul · Comrat

Novi Sad · Subotica · Zrenjanin · Pančevo · BEOGRAD (Belgrade) · Smederevo · Požarevac · Kragujevac · Čačak · Kraljevo · Niš · Zaječar · Vidin

Banja Luka · Doboj · Tuzla · Bijeljina · Zenica · Sarajevo · Višegrad

BULGARIA · Ruse · Varna · Dobrich · Razgrad · Silistra · Tutrakan · Zimnicea · Giurgiu

Zatoka Gdańska · Zalew Wiślany · Pojezierze Mazurski · Pripet · Dunărea (Danube) · Tisza · Mureş · Sava · Drava · Balaton · Neusiedler See · Carpaţii Meridionali · Nízke Tatry · Biele Karpaty · Vychodné Beskydy · Západné Beskydy · Dobrudja · Lacul Razelm · Ozero Sasyk

East from Greenwich

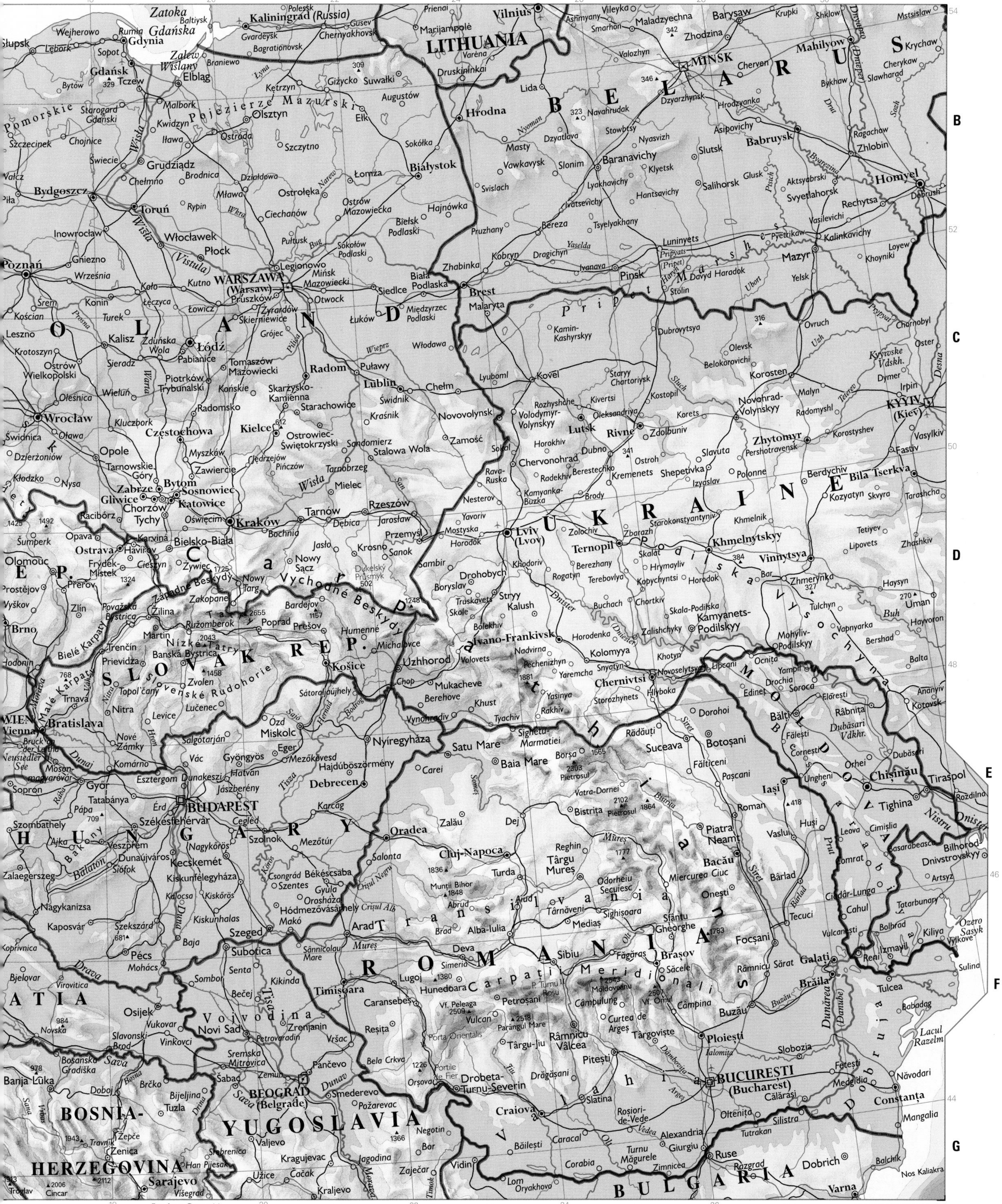

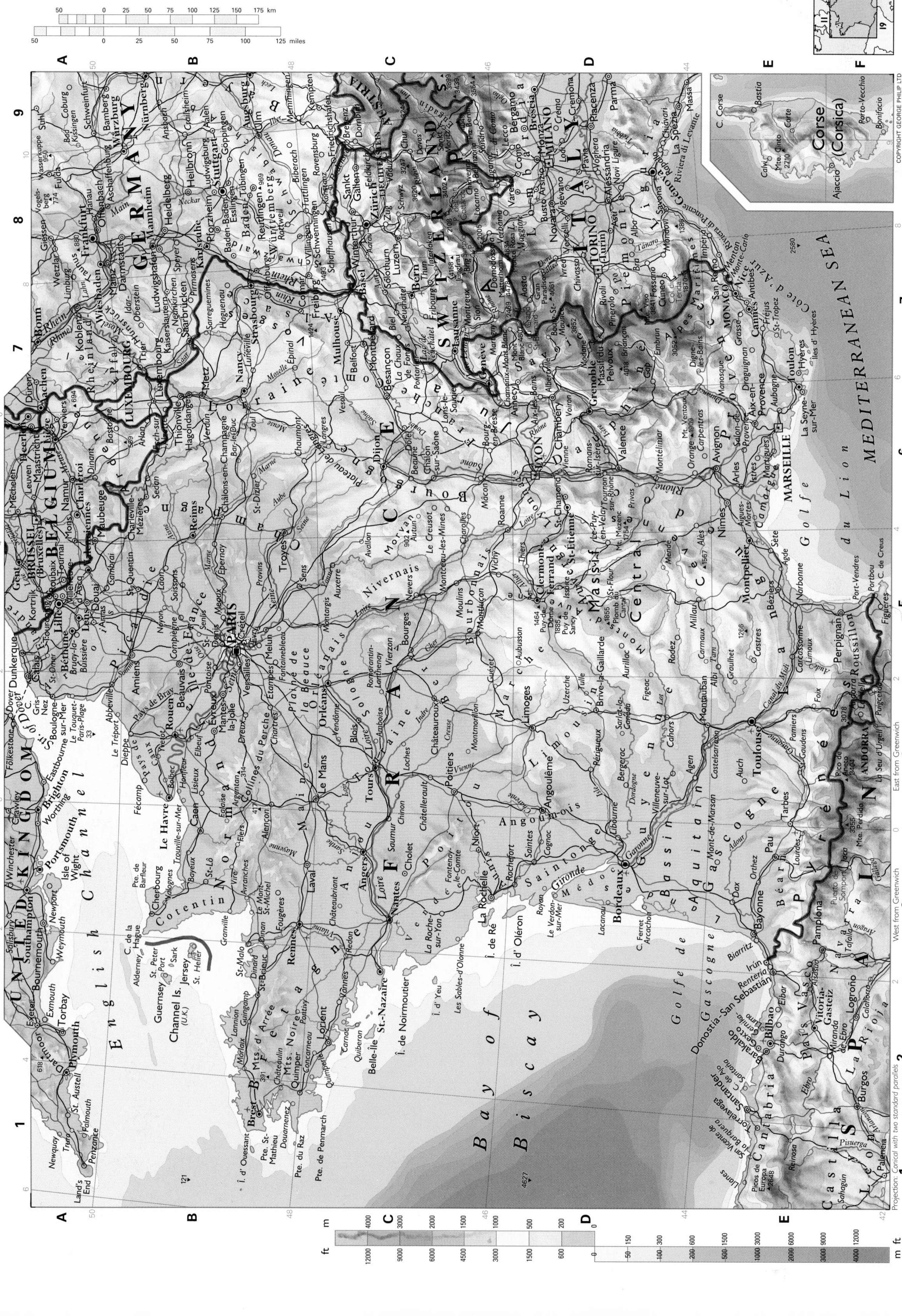
50 0 25 50 75 100 125 150 175 km
50 0 25 50 75 100 125 miles
FRANCE
PARIS
UNITED KINGDOM
BELGIUM
GERMANY
LUXEMBOURG
SWITZERLAND
ITALY
SPAIN
ANDORRA
MONACO
English Channel
Bay of Biscay
Golfe de Gascogne
Golfe du Lion
MEDITERRANEAN SEA
Massif Central
Pyrénées
Alpes
Corse (Corsica)
Channel Is. (U.K.)
Bretagne
Normandie
Bourgogne
Aquitaine
Provence
Lorraine
Champagne
Île-de-France
Picardie
Limousin
Auvergne
Languedoc
Gascogne
LYON
MARSEILLE
Bordeaux
Toulouse
Nantes
Lille
Strasbourg
Nice
Montpellier
Rennes
Reims
Le Havre
Dijon
Grenoble
Rouen
Limoges
Clermont-Ferrand
Orléans
Tours
Brest
Perpignan
Bayonne
Genève
Bern
Zürich
TORINO
MILANO
Projection: Conical with two standard parallels
West from Greenwich
East from Greenwich
COPYRIGHT GEORGE PHILIP LTD
m ft
12000 9000 6000 4500 3000 1500 600 0
4000 3000 2000 1500 1000 500 200 0
50 150 100 300 200 600 500 1500 1000 3000 2000 6000 3000 9000 4000 12000

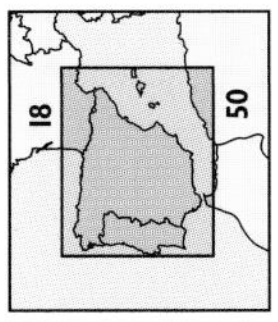

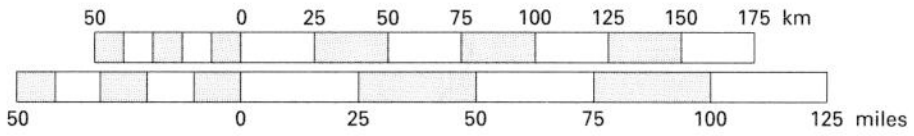

50 0 25 50 75 100 125 150 175 km
50 0 25 50 75 100 125 miles

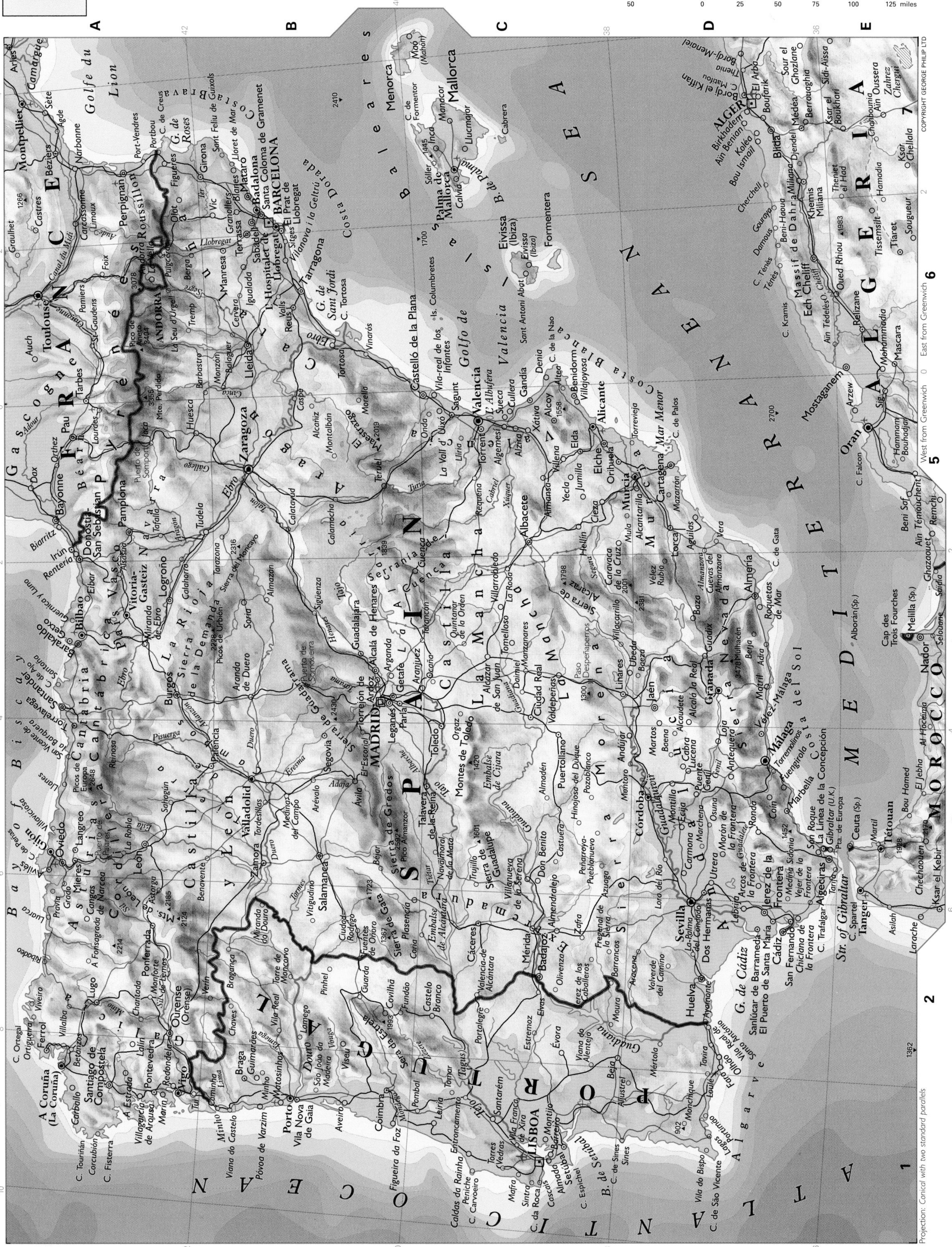

SPAIN

PORTUGAL

FRANCE

ALGERIA

MOROCCO

MADRID

BARCELONA

Valencia

Sevilla

Málaga

Zaragoza

LISBOA

Bilbao

Porto

ANDORRA

Mallorca

Menorca

Eivissa (Ibiza)

Formentera

ATLANTIC OCEAN

MEDITERRANEAN SEA

Balearic Is.

Golfe du Lion

Bay of Biscay

Pyrénées

Str. of Gibraltar

COPYRIGHT GEORGE PHILIP LTD

Projection: Conical with two standard parallels

West from Greenwich 0 East from Greenwich

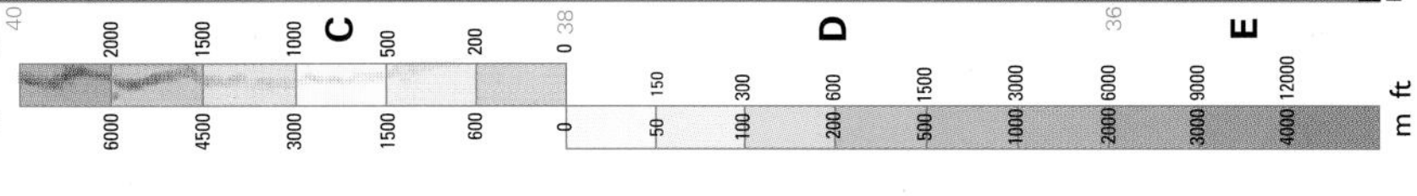

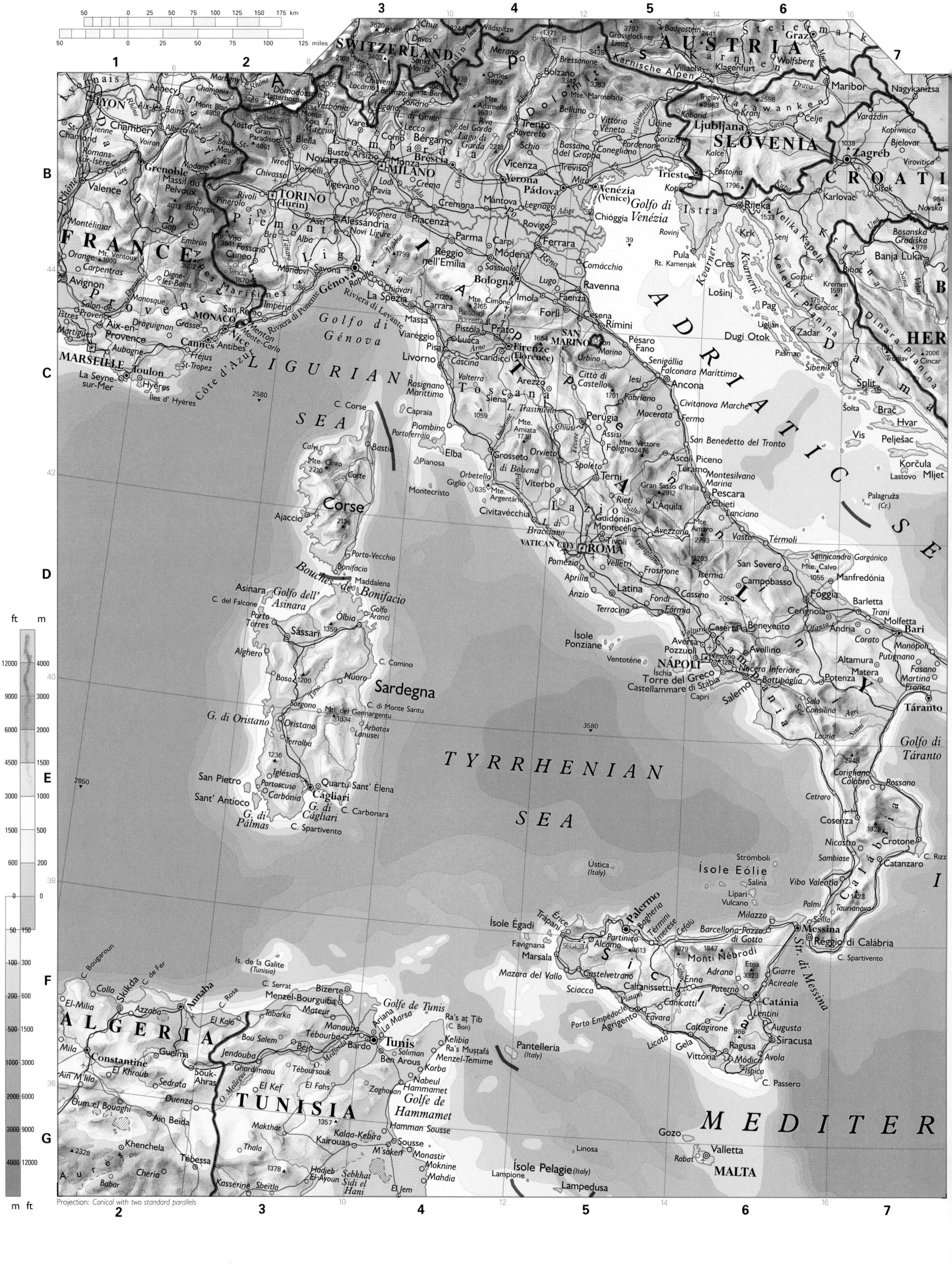

50 0 25 50 75 100 125 150 175 km
50 0 25 50 75 100 125 miles

SWITZERLAND
AUSTRIA
FRANCE
SLOVENIA
CROATIA
ALGERIA
TUNISIA
MALTA

Graz
Wolfsberg
Klagenfurt
Villach
Maribor
Nagykanizsa
Kobarid
Triglav 2863
Karawanken
Ljubljana
Celje
Varaždin
Kranj
Koprivnica
Bjelovar
Udine
Gorizia
Pordenone
Trieste
Postojna
Rijeka
Zagreb
Virovitica
Karlovac
Sisak
Bosanska Gradiška
Banja Luka
Bihać
Bolzano
Merano
Trento
Rovereto
Belluno
Vittório Véneto
Conegliano
Bassano del Grappa
Schio
Vicenza
Treviso
Venézia (Venice)
Golfo di Venézia
Verona
Padova
Mira
Chióggia
Rovigo
Legnago
Mantova
Adige
Pula
Cres
Krk
Lošinj
Pag
Zadar
Dugi Otok
Pašman
Šibenik
Split
Brač
Hvar
Vis
Korčula
Lastovo
Mljet
Peljesac
Palagruža

LYON
Chambéry
Grenoble
Annecy
Mont Blanc 4808
Aosta
Gran Paradiso 4061
TORINO (Turin)
Ivrea
Biella
Novara
Vercelli
Pavia
Lodi
Crema
Cremona
MILANO
Monza
Bérgamo
Brescia
Lago di Garda
Como
Lecco
Varese
Sondrio
Valence
Montélimar
Avignon
Carpentras
Orange
Gap
Briançon
Cuneo
Fossano
Savona
Génova
La Spézia
Massa
Carrara
Parma
Piacenza
Reggio nell'Emília
Módena
Bologna
Ferrara
Comácchio
Ravenna
Imola
Faenza
Forlì
Cesena
Rimini
MARSEILLE
Toulon
Nice
MONACO
Cannes
Antibes
San Remo
Impéria

LIGURIAN SEA
Golfo di Génova
ADRIATIC SEA
TYRRHENIAN SEA
MEDITER...

C. Corse
Calvi
Bastia
M. Cinto 2710
Corte
Ajaccio
Corse 2136
Porto-Vecchio
Bonifacio
Bouches de Bonifacio
Maddalena
Asinara
Golfo dell' Asinara
Porto Tórres
Sássari
Álghero
Bosa
Nuoro
Oristano
G. di Oristano
Terralba
Iglésias
San Pietro
Sant' Antíoco
Carbónia
Cágliari
G. di Cágliari
C. Spartivento
Sardegna
Elba
Piombino
Portoferráio
Capraia
Pianosa
Montecristo
Giglio
Livorno
Pisa
Lucca
Pistóia
Prato
Firenze (Florence)
Siena
Arezzo
Perúgia
Assisi
L. Trasimeno
Grosseto
Orbetello
Orvieto
Viterbo
Terni
Spoleto
Rieti
L'Aquila
ROMA
VATICAN CITY
Civitavécchia
L. di Bracciano
Tívoli
Frosinone
Latina
Ánzio
Terracina
Fondi
Cassino
Formia
Gaeta
Ancona
Macerata
Fermo
Ascoli Piceno
Teramo
Pescara
Chieti
Lanciano
Vasto
Térmoli
Campobasso
Isérnia
Foggia
Manfredónia
Barletta
Trani
Andria
Bari
Molfetta
Monópoli
Cerignola
Benevento
NÁPOLI
Avellino
Salerno
Capri
Ischia
Caserta
Aversa
Pozzuoli
Torre del Greco
Castellammare di Stábia
Nocera Inferiore
Battipáglia
Potenza
Matera
Altamura
Putignano
Fasano
Martina Franca
Táranto
Golfo di Táranto
Coriglano Cálabro
Rossano
Cosenza
Cetraro
Nicastro
Crotone
Catanzaro
Vibo Valéntia
Palmi
Réggio di Calábria
Messina
Str. di Messina
Sicília
Palermo
Trápani
Marsala
Mazara del Vallo
Castelvetrano
Sciacca
Agrigento
Caltanissetta
Enna
Caltagirone
Gela
Ragusa
Módica
Siracusa
Augusta
Catánia
Etna 3323
Acireale
Giarre
Paternò
Ísole Eólie
Strómboli
Lípari
Vulcano
Salina
Ústica
Pantelleria
Ísole Pelagie
Lampedusa
Linosa
Gozo
Valletta
MALTA

Annaba
Constantine
Skikda
Collo
El Kala
Tabarka
Bizerte
Menzel-Bourguiba
Mateur
Tunis
Golfe de Tunis
Ariana
La Marsa
Béja
Jendouba
El Kef
Kairouan
Sousse
Monastir
Mahdia
El Jem
Kasserine
Thala
Gafsa
Makthar
Sfax
Golfe de Hammamet
Hammamet
Nabeul
Korba
Kélibia
Ra's aṭ Ṭib (C. Bon)

ft m
12000 4000
9000 3000
6000 2000
4500 1500
3000 1000
1500 500
600 200
0 0

Projection: Conical with two standard parallels

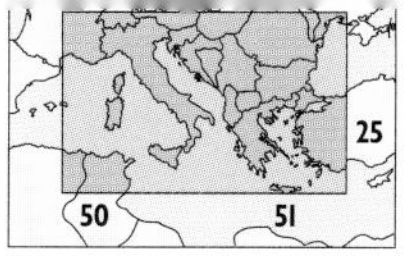
25
50
51

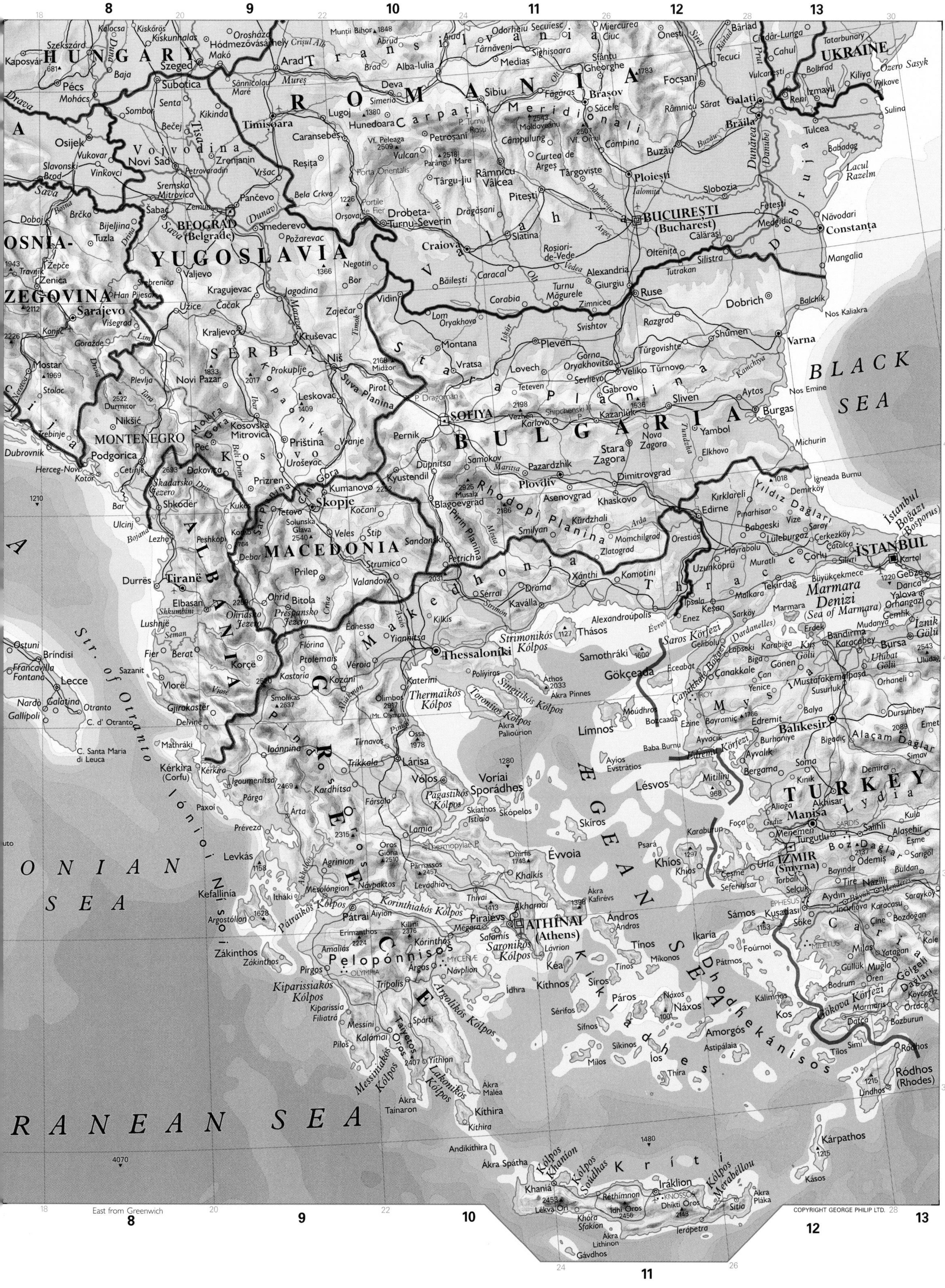
8
9
10
11
12
13
B
C
D
E
F
G
HUNGARY
ROMANIA
UKRAINE
YUGOSLAVIA
BOSNIA-HERZEGOVINA
SERBIA
MONTENEGRO
Kosovo
MACEDONIA
ALBANIA
BULGARIA
GREECE
TURKEY
Transilvania
Carpații Meridionali
Vojvodina
Walachia
Dobruja
Stara Planina
Rhodopi Planina
Thrace
Makedhonía
Pindhos
Kikládhes
Dhodhekánisos
Kríti
Pelopónnisos
Mysia
Lydia
Caria
BLACK SEA
AEGEAN SEA
IONIAN SEA
MEDITERRANEAN SEA
Str. of Otranto
Iónioi Nísoi
Marmara Denizi (Sea of Marmara)
BEOGRAD (Belgrade)
BUCUREȘTI (Bucharest)
SOFIYA
ATHÍNAI (Athens)
İSTANBUL
Skopje
Tiranë
Sarajevo
Podgorica
Szeged
Pécs
Mohács
Kaposvár
Kalocsa
Baja
Makó
Hódmezővásárhely
Arad
Timișoara
Lugoj
Deva
Hunedoara
Alba-Iulia
Sibiu
Brașov
Făgăraș
Sighișoara
Mediaș
Ploiești
Pitești
Râmnicu Vâlcea
Târgu-Jiu
Craiova
Drobeta-Turnu-Severin
Slatina
Caracal
Alexandria
Giurgiu
Ruse
Buzău
Brăila
Galați
Focșani
Tulcea
Constanța
Mangalia
Călărași
Slobozia
Medgidia
Sulina
Izmail
Reni
Chișinău
Subotica
Novi Sad
Zrenjanin
Pančevo
Smederevo
Kragujevac
Niš
Kraljevo
Čačak
Užice
Valjevo
Šabac
Novi Pazar
Priština
Prizren
Peć
Kosovska Mitrovica
Uroševac
Vranje
Leskovac
Pirot
Osijek
Vukovar
Vinkovci
Tuzla
Zenica
Mostar
Dubrovnik
Nikšić
Kotor
Bar
Ulcinj
Shkodër
Durrës
Elbasan
Berat
Fier
Vlorë
Korçë
Gjirokastër
Tetovo
Kumanovo
Veles
Štip
Prilep
Bitola
Ohrid
Strumica
Vidin
Lom
Montana
Vratsa
Pleven
Lovech
Gabrovo
Veliko Tŭrnovo
Razgrad
Shumen
Dobrich
Varna
Burgas
Sliven
Yambol
Kazanlŭk
Stara Zagora
Plovdiv
Pazardzhik
Pernik
Kyustendil
Blagoevgrad
Dimitrovgrad
Khaskovo
Kŭrdzhali
Edirne
Kırklareli
Lüleburgaz
Tekirdağ
Çorlu
Gebze
Bursa
Bandırma
Balıkesir
Çanakkale
Edremit
Manisa
İZMIR (Smyrna)
Aydın
Muğla
Bodrum
Marmaris
Thessaloníki
Kavála
Dráma
Sérrai
Xánthi
Komotiní
Alexandroúpolis
Kozáni
Flórina
Kastoría
Ioánnina
Kérkira (Corfu)
Préveza
Árta
Tríkkala
Lárisa
Vólos
Lamía
Kardhítsa
Agrínion
Mesolóngion
Pátrai
Kórinthos
Árgos
Náfplion
Trípolis
Kalámai
Spárti
Pírgos
Piraiévs
Khalkís
Thásos
Samothráki
Gökçeada
Límnos
Lésvos
Mitilíni
Khíos
Sámos
Ikaría
Skíros
Évvoia
Ándros
Tínos
Síros
Páros
Náxos
Mílos
Thíra
Amorgós
Kos
Ródhos (Rhodes)
Kárpathos
Kásos
Kíthira
Zákinthos
Kefallinía
Levkás
Khaniá
Réthimnon
Iráklion
Ierápetra
Gávdhos
Thermaïkós Kólpos
Saronikós Kólpos
Korinthiakós Kólpos
Patraikós Kólpos
Argolikós Kólpos
Lakonikós Kólpos
Messiniakós Kólpos
Kiparissiakós Kólpos
Saros Körfezi
Edremit Körfezi
Gökova Körfezi
Dunărea (Danube)
Sava
Drava
Olympus
Thermopylae
Troy
Knossos
Mycenae
Olympia
East from Greenwich
COPYRIGHT GEORGE PHILIP LTD.

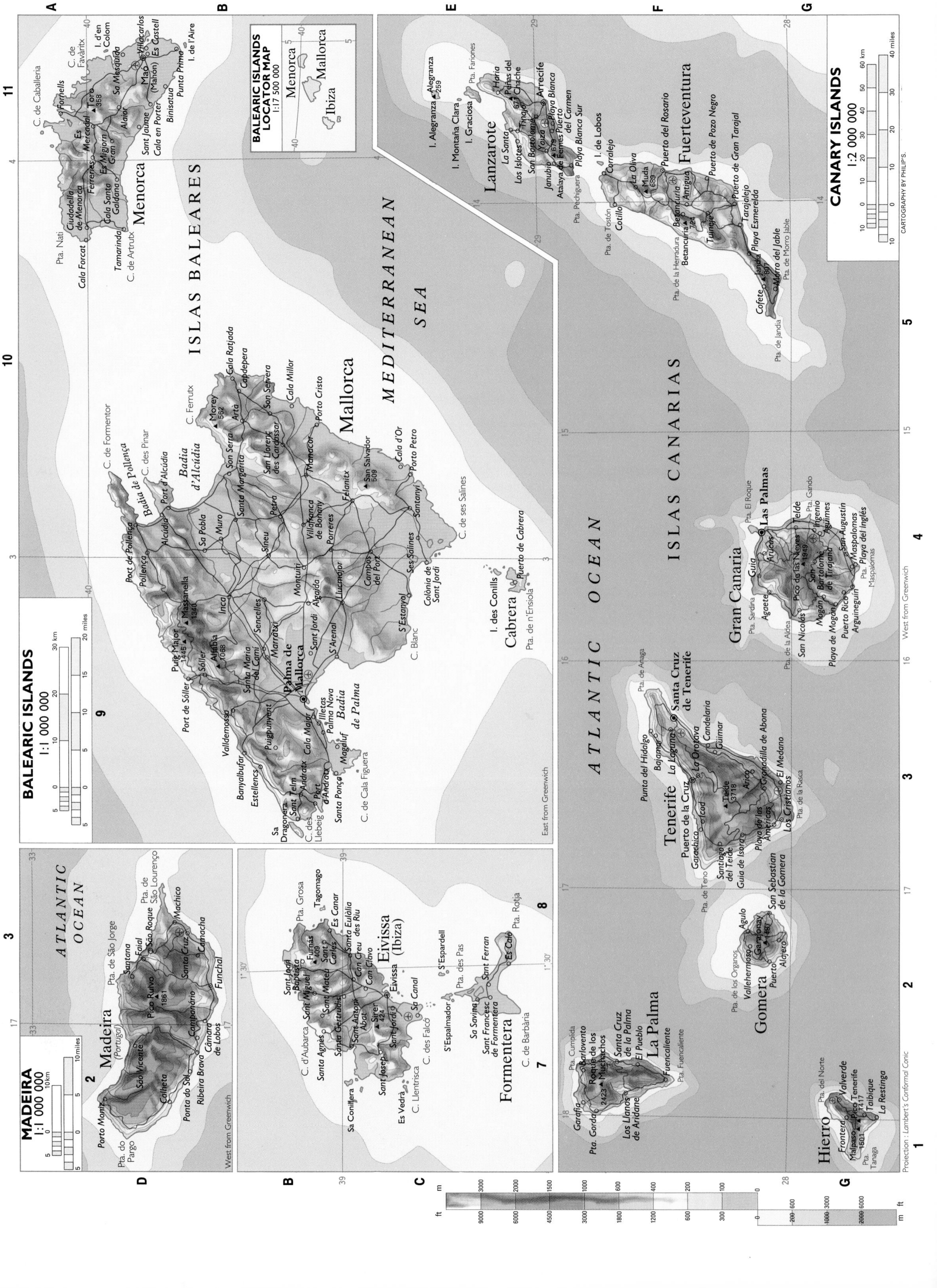

BALEARIC ISLANDS LOCATOR MAP
1:17 500 000
Menorca
Mallorca
Ibiza

MADEIRA
1:1 000 000

BALEARIC ISLANDS
1:1 000 000

CANARY ISLANDS
1:2 000 000

CARTOGRAPHY BY PHILIP'S.

Projection: Lambert's Conformal Conic

ISLAS BALEARES

Menorca

MEDITERRANEAN SEA

Mallorca

Lanzarote

Fuerteventura

ISLAS CANARIAS

ATLANTIC OCEAN

Gran Canaria

Las Palmas

Tenerife

Santa Cruz de Tenerife

Gomera

La Palma

Hierro

Madeira (Portugal)

Funchal

Eivissa (Ibiza)

Formentera

Cabrera

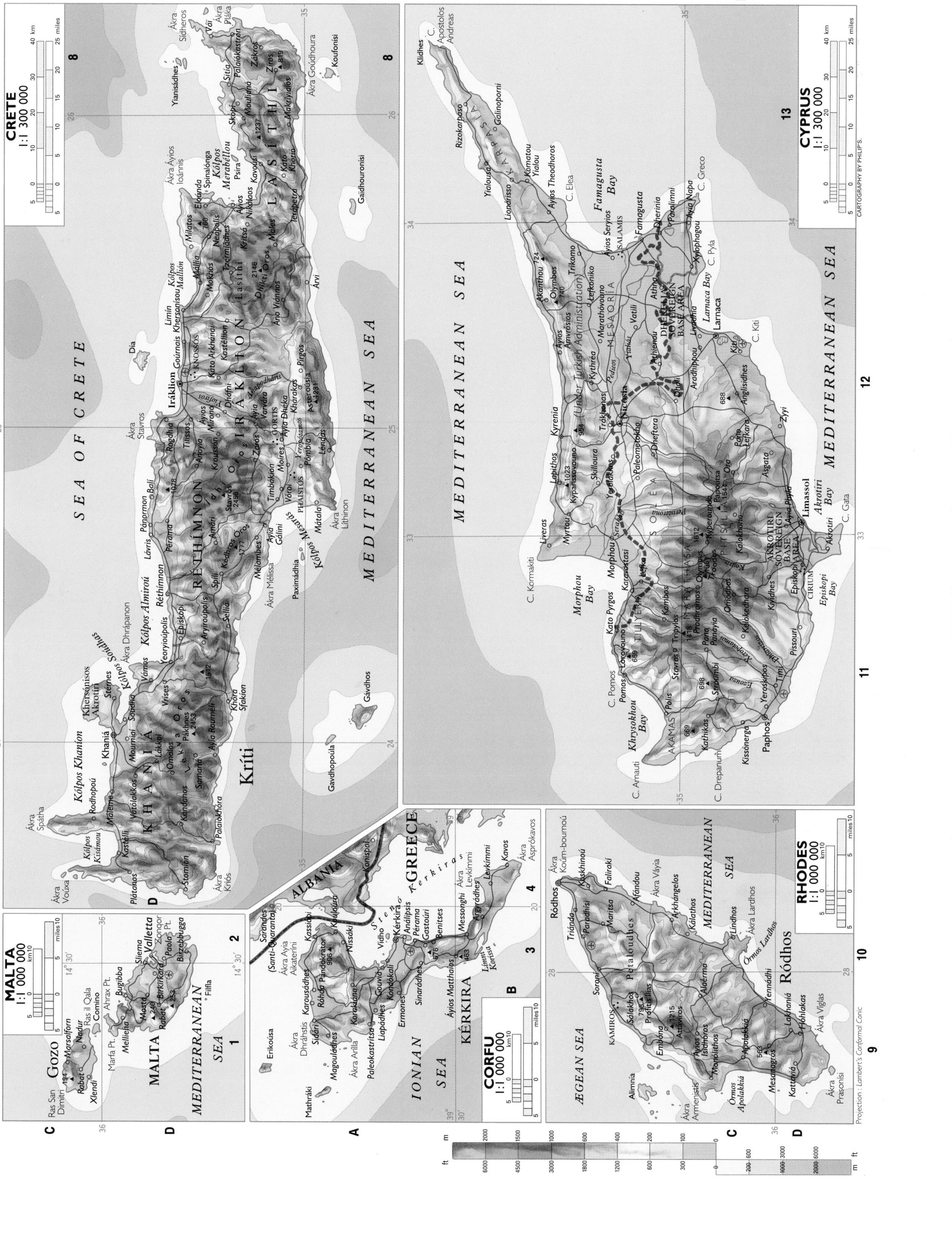

CRETE
1:1 300 000

MALTA
1:1 000 000

CORFU
1:1 000 000

RHODES
1:1 000 000

CYPRUS
1:1 300 000

CARTOGRAPHY BY PHILIP'S.

Projection : Lambert's Conformal Conic

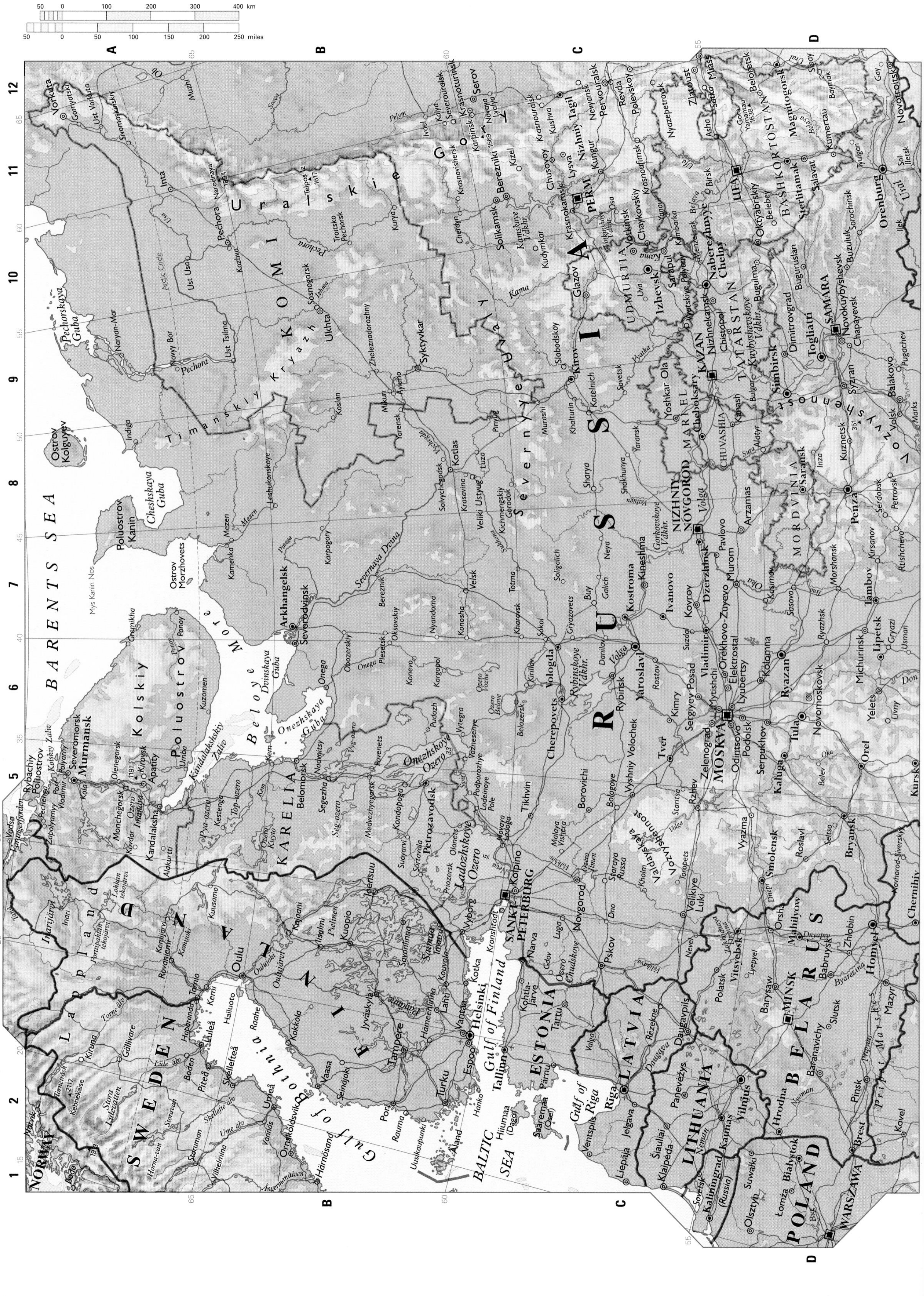

50   0   100   200   300   400 km
50   0   50   100   150   200   250 miles

NORWAY

SWEDEN

Lappland

FINLAND

Gulf of Bothnia

BALTIC SEA

Åland

Gulf of Finland

Helsinki
Espoo
Vantaa
Turku
Tampere

ESTONIA
Tallinn
Tartu
Pärnu

Gulf of Riga
Hiiumaa (Dago)
Saaremaa

LATVIA
Riga
Ventspils
Liepāja

LITHUANIA
Kaunas
Vilnius
Klaipėda
Šiauliai
Panevėžys
Jelgava
Daugavpils

Kaliningrad (Russia)

POLAND
WARSZAWA
Białystok
Brest

BELARUS
MINSK
Baranavichy
Homyel
Hrodna
Slutsk
Pinsk

BARENTS SEA

Ostrov Kolguyev

Poluostrov Kanin

Cheshskaya Guba

Mys Kanin Nos

Kolskiy Poluostrov

Murmansk
Severomorsk
Monchegorsk
Apatity
Kandalaksha
Kirovsk

KARELIA

Beloye More

Arkhangelsk
Severodvinsk

Onezhskaya Guba

Belomorsk
Petrozavodsk
Onezhskoye Ozero

Ladozhskoye Ozero

SANKT-PETERBURG
Narva
Pskov
Novgorod

KOMI

Timanskiy Kryazh

Uralskie Gory

Vorkuta
Inta
Pechora
Ukhta
Syktyvkar

Severnyye Uvaly

RUSSIA

Vologda
Cherepovets
Rybinsk
Yaroslavl
Kostroma
Ivanovo

MOSKVA
Tver
Smolensk
Bryansk
Tula
Kaluga
Orel
Kursk

NIZHNIY NOVGOROD
MARI EL
CHUVASHIA
MORDVINIA
Saransk
Penza
Tambov
Lipetsk

TATARSTAN
KAZAN
Ulyanovsk
Naberezhnyye Chelny
Cheboksary

UDMURTIA
Izhevsk
Kirov
Glazov

PERM
Nizhniy Tagil
Yekaterinburg

BASHKORTOSTAN
UFA
Sterlitamak
Magnitogorsk

SAMARA
Togliatti
Syzran
Orenburg

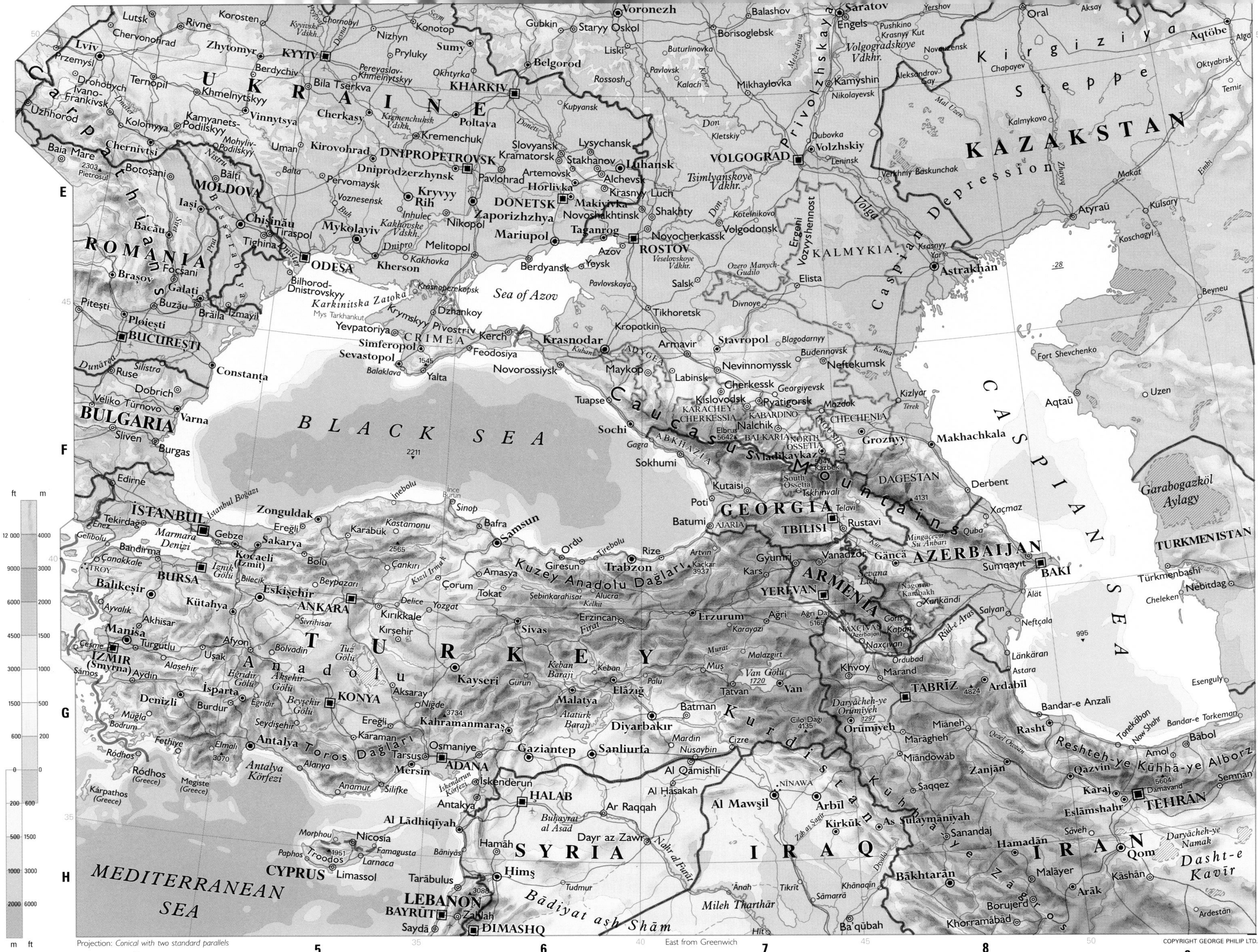

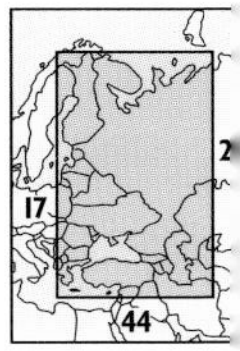

Projection: Conical with two standard parallels

East from Greenwich

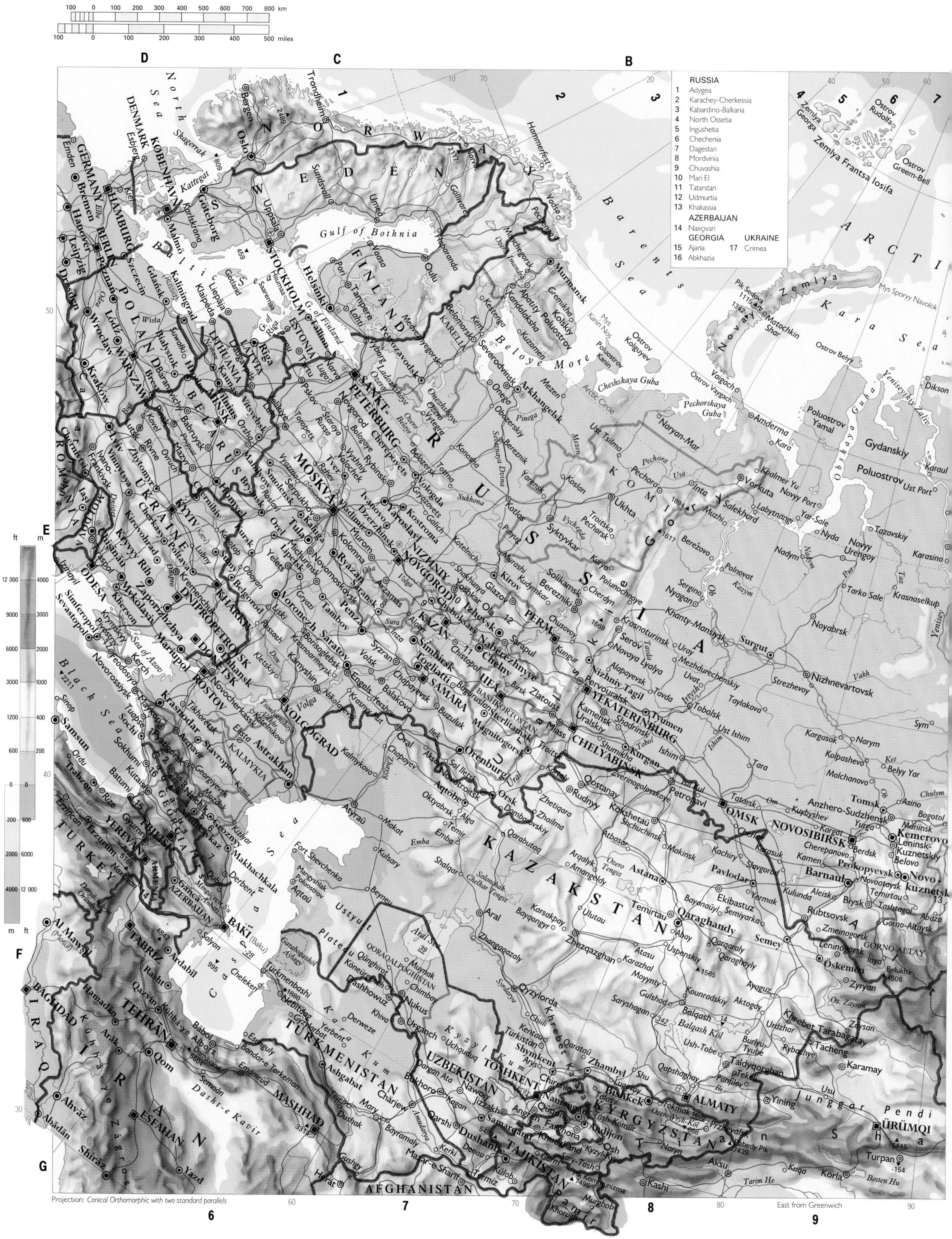

100 0 100 200 300 400 500 600 700 800 km
100 0 100 200 300 400 500 miles

RUSSIA
1 Adygea
2 Karachey-Cherkessia
3 Kabardino-Balkaria
4 North Ossetia
5 Ingushetia
6 Chechenia
7 Dagestan
8 Mordvinia
9 Chuvashia
10 Mari El
11 Tatarstan
12 Udmurtia
13 Khakassia

AZERBAIJAN
14 Naxçvan

GEORGIA
15 Ajaria
16 Abkhazia

UKRAINE
17 Crimea

Projection: Conical Orthomorphic with two standard parallels

East from Greenwich

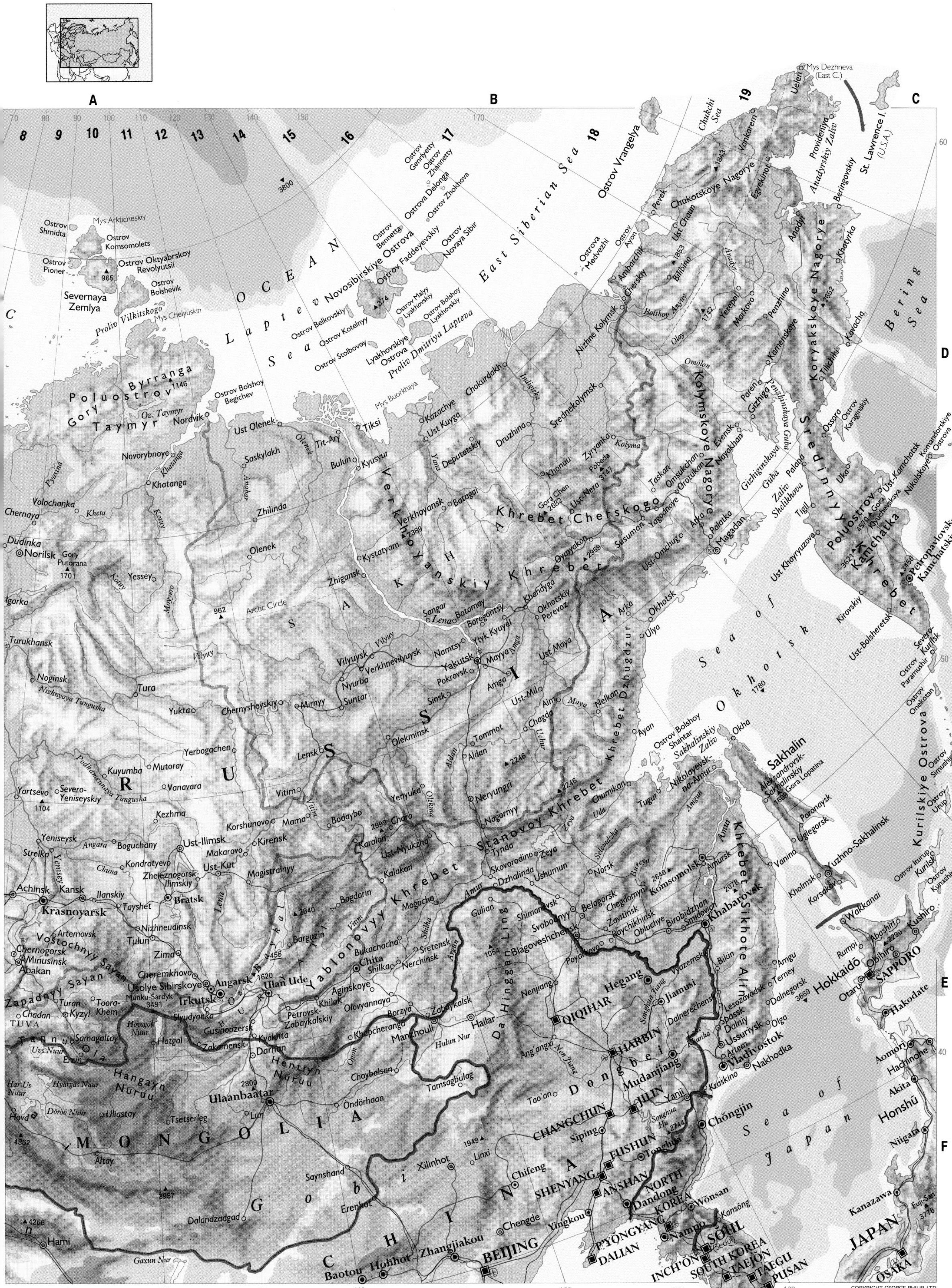
A
B
C
D
E
F
10
11
12
13
14
OCEAN
Laptev Sea
East Siberian Sea
Chukchi Sea
Bering Sea
Sea of Okhotsk
Sea of Japan
RUSSIA
MONGOLIA
CHINA
NORTH KOREA
SOUTH KOREA
JAPAN
Ostrov Shmidta
Mys Arkticheskiy
Ostrov Komsomolets
Ostrov Pioner
Ostrov Oktyabrskoy Revolyutsii
Ostrov Bolshevik
Severnaya Zemlya
Proliv Vilkitskogo
Mys Chelyuskin
Poluostrov Taymyr
Gory Byrranga
Oz. Taymyr
Ostrov Bolshoy Begichev
Nordvik
Novosibirskiye Ostrova
Ostrov Kotelnyy
Ostrov Belkovskiy
Ostrov Stolbovoy
Ostrov Faddeyevskiy
Ostrov Novaya Sibir
Ostrov Bennetta
Ostrova Delonga
Ostrov Zhokhova
Ostrov Genriyetty
Ostrov Zhannetty
Lyakhovskiye Ostrova
Ostrov Malyy Lyakhovskiy
Ostrov Bolshoy Lyakhovskiy
Proliv Dmitriya Lapteva
Mys Buorkhaya
Ostrov Vrangelya
Ostrova Medvezhi
Ostrov Ayon
Mys Dezhneva (East C.)
Uelen
St. Lawrence I. (U.S.A.)
Provideniya
Anadyrskiy Zaliv
Beringovskiy
Chukotskoye Nagorye
Vankarem
Egvekinot
Pevek
Ust Chaun
Bilibino
Ambarchik
Cherskiy
Nizhne Kolymsk
Anadyr
Koryakskoye Nagorye
Khatyrka
Markovo
Yeropol
Penzhino
Kamenskoye
Tilichiki
Korf
Omolon
Kolymskoye Nagorye
Srednekolymsk
Zyryanka
Kolyma
Chokurdakh
Indigirka
Kazachye
Ust Kuyga
Tiksi
Ust Olenek
Saskylakh
Tit-Ary
Bulun
Kyusyur
Deputatskiy
Druzhino
Khonuu
Pobeda 3147
Verkhoyansk
Batagai
Khrebet Cherskogo
Gora Chen 2682
Ust-Nera
Verkhoyanskiy Khrebet
Kystatyam
Zhigansk
Oymyakon
Susuman
Yagodnoye
Omsukchan
Evensk
Nayakhan
Gizhiga
Paren
Penzhinskaya Guba
Gizhiginskaya Guba
Zaliv Shelikhova
Palana
Sredinnyy Khrebet
Poluostrov Kamchatka
Ossora
Ostrov Karaginskiy
Ust-Kamchatsk
Komandorskiye Ostrova
Nikolskoye
Tigil
Ust Khayryuzovo
Petropavlovsk-Kamchatskiy
Kirovskiy
Ust-Bolsheretsk
Severo-Kurilsk
Ostrov Paramushir
Ostrov Onekotan
Ostrov Simushir
Kurilskiye Ostrova
Ostrov Urup
Ostrov Iturup
Kurilsk
Ostrov Kunashir
Magadan
Palatka
Atka
Ust-Omchug
Ola
Khandyga
Okhotskiy Perevoz
Okhotsk
Arka
Ulya
Ust Maya
Yakutsk
Mayya
Amga
Nyurba
Vilyuysk
Verkhnevilyuysk
Namtsy
Ytyk Kyuyel
Pokrovsk
Sangar
Batamay
Borogontsy
Suntar
Mirnyy
Sinsk
Olekminsk
Ust-Mil
Aim
Nelkan
Khrebet Dzhugdzur
Ayan
Ostrov Bolshoy Shantar
Okha
Sakhalinskiy Zaliv
Nikolayevsk-na-Amure
Sakhalin
Aleksandrovsk-Sakhalinskiy
Gora Lopatina
Poronaysk
Uglegorsk
Yuzhno-Sakhalinsk
Kholmsk
Korsakov
Wakkanai
Abashiri
Kushiro
Obihiro
Rumoi
SAPPORO
Hokkaido
Otaru
Hakodate
Aomori
Hachinohe
Akita
Honshū
Niigata
Kanazawa
Fuji-San 3776
ŌSAKA
Tommot
Aldan
Neryungri
Chumikan
Tugur
Uda
Stanovoy Khrebet
Tynda
Skovorodino
Zeya
Nagornyy
Olekma
Aldan
Uchur
Lensk
Vitim
Mama
Bodaybo
Chara
Kalakan
Ust-Nyukzha
Karalon
Yablonovyy Khrebet
Bagdarin
Barguzin
Ulan Ude
Chita
Shilka
Sretensk
Nerchinsk
Mogocha
Amur
Dzhalinda
Ushumun
Norsk
Selemdzha
Bureya
Komsomolsk
Amursk
Khabarovsk
Khrebet Sikhote Alin
Birobidzhan
Belogorsk
Svobodnyy
Blagoveshchensk
Shimanovsk
Gulian
Da Hinggan Ling
Vanino
Amgu
Terney
Dalnegorsk
Dalnerechensk
Lesozavodsk
Spassk
Ussuriysk
Vladivostok
Nakhodka
Artem
Kraskino
Chŏngjin
Tura
Yukta
Chernyshevskiy
Yerbogachen
Mutoray
Kuyumba
Vanavara
Podkamennaya Tunguska
Nizhnyaya Tunguska
Noginsk
Turukhansk
Igarka
Norilsk
Dudinka
Gory Putorana
Yessey
Olenek
Zhilinda
Khatanga
Novorybnoye
Volochanka
Chernaya
Kheta
Kotuy
Arctic Circle
Vilyuy
Yartsevo
Severo-Yeniseyskiy
Kezhma
Korshunovo
Kirensk
Ust-Ilimsk
Makarovo
Ust-Kut
Magistralnyy
Zheleznogorsk-Ilimskiy
Kondratyevo
Boguchany
Angara
Yeniseysk
Strelka
Yenisey
Chuna
Achinsk
Kansk
Ilanskiy
Tayshet
Bratsk
Krasnoyarsk
Nizhneudinsk
Tulun
Zima
Artemovsk
Vostochnyy Sayan
Chernogorsk
Minusinsk
Abakan
Cheremkhovo
Usolye Sibirskoye
Angarsk
Irkutsk
Munku-Sardyk 3491
Slyudyanka
Zapadnyy Sayan
Turan
Kyzyl
Toora-Khem
Chadan
TUVA
Samagaltay
Hövsgöl Nuur
Hatgal
Gusinoozersk
Kyakhta
Zakamensk
Darhan
Petrovsk-Zabaykalskiy
Khilok
Aginskoye
Olovyannaya
Borzya
Zabaykalsk
Krasnokamensk
Manzhouli
Hailar
Hulun Nur
Choybalsan
Tamsagbulag
Hentiyn Nuruu
Ulaanbaatar
Öndörhaan
Tsetserleg
Lun
Hangayn Nuruu
Uliastay
Hovd
Har Us Nuur
Hyargas Nuur
Uvs Nuur
Döröö Nuur
Altay
Saynshand
Dalandzadgad
Gobi
Erenhot
Hami
Gaxun Nur
Baotou
Hohhot
Zhangjiakou
BEIJING
Chengde
Chifeng
Xilinhot
Linxi
QIQIHAR
Nenjiang
Hegang
Jiamusi
HARBIN
Mudanjiang
Dongbei
Ang'angxi
Tao'an
JILIN
CHANGCHUN
Siping
FUSHUN
SHENYANG
ANSHAN
Tonghua
Yanji
Dandong
Yingkou
DALIAN
P'YŎNGYANG
Namp'o
Wŏnsan
Kansŏng
SŎUL
INCH'ŎN
TAEJŎN
TAEGU
PUSAN
COPYRIGHT GEORGE PHILIP LTD.

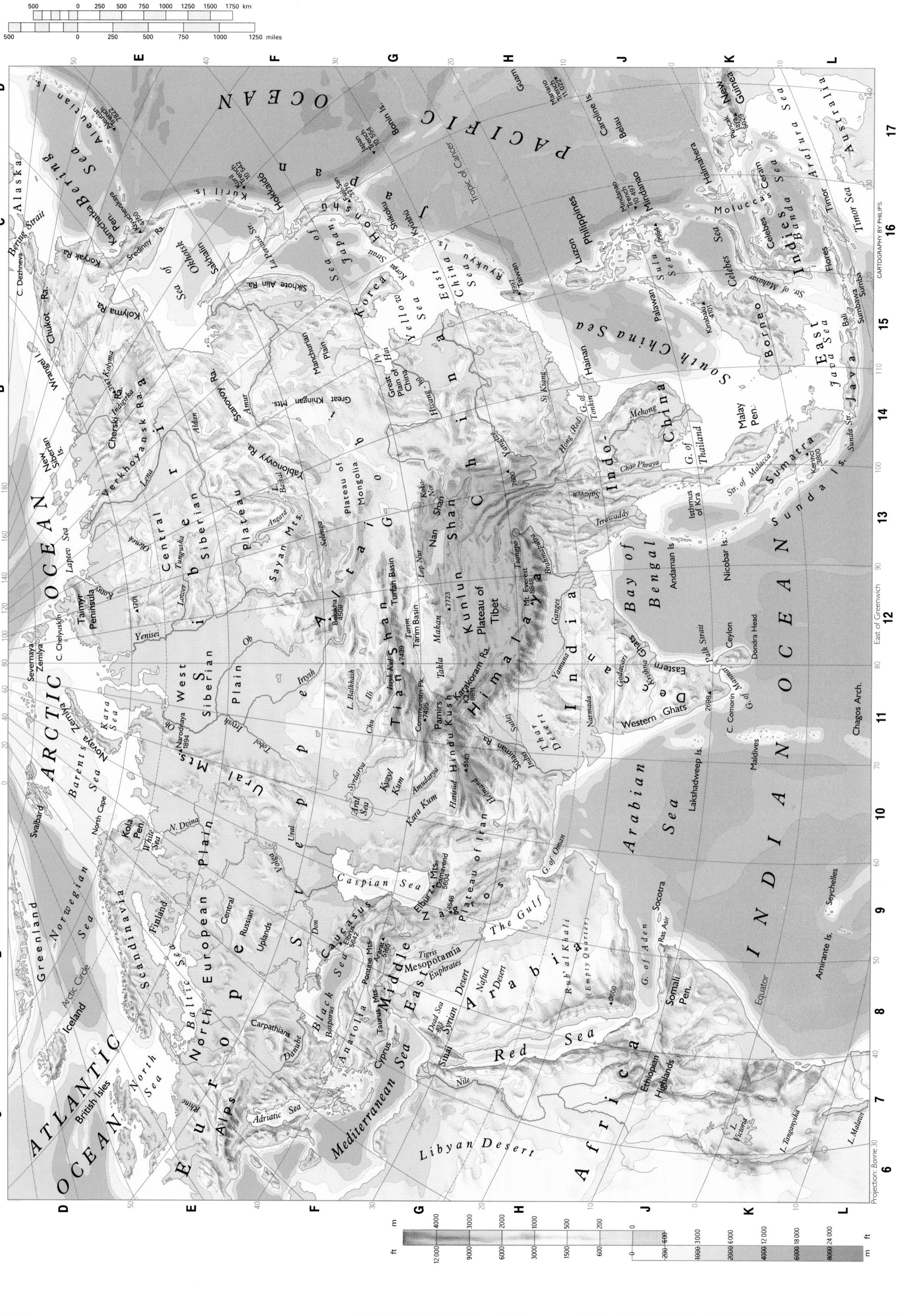

PACIFIC OCEAN

ARCTIC OCEAN

ATLANTIC OCEAN

INDIAN OCEAN

Europe

Asia

China

Africa

Australia

Bering Sea

Alaska

Kamchatka Pen.

Koryak Ra.

Sredinny Ra.

Sea of Okhotsk

Sakhalin

Hokkaido

Kuril Is.

Japan

Honshu

Shikoku

Kyushu

Korea

Yellow Sea

East China Sea

Ryukyu

Taiwan

Philippines

Luzon

Mindanao

Palawan

Sulu Sea

Celebes Sea

Borneo

Molucca Sea

Celebes

Halmahera

New Guinea

Arafura Sea

Timor Sea

Timor

Flores

Bali

Java

Sumatra

Malay Pen.

South China Sea

G. of Thailand

Indo-China

Mekong

Bay of Bengal

Andaman Is.

Nicobar Is.

Ceylon

India

Ganges

Brahmaputra

Himalaya

Mt. Everest 8848

Plateau of Tibet

Kunlun Shan

Tarim Basin

Takla Makan

Tian Shan

Turfan Basin

Altai

Plateau of Mongolia

Gobi

Manchurian Plain

Great Khingan Mts.

Yangtze

Nan Shan

Hwang Ho

Si Kiang

Hainan

G. of Tonkin

Irrawaddy

Chao Phraya

Salween

Isthmus of Kra

Str. of Malacca

Sunda Is.

Sunda Str.

Java Sea

Banda Sea

Indies

East Indies

Arabian Sea

Red Sea

G. of Aden

Socotra

Somali Pen.

Ethiopian Highlands

Nile

Libyan Desert

Sinai

Dead Sea

Syrian Desert

Mesopotamia

Tigris

Euphrates

The Gulf

G. of Oman

Arabia

Rub' al Khali (Empty Quarter)

Nafud Desert

Ras Asir

Caspian Sea

Elburz Mts.

Zagros

Plateau of Iran

Caucasus

Black Sea

Taurus Mts.

Anatolia

Cyprus

Mediterranean Sea

Middle East

Pontine Mts.

Ararat

Tabriz

Ural Mts.

West Siberian Plain

Central Siberian Plateau

Ob

Yenisei

Lena

Tunguska

Angara

Sayan Mts.

L. Baikal

Selenga

Yablonovyy Ra.

Stanovoy Ra.

Aldan

Amur

Sikhote Alin Ra.

Sea of Japan

La Pérouse Str.

Korea Str.

Verkhoyansk Ra.

Cherski Ra.

Kolyma Ra.

Chukot Pen.

C. Dezhnev

Bering Strait

Wrangel I.

New Siberian Is.

Taimyr Peninsula

C. Chelyuskin

Severnaya Zemlya

Novaya Zemlya

Kara Sea

Barents Sea

Kola Pen.

White Sea

N. Dvina

Volga

Don

Central Russian Uplands

North European Plain

Baltic Sea

Finland

Scandinavia

Norwegian Sea

Greenland

Iceland

British Isles

North Sea

Rhine

Alps

Danube

Carpathians

Adriatic Sea

Ural

Irtysh

Tobol

Ishim

Aral Sea

L. Balkhash

Syrdarya

Amudarya

Kara Kum

Kyzyl Kum

Chu

Ili

Pamirs

Communism Pk. 7495

Hindu Kush

Karakoram Ra.

Tsaidam

Lop Nor

Koko Nor

Hami

Narodnaya 1894

Iran

Thar Desert

Indus

Sutlej

Jhelum

Yamuna

Narmada

Godavari

Krishna

Eastern Ghats

Western Ghats

C. Comorin

G. of Mannar

Palk Strait

Dondra Head

Maldives

Lakshadweep Is.

Chagos Arch.

Seychelles

Amirante Is.

Equator

Tropic of Cancer

Arctic Circle

East of Greenwich

CARTOGRAPHY BY PHILIPS

Projection: Bonne

ft   m

12 000   4000
9000   3000
6000   2000
4500   1500
3000   1000
1500   600
600   200
0   0
200   600
4000   2000
6000   4000
8000   6000
m   ft

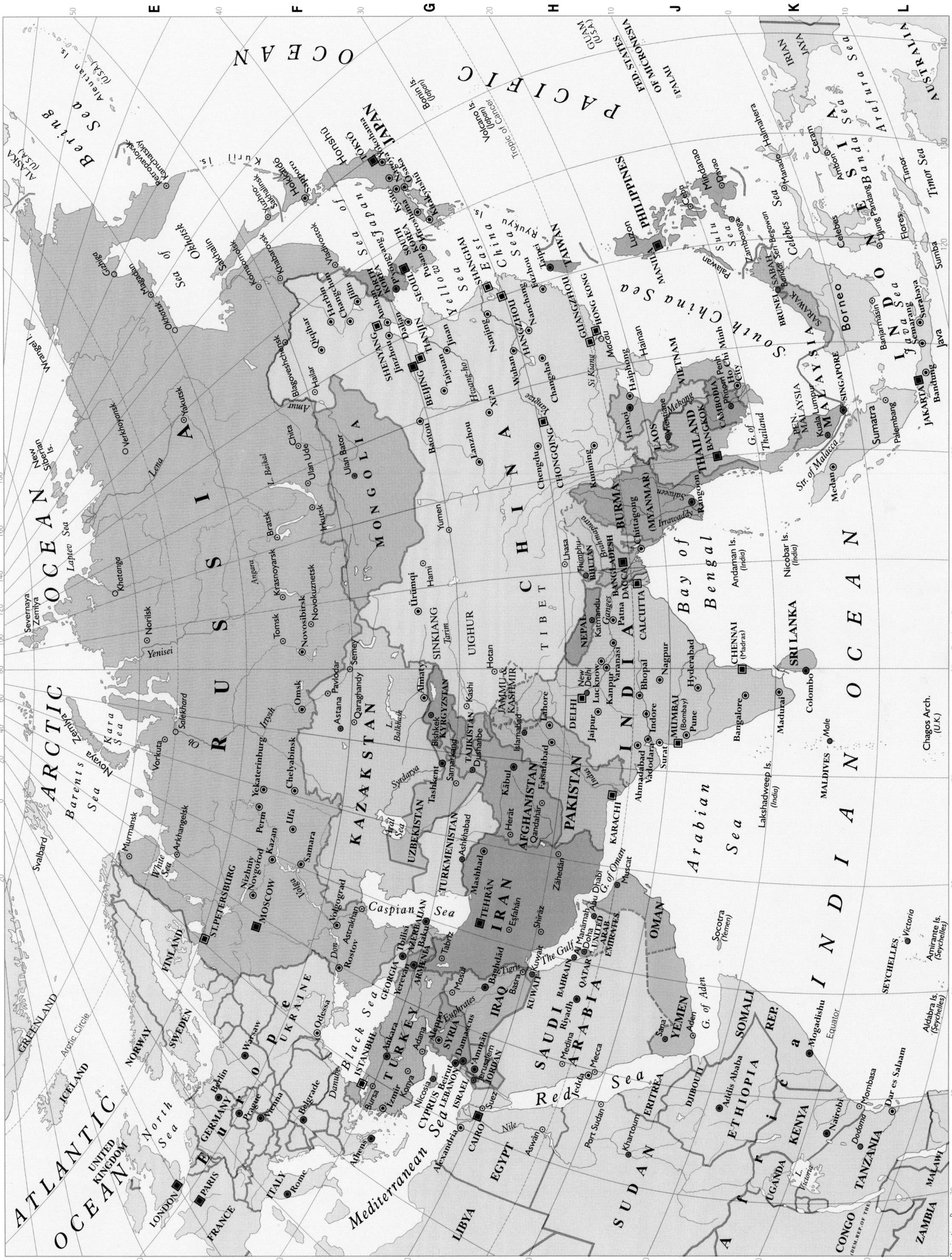

500   0   250 500 750 1000 1250 1500 1750 km
500   0   250   500   750   1000 miles

Projection: Bonne 30

COPYRIGHT GEORGE PHILIP LTD.

Hanoi ● Capital Cities

East from Greenwich

PACIFIC OCEAN

ARCTIC OCEAN

ATLANTIC OCEAN

INDIAN OCEAN

RUSSIA

KAZAKSTAN

MONGOLIA

CHINA

INDIA

IRAN

SAUDI ARABIA

MYANMAR (BURMA)

THAILAND

INDONESIA

AUSTRALIA

JAPAN

PHILIPPINES

MALAYSIA

JAPAN 1:5 000 000

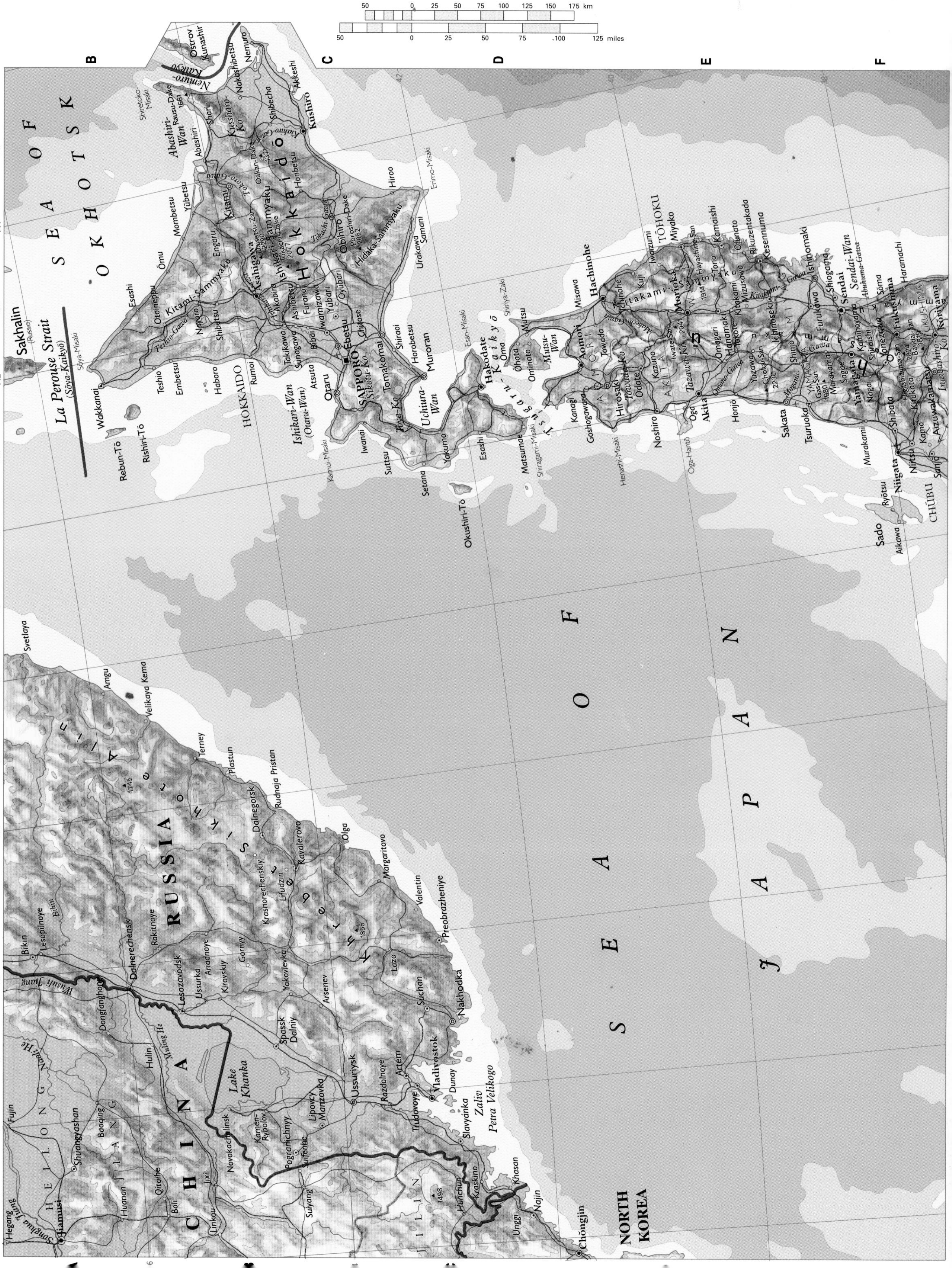
50 0 25 50 75 100 125 150 175 km
50 0 25 50 75 100 125 miles
SEA OF OKHOTSK
SEA OF JAPAN
La Perouse Strait (Sōya-Kaikyō)
Sakhalin (Russia)
Hokkaidō
HOKKAIDO
SAPPORO
Hakodate
Tsugaru-Kaikyō
TŌHOKU
Sendai
Niigata
Sado
Aomori
Akita
Morioka
Yamagata
Fukushima
Ishikari-Wan (Otaru-Wan)
Uchiura-Wan
Sendai-Wan
Nemuro-Kaikyō
Ostrov Kunashir
Kushiro
Obihiro
Asahikawa
Otaru
Muroran
Wakkanai
Rebun-Tō
Rishiri-Tō
Okushiri-Tō
RUSSIA
CHINA
NORTH KOREA
Vladivostok
Nakhodka
Ussuriysk
Lake Khanka
Zaliv Petra Velikogo
Sikhote Alin
Chŏngjin
Hachinohe
Miyako
Kamaishi
Ishinomaki
Noshiro
Hirosaki
Sakata
Shibata
Tsuruoka
Mutsu
Ōma

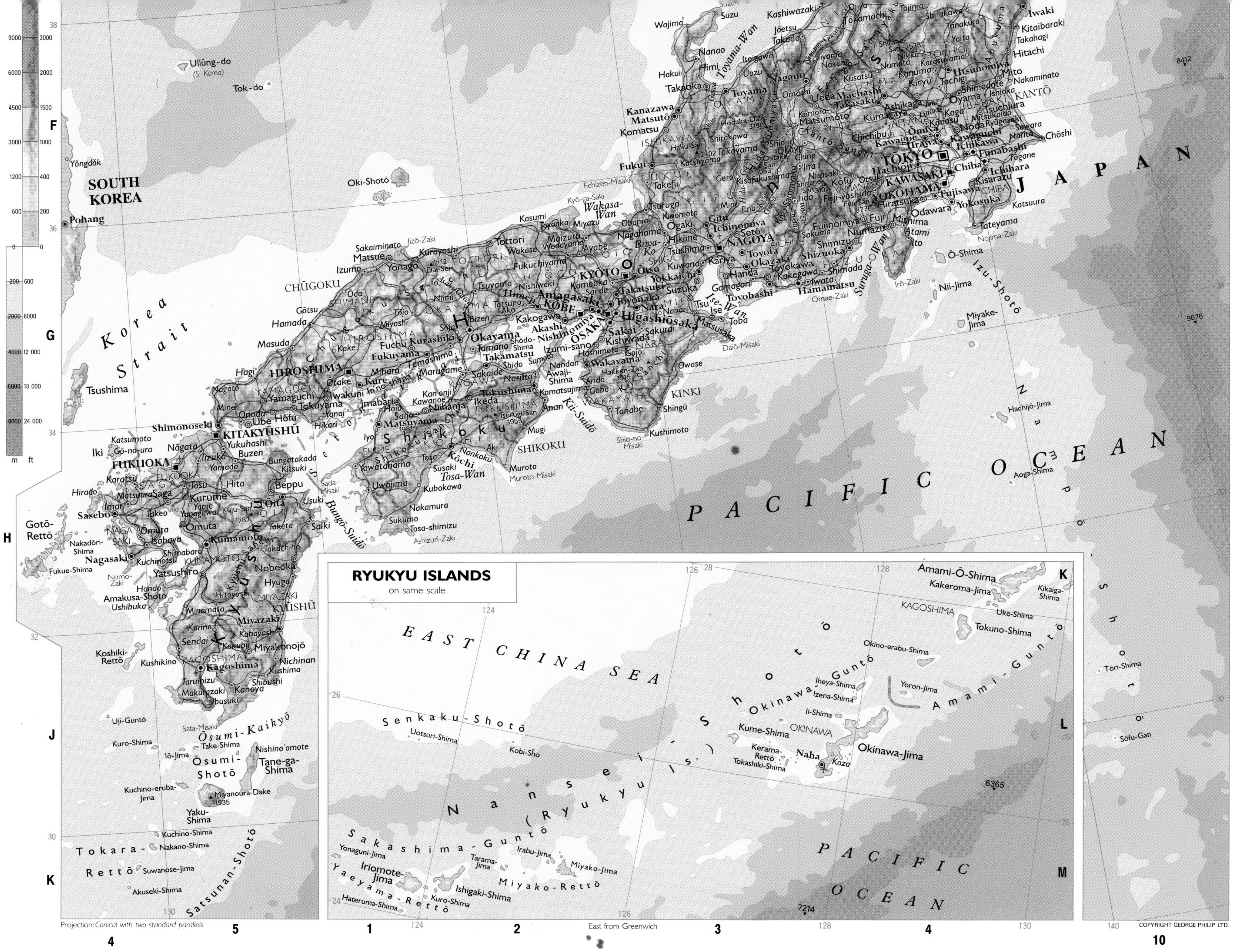

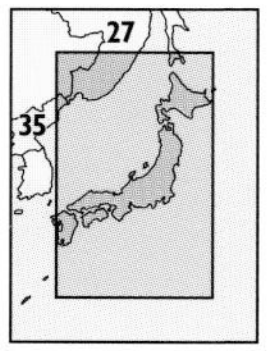

CHINA AND KOREA 1:15 000 000

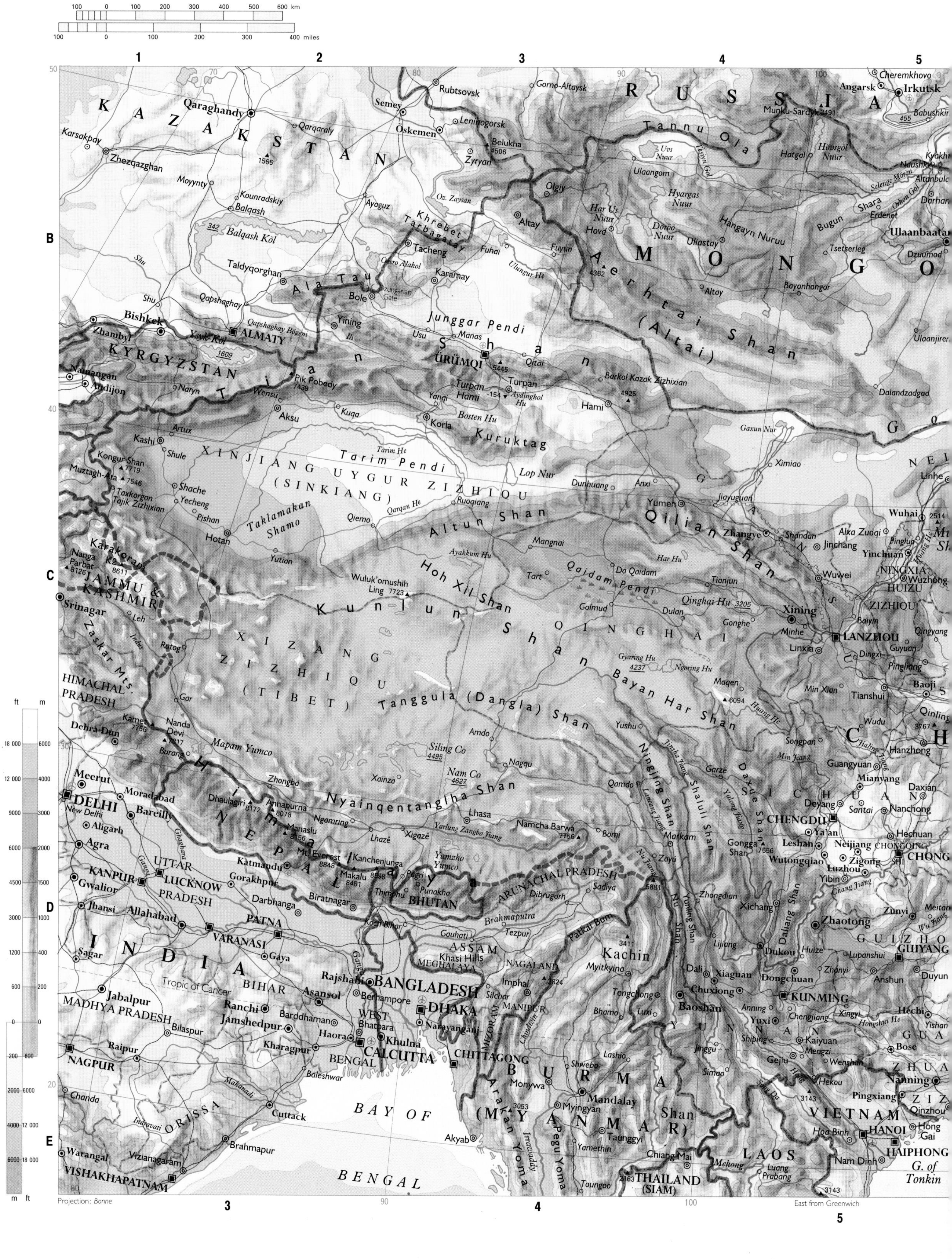
100 0 100 200 300 400 500 600 km
100 0 100 200 300 400 miles
1 2 3 4 5
B C D E
3 4 5
Projection: Bonne
East from Greenwich
ft m
18 000 6000
12 000 4000
9000 3000
6000 2000
4500 1500
3000 1000
1200 400
600 200
0 0
200 600
2000 6000
4000 12 000
6000 18 000
m ft
KAZAKSTAN
RUSSIA
MONGOLIA
KYRGYZSTAN
XINJIANG UYGUR ZIZHIQU
(SINKIANG)
XIZANG ZIZHIQU
(TIBET)
QINGHAI
SICHUAN
YUNNAN
GUIZHOU
NINGXIA HUIZU ZIZHIQU
JAMMU & KASHMIR
HIMACHAL PRADESH
UTTAR PRADESH
NEPAL
BHUTAN
ARUNACHAL PRADESH
ASSAM
MEGHALAYA
NAGALAND
MANIPUR
MIZORAM
BANGLADESH
WEST BENGAL
BIHAR
MADHYA PRADESH
ORISSA
INDIA
BURMA (MYANMAR)
THAILAND (SIAM)
LAOS
VIETNAM
Qaraghandy
Karsakpay
Zhezqazghan
Moyynty
Kounradskiy
Balqash
Balqash Köl
Taldyqorghan
Qapshaghay
Qapshaghay Bogeni
Ysyk-Köl
Bishkek
Zhambyl
ALMATY
Namangan
Andijon
Naryn
Semey
Rubtsovsk
Gorno-Altaysk
Leninogorsk
Öskemen
Qarqaraly
Belukha 4506
Zyryan
Oz. Zaysan
Ayaguz
Khrebet Tarbagatay
Tacheng
Ala Tau
Dzungarian Gate
Bole
Yining
Ili
Karamay
Fuhai
Ulungur He
Junggar Pendi
Tian Shan
Usu
Manas
ÜRÜMQI
Qitai
Turpan
Turpan Hami
Aydingkol Hu
Pik Pobedy 7439
Wensu
Aksu
Kuqa
Yanqi
Bosten Hu
Korla
Kuruktag
Kashi
Artux
Shule
Kongur Shan 7719
Muztagh-Ata 7546
Taxkorgan Tajik Zizhixian
Shache
Yecheng
Pishan
Hotan
Taklamakan Shamo
Tarim He
Tarim Pendi
Qiemo
Qarqan He
Ruoqiang
Lop Nur
Yutian
Altun Shan
Dunhuang
Anxi
Yumen
Jiayuguan
Hami
Barkol Kazak Zizhixian
4925
Gaxun Nur
Ximiao
Qilian Shan
Zhangye
Shandan
Jinchang
Wuwei
Alxa Zuoqi
Wuhai 2514
Linhe
Yinchuan
Wuzhong
Pingluo
Karakoram
Nanga Parbat 8126
K2 8611
Srinagar
Leh
Indus
Rutog
Zaskar Mts.
Ayakkum Hu
Mangnai
Wuluk'omushih Ling 7723
Hoh Xil Shan
Kunlun Shan
Tart
Da Qaidam
Qaidam Pendi
Golmud
Dulan
Tianjun
Qinghai Hu 3205
Xining
Gonghe
Minhe
LANZHOU
Baiyin
Linxia
Dingxi
Guyuan
Pingliang
Qingyang
Gyaring Hu 4237
Ngoring Hu
Maqen 6094
Bayan Har Shan
Huang He
Min Xian
Tianshui
Baoji
Qinling
Tanggula (Dangla) Shan
Gar
Kamet 7756
Nanda Devi 7817
Dehra Dun
Burang
Mapam Yumco
Amdo
Siling Co 4495
Nam Co 4627
Nagqu
Xainza
Zhongba
Nyainqentanglha Shan
Yushu
Qamdo
Ningjing Shan
Shaluli Shan
Jinsha Jiang
Lancang Jiang
Yalong Jiang
Garzê
Daxue Shan
Songpan
Min Jiang
Wudu
Jialing Jiang
Hanzhong
Guangyuan
Mianyang
Daxian
Nanchong
Deyang
Santai
CHENGDU
Ya'an
Leshan
Neijiang
Hechuan
CHONGQING SHI
Zigong
Luzhou
Yibin
Chang Jiang
Gongga Shan 7556
Wutongqiao
Markam
Meerut
Moradabad
DELHI
New Delhi
Bareilly
Aligarh
Agra
Ghaghara
Ganga
KANPUR
LUCKNOW
Gwalior
Jhansi
Allahabad
Gorakhpur
Dhaulagiri 8172
Annapurna 8078
Manaslu 8156
Himalaya
Katmandu
Mt. Everest 8848
Makalu 8481
Kanchenjunga 8598
Lhazê
Xigazê
Ngamring
Lhasa
Yarlung Zangbo Jiang
Yamzho Yumco
Namcha Barwa 7756
Bomi
Pagri
Thimphu
Punakha
Biratnagar
Darbhanga
Dibrugarh
Sadiya
Zayü
Nu Jiang
5881
Nu Shan
Yunling Shan
Zhongdian
Xichang
Daliang Shan
Lijiang
Zhaotong
Zunyi
Wu Jiang
Meitan
Dukou
Huize
Lupanshui
GUIYANG
Dali
Xiaguan
Chuxiong
Zhanyi
Anshun
Duyun
Dongchuan
KUNMING
Brahmaputra
Tezpur
Gauhati
Koch Bihar
Patkai Bum
3411
Kachin
Myitkyina
Khasi Hills
Imphal
3824
Silchar
Chindwin
Tengchong
Luxi
Baoshan
Bhamo
Anning
Yuxi
Chengjiang
Xingyi
Hongshui He
Hechi
Yishan
Shiping
Kaiyuan
Mengzi
Bose
Jinggu
Wenshan
Simao
Gejiu
Hekou
Song Da
3143
Lashio
Shwebo
Monywa
Mandalay
Myingyan
Meiktila
Taunggyi
Yamethin
Shan
Irrawaddy
Arakan Yoma
Pegu Yoma
3053
Chiang Mai
Toungoo
2163
Mekong
Luang Prabang
Hoa Binh
HANOI
Nam Dinh
HAIPHONG
Hong Gai
Pingxiang
Qinzhou
Nanning
G. of Tonkin
PATNA
VARANASI
Gaya
Sagar
Jabalpur
Ranchi
Jamshedpur
Asansol
Barddhaman
Bilaspur
Rajshahi
Berhampore
DHAKA
Narayanganj
Bhatpara
Haora
Khulna
CALCUTTA
Kharagpur
CHITTAGONG
Raipur
NAGPUR
Baleshwar
Mahanadi
Chanda
Cuttack
Indravati
Brahmapur
Vizianagaram
Warangal
VISHAKHAPATNAM
Akyab
BAY OF BENGAL
Tropic of Cancer
Angarsk
Irkutsk
Cheremkhovo
455
Babushkin
Munku-Sardyk 3491
Tannu Ola
Uvs Nuur
Ulaangom
Hatgal
Hövsgöl Nuur
Selenge Mörön
Orhon Gol
Kyakhta
Altanbulag
Darhan
Shara
Erdenet
Bugun
ULAANBAATAR
Dzuumod
Tsetserleg
Ölgiy
Altay
Hyargas Nuur
Har Us Nuur
Hovd
Dörgön Nuur
Uliastay
Hangayn Nuruu
Fuyun
4362
Aerhtai Shan (Altai)
Bayanhongor
Ulaanjirem
Dalandzadgad
1565
342
1609
5445
-154
70 80 90 100
50 40 30 20

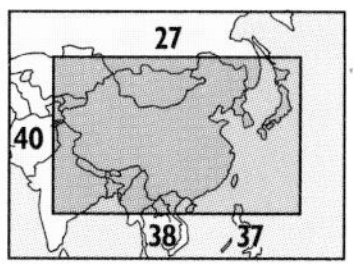

27
40
38 37

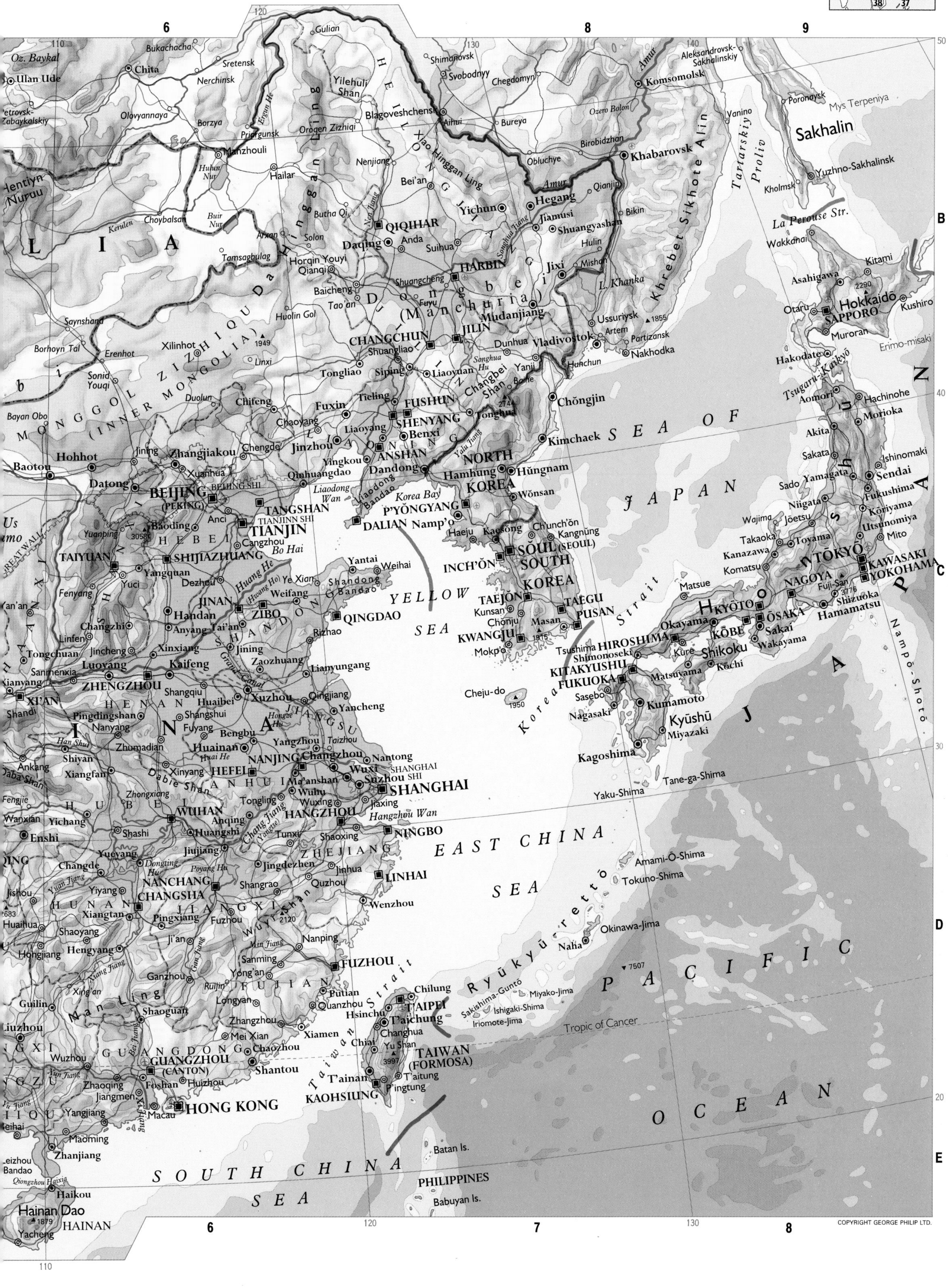

B

50

6 7 8 9

Oz. Baykal
Ulan Ude
Chita
Petrovsk-
Zabaykalskiy
Hentiyn
Nuruu
Bukachacha
Sretensk
Nerchinsk
Borzya
Olovyannaya
Manzhouli
Priargunsk
Choybalsan
Buir Nur
Huhun Nur
Hailar
Arxan
Solon
Horqin Youyi
Qianqi
Baicheng
Tao'an
Butha Qi
Nenjiang
Bei'an
Gulian
Shimanovsk
Svobodnyy
Blagoveshchensk
Aihui
Orogen Zizhiqi
Bureya
Chegdomyn
Komsomolsk
Ozero Bolon
Amur
Khabarovsk
Birobidzhan
Obluchye
Qianjin
Poronaysk
Mys Terpeniya
Sakhalin
Vanino
Aleksandrovsk-
Sakhalinskiy
Yuzhno-Sakhalinsk
Kholmsk
La Perouse Str.
Wakkanai

LIA

Saynshand
Borhoyn Tal
Bayan Obo
Baotou
Hohhot
Datong
Erenhot
Xilinhot
Sonid
Youqi
Duolun
Linxi
1949
Chifeng
Chaoyang
Jining
Zhangjiakou
Chengde
Xuanhua
Yuanping
Baoding
Anci
BEIJING
(PEKING)
BEIJING SHI
TANGSHAN
TIANJINN SHI
TIANJIN
Cangzhou
Huolin Gol
QIQIHAR
Daqing
Anda
Suihua
Shuangcheng
HARBIN
Fuyu
Jiamusi
Shuangyashan
Hulin
Mishan
L. Khanka
Jixi
Hegang
Yichun
Mudanjiang
JILIN
CHANGCHUN
Shuangliao
Liaoyuan
Siping
Tongliao
Tieling
Fuxin
FUSHUN
SHENYANG
Benxi
Liaoyang
ANSHAN
Jinzhou
Yingkou
Dandong
Qinhuangdao
Shijiazhuang
Dezhou
Ussuriysk
Artem
Vladivostok
Nakhodka
Partizansk
Hunchun
Yanji
Baihe
Changbai
Shan
Tonghua
Kimchaek
Chŏngjin
SEA OF
JAPAN
Hakodate
Aomori
Akita
Sakata
Morioka
Ishinomaki
Sendai
Fukushima
Kōriyama
Yamagata
Sado
Niigata
Wajima
Jōetsu
Takaoka
Kanazawa
Komatsu
Toyama
Utsunomiya
Mito
TŌKYŌ
KAWASAKI
YOKOHAMA
NAGOYA
Fuji-San
Shizuoka
Hamamatsu
ŌSAKA
KYŌTO
KŌBE
Sakai
Wakayama
HIROSHIMA
Okayama
Kure
Matsue
Kōchi
Matsuyama
Shikoku
SAPPORO
Asahigawa
Otaru
Muroran
HOKKAIDO
Kitami
Kushiro
Erimo-misaki
Tsugaru-Kaikyō

C

40

Hohhot
TAIYUAN
Fenyang
Yuci
Yangquan
Han Shui
Xianyang
Shandi
XI'AN
Weinan
Tongchuan
Jincheng
Linfen
Sanmenxia
Luoyang
Changzhi
HEBEI
Handan
Anyang
Tai'an
Jining
Xinxiang
ZHENGZHOU
HENAN
Nanyang
Pingdingshan
Zhumadian
Fuyang
Shangshui
Huaibei
Xuzhou
Kaifeng
Shangqiu
JINAN
ZIBO
QINGDAO
Weifang
Ye Xian
Weihai
Yantai
Bo Hai
Liaodong
Wan
Bohai
Dalian
P'YONGYANG
Namp'o
Haeju
Kaesong
INCH'ŎN
SŎUL (SEOUL)
Ch'unch'ŏn
Kangnŭng
Wŏnsan
Hamhung
Hŭngnam
NORTH
KOREA
SOUTH
KOREA
TAEJŎN
Kunsan
Chŏnju
KWANGJU
Mokp'o
Masan
PUSAN
TAEGU
Cheju-do
1950
Tsushima
Shimonoseki
KITAKYUSHU
FUKUOKA
Sasebo
Nagasaki
Kumamoto
Kyūshū
Miyazaki
Kagoshima
Yaku-Shima
Tane-ga-Shima
NAGOYA
Takaoka

Yellow Ho
(Huang Ho)
Huang He
Grand Canal
Hong Ze
Hu
Hongze
Lianyungang
Yancheng
Qinjiang
Huaian
Huai He
Bengbu
HEFEI
ANHUI
Ma'anshan
NANJING
Yangzhou
Changzhou
Taizhou
Wuxi
SHANGHAI SHI
Suzhou
SHANGHAI
Nantong
Haixing
Jiaxing
HANGZHOU
Hangzhou Wan
NINGBO
Shaoxing
ZHEJIANG
Jinhua
Quzhou
LINHAI
Wenzhou
Jingdezhen
Shangrao

Linshui
Changde
Yueyang
Dongting
Hu
Yiyang
Xiangtan
NANCHANG
CHANGSHA
Pingxiang
Poyang
Hu
Fuzhou
Ji'an
Nanping
Sanming
Yong'an
FUZHOU
Putian
Quanzhou
Longyan
Zhangzhou
FUJIAN
Xiamen
Ruijin
Ganzhou
Shaoguan
Mei Xian
Chaozhou
Shantou
GUANGDONG
GUANGZHOU
(CANTON)
Foshan
Huizhou
HONG KONG
Macau
Jiangmen
Yangjiang
Maoming
Zhanjiang
Zhaoqing
Wuzhou
Guilin
Liuzhou
Hengyang
Hongjiang
Shaoyang
HUNAN
Huaihua
Yuan Jiang
Xiang Jiang
Zhijiang

Shiyan
Xiangfan
Dabie Shan
Zhongxiang
WUHAN
Anqing
Huangshi
Jiujiang
Tongling
Wuhu
Wuxing
Chang Jiang
(Yangtze)
Tunxi

GREAT WALL
YELLOW
SEA
Shandong
Bandao
Rizhao
Zaozhuang

JAPAN
Korea
Strait
Nampō-Shotō

EAST CHINA
SEA
Amami-Ō-Shima
Tokuno-Shima
7507
Okinawa-Jima
Naha
Ryūkyū-rettō
Miyako-Jima
Sakishima-Guntō
Ishigaki-Shima
Iriomote-Jima
Tropic of Cancer

D

30

FUZHOU
Chilung
Hsinchu
TAIPEI
Taichung
Changhua
Chiai
Yu Shan
3997
TAIWAN
(FORMOSA)
T'ainan
P'aitung
KAOHSIUNG
Batan Is.
PHILIPPINES
Babuyan Is.

SOUTH CHINA
SEA
Haikou
Yacheng
HAINAN
Hainan Dao
1879
Qiongzhou Haixia
Beihai
Leizhou
Bandao

PACIFIC

OCEAN

E

20

6 120 7 130 8

110

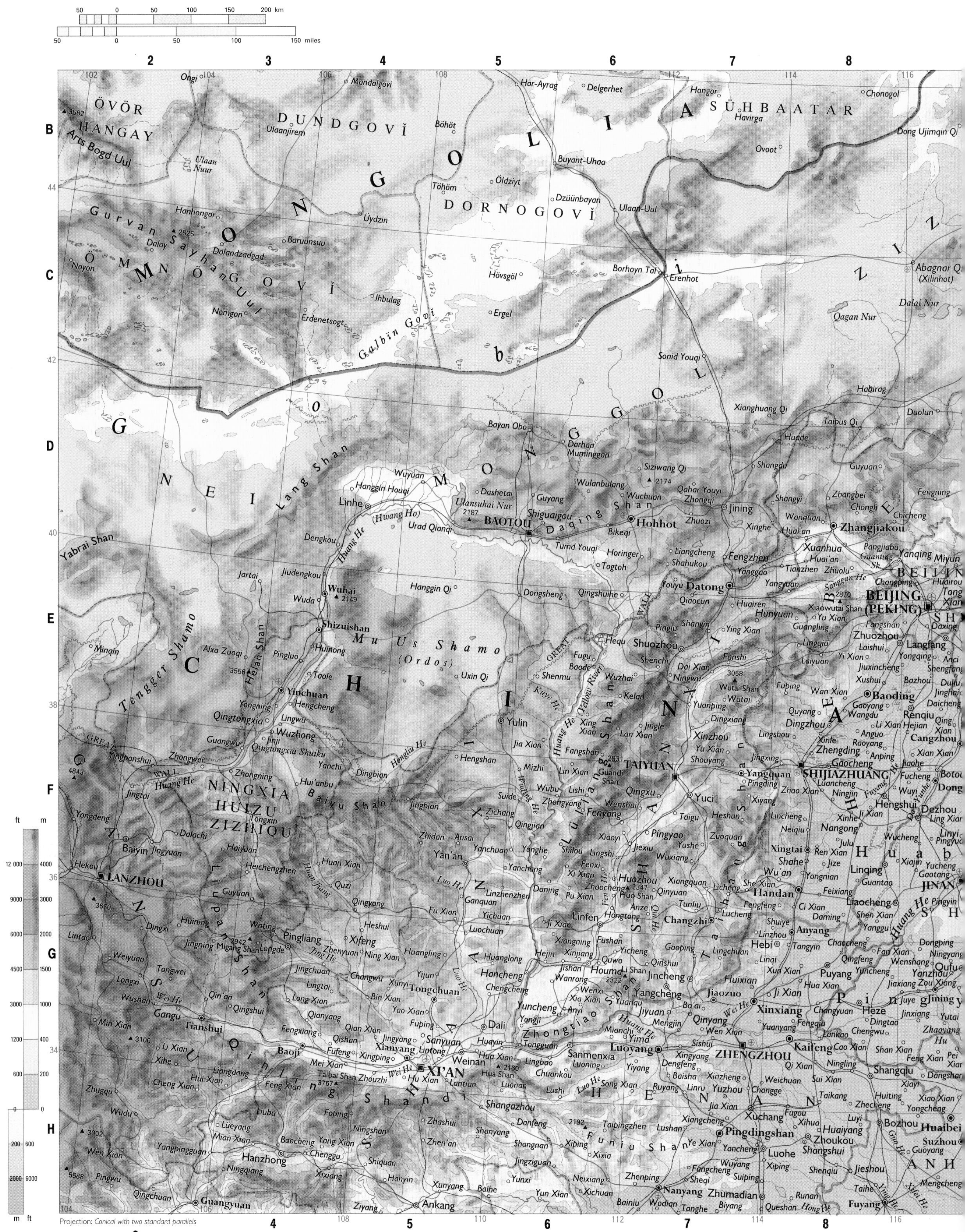

50 0 50 100 150 200 km
50 0 50 100 150 miles

Projection: Conical with two standard parallels

ft   m
12 000   4000
9000   3000
6000   2000
4500   1500
3000   1000
1200   400
600   200
0   0
200   600
2000   6000
m   ft

2 3 4 5 6 7 8

ÖVÖR
HANGAY
Arts Bogd Uul   ▲3582

D U N D G O V Ĭ
Ulaanjirem   Böhöt

Ongi   Ongor   Har-Ayrag   Delgerhet   Hongor   Chonogol

M O N G O L I A   SÜHBAATAR
Havirga   Dong Ujimqin Qi

Gurvan Sayhan Uul
Hanhongor   Ulaan Nuur
▲2825 Dalay   Baruunsuu
Ö M N Ö G O V Ĭ   Dalandzadgad
Noyon   Nomgon   Erdenetsogt   Ihbulag
Galbin Govi

Buyant-Uhaa   Ovoot
Öldziyt
Dzüünbayan   Ulaan-Uul
Hövsgöl   Ergel   Borhoyn Tal   Erenhot

D O R N O G O V Ĭ
Sonid Youqi   Habirag
Xianghuang Qi
Taibus Qi   Duolun
Huade
Bayan Obo   Darhan Muminggan   Siziwang Qi ▲2174   Qahar Youyi Zhongqi   Shangdu   Guyuan
Wuyuan   Dashetai   Guyang   Wulanbulang   Wuchuan   Daqing Shan   Xirighe   Zhangbei   Fengning
Hanggin Houqi   Ulansuhai Nur   Shiguaigou   Bikeqi   Hohhot   Zhuozi   Jining   Wanquan   Chongli   Chicheng
Linhe   ▲2187 BAOTOU   Tumd Youqi   Horinger   Togtoh   Liangcheng   Fengzhen   Xuanhua   Pangjiabu   Yanqing   Miyun
(Hwang Ho)   Urad Qianqi   Qingshuihe   Shahukou   Yanggao   Tianzhen   Zhuolu   Changping   BEIJING
Dengkou   Huang He   Hanggin Qi   Dongsheng   Youyu   Datong   Qiaocun   Hunyuan   Guangling   Zhuozhou
Jiudengkou   Wuhai ▲2149   Pingru   Shanyin   Yu Xian   Fangshan   Daxing
Wuda   Taole   M u   U s   S h a m o   Uxin Qi   Shenmu   Hequ   Shuozhou   Shenchi   Dai Xian   Wutai Shan ▲3058   Laishui   Baoding
Shizuishan   (Ordos)   Fugu   Baode   Wuzhai   Kelan   Ningwu   Fanshi   Fuping   Wan Xian
Huinong   Yulin   Xing Xian   Lan Xian   Dingxiang   Xinzhou   Yuanping   Wutai   Quyang   Gaoyang
Alxa Zuoqi   Pingluo   Jia Xian   Jiji Xian   Jingxing   Li Xian   Dingzhou
Minqin   Helan Shan   ▲3556   Hengshan   Mizhi   Lin Xian   Yu Xian   Shouyang   Lingshou   Xinfe   Anping   Xian   Suning
Yinchuan   Yongning   Hengcheng   Lishi   Guandi Shan   TAIYUAN ▲2831   Pingding   Yangquan   Zhengding   SHIJIAZHUANG   Raoyang
Qingtongxia   Lingwu   Suide   Wubu   Zhongyang   Qingxu   Yuci   Zhao Xian   Xingtai   Ningjin
Tengger Shamo   Wuzhong   Zichang   Qingjian   Fenyang   Wenshui   Taigu   Heshun   Lincheng   Nangong
Zhongwei   Jinji   Qingtongxia Shuiku   Yanchi   Dingbian   Ansai   Shilou   Lingshi   Jiexiu   Yushe   Zuoquan   Xingtai   Ren Xian   Shahe
Guangwu   Hongliu He   Yanchuan   Xiaoyi   Pingyao   Wuxiang   She Xian   Jize   Linqing
Yongdeng   Zhongning   Bai Yu Shan   Zhidan   Yan'an   Yonghe   Fenxi   Xi Xian   Xiangyuan   Huozhou   Wu'an   Yongnian   Guantao
Baiyin   Jingyuan   Huang He   Yanchang   Luo He   Fenxi   Hongtong   Qinyuan   Tunliu   Hebi   Handan   Feixiang   Liaocheng
Heichengzhen   Huan Xian   Ganquan   Ji Xian   Linfen   Daning   Pu Xian   Anze   Changzhi   Fengfeng   Ci Xian   Daming   Chaocheng   Dongping
Haiyuan   Quzi   Fu Xian   Yichuan   Huangling   Xiangning   Fushan   Yicheng   Lucheng   Linzhou   Tangyin   Shen Xian   Yanggu
Daluohi   Qingyang   Luochuan   Huanglong   Hejin   Xinjiang   Quwo   Gaoping   Lingchuan   Anyang   Fan Xian   Shangqiu

N I N G X I A   HUIZU   ZIZHIQU
Pingliang   Xifeng   Ning Xian   ▲2942 Migang Shan   Longde   Zhenyuan   Jingning   Jingchuan   Lingtai   Changwu   Xunyi   Tongchuan   Bin Xian   Yao Xian

L A N Z H O U
▲3670 Dingxi   Weiyuan   Tongwei   Longxi   Wushan   Gangu   Qin an   Qianyang   Long Xian   Fengxiang   Qishan
Lintao   Wei He   Tianshui   Liangdang   Qianyang   Fufeng   Xingping   Sanyuan   Dali   Huayin
Min Xian   ▲3100 Li Xian   Xihe   Hui Xian   Baoji   Mei Xian   Taibai Shan ▲3767   Zhouzhi   XI'AN   Weinan   Hua Xian   Lintong   Lantian   Huayin   Hua Shan ▲2160
Zhugqu   Cheng Xian   Liangdang   Feng Xian   Wei He   Chuankou
Q i n l i n g
Wudu   Lueyang   Mian Xian   Ningshan   Zhashui   Danfeng   Shangnan   ▲2192   Taipingzhen   Lushan
▲3002 Yangpingguan   Baocheng   Yang Xian   S h a n d i   Shangzhou   Shangnan   F u n i u   S h a n   Ye Xian   Yancheng
▲5588 Pingwu   Wen Xian   Hanzhong   Chenggu   Shiquan   Hanyin   Xunyang   Xiping   Nanzhao   Wuyang   Suiping
Qingchuan   Ningqiang   Xixiang   Baihe   Yunxi   Neixiang   Zhenping   Sheqi   Shenqiu
Guangyuan   Ziyang   Ankang   Xunyang   Yun Xian   Xichuan   Bainiu   Nanyang   Zhumadian   Runan
Taihe   Fuyang

Ongi   102   104   106   108   110   112   114   116

3   4   5   6   7   8

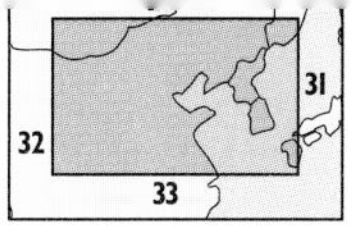
31
32
33

9 10 11 12 13 14 15 16

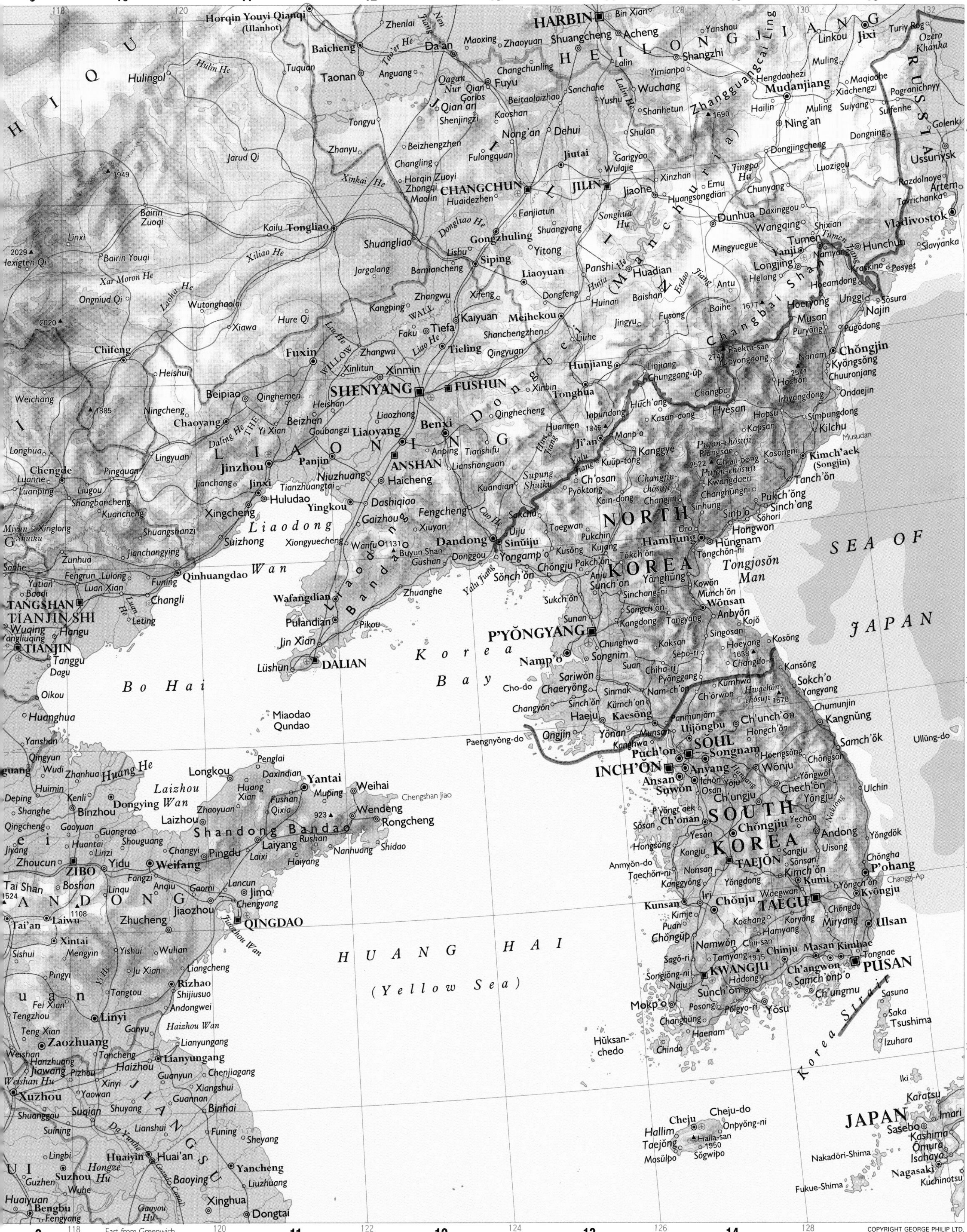
HARBIN
Bin Xian
Acheng
Shuangcheng
Zhaoyuan
Horqin Youyi Qianqi
(Ulanhot)
Zhenlai
Baicheng
Da'an
Maoxing
Taonan
Tuquan
Hulingol
Anguang
Qagan Nur
Qian Gorlos
Qian'an
Fuyu
Changchunling
Shenjingzi
Kaoshan
Beitaalaizhao
Sanchahe
Yushu
Wuchang
Lalin
Shangzhi
Yanshou
Yimianpo
Shanhetun
Zhangguangcai Ling
1690
Hengdaohezi
Mudanjiang
Linkou
Jixi
Muling
Maqiaohe
Xiachengzi
Pogranichnyy
Turiy Rog
Ozero Khanka
Hailin
Ning'an
Suiyang
Suifenhe
Golenki
Dongning
Ussuriysk
Tongyu
Nong'an
Dehui
Shulan
Beizhengzhen
Zhanyu
Changling
Fulongquan
Jiutai
Gangyao
Wulajie
Dongjingcheng
Luozigou
Razdolnoye
Artem
Tavrichanka
Vladivostok
Slavyanka
Jarud Qi
1949
Horqin Zuoyi Zhongqi
Maolin
CHANGCHUN
Huaidezhen
JILIN
Jiaohe
Xinzhan
Huangsongdian
Emu
Jingpo Hu
Chunyang
Xinkai He
Bairin Zuoqi
Kailu
Tongliao
Fanjiatun
Songhua Hu
Dunhua
Daxinggou
Wangqing
Shixian
Tumen
Hunchun
Linxi
2029
Hexigten Qi
Bairin Youqi
Xiliao He
Shuangliao
Dongliao He
Gongzhuling
Shuangyang
Yitong
Lishu
Siping
Jargalang
Bamiancheng
Mingyuegue
Yanji
Namyang
Longjing
Helong
Kraskino
Posyet
Xar Moron He
Laoha He
Liaoyuan
Panshi
Huadian
Antu
Hoeamdong
Ongniud Qi
Wutonghaolai
Zhangwu
Kangping
Xifeng
Dongfeng
Huinan
Baishan
Baihe
1677
Hoeryong
Unggi
Sosura
Najin
2020
Xiawa
Hure Qi
WALL
Faku
Tiefa
Kaiyuan
Meihekou
Jingyu
Fusong
Musan
Puryong
Pugodong
Chifeng
Fuxin
Liao He
Tieling
Shanchengzhen
Liuhe
Changbai Shan
Paektu-san
2744
Ch'ŏngjin
Kyŏngsŏng
Heishui
Zhangwu
Xinlitun
Xinmin
Qingyuan
Hunjiang
Linjiang
Chunggang-ŭp
Yŏnpyŏngdong
Nanam
2541
Chuuronjang
Weichang
Beipiao
Qinghemen
SHENYANG
FUSHUN
Xinbin
Tonghua
Hach'ŏn
Ondaejin
Irhyangdong
1885
Ningcheng
Chaoyang
Heishan
Liaozhong
Qingshecheng
Inpundong
Changbai
Hyesan
Simpundong
Yi Xian
Beizhen
Goubangzi
Liaoyang
Benxi
Huanren
Kasan-dong
Hapsu
Kapsan
Kilchu
Musudan
Longhua
Daling He
LIAONING
Anping
Tianshifu
1845
Manp'o
Pujon-chosuji
Kimch'aek
(Songjin)
Chengde
Pingquan
Lingyuan
Jinzhou
Panjin
ANSHAN
Lianshanguan
Ji'an
Kanggye
Pungsan
Ch'il-bong
Kosŏngni
Luanne
Luanping
Liugou
Jianchang
Jinxi
Niuzhuang
Haicheng
Kuandian
Ch'osan
2522
Pujŏn-chŏsuji
Kwangdaeri
Changhungni
Tanch'ŏn
Shangbancheng
Huludao
Tianzhuangtai
Yingkou
Dashiqiao
Supung Shuiku
Pyŏktong
Koin-dong
Changjin
Changjin-chŏsuji
Sinhung
Puk'ch'ŏng
Sinch'ang
Kuancheng
Xingcheng
Gaizhou
Fengcheng
Sakchu
NORTH
Sinp'o
Sŏhori
Miyun
Xinglong
Shuiku
Shuangshanzi
Liaodong
Xiongyuecheng
Xiuyan
Uiju
Taegwan
Hongwon
Zunhua
Jianchangying
Suizhong
Wanfu
1131
Buyun Shan
Dandong
Sinŭiju
Pukchin
Hamhung
Oro
Hŭngnam
SEA OF
Fengrun
Lulong
Funing
Qinhuangdao
Wan
Gushan
Donggou
Yongamp'o
Kusŏng
Kujang
Tŏkch'ŏn
Tongch'on-ni
Yutian
Luan Xian
Baodi
Changli
Wafangdian
Zhuanghe
Yalu Jiang
Sŏnch'ŏn
Chŏngju
Pakch'ŏn
Anju
KOREA
Yŏnghŭng
Tongjosŏn Man
TANGSHAN
TIANJIN SHI
Sunch'on
Sinchang-ni
Kowŏn
Munch'ŏn
Wŏnsan
Wuqing
Hangu
Leting
Pulandian
Sukch'ŏn
Sŏngch'ŏn
Anbyŏn
Kojŏ
JAPAN
TIANJIN
Pikou
P'YŎNGYANG
Sunan
Kangdong
Tongyang
Singosan
Kosŏng
Tanggu
Dagu
Jin Xian
Korea Bay
Chunghwa
Koksan
Sepo-ri
Hoeyang
Lüshun
DALIAN
Namp'o
Songnim
1638
Changdo-ri
Kansŏng
Bo Hai
Suan
Chiha-ri
Sariwŏn
Pyŏnggang
Kumhwa
Sokch'o
Oikou
Cho-do
Chaeryŏng
Sinmak
Nam-ch'on
Ch'ŏrwŏn
Hwach'ŏn-chŏsuji
1578
Yangyang
Changyŏn
Sinch'ŏn
Kŭmch'ŏn
Chumunjin
Miaodao Qundao
Haeju
Kaesŏng
Panmunjŏm
Ch'unch'ŏn
Kangnŭng
Huanghua
Ongjin
Yŏnan
Munsan
Uijŏngbu
Hongch'ŏn
Paengnyŏng-do
Kanghwa
SOUL
Samch'ŏk
Ullŭng-do
Yanshan
Songnam
Qingyun
Penglai
Puch'on
Hoengsŏng
Chŏngsŏn
Wudi
Zhanhua
Huang He
Longkou
Daxindian
Yantai
INCH'ŎN
Anyang
Wŏnju
Huimin
Laizhou Wan
Huang Xian
Fushan
Muping
Weihai
Chengshan Jiao
Ansan
Suwŏn
Ich'ŏn
Yŏju
Osan
Yŏngwŏl
Chech'ŏn
Deping
Kenli
Dongying
Qixia
923
Wendeng
Ch'ungju
Yŏngju
Ulchin
Shanghe
Binzhou
Zhaoyuan
Laizhou
Shandong Bandao
Rongcheng
P'yŏngt'aek
SOUTH
Qingcheng
Gaoyuan
Guangrao
Sŏsan
Ch'ŏnan
Yech'ŏn
Nakdong
Shouguang
Huantai
Laiyang
Rushan
Shidao
Yesan
Andong
Yŏngdŏk
Linzi
Changyi
Pingdu
Nanhuang
Hongsŏng
Kongju
KOREA
Chŏngju
Sangju
Uisong
Zhoucun
ZIBO
Yidu
Weifang
Laixi
Haiyang
Anmyŏn-do
Nonsan
TAEJŎN
Sŏnsan
Chŏngha
P'ohang
Tai Shan
Boshan
Fangzi
Taechŏn-ni
Kimch'ŏn
Changgi-Ap
1524
Linqu
Anqiu
Gaomi
Lancun
Jimo
Kanggyŏng
Yŏngdong
Kumi
Yŏngch'ŏn
Kyŏngju
Laiwu
1108
Chengyang
Jiaozhou
Kunsan
Iri
Chŏnju
Waegwan
TAEGU
Tai'an
Zhucheng
QINGDAO
Jiaozhou Wan
Kimje
Kochang
Koryŏng
Chŏngdo
Miryang
Ulsan
Xintai
Puan
Chŏngŭp
Hamyang
Sishui
Mengyin
Yishui
Wulian
HUANG HAI
Namwŏn
Chii-san
Masan
Kimhae
Tongnae
Liangcheng
Sagŏ-ri
Tamyang
1915
Chinju
PUSAN
Pingyi
Ju Xian
Rizhao
Shijiusuo
Songjŏng-ni
KWANGJU
Ch'angwŏn
Samch'ŏnp'o
(Yellow Sea)
Hwasun
Naju
Ch'ungmu
Tangtou
Andongwei
Sunch'ŏn
Sasuna
Fei Xian
Tengzhou
Linyi
Mokp'o
Posŏng
Pŏlgyo-ri
Yŏsu
Saka
Tsushima
Haizhou Wan
Ganyu
Changhŭng
Teng Xian
Lianyungang
Haenam
Korea Strait
Zaozhuang
Hŭksan-chedo
Chindo
Izuhara
Weishan
Tancheng
Lianyungang
Hanzhuang
Jiawang
Pizhou
Haizhou
Chenjiagang
Guanyun
Iki
Weishan Hu
Xinyi
Xiangshui
Karatsu
Xuzhou
Yaowan
Guannan
Binhai
Cheju-do
Shuyang
Imari
Shuanggou
Suqian
JAPAN
Cheju
Onpyŏng-ni
Lianshui
Sasebo
Hallim
Halla-san
1950
Kashima
Funing
Suining
Sheyang
Taejŏng
Sŏgwipo
Omura
Mosŭlpo
Lingbi
Huaiyin
Huai'an
Yancheng
Nakadōri-Shima
Isahaya
Hongze
Suzhou
Hu
Baoying
Nagasaki
Guzhen
Liuzhuang
Wuhe
Kuchinotsu
Fukue-Shima
Huaiyuan
Xinghua
Bengbu
Gaoyou Hu
Fengyang
Dongtai
RUSSIA
HEILONGJIANG
JILIN
(Manchuria)
Dongbei
WILLOW
THE
SHANDONG
JIANGSU
Liaodong Bandao
118
120
122
124
126
128
130
132
44
42
40
38
36
34
East from Greenwich

9 10 11 12 13 14 15

B C D E F G H

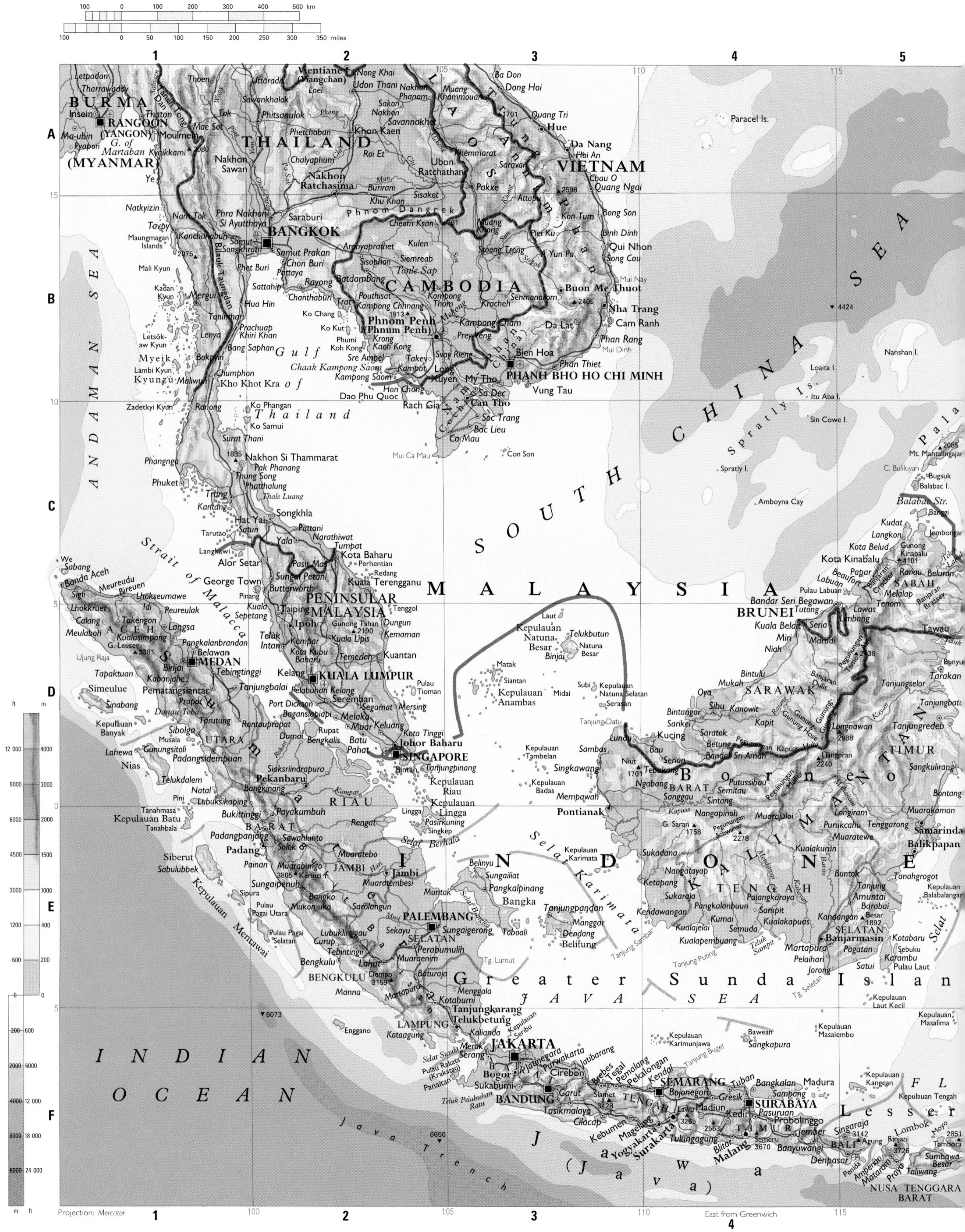
100 0 100 200 300 400 500 km
100 0 50 100 150 200 250 300 350 miles
BURMA (MYANMAR)
RANGOON (YANGON)
G. of Martaban
THAILAND
BANGKOK
LAOS
VIETNAM
Vientiane (Viangchan)
Hue
Da Nang
Qui Nhon
Nha Trang
CAMBODIA
Phnom Penh (Phnum Penh)
PHANH BHO HO CHI MINH
Gulf of Thailand
ANDAMAN SEA
SOUTH CHINA SEA
Paracel Is.
Spratly Is.
Strait of Malacca
MALAYSIA
PENINSULAR MALAYSIA
KUALA LUMPUR
SINGAPORE
Johor Baharu
George Town
Ipoh
BRUNEI
Bandar Seri Begawan
SABAH
Kota Kinabalu
SARAWAK
Kuching
Borneo
KALIMANTAN
TIMUR
BARAT
TENGAH
SELATAN
Pontianak
Samarinda
Balikpapan
Banjarmasin
INDONESIA
MEDAN
ACEH
Banda Aceh
Sumatera
Padang
Pekanbaru
Jambi
PALEMBANG
RIAU
Bangka
Belitung
Kepulauan Natuna
Kepulauan Anambas
Kepulauan Riau
Kepulauan Lingga
Selat Karimata
Greater Sunda Islands
JAVA SEA
JAKARTA
BANDUNG
SEMARANG
SURABAYA
Jawa (Java)
Madura
BALI
Lombok
NUSA TENGGARA BARAT
Lesser
INDIAN OCEAN
Java Trench
Kepulauan Mentawai
Siberut
Nias
Simeulue
Enggano
LAMPUNG
BENGKULU
Tanjungkarang Telukbetung
Denpasar
ft m
12 000 4000
9000 3000
6000 2000
4500 1500
3000 1000
1200 400
600 200
0 0
200 600
2000 6000
4000 12 000
6000 18 000
8000 24 000
m ft
Projection: Mercator
East from Greenwich
1 2 3 4 5
A B C D E F
100 105 110 115
15 10 5 0 5

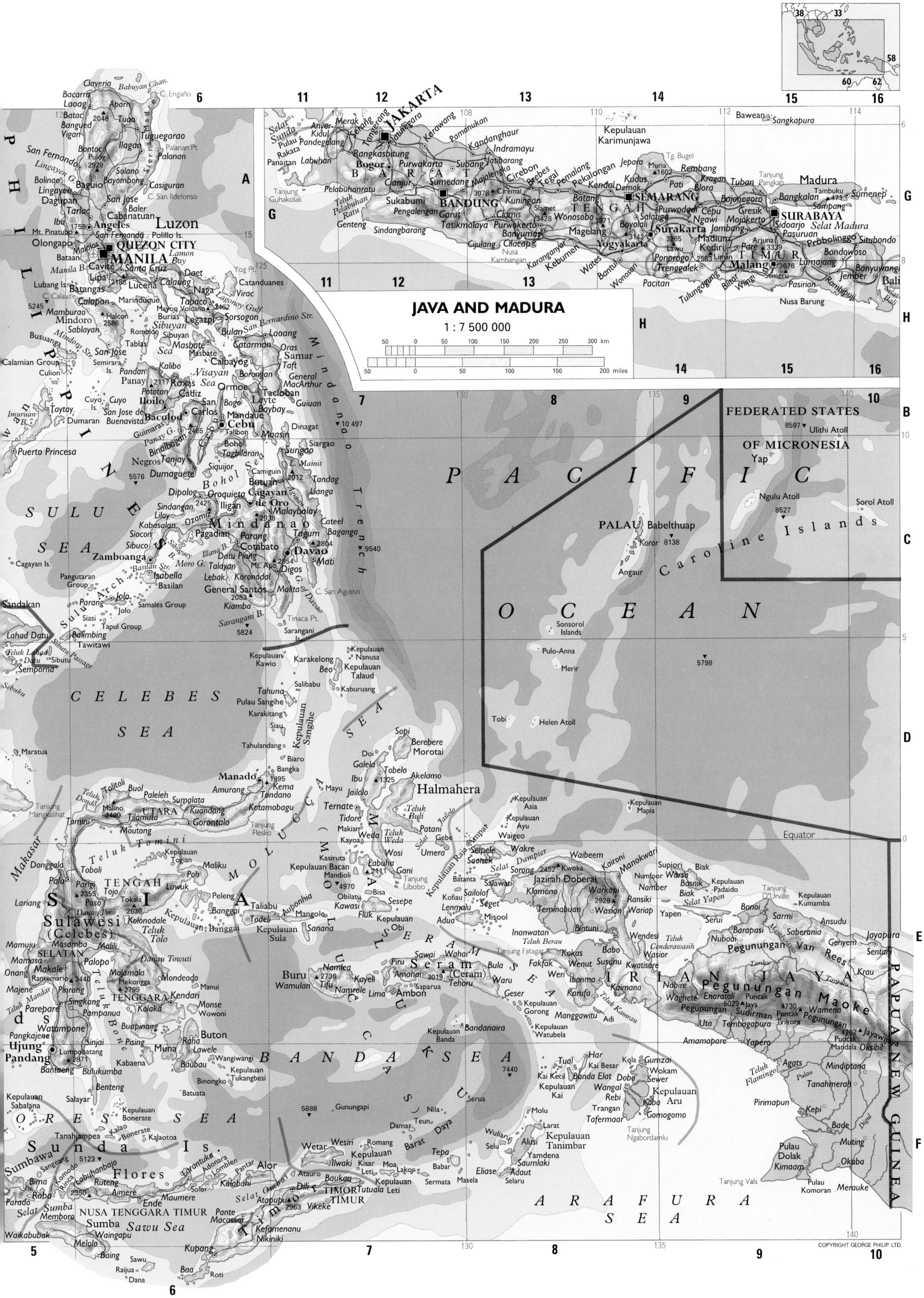

38 33
58
60 62
15 16

6 11 12 JAKARTA 13 14 15 16

PHILIPPINE

Clayeria
Bacarra
Laoag
Aparri C. Engaño
Babuyan Chan.
Batac Tuao
Bangued 2048 Tuguegarao
Vigan Bontoc Ilagan Palanan Pt.
San Fernando Pulog 2929 Solano Palanan
Lingayen G. Baguio Bayombong Casiguran
Bolinao Lingayen Dagupan San Jose C. San Ildefonso
Iba Tarlac Cabanatuan
Mt. Pinatubo 1759 San Fernando Baler
Olongapo Angeles Polillo Is.
QUEZON CITY Lamon
Cavite MANILA Bay
Lubang Is. Santa Cruz Daet
Batangas Lucena Calauag Virac
Calapan Naga Catanduanes
Mindoro Marinduque Tabaco Legazpi Sorsogon
Halcon 2586 Sibuyan San Bernardino Str.
Tablas Masbate Bulan Catarman Laoang
Romblon Oras
Semirara Is. Masbate Calbayog Taft
Pandan Sea Catbalogan General MacArthur
Cuyo Panay Roxas Borongan Guiuan
Is. Iloilo Cadiz Tacloban
San Jose de Bacolod San Carlos Leyte Baybay
Buenavista Bago Ormoc
Guimaras Bohol Sea Maasin
Negros Fanjay Dumaguete Tagbilaran
Bohol Surigao Siargao
Siquijor L. Mainit
Camiguin Butuan Tandag
Dipolog Oroquieta Cagayan 2012
Liloy de Oro Lianga
Dapitan Iligan Malaybalay
Siocon Ozamiz Cateel
Zamboanga Kabasalan Pagadian Parang Baganga
Sibuco Cotabato 2804
Basilan Str. Ilian Dau Piang Davao Mati
Isabella Moro G. Talayan Mt. Apo 2954
Lebak Koronadal Malita C. San Agustin
General Santos
Kiamba
Sarangani B.

SULU SEA
Cagayan Is.
Sandakan
Lahad Datu
Semporna

CELEBES SEA

PACIFIC OCEAN

FEDERATED STATES OF MICRONESIA
Yap
Ulithi Atoll 8597
Ngulu Atoll 8527
Sorol Atoll
Caroline Islands
PALAU Babelthuap
Koror 8138
Angaur

Sonsorol Islands
Pulo-Anna 5798
Merir
Tobi Helen Atoll

Karakelong Kepulauan Nanusa
Kawio Beo Kepulauan Talaud
Tahuna Salibabu Kaburuang
Pulau Sangihe
Karakitang Siau
Kepulauan Sanghe
Tahulandang

Sopi Morotai
Berebere
Doi Galela
Bangka Tobelo
Biaro Ibu Akelamo
Mayu Jailolo 1325
Ternate Halmahera
Tidore Teluk Buli
Makian Patani
Kayoa Weda Gebe

MOLUCCA SEA

Kepulauan Asia
Kepulauan Ayu
Kepulauan Mapia
Waigeo
Kepulauan Raja Ampat
Salawati Sorong Jazirah Doberai
Batanta

COPYRIGHT GEORGE PHILIP LTD.

5 7 130 8 135 9 10

6

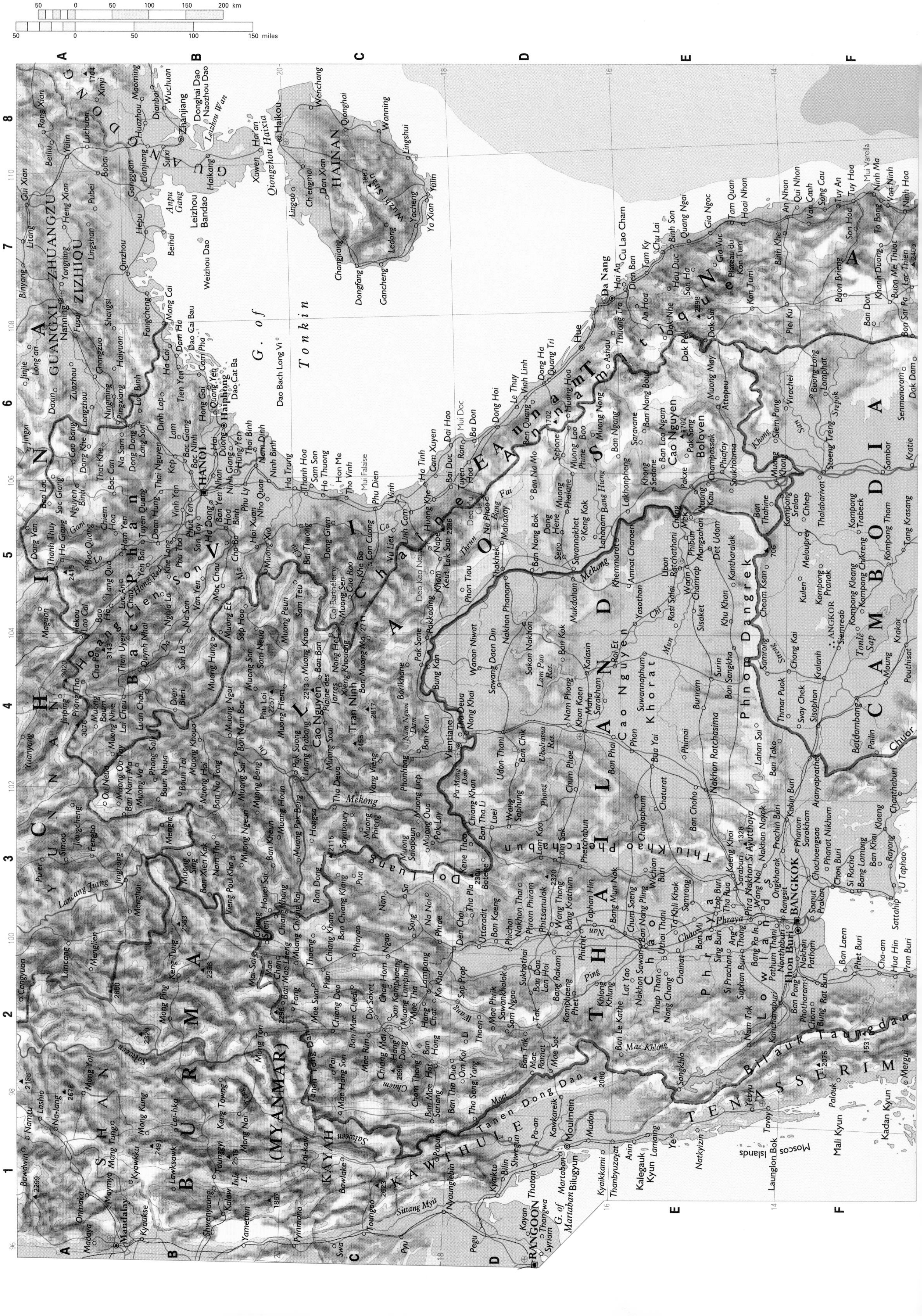

50 0 50 100 150 200 km
50 0 50 100 150 miles
G. of Tonkin
HAINAN
CAMBODIA
THAILAND
LAOS
BURMA (MYANMAR)
YUNNAN
GUANGXI ZHUANGZU ZIZHIQU
HANOI
BANGKOK
RANGOON
Vientiane
Mandalay
Haikou
Da Nang
Hue
Mekong
Khorat
Cao Nguyen Khorat
Phnom Dangrek
Gulf of Martaban

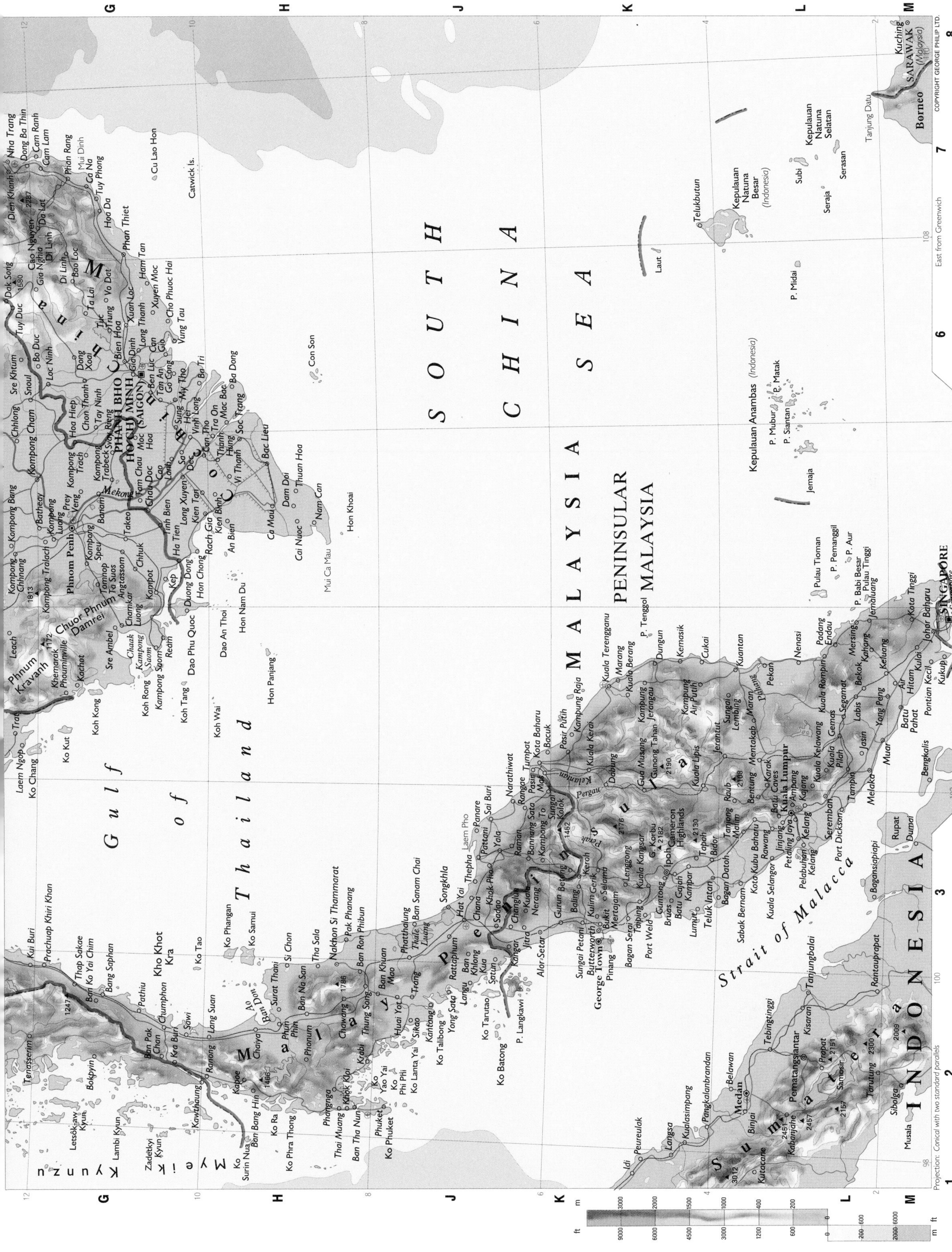
SOUTH CHINA SEA
Gulf of Thailand
MALAYSIA
PENINSULAR MALAYSIA
INDONESIA
Strait of Malacca
Sumatera
SINGAPORE
Kuala Lumpur
PHNOM PENH
THANH PHO HO CHI MINH (SAIGON)
Mekong
Borneo
SARAWAK (Malaysia)
Kuching
Kepulauan Anambas (Indonesia)
Kepulauan Natuna Besar (Indonesia)
Kepulauan Natuna Selatan
Pulau Tioman
Medan
Pinang
George Town
Ipoh
Melaka
Kuantan
Kuala Terengganu
Kota Baharu
Hat Yai
Songkhla
Surat Thani
Phuket
Ko Samui
Ko Phangan
Nakhon Si Thammarat
Kampot
Kep
Ha Tien
Rach Gia
Can Tho
Ca Mau
Mui Ca Mau
Con Son
Nha Trang
Cam Ranh
Phan Rang
Phan Thiet
Vung Tau
Da Lat
Bac Lieu
Soc Trang
Cameron Highlands
Gunong Tahan
Phnum Kravanh
Chuor Phnum Damrei
Kho Khot Kra
East from Greenwich
Projection: Conical with two standard parallels
COPYRIGHT GEORGE PHILIP LTD.
m
ft
3000
2000
1500
1000
400
200
0
9000
6000
4500
3000
1200
600
200
2000
6000

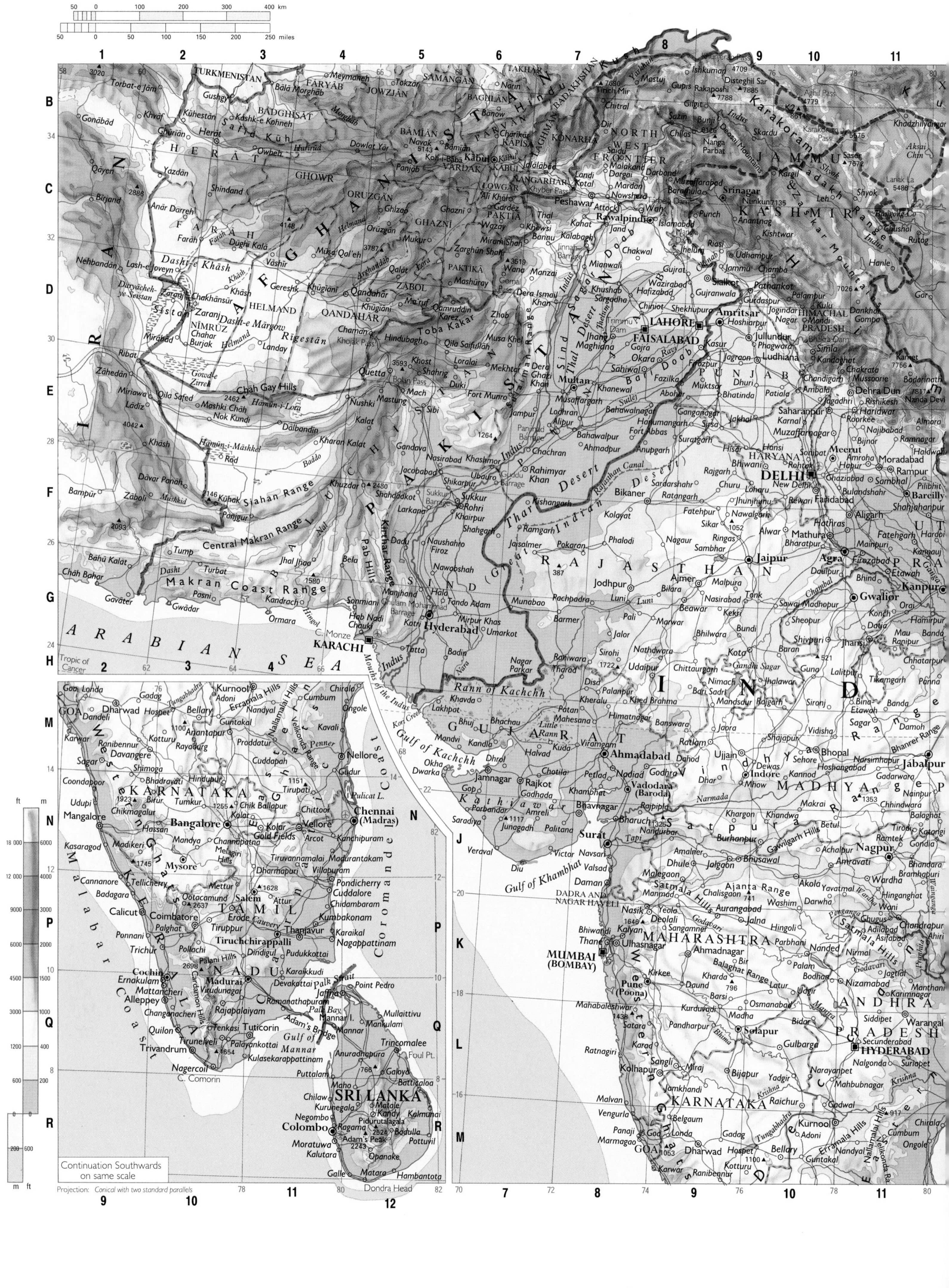

km
miles
TURKMENISTAN
AFGHANISTAN
HERĀT
FARĀH
HELMAND
NĪMRŪZ
QANDAHĀR
ORUZGĀN
GHAZNĪ
ZĀBOL
PAKTĪKĀ
Kabul
Herāt
Qandahār
Kandahār
IRAN
Zāhedān
Bampūr
PAKISTAN
NORTH WEST FRONTIER
Peshawar
Rawalpindi
Islamabad
Quetta
Multan
LAHORE
FAISALABAD
Hyderabad
KARACHI
Sukkur
SIND
Makran Coast Range
Central Makran Range
Siahan Range
Toba Kakar
Kirthar Range
Sulaiman Range
Thal Desert
Thar Desert
Great Indian Desert
Hindu Kush
Karakoram
JAMMU & KASHMIR
Srinagar
Ladakh
Zaskar Mountains
HIMACHAL PRADESH
PUNJAB
HARYANA
DELHI
New Delhi
RAJASTHAN
Jaipur
Agra
Kanpur
Gwalior
Bhopal
Indore
Jabalpur
Nagpur
MADHYA PRADESH
GUJARAT
Ahmadabad
Vadodara (Baroda)
Surat
Rann of Kachchh
Gulf of Kachchh
Kathiawar
Gulf of Khambhat
DADRA AND NAGAR HAVELI
MAHARASHTRA
MUMBAI (BOMBAY)
Pune (Poona)
Satpura Range
Vindhya Range
Western Ghats
ANDHRA PRADESH
HYDERABAD
Secunderabad
KARNATAKA
INDIA
ARABIAN SEA
Mouths of the Indus
Tropic of Cancer
KARNATAKA
Bangalore
Mysore
Mangalore
TAMIL NADU
Chennai (Madras)
Coimbatore
Madurai
Tiruchchirappalli
Pondicherry
KERALA
Cochin
Trivandrum
Calicut
Malabar Coast
Coromandel Coast
Eastern Ghats
Palk Strait
Palk Bay
Adam's Bridge
Gulf of Mannar
SRI LANKA
Colombo
Kandy
Jaffna
Trincomalee
Galle
Dondra Head
C. Comorin
Continuation Southwards on same scale
Projection: Conical with two standard parallels

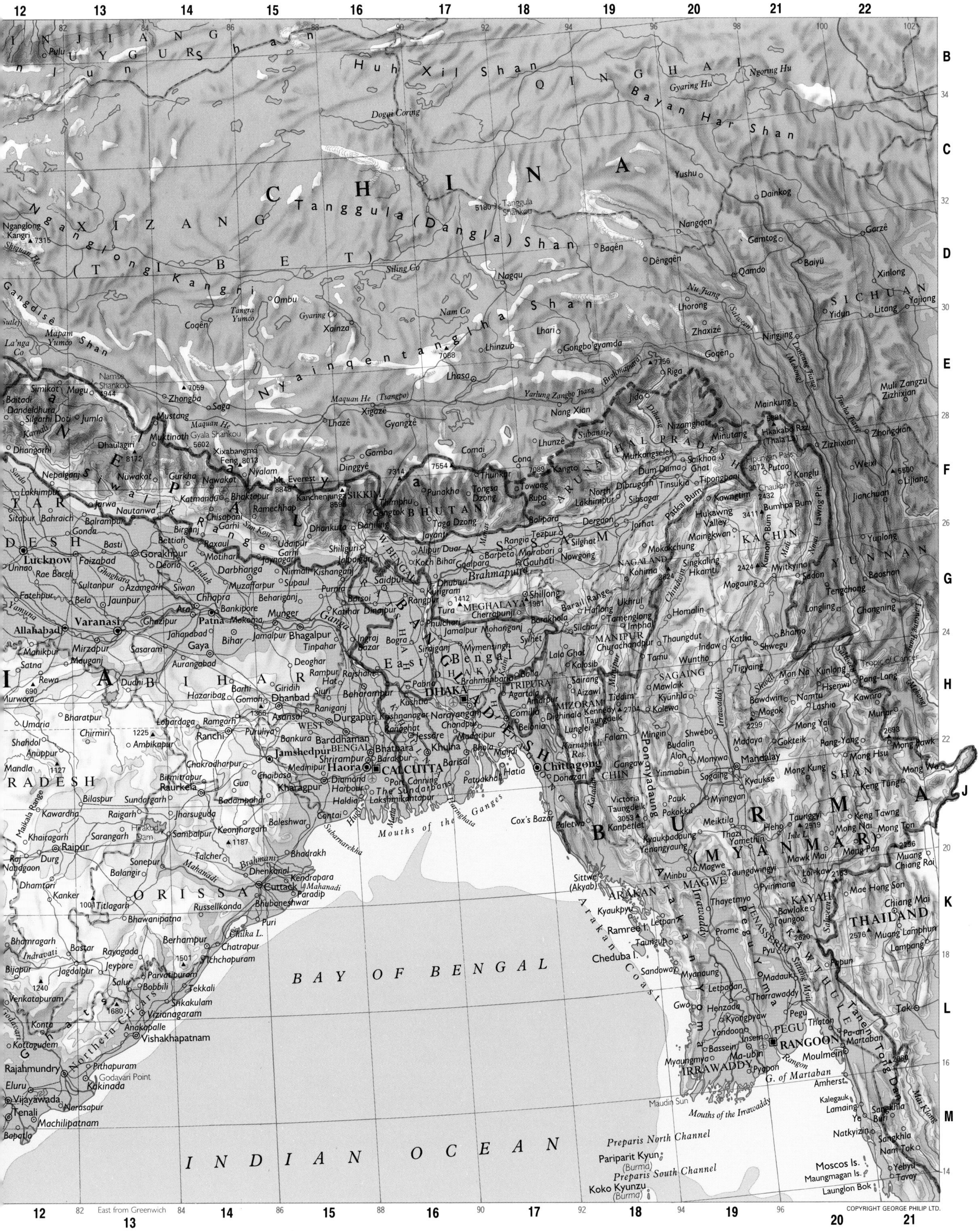

45 32
38

B
12 13 14 15 16 17 18 19 20 21 22

X I N J I A N G
U Y G U R
Pulu
Iun

34

Huh Xil Shan
Dogai Coring
QINGHAI
Gyaring Hu
Ngoring Hu

C
C H I N A
Yushu
Dainkog

32

Tanggula (Dangla) Shan
5180 Tanggula Shankou
Bayan Har Shan
Bagên
Dêngqên
Nangqên
Garntog
Qamdo
Garzê

Siling Co
Nagqu
Lhorong
Zhaxizê
Ningjing
Yidun
Litang
Yajiang
SICHUAN
Baiyü
Xinlong

D
X I Z A N G
(T i b e t)
Ngang long Kangri 7315
Kanghi
Ombu
Tangra Yumco
Gyaring Co
Xainza
Nam Co
Nainqentanglha Shan
Lhinzub
Gongbo'gyamda
Gogên
Qamdo

30

Mapam Yumco
La'nga Co
Gangdisê Shan
Sutlej
Coqên
Lhasa
Lhari
Brahmaputra
Riga
Jido
7756
Muli Zangzu Zizhixian

E
Namse Shankou
Simikot
Mugu 4944
Zhongba
Saga
Xigazê
Xigazê
Lhazê
Gyangzê
Gamba
Yarlung Zangbo Jiang
Nang Xian
Subansiri
Nizamghat
Zhongdran
Zhongdran

28

Baitadi
Dandeldhura
Silgarhi Doti
Jumla
Dhangarhi
Mustang
8172
Maquan He
7088
Lhari
Mürkongselek
Dibrugarh
Tinsukia
Tipongpani
Weixi
5500
Lijiang

F
N E P A L
Dhaulagiri
Muktinath
Gyala Shankou
5602
Xixabangma Feng 8013
Dinggyê
7314
7554
Thunkar
7089
Kangto
Towang
Rupa
A R U N A C H A L P R A D E S H
Dum Duma Ghat
Saikhoa Ghat
3072 Putao
Hpungan Pass
Chaukan Pass
Konglu
Jianchuan

26

Nepalganj
Nuwakot
Ngwakot
Gurkha
Katmandu
Ramechhap
Chisapani
Kancherjunga
8585
8845 Mt Everest
Sikkim
Gangtok
Thimphu
B H U T A N
Taga Dzong
Punakha
Tongsa Dzong
North Lakhimpur
Silsagar
Dergaon
Jorhat
Patkai Bum
Hukawng Valley
2432
Bumha Bum
3411
Yunlong
Yunnan

G
F A R
Sitapur
Bahraich
Balrampur
Gonda
Basti
Gorakhpur
Deoria
Siwan
Chhapra
Bettiah
Raxaul
Motihari
Darbhanga
Muzaffarpur
Supaul
Purnia
Kishanganj
Jalpaiguri
Shiliguri
Darjiling
Jayanti
Alipur Duar
Koch Bihar
Kurigram
1412
Dhubri
Rangia
Tezpur
Balipara
Mangaldai
Barpeta
Gauhati
Nowgong
Mokokchung
NAGALAND
Kohima
3824
Singkaling Hkamti
Mogaung
Myitkyina
K A C H I N
Maingkwan
Homalin
Tamenglong
Imphal
2424
Bhamo
Shwegu
Tengchong
Longling
Changning

24

Lucknow
Faizabad
Unnao
Rae Bareli
Ghaghara
Sultanpur
Azamgarh
Ara
Bankipore
Patna
Mokama
Munger
Ganga
Deoghar
Siri
Jamalpur
Bhagalpur
Tinpahar
Rajshahi
Bogra
Sirajganj
Mymensingh
Jamalpur
Mohanganj
Sylhet
Lala Ghat
Kolasib
Silchar
Haflong
Borakhola
Barail Range
Ukhrul
MANIPUR
Churachandpur
Thaungdut
Indaw
Katha
SAGAING
Tamu
Wuntho
Tigyaing
Kunlong
Tropic of Cancer

22

Allahabad
Varanasi
Mirzapur
Ghazipur
Jaunpur
Sasaram
Jahanabad
Gaya
Bela
Aurangabad
Bihar
Jamalpur
Rampur Hat
Barddhaman
Behrampur
Baharampur
East Bengal
Pabna
DHAKA
Brahmanbaria
TRIPURA
Agartala
Belonia
Comilla
MIZORAM
Tiddim
2704
Kennedy
Taungdek
Falam
Mawlaik
Kyunhla
Kalewa
Shwebo
Budalin
Mingin
Bawdwin
Namtu
Hsenwi
Mong Yai
Mogok
Lashio
Lungleh
Man Na
Pang-Long
Namtu
2638
Mong Hawk

H
I N D I A
Fatehpur
Mohikar
Satna
690
Rewa
Murwora
Umaria
Mandla
1127
R A D E S H
Dudhi
B I H A R
Hazaribag
Giridih
Gomoh
Barhi
Dhanbad
1366
Asansol
Raniganj
Durgapur
WEST
BENGAL
Bankura
Puruliya
Jamshedpur
Medinipur
Haora
CALCUTTA
Kharagpur
Diamond Harbour
Krishnanagar
Jessore
Narayanganj
Chandpur
Madaripur
Khulna
Barisal
Bhola
Hatia
BANGLADESH
Chittagong
Dohazari
C H I N
Kaladan
Victoria 3053
Taungdeik
Kanpetlet
Pauk
Pakokku
Myingyan
Meiktila
Yamethin
Thazi
Heho
2519
Taunggyi
Kyaukpadaung
Yenangyaung
Minbu
Magwe
2299
Maddaya
Mandalay
Mong Kung
Keng Tung
Mong Yai
Mong Nai
Mong Ton
Loikaw
Mong Pan
Muang Chiang Rai
Mong Wa
Takaw
2296

J
Bharatpur
Chirmiri
1225
Ambikapur
Anuppur
Raurkela
Lohardaga
Ramgarh
Ranchi
Chakradharpur
Gua
Chaibasa
Baripada
Bhadrakh
Mandla
Bitmirapur
Raigarh
Sundargarh
Bilaspur
Raipur
Durg
Dhamtari
Kanker
Sonepur
Balangir
Sambalpur
1187
O R I S S A
Cuttack
Kendrapara
Paradip
Bhubaneswar
Russellkonda
Chilka L.
Puri
Contai
Haldia
Laksmikantapur
Port Canning
The Sundarbans
Patuakhali
Cox's Bazar
Paletwa
Kyaukpyu
Ramree I.
ARAKAN
Sittwe (Akyab)
Arakan Coast
Kanpetlet
Letpan
Taungup
Cheduba I.
Sandoway
Thayetmyo
Prome
B U R M A
(M Y A N M A R)
MAGWE
Taungdwingyi
Pyinmana
Toungoo
KAYAH
Bawlake
2620
KAYAH
Loikaw
Mae Hong Son
2576
THAILAND
Chiang Mai
Muang Lamphun
Lampang

K
Bhamragarh
Bastar
Rayagada
Jeypore
Indravati
Jagdalpur
Bijapur
1240
1501
Ichchapuram
Parvatipuram
Salur
Bobbili
Tekkali
Srikakulam
Vizianagaram
Anakapalle
Vishakhapatnam
1680
Northern Circars

L
B A Y   O F   B E N G A L
Myanaung
Letpadan
Thonze
Tharrawaddy
Henzada
Gwo
Yandoon
Kyonpyaw
Bassein
Ma-ubin
Insein
RANGOON
PEGU
Pegu
Thaton
Pa-an
Martaban
Moulmein
Amherst

M
Rajahmundry
Eluru
Vijayawada
Tenali
Machilipatnam
Bapatla
Kakinada
Pithapuram
Godavari Point
Narasapur
Maudin Sun
IRRAWADDY
Myaungmya
Pyapon
Mouths of the Irrawaddy
Kalegauk I.
Lamaing
Ye
Sangkhla Buri
Nam Tok
Yebyu
Tavoy

I N D I A N   O C E A N
Preparis North Channel
Pariparit Kyun (Burma)
Preparis South Channel
Koko Kyunzu (Burma)
Launglon Bok
Moscos Is.
Maungmagan Is.

14

13 20

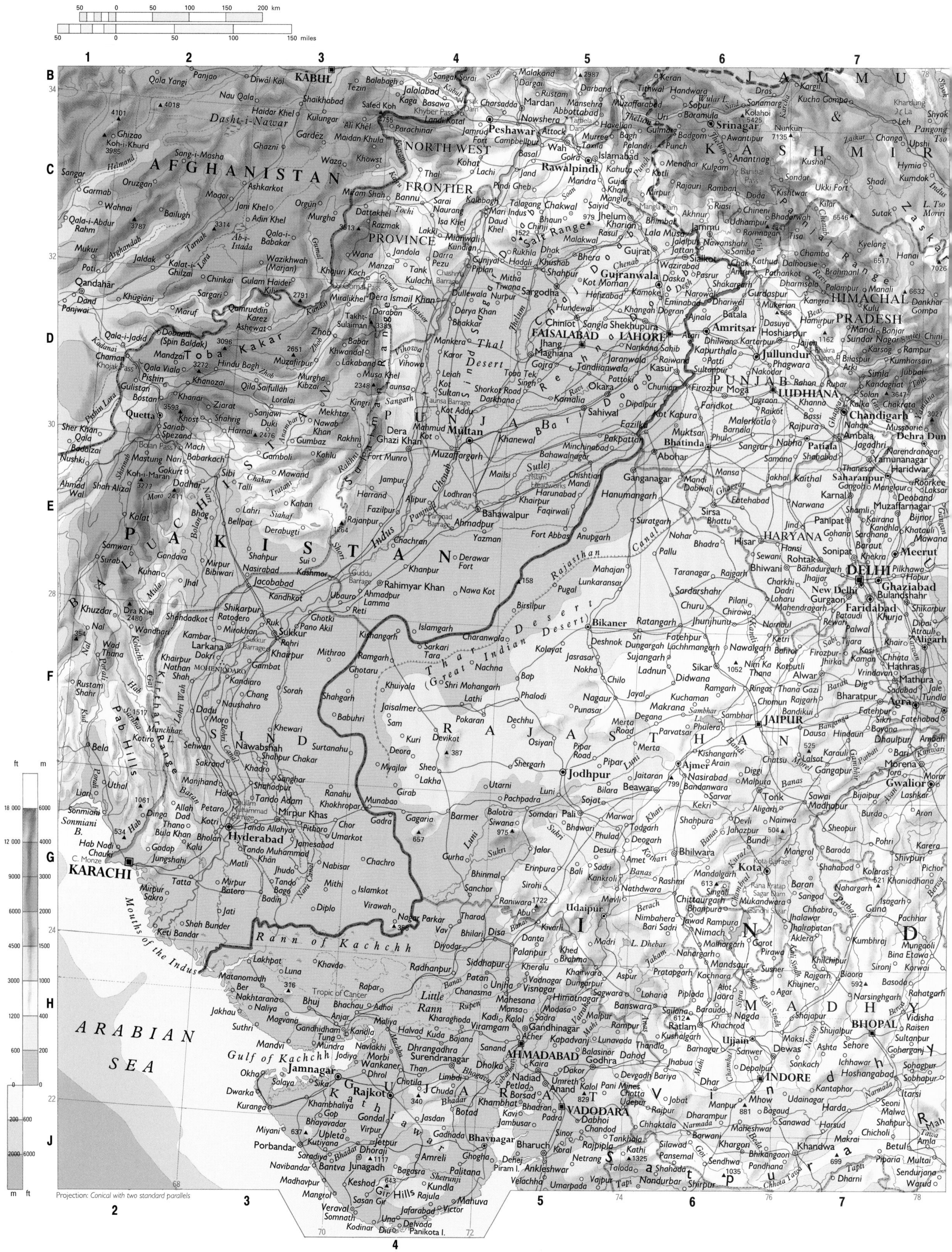

50 0 50 100 150 200 km
50 0 50 100 150 miles

AFGHANISTAN

PAKISTAN

BALUCHISTAN

SIND

PUNJAB

NORTH WEST FRONTIER PROVINCE

JAMMU & KASHMIR

HIMACHAL PRADESH

PUNJAB

HARYANA

RAJASTHAN

Thar Desert (Great Indian Desert)

MADHYA PRADESH

ARABIAN SEA

Gulf of Kachchh

Rann of Kachchh

Little Rann

Mouths of the Indus

Tropic of Cancer

KABUL
Peshawar
Rawalpindi
Islamabad
Srinagar
Quetta
FAISALABAD **LAHORE**
Amritsar
Jullundur
LUDHIANA
Chandigarh
Multan
Bhatinda
Patiala
Bahawalpur
DELHI
New Delhi
Ghaziabad
Meerut
Faridabad
Bikaner
Jaisalmer
Jodhpur
JAIPUR
Ajmer
Agra
Gwalior
Kota
Udaipur
KARACHI
Hyderabad
Jamnagar
Rajkot
AHMADABAD
Gandhinagar
VADODARA
Bhavnagar
INDORE
BHOPAL
Ujjain
Ratlam

ft m
18 000 6000
12 000 4000
9000 3000
6000 2000
4500 1500
3000 1000
1200 400
600 200
0 0
200 600
2000 6000
m ft

Projection: Conical with two standard parallels

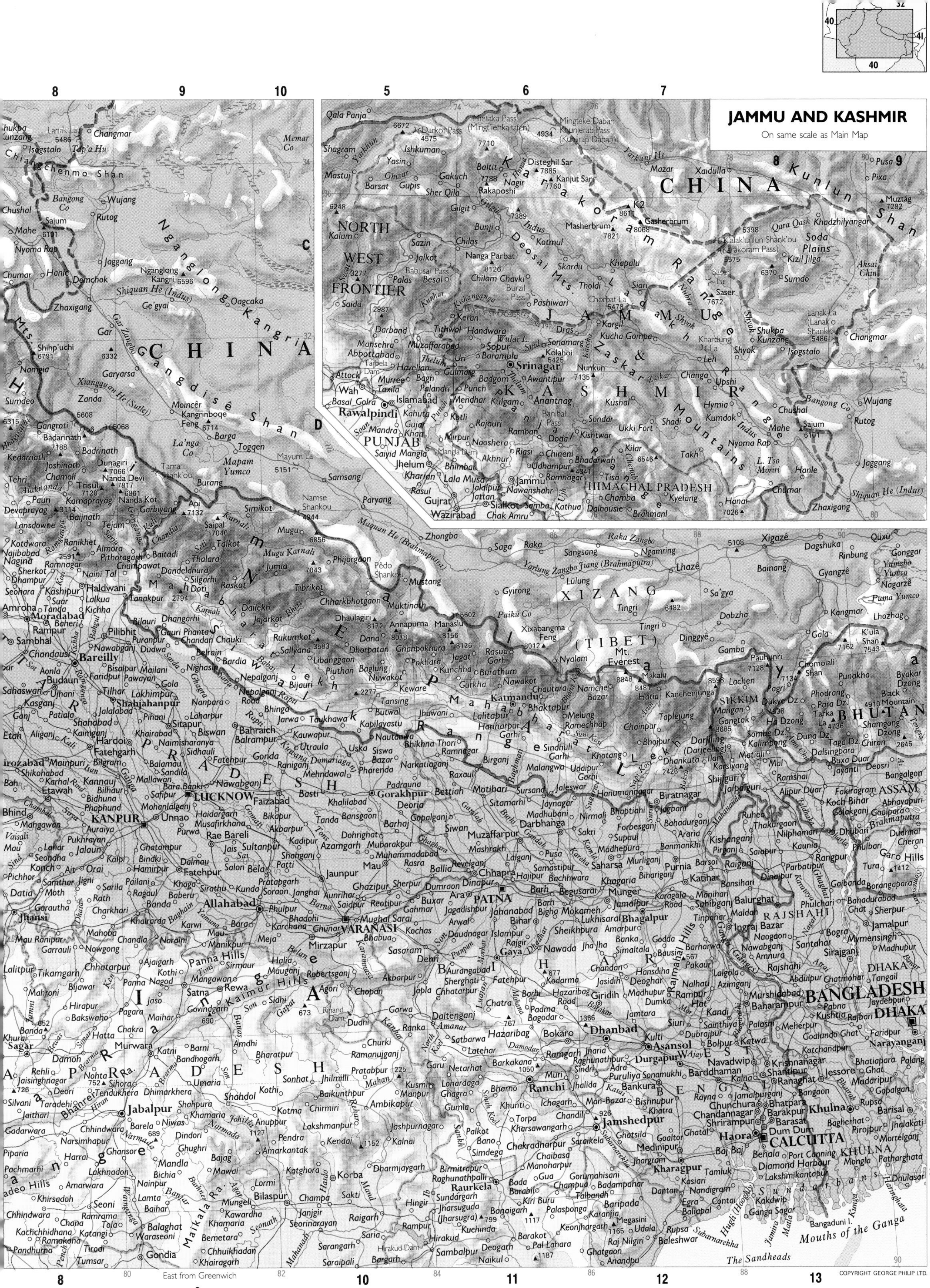

JAMMU AND KASHMIR
On same scale as Main Map
CHINA
NORTH WEST FRONTIER
PUNJAB
JAMMU & KASHMIR
HIMACHAL PRADESH
Karakoram Range
Zaskar Mountains
Ladakh Range
Kunlun Shan
Srinagar
Rawalpindi
Islamabad
Jammu
Gilgit
Leh
Kargil
K2 8611
Gasherbrum 8068
Nanga Parbat 8126
Soda Plains
Aksai Chin
CHINA
XIZANG (TIBET)
NEPAL
Mahabharat Lekh
Siwalik Range
Mt. Everest 8848
Kanchenjunga 8598
Annapurna 8078
Dhaulagiri 8172
Nanda Devi 7817
Katmandu
SIKKIM
BHUTAN
ASSAM
Garo Hills
BANGLADESH
DHAKA
RAJSHAHI
KHULNA
UTTAR PRADESH
MADHYA PRADESH
BIHAR
WEST BENGAL
LUCKNOW
KANPUR
Allahabad
VARANASI
PATNA
Gaya
Ranchi
Jamshedpur
Dhanbad
Asansol
CALCUTTA
Haora
Jabalpur
Bareilly
Moradabad
Gorakhpur
Darjeeling
Mouths of the Ganga
The Sandheads
Sundarbans
Kaimur Hills
Maikala Ra.
Rajmahal Hills
East from Greenwich

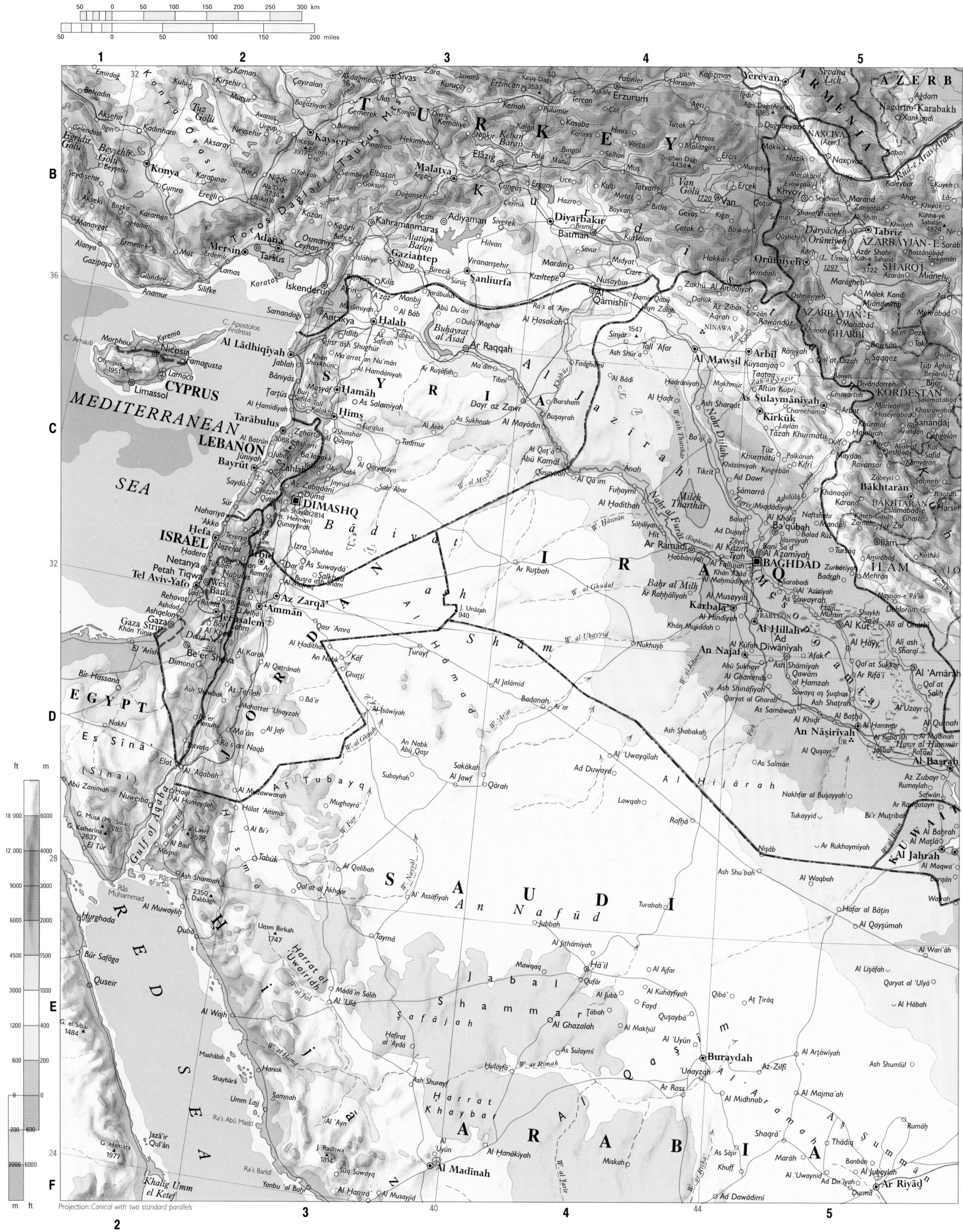

50 0 50 100 150 200 250 300 km
50 0 50 100 150 200 miles
TURKEY
SYRIA
IRAQ
JORDAN
SAUDI ARABIA
LEBANON
ISRAEL
CYPRUS
EGYPT
ARMENIA
KUWAIT
MEDITERRANEAN SEA
RED SEA
Es Sînâ' (Sinai)
Bādiyat ash Shām
Al Ḩamād
An Nafūd
Al Jazīrah
Mesopotamia
Al Ḩijārah
Jabal Shammar
Ḩarrat Khaybar
Al Ḩijāz
Ankara
Konya
Kayseri
Adana
Mersin
Tarsus
Malatya
Elâzığ
Diyarbakır
Gaziantep
Şanlıurfa
Erzurum
Sivas
Van
Van Gölü
Tuz Gölü
Beyşehir Gölü
Ağrı Dağı (Ararat) 5165
Yerevan
Nicosia
Limassol
Famagusta
Larnaca
Kyrenia
Antakya
İskenderun
Halab
Ḩamāh
Ḩimş
Al Lādhiqīyah
Tarābulus
Bayrūt
Ṣaydā
Zaḩlah
DIMASHQ
Jabal ash Shaykh (Mt. Hermon) 2814
Ar Raqqah
Dayr az Zawr
Tudmur
Al Ḩasakah
Al Qāmishlī
Buḩayrat al Asad
Ḩefa
Tel Aviv-Yafo
Jerusalem
Gaza
Gaza Strip
West Bank
Be'er Sheva
Dead Sea
Elat
Al 'Aqabah
'Ammān
Az Zarqā'
Irbid
Ma'ān
Gulf of Aqaba
BAGHDĀD
Al Mawşil
Arbīl
Kirkūk
As Sulaymānīyah
Ar Ramādī
Al Fallūjah
Karbalā'
Al Ḩillah
An Najaf
Ad Dīwānīyah
Al Kūt
Al 'Amārah
An Nāşirīyah
Al Başrah
Sāmarrā
Tikrīt
Nahr Dijlah (Tigris)
Nahr al Furāt (Euphrates)
Ar Ruţbah
Al Jahrah
Tabrīz
Orūmīyeh
Daryācheh-ye Orūmīyeh
Bākhtarān
Sanandaj
Ilām
Ḩā'il
Buraydah
'Unayzah
Al Madīnah
Ar Riyāḑ
Tabūk
Al Jawf
Sakākah
Taymā
Al 'Ulā
Al Wajh
Ḑubā
Yanbu 'al Baḩr
Hurghada
Quseir
Projection: Conical with two standard parallels

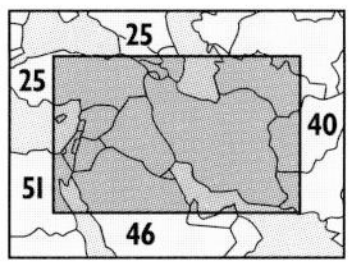

25
25
40
51
46

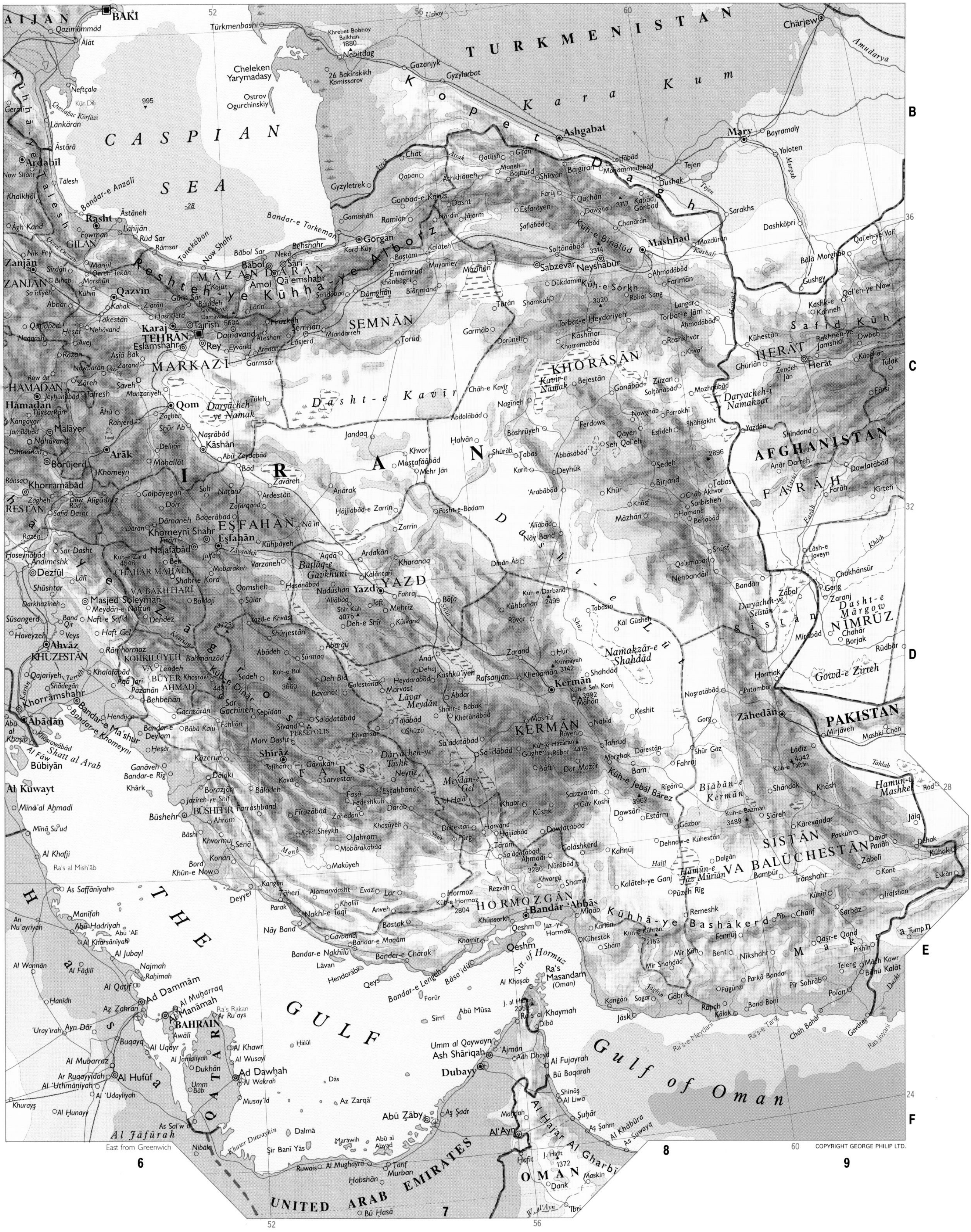

6
7
8
9
10
B
C
D
E
F
TURKMENISTAN
Kara Kum
Kopet Dagh
CASPIAN SEA
IRAN
AFGHANISTAN
PAKISTAN
THE GULF
Gulf of Oman
UNITED ARAB EMIRATES
OMAN
QATAR
BAHRAIN
BAKI
Türkmenbashi
Nebitdag
Ashgabat
Mary
Chärjew
Amudarya
Dasht-e Kavīr
Dasht-e Lūt
Reshteh-ye Kūhhā-ye Alborz
Kūhhā-ye Zāgros
Daryācheh-ye Namak
SEMNĀN
KHORĀSĀN
MĀZANDARĀN
GĪLĀN
ZANJĀN
HAMADĀN
MARKAZĪ
EŞFAHĀN
YAZD
KERMĀN
FĀRS
BŪSHEHR
KHŪZESTĀN
HORMOZGĀN
SĪSTĀN VA BALŪCHESTĀN
HERĀT
FARĀH
NĪMRŪZ
TEHRĀN
Tehrān
Karaj
Qom
Kāshān
Arāk
Mashhad
Neyshābūr
Sabzevār
Gorgān
Rasht
Qazvin
Ardabīl
Hamadān
Eşfahān
Yazd
Kermān
Shīrāz
Ahvāz
Ābādān
Khorramshahr
Būshehr
Bandar-e 'Abbās
Zāhedān
Zābol
Herāt
Shatt al Arab
Al Kuwayt
Ad Dammām
Al Manāmah
Ad Dawḩah
Al Hufūf
Dubayy
Abū Ẓaby
Ash Shāriqah
Al 'Ayn
Ra's al Khaymah
Str. of Hormuz
Qeshm
Chāh Bahār
Gowd-e Zirreh
Hamun-i Mashkel
Dasht-e Mārgow
Al Jāfūrah
Al Ḩajar Al Gharbī
East from Greenwich
COPYRIGHT GEORGE PHILIP LTD.

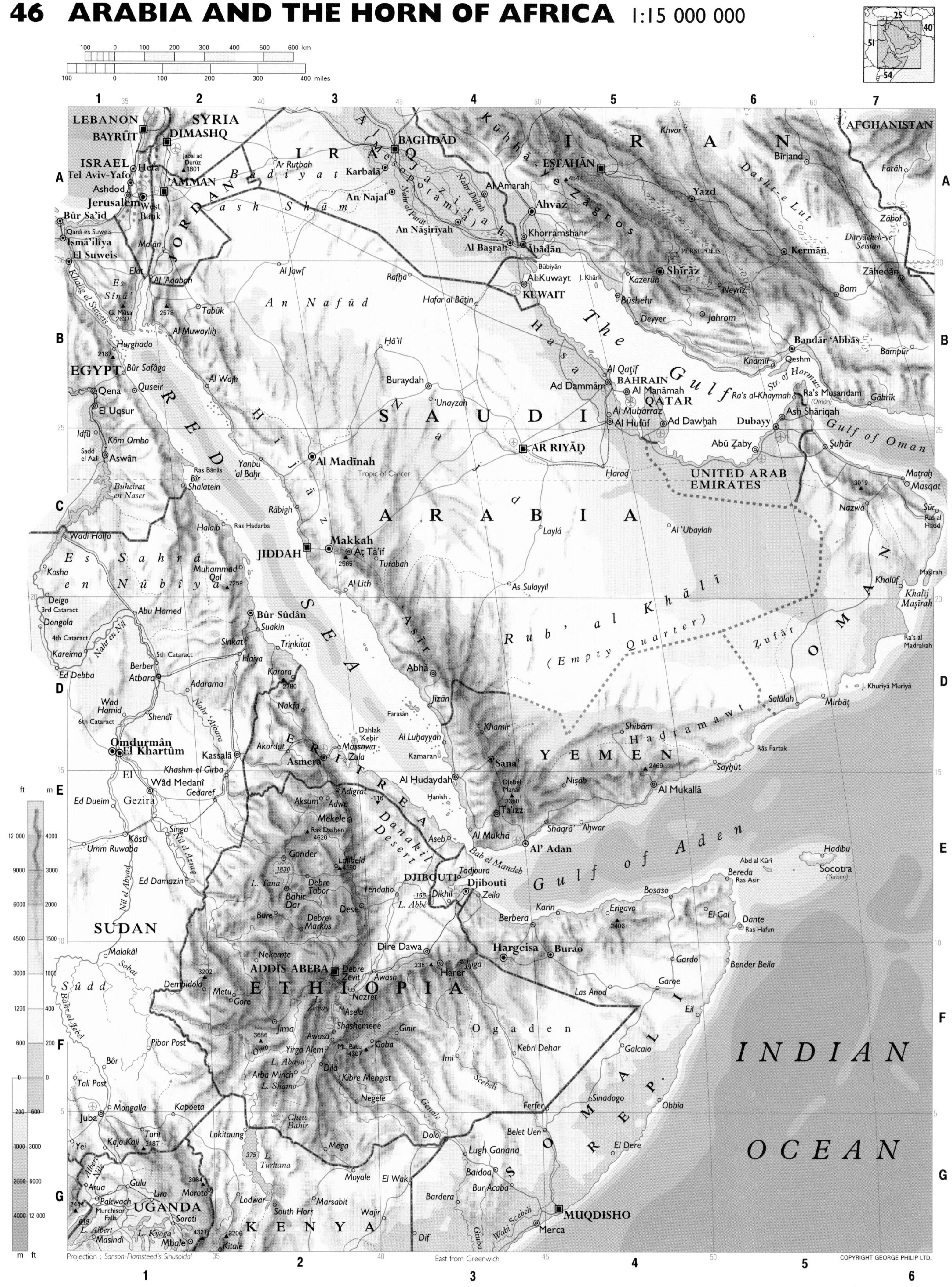

100 0 100 200 300 400 500 600 km
100 0 100 200 300 400 miles
LEBANON
BAYRŪT
SYRIA
DIMASHQ
ISRAEL
Tel Aviv-Yafo
Hefa
Ashdod
Jerusalem
West Bank
'AMMĀN
JORDAN
Jabal ad Durūz 1801
Bûr Sa'îd
Qanâ es Suweis
Ismâ'ilîya
El Suweis
Ma'ān
Elat
Al 'Aqabah
Es Sînâ'
G. Mûsa 2637
Khalîg el Suweis
Tabūk
2578
Bādiyat ash Shām
Ar Rutbah
IRAQ
BAGHDĀD
Karbalā'
An Najaf
Al Mesopotamia
Nahr Dijlah
Nahr al Furāt
Al 'Amarah
An Nāşirīyah
Al Başrah
IRAN
Kūhhā-ye Zāgros
EŞFAHĀN
4548
Ahvāz
Khorramshahr
Ābādān
Khvor
Bīrjand
Dasht-e Lut
Yazd
Kermān
PERSEPOLIS
Shīrāz
Kāzerūn
Būshehr
Neyrīz
Jahrom
Deyyer
Bam
Zāhedān
Zābol
Daryācheh-ye Sistan
Farāh
AFGHANISTAN
Būbiyān
Al Kuwayt
J. Khārk
KUWAIT
Hafar al Bāţin
Rafḩā'
Al Jawf
An Nafūd
Ḩā'il
Buraydah
'Unayzah
The Gulf
Al Hasa
Al Qaţīf
BAHRAIN
Al Manāmah
Ad Dammām
QATAR
Ad Dawḩah
Al Mubarraz
Al Hufūf
Bandar 'Abbās
Qeshm
Khamir
Str. of Hormuz
Ras al-Khaymah
Ra's Musandam
Bampūr
Gābrik
Ash Shāriqah
Dubayy
Abū Z̧aby
Şuḩār
Gulf of Oman
Maţraḩ
Masqat
3019
UNITED ARAB EMIRATES
SAUDI ARABIA
AR RIYĀD
Najd
Harad
Al Madīnah
Tropic of Cancer
Yanbu 'al Baḩr
Ḩijāz
Al Muwaylih
Al Wajh
Rābigh
Makkah
JIDDAH
Aţ Ţā'if
2565
Turabah
Al Līth
Laylá
Al 'Ubaylah
As Sulayyil
Rub' al Khālī (Empty Quarter)
'Asīr
Abhā
Jīzān
Farasān
Nazwá
Şūr
Ras al Hadd
Maşīrah
Khalūf
Khalīj Maşīrah
Ra's al Madrakah
OMAN
Z̧ufār
J. Khuriyā Muriyā
Salālah
Mirbāţ
Ḩaḑramawt
Shibām
YEMEN
Şan'ā'
2469
Ras Fartak
Sayhūt
Al Mukallā
Nişāb
Djebel Manar 3350
Ta'izz
Shaqrā'
Aḩwar
Al Ḩudaydah
Kamaran
Al Luḩayyah
Khamir
Ḩanish
Al Mukhā
Al 'Adan
Gulf of Aden
Bab el Mandeb
Hadibu
Abd al Kūrī
Socotra (Yemen)
Bereda
Ras Asir
EGYPT
Hurghada
2187
Bûr Safâga
Qena
Quseir
El Uqsur
Idfû
Kôm Ombo
Sadd el Aali
Aswân
Buheirat en Naser
Ras Bânâs
Bîr Shalatein
RED SEA
Halaib
Ras Hadarba
Wadi Halfa
Es Sahrâ en Nûbîya
Kosha
Muhammad Qol
2259
Delgo
3rd Cataract
Dongola
4th Cataract
Kareima
Nahr en Nîl
Abu Hamed
Bûr Sûdân
Suakin
Sinkat
Trinkitat
5th Cataract
Haiya
Ed Debba
Berber
Atbara
Adarama
Karora
2180
Nakfa
Wad Hamid
6th Cataract
Shendî
Nahr 'Atbara
Omdurmân
El Khartûm
Kassalâ
Khashm el Girba
El Gezira
Wâd Medanî
Gedaref
Ed Dueim
Kôstî
Singa
Umm Ruwaba
Nîl el Azraq
Nîl el Abyad
Ed Damazin
SUDAN
ERITREA
Akordat
Asmera
Massawa
Zula
Dahlak Kebir
Adigrat
Aksum
Adwa
Mekele
-116
Ras Dashen 4620
Gonder
Lalibela 4190
1830
L. Tana
Debre Tabor
Bahir Dar
Danakil Desert
Aseb
Tendaho
DJIBOUTI
Djibouti
Tadjoura
Dikhil
-155
L. Abbé
Zeila
Dese
Bure
Debre Markos
Berbera
Karin
Erigavo
2406
Bosaso
El Gal
Dante
Ras Hafun
Hargeisa
Burao
Dire Dawa
Harer
Jijiga
3381
ADDIS ABEBA
Debre Zevit
Nekemte
Awash
ETHIOPIA
3202
Dembidolo
Metu
Gore
L. Ziway
Nazret
Asela
Shashemene
Jima
Ginir
3686
Omo
Awasa
Yirga Alem
Mt. Batu 4307
Goba
L. Abaya
Arba Minch
L. Shamo
Dila
Kibre Mengist
Negele
Ogaden
Kebri Dehar
Imi
Scebeli
Gardo
Bender Beila
Garoe
Las Anod
Eil
Galcaio
SOMALI REP.
Sinadogo
Obbia
Ferfer
Belet Uen
El Dere
Lugh Ganana
Baidoa
Bur Acaba
Bardera
MUQDISHO
Merca
Wabi Scebeli
Giuba
Dif
Gandale
Dolo
Malakâl
Sobat
Sûdd
Bahr el Jebel
Pibor Post
Bôr
Tali Post
Mongalla
Kapoeta
Juba
Torit
Kajo Kaji
3187
Yei
Lokitaung
Chew Bahir
Mega
375
L. Turkana
Moyale
El Wak
Arua
Gulu
Lira
Moroto
3084
Albert Nile
Pakwach
Murchison Falls
UGANDA
Soroti
L. Albert
619
Masindi
L. Kyoga
Mbale
4321
3206
Kitale
Lodwar
South Horr
Marsabit
Wajir
KENYA
INDIAN OCEAN
ft m
12 000 4000
9000 3000
6000 2000
4500 1500
3000 1000
1200 400
600 200
0 0
200 600
1000 3000
2000 6000
4000 12 000
m ft
Projection : Sanson-Flamsteed's Sinusoidal
East from Greenwich
COPYRIGHT GEORGE PHILIP LTD.

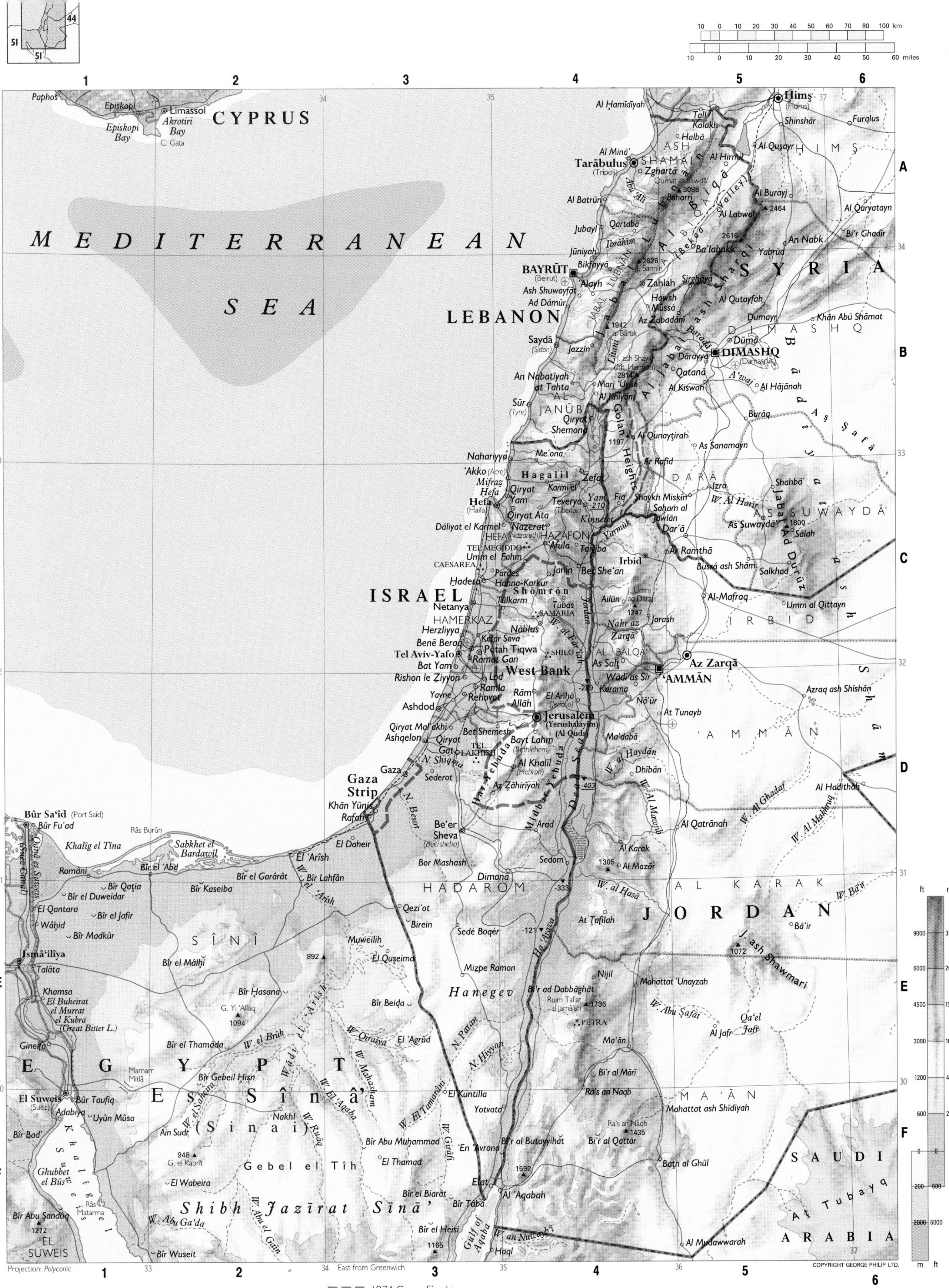

10 0 10 20 30 40 50 60 70 80 100 km
10 0 10 20 30 40 50 60 miles

1 2 3 4 5 6

Paphos
Episkopi
Episkopi Bay
Limassol
Akrotiri
Akrotiri Bay
C. Gata
CYPRUS

Al Ḥamīdīyah
●**Ḥimṣ** (Homs)
Tall
Kalakh
Shinshār
Furqlus

M E D I T E R R A N E A N

Al Mīnā'
Ṭarābulus (Tripoli)
Zghartā
Qurnat as Sawdā' 3088
Al Baṭrūn
Ibrāhīm
Jubayl
Qartabā
ASH SHAMĀL
Ḥalbā
Al Hirmil
Al Qusayr
Al Buṛayj
2464
Al Qaryatayn
2616
An Nabk
Bi'r Ghadīr

S E A

Jūniyah
Bikfayyā
BAYRŪT (Beirut)
'Alayh
Ash Shuwayfāt
Ad Dāmūr
2628 Sannīn
Ba'labakk
Sirghāyā
Az Zabadānī
Barādā
Yabrūd
Khān Abū Shāmat
Dumayr
Al Qutayfah
2814
'Ayn ash Shayr (Mt. Hermon)
Ḥawsh Mūssā
Zaḥlah
SYRIA
DIMASHQ

LEBANON

Saydā (Sidon)
Jazzīn
1942 al Bārūk
Dūmā
Darāyyā
●**DIMASHQ** (Damascus)
A'waj
Al Hājānah
As Safā

An Nabaṭīyah at Taḥta
Marj 'Uyūn
Al Khiyām
Al Kiswah
Burāq

Sūr (Tyre)
AL JANŪB
Qiryat Shemona
Golan Heights
Al Qunaytirah
As Sanamayn
Jabal ad Durūz

Nahariyya
Me'ona
1197
Ar Rafīd
DARĀ
Izra'
Shahbā
As Suwaydā'
1800 'Ād
Sālah

'Akko (Acre)
Hagalil
Zefat
Yam
Fiq
Shaykh Miskin
Saḥam al Jawlān
W. Al Harīr
SUWAYDĀ'
Mifraz Hefa
Qiryat Yam
Karmi'el
Teverya
Yam -210
Dar'ā
Salkhad
Hefa (Haifa)
Qiryat Ata
Nazerat
Kinneret
Yarmūk
Busrā ash Shām

Dāliyat el Karmel
Nazareth
HAZAFON
Afula
Ṭaiba
Ar Ramthā
Al-Mafraq
TEL MEGIDDO
HEFA
Bet She'an
Ailūn
J. Umm ad Daraj
Umm al Qittayn
CAESAREA
Umm el Fahm
Jarīn
1247
Hadera
Hanna-Karkur
Pardes
Shōmrōn
Ṭūbās
SAMARIA
Jarash
IRBID
ISRAEL
Tulkarm
Irbid

Netanya
HAMERKAZ
Nāblus
Nahr az Zarqā'
Herzliyya
Kefar Sava
W. al Fār'ah
Benē Beraq
Petaḥ Tiqwa
SHILO
As Salṭ
Az Zarqā'
Tel Aviv-Yafo
Ramat Gan
AL BALQĀ
●**AMMĀN**
Bat Yam
Wādī as Sīr
Rishon le Ziyyon
West Bank
Rām Allāh
-250
Karāma
Azraq ash Shīshān
Yavne
El Arīḥā (Jericho)
Na'ūr
Ramla
Rehovot
At Tunayb
Ashdod
Lod
'AMMĀN
Qiryat Mal'akhi
TEL LAKHISH
●**Jerusalem** (Yerushalayim) (Al Quds)
Ma'dabā
Ashqelon
Bet Shemesh
Bayt Laḥm (Bethlehem)
Qiryat Gat
Har Yehuda
W. al Haydān
Al Khalīl (Hebron)
Dhībān
Gaza
N. Shiqma
Az Ẓāhirīyah
Midbar Yehuda
W. al Maqrib
Gaza Strip
Sederot
-403
Al Hadithah
Khān Yūnis
Rafaḥ
N. Besor
Arad
Al Karak
W. Al Ghadaf

Be'er Sheva (Beersheba)
Sedom
Al Qaṭrānah
W. al Maqib
W. al Mabnud
El Daheir
Bor Mashash
1305
Al Mazār
W. al Maqrib
Bûr Sa'îd (Port Said)
Bûr Fu'ad
Râs Burûn
Dimona
KARAK
Bîr el 'Abd
HADAROM
-333
AL
Khalîg el Tîna
Sabkhet el Bardawîl
Bîr el Garârât
Bîr Lahfân
At Ṭafīlah
JORDAN
W. Bâ'ir
Români
Bîr el Mazâr
W. al Hasa
Bâ'ir

Qanâ es Sueis (Suez Canal)
Bîr Qatia
Bîr Kaseiba
Qezi'ot
W. 'Arîsh
Birein
El Qantara
Bîr el Duweidar
Bîr el Jafir
El Thamâda
892
Muweilih
Sedé Boqér
-121
SÎNÎ
Mizpe Ramon
Ra's an Naqb
Wâhid
Bîr Madkûr
W. el Brûk
Bîr Beiqa
J. ash Shawmari
1072
Ismâ'ilîya
Bîr Hasana
Bîr Beiqa
Hanegev
Bi'r ad Dabbâghât
Mahattat 'Unayzah
Talâta
G. Yi 'Allaq
1094
Khamsa
W. Qeraiya
Rujm Tal'at al Jamâ'ah
1736
El Buheirat el Murrat el Kubra (Great Bitter L.)
W. Abu Safâr
W. el Mahashim
El Agrûd
N. Paran
Nijil
Qa'el Jafr
Gineifa
Mamarr Mitlâ
Bîr Gebeil Hisn
Ma'ân
Bîr el Thamâda
W. el Sahara
El Kuntilla
Ra's an Naqb
1435
Yotvata
MA'ĀN
El Suweis (Suez)
Bûr Taufiq
Adabiya
Uyûn Mûsa
Âin Sudr
Nakhl
W. Ruqâ
Ma'ân
Mahattat ash Shîdîyah
EGYPT
Sînâ' (Sinai)
W. El 'Aqaba
Bîr Abu Muhammad
W. Girâfi
Bi'r al Mârî
Bîr Bad'
948 G. el Kabrît
Bîr Abu Muhammad
El Thamad
Bîr al Butaywihât
Bi'r al Qattâr
'En 'Avrona
Baṭn al Ghûl
SAUDI
Ghubbet el Bûs
1272 EL SUWEIS
Gebel el Tîh
El Wabeira
Bîr el Biarât
1592
Elat
Al 'Aqabah
ARABIA
Bîr Abu Sandûq
Râs Matarma
W. Abu Ga'da
W. Abu el Gân
Bîr el Heisi
1165
Gulf of Aqaba
W. an Nutwâ'
Ḥaql
Al Mudawwarah
Aṭ Ṭubayq
Shibh Jazîrat Sînâ'
Bîr Wuseit
Bîr Tâba

Projection: Polyconic
33 34 East from Greenwich 35 36 37
COPYRIGHT GEORGE PHILIP LTD.

1 2 3 4 5 6

ft m
9000 3000
6000 2000
4500 1500
3000 1000
1200 400
600 200
0 0
200 600
2000 6000
m ft

〓〓〓 1974 Cease Fire Lines

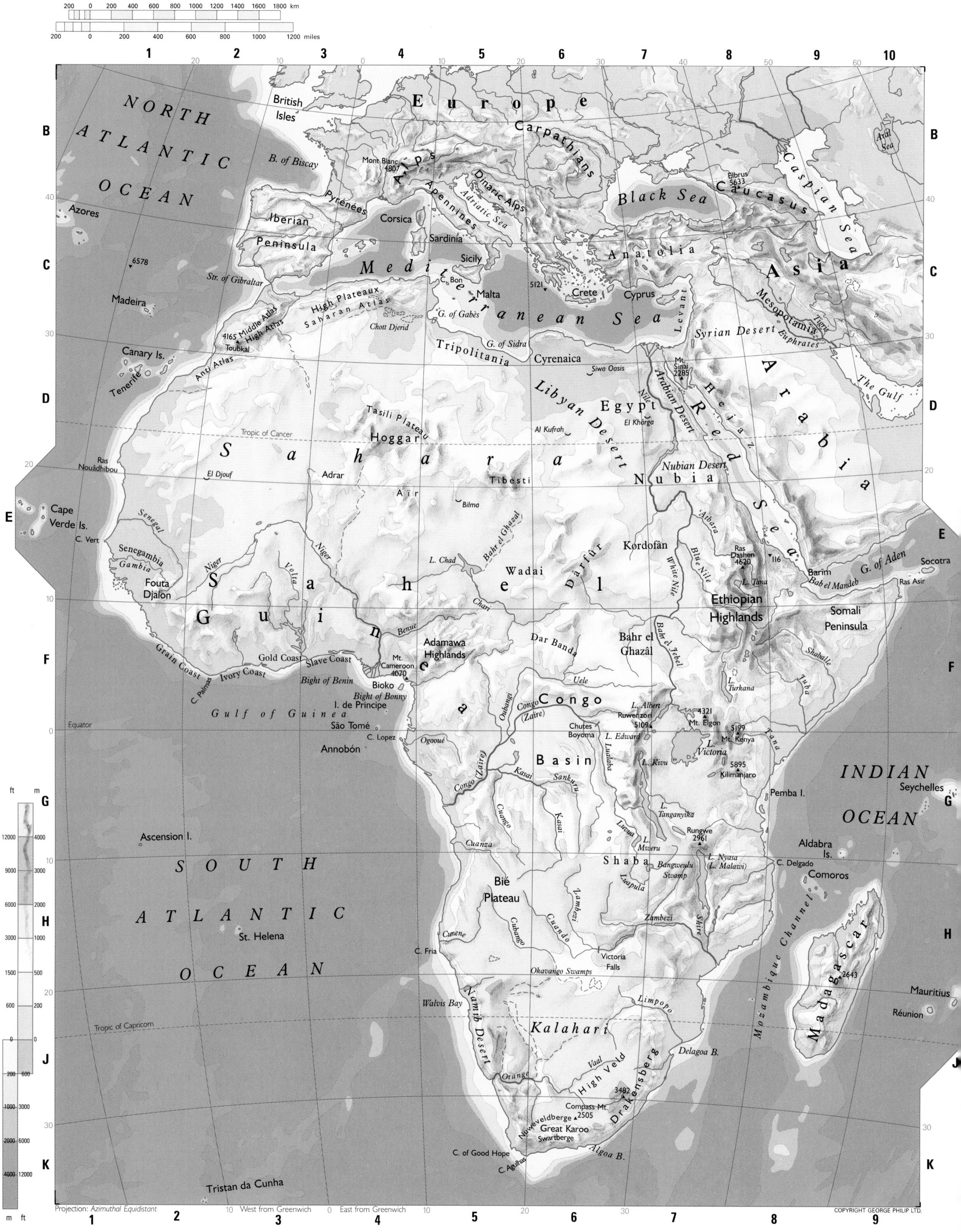

AFRICA : Physical 1:42 000 000

200 0 200 400 600 800 1000 1200 1400 1600 1800 km

200 0 200 400 600 800 1000 1200 miles

NORTH ATLANTIC OCEAN

British Isles

E u r o p e

Carpathians

Caspian Sea

Aral Sea

B. of Biscay

Mont Blanc 4807

Alps

Dinaric Alps

Black Sea

Elbrus 5633

Caucasus

Azores

Pyrénées

Apennines

Adriatic Sea

Anatolia

Asia

Iberian Peninsula

Corsica

Sardinia

Sicily

Crete

Cyprus

Mesopotamia

6578

Madeira

Str. of Gibraltar

Mediterranean Sea

C. Bon

Malta

5121

Levant

Tigris

Euphrates

Syrian Desert

The Gulf

Canary Is.

High Plateaux

High Atlas

Middle Atlas 4165

Saharan Atlas

Chott Djerid

G. of Gabès

G. of Sidra

Tripolitania

Cyrenaica

Siwa Oasis

Mt. Sinai 2285

Arabian Desert

Red Sea

Hejaz

Arabia

Tenerife

Anti Atlas

Toubkal

Ras Nouâdhibou

El Djouf

Adrar

Tasili Plateau

Hoggar

S a h a r a

Tropic of Cancer

Libyan Desert

Egypt

Al Kufrah

El Khârga

Nubian Desert

Nubia

Air

Tibesti

S a h e l

Bilma

Senegal

Cape Verde Is.

C. Vert

Senegambia

Gambia

Niger

Volta

Niger

Fouta Djalon

S u d a n

L. Chad

Bahr el Ghazal

Wadai

D a r f û r

Kordofàn

Atbara

Ras Dashen 4620

116

Barim

Bab el Mandeb

G. of Aden

Socotra

Ras Asir

Blue Nile

L. Tana

Ethiopian Highlands

Somali Peninsula

G u i n e a

Grain Coast

Gold Coast

Slave Coast

Ivory Coast

C. Palmas

Bight of Benin

Benue

Adamawa Highlands

Chari

Dar Banda

Uele

Bahr el Jebel

Bahr el Ghazâl

White Nile

Shabelle

L. Turkana

Juba

Mt. Cameroon 4070

Bioko

Bight of Bonny

I. de Principe

São Tomé

C. Lopez

Gulf of Guinea

Equator

Annobón

Ogooué

Oubangi

Congo (Zaïre)

C o n g o

Chutes Boyoma

L. Albert

Ruwenzori 5109

L. Edward

L. Kivu

Mt. Elgon 4321

Mt. Kenya 5199

L. Victoria

Kilimanjaro 5895

Tana

Pemba I.

Seychelles

INDIAN OCEAN

Ascension I.

SOUTH ATLANTIC OCEAN

Congo (Zaïre)

Kasai

Sankuru

Lualaba

Kasai

B a s i n

Cuanza

Cuango

L. Tanganyika

L. Mweru

Lugenga

Rungwe 2961

L. Nyasa (L. Malawi)

Aldabra Is.

C. Delgado

Comoros

St. Helena

Cuanza

Shaba

Bangweulu Swamp

Luapula

Bié Plateau

Zambezi

Cuando

Mozambique Channel

Madagascar

2643

Mauritius

Réunion

Cunene

Cubango

Zambezi

Shire

C. Fria

Okavango Swamps

Victoria Falls

Tropic of Capricorn

Namib Desert

K a l a h a r i

Limpopo

Delagoa B.

Walvis Bay

Vaal

High Veld

Orange

3482

Drakensberg

Compass Mt. 2505

Nuweveldberge

Great Karoo

Swartberge

Algoa B.

C. of Good Hope

C. Agulhas

Tristan da Cunha

Projection: Azimuthal Equidistant

West from Greenwich

East from Greenwich

ft | m

12000 | 4000

9000 | 3000

6000 | 2000

3000 | 1000

1500 | 500

600 | 200

0 | 0

600 | 200

3000 | 1000

6000 | 2000

12000 | 4000

m ft

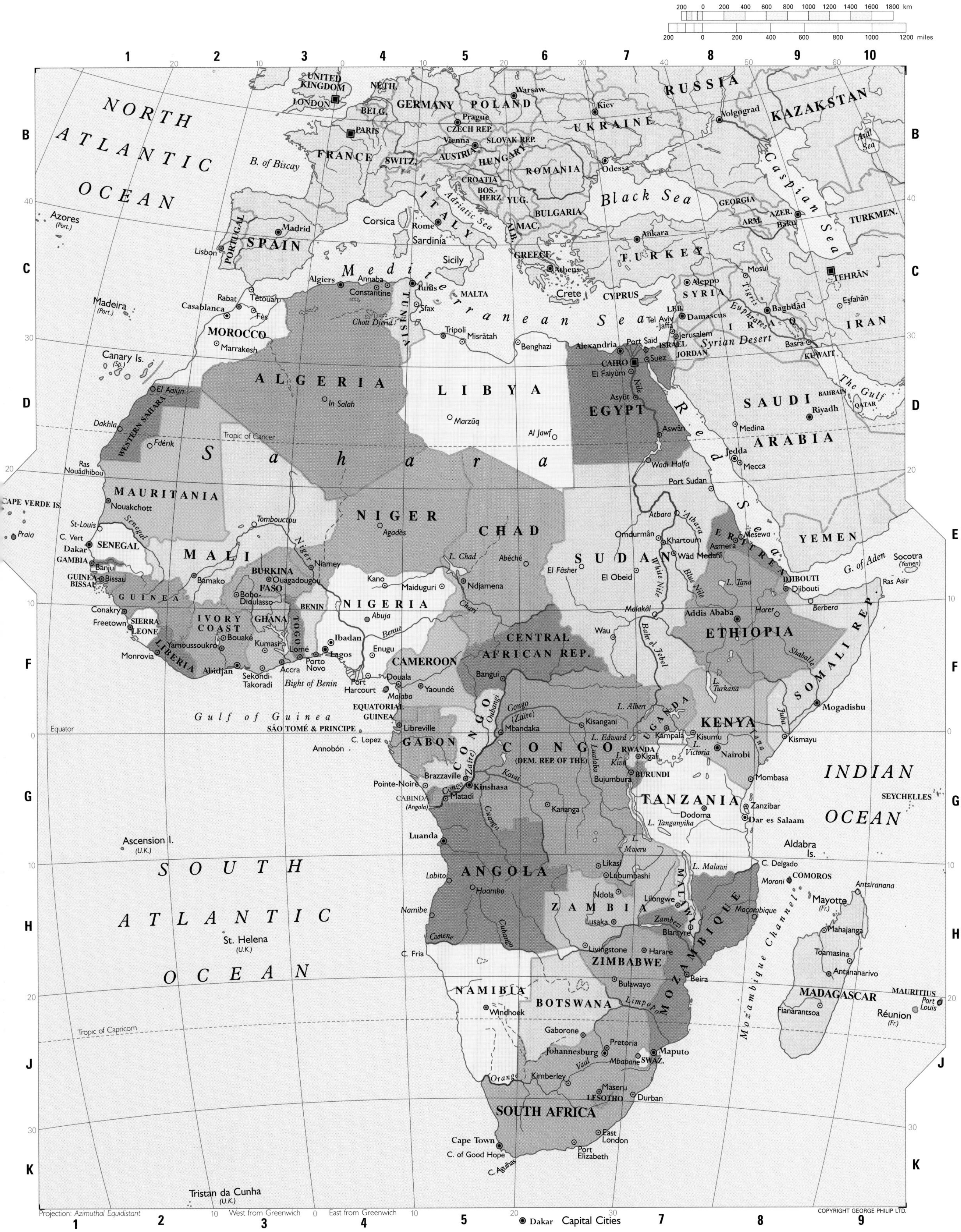

200 0 200 400 600 800 1000 1200 1400 1600 1800 km

200 0 200 400 600 800 1000 1200 miles

NORTH ATLANTIC OCEAN

SOUTH ATLANTIC OCEAN

INDIAN OCEAN

Mediterranean Sea

Black Sea

Caspian Sea

Red Sea

Gulf of Guinea

Bight of Benin

Mozambique Channel

The Gulf

G. of Aden

B. of Biscay

Adriatic Sea

Countries and regions:
UNITED KINGDOM, NETH., BELG., GERMANY, POLAND, FRANCE, SWITZ., ITALY, PORTUGAL, SPAIN, CZECH REP., SLOVAK REP., AUSTRIA, HUNGARY, CROATIA, BOS.-HERZ., YUG., ALB., MAC., BULGARIA, ROMANIA, UKRAINE, RUSSIA, KAZAKSTAN, GREECE, TURKEY, CYPRUS, SYRIA, LEB., ISRAEL, JORDAN, IRAQ, IRAN, SAUDI ARABIA, BAHRAIN, QATAR, KUWAIT, YEMEN, GEORGIA, ARM., AZER., TURKMEN.

MOROCCO, WESTERN SAHARA, ALGERIA, LIBYA, EGYPT, TUNISIA, MAURITANIA, MALI, NIGER, CHAD, SUDAN, ERITREA, DJIBOUTI, SOMALI REP., ETHIOPIA, SENEGAL, GAMBIA, GUINEA BISSAU, GUINEA, SIERRA LEONE, LIBERIA, IVORY COAST, GHANA, TOGO, BENIN, BURKINA FASO, NIGERIA, CAMEROON, CENTRAL AFRICAN REP., EQUATORIAL GUINEA, SÃO TOMÉ & PRINCIPE, GABON, CONGO, CONGO (DEM. REP. OF THE), UGANDA, KENYA, RWANDA, BURUNDI, TANZANIA, ANGOLA, CABINDA (Angola), ZAMBIA, MALAWI, MOZAMBIQUE, ZIMBABWE, NAMIBIA, BOTSWANA, SOUTH AFRICA, LESOTHO, SWAZ., MADAGASCAR, COMOROS, SEYCHELLES, MAURITIUS

Deserts/features:
Sahara, Syrian Desert, Tropic of Cancer, Tropic of Capricorn, Equator, Chott Djerid

Cities:
London, Paris, Madrid, Lisbon, Rabat, Casablanca, Fès, Tétouán, Marrakesh, Algiers, Annaba, Constantine, Tunis, Sfax, Tripoli, Misrátah, Benghazi, Alexandria, Port Said, Cairo, El Faiyûm, Suez, Asyût, Aswân, Wadi Halfa, Rome, Corsica, Sardinia, Sicily, Malta, Crete, Athens, Ankara, Aleppo, Mosul, Tehrán, Esfahán, Baghdád, Basra, Damascus, Jerusalem, Tel Aviv-Jaffa, Medina, Mecca, Jedda, Riyadh, Prague, Vienna, Warsaw, Kiev, Volgograd, Odessa, Baku, Aral Sea

Madeira (Port.), Azores (Port.), Canary Is. (Sp.), Cape Verde Is., Praia, Dakhla, El Aaiún, Fdérik, Ras Nouâdhibou, Nouakchott, Tombouctou, Agadès, In Salah, Marzûq, Al Jawf, L. Chad, Kano, Maiduguri, Ndjamena, Abéché, El Fâsher, El Obeid, Khartoum, Omdurmân, Atbara, Port Sudan, Mesewa, Asmera, Djibouti, Berbera, Ras Asir, Socotra (Yemen), Wâd Medani, Malakâl, Wau, Addis Ababa, Harer, L. Tana, Mogadishu, Kismayu

St-Louis, C. Vert, Dakar, Banjul, Bissau, Conakry, Freetown, Monrovia, Yamoussoukro, Abidjan, Bouaké, Kumasi, Accra, Sekondi-Takoradi, Bamako, Ouagadougou, Bobo-Dioulasso, Niamey, Lomé, Porto Novo, Ibadan, Lagos, Enugu, Abuja, Benin, Malabo, Libreville, Annobón, C. Lopez, Douala, Yaoundé, Port Harcourt, Bangui, Mbandaka, Kisangani, Kampala, Kisumu, Nairobi, Mombasa, Brazzaville, Kinshasa, Matadi, Pointe-Noire, Kananga, Bujumbura, Kigali, L. Kivu, L. Edward, L. Albert, L. Victoria, L. Turkana, Dodoma, Zanzibar, Dar es Salaam, Luanda, Lobito, Huambo, Namibe, Likasi, Lubumbashi, Ndola, Lusaka, Lilongwe, Blantyre, Moçambique, Moroni, Mayotte (Fr.), Antsiranana, Mahajanga, Toamasina, Antananarivo, Fianarantsoa, L. Malawi, L. Tanganyika, L. Mweru, Livingstone, Harare, Beira, Bulawayo, Windhoek, Gaborone, Pretoria, Johannesburg, Maputo, Mbabane, Maseru, Durban, East London, Port Elizabeth, Cape Town, C. of Good Hope, C. Agulhas, Kimberley, Réunion (Fr.), Port Louis, Aldabra Is., C. Delgado, C. Fria

Ascension I. (U.K.), St. Helena (U.K.), Tristan da Cunha (U.K.)

Rivers:
Nile, Blue Nile, White Nile, Bahr el Gebel, Senegal, Niger, Benue, Chari, Congo (Zaïre), Oubangui, Lualaba, Kasai, Cuango, Cunene, Cubango, Zambezi, Limpopo, Orange, Vaal, Euphrates, Tigris, Atbara, Shabeelle, Juba, Tana

West from Greenwich 0 East from Greenwich

Projection: Azimuthal Equidistant

● Dakar Capital Cities

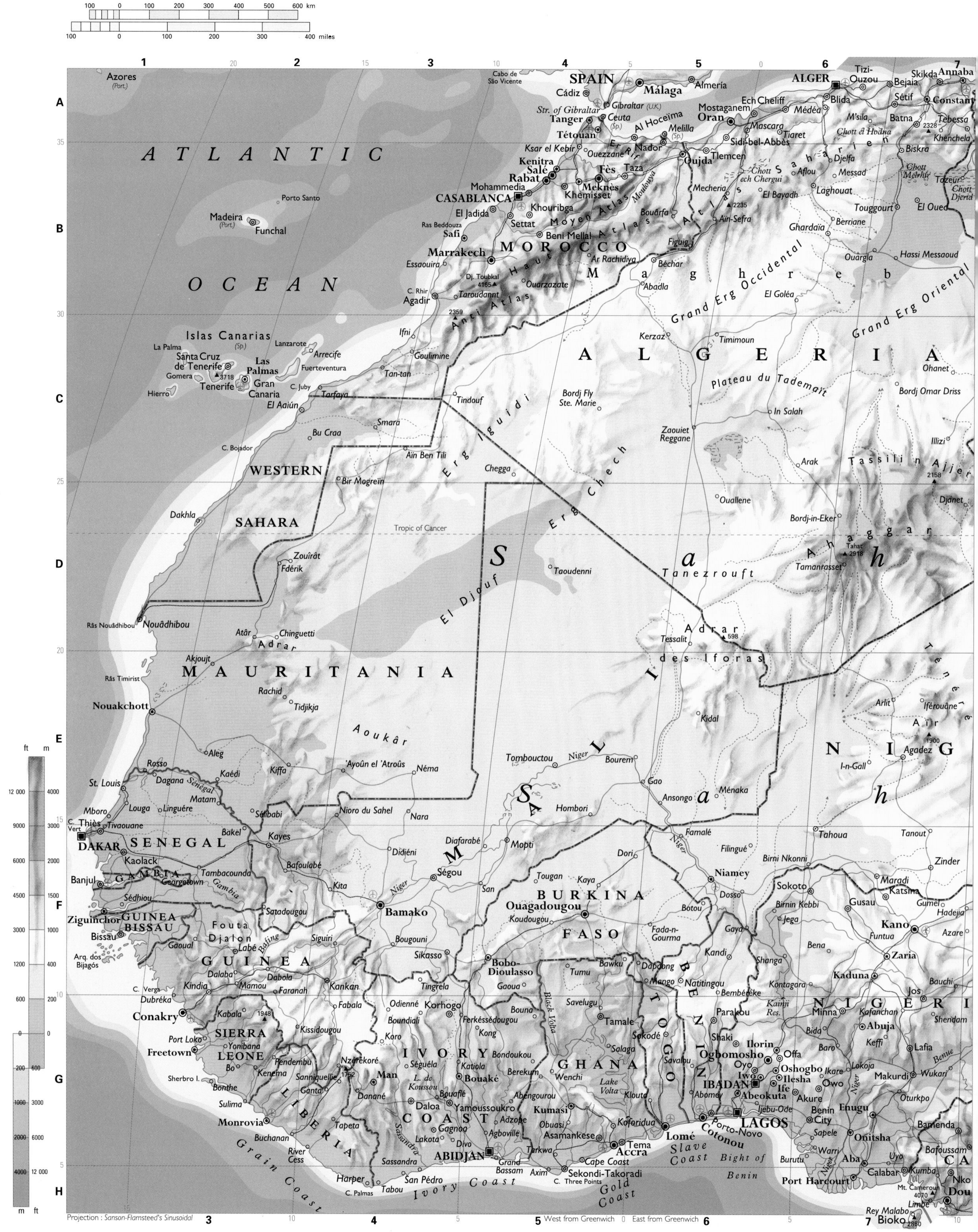

100 0 100 200 300 400 500 600 km
100 0 100 200 300 400 miles

ATLANTIC

OCEAN

Azores
(Port.)

Cabo de
São Vicente

SPAIN

Cádiz Málaga Almería
Str. of Gibraltar Gibraltar (U.K.)
Tanger Ceuta (Sp.) Al Hoceïma Melilla (Sp.)
Tétouan Nador
Ksar el Kebir Ouezzane Oujda
Kenitra Fès Taza
Salé Meknès
Rabat Khémisset
CASABLANCA Khouribga
Mohammedia Settat
El Jadida
Ras Beddouza Beni Mellal
Safi
Marrakech
Essaouira
C. Rhir Dj. Toubkal Ar Rachidia
Agadir 4165 Ouarzazate
Ifni Taroudannt
Goulimine 2359
Tan-tan
Tarfaya
El Aaiún
Smara
Bu Craa
C. Bojador
WESTERN
Ain Ben Tili
Bir Mogreïn
SAHARA
Dakhla
Zouîrât
Fdérik

ALGER Tizi-Ouzou Skikda Annaba
Bejaïa Sétif Constant
Ech Cheliff Blida M'sila Batna 2328 Tebessa
Mostaganem Médéa Khenchela
Oran Mascara Tiaret Chott el Hodna Biskra
Sidi-bel-Abbès Djelfa Messad Chott Melrhir
Tlemcen Aflou Chott
Saïss ech Chergui Laghouat Djerid
Mecheria El Bayadh El Oued
Ain-Sefra Ghardaïa Berriane Touggourt
Figuig Bouârfa Ouargla Hassi Messaoud
Béchar El Goléa
Abadla Grand Erg Occidental
Grand Erg Oriental
MAGHREB
Kerzaz
Timimoun
Bordj Fly Ohanet
Ste. Marie
Plateau du Tademaït Bordj Omar Driss
Tindouf
In Salah Illizi
Zaouiet
Reggane Tassili n Ajjer
Chegga 2158
Arak
Ouallene Bordj-in-Eker Djanet
Tropic of Cancer
SAHARA
Taoudenni Ahaggar Tahat 2918
Tanezrouft Tamanrasset
El Djouf

Ràs Nouâdhibou Nouâdhibou
Atâr Chinguetti
Adrar
Akjoujt
Ràs Timirist
MAURITANIA
Rachid
Tidjikja Adrar
des Iforas
Tessalit Adrar 598
Kidal
Aoukâr Arlit
Iférouâne
NIGER Aïr 1900
Agadez
I-n-Gall
Nouakchott

St. Louis Rosso
Dagana Aleg Kaédi Kiffa
Louga Linguère 'Ayoûn el 'Atroûs Néma
Mboro Matam Sélibabi Nioro du Sahel Nara
C. Vert Thiès Tiaouane Bakel
DAKAR Tombouctou Niger Bourem
Kayes Gao Ansongo Ménaka
SENEGAL Diafarabé Hombori Tahoua Tanout
Kaolack Tambacounda Mopti Famalé
Banjul Georgetown Kita Didiéni Ségou Dori Filingué Birni Nkonni
GAMBIA Bafoulabé San Tougan Kaya Niamey Sokoto Zinder
Sédhiou Satadougou Bamako Kita BURKINA Maradi Katsina
Ziguinchor GUINEA Ouagadougou Dosso Birnin Kebbi Gusau
BISSAU Fouta Siguiri Bougouni FASO Gaya Jega Funtua Kano
Bissau Djalon Labé Sikasso Fada-n- Kandi Bena Azare
Arq. dos Gaoual Koudougou Gourma Bawku Shanga Kaduna
Bijagós GUINEA Bobo- Tumu Dapong Kontagara Zaria
C. Verga Kindia Dalaba Dioulasso Gaoua Mango Bauchi
Dubréka Mamou Faranah Tingrela Natitingou NIGERIA
Conakry Kabala 1948 Fabala Odienné Korhogo Bembéréké Minna Kafanchan
Port Loko Kissidougou Boundiali Bouna Savelugu Parakou Bida Abuja Jos
SIERRA Kenema Koro Ferkéssédougou Kong Tamale Shaki Ilorin Keffi Lafia Shendam
Freetown LEONE Séguéla Katiola Bondoukou Salaga Sekodé Savalou Ogbomosho Offa Baro
Bo Sherbro I. Pendembu IVORY Berekum Wenchi TOGO Oyo Oshogbo Ikare Lokoja Wukari
Bonthe Nzérékoré Man L. de Bouaké Abengourou Lake BENIN Abomey Ibadan Ilesha Ife Owo Makurdi
Sulima Danané Koussou Kumasi Volta Savalou Iwo Akure Benin Oturkpo
Monrovia LIBERIA Tapeta GHANA Obuasi Kloute Porto- City Enugu
Buchanan COAST Yamoussoukro Adzope Koforidua Novo LAGOS Onitsha
River Cess Gagnoa Divo Asamankese Tema Lomé Cotonou Sapele Aba
Harper Sassandra Lakota Agboville Accra Slave Uyo Bafoussam
San Pédro ABIDJAN Grand Cape Coast Coast Warri Calabar Kumba
Tabou Bassam Gold Port Harcourt CAMEROON
C. Palmas Ivory Coast Axim Coast Bight of Nko
Grain Coast Sekondi-Takoradi Benin Mt. Cameroun Dou
C. Three Points 4070 Rey Malabo Limbe
Bioko

Islas Canarias
(Sp.)
La Palma Lanzarote
Santa Cruz Arrecife
de Tenerife Fuerteventura
Gomera 3718
Tenerife Las Palmas C. Juby
Hierro Gran Tarfaya
Canaria El Aaiún

Madeira
(Port.) Porto Santo
Funchal

West from Greenwich 0 East from Greenwich

Projection: Sanson-Flamsteed's Sinusoidal

ft m
12 000 4000
9000 3000
6000 2000
4500 1500
3000 1000
1200 400
600 200
0 0
200 600
1000 3000
2000 6000
4000 12 000
m ft

46
52

8
9
10
11
12
13
14
15
20
25
30
35
40
A
B
C
D
E
F
G
H
MEDITERRANEAN SEA
GREECE
TURKEY
CYPRUS
SYRIA
LEBANON
ISRAEL
JORDAN
IRAQ
SAUDI ARABIA
LIBYA
EGYPT
SUDAN
CHAD
CENTRAL AFRICAN REPUBLIC
ETHIOPIA
ERITREA
MEROON
MALTA
Valletta
Sicilia
Bizerte
CARTHAGE
Ariana
TUNIS
Béja
Nabeul
Sousse
Kairouan
Mahdia
Sfax
Gafsa
Golfe de Gabès
Gabès
Île de Djerba
Zarzis
Médenine
Tatahouine
Dehibat
Zuwārah
Tarābulus
Al Khums
Az Zāwiyah
Gharyān
968
Misrātah
Mizdah
Tripolitania
Surt
Khalīj Surt
Darnah
Zāwiyat al Baydā
Al Marj
Banghāzī
Suluq
Ajdābiyah
Tubruq
Bardīyah
Salûm
Cyrenaica
Al Jaghbūb
Awjilah
Daraj
Ghudāmis
Hūn
Zillah
Idehan Awbārī
Brach
Sabhah
1200
Awbārī
Marzūq
Fezzan
Wāw al Kabīr
Ghat
Al Qaṭrūn
Sahrâ' Libîya
Sahrâ' Rebiana
Al Kufrah
Al Jawf
Sahara
1082
J. Uweinat 1893
Ma'tan as Sarra
Toummo
Madama
Bardai
Aozou
Pic Toussidé 3265
3150 Tarso Emissi
Tibesti
Zouar
Emi Koussi 3415
Chirfa
Bilma
Fachi
Grand Erg du Bilma
Borkou
Ounianga Sérir
Dépression du Mourdi
Faya-Largeau
Fada
Ennedi
1310
Erg du Djourab
Zagaoua
Oum Chalouba
Biltine
ERG
Boultoum
Nguigmi
Zigey
Mao
Lac Tchad
Bahr el Ghazal
Moussoro
Bosso
Gashua
Nguru
Geidam
Massakory
Ati
Abéché
Oum Hadjer
Maiduguri
Ndjamena
Bokoro
Mongo
Goz Beïda
Zalingei
Kousseri
Potiskum
Massenya
Abou-Deïa
Bama
Chari
Am-Timan
Duku
Bajoga
Gombe
Maroua
Bongor
Biu
Kumo
Mubi
Guider
Numan
Garoua
Yola
Pala
Logone
Laï
Sarh
Moundou
Koumra
Doba
Birao
1226
Ndélé
Baïbokoum
Gashaka
Ngaoundéré
Banyo
Massif de l'Adamaoua
Paoua
Kaga Bandoro
Bossangoa
Yalinga
Bozoum
Bouar
Bétaré Oya
Foumban
Yoko
Sibut
Ippy
Bakouma
Bambari
Carnot
Bossembélé
Bangassou
Ngsamba
Sanaga
Bertoua
Nanga-Eboko
Batouri
Abong-Mbang
Berbérati
Bangui
Zongo
Bosobolo
Oubangi
Mobaye
Mobayi
Bomu
Bondo
Mbaïki
Libenge
Yaoundé
Uele
Ango
Dungu
Faradje
Antalya
ADANA
Antakya
HALAB
Nahr al Furāt
Ródhos
Iráklion
Kríti
Al Lādhiqīyah
Nicosia
Tarābulus
Ḥimṣ
BAYRŪT
DIMASHQ
Jabal ad Durūz
1801
Ar Ruṭbah
Bādiyat ash Shām
Hefa
Tel Aviv-Yafo
Ashdod
Jerusalem
West Bank
'AMMĀN
El Mahalla el Kubra
Damanhûr
EL ISKANDARÎYA
Dumyât
Bûr Sa'îd
Marsâ Matrûh
El Alamein
Tanta
El Mansûra
Zagazig
Qanâ es Suweis
Ismâ'îliya
EL GÎZA
EL QÂHIRA
El Suweis
Ma'ān
Al Jawf
Helwân
El Faiyûm
Beni Suef
Maghâgha
El Minyâ
Mallawi
Manfalût
Asyût
Tahta
Sohâg
Girga
Qena
THEBES
KARNAK
El Uqsur
Nahr en Nîl
Khalîg el Suweis
Es Sînâ'
G. Mûsa 2637
Elat
Al 'Aqabah
2578
Tabūk
Al Muwayliḥ
Es Sahrâ esh Sharqîya
Hurghada
2187
Bûr Safâga
Quseir
Al Wajh
Hijaz
RED SEA
-133
Munkhafed el Qattâra
Sîwa
Qasr Farâfra
Mût
El Wâhât el-Dakhla
El Khârga
El Wâhât el-Khârga
Idfû
Kom Ombo
Aswân
Sadd el Aali
Buheirat en Naser
ABU SIMBEL
Ras Bânâs
Bîr Shalatein
Yanbu 'al Baḥr
Rābigh
Halaib
Ras Hadarba
Wadi Halfa
El Wâhât el Selîma
Es Sahrâ en Nûbîya
Kosha
Delgo
Muhammad Qol
2259
3rd Cataract
Dongola
Abu Hamed
Bûr Sûdân
Suakin
Trinkitat
Sinkat
Haiya
4th Cataract
Kareima
5th Cataract
Berber
Atbara
Bir 'Atrun
Ed Debba
Nahr en Nîl
Karora
2180
Nakfa
Adarama
Nahr Atbara
Wad Hamid
Shendî
6th Cataract
Omdurmân
El Khartûm
Akordat
Kassalâ
Khashm el Girba
Malha
El Wuz
1954
Kutum
Sodiri
Umm Keddada
Al Junaynah
Dârfûr
Djebel Mara 3088
El Fâsher
Nyâlâ
Kordofân
El Gezira
Wad Medanî
Gedaref
Ed Dueim
El Obeid
Kôstî
Singa
Umm Ruwaba
En Nahud
Er Rahad
Abû Zabad
El Odaiya
Nîl el Azraq
Nîl el Abyad
Ed Damazin
Gonder
1830
L. Tana
Bahir Dar
Bure
Debre Markos
1325
Kâdugli
Bahr el Arab
Songo
Malakâl
Nekemte
Sobat
Said Bundas
Bahr el Ghazâl
Jur
Bahr el Jebel
Sûdd
Raga
Gogriâl
Wâw
Tonj
Rumbêk
Dembidolo
3202
Metu
Gore
Jima
3686
Omo
Pibor Post
Toinya
Bôr
Amâdi
Tali Post
L. Abaya
Arba Minch
L. Shamo
Obo
El Istiwa'iya
Yambiô
Juba
Mongalla
Kapoeta
Chew Bahir
Yei
Kajo Kaji
Torit
3187
Lokitaung
L. Turkana
375

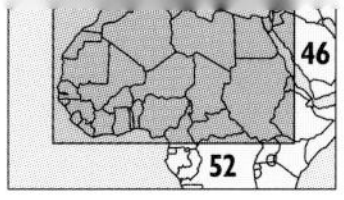

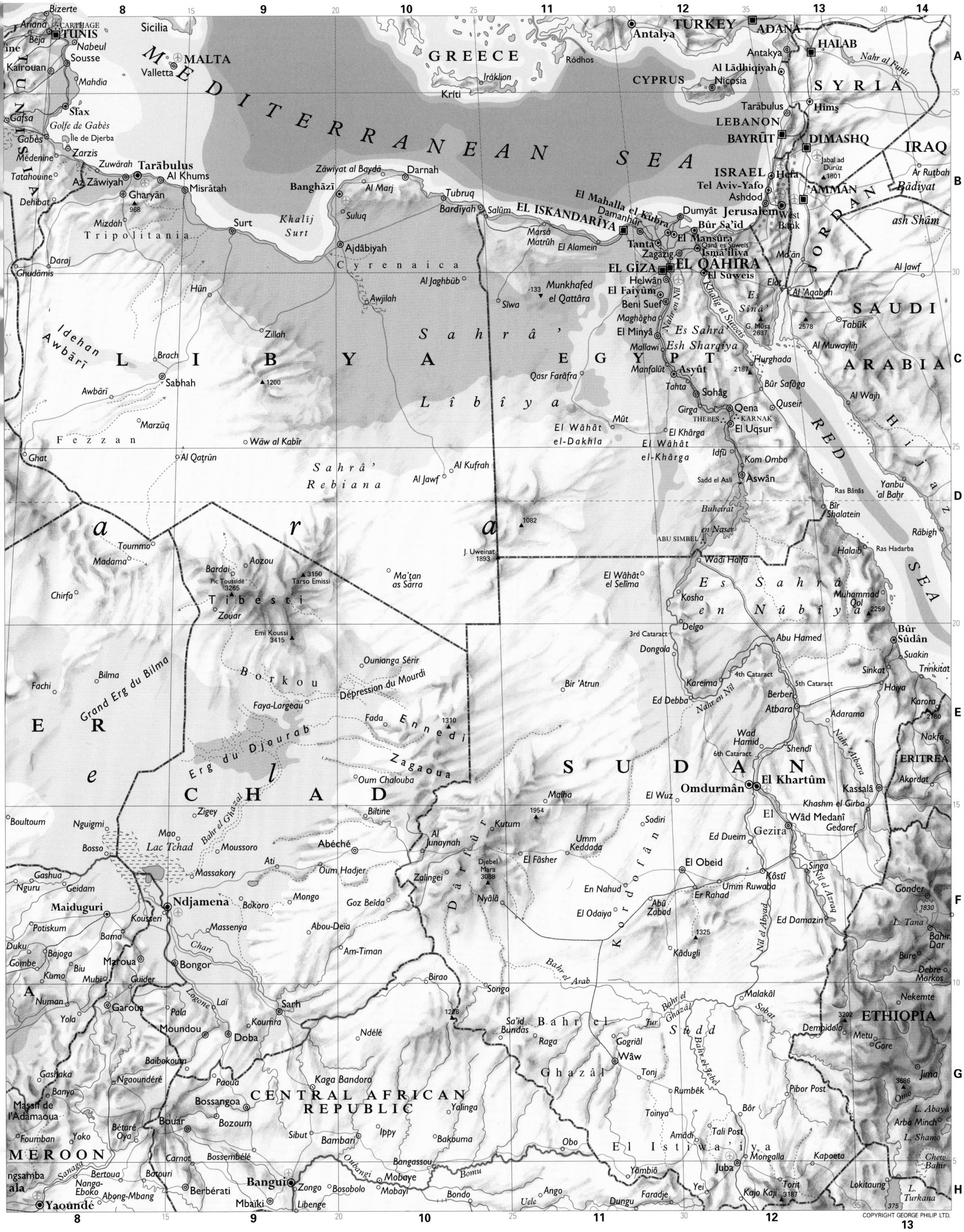

COPYRIGHT GEORGE PHILIP LTD.

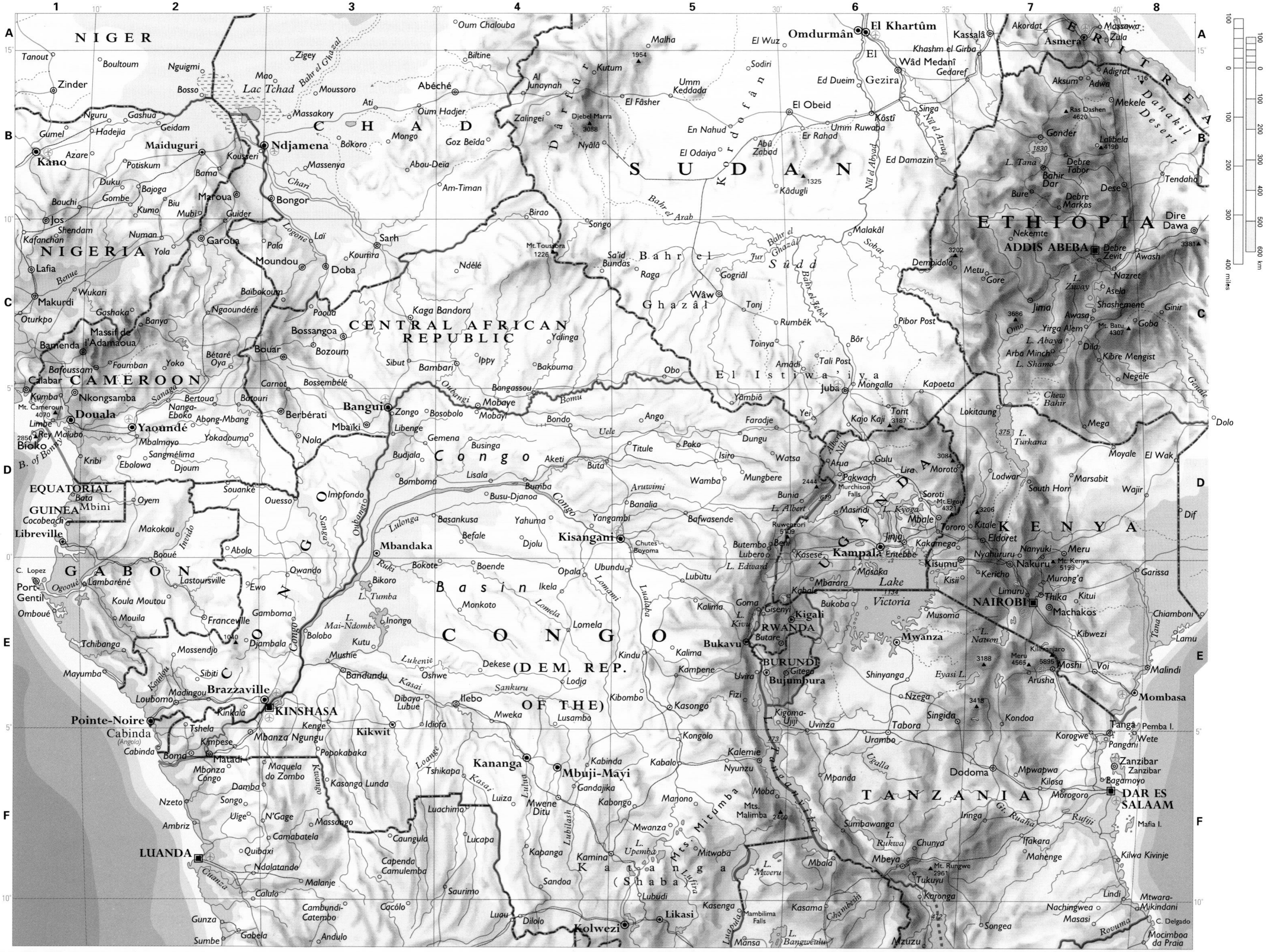

Scale: 100 0 100 200 300 400 500 600 km
100 0 100 200 300 400 miles

Countries and major regions:

NIGER

NIGERIA

CHAD

CAMEROON

CENTRAL AFRICAN REPUBLIC

SUDAN

ETHIOPIA

ERITREA

KENYA

UGANDA

RWANDA

BURUNDI

TANZANIA

CONGO (DEM. REP.)

CONGO

GABON

EQUATORIAL GUINEA

ANGOLA

Darfur
Kordofan
Sudd
Bahr el Ghazal
Congo Basin
Shaba (Katanga)
Danakil Desert
Mitumba Mts.

Selected cities and towns:

El Khartûm, Omdurmân, Kano, Ndjamena, Maiduguri, Yaoundé, Douala, Libreville, Bangui, Brazzaville, KINSHASA, Pointe-Noire, Cabinda, LUANDA, Kananga, Mbuji-Mayi, Kisangani, Bukavu, Kigali, Bujumbura, Kampala, NAIROBI, Mombasa, DAR ES SALAAM, Zanzibar, Dodoma, Mwanza, Tanga, ADDIS ABEBA, Asmera, Kassalâ, El Obeid, El Fâsher, Nyala, Addis Abeba, Dire Dawa, Nazret, Gonder, Mekele

Lake Victoria
Lake Tanganyika
L. Albert
L. Edward
L. Kivu
L. Turkana
L. Chad / Lac Tchad
Blue Nile / Bahr el Azraq
White Nile / Bahr el Jebel
Congo River
Lualaba
Kasai
Ubangi

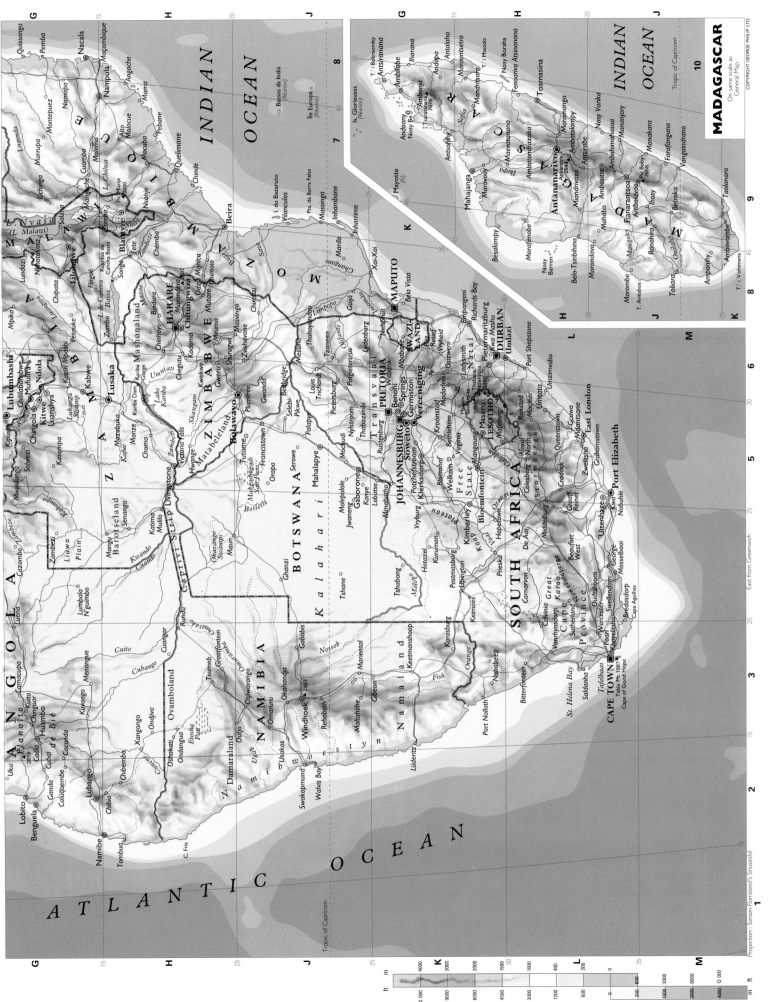

MADAGASCAR

On same scale as General Map

COPYRIGHT GEORGE PHILIP LTD.

EAST AFRICA 1:8 000 000

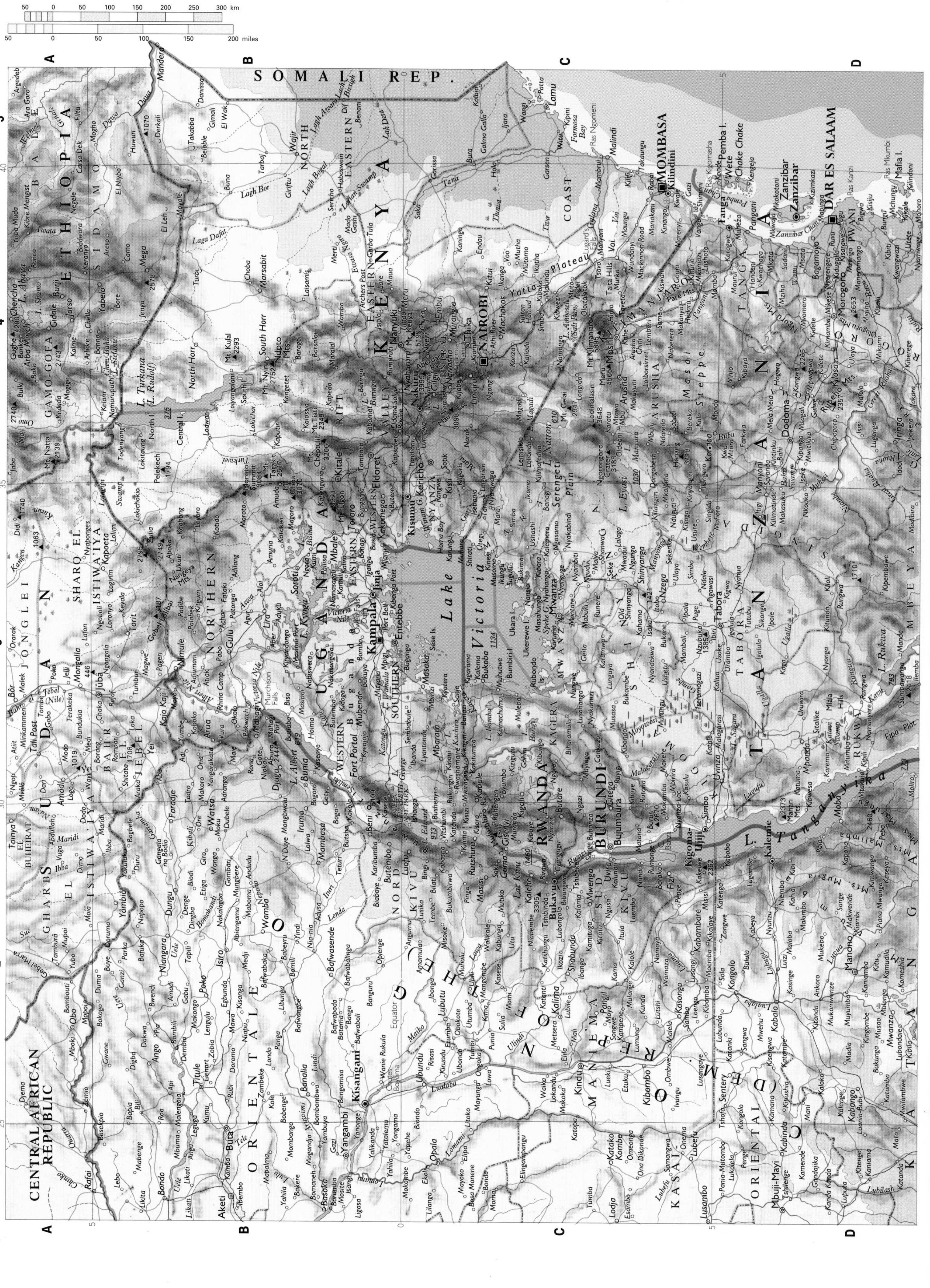
50 0 50 100 150 200 250 300 km
50 0 50 100 150 200 miles
SOMALI REP.
ETHIOPIA
KENYA
UGANDA
TANZANIA
RWANDA
BURUNDI
CENTRAL AFRICAN REPUBLIC
NAIROBI
MOMBASA
DAR ES SALAAM
Zanzibar
Kampala
Lake Victoria
L. Turkana (L. Rudolf)
L. Tanganyika
Pemba I.
Mafia I.

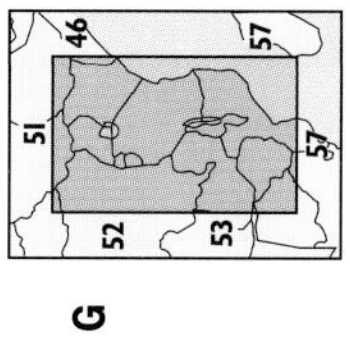

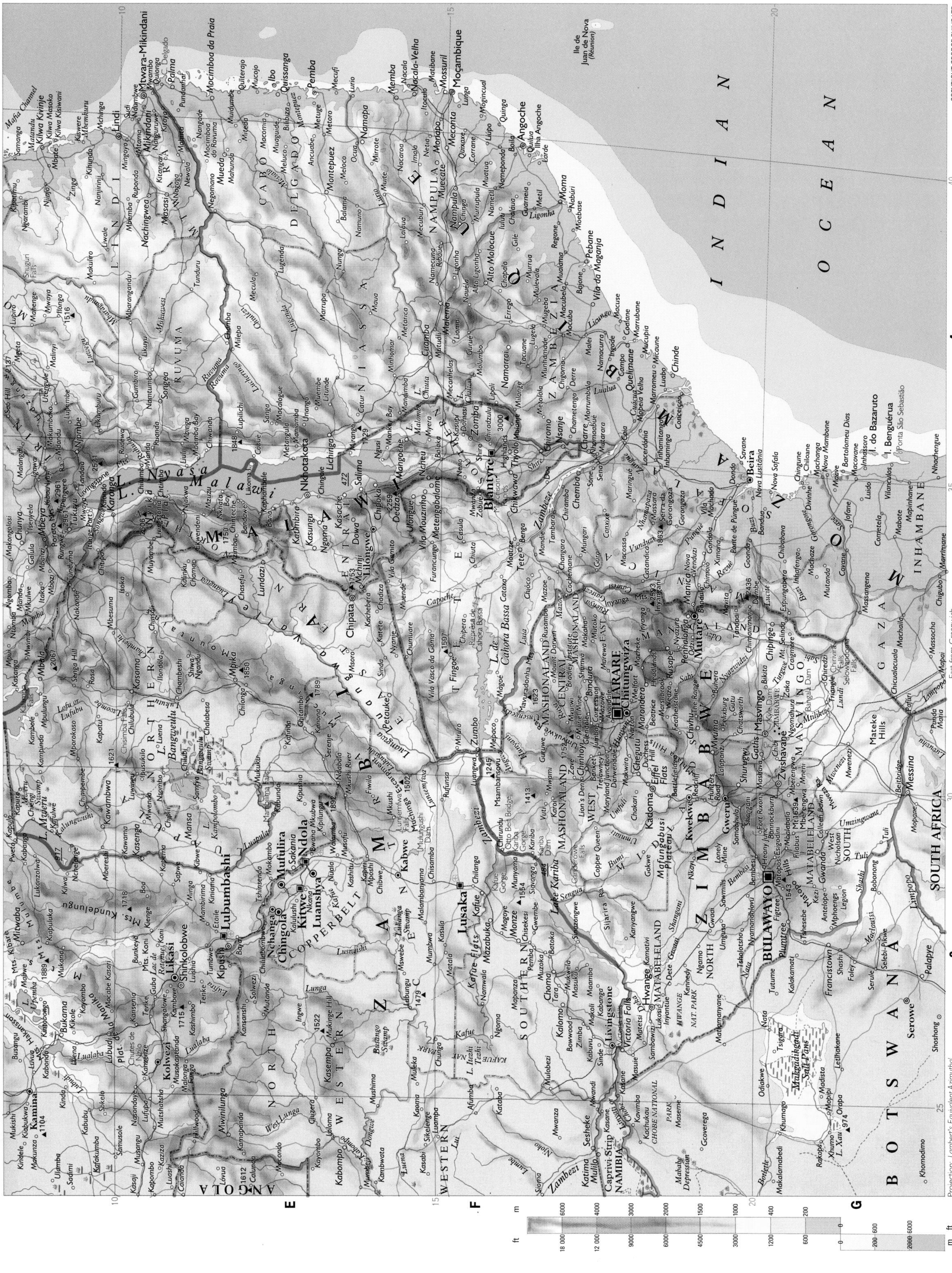

I N D I A N

O C E A N

East from Greenwich

Projection: Lambert's Equivalent Azimuthal

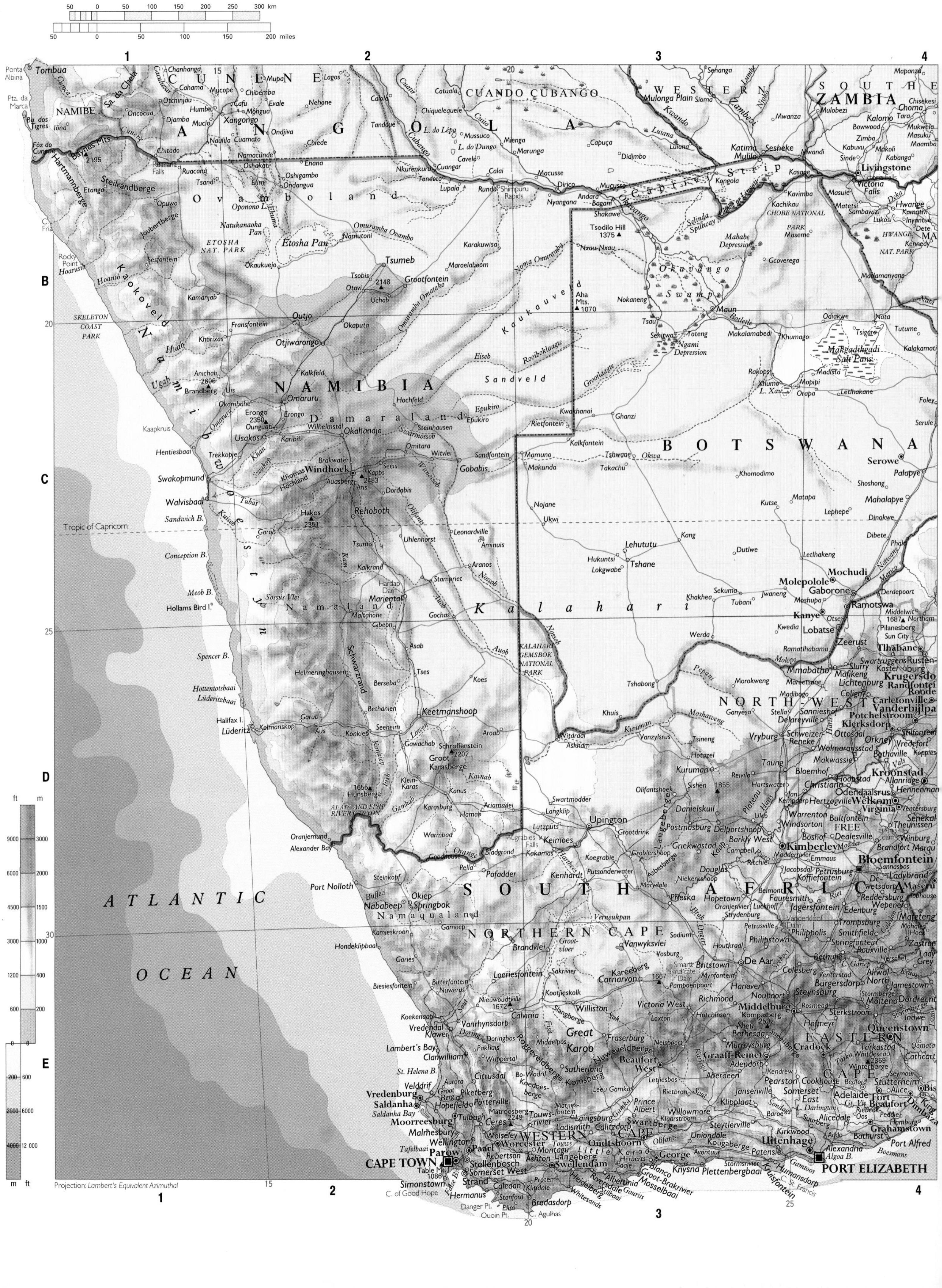
50 0 50 100 150 200 250 300 km
50 0 50 100 150 200 miles
ATLANTIC OCEAN
ANGOLA
CUNENE
CUANDO CUBANGO
ZAMBIA
WESTERN
SOUTHERN
NAMIBIA
BOTSWANA
SOUTH AFRICA
NORTHERN CAPE
WESTERN CAPE
EASTERN CAPE
FREE STATE
NORTH-WEST
Tropic of Capricorn
Kalahari
Namib Desert
Kaokoveld
Ovamboland
Damaraland
Namaland
Namaqualand
Sandveld
Great Karoo
Little Karoo
Caprivi Strip
Okavango Swamps
Makgadikgadi Salt Pans
Etosha Pan
ETOSHA NAT. PARK
SKELETON COAST PARK
KALAHARI GEMSBOK NATIONAL PARK
CHOBE NATIONAL PARK
HWANGE NAT. PARK
Windhoek
Walvisbaai
Swakopmund
Lüderitz
Keetmanshoop
Rehoboth
Tsumeb
Grootfontein
Otjiwarongo
Outjo
Okahandja
Gobabis
Mariental
Gaborone
Molepolole
Mochudi
Francistown
Serowe
Palapye
Mahalapye
Maun
Ghanzi
Tshane
Lobatse
Kanye
Livingstone
Victoria Falls
Kimberley
Bloemfontein
Upington
Kuruman
Vryburg
Mmabatho
Welkom
Kroonstad
De Aar
Middelburg
Graaff-Reinet
Beaufort West
Oudtshoorn
George
Knysna
Mosselbaai
Uitenhage
Grahamstown
Queenstown
CAPE TOWN
Simonstown
Stellenbosch
Paarl
Worcester
Swellendam
Saldanha
Vredenburg
Springbok
Port Nolloth
Oranjemund
PORT ELIZABETH
Port Alfred
C. of Good Hope
C. Agulhas
Orange
Molopo
Nossob
Auob
Fish
Okavango
Zambezi
Cunene
Projection: Lambert's Equivalent Azimuthal
ft m
9000 3000
6000 2000
4500 1500
3000 1000
1200 400
600 200
0 0
200 600
2000 6000
4000 12 000
m ft
1 2 3 4
B C D E
15 20 25 30

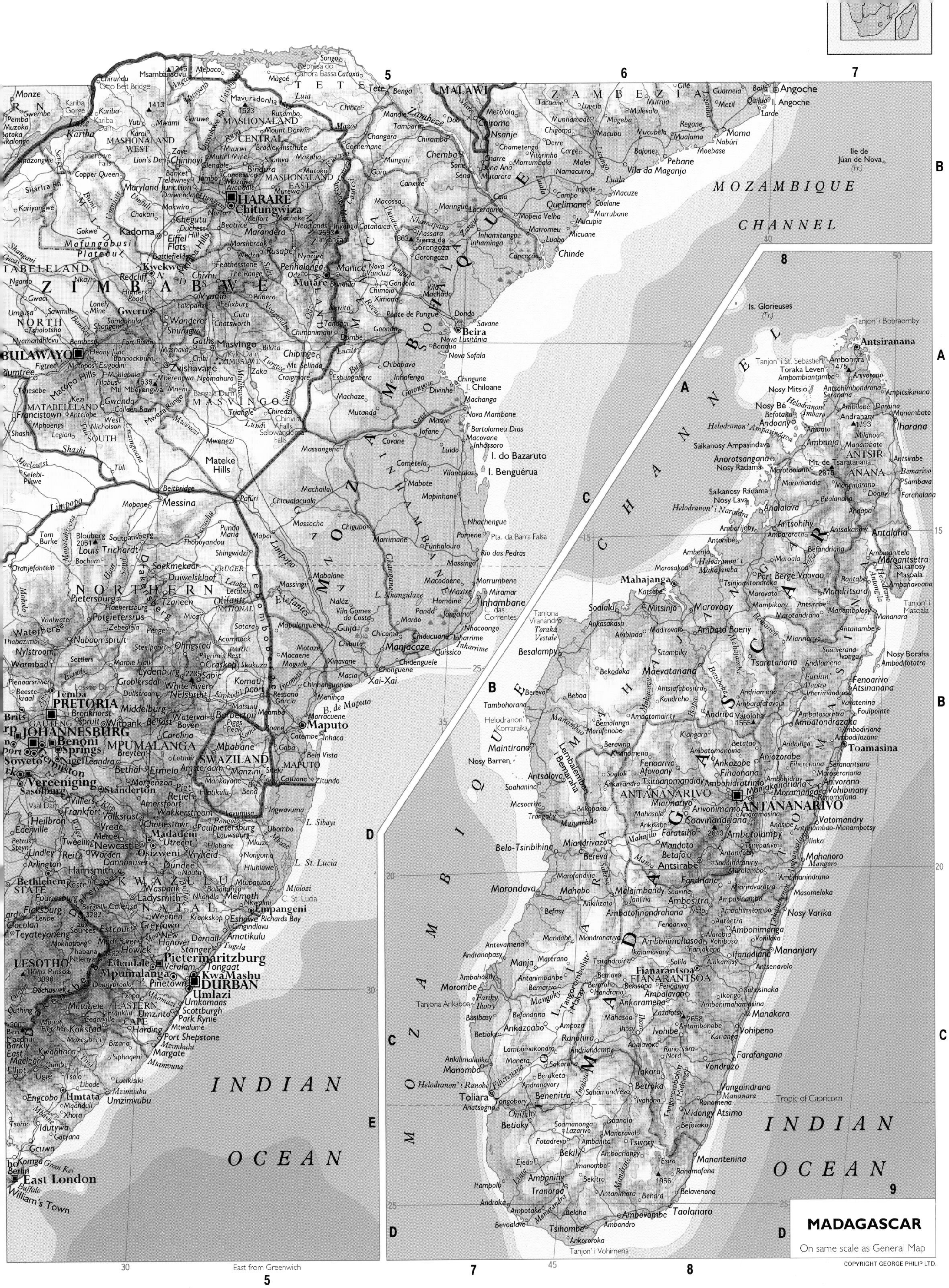

5 **6** **7**

MONZE

Kariba Gorge Kariba Dam Lake Kariba

Msambansovu 1245 Mepaco Mavuradonha Mts Songo Represa do Cahora Bassa Cataxa

Chirundu Otto Beit Bridge 1623 Mwami Guruwe Chioco

TETE Tete Benga Lúria

MALAWI

Z A M B E Z I A

Metolola Lugela Gilé Guarneia Boila Angoche

Mandie Mungari Macubu Mucubela Regone Moma

Chemba Mopeia Velha Marromeu Luabo

Quelimane Coalane Marrubane Mucupia

MOZAMBIQUE CHANNEL

Ile de Júan de Nova (Fr.)

B

Beira

Nova Lusitânia Nova Sofala Bandua

Savane Dondo

8

Is. Glorieuses (Fr.)

Tanjon' i Bobraomby

Antsiranana

A

Nosy Mitsio

Nosy Be Befotaka Andoany Ambilobe Daraina

MADAGASCAR

INDIAN OCEAN

MADAGASCAR

On same scale as General Map

COPYRIGHT GEORGE PHILIP LTD.

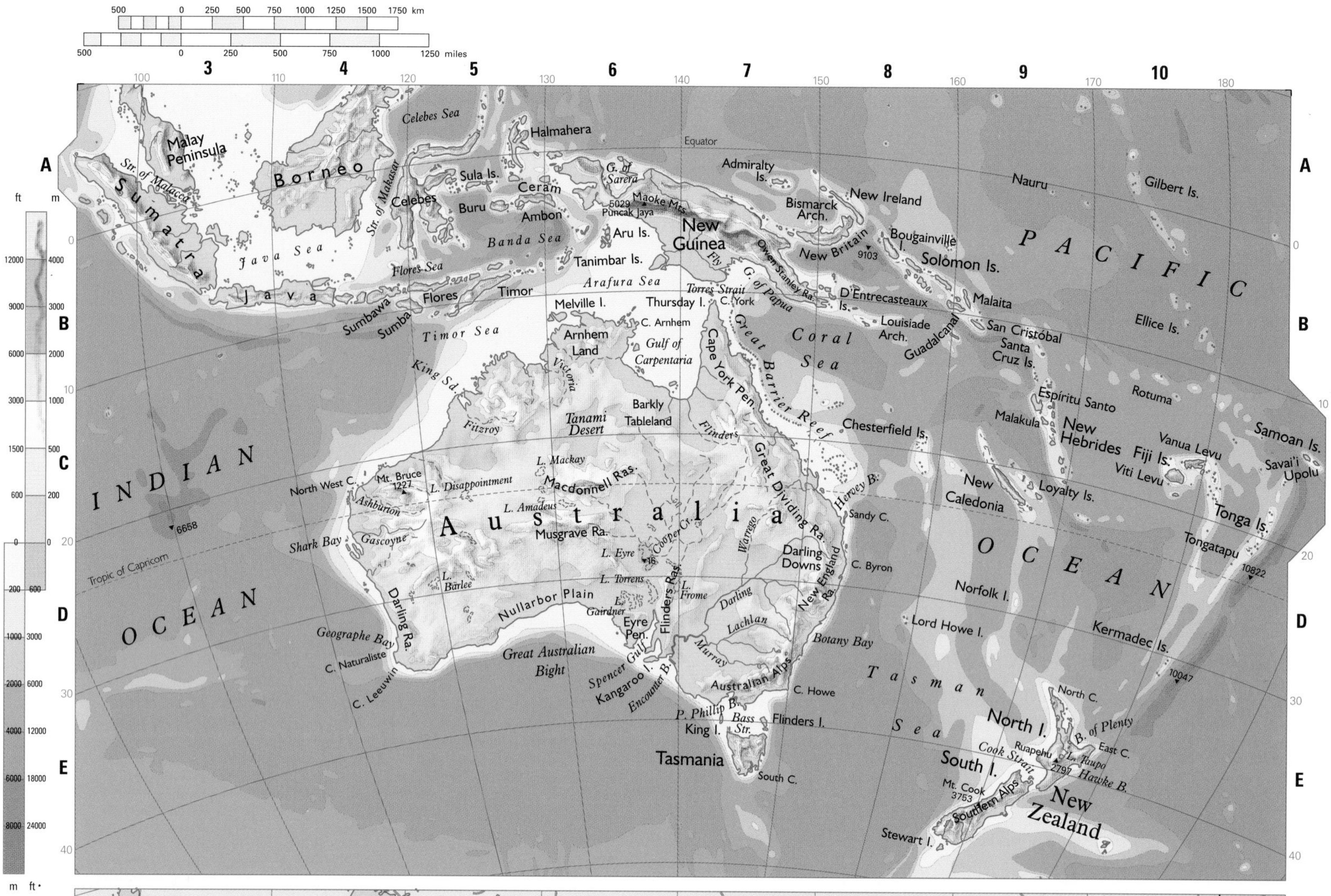

Top map (physical)

Scale bars:
500 250 0 250 500 750 1000 1250 1500 1750 km
3   4   5   6   7   8   9   10
500 0 250 500 750 1000 1250 miles

ft m
12000 4000
9000 3000
6000 2000
3000 1000
1500 500
600 200
0 0
200 600
1000 3000
2000 6000
4000 12000
6000 18000
8000 24000

Malay Peninsula
Celebes Sea
Borneo
Halmahera
Equator
Admiralty Is.
Nauru
Gilbert Is.
Str. of Malacca
Sula Is.
Ceram
G. of Sarera
Bismarck Arch.
New Ireland
PACIFIC
Sumatra
Str. of Makassar
Celebes
Buru
Ambon
5029 Puncak Jaya
Maoke Mts.
Owen Stanley Ra.
New Britain
9103
Bougainville
Solomon Is.
Java Sea
Banda Sea
Aru Is.
New Guinea
Fly
D'Entrecasteaux
Malaita
Ellice Is.
Java
Flores Sea
Tanimbar Is.
Arafura Sea
Torres Strait
G. of Papua
C. York
Coral Sea
San Cristóbal
Santa Cruz Is.
Sumbawa
Sumba
Flores
Timor
Melville I.
Thursday I.
Great Barrier Reef
Espíritu Santo
Rotuma
Samoan Is.
Timor Sea
C. Arnhem
Arnhem Land
Gulf of Carpentaria
Cape York Pen.
Great Dividing Ra.
Chesterfield Is.
Malakula
New Hebrides
Fiji Is.
Vanua Levu
Savai'i
Upolu
King Sd.
Victoria
Barkly Tableland
Loyalty Is.
Viti Levu
Fitzroy
Tanami Desert
Flinders
Hervey B.
New Caledonia
OCEAN
Tonga Is.
INDIAN
North West C.
Mt. Bruce 1227
L. Disappointment
L. Mackay
Macdonnell Ras.
Warrego
Darling Downs
New England
Sandy C.
Tongatapu
10822
Ashburton
L. Amadeus
Musgrave Ra.
L. Eyre
Cooper Cr.
C. Byron
Norfolk I.
6658
Shark Bay
Gascoyne
L. Torrens
New England Ra.
Darling
Lachlan
Lord Howe I.
Kermadec Is.
Tropic of Capricorn
L. Barlee
Eyre Pen.
L. Frome
Flinders Ras.
Murray
Botany Bay
OCEAN
Geographe Bay
Nullarbor Plain
L. Gairdner
Darling Ra.
Spencer Gulf
Kangaroo I.
Australian Alps
Tasman Sea
North C.
10047
C. Naturaliste
Great Australian Bight
Encounter B.
C. Howe
North I.
B. of Plenty
East C.
C. Leeuwin
P. Phillip B.
Bass Str.
Flinders I.
Ruapehu 2797
L. Taupo
Hawke B.
King I.
South C.
Cook Strait
Tasmania
Mt. Cook 3753
Southern Alps
New Zealand
Stewart I.

Australia

Bottom map (political)

m ft
Projection: Bonne
90 East from Greenwich 100
1 2 3 4 5 6 Canberra Capital Cities 8 9 10 11

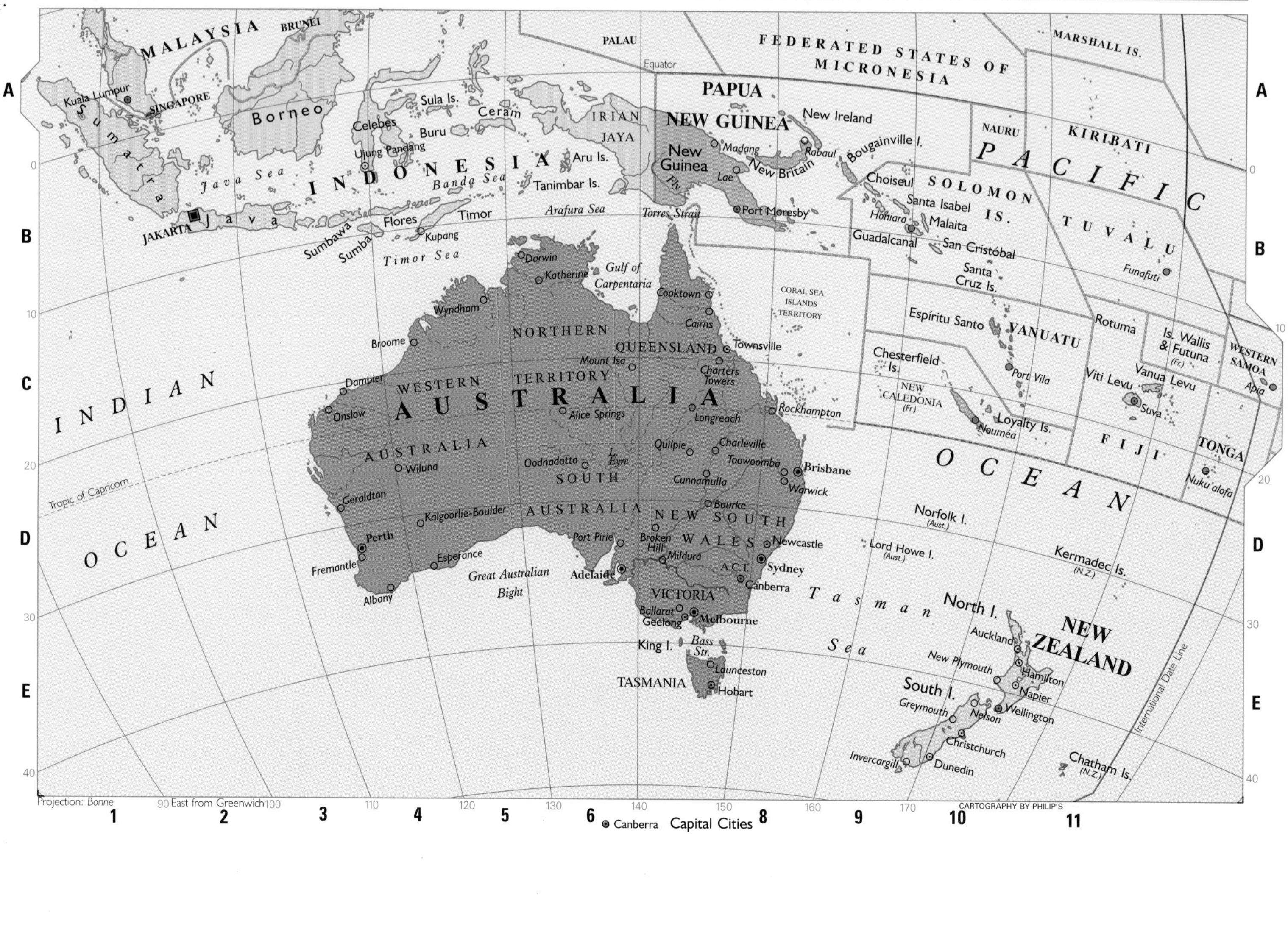

MALAYSIA BRUNEI
PALAU
FEDERATED STATES OF MICRONESIA
MARSHALL IS.
Kuala Lumpur
SINGAPORE
Borneo
Sula Is.
Ceram
Equator
PAPUA
NEW GUINEA
New Ireland
NAURU
KIRIBATI
Sumatra
Celebes
Buru
IRIAN JAYA
New Guinea
Madang
Rabaul
PACIFIC
Ujung Pandang
INDONESIA
Lae
New Britain
Bougainville I.
Choiseul
SOLOMON IS.
Java Sea
Banda Sea
Fly
Santa Isabel
TUVALU
JAKARTA
Java
Tanimbar Is.
Aru Is.
Port Moresby
Honiara
Malaita
Funafuti
Sumbawa
Sumba
Flores
Kupang
Timor
Arafura Sea
Torres Strait
Guadalcanal
San Cristóbal
Timor Sea
Darwin
Katherine
Gulf of Carpentaria
CORAL SEA ISLANDS TERRITORY
Santa Cruz Is.
Rotuma
WESTERN SAMOA
Cooktown
Espíritu Santo
VANUATU
Is. Wallis & Futuna (Fr.)
Wyndham
NORTHERN
Cairns
Chesterfield Is.
Port Vila
Vanua Levu
Apia
Broome
TERRITORY
QUEENSLAND
Townsville
NEW CALEDONIA (Fr.)
Viti Levu
Dampier
WESTERN
Mount Isa
Charters Towers
Suva
Onslow
AUSTRALIA
Alice Springs
Longreach
Rockhampton
Loyalty Is.
FIJI
TONGA
AUSTRALIA
Quilpie
Charleville
Nouméa
INDIAN
Wiluna
L. Eyre
SOUTH
Toowoomba
Brisbane
OCEAN
Nuku'alofa
Geraldton
Oodnadatta
AUSTRALIA
Cunnamulla
Warwick
Norfolk I. (Aust.)
Kalgoorlie-Boulder
Bourke
NEW SOUTH
Lord Howe I. (Aust.)
Kermadec Is. (N.Z.)
Perth
Port Pirie
Broken Hill
WALES
Newcastle
Fremantle
Esperance
Mildura
A.C.T.
Sydney
Adelaide
Canberra
North I.
Albany
Great Australian Bight
VICTORIA
Tasman Sea
NEW ZEALAND
Ballarat
Geelong
Melbourne
Auckland
King I.
Bass Str.
New Plymouth
Hamilton
TASMANIA
Launceston
South I.
Napier
Greymouth
Nelson
Wellington
Hobart
Invercargill
Dunedin
Christchurch
Chatham Is. (N.Z.)

CARTOGRAPHY BY PHILIP'S

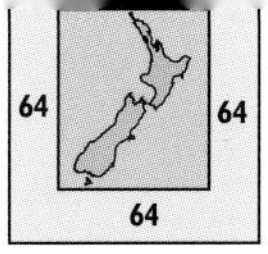

64

50 0 50 100 150 200 km
50 0 50 100 150 miles

PACIFIC

OCEAN

C. Reinga
C. Maria
van Diemen
North C.
Houhora Heads
Rangaunu B.
Doubtless B.
Mongonui
Whangaroa Harb.
Ahipara B.
Kaitaia
Tauroa Pt.
Okaihau
B. of Islands
C. Brett
Hokianga Harbour
Rawene
Hikurangi
Kaikohe
Kerikeri
Opua
Whangarei
Donnelly's Crossing
Whangarei Harb.
Bream Hd.
Bream B.
Dargaville
Waipu
Little
Barrier I.
Kaipara Harbour
Warkworth
C. Rodney
Great Barrier I.
C. Colville
Cuvier I.
Helensville
Hauraki
Gulf
Coromandel
Cuvier I.
Takapuna
Devonport
Whitianga
AUCKLAND
Manukau
Papakura
Thames
Mayor I.
Waiuku
Pukekohe
Mercer
Waihi
C. Runaway
Waikato
Paeroa
Tauranga Harb.
White I.
Huntly
Te Aroha
Mount
Morrinsville
Maunganui
Bay of Plenty
East C.

North
Island

Hamilton
Raglan
Cambridge
Whakatane
Opotiki
Te Awamutu
Putaruru
Kawerau
Mt. Hikurangi
Kawhia Harbour
Te Puke
Taneatua
1753
Otorohanga
Tokoroa
Rotorua
Rotorua
Motu
Te Kuiti
Kinleith
Taratera L.
Murupara
Tolaga Bay
Mokau
Mokau
Mokai
Kaingaroa
Ormond
Waipiro
North Taranaki
Wairakei
Forest
Waikaremoana
Bight
Ongarue
L. Taupo
Rangitaiki
Gisborne
Waitara
Taumarunui
Taupo
Poverty Bay
New Plymouth
Turangi
Tongariro
Waikokopu
Inglewood
Whangamomona
Ruapehu
Mahia Pen.
Mt. Egmont
Stratford
Ohakune
2797
Wairoa
C. Egmont
2518
Eltham
Raetihi
Waiouru
Bay
Hawke Bay
Opunake
Kapuni
Taihape
View
Hawera
Waverley
Mangaweka
Napier
C. Kidnappers
South Taranaki
Patea
Hastings
Bight
Wanganui
Hunterville
Waipawa
Marton
Halcombe
Waipukurau
Bulls
Feilding
Danneyirke
Palmerston
Woodville
C. Turnagain
North
Pahiatua
Foxton
Shannon
Sanson
Levin
C. Farewell
Otaki
Eketahuna
Collingwood
Golden
Paraparauma
Takaka
B.
D'Urville I.
Kapiti I.
Masterton
Tasman
B.
Pelorus Sd.
Carterton
Mts.
Motueka
Upper Hutt
Greytown
Karamea
Nelson
Havelock
Petone
Martinborough
Karamea
Richmond
Picton
WELLINGTON
Wairarapa
Bight
Tadmor
Wakefield
Lower Hutt
Seddonville
Matiri Ra.
Blenheim
Eastbourne
Granity
Lyell
Seddon
Strait
Westport
Murchison
Ward
Reefton
Inangahua
Rotoroa
2885 Mt. Tapuaenuku
Junction
Mt. Travers 2338
Blackball
Gr.
Spenser
Kaikoura
Runanga
Stillwater
Mts.
Greymouth
Hanmer
Kaikoura
Kumara
Springs
L. Brunner
Arthur's
Waiau
Hokitika
Jacksons
Pass
Culverden
Ross
Waikari
Hurunui
Waipara
Amberley
Oxford
Rangiora
Pegasus Bay
Coleridge
Kaiapoi
Springfield
New Brighton
Whitecliffs
Christchurch
Methven
Riccarton
Lyttelton
Staveley
Lincoln
Banks Pen.
Lake River
Akaroa

South
Island

Westland Bight
Mt. Cook
3753
Jackson B.
Haast
Okuru
Temuka
Okuru
Timaru
Milford Sd.
Aspiring
St.
Bligh Sound
3027
L.
Andrews
George Sound
Earnslaw
Pukaki
Waimate
2818
L. Tekapo
Fairlie
Wanaka
Ohau
L.
Wanaka
Ngapara
Cromwell
Kurow
Tokarahi
Secretary I.
Arrowtown
L.
Oamaru
Doubtful Sd.
Queenstown
Naseby
Maheno
Clyde
Hampden
Wakatipu
Alexandra
Dunback
Te Anau
Kingston
Roxburgh
Palmerston
L.
Waikouaiti
Breaksea Sd.
Manapouri
Lawrence
Port Chalmers
Dusky Sd.
Mossburn
Edievale
Kelso
Otago Harbour
Resolution I.
Lumsden
Tapanui
Saunders Pt.
Clifden
Ohai
Milton
Dunedin
Tuatapere
Winton
Fairfield
Gore
Clinton
Balclutha
Egenton
Mataura
Kaitangata
Te Waewae B.
Orepuki
Riverton
Wyndham
Owaka
Hedgehope
Nugget Pt.
Invercargill
Tokanui
Bluff
South Invercargill
Ruapuke I.
Halfmoon Bay
Foveaux Str.
Southwest C.
Stewart I.
Port Pegasus

TASMAN

SEA

SAMOA ISLANDS
1:12 000 000

WESTERN
SAMOA
AMERICAN
SAMOA
Savai'i
Apia
Upolu
Pago Pago
Tutuila
West from
Greenwich

Wallis & Futuna (Fr.)
Futuna

Niuafo'ou
(Tonga)
Thikombia
Lambasa
Vanua Levu
Yasawa Group
Lautoka
Taveuni
FIJI
Koro
Vanua Mbalavu
Nandi
1323
Levuka
Viti Levu
Ovalau
Koro Sea
Lakemba
TONGA
(Friendly Is.)
Suva
Gau
Vava'u
Moala
Kandavu
Lau Group
Vatoa
Tofua
Tongatapu
Nuku'alofa

FIJI AND TONGA
ISLANDS
1:12 000 000

50 0 50 100 150 200 km
50 0 50 100 150 miles

East from Greenwich
West from Greenwich
COPYRIGHT GEORGE PHILIP LTD.

ft   m
9000   3000
6000   2000
3000   1000
1200   400
600   200
0   0
200   600
2000   6000
4000   12 000
6000   18 000
m   ft

Projection : Conical with two standard parallels
East from Greenwich

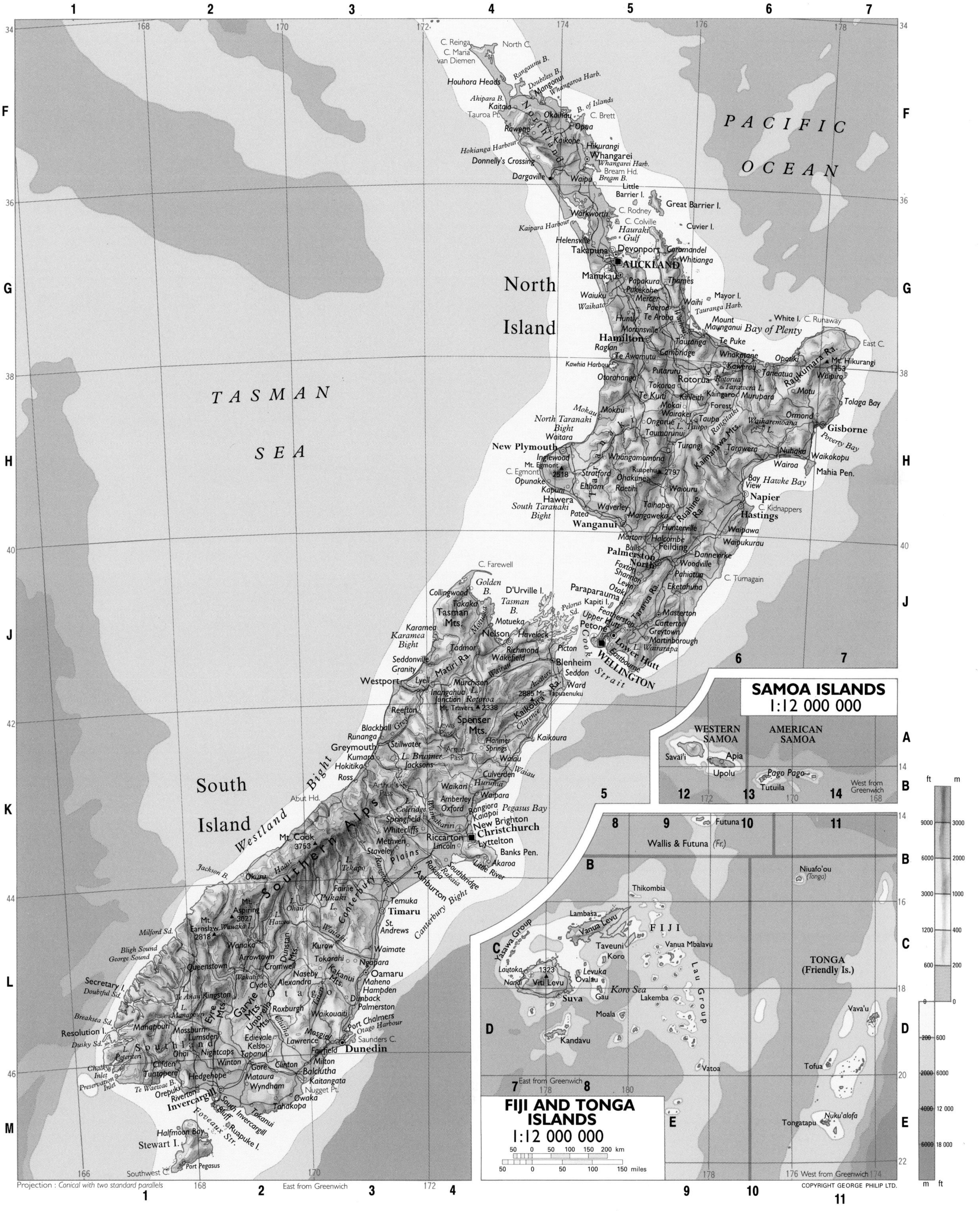

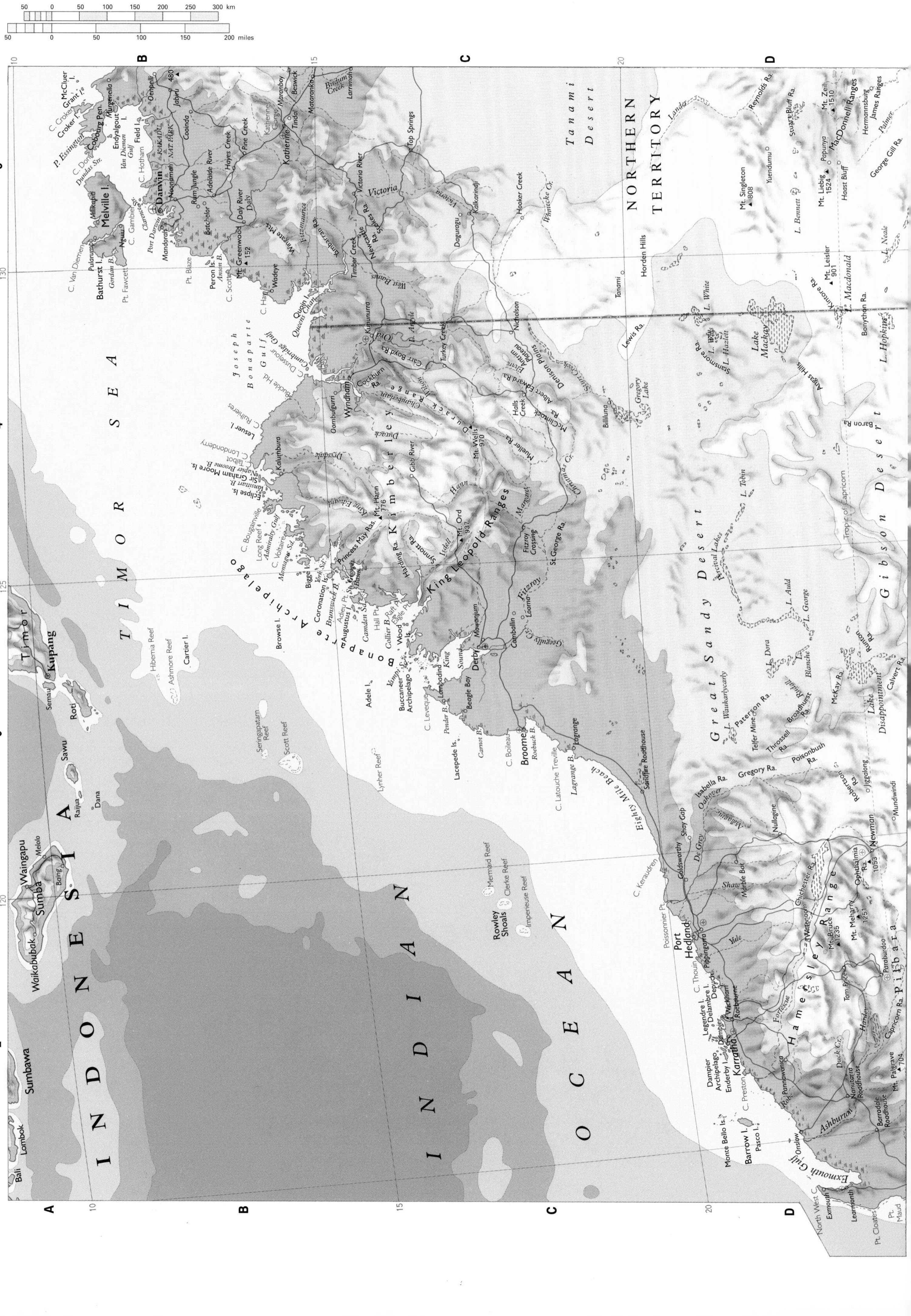

50 0 50 100 150 200 250 300 km
50 0 50 100 150 200 miles

INDIAN OCEAN

TIMOR SEA

INDONESIA

NORTHERN TERRITORY

Tanami Desert

Great Sandy Desert

Gibson Desert

Kimberley

King Leopold Ranges

Bonaparte Archipelago

Joseph Bonaparte Gulf

Hamersley Range

Pilbara

Bali
Lombok
Sumbawa
Sumba
Waingapu
Waikabubak
Lombok
Timor
Kupang
Semau
Roti
Sawu
Raijua
Dana
Melolo
Boing
Dampier Archipelago
Monte Bello Is.
Barrow I.
Pasco I.
C. Preston
Enderby I.
Legendre I.
C. Thouin
Dampier
Delambre I.
Karratha
Roebourne
Whim Creek
Port Hedland
Poissonnier Pt.
Goldsworthy
Shay Gap
Marble Bar
Nullagine
Newman
Mundiwindi
Mt. Bruce 1235
Mt. Meharry 1251
Wittenoom
Chichester Ra.
Ophthalmia Ra.
Tropic of Capricorn
Ashburton
Onslow
Exmouth Gulf
North West C.
Exmouth
Learmonth
Pt. Cloates
Pt. Maud
Barradale Roadhouse
Nanutarra Roadhouse
Mt. Palgrave

Broome
Roebuck B.
Eighty Mile Beach
Cape Keraudren
Sandfire Roadhouse
Lagrange B.
C. Latouche Treville
Lagrange
Carnot B.
C. Boileau
Lacepede Is.
Pender B.
Beagle Bay
Cape Leveque
Cape Borda
Buccaneer Archipelago
Adele I.
Sunday Str.
Cockatoo I.
Derby
King Sound
Yampi Sd.
Camden Sd.
Kimbolton
Fitzroy Crossing
Fitzroy
Looma
Christmas Cr.
Camballin
Noonkanbah
Mowanjum
Liveringa
Geegully Cr.
Gogo

Mt. Hann 776
Mt. Ord 937
Mt. Wells 970
Hann R.
Lennard R.
Isdell R.
Charnley R.
Durack R.
Durack Ra.
Chamberlain Ra.
Carr Boyd Ra.
Albert Edward Ra.
Mueller Ra.
McClintock Ra.
Lewis Ra.
Gregory Ra.
Paterson Ra.
Throssell Ra.
McKay Ra.
Broadhurst Ra.
Teller Mine Cr.
Poisonbush Ra.
Isabella Ra.
Oakover
De Grey
Shaw
Yule

Oombulgurri
Wyndham
Cambridge Gulf
Cockburn Ra.
Cambridge
C. Dussejour
Cape Londonderry
C. Rulhieres
C. Talbot
Napier Broome B.
Kalumburu
Bigge I.
Eclipse Is.
Sir Graham Moore Is.
Lesueur I.
King Edward R.
Prince Regent R.
Montague Sd.
C. Voltaire
Mitchell
Coronation Is.
Augustus I.
Brunswick B.
Secure B.
Collier B.
Wood
Sale R.
Hall Pt.
Long Reef
Admiralty Gulf
Kolumburu
Drysdale
Drysdale R.
Gibb River
C. Bougainville
Osborn Is.
Princess May Ras.

Kununurra
Lake Argyle
Turkey Creek
Ord
Halls Creek
Denison Plains
Sturt Cr.
Gordon Downs
Nicholson
Billiluna
Gregory Lake
Lake Gregory
Stansmore Ra.
L. White
Tanami
Lake Mackay

Darwin
Melville I.
Bathurst I.
C. Van Diemen
Pularumpi
Milikapiti
Nguiu
C. Gambier
C. Fourcroy
C. Helvetius
Cobourg Pen.
Croker I.
C. Croker
C. Don
Grant I.
C. McCluer
P. Essington
Dundas Str.
Van Diemen Gulf
Mt. Bundey
Pt. Fawcett
Gordon B.
Murgenella
Minjilang
Oenpelli
Jabiru
480
Cooinda
Cooinda
Hayes Creek
Adelaide River
Batchelor
Pine Creek
Ram Jungle
Katherine
Katherine Gorge
Tindal
Mataranka
Larrimah
Birdum Creek
Beswick
Maranboy
Victoria River
Daly River
Daly
Daly Waters
Newcastle Waters
Timber Creek
Top Springs
Hooker Creek
Kalkaringi
Wave Hill
Kirkimbie
West Baines
Limbunya
Inverway
Waterloo
Rosewood
Argyle
Kununurra
Nathan River
Port Darwin
Noonamah
Noogumbah
Wadeye
Pt. Keats
Peron Is.
Anson B.
C. Scott
Pt. Blaze
C. Hay
Fitzmaurice
Queens Channel
Bonaparte Gulf
Wyndham

Mt. Greenwood 152
Mt. Singleton 808
Horden Hills
Doguorgu
Tanami Desert
Mt. Leisler
Mt. Liebig 1524
Mt. Zeil 1510
Reynolds Ra.
Papunya
Yuendumu
L. Bennett
Hermannsburg
James Ranges
MacDonnell Ranges
Stuart Bluff Ra.
Hoast Bluff
George Gill Ra.
Mt. Hopkins
L. Neale
Baron Ra.
Banython Ra.
L. Hopkins
Lake Disappointment
Lake Auld
L. Dora
L. George
L. Blanche
L. Waukarlycarly
Percival Lakes
Rudall R.
Calver Ra.
Robertson Ra.
Jigalong
Balfour Downs
Roy Hill
Ethel Creek
Capricorn Ra. 704
Hinds
Tom Price
Paraburdoo
Duck Cr.
Rocklea
Wyloo
Forrest
Mt. Brockman
Mt. Watercombe
1053

Rowley Shoals
Mermaid Reef
Clerke Reef
Imperieuse Reef
Scott Reef
Seringapatam Reef
Ashmore Reef
Hibernia Reef
Cartier I.
Browse I.
Lynher Reef

37

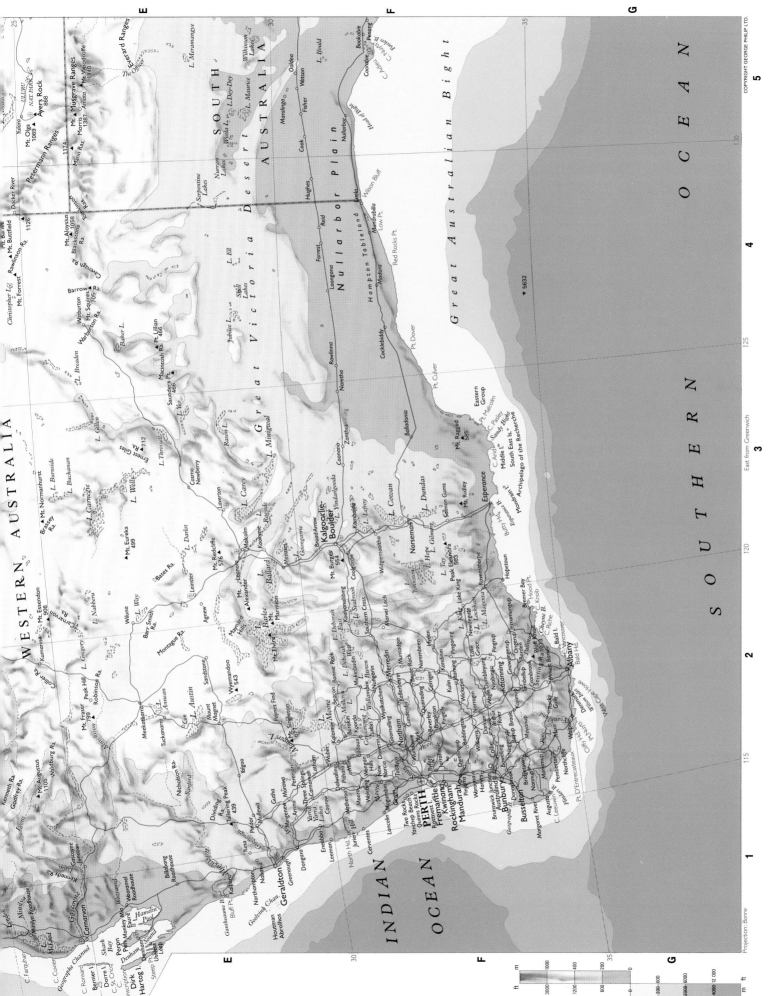

WESTERN AUSTRALIA

SOUTH AUSTRALIA

INDIAN OCEAN

SOUTHERN OCEAN

Great Australian Bight

Great Victoria Desert

Nullarbor Plain

Hampton Tableland

PERTH

Projection: Bonne

East from Greenwich

ft   m
3000
1200
600
0
m
1000
400
200

ft
200-600
2000 6000
4000 12 000
m

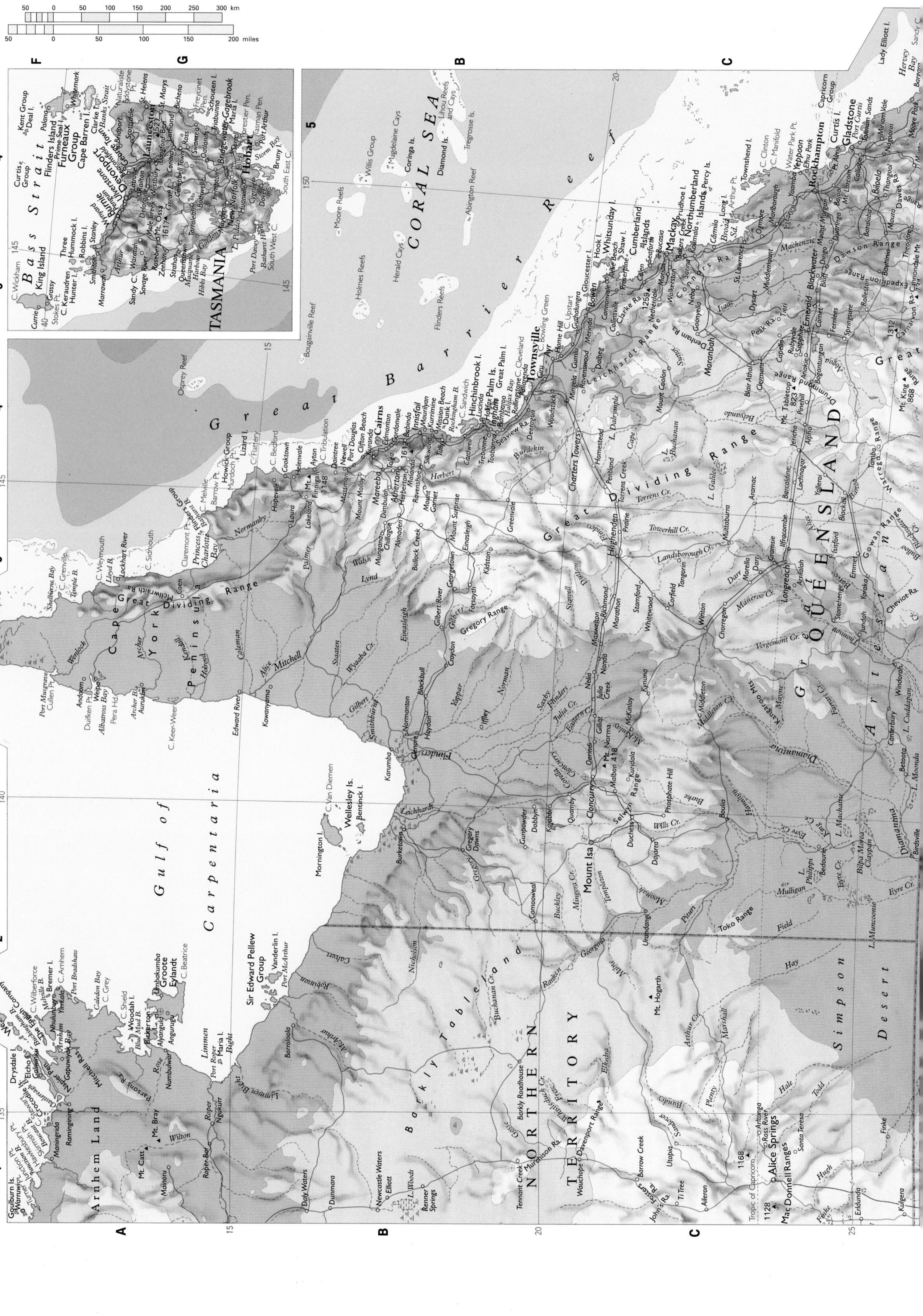

50 0 50 100 150 200 250 300 km
50 0 50 100 150 200 miles

TASMANIA

Bass Strait

CORAL SEA

Great Barrier Reef

Gulf of Carpentaria

Cape York Peninsula

Great Dividing Range

NORTHERN TERRITORY

QUEENSLAND

Simpson Desert

Barkly Tableland

Arnhem Land

Townsville
Cairns
Mackay
Rockhampton
Gladstone
Mount Isa
Cloncurry
Alice Springs
Flinders
Normanton
Longreach

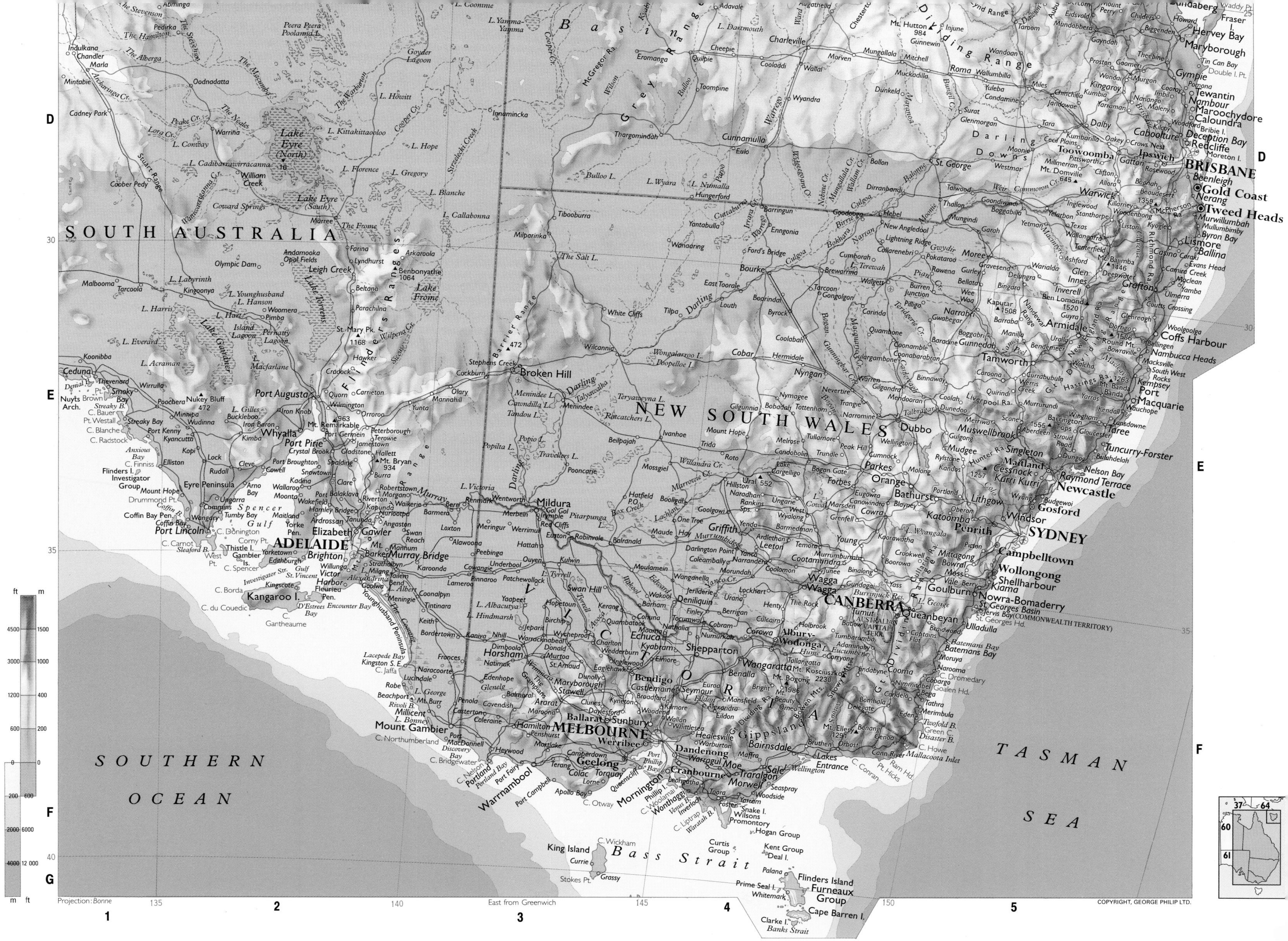
SOUTH AUSTRALIA
NEW SOUTH WALES
VICTORIA
AUSTRALIAN CAPITAL TERR. (COMMONWEALTH TERRITORY)
SOUTHERN OCEAN
TASMAN SEA
Bass Strait
ADELAIDE
MELBOURNE
SYDNEY
CANBERRA
BRISBANE
Gold Coast
Tweed Heads
Newcastle
Wollongong
Geelong
Ballarat
Bendigo
Broken Hill
Mildura
Port Augusta
Port Pirie
Whyalla
Port Lincoln
Mount Gambier
Kangaroo I.
King Island
Flinders Island
Furneaux Group
Cape Barren I.
Lake Eyre (North)
Lake Eyre (South)
Lake Torrens
Lake Gairdner
Lake Frome
Flinders Ranges
Barrier Range
Grey Range
Great Dividing Range
Darling Downs
Darling
Murray
Murrumbidgee
Lachlan
Toowoomba
Ipswich
Dubbo
Orange
Bathurst
Tamworth
Armidale
Coffs Harbour
Port Macquarie
Wagga Wagga
Albury
Wodonga
Shepparton
Warrnambool
Portland
Ceduna
Eyre Peninsula
Yorke Pen.
Spencer Gulf
Gulf St. Vincent
Wilsons Promontory
Projection: Bonne
East from Greenwich
135
140
145
150
30
35
40
D
E
F
G
1
2
3
4
5
ft
m
4500
3000
1200
600
0
200
2000
6000
12 000
1500
1000
400
37
60
61
64
COPYRIGHT, GEORGE PHILIP LTD.

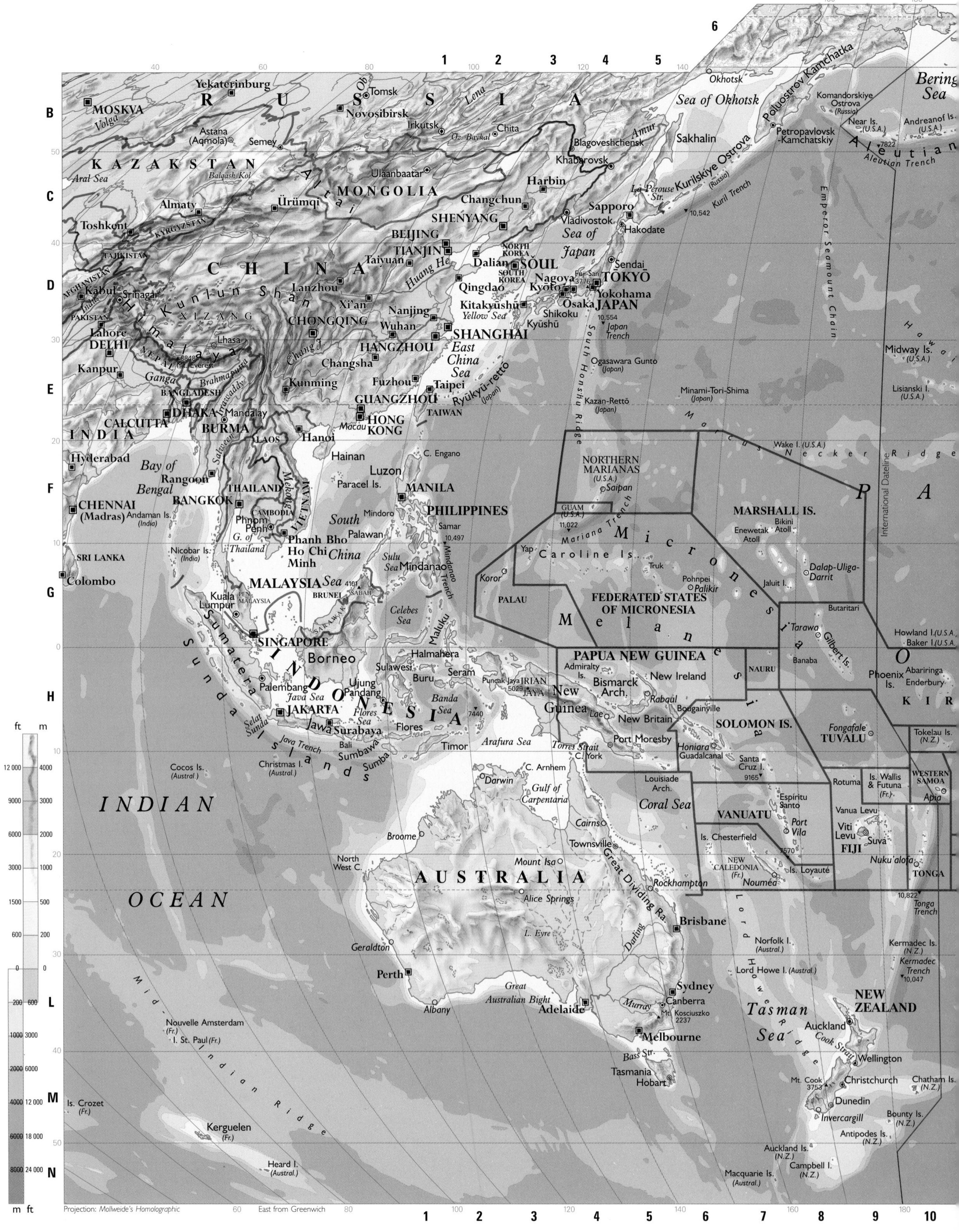

Projection: Mollweide's Homolographic   East from Greenwich

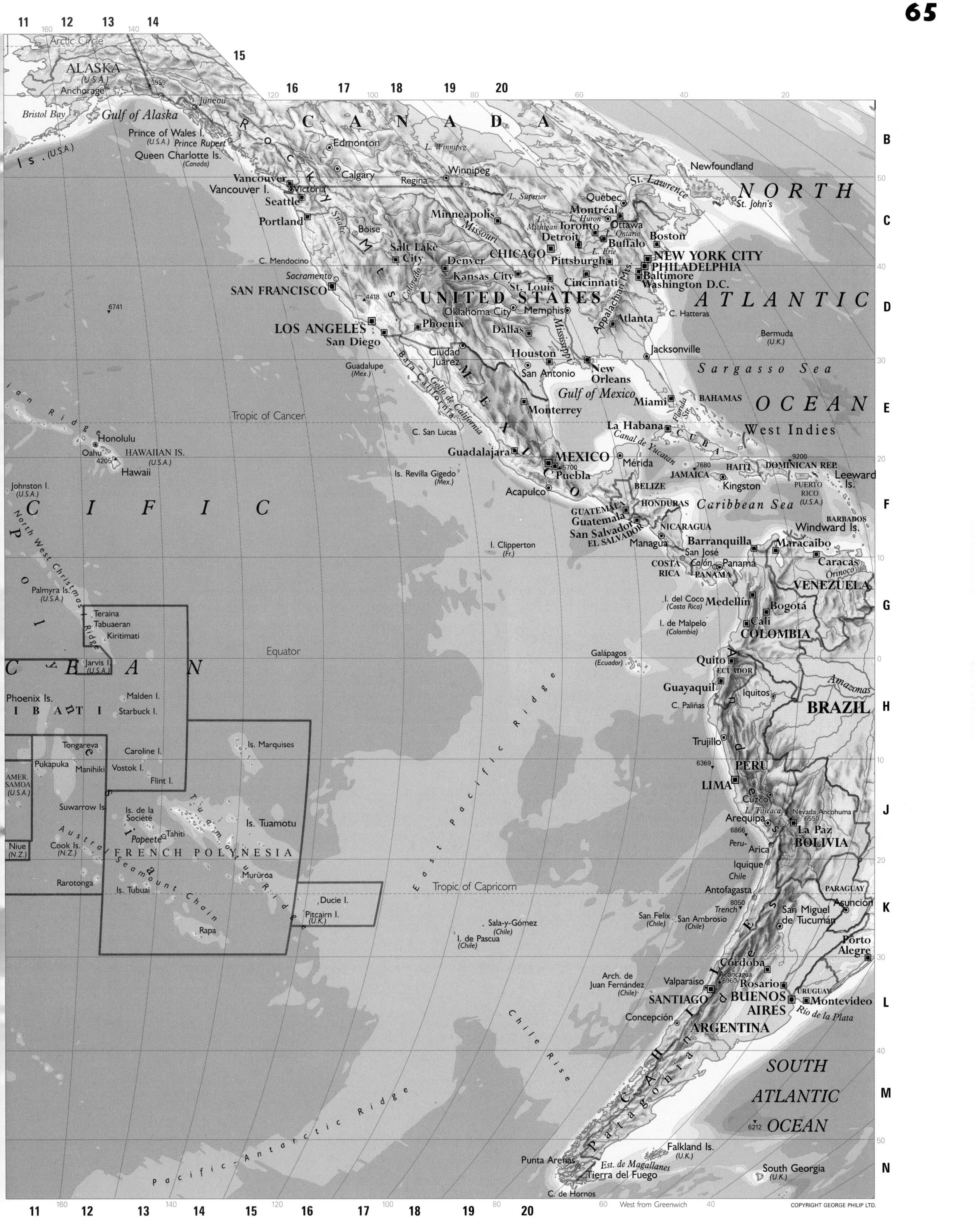

Arctic Circle

ALASKA
(U.S.A.)
Anchorage

Bristol Bay   *Gulf of Alaska*   Juneau

Is. *(U.S.A.)*

C A N A D A

Prince of Wales I.
(U.S.A.) Prince Rupert
Queen Charlotte Is.
(Canada)

Edmonton

L. Winnipeg

Calgary   Regina   Winnipeg

Newfoundland

Vancouver
Vancouver I.
Victoria
Seattle
Portland
Boise

N O R T H

L. Superior   Québec   St. Lawrence   St. John's
Minneapolis   Montréal
L. Huron   Toronto   Ottawa
L. Michigan   Detroit   Buffalo   Boston
Missouri   L. Ontario   L. Erie
Salt Lake   Denver   CHICAGO   Pittsburgh   **NEW YORK CITY**
City   Kansas City   St. Louis   Cincinnati   **PHILADELPHIA**
Baltimore
SAN FRANCISCO   Colorado   **UNITED STATES**   Washington D.C.

C. Mendocino
Sacramento

4418

Oklahoma City   Memphis   *A T L A N T I C*
LOS ANGELES   Phoenix   Dallas   Atlanta   C. Hatteras
San Diego   Ciudad   Houston   Jacksonville
Juárez   New   Bermuda
Guadalupe   San Antonio   Orleans   *(U.K.)*
(Mex.)   Gulf of Mexico   Miami   *Sargasso Sea*
Tropic of Cancer   Monterrey   BAHAMAS   *O C E A N*
C. San Lucas   La Habana   CUBA   *West Indies*

6741

Honolulu   Golfo de California   Mérida   7680   HAITI   DOMINICAN REP.   9200   Leeward
Oahu   HAWAIIAN IS.   C. San Lucas   Guadalajara   MEXICO   JAMAICA   Kingston   PUERTO   Is.
4205   *(U.S.A.)*   Is. Revilla Gigedo   Puebla   Canal de Yucatán   RICO   BARBADOS
Hawaii   *(Mex.)*   Acapulco   BELIZE   *Caribbean Sea*   *(U.S.A.)*   Windward Is.
GUATEMALA   HONDURAS
C I F I C   Guatemala   NICARAGUA   Barranquilla   Maracaibo
San Salvador   Managua   Caracas
Johnston I.   EL SALVADOR   San José   Barranquilla   Orinoco
(U.S.A.)   I. Clipperton   COSTA   Colón   Panamá   **VENEZUELA**
(Fr.)   RICA   PANAMA

Palmyra Is.   I. del Coco   Medellín   **COLOMBIA**
(U.S.A.)   *(Costa Rica)*   Bogotá
Teraina   I. de Malpelo   Cali
Tabuaeran   *(Colombia)*
Kiritimati   Galápagos   Quito
Equator   *(Ecuador)*   ECUADOR   Amazonas
Jarvis I.   Guayaquil   Iquitos   **BRAZIL**
(U.S.A.)   C. Palinas

Phoenix Is.   Malden I.   Trujillo
I B A   T I   Starbuck I.
Caroline I.   6369   **PERU**
Tongareva   Vostok I.   **LIMA**   Cuzco
Pukapuka   Manihiki   Flint I.   L. Titicaca   Nevada Ancohuma
AMER.   6550
SAMOA   Suwarrow Is   Arequipa
(U.S.A.)   Is. de la   6866   **La Paz**
Société   Tahiti   Peru-   Arica   **BOLIVIA**
Niue   Cook Is.   Papeete   Iquique   PARAGUAY
(N.Z.)   *(N.Z.)*   **F R E N C H   P O L Y N E S I A**   Chile   Asunción
Rarotonga   Is. Tuamotu   Antofagasta
Is. Tubuai   Mururoa   Tropic of Capricorn   8050   San Miguel
Ducie I.   Trench   San Felix   de Tucumán   Porto
Rapa   Pitcairn I.   *(Chile)*   San Ambrosio   Alegre
(U.K.)   *(Chile)*   Córdoba   URUGUAY
Sala-y-Gómez   Aconcagua   Rosario   Montevideo
(Chile)   Arch. de   6960   **BUENOS**   Rio de la Plata
I. de Pascua   Juan Fernández   Valparaíso   **AIRES**
(Chile)   *(Chile)*   **SANTIAGO**
Concepción   **ARGENTINA**

SOUTH

Chile Rise   *ATLANTIC*

OCEAN
6212
Falkland Is.
Punta Arenas   *(U.K.)*   South Georgia
Est. de Magallanes   *(U.K.)*
Tierra del Fuego
C. de Hornos

West from Greenwich   COPYRIGHT GEORGE PHILIP LTD.

B C D E F G H J K L M N

 NORTH AMERICA : Physical 1:35 000 000

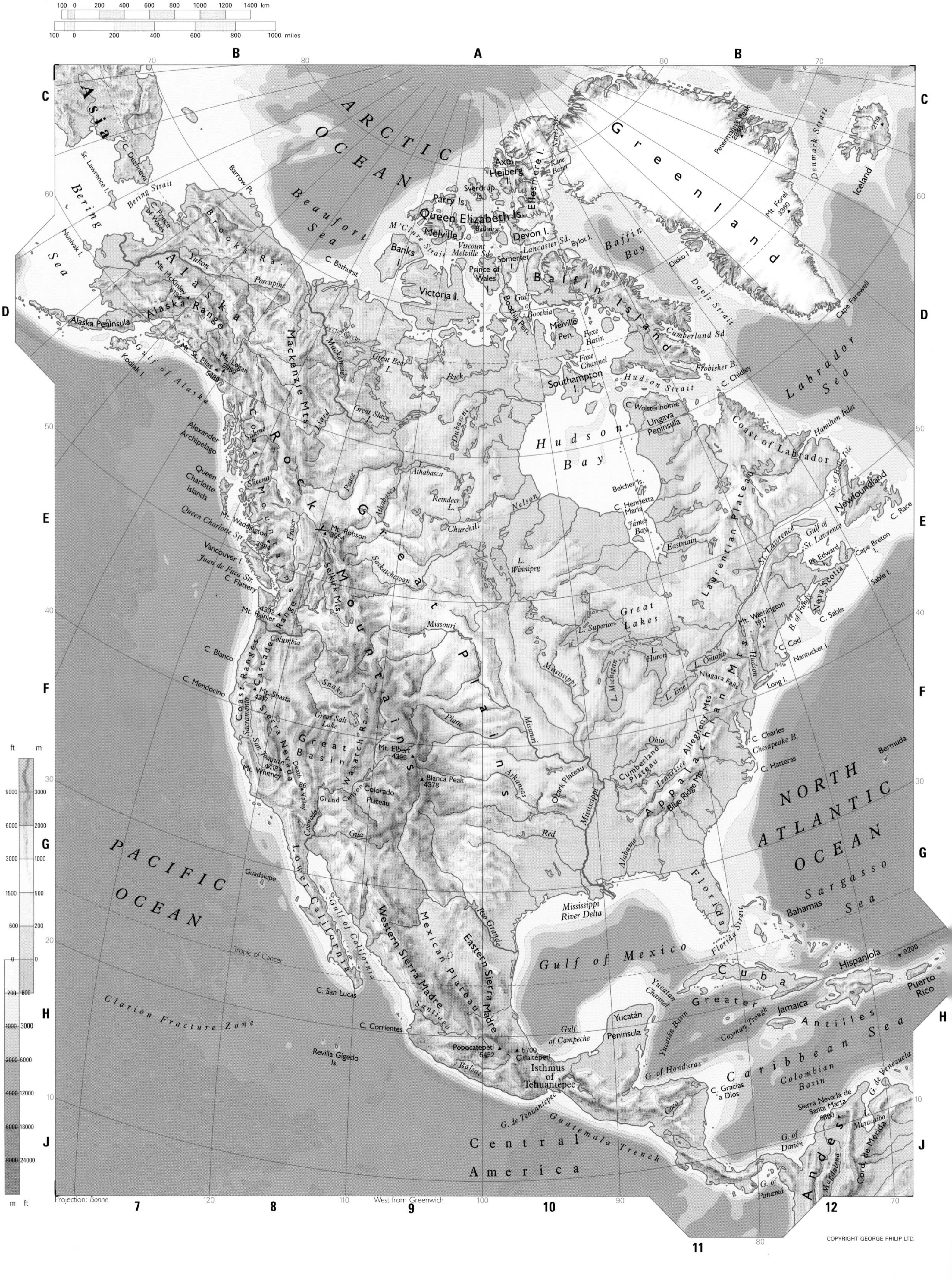
100 0 200 400 600 800 1000 1200 1400 km
100 0 200 400 600 800 1000 miles
ARCTIC OCEAN
Asia
C. Dezhneva
St. Lawrence I.
Bering Strait
Bering Sea
Nunivak I.
Barrow Pt.
Beaufort Sea
Brooks Ra.
C. Prince of Wales
Alaska
Yukon
Porcupine
Mt. McKinley 6194
Alaska Range
Alaska Peninsula
Kodiak I.
Gulf of Alaska
Mt. St. Elias 5489
Mt. Logan 5950
Mackenzie Mts
Mackenzie
Arctic Circle
C. Bathurst
Banks I.
M'Clure Strait
Victoria I.
Great Bear L.
Back
Great Slave L.
Liard
Dubawnt
Axel Heiberg I.
Sverdrup Is.
Parry Is.
Queen Elizabeth Is.
Melville I.
Bathurst I.
Viscount Melville Sd.
Devon I.
Ellesmere I.
Kane Basin
Lancaster Sd.
Bylot I.
Somerset I.
Prince of Wales I.
Gulf of Boothia
Boothia Pen.
Baffin Island
Baffin Bay
Melville Pen.
Foxe Basin
Foxe Channel
Southampton I.
Hudson Strait
Frobisher B.
Cumberland Sd.
Greenland
Petermann Peak 2940
Mt. Forel 3360
Disko I.
Davis Strait
Denmark Strait
Iceland
2119
Cape Farewell
Labrador Sea
C. Chidley
C. Wolstenholme
Ungava Peninsula
Hudson Bay
Belcher Is.
C. Henrietta Maria
James Bay
Eastmain
Coast of Labrador
Hamilton Inlet
Str. of Belle Isle
Newfoundland
C. Race
Laurentian Plateau
Nelson
Churchill
Reindeer L.
Athabasca
Peace
Alexander Archipelago
Stikine
Coast Mountains
Rocky Mountains
Skeena
Queen Charlotte Islands
Queen Charlotte Str.
Mt. Waddington 3994
Fraser
Mt. Robson 3954
Selkirk Mts
Great Plains
Saskatchewan
L. Winnipeg
Vancouver I.
Juan de Fuca Str.
C. Flattery
Mt. Rainier 4392
Cascade Range
Columbia
C. Blanco
C. Mendocino
Coast Ranges
Mt. Shasta 4317
Sacramento
Sierra Nevada
San Joaquin
Mt. Whitney 4418
Death Valley -86
Snake
Great Salt Lake
Great Basin
Wasatch Ra.
Mt. Elbert 4399
Blanca Peak 4378
Platte
Missouri
Grand Canyon
Colorado Plateau
Colorado
Gila
L. Superior
Great Lakes
L. Michigan
L. Huron
L. Erie
L. Ontario
Niagara Falls
Mississippi
Ohio
Cumberland Plateau
Tennessee
Allegheny Mts.
Appalachian Mts.
Blue Ridge Mts.
Ozark Plateau
Arkansas
Red
Alabama
St. Lawrence
Gulf of St. Lawrence
Pr. Edward I.
Cape Breton I.
Nova Scotia
Sable I.
B. of Fundy
C. Sable
Mt. Washington 1917
Hudson
C. Cod
Nantucket I.
Long I.
C. Charles
Chesapeake B.
C. Hatteras
Bermuda
NORTH ATLANTIC OCEAN
Sargasso Sea
Bahamas
Florida
Florida Strait
Mississippi River Delta
Gulf of Mexico
Rio Grande
PACIFIC OCEAN
Guadalupe
Lower California
Gulf of California
Western Sierra Madre
Mexican Plateau
Eastern Sierra Madre
Tropic of Cancer
C. San Lucas
Clarion Fracture Zone
C. Corrientes
Santiago
Revilla Gigedo Is.
Popocatepetl 5452
5700 Citlaltépetl
Balsas
Isthmus of Tehuantepec
Gulf of Campeche
Yucatán Peninsula
Yucatan Channel
Yucatan Basin
Cuba
Greater Antilles
Cayman Trough
Jamaica
Hispaniola
9200
Puerto Rico
Caribbean Sea
Colombian Basin
G. of Honduras
C. Gracias a Dios
Coco
G. de Tehuantepec
Guatemala Trench
Central America
G. of Darién
G. of Panamá
Sierra Nevada de Santa Marta 5800
G. de Venezuela
Maracaibo
Cord. de Mérida
Magdalena
Andes
ft m
9000 3000
6000 2000
3000 1000
1500 500
600 200
0 0
200 600
1000 3000
2000 6000
4000 12000
6000 18000
8000 24000
m ft
Projection: Bonne
West from Greenwich
COPYRIGHT GEORGE PHILIP LTD.

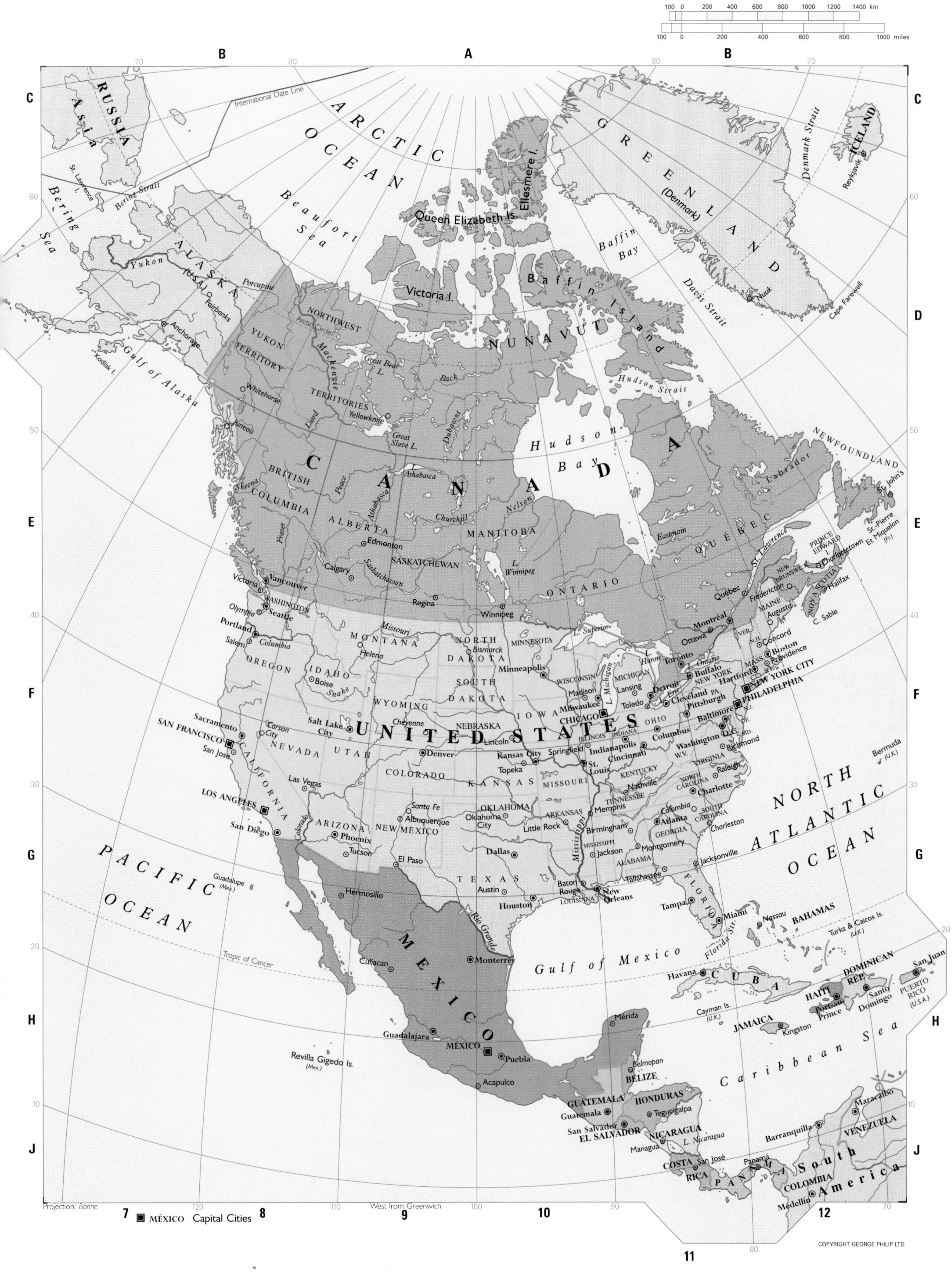

100 0 200 400 600 800 1000 1200 1400 km
100 0 200 400 600 800 1000 miles
ARCTIC OCEAN
RUSSIA
Asia
International Date Line
Bering Strait
Bering Sea
St. Lawrence I.
Beaufort Sea
Queen Elizabeth Is.
Ellesmere I.
GREENLAND (Denmark)
Denmark Strait
ICELAND
Reykjavik
Baffin Bay
Baffin Island
Davis Strait
Nuuk
Cape Farewell
ALASKA (U.S.A.)
Yukon
Porcupine
Fairbanks
Anchorage
Kodiak I.
Gulf of Alaska
Victoria I.
NORTHWEST TERRITORIES
Arctic Circle
YUKON TERRITORY
Mackenzie
Great Bear L.
Back
NUNAVUT
Hudson Strait
Whitehorse
Juneau
Yellowknife
Liard
Great Slave L.
Dubawnt
Hudson Bay
CANADA
NEWFOUNDLAND
Labrador
St. John's
BRITISH COLUMBIA
Skeena
Peace
Athabasca
Churchill
Nelson
ALBERTA
MANITOBA
Fraser
Edmonton
SASKATCHEWAN
Saskatchewan
Calgary
L. Winnipeg
Eastmain
QUÉBEC
St. Lawrence
PRINCE EDWARD I.
Charlottetown
St.-Pierre Et Miquelon (Fr.)
NEW BRUNSWICK
NOVA SCOTIA
Halifax
Fredericton
Québec
Victoria
Vancouver
Regina
Winnipeg
ONTARIO
MAINE
Augusta
C. Sable
WASHINGTON
Olympia
Seattle
Missouri
L. Superior
Montréal
Ottawa
Portland
Salem
Columbia
MONTANA
Helena
NORTH DAKOTA
Bismarck
MINNESOTA
OREGON
IDAHO
Boise
Snake
SOUTH DAKOTA
Minneapolis
WISCONSIN
L. Michigan
MICHIGAN
L. Huron
Toronto
L. Ontario
Buffalo
NEW YORK
Concord
Boston
Providence
Hartford
NEW YORK CITY
PHILADELPHIA
WYOMING
Madison
Lansing
Detroit
Toledo
L. Erie
Cleveland
Pittsburgh
PA.
Milwaukee
CHICAGO
IOWA
OHIO
Baltimore
Sacramento
SAN FRANCISCO
San José
Carson City
NEVADA
Salt Lake City
UNITED STATES
Cheyenne
NEBRASKA
Lincoln
ILLINOIS
INDIANA
Indianapolis
Columbus
Washington D.C.
Richmond
UTAH
Denver
Kansas City
Springfield
Cincinnati
W.V.
VIRGINIA
Bermuda (U.K.)
CALIFORNIA
COLORADO
Topeka
St. Louis
KENTUCKY
Raleigh
NORTH CAROLINA
Charlotte
Las Vegas
KANSAS
MISSOURI
Nashville
TENNESSEE
NORTH ATLANTIC OCEAN
LOS ANGELES
Santa Fe
OKLAHOMA
Oklahoma City
ARKANSAS
Memphis
Columbia
SOUTH CAROLINA
Albuquerque
Atlanta
San Diego
Colorado
ARIZONA
NEW MEXICO
Little Rock
Birmingham
GEORGIA
Charleston
Phoenix
MISSISSIPPI
Mississippi
Jackson
Montgomery
Tucson
El Paso
Dallas
ALABAMA
Jacksonville
PACIFIC OCEAN
Guadalupe (Mex.)
TEXAS
Tallahassee
Austin
Baton Rouge
New Orleans
LOUISIANA
FLORIDA
Hermosillo
Houston
Tampa
Miami
Nassau
BAHAMAS
Rio Grande
Florida Str.
Turks & Caicos Is. (U.K.)
Tropic of Cancer
MEXICO
Culiacan
Monterrey
Gulf of Mexico
Havana
CUBA
DOMINICAN REP.
San Juan
HAITI
Port-au-Prince
Santo Domingo
PUERTO RICO (U.S.A.)
Cayman Is. (U.K.)
Mérida
JAMAICA
Kingston
Guadalajara
MÉXICO
Puebla
Caribbean Sea
Revilla Gigedo Is. (Mex.)
Belmopan
BELIZE
Acapulco
GUATEMALA
HONDURAS
Maracaibo
Guatemala
Tegucigalpa
VENEZUELA
San Salvador
EL SALVADOR
NICARAGUA
L. Nicaragua
Barranquilla
Managua
COSTA RICA
San José
Panamá
PANAMA
South America
COLOMBIA
Medellín
Projection: Bonne
West from Greenwich
■ MÉXICO Capital Cities
COPYRIGHT GEORGE PHILIP LTD.

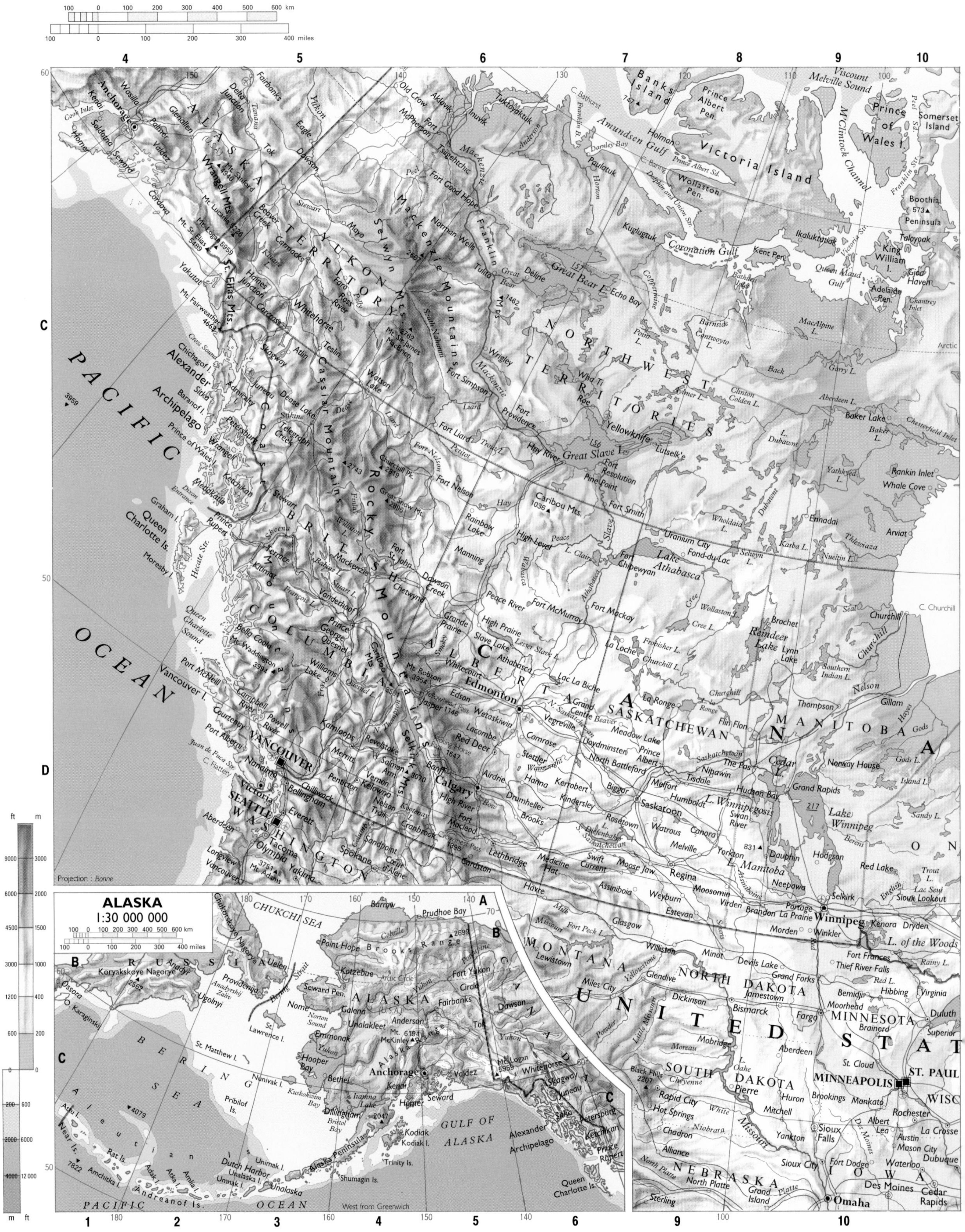

PACIFIC OCEAN

ALASKA

YUKON TERRITORY

NORTHWEST TERRITORIES

Victoria Island

Banks Island

Prince of Wales I.

Somerset Island

Boothia Peninsula

Great Bear L.

Great Slave L.

BRITISH COLUMBIA

ALBERTA

SASKATCHEWAN

MANITOBA

Lake Athabasca

Reindeer Lake

L. Winnipeg

Edmonton

Calgary

VANCOUVER

SEATTLE

WASHINGTON

MONTANA

NORTH DAKOTA

SOUTH DAKOTA

NEBRASKA

MINNESOTA

IOWA

WINNIPEG

MINNEAPOLIS ST. PAUL

UNITED STATES

Omaha

ALASKA
1:30 000 000

RUSSIA

CHUKCHI SEA

BERING SEA

ALASKA (U.S.A.)

Anchorage

GULF OF ALASKA

PACIFIC OCEAN

West from Greenwich

Projection : Bonne

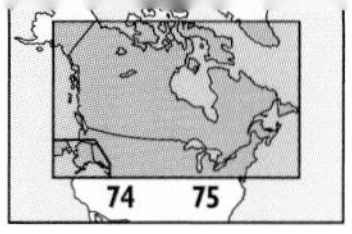

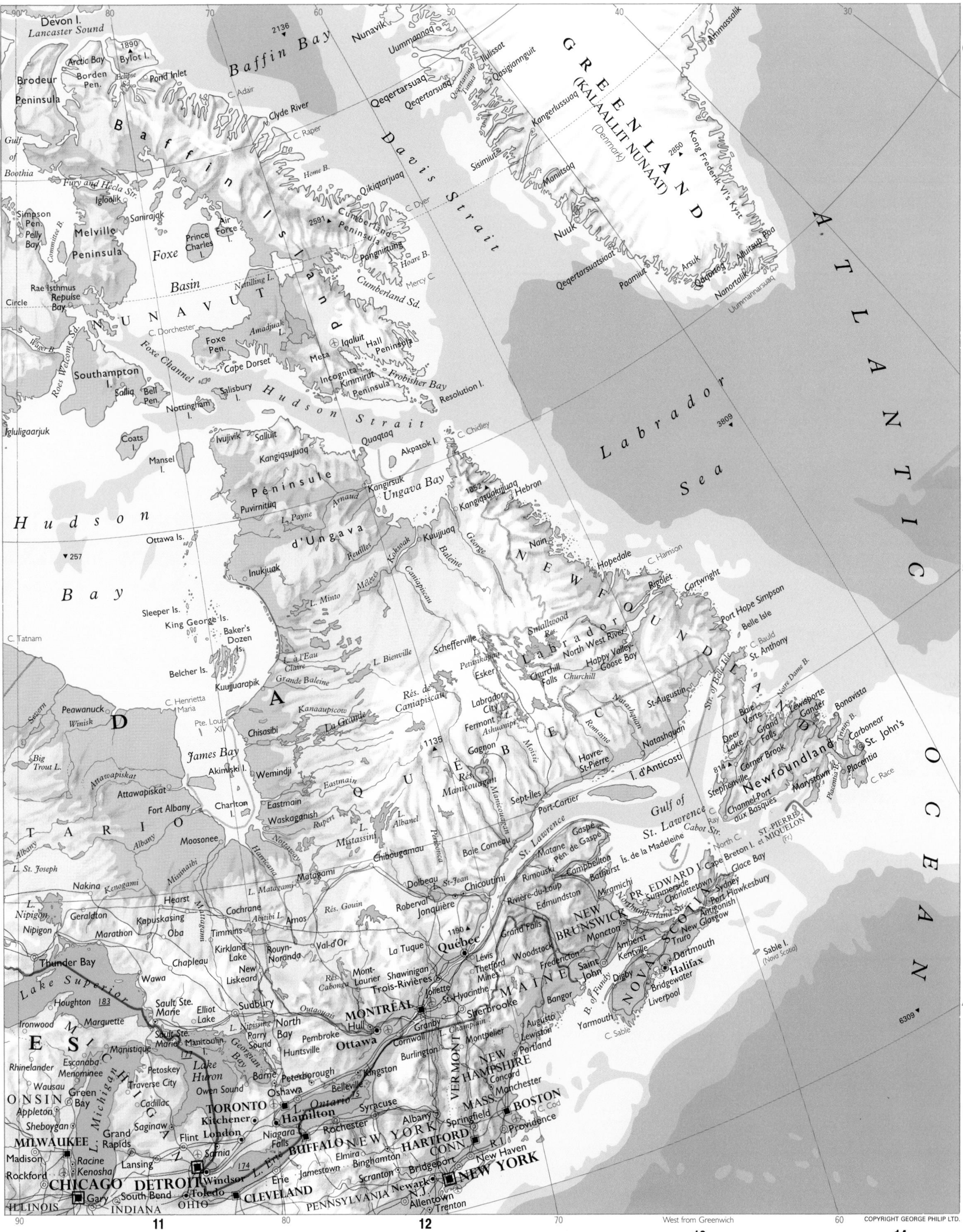

B

Devon I.
Lancaster Sound
2136
1890 Bylot I.
Baffin Bay
Nunavik
Uummannad
Upernavik
Ilulissat
Qasigiannguit
Ahmassalik
60

Arctic Bay
Borden
Pen.
Brodeur
Peninsula
Pond Inlet
C. Adair
Clyde River
Qeqertarsuaq
Qeqertarsuaq
Ritenbenk
Qasigiannguit
G R E E N L A N D
(KALAALLIT NUNAAT)
(Denmark)
2850
Kong Frederik VI's Kyst
Ahmassalik

Gulf
of
Boothia
Fury and Hecla Str.
Igloolik
C. Raper
Home B.
Qikiqtarjuaq
Sisimiut
Kangerlussuaq
Maniitsoq
Arsuk

Simpson
Pen.
Pelly
Bay
Melville
Peninsula
Sanirajak
Air
Force I.
Prince
Charles
I.
Cumberland
Peninsula
2591
C. Dyer
Pangnirtung
Hoare B.
Nuuk
Qeqertarsuatsiaat
Paamiut
Qaqortoq
Nanortalik
Muttsub Baa
Uummannarsuaq
C

Repulse
Bay
Rae Isthmus
Circle
C. Dorchester
Foxe
Basin
Southampton
I.
Nettilling L.
Amadjuak
Foxe
Pen.
Iqaluit
Meta
Incognita
Kimmirut
Peninsula
Hall
Peninsula
Cumberland Sd.
Mercy C.
Frobisher Bay
Resolution I.

D a v i s S t r a i t

A T L A N T I C

Wager B.
Iglugaarjuk
Coats
I.
Mansel
I.
Cape Dorset
Salisbury
I.
Nottingham
I.
Ivujivik
Salluit
Quaqtaq
C. Chidley
Akpatok I.
H u d s o n S t r a i t
Labrador
Sea
3809
50

Iglugaarjuk
Southampton
I.
Salliq
Bell
Pen.
King George Is.
Baker's
Dozen
Is.
Kangiqsujuaq
Kangirsuk
Ungava Bay
Kangiqsualujjuaq
Hebron
1852
Nain
Hopedale
C. Harrison
Cartwright

C. Tatnam
Peawanuck
Winisk
C. Henrietta
Maria
Sleeper Is.
Belcher Is.
P é n i n s u l e
d'U n g a v a
Puvirnituq
Inukjuak
Arnaud
L. Payne
Renilles
Kuujjuaq
Balene
George
N
E
W
F
O
U
N
D
L
A
N
D
Rigolet
Port Hope Simpson
Belle Isle

H u d s o n
B a y
257
Ottawa Is.
L. Minto
L. Bienville
Scefferville
Esker
Smallwood
Res.
North West River
Happy Valley
Goose Bay
Churchill
St-Augustin
L
A
B
R
A
D
O
R
St. Anthony
Strait of Belle Isle
Notre Dame B.
Lewisporte
Gander
Bonavista

Big
Trout L.
Kuujjuarapik
I. à l'Eau Claire
La Grande
Rés. de
Caniapiscau
Labrador
City
Fermont
Ashuanipi
Romaine
Natashquan
Deer
Lake
Baie
Verte
Grand
Falls
Carbonear
St. John's

Severn
Attawapiskat
C. Tatnam
James Bay
Akimiski I.
Grande Baleine
Chisasibi
Eastmain
Wemindji
Kanaaupscow
Q U É B E C
1135
Gagnon
Havre-
St-Pierre
I. d'Anticosti
Corner Brook
Stephenville
Channel-Port
aux Basques
Marystown
Placentia
C. Race

Albany
L. St. Joseph
Fort Albany
Moosonee
Waskaganish
Charlton
Eastmain
Rupert
Albanel
Mistassini
Chibougamau
Pontbriand
Manicouagan
Baie Comeau
Sept-Îles
Port-Cartier
Gaspé
Pen. de Gaspé
Gulf of
St. Lawrence
Îs. de la Madeleine
North C.
Cabot Str.
Glace Bay
ST-PIERRE
et MIQUELON
(Fr)

O N T A R I O
Nakina
Kenogami
Hearst
Cochrane
L. Matagami
Amos
Rés. Gouin
Roberval
St-Jean
Chicoutimi
Jonquière
Rimouski
Matane
Campbellton
Bathurst
Miramichi
PR. EDWARD I.
Summerside
Charlottetown
Northumberland Str.
Sydney
Antigonish
Port Hawkesbury
Sable I.
(Nova Scotia)
6309
40

L. Nipigon
Geraldton
Marathon
Nipigon
Oba
Timmins
Kirkland
Lake
New
Liskeard
Val-d'Or
La Tuque
Québec
Lévis
Thetford
Mines
Grand Falls
Woodstock
Edmundston
Fredericton
N E W
B R U N S W I C K
Moncton
Amherst
Kentville
New Glasgow
N
O
V
A
S
C
O
T
I
A
Dartmouth
Halifax

Thunder Bay
Lake Superior
Houghton 183
Marquette
Sault Ste.
Marie
Elliot
Lake
Sudbury
Chapleau
Wawa
Rouyn-
Noranda
Rés.
Mont-
Cabonga
Mont-
Laurier
Shawinigan
Trois-Rivières
Joliette
St-Hyacinthe
Sherbrooke
Granby
M
A
I
N
E
Bangor
Augusta
Saint
John
B. of Fundy
Bridgewater
Digby
Liverpool
Yarmouth
C. Sable

M I C H I G A N
Ironwood
Marquette
Escanaba
Manistique
Sault Ste.
Marie
Manitoulin
Georgian
Bay
North
Bay
Parry
Sound
Pembroke
Huntsville
MONTRÉAL
Hull
Ottawa
Cornwall
Burlington
Montpelier
VERMONT
NEW
HAMPSHIRE
Concord
Manchester
Portland
Lewiston
C. Cod

E S
Rhinelander
Menominee
Green
Bay
Traverse City
Cadillac
L.
Huron
Owen Sound
Barrie
Peterborough
Belleville
L. Ontario
Oshawa
TORONTO
Kingston
Syracuse
Albany
Springfield
MASS.
BOSTON
Providence
E

W I S C O N S I N
Appleton
Sheboygan
Green
Bay
Petoskey
L. Michigan
Saginaw
Flint
Kitchener
Hamilton
London
Niagara
Falls
Rochester
Elmira
Binghamton
NEW YORK
Scranton
Springfield
HARTFORD
CONN.
Bridgeport
New Haven
R.I.

Madison
MILWAUKEE
Racine
Kenosha
Lansing
Grand
Rapids
Sarnia
Flint
Windsor
Erie
BUFFALO
Jamestown
Binghamton
Newark
N.J.
NEW YORK

Rockford
CHICAGO
DETROIT
Toledo
CLEVELAND
PENNSYLVANIA
Allentown
Trenton
ILLINOIS
Gary
South Bend
INDIANA
OHIO
174

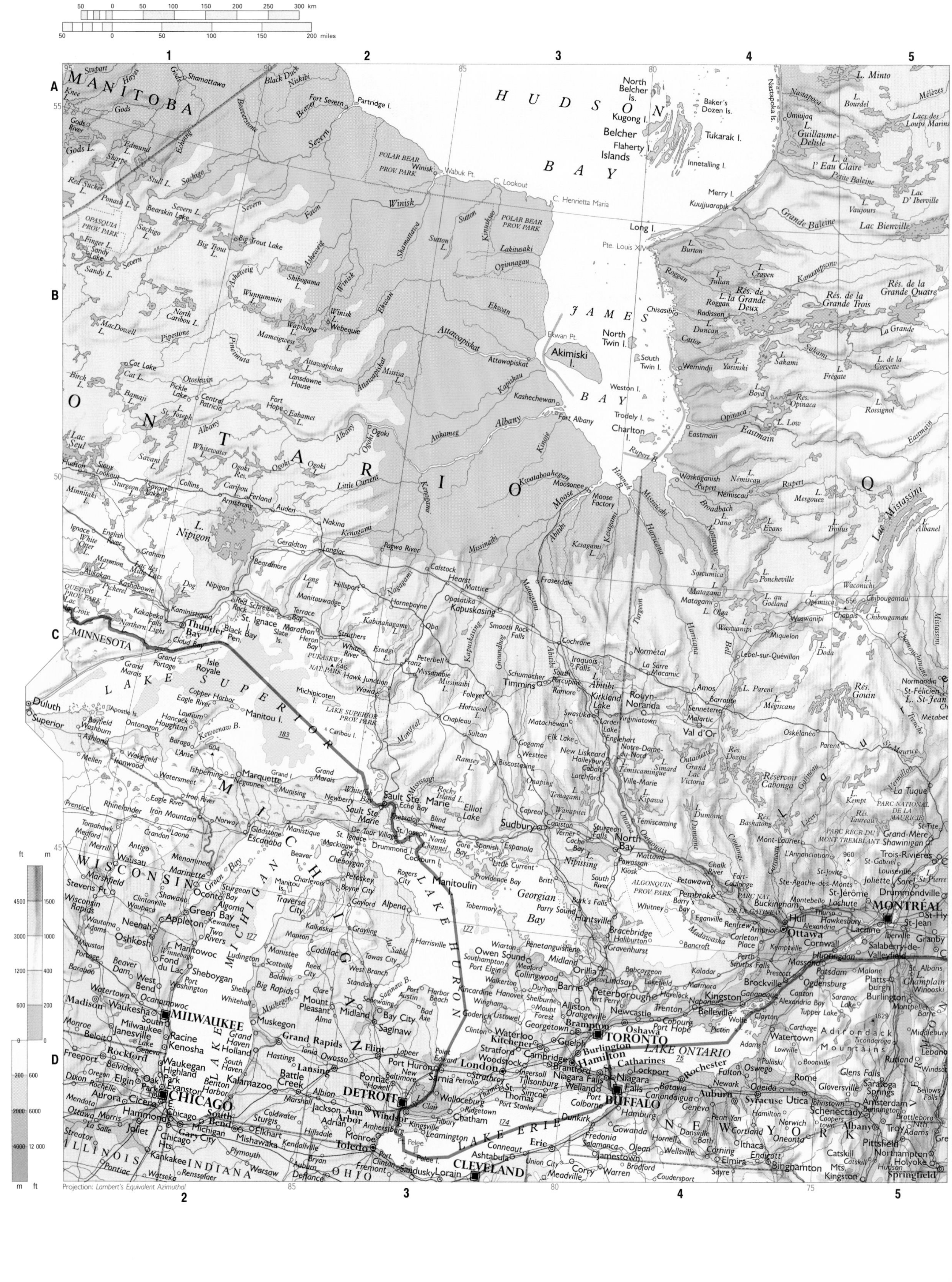
50 0 50 100 150 200 250 300 km
50 0 50 100 150 200 miles
1 2 3 4 5
A B C D
MANITOBA
ONTARIO
HUDSON BAY
JAMES BAY
MINNESOTA
WISCONSIN
MICHIGAN
ILLINOIS
INDIANA
OHIO
NEW YORK
LAKE SUPERIOR
LAKE MICHIGAN
LAKE HURON
LAKE ONTARIO
LAKE ERIE
Georgian Bay
Belcher Islands
Akimiski I.
North Belcher Is.
Flaherty I.
Kugong I.
Tukarak I.
Baker's Dozen Is.
Long I.
Charlton I.
North Twin I.
South Twin I.
C. Henrietta Maria
C. Lookout
POLAR BEAR PROV. PARK
OPASQUIA PROV. PARK
QUETICO PROV. PARK
PUKASKWA NAT. PARK
LAKE SUPERIOR PROV. PARK
ALGONQUIN PROV. PARK
Gods L.
Big Trout Lake
Sandy Lake
Pickle Lake
Fort Severn
Winisk
Attawapiskat
Fort Albany
Moosonee
Moose Factory
Kashechewan
Lac Seul
Sioux Lookout
L. Nipigon
Nipigon
Thunder Bay
Geraldton
Longlac
Hearst
Kapuskasing
Cochrane
Timmins
Kirkland Lake
Rouyn-Noranda
Val d'Or
Amos
Chibougamau
Chisasibi
Radisson
Eastmain
Wemindji
Kuujjuarapik
Umiujaq
Lac Mistassini
Rés. Gouin
Réservoir Cabonga
Duluth
Superior
Marquette
Sault Ste Marie
Sudbury
North Bay
Timiskaming
Manitoulin
Parry Sound
Huntsville
Pembroke
Ottawa
Hull
MONTRÉAL
Trois-Rivières
La Tuque
Shawinigan
Sherbrooke
Kingston
Belleville
Peterborough
Barrie
Orillia
Owen Sound
TORONTO
Oshawa
Hamilton
Brampton
Kitchener
Waterloo
Guelph
London
Sarnia
Windsor
DETROIT
Flint
Saginaw
Lansing
Grand Rapids
Kalamazoo
MILWAUKEE
Madison
CHICAGO
Gary
Toledo
CLEVELAND
Erie
BUFFALO
Niagara Falls
St. Catharines
Rochester
Syracuse
Utica
Albany
Schenectady
Watertown
Binghamton
Green Bay
Appleton
Oshkosh
Sheboygan
Ft. Pittsfield
Springfield
Adirondack Mountains
Projection: Lambert's Equivalent Azimuthal
95 90 85 80 75
55 50 45
ft m
4500 1500
3000 1000
1200 400
600 200
0 0
200 600
2000 6000
4000 12 000

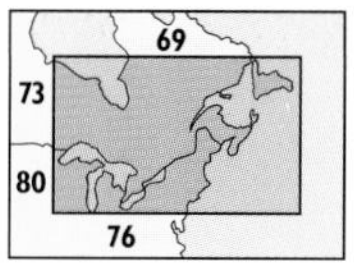
69
73
80
76

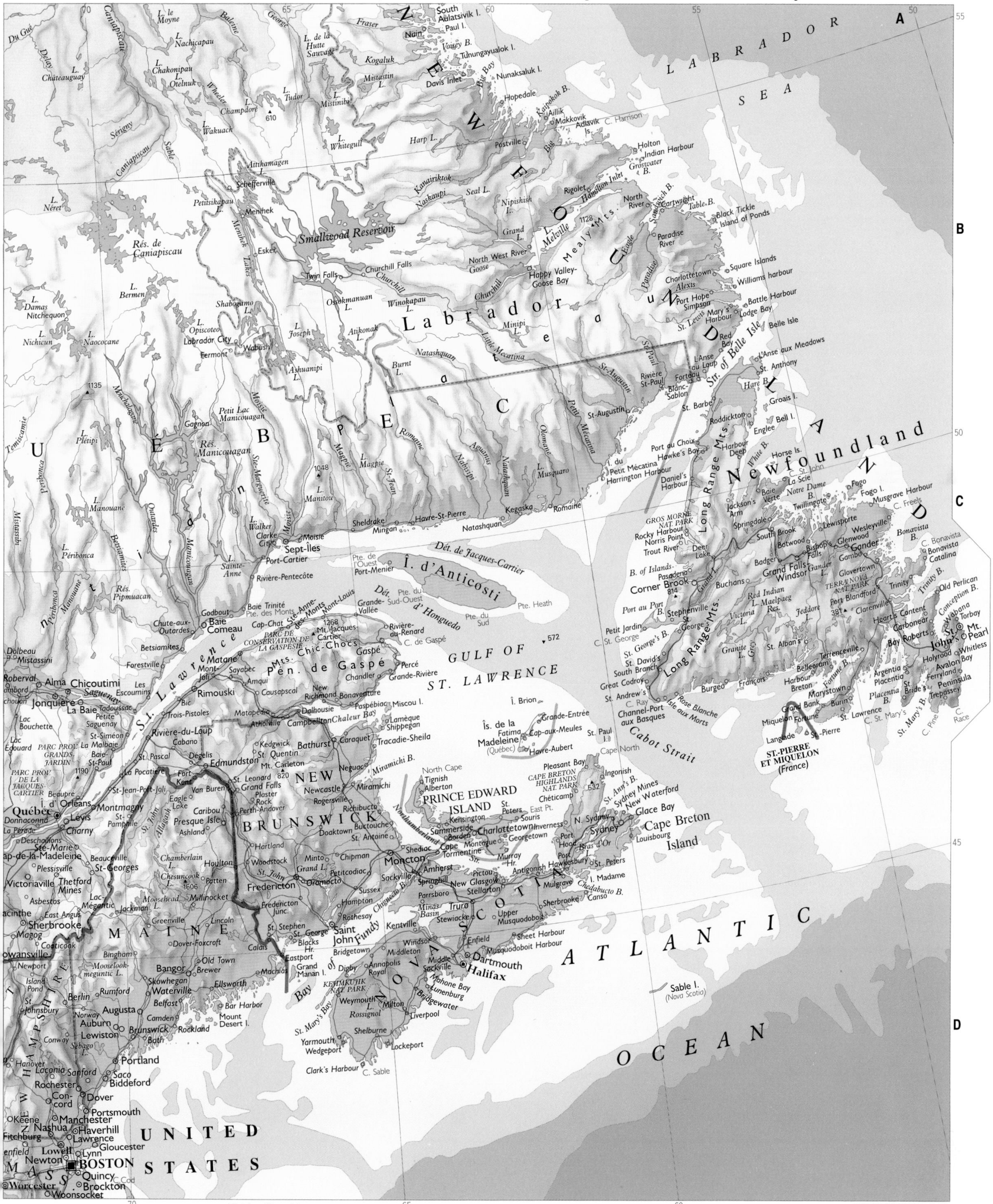
6
7
8
9
A
B
C
D
L A B R A D O R
S E A
N E W F O U N D L A N D
Labrador
Newfoundland
Q U É B E C
GULF OF
ST. LAWRENCE
Î. d'Anticosti
NEW
BRUNSWICK
PRINCE EDWARD
ISLAND
NOVA SCOTIA
Cape Breton
Island
M A I N E
UNITED
STATES
A T L A N T I C
O C E A N
ST.-PIERRE
ET MIQUELON
(France)
Smallwood Reservoir
St. Lawrence
Cabot Strait
Str. of Belle Isle
Bay of Fundy
Long Range Mts.
Mealy Mts.
Nain
Hopedale
Postville
Happy Valley-
Goose Bay
Churchill Falls
Labrador City
Schefferville
Sept-Îles
Baie Comeau
Chicoutimi
Québec
Rimouski
Gaspé
Moncton
Fredericton
Saint John
Charlottetown
Halifax
Dartmouth
Sydney
Corner Brook
Gander
St. John's
Grand Falls
Windsor
Stephenville
Bangor
Augusta
Portland
BOSTON
Sable I.
(Nova Scotia)
Î[s]. de la
Madeleine
(Québec)
West from Greenwich
70
65
60
55
50
45

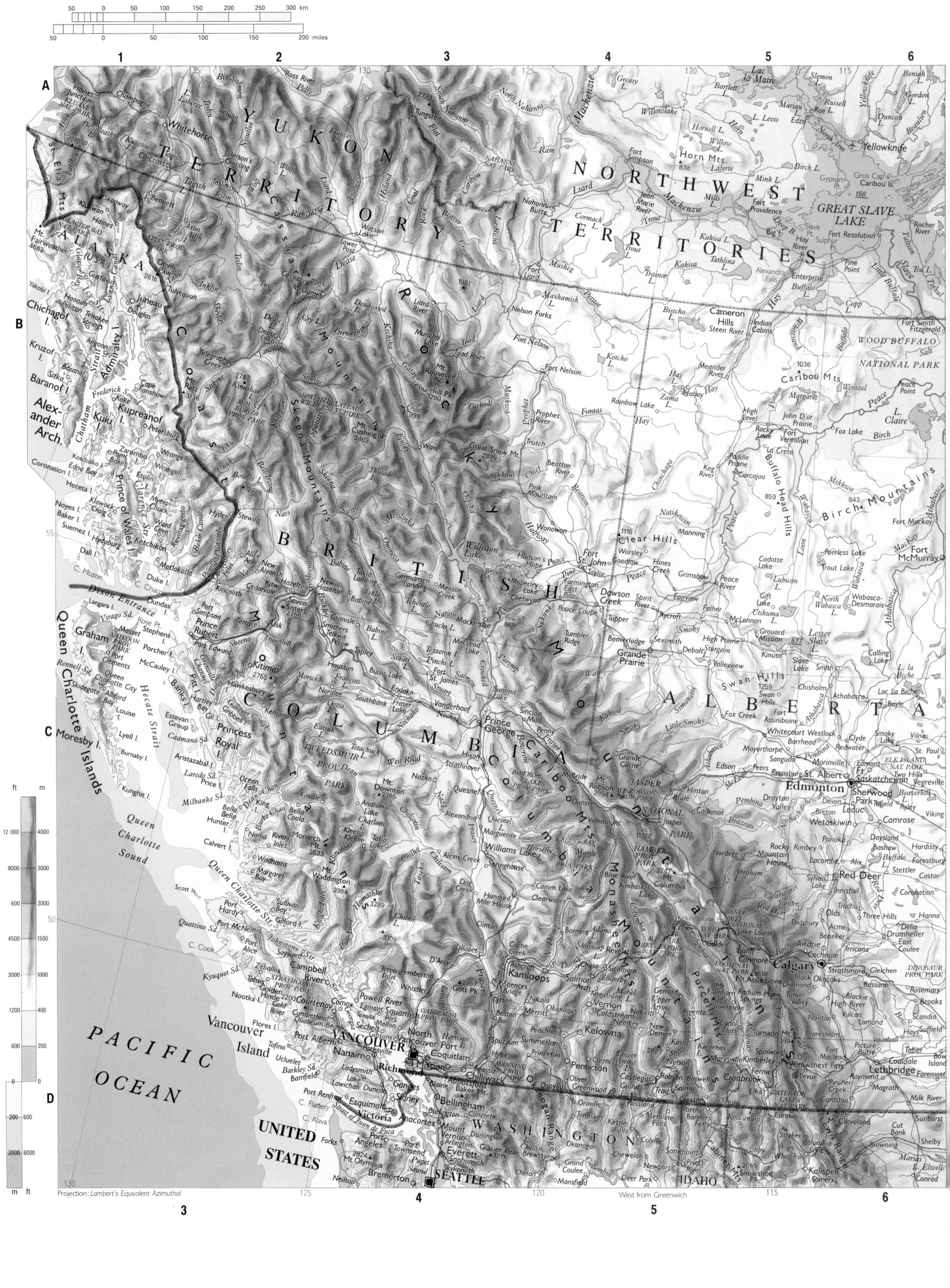

PACIFIC

OCEAN

UNITED

STATES

Projection: Lambert's Equivalent Azimuthal

West from Greenwich

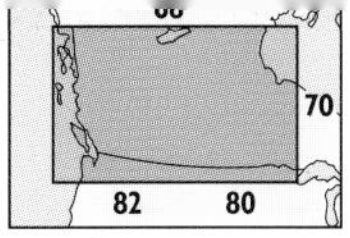

A

B

C

D

HUDSON

BAY

NUNAVUT

MANITOBA

SASKATCHEWAN

ONTARIO

MINNESOTA

NORTH DAKOTA

MONTANA

Lake Athabasca

LAKE WINNIPEG

Lake Winnipegosis

Cedar Lake

Winnipeg

Regina

Saskatoon

Prince Albert

Moose Jaw

Medicine Hat

Reindeer Lake

Brandon

Churchill

Thompson

Yorkton

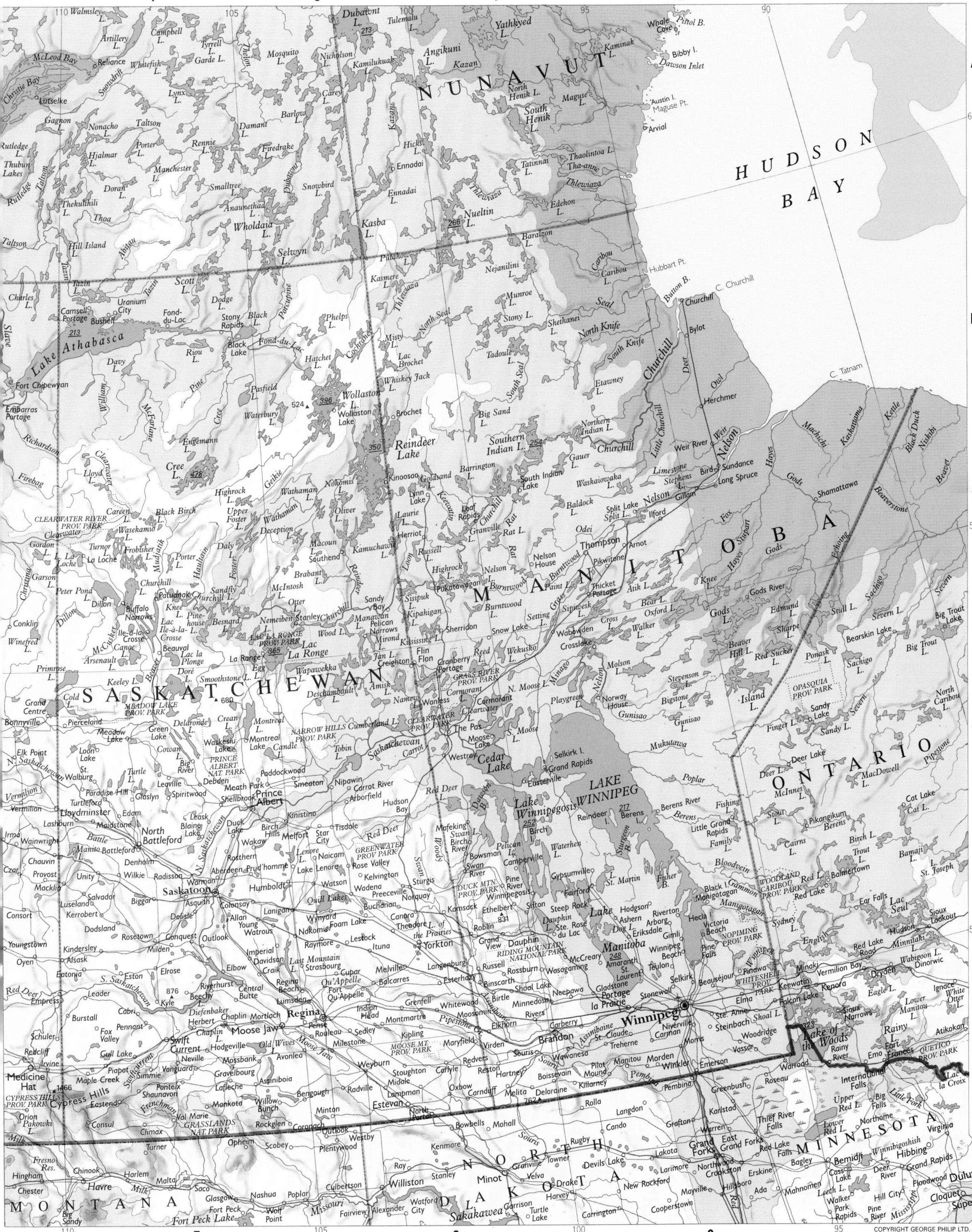

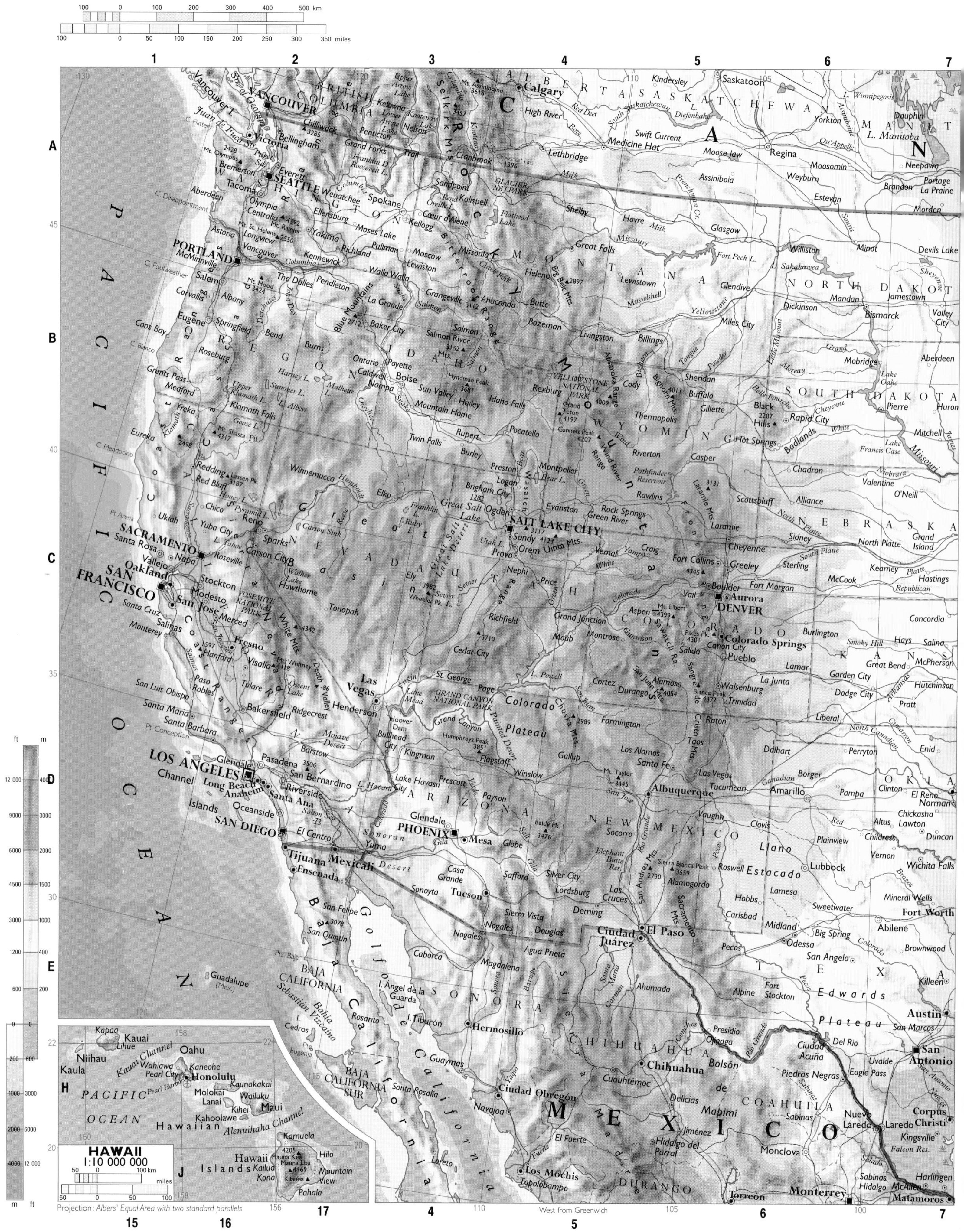

100 0 100 200 300 400 500 km
100 0 50 100 150 200 250 300 350 miles

| | 1 | 2 | 3 | 4 | 5 | 6 | 7 |

CANADA

BRITISH COLUMBIA · ALBERTA · SASKATCHEWAN · MANITOBA

Vancouver I. · VANCOUVER · Victoria · Bellingham · Kelowna · Penticton · Grand Forks · Trail · Cranbrook · Calgary · High River · Lethbridge · Medicine Hat · Swift Current · Moose Jaw · Regina · Moosomin · Yorkton · Neepawa · L. Manitoba · Brandon · La Prairie · Portage · Morden

Kindersley · Saskatoon · Diefenbaker · Red Deer · Assiniboia · Weyburn · Estevan · Williston · Minot · Devils Lake

WASHINGTON

Aberdeen · Olympia · Centralia · SEATTLE · Tacoma · Everett · Bremerton · Mt. Olympus 2428 · Wenatchee · Spokane · Sandpoint · Kalispell · Shelby · Havre · Glasgow · Glendive

OREGON

PORTLAND · Salem · McMinnville · Corvallis · Albany · Eugene · Springfield · Bend · Burns · Roseburg · Coos Bay · Grants Pass · Medford · Klamath Falls · Ontario · Caldwell · Nampa · Boise · Mountain Home

Astoria · Vancouver · The Dalles · Pendleton · Walla Walla · Lewiston · Moscow · Pullman · Grangeville · La Grande · Baker City · Salmon · Anaconda · Butte · Bozeman · Livingston · Billings · Miles City · Dickinson · Mandan · Bismarck · Jamestown · Valley City · Aberdeen

MONTANA · Great Falls · Helena · Lewistown · Musselshell · Sheridan · Buffalo · Gillette · Rapid City

IDAHO · Salmon River · Sun Valley · Hailey · Idaho Falls · Rexburg · Twin Falls · Burley · Rupert · Pocatello · Preston · Montpelier

WYOMING · Yellowstone National Park · Grand Teton 4197 · Gannett Peak 4207 · Cody · Thermopolis · Hot Springs · Riverton · Casper · Rawlins · Laramie · Cheyenne

NORTH DAKOTA · **SOUTH DAKOTA** · Pierre · Huron · Mitchell · Chadron · Valentine · O'Neill

NEBRASKA · Scottsbluff · Alliance · North Platte · Kearney · Hastings · McCook · Grand Island

CALIFORNIA

Eureka · Redding · Red Bluff · Chico · Ukiah · Santa Rosa · Napa · Vallejo · SACRAMENTO · Stockton · Roseville · Oakland · SAN FRANCISCO · San Jose · Modesto · Merced · Santa Cruz · Salinas · Monterey · Fresno · Visalia · Hanford · Tulare · Bakersfield · Ridgecrest · San Luis Obispo · Paso Robles · Santa Maria · Santa Barbara · LOS ANGELES · Glendale · Pasadena · San Bernardino · Riverside · Long Beach · Anaheim · Santa Ana · Oceanside · SAN DIEGO · El Centro · Mt. Whitney 4418

NEVADA · Reno · Sparks · Carson City · Winnemucca · Elko · Ely · Tonopah · Las Vegas · Henderson

UTAH · Great Salt Lake · Ogden · SALT LAKE CITY · Sandy · Orem · Provo · Nephi · Price · Richfield · Cedar City · St. George · Moab

COLORADO · Grand Junction · Montrose · Aspen · Vail · Boulder · Aurora · DENVER · Fort Collins · Greeley · Sterling · Colorado Springs · Pueblo · Cañon City · Alamosa · Durango · Cortez · Trinidad · Walsenburg · La Junta · Lamar

KANSAS · Garden City · Dodge City · Liberal · Hutchinson · Pratt · Great Bend · McPherson · Salina · Hays · Burlington

ARIZONA · Kingman · Lake Havasu City · Bullhead City · Flagstaff · Prescott · Winslow · Payson · Globe · PHOENIX · Glendale · Mesa · Yuma · Casa Grande · Tucson · Safford · Nogales · Sierra Vista · Douglas · Grand Canyon National Park · Humphreys Peak 3851 · Mt. Taylor 3445

NEW MEXICO · Gallup · Los Alamos · Santa Fe · Las Vegas · Albuquerque · Socorro · Silver City · Lordsburg · Deming · Las Cruces · Alamogordo · Roswell · Carlsbad · Hobbs · Clovis · Tucumcari · Raton

TEXAS · El Paso · Dalhart · Amarillo · Pampa · Borger · Perryton · Lubbock · Midland · Odessa · Big Spring · San Angelo · Abilene · Sweetwater · Fort Worth · Wichita Falls · Vernon · Childress · Plainview · Lamesa · Pecos · Fort Stockton · Alpine · Del Rio · Austin · San Antonio · Corpus Christi · Brownsville · Harlingen · McAllen · Matamoros · Laredo · Nuevo Laredo

OKLAHOMA · El Reno · Norman · Chickasha · Lawton · Altus · Duncan · Clinton · Enid

MEXICO

BAJA CALIFORNIA · BAJA CALIFORNIA SUR · Tijuana · Mexicali · Ensenada · San Felipe · San Quintin · Guadalupe (Mex.) · Isla Cedros · Bahía Vizcaíno · Santa Rosalía · Loreto

SONORA · Nogales · Caborca · Magdalena · Hermosillo · Guaymas · Ciudad Obregón · Navojoa · Los Mochis · Topolobampo · El Fuerte

CHIHUAHUA · Ciudad Juárez · Chihuahua · Cuauhtémoc · Delicias · Hidalgo del Parral · Ojinaga · Presidio

COAHUILA · Ciudad Acuña · Piedras Negras · Eagle Pass · Nuevo Laredo · Monclova · Sabinas · Torreón · Bolsón de Mapimí

DURANGO · NUEVO LEÓN · Monterrey

PACIFIC OCEAN

HAWAII 1:10 000 000

Kauai · Kapaa · Lihue · Niihau · Kaula · Oahu · Wahiawa · Pearl City · Honolulu · Kaneohe · Kaunakakai · Molokai · Lanai · Wailuku · Kihei · Maui · Kahoolawe · Hawaiian Islands · Mauna Kea 4205 · Mauna Loa 4169 · Kilauea · Hilo · Mountain View · Pahala · Kona · Kailua · Kamuela

PACIFIC OCEAN

Kauai Channel · Kaiwi Channel · Pailolo Channel · Alenuihaha Channel

Projection: Albers' Equal Area with two standard parallels

West from Greenwich

ft / m elevation scale: 12 000 / 4000 · 9000 / 3000 · 6000 / 2000 · 4500 / 1500 · 3000 / 1000 · 1200 / 400 · 0 / 0 · 200 / 600 · 600 / 2000 · 1000 / 3000 · 2000 / 6000 · 4000 / 12 000

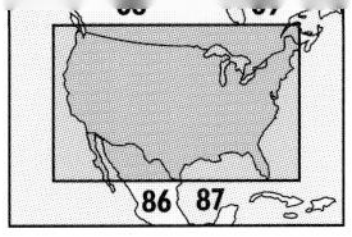
86 87

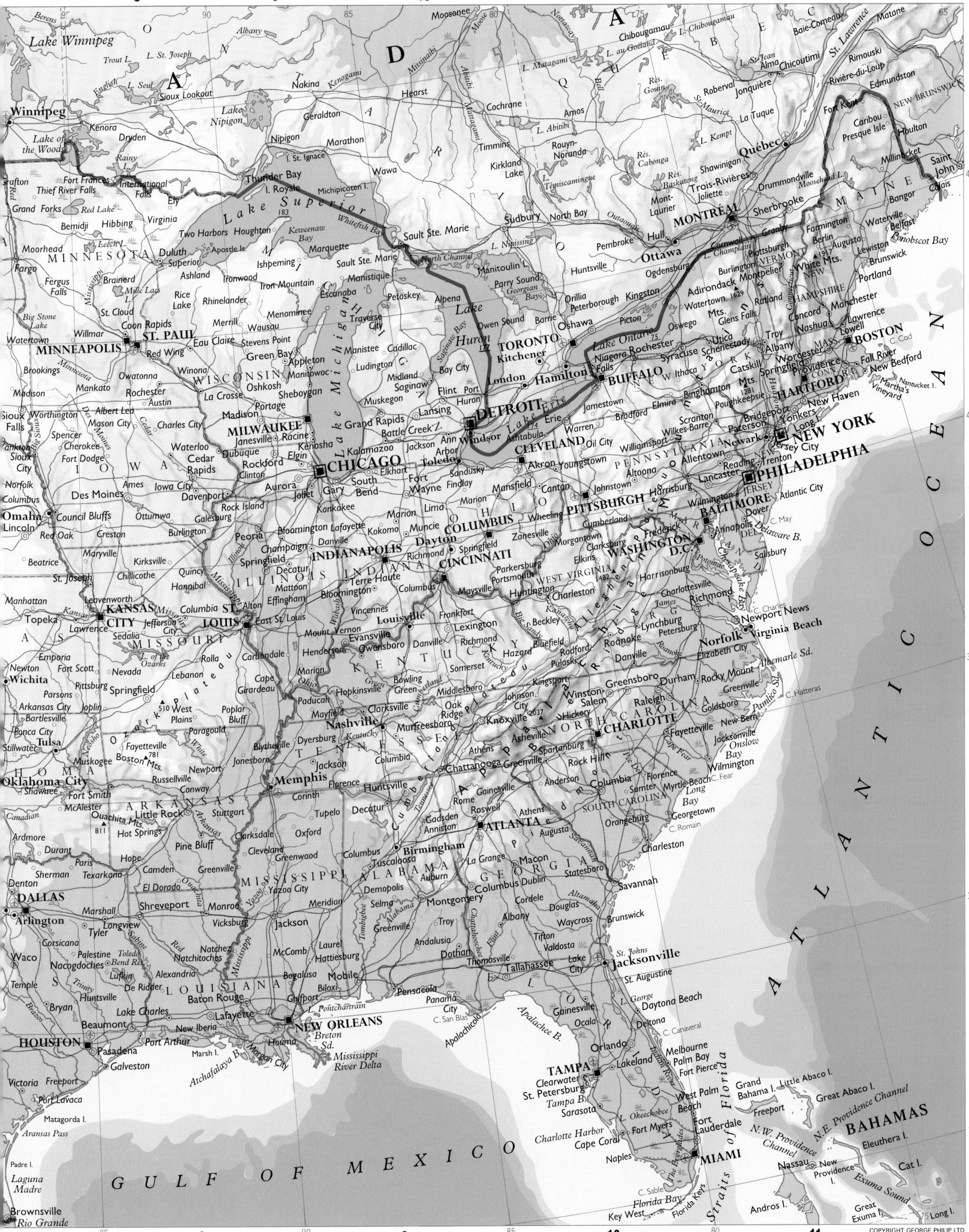
8 9 10 11 12 13
A B C D E F
CANADA
ONTARIO
QUEBEC
NEW BRUNSWICK
Lake Winnipeg
Winnipeg
Lake of the Woods
Kenora
Dryden
Sioux Lookout
Lake Nipigon
Nipigon
Thunder Bay
Lake Superior
Geraldton
Hearst
Marathon
Wawa
Moosonee
Cochrane
Timmins
Kirkland Lake
Amos
Rouyn-Noranda
Chibougamau
Roberval
Jonquière
Chicoutimi
Baie-Comeau
Rimouski
Rivière-du-Loup
Edmundston
Matane
St. Lawrence
La Tuque
Québec
Trois-Rivières
Drummondville
Sherbrooke
Shawinigan
MONTRÉAL
Ottawa
Hull
Pembroke
North Bay
Sudbury
Sault Ste. Marie
Huntsville
Parry Sound
Georgian Bay
Owen Sound
Barrie
Orillia
Peterborough
Kingston
Oshawa
TORONTO
Kitchener
Hamilton
London
Windsor
Lake Huron
Lake Ontario
Lake Erie
Lake Michigan
MINNESOTA
WISCONSIN
MICHIGAN
IOWA
ILLINOIS
INDIANA
OHIO
MISSOURI
KENTUCKY
TENNESSEE
ARKANSAS
MISSISSIPPI
ALABAMA
GEORGIA
LOUISIANA
FLORIDA
NORTH CAROLINA
SOUTH CAROLINA
VIRGINIA
WEST VIRGINIA
PENNSYLVANIA
NEW YORK
VERMONT
NEW HAMPSHIRE
MAINE
MASS.
CONN.
R.I.
NEW JERSEY
DEL.
MD.
MINNEAPOLIS
ST. PAUL
Duluth
Superior
Fargo
Moorhead
Grand Forks
Bemidji
Hibbing
Virginia
Brainerd
St. Cloud
Rochester
Mankato
Austin
Eau Claire
La Crosse
Green Bay
Appleton
Oshkosh
Manitowoc
Sheboygan
Madison
MILWAUKEE
Racine
Kenosha
CHICAGO
Rockford
Aurora
Joliet
Gary
South Bend
Elkhart
Fort Wayne
Toledo
DETROIT
Flint
Saginaw
Lansing
Grand Rapids
Kalamazoo
Battle Creek
Ann Arbor
Jackson
CLEVELAND
Akron
Youngstown
Canton
Mansfield
Erie
Buffalo
Niagara Falls
Rochester
Syracuse
Utica
Schenectady
Albany
Troy
Binghamton
Elmira
Ithaca
Plattsburgh
Burlington
Montpelier
Portland
Augusta
Bangor
Lewiston
BOSTON
Worcester
Springfield
Providence
HARTFORD
New Haven
Bridgeport
Yonkers
NEW YORK
Jersey City
Newark
Paterson
Trenton
PHILADELPHIA
Allentown
Reading
Lancaster
Harrisburg
Scranton
Wilkes-Barre
Williamsport
Altoona
Johnstown
PITTSBURGH
Wheeling
Wilmington
BALTIMORE
Dover
Atlantic City
Annapolis
WASHINGTON D.C.
Frederick
Cumberland
Morgantown
Clarksburg
Elkins
Parkersburg
Charleston
Huntington
Richmond
Charlottesville
Harrisonburg
Lynchburg
Roanoke
Petersburg
Newport News
Norfolk
Virginia Beach
Elizabeth City
Durham
Raleigh
Greensboro
Winston-Salem
CHARLOTTE
Fayetteville
Wilmington
Goldsboro
Greenville
New Bern
Jacksonville
Asheville
Knoxville
Chattanooga
Nashville
Murfreesboro
Clarksville
Jackson
Memphis
Huntsville
Birmingham
Tuscaloosa
Montgomery
Mobile
Dothan
ATLANTA
Athens
Macon
Augusta
Columbus
Savannah
Columbia
Charleston
Greenville
Spartanburg
Brunswick
Jacksonville
Tallahassee
Pensacola
Gainesville
Ocala
Daytona Beach
Orlando
TAMPA
St. Petersburg
Lakeland
Sarasota
Fort Myers
Cape Coral
Naples
West Palm Beach
Fort Lauderdale
MIAMI
Key West
Florida Keys
Straits of Florida
L. Okeechobee
C. Canaveral
C. Sable
Florida Bay
BAHAMAS
Grand Bahama I.
Freeport
Great Abaco I.
Nassau
New Providence I.
Eleuthera I.
Cat I.
Exuma Sound
Andros I.
Long I.
N.W. Providence Channel
N.E. Providence Channel
ATLANTIC OCEAN
GULF OF MEXICO
Mississippi River Delta
NEW ORLEANS
Baton Rouge
Lafayette
Lake Charles
Beaumont
Port Arthur
HOUSTON
Pasadena
Galveston
Freeport
Port Lavaca
Victoria
Matagorda I.
Aransas Pass
Padre I.
Laguna Madre
Brownsville
Rio Grande
DALLAS
Arlington
Denton
Sherman
Paris
Texarkana
Tyler
Longview
Marshall
Shreveport
Monroe
Alexandria
Natchez
Vicksburg
Jackson
Hattiesburg
Laurel
Meridian
Gulfport
Biloxi
Little Rock
Pine Bluff
Hot Springs
Fort Smith
Fayetteville
Jonesboro
Oklahoma City
Tulsa
Muskogee
Wichita
Topeka
KANSAS CITY
ST. LOUIS
Springfield
Columbia
Jefferson City
St. Joseph
Omaha
Lincoln
Council Bluffs
Des Moines
Cedar Rapids
Waterloo
Iowa City
Davenport
Dubuque
Sioux City
Sioux Falls
Peoria
Springfield
Champaign
Bloomington
Decatur
INDIANAPOLIS
Terre Haute
Bloomington
Evansville
Louisville
Lexington
Frankfort
CINCINNATI
Dayton
COLUMBUS
Springfield
Lima
Marion
Muncie
Kokomo
Lafayette
Paducah
Bowling Green
Owensboro
Ozark Plateau
Boston Mts.
Ouachita Mts.
Appalachian Mountains
Cumberland Plateau
Allegheny Mts.
Adirondack Mts.
Catskill Mts.
White Mts.
Green Mts.
Cape Cod
Nantucket I.
Martha's Vineyard
Long I.
Cape May
Delaware B.
Chesapeake Bay
C. Charles
Albemarle Sd.
Pamlico Sd.
C. Hatteras
C. Fear
Onslow Bay
Long Bay
C. Romain
Apalachee B.
C. San Blas
Tampa B.
Charlotte Harbor
Breton Sd.
L. Pontchartrain
Atchafalaya B.
Marsh I.
Penobscot Bay
Saint John
Calais
Houlton
Presque Isle
Caribou
45 40 35 30 25
95 90 85 80 75 65
8 9 10 11 12

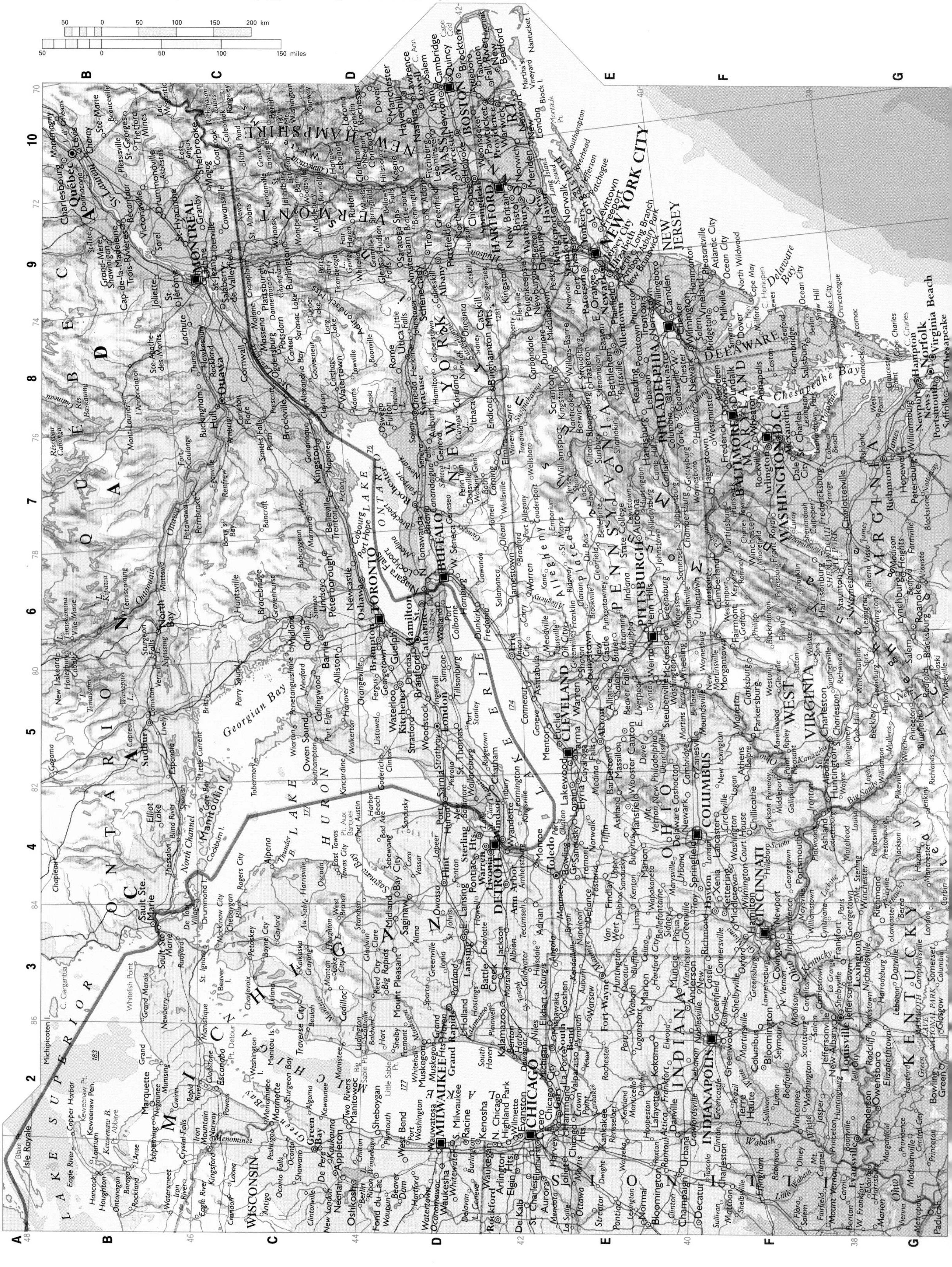
0 50 100 150 200 km
0 50 100 150 miles
ONTARIO
QUÉBEC
NEW YORK
PENNSYLVANIA
OHIO
INDIANA
ILLINOIS
MICHIGAN
WISCONSIN
KENTUCKY
WEST VIRGINIA
VIRGINIA
MARYLAND
DELAWARE
NEW JERSEY
NEW HAMPSHIRE
VERMONT
MASS.
CONN.
R.I.
LAKE SUPERIOR
LAKE MICHIGAN
LAKE HURON
LAKE ERIE
LAKE ONTARIO
Georgian Bay
Chesapeake Bay
Delaware Bay
NEW YORK CITY
PHILADELPHIA
BALTIMORE
WASHINGTON D.C.
BOSTON
HARTFORD
MONTRÉAL
Québec
Ottawa
TORONTO
BUFFALO
PITTSBURGH
CLEVELAND
DETROIT
COLUMBUS
CINCINNATI
INDIANAPOLIS
CHICAGO
MILWAUKEE
Norfolk
Richmond
Virginia Beach

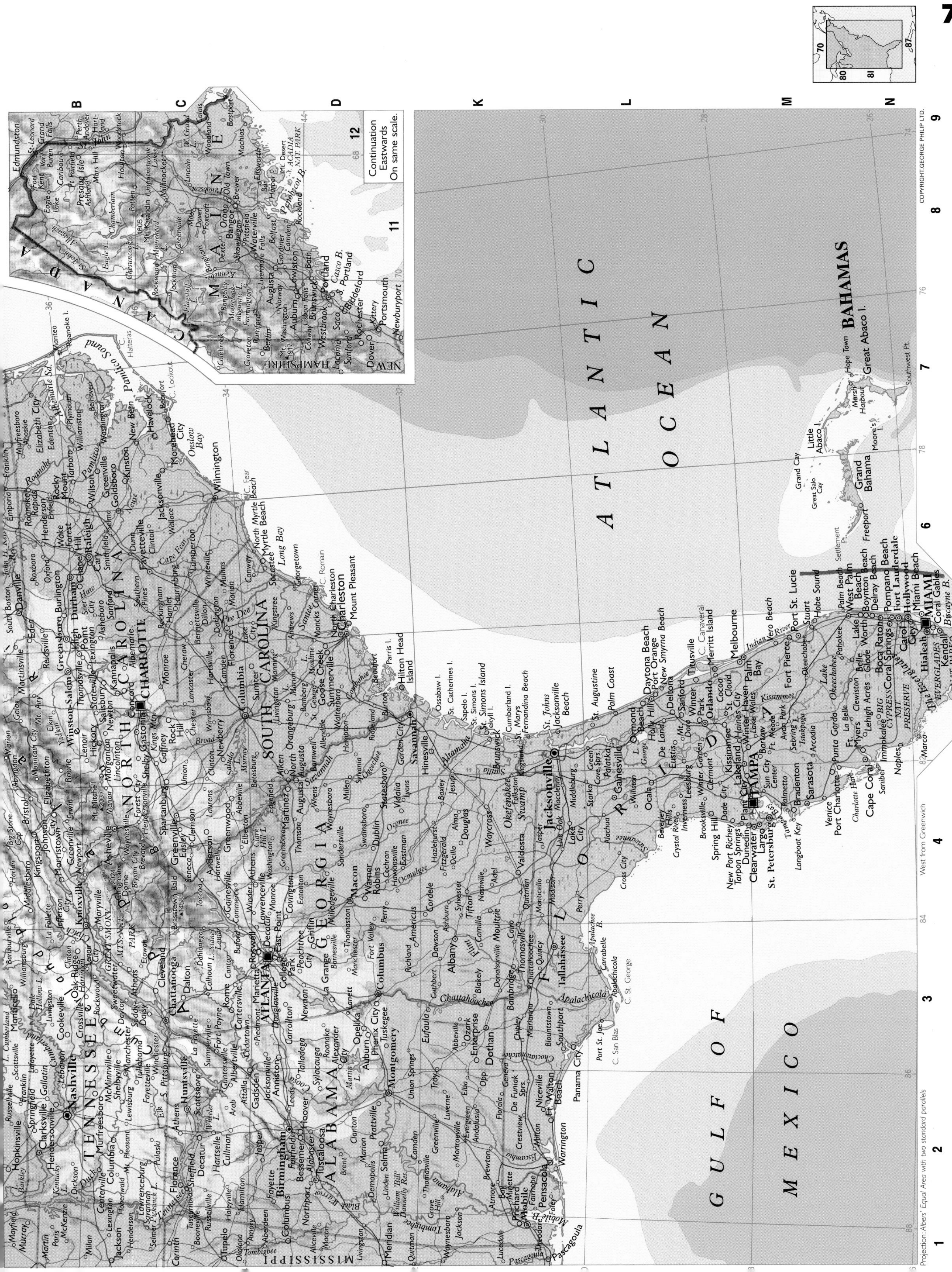
TENNESSEE
NORTH CAROLINA
SOUTH CAROLINA
GEORGIA
ALABAMA
MISSISSIPPI
FLORIDA
MAINE
NEW HAMPSHIRE
CANADA
BAHAMAS
ATLANTIC OCEAN
GULF OF MEXICO
Nashville
Knoxville
Chattanooga
Huntsville
Birmingham
Montgomery
Mobile
Pensacola
Tallahassee
ATLANTA
Macon
Columbus
Augusta
Savannah
Columbia
Charleston
CHARLOTTE
Raleigh
Durham
Greensboro
Winston-Salem
Wilmington
Jacksonville
Orlando
TAMPA
St. Petersburg
MIAMI
Fort Lauderdale
West Palm Beach
Daytona Beach
Gainesville
Portland
Bangor
Augusta
Lewiston
Grand Bahama
Great Abaco I.
Continuation Eastwards On same scale.
Projection: Albers' Equal Area with two standard parallels
West from Greenwich
COPYRIGHT.GEORGE PHILIP LTD.

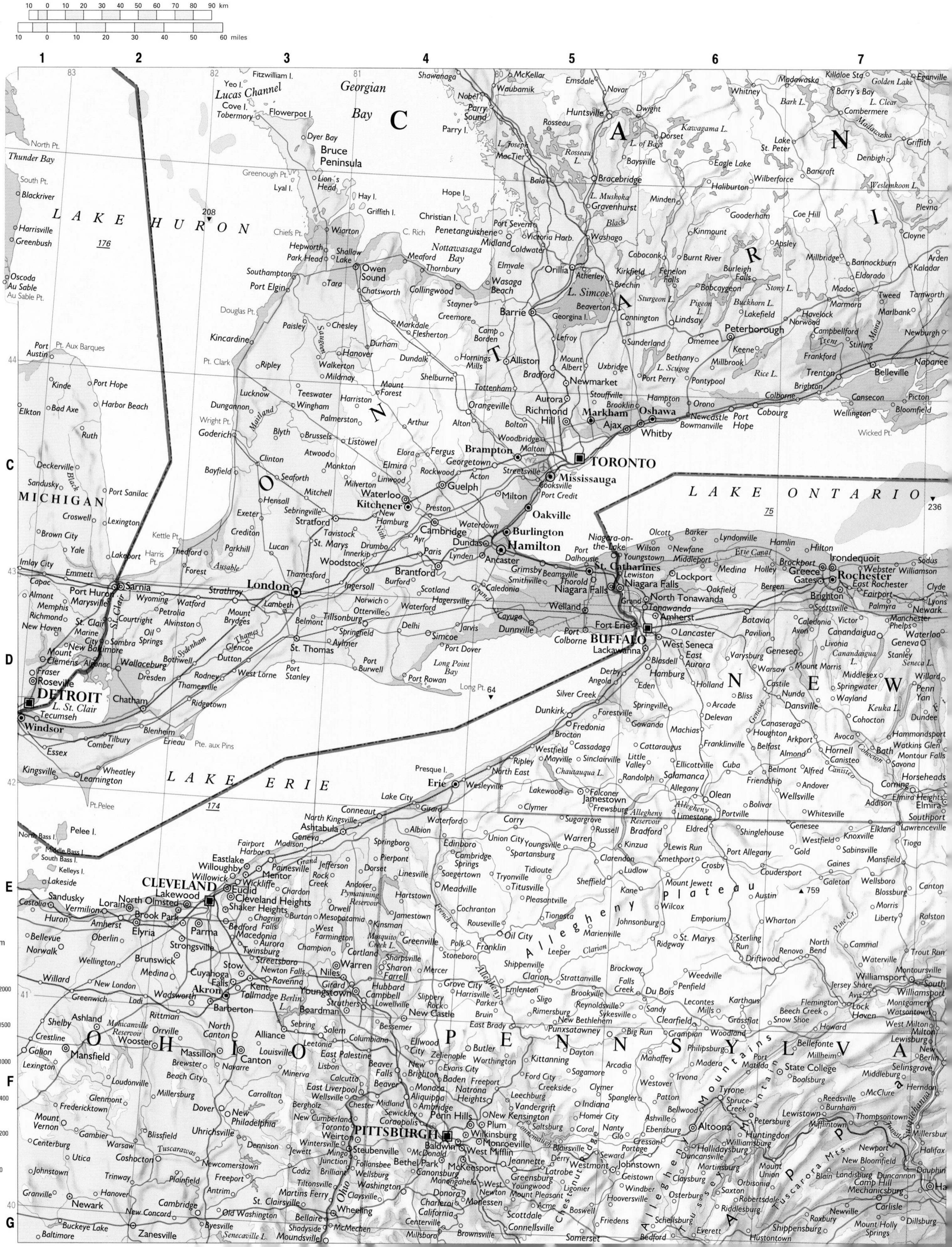

LAKE HURON
Georgian Bay
Bruce Peninsula
CANADA
ONTARIO
MICHIGAN
LAKE ONTARIO
LAKE ERIE
NEW YORK
OHIO
PENNSYLVANIA
Allegheny Plateau
Allegheny Mountains
TORONTO
Mississauga
Hamilton
London
Kitchener
BUFFALO
Rochester
DETROIT
Windsor
CLEVELAND
Akron
Youngstown
Erie
PITTSBURGH
Canton
Altoona
Oshawa
Peterborough
Barrie
St. Catharines
Niagara Falls
Sarnia
Port Huron

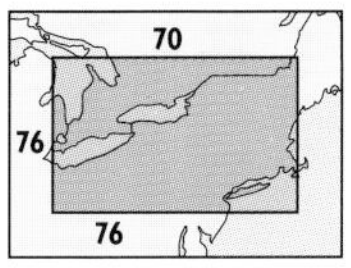

70
76
76

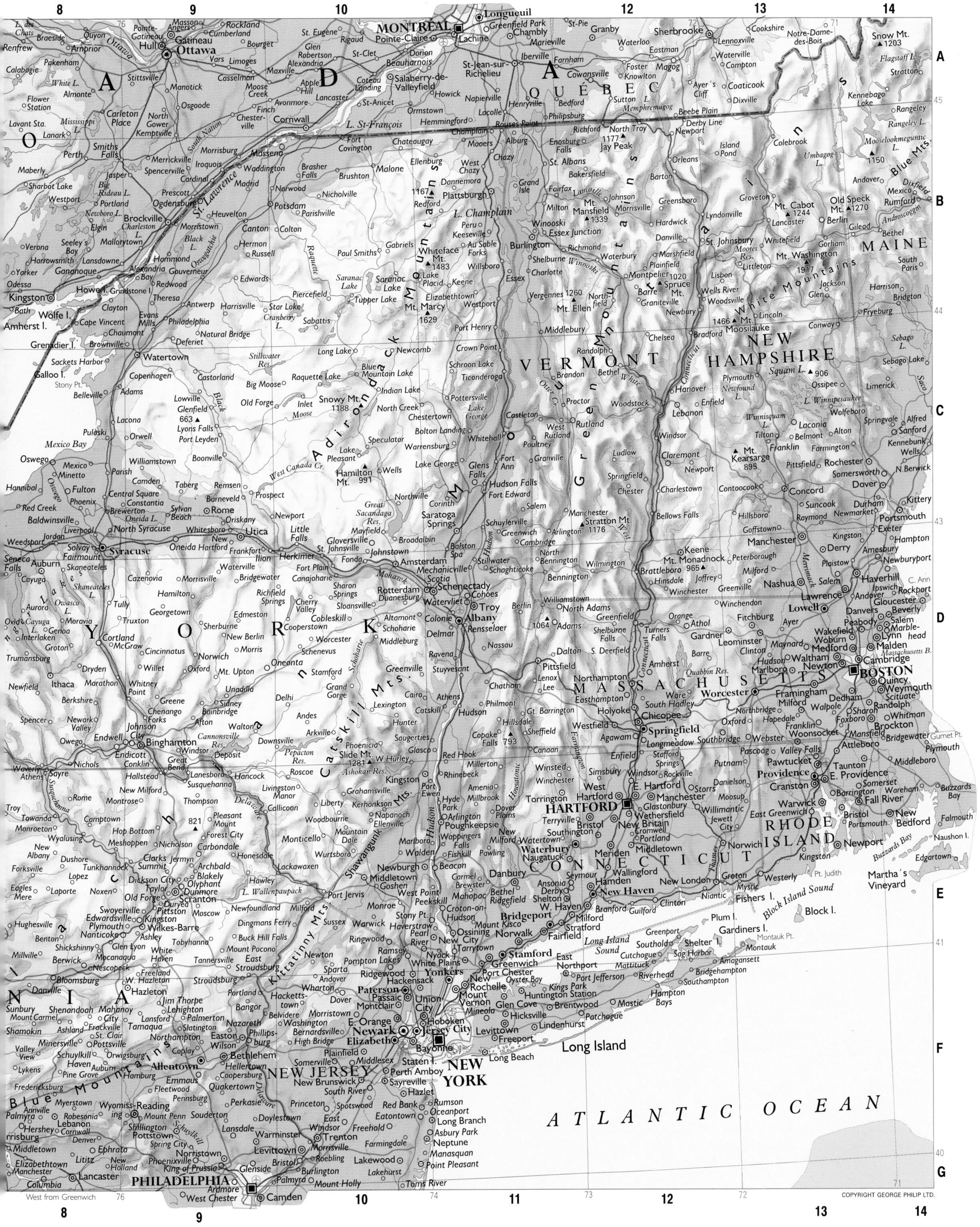

MONTREAL
Ottawa
QUÉBEC
MAINE
NEW HAMPSHIRE
VERMONT
MASSACHUSETTS
CONNECTICUT
RHODE ISLAND
NEW JERSEY
NEW YORK
HARTFORD
BOSTON
PHILADELPHIA
Providence
Springfield
Worcester
New Haven
Albany
Schenectady
Syracuse
Utica
Binghamton
Scranton
Allentown
Trenton
Newark
Jersey City
Yonkers
Paterson
Bridgeport
Stamford
Burlington
Plattsburgh
Sherbrooke
Manchester
Concord
Portsmouth
Lowell
Cambridge
Kingston
Camden
Long Island
Long Island Sound
Block Island Sound
Martha´s Vineyard
ATLANTIC OCEAN
L. Champlain
L. St-François
Adirondack Mountains
Green Mountains
White Mountains
Catskill Mts.
Blue Mountains
Kittatinny Mts.
Shawangunk Mts.
Mt. Marcy 1629
Mt. Washington 1917
West from Greenwich

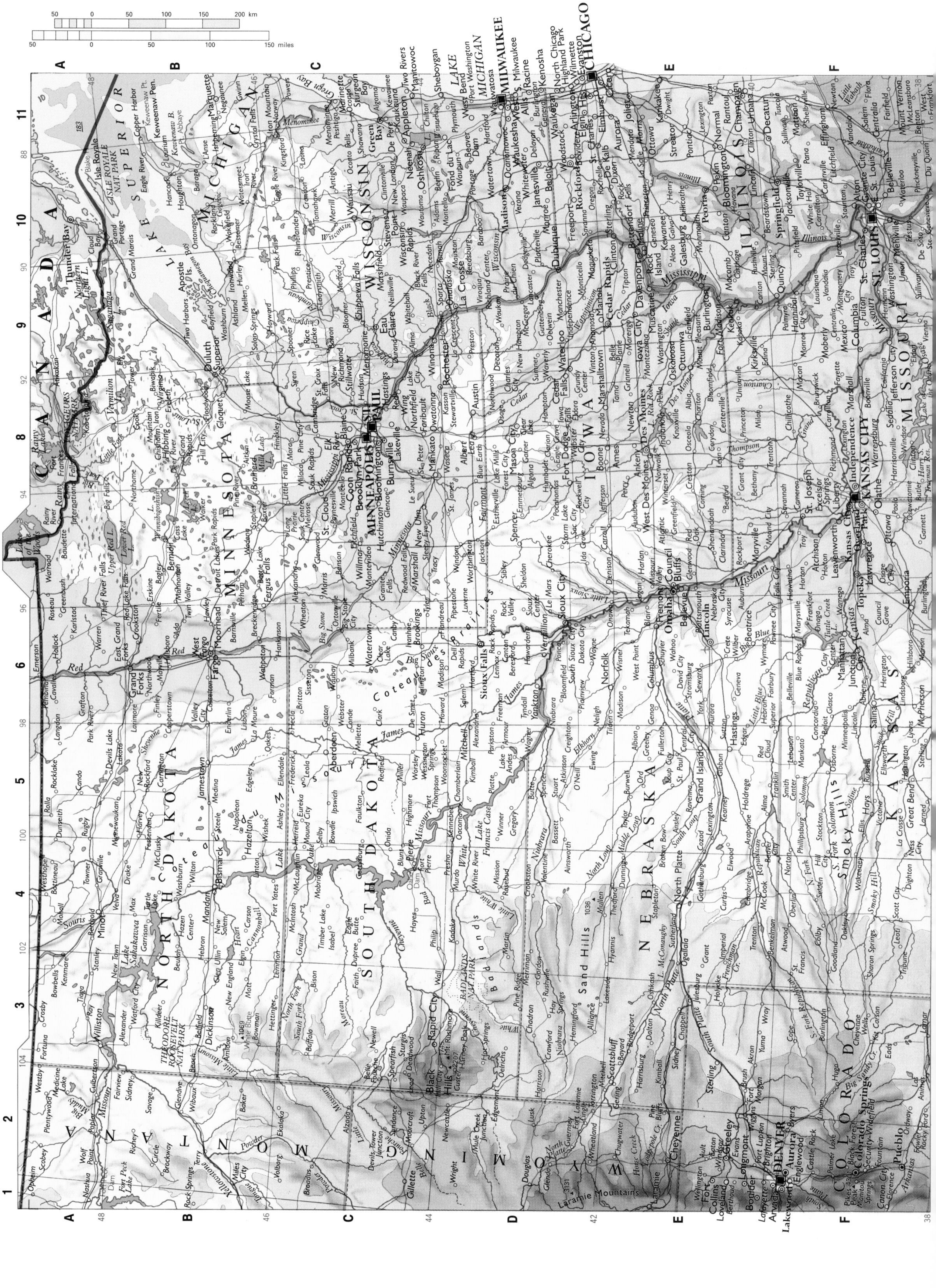
50 0 50 100 150 200 km
50 0 50 100 150 miles
C A N A D A
NORTH DAKOTA
SOUTH DAKOTA
NEBRASKA
KANSAS
MINNESOTA
WISCONSIN
IOWA
ILLINOIS
MISSOURI
MONTANA
WYOMING
COLORADO
LAKE SUPERIOR
LAKE MICHIGAN
MINNEAPOLIS
ST. PAUL
MILWAUKEE
CHICAGO
ST. LOUIS
KANSAS CITY
DENVER
Omaha
Des Moines
Sioux Falls
Lincoln
Topeka
Cheyenne
Rapid City
Bismarck
Fargo
Duluth
Madison
Pierre
Colorado Springs
Pueblo

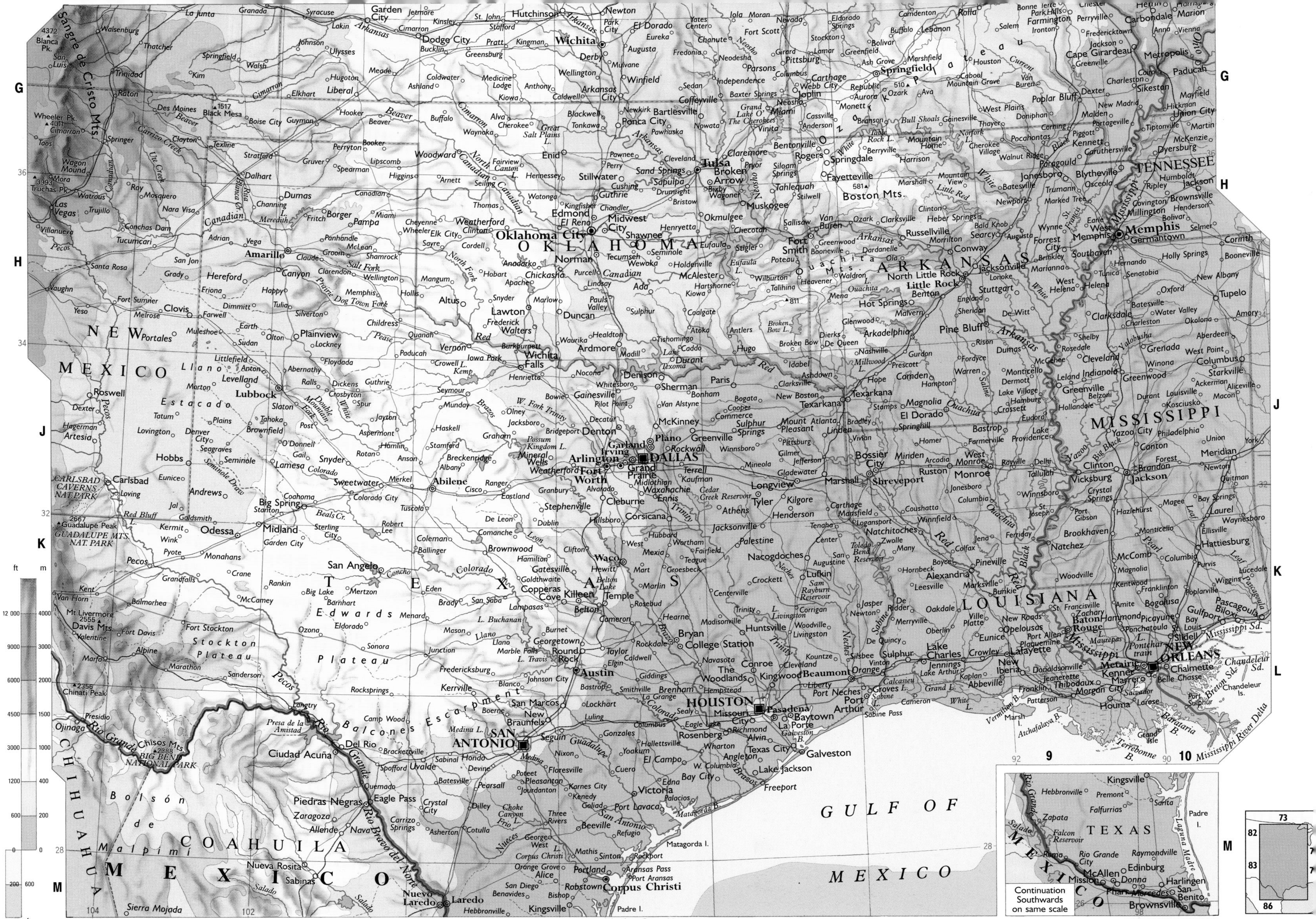

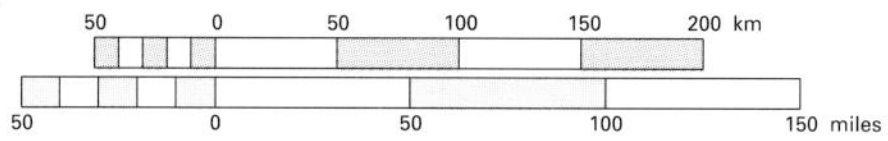
50 0 50 100 150 200 km
50 0 50 100 150 miles

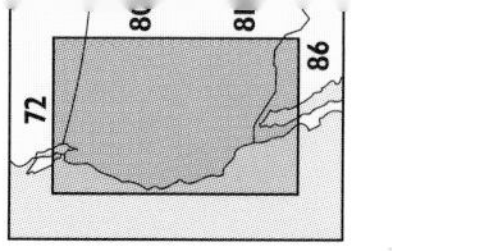

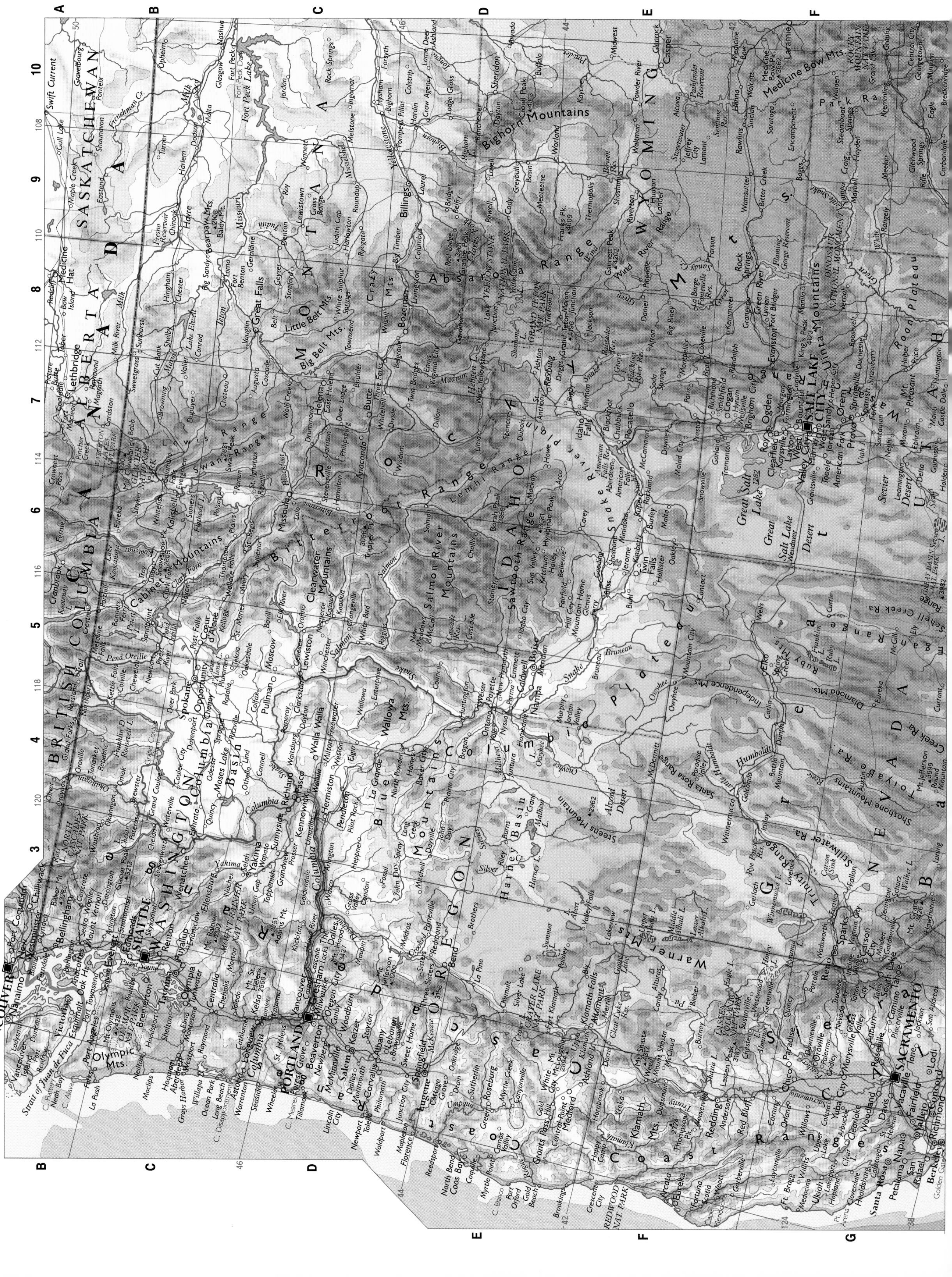
BRITISH COLUMBIA
ALBERTA
SASKATCHEWAN
CANADA
WASHINGTON
OREGON
IDAHO
MONTANA
WYOMING
NEVADA
UTAH
VANCOUVER
SEATTLE
PORTLAND
SACRAMENTO
SALT LAKE CITY
Spokane
Boise
Great Falls
Billings
Casper
Eugene
Reno
Ogden
Pocatello
Missoula
Helena
Butte
Bozeman
Medford
Redding
Yakima
Walla Walla
Lewiston
Idaho Falls
Twin Falls
Salem
Olympia
Tacoma
Bellingham
Victoria
Nanaimo
Lethbridge
Medicine Hat
Cranbrook
Great Salt Lake
Bighorn Mountains
Salmon River Mountains
Blue Mountains
Cascade Range
Snake River Plain
Columbia Basin
Harney Basin
Great Basin
Medicine Bow Mts.
Uinta Mountains
Wind River Range
Bitterroot Range
Clearwater Mountains
Sawtooth Range
Olympic Mts.
Wallowa Mts.
Steens Mountain
Warner Mts.
Sierra Nevada
Great Salt Lake Desert
Alvord Desert
Black Rock Desert
Roan Plateau
YELLOWSTONE NATIONAL PARK
GRAND TETON NAT. PARK
CRATER LAKE NAT. PARK
REDWOOD NAT. PARK
Strait of Juan de Fuca

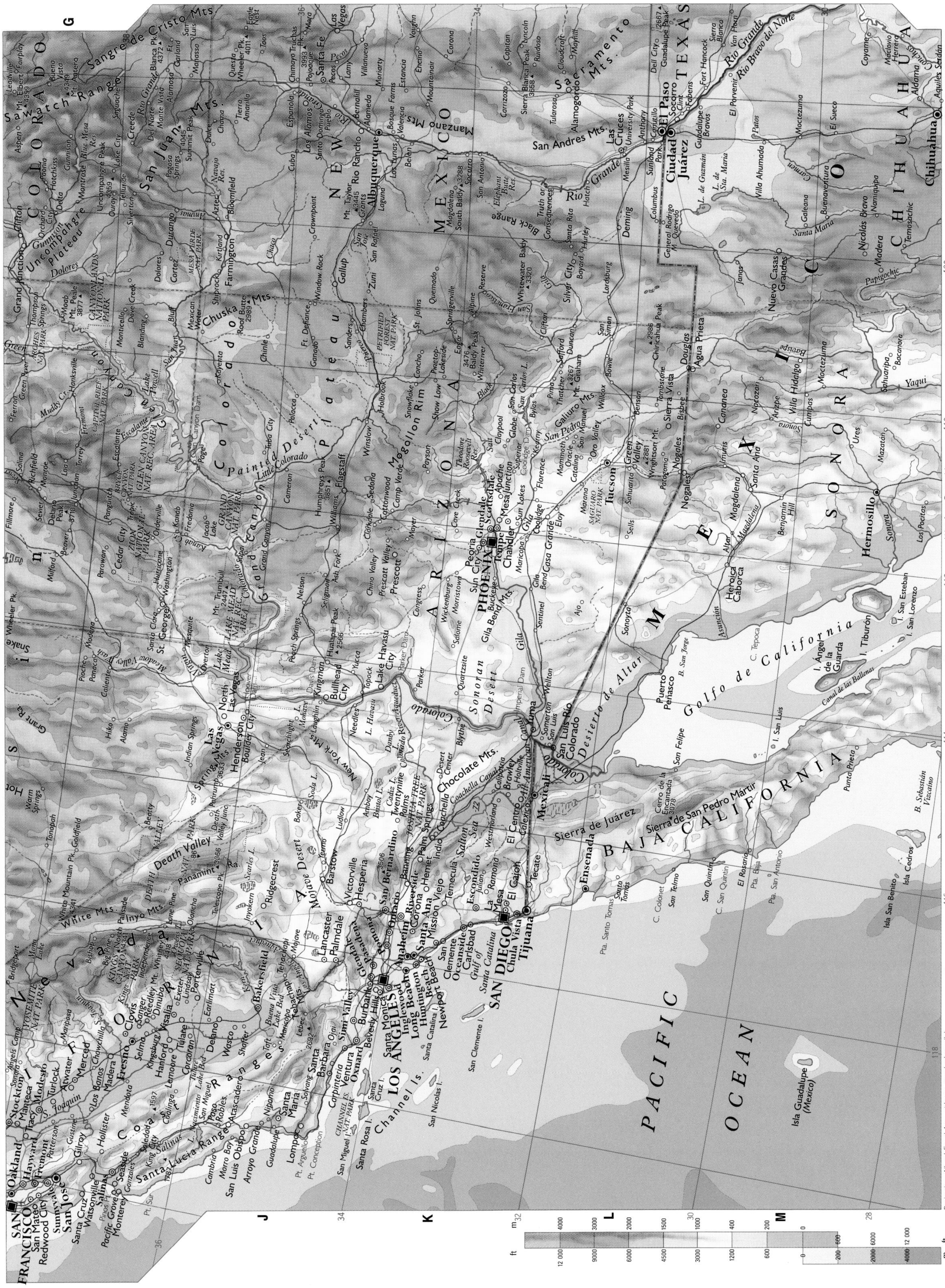

PACIFIC

OCEAN

BAJA CALIFORNIA

Golfo de California

SONORA

CHIHUAHUA

MEXICO

TEXAS

NEW MEXICO

ARIZONA

COLORADO

NEVADA

CALIFORNIA

LOS ANGELES

SAN DIEGO

SAN FRANCISCO

Phoenix

Tucson

Las Vegas

Albuquerque

Santa Fe

El Paso

Ciudad Juárez

Chihuahua

Hermosillo

Grand Canyon

Death Valley

Isla Guadalupe (Mexico)

Projection: Albers' Equal Area with two standard parallels

COPYRIGHT GEORGE PHILIP LTD.

West from Greenwich

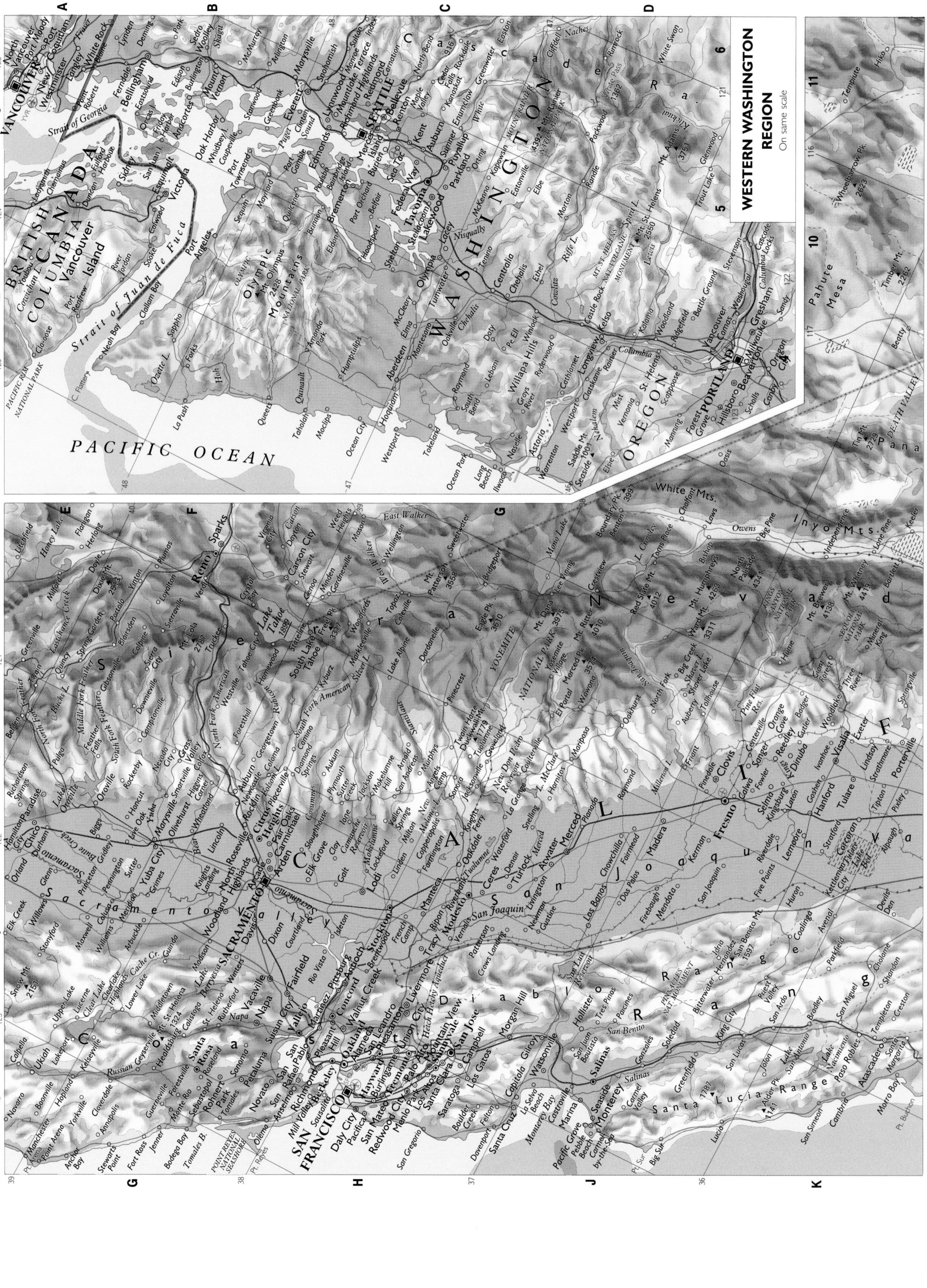

WESTERN WASHINGTON
REGION
On same scale

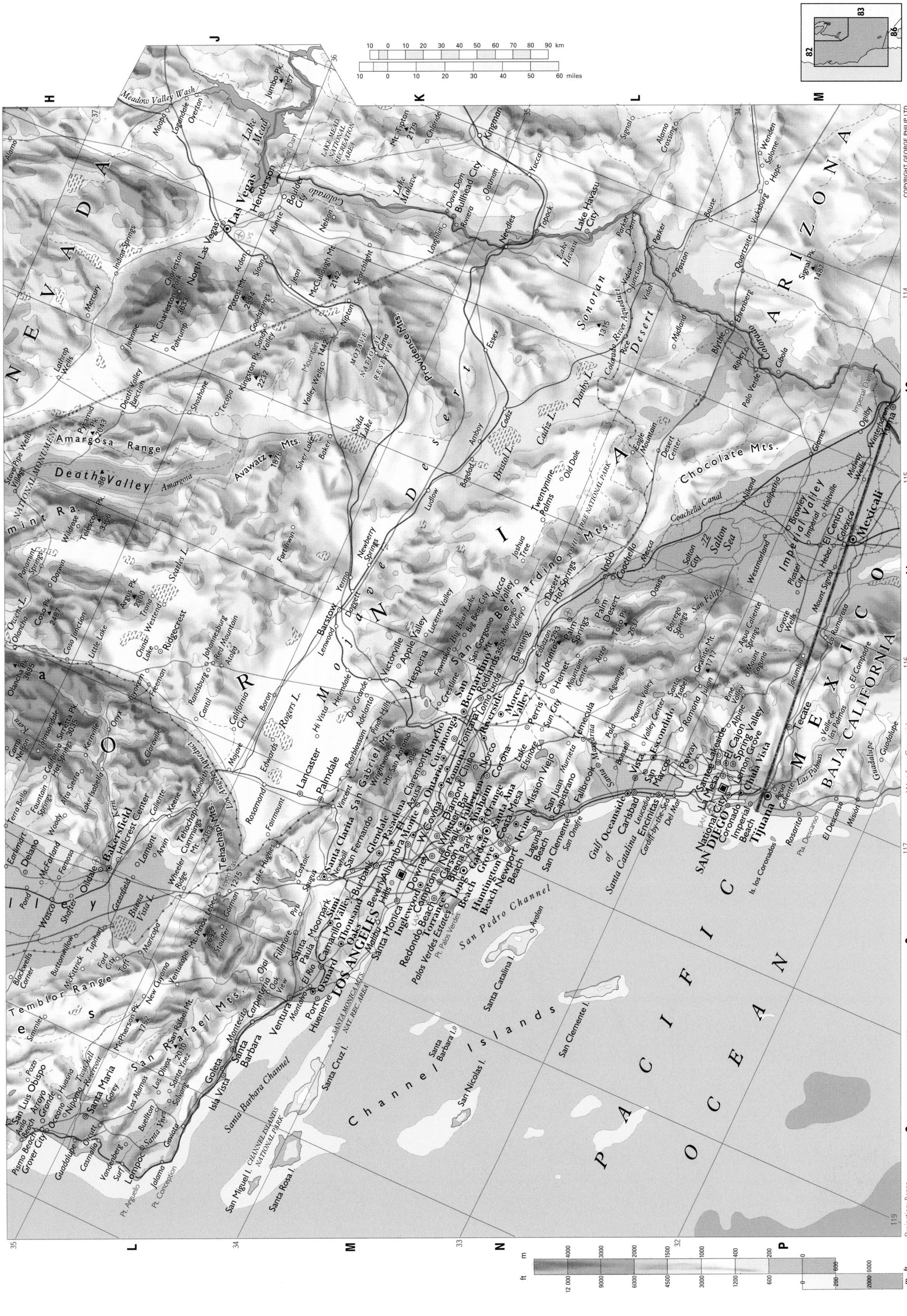

NEVADA
ARIZONA
MEXICO
BAJA CALIFORNIA
PACIFIC OCEAN
Channel Islands
Mojave Desert
Sonoran Desert
Las Vegas
Henderson
North Las Vegas
Lake Mead
Boulder City
Kingman
Needles
Lake Havasu City
Bullhead City
Parker
Blythe
Yuma
Mexicali
Calexico
El Centro
Brawley
Imperial Valley
Salton Sea
Indio
Palm Springs
Palm Desert
San Bernardino
Riverside
Barstow
Victorville
Hesperia
Lancaster
Palmdale
Santa Clarita
LOS ANGELES
Long Beach
Santa Ana
Anaheim
Irvine
Oxnard
Ventura
Santa Barbara
Lompoc
Santa Maria
San Luis Obispo
Bakersfield
Ridgecrest
Death Valley
Amargosa Range
Chocolate Mts.
San Bernardino Mts.
San Gabriel Mts.
Tehachapi Mts.
San Rafael Mts.
Temblor Range
SAN DIEGO
Chula Vista
Tijuana
Tecate
Ensenada
Escondido
Oceanside
Temecula
Santa Catalina I.
San Clemente I.
San Nicolas I.
Santa Cruz I.
Santa Rosa I.
San Miguel I.
Santa Barbara Channel
San Pedro Channel
Gulf of Santa Catalina
Projection: Bonne
West from Greenwich
COPYRIGHT GEORGE PHILIP LTD.

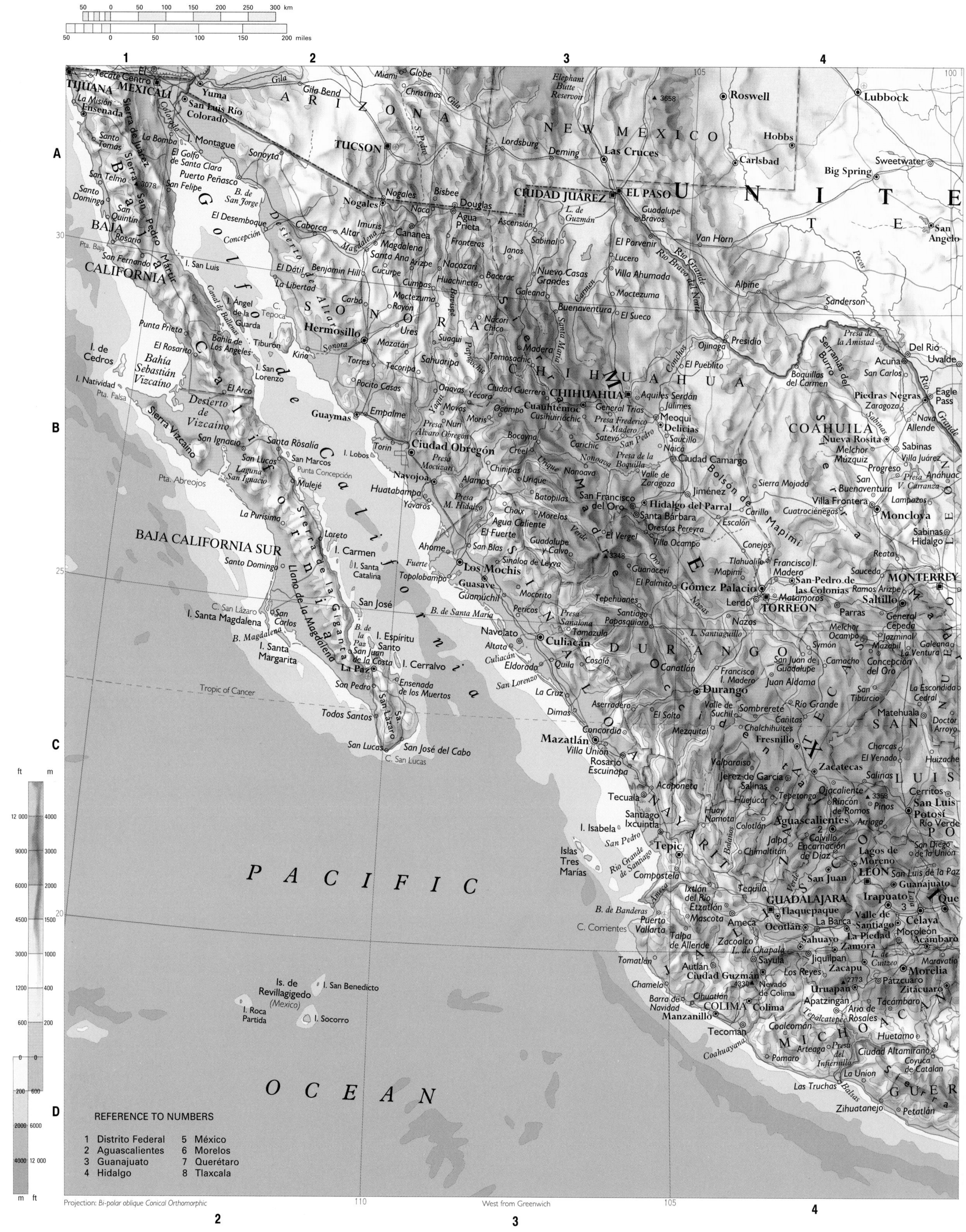

50 0 50 100 150 200 250 300 km
50 0 50 100 150 200 miles

REFERENCE TO NUMBERS

1 Distrito Federal   5 México
2 Aguascalientes   6 Morelos
3 Guanajuato   7 Querétaro
4 Hidalgo   8 Tlaxcala

Projection: Bi-polar oblique Conical Orthomorphic

West from Greenwich

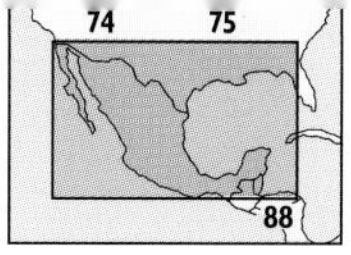

GULF OF MEXICO

M E X I C O

Tropic of Cancer

CUBA
Guane
La Fé

GULF OF

Golfo
de
Campeche

ARKANSAS
MISSISSIPPI
ALABAMA
GEORGIA
FLORIDA
LOUISIANA
TEXAS

Wichita Falls
Denison
Sherman
Paris
Red
Hope
Camden
Greenville
Texarkana
El Dorado
Tuscaloosa
Opelika
Columbus
McRae
Omutee

Denton
Greenville
Monroe
Vicksburg
Meridian
Phenix City
Montgomery
Americus
Cordele

FORT WORTH
DALLAS
Marshall
Longview
Shreveport
Jackson
Selma
Troy
Albany
GEORGIA
Tifton

Ranger
Cleburne
Tyler
Corsicana
Natchez
Laurel
Hattiesburg
Flomaton
Dothan
Chattahoochee
Valdosta
Waycross

Abilene
Hillsboro
Palestine
McComb
Jim Woodruff Res.
Tallahassee
Lake City

Brownwood
Waco
Nacogdoches
Alexandria
Bogalusa
Biloxi
MOBILE
Pensacola
Panama City
FLORIDA

Temple
Jewett
San Rayburn Reservoir
Baton Rouge
Hammond
Gulfport
C. San Blas
Apalachee Bay

Austin
Huntsville
Bryan
Lake Charles
NEW ORLEANS
Suwannee

San Antonio
Navasota
HOUSTON
Port Arthur
Lafayette
Atchafalaya Bay
Mississippi River Delta
Breton Sd.
Clearwater

Dilley
Rosenberg
Galveston
Terrebonne Bay

Nueces
Victoria
Corpus Christi

Laredo
Kingsville
Alice

Nuevo Laredo
Zapata
Laguna Madre

Presa Falcón
Nuevo Guerrero
Camargo
McAllen
Harlingen
Brownsville

General Treviño
Presa M.R. Gómez
Reynosa
Matamoros

Cadereyta
China
Valle Hermoso
Santa Teresa
Laguna Madre

Montemorelos
Mendez
San Fernando

Linares
Villagrán
Hidalgo
Santander Jiménez

Zaragoza
La Pesca
Soto la Marina

Ciudad Victoria
Llera
Calles

Tula
Ocampo
Ciudad Mante
Aldama
Pta. Jerez

I. Desterrada
I. Pérez (Mexico)

Ciudad Madero
Tampico
Pta. Yalkubul
Río Lagartos
C. Catoche
Cancún

Cárdenas de Valles
Pánuco
Progreso
Dzilam de Bravo
El Cuyo
Tizimín
Puerto Juárez

Ozuluama
L. de Tamiahua
Mérida
Motul
Temax
Izamal
Espita
Puerto Morelos

Tempoal
C. Rojo
YUCATÁN
Sotuta
Valladolid
Cozumel
Isla Cozumel

Tamazunchale
Chicontepec
Maxcanú
Ticul
Peto

Tuxpan
Tenabo
Tekax
Vigía Chico
B. de la Ascensión

Zimapán
Zacualtipán
Poza Rica
Papantla
UXMAL
Bolonchenticul
QUINTANA

San Juan del Río
Nautla
Campeche
Hopelchén
B. del Espíritu Santo

Huichapan
Pachuca
Huauchinango
Misantla
ETZNA
ROO

Tula
Tulancingo
Champotón
Felipe Carrillo Puerto
Banco Chinchorro

El Oro
Zumpango
Teziutlán
Jalapa Enríquez
Chenkán
Bacalar
B. de Chetumal

MÉXICO
Apizaco
ZEMPOALA
Veracruz
Chetumal

Toluca
Tlaxcala
Amecameca
Coatepec
Ciudad del Carmen
Matamoros
Corozal

PUEBLA
Citlaltépetl
L. de Términos
CAMPECHE
Orange Walk
Ambergris Cay

Cuernavaca
Córdoba
Alvarado
Frontera
Concepción
Turneffe Is.

Taxco
Izúcar de Matamoros
Orizaba
Tlacotalpan
Paraíso
Palizada
Belize City
BELIZE

Iguala
Chilapa
Chiautla
Cosamaloapan
San Andrés Tuxtla
Comalcalco
Villahermosa
Balancán
Belmopan
Dangriga

Tlaxiaco
Huautla de Jiménez
Tres Valles
Coatzacoalcos
TABASCO
Uaxactún
Benque Viejo
Is. de la Bahía

Chilpancingo
Acayucan
Minatitlán
Cárdenas
Tenosique
TIKAL
Maya Mts.
Roatán

Chilapa
Asunción Nochixtlán
Istmo de Tehuantepec
Macuspana
PALENQUE
Golfo de Honduras
Monkey River

Madre del Sur
Tlacolula
Jesús Carranza
Teapa
L. Petén Itzá
Flores

Acapulco
Ometepec
OAXACA
Tehuantepec
Chiapa de Corzo
La Concordia
San Luis
San Antonio
BELIZE

Pinotepa Nacional
MONTE ALBÁN
Matías Romero
San Cristóbal de las Casas
Punta Gorda
Puerto Barrios
Livingston

Jamiltepec
Ejutla
Ixtepec
Comitán
GUATEMALA
HONDURAS

Miahuatlán
Tehuantepec
Juchitán
Tonalá
Arriaga
Cuilco
Huehuetenango
Zacapa
San Pedro Sula

Puerto Escondido
Puerto Ángel
Salina Cruz
Pijijiapan
Motozintla
Cobán
El Progreso
Tela

Tututepec
San Pedro Mixtepec
Golfo de Tehuantepec
Mapastepec
Tapachula
Coatepeque
Retalhuleu
GUATEMALA
La Esperanza
Tegucigalpa

Tehuantepec
Huixtla
San Marcos
Totonicapán
Jalapa
Chiquimula
Comayagua

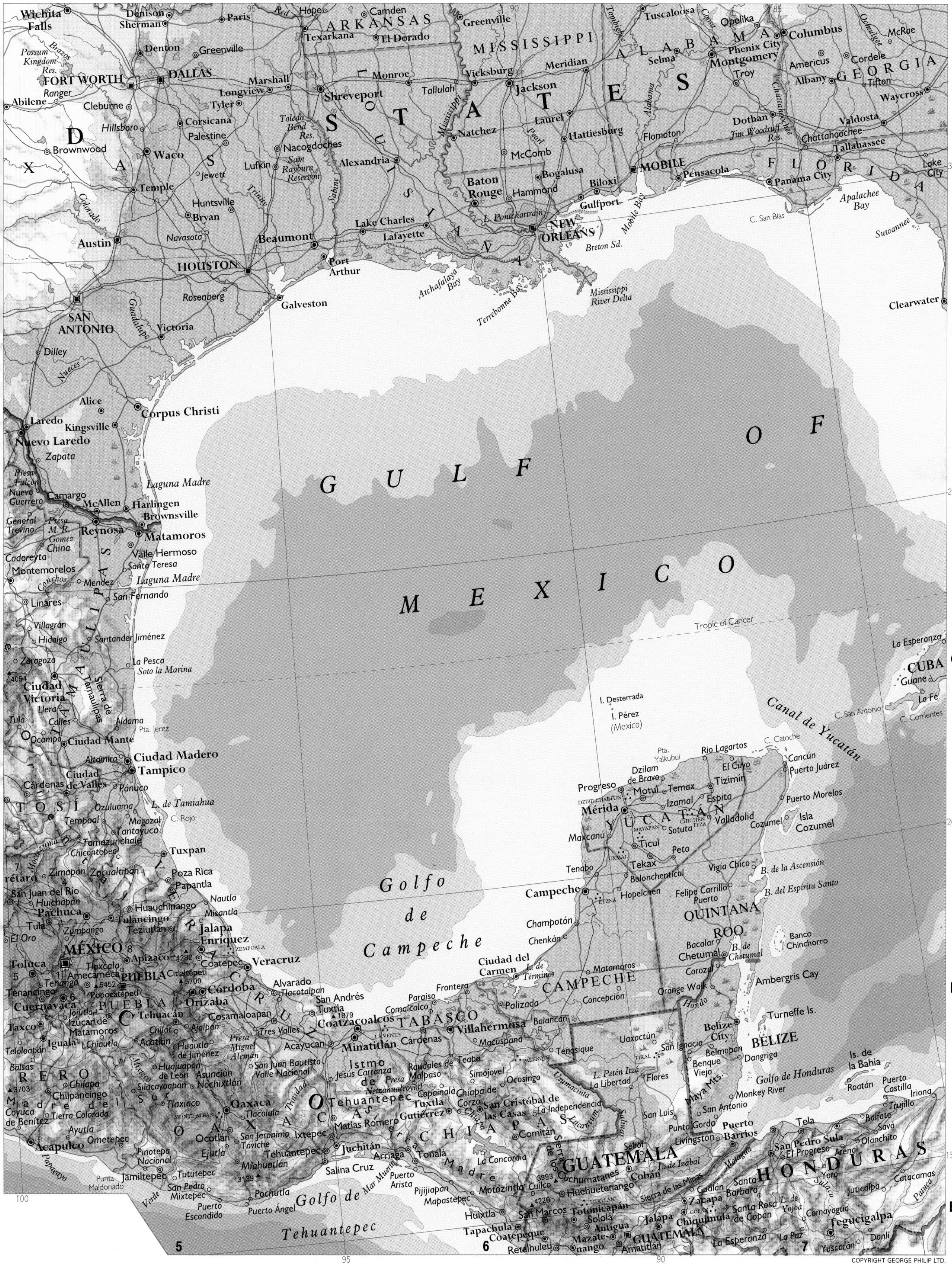

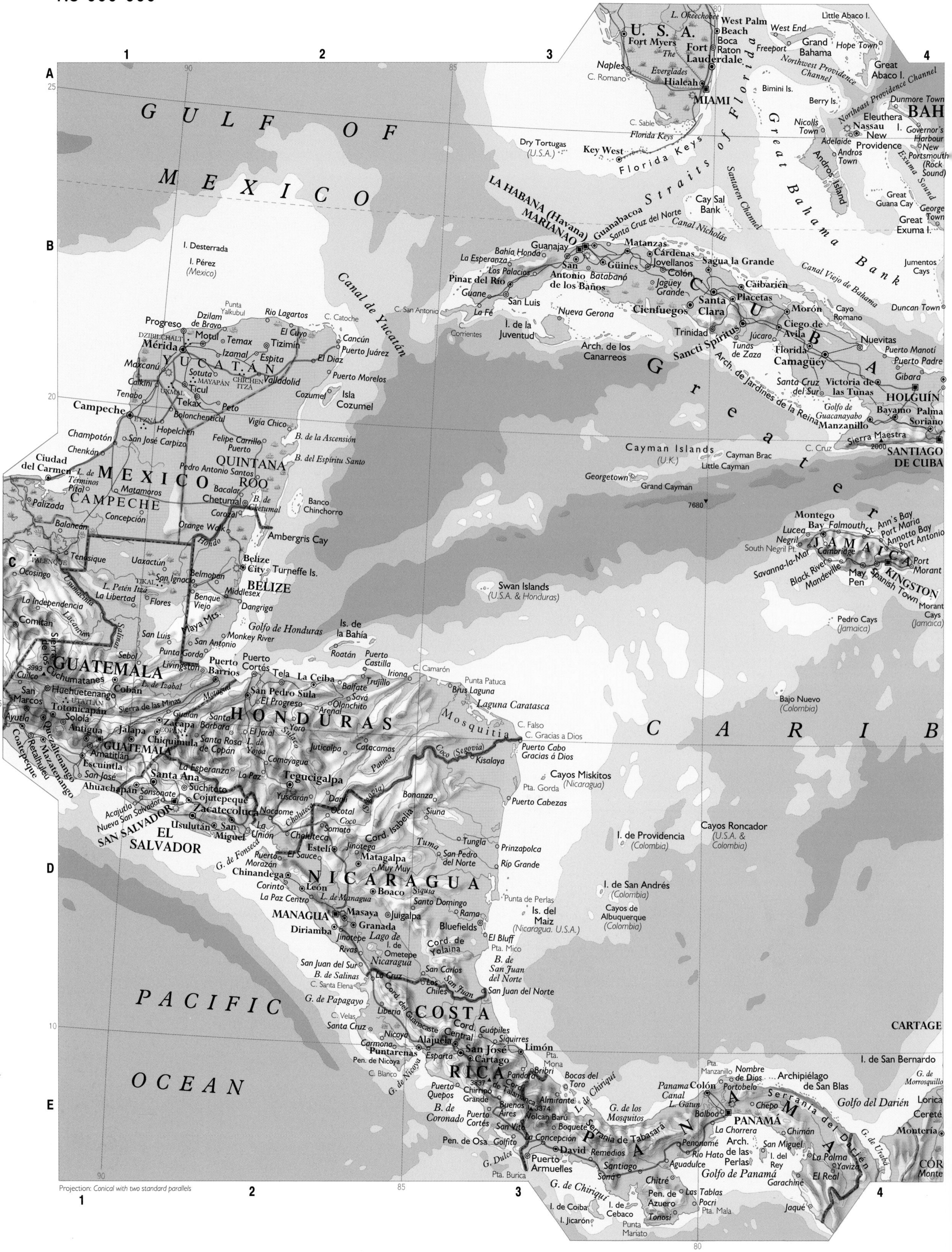

GULF OF MEXICO

PACIFIC OCEAN

CARIB

Projection: Conical with two standard parallels

MEXICO
YUCATÁN
CAMPECHE
QUINTANA ROO
Mérida
Campeche
Progreso
Motul
Valladolid
Cancún
Cozumel
Isla Cozumel

BELIZE
Belize City
Belmopan
Maya Mts.

GUATEMALA
GUATEMALA
HONDURAS
San Pedro Sula
Tegucigalpa

EL SALVADOR
SAN SALVADOR

NICARAGUA
MANAGUA
León
Masaya
Granada
Bluefields
Lago de Nicaragua

COSTA RICA
San José
Cartago
Limón

PANAMÁ
Panamá
Colón
Panama Canal
Golfo de Panamá

U.S.A.
MIAMI
Fort Lauderdale
West Palm Beach
Key West
Florida Keys
Straits of Florida

CUBA
LA HABANA (Havana)
MARIANAO
Matanzas
Cárdenas
Santa Clara
Cienfuegos
Camagüey
HOLGUÍN
SANTIAGO DE CUBA
Sierra Maestra

BAH
Grand Bahama
Great Abaco I.
Eleuthera
Nassau
New Providence
Great Exuma I.
Great Bahama Bank

JAMAICA
KINGSTON
Montego Bay

Cayman Islands (U.K.)
Grand Cayman
Little Cayman
Cayman Brac

Swan Islands (U.S.A. & Honduras)

I. de Providencia (Colombia)
Cayos Roncador (U.S.A. & Colombia)
I. de San Andrés (Colombia)
Cayos de Albuquerque (Colombia)
Is. del Maiz (Nicaragua, U.S.A.)

Cayos Miskitos (Nicaragua)
Mosquitia

CARTAGE

COR Monte

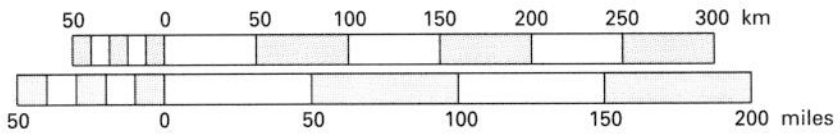

87

92 93

5   **6**   **7**   **8**

AMAS

A T L A N T I C

Arthur's Town
The Bight
Cat I.
San Salvador I.
Conception I.
Rum Cay
Long I.
Sandy Cay
Clarence Town
Samana Cay
Crooked I. Passage
Crooked I.
Albert Town
Snug Corner
Acklins I.
Cay Verde
Mira por vos Cay
Mayaguana I.
Caicos Passage
Cay Santa Domingo
Hogsty Reef
Little Inagua I.
Turks & Caicos (U.K.)
Caicos Is.
Turks Island Passage
Turks Is.

O C E A N

Tropic of Cancer

Banes
Antilla
Mayari
Moa
Baracoa
Lake Rose
Great Inagua I.
Matthew Town
Guantánamo
Pta. de Maisi
Maisi
Paso de los Vientos
(Windward Passage)
Î. de la Tortue
Cap-Haïtien
Monte Cristi
LA ISABELA
Santiago de los Cabelleros
San Francisco de Macorís
Puerto Rico Trench
Jean Rabel
Port-de-Paix
Puerto Plata
La Vega
Nagua
Samana
Milwaukee Deep 9200
Cap-à-Foux
G. de la Gonâve
Gonaïves
Hinche
Cord. Central
3175
Sánchez
Sabana de la Mar
Virgin Is.
Anegada Virgin Is. (U.K.)
Anegada Passage
Sombrero (U.K.)
St-Marc
HAITI
DOMINICAN REP.
San Pedro de Macorís
Hato Mayor
C. Engaño
Bayamón
SAN JUAN
Carolina
St. Thomas
Tortola (U.K.)
Road Town
Virgin Is. (U.S.A.)
Charlotte Amalie
Anguilla (U.K.)
St.-Martin (Fr.)
St.-Barthélemy (Fr.)
Jérémie
Î. de la Gonâve
PORT-AU-PRINCE
San Juan
L. Enriquillo
Higuey
Aguadilla
Arecibo
1338
Ponce
Fajardo
Carolina
Aguas
Christiansted
St. Maarten (Neth.)
Saba (Neth.)
Barbuda
Navassa I. (U.S.A.)
Dame Marie
C. Carcasse
Massif de la Hotte
2280
Petit Goâve
Jacmel
Barahona
San Cristóbal
SANTO DOMINGO
La Romana
B. de Yuma
I. Saona
Mayagüez
PUERTO RICO (U.S.A.)
Guayama
Frederiksted
St. Croix
St. Eustatius (Neth.)
ANTIGUA & BARBUDA
St. John's
Antigua
Les Cayes
Aquin
Azua
Compostela
Bani
Pedernales
Isla Mona (U.S.A.)
ST. KITTS & NEVIS
Basseterre
Nevis
Redonda
Montserrat (U.K.)
Pointe-à-Gravois
I. Beata
C. Beata
Hispaniola
Antilles
Antilles
Guadeloupe Passage
Ste.-Rose
Le Moule
La Désirade
GUADELOUPE (Fr.)
Pointe-à-Pitre (Fr.)
Basse-Terre
Marie-Galante
Grand-Bourg
I. des Saintes (Fr.)
Dominica Passage
Portsmouth
DOMINICA
Roseau
I. de Aves (Venezuela)
Martinique Passage
Mt. Pelée
Ste.-Marie
1397
Le François
Fort-de-France
Rivière-Pilote
MARTINIQUE (Fr.)
B E A N   S E A
St. Lucia Channel
Castries
Soufrière
ST. LUCIA
St. Vincent Passage
Soufrière 1234
ST. VINCENT
Speightstown
Bridgetown
Kingstown
& THE BARBADOS
Windward Islands
Leeward Islands
Lesser Antilles
Hillsborough
Grenadines
GRENADINES
St. George's
GRENADA

L e s s e r   A n t i l l e s

Aruba (Neth.)
Curaçao
Bonaire
Pta. Gallinas
C. San Román
Pen. de Paraguaná
Willemstad
NETH. ANTILLES
Is. Las Aves (Ven.)
I. Orchila (Ven.)
I. Blanquilla (Ven.)
Tobago
Pen. de la Guajira
Pta. Espada
Pen. de Paraguaná
Punta Fijo
Is. Los Roques (Ven.)
I. Los Hermanos (Ven.)
Is. Los Testigos (Ven.)
Dragon's Mouth
Scarborough
Ríohacha
Uribia
Punta Cardón
Puerto Cumarebo
I. de Margarita
La Asunción
Port of Spain
Galera Point
SANTA MARTA
GUAJIRA
Golfo de Venezuela
Coro
La Vela de Coro
La Tortuga (Ven.)
NUEVA ESPARTA
Porlamar
Pen. de Paria
Caribe
Arima
Rio Claro
BARRAN-QUILLA
Baranoa
Soledad
San Rafael
Altagracia
FALCÓN
Tucacas
Maracay
La Guaira
CARACAS
Cumaná
Carúpano
Güiria
TRINIDAD & TOBAGO
San Fernando
ATLÁNTICO
Ciénaga
Sabanalarga
Mene de Mauroa
Puerto Cabello
DISTRITO FEDERAL
MIRANDA
Higuerote
Río Chico
La Cruz
SUCRE
Caripito
Serpent's Mouth
NA
Sierra Nevada de Santa Marta
MARACAIBO
Santa Rita
Baragua
San Felipe
Carora
CARABOBO
Valencia
Villa de Cura
Los Teques
Puerto La Cruz
Barcelona
Caicara
Maturín
Fundación
Calamar
Valledupar
Villa del Rosario
Cabimas
LARA
YARACUY
Cantaura
MONAGAS
DELTA
Magdalena
Plato
Codazzi
Ciudad Ojeda
Machiques
BARQUISIMETO
Yaritagua
San Juan de los Morros de Orituco
Altagracia de Orituco
Aragua de Barcelona
Anaco
Tucupita
Carmen
Zambrano
CÉSAR
ZULIA
Lago de Maracaibo
Mene Grande
Acarigua
COJEDES
San Carlos
El Sombrero
Valle de la Pascua
ANZOÁTEGUI
El Tigre
AMACURO
Since-lejo
Corozal
Mompós
El Banco
Betijoque
Trujillo
TRUJILLO
PORTUGUESA
El Baúl
Calabozo
GUÁRICO
Santa María de Ipire
Ciudad Guayana
Soledad
Sincé
Magangué
Sahagún
San Carlos del Zulia
Valera
Guanare
Portuguesa
Pariaguán
El Pao
Sierra Imataca
San Marcos
Planeta Rica
El Barco
Encontrados
MÉRIDA
Barinas
BARINAS
Guárico
Manapire
Upata
Majagual
Ayapel
NORTE DE OCAÑA
Libertad
Puerto de Nutrias
San Fernando de Apure
Los Barrancos
DOBA
Caucasia
SANTANDER
Cúcuta
Ciudad Bolivia
Bruzual
Achaguas
Apure
Caicara
Mapire
Ciudad Bolívar
Guasipati
El Callao
libano
Simití
TÁCHIRA
Cord. de Santa Bárbara
V E N E Z U E L A
Orinoco
Embalse de Guri
Caroní
Tumeremo

75   **70**   **6**   **65**   **7**

West from Greenwich

5

COPYRIGHT GEORGE PHILIP LTD

A
B
C
D
E

ft   m
12 000 4000
9000 3000
6000 2000
4500 1500
3000 1000
1200 400
600 200
0   0
200 600
2000 6000
4000 12 000
6000 18 000
8000 24 000
m   ft

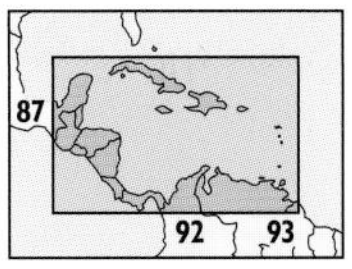

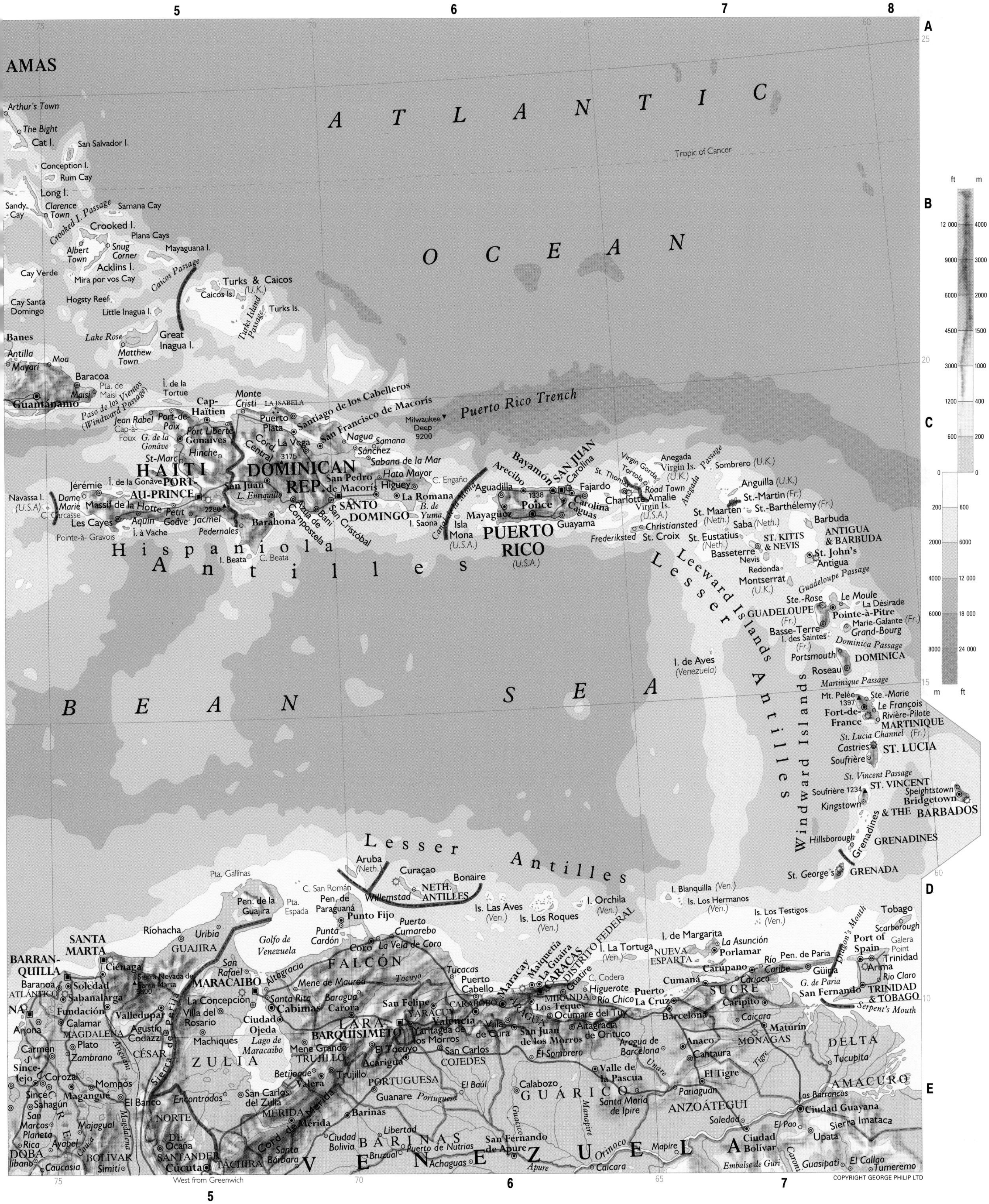

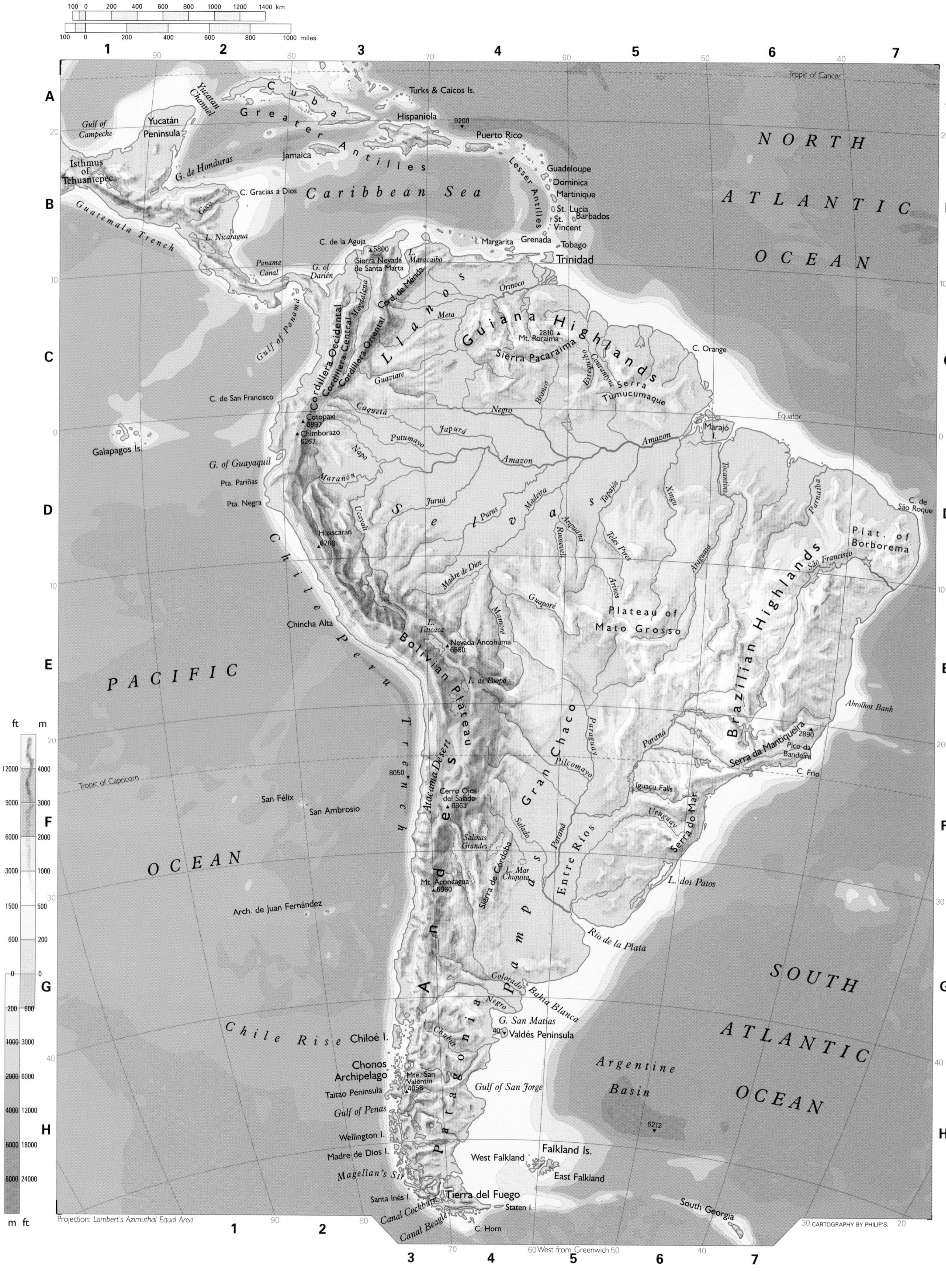

Projection: Lambert's Azimuthal Equal Area

CARTOGRAPHY BY PHILIP'S

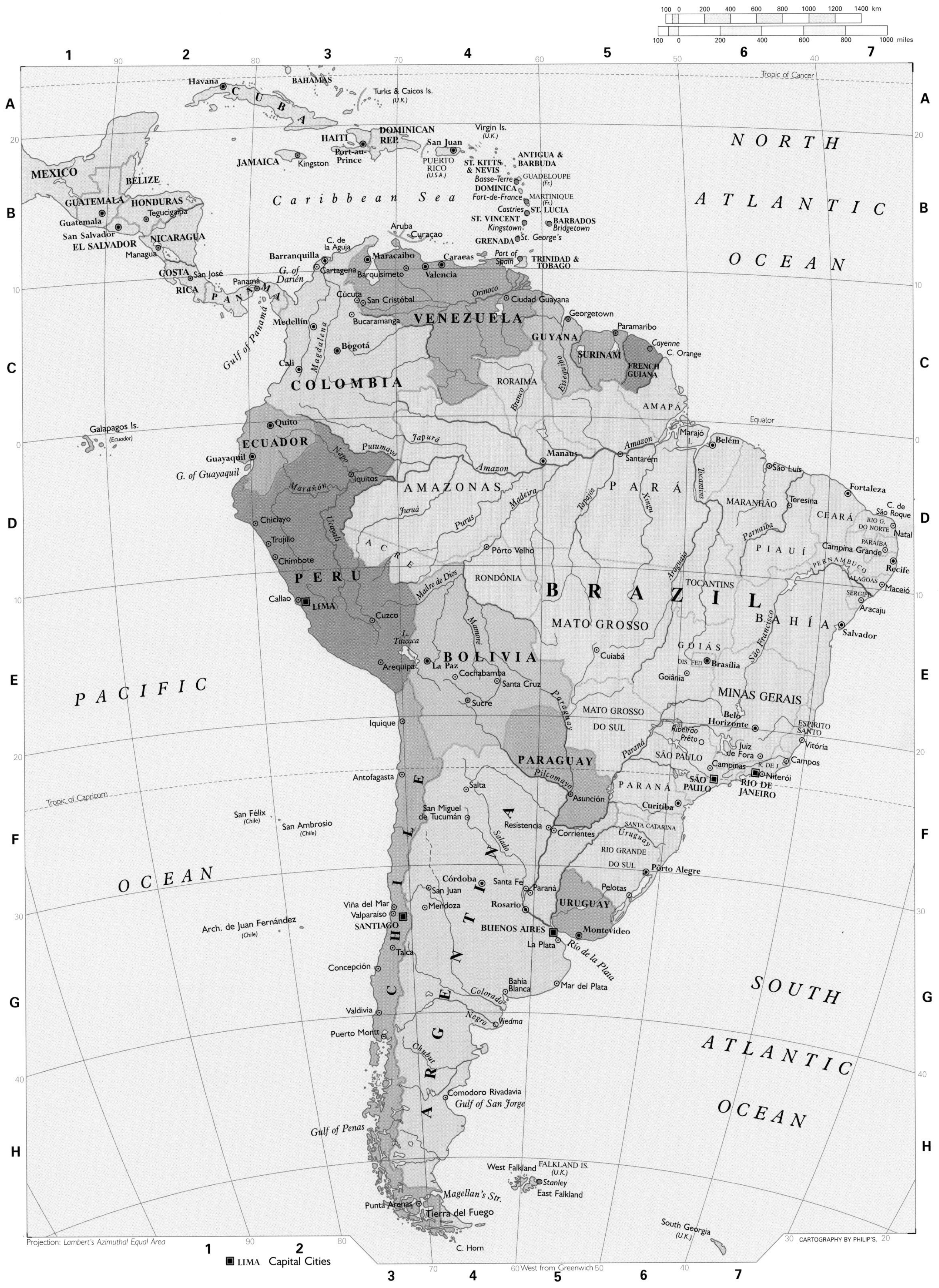

100 0 200 400 600 800 1000 1200 1400 km
100 0 200 400 600 800 1000 miles

Tropic of Cancer

A

Havana
CUBA
BAHAMAS
Turks & Caicos Is.
(U.K.)

MEXICO

HAITI
Port-au-Prince
DOMINICAN REP.
San Juan
Virgin Is.
(U.K.)

JAMAICA
Kingston
PUERTO RICO
(U.S.A.)
ST. KITTS & NEVIS
Basse-Terre
ANTIGUA & BARBUDA
GUADELOUPE
(Fr.)

B

BELIZE
GUATEMALA
Guatemala
HONDURAS
Tegucigalpa
San Salvador
EL SALVADOR
NICARAGUA
Managua
Caribbean Sea
DOMINICA
Fort-de-France
MARTINIQUE
(Fr.)
Castries **ST. LUCIA**
ST. VINCENT
Kingstown
BARBADOS
Bridgetown

NORTH

ATLANTIC

OCEAN

COSTA RICA
San José
Panamá
P A N A M A
Barranquilla
Cartagena
Aruba
Curaçao
C. de la Aguja
Maracaibo
Barquisimeto
Caracas
Valencia
Port of Spain
GRENADA
St. George's
TRINIDAD & TOBAGO

Cúcuta
San Cristóbal
Orinoco
Ciudad Guayana
Georgetown
Paramaribo
Cayenne
C. Orange

Medellín
Bucaramanga
G. of Darién
Gulf of Panamá
VENEZUELA
GUYANA
SURINAM
FRENCH GUIANA

C

Cali
Bogotá
C O L O M B I A
RORAIMA
Branco
Essequibo
AMAPÁ

Gulf of Guayaquil
Galapagos Is.
(Ecuador)
Quito
ECUADOR
Guayaquil
Napo
Putumayo
Japurá
Amazon
Marajó I.
Belém
Equator

Iquitos
Marañón
Amazon
Manaus
Santarém
São Luís
Fortaleza
C. de São Roque

D

Chiclayo
Trujillo
A M A Z O N A S
Juruá
Purus
Madeira
P A R Á
Tapajós
Xingu
Tocantins
MARANHÃO
Teresina
CEARÁ
RIO G. DO NORTE
Natal
Campina Grande
Recife

Chimbote
Ucayali
A C R E
Pôrto Velho
RONDÔNIA
B R A Z I L
PIAUÍ
Parnaíba
PERNAMBUCO
PARAÍBA
ALAGOAS
SERGIPE
Maceió

Callao **LIMA**
P E R U
Cuzco
Madre de Dios
Mamoré
MATO GROSSO
TOCANTINS
São Francisco
BAHÍA
Aracaju
Salvador

E

P A C I F I C
Arequipa
La Paz
BOLIVIA
Cochabamba
Santa Cruz
L. Titicaca
Cuiabá
GOIÁS
Goiânia
DIS. FED. Brasília

Iquique
Sucre
MATO GROSSO DO SUL
Belo Horizonte
MINAS GERAIS
ESPÍRITO SANTO
Vitória

Antofagasta
Paraguay
Pilcomayo
PARAGUAY
Paraná
Ribeirão Prêto
Juiz de Fora
SÃO PAULO
Campinas
SÃO PAULO
R. DE J.
Niterói
RIO DE JANEIRO

Salta
Asunción
PARANÁ
Curitiba

F

San Félix
(Chile)
San Ambrosio
(Chile)
San Miguel de Tucumán
Resistencia
Corrientes
Salado
A R G E N T I N A
C H I L E
SANTA CATARINA
U R U G U A Y
RIO GRANDE DO SUL
Pôrto Alegre

OCEAN

Arch. de Juan Fernández
(Chile)
Córdoba
San Juan
Santa Fe
Paraná
Rosario
Pelotas
URUGUAY

Viña del Mar
Valparaíso
SANTIAGO
Mendoza
BUENOS AIRES
La Plata
Montevideo
Río de la Plata

G

Talca
Concepción
Bahía Blanca
Colorado
Mar del Plata

Valdivia
Negro
Viedma

SOUTH

ATLANTIC

Puerto Montt
Chubut
Comodoro Rivadavia
Gulf of San Jorge

OCEAN

Gulf of Penas

H

West Falkland
FALKLAND IS.
(U.K.)
Stanley
East Falkland

Magellan's Str.
Punta Arenas
Tierra del Fuego
South Georgia
(U.K.)
C. Horn

Projection: Lambert's Azimuthal Equal Area
■ LIMA Capital Cities
CARTOGRAPHY BY PHILIP'S.
60 West from Greenwich 50

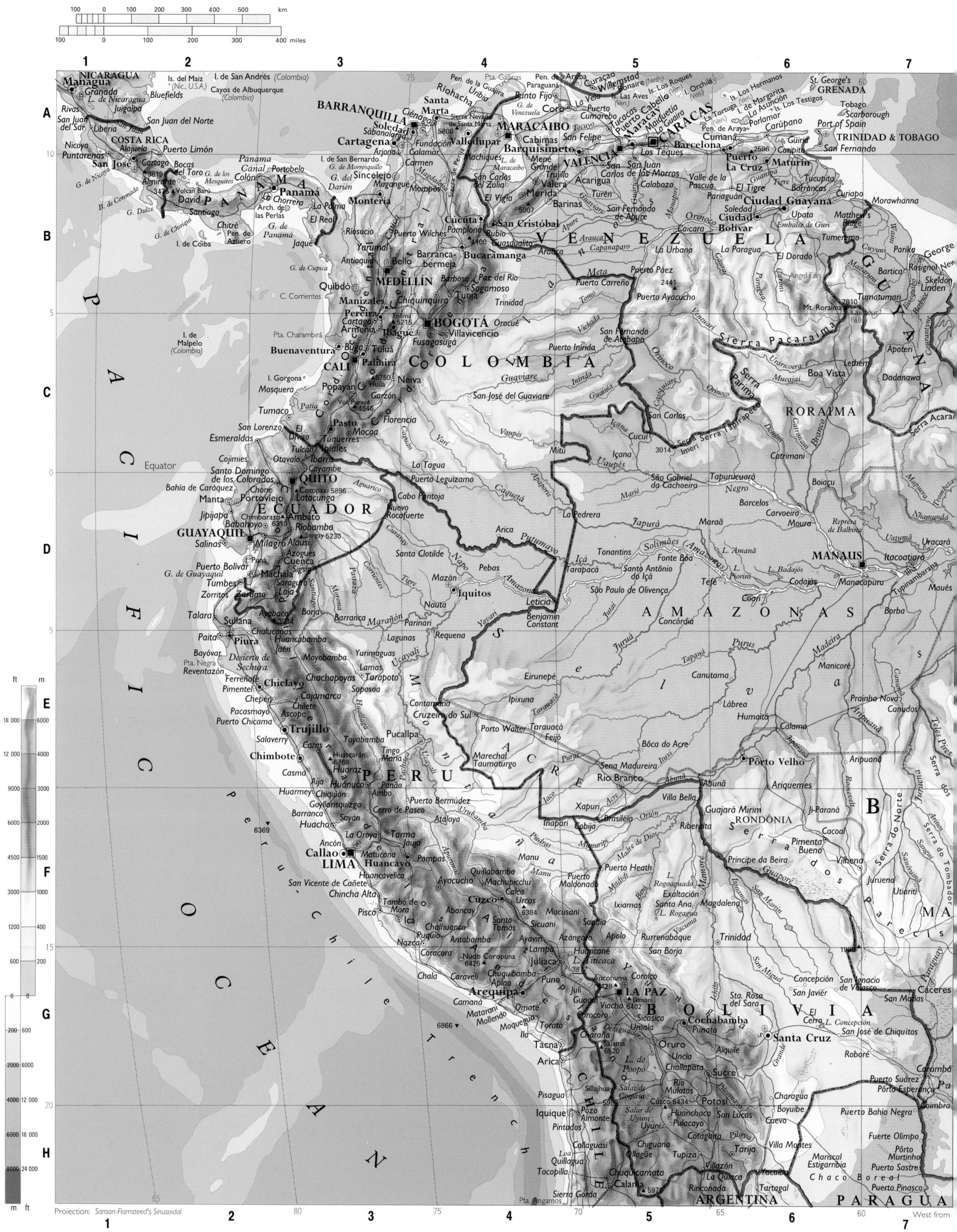
100 0 100 200 300 400 500 km
100 0 100 200 300 400 miles
1 2 3 4 5 6 7
A B C D E F G H
ft m
18 000 6000
12 000 4000
9000 3000
6000 2000
4500 1500
3000 1000
1200 400
600 200
0 0
200 600
2000 6000
4000 12 000
6000 18 000
8000 24 000
m ft
Projection: Sanson-Flamsteed's Sinusoidal
West from
NICARAGUA
Managua
Granada
L. de Nicaragua
Juigalpa
Bluefields
Is. del Maiz (Nic., U.S.A.)
I. de San Andrés (Colombia)
Cayos de Albuquerque (Colombia)
Rivas
San Juan del Sur
Liberia
San Juan del Norte
COSTA RICA
Alajuela
Puerto Limón
Nicoya
Puntarenas
San José
Cartago
Bocas del Toro
G. de los Mosquitos
Almirante
Volcan Barú
David
Santiago
G. de Nicoya
B. de Coronado
G. Dulce
G. de Chiriquí
Chitré
Pen. de Azuero
I. de Coiba
Panama Canal
Colón
Portobelo
PANAMA
Panamá
La Chorrera
Arch. de las Perlas
G. de Panamá
La Palma
El Real
Jaqué
BARRANQUILLA
Ciénaga
Santa Marta
Sierra Nevada de Santa Marta
Riohacha
Pen. de la Guajira
Uribia
Pta. Gallinas
Soledad
Sabanalarga
Cartagena
Fundación
Valledupar
Arjona
Calamar
I. de San Bernardo
G. de Morrosquillo
Sincelejo
Carmen
Magangué
Mompós
G. del Darién
Montería
Ríosucio
Puerto Wilches
Yarumal
Antioquia
Bello
MEDELLÍN
Barrancabermeja
Bucaramanga
G. de Cupica
Quibdó
C. Corrientes
Barbosa
Paz del Río
Sogamoso
Tunja
Chiquinquirá
Manizales
Pereira
Cartago
Armenia
Ibagué
Tolima
BOGOTÁ
Villavicencio
Fusagasugá
Orocué
Trinidad
Pta. Charambirá
I. de Malpelo (Colombia)
Buenaventura
Buga
Tuluá
Palmira
CALI
COLOMBIA
I. Gorgona
Mosquera
Popayán
Huila
Neiva
Garzón
Volc Puracé
Tumaco
Patía
San Lorenzo
Esmeraldas
Pasto
Mocoa
Florencia
El Diviso
Tulcán
Túquerres
Ipiales
Cojimies
Otavalo
Ibarra
Equator
Santo Domingo de los Colorados
QUITO
Cotopaxi
Latacunga
Bahía de Caráquez
Chone
Manta
Portoviejo
ECUADOR
Jipijapa
Chimborazo
Ambato
Babahoyo
Riobamba
Sangay
GUAYAQUIL
Salinas
Milagro
Alausí
Azogues
Cuenca
Sigsig
Puerto Bolívar
G. de Guayaquil
I. Puná
Machala
Tumbes
Zorritos
Zaruma
Saraguro
Loja
Talara
Sullana
Ayabaca
Borja
Paita
Piura
Chulucanas
Huancabamba
Jaén
Bayóvar
Pta. Negra
Reventazón
Desierto de Sechura
Moyobamba
Yurimaguas
Ferreñafe
Pimentel
Chiclayo
Chachapoyas
Lamas
Tarapoto
Saposoa
Chepén
Cajamarca
Chilete
Pacasmayo
Ascope
Puerto Chicama
Trujillo
Salaverry
Tayabamba
Chimbote
Caraz
Huascarán
Huaraz
Casma
Aija
Huánuco
Tingo María
Pucallpa
Panao
Ambo
Huarmey
Chiquián
Goyllarisquizga
Cerro de Pasco
Barranca
Huacho
Sayán
PERU
Puerto Bermúdez
Atalaya
La Oroya
Tarma
Jauja
Ancón
Callao
LIMA
Matucana
Huancayo
Pampas
Huancavelica
San Vicente de Cañete
Chincha Alta
Pisco
Ayacucho
Tambo de Mora
Ica
Quillabamba
Machupicchu
Calca
Cuzco
Urcos
Abancay
Santo Tomás
Chalhuanca
Puquio
Nazca
Antabamba
Coracora
Sicuani
Macusani
Ayaviri
Lampa
Juliaca
Nudo Coropuna
Chala
Caravelí
Chuquibamba
Aplao
Puno
Camaná
Arequipa
Matarani
Mollendo
Omate
Moquegua
Ilo
Torata
Tacna
Arica
Pisagua
Iquique
Pozo Almonte
Pintados
Collaguasi
Quillagua
Tocopilla
Chuquicamata
Calama
Sierra Gorda
Pta. Angamos
CHILE
Peru-Chile Trench
PACIFIC OCEAN
Pen. de Paraguaná
Aruba
Curaçao
Willemstad
Bonaire (Neth.)
Is. Los Roques
I. Orchila
Punto Fijo
G. de Venezuela
Coro
La Vela
Is. Las Aves
Puerto Cumarebo
Tucacas
Puerto Cabello
Maiquetía
La Guaira
CARACAS
MARACAIBO
Cabimas
Barquisimeto
San Felipe
Maracay
Valencia
Los Teques
Barcelona
Cumaná
Pen. de Araya
Carúpano
Is. Los Hermanos
I. de Margarita
La Asunción
Porlamar
Is. Los Testigos
La Tortuga
St. George's
GRENADA
Tobago
Scarborough
Port of Spain
TRINIDAD & TOBAGO
San Fernando
Güiria
Caripito
Maturín
Puerto La Cruz
Tucupita
Barrancas
Curiapo
L. de Maracaibo
Machiques
Mene Grande
Trujillo
Valera
Acarigua
San Juan de los Morros
Calabozo
Valle de la Pascua
El Tigre
San Carlos del Zulia
El Vigía
Mérida
Barinas
Guanare
Turén
San Fernando de Apure
Pariaguán
Soledad
Ciudad Guayana
Ciudad Bolívar
Caicara
Upata
Embalse de Guri
Tumeremo
Morawhanna
Matthew's Ridge
Cúcuta
Pamplona
San Cristóbal
Rubio
Guasdualito
Arauca
Capanaparo
La Urbana
La Paragua
VENEZUELA
El Dorado
Puerto Páez
Meta
Puerto Carreño
Angel Falls
Puerto Ayacucho
Mt. Roraima
Sierra Pacaraima
San Fernando de Atabapo
Puerto Inírida
Guaviare
San José del Guaviare
Inírida
Vaupés
Serra Parima
Uraricoera
Boa Vista
Mucajaí
RORAIMA
Lethem
Apoteri
Dadanawa
GUYANA
Bartica
Linden
Skeldon
Tumatumari
Parika
Rosignol
San Carlos
Cucuí
Serra Imeri
Serra Tapirapecó
Mitú
Içana
Uaupés
São Gabriel da Cachoeira
Tapurucuará
Negro
Caracaraí
Catrimani
Boiaçu
Barcelos
Carvoeiro
Moura
Represa de Balbina
Uatumã
Uracará
Caquetá
Apaporis
Aguarico
Cabo Pantoja
Nuevo Rocafuerte
Curaray
La Pedrera
Japurá
Maraã
Arica
Putumayo
Santa Clotilde
Napo
Pebas
Tonantins
Solimões
Amazonas
Fonte Boa
L. Amanã
MANAUS
Itacoatiara
Manacapuru
Mazán
Iquitos
Içá
Tarapacá
Santo Antônio do Içá
São Paulo de Olivença
Tefé
Codajás
Coari
Maués
Nauta
Leticia
Benjamin Constant
AMAZONAS
Borba
Barranca
Marañón
Parinari
Lagunas
Requena
Ucayali
Javari
Concórdia
Juruá
Purus
Madeira
Manicoré
Eirunepé
Canutama
Lábrea
Ipixuna
Contamana
Cruzeiro do Sul
Tarauacá
Feijó
Humaitá
Porto Walter
Marechal Taumaturgo
Sena Madureira
Rio Branco
Bôca do Acre
Porto Velho
ACRE
Calama
Ariquemes
Abunã
Xapuri
Brasiléia
Cobija
Villa Bella
Guajará Mirim
Riberalta
RONDÔNIA
Ji-Paraná
Inapari
Pimenta Bueno
Cacoal
Vilhena
Principe da Beira
Guaporé
Serra dos Parecis
Juruena
Utiariti
Aripuanã
Prainha Nova
Canudos
Manu
Puerto Maldonado
Puerto Heath
Madre de Dios
L. Rogoaguado
Exaltación
Santa Ana
Ixiamas
Magdalena
L. Rogagua
Sandia
Azángaro
Apolo
Rurrenabaque
San Borja
Trinidad
Huancané
L. Titicaca
Ancohuma
Coroico
LA PAZ
Illimani
Viacha
Juli
Guaqui
Corocoro
Sicasica
Umala
BOLIVIA
Cochabamba
Punata
Sta. Rosa del Sara
Concepción
San Ignacio de Velasco
San Javier
Cáceres
San Matías
Santa Cruz
El Cerro
L. Concepción
San José de Chiquitos
Roboré
Charaña
Sajama
Oruro
Aiquile
Uncía
Challapata
L. de Poopó
Sucre
Sillajhuay
Salar de Coipasa
Río Mulatos
Potosí
Salar de Uyuni
Uyuni
Huanchaca
Pulacayo
San Lucas
Cotagaita
Chiguana
Ollagüe
Tupiza
Tarija
Charagua
Boyuibe
Cuevo
Villa Montes
Villazón
La Quiaca
Yacuiba
Rinconada
Tartagal
ARGENTINA
Corumbá
Puerto Suárez
Porto Esperança
Coimbra
Puerto Bahía Negra
Fuerte Olimpo
Pôrto Murtinho
Mariscal Estigarribia
Puerto Sastre
Chaco Boreal
Puerto Pinasco
PARAGUAY

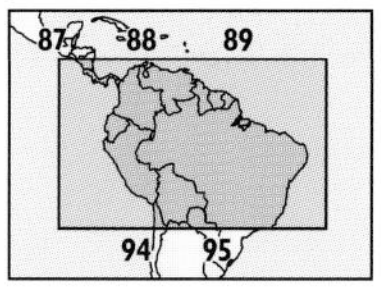
87
88
89
94
95

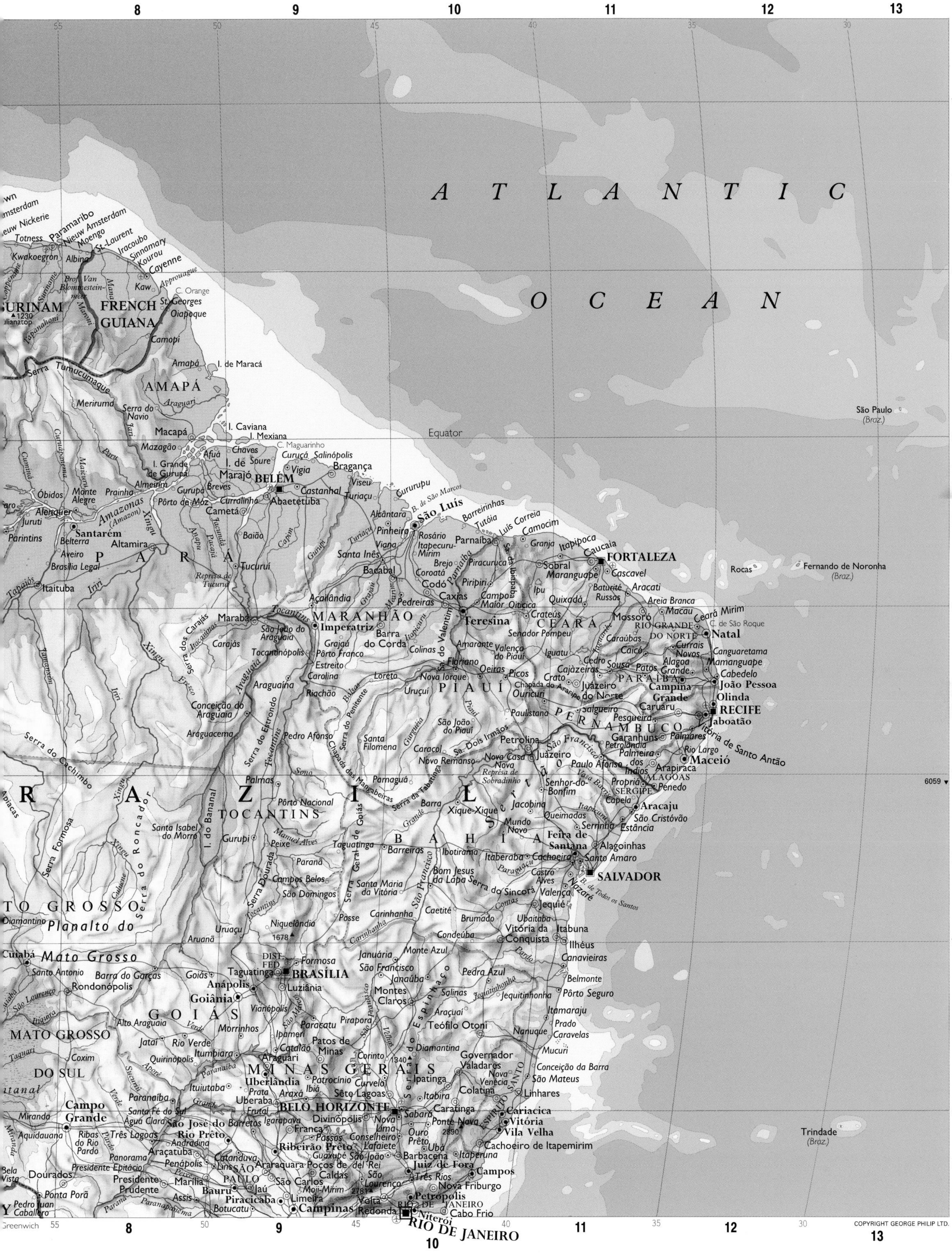
ATLANTIC
OCEAN
Equator
SURINAM
FRENCH GUIANA
Paramaribo
Nieuw Amsterdam
Moengo
St-Laurent
Iracoubo
Sinnamary
Kourou
Cayenne
Albina
Kwakoegron
Totness
Nieuw Nickerie
C. Orange
St-Georges
Oiapoque
Camopi
AMAPÁ
Amapá
I. de Maracá
Serra Tumucumaque
Merirumã
Serra do Navio
Macapá
I. Caviana
I. Mexiana
C. Maguarinho
Mazagão
Chaves
Afuá
I. de Marajó
I. Grande de Gurupá
Soure
Curuçá
Salinópolis
Vigia
Bragança
BELÉM
Castanhal
Abaetetuba
Viseu
Turiaçu
Cururupu
Almeirim
Monte Alegre
Prainha
Gurupá
Breves
Pôrto de Moz
Curralinho
Cametá
Óbidos
Juruti
Parintins
Santarém
Belterra
Aveiro
Brasília Legal
Itaituba
Altamira
Baião
Tucuruí
Represa de Tucuruí
PARÁ
Amazonas (Amazon)
Xingu
Tapajós
Iriri
Alcântara
São Luís
B. de São Marcos
Barreirinhas
Tutóia
Luís Correia
Camocim
Granja
Itapipoca
Caucaia
FORTALEZA
Sobral
Maranguape
Cascavel
Aracati
Baturité
Russas
Quixadá
Ipu
Areia Branca
Mossoró
Macau
Ceará Mirim
C. de São Roque
Natal
Pinheiro
Viana
Rosário
Itapecuru-Mirim
Parnaíba
Santa Inês
Brejo
Piracuruca
Bacabal
Coroatá
Codó
Piripiri
Caxias
Campo Maior
Pedreiras
Açailândia
Teresina
MARANHÃO
Imperatriz
Marabá
São João do Araguaia
Carajás
Serra dos Carajás
Tocantinópolis
Barra do Corda
Grajaú
Pôrto Franco
Estreito
Carolina
Colinas
Riachão
Araguaína
Conceição do Araguaia
Araguacema
Pedro Afonso
Amarante
Valença do Piauí
Floriano
Oeiras
Picos
Crateús
Senador Pompeu
CEARÁ
Iguatu
Crato
Juàzeiro do Norte
Cajàzeiras
Sousa
Patos
Caicó
Caraúbas
RIO GRANDE DO NORTE
Currais Novos
Alagoa Grande
Canguaretama
Mamanguape
Cabedelo
João Pessoa
PARAÍBA
Campina Grande
Caruaru
Olinda
RECIFE
Jaboatão
Vitória de Santo Antão
Pesqueira
Garanhuns
Palmares
Salgueiro
Paulistana
Ouricuri
PERNAMBUCO
PIAUÍ
Uruçuí
Loreto
Nova Iorque
São João do Piauí
Santa Filomena
Caracol
Novo Remanso
Sa. Dois Irmãos
Petrolina
Juàzeiro
Paulo Afonso
Palmeira dos Índios
Arapiraca
Rio Largo
Maceió
ALAGOAS
Penedo
Propriá
SERGIPE
Aracaju
São Cristóvão
Estância
Senhor-do-Bonfim
Represa de Sobradinho
Jacobina
Xique-Xique
Mundo Novo
Queimadas
Serrinha
Feira de Santana
Alagoinhas
Santo Amaro
SALVADOR
Cachoeira
Itaberaba
Castro Alves
Valença
Nazaré
B. de Todos os Santos
Jequié
Ubaitaba
Itabuna
Vitória da Conquista
Ilhéus
Canavieiras
Belmonte
Pôrto Seguro
BAHIA
Barreiras
Ibotirama
Bom Jesus da Lapa
Serra do Sincorá
Santa Maria da Vitória
Carinhanha
Caetité
Brumado
Condeúba
Parnaguá
Barra
Palmas
Pôrto Nacional
TOCANTINS
Gurupi
Peixe
Paranã
Campos Belos
São Domingos
Taguatinga
Santa Isabel do Morro
Serra do Roncador
Serra Formosa
Serra do Cachimbo
I. do Bananal
MATO GROSSO
Planalto do Mato Grosso
Cuiabá
Diamantino
Santo Antonio
Barra do Garças
Rondonópolis
Niquelândia
Uruaçu
Aruanã
Formosa
BRASÍLIA
DIST. FED.
Luziânia
Taguatinga
Goiás
Anápolis
Goiânia
GOIÁS
Vianópolis
Paracatu
Pirapora
Morrinhos
Ipameri
Alto Araguaia
Jataí
Rio Verde
Itumbiara
Quirinópolis
Catalão
Araguari
Coxim
MATO GROSSO DO SUL
Patos de Minas
Corinto
Diamantina
MINAS GERAIS
Uberlândia
Patrocínio
Curvelo
Ituiutaba
Prata
Araxá
Ibiá
Sete Lagoas
Itabira
Uberaba
Frutal
BELO HORIZONTE
Sabará
Divinópolis
Nova Lima
Ouro Prêto
Barbacena
Juiz de Fora
Januária
São Francisco
Janaúba
Montes Claros
Monte Azul
Pedra Azul
Salinas
Jequitinhonha
Araçuaí
Teófilo Otoni
Nanuque
Itamaraju
Prado
Caravelas
Mucuri
Governador Valadares
Nova Venécia
Conceição da Barra
São Mateus
Colatina
Linhares
ESPÍRITO SANTO
Caratinga
Ponte Nova
Cariacica
Vitória
Vila Velha
Cachoeiro de Itapemirim
Itaperuna
Campos
Nova Friburgo
Três Rios
Petrópolis
Niterói
RIO DE JANEIRO
Cabo Frio
Volta Redonda
Campo Grande
Miranda
Aquidauana
Ribas do Rio Pardo
Três Lagoas
Paranaíba
Santa Fé do Sul
Água Clara
São José do Rio Prêto
Barretos
Franca
Passos
Ribeirão Prêto
Araçatuba
Andradina
Panorama
Presidente Epitácio
Presidente Prudente
Penápolis
Marília
Catanduva
Lins
SÃO PAULO
Araraquara
São Carlos
Poços de Caldas
Jaú
Bauru
Assis
Piracicaba
Limeira
Campinas
Botucatu
Moji-Mirim
Dourados
Ponta Porã
Pedro Juan Caballero
Rocas
Fernando de Noronha (Braz.)
São Paulo (Braz.)
Trindade (Braz.)
6059
1230
1678
1340
2787
2890
Greenwich
55
50
45
40
35
30
10
5
0
15
20
A
B
C
D
E
F
G
H
8
9
10
11
12
13
COPYRIGHT GEORGE PHILIP LTD.

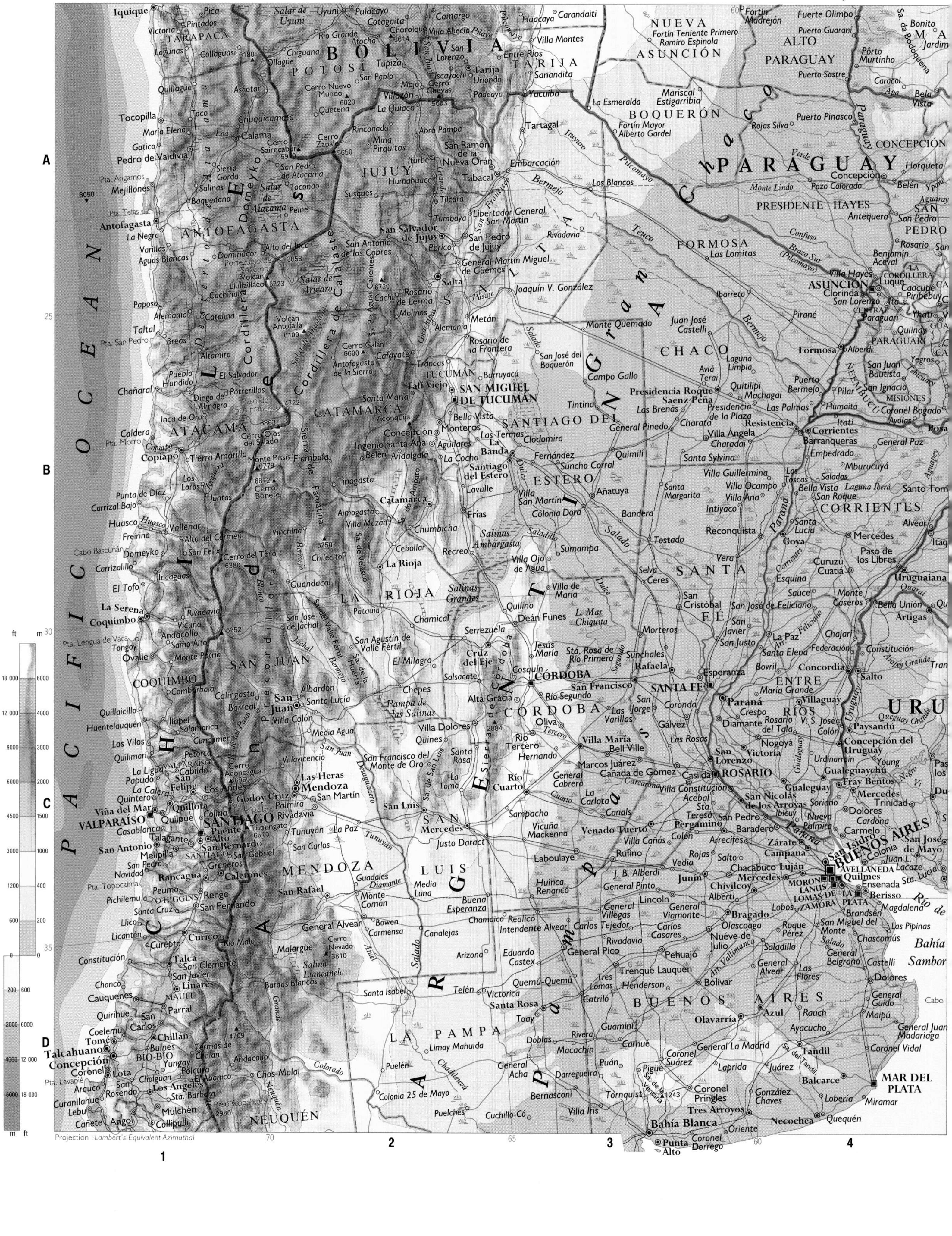

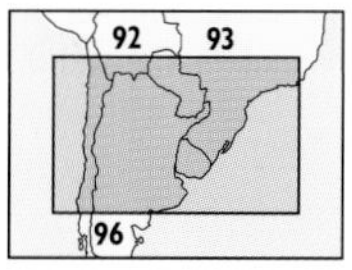

92 93
96

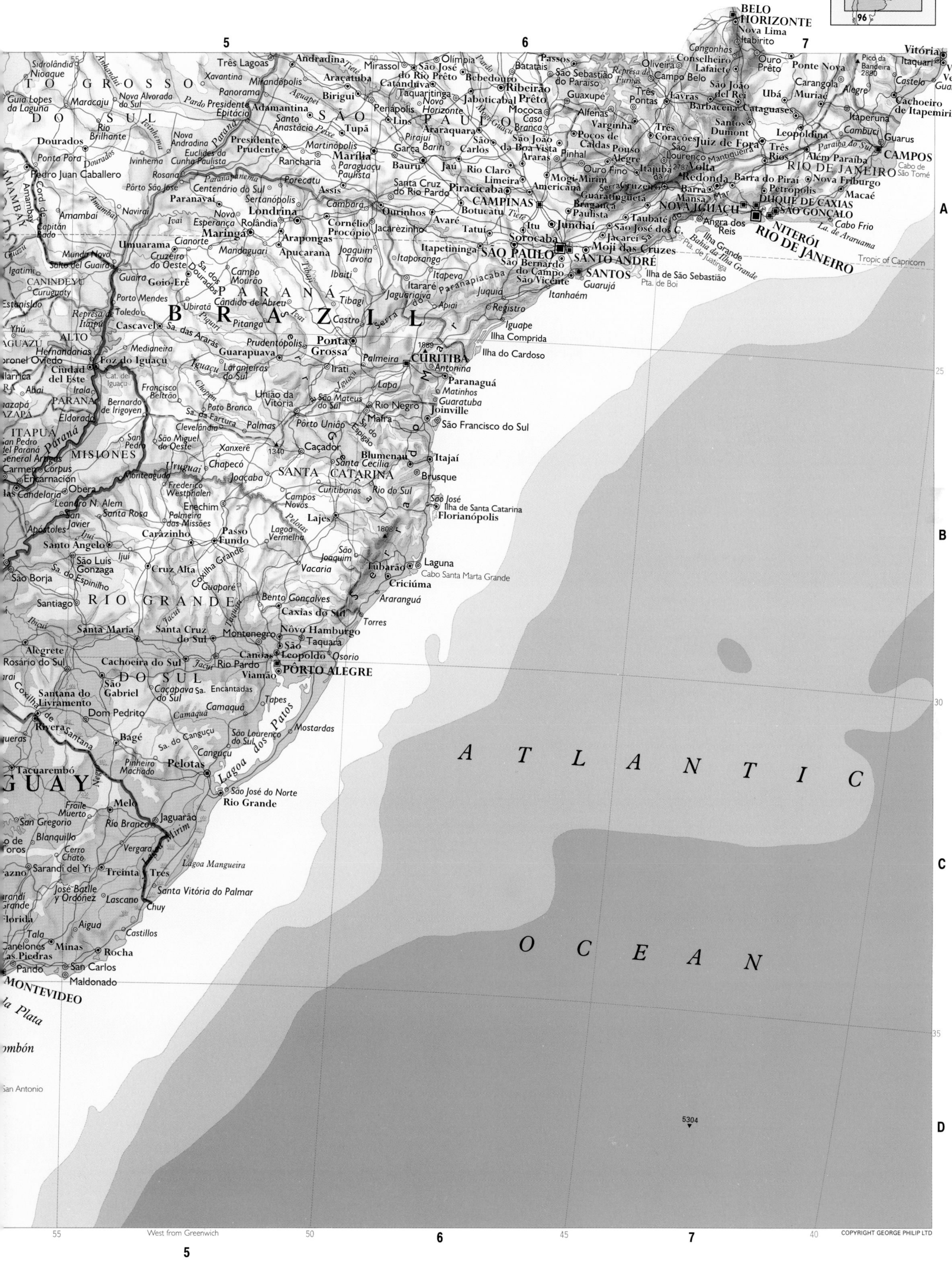

5

6

7

MATO GROSSO
DO SUL

Sidrolândia
Nioaque
Guia Lopes
da Laguna
Maracaju
Nova Alvorada
do Sul
Panorama
Três Lagoas
Andradina
Mirassol
Olímpia
São José
do Rio Prêto
Passos
Batatais
Olivera
Conselheiro
Lafaiete
Ponte Nova

BELO
HORIZONTE
Nova Lima
Itabirito
Congonhas
Ouro
Prêto
Carangola

Vitória
Itaquari
Vila
Velha
Guarapari

Dourados
Ponta Porã
Pedro Juan Caballero

Nova
Andradina
Aracatuba
Bebedouro
Ribeirão
Guaxupé
Campo Belo
São João
del Rei
Ubá
Muriaé
Pico da
Bandeira
2880
Cachoeiro
de Itapemirim

Castelo

Dourados
Rio
Brilhante
Adamantina
SÃO
Penápolis
do Rio Prêto
Mococa
Casa
Branca
Alfenas
Varginha
Três
Pontas
Barbacena
Cataguases
Itaperuna

Nova
do Sul
Pardo
Presidente
Epitácio
Martinópolis
Lins
PAULO
Araraquara
Garça
Bauru
Pouso
Alegre
Leopoldina
Cambuci
Guarus

Ponta Pora
Ivinhema
Presidente
Prudente
Tupã
Marília
Paraguaçu
Paulista
São
Carlos
Rio Claro
da Boa Vista
Araras
Pinhal
Ouro
Fino
São
Lourenço
Volta
Santos
Dumont
Juiz de Fora
Três
Rios
CAMPOS
Cabo de
São Tomé

Amambaí
Navirai
Rancharia
Assis
Piracicaba
Mogi-Mirim
Americana
Guaratinguetá
Redonda
Barra do Piraí
Nova Friburgo
Macaé

Mundo Nova
Umuarama
Londrina
Santa Cruz
do Rio Pardo
Ourinhos
CAMPINAS
Botucatu
Itu
Jundiaí
Bragança
Paulista
Taubaté
Mansa
RIO DE JANEIRO

CANINDEYU
Curuguaty
Guaira
Goio-Erê
Maringá
Apucarana
Joaquim
Távora
Avaré
Sorocaba
Jacareí
Moji das Cruzes
NOVA IGUAÇU
NITERÓI
Cabo Frio

Igatimi
Campo
Mourão
Itapetininga
SÃO PAULO
SANTO ANDRÉ
DUQUE DE CAXIAS
SÃO GONÇALO
La. de Araruama

BRAZIL
PARANÁ
São Bernardo
do Campo
Santos
São Vicente
Guarujá
Angra dos
Reis
RIO DE JANEIRO

Yhú
ALTO
Cascavel
Pitanga
Ponta
Grossa
CURITIBA
Paranapiacaba
Ilha de São Sebastião

Tropic of Capricorn

Foz do Iguaçu
Ciudad
del Este
Guarapuava
Palmeira
Antonina
Paranaguá
Pta. de Boi

Eldorado
PARANÁ
União da
Vitória
São Mateus
do Sul
Guaratuba

ITAPUA
MISIONES
Pato Branco
Pôrto União
Rio Negro
Joinville
São Francisco do Sul

Chapecó
Caçador
Itajaí
Blumenau

SANTA CATARINA
Brusque
Florianópolis
Ilha de Santa Catarina

RIO GRANDE

Lajes
Tubarão
Laguna
Cabo Santa Marta Grande

Caxias do Sul

DO SUL
Canoas
São
Leopoldo
Osorio

Pôrto Alegre
Viamão

Pelotas

Rio Grande

A T L A N T I C

O C E A N

5304

MONTEVIDEO

West from Greenwich

50

6

45

7

40

COPYRIGHT GEORGE PHILIP LTD

5

A

B

C

D

55

50

45

40

25

30

35

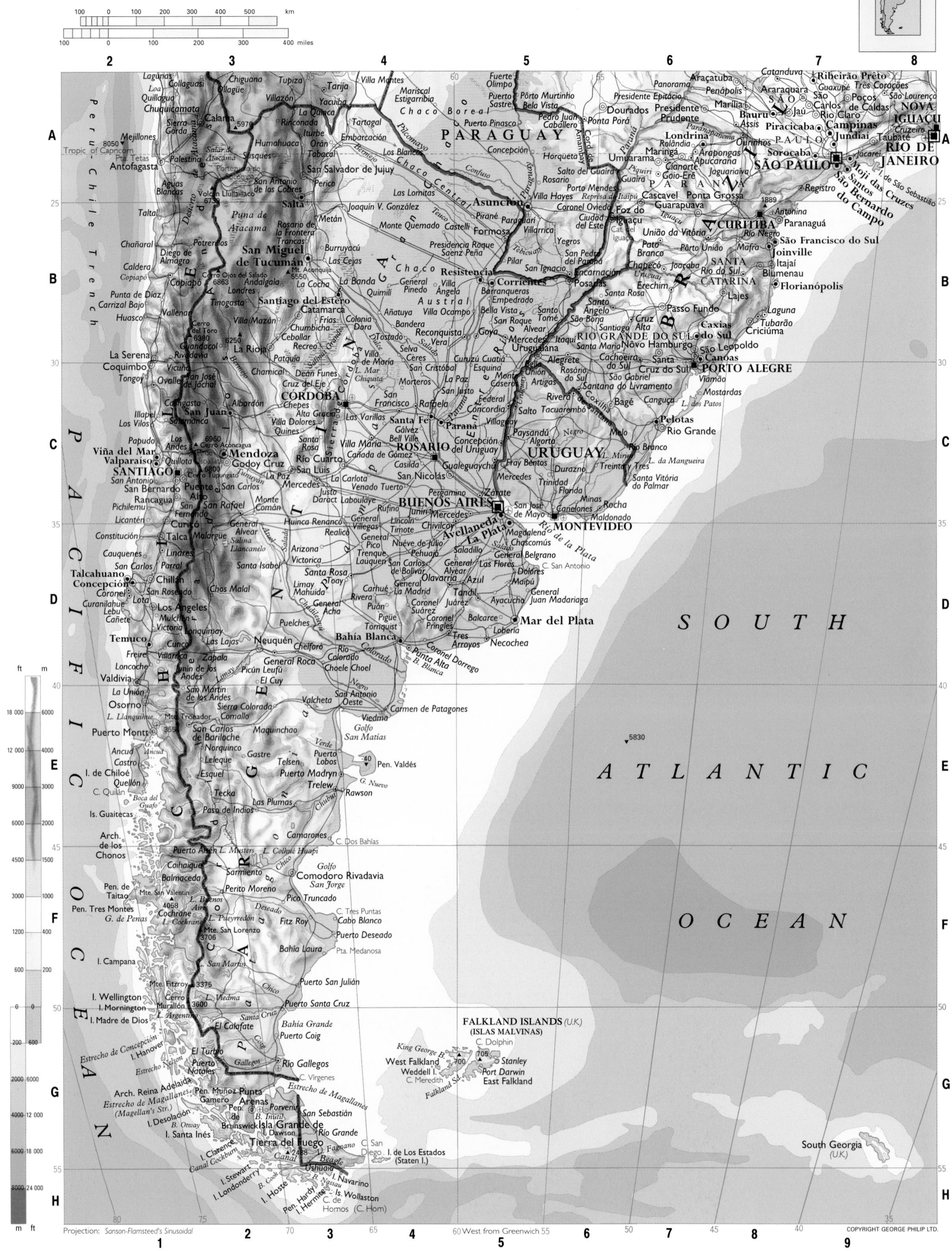
km
miles
Tropic of Capricorn
PACIFIC OCEAN
Peru-Chile Trench
SOUTH ATLANTIC OCEAN
PARAGUAY
URUGUAY
BRAZIL
ARGENTINA
CHILE
PATAGONIA
Chaco Boreal
Chaco Austral
Gran Chaco
Puna de Atacama
Desierto de Atacama
Antofagasta
Mejillones
Calama
Chuquicamata
Tocopilla
Taltal
Chañaral
Copiapó
Caldera
Vallenar
Huasco
La Serena
Coquimbo
Ovalle
Illapel
Los Vilos
Viña del Mar
Valparaíso
SANTIAGO
San Antonio
San Bernardo
Rancagua
Curicó
Talca
Constitución
Cauquenes
Chillán
Talcahuano
Concepción
Coronel
Lota
Los Ángeles
Temuco
Valdivia
Osorno
Puerto Montt
I. de Chiloé
Castro
Quellón
Is. Guaitecas
Arch. de los Chonos
Puerto Aisén
Coihaique
Pen. de Taitao
Pen. Tres Montes
G. de Penas
I. Campana
I. Wellington
Puerto Natales
Punta Arenas
Estrecho de Magallanes (Magellan's Str.)
Isla Grande de Tierra del Fuego
Ushuaia
Río Grande
I. de Los Estados (Staten I.)
C. de Hornos (C. Horn)
I. Navarino
Is. Wollaston
I. Hoste
Tarija
Yacuiba
Villa Montes
Mariscal Estigarribia
Humahuaca
San Salvador de Jujuy
Salta
San Miguel de Tucumán
Santiago del Estero
Catamarca
La Rioja
San Juan
Mendoza
Cerro Aconcagua 6960
San Luis
Río Cuarto
CÓRDOBA
Santa Fe
Paraná
ROSARIO
San Nicolás
Resistencia
Corrientes
Posadas
Formosa
Asunción
Encarnación
Concepción
BUENOS AIRES
La Plata
Avellaneda
MONTEVIDEO
Río de la Plata
Mar del Plata
Bahía Blanca
Santa Rosa
Neuquén
Viedma
Carmen de Patagones
Golfo San Matías
Pen. Valdés
Puerto Madryn
Trelew
Rawson
Comodoro Rivadavia
Golfo San Jorge
Puerto Deseado
Puerto San Julián
Puerto Santa Cruz
Río Gallegos
El Calafate
Salto
Paysandú
Rivera
Rio Grande
Pelotas
PORTO ALEGRE
Caxias do Sul
RIO GRANDE DO SUL
SANTA CATARINA
Florianópolis
Blumenau
Joinville
CURITIBA
PARANÁ
Londrina
Maringá
SÃO PAULO
Campinas
Santos
RIO DE JANEIRO
NOVA IGUAÇU
Foz do Iguaçu
Campo Grande
FALKLAND ISLANDS (U.K.) (ISLAS MALVINAS)
West Falkland
East Falkland
Stanley
South Georgia (U.K.)
Projection: Sanson-Flamsteed's Sinusoidal
West from Greenwich

INDEX

The index contains the names of all the principal places and features shown on the World Maps. Each name is followed by an additional entry in italics giving the country or region within which it is located. The alphabetical order of names composed of two or more words is governed primarily by the first word and then by the second. This is an example of the rule:

Mīr Kūh, *Iran*	**45 E8**	26 22N	58 55 E
Mīr Shahdād, *Iran*	**45 E8**	26 15N	58 29 E
Mira, *Italy*	**20 B5**	45 26N	12 8 E
Mira por vos Cay, *Bahamas* .	**89 B5**	22 9N	74 30W
Miraj, *India*	**40 L9**	16 50N	74 45 E

Physical features composed of a proper name (Erie) and a description (Lake) are positioned alphabetically by the proper name. The description is positioned after the proper name and is usually abbreviated:

Erie, L., *N. Amer.*	**78 D4**	42 15N	81 0W

Where a description forms part of a settlement or administrative name however, it is always written in full and put in its true alphabetic position:

Mount Morris, *U.S.A.*	**78 D7**	42 44N	77 52W

Names beginning with M' and Mc are indexed as if they were spelled Mac. Names beginning St. are alphabetised under Saint, but Sankt, Sint, Sant', Santa and San are all spelt in full and are alphabetised accordingly. If the same place name occurs two or more times in the index and all are in the same country, each is followed by the name of the administrative subdivision in which it is located. The names are placed in the alphabetical order of the subdivisions. For example:

Jackson, *Ky., U.S.A.*	**76 G4**	37 33N	83 23W
Jackson, *Mich., U.S.A.*	**76 D3**	42 15N	84 24W
Jackson, *Minn., U.S.A.*	**80 D7**	43 37N	95 1W

The number in bold type which follows each name in the index refers to the number of the map page where that feature or place will be found. This is usually the largest scale at which the place or feature appears.

The letter and figure which are in bold type immediately after the page number give the grid square on the map page, within which the feature is situated. The letter represents the latitude and the figure the longitude.

In some cases the feature itself may fall within the specified square, while the name is outside. This is usually the case only with features which are larger than a grid square.

For a more precise location the geographical coordinates which follow the letter/figure references give the latitude and the longitude of each place. The first set of figures represent the latitude which is the distance north or south of the Equator measured as an angle at the centre of the earth. The Equator is latitude 0°, the North Pole is 90°N, and the South Pole 90°S.

The second set of figures represent the longitude, which is the distance East or West of the prime meridian, which runs through Greenwich, England. Longitude is also measured as an angle at the centre of the earth and is given East or West of the prime meridian, from 0° to 180° in either direction.

The unit of measurement for latitude and longitude is the degree, which is subdivided into 60 minutes. Each index entry states the position of a place in degrees and minutes, a space being left between the degrees and the minutes.

The latitude is followed by N(orth) or S(outh) and the longitude by E(ast) or W(est).

Rivers are indexed to their mouths or confluences, and carry the symbol → after their names. A solid square ■ follows the name of a country, while an open square □ refers to a first order administrative area.

Abbreviations used in the index

A.C.T. – Australian Capital Territory
Afghan. – Afghanistan
Ala. – Alabama
Alta. – Alberta
Amer. – America(n)
Arch. – Archipelago
Ariz. – Arizona
Ark. – Arkansas
Atl. Oc. – Atlantic Ocean
B. – Baie, Bahía, Bay, Bucht, Bugt
B.C. – British Columbia
Bangla. – Bangladesh
Barr. – Barrage
Bos.-H. – Bosnia-Herzegovina
C. – Cabo, Cap, Cape, Coast
C.A.R. – Central African Republic
C. Prov. – Cape Province
Calif. – California
Cent. – Central
Chan. – Channel
Colo. – Colorado
Conn. – Connecticut
Cord. – Cordillera
Cr. – Creek
Czech. – Czech Republic
D.C. – District of Columbia
Del. – Delaware
Dep. – Dependency
Des. – Desert
Dist. – District
Dj. – Djebel
Domin. – Dominica
Dom. Rep. – Dominican Republic
E. – East

E. Salv. – El Salvador
Eq. Guin. – Equatorial Guinea
Fla. – Florida
Falk. Is. – Falkland Is.
G. – Golfe, Golfo, Gulf, Guba, Gebel
Ga. – Georgia
Gt. – Great, Greater
Guinea-Biss. – Guinea-Bissau
H.K. – Hong Kong
H.P. – Himachal Pradesh
Hants. – Hampshire
Harb. – Harbor, Harbour
Hd. – Head
Hts. – Heights
I.(s). – Île, Ilha, Insel, Isla, Island, Isle
Ill. – Illinois
Ind. – Indiana
Ind. Oc. – Indian Ocean
Ivory C. – Ivory Coast
J. – Jabal, Jebel, Jazira
Junc. – Junction
K. – Kap, Kapp
Kans. – Kansas
Kep. – Kepulauan
Ky. – Kentucky
L. – Lac, Lacul, Lago, Lagoa, Lake, Limni, Loch, Lough
La. – Louisiana
Liech. – Liechtenstein
Lux. – Luxembourg
Mad. P. – Madhya Pradesh
Madag. – Madagascar
Man. – Manitoba
Mass. – Massachusetts

Md. – Maryland
Me. – Maine
Medit. S. – Mediterranean Sea
Mich. – Michigan
Minn. – Minnesota
Miss. – Mississippi
Mo. – Missouri
Mont. – Montana
Mozam. – Mozambique
Mt.(e) – Mont, Monte, Monti, Montaña, Mountain
N. – Nord, Norte, North, Northern, Nouveau
N.B. – New Brunswick
N.C. – North Carolina
N. Cal. – New Caledonia
N. Dak. – North Dakota
N.H. – New Hampshire
N.I. – North Island
N.J. – New Jersey
N. Mex. – New Mexico
N.S. – Nova Scotia
N.S.W. – New South Wales
N.W.T. – North West Territory
N.Y. – New York
N.Z. – New Zealand
Nebr. – Nebraska
Neths. – Netherlands
Nev. – Nevada
Nfld. – Newfoundland
Nic. – Nicaragua
O. – Oued, Ouadi
Occ. – Occidentale
Okla. – Oklahoma
Ont. – Ontario
Or. – Orientale

Oreg. – Oregon
Os. – Ostrov
Oz. – Ozero
P. – Pass, Passo, Pasul, Pulau
P.E.I. – Prince Edward Island
Pa. – Pennsylvania
Pac. Oc. – Pacific Ocean
Papua N.G. – Papua New Guinea
Pass. – Passage
Pen. – Peninsula, Péninsule
Phil. – Philippines
Pk. – Park, Peak
Plat. – Plateau
Prov. – Province, Provincial
Pt. – Point
Pta. – Ponta, Punta
Pte. – Pointe
Qué. – Québec
Queens. – Queensland
R. – Rio, River
R.I. – Rhode Island
Ra.(s). – Range(s)
Raj. – Rajasthan
Reg. – Region
Rep. – Republic
Res. – Reserve, Reservoir
S. – San, South, Sea
Si. Arabia – Saudi Arabia
S.C. – South Carolina
S. Dak. – South Dakota
S.I. – South Island
S. Leone – Sierra Leone
Sa. – Serra, Sierra
Sask. – Saskatchewan
Scot. – Scotland
Sd. – Sound

Sev. – Severnaya
Sib. – Siberia
Sprs. – Springs
St. – Saint
Sta. – Santa, Station
Ste. – Sainte
Sto. – Santo
Str. – Strait, Stretto
Switz. – Switzerland
Tas. – Tasmania
Tenn. – Tennessee
Tex. – Texas
Tg. – Tanjung
Trin. & Tob. – Trinidad & Tobago
U.A.E. – United Arab Emirates
U.K. – United Kingdom
U.S.A. – United States of America
Ut. P. – Uttar Pradesh
Va. – Virginia
Vdkhr. – Vodokhranilishche
Vf. – Vírful
Vic. – Victoria
Vol. – Volcano
Vt. – Vermont
W. – Wadi, West
W. Va. – West Virginia
Wash. – Washington
Wis. – Wisconsin
Wlkp. – Wielkopolski
Wyo. – Wyoming
Yorks. – Yorkshire
Yug. – Yugoslavia

A Coruña

A

A Coruña, Spain 19 A1 43 20N 8 25W
A Estrada, Spain 19 A1 42 43N 8 27W
A Fonsagrada, Spain 19 A2 43 8N 7 4W
Aachen, Germany 16 C4 50 45N 6 6 E
Aalborg = Ålborg, Denmark 9 H13 57 2N 9 54 E
Aalen, Germany 16 D6 48 51N 10 6 E
Aalst, Belgium 15 D4 50 56N 4 2 E
Aalten, Neths. 15 C6 51 56N 6 35 E
Aalter, Belgium 15 C3 51 5N 3 28 E
Äänekoski, Finland 9 E21 62 36N 25 44 E
Aarau, Switz. 18 C8 47 23N 8 4 E
Aare →, Switz. 18 C8 47 33N 8 14 E
Aarhus = Århus, Denmark 9 H14 56 8N 10 11 E
Aarschot, Belgium 15 D4 50 59N 4 49 E
Aba, Dem. Rep. of the Congo 54 B3 3 58N 30 17 E
Aba, Nigeria 50 G7 5 10N 7 19 E
Ābādān, Iran 45 D6 30 22N 48 20 E
Ābādeh, Iran 45 D7 31 8N 52 40 E
Abadla, Algeria 50 B5 31 2N 2 45W
Abaetetuba, Brazil 93 D9 1 40S 48 50W
Abagnar Qi, China 34 C9 43 52N 116 2 E
Abai, Paraguay 95 B4 25 58S 55 54W
Abakan, Russia 27 D10 53 40N 91 10 E
Abancay, Peru 92 F4 13 35S 72 55W
Abariringa, Kiribati 64 H10 2 50S 171 40W
Abarqū, Iran 45 D7 31 10N 53 20 E
Abashiri, Japan 30 C12 44 0N 144 15 E
Abashiri-Wan, Japan 30 C12 44 0N 144 30 E
Abay, Kazakstan 26 E8 49 38N 72 53 E
Abaya, L., Ethiopia 46 F2 6 30N 37 50 E
Abaza, Russia 26 D10 52 39N 90 6 E
'Abbāsābād, Iran 45 C8 33 34N 58 23 E
Abbay = Nîl el Azraq →, Sudan 51 E12 15 38N 32 31 E
Abbaye, Pt., U.S.A. 76 B1 46 58N 88 8W
Abbé, L., Ethiopia 46 E3 11 8N 41 47 E
Abbeville, France 18 A4 50 6N 1 49 E
Abbeville, Ala., U.S.A. 77 K3 31 34N 85 15W
Abbeville, La., U.S.A. 81 L8 29 58N 92 8W
Abbeville, S.C., U.S.A. 77 H4 34 11N 82 23W
Abbot Ice Shelf, Antarctica 5 D16 73 0S 92 0W
Abbottabad, Pakistan 42 B5 34 10N 73 15 E
Abd al Kūrī, Ind. Oc. 46 E5 12 5N 52 20 E
Ābdar, Iran 45 D7 30 16N 55 19 E
'Abdolābād, Iran 45 C8 34 12N 56 30 E
Abdulpur, Bangla. 43 G13 24 15N 88 59 E
Abéché, Chad 51 F10 13 50N 20 35 E
Abengourou, Ivory C. 50 G5 6 42N 3 27W
Åbenrå, Denmark 9 J13 55 3N 9 25 E
Abeokuta, Nigeria 50 G6 7 3N 3 19 E
Aber, Uganda 54 B3 2 12N 32 25 E
Aberaeron, U.K. 11 E3 52 15N 4 15W
Aberayron = Aberaeron, U.K. 11 E3 52 15N 4 15W
Aberchirder, U.K. 12 D6 57 34N 2 37W
Abercorn = Mbala, Zambia 55 D3 8 46S 31 24 E
Abercorn, Australia 63 D5 25 12S 151 5 E
Aberdare, U.K. 11 F4 51 43N 3 27W
Aberdare Ra., Kenya 54 C4 0 15S 36 50 E
Aberdeen, Australia 63 E5 32 9S 150 56 E
Aberdeen, Canada 73 C7 52 20N 106 8W
Aberdeen, S. Africa 56 E3 32 28S 24 2 E
Aberdeen, U.K. 12 D6 57 9N 2 5W
Aberdeen, Ala., U.S.A. 77 J1 33 49N 88 33W
Aberdeen, Idaho, U.S.A. 82 E7 42 57N 112 50W
Aberdeen, Md., U.S.A. 76 F7 39 31N 76 10W
Aberdeen, S. Dak., U.S.A. 80 C5 45 28N 98 29W
Aberdeen, Wash., U.S.A. 84 D3 46 59N 123 50W
Aberdeen, City of □, U.K. 12 D6 57 10N 2 10W
Aberdeenshire □, U.K. 12 D6 57 17N 2 36W
Aberdovey = Aberdyfi, U.K. 11 E3 52 33N 4 3W
Aberdyfi, U.K. 11 E3 52 33N 4 3W
Aberfeldy, U.K. 12 E5 56 37N 3 51W
Abergavenny, U.K. 11 F4 51 49N 3 1W
Abergele, U.K. 10 D4 53 17N 3 35W
Abernathy, U.S.A. 81 J4 33 50N 101 51W
Abert, L., U.S.A. 82 E3 42 38N 120 14W
Aberystwyth, U.K. 11 E3 52 25N 4 5W
Abhā, Si. Arabia 46 D3 18 0N 42 34 E
Abhar, Iran 45 B6 36 9N 49 13 E
Abhayapuri, India 43 F14 26 24N 90 38 E
Abidjan, Ivory C. 50 G5 5 26N 3 58W
Abilene, Kans., U.S.A. 80 F6 38 55N 97 13W
Abilene, Tex., U.S.A. 81 J5 32 28N 99 43W
Abingdon, U.K. 11 F6 51 40N 1 17W
Abingdon, U.S.A. 77 G5 36 43N 81 59W
Abington Reef, Australia 62 B4 18 0S 149 35 E
Abitau →, Canada 73 B7 59 53N 109 3W
Abitibi →, Canada 70 B3 51 3N 80 55W
Abitibi, L., Canada 70 C4 48 40N 79 40W
Abkhaz Republic = Abkhazia □, Georgia 25 F7 43 12N 41 5 E
Abkhazia □, Georgia 25 F7 43 12N 41 5 E
Abminga, Australia 63 D1 26 8S 134 51 E
Åbo = Turku, Finland 9 F20 60 30N 22 19 E
Abohar, India 42 D6 30 10N 74 10 E
Abolo, Congo 52 D2 0 8N 14 16 E
Abomey, Benin 50 G6 7 10N 2 5 E
Abong-Mbang, Cameroon 52 D2 4 0N 13 8 E
Abou-Deïa, Chad 51 F9 11 20N 19 20 E
Aboyne, U.K. 12 D6 57 4N 2 47W
Abra Pampa, Argentina 94 A2 22 43S 65 42W
Abraham L., Canada 72 C5 52 15N 116 35W
Abreojos, Pta., Mexico 86 B2 26 50N 113 40W
Abrud, Romania 17 E12 46 19N 23 5 E
Absaroka Range, U.S.A. 82 D9 44 45N 109 50W
Abu, India 42 G5 24 41N 72 50 E
Abu al Abyad, U.A.E. 45 E7 24 11N 53 50 E
Abū al Khaşīb, Iraq 45 D6 30 25N 48 0 E
Abū 'Alī, Si. Arabia 45 E6 27 20N 49 27 E
Abū 'Alī →, Lebanon 47 A4 34 25N 35 50 E
Abu Dhabi = Abū Z̧āby, U.A.E. 45 E7 24 28N 54 22 E
Abū Du'ān, Syria 44 B3 36 25N 38 15 E
Abu el Gairi, W. →, Egypt 47 F2 29 35N 33 30 E
Abu Ga'da, W. →, Egypt 47 F1 29 15N 32 53 E
Abū Ḩadrīyah, Si. Arabia 45 E6 27 20N 48 58 E
Abu Hamed, Sudan 51 E12 19 32N 33 13 E
Abū Kamāl, Syria 44 C4 34 30N 41 0 E
Abū Madd, Ra's, Si. Arabia 44 E3 24 50N 37 7 E
Abū Mūsā, U.A.E. 45 E7 25 52N 55 3 E
Abu Şafāt, W. →, Jordan 47 E5 30 24N 36 7 E
Abu Simbel, Egypt 51 D12 22 18N 31 40 E
Abū Şukhayr, Iraq 44 D5 31 54N 44 30 E
Abû Zabad, Sudan 51 F11 12 25N 29 10 E
Abū Z̧āby, U.A.E. 45 E7 24 28N 54 22 E
Abū Zeydābād, Iran 45 C6 33 54N 51 45 E
Abuja, Nigeria 50 G7 9 16N 7 2 E
Abukuma-Gawa →, Japan 30 E10 38 6N 140 52 E
Abukuma-Sammyaku, Japan 30 F10 37 30N 140 45 E
Abunã, Brazil 92 E5 9 40S 65 20W
Abunã →, Brazil 92 E5 9 41S 65 20W
Aburo, Dem. Rep. of the Congo 54 B3 2 4N 30 53 E
Abut Hd., N.Z. 59 K3 43 7S 170 15 E
Acadia National Park, U.S.A. 77 C11 44 20N 68 13W
Açailândia, Brazil 93 D9 4 57S 47 0W
Acajutla, El Salv. 88 D2 13 36N 89 50W
Acámbaro, Mexico 86 D4 20 0N 100 40W
Acaponeta, Mexico 86 C3 22 30N 105 20W
Acapulco, Mexico 87 D5 16 51N 99 56W
Acarai, Serra, Brazil 92 C7 1 50N 57 50W
Acarigua, Venezuela 92 B5 9 33N 69 12W
Acatlán, Mexico 87 D5 18 10N 98 3W
Acayucan, Mexico 87 D6 17 59N 94 58W
Accomac, U.S.A. 76 G8 37 43N 75 40W
Accra, Ghana 50 G5 5 35N 0 6W
Accrington, U.K. 10 D5 53 45N 2 22W
Acebal, Argentina 94 C3 33 20S 60 50W
Aceh □, Indonesia 36 D1 4 15N 97 30 E
Achalpur, India 40 J10 21 22N 77 32 E
Acheng, China 35 B14 45 30N 126 58 E
Acher, India 42 H5 23 10N 72 32 E
Achill Hd., Ireland 13 C1 53 58N 10 15W
Achill I., Ireland 13 C1 53 58N 10 1W
Achinsk, Russia 27 D10 56 20N 90 20 E
Acireale, Italy 20 F6 37 37N 15 10 E
Ackerman, U.S.A. 81 J10 33 19N 89 11W
Acklins I., Bahamas 89 B5 22 30N 74 0W
Acme, Canada 72 C6 51 33N 113 30W
Acme, U.S.A. 78 F5 40 8N 79 26W
Aconcagua, Cerro, Argentina 94 C2 32 39S 70 0W
Aconquija, Mt., Argentina 94 B2 27 0S 66 0W
Açores, Is. dos = Azores, Atl. Oc. 50 A1 38 44N 29 0W
Acraman, L., Australia 63 E2 32 2S 135 23 E
Acre = 'Akko, Israel 47 C4 32 55N 35 4 E
Acre □, Brazil 92 E4 9 1S 71 0W
Acre →, Brazil 92 E5 8 45S 67 22W
Acton, Canada 78 C4 43 38N 80 3W
Acuña, Mexico 86 B4 29 18N 100 55W
Ad Dammām, Si. Arabia 45 E6 26 20N 50 5 E
Ad Dāmūr, Lebanon 47 B4 33 44N 35 27 E
Ad Dawādimī, Si. Arabia 44 E5 24 35N 44 15 E
Ad Dawḩah, Qatar 45 E6 25 15N 51 35 E
Ad Dawr, Iraq 44 C4 34 27N 43 47 E
Ad Dir'īyah, Si. Arabia 44 E5 24 44N 46 35 E
Ad Dīwānīyah, Iraq 44 D5 32 0N 45 0 E
Ad Dujayl, Iraq 44 C5 33 51N 44 14 E
Ad Duwayd, Si. Arabia 44 D4 30 15N 42 17 E
Ada, Minn., U.S.A. 80 B6 47 18N 96 31W
Ada, Okla., U.S.A. 81 H6 34 46N 96 41W
Adabiya, Egypt 47 F1 29 53N 32 28 E
Adair, C., Canada 69 A12 71 31N 71 24W
Adaja →, Spain 19 B3 41 32N 4 52W
Adak I., U.S.A. 68 C2 51 45N 176 45W
Adamaoua, Massif de l', Cameroon 52 C2 7 20N 12 20 E
Adamawa Highlands = Adamaoua, Massif de l', Cameroon 52 C2 7 20N 12 20 E
Adamello, Mte., Italy 18 C9 46 9N 10 30 E
Adaminaby, Australia 63 F4 36 0S 148 45 E
Adams, Mass., U.S.A. 79 D11 42 38N 73 7W
Adams, N.Y., U.S.A. 79 C8 43 49N 76 1W
Adams, Wis., U.S.A. 80 D10 43 57N 89 49W
Adam's Bridge, Sri Lanka 40 Q11 9 15N 79 40 E
Adams L., Canada 72 C5 51 10N 119 40W
Adams Mt., U.S.A. 84 D5 46 12N 121 30W
Adam's Peak, Sri Lanka 40 R12 6 48N 80 30 E
Adana, Turkey 25 G6 37 0N 35 16 E
Adapazarı = Sakarya, Turkey 25 F5 40 48N 30 25 E
Adarama, Sudan 51 E12 17 10N 34 52 E
Adare, C., Antarctica 5 D11 71 0S 171 0 E
Adaut, Indonesia 37 F8 8 8S 131 7 E
Adavale, Australia 63 D3 25 52S 144 32 E
Adda →, Italy 18 D8 45 8N 9 53 E
Addis Ababa = Addis Abeba, Ethiopia 46 F2 9 2N 38 42 E
Addis Abeba, Ethiopia 46 F2 9 2N 38 42 E
Addison, U.S.A. 78 D7 42 1N 77 14W
Addo, S. Africa 56 E4 33 32S 25 45 E
Ādeh, Iran 44 B5 37 42N 45 11 E
Adel, U.S.A. 77 K4 31 8N 83 25W
Adelaide, Australia 63 E2 34 52S 138 30 E
Adelaide, Bahamas 88 A4 25 4N 77 31W
Adelaide, S. Africa 56 E4 32 42S 26 20 E
Adelaide I., Antarctica 5 C17 67 15S 68 30W
Adelaide Pen., Canada 68 B10 68 15N 97 30W
Adelaide River, Australia 60 B5 13 15S 131 7 E
Adelanto, U.S.A. 85 L9 34 35N 117 22W
Adele I., Australia 60 C3 15 32S 123 9 E
Adélie, Terre, Antarctica 5 C10 68 0S 140 0 E
Adélie Land = Adélie, Terre, Antarctica 5 C10 68 0S 140 0 E
Aden = Al 'Adan, Yemen 46 E4 12 45N 45 0 E
Aden, G. of, Asia 46 E4 12 30N 47 30 E
Adendorp, S. Africa 56 E3 32 15S 24 30 E
Adh Dhayd, U.A.E. 45 E7 25 17N 55 53 E
Adhoi, India 42 H4 23 26N 70 32 E
Adi, Indonesia 37 E8 4 15S 133 30 E
Adieu, C., Australia 61 F5 32 0S 132 10 E
Adieu Pt., Australia 60 C3 15 14S 124 35 E
Adige →, Italy 20 B5 45 9N 12 20 E
Adigrat, Ethiopia 46 E2 14 20N 39 26 E
Adilabad, India 40 K11 19 33N 78 20 E
Adin Khel, Afghan. 40 C6 32 45N 68 5 E
Adirondack Mts., U.S.A. 79 C10 44 0N 74 0W
Adjumani, Uganda 54 B3 3 20N 31 50 E
Adlavik Is., Canada 71 A8 55 2N 57 45W
Admiralty G., Australia 60 B4 14 20S 125 55 E
Admiralty I., U.S.A. 72 B2 57 30N 134 30W
Admiralty Is., Papua N. G. 64 H6 2 0S 147 0 E
Adonara, Indonesia 37 F6 8 15S 123 5 E
Adoni, India 40 M10 15 33N 77 18 E
Adour →, France 18 E3 43 32N 1 32W
Adra, India 43 H12 23 30N 86 42 E
Adra, Spain 19 D4 36 43N 3 3W
Adrano, Italy 20 F6 37 40N 14 50 E
Adrar, Algeria 48 D4 27 51N 0 11 E
Adrar, Mauritania 50 D3 20 30N 7 30 E
Adrian, Mich., U.S.A. 76 E3 41 54N 84 2W
Adrian, Tex., U.S.A. 81 H3 35 16N 102 40W
Adriatic Sea, Medit. S. 20 C6 43 0N 16 0 E
Adua, Indonesia 37 E7 1 45S 129 50 E
Adwa, Ethiopia 46 E2 14 15N 38 52 E
Adygea □, Russia 25 F7 45 0N 40 0 E
Adzhar Republic = Ajaria □, Georgia 25 F7 41 30N 42 0 E
Adzopé, Ivory C. 50 G5 6 7N 3 49W
Ægean Sea, Medit. S. 21 E11 38 30N 25 0 E
Aerhtai Shan, Mongolia 32 B4 46 40N 92 45 E
'Afak, Iraq 44 C5 32 4N 45 15 E
Afándou, Greece 23 C10 36 18N 28 12 E
Afghanistan ■, Asia 40 C4 33 0N 65 0 E
Aflou, Algeria 50 B6 34 7N 2 3 E
Africa 48 E6 10 0N 20 0 E
'Afrīn, Syria 44 B3 36 32N 36 50 E
Afton, N.Y., U.S.A. 79 D9 42 14N 75 32W
Afton, Wyo., U.S.A. 82 E8 42 44N 110 56W
Afuá, Brazil 93 D8 0 15S 50 20W
'Afula, Israel 47 C4 32 37N 35 17 E
Afyon, Turkey 25 G5 38 45N 30 33 E
Afyonkarahisar = Afyon, Turkey 25 G5 38 45N 30 33 E
Agadès = Agadez, Niger 50 E7 16 58N 7 59 E
Agadez, Niger 50 E7 16 58N 7 59 E
Agadir, Morocco 50 B4 30 28N 9 55W
Agaete, Canary Is. 22 F4 28 6N 15 43W
Agar, India 42 H7 23 40N 76 2 E
Agartala, India 41 H17 23 50N 91 23 E
Agassiz, Canada 72 D4 49 14N 121 46W
Agats, Indonesia 37 F9 5 33S 138 0 E
Agawam, U.S.A. 79 D12 42 5N 72 37W
Agboville, Ivory C. 50 G5 5 55N 4 15W
Ağdam, Azerbaijan 44 B5 40 0N 46 58 E
Agde, France 18 E5 43 19N 3 28 E
Agen, France 18 D4 44 12N 0 38 E
Āgh Kand, Iran 45 B6 37 15N 48 4 E
Aginskoye, Russia 27 D12 51 6N 114 32 E
Agnew, Australia 61 E3 28 1S 120 31 E
Agori, India 43 G10 24 33N 82 57 E
Agra, India 42 F7 27 17N 77 58 E
Ağrı, Turkey 25 G7 39 44N 43 3 E
Agri →, Italy 20 D7 40 13N 16 44 E
Ağrı Dağı, Turkey 25 G7 39 50N 44 15 E
Ağrı Karakose = Ağrı, Turkey 25 G7 39 44N 43 3 E
Agrigento, Italy 20 F5 37 19N 13 34 E
Agrínion, Greece 21 E9 38 37N 21 27 E
Agua Caliente, Baja Calif., Mexico 85 N10 32 29N 116 59W
Agua Caliente, Sinaloa, Mexico 86 B3 26 30N 108 20W
Agua Caliente Springs, U.S.A. 85 N10 32 56N 116 19W
Água Clara, Brazil 93 H8 20 25S 52 45W
Agua Hechicero, Mexico 85 N10 32 26N 116 14W
Agua Prieta, Mexico 86 A3 31 20N 109 32W
Aguadilla, Puerto Rico 89 C6 18 26N 67 10W
Aguadulce, Panama 88 E3 8 15N 80 32W
Aguanga, U.S.A. 85 M10 33 27N 116 51W
Aguanish, Canada 71 B7 50 14N 62 2W
Aguanus →, Canada 71 B7 50 13N 62 5W
Aguapey →, Argentina 94 B4 29 7S 56 36W
Aguaray Guazú →, Paraguay 94 A4 24 47S 57 19W
Aguarico →, Ecuador 92 D3 0 59S 75 11W
Aguas Blancas, Chile 94 A2 24 15S 69 55W
Aguas Calientes, Sierra de, Argentina 94 B2 25 26S 66 40W
Aguascalientes, Mexico 86 C4 21 53N 102 12W
Aguascalientes □, Mexico 86 C4 22 0N 102 20W
Aguilares, Argentina 94 B2 27 26S 65 35W
Aguilas, Spain 19 D5 37 23N 1 35W
Agüimes, Canary Is. 22 G4 27 58N 15 27W
Aguja, C. de la, Colombia 90 B3 11 18N 74 12W
Agulhas, C., S. Africa 56 E3 34 52S 20 0 E
Agulo, Canary Is. 22 F2 28 11N 17 12W
Agung, Indonesia 36 F5 8 20S 115 28 E
Agur, Uganda 54 B3 2 28N 32 55 E
Agusan →, Phil. 37 C7 9 0N 125 30 E
Aha Mts., Botswana 56 B3 19 45S 21 0 E
Ahaggar, Algeria 50 D7 23 0N 6 30 E
Ahar, Iran 44 B5 38 35N 47 0 E
Ahipara B., N.Z. 59 F4 35 5S 173 5 E
Ahiri, India 40 K12 19 30N 80 0 E
Ahmad Wal, Pakistan 42 E1 29 18N 65 58 E
Ahmadabad, India 42 H5 23 0N 72 40 E
Aḩmadābād, Khorāsān, Iran 45 C9 35 3N 60 50 E
Aḩmadābād, Khorāsān, Iran 45 C8 35 49N 59 42 E
Aḩmadī, Iran 45 E8 27 56N 56 42 E
Ahmadnagar, India 40 K9 19 7N 74 46 E
Ahmadpur, Pakistan 42 E4 29 12N 71 10 E
Ahmadpur Lamma, Pakistan 42 E4 28 19N 70 3 E
Ahmedabad = Ahmadabad, India 42 H5 23 0N 72 40 E
Ahmednagar = Ahmadnagar, India 40 K9 19 7N 74 46 E
Ahome, Mexico 86 B3 25 55N 109 11W
Ahoskie, U.S.A. 77 G7 36 17N 76 59W
Ahram, Iran 45 D6 28 52N 51 16 E
Ahrax Pt., Malta 23 D1 35 59N 14 22 E
Āhū, Iran 45 C6 34 33N 50 2 E
Ahuachapán, El Salv. 88 D2 13 54N 89 52W
Ahvāz, Iran 45 D6 31 20N 48 40 E
Ahvenanmaa = Åland, Finland 9 F19 60 15N 20 0 E
Aḩwar, Yemen 46 E4 13 30N 46 40 E
Ai →, India 43 F14 26 26N 90 44 E
Aichi □, Japan 31 G8 35 0N 137 15 E
Aigua, Uruguay 95 C5 34 13S 54 46W
Aigues-Mortes, France 18 E6 43 35N 4 12 E
Aihui, China 33 A7 50 10N 127 30 E
Aija, Peru 92 E3 9 50S 77 45W
Aikawa, Japan 30 E9 38 2N 138 15 E
Aiken, U.S.A. 77 J5 33 34N 81 43W
Aileron, Australia 62 C1 22 39S 133 20 E
Aillik, Canada 71 A8 55 11N 59 18W
Ailsa Craig, U.K. 12 F3 55 15N 5 6W
'Ailūn, Jordan 47 C4 32 18N 35 47 E
Aim, Russia 27 D14 59 0N 133 55 E
Aimere, Indonesia 37 F6 8 45S 121 3 E
Aimogasta, Argentina 94 B2 28 33S 66 50W
Aïn Ben Tili, Mauritania 50 C4 25 59N 9 27W
Aïn-Sefra, Algeria 50 B5 32 47N 0 37W
'Ain Sudr, Egypt 47 F2 29 50N 33 6 E
Ainaži, Latvia 9 H21 57 50N 24 24 E
Ainsworth, U.S.A. 80 D5 42 33N 99 52W
Aiquile, Bolivia 92 G5 18 10S 65 10W
Aïr, Niger 50 E7 18 30N 8 0 E
Air Force I., Canada 69 B12 67 58N 74 5W
Air Hitam, Malaysia 39 M4 1 55N 103 11 E
Airdrie, Canada 72 C6 51 18N 114 2W
Airdrie, U.K. 12 F5 55 52N 3 57W
Aire →, U.K. 10 D7 53 43N 0 55W
Aire, I. de l', Spain 22 B11 39 48N 4 16 E
Airlie Beach, Australia 62 C4 20 16S 148 43 E
Aisne →, France 18 B5 49 26N 2 50 E
Ait, India 43 G8 25 54N 79 14 E
Aitkin, U.S.A. 80 B8 46 32N 93 42W
Aiud, Romania 17 E12 46 19N 23 44 E
Aix-en-Provence, France 18 E6 43 32N 5 27 E
Aix-la-Chapelle = Aachen, Germany 16 C4 50 45N 6 6 E
Aix-les-Bains, France 18 D6 45 41N 5 53 E
Aíyion, Greece 21 E10 38 15N 22 5 E
Aizawl, India 41 H18 23 40N 92 44 E
Aizkraukle, Latvia 9 H21 56 36N 25 11 E
Aizpute, Latvia 9 H19 56 43N 21 40 E
Aizuwakamatsu, Japan 30 F9 37 30N 139 56 E
Ajaccio, France 18 F8 41 55N 8 40 E
Ajaigarh, India 43 G9 24 52N 80 16 E
Ajalpan, Mexico 87 D5 18 22N 97 15W
Ajanta Ra., India 40 J9 20 28N 75 50 E
Ajari Rep. = Ajaria □, Georgia 25 F7 41 30N 42 0 E
Ajaria □, Georgia 25 F7 41 30N 42 0 E
Ajax, Canada 78 C5 43 50N 79 1W
Ajdâbiyah, Libya 51 B10 30 54N 20 4 E
Ajka, Hungary 17 E9 47 4N 17 31 E
'Ajmān, U.A.E. 45 E7 25 25N 55 30 E
Ajmer, India 42 F6 26 28N 74 37 E
Ajnala, India 42 D6 31 50N 74 48 E
Ajo, U.S.A. 83 K7 32 22N 112 52W
Ajo, C. de, Spain 19 A4 43 31N 3 35W
Akabira, Japan 30 C11 43 33N 142 5 E
Akamas □, Cyprus 23 D11 35 3N 32 18 E
Akanthou, Cyprus 23 D12 35 22N 33 45 E
Akaroa, N.Z. 59 K4 43 49S 172 59 E
Akashi, Japan 31 G7 34 45N 134 58 E
Akbarpur, Bihar, India 43 G10 24 39N 83 58 E
Akbarpur, Ut. P., India 43 F10 26 25N 82 32 E
Akelamo, Indonesia 37 D7 1 35N 129 40 E
Aketi, Dem. Rep. of the Congo 52 D4 2 38N 23 47 E
Akharnaí, Greece 21 E10 38 5N 23 44 E
Akhelóös →, Greece 21 E9 38 19N 21 7 E
Akhisar, Turkey 21 E12 38 56N 27 48 E
Akhnur, India 43 C6 32 52N 74 45 E
Akhtyrka = Okhtyrka, Ukraine 25 D5 50 25N 35 0 E
Aki, Japan 31 H6 33 30N 133 54 E
Akimiski I., Canada 70 B3 52 50N 81 30W
Akita, Japan 30 E10 39 45N 140 7 E
Akita □, Japan 30 E10 39 40N 140 30 E
Akjoujt, Mauritania 50 E3 19 45N 14 15W
Akkeshi, Japan 30 C12 43 2N 144 51 E
'Akko, Israel 47 C4 32 55N 35 4 E
Aklavik, Canada 68 B6 68 12N 135 0W
Aklera, India 42 G7 24 26N 76 32 E
Akmolinsk = Astana, Kazakstan 26 D8 51 10N 71 30 E
Akō, Japan 31 G7 34 45N 134 24 E
Akola, India 40 J10 20 42N 77 2 E
Akordat, Eritrea 46 D2 15 30N 37 40 E
Akpatok I., Canada 69 B13 60 25N 68 8W
Åkrahamn, Norway 9 G11 59 15N 5 10 E
Akranes, Iceland 8 D2 64 19N 22 5W
Akron, Colo., U.S.A. 80 E3 40 10N 103 13W
Akron, Ohio, U.S.A. 78 E3 41 5N 81 31W
Akrotiri, Cyprus 23 E11 34 36N 32 57 E
Akrotiri Bay, Cyprus 23 E12 34 35N 33 10 E
Aksai Chin, India 43 B8 35 15N 79 55 E
Aksaray, Turkey 25 G5 38 25N 34 2 E
Aksay, Kazakstan 25 D9 51 11N 53 0 E
Akşehir, Turkey 44 B1 38 18N 31 30 E
Akşehir Gölü, Turkey 25 G5 38 30N 31 25 E
Aksu, China 32 B3 41 5N 80 10 E
Aksum, Ethiopia 46 E2 14 5N 38 40 E
Aktogay, Kazakstan 26 E8 46 57N 79 40 E
Aktsyabrski, Belarus 17 B15 52 38N 28 53 E
Aktyubinsk = Aqtöbe, Kazakstan 25 D10 50 17N 57 10 E
Akure, Nigeria 50 G7 7 15N 5 5 E
Akureyri, Iceland 8 D4 65 40N 18 6W
Akuseki-Shima, Japan 31 K4 29 27N 129 37 E
Akyab = Sittwe, Burma 41 J18 20 18N 92 45 E
Al 'Adan, Yemen 46 E4 12 45N 45 0 E
Al Aḩsā = Hasa □, Si. Arabia 45 E6 25 50N 49 0 E
Al Ajfar, Si. Arabia 44 E4 27 26N 43 0 E
Al Amādīyah, Iraq 44 B4 37 5N 43 30 E
Al 'Amārah, Iraq 44 D5 31 55N 47 15 E
Al 'Aqabah, Jordan 47 F4 29 31N 35 0 E
Al Arak, Syria 44 C3 34 38N 38 35 E
Al 'Aramah, Si. Arabia 44 E5 25 30N 46 0 E
Al Arţāwīyah, Si. Arabia 44 E5 26 31N 45 20 E
Al 'Āşimah = 'Ammān □, Jordan 47 D5 31 40N 36 30 E
Al 'Assāfīyah, Si. Arabia 44 D3 28 17N 38 59 E
Al 'Ayn, Oman 45 E7 24 15N 55 45 E
Al 'Ayn, Si. Arabia 44 E3 25 4N 38 6 E
Al 'Az̧amīyah, Iraq 44 C5 33 22N 44 22 E
Al 'Azīzīyah, Iraq 44 C5 32 54N 45 4 E
Al Bāb, Syria 44 B3 36 23N 37 29 E
Al Bad', Si. Arabia 44 D2 28 28N 35 1 E
Al Bādī, Iraq 44 C4 35 56N 41 32 E
Al Baḩrah, Kuwait 44 D5 29 40N 47 52 E
Al Baḩral Mayyit = Dead Sea, Asia 47 D4 31 30N 35 30 E
Al Balqā' □, Jordan 47 C4 32 5N 35 45 E
Al Bārūk, J., Lebanon 47 B4 33 39N 35 40 E
Al Başrah, Iraq 44 D5 30 30N 47 50 E
Al Baţḩā, Iraq 44 D5 31 6N 45 53 E
Al Batrūn, Lebanon 47 A4 34 15N 35 40 E
Al Bayḑā, Libya 51 B10 32 50N 21 44 E
Al Biqā, Lebanon 47 A5 34 10N 36 10 E
Al Bi'r, Si. Arabia 44 D3 28 51N 36 16 E
Al Burayj, Syria 47 A5 34 15N 36 46 E
Al Faḑilī, Si. Arabia 45 E6 26 58N 49 10 E

Amadeus, L.

Al Fallūjah, *Iraq* **44 C4** 33 20N 43 55 E
Al Fāw, *Iraq* **45 D6** 30 0N 48 30 E
Al Fujayrah, *U.A.E.* **45 E8** 25 7N 56 18 E
Al Ghadaf, W. →, *Jordan* **47 D5** 31 26N 36 43 E
Al Ghammās, *Iraq* **44 D5** 31 45N 44 37 E
Al Ghazālah, *Si. Arabia* **44 E4** 26 48N 41 19 E
Al Hābah, *Si. Arabia* **44 E5** 27 10N 47 0 E
Al Ḥadīthah, *Iraq* **44 C4** 34 0N 41 13 E
Al Ḥadīthah, *Si. Arabia* **47 D6** 31 28N 37 8 E
Al Ḥaḍr, *Iraq* **44 C4** 35 35N 42 44 E
Al Hājānah, *Syria* **47 B5** 33 20N 36 33 E
Al Hajar al Gharbī, *Oman* **45 E8** 24 10N 56 15 E
Al Hāmad, *Si. Arabia* **44 D3** 31 30N 39 30 E
Al Hamdānīyah, *Syria* **44 C3** 35 25N 36 50 E
Al Ḥamīdīyah, *Syria* **47 A4** 34 42N 35 57 E
Al Ḥammār, *Iraq* **44 D5** 30 57N 46 51 E
Al Ḥamrā', *Si. Arabia* **44 E3** 24 2N 38 55 E
Al Ḥanākīyah, *Si. Arabia* **44 E4** 24 51N 40 31 E
Al Harīr, W. →, *Syria* **47 C4** 32 44N 35 59 E
Al Ḥasā, W. →, *Jordan* **47 D4** 31 4N 35 29 E
Al Ḥasakah, *Syria* **44 B4** 36 35N 40 45 E
Al Haydān, W. →, *Jordan* **47 D4** 31 29N 35 34 E
Al Ḥayy, *Iraq* **44 C5** 32 5N 46 5 E
Al Ḥijarah, *Asia* **44 D4** 30 0N 44 0 E
Al Ḥillah, *Iraq* **44 C5** 32 30N 44 25 E
Al Hindīyah, *Iraq* **44 C5** 32 30N 44 10 E
Al Hirmil, *Lebanon* **47 A5** 34 26N 36 24 E
Al Hoceïma, *Morocco* **50 A5** 35 8N 3 58W
Al Ḥudaydah, *Yemen* **46 E3** 14 50N 43 0 E
Al Hufūf, *Si. Arabia* **45 E6** 25 25N 49 45 E
Al Ḥumayḍah, *Si. Arabia* **44 D2** 29 14N 34 56 E
Al Ḥunayy, *Si. Arabia* **45 E6** 25 58N 48 45 E
Al Īsāwīyah, *Si. Arabia* **44 D3** 30 43N 37 59 E
Al Jafr, *Jordan* **47 E5** 30 18N 36 14 E
Al Jāfūrah, *Si. Arabia* **45 E7** 25 0N 50 15 E
Al Jaghbūb, *Libya* **51 C10** 29 42N 24 38 E
Al Jahrah, *Kuwait* **44 D5** 29 25N 47 40 E
Al Jalāmīd, *Si. Arabia* **44 D3** 31 20N 40 6 E
Al Jamalīyah, *Qatar* **45 E6** 25 37N 51 5 E
Al Janūb □, *Lebanon* **47 B4** 33 20N 35 20 E
Al Jawf, *Libya* **51 D10** 24 10N 23 24 E
Al Jawf, *Si. Arabia* **44 D3** 29 55N 39 40 E
Al Jazirah, *Iraq* **44 C5** 33 30N 44 0 E
Al Jithāmīyah, *Si. Arabia* **44 E4** 27 41N 41 43 E
Al Jubayl, *Si. Arabia* **45 E6** 27 0N 49 50 E
Al Jubaylah, *Si. Arabia* **44 E5** 24 55N 46 25 E
Al Jubb, *Si. Arabia* **44 E4** 27 11N 42 17 E
Al Junaynah, *Sudan* **51 F10** 13 27N 22 45 E
Al Kabā'ish, *Iraq* **44 D5** 30 58N 47 0 E
Al Karak, *Jordan* **47 D4** 31 11N 35 42 E
Al Karak □, *Jordan* **47 E5** 31 0N 36 0 E
Al Kāzim Tyah, *Iraq* **44 C5** 33 22N 44 12 E
Al Khābūra, *Oman* **45 F8** 23 57N 57 5 E
Al Khafji, *Si. Arabia* **45 E6** 28 24N 48 29 E
Al Khalīl, *West Bank* **47 D4** 31 32N 35 6 E
Al Khāliṣ, *Iraq* **44 C5** 33 49N 44 32 E
Al Kharsānīyah, *Si. Arabia* **45 E6** 27 13N 49 18 E
Al Khaṣab, *Oman* **45 E8** 26 14N 56 15 E
Al Khawr, *Qatar* **45 E6** 25 41N 51 30 E
Al Khiḍr, *Iraq* **44 D5** 31 12N 45 33 E
Al Khiyām, *Lebanon* **47 B4** 33 20N 35 36 E
Al Khums, *Libya* **51 B8** 32 40N 14 17 E
Al Kiswah, *Syria* **47 B5** 33 23N 36 14 E
Al Kūfah, *Iraq* **44 C5** 32 2N 44 24 E
Al Kufrah, *Libya* **51 D10** 24 17N 23 15 E
Al Kuhayfiyah, *Si. Arabia* **44 E4** 27 12N 43 3 E
Al Kūt, *Iraq* **44 C5** 32 30N 46 0 E
Al Kuwayt, *Kuwait* **44 D5** 29 30N 48 0 E
Al Labwah, *Lebanon* **47 A5** 34 11N 36 20 E
Al Lādhiqīyah, *Syria* **44 C2** 35 30N 35 45 E
Al Līth, *Si. Arabia* **46 C3** 20 9N 40 15 E
Al Liwā', *Oman* **45 E8** 24 31N 56 36 E
Al Luḥayyah, *Yemen* **46 D3** 15 45N 42 40 E
Al Madīnah, *Iraq* **44 D5** 30 57N 47 16 E
Al Madīnah, *Si. Arabia* **46 C2** 24 35N 39 52 E
Al Mafraq, *Jordan* **47 C5** 32 17N 36 14 E
Al Maḥmūdīyah, *Iraq* **44 C5** 33 3N 44 21 E
Al Majma'ah, *Si. Arabia* **44 E5** 25 57N 45 22 E
Al Makhruq, W. →, *Jordan* **47 D6** 31 28N 37 0 E
Al Makḥūl, *Si. Arabia* **44 E4** 26 37N 42 39 E
Al Manāmah, *Bahrain* **45 E6** 26 10N 50 30 E
Al Maqwa', *Kuwait* **44 D5** 29 10N 47 59 E
Al Marj, *Libya* **51 B10** 32 25N 20 30 E
Al Maṭlā, *Kuwait* **44 D5** 29 24N 47 40 E
Al Mawjib, W. →, *Jordan* **47 D4** 31 28N 35 36 E
Al Mawṣil, *Iraq* **44 B4** 36 15N 43 5 E
Al Mayādin, *Syria* **44 C4** 35 1N 40 27 E
Al Mazār, *Jordan* **47 D4** 31 4N 35 41 E
Al Midhnab, *Si. Arabia* **44 E5** 25 50N 44 18 E
Al Minā', *Lebanon* **47 A4** 34 24N 35 49 E
Al Miqdādīyah, *Iraq* **44 C5** 34 0N 45 0 E
Al Mubarraz, *Si. Arabia* **45 E6** 25 30N 49 40 E
Al Mudawwarah, *Jordan* **47 F5** 29 19N 36 0 E
Al Mughayrā', *U.A.E.* **45 E7** 24 5N 53 32 E
Al Muḥarraq, *Bahrain* **45 E6** 26 15N 50 40 E
Al Mukallā, *Yemen* **46 E4** 14 33N 49 2 E
Al Mukhā, *Yemen* **46 E3** 13 18N 43 15 E
Al Musayjīd, *Si. Arabia* **44 E3** 24 5N 39 5 E
Al Musayyib, *Iraq* **44 C5** 32 49N 44 20 E
Al Muwayliḥ, *Si. Arabia* **44 E2** 27 40N 35 30 E
Al Qā'im, *Iraq* **44 C4** 34 21N 41 7 E
Al Qalībah, *Si. Arabia* **44 D3** 28 24N 37 42 E
Al Qāmishli, *Syria* **44 B4** 37 10N 41 10 E
Al Qaryatayn, *Syria* **47 A6** 34 12N 37 13 E
Al Qaṣīm, *Si. Arabia* **44 E4** 26 0N 43 0 E
Al Qaṭ'ā, *Syria* **44 C4** 34 40N 40 48 E
Al Qaṭīf, *Si. Arabia* **45 E6** 26 35N 50 0 E
Al Qatrānah, *Jordan* **47 D5** 31 12N 36 6 E
Al Qaṭrūn, *Libya* **51 D9** 24 56N 15 3 E
Al Qayṣūmah, *Si. Arabia* **44 D5** 28 20N 46 7 E
Al Quds = Jerusalem, *Israel* **47 D4** 31 47N 35 10 E
Al Qunayṭirah, *Syria* **47 C4** 32 55N 35 45 E
Al Qurnah, *Iraq* **44 D5** 31 1N 47 25 E
Al Quṣayr, *Iraq* **44 D5** 30 39N 45 50 E
Al Quṣayr, *Syria* **47 A5** 34 31N 36 34 E
Al Qutayfah, *Syria* **47 B5** 33 44N 36 36 E
Al 'Ubaylah, *Si. Arabia* **46 C5** 21 59N 50 57 E
Al 'Uḍaylīyah, *Si. Arabia* **45 E6** 25 8N 49 18 E
Al 'Ulā, *Si. Arabia* **44 E3** 26 35N 38 0 E
Al 'Uqayr, *Si. Arabia* **45 E6** 25 40N 50 15 E
Al 'Uthmānīyah, *Si. Arabia* **45 E6** 25 5N 49 22 E
Al 'Uwaynid, *Si. Arabia* **44 E5** 24 50N 46 0 E
Al 'Uwayqīlah, *Si. Arabia* **44 D4** 30 30N 42 10 E
Al 'Uyūn, Ḥijāz, *Si. Arabia* **44 E3** 24 33N 39 35 E
Al 'Uyūn, Najd, *Si. Arabia* **44 E4** 26 30N 43 50 E
Al 'Uzayr, *Iraq* **44 D5** 31 19N 47 25 E
Al Wajh, *Si. Arabia* **44 E3** 26 10N 36 30 E
Al Wakrah, *Qatar* **45 E6** 25 10N 51 40 E
Al Wannān, *Si. Arabia* **45 E6** 26 55N 48 24 E
Al Waqbah, *Si. Arabia* **44 D5** 28 48N 45 33 E
Al Wari'āh, *Si. Arabia* **44 E5** 27 51N 47 25 E
Al Wusayl, *Qatar* **45 E6** 25 29N 51 29 E
Ala Dağ, *Turkey* **44 B2** 37 44N 35 9 E
Ala Tau Shankou = Dzungarian Gates, *Kazakstan* **32 B3** 45 0N 82 0 E
Alabama □, *U.S.A.* **77 J2** 33 0N 87 0W
Alabama →, *U.S.A.* **77 K2** 31 8N 87 57W
Alabaster, *U.S.A.* **77 J2** 33 15N 86 49W
Alaçam Dağları, *Turkey* **21 E13** 39 18N 28 49 E
Alachua, *U.S.A.* **77 L4** 29 47N 82 30W
Alaérma, *Greece* **23 C9** 36 9N 27 57 E
Alagoa Grande, *Brazil* **93 E11** 7 3S 35 35W
Alagoas □, *Brazil* **93 E11** 9 0S 36 0W
Alagoinhas, *Brazil* **93 F11** 12 7S 38 20W
Alaior, *Spain* **22 B11** 39 57N 4 8 E
Alajero, *Canary Is.* **22 F2** 28 3N 17 13W
Alajuela, *Costa Rica* **88 D3** 10 2N 84 8W
Alakamisy, *Madag.* **57 C8** 21 19S 47 14 E
Alaknanda →, *India* **43 D8** 30 8N 78 36 E
Alakurtti, *Russia* **24 A5** 67 0N 30 30 E
Alamarvdasht, *Iran* **45 E7** 27 37N 52 59 E
Alameda, *Calif., U.S.A.* **84 H4** 37 46N 122 15W
Alameda, *N. Mex., U.S.A.* **83 J10** 35 11N 106 37W
Alamo, *U.S.A.* **85 J11** 37 22N 115 10W
Alamo Crossing, *U.S.A.* **85 L13** 34 16N 113 33W
Alamogordo, *U.S.A.* **83 K11** 32 54N 105 57W
Alamos, *Mexico* **86 B3** 27 0N 109 0W
Alamosa, *U.S.A.* **83 H11** 37 28N 105 52W
Åland, *Finland* **9 F19** 60 15N 20 0 E
Ålands hav, *Sweden* **9 F18** 60 0N 19 30 E
Alandur, *India* **40 N12** 13 0N 80 15 E
Alania = North Ossetia □, *Russia* **25 F7** 43 30N 44 30 E
Alanya, *Turkey* **25 G5** 36 38N 32 0 E
Alaotra, Farihin', *Madag.* **57 B8** 17 30S 48 30 E
Alapayevsk, *Russia* **26 D7** 57 52N 61 42 E
Alaşehir, *Turkey* **21 E13** 38 23N 28 30 E
Alaska □, *U.S.A.* **68 B5** 64 0N 154 0W
Alaska, G. of, *Pac. Oc.* **68 C5** 58 0N 145 0W
Alaska Peninsula, *U.S.A.* **68 C4** 56 0N 159 0W
Alaska Range, *U.S.A.* **68 B4** 62 50N 151 0W
Älät, *Azerbaijan* **25 G8** 39 58N 49 25 E
Alatyr, *Russia* **24 D8** 54 55N 46 35 E
Alausi, *Ecuador* **92 D3** 2 0S 78 50W
Alava, C., *U.S.A.* **82 B1** 48 10N 124 44W
Alavus, *Finland* **9 E20** 62 35N 23 36 E
Alawoona, *Australia* **63 E3** 34 45S 140 30 E
'Alayh, *Lebanon* **47 B4** 33 46N 35 33 E
Alba, *Italy* **18 D8** 44 42N 8 2 E
Alba-Iulia, *Romania* **17 E12** 46 8N 23 39 E
Albacete, *Spain* **19 C5** 39 0N 1 50W
Albacutya, L., *Australia* **63 F3** 35 45S 141 58 E
Albanel, L., *Canada* **70 B5** 50 55N 73 12W
Albania ■, *Europe* **21 D9** 41 0N 20 0 E
Albany, *Australia* **61 G2** 35 1S 117 58 E
Albany, *Ga., U.S.A.* **77 K3** 31 35N 84 10W
Albany, *N.Y., U.S.A.* **79 D11** 42 39N 73 45W
Albany, *Oreg., U.S.A.* **82 D2** 44 38N 123 6W
Albany, *Tex., U.S.A.* **81 J5** 32 44N 99 18W
Albany →, *Canada* **70 B3** 52 17N 81 31W
Albardón, *Argentina* **94 C2** 31 20S 68 30W
Albatross B., *Australia* **62 A3** 12 45S 141 30 E
Albemarle, *U.S.A.* **77 H5** 35 21N 80 11W
Albemarle Sd., *U.S.A.* **77 H7** 36 5N 76 0W
Alberche →, *Spain* **19 C3** 39 58N 4 46W
Alberdi, *Paraguay* **94 B4** 26 14S 58 20W
Albert, L., *Australia* **63 F2** 35 30S 139 10 E
Albert Edward Ra., *Australia* **60 C4** 18 17S 127 57 E
Albert L., *Africa* **54 B3** 1 30N 31 0 E
Albert Lea, *U.S.A.* **80 D8** 43 39N 93 22W
Albert Nile →, *Uganda* **54 B3** 3 36N 32 2 E
Albert Town, *Bahamas* **89 B5** 22 37N 74 33W
Alberta □, *Canada* **72 C6** 54 40N 115 0W
Alberti, *Argentina* **94 D3** 35 1S 60 16W
Albertinia, *S. Africa* **56 E3** 34 11S 21 34 E
Alberton, *Canada* **71 C7** 46 50N 64 0W
Albertville = Kalemie, *Dem. Rep. of the Congo* **54 D2** 5 55S 29 9 E
Albertville, *France* **18 D7** 45 40N 6 22 E
Albertville, *U.S.A.* **77 H2** 34 16N 86 13W
Albi, *France* **18 E5** 43 56N 2 9 E
Albia, *U.S.A.* **80 E8** 41 2N 92 48W
Albina, *Surinam* **93 B8** 5 37N 54 15W
Albina, Ponta, *Angola* **56 B1** 15 52S 11 44 E
Albion, *Mich., U.S.A.* **76 D3** 42 15N 84 45W
Albion, *Nebr., U.S.A.* **80 E6** 41 42N 98 0W
Albion, *Pa., U.S.A.* **78 E4** 41 53N 80 22W
Alborán, *Medit. S.* **19 E4** 35 57N 3 0W
Ålborg, *Denmark* **9 H13** 57 2N 9 54 E
Alborz, Reshteh-ye Kūhhā-ye, *Iran* **45 C7** 36 0N 52 0 E
Albuquerque, *U.S.A.* **83 J10** 35 5N 106 39W
Albuquerque, Cayos de, *Caribbean* **88 D3** 12 10N 81 50W
Alburg, *U.S.A.* **79 B11** 44 59N 73 18W
Albury-Wodonga, *Australia* **63 F4** 36 3S 146 56 E
Alcalá de Henares, *Spain* **19 B4** 40 28N 3 22W
Alcalá la Real, *Spain* **19 D4** 37 27N 3 57W
Álcamo, *Italy* **20 F5** 37 59N 12 55 E
Alcaníz, *Spain* **19 B5** 41 2N 0 8W
Alcântara, *Brazil* **93 D10** 2 20S 44 30W
Alcántara, Embalse de, *Spain* **19 C2** 39 44N 6 50W
Alcantarilla, *Spain* **19 D5** 37 59N 1 12W
Alcaraz, Sierra de, *Spain* **19 C4** 38 40N 2 20W
Alcaudete, *Spain* **19 D3** 37 35N 4 5W
Alcázar de San Juan, *Spain* **19 C4** 39 24N 3 12W
Alchevsk, *Ukraine* **25 E6** 48 30N 38 45 E
Alcira = Alzira, *Spain* **19 C5** 39 9N 0 30W
Alcova, *U.S.A.* **82 E10** 42 34N 106 43W
Alcoy, *Spain* **19 C5** 38 43N 0 30W
Alcúdia, *Spain* **22 B10** 39 51N 3 7 E
Alcúdia, B. d', *Spain* **22 B10** 39 47N 3 15 E
Aldabra Is., *Seychelles* **49 G8** 9 22S 46 28 E
Aldama, *Mexico* **87 C5** 23 0N 98 4W
Aldan, *Russia* **27 D13** 58 40N 125 30 E
Aldan →, *Russia* **27 C13** 63 28N 129 35 E
Aldea, Pta. de la, *Canary Is.* **22 G4** 28 0N 15 50W
Aldeburgh, *U.K.* **11 E9** 52 10N 1 37 E
Alder Pk., *U.S.A.* **84 K5** 35 53N 121 22W
Alderney, *U.K.* **11 H5** 49 42N 2 11W
Aldershot, *U.K.* **11 F7** 51 15N 0 44W
Aledo, *U.S.A.* **80 E9** 41 12N 90 45W
Aleg, *Mauritania* **50 E3** 17 3N 13 55W
Alegranza, *Canary Is.* **22 E6** 29 23N 13 32W
Alegranza, I., *Canary Is.* **22 E6** 29 23N 13 32W
Alegre, *Brazil* **95 A7** 20 50S 41 30W
Alegrete, *Brazil* **95 B4** 29 40S 56 0W
Aleisk, *Russia* **26 D9** 52 40N 83 0 E
Aleksandriya = Oleksandriya, *Ukraine* **17 C14** 50 37N 26 19 E
Aleksandrov Gay, *Russia* **25 D8** 50 9N 48 34 E
Aleksandrovsk-Sakhalinskiy, *Russia* **27 D15** 50 50N 142 20 E
Além Paraíba, *Brazil* **95 A7** 21 52S 42 41W
Alemania, *Argentina* **94 B2** 25 40S 65 30W
Alemania, *Chile* **94 B2** 25 10S 69 55W
Alençon, *France* **18 B4** 48 27N 0 4 E
Alenquer, *Brazil* **93 D8** 1 56S 54 46W
Alenuihaha Channel, *U.S.A.* **74 H17** 20 30N 156 0W
Aleppo = Ḥalab, *Syria* **44 B3** 36 10N 37 15 E
Alès, *France* **18 D6** 44 9N 4 5 E
Alessándria, *Italy* **18 D8** 44 54N 8 37 E
Ålesund, *Norway* **9 E12** 62 28N 6 12 E
Aleutian Is., *Pac. Oc.* **68 C2** 52 0N 175 0W
Aleutian Trench, *Pac. Oc.* **64 C10** 48 0N 180 0 E
Alexander, *U.S.A.* **80 B3** 47 51N 103 39W
Alexander, Mt., *Australia* **61 E3** 28 58S 120 16 E
Alexander Arch., *U.S.A.* **68 C6** 56 0N 136 0W
Alexander Bay, *S. Africa* **56 D2** 28 40S 16 30 E
Alexander City, *U.S.A.* **77 J3** 32 56N 85 58W
Alexander I., *Antarctica* **5 C17** 69 0S 70 0W
Alexandra, *Australia* **63 F4** 37 8S 145 40 E
Alexandra, *N.Z.* **59 L2** 45 14S 169 25 E
Alexandra Falls, *Canada* **72 A5** 60 29N 116 18W
Alexandria = El Iskandarîya, *Egypt* **51 B11** 31 13N 29 58 E
Alexandria, *B.C., Canada* **72 C4** 52 35N 122 27W
Alexandria, *Ont., Canada* **79 A10** 45 19N 74 38W
Alexandria, *Romania* **17 G13** 43 57N 25 24 E
Alexandria, *S. Africa* **56 E4** 33 38S 26 28 E
Alexandria, *U.K.* **12 F4** 55 59N 4 35W
Alexandria, *La., U.S.A.* **81 K8** 31 18N 92 27W
Alexandria, *Minn., U.S.A.* **80 C7** 45 53N 95 22W
Alexandria, *S. Dak., U.S.A.* **80 D6** 43 39N 97 47W
Alexandria, *Va., U.S.A.* **76 F7** 38 48N 77 3W
Alexandria Bay, *U.S.A.* **79 B9** 44 20N 75 55W
Alexandrina, L., *Australia* **63 F2** 35 25S 139 10 E
Alexandroúpolis, *Greece* **21 D11** 40 50N 25 54 E
Alexis →, *Canada* **71 B8** 52 33N 56 8W
Alexis Creek, *Canada* **72 C4** 52 10N 123 20W
Alfabia, *Spain* **22 B9** 39 44N 2 44 E
Alfenas, *Brazil* **95 A6** 21 20S 46 10W
Alford, *Aberds., U.K.* **12 D6** 57 14N 2 41W
Alford, *Lincs., U.K.* **10 D8** 53 15N 0 10 E
Alfred, *Maine, U.S.A.* **79 C14** 43 29N 70 43W
Alfred, *N.Y., U.S.A.* **78 D7** 42 16N 77 48W
Alfreton, *U.K.* **10 D6** 53 6N 1 24W
Alga, *Kazakstan* **25 E10** 49 53N 57 20 E
Algaida, *Spain* **22 B9** 39 33N 2 53 E
Ålgård, *Norway* **9 G11** 58 46N 5 53 E
Algarve, *Portugal* **19 D1** 36 58N 8 20W
Algeciras, *Spain* **19 D3** 36 9N 5 28W
Algemesí, *Spain* **19 C5** 39 11N 0 27W
Alger, *Algeria* **50 A6** 36 42N 3 8 E
Algeria ■, *Africa* **50 C6** 28 30N 2 0 E
Alghero, *Italy* **20 D3** 40 33N 8 19 E
Algiers = Alger, *Algeria* **50 A6** 36 42N 3 8 E
Algoa B., *S. Africa* **56 E4** 33 50S 25 45 E
Algoma, *U.S.A.* **76 C2** 44 36N 87 26W
Algona, *U.S.A.* **80 D7** 43 4N 94 14W
Algonac, *U.S.A.* **78 D2** 42 37N 82 32W
Algonquin Prov. Park, *Canada* **70 C4** 45 50N 78 30W
Algorta, *Uruguay* **96 C5** 32 25S 57 23W
Alhambra, *U.S.A.* **85 L8** 34 8N 118 6W
Alhucemas = Al Hoceïma, *Morocco* **50 A5** 35 8N 3 58W
'Alī al Gharbī, *Iraq* **44 C5** 32 30N 46 45 E
'Alī ash Sharqī, *Iraq* **44 C5** 32 7N 46 44 E
'Alī Khēl, *Afghan.* **42 C3** 33 57N 69 43 E
Alī Shāh, *Iran* **44 B5** 38 9N 45 50 E
'Alīābād, *Khorāsān, Iran* **45 C8** 32 30N 57 30 E
'Alīābād, *Kordestān, Iran* **44 C5** 35 4N 46 58 E
'Alīābād, *Yazd, Iran* **45 D7** 31 41N 53 49 E
Aliağa, *Turkey* **21 E12** 38 47N 26 59 E
Aliákmon →, *Greece* **21 D10** 40 30N 22 36 E
Alicante, *Spain* **19 C5** 38 23N 0 30W
Alice, *S. Africa* **56 E4** 32 48S 26 55 E
Alice, *U.S.A.* **81 M5** 27 45N 98 5W
Alice →, *Queens., Australia* **62 C3** 24 2S 144 50 E
Alice →, *Queens., Australia* **62 B3** 15 35S 142 20 E
Alice Arm, *Canada* **72 B3** 55 29N 129 31W
Alice Springs, *Australia* **62 C1** 23 40S 133 50 E
Alicedale, *S. Africa* **56 E4** 33 15S 26 4 E
Aliceville, *U.S.A.* **77 J1** 33 8N 88 9W
Aliganj, *India* **43 F8** 27 30N 79 10 E
Aligarh, *Raj., India* **42 G7** 25 55N 76 15 E
Aligarh, *Ut. P., India* **42 F8** 27 55N 78 10 E
Alīgūdarz, *Iran* **45 C6** 33 25N 49 45 E
Alimnía, *Greece* **23 C9** 36 16N 27 43 E
Alingsås, *Sweden* **9 H15** 57 56N 12 31 E
Alipur, *Pakistan* **42 E4** 29 25N 70 55 E
Alipur Duar, *India* **41 F16** 26 30N 89 35 E
Aliquippa, *U.S.A.* **78 F4** 40 37N 80 15W
Alitus = Alytus, *Lithuania* **9 J21** 54 24N 24 3 E
Aliwal North, *S. Africa* **56 E4** 30 45S 26 45 E
Alix, *Canada* **72 C6** 52 24N 113 11W
Aljustrel, *Portugal* **19 D1** 37 55N 8 10W
Alkmaar, *Neths.* **15 B4** 52 37N 4 45 E
All American Canal, *U.S.A.* **83 K6** 32 45N 115 15W
Allagash →, *U.S.A.* **77 B11** 47 5N 69 3W
Allah Dad, *Pakistan* **42 G2** 25 38N 67 34 E
Allahabad, *India* **43 G9** 25 25N 81 58 E
Allan, *Canada* **73 C7** 51 53N 106 4W
Allanmyo, *Burma* **41 K19** 19 30N 95 17 E
Allanridge, *S. Africa* **56 D4** 27 45S 26 40 E
Allegany, *U.S.A.* **78 D6** 42 6N 78 30W
Allegheny →, *U.S.A.* **78 F5** 40 27N 80 1W
Allegheny Mts., *U.S.A.* **76 G6** 38 15N 80 10W
Allegheny Reservoir, *U.S.A.* **78 E6** 41 50N 79 0W
Allen, Bog of, *Ireland* **13 C5** 53 15N 7 0W
Allen, L., *Ireland* **13 B3** 54 8N 8 4W
Allendale, *U.S.A.* **77 J5** 33 1N 81 18W
Allende, *Mexico* **86 B4** 28 20N 100 50W
Allentown, *U.S.A.* **79 F9** 40 37N 75 29W
Alleppey, *India* **40 Q10** 9 30N 76 28 E
Aller →, *Germany* **16 B5** 52 56N 9 12 E
Alliance, *Nebr., U.S.A.* **80 D3** 42 6N 102 52W
Alliance, *Ohio, U.S.A.* **78 F3** 40 55N 81 6W
Allier →, *France* **18 C5** 46 57N 3 4 E
Alliford Bay, *Canada* **72 C2** 53 12N 131 58W
Alliston, *Canada* **78 B5** 44 9N 79 52W
Alloa, *U.K.* **12 E5** 56 7N 3 47W
Allora, *Australia* **63 D5** 28 2S 152 0 E
Alluitsup Paa = Sydprøven, *Greenland* **4 C5** 60 30N 45 35W
Alma, *Canada* **71 C5** 48 35N 71 40W
Alma, *Ga., U.S.A.* **77 K4** 31 33N 82 28W
Alma, *Kans., U.S.A.* **80 F6** 39 1N 96 17W
Alma, *Mich., U.S.A.* **76 D3** 43 23N 84 39W
Alma, *Nebr., U.S.A.* **80 E5** 40 6N 99 22W
Alma Ata = Almaty, *Kazakstan* **26 E8** 43 15N 76 57 E
Almada, *Portugal* **19 C1** 38 40N 9 9W
Almaden, *Australia* **62 B3** 17 22S 144 40 E
Almadén, *Spain* **19 C3** 38 49N 4 52W
Almanor, L., *U.S.A.* **82 F3** 40 14N 121 9W
Almansa, *Spain* **19 C5** 38 51N 1 5W
Almanzor, Pico, *Spain* **19 B3** 40 15N 5 18W
Almanzora →, *Spain* **19 D5** 37 14N 1 46W
Almaty, *Kazakstan* **26 E8** 43 15N 76 57 E
Almazán, *Spain* **19 B4** 41 30N 2 30W
Almeirim, *Brazil* **93 D8** 1 30S 52 34W
Almelo, *Neths.* **15 B6** 52 22N 6 42 E
Almendralejo, *Spain* **19 C2** 38 41N 6 26W
Almere-Stad, *Neths.* **15 B5** 52 20N 5 15 E
Almería, *Spain* **19 D4** 36 52N 2 27W
Almirante, *Panama* **88 E3** 9 10N 82 30W
Almiroú, Kólpos, *Greece* **23 D6** 35 23N 24 20 E
Almond, *U.S.A.* **78 D7** 42 19N 77 44W
Almont, *U.S.A.* **78 D1** 42 55N 83 3W
Almonte, *Canada* **79 A8** 45 14N 76 12W
Almora, *India* **43 E8** 29 38N 79 40 E
Alness, *U.K.* **12 D4** 57 41N 4 16W
Alnmouth, *U.K.* **10 B6** 55 24N 1 37W
Alnwick, *U.K.* **10 B6** 55 24N 1 42W
Aloi, *Uganda* **54 B3** 2 16N 33 10 E
Alon, *Burma* **41 H19** 22 12N 95 5 E
Alor, *Indonesia* **37 F6** 8 15S 124 30 E
Alor Setar, *Malaysia* **39 J3** 6 7N 100 22 E
Alot, *India* **42 H6** 23 56N 75 40 E
Aloysius, Mt., *Australia* **61 E4** 26 0S 128 38 E
Alpaugh, *U.S.A.* **84 K7** 35 53N 119 29W
Alpena, *U.S.A.* **76 C4** 45 4N 83 27W
Alpha, *Australia* **62 C4** 23 39S 146 37 E
Alphen aan den Rijn, *Neths.* **15 B4** 52 7N 4 40 E
Alpine, *Ariz., U.S.A.* **83 K9** 33 51N 109 9W
Alpine, *Calif., U.S.A.* **85 N10** 32 50N 116 46W
Alpine, *Tex., U.S.A.* **81 K3** 30 22N 103 40W
Alps, *Europe* **18 C8** 46 30N 9 30 E
Alsace, *France* **18 B7** 48 15N 7 25 E
Alsask, *Canada* **73 C7** 51 21N 109 59W
Alsasua, *Spain* **19 A4** 42 54N 2 10W
Alsek →, *U.S.A.* **72 B1** 59 10N 138 12W
Alsten, *Norway* **8 D15** 65 58N 12 40 E
Alston, *U.K.* **10 C5** 54 49N 2 25W
Alta, *Norway* **8 B20** 69 57N 23 10 E
Alta Gracia, *Argentina* **94 C3** 31 40S 64 30W
Alta Sierra, *U.S.A.* **85 K8** 35 42N 118 33W
Altaelva →, *Norway* **8 B20** 69 54N 23 17 E
Altafjorden, *Norway* **8 A20** 70 5N 23 5 E
Altai = Aerhtai Shan, *Mongolia* **32 B4** 46 40N 92 45 E
Altamaha →, *U.S.A.* **77 K5** 31 20N 81 20W
Altamira, *Brazil* **93 D8** 3 12S 52 10W
Altamira, *Chile* **94 B2** 25 47S 69 51W
Altamira, *Mexico* **87 C5** 22 24N 97 55W
Altamont, *U.S.A.* **79 D10** 42 43N 74 3W
Altamura, *Italy* **20 D7** 40 49N 16 33 E
Altanbulag, *Mongolia* **32 A5** 50 16N 106 30 E
Altar, *Mexico* **86 A2** 30 40N 111 50W
Altar, Desierto de, *Mexico* **86 B2** 30 10N 112 0W
Altata, *Mexico* **86 C3** 24 30N 108 0W
Altavista, *U.S.A.* **76 G6** 37 6N 79 17W
Altay, *China* **32 B3** 47 48N 88 10 E
Altea, *Spain* **19 C5** 38 38N 0 2W
Altiplano = Bolivian Plateau, *S. Amer.* **90 E4** 20 0S 67 30W
Alto Araguaia, *Brazil* **93 G8** 17 15S 53 20W
Alto Cuchumatanes = Cuchumatanes, Sierra de los, *Guatemala* **88 C1** 15 35N 91 25W
Alto del Carmen, *Chile* **94 B1** 28 46S 70 30W
Alto del Inca, *Chile* **94 A2** 24 10S 68 10W
Alto Ligonha, *Mozam.* **55 F4** 15 30S 38 11 E
Alto Molocue, *Mozam.* **55 F4** 15 50S 37 35 E
Alto Paraguay □, *Paraguay* **94 A4** 21 0S 58 30W
Alto Paraná □, *Paraguay* **95 B5** 25 30S 54 50W
Alton, *Canada* **78 C4** 43 54N 80 5W
Alton, *U.K.* **11 F7** 51 9N 0 59W
Alton, *Ill., U.S.A.* **80 F9** 38 53N 90 11W
Alton, *N.H., U.S.A.* **79 C13** 43 27N 71 13W
Altoona, *U.S.A.* **78 F6** 40 31N 78 24W
Altūn Kūprī, *Iraq* **44 C5** 35 45N 44 9 E
Altun Shan, *China* **32 C3** 38 30N 88 0 E
Alturas, *U.S.A.* **82 F3** 41 29N 120 32W
Altus, *U.S.A.* **81 H5** 34 38N 99 20W
Alucra, *Turkey* **25 F6** 40 22N 38 47 E
Alūksne, *Latvia* **9 H22** 57 24N 27 3 E
Alunite, *U.S.A.* **85 K12** 35 59N 114 55W
Alusi, *Indonesia* **37 F8** 7 35S 131 40 E
Alva, *U.S.A.* **81 G5** 36 48N 98 40W
Alvarado, *Mexico* **87 D5** 18 40N 95 50W
Alvarado, *U.S.A.* **81 J6** 32 24N 97 13W
Alvaro Obregón, Presa, *Mexico* **86 B3** 27 55N 109 52W
Alvear, *Argentina* **94 B4** 29 5S 56 30W
Alvesta, *Sweden* **9 H16** 56 54N 14 35 E
Alvin, *U.S.A.* **81 L7** 29 26N 95 15W
Alvinston, *Canada* **78 D3** 42 49N 81 52W
Älvkarleby, *Sweden* **9 F17** 60 34N 17 26 E
Alvord Desert, *U.S.A.* **82 E4** 42 30N 118 25W
Älvsbyn, *Sweden* **8 D19** 65 40N 21 0 E
Alwar, *India* **42 F7** 27 38N 76 34 E
Alxa Zuoqi, *China* **34 E3** 38 50N 105 40 E
Alyangula, *Australia* **62 A2** 13 55S 136 30 E
Alyata = Älät, *Azerbaijan* **25 G8** 39 58N 49 25 E
Alyth, *U.K.* **12 E5** 56 38N 3 13W
Alytus, *Lithuania* **9 J21** 54 24N 24 3 E
Alzada, *U.S.A.* **80 C2** 45 2N 104 25W
Alzira, *Spain* **19 C5** 39 9N 0 30W
Am-Timan, *Chad* **51 F10** 11 0N 20 10 E
Amadeus, L., *Australia* **61 D5** 24 54S 131 0 E

Amadi

Amadi,
Dem. Rep. of the Congo . **54 B2** 3 40N 26 40 E
Amâdi, *Sudan* . . . . **51 G12** 5 29N 30 25 E
Amadjuak L., *Canada* **69 B12** 65 0N 71 8W
Amagansett, *U.S.A.* **79 F12** 40 59N 72 9W
Amagasaki, *Japan* . . . . **31 G7** 34 42N 135 20 E
Amahai, *Indonesia* . . . . **37 E7** 3 20S 128 55 E
Amakusa-Shotō, *Japan* . . . **31 H5** 32 15N 130 10 E
Åmål, *Sweden* . . . . **9 G15** 59 3N 12 42 E
Amaliás, *Greece* . . . . **21 F9** 37 47N 21 22 E
Amalner, *India* . . . . **40 J9** 21 5N 75 5 E
Amamapare, *Indonesia* . . . **37 E9** 4 53S 136 38 E
Amambaí, *Brazil* **95 A4** 23 5S 55 13W
Amambaí →, *Brazil* **95 A5** 23 22S 53 56W
Amambay □, *Paraguay* . . . **95 A4** 23 0S 56 0W
Amambay, Cordillera de,
S. Amer. **95 A4** 23 0S 55 45W
Amami-Guntō, *Japan* . . . . . **31 L4** 27 16N 129 21 E
Amami-Ō-Shima, *Japan* . . . **31 L4** 28 0N 129 0 E
Amanã, L., *Brazil* **92 D6** 2 35S 64 40W
Amanat →, *India* . . . . **43 G11** 24 7N 84 4 E
Amanda Park, *U.S.A.* **84 C3** 47 28N 123 55W
Amangeldy, *Kazakstan* . . . . **26 D7** 50 10N 65 10 E
Amapá, *Brazil* **93 C8** 2 5N 50 50W
Amapá □, *Brazil* **93 C8** 1 40N 52 0W
Amarante, *Brazil* **93 E10** 6 14S 42 50W
Amaranth, *Canada* **73 C9** 50 36N 98 43W
Amargosa →, *U.S.A.* **85 J10** 36 14N 116 51W
Amargosa Range, *U.S.A.* . . **85 J10** 36 20N 116 45W
Amári, *Greece* . . . . **23 D6** 35 13N 24 40 E
Amarillo, *U.S.A.* **81 H4** 35 13N 101 50W
Amarkantak, *India* . . . . **43 H9** 22 40N 81 45 E
Amaro, Mte., *Italy* . . . . **20 C6** 42 5N 14 5 E
Amarpur, *India* . . . . **43 G12** 25 5N 87 0 E
Amarwara, *India* . . . . **43 H8** 22 18N 79 10 E
Amasya □, *Turkey* . . . . **25 F6** 40 40N 35 50 E
Amata, *Australia* . . . . **61 E5** 26 9S 131 9 E
Amatikulu, *S. Africa* . . . . . . **57 D5** 29 3S 31 33 E
Amatitlán, *Guatemala* **88 D1** 14 29N 90 38W
Amay, *Belgium* . . . . **15 D5** 50 33N 5 19 E
Amazon = Amazonas →,
S. Amer. **93 D9** 0 5S 50 0W
Amazonas □, *Brazil* **92 E6** 5 0S 65 0W
Amazonas →, *S. Amer.* . . **93 D9** 0 5S 50 0W
Ambah, *India* . . . . **42 F8** 26 43N 78 13 E
Ambahakily, *Madag.* . . . . . . **57 C7** 21 36S 43 41 E
Ambala, *India* . . . . **42 D7** 30 23N 76 56 E
Ambalavao, *Madag.* . . . . . . **57 C8** 21 50S 46 56 E
Ambanja, *Madag.* . . . . **57 A8** 13 40S 48 27 E
Ambarchik, *Russia* . . . . **27 C17** 69 40N 162 20 E
Ambarijeby, *Madag.* . . . . . . **57 A8** 14 56S 47 41 E
Ambaro, Helodranon',
Madag. . . . . **57 A8** 13 23S 48 38 E
Ambato, *Ecuador* **92 D3** 1 5S 78 42W
Ambato, Sierra de,
Argentina **94 B2** 28 25S 66 10W
Ambato Boeny, *Madag.* . . . **57 B8** 16 28S 46 43 E
Ambatofinandrahana,
Madag. . . . . **57 C8** 20 33S 46 48 E
Ambatolampy, *Madag.* . . . . **57 B8** 19 20S 47 35 E
Ambatondrazaka, *Madag.* . **57 B8** 17 55S 48 28 E
Ambatosoratra, *Madag.* . . . **57 B8** 17 37S 48 31 E
Ambenja, *Madag.* . . . . **57 B8** 15 17S 46 58 E
Amberg, *Germany* . . . . **16 D6** 49 26N 11 52 E
Ambergris Cay, *Belize* **87 D7** 18 0N 88 0W
Amberley, *N.Z.* . . . . **59 K4** 43 9S 172 44 E
Ambikapur, *India* . . . . **43 H10** 23 15N 83 15 E
Ambilobé, *Madag.* . . . . **57 A8** 13 10S 49 3 E
Ambinanindrano, *Madag.* . . **57 C8** 20 5S 48 23 E
Amble, *U.K.* **10 B6** 55 20N 1 36W
Ambleside, *U.K.* **10 C5** 54 26N 2 58W
Ambo, *Peru* **92 F3** 10 5S 76 10W
Ambodifototra, *Madag.* . . . . **57 B8** 16 59S 49 52 E
Ambodilazana, *Madag.* . . . . **57 B8** 18 6S 49 10 E
Ambohimahasoa, *Madag.* . . **57 C8** 21 7S 47 13 E
Ambohimanga, *Madag.* . . . . **57 C8** 20 52S 47 36 E
Ambohitra, *Madag.* . . . . **57 A8** 12 30S 49 10 E
Amboise, *France* . . . . **18 C4** 47 24N 1 2 E
Ambon, *Indonesia* . . . . **37 E7** 3 35S 128 20 E
Amboseli, L., *Kenya* . . . . . . **54 C4** 2 40S 37 10 E
Ambositra, *Madag.* . . . . **57 C8** 20 31S 47 25 E
Ambovombe, *Madag.* . . . . . . **57 D8** 25 11S 46 5 E
Amboy, *U.S.A.* **85 L11** 34 33N 115 45W
Amboyna Cay, *S. China Sea* **36 C4** 7 50N 112 50 E
Ambridge, *U.S.A.* **78 F4** 40 36N 80 14W
Ambriz, *Angola* . . . . **52 F2** 7 48S 13 8 E
Amchitka I., *U.S.A.* . . . . . . **68 C1** 51 32N 179 0 E
Amderma, *Russia* . . . . **26 C7** 69 45N 61 30 E
Amdhi, *India* . . . . **43 H9** 23 51N 81 27 E
Ameca, *Mexico* **86 C4** 20 30N 104 0W
Ameca →, *Mexico* **86 C3** 20 40N 105 15W
Amecameca, *Mexico* **87 D5** 19 7N 98 46W
Ameland, *Neths.* . . . . **15 A5** 53 27N 5 45 E
Amenia, *U.S.A.* **79 E11** 41 51N 73 33W
American Falls, *U.S.A.* **82 E7** 42 47N 112 51W
American Falls Reservoir,
U.S.A. **82 E7** 42 47N 112 52W
American Fork, *U.S.A.* **82 F8** 40 23N 111 48W
American Highland,
Antarctica . . . . **5 D6** 73 0S 75 0 E
American Samoa ■,
Pac. Oc. **59 B13** 14 20S 170 40W
Americana, *Brazil* **95 A6** 22 45S 47 20W
Americus, *U.S.A.* **77 K3** 32 4N 84 14W
Amersfoort, *Neths.* . . . . **15 B5** 52 9N 5 23 E
Amersfoort, *S. Africa* . . . . . **57 D4** 26 59S 29 53 E
Amery Ice Shelf, *Antarctica* **5 C6** 69 30S 72 0 E
Ames, *U.S.A.* **80 E8** 42 2N 93 37W
Amesbury, *U.S.A.* **79 D14** 42 51N 70 56W
Amet, *India* . . . . **42 G5** 25 18N 73 56 E
Amga, *Russia* . . . . **27 C14** 60 50N 132 0 E
Amga →, *Russia* . . . . **27 C14** 62 38N 134 32 E
Amgu, *Russia* . . . . **27 E14** 45 45N 137 15 E
Amgun →, *Russia* . . . . . . **27 D14** 52 56N 139 38 E
Amherst, *Burma* . . . . **41 L20** 16 2N 97 20 E
Amherst, *Canada* **71 C7** 45 48N 64 8W
Amherst, *Mass., U.S.A.* . . . **79 D12** 42 23N 72 31W
Amherst, *N.Y., U.S.A.* **78 D6** 42 59N 78 48W
Amherst, *Ohio, U.S.A.* **78 E2** 41 24N 82 14W
Amherst I., *Canada* **79 B8** 44 8N 76 43W
Amherstburg, *Canada* **70 D3** 42 6N 83 6W
Amiata, Mte., *Italy* . . . . **20 C4** 42 53N 11 37 E
Amidon, *U.S.A.* **80 B3** 46 29N 103 19W
Amiens, *France* . . . . **18 B5** 49 54N 2 16 E
Amīrābād, *Iran* . . . . **44 C5** 33 20N 46 16 E
Amirante Is., *Seychelles* . . . **28 K9** 6 0S 53 0 E
Amisk L., *Canada* **73 C8** 54 35N 102 15W
Amistad, Presa de la,
Mexico **86 B4** 29 24N 101 0W
Amite, *U.S.A.* **81 K9** 30 44N 90 30W
Amla, *India* . . . . **42 J8** 21 56N 78 7 E
Amlia I., *U.S.A.* **68 C2** 52 4N 173 30W
Amlwch, *U.K.* **10 D3** 53 24N 4 20W
'Ammān, *Jordan* . . . . **47 D4** 31 57N 35 52 E
'Ammān □, *Jordan* . . . . . . **47 D5** 31 40N 36 30 E
Ammanford, *U.K.* **11 F4** 51 48N 3 59W
Ammassalik =
Angmagssalik, *Greenland* **4 C6** 65 40N 37 20W
Ammon, *U.S.A.* **82 E8** 43 28N 111 58W
Amnat Charoen, *Thailand* . **38 E5** 15 51N 104 38 E
Amnura, *Bangla.* . . . . **43 G13** 24 37N 88 25 E
Āmol, *Iran* . . . . **45 B7** 36 23N 52 20 E
Amorgós, *Greece* . . . . **21 F11** 36 50N 25 57 E
Amory, *U.S.A.* **77 J1** 33 59N 88 29W
Amos, *Canada* **70 C4** 48 35N 78 5W
Åmot, *Norway* . . . . **9 G13** 59 57N 9 54 E
Amoy = Xiamen, *China* . . . **33 D6** 24 25N 118 4 E
Ampang, *Malaysia* . . . . **39 L3** 3 8N 101 45 E
Ampanihy, *Madag.* . . . . **57 C7** 24 40S 44 45 E
Ampasindava, Helodranon',
Madag. . . . . **57 A8** 13 40S 48 15 E
Ampasindava, Saikanosy,
Madag. . . . . **57 A8** 13 42S 47 55 E
Ampenan, *Indonesia* . . . . . . **36 F5** 8 35S 116 13 E
Amper →, *Germany* . . . . . **16 D6** 48 29N 11 55 E
Ampotaka, *Madag.* . . . . **57 D7** 25 3S 44 41 E
Ampoza, *Madag.* . . . . **57 C7** 22 20S 44 44 E
Amqui, *Canada* **71 C6** 48 28N 67 27W
Amravati, *India* . . . . **40 J10** 20 55N 77 45 E
Amreli, *India* . . . . **42 J4** 21 35N 71 17 E
Amritsar, *India* . . . . **42 D6** 31 35N 74 57 E
Amroha, *India* . . . . **43 E8** 28 53N 78 30 E
Amsterdam, *Neths.* . . . . **15 B4** 52 23N 4 54 E
Amsterdam, *U.S.A.* **79 D10** 42 56N 74 11W
Amsterdam, I., *Ind. Oc.* . . . **3 F13** 38 30S 77 30 E
Amstetten, *Austria* . . . . **16 D8** 48 7N 14 51 E
Amudarya →, *Uzbekistan* **26 E6** 43 58N 59 34 E
Amundsen Gulf, *Canada* . . **68 A7** 71 0N 124 0W
Amundsen Sea, *Antarctica* **5 D15** 72 0S 115 0W
Amuntai, *Indonesia* . . . . . . **36 E5** 2 28S 115 25 E
Amur →, *Russia* . . . . **27 D15** 52 56N 141 10 E
Amurang, *Indonesia* . . . . . . **37 D6** 1 5N 124 40 E
Amuri Pass, *N.Z.* . . . . **59 K4** 42 31S 172 11 E
Amursk, *Russia* . . . . **27 D14** 50 14N 136 54 E
Amyderya = Amudarya →,
Uzbekistan . . . . **26 E6** 43 58N 59 34 E
An Bien, *Vietnam* . . . . **39 H5** 9 45N 105 0 E
An Hoa, *Vietnam* . . . . **38 E7** 15 40N 108 5 E
An Nabatīyah at Tahta,
Lebanon . . . . **47 B4** 33 23N 35 27 E
An Nabk, *Si. Arabia* . . . . . . **44 D3** 31 20N 37 20 E
An Nabk, *Syria* . . . . **47 A5** 34 2N 36 44 E
An Nabk Abū Qaşr,
Si. Arabia . . . . **44 D3** 30 21N 38 34 E
An Nafūd, *Si. Arabia* . . . . . **44 D4** 28 15N 41 0 E
An Najaf, *Iraq* . . . . **44 C5** 32 3N 44 15 E
An Nāşirīyah, *Iraq* . . . . **44 D5** 31 0N 46 15 E
An Nhon, *Vietnam* . . . . **38 F7** 13 55N 109 7 E
An Nu'ayrīyah, *Si. Arabia* . **45 E6** 27 30N 48 30 E
An Nuwaybʻī, W. →,
Si. Arabia . . . . **47 F3** 29 18N 34 57 E
An Thoi, Dao, *Vietnam* . . . . **39 H5** 9 58N 104 0 E
An Uaimh, *Ireland* **13 C5** 53 39N 6 41W
Anabar →, *Russia* . . . . . . **27 B12** 73 8N 113 36 E
'Anabtā, *West Bank* . . . . . . **47 C4** 32 19N 35 7 E
Anaconda, *U.S.A.* **82 C7** 46 8N 112 57W
Anacortes, *U.S.A.* **84 B4** 48 30N 122 37W
Anadarko, *U.S.A.* **81 H5** 35 4N 98 15W
Anadolu, *Turkey* . . . . **25 G5** 39 0N 30 0 E
Anadyr, *Russia* . . . . **27 C18** 64 35N 177 20 E
Anadyr →, *Russia* . . . . . . **27 C18** 64 55N 176 5 E
Anadyrskiy Zaliv, *Russia* . . **27 C19** 64 0N 180 0 E
Anaga, Pta. de, *Canary Is.* . **22 F3** 28 34N 16 9W
'Ānah, *Iraq* . . . . **44 C4** 34 25N 42 0 E
Anaheim, *U.S.A.* **85 M9** 33 50N 117 55W
Anahim Lake, *Canada* **72 C3** 52 28N 125 18W
Anáhuac, *Mexico* **86 B4** 27 14N 100 9W
Anakapalle, *India* . . . . **41 L13** 17 42N 83 6 E
Anakie, *Australia* . . . . **62 C4** 23 32S 147 45 E
Analalava, *Madag.* . . . . **57 A8** 14 35S 48 0 E
Análipsis, *Greece* . . . . **23 A3** 39 36N 19 55 E
Anambar →, *Pakistan* . . . **42 D3** 30 15N 68 50 E
Anambas, Kepulauan,
Indonesia . . . . **39 L6** 3 20N 106 30 E
Anambas Is. = Anambas,
Kepulauan, *Indonesia* . . . **39 L6** 3 20N 106 30 E
Anamosa, *U.S.A.* **80 D9** 42 7N 91 17W
Anamur, *Turkey* . . . . **25 G5** 36 8N 32 58 E
Anan, *Japan* . . . . **31 H7** 33 54N 134 40 E
Anand, *India* . . . . **42 H5** 22 32N 72 59 E
Anantnag, *India* . . . . **43 C6** 33 45N 75 10 E
Ananyiv, *Ukraine* . . . . **17 E15** 47 44N 29 58 E
Anapodháris →, *Greece* . . **23 E7** 34 59N 25 20 E
Anápolis, *Brazil* **93 G9** 16 15S 48 50W
Anapu →, *Brazil* **93 D8** 1 53S 50 53W
Anār, *Iran* . . . . **45 D7** 30 55N 55 13 E
Anārak, *Iran* . . . . **45 C7** 33 25N 53 40 E
Anas →, *India* . . . . **42 H5** 23 26N 74 0 E
Anatolia = Anadolu, *Turkey* **25 G5** 39 0N 30 0 E
Anatsogno, *Madag.* . . . . **57 C7** 23 33S 43 46 E
Añatuya, *Argentina* **94 B3** 28 20S 62 50W
Anaunethad L., *Canada* . . . **73 A8** 60 55N 104 25W
Anbyŏn, *N. Korea* . . . . **35 E14** 39 1N 127 35 E
Ancaster, *Canada* **78 C5** 43 13N 79 59W
Anchor Bay, *U.S.A.* **84 G3** 38 48N 123 34W
Anchorage, *U.S.A.* **68 B5** 61 13N 149 54W
Anci, *China* . . . . **34 E9** 39 20N 116 40 E
Ancohuma, Nevada, *Bolivia* **92 G5** 16 0S 68 50W
Ancón, *Peru* **92 F3** 11 50S 77 10W
Ancona, *Italy* . . . . **20 C5** 43 38N 13 30 E
Ancud, *Chile* **96 E2** 42 0S 73 50W
Ancud, G. de, *Chile* **96 E2** 42 0S 73 0W
Anda, *China* . . . . **33 B7** 46 24N 125 19 E
Andacollo, *Argentina* **94 D1** 37 10S 70 42W
Andacollo, *Chile* **94 C1** 30 14S 71 6W
Andalgalá, *Argentina* **94 B2** 27 40S 66 30W
Åndalsnes, *Norway* . . . . . . **9 E12** 62 35N 7 43 E
Andalucía □, *Spain* **19 D3** 37 35N 5 0W
Andalusia = Andalucía □,
Spain **19 D3** 37 35N 5 0W
Andalusia, *U.S.A.* **77 K2** 31 18N 86 29W
Andaman Is., *Ind. Oc.* . . . . **28 H13** 12 30N 92 30 E
Andaman Sea, *Ind. Oc.* . . . **36 B1** 13 0N 96 0 E
Andamooka Opal Fields,
Australia . . . . **63 E2** 30 27S 137 9 E
Andapa, *Madag.* . . . . **57 A8** 14 39S 49 39 E
Andara, *Namibia* . . . . **56 B3** 18 2S 21 9 E
Andenes, *Norway* . . . . **8 B17** 69 19N 16 18 E
Andenne, *Belgium* . . . . **15 D5** 50 28N 5 5 E
Anderson, *Alaska, U.S.A.* . . **68 B5** 64 25N 149 15W
Anderson, *Calif., U.S.A.* . . . **82 F2** 40 27N 122 18W
Anderson, *Ind., U.S.A.* **76 E3** 40 10N 85 41W
Anderson, *Mo., U.S.A.* **81 G7** 36 39N 94 27W
Anderson, *S.C., U.S.A.* **77 H4** 34 31N 82 39W
Anderson →, *Canada* **68 B7** 69 42N 129 0W
Andes, *U.S.A.* **79 D10** 42 12N 74 47W
Andes, Cord. de los,
S. Amer. **92 H5** 20 0S 68 0W
Andfjorden, *Norway* . . . . . . **8 B17** 69 10N 16 20 E
Andhra Pradesh □, *India* . . **40 L11** 18 0N 79 0 E
Andijon, *Uzbekistan* . . . . . . **26 E8** 41 10N 72 15 E
Andikíthira, *Greece* . . . . . . **21 G10** 35 52N 23 15 E
Andīmeshk, *Iran* . . . . **45 C6** 32 27N 48 21 E
Andizhan = Andijon,
Uzbekistan . . . . **26 E8** 41 10N 72 15 E
Andoany, *Madag.* . . . . **57 A8** 13 25S 48 16 E
Andong, *S. Korea* . . . . **35 F15** 36 40N 128 43 E
Andongwei, *China* . . . . **35 G10** 35 6N 119 20 E
Andoom, *Australia* . . . . **62 A3** 12 25S 141 53 E
Andorra ■, *Europe* . . . . . . **18 E4** 42 30N 1 30 E
Andorra La Vella, *Andorra* . **18 E4** 42 31N 1 32 E
Andover, *U.K.* **11 F6** 51 12N 1 29W
Andover, *Maine, U.S.A.* . . . **79 B14** 44 38N 70 45W
Andover, *Mass., U.S.A.* . . . **79 D13** 42 40N 71 8W
Andover, *N.J., U.S.A.* **79 F10** 40 59N 74 45W
Andover, *N.Y., U.S.A.* **78 D7** 42 10N 77 48W
Andover, *Ohio, U.S.A.* **78 E4** 41 36N 80 34W
Andøya, *Norway* . . . . **8 B16** 69 10N 15 50 E
Andradina, *Brazil* **93 H8** 20 54S 51 23W
Andrahary, Mt., *Madag.* . . . **57 A8** 13 37S 49 17 E
Andramasina, *Madag.* . . . . . **57 B8** 19 11S 47 35 E
Andranopasy, *Madag.* . . . . **57 C7** 21 17S 43 44 E
Andratx, *Spain* . . . . **22 B9** 39 39N 2 25 E
Andreanof Is., *U.S.A.* **68 C2** 51 30N 176 0W
Andrews, *S.C., U.S.A.* **77 J6** 33 27N 79 34W
Andrews, *Tex., U.S.A.* **81 J3** 32 19N 102 33W
Ándria, *Italy* . . . . **20 D7** 41 13N 16 17 E
Andriba, *Madag.* . . . . **57 B8** 17 30S 46 58 E
Androka, *Madag.* . . . . **57 C7** 24 58S 44 2 E
Andropov = Rybinsk, *Russia* **24 C6** 58 5N 38 50 E
Ándros, *Greece* . . . . **21 F11** 37 50N 24 57 E
Andros I., *Bahamas* **88 B4** 24 30N 78 0W
Andros Town, *Bahamas* . . . **88 B4** 24 43N 77 47W
Androscoggin →, *U.S.A.* . **79 C14** 43 58N 70 0W
Andselv, *Norway* . . . . **8 B18** 69 4N 18 34 E
Andújar, *Spain* **19 C3** 38 3N 4 5W
Andulo, *Angola* . . . . **52 G3** 11 25S 16 45 E
Anegada I., *Virgin Is.* **89 C7** 18 45N 64 20W
Anegada Passage, *W. Indies* **89 C7** 18 15N 63 45W
Aneto, Pico de, *Spain* . . . . . **19 A6** 42 37N 0 40 E
Ang Thong, *Thailand* . . . . . **38 E3** 14 35N 100 31 E
Angamos, Punta, *Chile* **94 A1** 23 1S 70 32W
Angara →, *Russia* . . . . . . **27 D10** 58 5N 94 20 E
Angarsk, *Russia* . . . . **27 D11** 52 30N 104 0 E
Angas Hills, *Australia* . . . . **60 D4** 23 0S 127 50 E
Angaston, *Australia* . . . . . . **63 E2** 34 30S 139 8 E
Angaur I., *Pac. Oc.* . . . . . . **37 C8** 6 54N 134 9 E
Ånge, *Sweden* . . . . **9 E16** 62 31N 15 35 E
Ángel, Salto = Angel Falls,
Venezuela **92 B6** 5 57N 62 30W
Ángel de la Guarda, I.,
Mexico **86 B2** 29 30N 113 30W
Angel Falls, *Venezuela* . . . **92 B6** 5 57N 62 30W
Angeles, *Phil.* . . . . **37 A6** 15 9N 120 33 E
Ängelholm, *Sweden* . . . . . . **9 H15** 56 15N 12 58 E
Angels Camp, *U.S.A.* **84 G6** 38 4N 120 32W
Ångermanälven →,
Sweden . . . . **8 E17** 62 40N 18 0 E
Ångermanland, *Sweden* . . . **8 E18** 63 36N 17 45 E
Angers, *Canada* **79 A9** 45 31N 75 29W
Angers, *France* **18 C3** 47 30N 0 35W
Ängesån →, *Sweden* . . . . . **8 C20** 66 16N 22 47 E
Angikuni L., *Canada* **73 A9** 62 0N 100 0W
Angkor, *Cambodia* . . . . **38 F4** 13 22N 103 50 E
Anglesey, *U.K.* **10 D3** 53 17N 4 20W
Anglesey, Isle of □, *U.K.* . . **10 D3** 53 16N 4 18W
Angleton, *U.S.A.* **81 L7** 29 10N 95 26W
Anglisidhes, *Cyprus* . . . . . . **23 E12** 34 51N 33 27 E
Angmagssalik, *Greenland* . . **4 C6** 65 40N 37 20W
Ango,
Dem. Rep. of the Congo . **54 B2** 4 10N 26 5 E
Angoche, *Mozam.* . . . . **55 F4** 16 8S 39 55 E
Angoche, I., *Mozam.* . . . . . . **55 F4** 16 20S 39 50 E
Angol, *Chile* **94 D1** 37 56S 72 45W
Angola, *Ind., U.S.A.* **76 E3** 41 38N 85 0W
Angola, *N.Y., U.S.A.* **78 D5** 42 38N 79 2W
Angola ■, *Africa* . . . . **53 G3** 12 0S 18 0 E
Angoulême, *France* . . . . **18 D4** 45 39N 0 10 E
Angoumois, *France* . . . . **18 D3** 45 50N 0 25 E
Angra dos Reis, *Brazil* **95 A7** 23 0S 44 10W
Angren, *Uzbekistan* . . . . . . **26 E8** 41 1N 70 12 E
Angtassom, *Cambodia* . . . . **39 G5** 11 1N 104 41 E
Angu,
Dem. Rep. of the Congo . **54 B1** 3 25N 24 28 E
Anguang, *China* . . . . **35 B12** 45 15N 123 45 E
Anguilla ■, *W. Indies* **89 C7** 18 14N 63 5W
Anguo, *China* . . . . **34 E8** 38 28N 115 15 E
Angurugu, *Australia* . . . . . . **62 A2** 14 0S 136 25 E
Angus □, *U.K.* **12 E6** 56 46N 2 56W
Anhanduí →, *Brazil* **95 A5** 21 46S 52 9W
Anholt, *Denmark* . . . . **9 H14** 56 42N 11 33 E
Anhui □, *China* . . . . **33 C6** 32 0N 117 0 E
Anhwei = Anhui □, *China* . **33 C6** 32 0N 117 0 E
Anichab, *Namibia* . . . . **56 C1** 21 0S 14 46 E
Animas →, *U.S.A.* **83 H9** 36 43N 108 13W
Anivorano, *Madag.* . . . . **57 B8** 18 44S 48 58 E
Anjalankoski, *Finland* . . . . **9 F22** 60 45N 26 51 E
Anjar, *India* . . . . **42 H4** 23 6N 70 10 E
Anjidiv I., *India* . . . . **40 M9** 14 40N 74 10 E
Anjou, *France* **18 C3** 47 20N 0 15W
Anjozorobe, *Madag.* . . . . . . **57 B8** 18 22S 47 52 E
Anju, *N. Korea* . . . . **35 E13** 39 36N 125 40 E
Ankaboa, Tanjon, *Madag.* . . **57 C7** 21 58S 43 20 E
Ankang, *China* . . . . **34 H5** 32 40N 109 1 E
Ankara, *Turkey* . . . . **25 G5** 39 57N 32 54 E
Ankaramena, *Madag.* . . . . . **57 C8** 21 57S 46 39 E
Ankaratra, *Madag.* . . . . **53 H9** 19 25S 47 12 E
Ankazoabo, *Madag.* . . . . . . **57 C7** 22 18S 44 31 E
Ankazobe, *Madag.* . . . . **57 B8** 18 20S 47 10 E
Ankeny, *U.S.A.* **80 E8** 41 44N 93 36W
Ankisabe, *Madag.* . . . . **57 B8** 19 17S 46 29 E
Ankoro,
Dem. Rep. of the Congo . **54 D2** 6 45S 26 55 E
Anmyŏn-do, *S. Korea* . . . . . **35 F14** 36 25N 126 25 E
Ann, C., *U.S.A.* **79 D14** 42 38N 70 35W
Ann Arbor, *U.S.A.* **76 D4** 42 17N 83 45W
Anna, *U.S.A.* **81 G10** 37 28N 89 15W
Annaba, *Algeria* . . . . **50 A7** 36 50N 7 46 E
Annalee →, *Ireland* **13 B4** 54 2N 7 24W
Annam, *Vietnam* . . . . **38 E7** 16 0N 108 0 E
Annamitique, Chaîne, *Asia* **38 D6** 17 0N 106 0 E
Annan, *U.K.* **12 G5** 54 59N 3 16W
Annan →, *U.K.* **12 G5** 54 58N 3 16W
Annapolis, *U.S.A.* **76 F7** 38 59N 76 30W
Annapolis Royal, *Canada* . . **71 D6** 44 44N 65 32W
Annapurna, *Nepal* . . . . **43 E10** 28 34N 83 50 E
Annean, L., *Australia* . . . . . **61 E2** 26 54S 118 14 E
Annecy, *France* . . . . **18 D7** 45 55N 6 8 E
Anning, *China* . . . . **32 D5** 24 55N 102 26 E
Anniston, *U.S.A.* **77 J3** 33 39N 85 50W
Annobón, *Atl. Oc.* . . . . **49 G4** 1 25S 5 36 E
Annotto Bay, *Jamaica* **88 C4** 18 17N 76 45W
Annville, *U.S.A.* **79 F8** 40 20N 76 31W
Áno Viánnos, *Greece* . . . . . **23 D7** 35 2N 25 21 E
Anorotsangana, *Madag.* . . . **57 A8** 13 56S 47 55 E
Anóyia, *Greece* . . . . **23 D6** 35 16N 24 52 E
Anping, *Hebei, China* . . . . . **34 E8** 38 15N 115 30 E
Anping, *Liaoning, China* . . . **35 D12** 41 5N 123 30 E
Anqing, *China* . . . . **33 C6** 30 30N 117 3 E
Anqiu, *China* . . . . **35 F10** 36 25N 119 10 E
Ansai, *China* . . . . **34 F5** 36 50N 109 20 E
Ansbach, *Germany* . . . . **16 D6** 49 28N 10 34 E
Anshan, *China* . . . . **35 D12** 41 5N 122 58 E
Anshun, *China* . . . . **32 D5** 26 18N 105 57 E
Ansley, *U.S.A.* **80 E5** 41 18N 99 23W
Anson, *U.S.A.* **81 J5** 32 45N 99 54W
Anson B., *Australia* . . . . . . **60 B5** 13 20S 130 6 E
Ansongo, *Mali* . . . . **50 E6** 15 25N 0 35 E
Ansonia, *U.S.A.* **79 E11** 41 21N 73 5W
Anstruther, *U.K.* **12 E6** 56 14N 2 41W
Ansudu, *Indonesia* . . . . **37 E9** 2 11S 139 22 E
Antabamba, *Peru* **92 F4** 14 40S 73 0W
Antakya, *Turkey* . . . . **25 G6** 36 14N 36 10 E
Antalaha, *Madag.* . . . . **57 A9** 14 57S 50 20 E
Antalya, *Turkey* . . . . **25 G5** 36 52N 30 45 E
Antalya Körfezi, *Turkey* . . . **25 G5** 36 15N 31 30 E
Antananarivo, *Madag.* . . . . **57 B8** 18 55S 47 31 E
Antananarivo □, *Madag.* . . **57 B8** 19 0S 47 0 E
Antanimbaribe, *Madag.* . . . **57 C7** 21 30S 44 48 E
Antarctic Pen., *Antarctica* . . **5 C18** 67 0S 60 0W
Antarctica . . . . **5 E3** 90 0S 0 0 E
Antelope, *Zimbabwe* . . . . . . **55 G2** 21 2S 28 31 E
Antequera, *Paraguay* **94 A4** 24 8S 57 7W
Antequera, *Spain* **19 D3** 37 5N 4 33W
Antero, Mt., *U.S.A.* **83 G10** 38 41N 106 15W
Anthony, *Kans., U.S.A.* **81 G5** 37 9N 98 2W
Anthony, *N. Mex., U.S.A.* . . **83 K10** 32 0N 106 36W
Anti Atlas, *Morocco* **50 C4** 30 0N 8 30W
Anti-Lebanon = Ash Sharqi,
Al Jabal, *Lebanon* . . . . . . **47 B5** 33 40N 36 10 E
Antibes, *France* . . . . **18 E7** 43 34N 7 6 E
Anticosti, Î. d', *Canada* . . . **71 C7** 49 30N 63 0W
Antigo, *U.S.A.* **80 C10** 45 9N 89 9W
Antigonish, *Canada* **71 C7** 45 38N 61 58W
Antigua, *Canary Is.* **22 F5** 28 24N 14 1W
Antigua, *W. Indies* **89 C7** 17 0N 61 50W
Antigua & Barbuda ■,
W. Indies **89 C7** 17 20N 61 48W
Antigua Guatemala,
Guatemala **88 D1** 14 34N 90 41W
Antilla, *Cuba* **88 B4** 20 40N 75 50W
Antilles = West Indies,
Cent. Amer. **89 D7** 15 0N 65 0W
Antioch, *U.S.A.* **84 G5** 38 1N 121 48W
Antioquia, *Colombia* **92 B3** 6 40N 75 55W
Antipodes Is., *Pac. Oc.* . . . . **64 M9** 49 45S 178 40 E
Antlers, *U.S.A.* **81 H7** 34 14N 95 37W
Antofagasta, *Chile* **94 A1** 23 50S 70 30W
Antofagasta □, *Chile* **94 A2** 24 0S 69 0W
Antofagasta de la Sierra,
Argentina **94 B2** 26 5S 67 20W
Antofalla, *Argentina* **94 B2** 25 30S 68 5W
Antofalla, Salar de,
Argentina **94 B2** 25 40S 67 45W
Anton, *U.S.A.* **81 J3** 33 49N 102 10W
Antongila, Helodrano,
Madag. . . . . **57 B8** 15 30S 49 50 E
Antonibé, *Madag.* . . . . **57 B8** 15 7S 47 24 E
Antonibé, Presqu'île d',
Madag. . . . . **57 A8** 14 55S 47 20 E
Antonina, *Brazil* **95 B6** 25 26S 48 42W
Antrim, *U.K.* **13 B5** 54 43N 6 14W
Antrim, *U.S.A.* **78 F3** 40 7N 81 21W
Antrim □, *U.K.* **13 B5** 54 56N 6 25W
Antrim, Mts. of, *U.K.* **13 A5** 55 3N 6 14W
Antrim Plateau, *Australia* . . **60 C4** 18 8S 128 20 E
Antsalova, *Madag.* . . . . **57 B7** 18 40S 44 37 E
Antsirabe, *Madag.* . . . . **57 B8** 19 55S 47 2 E
Antsiranana, *Madag.* . . . . . **57 A8** 12 25S 49 20 E
Antsohihy, *Madag.* . . . . **57 A8** 14 50S 47 59 E
Antsohimbondrona
Seranana, *Madag.* . . . . . . **57 A8** 13 7S 48 48 E
Antu, *China* . . . . **35 C15** 42 30N 128 20 E
Antwerp = Antwerpen,
Belgium . . . . **15 C4** 51 13N 4 25 E
Antwerp, *U.S.A.* **79 B9** 44 12N 75 37W
Antwerpen, *Belgium* . . . . . . **15 C4** 51 13N 4 25 E
Antwerpen □, *Belgium* . . . . **15 C4** 51 15N 4 40 E
Anupgarh, *India* . . . . **42 E5** 29 10N 73 10 E
Anuppur, *India* . . . . **43 H9** 23 6N 81 41 E
Anuradhapura, *Sri Lanka* . . **40 Q12** 8 22N 80 28 E
Anveh, *Iran* . . . . **45 E7** 27 23N 54 11 E
Anvers = Antwerpen,
Belgium . . . . **15 C4** 51 13N 4 25 E
Anvers I., *Antarctica* **5 C17** 64 30S 63 40W
Anxi, *China* . . . . **32 B4** 40 30N 95 43 E
Anxious B., *Australia* . . . . . **63 E1** 33 24S 134 45 E
Anyang, *China* . . . . **34 F8** 36 5N 114 21 E
Anyer-Kidul, *Indonesia* . . . . **37 G11** 6 4S 105 53 E
Anyi, *China* . . . . **34 G6** 35 2N 111 2 E
Anza, *U.S.A.* **85 M10** 33 35N 116 39W
Anze, *China* . . . . **34 F7** 36 10N 112 12 E
Anzhero-Sudzhensk, *Russia* **26 D9** 56 10N 86 0 E
Ánzio, *Italy* . . . . **20 D5** 41 27N 12 37 E
Aoga-Shima, *Japan* . . . . . . **31 H9** 32 28N 139 46 E
Aomen = Macau, *China* . . . **33 D6** 22 16N 113 35 E
Aomori, *Japan* . . . . **30 D10** 40 45N 140 45 E

Asmera

Asmera, Eritrea 46 D2 15 19N 38 55 E
Åsnen, Sweden 9 H16 56 37N 14 45 E
Aspen, U.S.A. 83 G10 39 11N 106 49W
Aspermont, U.S.A. 81 J4 33 8N 100 14W
Aspiring, Mt., N.Z. 59 L2 44 23S 168 46 E
Asprókavos, Ákra, Greece 23 B4 39 21N 20 6 E
Aspur, India 42 H6 23 58N 74 7 E
Asquith, Canada 73 C7 52 8N 107 13W
Assam □, India 41 G18 26 0N 93 0 E
Asse, Belgium 15 D4 50 24N 4 10 E
Assen, Neths. 15 A6 53 0N 6 35 E
Assiniboia, Canada 73 D7 49 40N 105 59W
Assiniboine →, Canada 73 D9 49 53N 97 8W
Assiniboine, Mt., Canada 72 C5 50 52N 115 39W
Assis, Brazil 95 A5 22 40S 50 20W
Assisi, Italy 20 C5 43 4N 12 37 E
Assynt, L., U.K. 12 C3 58 10N 5 3W
Astana, Kazakstan 26 D8 51 10N 71 30 E
Āstāneh, Iran 45 B6 37 17N 49 59 E
Astara, Azerbaijan 25 G8 38 30N 48 50 E
Asteroúsia, Greece 23 E7 34 59N 25 3 E
Asti, Italy 18 D8 44 54N 8 12 E
Astipálaia, Greece 21 F12 36 32N 26 22 E
Astorga, Spain 19 A2 42 29N 6 8W
Astoria, U.S.A. 84 D3 46 11N 123 50W
Astrakhan, Russia 25 E8 46 25N 48 5 E
Asturias □, Spain 19 A3 43 15N 6 0W
Asunción, Paraguay 94 B4 25 10S 57 30W
Asunción Nochixtlán, Mexico 87 D5 17 28N 97 14W
Aswa →, Uganda 54 B3 3 43N 31 55 E
Aswân, Egypt 51 D12 24 4N 32 57 E
Aswân High Dam = Sadd el Aali, Egypt 51 D12 23 54N 32 54 E
Asyût, Egypt 51 C12 27 11N 31 4 E
At Țafilah, Jordan 47 E4 30 45N 35 30 E
Aț Ța'if, Si. Arabia 46 C3 21 5N 40 27 E
Aț Țirāq, Si. Arabia 44 E5 27 19N 44 33 E
Aț Tubayq, Si. Arabia 44 D3 29 30N 37 0 E
Atacama □, Chile 94 B2 27 30S 70 0W
Atacama, Desierto de, Chile 94 A2 24 0S 69 20W
Atacama, Salar de, Chile 94 A2 23 30S 68 20W
Atalaya, Peru 92 F4 10 45S 73 50W
Atalaya de Femes, Canary Is. 22 F6 28 56N 13 47W
Atami, Japan 31 G9 35 5N 139 4 E
Atapupu, Indonesia 37 F6 9 0S 124 51 E
Atâr, Mauritania 50 D3 20 30N 13 5W
Atari, Pakistan 42 D6 30 56N 74 2 E
Atascadero, U.S.A. 84 K6 35 29N 120 40W
Atasu, Kazakstan 26 E8 48 30N 71 0 E
Atatürk Barajı, Turkey 25 G6 37 28N 38 30 E
Atauro, Indonesia 37 F7 8 10S 125 30 E
Atbara, Sudan 51 E12 17 42N 33 59 E
'Atbara →, Sudan 51 E12 17 40N 33 56 E
Atbasar, Kazakstan 26 D7 51 48N 68 20 E
Atchafalaya B., U.S.A. 81 L9 29 25N 91 25W
Atchison, U.S.A. 80 F7 39 34N 95 7W
Āteshān, Iran 45 C7 35 35N 52 37 E
Ath, Belgium 15 D3 50 38N 3 47 E
Athabasca, Canada 72 C6 54 45N 113 20W
Athabasca →, Canada 73 B6 58 40N 110 50W
Athabasca, L., Canada 73 B7 59 15N 109 15W
Athboy, Ireland 13 C5 53 37N 6 56W
Athenry, Ireland 13 C3 53 18N 8 44W
Athens = Athínai, Greece 21 F10 37 58N 23 46 E
Athens, Ala., U.S.A. 77 H2 34 48N 86 58W
Athens, Ga., U.S.A. 77 J4 33 57N 83 23W
Athens, N.Y., U.S.A. 79 D11 42 16N 73 49W
Athens, Ohio, U.S.A. 76 F4 39 20N 82 6W
Athens, Pa., U.S.A. 79 E8 41 57N 76 31W
Athens, Tenn., U.S.A. 77 H3 35 27N 84 36W
Athens, Tex., U.S.A. 81 J7 32 12N 95 51W
Atherley, Canada 78 B5 44 37N 79 20W
Atherton, Australia 62 B4 17 17S 145 30 E
Athienou, Cyprus 23 D12 35 3N 33 32 E
Athínai, Greece 21 F10 37 58N 23 46 E
Athlone, Ireland 13 C4 53 25N 7 56W
Athna, Cyprus 23 D12 35 3N 33 47 E
Athol, U.S.A. 79 D12 42 36N 72 14W
Atholl, Forest of, U.K. 12 E5 56 51N 3 50W
Atholville, Canada 71 C6 47 59N 66 43W
Áthos, Greece 21 D11 40 9N 24 22 E
Athy, Ireland 13 C5 53 0N 7 0W
Ati, Chad 51 F9 13 13N 18 20 E
Atiak, Uganda 54 B3 3 12N 32 2 E
Atik L., Canada 73 B9 55 15N 96 0W
Atikameg →, Canada 70 B3 52 30N 82 46W
Atikokan, Canada 70 C1 48 45N 91 37W
Atikonak L., Canada 71 B7 52 40N 64 32W
Atka, Russia 27 C16 60 50N 151 48 E
Atka I., U.S.A. 68 C2 52 7N 174 30W
Atkinson, U.S.A. 80 D5 42 32N 98 59W
Atlanta, Ga., U.S.A. 77 J3 33 45N 84 23W
Atlanta, Tex., U.S.A. 81 J7 33 7N 94 10W
Atlantic, U.S.A. 80 E7 41 24N 95 1W
Atlantic City, U.S.A. 76 F8 39 21N 74 27W
Atlantic Ocean 2 E9 0 0 20 0W
Atlas Mts. = Haut Atlas, Morocco 50 B4 32 30N 5 0W
Atlin, Canada 72 B2 59 31N 133 41W
Atlin, L., Canada 72 B2 59 26N 133 45W
Atlin Prov. Park, Canada 72 B2 59 10N 134 30W
Atmore, U.S.A. 77 K2 31 2N 87 29W
Atoka, U.S.A. 81 H6 34 23N 96 8W
Atolia, U.S.A. 85 K9 35 19N 117 37W
Atrai →, Bangla. 43 G13 24 7N 89 22 E
Atrak = Atrek →, Turkmenistan 45 B8 37 35N 53 58 E
Atrauli, India 42 E8 28 2N 78 20 E
Atrek →, Turkmenistan 45 B8 37 35N 53 58 E
Atsuta, Japan 30 C10 43 24N 141 26 E
Attalla, U.S.A. 77 H2 34 1N 86 6W
Attapu, Laos 38 E6 14 48N 106 50 E
Attáviros, Greece 23 C9 36 12N 27 50 E
Attawapiskat, Canada 70 B3 52 56N 82 24W
Attawapiskat →, Canada 70 B3 52 57N 82 18W
Attawapiskat L., Canada 70 B2 52 18N 87 54W
Attica, Ind., U.S.A. 76 E2 40 18N 87 15W
Attica, Ohio, U.S.A. 78 E2 41 4N 82 53W
Attikamagen L., Canada 71 B6 55 0N 66 30W
Attleboro, U.S.A. 79 E13 41 57N 71 17W
Attock, Pakistan 42 C5 33 52N 72 20 E
Attopeu = Attapu, Laos 38 E6 14 48N 106 50 E
Attu I., U.S.A. 68 C1 52 55N 172 55 E
Attur, India 40 P11 11 35N 78 30 E
Atuel →, Argentina 94 D2 36 17S 66 50W
Åtvidaberg, Sweden 9 G17 58 12N 16 0 E
Atwater, U.S.A. 84 H6 37 21N 120 37W
Atwood, Canada 78 C3 43 40N 81 1W
Atwood, U.S.A. 80 F4 39 48N 101 3W
Atyraū, Kazakstan 25 E9 47 5N 52 0 E
Au Sable, U.S.A. 78 B1 44 25N 83 20W
Au Sable →, U.S.A. 76 C4 44 25N 83 20W
Au Sable Forks, U.S.A. 79 B11 44 27N 73 41W
Au Sable Pt., U.S.A. 78 B1 44 20N 83 20W
Aubagne, France 18 E6 43 17N 5 37 E
Aubarca, C. d', Spain 22 B7 39 4N 1 22 E
Aube →, France 18 B5 48 34N 3 43 E
Auberry, U.S.A. 84 H7 37 7N 119 29W
Auburn, Ala., U.S.A. 77 J3 32 36N 85 29W
Auburn, Calif., U.S.A. 84 G5 38 54N 121 4W
Auburn, Ind., U.S.A. 76 E3 41 22N 85 4W
Auburn, Maine, U.S.A. 77 C10 44 6N 70 14W
Auburn, N.Y., U.S.A. 79 D8 42 56N 76 34W
Auburn, Nebr., U.S.A. 80 E7 40 23N 95 51W
Auburn, Pa., U.S.A. 79 F8 40 36N 76 6W
Auburn, Wash., U.S.A. 84 C4 47 18N 122 14W
Auburn Ra., Australia 63 D5 25 15S 150 30 E
Aubusson, France 18 D5 45 57N 2 11 E
Auch, France 18 E4 43 39N 0 36 E
Auckland, N.Z. 59 G5 36 52S 174 46 E
Auckland Is., Pac. Oc. 64 N8 50 40S 166 5 E
Aude →, France 18 E5 43 13N 3 14 E
Auden, Canada 70 B2 50 14N 87 53W
Audubon, U.S.A. 80 E7 41 43N 94 56W
Augathella, Australia 63 D4 25 48S 146 35 E
Aughnacloy, U.K. 13 B5 54 25N 6 59W
Augrabies Falls, S. Africa 56 D3 28 35S 20 20 E
Augsburg, Germany 16 D6 48 25N 10 52 E
Augusta, Australia 61 F2 34 19S 115 9 E
Augusta, Italy 20 F6 37 13N 15 13 E
Augusta, Ark., U.S.A. 81 H9 35 17N 91 22W
Augusta, Ga., U.S.A. 77 J5 33 28N 81 58W
Augusta, Kans., U.S.A. 81 G6 37 41N 96 59W
Augusta, Maine, U.S.A. 69 D13 44 19N 69 47W
Augusta, Mont., U.S.A. 82 C7 47 30N 112 24W
Augustów, Poland 17 B12 53 51N 23 0 E
Augustus, Mt., Australia 61 D2 24 20S 116 50 E
Augustus I., Australia 60 C3 15 20S 124 30 E
Aukum, U.S.A. 84 G6 38 34N 120 43W
Auld, L., Australia 60 D3 22 25S 123 50 E
Ault, U.S.A. 80 E2 40 35N 104 44W
Aunis, France 18 C3 46 5N 0 50W
Auponhia, Indonesia 37 E7 1 58S 125 27 E
Aur, Pulau, Malaysia 39 L5 2 35N 104 10 E
Auraiya, India 43 F8 26 28N 79 33 E
Aurangabad, Bihar, India 43 G11 24 45N 84 18 E
Aurangabad, Maharashtra, India 40 K9 19 50N 75 23 E
Aurich, Germany 16 B4 53 28N 7 28 E
Aurillac, France 18 D5 44 55N 2 26 E
Aurora, Canada 78 C5 44 0N 79 28W
Aurora, S. Africa 56 E2 32 40S 18 29 E
Aurora, Colo., U.S.A. 80 F2 39 44N 104 52W
Aurora, Ill., U.S.A. 76 E1 41 45N 88 19W
Aurora, Mo., U.S.A. 81 G8 36 58N 93 43W
Aurora, N.Y., U.S.A. 79 D8 42 45N 76 42W
Aurora, Nebr., U.S.A. 80 E6 40 52N 98 0W
Aurora, Ohio, U.S.A. 78 E3 41 21N 81 20W
Aurukun, Australia 62 A3 13 20S 141 45 E
Aus, Namibia 56 D2 26 35S 16 12 E
Ausable →, Canada 78 C3 43 19N 81 46W
Auschwitz = Oświęcim, Poland 17 C10 50 2N 19 11 E
Austin, Minn., U.S.A. 80 D8 43 40N 92 58W
Austin, Nev., U.S.A. 82 G5 39 30N 117 4W
Austin, Pa., U.S.A. 78 E6 41 38N 78 6W
Austin, Tex., U.S.A. 81 K6 30 17N 97 45W
Austin, L., Australia 61 E2 27 40S 118 0 E
Austin I., Canada 73 A10 61 10N 94 0W
Austra, Norway 8 D14 65 8N 11 55 E
Austral Is. = Tubuai Is., Pac. Oc. 65 K13 25 0S 150 0W
Austral Seamount Chain, Pac. Oc. 65 K13 24 0S 150 0W
Australia ■, Oceania 64 K5 23 0S 135 0 E
Australian Capital Territory □, Australia 63 F4 35 30S 149 0 E
Australind, Australia 61 F2 33 17S 115 42 E
Austria ■, Europe 16 E8 47 0N 14 0 E
Austvågøy, Norway 8 B16 68 20N 14 40 E
Autlán, Mexico 86 D4 19 40N 104 30W
Autun, France 18 C6 46 58N 4 17 E
Auvergne, France 18 D5 45 20N 3 15 E
Auvergne, Mts. d', France 18 D5 45 20N 2 55 E
Auxerre, France 18 C5 47 48N 3 32 E
Ava, U.S.A. 81 G8 36 57N 92 40W
Avallon, France 18 C5 47 30N 3 53 E
Avalon, U.S.A. 85 M8 33 21N 118 20W
Avalon Pen., Canada 71 C9 47 30N 53 20W
Avanos, Turkey 44 B2 38 43N 34 51 E
Avaré, Brazil 95 A6 23 4S 48 58W
Avawatz Mts., U.S.A. 85 K10 35 40N 116 30W
Aveiro, Brazil 93 D7 3 10S 55 5W
Aveiro, Portugal 19 B1 40 37N 8 38W
Āvej, Iran 45 C6 35 40N 49 15 E
Avellaneda, Argentina 94 C4 34 50S 58 10W
Avellino, Italy 20 D6 40 54N 14 47 E
Avenal, U.S.A. 84 K6 36 0N 120 8W
Aversa, Italy 20 D6 40 58N 14 12 E
Avery, U.S.A. 82 C6 47 15N 115 49W
Aves, Is. las, Venezuela 89 D6 12 0N 67 30W
Avesta, Sweden 9 F17 60 9N 16 10 E
Avezzano, Italy 20 C5 42 2N 13 25 E
Aviá Terai, Argentina 94 B3 26 45S 60 50W
Aviemore, U.K. 12 D5 57 12N 3 50W
Avignon, France 18 E6 43 57N 4 50 E
Ávila, Spain 19 B3 40 39N 4 43W
Avila Beach, U.S.A. 85 K6 35 11N 120 44W
Avilés, Spain 19 A3 43 35N 5 57W
Avis, U.S.A. 78 E7 41 11N 77 19W
Avoca, U.S.A. 78 D7 42 25N 77 25W
Avoca →, Australia 63 F3 35 40S 143 43 E
Avoca →, Ireland 13 D5 52 48N 6 10W
Avola, Canada 72 C5 51 45N 119 19W
Avola, Italy 20 F6 36 56N 15 7 E
Avon, U.S.A. 78 D7 42 55N 77 45W
Avon →, Australia 61 F2 31 40S 116 7 E
Avon →, Bristol, U.K. 11 F5 51 29N 2 41W
Avon →, Dorset, U.K. 11 G6 50 44N 1 46W
Avon →, Warks., U.K. 11 E5 52 0N 2 8W
Avon Park, U.S.A. 77 M5 27 36N 81 31W
Avondale, Zimbabwe 55 F3 17 43S 30 58 E
Avonlea, Canada 73 D8 50 0N 105 0W
Avonmore, Canada 79 A10 45 10N 74 58W
Avranches, France 18 B3 48 40N 1 20W
A'waj →, Syria 47 B5 33 23N 36 20 E
Awaji-Shima, Japan 31 G7 34 30N 134 50 E
'Awālī, Bahrain 45 E6 26 0N 50 30 E
Awantipur, India 43 C6 33 55N 75 3 E
Awasa, Ethiopia 46 F2 7 3N 38 28 E
Awash, Ethiopia 46 F3 9 1N 40 10 E
Awatere →, N.Z. 59 J5 41 37S 174 10 E
Awbārī, Libya 51 C8 26 46N 12 57 E
Awe, L., U.K. 12 E3 56 17N 5 16W
Awjilah, Libya 51 C10 29 8N 21 7 E
Axe →, U.K. 11 F5 50 42N 3 4W
Axel Heiberg I., Canada 4 B3 80 0N 90 0W
Axim, Ghana 50 H5 4 51N 2 15W
Axiós →, Greece 21 D10 40 57N 22 35 E
Axminster, U.K. 11 G4 50 46N 3 0W
Ayabaca, Peru 92 D3 4 40S 79 53W
Ayabe, Japan 31 G7 35 20N 135 20 E
Ayacucho, Argentina 94 D4 37 5S 58 20W
Ayacucho, Peru 92 F4 13 0S 74 0W
Ayaguz, Kazakstan 26 E9 48 10N 80 10 E
Ayamonte, Spain 19 D2 37 12N 7 24W
Ayan, Russia 27 D14 56 30N 138 16 E
Ayaviri, Peru 92 F4 14 50S 70 35W
Aydın, Turkey 21 F12 37 51N 27 51 E
Aydin □, Turkey 25 G4 37 50N 28 0 E
Ayer, U.S.A. 79 D13 42 34N 71 35W
Ayer's Cliff, Canada 79 A12 45 10N 72 3W
Ayers Rock, Australia 61 E5 25 23S 131 5 E
Ayia Aikateríni, Ákra, Greece 23 A3 39 50N 19 50 E
Ayia Dhéka, Greece 23 D6 35 3N 24 58 E
Ayia Gálini, Greece 23 D6 35 6N 24 41 E
Ayia Napa, Cyprus 23 E13 34 59N 34 0 E
Ayia Phyla, Cyprus 23 E12 34 43N 33 1 E
Ayia Varvára, Greece 23 D7 35 8N 25 1 E
Áyios Amvrósios, Cyprus 23 D12 35 20N 33 35 E
Áyios Evstrátios, Greece 21 E11 39 34N 24 58 E
Áyios Ioánnis, Ákra, Greece 23 D7 35 20N 25 40 E
Áyios Isidhoros, Greece 23 C9 36 9N 27 51 E
Áyios Matthaíos, Greece 23 B3 39 30N 19 47 E
Áyios Nikólaos, Greece 23 D7 35 11N 25 41 E
Áyios Seryios, Cyprus 23 D12 35 12N 33 53 E
Ayios Theodhoros, Cyprus 23 D13 35 22N 34 1 E
Aykino, Russia 24 B8 62 15N 49 56 E
Aylesbury, U.K. 11 F7 51 49N 0 49W
Aylmer, Canada 78 D4 42 46N 80 59W
Aylmer, L., Canada 68 B8 64 0N 110 8W
'Ayn, Wādī al, Oman 45 F7 22 15N 55 28 E
Ayn Dār, Si. Arabia 45 E7 25 55N 49 10 E
Ayn Zālah, Iraq 44 B4 36 45N 42 35 E
Ayolas, Paraguay 94 B4 27 10S 56 59W
Ayon, Ostrov, Russia 27 C17 69 50N 169 0 E
'Ayoûn el 'Atroûs, Mauritania 50 E4 16 40N 9 37W
Ayr, Australia 62 B4 19 35S 147 25 E
Ayr, Canada 78 C4 43 17N 80 27W
Ayr, U.K. 12 F4 55 28N 4 38W
Ayr →, U.K. 12 F4 55 28N 4 38W
Ayre, Pt. of, U.K. 10 C3 54 25N 4 21W
Ayton, Australia 62 B4 15 56S 145 22 E
Aytos, Bulgaria 21 C12 42 42N 27 16 E
Ayu, Kepulauan, Indonesia 37 D8 0 35N 131 5 E
Ayutla, Guatemala 88 D1 14 40N 92 10W
Ayutla, Mexico 87 D5 16 58N 99 17W
Ayvacık, Turkey 21 E12 39 36N 26 24 E
Ayvalık, Turkey 21 E12 39 20N 26 46 E
Az Zabadānī, Syria 47 B5 33 43N 36 5 E
Az Zāhirīyah, West Bank 47 D3 31 25N 34 58 E
Az Zahrān, Si. Arabia 45 E6 26 10N 50 7 E
Az Zarqā, Jordan 47 C5 32 5N 36 4 E
Az Zarqā', U.A.E. 45 E7 24 53N 53 4 E
Az Zāwiyah, Libya 51 B8 32 52N 12 56 E
Az Zibār, Iraq 44 B5 36 52N 44 4 E
Az-Zilfī, Si. Arabia 44 E5 26 12N 44 52 E
Az Zubayr, Iraq 44 D5 30 26N 47 40 E
Azamgarh, India 43 F10 26 5N 83 13 E
Azangaro, Peru 92 F4 14 55S 70 13W
Āzār Shahr, Iran 44 B5 37 45N 45 59 E
Azarān, Iran 44 B5 37 25N 47 16 E
Azärbayjan = Azerbaijan ■, Asia 25 F8 40 20N 48 0 E
Āzarbāyjān-e Gharbī □, Iran 44 B5 37 0N 44 30 E
Āzarbāyjān-e Sharqī □, Iran 44 B5 37 20N 47 0 E
Azare, Nigeria 50 F8 11 55N 10 10 E
A'zāz, Syria 44 B3 36 36N 37 4 E
Azbine = Aïr, Niger 50 E7 18 30N 8 0 E
Azerbaijan ■, Asia 25 F8 40 20N 48 0 E
Azerbaijchan = Azerbaijan ■, Asia 25 F8 40 20N 48 0 E
Azimganj, India 43 G13 24 14N 88 16 E
Azogues, Ecuador 92 D3 2 35S 78 0W
Azores, Atl. Oc. 50 A1 38 44N 29 0W
Azov, Russia 25 E6 47 3N 39 25 E
Azov, Sea of, Europe 25 E6 46 0N 36 30 E
Azovskoye More = Azov, Sea of, Europe 25 E6 46 0N 36 30 E
Azraq ash Shīshān, Jordan 47 D5 31 50N 36 49 E
Aztec, U.S.A. 83 H10 36 49N 107 59W
Azúa de Compostela, Dom. Rep. 89 C5 18 25N 70 44W
Azuaga, Spain 19 C3 38 16N 5 39W
Azuero, Pen. de, Panama 88 E3 7 30N 80 30W
Azul, Argentina 94 D4 36 42S 59 43W
Azusa, U.S.A. 85 L9 34 8N 117 52W

B

Ba Don, Vietnam 38 D6 17 45N 106 26 E
Ba Dong, Vietnam 39 H6 9 40N 106 33 E
Ba Ngoi = Cam Lam, Vietnam 39 G7 11 54N 109 10 E
Ba Tri, Vietnam 39 G6 10 2N 106 36 E
Ba Xian = Bazhou, China 34 E9 39 8N 116 22 E
Baa, Indonesia 37 F6 10 50S 123 0 E
Baarle-Nassau, Belgium 15 C4 51 27N 4 56 E
Bab el Mandeb, Red Sea 46 E3 12 35N 43 25 E
Baba Burnu, Turkey 21 E12 39 29N 26 2 E
Bābā Kalū, Iran 45 D6 30 7N 50 49 E
Babadag, Romania 17 F15 44 53N 28 44 E
Babadayhan, Turkmenistan 26 F7 37 42N 60 23 E
Babaeski, Turkey 21 D12 41 26N 27 6 E
Babahoyo, Ecuador 92 D3 1 40S 79 30W
Babai = Sarju →, India 43 F9 27 21N 81 23 E
Babar, Indonesia 37 F7 8 0S 129 30 E
Babar, Pakistan 42 D3 31 7N 69 32 E
Babarkach, Pakistan 42 E3 29 45N 68 0 E
Babb, U.S.A. 82 B7 48 51N 113 27W
Babelthuap, Pac. Oc. 37 C8 7 30N 134 30 E
Baberu, India 43 G9 25 33N 80 43 E
Babi Besar, Pulau, Malaysia 39 L4 2 25N 103 59 E
Babinda, Australia 62 B4 17 20S 145 56 E
Babine, Canada 72 B3 55 22N 126 37W
Babine →, Canada 72 B3 55 45N 127 44W
Babine L., Canada 72 C3 54 48N 126 0W
Babo, Indonesia 37 E8 2 30S 133 30 E
Bābol, Iran 45 B7 36 40N 52 50 E
Bābol Sar, Iran 45 B7 36 45N 52 45 E
Babruysk, Belarus 17 B15 53 10N 29 15 E
Babuhri, India 42 F3 26 49N 69 43 E
Babusar Pass, Pakistan 43 B5 35 12N 73 59 E
Babuyan Chan., Phil. 37 A6 18 40N 121 30 E
Babylon, Iraq 44 C5 32 34N 44 22 E
Bac Lieu, Vietnam 39 H5 9 17N 105 43 E
Bac Phan, Vietnam 38 B5 22 0N 105 0 E
Bacabal, Brazil 93 D10 4 15S 44 45W
Bacalar, Mexico 87 D7 18 50N 87 27W
Bacan, Kepulauan, Indonesia 37 E7 0 35S 127 30 E
Bacarra, Phil. 37 A6 18 15N 120 37 E
Bacău, Romania 17 E14 46 35N 26 55 E
Bacerac, Mexico 86 A3 30 18N 108 50W
Bach Long Vi, Dao, Vietnam 38 B6 20 10N 107 40 E
Bachelina, Russia 26 D7 57 45N 67 20 E
Bachhwara, India 43 G11 25 35N 85 54 E
Back →, Canada 68 B9 65 10N 104 0W
Bacolod, Phil. 37 B6 10 40N 122 57 E
Bacuk, Malaysia 39 J4 6 4N 102 25 E
Bād, Iran 45 C7 33 41N 52 1 E
Bad →, U.S.A. 80 C4 44 21N 100 22W
Bad Axe, U.S.A. 78 C2 43 48N 83 0W
Bad Ischl, Austria 16 E7 47 44N 13 38 E
Bad Kissingen, Germany 16 C6 50 11N 10 4 E
Bad Lands, U.S.A. 80 D3 43 40N 102 10W
Bada Barabil, India 43 H11 22 7N 85 24 E
Badagara, India 40 P9 11 35N 75 40 E
Badajós, L., Brazil 92 D6 3 15S 62 50W
Badajoz, Spain 19 C2 38 50N 6 59W
Badalona, Spain 19 B7 41 26N 2 15 E
Badalzai, Afghan. 42 E1 29 50N 65 35 E
Badampahar, India 41 H15 22 10N 86 10 E
Badanah, Si. Arabia 44 D4 30 58N 41 30 E
Badarinath, India 43 D8 30 45N 79 30 E
Badas, Kepulauan, Indonesia 36 D3 0 45N 107 5 E
Baddo →, Pakistan 40 F4 28 0N 64 20 E
Bade, Indonesia 37 F9 7 10S 139 35 E
Baden, Austria 16 D9 48 1N 16 13 E
Baden, U.S.A. 78 F4 40 38N 80 14W
Baden-Baden, Germany 16 D5 48 44N 8 13 E
Baden-Württemberg □, Germany 16 D5 48 20N 8 40 E
Badgastein, Austria 16 E7 47 7N 13 9 E
Badger, Canada 71 C8 49 0N 56 4W
Badger, U.S.A. 84 J7 36 38N 119 1W
Bādghīsāt □, Afghan. 40 B3 35 0N 63 0 E
Badgom, India 43 B6 34 1N 74 45 E
Badin, Pakistan 42 G3 24 38N 68 54 E
Badlands National Park, U.S.A. 80 D3 43 38N 102 56W
Badrah, Iraq 44 C5 33 6N 45 58 E
Badrinath, India 43 D8 30 44N 79 29 E
Badulla, Sri Lanka 40 R12 7 1N 81 7 E
Baena, Spain 19 D3 37 37N 4 20W
Baeza, Spain 19 D4 37 57N 3 25W
Baffin B., Canada 4 B4 72 0N 64 0W
Baffin I., Canada 69 B12 68 0N 75 0W
Bafing →, Mali 50 F3 13 49N 10 50W
Bafliyūn, Syria 44 B3 36 37N 36 59 E
Bafoulabé, Mali 50 F3 13 50N 10 55W
Bafoussam, Cameroon 52 C2 5 28N 10 25 E
Bāfq, Iran 45 D7 31 40N 55 25 E
Bafra, Turkey 25 F6 41 34N 35 54 E
Bāft, Iran 45 D8 29 15N 56 38 E
Bafwasende, Dem. Rep. of the Congo 54 B2 1 3N 27 5 E
Bagamoyo, Tanzania 54 D4 6 28S 38 55 E
Bagan Datoh, Malaysia 39 L3 3 59N 100 47 E
Bagan Serai, Malaysia 39 K3 5 1N 100 32 E
Baganga, Phil. 37 C7 7 34N 126 33 E
Bagani, Namibia 56 B3 18 7S 21 41 E
Bagansiapiapi, Indonesia 36 D2 2 12N 100 50 E
Bagasra, India 42 J4 21 30N 71 0 E
Bagaud, India 42 H6 22 19N 75 53 E
Bagdad, U.S.A. 85 L11 34 35N 115 53W
Bagdarin, Russia 27 D12 54 26N 113 36 E
Bagé, Brazil 95 C5 31 20S 54 15W
Bagenalstown = Muine Bheag, Ireland 13 D5 52 42N 6 58W
Baggs, U.S.A. 82 F10 41 2N 107 39W
Bagh, Pakistan 43 C5 33 59N 73 45 E
Baghain →, India 43 G9 25 32N 81 1 E
Baghdād, Iraq 44 C5 33 20N 44 30 E
Bagheria, Italy 20 E5 38 5N 13 30 E
Baghlān, Afghan. 40 A6 36 12N 69 0 E
Bagley, U.S.A. 80 B7 47 32N 95 24W
Bagodar, India 43 G11 24 5N 85 52 E
Bagrationovsk, Russia 9 J19 54 23N 20 39 E
Baguio, Phil. 37 A6 16 26N 120 34 E
Bah, India 43 F8 26 53N 78 36 E
Bahadurganj, India 43 F12 26 16N 87 49 E
Bahadurgarh, India 42 E7 28 40N 76 57 E
Bahama, Canal Viejo de, W. Indies 88 B4 22 10N 77 30W
Bahamas ■, N. Amer. 89 B5 24 0N 75 0W
Baharampur, India 43 G13 24 2N 88 27 E
Bahawalnagar, Pakistan 42 E5 30 0N 73 15 E
Bahawalpur, Pakistan 42 E4 29 24N 71 40 E
Baheri, India 43 E8 28 45N 79 34 E
Bahgul →, India 43 F8 27 45N 79 36 E
Bahi, Tanzania 54 D4 5 58S 35 21 E
Bahi Swamp, Tanzania 54 D4 6 10S 35 0 E
Bahía = Salvador, Brazil 93 F11 13 0S 38 30W
Bahía □, Brazil 93 F10 12 0S 42 0W
Bahía, Is. de la, Honduras 88 C2 16 45N 86 15W
Bahía Blanca, Argentina 94 D3 38 35S 62 13W
Bahía de Caráquez, Ecuador 92 D2 0 40S 80 27W
Bahía Honda, Cuba 88 B3 22 54N 83 10W
Bahía Laura, Argentina 96 F3 48 10S 66 30W
Bahía Negra, Paraguay 92 H7 20 5S 58 5W

Bardstown

Bahir Dar, *Ethiopia* **46 E2** 11 37N 37 10 E
Bahmanzād, *Iran* **45 D6** 31 15N 51 47 E
Bahr el Ghazâl □, *Sudan* **51 G11** 7 0N 28 0 E
Bahraich, *India* **43 F9** 27 38N 81 37 E
Bahrain ■, *Asia* **45 E6** 26 0N 50 35 E
Bahror, *India* **42 F7** 27 51N 76 20 E
Bāhū Kalāt, *Iran* **45 E9** 25 43N 61 25 E
Bai Bung, Mui = Ca Mau, Mui, *Vietnam* **39 H5** 8 38N 104 44 E
Bai Duc, *Vietnam* **38 C5** 18 3N 105 49 E
Bai Thuong, *Vietnam* **38 C5** 19 54N 105 23 E
Baia Mare, *Romania* **17 E12** 47 40N 23 35 E
Baião, *Brazil* **93 D9** 2 40S 49 40W
Baïbokoum, *Chad* **51 G9** 7 46N 15 43 E
Baicheng, *China* **35 B12** 45 38N 122 42 E
Baidoa, *Somali Rep.* **46 G3** 3 8N 43 30 E
Baie Comeau, *Canada* **71 C6** 49 12N 68 10W
Baie-St-Paul, *Canada* **71 C5** 47 28N 70 32W
Baie Trinité, *Canada* **71 C6** 49 25N 67 20W
Baie Verte, *Canada* **71 C8** 49 55N 56 12W
Baihar, *India* **43 H9** 22 6N 80 33 E
Baihe, *China* **34 H6** 32 50N 110 5 E
Ba'ījī, *Iraq* **44 C4** 35 0N 43 30 E
Baijnath, *India* **43 E8** 29 55N 79 37 E
Baikal, L. = Baykal, Oz., *Russia* **27 D11** 53 0N 108 0 E
Baikunthpur, *India* **43 H10** 23 15N 82 33 E
Baile Atha Cliath = Dublin, *Ireland* **13 C5** 53 21N 6 15W
Băileşti, *Romania* **17 F12** 44 1N 23 20 E
Bainbridge, *Ga., U.S.A.* **77 K3** 30 55N 84 35W
Bainbridge, *N.Y., U.S.A.* **79 D9** 42 18N 75 29W
Baing, *Indonesia* **37 F6** 10 14S 120 34 E
Bainiu, *China* **34 H7** 32 50N 112 15 E
Bâ'ir, *Jordan* **47 E5** 30 45N 36 55 E
Bairin Youqi, *China* **35 C10** 43 30N 118 35 E
Bairin Zuoqi, *China* **35 C10** 43 58N 119 15 E
Bairnsdale, *Australia* **63 F4** 37 48S 147 36 E
Baisha, *China* **34 G7** 34 20N 112 32 E
Baitadi, *Nepal* **43 E9** 29 35N 80 25 E
Baiyin, *China* **34 F3** 36 45N 104 14 E
Baiyu Shan, *China* **34 F4** 37 15N 107 30 E
Baj Baj, *India* **43 H13** 22 30N 88 5 E
Baja, *Hungary* **17 E10** 46 12N 18 59 E
Baja, Pta., *Mexico* **86 B1** 29 50N 116 0W
Baja California, *Mexico* **86 A1** 31 10N 115 12W
Baja California □, *Mexico* **86 B2** 30 0N 115 0W
Baja California Sur □, *Mexico* **86 B2** 25 50N 111 50W
Bajag, *India* **43 H9** 22 40N 81 21 E
Bajamar, *Canary Is.* **22 F3** 28 33N 16 20W
Bajana, *India* **42 H4** 23 7N 71 49 E
Bājgīrān, *Iran* **45 B8** 37 36N 58 24 E
Bajimba, Mt., *Australia* **63 D5** 29 17S 152 6 E
Bajo Nuevo, *Caribbean* **88 C4** 15 40N 78 50W
Bajoga, *Nigeria* **51 F8** 10 57N 11 20 E
Bajool, *Australia* **62 C5** 23 40S 150 35 E
Bakel, *Senegal* **50 F3** 14 56N 12 20W
Baker, *Calif., U.S.A.* **85 K10** 35 16N 116 4W
Baker, *Mont., U.S.A.* **80 B2** 46 22N 104 17W
Baker, L., *Canada* **68 B10** 64 0N 96 0W
Baker City, *U.S.A.* **82 D5** 44 47N 117 50W
Baker I., *Pac. Oc.* **64 G10** 0 10N 176 35W
Baker I., *U.S.A.* **72 B2** 55 20N 133 40W
Baker L., *Australia* **61 E4** 26 54S 126 5 E
Baker Lake, *Canada* **68 B10** 64 20N 96 3W
Baker Mt., *U.S.A.* **82 B3** 48 50N 121 49W
Bakers Creek, *Australia* **62 C4** 21 13S 149 7 E
Baker's Dozen Is., *Canada* **70 A4** 56 45N 78 45W
Bakersfield, *Calif., U.S.A.* **85 K8** 35 23N 119 1W
Bakersfield, *Vt., U.S.A.* **79 B12** 44 45N 72 48W
Bākhtarān, *Iran* **44 C5** 34 23N 47 0 E
Bākhtarān □, *Iran* **44 C5** 34 0N 46 30 E
Bakı, *Azerbaijan* **25 F8** 40 29N 49 56 E
Bakkafjörður, *Iceland* **8 C6** 66 2N 14 48W
Bakony, *Hungary* **17 E9** 47 10N 17 30 E
Bakony Forest = Bakony, *Hungary* **17 E9** 47 10N 17 30 E
Bakouma, *C.A.R.* **52 C4** 5 40N 22 56 E
Bakswaho, *India* **43 G8** 24 15N 79 18 E
Baku = Bakı, *Azerbaijan* **25 F8** 40 29N 49 56 E
Bakutis Coast, *Antarctica* **5 D15** 74 0S 120 0W
Baky = Bakı, *Azerbaijan* **25 F8** 40 29N 49 56 E
Bala, *Canada* **78 A5** 45 1N 79 37W
Bala, *U.K.* **10 E4** 52 54N 3 36W
Bala, L., *U.K.* **10 E4** 52 53N 3 37W
Balabac I., *Phil.* **36 C5** 8 0N 117 0 E
Balabac Str., *E. Indies* **36 C5** 7 53N 117 5 E
Balabagh, *Afghan.* **42 B4** 34 25N 70 12 E
Ba'labakk, *Lebanon* **47 B5** 34 0N 36 10 E
Balabalangan, Kepulauan, *Indonesia* **36 E5** 2 20S 117 30 E
Balad, *Iraq* **44 C5** 34 1N 44 9 E
Balad Rūz, *Iraq* **44 C5** 33 42N 45 5 E
Bālādeh, *Fārs, Iran* **45 D6** 29 17N 51 56 E
Bālādeh, *Māzandaran, Iran* **45 B6** 36 12N 51 48 E
Balaghat, *India* **40 J12** 21 49N 80 12 E
Balaghat Ra., *India* **40 K10** 18 50N 76 30 E
Balaguer, *Spain* **19 B6** 41 50N 0 50 E
Balaklava, *Ukraine* **25 F5** 44 30N 33 30 E
Balakovo, *Russia* **24 D8** 52 4N 47 55 E
Balamau, *India* **43 F9** 27 10N 80 21 E
Balancán, *Mexico* **87 D6** 17 48N 91 32W
Balashov, *Russia* **25 D7** 51 30N 43 10 E
Balasinor, *India* **42 H5** 22 57N 73 23 E
Balasore = Baleshwar, *India* **41 J15** 21 35N 87 3 E
Balaton, *Hungary* **17 E9** 46 50N 17 40 E
Balbina, Represa de, *Brazil* **92 D7** 2 0S 59 30W
Balboa, *Panama* **88 E4** 8 57N 79 34W
Balbriggan, *Ireland* **13 C5** 53 37N 6 11W
Balcarce, *Argentina* **94 D4** 38 0S 58 10W
Balcarres, *Canada* **73 C8** 50 50N 103 35W
Balchik, *Bulgaria* **21 C13** 43 28N 28 11 E
Balclutha, *N.Z.* **59 M2** 46 15S 169 45 E
Balcones Escarpment, *U.S.A.* **81 L5** 29 30N 99 15W
Bald Hd., *Australia* **61 G2** 35 6S 118 1 E
Bald I., *Australia* **61 F2** 34 57S 118 27 E
Bald Knob, *U.S.A.* **81 H9** 35 19N 91 34W
Baldock L., *Canada* **73 B9** 56 33N 97 57W
Baldwin, *Mich., U.S.A.* **76 D3** 43 54N 85 51W
Baldwin, *Pa., U.S.A.* **78 F5** 40 23N 79 59W
Baldwinsville, *U.S.A.* **79 C8** 43 10N 76 20W
Baldy Mt., *U.S.A.* **82 B9** 48 9N 109 39W
Baldy Peak, *U.S.A.* **83 K9** 33 54N 109 34W
Baleares, Is., *Spain* **22 B10** 39 30N 3 0 E
Balearic Is. = Baleares, Is., *Spain* **22 B10** 39 30N 3 0 E
Baleine = Whale →, *Canada* **71 A6** 58 15N 67 40W
Baler, *Phil.* **37 A6** 15 46N 121 34 E
Baleshare, *U.K.* **12 D1** 57 31N 7 22W
Baleshwar, *India* **41 J15** 21 35N 87 3 E
Balfate, *Honduras* **88 C2** 15 48N 86 25W
Balí, *Greece* **23 D6** 35 25N 24 47 E
Bali, *India* **42 G5** 25 11N 73 17 E
Bali □, *Indonesia* **36 F5** 8 20S 115 0 E
Bali, Selat, *Indonesia* **37 H16** 8 18S 114 25 E
Baliapal, *India* **43 J12** 21 40N 87 17 E
Balikeşir, *Turkey* **21 E12** 39 39N 27 53 E
Balikpapan, *Indonesia* **36 E5** 1 10S 116 55 E
Balimbing, *Phil.* **37 C5** 5 5N 119 58 E
Baling, *Malaysia* **39 K3** 5 41N 100 55 E
Balipara, *India* **41 F18** 26 50N 92 45 E
Balkan Mts. = Stara Planina, *Bulgaria* **21 C10** 43 15N 23 0 E
Balkhash = Balqash, *Kazakstan* **26 E8** 46 50N 74 50 E
Balkhash, Ozero = Balqash Köl, *Kazakstan* **26 E8** 46 0N 74 50 E
Balla, *Bangla.* **41 G17** 24 10N 91 35 E
Ballachulish, *U.K.* **12 E3** 56 41N 5 8W
Balladonia, *Australia* **61 F3** 32 27S 123 51 E
Ballaghaderreen, *Ireland* **13 C3** 53 55N 8 34W
Ballarat, *Australia* **63 F3** 37 33S 143 50 E
Ballard, L., *Australia* **61 E3** 29 20S 120 40 E
Ballater, *U.K.* **12 D5** 57 3N 3 3W
Ballenas, Canal de, *Mexico* **86 B2** 29 10N 113 45W
Balleny Is., *Antarctica* **5 C11** 66 30S 163 0 E
Ballia, *India* **43 G11** 25 46N 84 12 E
Ballina, *Australia* **63 D5** 28 50S 153 31 E
Ballina, *Ireland* **13 B2** 54 7N 9 9W
Ballinasloe, *Ireland* **13 C3** 53 20N 8 13W
Ballinger, *U.S.A.* **81 K5** 31 45N 99 57W
Ballinrobe, *Ireland* **13 C2** 53 38N 9 13W
Ballinskelligs B., *Ireland* **13 E1** 51 48N 10 13W
Ballston Spa, *U.S.A.* **79 D11** 43 0N 73 51W
Ballycastle, *U.K.* **13 A5** 55 12N 6 15W
Ballyclare, *U.K.* **13 B5** 54 46N 6 0W
Ballyhaunis, *Ireland* **13 C3** 53 46N 8 46W
Ballymena, *U.K.* **13 B5** 54 52N 6 17W
Ballymoney, *U.K.* **13 A5** 55 5N 6 31W
Ballymote, *Ireland* **13 B3** 54 5N 8 31W
Ballynahinch, *U.K.* **13 B6** 54 24N 5 54W
Ballyquintin Pt., *U.K.* **13 B6** 54 20N 5 30W
Ballyshannon, *Ireland* **13 B3** 54 30N 8 11W
Balmaceda, *Chile* **96 F2** 46 0S 71 50W
Balmertown, *Canada* **73 C10** 51 4N 93 41W
Balmoral, *Australia* **63 F3** 37 15S 141 48 E
Balmorhea, *U.S.A.* **81 K3** 30 59N 103 45W
Balonne →, *Australia* **63 D4** 28 47S 147 56 E
Balotra, *India* **42 G5** 25 50N 72 14 E
Balqash, *Kazakstan* **26 E8** 46 50N 74 50 E
Balqash Köl, *Kazakstan* **26 E8** 46 0N 74 50 E
Balrampur, *India* **43 F10** 27 30N 82 20 E
Balranald, *Australia* **63 E3** 34 38S 143 33 E
Balsas, *Mexico* **87 D5** 18 0N 99 40W
Balsas →, *Brazil* **93 E9** 7 15S 44 35W
Balsas →, *Mexico* **86 D4** 17 55N 102 10W
Balston Spa, *U.S.A.* **79 D11** 43 0N 73 52W
Balta, *Ukraine* **17 D15** 48 2N 29 45 E
Bălţi, *Moldova* **17 E14** 47 48N 27 58 E
Baltic Sea, *Europe* **9 H18** 57 0N 19 0 E
Baltimore, *Ireland* **13 E2** 51 29N 9 22W
Baltimore, *Md., U.S.A.* **76 F7** 39 17N 76 37W
Baltimore, *Ohio, U.S.A.* **78 G2** 39 51N 82 36W
Baltit, *Pakistan* **43 A6** 36 15N 74 40 E
Baltiysk, *Russia* **9 J18** 54 41N 19 58 E
Baluchistan □, *Pakistan* **40 F4** 27 30N 65 0 E
Balurghat, *India* **43 G13** 25 15N 88 44 E
Balvi, *Latvia* **9 H22** 57 8N 27 15 E
Balya, *Turkey* **21 E12** 39 44N 27 35 E
Bam, *Iran* **45 D8** 29 7N 58 14 E
Bama, *Nigeria* **51 F8** 11 33N 13 41 E
Bamaga, *Australia* **62 A3** 10 50S 142 25 E
Bamaji L., *Canada* **70 B1** 51 9N 91 25W
Bamako, *Mali* **50 F4** 12 34N 7 55W
Bambari, *C.A.R.* **52 C4** 5 40N 20 35 E
Bambaroo, *Australia* **62 B4** 18 50S 146 10 E
Bamberg, *Germany* **16 D6** 49 54N 10 54 E
Bamberg, *U.S.A.* **77 J5** 33 18N 81 2W
Bambili, *Dem. Rep. of the Congo* **54 B2** 3 40N 26 0 E
Bamenda, *Cameroon* **52 C1** 5 57N 10 11 E
Bamfield, *Canada* **72 D3** 48 45N 125 10W
Bāmīān □, *Afghan.* **40 B5** 35 0N 67 0 E
Bamiancheng, *China* **35 C13** 43 15N 124 2 E
Bampūr, *Iran* **45 E9** 27 15N 60 21 E
Ban Ban, *Laos* **38 C4** 19 31N 103 30 E
Ban Bang Hin, *Thailand* **39 H2** 9 32N 98 35 E
Ban Chiang Klang, *Thailand* **38 C3** 19 25N 100 55 E
Ban Chik, *Laos* **38 D4** 17 15N 102 22 E
Ban Choho, *Thailand* **38 E4** 15 2N 102 9 E
Ban Dan Lan Hoi, *Thailand* **38 D2** 17 0N 99 35 E
Ban Don = Surat Thani, *Thailand* **39 H2** 9 6N 99 20 E
Ban Don, *Vietnam* **38 F6** 12 53N 107 48 E
Ban Don, Ao →, *Thailand* **39 H2** 9 20N 99 25 E
Ban Dong, *Thailand* **38 C3** 19 30N 100 59 E
Ban Hong, *Thailand* **38 C2** 18 18N 98 50 E
Ban Kaeng, *Thailand* **38 D3** 17 29N 100 7 E
Ban Kantang, *Thailand* **39 J2** 7 25N 99 31 E
Ban Keun, *Laos* **38 C4** 18 22N 102 35 E
Ban Khai, *Thailand* **38 F3** 12 46N 101 18 E
Ban Kheun, *Laos* **38 B3** 20 13N 101 7 E
Ban Khlong Kua, *Thailand* **39 J3** 6 57N 100 8 E
Ban Khuan Mao, *Thailand* **39 J2** 7 50N 99 37 E
Ban Ko Yai Chim, *Thailand* **39 G2** 11 17N 99 26 E
Ban Kok, *Thailand* **38 D4** 16 40N 103 40 E
Ban Laem, *Thailand* **38 F2** 13 13N 99 59 E
Ban Lao Ngam, *Laos* **38 E6** 15 28N 106 10 E
Ban Le Kathe, *Thailand* **38 E2** 15 49N 98 53 E
Ban Mae Chedi, *Thailand* **38 C2** 19 11N 99 31 E
Ban Mae Laeng, *Thailand* **38 B2** 20 1N 99 17 E
Ban Mae Sariang, *Thailand* **38 C1** 18 10N 97 56 E
Ban Mê Thuôt = Buon Ma Thuot, *Vietnam* **38 F7** 12 40N 108 3 E
Ban Mi, *Thailand* **38 E3** 15 3N 100 32 E
Ban Muong Mo, *Laos* **38 C4** 19 4N 103 58 E
Ban Na Mo, *Laos* **38 D5** 17 7N 105 40 E
Ban Na San, *Thailand* **39 H2** 8 53N 99 52 E
Ban Na Tong, *Laos* **38 B3** 20 56N 101 47 E
Ban Nam Bac, *Laos* **38 B4** 20 38N 102 20 E
Ban Nam Ma, *Laos* **38 A3** 22 2N 101 37 E
Ban Ngang, *Laos* **38 E6** 15 59N 106 11 E
Ban Nong Bok, *Laos* **38 D5** 17 5N 104 48 E
Ban Nong Boua, *Laos* **38 E6** 15 40N 106 33 E
Ban Nong Pling, *Thailand* **38 E3** 15 40N 100 10 E
Ban Pak Chan, *Thailand* **39 G2** 10 32N 98 51 E
Ban Phai, *Thailand* **38 D4** 16 4N 102 44 E
Ban Pong, *Thailand* **38 F2** 13 50N 99 55 E
Ban Ron Phibun, *Thailand* **39 H2** 8 9N 99 51 E
Ban Sanam Chai, *Thailand* **39 J3** 7 33N 100 25 E
Ban Sangkha, *Thailand* **38 E4** 14 37N 103 52 E
Ban Tak, *Thailand* **38 D2** 17 2N 99 4 E
Ban Tako, *Thailand* **38 E4** 14 5N 102 40 E
Ban Tha Dua, *Thailand* **38 D2** 17 59N 98 39 E
Ban Tha Li, *Thailand* **38 D3** 17 37N 101 25 E
Ban Tha Nun, *Thailand* **39 H2** 8 12N 98 18 E
Ban Thahine, *Laos* **38 E5** 14 12N 105 33 E
Ban Xien Kok, *Laos* **38 B3** 20 54N 100 39 E
Ban Yen Nhan, *Vietnam* **38 B6** 20 57N 106 2 E
Banaba, *Kiribati* **64 H8** 0 45S 169 50 E
Banalia, *Dem. Rep. of the Congo* **54 B2** 1 32N 25 5 E
Banam, *Cambodia* **39 G5** 11 20N 105 17 E
Bananal, I. do, *Brazil* **93 F8** 11 30S 50 30W
Banaras = Varanasi, *India* **43 G10** 25 22N 83 0 E
Banas →, *Gujarat, India* **42 H4** 23 45N 71 25 E
Banas →, *Mad. P., India* **43 G9** 24 15N 81 30 E
Bânâs, Ras, *Egypt* **51 D13** 23 57N 35 59 E
Banbān, *Si. Arabia* **44 E5** 25 1N 46 35 E
Banbridge, *U.K.* **13 B5** 54 22N 6 16W
Banbury, *U.K.* **11 E6** 52 4N 1 20W
Banchory, *U.K.* **12 D6** 57 3N 2 29W
Bancroft, *Canada* **78 A7** 45 3N 77 51W
Band Bonī, *Iran* **45 E8** 25 30N 59 33 E
Band Qīr, *Iran* **45 D6** 31 39N 48 53 E
Banda, *India* **43 G9** 25 30N 80 26 E
Banda, *Mad. P., India* **43 G8** 24 3N 78 57 E
Banda, Kepulauan, *Indonesia* **37 E7** 4 37S 129 50 E
Banda Aceh, *Indonesia* **36 C1** 5 35N 95 20 E
Banda Banda, Mt., *Australia* **63 E5** 31 10S 152 28 E
Banda Elat, *Indonesia* **37 F8** 5 40S 133 5 E
Banda Is. = Banda, Kepulauan, *Indonesia* **37 E7** 4 37S 129 50 E
Banda Sea, *Indonesia* **37 F8** 6 0S 130 0 E
Bandai-San, *Japan* **30 F10** 37 36N 140 4 E
Bandān, *Iran* **45 D9** 31 23N 60 44 E
Bandanaira, *Indonesia* **37 E7** 4 32S 129 54 E
Bandanwara, *India* **42 F6** 26 9N 74 38 E
Bandar = Machilipatnam, *India* **41 L12** 16 12N 81 8 E
Bandār 'Abbās, *Iran* **45 E8** 27 15N 56 15 E
Bandar-e Anzalī, *Iran* **45 B6** 37 30N 49 30 E
Bandar-e Bushehr = Būshehr, *Iran* **45 D6** 28 55N 50 55 E
Bandar-e Chārak, *Iran* **45 E7** 26 45N 54 20 E
Bandar-e Deylam, *Iran* **45 D6** 30 5N 50 10 E
Bandar-e Khomeynı, *Iran* **45 D6** 30 30N 49 5 E
Bandar-e Lengeh, *Iran* **45 E7** 26 35N 54 58 E
Bandar-e Maqām, *Iran* **45 E7** 26 56N 53 29 E
Bandar-e Ma'shur, *Iran* **45 D6** 30 35N 49 10 E
Bandar-e Nakhīlū, *Iran* **45 E7** 26 58N 53 30 E
Bandar-e Rīg, *Iran* **45 D6** 29 29N 50 38 E
Bandar-e Torkeman, *Iran* **45 B7** 37 0N 54 10 E
Bandar Maharani = Muar, *Malaysia* **39 L4** 2 3N 102 34 E
Bandar Penggaram = Batu Pahat, *Malaysia* **39 M4** 1 50N 102 56 E
Bandar Seri Begawan, *Brunei* **36 D5** 4 52N 115 0 E
Bandar Sri Aman, *Malaysia* **36 D4** 1 15N 111 32 E
Bandawe, *Malawi* **55 E3** 11 58S 34 5 E
Bandeira, Pico da, *Brazil* **95 A7** 20 26S 41 47W
Bandera, *Argentina* **94 B3** 28 55S 62 20W
Banderas, B. de, *Mexico* **86 C3** 20 40N 105 30W
Bandhogarh, *India* **43 H9** 23 40N 81 2 E
Bandi →, *India* **42 F6** 26 12N 75 47 E
Bandikui, *India* **42 F7** 27 3N 76 34 E
Bandırma, *Turkey* **21 D13** 40 20N 28 0 E
Bandon, *Ireland* **13 E3** 51 44N 8 44W
Bandon →, *Ireland* **13 E3** 51 43N 8 37W
Bandula, *Mozam.* **55 F3** 19 0S 33 7 E
Bandundu, *Dem. Rep. of the Congo* **52 E3** 3 15S 17 22 E
Bandung, *Indonesia* **37 G12** 6 54S 107 36 E
Bāneh, *Iran* **44 C5** 35 59N 45 53 E
Banes, *Cuba* **89 B4** 21 0N 75 42W
Banff, *Canada* **72 C5** 51 10N 115 34W
Banff, *U.K.* **12 D6** 57 40N 2 33W
Banff Nat. Park, *Canada* **72 C5** 51 30N 116 15W
Bang Fai →, *Laos* **38 D5** 16 57N 104 45 E
Bang Hieng →, *Laos* **38 D5** 16 10N 105 10 E
Bang Krathum, *Thailand* **38 D3** 16 34N 100 18 E
Bang Lamung, *Thailand* **38 F3** 13 3N 100 56 E
Bang Mun Nak, *Thailand* **38 D3** 16 2N 100 23 E
Bang Pa In, *Thailand* **38 E3** 14 14N 100 35 E
Bang Rakam, *Thailand* **38 D3** 16 45N 100 7 E
Bang Saphan, *Thailand* **39 G2** 11 14N 99 28 E
Bangaduni I., *India* **43 J13** 21 34N 88 52 E
Bangala Dam, *Zimbabwe* **55 G3** 21 7S 31 25 E
Bangalore, *India* **40 N10** 12 59N 77 40 E
Banganga →, *India* **42 F6** 27 6N 77 25 E
Bangaon, *India* **43 H13** 23 0N 88 47 E
Bangassou, *C.A.R.* **52 D4** 4 55N 23 7 E
Banggai, *Indonesia* **37 E6** 1 34S 123 30 E
Banggai, Kepulauan, *Indonesia* **37 E6** 1 40S 123 30 E
Banggai Arch. = Banggai, Kepulauan, *Indonesia* **37 E6** 1 40S 123 30 E
Banggi, *Malaysia* **36 C5** 7 17N 117 12 E
Banghāzī, *Libya* **51 B10** 32 11N 20 3 E
Bangka, *Sulawesi, Indonesia* **37 D7** 1 50N 125 5 E
Bangka, *Sumatera, Indonesia* **36 E3** 2 0S 105 50 E
Bangka, Selat, *Indonesia* **36 E3** 2 30S 105 30 E
Bangkalan, *Indonesia* **37 G15** 7 2S 112 46 E
Bangkinang, *Indonesia* **36 D2** 0 18N 101 5 E
Bangko, *Indonesia* **36 E2** 2 5S 102 9 E
Bangkok, *Thailand* **38 F3** 13 45N 100 35 E
Bangladesh ■, *Asia* **41 H17** 24 0N 90 0 E
Bangong Co, *India* **43 B8** 35 50N 79 20 E
Bangor, *Down, U.K.* **13 B6** 54 40N 5 40W
Bangor, *Gwynedd, U.K.* **10 D3** 53 14N 4 8W
Bangor, *Maine, U.S.A.* **69 D13** 44 48N 68 46W
Bangor, *Pa., U.S.A.* **79 F9** 40 52N 75 13W
Bangued, *Phil.* **37 A6** 17 40N 120 37 E
Bangui, *C.A.R.* **52 D3** 4 23N 18 35 E
Banguru, *Dem. Rep. of the Congo* **54 B2** 0 30N 27 10 E
Bangweulu, L., *Zambia* **55 E3** 11 0S 30 0 E
Bangweulu Swamp, *Zambia* **55 E3** 11 20S 30 15 E
Bani, *Dom. Rep.* **89 C5** 18 16N 70 22W
Banī Sa'd, *Iraq* **44 C5** 33 34N 44 32 E
Banihal Pass, *India* **43 C6** 33 30N 75 12 E
Bāniyās, *Syria* **44 C3** 35 10N 36 0 E
Banja Luka, *Bos.-H.* **20 B7** 44 49N 17 11 E
Banjar, *India* **42 D7** 31 38N 77 21 E
Banjar →, *India* **43 H9** 22 36N 80 22 E
Banjarmasin, *Indonesia* **36 E4** 3 20S 114 35 E
Banjul, *Gambia* **50 F2** 13 28N 16 40W
Banka, *India* **43 G12** 24 53N 86 55 E
Banket, *Zimbabwe* **55 F3** 17 27S 30 19 E
Bankipore, *India* **41 G14** 25 35N 85 10 E
Banks I., *B.C., Canada* **72 C3** 53 20N 130 0W
Banks I., *N.W.T., Canada* **68 A7** 73 15N 121 30W
Banks Pen., *N.Z.* **59 K4** 43 45S 173 15 E
Banks Str., *Australia* **62 G4** 40 40S 148 10 E
Bankura, *India* **43 H12** 23 11N 87 18 E
Banmankhi, *India* **43 G12** 25 53N 87 11 E
Bann →, *Arm., U.K.* **13 B5** 54 30N 6 31W
Bann →, *L'derry., U.K.* **13 A5** 55 8N 6 41W
Bannang Sata, *Thailand* **39 J3** 6 16N 101 16 E
Banning, *U.S.A.* **85 M10** 33 56N 116 53W
Banningville = Bandundu, *Dem. Rep. of the Congo* **52 E3** 3 15S 17 22 E
Bannockburn, *Canada* **78 B7** 44 39N 77 33W
Bannockburn, *U.K.* **12 E5** 56 5N 3 55W
Bannockburn, *Zimbabwe* **55 G2** 20 17S 29 48 E
Bannu, *Pakistan* **40 C7** 33 0N 70 18 E
Bano, *India* **43 H11** 22 40N 84 55 E
Bansgaon, *India* **43 F10** 26 33N 83 21 E
Banská Bystrica, *Slovak Rep.* **17 D10** 48 46N 19 14 E
Banswara, *India* **42 H6** 23 32N 74 24 E
Bantaeng, *Indonesia* **37 F5** 5 32S 119 56 E
Bantry, *Ireland* **13 E2** 51 41N 9 27W
Bantry B., *Ireland* **13 E2** 51 37N 9 44W
Bantul, *Indonesia* **37 G14** 7 55S 110 19 E
Bantva, *India* **42 J4** 21 29N 70 12 E
Banu, *Afghan.* **40 B6** 35 35N 69 5 E
Banyak, Kepulauan, *Indonesia* **36 D1** 2 10N 97 10 E
Banyalbufar, *Spain* **22 B9** 39 42N 2 31 E
Banyo, *Cameroon* **52 C2** 6 52N 11 45 E
Banyumas, *Indonesia* **37 G13** 7 32S 109 18 E
Banyuwangi, *Indonesia* **37 H16** 8 13S 114 21 E
Banzare Coast, *Antarctica* **5 C9** 68 0S 125 0 E
Banzyville = Mobayi, *Dem. Rep. of the Congo* **52 D4** 4 15N 21 8 E
Bao Lac, *Vietnam* **38 A5** 22 57N 105 40 E
Bao Loc, *Vietnam* **39 G6** 11 32N 107 48 E
Baocheng, *China* **34 H4** 33 12N 106 56 E
Baode, *China* **34 E6** 39 1N 111 5 E
Baodi, *China* **35 E9** 39 38N 117 20 E
Baoding, *China* **34 E8** 38 50N 115 28 E
Baoji, *China* **34 G4** 34 20N 107 5 E
Baoshan, *China* **32 D4** 25 10N 99 5 E
Baotou, *China* **34 D6** 40 32N 110 2 E
Baoying, *China* **35 H10** 33 17N 119 20 E
Bap, *India* **42 F5** 27 23N 72 18 E
Bapatla, *India* **41 M12** 15 55N 80 30 E
Bāqerābād, *Iran* **45 C6** 33 2N 51 58 E
Ba'qūbah, *Iraq* **44 C5** 33 45N 44 50 E
Baquedano, *Chile* **94 A2** 23 20S 69 52W
Bar, *Montenegro, Yug.* **21 C8** 42 8N 19 6 E
Bar, *Ukraine* **17 D14** 49 4N 27 40 E
Bar Bigha, *India* **43 G11** 25 21N 85 47 E
Bar Harbor, *U.S.A.* **77 C11** 44 23N 68 13W
Bar-le-Duc, *France* **18 B6** 48 47N 5 10 E
Bara, *India* **43 G9** 25 16N 81 43 E
Bara Banki, *India* **43 F9** 26 55N 81 12 E
Barabai, *Indonesia* **36 E5** 2 32S 115 34 E
Baraboo, *U.S.A.* **80 D10** 43 28N 89 45W
Baracoa, *Cuba* **89 B5** 20 20N 74 30W
Baradā →, *Syria* **47 B5** 33 33N 36 34 E
Baradero, *Argentina* **94 C4** 33 52S 59 29W
Baradine, *Australia* **63 E4** 30 56S 149 4 E
Baraga, *U.S.A.* **80 B10** 46 47N 88 30W
Barah →, *India* **42 F6** 27 42N 77 5 E
Barahona, *Dom. Rep.* **89 C5** 18 13N 71 7W
Barail Range, *India* **41 G18** 25 15N 93 20 E
Barakaldo, *Spain* **19 A4** 43 18N 2 59W
Barakar →, *India* **43 G12** 24 7N 86 14 E
Barakhola, *India* **41 G18** 25 0N 92 45 E
Barakot, *India* **43 J11** 21 33N 84 59 E
Barakpur, *India* **43 H13** 22 44N 88 30 E
Baralaba, *Australia* **62 C4** 24 13S 149 50 E
Baralzon L., *Canada* **73 B9** 60 0N 98 3W
Baramula, *India* **43 B6** 34 15N 74 20 E
Baran, *India* **42 G7** 25 9N 76 40 E
Baran →, *Pakistan* **42 G3** 25 13N 68 17 E
Baranavichy, *Belarus* **17 B14** 53 10N 26 0 E
Baranof, *U.S.A.* **72 B2** 57 5N 134 50W
Baranof I., *U.S.A.* **68 C6** 57 0N 135 0W
Barapasi, *Indonesia* **37 E9** 2 15S 137 5 E
Barasat, *India* **43 H13** 22 46N 88 31 E
Barat Daya, Kepulauan, *Indonesia* **37 F7** 7 30S 128 0 E
Barataria B., *U.S.A.* **81 L10** 29 20N 89 55W
Barauda, *India* **42 H6** 23 33N 75 15 E
Baraut, *India* **42 E7** 29 13N 77 7 E
Barbacena, *Brazil* **95 A7** 21 15S 43 56W
Barbados ■, *W. Indies* **89 D8** 13 10N 59 30W
Barbària, C. de, *Spain* **22 C7** 38 39N 1 24 E
Barbastro, *Spain* **19 A6** 42 2N 0 5 E
Barberton, *S. Africa* **57 D5** 25 42S 31 2 E
Barberton, *U.S.A.* **78 E3** 41 0N 81 39W
Barbosa, *Colombia* **92 B4** 5 57N 73 37W
Barbourville, *U.S.A.* **77 G4** 36 52N 83 53W
Barbuda, *W. Indies* **89 C7** 17 30N 61 40W
Barcaldine, *Australia* **62 C4** 23 43S 145 6 E
Barcellona Pozzo di Gotto, *Italy* **20 E6** 38 9N 15 13 E
Barcelona, *Spain* **19 B7** 41 21N 2 10 E
Barcelona, *Venezuela* **92 A6** 10 10N 64 40W
Barcelos, *Brazil* **92 D6** 1 0S 63 0W
Barcoo →, *Australia* **62 D3** 25 30S 142 50 E
Bardaï, *Chad* **51 D9** 21 25N 17 0 E
Bardas Blancas, *Argentina* **94 D2** 35 49S 69 45W
Barddhaman, *India* **43 H12** 23 14N 87 39 E
Bardejov, *Slovak Rep.* **17 D11** 49 18N 21 15 E
Bardera, *Somali Rep.* **46 G3** 2 20N 42 27 E
Bardīyah, *Libya* **51 B10** 31 45N 25 5 E
Bardsey I., *U.K.* **10 E3** 52 45N 4 47W
Bardstown, *U.S.A.* **76 G3** 37 49N 85 28W

Big Timber

Belfast, *Maine, U.S.A.* 77 C11 44 26N 69 1W
Belfast, *N.Y., U.S.A.* 78 D6 42 21N 78 7W
Belfast L., *U.K.* 13 B6 54 40N 5 50W
Belfield, *U.S.A.* 80 B3 46 53N 103 12W
Belfort, *France* 18 C7 47 38N 6 50 E
Belfry, *U.S.A.* 82 D9 45 9N 109 1W
Belgaum, *India* 40 M9 15 55N 74 35 E
Belgium ■, *Europe* 15 D4 50 30N 5 0 E
Belgorod, *Russia* 25 D6 50 35N 36 35 E
Belgorod-Dnestrovskiy = Bilhorod-Dnistrovskyy, *Ukraine* 25 E5 46 11N 30 23 E
Belgrade = Beograd, *Serbia, Yug.* 21 B9 44 50N 20 37 E
Belgrade, *U.S.A.* 82 D8 45 47N 111 11W
Belhaven, *U.S.A.* 77 H7 35 33N 76 37W
Beli Drim —►, *Europe* 21 C9 42 6N 20 25 E
Belinyu, *Indonesia* 36 E3 1 35S 105 50 E
Beliton Is. = Belitung, *Indonesia* 36 E3 3 10S 107 50 E
Belitung, *Indonesia* 36 E3 3 10S 107 50 E
Belize ■, *Cent. Amer.* 87 D7 17 0N 88 30W
Belize City, *Belize* 87 D7 17 25N 88 0W
Belkovskiy, Ostrov, *Russia* 27 B14 75 32N 135 44 E
Bell —►, *Canada* 70 C4 49 48N 77 38W
Bell I., *Canada* 71 B8 50 46N 55 35W
Bell-Irving —►, *Canada* 72 B3 56 12N 129 5W
Bell Peninsula, *Canada* 69 B11 63 50N 82 0W
Bell Ville, *Argentina* 94 C3 32 40S 62 40W
Bella Bella, *Canada* 72 C3 52 10N 128 10W
Bella Coola, *Canada* 72 C3 52 25N 126 40W
Bella Unión, *Uruguay* 94 C4 30 15S 57 40W
Bella Vista, *Corrientes, Argentina* 94 B4 28 33S 59 0W
Bella Vista, *Tucuman, Argentina* 94 B2 27 10S 65 25W
Bellaire, *U.S.A.* 78 F4 40 1N 80 45W
Bellary, *India* 40 M10 15 10N 76 56 E
Bellata, *Australia* 63 D4 29 53S 149 46 E
Belle-Chasse, *U.S.A.* 81 L10 29 51N 89 59W
Belle Fourche, *U.S.A.* 80 C3 44 40N 103 51W
Belle Fourche —►, *U.S.A.* 80 C3 44 26N 102 18W
Belle Glade, *U.S.A.* 77 M5 26 41N 80 40W
Belle-Île, *France* 18 C2 47 20N 3 10W
Belle Isle, *Canada* 71 B8 51 57N 55 25W
Belle Isle, Str. of, *Canada* 71 B8 51 30N 56 30W
Belle Plaine, *U.S.A.* 80 E8 41 54N 92 17W
Bellefontaine, *U.S.A.* 76 E4 40 22N 83 46W
Bellefonte, *U.S.A.* 78 F7 40 55N 77 47W
Belleoram, *Canada* 71 C8 47 31N 55 25W
Belleville, *Canada* 78 B7 44 10N 77 23W
Belleville, *Ill., U.S.A.* 80 F10 38 31N 89 59W
Belleville, *Kans., U.S.A.* 80 F6 39 50N 97 38W
Belleville, *N.Y., U.S.A.* 79 C8 43 46N 76 10W
Bellevue, *Canada* 72 D6 49 35N 114 22W
Bellevue, *Idaho, U.S.A.* 82 E6 43 28N 114 16W
Bellevue, *Nebr., U.S.A.* 80 E7 41 8N 95 53W
Bellevue, *Ohio, U.S.A.* 78 E2 41 17N 82 51W
Bellevue, *Wash., U.S.A.* 84 C4 47 37N 122 12W
Bellin = Kangirsuk, *Canada* 69 C13 60 0N 70 0W
Bellingen, *Australia* 63 E5 30 25S 152 50 E
Bellingham, *U.S.A.* 68 D7 48 46N 122 29W
Bellingshausen Sea, *Antarctica* 5 C17 66 0S 80 0W
Bellinzona, *Switz.* 18 C8 46 11N 9 1 E
Bello, *Colombia* 92 B3 6 20N 75 33W
Bellows Falls, *U.S.A.* 79 C12 43 8N 72 27W
Bellpat, *Pakistan* 42 E3 29 0N 68 5 E
Belluno, *Italy* 20 A5 46 9N 12 13 E
Bellwood, *U.S.A.* 78 F6 40 36N 78 20W
Belmont, *Canada* 78 D3 42 53N 81 5W
Belmont, *S. Africa* 56 D3 29 28S 24 22 E
Belmont, *U.S.A.* 78 D6 42 14N 78 2W
Belmonte, *Brazil* 93 G11 16 0S 39 0W
Belmopan, *Belize* 87 D7 17 18N 88 30W
Belmullet, *Ireland* 13 B2 54 14N 9 58W
Belo Horizonte, *Brazil* 93 G10 19 55S 43 56W
Belo-sur-Mer, *Madag.* 57 C7 20 42S 44 0 E
Belo-Tsiribihina, *Madag.* 57 B7 19 40S 44 30 E
Belogorsk, *Russia* 27 D13 51 0N 128 20 E
Beloha, *Madag.* 57 D8 25 10S 45 3 E
Beloit, *Kans., U.S.A.* 80 F5 39 28N 98 6W
Beloit, *Wis., U.S.A.* 80 D10 42 31N 89 2W
Belokorovichi, *Ukraine* 17 C15 51 7N 28 2 E
Belomorsk, *Russia* 24 B5 64 35N 34 54 E
Belonia, *India* 41 H17 23 15N 91 30 E
Beloretsk, *Russia* 24 D10 53 58N 58 24 E
Belorussia = Belarus ■, *Europe* 17 B14 53 30N 27 0 E
Belovo, *Russia* 26 D9 54 30N 86 0 E
Beloye, Ozero, *Russia* 24 B6 60 10N 37 35 E
Beloye More, *Russia* 24 A6 66 30N 38 0 E
Belozersk, *Russia* 24 B6 60 1N 37 45 E
Belpre, *U.S.A.* 76 F5 39 17N 81 34W
Belrain, *India* 43 E9 28 23N 80 55 E
Belt, *U.S.A.* 82 C8 47 23N 110 55W
Beltana, *Australia* 63 E2 30 48S 138 25 E
Belterra, *Brazil* 93 D8 2 45S 55 0W
Belton, *U.S.A.* 81 K6 31 3N 97 28W
Belton L., *U.S.A.* 81 K6 31 8N 97 32W
Beltsy = Bălţi, *Moldova* 17 E14 47 48N 27 58 E
Belturbet, *Ireland* 13 B4 54 6N 7 26W
Belukha, *Russia* 26 E9 49 50N 86 50 E
Beluran, *Malaysia* 36 C5 5 48N 117 35 E
Belvidere, *Ill., U.S.A.* 80 D10 42 15N 88 50W
Belvidere, *N.J., U.S.A.* 79 F9 40 50N 75 5W
Belyando —►, *Australia* 62 C4 21 38S 146 50 E
Belyy, Ostrov, *Russia* 26 B8 73 30N 71 0 E
Belyy Yar, *Russia* 26 D9 58 26N 84 39 E
Belzoni, *U.S.A.* 81 J9 33 11N 90 29W
Bemaraha, Lembalemban' i, *Madag.* 57 B7 18 40S 44 45 E
Bemarivo, *Madag.* 57 C7 21 45S 44 45 E
Bemarivo —►, *Madag.* 57 B8 15 27S 47 40 E
Bemavo, *Madag.* 57 C8 21 33S 45 25 E
Bembéréke, *Benin* 50 F6 10 11N 2 43 E
Bembesi, *Zimbabwe* 55 G2 20 0S 28 58 E
Bembesi —►, *Zimbabwe* 55 F2 18 57S 27 47 E
Bemetara, *India* 43 J9 21 42N 81 32 E
Bemidji, *U.S.A.* 80 B7 47 28N 94 53W
Ben, *Iran* 45 C6 32 32N 50 45 E
Ben Cruachan, *U.K.* 12 E3 56 26N 5 8W
Ben Dearg, *U.K.* 12 D4 57 47N 4 56W
Ben Hope, *U.K.* 12 C4 58 25N 4 36W
Ben Lawers, *U.K.* 12 E4 56 32N 4 14W
Ben Lomond, *N.S.W., Australia* 63 E5 30 1S 151 43 E
Ben Lomond, *Tas., Australia* 62 G4 41 38S 147 42 E
Ben Lomond, *U.K.* 12 E4 56 11N 4 38W
Ben Luc, *Vietnam* 39 G6 10 39N 106 29 E
Ben Macdhui, *U.K.* 12 D5 57 4N 3 40W
Ben Mhor, *U.K.* 12 D1 57 15N 7 18W
Ben More, *Arg. & Bute, U.K.* 12 E2 56 26N 6 1W
Ben More, *Stirl., U.K.* 12 E4 56 23N 4 32W
Ben More Assynt, *U.K.* 12 C4 58 8N 4 52W
Ben Nevis, *U.K.* 12 E3 56 48N 5 1W
Ben Quang, *Vietnam* 38 D6 17 3N 106 55 E
Ben Vorlich, *U.K.* 12 E4 56 21N 4 14W
Ben Wyvis, *U.K.* 12 D4 57 40N 4 35W
Bena, *Nigeria* 50 F7 11 20N 5 50 E
Benalla, *Australia* 63 F4 36 30S 146 0 E
Benares = Varanasi, *India* 43 G10 25 22N 83 0 E
Benavente, *Spain* 19 A3 42 2N 5 43W
Benavides, *U.S.A.* 81 M5 27 36N 98 25W
Benbecula, *U.K.* 12 D1 57 26N 7 21W
Benbonyathe, *Australia* 63 E2 30 25S 139 11 E
Bend, *U.S.A.* 82 D3 44 4N 121 19W
Bendemeer, *Australia* 63 E5 30 53S 151 8 E
Bender Beila, *Somali Rep.* 46 F5 9 30N 50 48 E
Bendery = Tighina, *Moldova* 17 E15 46 50N 29 30 E
Bendigo, *Australia* 63 F3 36 40S 144 15 E
Benē Beraq, *Israel* 47 C3 32 6N 34 51 E
Benenitra, *Madag.* 57 C8 23 27S 45 5 E
Benevento, *Italy* 20 D6 41 8N 14 45 E
Benga, *Mozam.* 55 F3 16 11S 33 40 E
Bengal, Bay of, *Ind. Oc.* 41 M17 15 0N 90 0 E
Bengbu, *China* 35 H9 32 58N 117 20 E
Benghazi = Banghāzī, *Libya* 51 B10 32 11N 20 3 E
Bengkalis, *Indonesia* 36 D2 1 30N 102 10 E
Bengkulu, *Indonesia* 36 E2 3 50S 102 12 E
Bengkulu □, *Indonesia* 36 E2 3 48S 102 16 E
Bengough, *Canada* 73 D7 49 25N 105 10W
Benguela, *Angola* 53 G2 12 37S 13 25 E
Benguérua, I., *Mozam.* 57 C6 21 58S 35 28 E
Beni, *Dem. Rep. of the Congo* 54 B2 0 30N 29 27 E
Beni —►, *Bolivia* 92 F5 10 23S 65 24W
Beni Mellal, *Morocco* 50 B4 32 21N 6 21W
Beni Suef, *Egypt* 51 C12 29 5N 31 6 E
Beniah L., *Canada* 72 A6 63 23N 112 17W
Benicia, *U.S.A.* 84 G4 38 3N 122 9W
Benidorm, *Spain* 19 C5 38 33N 0 9W
Benin ■, *Africa* 50 G6 10 0N 2 0 E
Benin, Bight of, *W. Afr.* 50 H6 5 0N 3 0 E
Benin City, *Nigeria* 50 G7 6 20N 5 31 E
Benitses, *Greece* 23 A3 39 32N 19 55 E
Benjamin Aceval, *Paraguay* 94 A4 24 58S 57 34W
Benjamin Constant, *Brazil* 92 D4 4 40S 70 15W
Benjamin Hill, *Mexico* 86 A2 30 10N 111 10W
Benkelman, *U.S.A.* 80 E4 40 3N 101 32W
Bennett, *Canada* 72 B2 59 56N 134 53W
Bennett, L., *Australia* 60 D5 22 50S 131 2 E
Bennetta, Ostrov, *Russia* 27 B15 76 21N 148 56 E
Bennettsville, *U.S.A.* 77 H6 34 37N 79 41W
Bennington, *N.H., U.S.A.* 79 D11 43 0N 71 55W
Bennington, *Vt., U.S.A.* 79 D11 42 53N 73 12W
Benoni, *S. Africa* 57 D4 26 11S 28 18 E
Benque Viejo, *Belize* 87 D7 17 5N 89 8W
Benson, *Ariz., U.S.A.* 83 L8 31 58N 110 18W
Benson, *Minn., U.S.A.* 80 C7 45 19N 95 36W
Bent, *Iran* 45 E8 26 20N 59 31 E
Benteng, *Indonesia* 37 F6 6 10S 120 30 E
Bentinck I., *Australia* 62 B2 17 3S 139 35 E
Bento Gonçalves, *Brazil* 95 B5 29 10S 51 31W
Benton, *Ark., U.S.A.* 81 H8 34 34N 92 35W
Benton, *Calif., U.S.A.* 84 H8 37 48N 118 32W
Benton, *Ill., U.S.A.* 80 G10 38 0N 88 55W
Benton, *Pa., U.S.A.* 79 E8 41 12N 76 23W
Benton Harbor, *U.S.A.* 76 D2 42 6N 86 27W
Bentonville, *U.S.A.* 81 G7 36 22N 94 13W
Bentung, *Malaysia* 39 L3 3 31N 101 55 E
Benue —►, *Nigeria* 50 G7 7 48N 6 46 E
Benxi, *China* 35 D12 41 20N 123 48 E
Beo, *Indonesia* 37 D7 4 25N 126 50 E
Beograd, *Serbia, Yug.* 21 B9 44 50N 20 37 E
Beppu, *Japan* 31 H5 33 15N 131 30 E
Beqaa Valley = Al Biqā, *Lebanon* 47 A5 34 10N 36 10 E
Ber Mota, *India* 42 H3 23 27N 68 34 E
Berach —►, *India* 42 G6 25 15N 75 2 E
Berati, *Albania* 21 D8 40 43N 19 59 E
Berau, Teluk, *Indonesia* 37 E8 2 30S 132 30 E
Berber, *Sudan* 51 E12 18 0N 34 0 E
Berbera, *Somali Rep.* 46 E4 10 30N 45 2 E
Berbérati, *C.A.R.* 52 D3 4 15N 15 40 E
Berbice —►, *Guyana* 92 B7 6 20N 57 32W
Berdichev = Berdychiv, *Ukraine* 17 D15 49 57N 28 30 E
Berdsk, *Russia* 26 D9 54 47N 83 2 E
Berdyansk, *Ukraine* 25 E6 46 45N 36 50 E
Berdychiv, *Ukraine* 17 D15 49 57N 28 30 E
Berea, *U.S.A.* 76 G3 37 34N 84 17W
Berebere, *Indonesia* 37 D7 2 25N 128 45 E
Bereda, *Somali Rep.* 46 E5 11 45N 51 0 E
Berehove, *Ukraine* 17 D12 48 15N 22 35 E
Berekum, *Ghana* 50 G5 7 29N 2 34W
Berens —►, *Canada* 73 C9 52 25N 97 2W
Berens I., *Canada* 73 C9 52 18N 97 18W
Berens River, *Canada* 73 C9 52 25N 97 0W
Beresford, *U.S.A.* 80 D6 43 5N 96 47W
Berestechko, *Ukraine* 17 C13 50 22N 25 5 E
Berevo, *Mahajanga, Madag.* 57 B7 17 14S 44 17 E
Berevo, *Toliara, Madag.* 57 B7 19 44S 44 58 E
Bereza, *Belarus* 17 B13 52 31N 24 51 E
Berezhany, *Ukraine* 17 D13 49 26N 24 58 E
Berezina = Byarezina —►, *Belarus* 17 B16 52 33N 30 14 E
Bereznik, *Russia* 24 B7 62 51N 42 40 E
Berezniki, *Russia* 24 C10 59 24N 56 46 E
Berezovo, *Russia* 26 C7 64 0N 65 0 E
Berga, *Spain* 19 A6 42 6N 1 48 E
Bergama, *Turkey* 21 E12 39 8N 27 11 E
Bergamo, *Italy* 18 D8 45 41N 9 43 E
Bergen, *Neths.* 15 B4 52 40N 4 43 E
Bergen, *Norway* 9 F11 60 20N 5 20 E
Bergen, *U.S.A.* 78 C7 43 5N 77 57W
Bergen op Zoom, *Neths.* 15 C4 51 28N 4 18 E
Bergerac, *France* 18 D4 44 51N 0 30 E
Bergholz, *U.S.A.* 78 F4 40 31N 80 53W
Bergisch Gladbach, *Germany* 15 D7 50 59N 7 8 E
Bergville, *S. Africa* 57 D4 28 52S 29 18 E
Berhala, Selat, *Indonesia* 36 E2 1 0S 104 15 E
Berhampore = Baharampur, *India* 43 G13 24 2N 88 27 E
Berhampur = Brahmapur, *India* 41 K14 19 15N 84 54 E
Bering Sea, *Pac. Oc.* 68 C1 58 0N 171 0 E
Bering Strait, *Pac. Oc.* 68 B3 65 30N 169 0W
Beringovskiy, *Russia* 27 C18 63 3N 179 19 E
Berisso, *Argentina* 94 C4 34 56S 57 50W
Berja, *Spain* 19 D4 36 50N 2 56W
Berkeley, *U.S.A.* 84 H4 37 52N 122 16W
Berkner I., *Antarctica* 5 D18 79 30S 50 0W
Berkshire, *U.S.A.* 79 D8 42 19N 76 11W
Berkshire Downs, *U.K.* 11 F6 51 33N 1 29W
Berlin, *Germany* 16 B7 52 30N 13 25 E
Berlin, *Md., U.S.A.* 76 F8 38 20N 75 13W
Berlin, *N.H., U.S.A.* 79 B13 44 28N 71 11W
Berlin, *N.Y., U.S.A.* 79 D11 42 42N 73 23W
Berlin, *Wis., U.S.A.* 76 D1 43 58N 88 57W
Berlin L., *U.S.A.* 78 E4 41 3N 81 0W
Bermejo —►, *Formosa, Argentina* 94 B4 26 51S 58 23W
Bermejo —►, *San Juan, Argentina* 94 C2 32 30S 67 30W
Bermen, L., *Canada* 71 B6 53 35N 68 55W
Bermuda ■, *Atl. Oc.* 66 F13 32 45N 65 0W
Bern, *Switz.* 18 C7 46 57N 7 28 E
Bernalillo, *U.S.A.* 83 J10 35 18N 106 33W
Bernardo de Irigoyen, *Argentina* 95 B5 26 15S 53 40W
Bernardo O'Higgins □, *Chile* 94 C1 34 15S 70 45W
Bernardsville, *U.S.A.* 79 F10 40 43N 74 34W
Bernasconi, *Argentina* 94 D3 37 55S 63 44W
Bernburg, *Germany* 16 C6 51 47N 11 44 E
Berne = Bern, *Switz.* 18 C7 46 57N 7 28 E
Berneray, *U.K.* 12 D1 57 43N 7 11W
Bernier I., *Australia* 61 D1 24 50S 113 12 E
Bernina, Piz, *Switz.* 18 C8 46 20N 9 54 E
Beroroha, *Madag.* 57 C8 21 40S 45 10 E
Beroun, *Czech Rep.* 16 D8 49 57N 14 5 E
Berri, *Australia* 63 E3 34 14S 140 35 E
Berriane, *Algeria* 50 B6 32 50N 3 46 E
Berrigan, *Australia* 63 F4 35 38S 145 49 E
Berry, *Australia* 63 E5 34 46S 150 43 E
Berry, *France* 18 C5 46 50N 2 0 E
Berry Is., *Bahamas* 88 A4 25 40N 77 50W
Berryessa L., *U.S.A.* 84 G4 38 31N 122 6W
Berryville, *U.S.A.* 81 G8 36 22N 93 34W
Bershad, *Ukraine* 17 D15 48 22N 29 31 E
Berthold, *U.S.A.* 80 A4 48 19N 101 44W
Berthoud, *U.S.A.* 80 E2 40 19N 105 5W
Bertoua, *Cameroon* 52 D2 4 30N 13 45 E
Bertraghboy B., *Ireland* 13 C2 53 22N 9 54W
Berwick, *U.S.A.* 79 E8 41 3N 76 14W
Berwick-upon-Tweed, *U.K.* 10 B6 55 46N 2 0W
Berwyn Mts., *U.K.* 10 E4 52 54N 3 26W
Besal, *Pakistan* 43 B5 35 4N 73 56 E
Besalampy, *Madag.* 57 B7 16 43S 44 29 E
Besançon, *France* 18 C7 47 15N 6 2 E
Besar, *Indonesia* 36 E5 2 40S 116 0 E
Besnard L., *Canada* 73 B7 55 25N 106 0W
Besni, *Turkey* 44 B3 37 41N 37 52 E
Besor, N. —►, *Egypt* 47 D3 31 28N 34 22 E
Bessarabiya, *Moldova* 17 E15 47 0N 28 10 E
Bessarabka = Basarabeasca, *Moldova* 17 E15 46 21N 28 58 E
Bessemer, *Ala., U.S.A.* 77 J2 33 24N 86 58W
Bessemer, *Mich., U.S.A.* 80 B9 46 29N 90 3W
Bessemer, *Pa., U.S.A.* 78 F4 40 59N 80 30W
Beswick, *Australia* 60 B5 14 34S 132 53 E
Bet She'an, *Israel* 47 C4 32 30N 35 30 E
Bet Shemesh, *Israel* 47 D4 31 44N 35 0 E
Betafo, *Madag.* 57 B8 19 50S 46 51 E
Betancuria, *Canary Is.* 22 F5 28 25N 14 3W
Betanzos, *Spain* 19 A1 43 15N 8 12W
Bétaré Oya, *Cameroon* 52 C2 5 40N 14 5 E
Bethal, *S. Africa* 57 D4 26 27S 29 28 E
Bethanien, *Namibia* 56 D2 26 31S 17 8 E
Bethany, *Canada* 78 B6 44 11N 78 34W
Bethany, *U.S.A.* 80 E7 40 16N 94 2W
Bethel, *Alaska, U.S.A.* 68 B3 60 48N 161 45W
Bethel, *Conn., U.S.A.* 79 E11 41 22N 73 25W
Bethel, *Maine, U.S.A.* 79 B14 44 25N 70 47W
Bethel, *Vt., U.S.A.* 79 C12 43 50N 72 38W
Bethel Park, *U.S.A.* 78 F4 40 20N 80 1W
Bethlehem = Bayt Lahm, *West Bank* 47 D4 31 43N 35 12 E
Bethlehem, *S. Africa* 57 D4 28 14S 28 18 E
Bethlehem, *U.S.A.* 79 F9 40 37N 75 23W
Bethulie, *S. Africa* 56 E4 30 30S 25 59 E
Béthune, *France* 18 A5 50 30N 2 38 E
Betioky, *Madag.* 57 C7 23 48S 44 20 E
Betong, *Thailand* 39 K3 5 45N 101 5 E
Betoota, *Australia* 62 D3 25 45S 140 42 E
Betroka, *Madag.* 57 C8 23 16S 46 0 E
Betsiamites, *Canada* 71 C6 48 56N 68 40W
Betsiamites —►, *Canada* 71 C6 48 56N 68 38W
Betsiboka —►, *Madag.* 57 B8 16 3S 46 36 E
Bettendorf, *U.S.A.* 80 E9 41 32N 90 30W
Bettiah, *India* 43 F11 26 48N 84 33 E
Betul, *India* 40 J10 21 58N 77 59 E
Betung, *Malaysia* 36 D4 1 24N 111 31 E
Betws-y-Coed, *U.K.* 10 D4 53 5N 3 48W
Beulah, *Mich., U.S.A.* 76 C2 44 38N 86 6W
Beulah, *N. Dak., U.S.A.* 80 B4 47 16N 101 47W
Beveren, *Belgium* 15 C4 51 12N 4 16 E
Beverley, *Australia* 61 F2 32 9S 116 56 E
Beverley, *U.K.* 10 D7 53 51N 0 26W
Beverley Hills, *U.S.A.* 77 L4 28 56N 82 28W
Beverly, *U.S.A.* 79 D14 42 33N 70 53W
Beverly Hills, *U.S.A.* 85 L8 34 4N 118 25W
Bewas —►, *India* 43 H8 23 59N 79 21 E
Bexhill, *U.K.* 11 G8 50 51N 0 29 E
Beyānlū, *Iran* 44 C5 36 0N 47 51 E
Beyneu, *Kazakstan* 25 E10 45 18N 55 9 E
Beypazarı, *Turkey* 25 F5 40 10N 31 56 E
Beyşehir Gölü, *Turkey* 25 G5 37 41N 31 33 E
Béziers, *France* 18 E5 43 20N 3 12 E
Bezwada = Vijayawada, *India* 41 L12 16 31N 80 39 E
Bhabua, *India* 43 G10 25 3N 83 37 E
Bhachau, *India* 40 H7 23 20N 70 16 E
Bhadar —►, *Gujarat, India* 42 H5 22 17N 72 20 E
Bhadar —►, *Gujarat, India* 42 J3 21 27N 69 47 E
Bhadarwah, *India* 43 C6 32 58N 75 46 E
Bhadohi, *India* 43 G10 25 25N 82 34 E
Bhadra, *India* 42 E6 29 8N 75 14 E
Bhadrakh, *India* 41 J15 21 10N 86 30 E
Bhadran, *India* 42 H5 22 19N 72 6 E
Bhadravati, *India* 40 N9 13 49N 75 40 E
Bhag, *Pakistan* 42 E2 29 2N 67 49 E
Bhagalpur, *India* 43 G12 25 10N 87 0 E
Bhagirathi —►, *Ut. P., India* 43 D8 30 8N 78 35 E
Bhagirathi —►, *W. Bengal, India* 43 H13 23 25N 88 23 E
Bhakkar, *Pakistan* 42 D4 31 40N 71 5 E
Bhakra Dam, *India* 42 D7 31 30N 76 45 E
Bhamo, *Burma* 41 G20 24 15N 97 15 E
Bhandara, *India* 40 J11 21 5N 79 42 E
Bhanpura, *India* 42 G6 24 31N 75 44 E
Bhanrer Ra., *India* 43 H8 23 40N 79 45 E
Bhaptiahi, *India* 43 F12 26 19N 86 44 E
Bharat = India ■, *Asia* 40 K11 20 0N 78 0 E
Bharatpur, *Mad. P., India* 43 H9 23 44N 81 46 E
Bharatpur, *Raj., India* 42 F7 27 15N 77 30 E
Bharno, *India* 43 H11 23 14N 84 53 E
Bhatinda, *India* 42 D6 30 15N 74 57 E
Bhatpara, *India* 43 H13 22 50N 88 25 E
Bhattu, *India* 42 E6 29 36N 75 19 E
Bhaun, *Pakistan* 42 C5 32 55N 72 40 E
Bhaunagar = Bhavnagar, *India* 40 J8 21 45N 72 10 E
Bhavnagar, *India* 40 J8 21 45N 72 10 E
Bhawanipatna, *India* 41 K12 19 55N 80 10 E
Bhawari, *India* 42 G5 25 42N 73 4 E
Bhayavadar, *India* 42 J4 21 51N 70 15 E
Bhera, *Pakistan* 42 C5 32 29N 72 57 E
Bhikangaon, *India* 42 J6 21 52N 75 57 E
Bhilsa = Vidisha, *India* 42 H7 23 28N 77 53 E
Bhilwara, *India* 42 G6 25 25N 74 38 E
Bhima —►, *India* 40 L10 16 25N 77 17 E
Bhimavaram, *India* 41 L12 16 30N 81 30 E
Bhimbar, *Pakistan* 43 C6 32 59N 74 3 E
Bhind, *India* 43 F8 26 30N 78 46 E
Bhinga, *India* 43 F9 27 43N 81 56 E
Bhinmal, *India* 42 G5 25 0N 72 15 E
Bhiwandi, *India* 40 K8 19 20N 73 0 E
Bhiwani, *India* 42 E7 28 50N 76 9 E
Bhogava —►, *India* 42 H5 22 26N 72 20 E
Bhola, *Bangla.* 41 H17 22 45N 90 35 E
Bholari, *Pakistan* 42 G3 25 19N 68 13 E
Bhopal, *India* 42 H7 23 20N 77 30 E
Bhubaneshwar, *India* 41 J14 20 15N 85 50 E
Bhuj, *India* 42 H3 23 15N 69 49 E
Bhusaval, *India* 40 J9 21 3N 75 46 E
Bhutan ■, *Asia* 41 F17 27 25N 90 30 E
Biafra, B. of = Bonny, Bight of, *Africa* 52 D1 3 30N 9 20 E
Biak, *Indonesia* 37 E9 1 10S 136 6 E
Biała Podlaska, *Poland* 17 B12 52 4N 23 6 E
Białogard, *Poland* 16 A8 54 2N 15 58 E
Białystok, *Poland* 17 B12 53 10N 23 10 E
Biaora, *India* 42 H7 23 56N 76 56 E
Bīārjmand, *Iran* 45 B7 36 6N 55 53 E
Biaro, *Indonesia* 37 D7 2 5N 125 26 E
Biarritz, *France* 18 E3 43 29N 1 33W
Bibai, *Japan* 30 C10 43 19N 141 52 E
Bibby I., *Canada* 73 A10 61 55N 93 0W
Biberach, *Germany* 16 D5 48 5N 9 47 E
Bibungwa, *Dem. Rep. of the Congo* 54 C2 2 40S 28 15 E
Bic, *Canada* 71 C6 48 20N 68 41W
Bicester, *U.K.* 11 F6 51 54N 1 9W
Bicheno, *Australia* 62 G4 41 52S 148 18 E
Bichia, *India* 43 H9 22 27N 80 42 E
Bickerton I., *Australia* 62 A2 13 45S 136 10 E
Bida, *Nigeria* 50 G7 9 3N 5 58 E
Bidar, *India* 40 L10 17 55N 77 35 E
Biddeford, *U.S.A.* 77 D10 43 30N 70 28W
Bideford, *U.K.* 11 F3 51 1N 4 13W
Bideford Bay, *U.K.* 11 F3 51 5N 4 20W
Bidhuna, *India* 43 F8 26 49N 79 31 E
Bidor, *Malaysia* 39 K3 4 6N 101 15 E
Bié, Planalto de, *Angola* 53 G3 12 0S 16 0 E
Bieber, *U.S.A.* 82 F3 41 7N 121 8W
Biel, *Switz.* 18 C7 47 8N 7 14 E
Bielefeld, *Germany* 16 B5 52 1N 8 33 E
Biella, *Italy* 18 D8 45 34N 8 3 E
Bielsk Podlaski, *Poland* 17 B12 52 47N 23 12 E
Bielsko-Biała, *Poland* 17 D10 49 50N 19 2 E
Bien Hoa, *Vietnam* 39 G6 10 57N 106 49 E
Bienne = Biel, *Switz.* 18 C7 47 8N 7 14 E
Bienville, L., *Canada* 70 A5 55 5N 72 40W
Biesiesfontein, *S. Africa* 56 E2 30 57S 17 58 E
Big —►, *Canada* 71 B8 54 50N 58 55W
Big B., *Canada* 71 A7 55 43N 60 35W
Big Bear City, *U.S.A.* 85 L10 34 16N 116 51W
Big Bear Lake, *U.S.A.* 85 L10 34 15N 116 56W
Big Belt Mts., *U.S.A.* 82 C8 46 30N 111 25W
Big Bend, *Swaziland* 57 D5 26 50S 31 58 E
Big Bend National Park, *U.S.A.* 81 L3 29 20N 103 5W
Big Black —►, *U.S.A.* 81 K9 32 3N 91 4W
Big Blue —►, *U.S.A.* 80 F6 39 35N 96 34W
Big Creek, *U.S.A.* 84 H7 37 11N 119 14W
Big Cypress National Preserve, *U.S.A.* 77 M5 26 0N 81 10W
Big Cypress Swamp, *U.S.A.* 77 M5 26 12N 81 10W
Big Falls, *U.S.A.* 80 A8 48 12N 93 48W
Big Fork —►, *U.S.A.* 80 A8 48 31N 93 43W
Big Horn Mts. = Bighorn Mts., *U.S.A.* 82 D10 44 30N 107 30W
Big I., *Canada* 72 A5 61 7N 116 45W
Big Lake, *U.S.A.* 81 K4 31 12N 101 28W
Big Moose, *U.S.A.* 79 C10 43 49N 74 58W
Big Muddy Cr. —►, *U.S.A.* 80 A2 48 8N 104 36W
Big Pine, *U.S.A.* 84 H8 37 10N 118 17W
Big Piney, *U.S.A.* 82 E8 42 32N 110 7W
Big Rapids, *U.S.A.* 76 D3 43 42N 85 29W
Big Rideau L., *Canada* 79 B8 44 40N 76 15W
Big River, *Canada* 73 C7 53 50N 107 0W
Big Run, *U.S.A.* 78 F6 40 57N 78 55W
Big Sable Pt., *U.S.A.* 76 C2 44 3N 86 1W
Big Salmon —►, *Canada* 72 A2 61 52N 134 55W
Big Sand L., *Canada* 73 B9 57 45N 99 45W
Big Sandy, *U.S.A.* 82 B8 48 11N 110 7W
Big Sandy —►, *U.S.A.* 76 F4 38 25N 82 36W
Big Sandy Cr. —►, *U.S.A.* 80 F3 38 7N 102 29W
Big Sioux —►, *U.S.A.* 80 D6 42 29N 96 27W
Big Spring, *U.S.A.* 81 J4 32 15N 101 28W
Big Stone City, *U.S.A.* 80 C6 45 18N 96 28W
Big Stone Gap, *U.S.A.* 77 G4 36 52N 82 47W
Big Stone L., *U.S.A.* 80 C6 45 30N 96 35W
Big Sur, *U.S.A.* 84 J5 36 15N 121 48W
Big Timber, *U.S.A.* 82 D9 45 50N 109 57W

Big Trout L.

Big Trout L., *Canada* 70 B2 53 40N 90 0W
Big Trout Lake, *Canada* 70 B2 53 45N 90 0W
Biğa, *Turkey* 21 D12 40 13N 27 14 E
Bigadiç, *Turkey* 21 E13 39 22N 28 7 E
Biggar, *Canada* 73 C7 52 4N 108 0W
Biggar, *U.K.* 12 F5 55 38N 3 32W
Bigge I., *Australia* 60 B4 14 35S 125 10 E
Biggenden, *Australia* 63 D5 25 31S 152 4 E
Biggleswade, *U.K.* 11 E7 52 5N 0 14W
Biggs, *U.S.A.* 84 F5 39 25N 121 43W
Bighorn, *U.S.A.* 82 C10 46 10N 107 27W
Bighorn →, *U.S.A.* 82 C10 46 10N 107 28W
Bighorn L., *U.S.A.* 82 D9 44 55N 108 15W
Bighorn Mts., *U.S.A.* 82 D10 44 30N 107 30W
Bigstone L., *Canada* 73 C9 53 42N 95 44W
Bigwa, *Tanzania* 54 D4 7 10S 39 10 E
Bihać, *Bos.-H.* 16 F8 44 49N 15 57 E
Bihar, *India* 43 G11 25 5N 85 40 E
Bihar □, *India* 43 G12 25 0N 86 0 E
Biharamulo, *Tanzania* 54 C3 2 25S 31 25 E
Bihariganj, *India* 43 G12 25 44N 86 59 E
Bihor, Munţii, *Romania* 17 E12 46 29N 22 47 E
Bijagós, Arquipélago dos, *Guinea-Biss.* 50 F2 11 15N 16 10W
Bijaipur, *India* 42 F7 26 2N 77 20 E
Bijapur, *Karnataka, India* 40 L9 16 50N 75 55 E
Bijapur, *Mad. P., India* 41 K12 18 50N 80 50 E
Bījār, *Iran* 44 C5 35 52N 47 35 E
Bijawar, *India* 43 G8 24 38N 79 30 E
Bijeljina, *Bos.-H.* 21 B8 44 46N 19 14 E
Bijnor, *India* 42 E8 29 27N 78 11 E
Bikaner, *India* 42 E5 28 2N 73 18 E
Bikapur, *India* 43 F10 26 30N 82 7 E
Bikeqi, *China* 34 D6 40 43N 111 20 E
Bikfayyā, *Lebanon* 47 B4 33 55N 35 41 E
Bikin, *Russia* 27 E14 46 50N 134 20 E
Bikin →, *Russia* 30 A7 46 51N 134 2 E
Bikini Atoll, *Marshall Is.* 64 F8 12 0N 167 30 E
Bikoro, *Dem. Rep. of the Congo* 52 E3 0 48S 18 15 E
Bila Tserkva, *Ukraine* 17 D16 49 45N 30 10 E
Bilara, *India* 42 F5 26 14N 73 53 E
Bilaspur, *Mad. P., India* 43 H10 22 2N 82 15 E
Bilaspur, *Punjab, India* 42 D7 31 19N 76 50 E
Bilauk Taungdan, *Thailand* 38 F2 13 0N 99 0 E
Bilbao, *Spain* 19 A4 43 16N 2 56W
Bilbo = Bilbao, *Spain* 19 A4 43 16N 2 56W
Bíldudalur, *Iceland* 8 D2 65 41N 23 36W
Bílé Karpaty, *Europe* 17 D9 49 5N 18 0 E
Bilecik, *Turkey* 25 F5 40 5N 30 5 E
Bilgram, *India* 43 F9 27 11N 80 2 E
Bilhaur, *India* 43 F9 26 51N 80 5 E
Bilhorod-Dnistrovskyy, *Ukraine* 25 E5 46 11N 30 23 E
Bilibino, *Russia* 27 C17 68 3N 166 20 E
Bilibiza, *Mozam.* 55 E5 12 30S 40 20 E
Billabalong Roadhouse, *Australia* 61 E2 27 25S 115 49 E
Billiluna, *Australia* 60 C4 19 37S 127 41 E
Billings, *U.S.A.* 82 D9 45 47N 108 30W
Billiton Is. = Belitung, *Indonesia* 36 E3 3 10S 107 50 E
Bilma, *Niger* 51 E8 18 50N 13 30 E
Biloela, *Australia* 62 C5 24 24S 150 31 E
Biloxi, *U.S.A.* 81 K10 30 24N 88 53W
Bilpa Morea Claypan, *Australia* 62 D3 25 0S 140 0 E
Biltine, *Chad* 51 F10 14 40N 20 50 E
Bima, *Indonesia* 37 F5 8 22S 118 49 E
Bimini Is., *Bahamas* 88 A4 25 42N 79 25W
Bin Xian, *Heilongjiang, China* 35 B14 45 42N 127 32 E
Bin Xian, *Shaanxi, China* 34 G5 35 2N 108 4 E
Bina-Etawah, *India* 42 G8 24 13N 78 14 E
Bināb, *Iran* 45 B6 36 35N 48 41 E
Binalbagan, *Phil.* 37 B6 10 12N 122 50 E
Binalong, *Australia* 63 E4 34 40S 148 39 E
Bīnālūd, Kūh-e, *Iran* 45 B8 36 30N 58 30 E
Binatang = Bintangor, *Malaysia* 36 D4 2 10N 111 40 E
Binche, *Belgium* 15 D4 50 26N 4 10 E
Bindki, *India* 43 F9 26 2N 80 36 E
Bindura, *Zimbabwe* 55 F3 17 18S 31 18 E
Bingara, *Australia* 63 D5 29 52S 150 36 E
Bingham, *U.S.A.* 77 C11 45 3N 69 53W
Binghamton, *U.S.A.* 79 D9 42 6N 75 55W
Bingöl, *Turkey* 44 B4 38 53N 40 29 E
Binh Dinh = An Nhon, *Vietnam* 38 F7 13 55N 109 7 E
Binh Khe, *Vietnam* 38 F7 13 57N 108 51 E
Binh Son, *Vietnam* 38 E7 15 20N 108 40 E
Binhai, *China* 35 G10 34 2N 119 49 E
Binisatua, *Spain* 22 B11 39 50N 4 11 E
Binjai, *Indonesia* 36 D1 3 20N 98 30 E
Binnaway, *Australia* 63 E4 31 28S 149 24 E
Binongko, *Indonesia* 37 F6 5 55S 123 55 E
Binscarth, *Canada* 73 C8 50 37N 101 17W
Bintan, *Indonesia* 36 D2 1 0N 104 0 E
Bintangor, *Malaysia* 36 D4 2 10N 111 40 E
Bintulu, *Malaysia* 36 D4 3 10N 113 0 E
Bintuni, *Indonesia* 37 E8 2 7S 133 32 E
Binzert = Bizerte, *Tunisia* 51 A7 37 15N 9 50 E
Binzhou, *China* 35 F10 37 20N 118 2 E
Bio Bío □, *Chile* 94 D1 37 35S 72 0W
Bioko, *Eq. Guin.* 52 D1 3 30N 8 40 E
Bir, *India* 40 K9 19 0N 75 54 E
Bîr Abu Muḥammad, *Egypt* 47 F3 29 44N 34 14 E
Bi'r ad Dabbāghāt, *Jordan* 47 E4 30 26N 35 32 E
Bi'r al Butayyihāt, *Jordan* 47 F4 29 47N 35 20 E
Bi'r al Mārī, *Jordan* 47 E4 30 4N 35 33 E
Bi'r al Qattār, *Jordan* 47 F4 29 47N 35 32 E
Bir 'Atrun, *Sudan* 51 E11 18 15N 26 40 E
Bîr Beiḍa, *Egypt* 47 E3 30 25N 34 29 E
Bîr el 'Abd, *Egypt* 47 D2 31 2N 33 0 E
Bîr el Biarât, *Egypt* 47 F3 29 30N 34 43 E
Bîr el Duweidar, *Egypt* 47 E1 30 56N 32 32 E
Bîr el Garârât, *Egypt* 47 D2 31 3N 33 34 E
Bîr el Heisi, *Egypt* 47 F3 29 22N 34 36 E
Bîr el Jafir, *Egypt* 47 E1 30 50N 32 41 E
Bîr el Mâlḥi, *Egypt* 47 E2 30 38N 33 19 E
Bîr el Thamâda, *Egypt* 47 E2 30 12N 33 27 E
Bîr Gebeil Ḥiṣn, *Egypt* 47 E2 30 2N 33 18 E
Bi'r Ghadīr, *Syria* 47 A6 34 6N 37 3 E
Bîr Ḥasana, *Egypt* 47 E2 30 29N 33 46 E
Bîr Kaseiba, *Egypt* 47 E2 31 0N 33 17 E
Bîr Lahfân, *Egypt* 47 E2 31 0N 33 51 E
Bîr Madkûr, *Egypt* 47 E1 30 44N 32 33 E
Bir Mogreïn, *Mauritania* 50 C3 25 10N 11 25W
Bi'r Muṭribah, *Kuwait* 44 D5 29 54N 47 17 E
Bîr Qaţia, *Egypt* 47 E1 30 58N 32 45 E
Bîr Shalatein, *Egypt* 51 D13 23 5N 35 25 E
Biratnagar, *Nepal* 43 F12 26 27N 87 17 E
Birawa, *Dem. Rep. of the Congo* 54 C2 2 20S 28 48 E
Birch →, *Canada* 72 B6 58 28N 112 17W
Birch Hills, *Canada* 73 C7 52 59N 105 25W
Birch I., *Canada* 73 C9 52 26N 99 54W
Birch L., *N.W.T., Canada* 72 A5 62 4N 116 33W
Birch L., *Ont., Canada* 70 B1 51 23N 92 18W
Birch Mts., *Canada* 72 B6 57 30N 113 10W
Birch River, *Canada* 73 C8 52 24N 101 6W
Birchip, *Australia* 63 F3 35 56S 142 55 E
Bird, *Canada* 73 B10 56 30N 94 13W
Bird I. = Las Aves, Is., *W. Indies* 89 C7 15 45N 63 55W
Birdsville, *Australia* 62 D2 25 51S 139 20 E
Birdum Cr., *Australia* 60 C5 15 14S 133 0 E
Birecik, *Turkey* 44 B3 37 2N 38 0 E
Birein, *Israel* 47 E3 30 50N 34 28 E
Bireuen, *Indonesia* 36 C1 5 14N 96 39 E
Birigui, *Brazil* 95 A5 21 18S 50 16W
Birjand, *Iran* 45 C8 32 53N 59 13 E
Birkenhead, *U.K.* 10 D4 53 23N 3 2W
Bîrlad = Bârlad, *Romania* 17 E14 46 15N 27 38 E
Birmingham, *U.K.* 11 E6 52 29N 1 52W
Birmingham, *U.S.A.* 77 J2 33 31N 86 48W
Birmitrapur, *India* 41 H14 22 24N 84 46 E
Birni Nkonni, *Niger* 50 F7 13 55N 5 15 E
Birnin Kebbi, *Nigeria* 50 F6 12 32N 4 12 E
Birobidzhan, *Russia* 27 E14 48 50N 132 50 E
Birr, *Ireland* 13 C4 53 6N 7 54W
Birrie →, *Australia* 63 D4 29 43S 146 37 E
Birsilpur, *India* 42 E5 28 11N 72 15 E
Birsk, *Russia* 24 C10 55 25N 55 30 E
Birtle, *Canada* 73 C8 50 30N 101 5W
Birur, *India* 40 N9 13 30N 75 55 E
Biržai, *Lithuania* 9 H21 56 11N 24 45 E
Birzebbugga, *Malta* 23 D2 35 49N 14 32 E
Bisa, *Indonesia* 37 E7 1 15S 127 28 E
Bisalpur, *India* 43 E8 28 14N 79 48 E
Bisbee, *U.S.A.* 83 L9 31 27N 109 55W
Biscay, B. of, *Atl. Oc.* 18 D1 45 0N 2 0W
Biscayne B., *U.S.A.* 77 N5 25 40N 80 12W
Biscoe Bay, *Antarctica* 5 D13 77 0S 152 0W
Biscoe Is., *Antarctica* 5 C17 66 0S 67 0W
Biscostasing, *Canada* 70 C3 47 18N 82 9W
Bishkek, *Kyrgyzstan* 26 E8 42 54N 74 46 E
Bishnupur, *India* 43 H12 23 8N 87 20 E
Bisho, *S. Africa* 57 E4 32 50S 27 23 E
Bishop, *Calif., U.S.A.* 84 H8 37 22N 118 24W
Bishop, *Tex., U.S.A.* 81 M6 27 35N 97 48W
Bishop Auckland, *U.K.* 10 C6 54 39N 1 40W
Bishop's Falls, *Canada* 71 C8 49 2N 55 30W
Bishop's Stortford, *U.K.* 11 F8 51 52N 0 10 E
Bisina, L., *Uganda* 54 B3 1 38N 33 56 E
Biskra, *Algeria* 50 B7 34 50N 5 44 E
Bismarck, *U.S.A.* 80 B4 46 48N 100 47W
Bismarck Arch., *Papua N. G.* 64 H7 2 30S 150 0 E
Biso, *Uganda* 54 B3 1 44N 31 26 E
Bison, *U.S.A.* 80 C3 45 31N 102 28W
Bīsotūn, *Iran* 44 C5 34 23N 47 26 E
Bissagos = Bijagós, Arquipélago dos, *Guinea-Biss.* 50 F2 11 15N 16 10W
Bissau, *Guinea-Biss.* 50 F2 11 45N 15 45W
Bistcho L., *Canada* 72 B5 59 45N 118 50W
Bistriţa, *Romania* 17 E13 47 9N 24 35 E
Bistriţa →, *Romania* 17 E14 46 30N 26 57 E
Biswan, *India* 43 F9 27 29N 81 2 E
Bitola, *Macedonia* 21 D9 41 1N 21 20 E
Bitolj = Bitola, *Macedonia* 21 D9 41 1N 21 20 E
Bitter Creek, *U.S.A.* 82 F9 41 33N 108 33W
Bitterfontein, *S. Africa* 56 E2 31 1S 18 32 E
Bitterroot →, *U.S.A.* 82 C6 46 52N 114 7W
Bitterroot Range, *U.S.A.* 82 D6 46 0N 114 20W
Bitterwater, *U.S.A.* 84 J6 36 23N 121 0W
Biu, *Nigeria* 51 F8 10 40N 12 3 E
Biwa-Ko, *Japan* 31 G8 35 15N 136 10 E
Biwabik, *U.S.A.* 80 B8 47 32N 92 21W
Bixby, *U.S.A.* 81 H7 35 57N 95 53W
Biyang, *China* 34 H7 32 38N 113 21 E
Biysk, *Russia* 26 D9 52 40N 85 0 E
Bizana, *S. Africa* 57 E4 30 50S 29 52 E
Bizen, *Japan* 31 G7 34 43N 134 8 E
Bizerte, *Tunisia* 51 A7 37 15N 9 50 E
Bjargtangar, *Iceland* 8 D1 65 30N 24 30W
Bjelovar, *Croatia* 20 B7 45 56N 16 49 E
Bjørnevatn, *Norway* 8 B23 69 40N 30 0 E
Bjørnøya, *Arctic* 4 B8 74 30N 19 0 E
Black →, *Canada* 78 B5 44 42N 79 19W
Black →, *Ariz., U.S.A.* 83 K8 33 44N 110 13W
Black →, *Ark., U.S.A.* 81 H9 35 38N 91 20W
Black →, *Mich., U.S.A.* 78 D2 42 59N 82 27W
Black →, *N.Y., U.S.A.* 79 C8 43 59N 76 4W
Black →, *Wis., U.S.A.* 80 D9 43 57N 91 22W
Black Bay Pen., *Canada* 70 C2 48 38N 88 21W
Black Birch L., *Canada* 73 B7 56 53N 107 45W
Black Diamond, *Canada* 72 C6 50 45N 114 14W
Black Duck →, *Canada* 70 A2 56 51N 89 2W
Black Forest = Schwarzwald, *Germany* 16 D5 48 30N 8 20 E
Black Forest, *U.S.A.* 80 F2 39 0N 104 43W
Black Hd., *Ireland* 13 C2 53 9N 9 16W
Black Hills, *U.S.A.* 80 D3 44 0N 103 45W
Black I., *Canada* 73 C9 51 12N 96 30W
Black L., *Canada* 73 B7 59 12N 105 15W
Black L., *Mich., U.S.A.* 76 C3 45 28N 84 16W
Black L., *N.Y., U.S.A.* 79 B9 44 31N 75 36W
Black Lake, *Canada* 73 B7 59 11N 105 20W
Black Mesa, *U.S.A.* 81 G3 36 58N 102 58W
Black Mt. = Mynydd Du, *U.K.* 11 F4 51 52N 3 50W
Black Mts., *U.K.* 11 F4 51 55N 3 7W
Black Range, *U.S.A.* 83 K10 33 15N 107 50W
Black River, *Jamaica* 88 C4 18 0N 77 50W
Black River Falls, *U.S.A.* 80 C9 44 18N 90 51W
Black Sea, *Eurasia* 25 F6 43 30N 35 0 E
Black Tickle, *Canada* 71 B8 53 28N 55 45W
Black Volta →, *Africa* 50 G5 8 41N 1 33W
Black Warrior →, *U.S.A.* 77 J2 32 32N 87 51W
Blackall, *Australia* 62 C4 24 25S 145 45 E
Blackball, *N.Z.* 59 K3 42 22S 171 26 E
Blackbull, *Australia* 62 B3 17 55S 141 45 E
Blackburn, *U.K.* 10 D5 53 45N 2 29W
Blackburn with Darwen □, *U.K.* 10 D5 53 45N 2 29W
Blackfoot, *U.S.A.* 82 E7 43 11N 112 21W
Blackfoot →, *U.S.A.* 82 C7 46 52N 113 53W
Blackfoot River Reservoir, *U.S.A.* 82 E8 43 0N 111 43W
Blackie, *Canada* 72 C6 50 36N 113 37W
Blackpool, *U.K.* 10 D4 53 49N 3 3W
Blackpool □, *U.K.* 10 D4 53 49N 3 3W
Blackriver, *U.S.A.* 78 B1 44 46N 83 17W
Blacks Harbour, *Canada* 71 C6 45 3N 66 49W
Blacksburg, *U.S.A.* 76 G5 37 14N 80 25W
Blacksod B., *Ireland* 13 B1 54 6N 10 0W
Blackstone, *U.S.A.* 76 G7 37 4N 78 0W
Blackstone Ra., *Australia* 61 E4 26 0S 128 30 E
Blackwater, *Australia* 62 C4 23 35S 148 53 E
Blackwater →, *Meath, Ireland* 13 C4 53 39N 6 41W
Blackwater →, *Waterford, Ireland* 13 D4 52 4N 7 52W
Blackwater →, *U.K.* 13 B5 54 31N 6 35W
Blackwell, *U.S.A.* 81 G6 36 48N 97 17W
Blackwells Corner, *U.S.A.* 85 K7 35 37N 119 47W
Blaenau Ffestiniog, *U.K.* 10 E4 53 0N 3 56W
Blaenau Gwent □, *U.K.* 11 F4 51 48N 3 12W
Blagodarnoye = Blagodarnyy, *Russia* 25 E7 45 7N 43 37 E
Blagodarnyy, *Russia* 25 E7 45 7N 43 37 E
Blagoevgrad, *Bulgaria* 21 C10 42 2N 23 5 E
Blagoveshchensk, *Russia* 27 D13 50 20N 127 30 E
Blain, *U.S.A.* 78 F7 40 20N 77 31W
Blaine, *Minn., U.S.A.* 80 C8 45 10N 93 13W
Blaine, *Wash., U.S.A.* 84 B4 48 59N 122 45W
Blaine Lake, *Canada* 73 C7 52 51N 106 52W
Blair, *U.S.A.* 80 E6 41 33N 96 8W
Blair Athol, *Australia* 62 C4 22 42S 147 31 E
Blair Atholl, *U.K.* 12 E5 56 46N 3 50W
Blairgowrie, *U.K.* 12 E5 56 35N 3 21W
Blairsden, *U.S.A.* 84 F6 39 47N 120 37W
Blairsville, *U.S.A.* 78 F5 40 26N 79 16W
Blake Pt., *U.S.A.* 80 A10 48 11N 88 25W
Blakely, *Ga., U.S.A.* 77 K3 31 23N 84 56W
Blakely, *Pa., U.S.A.* 79 E9 41 28N 75 37W
Blanc, C., *Spain* 22 B9 39 21N 2 51 E
Blanc, Mont, *Alps* 18 D7 45 48N 6 50 E
Blanc-Sablon, *Canada* 71 B8 51 24N 57 12W
Blanca, B., *Argentina* 96 D4 39 10S 61 30W
Blanca Peak, *U.S.A.* 83 H11 37 35N 105 29W
Blanche, C., *Australia* 63 E1 33 1S 134 9 E
Blanche, L., *S. Austral., Australia* 63 D2 29 15S 139 40 E
Blanche, L., *W. Austral., Australia* 60 D3 22 25S 123 17 E
Blanco, *S. Africa* 56 E3 33 55S 22 23 E
Blanco, *U.S.A.* 81 K5 30 6N 98 25W
Blanco →, *Argentina* 94 C2 30 20S 68 42W
Blanco, C., *Costa Rica* 88 E2 9 34N 85 8W
Blanco, C., *U.S.A.* 82 E1 42 51N 124 34W
Blanda →, *Iceland* 8 D3 65 37N 20 9W
Blandford Forum, *U.K.* 11 G5 50 51N 2 9W
Blanding, *U.S.A.* 83 H9 37 37N 109 29W
Blanes, *Spain* 19 B7 41 40N 2 48 E
Blankenberge, *Belgium* 15 C3 51 20N 3 9 E
Blanquilla, I., *Venezuela* 89 D7 11 51N 64 37W
Blanquillo, *Uruguay* 95 C4 32 53S 55 37W
Blantyre, *Malawi* 55 F4 15 45S 35 0 E
Blarney, *Ireland* 13 E3 51 56N 8 33W
Blasdell, *U.S.A.* 78 D6 42 48N 78 50W
Blåvands Huk, *Denmark* 9 J13 55 33N 8 4 E
Blaydon, *U.K.* 10 C6 54 58N 1 42W
Blayney, *Australia* 63 E4 33 32S 149 14 E
Blaze, Pt., *Australia* 60 B5 12 56S 130 11 E
Blekinge, *Sweden* 9 H16 56 25N 15 20 E
Blenheim, *Canada* 78 D3 42 20N 82 0W
Blenheim, *N.Z.* 59 J4 41 38S 173 57 E
Bletchley, *U.K.* 11 F7 51 59N 0 44W
Blida, *Algeria* 50 A6 36 30N 2 49 E
Bligh Sound, *N.Z.* 59 L1 44 47S 167 32 E
Blind River, *Canada* 70 C3 46 10N 82 58W
Bliss, *Idaho, U.S.A.* 82 E6 42 56N 114 57W
Bliss, *N.Y., U.S.A.* 78 D6 42 34N 78 15W
Blissfield, *U.S.A.* 78 F3 40 24N 81 58W
Blitar, *Indonesia* 37 H15 8 5S 112 11 E
Block I., *U.S.A.* 79 E13 41 11N 71 35W
Block Island Sd., *U.S.A.* 79 E13 41 15N 71 40W
Blodgett Iceberg Tongue, *Antarctica* 5 C9 66 8S 130 35 E
Bloemfontein, *S. Africa* 56 D4 29 6S 26 7 E
Bloemhof, *S. Africa* 56 D4 27 38S 25 32 E
Blois, *France* 18 C4 47 35N 1 20 E
Blönduós, *Iceland* 8 D3 65 40N 20 12W
Bloodvein →, *Canada* 73 C9 51 47N 96 43W
Bloody Foreland, *Ireland* 13 A3 55 10N 8 17W
Bloomer, *U.S.A.* 80 C9 45 6N 91 29W
Bloomfield, *Canada* 78 C7 43 59N 77 14W
Bloomfield, *Iowa, U.S.A.* 80 E8 40 45N 92 25W
Bloomfield, *N. Mex., U.S.A.* 83 H10 36 43N 107 59W
Bloomfield, *Nebr., U.S.A.* 80 D6 42 36N 97 39W
Bloomington, *Ill., U.S.A.* 80 E10 40 28N 89 0W
Bloomington, *Ind., U.S.A.* 76 F2 39 10N 86 32W
Bloomington, *Minn., U.S.A.* 80 C8 44 50N 93 17W
Bloomsburg, *U.S.A.* 79 F8 41 0N 76 27W
Blora, *Indonesia* 37 G14 6 57S 111 25 E
Blossburg, *U.S.A.* 78 E7 41 41N 77 4W
Blouberg, *S. Africa* 57 C4 23 8S 28 59 E
Blountstown, *U.S.A.* 77 K3 30 27N 85 3W
Blue Earth, *U.S.A.* 80 D8 43 38N 94 6W
Blue Mesa Reservoir, *U.S.A.* 83 G10 38 28N 107 20W
Blue Mountain Lake, *U.S.A.* 79 C10 43 52N 74 30W
Blue Mts., *Maine, U.S.A.* 79 B14 44 50N 70 35W
Blue Mts., *Oreg., U.S.A.* 82 D4 45 15N 119 0W
Blue Mts., *Pa., U.S.A.* 79 F8 40 30N 76 30W
Blue Mud B., *Australia* 62 A2 13 30S 136 0 E
Blue Nile = Nîl el Azraq →, *Sudan* 51 E12 15 38N 32 31 E
Blue Rapids, *U.S.A.* 80 F6 39 41N 96 39W
Blue Ridge Mts., *U.S.A.* 77 G5 36 30N 80 15W
Blue River, *Canada* 72 C5 52 6N 119 18W
Bluefield, *U.S.A.* 76 G5 37 15N 81 17W
Bluefields, *Nic.* 88 D3 12 20N 83 50W
Bluff, *Australia* 62 C4 23 35S 149 4 E
Bluff, *N.Z.* 59 M2 46 37S 168 20 E
Bluff, *U.S.A.* 83 H9 37 17N 109 33W
Bluff Knoll, *Australia* 61 F2 34 24S 118 15 E
Bluff Pt., *Australia* 61 E1 27 50S 114 5 E
Bluffton, *U.S.A.* 76 E3 40 44N 85 11W
Blumenau, *Brazil* 95 B6 27 0S 49 0W
Blunt, *U.S.A.* 80 C5 44 31N 99 59W
Bly, *U.S.A.* 82 E3 42 24N 121 3W
Blyth, *Canada* 78 C3 43 44N 81 26W
Blyth, *U.K.* 10 B6 55 8N 1 31W
Blythe, *U.S.A.* 85 M12 33 37N 114 36W
Blytheville, *U.S.A.* 81 H10 35 56N 89 55W
Bo, *S. Leone* 50 G3 7 55N 11 50W
Bo Duc, *Vietnam* 39 G6 11 58N 106 50 E
Bo Hai, *China* 35 E10 39 0N 119 0 E
Bo Xian = Bozhou, *China* 34 H8 33 55N 115 41 E
Boa Vista, *Brazil* 92 C6 2 48N 60 30W
Boaco, *Nic.* 88 D2 12 29N 85 35W
Bo'ai, *China* 34 G7 35 10N 113 3 E
Boalsburg, *U.S.A.* 78 F7 40 46N 77 47W
Boardman, *U.S.A.* 78 E4 41 2N 80 40W
Bobadah, *Australia* 63 E4 32 19S 146 41 E
Bobbili, *India* 41 K13 18 35N 83 30 E
Bobcaygeon, *Canada* 78 B6 44 33N 78 33W
Bobo-Dioulasso, *Burkina Faso* 50 F5 11 8N 4 13W
Bóbr →, *Poland* 16 B8 52 4N 15 4 E
Bobraomby, Tanjon' i, *Madag.* 57 A8 12 40S 49 10 E
Bobruysk = Babruysk, *Belarus* 17 B15 53 10N 29 15 E
Boby, Pic, *Madag.* 53 J9 22 12S 46 55 E
Bôca do Acre, *Brazil* 92 E5 8 50S 67 27W
Boca Raton, *U.S.A.* 77 M5 26 21N 80 5W
Bocas del Toro, *Panama* 88 E3 9 15N 82 20W
Bochnia, *Poland* 17 D11 49 58N 20 27 E
Bochum, *Germany* 16 C4 51 28N 7 13 E
Bocoyna, *Mexico* 86 B3 27 52N 107 35W
Bodaybo, *Russia* 27 D12 57 50N 114 0 E
Boddam, *U.K.* 12 B7 59 56N 1 17W
Boddington, *Australia* 61 F2 32 50S 116 30 E
Bodega Bay, *U.S.A.* 84 G3 38 20N 123 3W
Boden, *Sweden* 8 D19 65 50N 21 42 E
Bodensee, *Europe* 18 C8 47 35N 9 25 E
Bodhan, *India* 40 K10 18 40N 77 44 E
Bodmin, *U.K.* 11 G3 50 28N 4 43W
Bodmin Moor, *U.K.* 11 G3 50 33N 4 36W
Bodø, *Norway* 8 C16 67 17N 14 24 E
Bodrog →, *Hungary* 17 D11 48 11N 21 22 E
Bodrum, *Turkey* 21 F12 37 3N 27 30 E
Boende, *Dem. Rep. of the Congo* 52 E4 0 24S 21 12 E
Boerne, *U.S.A.* 81 L5 29 47N 98 44W
Bogalusa, *U.S.A.* 81 K10 30 47N 89 52W
Bogan →, *Australia* 63 D4 29 59S 146 17 E
Bogan Gate, *Australia* 63 E4 33 7S 147 49 E
Bogantungan, *Australia* 62 C4 23 41S 147 17 E
Bogata, *U.S.A.* 81 J7 33 28N 95 13W
Boggabilla, *Australia* 63 D5 28 36S 150 24 E
Boggabri, *Australia* 63 E5 30 45S 150 5 E
Boggeragh Mts., *Ireland* 13 D3 52 2N 8 55W
Boglan = Solhan, *Turkey* 44 B4 38 57N 41 3 E
Bognor Regis, *U.K.* 11 G7 50 47N 0 40W
Bogo, *Phil.* 37 B6 11 3N 124 0 E
Bogong, Mt., *Australia* 63 F4 36 47S 147 17 E
Bogor, *Indonesia* 37 G12 6 36S 106 48 E
Bogotá, *Colombia* 92 C4 4 34N 74 0W
Bogotol, *Russia* 26 D9 56 15N 89 50 E
Bogra, *Bangla.* 41 G16 24 51N 89 22 E
Boguchany, *Russia* 27 D10 58 40N 97 30 E
Bohemian Forest = Böhmerwald, *Germany* 16 D7 49 8N 13 14 E
Böhmerwald, *Germany* 16 D7 49 8N 13 14 E
Bohol, *Phil.* 37 C6 9 50N 124 10 E
Bohol Sea, *Phil.* 37 C6 9 0N 124 0 E
Bohuslän, *Sweden* 9 G14 58 25N 12 0 E
Boi, Pta. de, *Brazil* 95 A6 23 55S 45 15W
Boiaçu, *Brazil* 92 D6 0 27S 61 46W
Boileau, C., *Australia* 60 C3 17 40S 122 7 E
Boise, *U.S.A.* 82 E5 43 37N 116 13W
Boise City, *U.S.A.* 81 G3 36 44N 102 31W
Boissevain, *Canada* 73 D8 49 15N 100 5W
Bojador C., *W. Sahara* 50 C3 26 0N 14 30W
Bojana →, *Albania* 21 D8 41 52N 19 22 E
Bojnūrd, *Iran* 45 B8 37 30N 57 20 E
Bojonegoro, *Indonesia* 37 G14 7 11S 111 54 E
Bokaro, *India* 43 H11 23 46N 85 55 E
Bokhara →, *Australia* 63 D4 29 55S 146 42 E
Boknafjorden, *Norway* 9 G11 59 14N 5 40 E
Bokoro, *Chad* 51 F9 12 25N 17 14 E
Bokote, *Dem. Rep. of the Congo* 52 E4 0 12S 21 8 E
Bokpyin, *Burma* 39 G2 11 18N 98 42 E
Bolan →, *Pakistan* 42 E2 28 38N 67 42 E
Bolan Pass, *Pakistan* 40 E5 29 50N 67 20 E
Bolaños →, *Mexico* 86 C4 21 14N 104 8W
Bolbec, *France* 18 B4 49 30N 0 30 E
Boldājī, *Iran* 45 D6 31 56N 51 3 E
Bole, *China* 32 B3 45 11N 81 37 E
Bolekhiv, *Ukraine* 17 D12 49 0N 23 57 E
Bolesławiec, *Poland* 16 C8 51 17N 15 37 E
Bolgrad = Bolhrad, *Ukraine* 17 F15 45 40N 28 32 E
Bolhrad, *Ukraine* 17 F15 45 40N 28 32 E
Bolívar, *Argentina* 94 D3 36 15S 60 53W
Bolivar, *Mo., U.S.A.* 81 G8 37 37N 93 25W
Bolivar, *N.Y., U.S.A.* 78 D6 42 4N 78 10W
Bolivar, *Tenn., U.S.A.* 81 H10 35 12N 89 0W
Bolivia ■, *S. Amer.* 92 G6 17 6S 64 0W
Bolivian Plateau, *S. Amer.* 90 E4 20 0S 67 30W
Bollnäs, *Sweden* 9 F17 61 21N 16 24 E
Bollon, *Australia* 63 D4 28 2S 147 29 E
Bolmen, *Sweden* 9 H15 56 55N 13 40 E
Bolobo, *Dem. Rep. of the Congo* 52 E3 2 6S 16 20 E
Bologna, *Italy* 20 B4 44 29N 11 20 E
Bologoye, *Russia* 24 C5 57 55N 34 5 E
Bolonchenticul, *Mexico* 87 D7 20 0N 89 49W
Boloven, Cao Nguyen, *Laos* 38 E6 15 10N 106 30 E
Bolpur, *India* 43 H12 23 40N 87 45 E
Bolsena, L. di, *Italy* 20 C4 42 36N 11 56 E
Bolshevik, Ostrov, *Russia* 27 B11 78 30N 102 0 E
Bolshoi Kavkas = Caucasus Mountains, *Eurasia* 25 F7 42 50N 44 0 E
Bolshoy Anyuy →, *Russia* 27 C17 68 30N 160 49 E
Bolshoy Begichev, Ostrov, *Russia* 27 B12 74 20N 112 30 E
Bolshoy Lyakhovskiy, Ostrov, *Russia* 27 B15 73 35N 142 0 E
Bolshoy Tyuters, Ostrov, *Russia* 9 G22 59 51N 27 13 E
Bolsward, *Neths.* 15 A5 53 3N 5 32 E
Bolt Head, *U.K.* 11 G4 50 12N 3 48W
Bolton, *Canada* 78 C5 43 54N 79 45W

Broad Arrow

108

Cárdenas

Cabora Bassa Dam = Cahora Bassa, Reprêsa de, *Mozam.* **55 F3** 15 20S 32 50 E
Caborca, *Mexico* **86 A2** 30 40N 112 10W
Cabot, Mt., *U.S.A.* **79 B13** 44 30N 71 25W
Cabot Hd., *Canada* **78 A3** 45 14N 81 17W
Cabot Str., *Canada* **71 C8** 47 15N 59 40W
Cabra, *Spain* **19 D3** 37 30N 4 28W
Cabrera, *Spain* **22 B9** 39 8N 2 57 E
Cabri, *Canada* **73 C7** 50 35N 108 25W
Cabriel →, *Spain* **19 C5** 39 14N 1 3W
Caçador, *Brazil* **95 B5** 26 47S 51 0W
Čačak, *Serbia, Yug.* **21 C9** 43 54N 20 20 E
Caçapava do Sul, *Brazil* **95 C5** 30 30S 53 30W
Cáceres, *Brazil* **92 G7** 16 5S 57 40W
Cáceres, *Spain* **19 C2** 39 26N 6 23W
Cache Bay, *Canada* **70 C4** 46 22N 80 0W
Cache Cr. →, *U.S.A.* **84 G5** 38 42N 121 42W
Cache Creek, *Canada* **72 C4** 50 48N 121 19W
Cachi, *Argentina* **94 B2** 25 5S 66 10W
Cachimbo, Serra do, *Brazil* **93 E7** 9 30S 55 30W
Cachinal de la Sierra, *Chile* **94 A2** 24 58S 69 32W
Cachoeira, *Brazil* **93 F11** 12 30S 39 0W
Cachoeira de Itapemirim, *Brazil* **95 A7** 20 51S 41 7W
Cachoeira do Sul, *Brazil* **95 C5** 30 3S 52 53W
Cacoal, *Brazil* **92 F6** 11 32S 61 18W
Cacólo, *Angola* **52 G3** 10 9S 19 21 E
Caconda, *Angola* **53 G3** 13 48S 15 8 E
Caddo, *U.S.A.* **81 H6** 34 7N 96 16W
Cader Idris, *U.K.* **11 E4** 52 42N 3 53W
Cadereyta, *Mexico* **86 B5** 25 36N 100 0W
Cadibarrawirracanna, L., *Australia* **63 D2** 28 52S 135 27 E
Cadillac, *U.S.A.* **76 C3** 44 15N 85 24W
Cadiz, *Phil.* **37 B6** 10 57N 123 15 E
Cádiz, *Spain* **19 D2** 36 30N 6 20W
Cadiz, *Calif., U.S.A.* **85 L11** 34 30N 115 28W
Cadiz, *Ohio, U.S.A.* **78 F4** 40 22N 81 0W
Cádiz, G. de, *Spain* **19 D2** 36 40N 7 0W
Cadiz L., *U.S.A.* **83 J6** 34 18N 115 24W
Cadney Park, *Australia* **63 D1** 27 55S 134 3 E
Cadomin, *Canada* **72 C5** 53 2N 117 20W
Cadotte Lake, *Canada* **72 B5** 56 26N 116 23W
Cadoux, *Australia* **61 F2** 30 46S 117 7 E
Caen, *France* **18 B3** 49 10N 0 22W
Caernarfon, *U.K.* **10 D3** 53 8N 4 16W
Caernarfon B., *U.K.* **10 D3** 53 4N 4 40W
Caernarvon = Caernarfon, *U.K.* **10 D3** 53 8N 4 16W
Caerphilly, *U.K.* **11 F4** 51 35N 3 13W
Caerphilly □, *U.K.* **11 F4** 51 37N 3 12W
Caesarea, *Israel* **47 C3** 32 30N 34 53 E
Caetité, *Brazil* **93 F10** 13 50S 42 32W
Cafayate, *Argentina* **94 B2** 26 2S 66 0W
Cafu, *Angola* **56 B2** 16 30S 15 8 E
Cagayan de Oro, *Phil.* **37 C6** 8 30N 124 40 E
Cagayan Is., *Phil.* **37 C5** 9 40N 121 16 E
Cágliari, *Italy* **20 E3** 39 13N 9 7 E
Cágliari, G. di, *Italy* **20 E3** 39 8N 9 11 E
Caguán →, *Colombia* **92 D4** 0 8S 74 18W
Caguas, *Puerto Rico* **89 C6** 18 14N 66 2W
Caha Mts., *Ireland* **13 E2** 51 45N 9 40W
Cahama, *Angola* **56 B1** 16 17S 14 19 E
Caher, *Ireland* **13 D4** 52 22N 7 56W
Cahersiveen, *Ireland* **13 E1** 51 56N 10 14W
Cahora Bassa, Reprêsa de, *Mozam.* **55 F3** 15 20S 32 50 E
Cahore Pt., *Ireland* **13 D5** 52 33N 6 12W
Cahors, *France* **18 D4** 44 27N 1 27 E
Cahul, *Moldova* **17 F15** 45 50N 28 15 E
Cai Nuoc, *Vietnam* **39 H5** 8 56N 105 1 E
Caia, *Mozam.* **55 F4** 17 51S 35 24 E
Caianda, *Angola* **55 E1** 11 2S 23 31 E
Caibarién, *Cuba* **88 B4** 22 30N 79 30W
Caicara, *Venezuela* **92 B5** 7 38N 66 10W
Caicó, *Brazil* **93 E11** 6 20S 37 0W
Caicos Is., *W. Indies* **89 B5** 21 40N 71 40W
Caicos Passage, *W. Indies* **89 B5** 22 45N 72 45W
Caird Coast, *Antarctica* **5 D1** 75 0S 25 0W
Cairn Gorm, *U.K.* **12 D5** 57 7N 3 39W
Cairngorm Mts., *U.K.* **12 D5** 57 6N 3 42W
Cairnryan, *U.K.* **12 G3** 54 59N 5 1W
Cairns, *Australia* **62 B4** 16 57S 145 45 E
Cairns L., *Canada* **73 C10** 51 42N 94 30W
Cairo = El Qâhira, *Egypt* **51 B12** 30 1N 31 14 E
Cairo, *Ga., U.S.A.* **77 K3** 30 52N 84 13W
Cairo, *Ill., U.S.A.* **81 G10** 37 0N 89 11W
Cairo, *N.Y., U.S.A.* **79 D11** 42 18N 74 0W
Caithness, Ord of, *U.K.* **12 C5** 58 8N 3 36W
Cajamarca, *Peru* **92 E3** 7 5S 78 28W
Cajàzeiras, *Brazil* **93 E11** 6 52S 38 30W
Cala d'Or, *Spain* **22 B10** 39 23N 3 14 E
Cala en Porter, *Spain* **22 B11** 39 52N 4 8 E
Cala Figuera, C. de, *Spain* **22 B9** 39 27N 2 31 E
Cala Forcat, *Spain* **22 B10** 40 0N 3 47 E
Cala Major, *Spain* **22 B9** 39 33N 2 37 E
Cala Mezquida = Sa Mesquida, *Spain* **22 B11** 39 55N 4 16 E
Cala Millor, *Spain* **22 B10** 39 35N 3 22 E
Cala Ratjada, *Spain* **22 B10** 39 43N 3 27 E
Cala Santa Galdana, *Spain* **22 B10** 39 56N 3 58 E
Calabar, *Nigeria* **50 H7** 4 57N 8 20 E
Calabogie, *Canada* **79 A8** 45 18N 76 43W
Calabozo, *Venezuela* **92 B5** 9 0N 67 28W
Calábria □, *Italy* **20 E7** 39 0N 16 30 E
Calafate, *Argentina* **96 G2** 50 19S 72 15W
Calahorra, *Spain* **19 A5** 42 18N 1 59W
Calais, *France* **18 A4** 50 57N 1 56 E
Calais, *U.S.A.* **77 C12** 45 11N 67 17W
Calalaste, Cord. de, *Argentina* **94 B2** 25 0S 67 0W
Calama, *Brazil* **92 E6** 8 0S 62 50W
Calama, *Chile* **94 A2** 22 30S 68 55W
Calamar, *Colombia* **92 A4** 10 15N 74 55W
Calamian Group, *Phil.* **37 B5** 11 50N 119 55 E
Calamocha, *Spain* **19 B5** 40 50N 1 17W
Calang, *Indonesia* **36 D1** 4 37N 95 37 E
Calapan, *Phil.* **37 B6** 13 25N 121 7 E
Călăraşi, *Romania* **17 F14** 44 12N 27 20 E
Calatayud, *Spain* **19 B5** 41 20N 1 40W
Calauag, *Phil.* **37 B6** 13 55N 122 15 E
Calavite, C., *Phil.* **37 B6** 13 26N 120 20 E
Calbayog, *Phil.* **37 B6** 12 4N 124 38 E
Calca, *Peru* **92 F4** 13 22S 72 0W
Calcasieu L., *U.S.A.* **81 L8** 29 55N 93 18W
Calcutta, *India* **43 H13** 22 36N 88 24 E
Calcutta, *U.S.A.* **78 F4** 40 40N 80 34W
Caldas da Rainha, *Portugal* **19 C1** 39 24N 9 8W
Calder →, *U.K.* **10 D6** 53 44N 1 22W
Caldera, *Chile* **94 B1** 27 5S 70 55W
Caldwell, *Idaho, U.S.A.* **82 E5** 43 40N 116 41W
Caldwell, *Kans., U.S.A.* **81 G6** 37 2N 97 37W
Caldwell, *Tex., U.S.A.* **81 K6** 30 32N 96 42W
Caledon, *S. Africa* **56 E2** 34 14S 19 26 E
Caledon →, *S. Africa* **56 E4** 30 31S 26 5 E
Caledon B., *Australia* **62 A2** 12 45S 137 0 E
Caledonia, *Canada* **78 C5** 43 7N 79 58W
Caledonia, *U.S.A.* **78 D7** 42 58N 77 51W
Calemba, *Angola* **56 B2** 16 0S 15 44 E
Calen, *Australia* **62 C4** 20 56S 148 48 E
Caletones, *Chile* **94 C1** 34 6S 70 27W
Calexico, *U.S.A.* **85 N11** 32 40N 115 30W
Calf of Man, *U.K.* **10 C3** 54 3N 4 48W
Calgary, *Canada* **72 C6** 51 0N 114 10W
Calheta, *Madeira* **22 D2** 32 44N 17 11W
Calhoun, *U.S.A.* **77 H3** 34 30N 84 57W
Cali, *Colombia* **92 C3** 3 25N 76 35W
Calicut, *India* **40 P9** 11 15N 75 43 E
Caliente, *U.S.A.* **83 H6** 37 37N 114 31W
California, *Mo., U.S.A.* **80 F8** 38 38N 92 34W
California, *Pa., U.S.A.* **78 F5** 40 4N 79 54W
California □, *U.S.A.* **84 H7** 37 30N 119 30W
California, Baja, *Mexico* **86 A1** 32 10N 115 12W
California, Baja, T.N. = Baja California □, *Mexico* **86 B2** 30 0N 115 0W
California, Baja, T.S. = Baja California Sur □, *Mexico* **86 B2** 25 50N 111 50W
California, G. de, *Mexico* **86 B2** 27 0N 111 0W
California City, *U.S.A.* **85 K9** 35 10N 117 55W
California Hot Springs, *U.S.A.* **85 K8** 35 51N 118 41W
Calingasta, *Argentina* **94 C2** 31 15S 69 30W
Calipatria, *U.S.A.* **85 M11** 33 8N 115 31W
Calistoga, *U.S.A.* **84 G4** 38 35N 122 35W
Calitzdorp, *S. Africa* **56 E3** 33 33S 21 42 E
Callabonna, L., *Australia* **63 D3** 29 40S 140 5 E
Callan, *Ireland* **13 D4** 52 32N 7 24W
Callander, *U.K.* **12 E4** 56 15N 4 13W
Callao, *Peru* **92 F3** 12 0S 77 0W
Calles, *Mexico* **87 C5** 23 2N 98 42W
Callicoon, *U.S.A.* **79 E9** 41 46N 75 3W
Calling Lake, *Canada* **72 B6** 55 15N 113 12W
Calliope, *Australia* **62 C5** 24 0S 151 16 E
Calne, *U.K.* **11 F6** 51 26N 2 0W
Calola, *Angola* **56 B2** 16 25S 17 48 E
Caloundra, *Australia* **63 D5** 26 45S 153 10 E
Calpella, *U.S.A.* **84 F3** 39 14N 123 12W
Calpine, *U.S.A.* **84 F6** 39 40N 120 27W
Calstock, *Canada* **70 C3** 49 47N 84 9W
Caltagirone, *Italy* **20 F6** 37 14N 14 31 E
Caltanissetta, *Italy* **20 F6** 37 29N 14 4 E
Calulo, *Angola* **52 G2** 10 1S 14 56 E
Caluquembe, *Angola* **53 G2** 13 47S 14 44 E
Calvert →, *Australia* **62 B2** 16 17S 137 44 E
Calvert I., *Canada* **72 C3** 51 30N 128 0W
Calvert Ra., *Australia* **60 D3** 24 0S 122 30 E
Calvi, *France* **18 E8** 42 34N 8 45 E
Calviá, *Spain* **19 C7** 39 34N 2 31 E
Calvillo, *Mexico* **86 C4** 21 51N 102 43W
Calvinia, *S. Africa* **56 E2** 31 28S 19 45 E
Calwa, *U.S.A.* **84 J7** 36 42N 119 46W
Cam →, *U.K.* **11 E8** 52 21N 0 16 E
Cam Lam, *Vietnam* **39 G7** 11 54N 109 10 E
Cam Ranh, *Vietnam* **39 G7** 11 54N 109 12 E
Cam Xuyen, *Vietnam* **38 C6** 18 15N 106 0 E
Camabatela, *Angola* **52 F3** 8 20S 15 26 E
Camacha, *Madeira* **22 D3** 32 41N 16 49W
Camacho, *Mexico* **86 C4** 24 25N 102 18W
Camacupa, *Angola* **53 G3** 11 58S 17 22 E
Camagüey, *Cuba* **88 B4** 21 20N 78 0W
Camaná, *Peru* **92 G4** 16 30S 72 50W
Camanche Reservoir, *U.S.A.* **84 G6** 38 14N 121 1W
Camaquã, *Brazil* **95 C5** 30 51S 51 49W
Camaquã →, *Brazil* **95 C5** 31 17S 51 47W
Câmara de Lobos, *Madeira* **22 D3** 32 39N 16 59W
Camargo, *Mexico* **87 B5** 26 19N 98 50W
Camargue, *France* **18 E6** 43 34N 4 34 E
Camarillo, *U.S.A.* **85 L7** 34 13N 119 2W
Camarón, C., *Honduras* **88 C2** 16 0N 85 5W
Camarones, *Argentina* **96 E3** 44 50S 65 40W
Camas, *U.S.A.* **84 E4** 45 35N 122 24W
Camas Valley, *U.S.A.* **82 E2** 43 2N 123 40W
Camballin, *Australia* **60 C3** 17 59S 124 12 E
Cambará, *Brazil* **95 A5** 23 2S 50 5W
Cambay = Khambhat, *India* **42 H5** 22 23N 72 33 E
Cambay, G. of = Khambhat, G. of, *India* **40 J8** 20 45N 72 30 E
Cambodia ■, *Asia* **38 F5** 12 15N 105 0 E
Camborne, *U.K.* **11 G2** 50 12N 5 19W
Cambrai, *France* **18 A5** 50 11N 3 14 E
Cambria, *U.S.A.* **84 K5** 35 34N 121 5W
Cambrian Mts., *U.K.* **11 E4** 52 3N 3 57W
Cambridge, *Canada* **78 C4** 43 23N 80 15W
Cambridge, *Jamaica* **88 C4** 18 18N 77 54W
Cambridge, *N.Z.* **59 G5** 37 54S 175 29 E
Cambridge, *U.K.* **11 E8** 52 12N 0 8 E
Cambridge, *Mass., U.S.A.* **79 D13** 42 22N 71 6W
Cambridge, *Md., U.S.A.* **75 C11** 38 34N 76 5W
Cambridge, *Minn., U.S.A.* **80 C8** 45 34N 93 13W
Cambridge, *N.Y., U.S.A.* **79 C11** 43 2N 73 22W
Cambridge, *Nebr., U.S.A.* **80 E4** 40 17N 100 10W
Cambridge, *Ohio, U.S.A.* **78 F3** 40 2N 81 35W
Cambridge Bay = Ikaluktutiak, *Canada* **68 B9** 69 10N 105 0W
Cambridge G., *Australia* **60 B4** 14 55S 128 15 E
Cambridge Springs, *U.S.A.* **78 E4** 41 48N 80 4W
Cambridgeshire □, *U.K.* **11 E7** 52 25N 0 7W
Cambuci, *Brazil* **95 A7** 21 35S 41 55W
Cambundi-Catembo, *Angola* **52 G3** 10 10S 17 35 E
Camden, *Ala., U.S.A.* **77 K2** 31 59N 87 17W
Camden, *Ark., U.S.A.* **81 J8** 33 35N 92 50W
Camden, *Maine, U.S.A.* **77 C11** 44 13N 69 4W
Camden, *N.J., U.S.A.* **79 G9** 39 56N 75 7W
Camden, *N.Y., U.S.A.* **79 C9** 43 20N 75 45W
Camden, *S.C., U.S.A.* **77 H5** 34 16N 80 36W
Camden Sd., *Australia* **60 C3** 15 27S 124 25 E
Camdenton, *U.S.A.* **81 F8** 38 1N 92 45W
Cameron, *Ariz., U.S.A.* **83 J8** 35 53N 111 25W
Cameron, *La., U.S.A.* **81 L8** 29 48N 93 20W
Cameron, *Mo., U.S.A.* **80 F7** 39 44N 94 14W
Cameron, *Tex., U.S.A.* **81 K6** 30 51N 96 59W
Cameron Highlands, *Malaysia* **39 K3** 4 27N 101 22 E
Cameron Hills, *Canada* **72 B5** 59 48N 118 0W
Cameroon ■, *Africa* **52 C2** 6 0N 12 30 E
Cameroun, Mt., *Cameroon* **52 D1** 4 13N 9 10 E
Cametá, *Brazil* **93 D9** 2 12S 49 30W
Camiguin I., *Phil.* **37 C6** 18 56N 121 55 E
Camilla, *U.S.A.* **77 K3** 31 14N 84 12W
Caminha, *Portugal* **19 B1** 41 50N 8 50W
Camino, *U.S.A.* **84 G6** 38 44N 120 41W
Camira Creek, *Australia* **63 D5** 29 15S 152 58 E
Cammal, *U.S.A.* **78 E7** 41 24N 77 28W
Camocim, *Brazil* **93 D10** 2 55S 40 50W
Camooweal, *Australia* **62 B2** 19 56S 138 7 E
Camopi, *Fr. Guiana* **93 C8** 3 12N 52 17W
Camp Borden, *Canada* **78 B5** 44 18N 79 56W
Camp Hill, *U.S.A.* **78 F8** 40 14N 76 55W
Camp Nelson, *U.S.A.* **85 J8** 36 8N 118 39W
Camp Pendleton, *U.S.A.* **85 M9** 33 16N 117 23W
Camp Verde, *U.S.A.* **83 J8** 34 34N 111 51W
Camp Wood, *U.S.A.* **81 L5** 29 40N 100 1W
Campana, *Argentina* **94 C4** 34 10S 58 55W
Campana, I., *Chile* **96 F1** 48 20S 75 20W
Campanário, *Madeira* **22 D2** 32 39N 17 2W
Campánia □, *Italy* **20 D6** 41 0N 14 30 E
Campbell, *S. Africa* **56 D3** 28 48S 23 44 E
Campbell, *Calif., U.S.A.* **84 H5** 37 17N 121 57W
Campbell, *Ohio, U.S.A.* **78 E4** 41 5N 80 37W
Campbell I., *Pac. Oc.* **64 N8** 52 30S 169 0 E
Campbell L., *Canada* **73 A7** 63 14N 106 55W
Campbell River, *Canada* **72 C3** 50 5N 125 20W
Campbell Town, *Australia* **62 G4** 41 52S 147 30 E
Campbellford, *Canada* **78 B7** 44 18N 77 48W
Campbellpur, *Pakistan* **42 C5** 33 46N 72 26 E
Campbellsville, *U.S.A.* **76 G3** 37 21N 85 20W
Campbellton, *Canada* **71 C6** 47 57N 66 43W
Campbelltown, *Australia* **63 E5** 34 4S 150 49 E
Campbeltown, *U.K.* **12 F3** 55 26N 5 36W
Campeche, *Mexico* **87 D6** 19 50N 90 32W
Campeche □, *Mexico* **87 D6** 19 50N 90 32W
Campeche, Golfo de, *Mexico* **87 D6** 19 30N 93 0W
Camperdown, *Australia* **63 F3** 38 14S 143 9 E
Camperville, *Canada* **73 C8** 51 59N 100 9W
Câmpina, *Romania* **17 F13** 45 10N 25 45 E
Campina Grande, *Brazil* **93 E11** 7 20S 35 47W
Campinas, *Brazil* **95 A6** 22 50S 47 0W
Campo Grande, *Brazil* **93 H8** 20 25S 54 40W
Campo Maíor, *Brazil* **93 D10** 4 50S 42 12W
Campo Mourão, *Brazil* **95 A5** 24 3S 52 22W
Campobasso, *Italy* **20 D6** 41 34N 14 39 E
Campos, *Brazil* **95 A7** 21 50S 41 20W
Campos Belos, *Brazil* **93 F9** 13 10S 47 3W
Campos del Puerto, *Spain* **22 B10** 39 26N 3 1 E
Campos Novos, *Brazil* **95 B5** 27 21S 51 50W
Camptonville, *U.S.A.* **84 F5** 39 27N 121 3W
Camptown, *U.S.A.* **79 E8** 41 44N 76 14W
Câmpulung, *Romania* **17 F13** 45 17N 25 3 E
Camrose, *Canada* **72 C6** 53 0N 112 50W
Camsell Portage, *Canada* **73 B7** 59 37N 109 15W
Çan, *Turkey* **21 D12** 40 2N 27 3 E
Can Clavo, *Spain* **22 C7** 38 57N 1 27 E
Can Creu, *Spain* **22 C7** 38 58N 1 28 E
Can Gio, *Vietnam* **39 G6** 10 25N 106 58 E
Can Tho, *Vietnam* **39 G5** 10 2N 105 46 E
Canaan, *U.S.A.* **79 D11** 42 2N 73 20W
Canada ■, *N. Amer.* **68 C10** 60 0N 100 0W
Cañada de Gómez, *Argentina* **94 C3** 32 40S 61 30W
Canadian, *U.S.A.* **81 H4** 35 55N 100 23W
Canadian →, *U.S.A.* **81 H7** 35 28N 95 3W
Canajoharie, *U.S.A.* **79 D10** 42 54N 74 35W
Çanakkale, *Turkey* **21 D12** 40 8N 26 24 E
Çanakkale Boğazı, *Turkey* **21 D12** 40 17N 26 32 E
Canal Flats, *Canada* **72 C5** 50 10N 115 48W
Canalejas, *Argentina* **94 D2** 35 15S 66 34W
Canals, *Argentina* **94 C3** 33 35S 62 53W
Canandaigua, *U.S.A.* **78 D7** 42 54N 77 17W
Canandaigua L., *U.S.A.* **78 D7** 42 47N 77 19W
Cananea, *Mexico* **86 A2** 31 0N 110 20W
Canarias, Is., *Atl. Oc.* **22 F4** 28 30N 16 0W
Canarreos, Arch. de los, *Cuba* **88 B3** 21 35N 81 40W
Canary Is. = Canarias, Is., *Atl. Oc.* **22 F4** 28 30N 16 0W
Canaseraga, *U.S.A.* **78 D7** 42 27N 77 45W
Canatlán, *Mexico* **86 C4** 24 31N 104 47W
Canaveral, C., *U.S.A.* **77 L5** 28 27N 80 32W
Canavieiras, *Brazil* **93 G11** 15 39S 39 0W
Canberra, *Australia* **63 F4** 35 15S 149 8 E
Canby, *Calif., U.S.A.* **82 F3** 41 27N 120 52W
Canby, *Minn., U.S.A.* **80 C6** 44 43N 96 16W
Canby, *Oreg., U.S.A.* **84 E4** 45 16N 122 42W
Cancún, *Mexico* **87 C7** 21 8N 86 44W
Candelaria, *Argentina* **95 B4** 27 29S 55 44W
Candelaria, *Canary Is.* **22 F3** 28 22N 16 22W
Candelo, *Australia* **63 F4** 36 47S 149 43 E
Candia = Iráklion, *Greece* **23 D7** 35 20N 25 12 E
Candle L., *Canada* **73 C7** 53 50N 105 18W
Candlemas I., *Antarctica* **5 B1** 57 3S 26 40W
Cando, *U.S.A.* **80 A5** 48 32N 99 12W
Canea = Khaniá, *Greece* **23 D6** 35 30N 24 4 E
Canelones, *Uruguay* **95 C4** 34 32S 56 17W
Cañete, *Chile* **94 D1** 37 50S 73 30W
Cañete, *Peru* **92 F3** 13 8S 76 30W
Cangas de Narcea, *Spain* **19 A2** 43 10N 6 32W
Canguaretama, *Brazil* **93 E11** 6 20S 35 5W
Canguçu, *Brazil* **95 C5** 31 22S 52 43W
Canguçu, Serra do, *Brazil* **95 C5** 31 20S 52 40W
Cangzhou, *China* **34 E9** 38 19N 116 52 E
Caniapiscau →, *Canada* **71 A6** 56 40N 69 30W
Caniapiscau Rés. de, *Canada* **71 B6** 54 10N 69 55W
Canicattì, *Italy* **20 F5** 37 21N 13 51 E
Canim Lake, *Canada* **72 C4** 51 47N 120 54W
Canindeyu □, *Paraguay* **95 A5** 24 10S 55 0W
Canisteo, *U.S.A.* **78 D7** 42 16N 77 36W
Canisteo →, *U.S.A.* **78 D7** 42 7N 77 8W
Cañitas, *Mexico* **86 C4** 23 36N 102 43W
Çankırı, *Turkey* **25 F5** 40 40N 33 37 E
Cankuzo, *Burundi* **54 C3** 3 10S 30 31 E
Canmore, *Canada* **72 C5** 51 7N 115 18W
Cann River, *Australia* **63 F4** 37 35S 149 7 E
Canna, *U.K.* **12 D2** 57 3N 6 33W
Cannanore, *India* **40 P9** 11 53N 75 27 E
Cannes, *France* **18 E7** 43 32N 7 1 E
Canning Town = Port Canning, *India* **43 H13** 22 23N 88 40 E
Cannington, *Canada* **78 B5** 44 20N 79 2W
Cannock, *U.K.* **11 E5** 52 41N 2 1W
Cannon Ball →, *U.S.A.* **80 B4** 46 20N 100 38W
Cannondale Mt., *Australia* **62 D4** 25 13S 148 57 E
Cannonsville Reservoir, *U.S.A.* **79 D9** 42 4N 75 22W
Cannonvale, *Australia* **62 C4** 20 17S 148 43 E
Canoas, *Brazil* **95 B5** 29 56S 51 11W
Canoe L., *Canada* **73 B7** 55 10N 108 15W
Canon City, *U.S.A.* **80 F2** 38 27N 105 14W
Canora, *Canada* **73 C8** 51 40N 102 30W
Canowindra, *Australia* **63 E4** 33 35S 148 38 E
Canso, *Canada* **71 C7** 45 20N 61 0W
Cantabria □, *Spain* **19 A4** 43 10N 4 0W
Cantabrian Mts. = Cantábrica, Cordillera, *Spain* **19 A3** 43 0N 5 10W
Cantábrica, Cordillera, *Spain* **19 A3** 43 0N 5 10W
Cantal, Plomb du, *France* **18 D5** 45 3N 2 45 E
Canterbury, *Australia* **62 D3** 25 23S 141 53 E
Canterbury, *U.K.* **11 F9** 51 16N 1 6 E
Canterbury □, *N.Z.* **59 K3** 43 45S 171 19 E
Canterbury Bight, *N.Z.* **59 L3** 44 16S 171 55 E
Canterbury Plains, *N.Z.* **59 K3** 43 55S 171 22 E
Cantil, *U.S.A.* **85 K9** 35 18N 117 58W
Canton = Guangzhou, *China* **33 D6** 23 5N 113 10 E
Canton, *Ga., U.S.A.* **77 H3** 34 14N 84 29W
Canton, *Ill., U.S.A.* **80 E9** 40 33N 90 2W
Canton, *Miss., U.S.A.* **81 J9** 32 37N 90 2W
Canton, *Mo., U.S.A.* **80 E9** 40 8N 91 32W
Canton, *N.Y., U.S.A.* **79 B9** 44 36N 75 10W
Canton, *Ohio, U.S.A.* **78 F3** 40 48N 81 23W
Canton, *Pa., U.S.A.* **78 E8** 41 39N 76 51W
Canton, *S. Dak., U.S.A.* **80 D6** 43 18N 96 35W
Canton L., *U.S.A.* **81 G5** 36 6N 98 35W
Canudos, *Brazil* **92 E7** 7 13S 58 5W
Canumã →, *Brazil* **92 D7** 3 55S 59 10W
Canutama, *Brazil* **92 E6** 6 30S 64 20W
Canutillo, *U.S.A.* **83 L10** 31 55N 106 36W
Canvey, *U.K.* **11 F8** 51 31N 0 37 E
Canyon, *U.S.A.* **81 H4** 34 59N 101 55W
Canyonlands National Park, *U.S.A.* **83 G9** 38 15N 110 0W
Canyonville, *U.S.A.* **82 E2** 42 56N 123 17W
Cao He →, *China* **35 D13** 40 10N 124 32 E
Cao Lanh, *Vietnam* **39 G5** 10 27N 105 38 E
Cao Xian, *China* **34 G8** 34 50N 115 35 E
Cap-aux-Meules, *Canada* **71 C7** 47 23N 61 52W
Cap-Chat, *Canada* **71 C6** 49 6N 66 40W
Cap-de-la-Madeleine, *Canada* **70 C5** 46 22N 72 31W
Cap-Haïtien, *Haiti* **89 C5** 19 40N 72 20W
Capac, *U.S.A.* **78 C2** 43 1N 82 56W
Capanaparo →, *Venezuela* **92 B5** 7 1N 67 7W
Cape →, *Australia* **62 C4** 20 59S 146 51 E
Cape Barren I., *Australia* **62 G4** 40 25S 148 15 E
Cape Breton Highlands Nat. Park, *Canada* **71 C7** 46 50N 60 40W
Cape Breton I., *Canada* **71 C7** 46 0N 60 30W
Cape Charles, *U.S.A.* **76 G8** 37 16N 76 1W
Cape Coast, *Ghana* **50 G5** 5 5N 1 15W
Cape Coral, *U.S.A.* **77 M5** 26 33N 81 57W
Cape Dorset, *Canada* **69 B12** 64 14N 76 32W
Cape Fear →, *U.S.A.* **77 H6** 33 53N 78 1W
Cape Girardeau, *U.S.A.* **81 G10** 37 19N 89 32W
Cape May, *U.S.A.* **76 F8** 38 56N 74 56W
Cape May Point, *U.S.A.* **75 C12** 38 56N 74 58W
Cape Province □, *S. Africa* **53 L3** 32 0S 23 0 E
Cape Tormentine, *Canada* **71 C7** 46 8N 63 47W
Cape Town, *S. Africa* **56 E2** 33 55S 18 22 E
Cape Verde Is. ■, *Atl. Oc.* **49 E1** 17 10N 25 20W
Cape Vincent, *U.S.A.* **79 B8** 44 8N 76 20W
Cape York Peninsula, *Australia* **62 A3** 12 0S 142 30 E
Capela, *Brazil* **93 F11** 10 30S 37 0W
Capella, *Australia* **62 C4** 23 2S 148 1 E
Capenda Camulemba, *Angola* **52 F3** 9 24S 18 27 E
Capim →, *Brazil* **93 D9** 1 40S 47 47W
Capitan, *U.S.A.* **83 K11** 33 35N 105 35W
Capitol Reef National Park, *U.S.A.* **83 G8** 38 15N 111 10W
Capitola, *U.S.A.* **84 J5** 36 59N 121 57W
Capoche →, *Mozam.* **55 F3** 15 35S 33 0 E
Capraia, *Italy* **18 E8** 43 2N 9 50 E
Capreol, *Canada* **70 C3** 46 43N 80 56W
Capri, *Italy* **20 D6** 40 33N 14 14 E
Capricorn Group, *Australia* **62 C5** 23 30S 151 55 E
Capricorn Ra., *Australia* **60 D2** 23 20S 116 50 E
Caprivi Strip, *Namibia* **56 B3** 18 0S 23 0 E
Captain's Flat, *Australia* **63 F4** 35 35S 149 27 E
Caquetá →, *Colombia* **92 D5** 1 15S 69 15W
Caracal, *Romania* **17 F13** 44 8N 24 22 E
Caracas, *Venezuela* **92 A5** 10 30N 66 55W
Caracol, *Brazil* **94 A4** 22 18S 57 1W
Caracol, *Piauí, Brazil* **93 E10** 9 15S 43 22W
Carajas, *Brazil* **93 E8** 6 5S 50 23W
Carajás, Serra dos, *Brazil* **93 E8** 6 0S 51 30W
Carangola, *Brazil* **95 A7** 20 44S 42 5W
Caransebeş, *Romania* **17 F12** 45 28N 22 18 E
Caraquet, *Canada* **71 C6** 47 48N 64 57W
Caras, *Peru* **92 E3** 9 3S 77 47W
Caratasca, L., *Honduras* **88 C3** 15 20N 83 40W
Caratinga, *Brazil* **93 G10** 19 50S 42 10W
Caraúbas, *Brazil* **93 E11** 5 43S 37 33W
Caravaca = Caravaca de la Cruz, *Spain* **19 C5** 38 8N 1 52W
Caravaca de la Cruz, *Spain* **19 C5** 38 8N 1 52W
Caravelas, *Brazil* **93 G11** 17 45S 39 15W
Caraveli, *Peru* **92 G4** 15 45S 73 25W
Caràzinho, *Brazil* **95 B5** 28 16S 52 46W
Carballo, *Spain* **19 A1** 43 13N 8 41W
Carberry, *Canada* **73 D9** 49 50N 99 25W
Carbó, *Mexico* **86 B2** 29 42N 110 58W
Carbonara, C., *Italy* **20 E3** 39 6N 9 31 E
Carbondale, *Colo., U.S.A.* **82 G10** 39 24N 107 13W
Carbondale, *Ill., U.S.A.* **81 G10** 37 44N 89 13W
Carbondale, *Pa., U.S.A.* **79 E9** 41 35N 75 30W
Carbonear, *Canada* **71 C9** 47 42N 53 13W
Carbónia, *Italy* **20 E3** 39 10N 8 30 E
Carcajou, *Canada* **72 B5** 57 47N 117 6W
Carcarana →, *Argentina* **94 C3** 32 27S 60 48W
Carcasse, C., *Haiti* **89 C5** 18 30N 74 28W
Carcassonne, *France* **18 E5** 43 13N 2 20 E
Carcross, *Canada* **72 A2** 60 13N 134 45W
Cardamon Hills, *India* **40 Q10** 9 30N 77 15 E
Cárdenas, *Cuba* **88 B3** 23 0N 81 30W
Cárdenas, *San Luis Potosí, Mexico* **87 C5** 22 0N 99 41W

Chinchilla

Chamical, *Argentina* 94 **C2** 30 22S 66 27W
Chamkar Luong, *Cambodia* 39 **G4** 11 0N 103 45 E
Chamoli, *India* 43 **D8** 30 24N 79 21 E
Chamonix-Mont Blanc, *France* 18 **D7** 45 55N 6 51 E
Chamouchouane →, *Canada* 70 **C5** 48 37N 72 20W
Champa, *India* 43 **H10** 22 2N 82 43 E
Champagne, *Canada* 72 **A1** 60 49N 136 30W
Champagne, *France* 18 **B6** 48 40N 4 20 E
Champaign, *U.S.A.* 76 **E1** 40 7N 88 15W
Champassak, *Laos* 38 **E5** 14 53N 105 52 E
Champawat, *India* 43 **E9** 29 20N 80 6 E
Champdoré, L., *Canada* 71 **A6** 55 55N 65 49W
Champion, *U.S.A.* 78 **E4** 41 19N 80 51W
Champlain, *U.S.A.* 79 **B11** 44 59N 73 27W
Champlain, L., *U.S.A.* 79 **B11** 44 40N 73 20W
Champotón, *Mexico* 87 **D6** 19 20N 90 50W
Champua, *India* 43 **H11** 22 5N 85 40 E
Chana, *Thailand* 39 **J3** 6 55N 100 44 E
Chañaral, *Chile* 94 **B1** 26 23S 70 40W
Chanārān, *Iran* 45 **B8** 36 39N 59 6 E
Chanasma, *India* 42 **H5** 23 44N 72 5 E
Chanco, *Chile* 94 **D1** 35 44S 72 32W
Chand, *India* 43 **J8** 21 57N 79 7 E
Chandan, *India* 43 **G12** 24 38N 86 40 E
Chandan Chauki, *India* 43 **E9** 28 33N 80 47 E
Chandannagar, *India* 43 **H13** 22 52N 88 24 E
Chandausi, *India* 43 **E8** 28 27N 78 49 E
Chandeleur Is., *U.S.A.* 81 **L10** 29 55N 88 57W
Chandeleur Sd., *U.S.A.* 81 **L10** 29 55N 89 0W
Chandigarh, *India* 42 **D7** 30 43N 76 47 E
Chandil, *India* 43 **H12** 22 58N 86 3 E
Chandler, *Australia* 63 **D1** 27 0S 133 19 E
Chandler, *Canada* 71 **C7** 48 18N 64 46W
Chandler, *Ariz., U.S.A.* 83 **K8** 33 18N 111 50W
Chandler, *Okla., U.S.A.* 81 **H6** 35 42N 96 53W
Chandod, *India* 42 **J5** 21 59N 73 28 E
Chandpur, *Bangla.* 41 **H17** 23 8N 90 45 E
Chandrapur, *India* 40 **K11** 19 57N 79 25 E
Chānf, *Iran* 45 **E9** 26 38N 60 29 E
Chang, *Pakistan* 42 **F3** 26 59N 68 30 E
Chang, Ko, *Thailand* 39 **G4** 12 0N 102 23 E
Ch'ang Chiang = Chang Jiang →, *China* 33 **C7** 31 48N 121 10 E
Chang Jiang →, *China* 33 **C7** 31 48N 121 10 E
Changa, *India* 43 **C7** 33 53N 77 35 E
Changanacheri, *India* 40 **Q10** 9 25N 76 31 E
Changane →, *Mozam.* 57 **C5** 24 30S 33 30 E
Changbai, *China* 35 **D15** 41 25N 128 5 E
Changbai Shan, *China* 35 **C15** 42 20N 129 0 E
Changchiak'ou = Zhangjiakou, *China* 34 **D8** 40 48N 114 55 E
Ch'angchou = Changzhou, *China* 33 **C6** 31 47N 119 58 E
Changchun, *China* 35 **C13** 43 57N 125 17 E
Changchunling, *China* 35 **B13** 45 18N 125 27 E
Changde, *China* 33 **D6** 29 4N 111 35 E
Changdo-ri, *N. Korea* 35 **E14** 38 30N 127 40 E
Changhai = Shanghai, *China* 33 **C7** 31 15N 121 26 E
Changhua, *Taiwan* 33 **D7** 24 2N 120 30 E
Changhŭng, *S. Korea* 35 **G14** 34 41N 126 52 E
Changhŭngni, *N. Korea* 35 **D15** 40 24N 128 19 E
Changjiang, *China* 38 **C7** 19 20N 108 55 E
Changjin, *N. Korea* 35 **D14** 40 23N 127 15 E
Changjin-chŏsuji, *N. Korea* 35 **D14** 40 30N 127 15 E
Changli, *China* 35 **E10** 39 40N 119 13 E
Changling, *China* 35 **B12** 44 20N 123 58 E
Changlun, *Malaysia* 39 **J3** 6 25N 100 26 E
Changping, *China* 34 **D9** 40 14N 116 12 E
Changsha, *China* 33 **D6** 28 12N 113 0 E
Changwu, *China* 34 **G4** 35 10N 107 45 E
Changyi, *China* 35 **F10** 36 40N 119 30 E
Changyŏn, *N. Korea* 35 **E13** 38 15N 125 6 E
Changyuan, *China* 34 **G8** 35 15N 114 42 E
Changzhi, *China* 34 **F7** 36 10N 113 6 E
Changzhou, *China* 33 **C6** 31 47N 119 58 E
Chanhanga, *Angola* 56 **B1** 16 0S 14 8 E
Channapatna, *India* 40 **N10** 12 40N 77 15 E
Channel Is., *U.K.* 11 **H5** 49 19N 2 24W
Channel Is., *U.S.A.* 85 **M7** 33 40N 119 15W
Channel Islands National Park, *U.S.A.* 85 **M8** 33 30N 119 0W
Channel-Port aux Basques, *Canada* 71 **C8** 47 30N 59 9W
Channel Tunnel, *Europe* 11 **F9** 51 0N 1 30 E
Channing, *U.S.A.* 81 **H3** 35 41N 102 20W
Chantada, *Spain* 19 **A2** 42 36N 7 46W
Chanthaburi, *Thailand* 38 **F4** 12 38N 102 12 E
Chantrey Inlet, *Canada* 68 **B10** 67 48N 96 20W
Chanute, *U.S.A.* 81 **G7** 37 41N 95 27W
Chao Phraya →, *Thailand* 38 **F3** 13 32N 100 36 E
Chao Phraya Lowlands, *Thailand* 38 **E3** 15 30N 100 0 E
Chaocheng, *China* 34 **F8** 36 4N 115 37 E
Chaoyang, *China* 35 **D11** 41 35N 120 22 E
Chaozhou, *China* 33 **D6** 23 42N 116 32 E
Chapais, *Canada* 70 **C5** 49 47N 74 51W
Chapala, *Mozam.* 55 **F4** 15 50S 37 35 E
Chapala, L. de, *Mexico* 86 **C4** 20 10N 103 20W
Chapayev, *Kazakstan* 25 **D9** 50 25N 51 10 E
Chapayevsk, *Russia* 24 **D8** 53 0N 49 40 E
Chapecó, *Brazil* 95 **B5** 27 14S 52 41W
Chapel Hill, *U.S.A.* 77 **H6** 35 55N 79 4W
Chapleau, *Canada* 70 **C3** 47 50N 83 24W
Chaplin, *Canada* 73 **C7** 50 28N 106 40W
Chaplin L., *Canada* 73 **C7** 50 22N 106 36W
Chappell, *U.S.A.* 80 **E3** 41 6N 102 28W
Chapra = Chhapra, *India* 43 **G11** 25 48N 84 44 E
Chara, *Russia* 27 **D12** 56 54N 118 20 E
Charadai, *Argentina* 94 **B4** 27 35S 59 55W
Charagua, *Bolivia* 92 **G6** 19 45S 63 10W
Charambirá, Punta, *Colombia* 92 **C3** 4 16N 77 32W
Charaña, *Bolivia* 92 **G5** 17 30S 69 25W
Charanwala, *India* 42 **F5** 27 51N 72 10 E
Charata, *Argentina* 94 **B3** 27 13S 61 14W
Charcas, *Mexico* 86 **C4** 23 10N 101 20W
Chard, *U.K.* 11 **G5** 50 52N 2 58W
Chardon, *U.S.A.* 78 **E3** 41 35N 81 12W
Chardzhou = Chärjew, *Turkmenistan* 26 **F7** 39 6N 63 34 E
Charente →, *France* 18 **D3** 45 57N 1 5W
Chari →, *Chad* 51 **F8** 12 58N 14 31 E
Chārīkār, *Afghan.* 40 **B6** 35 0N 69 10 E
Chariton →, *U.S.A.* 80 **F8** 39 19N 92 58W
Chärjew, *Turkmenistan* 26 **F7** 39 6N 63 34 E
Charkhari, *India* 43 **G8** 25 24N 79 45 E
Charkhi Dadri, *India* 42 **E7** 28 37N 76 17 E
Charleroi, *Belgium* 15 **D4** 50 24N 4 27 E
Charleroi, *U.S.A.* 78 **F5** 40 9N 79 57W
Charles, C., *U.S.A.* 76 **G8** 37 7N 75 58W
Charles City, *U.S.A.* 80 **D8** 43 4N 92 41W
Charles L., *Canada* 73 **B6** 59 50N 110 33W
Charles Town, *U.S.A.* 76 **F7** 39 17N 77 52W
Charleston, *Ill., U.S.A.* 76 **F1** 39 30N 88 10W
Charleston, *Miss., U.S.A.* 81 **H9** 34 1N 90 4W
Charleston, *Mo., U.S.A.* 81 **G10** 36 55N 89 21W
Charleston, *S.C., U.S.A.* 77 **J6** 32 46N 79 56W
Charleston, *W. Va., U.S.A.* 76 **F5** 38 21N 81 38W
Charleston L., *Canada* 79 **B9** 44 32N 76 0W
Charleston Peak, *U.S.A.* 85 **J11** 36 16N 115 42W
Charlestown, *Ireland* 13 **C3** 53 58N 8 48W
Charlestown, *S. Africa* 57 **D4** 27 26S 29 53 E
Charlestown, *Ind., U.S.A.* 76 **F3** 38 27N 85 40W
Charlestown, *N.H., U.S.A.* 79 **C12** 43 14N 72 25W
Charleville = Rath Luirc, *Ireland* 13 **D3** 52 21N 8 40W
Charleville, *Australia* 63 **D4** 26 24S 146 15 E
Charleville-Mézières, *France* 18 **B6** 49 44N 4 40 E
Charlevoix, *U.S.A.* 76 **C3** 45 19N 85 16W
Charlotte, *Mich., U.S.A.* 76 **D3** 42 34N 84 50W
Charlotte, *N.C., U.S.A.* 77 **H5** 35 13N 80 51W
Charlotte, *Vt., U.S.A.* 79 **B11** 44 19N 73 14W
Charlotte Amalie, *Virgin Is.* 89 **C7** 18 21N 64 56W
Charlotte Harbor, *U.S.A.* 77 **M4** 26 50N 82 10W
Charlotte L., *Canada* 72 **C3** 52 12N 125 19W
Charlottesville, *U.S.A.* 76 **F6** 38 2N 78 30W
Charlottetown, *Nfld., Canada* 71 **B8** 52 46N 56 7W
Charlottetown, *P.E.I., Canada* 71 **C7** 46 14N 63 8W
Charlton, *Australia* 63 **F3** 36 16S 143 24 E
Charlton, *U.S.A.* 80 **E8** 40 59N 93 20W
Charlton I., *Canada* 70 **B4** 52 0N 79 20W
Charny, *Canada* 71 **C5** 46 43N 71 15W
Charolles, *France* 18 **C6** 46 27N 4 16 E
Charre, *Mozam.* 55 **F4** 17 13S 35 10 E
Charsadda, *Pakistan* 42 **B4** 34 7N 71 45 E
Charters Towers, *Australia* 62 **C4** 20 5S 146 13 E
Chartres, *France* 18 **B4** 48 29N 1 30 E
Chascomús, *Argentina* 94 **D4** 35 30S 58 0W
Chasefu, *Zambia* 55 **E3** 11 55S 33 8 E
Chashma Barrage, *Pakistan* 42 **C4** 32 27N 71 20 E
Chāt, *Iran* 45 **B7** 37 59N 55 16 E
Châteaubriant, *France* 18 **C3** 47 43N 1 23W
Chateaugay, *U.S.A.* 79 **B10** 44 56N 74 5W
Châteauguay, L., *Canada* 71 **A5** 56 26N 70 3W
Châteaulin, *France* 18 **B1** 48 11N 4 8W
Châteauroux, *France* 18 **C4** 46 50N 1 40 E
Châtellerault, *France* 18 **C4** 46 50N 0 30 E
Chatham = Miramichi, *Canada* 71 **C6** 47 2N 65 28W
Chatham, *Canada* 78 **D2** 42 24N 82 11W
Chatham, *U.K.* 11 **F8** 51 22N 0 32 E
Chatham, *U.S.A.* 79 **D11** 42 21N 73 36W
Chatham Is., *Pac. Oc.* 64 **M10** 44 0S 176 40W
Chatmohar, *Bangla.* 43 **G13** 24 15N 89 15 E
Chatra, *India* 43 **G11** 24 12N 84 56 E
Chatrapur, *India* 41 **K14** 19 22N 85 2 E
Chats, L. des, *Canada* 79 **A8** 45 30N 76 20W
Chatsu, *India* 42 **F6** 26 36N 75 57 E
Chatsworth, *Canada* 78 **B4** 44 27N 80 54W
Chatsworth, *Zimbabwe* 55 **F3** 19 38S 31 13 E
Chattahoochee, *U.S.A.* 77 **K3** 30 42N 84 51W
Chattahoochee →, *U.S.A.* 77 **K3** 30 54N 84 57W
Chattanooga, *U.S.A.* 77 **H3** 35 3N 85 19W
Chatteris, *U.K.* 11 **E8** 52 28N 0 2 E
Chaturat, *Thailand* 38 **E3** 15 40N 101 51 E
Chau Doc, *Vietnam* 39 **G5** 10 42N 105 7 E
Chauk, *Burma* 41 **J19** 20 53N 94 49 E
Chaukan La, *Burma* 41 **F20** 27 0N 97 15 E
Chaumont, *France* 18 **B6** 48 7N 5 8 E
Chaumont, *U.S.A.* 79 **B8** 44 4N 76 8W
Chautauqua L., *U.S.A.* 78 **D5** 42 10N 79 24W
Chauvin, *Canada* 73 **C6** 52 45N 110 10W
Chaves, *Brazil* 93 **D9** 0 15S 49 55W
Chaves, *Portugal* 19 **B2** 41 45N 7 32W
Chawang, *Thailand* 39 **H2** 8 25N 99 30 E
Chaykovskiy, *Russia* 24 **C9** 56 47N 54 9 E
Chazy, *U.S.A.* 79 **B11** 44 53N 73 26W
Cheb, *Czech Rep.* 16 **C7** 50 9N 12 28 E
Cheboksary, *Russia* 24 **C8** 56 8N 47 12 E
Cheboygan, *U.S.A.* 76 **C3** 45 39N 84 29W
Chech, Erg, *Africa* 50 **D5** 25 0N 2 15W
Chechenia □, *Russia* 25 **F8** 43 30N 45 29 E
Checheno-Ingush Republic = Chechenia □, *Russia* 25 **F8** 43 30N 45 29 E
Chechnya = Chechenia □, *Russia* 25 **F8** 43 30N 45 29 E
Chech'ŏn, *S. Korea* 35 **F15** 37 8N 128 12 E
Checotah, *U.S.A.* 81 **H7** 35 28N 95 31W
Chedabucto B., *Canada* 71 **C7** 45 25N 61 8W
Cheduba I., *Burma* 41 **K18** 18 45N 93 40 E
Cheepie, *Australia* 63 **D4** 26 33S 145 1 E
Chegdomyn, *Russia* 27 **D14** 51 7N 133 1 E
Chegga, *Mauritania* 50 **C4** 25 27N 5 40W
Chegutu, *Zimbabwe* 55 **F3** 18 10S 30 14 E
Chehalis, *U.S.A.* 84 **D4** 46 40N 122 58W
Chehalis →, *U.S.A.* 84 **D3** 46 57N 123 50W
Cheju do, *S. Korea* 35 **H14** 33 29N 126 34 E
Chekiang = Zhejiang □, *China* 33 **D7** 29 0N 120 0 E
Chela, Sa. da, *Angola* 56 **B1** 16 20S 13 20 E
Chelan, *U.S.A.* 82 **C4** 47 51N 120 1W
Chelan, L., *U.S.A.* 82 **B3** 48 11N 120 30W
Cheleken, *Turkmenistan* 25 **G9** 39 34N 53 16 E
Cheleken Yarymadasy, *Turkmenistan* 45 **B7** 39 30N 53 15 E
Chelforó, *Argentina* 96 **D3** 39 0S 66 33W
Chelkar = Shalqar, *Kazakstan* 26 **E6** 47 48N 59 39 E
Chelkar Tengiz, Solonchak, *Kazakstan* 26 **E7** 48 5N 63 7 E
Chełm, *Poland* 17 **C12** 51 8N 23 30 E
Chełmno, *Poland* 17 **B10** 53 20N 18 30 E
Chelmsford, *U.K.* 11 **F8** 51 44N 0 29 E
Chelsea, *U.S.A.* 79 **C12** 43 59N 72 27W
Cheltenham, *U.K.* 11 **F5** 51 54N 2 4W
Chelyabinsk, *Russia* 26 **D7** 55 10N 61 24 E
Chelyuskin, C., *Russia* 28 **B14** 77 30N 103 0 E
Chemainus, *Canada* 84 **B3** 48 55N 123 42W
Chemba, *Mozam.* 53 **H6** 17 9S 34 53 E
Chemnitz, *Germany* 16 **C7** 50 51N 12 54 E
Chemult, *U.S.A.* 82 **E3** 43 14N 121 47W
Chen, Gora, *Russia* 27 **C15** 65 16N 141 50 E
Chenab →, *Pakistan* 42 **D4** 30 23N 71 2 E
Chenango Forks, *U.S.A.* 79 **D9** 42 15N 75 51W
Cheney, *U.S.A.* 82 **C5** 47 30N 117 35W
Cheng Xian, *China* 34 **H3** 33 43N 105 42 E
Chengcheng, *China* 34 **G5** 35 8N 109 56 E
Chengchou = Zhengzhou, *China* 34 **G7** 34 45N 113 34 E
Chengde, *China* 35 **D9** 40 59N 117 58 E
Chengdu, *China* 32 **C5** 30 38N 104 2 E
Chenggu, *China* 34 **H4** 33 10N 107 21 E
Chengjiang, *China* 32 **D5** 24 39N 103 0 E
Ch'engmai, *China* 38 **C7** 19 50N 109 58 E
Ch'engtu = Chengdu, *China* 32 **C5** 30 38N 104 2 E
Chengwu, *China* 34 **G8** 34 58N 115 50 E
Chengyang, *China* 35 **F11** 36 18N 120 21 E
Chenjiagang, *China* 35 **G10** 34 23N 119 47 E
Chenkán, *Mexico* 87 **D6** 19 8N 90 58W
Chennai, *India* 40 **N12** 13 8N 80 19 E
Cheo Reo, *Vietnam* 36 **B3** 13 25N 108 28 E
Cheom Ksan, *Cambodia* 38 **E5** 14 13N 104 56 E
Chepén, *Peru* 92 **E3** 7 15S 79 23W
Chepes, *Argentina* 94 **C2** 31 20S 66 35W
Chepo, *Panama* 88 **E4** 9 10N 79 6W
Chepstow, *U.K.* 11 **F5** 51 38N 2 41W
Cheptulil, Mt., *Kenya* 54 **B4** 1 25N 35 35 E
Chequamegon B., *U.S.A.* 80 **B9** 46 40N 90 30W
Cher →, *France* 18 **C4** 47 21N 0 29 E
Cheraw, *U.S.A.* 77 **H6** 34 42N 79 53W
Cherbourg, *France* 18 **B3** 49 39N 1 40W
Cherdyn, *Russia* 24 **B10** 60 24N 56 29 E
Cheremkhovo, *Russia* 27 **D11** 53 8N 103 1 E
Cherepanovo, *Russia* 26 **D9** 54 15N 83 30 E
Cherepovets, *Russia* 24 **C6** 59 5N 37 55 E
Chergui, Chott ech, *Algeria* 50 **B6** 34 21N 0 25 E
Cherikov = Cherykaw, *Belarus* 17 **B16** 53 32N 31 20 E
Cherkasy, *Ukraine* 25 **E5** 49 27N 32 4 E
Cherkessk, *Russia* 25 **F7** 44 15N 42 5 E
Cherlak, *Russia* 26 **D8** 54 15N 74 55 E
Chernaya, *Russia* 27 **B9** 70 30N 89 10 E
Chernigov = Chernihiv, *Ukraine* 24 **D5** 51 28N 31 20 E
Chernihiv, *Ukraine* 24 **D5** 51 28N 31 20 E
Chernivtsi, *Ukraine* 17 **D13** 48 15N 25 52 E
Chernobyl = Chornobyl, *Ukraine* 17 **C16** 51 20N 30 15 E
Chernogorsk, *Russia* 27 **D10** 53 49N 91 18 E
Chernovtsy = Chernivtsi, *Ukraine* 17 **D13** 48 15N 25 52 E
Chernyakhovsk, *Russia* 9 **J19** 54 36N 21 48 E
Chernysheyskiy, *Russia* 27 **C12** 63 0N 112 30 E
Cherokee, *Iowa, U.S.A.* 80 **D7** 42 45N 95 33W
Cherokee, *Okla., U.S.A.* 81 **G5** 36 45N 98 21W
Cherokee Village, *U.S.A.* 81 **G9** 36 17N 91 30W
Cherokees, Grand Lake O' The, *U.S.A.* 81 **G7** 36 28N 95 2W
Cherrapunji, *India* 41 **G17** 25 17N 91 47 E
Cherry Valley, *Calif., U.S.A.* 85 **M10** 33 59N 116 57W
Cherry Valley, *N.Y., U.S.A.* 79 **D10** 42 48N 74 45W
Cherskiy, *Russia* 27 **C17** 68 45N 161 18 E
Cherskogo Khrebet, *Russia* 27 **C15** 65 0N 143 0 E
Cherven, *Belarus* 17 **B15** 53 45N 28 28 E
Chervonohrad, *Ukraine* 17 **C13** 50 25N 24 10 E
Cherwell →, *U.K.* 11 **F6** 51 44N 1 14W
Cherykaw, *Belarus* 17 **B16** 53 32N 31 20 E
Chesapeake, *U.S.A.* 76 **G7** 36 50N 76 17W
Chesapeake B., *U.S.A.* 76 **G7** 38 0N 76 10W
Cheshire □, *U.K.* 10 **D5** 53 14N 2 30W
Cheshskaya Guba, *Russia* 24 **A8** 67 20N 47 0 E
Cheshunt, *U.K.* 11 **F7** 51 43N 0 1W
Chesil Beach, *U.K.* 11 **G5** 50 37N 2 33W
Chesley, *Canada* 78 **B3** 44 17N 81 5W
Chester, *U.K.* 10 **D5** 53 12N 2 53W
Chester, *Calif., U.S.A.* 82 **F3** 40 19N 121 14W
Chester, *Ill., U.S.A.* 81 **G10** 37 55N 89 49W
Chester, *Mont., U.S.A.* 82 **B8** 48 31N 110 58W
Chester, *Pa., U.S.A.* 76 **F8** 39 51N 75 22W
Chester, *S.C., U.S.A.* 77 **H5** 34 43N 81 12W
Chester, *Vt., U.S.A.* 79 **C12** 43 16N 72 36W
Chester, *W. Va., U.S.A.* 78 **F4** 40 37N 80 34W
Chester-le-Street, *U.K.* 10 **C6** 54 51N 1 34W
Chesterfield, *U.K.* 10 **D6** 53 15N 1 25W
Chesterfield, Is., *N. Cal.* 64 **J7** 19 52S 158 15 E
Chesterfield Inlet, *Canada* 68 **B10** 63 30N 90 45W
Chesterton Ra., *Australia* 63 **D4** 25 30S 147 27 E
Chestertown, *U.S.A.* 79 **C11** 43 40N 73 48W
Chesterville, *Canada* 79 **A9** 45 6N 75 14W
Chestnut Ridge, *U.S.A.* 78 **F5** 40 20N 79 10W
Chesuncook L., *U.S.A.* 77 **C11** 46 0N 69 21W
Chéticamp, *Canada* 71 **C7** 46 37N 60 59W
Chetumal, *Mexico* 87 **D7** 18 30N 88 20W
Chetumal, B. de, *Mexico* 87 **D7** 18 40N 88 10W
Chetwynd, *Canada* 72 **B4** 55 45N 121 36W
Cheviot, The, *U.K.* 10 **B5** 55 29N 2 9W
Cheviot Hills, *U.K.* 10 **B5** 55 20N 2 30W
Cheviot Ra., *Australia* 62 **D3** 25 20S 143 45 E
Chew Bahir, *Ethiopia* 46 **G2** 4 40N 36 50 E
Chewelah, *U.S.A.* 82 **B5** 48 17N 117 43W
Cheyenne, *Okla., U.S.A.* 81 **H5** 35 37N 99 40W
Cheyenne, *Wyo., U.S.A.* 80 **E2** 41 8N 104 49W
Cheyenne →, *U.S.A.* 80 **C4** 44 41N 101 18W
Cheyenne Wells, *U.S.A.* 80 **F3** 38 49N 102 21W
Cheyne B., *Australia* 61 **F2** 34 35S 118 50 E
Chhabra, *India* 42 **G7** 24 40N 76 54 E
Chhaktala, *India* 42 **H6** 22 6N 74 11 E
Chhapra, *India* 43 **G11** 25 48N 84 44 E
Chhata, *India* 42 **F7** 27 42N 77 30 E
Chhatarpur, *Bihar, India* 43 **G11** 24 23N 84 11 E
Chhatarpur, *Mad. P., India* 43 **G8** 24 55N 79 35 E
Chhep, *Cambodia* 38 **F5** 13 45N 105 24 E
Chhindwara, *Mad. P., India* 43 **H8** 23 3N 79 29 E
Chhindwara, *Mad. P., India* 43 **H8** 22 2N 78 59 E
Chhlong, *Cambodia* 39 **F5** 12 15N 105 58 E
Chhota Tawa →, *India* 42 **H7** 22 14N 76 36 E
Chhoti Kali Sindh →, *India* 42 **G6** 24 2N 75 31 E
Chhuikhadan, *India* 43 **J9** 21 32N 80 59 E
Chhuk, *Cambodia* 39 **G5** 10 46N 104 28 E
Chi →, *Thailand* 38 **E5** 15 11N 104 43 E
Chiai, *Taiwan* 33 **D7** 23 29N 120 25 E
Chiamboni, *Somali Rep.* 52 **E8** 1 39S 41 35 E
Chiamussu = Jiamusi, *China* 33 **B8** 46 40N 130 26 E
Chiang Dao, *Thailand* 38 **C2** 19 22N 98 58 E
Chiang Kham, *Thailand* 38 **C3** 19 32N 100 18 E
Chiang Khan, *Thailand* 38 **D3** 17 52N 101 36 E
Chiang Mai, *Thailand* 38 **C2** 18 47N 98 59 E
Chiang Rai, *Thailand* 38 **C2** 19 52N 99 50 E
Chiapa →, *Mexico* 87 **D6** 16 42N 93 0W
Chiapa de Corzo, *Mexico* 87 **D6** 16 42N 93 0W
Chiapas □, *Mexico* 87 **D6** 17 0N 92 45W
Chiautla, *Mexico* 87 **D5** 18 18N 98 34W
Chiávari, *Italy* 18 **D8** 44 19N 9 19 E
Chiavenna, *Italy* 18 **C8** 46 19N 9 24 E
Chiba, *Japan* 31 **G10** 35 30N 140 7 E
Chiba □, *Japan* 31 **G10** 35 30N 140 20 E
Chibabava, *Mozam.* 57 **C5** 20 17S 33 35 E
Chibemba, *Cunene, Angola* 53 **H2** 15 48S 14 8 E
Chibemba, *Huila, Angola* 56 **B2** 16 20S 15 20 E
Chibia, *Angola* 53 **H2** 15 10S 13 42 E
Chibougamau, *Canada* 70 **C5** 49 56N 74 24W
Chibougamau, L., *Canada* 70 **C5** 49 50N 74 20W
Chic-Chocs, Mts., *Canada* 71 **C6** 48 55N 66 0W
Chicacole = Srikakulam, *India* 41 **K13** 18 14N 83 58 E
Chicago, *U.S.A.* 76 **E2** 41 53N 87 38W
Chicago Heights, *U.S.A.* 76 **E2** 41 30N 87 38W
Chichagof I., *U.S.A.* 68 **C6** 57 30N 135 30W
Chichén-Itzá, *Mexico* 87 **C7** 20 40N 88 36W
Chicheng, *China* 34 **D8** 40 55N 115 55 E
Chichester, *U.K.* 11 **G7** 50 50N 0 47W
Chichester Ra., *Australia* 60 **D2** 22 12S 119 15 E
Chichibu, *Japan* 31 **F9** 36 5N 139 10 E
Ch'ich'ihaerh = Qiqihar, *China* 27 **E13** 47 26N 124 0 E
Chicholi, *India* 42 **H8** 22 1N 77 40 E
Chickasha, *U.S.A.* 81 **H6** 35 3N 97 58W
Chiclana de la Frontera, *Spain* 19 **D2** 36 26N 6 9W
Chiclayo, *Peru* 92 **E3** 6 42S 79 50W
Chico, *U.S.A.* 84 **F5** 39 44N 121 50W
Chico →, *Chubut, Argentina* 96 **E3** 44 0S 67 0W
Chico →, *Santa Cruz, Argentina* 96 **G3** 50 0S 68 30W
Chicomo, *Mozam.* 57 **C5** 24 31S 34 6 E
Chicontepec, *Mexico* 87 **C5** 20 58N 98 10W
Chicopee, *U.S.A.* 79 **D12** 42 9N 72 37W
Chicoutimi, *Canada* 71 **C5** 48 28N 71 5W
Chicualacuala, *Mozam.* 57 **C5** 22 6S 31 42 E
Chidambaram, *India* 40 **P11** 11 20N 79 45 E
Chidenguele, *Mozam.* 57 **C5** 24 55S 34 11 E
Chidley, C., *Canada* 69 **B13** 60 23N 64 26W
Chiede, *Angola* 56 **B2** 17 15S 16 22 E
Chiefs Pt., *Canada* 78 **B3** 44 41N 81 18W
Chiem Hoa, *Vietnam* 38 **A5** 22 12N 105 17 E
Chiemsee, *Germany* 16 **E7** 47 53N 12 28 E
Chiengi, *Zambia* 55 **D2** 8 45S 29 10 E
Chiengmai = Chiang Mai, *Thailand* 38 **C2** 18 47N 98 59 E
Chiese →, *Italy* 18 **D9** 45 8N 10 25 E
Chieti, *Italy* 20 **C6** 42 21N 14 10 E
Chifeng, *China* 35 **C10** 42 18N 118 58 E
Chignecto B., *Canada* 71 **C7** 45 30N 64 40W
Chiguana, *Bolivia* 94 **A2** 21 0S 67 58W
Chigwell, *U.K.* 11 **F8** 51 37N 0 5 E
Chiha-ri, *N. Korea* 35 **E14** 38 40N 126 30 E
Chihli, G. of = Bo Hai, *China* 35 **E10** 39 0N 119 0 E
Chihuahua, *Mexico* 86 **B3** 28 40N 106 3W
Chihuahua □, *Mexico* 86 **B3** 28 40N 106 3W
Chiili, *Kazakstan* 26 **E7** 44 20N 66 15 E
Chik Bollapur, *India* 40 **N10** 13 25N 77 45 E
Chikmagalur, *India* 40 **N9** 13 15N 75 45 E
Chikwawa, *Malawi* 55 **F3** 16 2S 34 50 E
Chilac, *Mexico* 87 **D5** 18 20N 97 24W
Chilam Chavki, *Pakistan* 43 **B6** 35 5N 75 5 E
Chilanga, *Zambia* 55 **F2** 15 33S 28 16 E
Chilapa, *Mexico* 87 **D5** 17 40N 99 11W
Chilas, *Pakistan* 43 **B6** 35 25N 74 5 E
Chilaw, *Sri Lanka* 40 **R11** 7 30N 79 50 E
Chilcotin →, *Canada* 72 **C4** 51 44N 122 23W
Childers, *Australia* 63 **D5** 25 15S 152 17 E
Childress, *U.S.A.* 81 **H4** 34 25N 100 13W
Chile ■, *S. Amer.* 96 **D2** 35 0S 72 0W
Chile Rise, *Pac. Oc.* 65 **L18** 38 0S 92 0W
Chilecito, *Argentina* 94 **B2** 29 10S 67 30W
Chilete, *Peru* 92 **E3** 7 10S 78 50W
Chililabombwe, *Zambia* 55 **E2** 12 18S 27 43 E
Chilin = Jilin, *China* 35 **C14** 43 44N 126 30 E
Chilka L., *India* 41 **K14** 19 40N 85 25 E
Chilko →, *Canada* 72 **C4** 52 0N 123 40W
Chilko L., *Canada* 72 **C4** 51 20N 124 10W
Chillagoe, *Australia* 62 **B3** 17 7S 144 33 E
Chillán, *Chile* 94 **D1** 36 40S 72 10W
Chillicothe, *Ill., U.S.A.* 80 **E10** 40 55N 89 29W
Chillicothe, *Mo., U.S.A.* 80 **F8** 39 48N 93 33W
Chillicothe, *Ohio, U.S.A.* 76 **F4** 39 20N 82 59W
Chilliwack, *Canada* 72 **D4** 49 10N 121 54W
Chilo, *India* 42 **F5** 27 25N 73 32 E
Chiloane, I., *Mozam.* 57 **C5** 20 40S 34 55 E
Chiloé, I. de, *Chile* 96 **E2** 42 30S 73 50W
Chilpancingo, *Mexico* 87 **D5** 17 30N 99 30W
Chiltern Hills, *U.K.* 11 **F7** 51 40N 0 53W
Chilton, *U.S.A.* 76 **C1** 44 2N 88 10W
Chilubi, *Zambia* 55 **E2** 11 5S 29 58 E
Chilubula, *Zambia* 55 **E3** 10 14S 30 51 E
Chilumba, *Malawi* 55 **E3** 10 28S 34 12 E
Chilung, *Taiwan* 33 **D7** 25 3N 121 45 E
Chilwa, L., *Malawi* 55 **F4** 15 15S 35 40 E
Chimaltitán, *Mexico* 86 **C4** 21 46N 103 50W
Chimán, *Panama* 88 **E4** 8 45N 78 40W
Chimay, *Belgium* 15 **D4** 50 3N 4 20 E
Chimayo, *U.S.A.* 83 **H11** 36 0N 105 56W
Chimbay, *Uzbekistan* 26 **E6** 42 57N 59 47 E
Chimborazo, *Ecuador* 92 **D3** 1 29S 78 55W
Chimbote, *Peru* 92 **E3** 9 0S 78 35W
Chimkent = Shymkent, *Kazakstan* 26 **E7** 42 18N 69 36 E
Chimoio, *Mozam.* 55 **F3** 19 4S 33 30 E
Chimpembe, *Zambia* 55 **D2** 9 31S 29 33 E
Chin □, *Burma* 41 **J18** 22 0N 93 0 E
Chin Ling Shan = Qinling Shandi, *China* 34 **H5** 33 50N 108 10 E
China, *Mexico* 87 **B5** 25 40N 99 20W
China ■, *Asia* 33 **D6** 30 0N 110 0 E
China Lake, *U.S.A.* 85 **K9** 35 44N 117 37W
Chinan = Jinan, *China* 34 **F9** 36 38N 117 1 E
Chinandega, *Nic.* 88 **D2** 12 35N 87 12W
Chinati Peak, *U.S.A.* 81 **L2** 29 57N 104 29W
Chincha Alta, *Peru* 92 **F3** 13 25S 76 7W
Chinchaga →, *Canada* 72 **B5** 58 53N 118 20W
Chinchilla, *Australia* 63 **D5** 26 45S 150 38 E

Corrientes

Corrientes □, *Argentina* **94 B4** 28 0S 57 0W
Corrientes →, *Argentina* **94 C4** 30 42S 59 38W
Corrientes →, *Peru* **92 D4** 3 43S 74 35W
Corrientes, C., *Colombia* **92 B3** 5 30N 77 34W
Corrientes, C., *Cuba* **88 B3** 21 43N 84 30W
Corrientes, C., *Mexico* **86 C3** 20 25N 105 42W
Corrigan, *U.S.A.* **81 K7** 31 0N 94 52W
Corrigin, *Australia* **61 F2** 32 20S 117 53 E
Corry, *U.S.A.* **78 E5** 41 55N 79 39W
Corryong, *Australia* **63 F4** 36 12S 147 53 E
Corse, *France* **18 F8** 42 0N 9 0 E
Corse, C., *France* **18 E8** 43 1N 9 25 E
Corsica = Corse, *France* **18 F8** 42 0N 9 0 E
Corsicana, *U.S.A.* **81 J6** 32 6N 96 28W
Corte, *France* **18 E8** 42 19N 9 11 E
Cortez, *U.S.A.* **83 H9** 37 21N 108 35W
Cortland, *N.Y., U.S.A.* **79 D8** 42 36N 76 11W
Cortland, *Ohio, U.S.A.* **78 E4** 41 20N 80 44W
Çorum, *Turkey* **25 F5** 40 30N 34 57 E
Corumbá, *Brazil* **92 G7** 19 0S 57 30W
Corunna = A Coruña, *Spain* **19 A1** 43 20N 8 25W
Corvallis, *U.S.A.* **82 D2** 44 34N 123 16W
Corvette, L. de la, *Canada* **70 B5** 53 25N 74 3W
Corydon, *U.S.A.* **80 E8** 40 46N 93 19W
Cosalá, *Mexico* **86 C3** 24 28N 106 40W
Cosamaloapan, *Mexico* **87 D5** 18 23N 95 50W
Cosenza, *Italy* **20 E7** 39 18N 16 15 E
Coshocton, *U.S.A.* **78 F3** 40 16N 81 51W
Cosmo Newberry, *Australia* **61 E3** 28 0S 122 54 E
Coso Junction, *U.S.A.* **85 J9** 36 3N 117 57W
Coso Pk., *U.S.A.* **85 J9** 36 13N 117 44W
Cosquín, *Argentina* **94 C3** 31 15S 64 30W
Costa Blanca, *Spain* **19 C5** 38 25N 0 10W
Costa Brava, *Spain* **19 B7** 41 30N 3 0 E
Costa del Sol, *Spain* **19 D3** 36 30N 4 30W
Costa Dorada, *Spain* **19 B6** 41 12N 1 15 E
Costa Mesa, *U.S.A.* **85 M9** 33 38N 117 55W
Costa Rica ■, *Cent. Amer.* **88 E3** 10 0N 84 0W
Cosumnes →, *U.S.A.* **84 G5** 38 16N 121 26W
Cotabato, *Phil.* **37 C6** 7 14N 124 15 E
Cotagaita, *Bolivia* **94 A2** 20 45S 65 40W
Côte d'Azur, *France* **18 E7** 43 25N 7 10 E
Côte-d'Ivoire = Ivory Coast ■, *Africa* **50 G4** 7 30N 5 0W
Coteau des Prairies, *U.S.A.* **80 C6** 45 20N 97 50W
Coteau du Missouri, *U.S.A.* **80 B4** 47 0N 100 0W
Coteau Landing, *Canada* **79 A10** 45 15N 74 13W
Cotentin, *France* **18 B3** 49 15N 1 30W
Cotillo, *Canary Is.* **22 F5** 28 41N 14 1W
Cotonou, *Benin* **50 G6** 6 20N 2 25 E
Cotopaxi, *Ecuador* **92 D3** 0 40S 78 30W
Cotswold Hills, *U.K.* **11 F5** 51 42N 2 10W
Cottage Grove, *U.S.A.* **82 E2** 43 48N 123 3W
Cottbus, *Germany* **16 C8** 51 45N 14 20 E
Cottonwood, *U.S.A.* **83 J7** 34 45N 112 1W
Cotulla, *U.S.A.* **81 L5** 28 26N 99 14W
Coudersport, *U.S.A.* **78 E6** 41 46N 78 1W
Couedic, C. du, *Australia* **63 F2** 36 5S 136 40 E
Coulee City, *U.S.A.* **82 C4** 47 37N 119 17W
Coulman I., *Antarctica* **5 D11** 73 35S 170 0 E
Coulonge →, *Canada* **70 C4** 45 52N 76 46W
Coulterville, *U.S.A.* **84 H6** 37 43N 120 12W
Council, *U.S.A.* **82 D5** 44 44N 116 26W
Council Bluffs, *U.S.A.* **80 E7** 41 16N 95 52W
Council Grove, *U.S.A.* **80 F6** 38 40N 96 29W
Coupeville, *U.S.A.* **84 B4** 48 13N 122 41W
Courantyne →, *S. Amer.* **92 B7** 5 55N 57 5W
Courcelles, *Belgium* **15 D4** 50 28N 4 22 E
Courtenay, *Canada* **72 D4** 49 45N 125 0W
Courtland, *U.S.A.* **84 G5** 38 20N 121 34W
Courtrai = Kortrijk, *Belgium* **15 D3** 50 50N 3 17 E
Courtright, *Canada* **78 D2** 42 49N 82 28W
Coushatta, *U.S.A.* **81 J8** 32 1N 93 21W
Coutts Crossing, *Australia* **63 D5** 29 49S 152 55 E
Couvin, *Belgium* **15 D4** 50 3N 4 29 E
Cove I., *Canada* **78 A3** 45 17N 81 44W
Coventry, *U.K.* **11 E6** 52 25N 1 28W
Covilhã, *Portugal* **19 B2** 40 17N 7 31W
Covington, *Ga., U.S.A.* **77 J4** 33 36N 83 51W
Covington, *Ky., U.S.A.* **76 F3** 39 5N 84 31W
Covington, *Okla., U.S.A.* **81 G6** 36 18N 97 35W
Covington, *Tenn., U.S.A.* **81 H10** 35 34N 89 39W
Covington, *Va., U.S.A.* **76 G5** 37 47N 79 59W
Cowal, L., *Australia* **63 E4** 33 40S 147 25 E
Cowan, L., *Australia* **61 F3** 31 45S 121 45 E
Cowan L., *Canada* **73 C7** 54 0N 107 15W
Cowangie, *Australia* **63 F3** 35 12S 141 26 E
Cowansville, *Canada* **79 A12** 45 14N 72 46W
Coward Springs, *Australia* **63 D2** 29 24S 136 49 E
Cowcowing Lakes, *Australia* **61 F2** 30 55S 117 20 E
Cowdenbeath, *U.K.* **12 E5** 56 7N 3 21W
Cowell, *Australia* **63 E2** 33 39S 136 56 E
Cowes, *U.K.* **11 G6** 50 45N 1 18W
Cowichan L., *Canada* **84 B2** 48 53N 124 17W
Cowlitz →, *U.S.A.* **84 D4** 46 6N 122 55W
Cowra, *Australia* **63 E4** 33 49S 148 42 E
Coxilha Grande, *Brazil* **95 B5** 28 18S 51 30W
Coxim, *Brazil* **93 G8** 18 30S 54 55W
Cox's Bazar, *Bangla.* **41 J17** 21 26N 91 59 E
Coyote Wells, *U.S.A.* **85 N11** 32 44N 115 58W
Coyuca de Benítez, *Mexico* **87 D4** 17 1N 100 8W
Coyuca de Catalan, *Mexico* **86 D4** 18 18N 100 41W
Cozad, *U.S.A.* **80 E5** 40 52N 99 59W
Cozumel, *Mexico* **87 C7** 20 31N 86 55W
Cozumel, Isla, *Mexico* **87 C7** 20 30N 86 40W
Cracow = Kraków, *Poland* **17 C10** 50 4N 19 57 E
Cracow, *Australia* **63 D5** 25 17S 150 17 E
Cradock, *Australia* **63 E2** 32 6S 138 31 E
Cradock, *S. Africa* **56 E4** 32 8S 25 36 E
Craig, *U.S.A.* **82 F10** 40 31N 107 33W
Craigavon, *U.K.* **13 B5** 54 27N 6 23W
Craigmore, *Zimbabwe* **55 G3** 20 28S 32 50 E
Craik, *Canada* **73 C7** 51 3N 105 49W
Crailsheim, *Germany* **16 D6** 49 8N 10 5 E
Craiova, *Romania* **17 F12** 44 21N 23 48 E
Cramsie, *Australia* **62 C3** 23 20S 144 15 E
Cranberry L., *U.S.A.* **79 B10** 44 11N 74 50W
Cranberry Portage, *Canada* **73 C8** 54 35N 101 23W
Cranbrook, *Australia* **61 F2** 34 18S 117 33 E
Cranbrook, *Canada* **72 D5** 49 30N 115 46W
Crandon, *U.S.A.* **80 C10** 45 34N 88 54W
Crane, *Oreg., U.S.A.* **82 E4** 43 25N 118 35W
Crane, *Tex., U.S.A.* **81 K3** 31 24N 102 21W
Cranston, *U.S.A.* **79 E13** 41 47N 71 26W
Crater L., *U.S.A.* **82 E2** 42 56N 122 6W
Crater Lake National Park, *U.S.A.* **82 E2** 42 55N 122 10W
Crateús, *Brazil* **93 E10** 5 10S 40 39W
Crato, *Brazil* **93 E11** 7 10S 39 25W
Craven, L., *Canada* **70 B4** 54 20N 76 56W
Crawford, *U.S.A.* **80 D3** 42 41N 103 25W
Crawfordsville, *U.S.A.* **76 E2** 40 2N 86 54W
Crawley, *U.K.* **11 F7** 51 7N 0 11W
Crazy Mts., *U.S.A.* **82 C8** 46 12N 110 20W
Crean L., *Canada* **73 C7** 54 5N 106 9W
Crediton, *Canada* **78 C3** 43 17N 81 33W
Cree →, *Canada* **73 B7** 58 57N 105 47W
Cree →, *U.K.* **12 G4** 54 55N 4 25W
Cree L., *Canada* **73 B7** 57 30N 106 30W
Creede, *U.S.A.* **83 H10** 37 51N 106 56W
Creekside, *U.S.A.* **78 F5** 40 40N 79 11W
Creel, *Mexico* **86 B3** 27 45N 107 38W
Creemore, *Canada* **78 B4** 44 19N 80 6W
Creighton, *Canada* **73 C8** 54 45N 101 54W
Creighton, *U.S.A.* **80 D6** 42 28N 97 54W
Crema, *Italy* **18 D8** 45 22N 9 41 E
Cremona, *Italy* **18 D9** 45 7N 10 2 E
Cres, *Croatia* **16 F8** 44 58N 14 25 E
Crescent City, *U.S.A.* **82 F1** 41 45N 124 12W
Crespo, *Argentina* **94 C3** 32 2S 60 19W
Cresson, *U.S.A.* **78 F6** 40 28N 78 36W
Crestline, *Calif., U.S.A.* **85 L9** 34 14N 117 18W
Crestline, *Ohio, U.S.A.* **78 F2** 40 47N 82 44W
Creston, *Canada* **72 D5** 49 10N 116 31W
Creston, *Calif., U.S.A.* **84 K6** 35 32N 120 33W
Creston, *Iowa, U.S.A.* **80 E7** 41 4N 94 22W
Crestview, *Calif., U.S.A.* **84 H8** 37 46N 118 58W
Crestview, *Fla., U.S.A.* **77 K2** 30 46N 86 34W
Crete = Kríti, *Greece* **23 D7** 35 15N 25 0 E
Crete, *U.S.A.* **80 E6** 40 38N 96 58W
Créteil, *France* **18 B5** 48 47N 2 28 E
Creus, C. de, *Spain* **19 A7** 42 20N 3 19 E
Creuse →, *France* **18 C4** 47 0N 0 34 E
Crewe, *U.K.* **10 D5** 53 6N 2 26W
Crewkerne, *U.K.* **11 G5** 50 53N 2 48W
Criciúma, *Brazil* **95 B6** 28 40S 49 23W
Crieff, *U.K.* **12 E5** 56 22N 3 50W
Crimea □, *Ukraine* **25 E5** 45 30N 33 10 E
Crimean Pen. = Krymskyy Pivostriv, *Ukraine* **25 F5** 45 0N 34 0 E
Crişul Alb →, *Romania* **17 E11** 46 42N 21 17 E
Crişul Negru →, *Romania* **17 E11** 46 42N 21 16 E
Crna →, *Macedonia* **21 D9** 41 33N 21 59 E
Crna Gora = Montenegro □, *Yugoslavia* **21 C8** 42 40N 19 20 E
Crna Gora, *Macedonia* **21 C9** 42 10N 21 30 E
Crna Reka = Crna →, *Macedonia* **21 D9** 41 33N 21 59 E
Croagh Patrick, *Ireland* **13 C2** 53 46N 9 40W
Croatia ■, *Europe* **16 F9** 45 20N 16 0 E
Crocker, Banjaran, *Malaysia* **36 C5** 5 40N 116 30 E
Crockett, *U.S.A.* **81 K7** 31 19N 95 27W
Crocodile = Krokodil →, *Mozam.* **57 D5** 25 14S 32 18 E
Crocodile Is., *Australia* **62 A1** 12 3S 134 58 E
Crohy Hd., *Ireland* **13 B3** 54 55N 8 26W
Croix, L. La, *Canada* **70 C1** 48 20N 92 15W
Croker, C., *Australia* **60 B5** 10 58S 132 35 E
Croker, C., *Canada* **78 B4** 44 58N 80 59W
Croker I., *Australia* **60 B5** 11 12S 132 32 E
Cromarty, *U.K.* **12 D4** 57 40N 4 2W
Cromer, *U.K.* **10 E9** 52 56N 1 17 E
Cromwell, *N.Z.* **59 L2** 45 3S 169 14 E
Cromwell, *U.S.A.* **79 E12** 41 36N 72 39W
Crook, *U.K.* **10 C6** 54 43N 1 45W
Crooked →, *Canada* **72 C4** 54 50N 122 54W
Crooked →, *U.S.A.* **82 D3** 44 32N 121 16W
Crooked I., *Bahamas* **89 B5** 22 50N 74 10W
Crooked Island Passage, *Bahamas* **89 B5** 23 0N 74 30W
Crookston, *Minn., U.S.A.* **80 B6** 47 47N 96 37W
Crookston, *Nebr., U.S.A.* **80 D4** 42 56N 100 45W
Crookwell, *Australia* **63 E4** 34 28S 149 24 E
Crosby, *U.K.* **10 D4** 53 30N 3 3W
Crosby, *U.S.A.* **78 E6** 41 45N 78 23W
Crosbyton, *U.S.A.* **81 J4** 33 40N 101 14W
Cross City, *U.S.A.* **77 L4** 29 38N 83 7W
Cross Fell, *U.K.* **10 C5** 54 43N 2 28W
Cross L., *Canada* **73 C9** 54 45N 97 30W
Cross Lake, *Canada* **73 C9** 54 37N 97 47W
Cross Sound, *U.S.A.* **68 C6** 58 0N 135 0W
Crossett, *U.S.A.* **81 J9** 33 8N 91 58W
Crosshaven, *Ireland* **13 E3** 51 47N 8 17W
Crossville, *U.S.A.* **77 G3** 35 57N 85 2W
Croswell, *U.S.A.* **78 C2** 43 16N 82 37W
Croton-on-Hudson, *U.S.A.* **79 E11** 41 12N 73 55W
Crotone, *Italy* **20 E7** 39 5N 17 8 E
Crow →, *Canada* **72 B4** 59 41N 124 20W
Crow Agency, *U.S.A.* **82 D10** 45 36N 107 28W
Crow Hd., *Ireland* **13 E1** 51 35N 10 9W
Crowell, *U.S.A.* **81 J5** 33 59N 99 43W
Crowley, *U.S.A.* **81 K8** 30 13N 92 22W
Crowley, L., *U.S.A.* **84 H8** 37 35N 118 42W
Crown Point, *Ind., U.S.A.* **76 E2** 41 25N 87 22W
Crown Point, *N.Y., U.S.A.* **79 C11** 43 57N 73 26W
Crownpoint, *U.S.A.* **83 J9** 35 41N 108 9W
Crows Landing, *U.S.A.* **84 H5** 37 23N 121 6W
Crows Nest, *Australia* **63 D5** 27 16S 152 4 E
Crowsnest Pass, *Canada* **72 D6** 49 40N 114 40W
Croydon, *Australia* **62 B3** 18 13S 142 14 E
Croydon, *U.K.* **11 F7** 51 22N 0 5W
Crozet Is., *Ind. Oc.* **3 G12** 46 27S 52 0 E
Cruz, C., *Cuba* **88 C4** 19 50N 77 50W
Cruz Alta, *Brazil* **95 B5** 28 45S 53 40W
Cruz del Eje, *Argentina* **94 C3** 30 45S 64 50W
Cruzeiro, *Brazil* **95 A7** 22 33S 45 0W
Cruzeiro do Oeste, *Brazil* **95 A5** 23 46S 53 4W
Cruzeiro do Sul, *Brazil* **92 E4** 7 35S 72 35W
Cry L., *Canada* **72 B3** 58 45N 129 0W
Crystal Bay, *U.S.A.* **84 F7** 39 15N 120 0W
Crystal Brook, *Australia* **63 E2** 33 21S 138 12 E
Crystal City, *U.S.A.* **81 L5** 28 41N 99 50W
Crystal Falls, *U.S.A.* **76 B1** 46 5N 88 20W
Crystal River, *U.S.A.* **77 L4** 28 54N 82 35W
Crystal Springs, *U.S.A.* **81 K9** 31 59N 90 21W
Csongrád, *Hungary* **17 E11** 46 43N 20 12 E
Cu Lao Hon, *Vietnam* **39 G7** 10 54N 108 18 E
Cua Rao, *Vietnam* **38 C5** 19 16N 104 27 E
Cuácua →, *Mozam.* **55 F4** 17 54S 37 0 E
Cuamato, *Angola* **56 B2** 17 2S 15 7 E
Cuamba, *Mozam.* **55 E4** 14 45S 36 22 E
Cuando →, *Angola* **53 H4** 17 30S 23 15 E
Cuando Cubango □, *Angola* **56 B3** 16 25S 20 0 E
Cuangar, *Angola* **56 B2** 17 36S 18 39 E
Cuanza →, *Angola* **52 F2** 9 2S 13 30 E
Cuarto →, *Argentina* **94 C3** 33 25S 63 2W
Cuatrociénegas, *Mexico* **86 B4** 26 59N 102 5W
Cuauhtémoc, *Mexico* **86 B3** 28 25N 106 52W
Cuba, *N. Mex., U.S.A.* **83 J10** 36 1N 107 4W
Cuba, *N.Y., U.S.A.* **78 D6** 42 13N 78 17W
Cuba ■, *W. Indies* **88 B4** 22 0N 79 0W
Cubal, *Angola* **53 G2** 12 26S 14 3 E
Cubango →, *Africa* **56 B3** 18 50S 22 25 E
Cuchumatanes, Sierra de los, *Guatemala* **88 C1** 15 35N 91 25W
Cuckfield, *U.K.* **11 F7** 51 1N 0 8W
Cucuí, *Brazil* **92 C5** 1 12N 66 50W
Cucurpe, *Mexico* **86 A2** 30 20N 110 43W
Cúcuta, *Colombia* **92 B4** 7 54N 72 31W
Cuddalore, *India* **40 P11** 11 46N 79 45 E
Cuddapah, *India* **40 M11** 14 30N 78 47 E
Cuddapan, L., *Australia* **62 D3** 25 45S 141 26 E
Cue, *Australia* **61 E2** 27 25S 117 54 E
Cuenca, *Ecuador* **92 D3** 2 50S 79 9W
Cuenca, *Spain* **19 B4** 40 5N 2 10W
Cuenca, Serranía de, *Spain* **19 C5** 39 55N 1 50W
Cuernavaca, *Mexico* **87 D5** 18 55N 99 15W
Cuero, *U.S.A.* **81 L6** 29 6N 97 17W
Cuevas del Almanzora, *Spain* **19 D5** 37 18N 1 58W
Cuevo, *Bolivia* **92 H6** 20 15S 63 30W
Cuiabá, *Brazil* **93 G7** 15 30S 56 0W
Cuiabá →, *Brazil* **93 G7** 17 5S 56 36W
Cuijk, *Neths.* **15 C5** 51 44N 5 50 E
Cuilco, *Guatemala* **88 C1** 15 24N 91 58W
Cuillin Hills, *U.K.* **12 D2** 57 13N 6 15W
Cuillin Sd., *U.K.* **12 D2** 57 4N 6 20W
Cuito →, *Angola* **56 B3** 18 1S 20 48 E
Cuitzeo, L. de, *Mexico* **86 D4** 19 55N 101 5W
Cukai, *Malaysia* **39 K4** 4 13N 103 25 E
Culbertson, *U.S.A.* **80 A2** 48 9N 104 31W
Culcairn, *Australia* **63 F4** 35 41S 147 3 E
Culgoa →, *Australia* **63 D4** 29 56S 146 20 E
Culiacán, *Mexico* **86 C3** 24 50N 107 23W
Culiacán →, *Mexico* **86 C3** 24 30N 107 42W
Culion, *Phil.* **37 B6** 11 54N 119 58 E
Cullarin Ra., *Australia* **63 E4** 34 30S 149 30 E
Cullen, *U.K.* **12 D6** 57 42N 2 49W
Cullen Pt., *Australia* **62 A3** 11 57S 141 54 E
Cullera, *Spain* **19 C5** 39 9N 0 17W
Cullman, *U.S.A.* **77 H2** 34 11N 86 51W
Culpeper, *U.S.A.* **76 F7** 38 30N 78 0W
Culuene →, *Brazil* **93 F8** 12 56S 52 51W
Culver, Pt., *Australia* **61 F3** 32 54S 124 43 E
Culverden, *N.Z.* **59 K4** 42 47S 172 49 E
Cumaná, *Venezuela* **92 A6** 10 30N 64 5W
Cumberland, *B.C., Canada* **72 D4** 49 40N 125 0W
Cumberland, *Ont., Canada* **79 A9** 45 29N 75 24W
Cumberland, *U.S.A.* **76 F6** 39 39N 78 46W
Cumberland →, *U.S.A.* **77 G2** 36 15N 87 0W
Cumberland, L., *U.S.A.* **77 G3** 36 57N 84 55W
Cumberland I., *U.S.A.* **77 K5** 30 50N 81 25W
Cumberland Is., *Australia* **62 C4** 20 35S 149 10 E
Cumberland L., *Canada* **73 C8** 54 3N 102 18W
Cumberland Pen., *Canada* **69 B13** 67 0N 64 0W
Cumberland Plateau, *U.S.A.* **77 H3** 36 0N 85 0W
Cumberland Sd., *Canada* **69 B13** 65 30N 66 0W
Cumbernauld, *U.K.* **12 F5** 55 57N 3 58W
Cumborah, *Australia* **63 D4** 29 40S 147 45 E
Cumbria □, *U.K.* **10 C5** 54 42N 2 52W
Cumbrian Mts., *U.K.* **10 C5** 54 30N 3 0W
Cumbum, *India* **40 M11** 15 40N 79 10 E
Cuminá →, *Brazil* **93 D7** 1 30S 56 0W
Cummings Mt., *U.S.A.* **85 K8** 35 2N 118 34W
Cummins, *Australia* **63 E2** 34 16S 135 43 E
Cumnock, *Australia* **63 E4** 32 59S 148 46 E
Cumnock, *U.K.* **12 F4** 55 28N 4 17W
Cumpas, *Mexico* **86 B3** 30 0N 109 48W
Cumplida, Pta., *Canary Is.* **22 F2** 28 50N 17 48W
Cunco, *Chile* **96 D2** 38 55S 72 2W
Cuncumén, *Chile* **94 C1** 31 53S 70 38W
Cunderdin, *Australia* **61 F2** 31 37S 117 12 E
Cunene →, *Angola* **56 B1** 17 20S 11 50 E
Cúneo, *Italy* **18 D7** 44 23N 7 32 E
Çüngüş, *Turkey* **44 B3** 38 13N 39 17 E
Cunillera, I. = Sa Conillera, *Spain* **22 C7** 38 59N 1 13 E
Cunnamulla, *Australia* **63 D4** 28 2S 145 38 E
Cupar, *Canada* **73 C8** 50 57N 104 10W
Cupar, *U.K.* **12 E5** 56 19N 3 1W
Cupica, G. de, *Colombia* **92 B3** 6 25N 77 30W
Curaçao, *Neth. Ant.* **89 D6** 12 10N 69 0W
Curanilahue, *Chile* **94 D1** 37 29S 73 28W
Curaray →, *Peru* **92 D4** 2 20S 74 5W
Curepto, *Chile* **94 D1** 35 8S 72 1W
Curiapo, *Venezuela* **92 B6** 8 33N 61 5W
Curicó, *Chile* **94 C1** 34 55S 71 20W
Curitiba, *Brazil* **95 B6** 25 20S 49 10W
Curitibanos, *Brazil* **95 B5** 27 18S 50 36W
Currabubula, *Australia* **63 E5** 31 16S 150 44 E
Currais Novos, *Brazil* **93 E11** 6 13S 36 30W
Curralinho, *Brazil* **93 D9** 1 45S 49 46W
Currant, *U.S.A.* **82 G6** 38 51N 115 32W
Current →, *U.S.A.* **81 G9** 36 15N 90 55W
Currie, *Australia* **62 F3** 39 56S 143 53 E
Currie, *U.S.A.* **82 F6** 40 16N 114 45W
Curtea de Argeş, *Romania* **17 F13** 45 12N 24 42 E
Curtis, *U.S.A.* **80 E4** 40 38N 100 31W
Curtis Group, *Australia* **62 F4** 39 30S 146 37 E
Curtis I., *Australia* **62 C5** 23 35S 151 10 E
Curuápanema →, *Brazil* **93 D7** 2 25S 55 2W
Curuçá, *Brazil* **93 D9** 0 43S 47 50W
Curuguaty, *Paraguay* **95 A4** 24 31S 55 42W
Curup, *Indonesia* **36 E2** 4 26S 102 13 E
Cururupu, *Brazil* **93 D10** 1 50S 44 50W
Curuzú Cuatiá, *Argentina* **94 B4** 29 50S 58 5W
Curvelo, *Brazil* **93 G10** 18 45S 44 27W
Cushing, *U.S.A.* **81 H6** 35 59N 96 46W
Cushing, Mt., *Canada* **72 B3** 57 35N 126 57W
Cusihuiriáchic, *Mexico* **86 B3** 28 10N 106 50W
Custer, *U.S.A.* **80 D3** 43 46N 103 36W
Cut Bank, *U.S.A.* **82 B7** 48 38N 112 20W
Cutchogue, *U.S.A.* **79 E12** 41 1N 72 30W
Cuthbert, *U.S.A.* **77 K3** 31 46N 84 48W
Cutler, *U.S.A.* **84 J7** 36 31N 119 17W
Cuttaburra →, *Australia* **63 D3** 29 43S 144 22 E
Cuttack, *India* **41 J14** 20 25N 85 57 E
Cuvier, C., *Australia* **61 D1** 23 14S 113 22 E
Cuvier I., *N.Z.* **59 G5** 36 27S 175 50 E
Cuxhaven, *Germany* **16 B5** 53 51N 8 41 E
Cuyahoga Falls, *U.S.A.* **78 E3** 41 8N 81 29W
Cuyo, *Phil.* **37 B6** 10 50N 121 5 E
Cuyuni →, *Guyana* **92 B7** 6 23N 58 41W
Cuzco, *Bolivia* **92 H5** 20 0S 66 50W
Cuzco, *Peru* **92 F4** 13 32S 72 0W
Cwmbran, *U.K.* **11 F4** 51 39N 3 2W
Cyangugu, *Rwanda* **54 C2** 2 29S 28 54 E
Cyclades = Kikládhes, *Greece* **21 F11** 37 0N 24 30 E
Cygnet, *Australia* **62 G4** 43 8S 147 1 E
Cynthiana, *U.S.A.* **76 F3** 38 23N 84 18W
Cypress Hills, *Canada* **73 D7** 49 40N 109 30W
Cypress Hills Prov. Park, *Canada* **73 D7** 49 40N 109 30W
Cyprus ■, *Asia* **23 E12** 35 0N 33 0 E
Cyrenaica, *Libya* **51 C10** 27 0N 23 0 E
Czar, *Canada* **73 C6** 52 27N 110 50W
Czech Rep. ■, *Europe* **16 D8** 50 0N 15 0 E
Częstochowa, *Poland* **17 C10** 50 49N 19 7 E

D

Da Hinggan Ling, *China* **33 B7** 48 0N 121 0 E
Da Lat, *Vietnam* **39 G7** 11 56N 108 25 E
Da Nang, *Vietnam* **38 D7** 16 4N 108 13 E
Da Qaidam, *China* **32 C4** 37 50N 95 15 E
Da Yunhe →, *China* **35 G11** 34 25N 120 5 E
Da'an, *China* **35 B13** 45 30N 124 7 E
Daba Shan, *China* **33 C5** 32 0N 109 0 E
Dabbagh, Jabal, *Si. Arabia* **44 E2** 27 52N 35 45 E
Dabhoi, *India* **42 H5** 22 10N 73 20 E
Dabo = Pasirkuning, *Indonesia* **36 E2** 0 30S 104 33 E
Dabola, *Guinea* **50 F3** 10 50N 11 5W
Dabung, *Malaysia* **39 K4** 5 23N 102 1 E
Dacca = Dhaka, *Bangla.* **43 H14** 23 43N 90 26 E
Dacca = Dhaka □, *Bangla.* **43 G14** 24 25N 90 25 E
Dachau, *Germany* **16 D6** 48 15N 11 26 E
Dadanawa, *Guyana* **92 C7** 2 50N 59 30W
Dade City, *U.S.A.* **77 L4** 28 22N 82 11W
Dadhar, *Pakistan* **42 E2** 29 28N 67 39 E
Dadra & Nagar Haveli □, *India* **40 J8** 20 5N 73 0 E
Dadri = Charkhi Dadri, *India* **42 E7** 28 37N 76 17 E
Dadu, *Pakistan* **42 F2** 26 45N 67 45 E
Daet, *Phil.* **37 B6** 14 2N 122 55 E
Dagana, *Senegal* **50 E2** 16 30N 15 35W
Dagestan □, *Russia* **25 F8** 42 30N 47 0 E
Daggett, *U.S.A.* **85 L10** 34 52N 116 52W
Daghestan Republic = Dagestan □, *Russia* **25 F8** 42 30N 47 0 E
Dağliq Qarabağ = Nagorno-Karabakh, *Azerbaijan* **25 F8** 39 55N 46 45 E
Dagö = Hiiumaa, *Estonia* **9 G20** 58 50N 22 45 E
Dagu, *China* **35 E9** 38 59N 117 40 E
Dagupan, *Phil.* **37 A6** 16 3N 120 20 E
Daguragu, *Australia* **60 C5** 17 33S 130 30 E
Dahlak Kebir, *Eritrea* **46 D3** 15 50N 40 10 E
Dahlonega, *U.S.A.* **77 H4** 34 32N 83 59W
Dahod, *India* **42 H6** 22 50N 74 15 E
Dahomey = Benin ■, *Africa* **50 G6** 10 0N 2 0 E
Dahūk, *Iraq* **44 B3** 36 50N 43 1 E
Dai Hao, *Vietnam* **38 C6** 18 1N 106 25 E
Dai-Sen, *Japan* **31 G6** 35 22N 133 32 E
Dai Xian, *China* **34 E7** 39 4N 112 58 E
Daicheng, *China* **34 E9** 38 42N 116 38 E
Daingean, *Ireland* **13 C4** 53 18N 7 17W
Daintree, *Australia* **62 B4** 16 20S 145 20 E
Daiō-Misaki, *Japan* **31 G8** 34 15N 136 45 E
Daisetsu-Zan, *Japan* **30 C11** 43 30N 142 57 E
Dajarra, *Australia* **62 C2** 21 42S 139 30 E
Dak Dam, *Cambodia* **38 F6** 12 20N 107 21 E
Dak Nhe, *Vietnam* **38 E6** 15 28N 107 48 E
Dak Pek, *Vietnam* **38 E6** 15 4N 107 44 E
Dak Song, *Vietnam* **39 F6** 12 19N 107 35 E
Dak Sui, *Vietnam* **38 E6** 14 55N 107 43 E
Dakar, *Senegal* **50 F2** 14 34N 17 29W
Dakhla, *W. Sahara* **50 D2** 23 50N 15 53W
Dakhla, El Wâhât el-, *Egypt* **51 C11** 25 30N 28 50 E
Dakor, *India* **42 H5** 22 45N 73 11 E
Dakota City, *U.S.A.* **80 D6** 42 25N 96 25W
Đakovica, *Yugoslavia* **21 C9** 42 22N 20 26 E
Dalachi, *China* **34 F3** 36 48N 105 0 E
Dalai Nur, *China* **34 C9** 43 20N 116 45 E
Dālakī, *Iran* **45 D6** 29 26N 51 17 E
Dalälven, *Sweden* **9 F17** 60 12N 16 43 E
Dalaman →, *Turkey* **21 F13** 36 41N 28 43 E
Dalandzadgad, *Mongolia* **34 C3** 43 27N 104 30 E
Dalap-Uliga-Darrit, *Marshall Is.* **64 G9** 7 7N 171 24 E
Dalarna, *Sweden* **9 F16** 61 0N 14 0 E
Dālbandīn, *Pakistan* **40 E4** 29 0N 64 23 E
Dalbeattie, *U.K.* **12 G5** 54 56N 3 50W
Dalbeg, *Australia* **62 C4** 20 16S 147 18 E
Dalby, *Australia* **63 D5** 27 10S 151 17 E
Dale City, *U.S.A.* **76 F7** 38 38N 77 18W
Dale Hollow L., *U.S.A.* **77 G3** 36 32N 85 27W
Dalgān, *Iran* **45 E8** 27 31N 59 19 E
Dalhart, *U.S.A.* **81 G3** 36 4N 102 31W
Dalhousie, *Canada* **71 C6** 48 5N 66 26W
Dalhousie, *India* **42 C6** 32 38N 75 58 E
Dali, *Shaanxi, China* **34 G5** 34 48N 109 58 E
Dali, *Yunnan, China* **32 D5** 25 40N 100 10 E
Dalian, *China* **35 E11** 38 50N 121 40 E
Daliang Shan, *China* **32 D5** 28 0N 102 45 E
Daling He →, *China* **35 D11** 40 55N 121 40 E
Dāliyat el Karmel, *Israel* **47 C4** 32 43N 35 2 E
Dalkeith, *U.K.* **12 F5** 55 54N 3 4W
Dallas, *Oreg., U.S.A.* **82 D2** 44 55N 123 19W
Dallas, *Tex., U.S.A.* **81 J6** 32 47N 96 49W
Dalmā, *U.A.E.* **45 E7** 24 30N 52 20 E
Dalmacija, *Croatia* **20 C7** 43 20N 17 0 E
Dalmas, L., *Canada* **71 B5** 53 30N 71 50W
Dalmatia = Dalmacija, *Croatia* **20 C7** 43 20N 17 0 E
Dalmau, *India* **43 F9** 26 4N 81 2 E
Dalmellington, *U.K.* **12 F4** 55 19N 4 23W
Dalnegorsk, *Russia* **27 E14** 44 32N 135 33 E
Dalnerechensk, *Russia* **27 E14** 45 55N 133 40 E
Daloa, *Ivory C.* **50 G4** 7 0N 6 30W
Dalry, *U.K.* **12 F4** 55 42N 4 43W
Dalrymple, L., *Australia* **62 C4** 20 40S 147 0 E
Dalsland, *Sweden* **9 G14** 58 50N 12 15 E
Daltenganj, *India* **43 H11** 24 0N 84 4 E
Dalton, *Ga., U.S.A.* **77 H3** 34 46N 84 58W

Despeñaperros, Paso

Despeñaperros, Paso, *Spain* **19 C4** 38 24N 3 30W
Dessau, *Germany* **16 C7** 51 51N 12 14 E
Dessye = Dese, *Ethiopia* **46 E2** 11 5N 39 40 E
D'Estrees B., *Australia* **63 F2** 35 55S 137 45 E
Desuri, *India* **42 G5** 25 18N 73 35 E
Det Udom, *Thailand* **38 E5** 14 54N 105 5 E
Dete, *Zimbabwe* **55 F2** 18 38S 26 50 E
Detmold, *Germany* **16 C5** 51 56N 8 52 E
Detour, Pt., *U.S.A.* **76 C2** 45 40N 86 40W
Detroit, *U.S.A.* **78 D1** 42 20N 83 3W
Detroit Lakes, *U.S.A.* **80 B7** 46 49N 95 51W
Deurne, *Neths.* **15 C5** 51 27N 5 49 E
Deutsche Bucht, *Germany* **16 A5** 54 15N 8 0 E
Deva, *Romania* **17 F12** 45 53N 22 55 E
Devakottai, *India* **40 Q11** 9 55N 78 45 E
Devaprayag, *India* **43 D8** 30 13N 78 35 E
Deventer, *Neths.* **15 B6** 52 15N 6 10 E
Deveron →, *U.K.* **12 D6** 57 41N 2 32W
Devgadh Bariya, *India* **42 H5** 22 40N 73 55 E
Devikot, *India* **42 F4** 26 42N 71 12 E
Devils Den, *U.S.A.* **84 K7** 35 46N 119 58W
Devils Lake, *U.S.A.* **80 A5** 48 7N 98 52W
Devils Paw, *Canada* **72 B2** 58 47N 134 0W
Devils Tower Junction, *U.S.A.* **80 C2** 44 31N 104 57W
Devine, *U.S.A.* **81 L5** 29 8N 98 54W
Devizes, *U.K.* **11 F6** 51 22N 1 58W
Devli, *India* **42 G6** 25 50N 75 20 E
Devon, *Canada* **72 C6** 53 24N 113 44W
Devon □, *U.K.* **11 G4** 50 50N 3 40W
Devon I., *Canada* **4 B3** 75 10N 85 0W
Devonport, *Australia* **62 G4** 41 10S 146 22 E
Devonport, *N.Z.* **59 G5** 36 49S 174 49 E
Dewas, *India* **42 H7** 22 59N 76 3 E
Dewetsdorp, *S. Africa* **56 D4** 29 33S 26 39 E
Dexter, *Maine, U.S.A.* **77 C11** 45 1N 69 18W
Dexter, *Mo., U.S.A.* **81 G10** 36 48N 89 57W
Dexter, *N. Mex., U.S.A.* **81 J2** 33 12N 104 22W
Dey-Dey, L., *Australia* **61 E5** 29 12S 131 4 E
Deyhūk, *Iran* **45 C8** 33 15N 57 30 E
Deyyer, *Iran* **45 E6** 27 55N 51 55 E
Dezadeash L., *Canada* **72 A1** 60 28N 136 58W
Dezfūl, *Iran* **45 C6** 32 20N 48 30 E
Dezhneva, Mys, *Russia* **27 C19** 66 5N 169 40W
Dezhou, *China* **34 F9** 37 26N 116 18 E
Dhadhar →, *India* **43 G11** 24 56N 85 24 E
Dháfni, *Greece* **23 D7** 35 13N 25 3 E
Dhahiriya = Aẓ Ẓāhirīyah, *West Bank* **47 D3** 31 25N 34 58 E
Dhahran = Aẓ Ẓahrān, *Si. Arabia* **45 E6** 26 10N 50 7 E
Dhak, *Pakistan* **42 C5** 32 25N 72 33 E
Dhaka, *Bangla.* **43 H14** 23 43N 90 26 E
Dhaka □, *Bangla.* **43 G14** 24 25N 90 25 E
Dhali, *Cyprus* **23 D12** 35 1N 33 25 E
Dhampur, *India* **43 E8** 29 19N 78 33 E
Dhamtari, *India* **41 J12** 20 42N 81 35 E
Dhanbad, *India* **43 H12** 23 50N 86 30 E
Dhangarhi, *Nepal* **41 E12** 28 55N 80 40 E
Dhankuta, *Nepal* **43 F12** 26 55N 87 40 E
Dhar, *India* **42 H6** 22 35N 75 26 E
Dharampur, *India* **42 H6** 22 13N 75 18 E
Dharamsala = Dharmsala, *India* **42 C7** 32 16N 76 23 E
Dhariwal, *India* **42 D6** 31 57N 75 19 E
Dharla →, *Bangla.* **43 G13** 25 46N 89 42 E
Dharmapuri, *India* **40 N11** 12 10N 78 10 E
Dharmjaygarh, *India* **43 H10** 22 28N 83 13 E
Dharmsala, *India* **42 C7** 32 16N 76 23 E
Dharni, *India* **42 J7** 21 33N 76 53 E
Dhasan →, *India* **43 G8** 25 48N 79 24 E
Dhaulagiri, *Nepal* **43 E10** 28 39N 83 28 E
Dhebar, L., *India* **42 G6** 24 10N 74 0 E
Dheftera, *Cyprus* **23 D12** 35 5N 33 16 E
Dhenkanal, *India* **41 J14** 20 45N 85 35 E
Dherinia, *Cyprus* **23 D12** 35 3N 33 57 E
Dhiarrizos →, *Cyprus* **23 E11** 34 41N 32 34 E
Dhībān, *Jordan* **47 D4** 31 30N 35 46 E
Dhíkti Óros, *Greece* **23 D7** 35 8N 25 30 E
Dhilwan, *India* **42 D6** 31 31N 75 21 E
Dhimarkhera, *India* **43 H9** 23 28N 80 22 E
Dhírfis = Dhírfis Óros, *Greece* **21 E10** 38 40N 23 54 E
Dhírfis Óros, *Greece* **21 E10** 38 40N 23 54 E
Dhodhekánisos, *Greece* **21 F12** 36 35N 27 0 E
Dholka, *India* **42 H5** 22 44N 72 29 E
Dhoraji, *India* **42 J4** 21 45N 70 37 E
Dhráhstis, Ákra, *Greece* **23 A3** 39 48N 19 40 E
Dhrangadhra, *India* **42 H4** 22 59N 71 31 E
Dhrápanon, Ákra, *Greece* **23 D6** 35 28N 24 14 E
Dhrol, *India* **42 H4** 22 33N 70 25 E
Dhuburi, *India* **41 F16** 26 2N 89 59 E
Dhule, *India* **40 J9** 20 58N 74 50 E
Di Linh, *Vietnam* **39 G7** 11 35N 108 4 E
Di Linh, Cao Nguyen, *Vietnam* **39 G7** 11 30N 108 0 E
Día, *Greece* **23 D7** 35 28N 25 14 E
Diablo, Mt., *U.S.A.* **84 H5** 37 53N 121 56W
Diablo Range, *U.S.A.* **84 J5** 37 20N 121 25W
Diafarabé, *Mali* **50 F5** 14 9N 4 57W
Diamante, *Argentina* **94 C3** 32 5S 60 40W
Diamante →, *Argentina* **94 C2** 34 30S 66 46W
Diamantina, *Brazil* **93 G10** 18 17S 43 40W
Diamantina →, *Australia* **63 D2** 26 45S 139 10 E
Diamantino, *Brazil* **93 F7** 14 30S 56 30W
Diamond Bar, *U.S.A.* **85 L9** 34 1N 117 48W
Diamond Harbour, *India* **43 H13** 22 11N 88 14 E
Diamond Is., *Australia* **62 B5** 17 25S 151 5 E
Diamond Mts., *U.S.A.* **82 G6** 39 50N 115 30W
Diamond Springs, *U.S.A.* **84 G6** 38 42N 120 49W
Dībā, *Oman* **45 E8** 25 45N 56 16 E
Dibai, *India* **42 E8** 28 13N 78 15 E
Dibaya-Lubue, *Dem. Rep. of the Congo* **52 E3** 4 12S 19 54 E
Dibete, *Botswana* **56 C4** 23 45S 26 32 E
Dibrugarh, *India* **41 F19** 27 29N 94 55 E
Dickens, *U.S.A.* **81 J4** 33 37N 100 50W
Dickinson, *U.S.A.* **80 B3** 46 53N 102 47W
Dickson = Dikson, *Russia* **26 B9** 73 40N 80 5 E
Dickson, *U.S.A.* **77 G2** 36 5N 87 23W
Dickson City, *U.S.A.* **79 E9** 41 29N 75 40W
Didiéni, *Mali* **50 F4** 13 53N 8 6W
Didsbury, *Canada* **72 C6** 51 35N 114 10W
Didwana, *India* **42 F6** 27 23N 74 36 E
Diefenbaker, L., *Canada* **73 C7** 51 0N 106 55W
Diego de Almagro, *Chile* **94 B1** 26 22S 70 3W
Diego Garcia, *Ind. Oc.* **3 E13** 7 50S 72 50 E
Diekirch, *Lux.* **15 E6** 49 52N 6 10 E
Dien Ban, *Vietnam* **38 E7** 15 53N 108 16 E
Dien Khanh, *Vietnam* **39 F7** 12 15N 109 6 E
Dieppe, *France* **18 B4** 49 54N 1 4 E
Dierks, *U.S.A.* **81 H8** 34 7N 94 1W
Diest, *Belgium* **15 D5** 50 58N 5 4 E
Dif, *Somali Rep.* **46 G3** 0 59N 0 56 E
Differdange, *Lux.* **15 E5** 49 31N 5 54 E
Dig, *India* **42 F7** 27 28N 77 20 E
Digba, *Dem. Rep. of the Congo* **54 B2** 4 25N 25 48 E
Digby, *Canada* **71 D6** 44 38N 65 50W
Diggi, *India* **42 F6** 26 22N 75 26 E
Dighinala, *Bangla.* **41 H18** 23 15N 92 5 E
Dighton, *U.S.A.* **80 F4** 38 29N 100 28W
Digne-les-Bains, *France* **18 D7** 44 5N 6 12 E
Digos, *Phil.* **37 C7** 6 45N 125 20 E
Digranes, *Iceland* **8 C6** 66 4N 14 44W
Digul →, *Indonesia* **37 F9** 7 7S 138 42 E
Dihang →, *India* **41 F19** 27 48N 95 30 E
Dijlah, Nahr →, *Asia* **44 D5** 31 0N 47 25 E
Dijon, *France* **18 C6** 47 20N 5 3 E
Dikkil, *Djibouti* **46 E3** 11 8N 42 20 E
Dikomu di Kai, *Botswana* **56 C3** 24 58S 24 36 E
Diksmuide, *Belgium* **15 C2** 51 2N 2 52 E
Dikson, *Russia* **26 B9** 73 40N 80 5 E
Dila, *Ethiopia* **46 F2** 6 21N 38 22 E
Dili, *Indonesia* **37 F7** 8 39S 125 34 E
Dilley, *U.S.A.* **81 L5** 28 40N 99 10W
Dillingham, *U.S.A.* **68 C4** 59 3N 158 28W
Dillon, *Canada* **73 B7** 55 56N 108 35W
Dillon, *Mont., U.S.A.* **82 D7** 45 13N 112 38W
Dillon, *S.C., U.S.A.* **77 H6** 34 25N 79 22W
Dillon →, *Canada* **73 B7** 55 56N 108 56W
Dillsburg, *U.S.A.* **78 F7** 40 7N 77 2W
Dilolo, *Dem. Rep. of the Congo* **52 G4** 10 28S 22 18 E
Dimas, *Mexico* **86 C3** 23 43N 106 47W
Dimashq, *Syria* **47 B5** 33 30N 36 18 E
Dimashq □, *Syria* **47 B5** 33 30N 36 30 E
Dimbaza, *S. Africa* **57 E4** 32 50S 27 14 E
Dimboola, *Australia* **63 F3** 36 28S 142 7 E
Dîmboviţa = Dâmboviţa →, *Romania* **17 F14** 44 12N 26 26 E
Dimbulah, *Australia* **62 B4** 17 8S 145 4 E
Dimitrovgrad, *Bulgaria* **21 C11** 42 5N 25 35 E
Dimitrovgrad, *Russia* **24 D8** 54 14N 49 39 E
Dimitrovo = Pernik, *Bulgaria* **21 C10** 42 35N 23 2 E
Dimmitt, *U.S.A.* **81 H3** 34 33N 102 19W
Dimona, *Israel* **47 D4** 31 2N 35 1 E
Dinagat, *Phil.* **37 B7** 10 10N 125 40 E
Dinajpur, *Bangla.* **41 G16** 25 33N 88 43 E
Dinan, *France* **18 B2** 48 28N 2 2W
Dīnān Āb, *Iran* **45 C8** 32 4N 56 49 E
Dinant, *Belgium* **15 D4** 50 16N 4 55 E
Dinapur, *India* **43 G11** 25 38N 85 5 E
Dīnār, Kūh-e, *Iran* **45 D6** 30 42N 51 46 E
Dinara Planina, *Croatia* **20 C7** 44 0N 16 30 E
Dinard, *France* **18 B2** 48 38N 2 6W
Dinaric Alps = Dinara Planina, *Croatia* **20 C7** 44 0N 16 30 E
Dindigul, *India* **40 P11** 10 25N 78 0 E
Dindori, *India* **43 H9** 22 57N 81 5 E
Ding Xian = Dingzhou, *China* **34 E8** 38 30N 114 59 E
Dinga, *Pakistan* **42 G2** 25 26N 67 10 E
Dingbian, *China* **34 F4** 37 35N 107 32 E
Dingle, *Ireland* **13 D1** 52 9N 10 17W
Dingle B., *Ireland* **13 D1** 52 3N 10 20W
Dingmans Ferry, *U.S.A.* **79 E10** 41 13N 74 55W
Dingo, *Australia* **62 C4** 23 38S 149 19 E
Dingtao, *China* **34 G8** 35 5N 115 35 E
Dingwall, *U.K.* **12 D4** 57 36N 4 26W
Dingxi, *China* **34 G3** 35 30N 104 33 E
Dingxiang, *China* **34 E7** 38 30N 112 58 E
Dingzhou, *China* **34 E8** 38 30N 114 59 E
Dinh, Mui, *Vietnam* **39 G7** 11 22N 109 1 E
Dinokwe, *Botswana* **56 C4** 23 29S 26 37 E
Dinorwic, *Canada* **73 D10** 49 41N 92 30W
Dinosaur National Monument, *U.S.A.* **82 F9** 40 30N 108 45W
Dinosaur Prov. Park, *Canada* **72 C6** 50 47N 111 30W
Dinuba, *U.S.A.* **84 J7** 36 32N 119 23W
Dipalpur, *Pakistan* **42 D5** 30 40N 73 39 E
Diplo, *Pakistan* **42 G3** 24 35N 69 35 E
Dipolog, *Phil.* **37 C6** 8 36N 123 20 E
Dir, *Pakistan* **40 B7** 35 8N 71 59 E
Dire Dawa, *Ethiopia* **46 F3** 9 35N 41 45 E
Diriamba, *Nic.* **88 D2** 11 51N 86 19W
Dirk Hartog I., *Australia* **61 E1** 25 50S 113 5 E
Dirranbandi, *Australia* **63 D4** 28 33S 148 17 E
Disa, *India* **42 G5** 24 18N 72 10 E
Disappointment, C., *U.S.A.* **82 C2** 46 18N 124 5W
Disappointment, L., *Australia* **60 D3** 23 20S 122 40 E
Disaster B., *Australia* **63 F4** 37 15S 149 58 E
Discovery B., *Australia* **63 F3** 38 10S 140 40 E
Disko, *Greenland* **4 C5** 69 45N 53 30W
Disko Bugt, *Greenland* **4 C5** 69 10N 52 0W
Diss, *U.K.* **11 E9** 52 23N 1 7 E
Disteghil Sar, *Pakistan* **43 A6** 36 20N 75 12 E
Distrito Federal □, *Brazil* **93 G9** 15 45S 47 45W
Distrito Federal □, *Mexico* **87 D5** 19 15N 99 10W
Diu, *India* **42 J4** 20 45N 70 58 E
Dīvāndarreh, *Iran* **44 C5** 35 55N 47 2 E
Divide, *U.S.A.* **82 D7** 45 45N 112 45W
Dividing Ra., *Australia* **61 E2** 27 45S 116 0 E
Divinópolis, *Brazil* **93 H10** 20 10S 44 54W
Divnoye, *Russia* **25 E7** 45 55N 43 21 E
Divo, *Ivory C.* **50 G4** 5 48N 5 15W
Dīwāl Kol, *Afghan.* **42 B2** 34 23N 67 52 E
Dixie Mt., *U.S.A.* **84 F6** 39 55N 120 16W
Dixon, *Calif., U.S.A.* **84 G5** 38 27N 121 49W
Dixon, *Ill., U.S.A.* **80 E10** 41 50N 89 29W
Dixon Entrance, *U.S.A.* **68 C6** 54 30N 132 0W
Dixville, *Canada* **79 A13** 45 4N 71 46W
Diyālā →, *Iraq* **44 C5** 33 14N 44 31 E
Diyarbakır, *Turkey* **25 G7** 37 55N 40 18 E
Diyodar, *India* **42 G4** 24 8N 71 50 E
Djakarta = Jakarta, *Indonesia* **37 G12** 6 9S 106 49 E
Djamba, *Angola* **56 B1** 16 45S 13 58 E
Djambala, *Congo* **52 E2** 2 32S 14 30 E
Djanet, *Algeria* **50 D7** 24 35N 9 32 E
Djawa = Jawa, *Indonesia* **37 G14** 7 0S 110 0 E
Djelfa, *Algeria* **50 B6** 34 40N 3 15 E
Djema, *C.A.R.* **54 A2** 6 3N 25 15 E
Djerba, I. de, *Tunisia* **51 B8** 33 50N 10 48 E
Djerid, Chott, *Tunisia* **50 B7** 33 42N 8 30 E
Djibouti, *Djibouti* **46 E3** 11 30N 43 5 E
Djibouti ■, *Africa* **46 E3** 12 0N 43 0 E
Djolu, *Dem. Rep. of the Congo* **52 D4** 0 35N 22 5 E
Djoum, *Cameroon* **52 D2** 2 41N 12 35 E
Djourab, Erg du, *Chad* **51 E9** 16 40N 18 50 E
Djugu, *Dem. Rep. of the Congo* **54 B3** 1 55N 30 35 E
Djúpivogur, *Iceland* **8 D6** 64 39N 14 17W
Dmitriya Lapteva, Proliv, *Russia* **27 B15** 73 0N 140 0 E
Dnepr = Dnipro →, *Ukraine* **25 E5** 46 30N 32 18 E
Dneprodzerzhinsk = Dniprodzerzhynsk, *Ukraine* **25 E5** 48 32N 34 37 E
Dnepropetrovsk = Dnipropetrovsk, *Ukraine* **25 E6** 48 30N 35 0 E
Dnestr = Dnister →, *Europe* **17 E16** 46 18N 30 17 E
Dnestrovski = Belgorod, *Russia* **25 D6** 50 35N 36 35 E
Dnieper = Dnipro →, *Ukraine* **25 E5** 46 30N 32 18 E
Dniester = Dnister →, *Europe* **17 E16** 46 18N 30 17 E
Dnipro →, *Ukraine* **25 E5** 46 30N 32 18 E
Dniprodzerzhynsk, *Ukraine* **25 E5** 48 32N 34 37 E
Dnipropetrovsk, *Ukraine* **25 E6** 48 30N 35 0 E
Dnister →, *Europe* **17 E16** 46 18N 30 17 E
Dnistrovskyy Lyman, *Ukraine* **17 E16** 46 15N 30 17 E
Dno, *Russia* **24 C4** 57 50N 29 58 E
Dnyapro = Dnipro →, *Ukraine* **25 E5** 46 30N 32 18 E
Doaktown, *Canada* **71 C6** 46 33N 66 8W
Doba, *Chad* **51 G9** 8 40N 16 50 E
Dobandi, *Pakistan* **42 D2** 31 13N 66 50 E
Dobbyn, *Australia* **62 B3** 19 44S 140 2 E
Dobele, *Latvia* **9 H20** 56 37N 23 16 E
Doberai, Jazirah, *Indonesia* **37 E8** 1 25S 133 0 E
Doblas, *Argentina* **94 D3** 37 5S 64 0W
Dobo, *Indonesia* **37 F8** 5 45S 134 15 E
Doboj, *Bos.-H.* **21 B8** 44 46N 18 4 E
Dobreta-Turnu Severin, *Romania* **17 F12** 44 39N 22 41 E
Dobrich, *Bulgaria* **21 C12** 43 37N 27 49 E
Dobruja, *Europe* **17 F15** 44 30N 28 15 E
Dobrush, *Belarus* **17 B16** 52 25N 31 22 E
Doc, Mui, *Vietnam* **38 D6** 17 58N 106 30 E
Docker River, *Australia* **61 D4** 24 52S 129 5 E
Doctor Arroyo, *Mexico* **86 C4** 23 40N 100 11W
Doda, *India* **43 C6** 33 10N 75 34 E
Doda, L., *Canada* **70 C4** 49 25N 75 13W
Dodecanese = Dhodhekánisos, *Greece* **21 F12** 36 35N 27 0 E
Dodge City, *U.S.A.* **81 G5** 37 45N 100 1W
Dodge L., *Canada* **73 B7** 59 50N 105 36W
Dodgeville, *U.S.A.* **80 D9** 42 58N 90 8W
Dodoma, *Tanzania* **54 D4** 6 8S 35 45 E
Dodoma □, *Tanzania* **54 D4** 6 0S 36 0 E
Dodsland, *Canada* **73 C7** 51 50N 108 45W
Dodson, *U.S.A.* **82 B9** 48 24N 108 15W
Doesburg, *Neths.* **15 B6** 52 1N 6 9 E
Doetinchem, *Neths.* **15 C6** 51 59N 6 18 E
Dog Creek, *Canada* **72 C4** 51 35N 122 14W
Dog L., *Man., Canada* **73 C9** 51 2N 98 31W
Dog L., *Ont., Canada* **70 C2** 48 48N 89 30W
Dogi, *Afghan.* **40 C3** 32 20N 62 50 E
Dogran, *Pakistan* **42 D5** 31 48N 73 35 E
Doğubayazıt, *Turkey* **44 B5** 39 31N 44 5 E
Doha = Ad Dawḩah, *Qatar* **45 E6** 25 15N 51 35 E
Dohazari, *Bangla.* **41 H18** 22 10N 92 5 E
Dohrighat, *India* **43 F10** 26 16N 83 31 E
Doi, *Indonesia* **37 D7** 2 14N 127 49 E
Doi Luang, *Thailand* **38 C3** 18 30N 101 0 E
Doi Saket, *Thailand* **38 C2** 18 52N 99 9 E
Dois Irmãos, Sa., *Brazil* **93 E10** 9 0S 42 30W
Dokkum, *Neths.* **15 A5** 53 20N 5 59 E
Dokri, *Pakistan* **42 F3** 27 25N 68 7 E
Dolak, Pulau, *Indonesia* **37 F9** 8 0S 138 30 E
Dolbeau, *Canada* **71 C5** 48 53N 72 18W
Dole, *France* **18 C6** 47 7N 5 31 E
Dolgellau, *U.K.* **10 E4** 52 45N 3 53W
Dolgelley = Dolgellau, *U.K.* **10 E4** 52 45N 3 53W
Dollard, *Neths.* **15 A7** 53 20N 7 10 E
Dolo, *Ethiopia* **46 G3** 4 11N 42 3 E
Dolomites = Dolomiti, *Italy* **20 A4** 46 23N 11 51 E
Dolomiti, *Italy* **20 A4** 46 23N 11 51 E
Dolores, *Argentina* **94 D4** 36 20S 57 40W
Dolores, *Uruguay* **94 C4** 33 34S 58 15W
Dolores, *U.S.A.* **83 H9** 37 28N 108 30W
Dolores →, *U.S.A.* **83 G9** 38 49N 109 17W
Dolphin, C., *Falk. Is.* **96 G5** 51 10S 59 0W
Dolphin and Union Str., *Canada* **68 B8** 69 5N 114 45W
Dom Pedrito, *Brazil* **95 C5** 31 0S 54 40W
Domariaganj →, *India* **43 F10** 26 17N 83 44 E
Domasi, *Malawi* **55 F4** 15 15S 35 22 E
Dombarovskiy, *Russia* **26 D6** 50 46N 59 32 E
Dombås, *Norway* **9 E13** 62 4N 9 8 E
Domel I. = Letsôk-aw Kyun, *Burma* **39 G2** 11 30N 98 25 E
Domeyko, *Chile* **94 B1** 29 0S 71 0W
Domeyko, Cordillera, *Chile* **94 A2** 24 30S 69 0W
Dominador, *Chile* **94 A2** 24 21S 69 20W
Dominica ■, *W. Indies* **89 C7** 15 20N 61 20W
Dominica Passage, *W. Indies* **89 C7** 15 10N 61 20W
Dominican Rep. ■, *W. Indies* **89 C5** 19 0N 70 30W
Domodóssola, *Italy* **18 C8** 46 7N 8 17 E
Domville, Mt., *Australia* **63 D5** 28 1S 151 15 E
Don →, *Russia* **25 E6** 47 4N 39 18 E
Don →, *Aberds., U.K.* **12 D6** 57 11N 2 5W
Don →, *S. Yorks., U.K.* **10 D7** 53 41N 0 52W
Don, C., *Australia* **60 B5** 11 18S 131 46 E
Don Benito, *Spain* **19 C3** 38 53N 5 51W
Dona Ana = Nhamaabué, *Mozam.* **55 F4** 17 25S 35 5 E
Donaghadee, *U.K.* **13 B6** 54 39N 5 33W
Donald, *Australia* **63 F3** 36 23S 143 0 E
Donaldsonville, *U.S.A.* **81 K9** 30 6N 90 59W
Donalsonville, *U.S.A.* **77 K3** 31 3N 84 53W
Donau = Dunărea →, *Europe* **17 F15** 45 20N 29 40 E
Donau →, *Austria* **15 D3** 48 10N 17 0 E
Donauwörth, *Germany* **16 D6** 48 43N 10 47 E
Doncaster, *U.K.* **10 D6** 53 32N 1 6W
Dondo, *Mozam.* **55 F3** 19 33S 34 46 E
Dondo, Teluk, *Indonesia* **37 D6** 0 50N 120 30 E
Dondra Head, *Sri Lanka* **40 S12** 5 55N 80 40 E
Donegal, *Ireland* **13 B3** 54 39N 8 5W
Donegal □, *Ireland* **13 B4** 54 53N 8 0W
Donegal B., *Ireland* **13 B3** 54 31N 8 49W
Donets →, *Russia* **25 E7** 47 33N 40 55 E
Donetsk, *Ukraine* **25 E6** 48 0N 37 45 E
Dong Ba Thin, *Vietnam* **39 F7** 12 8N 109 13 E
Dong Dang, *Vietnam* **38 B6** 21 54N 106 42 E
Dong Giam, *Vietnam* **38 C5** 19 25N 105 31 E
Dong Ha, *Vietnam* **38 D6** 16 55N 107 8 E
Dong Hene, *Laos* **38 D5** 16 40N 105 18 E
Dong Hoi, *Vietnam* **38 D6** 17 29N 106 36 E
Dong Khe, *Vietnam* **38 A6** 22 26N 106 27 E
Dong Ujimqin Qi, *China* **34 B9** 45 32N 116 55 E
Dong Van, *Vietnam* **38 A5** 23 16N 105 22 E
Dong Xoai, *Vietnam* **39 G6** 11 32N 106 55 E
Dongara, *Australia* **61 E1** 29 14S 114 57 E
Dongbei, *China* **35 D13** 45 0N 125 0 E
Dongchuan, *China* **32 D5** 26 8N 103 1 E
Dongfang, *China* **38 C7** 18 50N 108 33 E
Dongfeng, *China* **35 C13** 42 40N 125 34 E
Donggala, *Indonesia* **37 E5** 0 30S 119 40 E
Donggou, *China* **35 E13** 39 52N 124 10 E
Dongguang, *China* **34 F9** 37 50N 116 30 E
Dongjingcheng, *China* **35 B15** 44 5N 129 10 E
Dongning, *China* **35 B16** 44 2N 131 5 E
Dongola, *Sudan* **51 E12** 19 9N 30 22 E
Dongping, *China* **34 G9** 35 55N 116 20 E
Dongsheng, *China* **34 E6** 39 50N 110 0 E
Dongtai, *China* **35 H11** 32 51N 120 21 E
Dongting Hu, *China* **33 D6** 29 18N 112 45 E
Donington, C., *Australia* **63 E2** 34 45S 136 0 E
Doniphan, *U.S.A.* **81 G9** 36 37N 90 50W
Dønna, *Norway* **8 C15** 66 6N 12 30 E
Donna, *U.S.A.* **81 M5** 26 9N 98 4W
Donnaconna, *Canada* **71 C5** 46 41N 71 41W
Donnelly's Crossing, *N.Z.* **59 F4** 35 42S 173 38 E
Donnybrook, *Australia* **61 F2** 33 34S 115 48 E
Donnybrook, *S. Africa* **57 D4** 29 59S 29 48 E
Donora, *U.S.A.* **78 F5** 40 11N 79 52W
Donostia = Donostia-San Sebastián, *Spain* **19 A5** 43 17N 1 58W
Donostia-San Sebastián, *Spain* **19 A5** 43 17N 1 58W
Doon →, *U.K.* **12 F4** 55 27N 4 39W
Dora, L., *Australia* **60 D3** 22 0S 123 0 E
Dora Báltea →, *Italy* **18 D8** 45 11N 8 3 E
Doran L., *Canada* **73 A7** 61 13N 108 6W
Dorchester, *U.K.* **11 G5** 50 42N 2 27W
Dorchester, C., *Canada* **69 B12** 65 27N 77 27W
Dordogne →, *France* **18 D3** 45 2N 0 36W
Dordrecht, *Neths.* **15 C4** 51 48N 4 39 E
Dordrecht, *S. Africa* **56 E4** 31 20S 27 3 E
Doré L., *Canada* **73 C7** 54 46N 107 17W
Doré Lake, *Canada* **73 C7** 54 38N 107 36W
Dori, *Burkina Faso* **50 F5** 14 3N 0 2W
Doring →, *S. Africa* **56 E2** 31 54S 18 39 E
Doringbos, *S. Africa* **56 E2** 31 59S 19 16 E
Dorion, *Canada* **79 A10** 45 23N 74 3W
Dornbirn, *Austria* **16 E5** 47 25N 9 45 E
Dornie, *U.K.* **12 D3** 57 17N 5 31W
Dornoch, *U.K.* **12 D4** 57 53N 4 2W
Dornoch Firth, *U.K.* **12 D4** 57 51N 4 4W
Dornogovĭ □, *Mongolia* **34 C6** 44 0N 110 0 E
Dorohoi, *Romania* **17 E14** 47 56N 26 23 E
Döröö Nuur, *Mongolia* **32 B4** 48 0N 93 0 E
Dorr, *Iran* **45 C6** 33 17N 50 38 E
Dorre I., *Australia* **61 E1** 25 13S 113 12 E
Dorrigo, *Australia* **63 E5** 30 20S 152 44 E
Dorris, *U.S.A.* **82 F3** 41 58N 121 55W
Dorset, *Canada* **78 A6** 45 14N 78 54W
Dorset, *U.S.A.* **78 E4** 41 40N 80 40W
Dorset □, *U.K.* **11 G5** 50 45N 2 26W
Dortmund, *Germany* **16 C4** 51 30N 7 28 E
Doruma, *Dem. Rep. of the Congo* **54 B2** 4 42N 27 33 E
Dorūneh, *Iran* **45 C8** 35 10N 57 18 E
Dos Bahías, C., *Argentina* **96 E3** 44 58S 65 32W
Dos Hermanas, *Spain* **19 D3** 37 16N 5 55W
Dos Palos, *U.S.A.* **84 J6** 36 59N 120 37W
Dosso, *Niger* **50 F6** 13 0N 3 13 E
Dothan, *U.S.A.* **77 K3** 31 13N 85 24W
Doty, *U.S.A.* **84 D3** 46 38N 123 17W
Douai, *France* **18 A5** 50 21N 3 4 E
Douala, *Cameroon* **52 D1** 4 0N 9 45 E
Douarnenez, *France* **18 B1** 48 6N 4 21W
Double Island Pt., *Australia* **63 D5** 25 56S 153 11 E
Double Mountain Fork →, *U.S.A.* **81 J4** 33 16N 100 0W
Doubs →, *France* **18 C6** 46 53N 5 1 E
Doubtful Sd., *N.Z.* **59 L1** 45 20S 166 49 E
Doubtless B., *N.Z.* **59 F4** 34 55S 173 26 E
Douglas, *S. Africa* **56 D3** 29 4S 23 46 E
Douglas, *U.K.* **10 C3** 54 10N 4 28W
Douglas, *Ariz., U.S.A.* **83 L9** 31 21N 109 33W
Douglas, *Ga., U.S.A.* **77 K4** 31 31N 82 51W
Douglas, *Wyo., U.S.A.* **80 D2** 42 45N 105 24W
Douglas Chan., *Canada* **72 C3** 53 40N 129 20W
Douglas Pt., *Canada* **78 B3** 44 19N 81 37W
Douglasville, *U.S.A.* **77 J3** 33 45N 84 45W
Dounreay, *U.K.* **12 C5** 58 35N 3 44W
Dourada, Serra, *Brazil* **93 F9** 13 10S 48 45W
Dourados, *Brazil* **95 A5** 22 9S 54 50W
Dourados →, *Brazil* **95 A5** 21 58S 54 18W
Dourados, Serra dos, *Brazil* **95 A5** 23 30S 53 30W
Douro →, *Europe* **19 B1** 41 8N 8 40W
Dove →, *U.K.* **10 E6** 52 51N 1 36W
Dove Creek, *U.S.A.* **83 H9** 37 46N 108 54W
Dover, *Australia* **62 G4** 43 18S 147 2 E
Dover, *U.K.* **11 F9** 51 7N 1 19 E
Dover, *Del., U.S.A.* **76 F8** 39 10N 75 32W
Dover, *N.H., U.S.A.* **79 C14** 43 12N 70 56W
Dover, *N.J., U.S.A.* **79 F10** 40 53N 74 34W
Dover, *Ohio, U.S.A.* **78 F3** 40 32N 81 29W
Dover, Pt., *Australia* **61 F4** 32 32S 125 32 E
Dover, Str. of, *Europe* **11 G9** 51 0N 1 30 E
Dover-Foxcroft, *U.S.A.* **77 C11** 45 11N 69 13W
Dover Plains, *U.S.A.* **79 E11** 41 43N 73 35W
Dovey = Dyfi →, *U.K.* **11 E3** 52 32N 4 3W
Dovrefjell, *Norway* **9 E13** 62 15N 9 33 E
Dow Rūd, *Iran* **45 C6** 33 28N 49 4 E
Dowa, *Malawi* **55 E3** 13 38S 33 58 E
Dowagiac, *U.S.A.* **76 E2** 41 59N 86 6W

Feldkirch

Erfenisdam, S. Africa 56 D4 28 30S 26 50 E
Erfurt, Germany 16 C6 50 58N 11 2 E
Erg Iguidi, Africa 50 C4 27 0N 7 0 E
Ergani, Turkey 44 B3 38 17N 39 49 E
Ergel, Mongolia 34 C5 43 8N 109 5 E
Ergeni Vozvyshennost, Russia 25 E7 47 0N 44 0 E
Ērgli, Latvia 9 H21 56 54N 25 38 E
Eriboll, L., U.K. 12 C4 58 30N 4 42W
Érice, Italy 20 E5 38 2N 12 35 E
Erie, U.S.A. 78 D4 42 8N 80 5W
Erie, L., N. Amer. 78 D4 42 15N 81 0W
Erie Canal, U.S.A. 78 C7 43 5N 78 43W
Erieau, Canada 78 D3 42 16N 81 57W
Erigavo, Somali Rep. 46 E4 10 35N 47 20 E
Erikoúsa, Greece 23 A3 39 53N 19 34 E
Eriksdale, Canada 73 C9 50 52N 98 7W
Erímanthos, Greece 21 F9 37 57N 21 50 E
Erimo-misaki, Japan 30 D11 41 50N 143 15 E
Erinpura, India 42 G5 25 9N 73 3 E
Eriskay, U.K. 12 D1 57 4N 7 18W
Eritrea ■, Africa 46 D2 14 0N 38 30 E
Erlangen, Germany 16 D6 49 36N 11 0 E
Erldunda, Australia 62 D1 25 14S 133 12 E
Ermelo, Neths. 15 B5 52 18N 5 35 E
Ermelo, S. Africa 57 D4 26 31S 29 59 E
Ermenek, Turkey 44 B2 36 38N 33 0 E
Ermones, Greece 23 A3 39 37N 19 46 E
Ermoúpolis = Síros, Greece 21 F11 37 28N 24 57 E
Ernakulam = Cochin, India 40 Q10 9 59N 76 22 E
Erne →, Ireland 13 B3 54 30N 8 16W
Erne, Lower L., U.K. 13 B4 54 28N 7 47W
Erne, Upper L., U.K. 13 B4 54 14N 7 32W
Ernest Giles Ra., Australia 61 E3 27 0S 123 45 E
Erode, India 40 P10 11 24N 77 45 E
Eromanga, Australia 63 D3 26 40S 143 11 E
Erongo, Namibia 56 C2 21 39S 15 58 E
Erramala Hills, India 40 M11 15 30N 78 15 E
Errigal, Ireland 13 A3 55 2N 8 6W
Erris Hd., Ireland 13 B1 54 19N 10 0W
Erskine, U.S.A. 80 B7 47 40N 96 0W
Ertis = Irtysh →, Russia 26 C7 61 4N 68 52 E
Erwin, U.S.A. 77 G4 36 9N 82 25W
Erzgebirge, Germany 16 C7 50 27N 12 55 E
Erzin, Russia 27 D10 50 15N 95 10 E
Erzincan, Turkey 25 G6 39 46N 39 30 E
Erzurum, Turkey 25 G7 39 57N 41 15 E
Es Caló, Spain 22 C8 38 40N 1 30 E
Es Canar, Spain 22 B8 39 2N 1 36 E
Es Mercadal, Spain 22 B11 39 59N 4 5 E
Es Migjorn Gran, Spain 22 B11 39 57N 4 3 E
Es Sahrâ' Esh Sharqîya, Egypt 51 C12 27 30N 32 30 E
Es Sînâ', Egypt 47 F3 29 0N 34 0 E
Es Vedrà, Spain 22 C7 38 52N 1 12 E
Esambo, Dem. Rep. of the Congo 54 C1 3 48S 23 30 E
Esan-Misaki, Japan 30 D10 41 40N 141 10 E
Esashi, Hokkaidō, Japan 30 B11 44 56N 142 35 E
Esashi, Hokkaidō, Japan 30 D10 41 52N 140 7 E
Esbjerg, Denmark 9 J13 55 29N 8 29 E
Escalante, U.S.A. 83 H8 37 47N 111 36W
Escalante →, U.S.A. 83 H8 37 24N 110 57W
Escalón, Mexico 86 B4 26 46N 104 20W
Escambia →, U.S.A. 77 K2 30 32N 87 11W
Escanaba, U.S.A. 76 C2 45 45N 87 4W
Esch-sur-Alzette, Lux. 18 B6 49 32N 6 0 E
Escondido, U.S.A. 85 M9 33 7N 117 5W
Escuinapa, Mexico 86 C3 22 50N 105 50W
Escuintla, Guatemala 88 D1 14 20N 90 48W
Esenguly, Turkmenistan 26 F6 37 37N 53 59 E
Eşfahān, Iran 45 C6 32 39N 51 43 E
Eşfahān □, Iran 45 C6 32 50N 51 50 E
Esfarāyen, Iran 45 B8 37 4N 57 30 E
Esfideh, Iran 45 C8 33 39N 59 46 E
Esh Sham = Dimashq, Syria 47 B5 33 30N 36 18 E
Esha Ness, U.K. 12 A7 60 29N 1 38W
Esher, U.K. 11 F7 51 21N 0 20W
Eshowe, S. Africa 57 D5 28 50S 31 30 E
Esil = Ishim →, Russia 26 D8 57 45N 71 10 E
Esk →, Cumb., U.K. 12 G5 54 58N 3 2W
Esk →, N. Yorks., U.K. 10 C7 54 30N 0 37W
Eskān, Iran 45 E9 26 48N 63 9 E
Esker, Canada 71 B6 53 53N 66 25W
Eskifjörður, Iceland 8 D7 65 3N 13 55W
Eskilstuna, Sweden 9 G17 59 22N 16 32 E
Eskimo Pt., Canada 68 B10 61 10N 94 15W
Eskişehir, Turkey 25 G5 39 50N 30 30 E
Esla →, Spain 19 B2 41 29N 6 3W
Eslāmābād-e Gharb, Iran 44 C5 34 10N 46 30 E
Eslāmshahr, Iran 45 C6 35 40N 51 10 E
Eşme, Turkey 21 E13 38 23N 28 58 E
Esmeraldas, Ecuador 92 C3 1 0N 79 40W
Esnagi L., Canada 70 C3 48 36N 84 33W
Espanola, Canada 70 C3 46 15N 81 46W
Espanola, U.S.A. 83 H10 35 59N 106 5W
Esparta, Costa Rica 88 E3 9 59N 84 40W
Esperance, Australia 61 F3 33 45S 121 55 E
Esperance B., Australia 61 F3 33 48S 121 55 E
Esperanza, Argentina 94 C3 31 29S 61 3W
Espichel, C., Portugal 19 C1 38 22N 9 16W
Espigão, Serra do, Brazil 95 B5 26 35S 50 30W
Espinazo, Sierra del = Espinhaço, Serra do, Brazil 93 G10 17 30S 43 30W
Espinhaço, Serra do, Brazil 93 G10 17 30S 43 30W
Espinilho, Serra do, Brazil 95 B5 28 30S 55 0W
Espírito Santo □, Brazil 93 H10 20 0S 40 45W
Espíritu Santo, Vanuatu 64 J8 15 15S 166 50 E
Espíritu Santo, B. del, Mexico 87 D7 19 15N 87 0W
Espíritu Santo, I., Mexico 86 C2 24 30N 110 23W
Espita, Mexico 87 C7 21 1N 88 19W
Espoo, Finland 9 F21 60 12N 24 40 E
Espungabera, Mozam. 57 C5 20 29S 32 45 E
Esquel, Argentina 96 E2 42 55S 71 20W
Esquimalt, Canada 72 D4 48 26N 123 25W
Esquina, Argentina 94 C4 30 0S 59 30W
Essaouira, Morocco 50 B4 31 32N 9 42W
Essebie, Dem. Rep. of the Congo 54 B3 2 58N 30 40 E
Essen, Belgium 15 C4 51 28N 4 28 E
Essen, Germany 16 C4 51 28N 7 2 E
Essendon, Mt., Australia 61 E3 25 0S 120 29 E
Essequibo →, Guyana 92 B7 6 50N 58 30W
Essex, Canada 78 D2 42 10N 82 49W
Essex, Calif., U.S.A. 85 L11 34 44N 115 15W
Essex, N.Y., U.S.A. 79 B11 44 19N 73 21W
Essex □, U.K. 11 F8 51 54N 0 27 E
Essex Junction, U.S.A. 79 B11 44 29N 73 7W
Esslingen, Germany 16 D5 48 44N 9 18 E
Estados, I. de Los, Argentina 96 G4 54 40S 64 30W
Eşṭahbānāt, Iran 45 D7 29 8N 54 4 E
Estância, Brazil 93 F11 11 16S 37 26W
Estancia, U.S.A. 83 J10 34 46N 106 4W
Estārm, Iran 45 D8 28 21N 58 21 E
Estcourt, S. Africa 57 D4 29 0S 29 53 E
Estelí, Nic. 88 D2 13 9N 86 22W
Estellencs, Spain 22 B9 39 39N 2 29 E
Esterhazy, Canada 73 C8 50 37N 102 5W
Estevan, Canada 73 D8 49 10N 102 59W
Estevan Group, Canada 72 C3 53 3N 129 38W
Estherville, U.S.A. 80 D7 43 24N 94 50W
Eston, Canada 73 C7 51 8N 108 40W
Estonia ■, Europe 9 G21 58 30N 25 30 E
Estreito, Brazil 93 E9 6 32S 47 25W
Estrela, Serra da, Portugal 19 B2 40 10N 7 45W
Estremoz, Portugal 19 C2 38 51N 7 39W
Estrondo, Serra do, Brazil 93 E9 7 20S 48 0W
Esztergom, Hungary 17 E10 47 47N 18 44 E
Etah, India 43 F8 27 35N 78 40 E
Étampes, France 18 B5 48 26N 2 10 E
Etanga, Namibia 56 B1 17 55S 13 0 E
Etawah, India 43 F8 26 48N 79 6 E
Etawney L., Canada 73 B9 57 50N 96 50W
Ethel, U.S.A. 84 D4 46 32N 122 46W
Ethelbert, Canada 73 C8 51 32N 100 25W
Ethiopia ■, Africa 46 F3 8 0N 40 0 E
Ethiopian Highlands, Ethiopia 28 J7 10 0N 37 0 E
Etive, L., U.K. 12 E3 56 29N 5 10W
Etna, Italy 20 F6 37 50N 14 55 E
Etoile, Dem. Rep. of the Congo 55 E2 11 33S 27 30 E
Etosha Pan, Namibia 56 B2 18 40S 16 30 E
Etowah, U.S.A. 77 H3 35 20N 84 32W
Ettelbruck, Lux. 15 E6 49 51N 6 5 E
Ettrick Water →, U.K. 12 F6 55 31N 2 55W
Etuku, Dem. Rep. of the Congo 54 C2 3 42S 25 45 E
Etzatlán, Mexico 86 C4 20 48N 104 5W
Etzná, Mexico 87 D6 19 35N 90 15W
Euboea = Évvoia, Greece 21 E11 38 30N 24 0 E
Eucla, Australia 61 F4 31 41S 128 52 E
Euclid, U.S.A. 78 E3 41 34N 81 32W
Eucumbene, L., Australia 63 F4 36 2S 148 40 E
Eudora, U.S.A. 81 J9 33 7N 91 16W
Eufaula, Ala., U.S.A. 77 K3 31 54N 85 9W
Eufaula, Okla., U.S.A. 81 H7 35 17N 95 35W
Eufaula L., U.S.A. 81 H7 35 18N 95 21W
Eugene, U.S.A. 82 E2 44 5N 123 4W
Eugowra, Australia 63 E4 33 22S 148 24 E
Eulo, Australia 63 D4 28 10S 145 3 E
Eunice, La., U.S.A. 81 K8 30 30N 92 25W
Eunice, N. Mex., U.S.A. 81 J3 32 26N 103 10W
Eupen, Belgium 15 D6 50 37N 6 3 E
Euphrates = Furāt, Nahr al →, Asia 44 D5 31 0N 47 25 E
Eureka, Canada 4 B3 80 0N 85 56W
Eureka, Calif., U.S.A. 82 F1 40 47N 124 9W
Eureka, Kans., U.S.A. 81 G6 37 49N 96 17W
Eureka, Mont., U.S.A. 82 B6 48 53N 115 3W
Eureka, Nev., U.S.A. 82 G5 39 31N 115 58W
Eureka, S. Dak., U.S.A. 80 C5 45 46N 99 38W
Eureka, Mt., Australia 61 E3 26 35S 121 35 E
Euroa, Australia 63 F4 36 44S 145 35 E
Europa, Île, Ind. Oc. 53 J8 22 20S 40 22 E
Europa, Picos de, Spain 19 A3 43 10N 4 49W
Europa, Pta. de, Gib. 19 D3 36 3N 5 21W
Europe 6 E10 50 0N 20 0 E
Europoort, Neths. 15 C4 51 57N 4 10 E
Eustis, U.S.A. 77 L5 28 51N 81 41W
Euston, Australia 63 E3 34 30S 142 46 E
Eutsuk L., Canada 72 C3 53 20N 126 45W
Evale, Angola 56 B2 16 33S 15 44 E
Evans, U.S.A. 80 E2 40 23N 104 41W
Evans, L., Canada 70 B4 50 50N 77 0W
Evans City, U.S.A. 78 F4 40 46N 80 4W
Evans Head, Australia 63 D5 29 7S 153 27 E
Evans Mills, U.S.A. 79 B9 44 6N 75 48W
Evansburg, Canada 72 C5 53 36N 114 59W
Evanston, Ill., U.S.A. 76 E2 42 3N 87 41W
Evanston, Wyo., U.S.A. 82 F8 41 16N 110 58W
Evansville, U.S.A. 76 G2 37 58N 87 35W
Evaz, Iran 45 E7 27 46N 53 59 E
Eveleth, U.S.A. 80 B8 47 28N 92 32W
Evensk, Russia 27 C16 62 12N 159 30 E
Everard, L., Australia 63 E2 31 30S 135 0 E
Everard Ranges, Australia 61 E5 27 5S 132 28 E
Everest, Mt., Nepal 43 E12 28 5N 86 58 E
Everett, Pa., U.S.A. 78 F6 40 1N 78 23W
Everett, Wash., U.S.A. 84 C4 47 59N 122 12W
Everglades, The, U.S.A. 77 N5 25 50N 81 0W
Everglades National Park, U.S.A. 77 N5 25 30N 81 0W
Evergreen, Ala., U.S.A. 77 K2 31 26N 86 57W
Evergreen, Mont., U.S.A. 82 B6 48 9N 114 13W
Evesham, U.K. 11 E6 52 6N 1 56W
Evje, Norway 9 G12 58 36N 7 51 E
Évora, Portugal 19 C2 38 33N 7 57W
Evowghlī, Iran 44 B5 38 43N 45 13 E
Évreux, France 18 B4 49 3N 1 8 E
Évros →, Bulgaria 21 D12 41 40N 26 34 E
Évry, France 18 B5 48 38N 2 27 E
Évvoia, Greece 21 E11 38 30N 24 0 E
Ewe, L., U.K. 12 D3 57 49N 5 38W
Ewing, U.S.A. 80 D5 42 16N 98 21W
Ewo, Congo 52 E2 0 48S 14 45 E
Exaltación, Bolivia 92 F5 13 10S 65 20W
Excelsior Springs, U.S.A. 80 F7 39 20N 94 13W
Exe →, U.K. 11 G4 50 41N 3 29W
Exeter, Canada 78 C3 43 21N 81 29W
Exeter, U.K. 11 G4 50 43N 3 31W
Exeter, Calif., U.S.A. 84 J7 36 18N 119 9W
Exeter, N.H., U.S.A. 79 D14 42 59N 70 57W
Exmoor, U.K. 11 F4 51 12N 3 45W
Exmouth, Australia 60 D1 21 54S 114 10 E
Exmouth, U.K. 11 G4 50 37N 3 25W
Exmouth G., Australia 60 D1 22 15S 114 15 E
Expedition Ra., Australia 62 C4 24 30S 149 12 E
Extremadura □, Spain 19 C2 39 30N 6 5W
Exuma Sound, Bahamas 88 B4 24 30N 76 20W
Eyasi, L., Tanzania 54 C4 3 30S 35 0 E
Eye Pen., U.K. 12 C2 58 13N 6 10W
Eyemouth, U.K. 12 F6 55 52N 2 5W
Eyjafjörður, Iceland 8 C4 66 15N 18 30W
Eyre (North), L., Australia 63 D2 28 30S 137 20 E
Eyre (South), L., Australia 63 D2 29 18S 137 25 E
Eyre Mts., N.Z. 59 L2 45 25S 168 25 E
Eyre Pen., Australia 63 E2 33 30S 136 17 E
Eysturoy, Færoe Is. 8 E9 62 13N 6 54W
Eyvānkī, Iran 45 C6 35 24N 51 56 E
Ezine, Turkey 21 E12 39 48N 26 20 E
Ezouza →, Cyprus 23 E11 34 44N 32 27 E

F

F.Y.R.O.M. = Macedonia ■, Europe 21 D9 41 53N 21 40 E
Fabala, Guinea 50 G4 9 44N 9 5W
Fabens, U.S.A. 83 L10 31 30N 106 10W
Fabriano, Italy 20 C5 43 20N 12 54 E
Fachi, Niger 51 E8 18 6N 11 34 E
Fada, Chad 51 E10 17 13N 21 34 E
Fada-n-Gourma, Burkina Faso 50 F6 12 10N 0 30 E
Faddeyevskiy, Ostrov, Russia 27 B15 76 0N 144 0 E
Fadghāmī, Syria 44 C4 35 53N 40 52 E
Faenza, Italy 20 B4 44 17N 11 53 E
Færoe Is. = Føroyar, Atl. Oc. 8 F9 62 0N 7 0W
Făgăras, Romania 17 F13 45 48N 24 58 E
Fagersta, Sweden 9 F16 60 1N 15 46 E
Fagnano, L., Argentina 96 G3 54 30S 68 0W
Fahliān, Iran 45 D6 30 11N 51 28 E
Fahraj, Kermān, Iran 45 D8 29 0N 59 0 E
Fahraj, Yazd, Iran 45 D7 31 46N 54 36 E
Faial, Madeira 22 D3 32 47N 16 53W
Fair Haven, U.S.A. 76 D9 43 36N 73 16W
Fair Hd., U.K. 13 A5 55 14N 6 9W
Fair Oaks, U.S.A. 84 G5 38 39N 121 16W
Fairbanks, U.S.A. 68 B5 64 51N 147 43W
Fairbury, U.S.A. 80 E6 40 8N 97 11W
Fairfax, U.S.A. 79 B11 44 40N 73 1W
Fairfield, Ala., U.S.A. 77 J2 33 29N 86 55W
Fairfield, Calif., U.S.A. 84 G4 38 15N 122 3W
Fairfield, Conn., U.S.A. 79 E11 41 9N 73 16W
Fairfield, Idaho, U.S.A. 82 E6 43 21N 114 44W
Fairfield, Ill., U.S.A. 76 F1 38 23N 88 22W
Fairfield, Iowa, U.S.A. 80 E9 40 56N 91 57W
Fairfield, Tex., U.S.A. 81 K7 31 44N 96 10W
Fairford, Canada 73 C9 51 37N 98 38W
Fairhope, U.S.A. 77 K2 30 31N 87 54W
Fairlie, N.Z. 59 L3 44 5S 170 49 E
Fairmead, U.S.A. 84 H6 37 5N 120 10W
Fairmont, Minn., U.S.A. 80 D7 43 39N 94 28W
Fairmont, W. Va., U.S.A. 76 F5 39 29N 80 9W
Fairmount, Calif., U.S.A. 85 L8 34 45N 118 26W
Fairmount, N.Y., U.S.A. 79 C8 43 5N 76 12W
Fairplay, U.S.A. 83 G11 39 15N 106 2W
Fairport, U.S.A. 78 C7 43 6N 77 27W
Fairport Harbor, U.S.A. 78 E3 41 45N 81 17W
Fairview, Canada 72 B5 56 5N 118 25W
Fairview, Mont., U.S.A. 80 B2 47 51N 104 3W
Fairview, Okla., U.S.A. 81 G5 36 16N 98 29W
Fairweather, Mt., U.S.A. 72 B1 58 55N 137 32W
Faisalabad, Pakistan 42 D5 31 30N 73 5 E
Faith, U.S.A. 80 C3 45 2N 102 2W
Faizabad, India 43 F10 26 45N 82 10 E
Fajardo, Puerto Rico 89 C6 18 20N 65 39W
Fajr, Wādī, Si. Arabia 44 D3 29 10N 38 10 E
Fakenham, U.K. 10 E8 52 51N 0 51 E
Fakfak, Indonesia 37 E8 3 0S 132 15 E
Faku, China 35 C12 42 32N 123 21 E
Falaise, France 18 B3 48 54N 0 12W
Falaise, Mui, Vietnam 38 C5 19 6N 105 45 E
Falam, Burma 41 H18 23 0N 93 45 E
Falcó, C. des, Spain 22 C7 38 50N 1 23 E
Falcón, Presa, Mexico 87 B5 26 35N 99 10W
Falcon Lake, Canada 73 D9 49 42N 95 15W
Falcon Reservoir, U.S.A. 81 M5 26 34N 99 10W
Falconara Marittima, Italy 20 C5 43 37N 13 24 E
Falcone, C. del, Italy 20 D3 40 58N 8 12 E
Falconer, U.S.A. 78 D5 42 7N 79 13W
Faleshty = Făleşti, Moldova 17 E14 47 32N 27 44 E
Făleşti, Moldova 17 E14 47 32N 27 44 E
Falfurrias, U.S.A. 81 M5 27 14N 98 9W
Falher, Canada 72 B5 55 44N 117 15W
Faliraki, Greece 23 C10 36 22N 28 12 E
Falkenberg, Sweden 9 H15 56 54N 12 30 E
Falkirk, U.K. 12 F5 56 0N 3 47W
Falkirk □, U.K. 12 F5 55 58N 3 49W
Falkland, U.K. 12 E5 56 16N 3 12W
Falkland Is. □, Atl. Oc. 96 G5 51 30S 59 0W
Falkland Sd., Falk. Is. 96 G5 52 0S 60 0W
Falköping, Sweden 9 G15 58 12N 13 33 E
Fall River, U.S.A. 79 E13 41 43N 71 10W
Fallbrook, U.S.A. 85 M9 33 23N 117 15W
Fallon, U.S.A. 82 G4 39 28N 118 47W
Falls City, U.S.A. 80 E7 40 3N 95 36W
Falls Creek, U.S.A. 78 E6 41 9N 78 48W
Falmouth, Jamaica 88 C4 18 30N 77 40W
Falmouth, U.K. 11 G2 50 9N 5 5W
Falmouth, U.S.A. 79 E14 41 33N 70 37W
Falsa, Pta., Mexico 86 B1 27 51N 115 3W
False B., S. Africa 56 E2 34 15S 18 40 E
Falso, C., Honduras 88 C3 15 12N 83 21W
Falster, Denmark 9 J14 54 45N 11 55 E
Falsterbo, Sweden 9 J15 55 23N 12 50 E
Fălticeni, Romania 17 E14 47 21N 26 20 E
Falun, Sweden 9 F16 60 37N 15 37 E
Famagusta, Cyprus 23 D12 35 8N 33 55 E
Famagusta Bay, Cyprus 23 D13 35 15N 34 0 E
Famalé, Niger 50 F6 14 33N 1 5 E
Famatina, Sierra de, Argentina 94 B2 27 30S 68 0W
Family L., Canada 73 C9 51 54N 95 27W
Famoso, U.S.A. 85 K7 35 37N 119 12W
Fan Xian, China 34 G8 35 55N 115 38 E
Fanad Hd., Ireland 13 A4 55 17N 7 38W
Fandriana, Madag. 57 C8 20 14S 47 21 E
Fangcheng, China 34 H7 33 18N 112 59 E
Fangshan, China 34 E6 38 3N 111 25 E
Fangzi, China 35 F10 36 33N 119 10 E
Fanjiatun, China 35 C13 43 40N 125 15 E
Fannich, L., U.K. 12 D4 57 38N 4 59W
Fannūj, Iran 45 E8 26 35N 59 38 E
Fanø, Denmark 9 J13 55 25N 8 25 E
Fano, Italy 20 C5 43 50N 13 1 E
Fanshi, China 34 E7 39 12N 113 20 E
Fao = Al Fāw, Iraq 45 D6 30 0N 48 30 E
Faqirwali, Pakistan 42 E5 29 27N 73 0 E
Faradje, Dem. Rep. of the Congo 54 B2 3 50N 29 45 E
Farafangana, Madag. 57 C8 22 49S 47 50 E
Farāh, Afghan. 40 C3 32 20N 62 7 E
Farāh □, Afghan. 40 C3 32 25N 62 10 E
Farahalana, Madag. 57 A9 14 26S 50 10 E
Faranah, Guinea 50 F3 10 3N 10 45W
Farasān, Jazā'ir, Si. Arabia 46 D3 16 45N 41 55 E
Farasan Is. = Farasān, Jazā'ir, Si. Arabia 46 D3 16 45N 41 55 E
Faratsiho, Madag. 57 B8 19 24S 46 57 E
Fareham, U.K. 11 G6 50 51N 1 11W
Farewell, C., N.Z. 59 J4 40 29S 172 43 E
Farewell C. = Farvel, Kap, Greenland 4 D5 59 48N 43 55W
Farghona, Uzbekistan 26 E8 40 23N 71 19 E
Fargo, U.S.A. 80 B6 46 53N 96 48W
Fār'iah, W. al →, West Bank 47 C4 32 12N 35 27 E
Faribault, U.S.A. 80 C8 44 18N 93 16W
Faridabad, India 42 E6 28 26N 77 19 E
Faridkot, India 42 D6 30 44N 74 45 E
Faridpur, Bangla. 43 H13 23 15N 89 55 E
Faridpur, India 43 E8 28 13N 79 33 E
Farīmān, Iran 45 C8 35 40N 59 49 E
Farina, Australia 63 E2 30 3S 138 15 E
Fariones, Pta., Canary Is. 22 E6 29 13N 13 28W
Farmerville, U.S.A. 81 J8 32 47N 92 24W
Farmingdale, U.S.A. 79 F10 40 12N 74 10W
Farmington, Canada 72 B4 55 54N 120 30W
Farmington, Calif., U.S.A. 84 H6 37 55N 120 59W
Farmington, Maine, U.S.A. 77 C10 44 40N 70 9W
Farmington, Mo., U.S.A. 81 G9 37 47N 90 25W
Farmington, N.H., U.S.A. 79 C13 43 24N 71 4W
Farmington, N. Mex., U.S.A. 83 H9 36 44N 108 12W
Farmington, Utah, U.S.A. 82 F8 41 0N 111 12W
Farmington →, U.S.A. 79 E12 41 51N 72 38W
Farmville, U.S.A. 76 G6 37 18N 78 24W
Farne Is., U.K. 10 B6 55 38N 1 37W
Farnham, Canada 79 A12 45 17N 72 59W
Farnham, Mt., Canada 72 C5 50 29N 116 30W
Faro, Brazil 93 D7 2 10S 56 39W
Faro, Canada 68 B6 62 11N 133 22W
Faro, Portugal 19 D2 37 2N 7 55W
Fårö, Sweden 9 H18 57 55N 19 5 E
Farquhar, C., Australia 61 D1 23 50S 113 36 E
Farrars Cr. →, Australia 62 D3 25 35S 140 43 E
Farrāshband, Iran 45 D7 28 57N 52 5 E
Farrell, U.S.A. 78 E4 41 13N 80 30W
Farrokhī, Iran 45 C8 33 50N 59 31 E
Farruch, C. = Ferrutx, C., Spain 22 B10 39 47N 3 21 E
Farrukhabad-cum-Fatehgarh, India 40 F11 27 30N 79 32 E
Fārs □, Iran 45 D7 29 30N 55 0 E
Fársala, Greece 21 E10 39 17N 22 23 E
Farson, U.S.A. 82 E9 42 6N 109 27W
Farsund, Norway 9 G12 58 5N 6 55 E
Fartak, Râs, Si. Arabia 44 D2 28 5N 34 34 E
Fartak, Ra's, Yemen 46 D5 15 38N 52 15 E
Fartura, Serra da, Brazil 95 B5 26 21S 52 52W
Fārūj, Iran 45 B8 37 14N 58 14 E
Farvel, Kap, Greenland 4 D5 59 48N 43 55W
Farwell, U.S.A. 81 H3 34 23N 103 2W
Fasā, Iran 45 D7 29 0N 53 39 E
Fasano, Italy 20 D7 40 50N 17 22 E
Fastiv, Ukraine 17 C15 50 7N 29 57 E
Fastov = Fastiv, Ukraine 17 C15 50 7N 29 57 E
Fatagar, Tanjung, Indonesia 37 E8 2 46S 131 57 E
Fatehabad, Haryana, India 42 E6 29 31N 75 27 E
Fatehabad, Ut. P., India 42 F8 27 1N 78 19 E
Fatehgarh, India 43 F8 27 25N 79 35 E
Fatehpur, Bihar, India 43 G11 24 38N 85 14 E
Fatehpur, Raj., India 42 F6 28 0N 74 40 E
Fatehpur, Ut. P., India 43 G9 25 56N 81 13 E
Fatehpur, Ut. P., India 43 F9 27 10N 81 13 E
Fatehpur Sikri, India 42 F6 27 6N 77 40 E
Fatima, Canada 71 C7 47 24N 61 53W
Faulkton, U.S.A. 80 C5 45 2N 99 8W
Faure I., Australia 61 E1 25 52S 113 50 E
Fauresmith, S. Africa 56 D4 29 44S 25 17 E
Fauske, Norway 8 C16 67 17N 15 25 E
Favara, Italy 20 F5 37 19N 13 39 E
Favàritx, C. de, Spain 22 B11 40 0N 4 15 E
Favignana, Italy 20 F5 37 56N 12 20 E
Fawcett, Pt., Australia 60 B5 11 46S 130 2 E
Fawn →, Canada 70 A2 55 20N 87 35W
Fawnskin, U.S.A. 85 L10 34 16N 116 56W
Faxaflói, Iceland 8 D2 64 29N 23 0W
Faya-Largeau, Chad 51 E9 17 58N 19 6 E
Fayd, Si. Arabia 44 E4 27 1N 42 52 E
Fayette, Ala., U.S.A. 77 J2 33 41N 87 50W
Fayette, Mo., U.S.A. 80 F8 39 9N 92 41W
Fayetteville, Ark., U.S.A. 81 G7 36 4N 94 10W
Fayetteville, N.C., U.S.A. 77 H6 35 3N 78 53W
Fayetteville, Tenn., U.S.A. 77 H2 35 9N 86 34W
Fazilka, India 42 D6 30 27N 74 2 E
Fazilpur, Pakistan 42 E4 29 18N 70 29 E
Fdérik, Mauritania 50 D3 22 40N 12 45W
Feale →, Ireland 13 D2 52 27N 9 37W
Fear, C., U.S.A. 77 J7 33 50N 77 58W
Feather →, U.S.A. 82 G3 38 47N 121 36W
Feather Falls, U.S.A. 84 F5 39 36N 121 16W
Featherston, N.Z. 59 J5 41 6S 175 20 E
Featherstone, Zimbabwe 55 F3 18 42S 30 55 E
Fécamp, France 18 B4 49 45N 0 22 E
Fedala = Mohammedia, Morocco 50 B4 33 44N 7 21W
Federación, Argentina 94 C4 31 0S 57 55W
Féderal, Argentina 96 C5 30 57S 58 48W
Federal Way, U.S.A. 84 C4 47 18N 122 19W
Fedeshkūh, Iran 45 D7 28 49N 53 50 E
Fehmarn, Germany 16 A6 54 27N 11 7 E
Fehmarn Bælt, Europe 9 J14 54 35N 11 20 E
Fehmarn Belt = Fehmarn Bælt, Europe 9 J14 54 35N 11 20 E
Fei Xian, China 35 G9 35 18N 117 59 E
Feijó, Brazil 92 E4 8 9S 70 21W
Feilding, N.Z. 59 J5 40 13S 175 35 E
Feira de Santana, Brazil 93 F11 12 15S 38 57W
Feixiang, China 34 F8 36 30N 114 45 E
Felanitx, Spain 22 B10 39 28N 3 9 E
Feldkirch, Austria 16 E5 47 15N 9 37 E

Gatton

Frankfurt, *Brandenburg, Germany* 16 B8 52 20N 14 32 E
Frankfurt, *Hessen, Germany* 16 C5 50 7N 8 41 E
Fränkische Alb, *Germany* 16 D6 49 10N 11 23 E
Frankland —►, *Australia* 61 G2 35 0S 116 48 E
Franklin, *Ky., U.S.A.* 77 G2 36 43N 86 35W
Franklin, *La., U.S.A.* 81 L9 29 48N 91 30W
Franklin, *Mass., U.S.A.* 79 D13 42 5N 71 24W
Franklin, *N.H., U.S.A.* 79 C13 43 27N 71 39W
Franklin, *Nebr., U.S.A.* 80 E5 40 6N 98 57W
Franklin, *Pa., U.S.A.* 78 E5 41 24N 79 50W
Franklin, *Va., U.S.A.* 77 G7 36 41N 76 56W
Franklin, *W. Va., U.S.A.* 76 F6 38 39N 79 20W
Franklin B., *Canada* 68 B7 69 45N 126 0W
Franklin D. Roosevelt L., *U.S.A.* 82 B4 48 18N 118 9W
Franklin I., *Antarctica* 5 D11 76 10S 168 30 E
Franklin L., *U.S.A.* 82 F6 40 25N 115 22W
Franklin Mts., *Canada* 68 B7 65 0N 125 0W
Franklin Str., *Canada* 68 A10 72 0N 96 0W
Franklinton, *U.S.A.* 81 K9 30 51N 90 9W
Franklinville, *U.S.A.* 78 D6 42 20N 78 27W
Franks Pk., *U.S.A.* 82 E9 43 58N 109 18W
Frankston, *Australia* 63 F4 38 8S 145 8 E
Frantsa Iosifa, Zemlya, *Russia* 26 A6 82 0N 55 0 E
Franz, *Canada* 70 C3 48 25N 84 30W
Franz Josef Land = Frantsa Iosifa, Zemlya, *Russia* 26 A6 82 0N 55 0 E
Fraser, *U.S.A.* 78 D2 42 32N 82 57W
Fraser —►, *B.C., Canada* 72 D4 49 7N 123 11W
Fraser —►, *Nfld., Canada* 71 A7 56 39N 62 10W
Fraser, Mt., *Australia* 61 E2 25 35S 118 20 E
Fraser I., *Australia* 63 D5 25 15S 153 10 E
Fraser Lake, *Canada* 72 C4 54 0N 124 50W
Fraserburg, *S. Africa* 56 E3 31 55S 21 30 E
Fraserburgh, *U.K.* 12 D6 57 42N 2 1W
Fraserdale, *Canada* 70 C3 49 55N 81 37W
Fray Bentos, *Uruguay* 94 C4 33 10S 58 15W
Fredericia, *Denmark* 9 J13 55 34N 9 45 E
Frederick, *Md., U.S.A.* 76 F7 39 25N 77 25W
Frederick, *Okla., U.S.A.* 81 H5 34 23N 99 1W
Frederick, *S. Dak., U.S.A.* 80 C5 45 50N 98 31W
Fredericksburg, *Pa., U.S.A.* 79 F8 40 27N 76 26W
Fredericksburg, *Tex., U.S.A.* 81 K5 30 16N 98 52W
Fredericksburg, *Va., U.S.A.* 76 F7 38 18N 77 28W
Fredericktown, *Mo., U.S.A.* 81 G9 37 34N 90 18W
Fredericktown, *Ohio, U.S.A.* 78 F2 40 29N 82 33W
Frederico I. Madero, Presa, *Mexico* 86 B3 28 7N 105 40W
Frederico Westphalen, *Brazil* 95 B5 27 22S 53 24W
Fredericton, *Canada* 71 C6 45 57N 66 40W
Fredericton Junction, *Canada* 71 C6 45 41N 66 40W
Frederikshåb, *Greenland* 4 C5 62 0N 49 43W
Frederikshavn, *Denmark* 9 H14 57 28N 10 31 E
Frederiksted, *Virgin Is.* 89 C7 17 43N 64 53W
Fredonia, *Ariz., U.S.A.* 83 H7 36 57N 112 32W
Fredonia, *Kans., U.S.A.* 81 G7 37 32N 95 49W
Fredonia, *N.Y., U.S.A.* 78 D5 42 26N 79 20W
Fredrikstad, *Norway* 9 G14 59 13N 10 57 E
Free State □, *S. Africa* 56 D4 28 30S 27 0 E
Freehold, *U.S.A.* 79 F10 40 16N 74 17W
Freel Peak, *U.S.A.* 84 G7 38 52N 119 54W
Freeland, *U.S.A.* 79 E9 41 1N 75 54W
Freels, C., *Canada* 71 C9 49 15N 53 30W
Freeman, *Calif., U.S.A.* 85 K9 35 35N 117 53W
Freeman, *S. Dak., U.S.A.* 80 D6 43 21N 97 26W
Freeport, *Bahamas* 88 A4 26 30N 78 47W
Freeport, *Ill., U.S.A.* 80 D10 42 17N 89 36W
Freeport, *N.Y., U.S.A.* 79 F11 40 39N 73 35W
Freeport, *Ohio, U.S.A.* 78 F3 40 12N 81 15W
Freeport, *Pa., U.S.A.* 78 F5 40 41N 79 41W
Freeport, *Tex., U.S.A.* 81 L7 28 57N 95 21W
Freetown, *S. Leone* 50 G3 8 30N 13 17W
Frégate, L., *Canada* 70 B5 53 15N 74 45W
Fregenal de la Sierra, *Spain* 19 C2 38 10N 6 39W
Freibourg = Fribourg, *Switz.* 18 C7 46 49N 7 9 E
Freiburg, *Germany* 16 E4 47 59N 7 51 E
Freire, *Chile* 96 D2 38 54S 72 38W
Freirina, *Chile* 94 B1 28 30S 71 10W
Freising, *Germany* 16 D6 48 24N 11 45 E
Freistadt, *Austria* 16 D8 48 30N 14 30 E
Fréjus, *France* 18 E7 43 25N 6 44 E
Fremantle, *Australia* 61 F2 32 7S 115 47 E
Fremont, *Calif., U.S.A.* 84 H4 37 32N 121 57W
Fremont, *Mich., U.S.A.* 76 D3 43 28N 85 57W
Fremont, *Nebr., U.S.A.* 80 E6 41 26N 96 30W
Fremont, *Ohio, U.S.A.* 76 E4 41 21N 83 7W
Fremont —►, *U.S.A.* 83 G8 38 24N 110 42W
French Camp, *U.S.A.* 84 H5 37 53N 121 16W
French Creek —►, *U.S.A.* 78 E5 41 24N 79 50W
French Guiana ■, *S. Amer.* 93 C8 4 0N 53 0W
French Pass, *N.Z.* 59 J4 40 55S 173 55 E
French Polynesia ■, *Pac. Oc.* 65 K13 20 0S 145 0W
Frenchman Cr. —►, *N. Amer.* 82 B10 48 31N 107 10W
Frenchman Cr. —►, *U.S.A.* 80 E4 40 14N 100 50W
Fresco —►, *Brazil* 93 E8 7 15S 51 30W
Freshfield, C., *Antarctica* 5 C10 68 25S 151 10 E
Fresnillo, *Mexico* 86 C4 23 10N 103 0W
Fresno, *U.S.A.* 84 J7 36 44N 119 47W
Fresno Reservoir, *U.S.A.* 82 B9 48 36N 109 57W
Frew —►, *Australia* 62 C2 20 0S 135 38 E
Frewsburg, *U.S.A.* 78 D5 42 3N 79 10W
Freycinet Pen., *Australia* 62 G4 42 10S 148 25 E
Fria, C., *Namibia* 56 B1 18 0S 12 0 E
Friant, *U.S.A.* 84 J7 36 59N 119 43W
Frías, *Argentina* 94 B2 28 40S 65 5W
Fribourg, *Switz.* 18 C7 46 49N 7 9 E
Friday Harbor, *U.S.A.* 84 B3 48 32N 123 1W
Friedens, *U.S.A.* 78 F6 40 3N 78 59W
Friedrichshafen, *Germany* 16 E5 47 39N 9 30 E
Friendly Is. = Tonga ■, *Pac. Oc.* 59 D11 19 50S 174 30W
Friendship, *U.S.A.* 78 D6 42 12N 78 8W
Friesland □, *Neths.* 15 A5 53 5N 5 50 E
Frio —►, *U.S.A.* 81 L5 28 26N 98 11W
Frio, C., *Brazil* 90 F6 22 50S 41 50W
Friona, *U.S.A.* 81 H3 34 38N 102 43W
Fritch, *U.S.A.* 81 H4 35 38N 101 36W
Frobisher B., *Canada* 69 B13 62 30N 66 0W
Frobisher Bay = Iqaluit, *Canada* 69 B13 63 44N 68 31W
Frobisher L., *Canada* 73 B7 56 20N 108 15W
Frohavet, *Norway* 8 E13 64 0N 9 30 E
Frome, *U.K.* 11 F5 51 14N 2 19W
Frome —►, *U.K.* 11 G5 50 41N 2 6W
Frome, L., *Australia* 63 E2 30 45S 139 45 E
Front Range, *U.S.A.* 74 C5 40 25N 105 45W
Front Royal, *U.S.A.* 76 F6 38 55N 78 12W
Frontera, *Canary Is.* 22 G2 27 47N 17 59W
Frontera, *Mexico* 87 D6 18 30N 92 40W
Fronteras, *Mexico* 86 A3 30 56N 109 31W
Frosinone, *Italy* 20 D5 41 38N 13 19 E
Frostburg, *U.S.A.* 76 F6 39 39N 78 56W
Frostisen, *Norway* 8 B17 68 14N 17 10 E
Frøya, *Norway* 8 E13 63 43N 8 40 E
Frunze = Bishkek, *Kyrgyzstan* 26 E8 42 54N 74 46 E
Frutal, *Brazil* 93 H9 20 0S 49 0W
Frýdek-Místek, *Czech Rep.* 17 D10 49 40N 18 20 E
Fryeburg, *U.S.A.* 79 B14 44 1N 70 59W
Fu Xian = Wafangdian, *China* 35 E11 39 38N 121 58 E
Fu Xian, *China* 34 G5 36 0N 109 20 E
Fucheng, *China* 34 F9 37 50N 116 10 E
Fuchou = Fuzhou, *China* 33 D6 26 5N 119 16 E
Fuchū, *Japan* 31 G6 34 34N 133 14 E
Fuencaliente, *Canary Is.* 22 F2 28 28N 17 50W
Fuencaliente, Pta., *Canary Is.* 22 F2 28 27N 17 51W
Fuengirola, *Spain* 19 D3 36 32N 4 41W
Fuentes de Oñoro, *Spain* 19 B2 40 33N 6 52W
Fuerte —►, *Mexico* 86 B3 25 50N 109 25W
Fuerte Olimpo, *Paraguay* 94 A4 21 0S 57 51W
Fuerteventura, *Canary Is.* 22 F6 28 30N 14 0W
Fufeng, *China* 34 G5 34 22N 108 0 E
Fugou, *China* 34 G8 34 3N 114 25 E
Fugu, *China* 34 E6 39 2N 111 3 E
Fuhai, *China* 32 B3 47 2N 87 25 E
Fuḩaymī, *Iraq* 44 C4 34 16N 42 10 E
Fuji, *Japan* 31 G9 35 9N 138 39 E
Fuji-San, *Japan* 31 G9 35 22N 138 44 E
Fuji-yoshida, *Japan* 31 G9 35 30N 138 46 E
Fujian □, *China* 33 D6 26 0N 118 0 E
Fujinomiya, *Japan* 31 G9 35 10N 138 40 E
Fujisawa, *Japan* 31 G9 35 22N 139 29 E
Fujiyama, Mt. = Fuji-San, *Japan* 31 G9 35 22N 138 44 E
Fukien = Fujian □, *China* 33 D6 26 0N 118 0 E
Fukuchiyama, *Japan* 31 G7 35 19N 135 9 E
Fukue-Shima, *Japan* 31 H4 32 40N 128 45 E
Fukui, *Japan* 31 F8 36 5N 136 10 E
Fukui □, *Japan* 31 G8 36 0N 136 12 E
Fukuoka, *Japan* 31 H5 33 39N 130 21 E
Fukuoka □, *Japan* 31 H5 33 30N 131 0 E
Fukushima, *Japan* 30 F10 37 44N 140 28 E
Fukushima □, *Japan* 30 F10 37 30N 140 15 E
Fukuyama, *Japan* 31 G6 34 35N 133 20 E
Fulda, *Germany* 16 C5 50 32N 9 40 E
Fulda —►, *Germany* 16 C5 51 25N 9 39 E
Fulford Harbour, *Canada* 84 B3 48 47N 123 27W
Fullerton, *Calif., U.S.A.* 85 M9 33 53N 117 56W
Fullerton, *Nebr., U.S.A.* 80 E6 41 22N 97 58W
Fulongquan, *China* 35 B13 44 20N 124 42 E
Fulton, *Mo., U.S.A.* 80 F9 38 52N 91 57W
Fulton, *N.Y., U.S.A.* 79 C8 43 19N 76 25W
Funabashi, *Japan* 31 G10 35 45N 140 0 E
Funchal, *Madeira* 22 D3 32 38N 16 54W
Fundación, *Colombia* 92 A4 10 31N 74 11W
Fundão, *Portugal* 19 B2 40 8N 7 30W
Fundy, B. of, *Canada* 71 D6 45 0N 66 0W
Funing, *Hebei, China* 35 E10 39 53N 119 12 E
Funing, *Jiangsu, China* 35 H10 33 45N 119 50 E
Funiu Shan, *China* 34 H7 33 30N 112 20 E
Funtua, *Nigeria* 50 F7 11 30N 7 18 E
Fuping, *Hebei, China* 34 E8 38 48N 114 12 E
Fuping, *Shaanxi, China* 34 G5 34 42N 109 10 E
Furano, *Japan* 30 C11 43 21N 142 23 E
Furāt, Nahr al —►, *Asia* 44 D5 31 0N 47 25 E
Fūrg, *Iran* 45 D7 28 18N 55 13 E
Furnás, *Spain* 22 B8 39 3N 1 32 E
Furnas, Reprêsa de, *Brazil* 95 A6 20 50S 45 30W
Furneaux Group, *Australia* 62 G4 40 10S 147 50 E
Furqlus, *Syria* 47 A6 34 36N 37 8 E
Fürstenwalde, *Germany* 16 B8 52 22N 14 3 E
Fürth, *Germany* 16 D6 49 28N 10 59 E
Furukawa, *Japan* 30 E10 38 34N 140 58 E
Fury and Hecla Str., *Canada* 69 B11 69 56N 84 0W
Fusagasuga, *Colombia* 92 C4 4 21N 74 22W
Fushan, *Shandong, China* 35 F11 37 30N 121 15 E
Fushan, *Shanxi, China* 34 G6 35 58N 111 51 E
Fushun, *China* 35 D12 41 50N 123 56 E
Fusong, *China* 35 C14 42 20N 127 15 E
Futuna, *Wall. & F. Is.* 59 B8 14 25S 178 20 E
Fuxin, *China* 35 C11 42 5N 121 48 E
Fuyang, *China* 34 H8 33 0N 115 48 E
Fuyang He —►, *China* 34 E9 38 12N 117 0 E
Fuyu, *China* 35 B13 45 12N 124 43 E
Fuzhou, *China* 33 D6 26 5N 119 16 E
Fylde, *U.K.* 10 D5 53 50N 2 58W
Fyn, *Denmark* 9 J14 55 20N 10 30 E
Fyne, L., *U.K.* 12 F3 55 59N 5 23W

G

Gabela, *Angola* 52 G2 11 0S 14 24 E
Gabès, *Tunisia* 51 B8 33 53N 10 2 E
Gabès, G. de, *Tunisia* 51 B8 34 0N 10 30 E
Gabon ■, *Africa* 52 E2 0 10S 10 0 E
Gaborone, *Botswana* 56 C4 24 45S 25 57 E
Gabriels, *U.S.A.* 79 B10 44 26N 74 12W
Gābrīk, *Iran* 45 E8 25 44N 58 28 E
Gabrovo, *Bulgaria* 21 C11 42 52N 25 19 E
Gāch Sār, *Iran* 45 B6 36 7N 51 19 E
Gachsārān, *Iran* 45 D6 30 15N 50 45 E
Gadag, *India* 40 M9 15 30N 75 45 E
Gadap, *Pakistan* 42 G2 25 5N 67 28 E
Gadarwara, *India* 43 H8 22 50N 78 50 E
Gadhada, *India* 42 J4 22 0N 71 35 E
Gadra, *Pakistan* 42 G4 25 40N 70 38 E
Gadsden, *U.S.A.* 77 H3 34 1N 86 1W
Gadwal, *India* 40 L10 16 10N 77 50 E
Gaffney, *U.S.A.* 77 H5 35 5N 81 39W
Gafsa, *Tunisia* 50 B7 34 24N 8 43 E
Gagaria, *India* 42 G4 25 43N 70 46 E
Gagnoa, *Ivory C.* 50 G4 6 56N 5 16W
Gagnon, *Canada* 71 B6 51 50N 68 5W
Gagnon, L., *Canada* 73 A6 62 3N 110 27W
Gahini, *Rwanda* 54 C3 1 50S 30 30 E
Gahmar, *India* 43 G10 25 27N 83 49 E
Gai Xian = Gaizhou, *China* 35 D12 40 22N 122 20 E
Gaïdhouronísi, *Greece* 23 E7 34 53N 25 41 E
Gail, *U.S.A.* 81 J4 32 46N 101 27W
Gaillimh = Galway, *Ireland* 13 C2 53 17N 9 3W
Gaines, *U.S.A.* 78 E7 41 46N 77 35W
Gainesville, *Fla., U.S.A.* 77 L4 29 40N 82 20W
Gainesville, *Ga., U.S.A.* 77 H4 34 18N 83 50W
Gainesville, *Mo., U.S.A.* 81 G8 36 36N 92 26W
Gainesville, *Tex., U.S.A.* 81 J6 33 38N 97 8W
Gainsborough, *U.K.* 10 D7 53 24N 0 46W
Gairdner, L., *Australia* 63 E2 31 30S 136 0 E
Gairloch, L., *U.K.* 12 D3 57 43N 5 45W
Gaizhou, *China* 35 D12 40 22N 122 20 E
Gaj —►, *Pakistan* 42 F2 26 26N 67 21 E
Gakuch, *Pakistan* 43 A5 36 7N 73 45 E
Galán, Cerro, *Argentina* 94 B2 25 55S 66 52W
Galana —►, *Kenya* 54 C5 3 9S 40 8 E
Galápagos, *Pac. Oc.* 90 D1 0 0 91 0W
Galashiels, *U.K.* 12 F6 55 37N 2 49W
Galați, *Romania* 17 F15 45 27N 28 2 E
Galatina, *Italy* 21 D8 40 10N 18 10 E
Galax, *U.S.A.* 77 G5 36 40N 80 56W
Galcaio, *Somali Rep.* 46 F4 6 30N 47 30 E
Galdhøpiggen, *Norway* 9 F12 61 38N 8 18 E
Galeana, *Mexico* 86 C4 24 50N 100 4W
Galeana, *Nuevo León, Mexico* 86 A3 24 50N 100 4W
Galela, *Indonesia* 37 D7 1 50N 127 49 E
Galena, *U.S.A.* 68 B4 64 44N 156 56W
Galera Point, *Trin. & Tob.* 89 D7 10 8N 61 0W
Galesburg, *U.S.A.* 80 E9 40 57N 90 22W
Galeton, *U.S.A.* 78 E7 41 44N 77 39W
Galich, *Russia* 24 C7 58 22N 42 24 E
Galicia □, *Spain* 19 A2 42 43N 7 45W
Galilee = Hagalil, *Israel* 47 C4 32 53N 35 18 E
Galilee, L., *Australia* 62 C4 22 20S 145 50 E
Galilee, Sea of = Yam Kinneret, *Israel* 47 C4 32 45N 35 35 E
Galinoporni, *Cyprus* 23 D13 35 31N 34 18 E
Galion, *U.S.A.* 78 F2 40 44N 82 47W
Galiuro Mts., *U.S.A.* 83 K8 32 30N 110 20W
Galiwinku, *Australia* 62 A2 12 2S 135 34 E
Gallan Hd., *U.K.* 12 C1 58 15N 7 2W
Gallatin, *U.S.A.* 77 G2 36 24N 86 27W
Galle, *Sri Lanka* 40 R12 6 5N 80 10 E
Gállego —►, *Spain* 19 B5 41 39N 0 51W
Gallegos —►, *Argentina* 96 G3 51 35S 69 0W
Galley Hd., *Ireland* 13 E3 51 32N 8 55W
Gallinas, Pta., *Colombia* 92 A4 12 28N 71 40W
Gallipoli = Gelibolu, *Turkey* 21 D12 40 28N 26 43 E
Gallípoli, *Italy* 21 D8 40 3N 17 58 E
Gallipolis, *U.S.A.* 76 F4 38 49N 82 12W
Gällivare, *Sweden* 8 C19 67 9N 20 40 E
Galloo I., *U.S.A.* 79 C8 43 55N 76 25W
Galloway, *U.K.* 12 F4 55 1N 4 29W
Galloway, Mull of, *U.K.* 12 G4 54 39N 4 52W
Gallup, *U.S.A.* 83 J9 35 32N 108 45W
Galoya, *Sri Lanka* 40 Q12 8 10N 80 55 E
Galt, *U.S.A.* 84 G5 38 15N 121 18W
Galty Mts., *Ireland* 13 D3 52 22N 8 10W
Galtymore, *Ireland* 13 D3 52 21N 8 11W
Galva, *U.S.A.* 80 E9 41 10N 90 3W
Galveston, *U.S.A.* 81 L7 29 18N 94 48W
Galveston B., *U.S.A.* 81 L7 29 36N 94 50W
Gálvez, *Argentina* 94 C3 32 0S 61 14W
Galway, *Ireland* 13 C2 53 17N 9 3W
Galway □, *Ireland* 13 C2 53 22N 9 1W
Galway B., *Ireland* 13 C2 53 13N 9 10W
Gam —►, *Vietnam* 38 B5 21 55N 105 12 E
Gamagori, *Japan* 31 G8 34 50N 137 14 E
Gambat, *Pakistan* 42 F3 27 17N 68 26 E
Gambhir —►, *India* 42 F6 26 58N 77 27 E
Gambia ■, *W. Afr.* 50 F2 13 25N 16 0W
Gambia —►, *W. Afr.* 50 F2 13 28N 16 34W
Gambier, *U.S.A.* 78 F2 40 22N 82 23W
Gambier, C., *Australia* 60 B5 11 56S 130 57 E
Gambier Is., *Australia* 63 F2 35 3S 136 30 E
Gambo, *Canada* 71 C9 48 47N 54 13W
Gamboli, *Pakistan* 42 E3 29 53N 68 24 E
Gamboma, *Congo* 52 E3 1 55S 15 52 E
Gamlakarleby = Kokkola, *Finland* 8 E20 63 50N 23 8 E
Gammon —►, *Canada* 73 C9 51 24N 95 44W
Gan Jiang —►, *China* 33 D6 29 15N 116 0 E
Ganado, *U.S.A.* 83 J9 35 43N 109 33W
Gananoque, *Canada* 79 B8 44 20N 76 10W
Ganāveh, *Iran* 45 D6 29 35N 50 35 E
Gäncä, *Azerbaijan* 25 F8 40 45N 46 20 E
Gancheng, *China* 38 C7 18 51N 108 37 E
Gand = Gent, *Belgium* 15 C3 51 2N 3 42 E
Ganda, *Angola* 53 G2 13 3S 14 35 E
Gandajika, *Dem. Rep. of the Congo* 52 F4 6 45S 23 57 E
Gandak —►, *India* 43 G11 25 39N 85 13 E
Gandava, *Pakistan* 42 E2 28 32N 67 32 E
Gander, *Canada* 71 C9 48 58N 54 35W
Gander L., *Canada* 71 C9 48 58N 54 35W
Ganderowe Falls, *Zimbabwe* 55 F2 17 20S 29 10 E
Gandhi Sagar, *India* 42 G6 24 40N 75 40 E
Gandhinagar, *India* 42 H5 23 15N 72 45 E
Gandía, *Spain* 19 C5 38 58N 0 9W
Gando, Pta., *Canary Is.* 22 G4 27 55N 15 22W
Ganedidalem = Gani, *Indonesia* 37 E7 0 48S 128 14 E
Ganga —►, *India* 43 H14 23 20N 90 30 E
Ganga Sagar, *India* 43 J13 21 38N 88 5 E
Gangan —►, *India* 43 E8 28 38N 78 58 E
Ganganagar, *India* 42 E5 29 56N 73 56 E
Gangapur, *India* 42 F7 26 32N 76 49 E
Gangaw, *Burma* 41 H19 22 5N 94 5 E
Gangdisê Shan, *China* 41 D12 31 20N 81 0 E
Ganges = Ganga —►, *India* 43 H14 23 20N 90 30 E
Ganges, *Canada* 72 D4 48 51N 123 31W
Ganges, Mouths of the, *India* 43 J14 21 30N 90 0 E
Gangoh, *India* 42 E7 29 46N 77 18 E
Gangroti, *India* 43 D8 30 50N 79 10 E
Gangtok, *India* 41 F16 27 20N 88 37 E
Gangu, *China* 34 G3 34 40N 105 15 E
Gangyao, *China* 35 B14 44 12N 126 37 E
Gani, *Indonesia* 37 E7 0 48S 128 14 E
Ganj, *India* 43 F8 27 45N 78 57 E
Gannett Peak, *U.S.A.* 82 E9 43 11N 109 39W
Ganquan, *China* 34 F5 36 20N 109 20 E
Gansu □, *China* 34 G3 36 0N 104 0 E
Ganta, *Liberia* 50 G4 7 15N 8 59W
Gantheaume, C., *Australia* 63 F2 36 4S 137 32 E
Gantheaume B., *Australia* 61 E1 27 40S 114 10 E
Gantsevichi = Hantsavichy, *Belarus* 17 B14 52 49N 26 30 E
Ganyem = Genyem, *Indonesia* 37 E10 2 46S 140 12 E
Ganyu, *China* 35 G10 34 50N 119 8 E
Ganzhou, *China* 33 D6 25 51N 114 56 E
Gao, *Mali* 50 E5 16 15N 0 5W
Gaomi, *China* 35 F10 36 20N 119 42 E
Gaoping, *China* 34 G7 35 45N 112 55 E
Gaotang, *China* 34 F9 36 50N 116 15 E
Gaoua, *Burkina Faso* 50 F5 10 20N 3 8W
Gaoual, *Guinea* 50 F3 11 45N 13 25W
Gaoxiong = Kaohsiung, *Taiwan* 33 D7 22 35N 120 16 E
Gaoyang, *China* 34 E8 38 40N 115 45 E
Gaoyou Hu, *China* 35 H10 32 45N 119 20 E
Gaoyuan, *China* 35 F9 37 8N 117 58 E
Gap, *France* 18 D7 44 33N 6 5 E
Gapat —►, *India* 43 G10 24 30N 82 28 E
Gapuwiyak, *Australia* 62 A2 12 25S 135 43 E
Gar, *China* 32 C2 32 10N 79 58 E
Garabogazköl Aylagy, *Turkmenistan* 25 F9 41 0N 53 30 E
Garachico, *Canary Is.* 22 F3 28 22N 16 46W
Garachiné, *Panama* 88 E4 8 0N 78 12W
Garafia, *Canary Is.* 22 F2 28 48N 17 57W
Garah, *Australia* 63 D4 29 5S 149 38 E
Garajonay, *Canary Is.* 22 F2 28 7N 17 14W
Garanhuns, *Brazil* 93 E11 8 50S 36 30W
Garautha, *India* 43 G8 25 34N 79 18 E
Garba Tula, *Kenya* 54 B4 0 30N 38 32 E
Garberville, *U.S.A.* 82 F2 40 6N 123 48W
Garbiyang, *India* 43 D9 30 8N 80 54 E
Garda, L. di, *Italy* 20 B4 45 40N 10 41 E
Garde L., *Canada* 73 A7 62 50N 106 13W
Garden City, *Ga., U.S.A.* 77 J5 32 6N 81 9W
Garden City, *Kans., U.S.A.* 81 G4 37 58N 100 53W
Garden City, *Tex., U.S.A.* 81 K4 31 52N 101 29W
Garden Grove, *U.S.A.* 85 M9 33 47N 117 55W
Gardēz, *Afghan.* 42 C3 33 37N 69 9 E
Gardiner, *Maine, U.S.A.* 77 C11 44 14N 69 47W
Gardiner, *Mont., U.S.A.* 82 D8 45 2N 110 22W
Gardiners I., *U.S.A.* 79 E12 41 6N 72 6W
Gardner, *U.S.A.* 79 D13 42 34N 71 59W
Gardner Canal, *Canada* 72 C3 53 27N 128 8W
Gardnerville, *U.S.A.* 84 G7 38 56N 119 45W
Gardo, *Somali Rep.* 46 F4 9 30N 49 6 E
Garey, *U.S.A.* 85 L6 34 53N 120 19W
Garfield, *U.S.A.* 82 C5 47 1N 117 9W
Garforth, *U.K.* 10 D6 53 47N 1 24W
Gargano, Mte., *Italy* 20 D6 41 43N 15 43 E
Garibaldi Prov. Park, *Canada* 72 D4 49 50N 122 40W
Garies, *S. Africa* 56 E2 30 32S 17 59 E
Garigliano —►, *Italy* 20 D5 41 13N 13 45 E
Garissa, *Kenya* 54 C4 0 25S 39 40 E
Garland, *Tex., U.S.A.* 81 J6 32 55N 96 38W
Garland, *Utah, U.S.A.* 82 F7 41 47N 112 10W
Garm, *Tajikistan* 26 F8 39 0N 70 20 E
Garmāb, *Iran* 45 C8 35 25N 56 45 E
Garmisch-Partenkirchen, *Germany* 16 E6 47 30N 11 6 E
Garmsār, *Iran* 45 C7 35 20N 52 25 E
Garner, *U.S.A.* 80 D8 43 6N 93 36W
Garnett, *U.S.A.* 80 F7 38 17N 95 14W
Garo Hills, *India* 43 G14 25 30N 90 30 E
Garoe, *Somali Rep.* 46 F4 8 25N 48 33 E
Garonne —►, *France* 18 D3 45 2N 0 36W
Garot, *India* 42 G6 24 19N 75 41 E
Garoua, *Cameroon* 51 G8 9 19N 13 21 E
Garrauli, *India* 43 G8 25 5N 79 22 E
Garrison, *Mont., U.S.A.* 82 C7 46 31N 112 49W
Garrison, *N. Dak., U.S.A.* 80 B4 47 40N 101 25W
Garrison Res. = Sakakawea, L., *U.S.A.* 80 B4 47 30N 101 25W
Garron Pt., *U.K.* 13 A6 55 3N 5 59W
Garry —►, *U.K.* 12 E5 56 44N 3 47W
Garry, L., *Canada* 68 B9 65 58N 100 18W
Garsen, *Kenya* 54 C5 2 20S 40 5 E
Garson L., *Canada* 73 B6 56 19N 110 2W
Garu, *India* 43 H11 23 40N 84 14 E
Garub, *Namibia* 56 D2 26 37S 16 0 E
Garut, *Indonesia* 37 G12 7 14S 107 53 E
Garvie Mts., *N.Z.* 59 L2 45 30S 168 50 E
Garwa = Garoua, *Cameroon* 51 G8 9 19N 13 21 E
Garwa, *India* 43 G10 24 11N 83 47 E
Gary, *U.S.A.* 76 E2 41 36N 87 20W
Garzê, *China* 32 C5 31 38N 100 1 E
Garzón, *Colombia* 92 C3 2 10N 75 40W
Gas-San, *Japan* 30 E10 38 32N 140 1 E
Gasan Kuli = Esenguly, *Turkmenistan* 26 F6 37 37N 53 59 E
Gascogne, *France* 18 E4 43 45N 0 20 E
Gascogne, G. de, *Europe* 18 D2 44 0N 2 0W
Gascony = Gascogne, *France* 18 E4 43 45N 0 20 E
Gascoyne —►, *Australia* 61 D1 24 52S 113 37 E
Gascoyne Junction, *Australia* 61 E2 25 2S 115 17 E
Gashaka, *Nigeria* 51 G8 7 20N 11 29 E
Gasherbrum, *Pakistan* 43 B7 35 40N 76 40 E
Gashua, *Nigeria* 51 F8 12 54N 11 0 E
Gaspé, *Canada* 71 C7 48 52N 64 30W
Gaspé, C. de, *Canada* 71 C7 48 48N 64 7W
Gaspé, Pén. de, *Canada* 71 C6 48 45N 65 40W
Gaspésie, Parc de Conservation de la, *Canada* 71 C6 48 55N 65 50W
Gasteiz = Vitoria-Gasteiz, *Spain* 19 A4 42 50N 2 41W
Gastonia, *U.S.A.* 77 H5 35 16N 81 11W
Gastre, *Argentina* 96 E3 42 20S 69 15W
Gata, C., *Cyprus* 23 E12 34 34N 33 2 E
Gata, C. de, *Spain* 19 D4 36 41N 2 13W
Gata, Sierra de, *Spain* 19 B2 40 20N 6 45W
Gataga —►, *Canada* 72 B3 58 35N 126 59W
Gatehouse of Fleet, *U.K.* 12 G4 54 53N 4 12W
Gates, *U.S.A.* 78 C7 43 9N 77 42W
Gateshead, *U.K.* 10 C6 54 57N 1 35W
Gatesville, *U.S.A.* 81 K6 31 26N 97 45W
Gaths, *Zimbabwe* 55 G3 20 2S 30 32 E
Gatico, *Chile* 94 A1 22 29S 70 20W
Gatineau, *Canada* 79 A9 45 29N 75 38W
Gatineau —►, *Canada* 70 C4 45 27N 75 42W
Gatineau, Parc Nat. de la, *Canada* 70 C4 45 40N 76 0W
Gatton, *Australia* 63 D5 27 32S 152 17 E

Gatun, L.

Gatun, L., Panama 88 E4 9 7N 79 56W
Gatyana, S. Africa 57 E4 32 16S 28 31 E
Gau, Fiji 59 D8 18 2S 179 18 E
Gauer L., Canada 73 B9 57 0N 97 50W
Gauhati, India 41 F17 26 10N 91 45 E
Gauja →, Latvia 9 H21 57 10N 24 16 E
Gaula →, Norway 8 E14 63 21N 10 14 E
Gauri Phanta, India 43 E9 28 41N 80 36 E
Gausta, Norway 9 G13 59 48N 8 40 E
Gauteng □, S. Africa 57 D4 26 0S 28 0 E
Gāv Koshī, Iran 45 D8 28 38N 57 12 E
Gāvakān, Iran 45 D7 29 37N 53 10 E
Gavāter, Iran 45 E9 25 10N 61 31 E
Gāvbandī, Iran 45 E7 27 12N 53 4 E
Gavdhopoúla, Greece 23 E6 34 56N 24 0 E
Gávdhos, Greece 23 E6 34 50N 24 5 E
Gaviota, U.S.A. 85 L6 34 29N 120 13W
Gāvkhūnī, Bāţlāq-e, Iran 45 C7 32 6N 52 52 E
Gävle, Sweden 9 F17 60 40N 17 9 E
Gawachab, Namibia 56 D2 27 4S 17 55 E
Gawilgarh Hills, India 40 J10 21 15N 76 45 E
Gawler, Australia 63 E2 34 30S 138 42 E
Gaxun Nur, China 32 B5 42 22N 100 30 E
Gay, Russia 24 D10 51 27N 58 27 E
Gaya, India 43 G11 24 47N 85 4 E
Gaya, Niger 50 F6 11 52N 3 28 E
Gaylord, U.S.A. 76 C3 45 2N 84 41W
Gayndah, Australia 63 D5 25 35S 151 32 E
Gaysin = Haysyn, Ukraine 17 D15 48 57N 29 25 E
Gayvoron = Hayvoron, Ukraine 17 D15 48 22N 29 52 E
Gaza, Gaza Strip 47 D3 31 30N 34 28 E
Gaza □, Mozam. 57 C5 23 10S 32 45 E
Gaza Strip □, Asia 47 D3 31 29N 34 25 E
Gazanjyk, Turkmenistan 45 B7 39 16N 55 32 E
Gāzbor, Iran 45 D8 28 5N 58 51 E
Gazi, Dem. Rep. of the Congo 54 B1 1 3N 24 30 E
Gaziantep, Turkey 25 G6 37 6N 37 23 E
Gcuwa, S. Africa 57 E4 32 20S 28 11 E
Gdańsk, Poland 17 A10 54 22N 18 40 E
Gdańska, Zatoka, Poland 17 A10 54 30N 19 20 E
Gdov, Russia 9 G22 58 48N 27 55 E
Gdynia, Poland 17 A10 54 35N 18 33 E
Gebe, Indonesia 37 D7 0 5N 129 25 E
Gebze, Turkey 21 D13 40 47N 29 25 E
Gedaref, Sudan 51 F13 14 2N 35 28 E
Gediz →, Turkey 21 E12 38 35N 26 48 E
Gedser, Denmark 9 J14 54 35N 11 55 E
Geegully Cr. →, Australia 60 C3 18 32S 123 41 E
Geel, Belgium 15 C4 51 10N 4 59 E
Geelong, Australia 63 F3 38 10S 144 22 E
Geelvink B. = Cenderwasih, Teluk, Indonesia 37 E9 3 0S 135 20 E
Geelvink Chan., Australia 61 E1 28 30S 114 0 E
Geesthacht, Germany 16 B6 53 26N 10 22 E
Geidam, Nigeria 51 F8 12 57N 11 57 E
Geikie →, Canada 73 B8 57 45N 103 52W
Geistown, U.S.A. 78 F6 40 18N 78 52W
Geita, Tanzania 54 C3 2 48S 32 12 E
Gejiu, China 32 D5 23 20N 103 10 E
Gel, Meydān-e, Iran 45 D7 29 4N 54 50 E
Gela, Italy 20 F6 37 4N 14 15 E
Gelderland □, Neths. 15 B6 52 5N 6 10 E
Geldrop, Neths. 15 C5 51 25N 5 32 E
Geleen, Neths. 15 D5 50 57N 5 49 E
Gelibolu, Turkey 21 D12 40 28N 26 43 E
Gelsenkirchen, Germany 16 C4 51 32N 7 6 E
Gemas, Malaysia 39 L4 2 37N 102 36 E
Gembloux, Belgium 15 D4 50 34N 4 43 E
Gemena, Dem. Rep. of the Congo 52 D3 3 13N 19 48 E
Gemerek, Turkey 44 B3 39 15N 36 10 E
Gemlik, Turkey 21 D13 40 26N 29 9 E
Genale, Ethiopia 46 F2 6 0N 39 30 E
General Acha, Argentina 94 D3 37 20S 64 38W
General Alvear, Buenos Aires, Argentina 94 D4 36 0S 60 0W
General Alvear, Mendoza, Argentina 94 D2 35 0S 67 40W
General Artigas, Paraguay 94 B4 26 52S 56 16W
General Belgrano, Argentina 94 D4 36 35S 58 47W
General Cabrera, Argentina 94 C3 32 53S 63 52W
General Cepeda, Mexico 86 B4 25 23N 101 27W
General Guido, Argentina 94 D4 36 40S 57 50W
General Juan Madariaga, Argentina 94 D4 37 0S 57 0W
General La Madrid, Argentina 94 D3 37 17S 61 20W
General MacArthur, Phil. 37 B7 11 18N 125 28 E
General Martin Miguel de Güemes, Argentina 94 A3 24 50S 65 0W
General Paz, Argentina 94 B4 27 45S 57 36W
General Pico, Argentina 94 D3 35 45S 63 50W
General Pinedo, Argentina 94 B3 27 15S 61 20W
General Pinto, Argentina 94 C3 34 45S 61 50W
General Roca, Argentina 96 D3 39 2S 67 35W
General Santos, Phil. 37 C7 6 5N 125 14 E
General Trevino, Mexico 87 B5 26 14N 99 29W
General Trias, Mexico 86 B3 28 21N 106 22W
General Viamonte, Argentina 94 D3 35 1S 61 3W
General Villegas, Argentina 94 D3 35 5S 63 0W
Genesee, Idaho, U.S.A. 82 C5 46 33N 116 56W
Genesee, Pa., U.S.A. 78 E7 41 59N 77 54W
Genesee →, U.S.A. 78 C7 43 16N 77 36W
Geneseo, Ill., U.S.A. 80 E9 41 27N 90 9W
Geneseo, N.Y., U.S.A. 78 D7 42 48N 77 49W
Geneva = Genève, Switz. 18 C7 46 12N 6 9 E
Geneva, Ala., U.S.A. 77 K3 31 2N 85 52W
Geneva, N.Y., U.S.A. 78 D8 42 52N 76 59W
Geneva, Nebr., U.S.A. 80 E6 40 32N 97 36W
Geneva, Ohio, U.S.A. 78 E4 41 48N 80 57W
Geneva, L. = Léman, L., Europe 18 C7 46 26N 6 30 E
Geneva, L., U.S.A. 76 D1 42 38N 88 30W
Genève, Switz. 18 C7 46 12N 6 9 E
Genil →, Spain 19 D3 37 42N 5 19W
Genk, Belgium 15 D5 50 58N 5 32 E
Gennargentu, Mti. del, Italy 20 D3 40 1N 9 19 E
Genoa = Génova, Italy 18 D8 44 25N 8 57 E
Genoa, Australia 63 F4 37 29S 149 35 E
Genoa, N.Y., U.S.A. 79 D8 42 40N 76 32W
Genoa, Nebr., U.S.A. 80 E6 41 27N 97 44W
Genoa, Nev., U.S.A. 84 F7 39 2N 119 50W
Génova, Italy 18 D8 44 25N 8 57 E
Génova, G. di, Italy 20 C3 44 0N 9 0 E
Genriyetty, Ostrov, Russia 27 B16 77 6N 156 30 E
Gent, Belgium 15 C3 51 2N 3 42 E
Genteng, Indonesia 37 G12 7 22S 106 24 E
Genyem, Indonesia 37 E10 2 46S 140 12 E
Geographe B., Australia 61 F2 33 30S 115 15 E
Geographe Chan., Australia 61 D1 24 30S 113 0 E
Georga, Zemlya, Russia 26 A5 80 30N 49 0 E
George, S. Africa 56 E3 33 58S 22 29 E
George →, Canada 71 A6 58 49N 66 10W
George, L., N.S.W., Australia 63 F4 35 10S 149 25 E
George, L., S. Austral., Australia 63 F3 37 25S 140 0 E
George, L., W. Austral., Australia 60 D3 22 45S 123 40 E
George, L., Uganda 54 B3 0 5N 30 10 E
George, L., Fla., U.S.A. 77 L5 29 17N 81 36W
George, L., N.Y., U.S.A. 79 C11 43 37N 73 33W
George Gill Ra., Australia 60 D5 24 22S 131 45 E
George River = Kangiqsualujjuaq, Canada 69 C13 58 30N 65 59W
George Sound, N.Z. 59 L1 44 52S 167 25 E
George Town, Australia 62 G4 41 6S 146 49 E
George Town, Bahamas 88 B4 23 33N 75 47W
George Town, Malaysia 39 K3 5 25N 100 15 E
George V Land, Antarctica 5 C10 69 0S 148 0 E
George VI Sound, Antarctica 5 D17 71 0S 68 0W
George West, U.S.A. 81 L5 28 20N 98 7W
Georgetown, Australia 62 B3 18 17S 143 33 E
Georgetown, Ont., Canada 78 C5 43 40N 79 56W
Georgetown, P.E.I., Canada 71 C7 46 13N 62 24W
Georgetown, Cayman Is. 88 C3 19 20N 81 24W
Georgetown, Gambia 50 F3 13 30N 14 47W
Georgetown, Guyana 92 B7 6 50N 58 12W
Georgetown, Calif., U.S.A. 84 G6 38 54N 120 50W
Georgetown, Colo., U.S.A. 82 G11 39 42N 105 42W
Georgetown, Ky., U.S.A. 76 F3 38 13N 84 33W
Georgetown, N.Y., U.S.A. 79 D9 42 46N 75 44W
Georgetown, Ohio, U.S.A. 76 F4 38 52N 83 54W
Georgetown, S.C., U.S.A. 77 J6 33 23N 79 17W
Georgetown, Tex., U.S.A. 81 K6 30 38N 97 41W
Georgia □, U.S.A. 77 K5 32 50N 83 15W
Georgia ■, Asia 25 F7 42 0N 43 0 E
Georgia, Str. of, Canada 72 D4 49 25N 124 0W
Georgian B., Canada 78 A4 45 15N 81 0W
Georgina →, Australia 62 C2 23 30S 139 47 E
Georgina I., Canada 78 B5 44 22N 79 17W
Georgiu-Dezh = Liski, Russia 25 D6 51 3N 39 30 E
Georgiyevsk, Russia 25 F7 44 12N 43 28 E
Gera, Germany 16 C7 50 53N 12 4 E
Geraardsbergen, Belgium 15 D3 50 45N 3 53 E
Geral, Serra, Brazil 95 B6 26 25S 50 0W
Geral de Goiás, Serra, Brazil 93 F9 12 0S 46 0W
Geraldine, U.S.A. 82 C8 47 36N 110 16W
Geraldton, Australia 61 E1 28 48S 114 32 E
Geraldton, Canada 70 C2 49 44N 86 59W
Gereshk, Afghan. 40 D4 31 47N 64 35 E
Gerik, Malaysia 39 K3 5 50N 101 15 E
Gering, U.S.A. 80 E3 41 50N 103 40W
Gerlach, U.S.A. 82 F4 40 39N 119 21W
Germansen Landing, Canada 72 B4 55 43N 124 40W
Germantown, U.S.A. 81 M10 35 5N 89 49W
Germany ■, Europe 16 C6 51 0N 10 0 E
Germī, Iran 45 B6 39 1N 48 3 E
Germiston, S. Africa 57 D4 26 15S 28 10 E
Gernika-Lumo, Spain 19 A4 43 19N 2 40W
Gero, Japan 31 G8 35 48N 137 14 E
Gerona = Girona, Spain 19 B7 41 58N 2 46 E
Gerrard, Canada 72 C5 50 30N 117 17W
Geser, Indonesia 37 E8 3 50S 130 54 E
Getafe, Spain 19 B4 40 18N 3 44W
Gettysburg, Pa., U.S.A. 76 F7 39 50N 77 14W
Gettysburg, S. Dak., U.S.A. 80 C5 45 1N 99 57W
Getxo, Spain 19 A4 43 21N 2 59W
Getz Ice Shelf, Antarctica 5 D14 75 0S 130 0W
Geyser, U.S.A. 82 C8 47 16N 110 30W
Geyserville, U.S.A. 84 G4 38 42N 122 54W
Ghaggar →, India 42 E6 29 30N 74 53 E
Ghaghara →, India 43 G11 25 45N 84 40 E
Ghaghat →, Bangla. 43 G13 25 19N 89 38 E
Ghagra, India 43 H11 23 17N 84 33 E
Ghagra →, India 43 F9 27 29N 81 9 E
Ghana ■, W. Afr. 50 G5 8 0N 1 0W
Ghansor, India 43 H9 22 39N 80 1 E
Ghanzi, Botswana 56 C3 21 50S 21 34 E
Ghanzi □, Botswana 56 C3 21 50S 21 45 E
Ghardaïa, Algeria 50 B6 32 20N 3 37 E
Gharyān, Libya 51 B8 32 10N 13 0 E
Ghat, Libya 51 D8 24 59N 10 11 E
Ghatal, India 43 H12 22 40N 87 46 E
Ghatampur, India 43 F9 26 8N 80 13 E
Ghatsila, India 43 H12 22 36N 86 29 E
Ghaţţī, Si. Arabia 44 D3 31 16N 37 31 E
Ghawdex = Gozo, Malta 23 C1 36 3N 14 13 E
Ghazal, Bahr el →, Chad 51 F9 13 0N 15 47 E
Ghazâl, Bahr el →, Sudan 51 G12 9 31N 30 25 E
Ghaziabad, India 42 E7 28 42N 77 26 E
Ghazipur, India 43 G10 25 38N 83 35 E
Ghaznī, Afghan. 42 C3 33 30N 68 28 E
Ghaznī □, Afghan. 40 C6 32 10N 68 20 E
Ghent = Gent, Belgium 15 C3 51 2N 3 42 E
Ghīnah, Wādī al, Si. Arabia 44 D3 30 27N 38 14 E
Ghizao, Afghan. 42 C1 33 20N 65 44 E
Ghizar →, Pakistan 43 A5 36 15N 73 43 E
Ghotaru, India 42 F4 27 20N 70 1 E
Ghotki, Pakistan 42 E3 28 5N 69 21 E
Ghowr □, Afghan. 40 C4 34 0N 64 20 E
Ghudaf, W. al →, Iraq 44 C4 32 56N 43 30 E
Ghudāmis, Libya 51 B7 30 11N 9 29 E
Ghughri, India 43 H9 22 39N 80 41 E
Ghugus, India 40 K11 19 58N 79 12 E
Ghulam Mohammad Barrage, Pakistan 42 G3 25 30N 68 20 E
Ghūrīān, Afghan. 40 B2 34 17N 61 25 E
Gia Dinh, Vietnam 39 G6 10 49N 106 42 E
Gia Lai = Plei Ku, Vietnam 38 F7 13 57N 108 0 E
Gia Nghia, Vietnam 39 G6 11 58N 107 42 E
Gia Ngoc, Vietnam 38 E7 14 50N 108 58 E
Gia Vuc, Vietnam 38 E7 14 42N 108 34 E
Giant Forest, U.S.A. 84 J8 36 36N 118 43W
Giants Causeway, U.K. 13 A5 55 16N 6 29W
Giarabub = Al Jaghbūb, Libya 51 C10 29 42N 24 38 E
Giarre, Italy 20 F6 37 43N 15 11 E
Gibara, Cuba 88 B4 21 9N 76 11W
Gibb River, Australia 60 C4 16 26S 126 26 E
Gibbon, U.S.A. 80 E5 40 45N 98 51W
Gibeon, Namibia 56 D2 25 7S 17 45 E
Gibraltar ■, Europe 19 D3 36 7N 5 22W
Gibraltar, Str. of, Medit. S. 19 E3 35 55N 5 40W
Gibson Desert, Australia 60 D4 24 0S 126 0 E
Gibsons, Canada 72 D4 49 24N 123 32W
Gibsonville, U.S.A. 84 F6 39 46N 120 54W
Giddings, U.S.A. 81 K6 30 11N 96 56W
Giessen, Germany 16 C5 50 34N 8 41 E
Gīfān, Iran 45 B8 37 54N 57 28 E
Gift Lake, Canada 72 B5 55 53N 115 49W
Gifu, Japan 31 G8 35 30N 136 45 E
Gifu □, Japan 31 G8 35 40N 137 0 E
Giganta, Sa. de la, Mexico 86 B2 25 30N 111 30W
Gigha, U.K. 12 F3 55 42N 5 44W
Giglio, Italy 20 C4 42 20N 10 52 E
Gijón, Spain 19 A3 43 32N 5 42W
Gil I., Canada 72 C3 53 12N 129 15W
Gila →, U.S.A. 83 K6 32 43N 114 33W
Gila Bend, U.S.A. 83 K7 32 57N 112 43W
Gila Bend Mts., U.S.A. 83 K7 33 10N 113 0W
Gīlān □, Iran 45 B6 37 0N 50 0 E
Gilbert →, Australia 62 B3 16 35S 141 15 E
Gilbert Is., Kiribati 64 G9 1 0N 172 0 E
Gilbert River, Australia 62 B3 18 9S 142 52 E
Gilead, U.S.A. 79 B14 44 24N 70 59W
Gilford I., Canada 72 C3 50 40N 126 30W
Gilgandra, Australia 63 E4 31 43S 148 39 E
Gilgil, Kenya 54 C4 0 30S 36 20 E
Gilgit, India 43 B6 35 50N 74 15 E
Gilgit →, Pakistan 43 B6 35 44N 74 37 E
Gilgunnia, Australia 63 E4 32 26S 146 2 E
Gillam, Canada 73 B10 56 20N 94 40W
Gillen, L., Australia 61 E3 26 11S 124 38 E
Gilles, L., Australia 63 E2 32 50S 136 45 E
Gillette, U.S.A. 80 C2 44 18N 105 30W
Gilliat, Australia 62 C3 20 40S 141 28 E
Gillingham, U.K. 11 F8 51 23N 0 33 E
Gilmer, U.S.A. 81 J7 32 44N 94 57W
Gilmore, L., Australia 61 F3 32 29S 121 37 E
Gilroy, U.S.A. 84 H5 37 1N 121 34W
Gimli, Canada 73 C9 50 40N 97 0W
Gin Gin, Australia 63 D5 25 0S 151 58 E
Gingin, Australia 61 F2 31 22S 115 54 E
Ginir, Ethiopia 46 F3 7 6N 40 40 E
Gióna, Óros, Greece 21 E10 38 38N 22 14 E
Gippsland, Australia 63 F4 37 52S 147 0 E
Gir Hills, India 42 J4 21 0N 71 0 E
Girab, India 42 F4 26 2N 70 38 E
Girâfi, W. →, Egypt 47 F3 29 58N 34 39 E
Girard, Kans., U.S.A. 81 G7 37 31N 94 51W
Girard, Ohio, U.S.A. 78 E4 41 9N 80 42W
Girard, Pa., U.S.A. 78 D4 42 0N 80 19W
Girard, Pa., U.S.A. 78 E4 42 0N 80 19W
Girdle Ness, U.K. 12 D6 57 9N 2 3W
Giresun, Turkey 25 F6 40 55N 38 30 E
Girga, Egypt 51 C12 26 17N 31 55 E
Giri →, India 42 D7 30 28N 77 41 E
Giridih, India 43 G12 24 10N 86 21 E
Girne = Kyrenia, Cyprus 23 D12 35 20N 33 20 E
Girona, Spain 19 B7 41 58N 2 46 E
Gironde →, France 18 D3 45 32N 1 7W
Giru, Australia 62 B4 19 30S 147 5 E
Girvan, U.K. 12 F4 55 14N 4 51W
Gisborne, N.Z. 59 H7 38 39S 178 5 E
Gisenyi, Rwanda 54 C2 1 41S 29 15 E
Gislaved, Sweden 9 H15 57 19N 13 32 E
Gitega, Burundi 54 C2 3 26S 29 56 E
Giuba →, Somali Rep. 46 G3 1 30N 42 35 E
Giurgiu, Romania 17 G13 43 52N 25 57 E
Giza = El Gîza, Egypt 51 C12 30 0N 31 10 E
Gizhiga, Russia 27 C17 62 3N 160 30 E
Gizhiginskaya Guba, Russia 27 C16 61 0N 158 0 E
Giżycko, Poland 17 A11 54 2N 21 48 E
Gjirokastra, Albania 21 D9 40 7N 20 10 E
Gjoa Haven, Canada 68 B10 68 20N 96 8W
Gjøvik, Norway 9 F14 60 47N 10 43 E
Glace Bay, Canada 71 C8 46 11N 59 58W
Glacier Bay National Park and Preserve, U.S.A. 72 B1 58 45N 136 30W
Glacier National Park, Canada 72 C5 51 15N 117 30W
Glacier National Park, U.S.A. 82 B7 48 30N 113 18W
Glacier Peak, U.S.A. 82 B3 48 7N 121 7W
Gladewater, U.S.A. 81 J7 32 33N 94 56W
Gladstone, Queens., Australia 62 C5 23 52S 151 16 E
Gladstone, S. Austral., Australia 63 E2 33 15S 138 22 E
Gladstone, Canada 73 C9 50 13N 98 57W
Gladstone, U.S.A. 76 C2 45 51N 87 1W
Gladwin, U.S.A. 76 D3 43 59N 84 29W
Glåma = Glomma →, Norway 9 G14 59 12N 10 57 E
Gláma, Iceland 8 D2 65 48N 23 0W
Glamis, U.S.A. 85 N11 32 55N 115 5W
Glasco, Kans., U.S.A. 80 F6 39 22N 97 50W
Glasco, N.Y., U.S.A. 79 D11 42 3N 73 57W
Glasgow, U.K. 12 F4 55 51N 4 15W
Glasgow, Ky., U.S.A. 76 G3 37 0N 85 55W
Glasgow, Mont., U.S.A. 82 B10 48 12N 106 38W
Glaslyn, Canada 73 C7 53 22N 108 21W
Glastonbury, U.K. 11 F5 51 9N 2 43W
Glastonbury, U.S.A. 79 E12 41 43N 72 37W
Glazov, Russia 24 C9 58 9N 52 40 E
Gleichen, Canada 72 C6 50 52N 113 3W
Gleiwitz = Gliwice, Poland 17 C10 50 22N 18 41 E
Glen, U.S.A. 79 B13 44 7N 71 11W
Glen Affric, U.K. 12 D3 57 17N 5 1W
Glen Canyon, U.S.A. 83 H8 37 30N 110 40W
Glen Canyon Dam, U.S.A. 83 H8 36 57N 111 29W
Glen Canyon National Recreation Area, U.S.A. 83 H8 37 15N 111 0W
Glen Coe, U.K. 12 E3 56 40N 5 0W
Glen Cove, U.S.A. 79 F11 40 52N 73 38W
Glen Garry, U.K. 12 D3 57 3N 5 7W
Glen Innes, Australia 63 D5 29 44S 151 44 E
Glen Lyon, U.S.A. 79 E8 41 10N 76 5W
Glen Mor, U.K. 12 D4 57 9N 4 37W
Glen Moriston, U.K. 12 D4 57 11N 4 52W
Glen Robertson, Canada 79 A10 45 22N 74 30W
Glen Spean, U.K. 12 E4 56 53N 4 40W
Glen Ullin, U.S.A. 80 B4 46 49N 101 50W
Glencoe, Canada 78 D3 42 45N 81 43W
Glencoe, S. Africa 57 D5 28 11S 30 11 E
Glencoe, U.S.A. 80 C7 44 46N 94 9W
Glendale, Ariz., U.S.A. 83 K7 33 32N 112 11W
Glendale, Calif., U.S.A. 85 L8 34 9N 118 15W
Glendale, Zimbabwe 55 F3 17 22S 31 5 E
Glendive, U.S.A. 80 B2 47 7N 104 43W
Glendo, U.S.A. 80 D2 42 30N 105 2W
Glenelg →, Australia 63 F3 38 4S 140 59 E
Glenfield, U.S.A. 79 C9 43 43N 75 24W
Glengarriff, Ireland 13 E2 51 45N 9 34W
Glenmont, U.S.A. 78 F2 40 31N 82 6W
Glenmorgan, Australia 63 D4 27 14S 149 42 E
Glenn, U.S.A. 84 F4 39 31N 122 1W
Glennallen, U.S.A. 68 B5 62 0N 145 50W
Glennamaddy, Ireland 13 C3 53 37N 8 33W
Glenns Ferry, U.S.A. 82 E6 42 57N 115 18W
Glenore, Australia 62 B3 17 50S 141 12 E
Glenreagh, Australia 63 E5 30 2S 153 1 E
Glenrock, U.S.A. 82 E11 42 52N 105 52W
Glenrothes, U.K. 12 E5 56 12N 3 10W
Glens Falls, U.S.A. 79 C11 43 19N 73 39W
Glenside, U.S.A. 79 F9 40 6N 75 9W
Glenties, Ireland 13 B3 54 49N 8 16W
Glenville, U.S.A. 76 F5 38 56N 80 50W
Glenwood, Canada 71 C9 49 0N 54 58W
Glenwood, Ark., U.S.A. 81 H8 34 20N 93 33W
Glenwood, Hawaii, U.S.A. 74 J17 19 29N 155 9W
Glenwood, Iowa, U.S.A. 80 E7 41 3N 95 45W
Glenwood, Minn., U.S.A. 80 C7 45 39N 95 23W
Glenwood, Wash., U.S.A. 84 D5 46 1N 121 17W
Glenwood Springs, U.S.A. 82 G10 39 33N 107 19W
Glettinganes, Iceland 8 D7 65 30N 13 37W
Gliwice, Poland 17 C10 50 22N 18 41 E
Globe, U.S.A. 83 K8 33 24N 110 47W
Głogów, Poland 16 C9 51 37N 16 5 E
Glomma →, Norway 9 G14 59 12N 10 57 E
Glorieuses, Is., Ind. Oc. 57 A8 11 30S 47 20 E
Glossop, U.K. 10 D6 53 27N 1 56W
Gloucester, Australia 63 E5 32 0S 151 59 E
Gloucester, U.K. 11 F5 51 53N 2 15W
Gloucester, U.S.A. 79 D14 42 37N 70 40W
Gloucester I., Australia 62 C4 20 0S 148 30 E
Gloucester Point, U.S.A. 76 G7 37 15N 76 29W
Gloucestershire □, U.K. 11 F5 51 46N 2 15W
Gloversville, U.S.A. 79 C10 43 3N 74 21W
Glovertown, Canada 71 C9 48 40N 54 3W
Glusk, Belarus 17 B15 52 53N 28 41 E
Gmünd, Austria 16 D8 48 45N 15 0 E
Gmunden, Austria 16 E7 47 55N 13 48 E
Gniezno, Poland 17 B9 52 30N 17 35 E
Gnowangerup, Australia 61 F2 33 58S 117 59 E
Go Cong, Vietnam 39 G6 10 22N 106 40 E
Gō-no-ura, Japan 31 H4 33 44N 129 40 E
Goa, India 40 M8 15 33N 73 59 E
Goa □, India 40 M8 15 33N 73 59 E
Goalen Hd., Australia 63 F5 36 33S 150 4 E
Goalpara, India 41 F17 26 10N 90 40 E
Goaltor, India 43 H12 22 43N 87 10 E
Goalundo Ghat, Bangla. 43 H13 23 50N 89 47 E
Goat Fell, U.K. 12 F3 55 38N 5 11W
Goba, Ethiopia 46 F2 7 1N 39 59 E
Goba, Mozam. 57 D5 26 15S 32 13 E
Gobabis, Namibia 56 C2 22 30S 19 0 E
Gobi, Asia 34 C6 44 0N 110 0 E
Gobō, Japan 31 H7 33 53N 135 10 E
Gochas, Namibia 56 C2 24 59S 18 55 E
Godavari →, India 41 L13 16 25N 82 18 E
Godavari Pt., India 41 L13 17 0N 82 20 E
Godbout, Canada 71 C6 49 20N 67 38W
Godda, India 43 G12 24 50N 87 13 E
Goderich, Canada 78 C3 43 45N 81 41W
Godfrey Ra., Australia 61 D2 24 0S 117 0 E
Godhavn, Greenland 4 C5 69 15N 53 38W
Godhra, India 42 H5 22 49N 73 40 E
Godoy Cruz, Argentina 94 C2 32 56S 68 52W
Gods →, Canada 70 A1 56 22N 92 51W
Gods L., Canada 70 B1 54 40N 94 15W
Gods River, Canada 73 C10 54 50N 94 5W
Godthåb = Nuuk, Greenland 69 B14 64 10N 51 35W
Godwin Austen = K2, Pakistan 43 B7 35 58N 76 32 E
Goeie Hoop, Kaap die = Good Hope, C. of, S. Africa 56 E2 34 24S 18 30 E
Goéland, L. au, Canada 70 C4 49 50N 76 48W
Goeree, Neths. 15 C3 51 50N 4 0 E
Goes, Neths. 15 C3 51 30N 3 55 E
Goffstown, U.S.A. 79 C13 43 1N 71 36W
Gogama, Canada 70 C3 47 35N 81 43W
Gogebic, L., U.S.A. 80 B10 46 30N 89 35W
Gogra = Ghaghara →, India 43 G11 25 45N 84 40 E
Gogriāl, Sudan 51 G11 8 30N 28 8 E
Gohana, India 42 E7 29 8N 76 42 E
Goharganj, India 42 H7 23 1N 77 41 E
Goi →, India 42 H6 22 4N 74 46 E
Goiânia, Brazil 93 G9 16 43S 49 20W
Goiás, Brazil 93 G8 15 55S 50 10W
Goiás □, Brazil 93 F9 12 10S 48 0W
Goio-Ere, Brazil 95 A5 24 12S 53 1W
Gojō, Japan 31 G7 34 21N 135 42 E
Gojra, Pakistan 42 D5 31 10N 72 40 E
Gökçeada, Turkey 21 D11 40 10N 25 50 E
Gökova Körfezi, Turkey 21 F12 36 55N 27 50 E
Gokteik, Burma 41 H20 22 26N 97 0 E
Gokurt, Pakistan 42 E2 29 40N 67 26 E
Gol Gol, Australia 63 E3 34 12S 142 14 E
Gola, India 43 E9 28 3N 80 32 E
Golakganj, India 43 F13 26 8N 89 52 E
Golan Heights = Hagolan, Syria 47 C4 33 0N 35 45 E
Golāshkerd, Iran 45 E8 27 59N 57 16 E
Golchikha, Russia 4 B12 71 45N 83 30 E
Golconda, U.S.A. 82 F5 40 58N 117 30W
Gold, U.S.A. 78 E7 41 52N 77 50W
Gold Beach, U.S.A. 82 E1 42 25N 124 25W
Gold Coast, W. Afr. 50 H5 4 0N 1 40W
Gold Hill, U.S.A. 82 E2 42 26N 123 3W
Gold River, Canada 72 D3 49 46N 126 3W
Golden, Canada 72 C5 51 20N 116 59W
Golden B., N.Z. 59 J4 40 40S 172 50 E
Golden Gate, U.S.A. 82 H2 37 54N 122 30W
Golden Hinde, Canada 72 D3 49 40N 125 44W
Golden Lake, Canada 78 A7 45 34N 77 21W
Golden Vale, Ireland 13 D3 52 33N 8 17W
Goldendale, U.S.A. 82 D3 45 49N 120 50W
Goldfield, U.S.A. 83 H5 37 42N 117 14W
Goldsand L., Canada 73 B8 57 2N 101 8W
Goldsboro, U.S.A. 77 H7 35 23N 77 59W
Goldsmith, U.S.A. 81 K3 31 59N 102 37W

Grenadines

Goldsworthy, Australia 60 D2 20 21S 119 30 E
Goldthwaite, U.S.A. 81 K5 31 27N 98 34W
Goleniów, Poland 16 B8 53 35N 14 50 E
Golestānak, Iran 45 D7 30 36N 54 14 E
Goleta, U.S.A. 85 L7 34 27N 119 50W
Golfito, Costa Rica 88 E3 8 41N 83 5W
Golfo Aranci, Italy 20 D3 40 59N 9 38 E
Goliad, U.S.A. 81 L6 28 40N 97 23W
Golpāyegān, Iran 45 C6 33 27N 50 18 E
Golra, Pakistan 42 C5 33 37N 72 56 E
Golspie, U.K. 12 D5 57 58N 3 59W
Goma, Dem. Rep. of the Congo 54 C2 1 37S 29 10 E
Gomal Pass, Pakistan 42 D3 31 56N 69 20 E
Gomati →, India 43 G10 25 32N 83 11 E
Gombari, Dem. Rep. of the Congo 54 B2 2 45N 29 3 E
Gombe, Nigeria 51 F8 10 19N 11 2 E
Gombe →, Tanzania 54 C3 4 38S 31 40 E
Gomel = Homyel, Belarus 17 B16 52 28N 31 0 E
Gomera, Canary Is. 22 F2 28 7N 17 14W
Gómez Palacio, Mexico 86 B4 25 40N 104 0W
Gomīshān, Iran 45 B7 37 4N 54 6 E
Gomogomo, Indonesia 37 F8 6 39S 134 43 E
Gomoh, India 41 H15 23 52N 86 10 E
Gompa = Ganta, Liberia 50 G4 7 15N 8 59W
Gonābād, Iran 45 C8 34 15N 58 45 E
Gonaïves, Haiti 89 C5 19 20N 72 42W
Gonâve, G. de la, Haiti 89 C5 19 29N 72 42W
Gonâve, I. de la, Haiti 89 C5 18 45N 73 0W
Gonbad-e Kāvūs, Iran 45 B7 37 20N 55 25 E
Gonda, India 43 F9 27 9N 81 58 E
Gondal, India 42 J4 21 58N 70 52 E
Gonder, Ethiopia 46 E2 12 39N 37 30 E
Gondia, India 40 J12 21 23N 80 10 E
Gondola, Mozam. 55 F3 19 10S 33 37 E
Gönen, Turkey 21 D12 40 6N 27 39 E
Gonghe, China 32 C5 36 18N 100 32 E
Gongolgon, Australia 63 E4 30 21S 146 54 E
Gongzhuling, China 35 C13 43 30N 124 40 E
Gonzales, Calif., U.S.A. 84 J5 36 30N 121 26W
Gonzales, Tex., U.S.A. 81 L6 29 30N 97 27W
González Chaves, Argentina 94 D3 38 2S 60 5W
Good Hope, C. of, S. Africa 56 E2 34 24S 18 30 E
Gooderham, Canada 78 B6 44 54N 78 21W
Gooding, U.S.A. 82 E6 42 56N 114 43W
Goodland, U.S.A. 80 F4 39 21N 101 43W
Goodlow, Canada 72 B4 56 20N 120 8W
Goodooga, Australia 63 D4 29 3S 147 28 E
Goodsprings, U.S.A. 85 K11 35 49N 115 27W
Goole, U.K. 10 D7 53 42N 0 53W
Goolgowi, Australia 63 E4 33 58S 145 41 E
Goolwa, Australia 63 F2 35 30S 138 47 E
Goomalling, Australia 61 F2 31 15S 116 49 E
Goomeri, Australia 63 D5 26 12S 152 6 E
Goonda, Mozam. 55 F3 19 48S 33 57 E
Goondiwindi, Australia 63 D5 28 30S 150 21 E
Goongarrie, L., Australia 61 F3 30 3S 121 9 E
Goonyella, Australia 62 C4 21 47S 147 58 E
Goose →, Canada 71 B7 53 20N 60 35W
Goose Creek, U.S.A. 77 J5 32 59N 80 2W
Goose L., U.S.A. 82 F3 41 56N 120 26W
Gop, India 40 H6 22 5N 69 50 E
Gopalganj, India 43 F11 26 28N 84 30 E
Göppingen, Germany 16 D5 48 42N 9 39 E
Gorakhpur, India 43 F10 26 47N 83 23 E
Goražde, Bos.-H. 21 C8 43 38N 18 58 E
Gorda, U.S.A. 84 K5 35 53N 121 26W
Gorda, Pta., Canary Is. 22 F2 28 45N 18 0W
Gorda, Pta., Nic. 88 D3 14 20N 83 10W
Gordan B., Australia 60 B5 11 35S 130 10 E
Gordon, U.S.A. 80 D3 42 48N 102 12W
Gordon →, Australia 62 G4 42 27S 145 30 E
Gordon L., Alta., Canada 73 B6 56 30N 110 25W
Gordon L., N.W.T., Canada 72 A6 63 5N 113 11W
Gordonvale, Australia 62 B4 17 5S 145 50 E
Gore, Ethiopia 46 F2 8 12N 35 32 E
Gore, N.Z. 59 M2 46 5S 168 58 E
Gore Bay, Canada 70 C3 45 57N 82 28W
Gorey, Ireland 13 D5 52 41N 6 18W
Gorg, Iran 45 D8 29 29N 59 43 E
Gorgān, Iran 45 B7 36 50N 54 29 E
Gorgona, I., Colombia 92 C3 3 0N 78 10W
Gorham, U.S.A. 79 B13 44 23N 71 10W
Goriganga →, India 43 E9 29 45N 80 23 E
Gorinchem, Neths. 15 C4 51 50N 4 59 E
Goris, Armenia 25 G8 39 31N 46 22 E
Gorízia, Italy 20 B5 45 56N 13 37 E
Gorki = Nizhniy Novgorod, Russia 24 C7 56 20N 44 0 E
Gorkiy = Nizhniy Novgorod, Russia 24 C7 56 20N 44 0 E
Gorkovskoye Vdkhr., Russia 24 C7 57 2N 43 4 E
Görlitz, Germany 16 C8 51 9N 14 58 E
Gorlovka = Horlivka, Ukraine 25 E6 48 19N 38 5 E
Gorman, U.S.A. 85 L8 34 47N 118 51W
Gorna Dzhumayo = Blagoevgrad, Bulgaria 21 C10 42 2N 23 5 E
Gorna Oryakhovitsa, Bulgaria 21 C11 43 7N 25 40 E
Gorno-Altay □, Russia 26 D9 51 0N 86 0 E
Gorno-Altaysk, Russia 26 D9 51 50N 86 5 E
Gornyatski, Russia 24 A11 67 32N 64 3 E
Gornyy, Russia 30 B6 44 57N 133 59 E
Gorodenka = Horodenka, Ukraine 17 D13 48 41N 25 29 E
Gorodok = Horodok, Ukraine 17 D12 49 46N 23 32 E
Gorokhov = Horokhiv, Ukraine 17 C13 50 30N 24 45 E
Goromonzi, Zimbabwe 55 F3 17 52S 31 22 E
Gorong, Kepulauan, Indonesia 37 E8 3 59S 131 25 E
Gorongose →, Mozam. 57 C5 20 30S 34 40 E
Gorongoza, Mozam. 55 F3 18 44S 34 2 E
Gorongoza, Sa. da, Mozam. 55 F3 18 27S 34 2 E
Gorontalo, Indonesia 37 D6 0 35N 123 5 E
Gort, Ireland 13 C3 53 3N 8 49W
Gortis, Greece 23 D6 35 4N 24 58 E
Gorzów Wielkopolski, Poland 16 B8 52 43N 15 15 E
Gosford, Australia 63 E5 33 23S 151 18 E
Goshen, Calif., U.S.A. 84 J7 36 21N 119 25W
Goshen, Ind., U.S.A. 76 E3 41 35N 85 50W
Goshen, N.Y., U.S.A. 79 E10 41 24N 74 20W
Goshogawara, Japan 30 D10 40 48N 140 27 E
Goslar, Germany 16 C6 51 54N 10 25 E
Gospič, Croatia 16 F8 44 35N 15 23 E
Gosport, U.K. 11 G6 50 48N 1 9W
Gosse →, Australia 62 B1 19 32S 134 37 E
Göta älv →, Sweden 9 H14 57 42N 11 54 E
Göta kanal, Sweden 9 G16 58 30N 15 58 E
Götaland, Sweden 9 G15 57 30N 14 30 E
Göteborg, Sweden 9 H14 57 43N 11 59 E
Gotha, Germany 16 C6 50 56N 10 42 E
Gothenburg = Göteborg, Sweden 9 H14 57 43N 11 59 E
Gothenburg, U.S.A. 80 E4 40 56N 100 10W
Gotland, Sweden 9 H18 57 30N 18 33 E
Gotō-Rettō, Japan 31 H4 32 55N 129 5 E
Gotska Sandön, Sweden 9 G18 58 24N 19 15 E
Gōtsu, Japan 31 G6 35 0N 132 14 E
Gott Pk., Canada 72 C4 50 18N 122 16W
Göttingen, Germany 16 C5 51 31N 9 55 E
Gottwaldov = Zlín, Czech Rep. 17 D9 49 14N 17 40 E
Goubangzi, China 35 D11 41 20N 121 52 E
Gouda, Neths. 15 B4 52 1N 4 42 E
Goúdhoura, Ákra, Greece 23 E8 34 59N 26 6 E
Gough I., Atl. Oc. 2 G9 40 10S 9 45W
Gouin, Rés., Canada 70 C5 48 35N 74 40W
Goulburn, Australia 63 E4 34 44S 149 44 E
Goulburn Is., Australia 62 A1 11 40S 133 20 E
Goulimine, Morocco 50 C3 28 56N 10 0W
Gourits →, S. Africa 56 E3 34 21S 21 52 E
Goúrnais, Greece 23 D7 35 19N 25 16 E
Gouverneur, U.S.A. 79 B9 44 20N 75 28W
Gouviá, Greece 23 A3 39 39N 19 50 E
Governador Valadares, Brazil 93 G10 18 15S 41 57W
Governor's Harbour, Bahamas 88 A4 25 10N 76 14W
Govindgarh, India 43 G9 24 23N 81 18 E
Gowan Ra., Australia 62 D4 25 0S 145 0 E
Gowanda, U.S.A. 78 D6 42 28N 78 56W
Gowd-e Zirreh, Afghan. 40 E3 29 45N 62 0 E
Gower, U.K. 11 F3 51 35N 4 10W
Gowna, L., Ireland 13 C4 53 51N 7 34W
Goya, Argentina 94 B4 29 10S 59 10W
Goyder Lagoon, Australia 63 D2 27 3S 138 58 E
Goyllarisquisga, Peru 92 F3 10 31S 76 24W
Goz Beïda, Chad 51 F10 12 10N 21 20 E
Gozo, Malta 23 C1 36 3N 14 13 E
Graaff-Reinet, S. Africa 56 E3 32 13S 24 32 E
Gračac, Croatia 16 F8 44 18N 15 57 E
Gracias a Dios, C., Honduras 88 D3 15 0N 83 10W
Graciosa, I., Canary Is. 22 E6 29 15N 13 32W
Grado, Spain 19 A2 43 23N 6 4W
Grady, U.S.A. 81 H3 34 49N 103 19W
Grafham Water, U.K. 11 E7 52 19N 0 18W
Grafton, Australia 63 D5 29 38S 152 58 E
Grafton, N. Dak., U.S.A. 80 A6 48 25N 97 25W
Grafton, W. Va., U.S.A. 76 F5 39 21N 80 2W
Graham, Canada 70 C1 49 20N 90 30W
Graham, U.S.A. 81 J5 33 6N 98 35W
Graham, Mt., U.S.A. 83 K9 32 42N 109 52W
Graham Bell, Ostrov = Greem-Bell, Ostrov, Russia 26 A7 81 0N 62 0 E
Graham I., B.C., Canada 72 C2 53 40N 132 30W
Graham I., N.W.T., Canada 68 C6 77 25N 90 30W
Graham Land, Antarctica 5 C17 65 0S 64 0W
Grahamstown, S. Africa 56 E4 33 19S 26 31 E
Grahamsville, U.S.A. 79 E10 41 51N 74 33W
Grain Coast, W. Afr. 50 H3 4 20N 10 0W
Grajaú, Brazil 93 E9 5 50S 46 4W
Grajaú →, Brazil 93 D10 3 41S 44 48W
Grampian, U.S.A. 78 F6 40 58N 78 37W
Grampian Highlands = Grampian Mts., U.K. 12 E5 56 50N 4 0W
Grampian Mts., U.K. 12 E5 56 50N 4 0W
Grampians, The, Australia 63 F3 37 0S 142 20 E
Gran Canaria, Canary Is. 22 G4 27 55N 15 35W
Gran Chaco, S. Amer. 94 B3 25 0S 61 0W
Gran Paradiso, Italy 18 D7 45 33N 7 17 E
Gran Sasso d'Itália, Italy 20 C5 42 27N 13 42 E
Granada, Nic. 88 D2 11 58N 86 0W
Granada, Spain 19 D4 37 10N 3 35W
Granada, U.S.A. 81 F3 38 4N 102 19W
Granadilla de Abona, Canary Is. 22 F3 28 7N 16 33W
Granard, Ireland 13 C4 53 47N 7 30W
Granbury, U.S.A. 81 J6 32 27N 97 47W
Granby, Canada 79 A12 45 25N 72 45W
Granby, U.S.A. 82 F11 40 5N 105 56W
Grand →, Canada 78 D5 42 51N 79 34W
Grand →, Mo., U.S.A. 80 F8 39 23N 93 7W
Grand →, S. Dak., U.S.A. 80 C4 45 40N 100 45W
Grand Bahama, Bahamas 88 A4 26 40N 78 30W
Grand Bank, Canada 71 C8 47 6N 55 48W
Grand Bassam, Ivory C. 50 G5 5 10N 3 49W
Grand-Bourg, Guadeloupe 89 C7 15 53N 61 19W
Grand Canal = Yun Ho →, China 35 E9 39 10N 117 10 E
Grand Canyon, U.S.A. 83 H7 36 3N 112 9W
Grand Canyon National Park, U.S.A. 83 H7 36 15N 112 30W
Grand Cayman, Cayman Is. 88 C3 19 20N 81 20W
Grand Centre, Canada 73 C6 54 25N 110 13W
Grand Coulee, U.S.A. 82 C4 47 57N 119 0W
Grand Coulee Dam, U.S.A. 82 C4 47 57N 118 59W
Grand Erg du Bilma, Niger 51 E8 18 30N 14 0 E
Grand Erg Occidental, Algeria 50 B6 30 20N 1 0 E
Grand Erg Oriental, Algeria 50 B7 30 0N 6 30 E
Grand Falls, Canada 71 C6 47 3N 67 44W
Grand Falls-Windsor, Canada 71 C8 48 56N 55 40W
Grand Forks, Canada 72 D5 49 0N 118 30W
Grand Forks, U.S.A. 80 B6 47 55N 97 3W
Grand Gorge, U.S.A. 79 D10 42 21N 74 29W
Grand Haven, U.S.A. 76 D2 43 4N 86 13W
Grand I., Mich., U.S.A. 76 B2 46 31N 86 40W
Grand I., N.Y., U.S.A. 78 D6 43 0N 78 58W
Grand Island, U.S.A. 80 E5 40 55N 98 21W
Grand Isle, La., U.S.A. 81 L9 29 14N 90 0W
Grand Isle, Vt., U.S.A. 79 B11 44 43N 73 18W
Grand Junction, U.S.A. 83 G9 39 4N 108 33W
Grand L., N.B., Canada 71 C6 45 57N 66 7W
Grand L., Nfld., Canada 71 C8 49 0N 57 30W
Grand L., Nfld., Canada 71 B7 53 40N 60 30W
Grand L., U.S.A. 81 L8 29 55N 92 47W
Grand Lake, U.S.A. 82 F11 40 15N 105 49W
Grand Manan I., Canada 71 D6 44 45N 66 52W
Grand Marais, Canada 80 B9 47 45N 90 25W
Grand Marais, U.S.A. 76 B3 46 40N 85 59W
Grand-Mère, Canada 70 C5 46 36N 72 40W
Grand Prairie, U.S.A. 81 J6 32 47N 97 0W
Grand Rapids, Canada 73 C9 53 12N 99 19W
Grand Rapids, Mich., U.S.A. 76 D2 42 58N 85 40W
Grand Rapids, Minn., U.S.A. 80 B8 47 14N 93 31W
Grand St-Bernard, Col du, Europe 18 D7 45 50N 7 10 E
Grand Teton, U.S.A. 82 E8 43 54N 111 50W
Grand Teton National Park, U.S.A. 82 D8 43 50N 110 50W
Grand Union Canal, U.K. 11 E7 52 7N 0 53W
Grand View, Canada 73 C8 51 10N 100 42W
Grande →, Jujuy, Argentina 94 A2 24 20S 65 2W
Grande →, Mendoza, Argentina 94 D2 36 52S 69 45W
Grande →, Bolivia 92 G6 15 51S 64 39W
Grande →, Bahia, Brazil 93 F10 11 30S 44 30W
Grande →, Minas Gerais, Brazil 93 H8 20 6S 51 4W
Grande, B., Argentina 96 G3 50 30S 68 20W
Grande, Rio →, U.S.A. 81 N6 25 58N 97 9W
Grande Baleine, R. de la →, Canada 70 A4 55 16N 77 47W
Grande Cache, Canada 72 C5 53 53N 119 8W
Grande-Entrée, Canada 71 C7 47 30N 61 40W
Grande Prairie, Canada 72 B5 55 10N 118 50W
Grande-Rivière, Canada 71 C7 48 26N 64 30W
Grande-Vallée, Canada 71 C6 49 14N 65 8W
Grandfalls, U.S.A. 81 K3 31 20N 102 51W
Grandview, U.S.A. 82 C4 46 15N 119 54W
Graneros, Chile 94 C1 34 5S 70 45W
Grangemouth, U.K. 12 E5 56 1N 3 42W
Granger, U.S.A. 82 F9 41 35N 109 58W
Grangeville, U.S.A. 82 D5 45 56N 116 7W
Granisle, Canada 72 C3 54 53N 126 13W
Granite City, U.S.A. 80 F9 38 42N 90 9W
Granite Falls, U.S.A. 80 C7 44 49N 95 33W
Granite L., Canada 71 C8 48 8N 57 5W
Granite Mt., U.S.A. 85 M10 33 5N 116 28W
Granite Pk., U.S.A. 82 D9 45 10N 109 48W
Graniteville, U.S.A. 79 B12 44 8N 72 29W
Granity, N.Z. 59 J3 41 39S 171 51 E
Granja, Brazil 93 D10 3 7S 40 50W
Granollers, Spain 19 B7 41 39N 2 18 E
Grant, U.S.A. 80 E4 40 53N 101 42W
Grant, Mt., U.S.A. 82 G4 38 34N 118 48W
Grant City, U.S.A. 80 E7 40 29N 94 25W
Grant I., Australia 60 B5 11 10S 132 52 E
Grant Range, U.S.A. 83 G6 38 30N 115 25W
Grantham, U.K. 10 E7 52 55N 0 38W
Grantown-on-Spey, U.K. 12 D5 57 20N 3 36W
Grants, U.S.A. 83 J10 35 9N 107 52W
Grants Pass, U.S.A. 82 E2 42 26N 123 19W
Grantsville, U.S.A. 82 F7 40 36N 112 28W
Granville, France 18 B3 48 50N 1 35W
Granville, N. Dak., U.S.A. 80 A4 48 16N 100 47W
Granville, N.Y., U.S.A. 79 C11 43 24N 73 16W
Granville, Ohio, U.S.A. 78 F2 40 4N 82 31W
Granville L., Canada 73 B8 56 18N 100 30W
Graskop, S. Africa 57 C5 24 56S 30 49 E
Grass →, Canada 73 B9 56 3N 96 33W
Grass Range, U.S.A. 82 C9 47 0N 109 0W
Grass River Prov. Park, Canada 73 C8 54 40N 100 50W
Grass Valley, Calif., U.S.A. 84 F6 39 13N 121 4W
Grass Valley, Oreg., U.S.A. 82 D3 45 22N 120 47W
Grasse, France 18 E7 43 38N 6 56 E
Grassflat, U.S.A. 78 F6 41 0N 78 6W
Grasslands Nat. Park, Canada 73 D7 49 11N 107 38W
Grassy, Australia 62 G3 40 3S 144 5 E
Graulhet, France 18 E4 43 45N 1 59 E
Gravelbourg, Canada 73 D7 49 50N 106 35W
's-Gravenhage, Neths. 15 B4 52 7N 4 17 E
Gravenhurst, Canada 78 B5 44 52N 79 20W
Gravesend, Australia 63 D5 29 35S 150 20 E
Gravesend, U.K. 11 F8 51 26N 0 22 E
Gravois, Pointe-à-, Haiti 89 C5 18 15N 73 56W
Grayling, U.S.A. 76 C3 44 40N 84 43W
Grays Harbor, U.S.A. 82 C1 46 59N 124 1W
Grays L., U.S.A. 82 E8 43 4N 111 26W
Grays River, U.S.A. 84 D3 46 21N 123 37W
Graz, Austria 16 E8 47 4N 15 27 E
Greasy L., Canada 72 A4 62 55N 122 12W
Great Abaco I., Bahamas 88 A4 26 25N 77 10W
Great Artesian Basin, Australia 62 C3 23 0S 144 0 E
Great Australian Bight, Australia 61 F5 33 30S 130 0 E
Great Bahama Bank, Bahamas 88 B4 23 15N 78 0W
Great Barrier I., N.Z. 59 G5 36 11S 175 25 E
Great Barrier Reef, Australia 62 B4 18 0S 146 50 E
Great Barrington, U.S.A. 79 D11 42 12N 73 22W
Great Basin, U.S.A. 82 G5 40 0N 117 0W
Great Basin Nat. Park, U.S.A. 82 G6 38 55N 114 14W
Great Bear →, Canada 68 B7 65 0N 124 0W
Great Bear L., Canada 68 B8 65 30N 120 0W
Great Belt = Store Bælt, Denmark 9 J14 55 20N 11 0 E
Great Bend, Kans., U.S.A. 80 F5 38 22N 98 46W
Great Bend, Pa., U.S.A. 79 E9 41 58N 75 45W
Great Blasket I., Ireland 13 D1 52 6N 10 32W
Great Britain, Europe 6 E5 54 0N 2 15W
Great Codroy, Canada 71 C8 47 51N 59 16W
Great Dividing Ra., Australia 62 C4 23 0S 146 0 E
Great Driffield = Driffield, U.K. 10 C7 54 0N 0 26W
Great Exuma I., Bahamas 88 B4 23 30N 75 50W
Great Falls, U.S.A. 82 C8 47 30N 111 17W
Great Fish = Groot Vis →, S. Africa 56 E4 33 28S 27 5 E
Great Guana Cay, Bahamas 88 B4 24 0N 76 20W
Great Inagua I., Bahamas 89 B5 21 0N 73 20W
Great Indian Desert = Thar Desert, India 42 F5 28 0N 72 0 E
Great Karoo, S. Africa 56 E3 31 55S 21 0 E
Great Lake, Australia 62 G4 41 50S 146 40 E
Great Lakes, N. Amer. 66 E11 46 0N 84 0W
Great Malvern, U.K. 11 E5 52 7N 2 18W
Great Miami →, U.S.A. 76 F3 39 20N 84 40W
Great Ormes Head, U.K. 10 D4 53 20N 3 52W
Great Ouse →, U.K. 10 E8 52 48N 0 21 E
Great Palm I., Australia 62 B4 18 45S 146 40 E
Great Plains, N. Amer. 74 A6 47 0N 105 0W
Great Ruaha →, Tanzania 54 D4 7 56S 37 52 E
Great Sacandaga Res., U.S.A. 79 C10 43 6N 74 16W
Great Saint Bernard Pass = Grand St-Bernard, Col du, Europe 18 D7 45 50N 7 10 E
Great Salt L., U.S.A. 82 F7 41 15N 112 40W
Great Salt Lake Desert, U.S.A. 82 F7 40 50N 113 30W
Great Salt Plains L., U.S.A. 81 G5 36 45N 98 8W
Great Sandy Desert, Australia 60 D3 21 0S 124 0 E
Great Sangi = Sangihe, Pulau, Indonesia 37 D7 3 45N 125 30 E
Great Skellig, Ireland 13 E1 51 47N 10 33W
Great Slave L., Canada 72 A5 61 23N 115 38W
Great Smoky Mts. Nat. Park, U.S.A. 77 H4 35 40N 83 40W
Great Snow Mt., Canada 72 B4 57 26N 124 0W
Great Stour = Stour →, U.K. 11 F9 51 18N 1 22 E
Great Victoria Desert, Australia 61 E4 29 30S 126 30 E
Great Wall, China 34 E5 38 30N 109 30 E
Great Whernside, U.K. 10 C6 54 10N 1 58W
Great Yarmouth, U.K. 11 E9 52 37N 1 44 E
Greater Antilles, W. Indies 89 C5 17 40N 74 0W
Greater London □, U.K. 11 F7 51 31N 0 6W
Greater Manchester □, U.K. 10 D5 53 30N 2 15W
Greater Sunda Is., Indonesia 36 F4 7 0S 112 0 E
Greco, C., Cyprus 23 E13 34 57N 34 5 E
Gredos, Sierra de, Spain 19 B3 40 20N 5 0W
Greece, U.S.A. 78 C7 43 13N 77 41W
Greece ■, Europe 21 E9 40 0N 23 0 E
Greeley, Colo., U.S.A. 80 E2 40 25N 104 42W
Greeley, Nebr., U.S.A. 80 E5 41 33N 98 32W
Greem-Bell, Ostrov, Russia 26 A7 81 0N 62 0 E
Green, U.S.A. 82 E2 43 9N 123 22W
Green →, Ky., U.S.A. 76 G2 37 54N 87 30W
Green →, Utah, U.S.A. 83 G9 38 11N 109 53W
Green B., U.S.A. 76 C2 45 0N 87 30W
Green Bay, U.S.A. 76 C2 44 31N 88 0W
Green C., Australia 63 F5 37 13S 150 1 E
Green Cove Springs, U.S.A. 77 L5 29 59N 81 42W
Green Lake, Canada 73 C7 54 17N 107 47W
Green Mts., U.S.A. 79 C12 43 45N 72 45W
Green River, Utah, U.S.A. 83 G8 38 59N 110 10W
Green River, Wyo., U.S.A. 82 F9 41 32N 109 28W
Green Valley, U.S.A. 83 L8 31 52N 110 56W
Greenbank, U.S.A. 84 B4 48 6N 122 34W
Greenbush, Mich., U.S.A. 78 B1 44 35N 83 19W
Greenbush, Minn., U.S.A. 80 A6 48 42N 96 11W
Greencastle, U.S.A. 76 F2 39 38N 86 52W
Greene, U.S.A. 79 D9 42 20N 75 46W
Greenfield, Calif., U.S.A. 84 J5 36 19N 121 15W
Greenfield, Calif., U.S.A. 85 K8 35 15N 119 0W
Greenfield, Ind., U.S.A. 76 F3 39 47N 85 46W
Greenfield, Iowa, U.S.A. 80 E7 41 18N 94 28W
Greenfield, Mass., U.S.A. 79 D12 42 35N 72 36W
Greenfield, Mo., U.S.A. 81 G8 37 25N 93 51W
Greenfield Park, Canada 79 A11 45 29N 73 29W
Greenland ■, N. Amer. 4 C5 66 0N 45 0W
Greenland Sea, Arctic 4 B7 73 0N 10 0W
Greenock, U.K. 12 F4 55 57N 4 46W
Greenore, Ireland 13 B5 54 2N 6 8W
Greenore Pt., Ireland 13 D5 52 14N 6 19W
Greenough, Australia 61 E1 28 58S 114 43 E
Greenough →, Australia 61 E1 28 51S 114 38 E
Greenough Pt., Canada 78 B3 44 58N 81 26W
Greenport, U.S.A. 79 E12 41 6N 72 22W
Greensboro, Ga., U.S.A. 77 J4 33 35N 83 11W
Greensboro, N.C., U.S.A. 77 G6 36 4N 79 48W
Greensboro, Vt., U.S.A. 79 B12 44 36N 72 18W
Greensburg, Ind., U.S.A. 76 F3 39 20N 85 29W
Greensburg, Kans., U.S.A. 81 G5 37 36N 99 18W
Greensburg, Pa., U.S.A. 78 F5 40 18N 79 33W
Greenstone Pt., U.K. 12 D3 57 55N 5 37W
Greenvale, Australia 62 B4 18 59S 145 7 E
Greenville, Ala., U.S.A. 77 K2 31 50N 86 38W
Greenville, Calif., U.S.A. 84 E6 40 8N 120 57W
Greenville, Maine, U.S.A. 77 C11 45 28N 69 35W
Greenville, Mich., U.S.A. 76 D3 43 11N 85 15W
Greenville, Miss., U.S.A. 81 J9 33 24N 91 4W
Greenville, Mo., U.S.A. 81 G9 37 8N 90 27W
Greenville, N.C., U.S.A. 77 H7 35 37N 77 23W
Greenville, N.H., U.S.A. 79 D13 42 46N 71 49W
Greenville, N.Y., U.S.A. 79 D10 42 25N 74 1W
Greenville, Ohio, U.S.A. 76 E3 40 6N 84 38W
Greenville, Pa., U.S.A. 78 E4 41 24N 80 23W
Greenville, S.C., U.S.A. 77 H4 34 51N 82 24W
Greenville, Tenn., U.S.A. 77 G4 36 13N 82 51W
Greenville, Tex., U.S.A. 81 J6 33 8N 96 7W
Greenwater Lake Prov. Park, Canada 73 C8 52 32N 103 30W
Greenwich, U.K. 11 F8 51 29N 0 1 E
Greenwich, Conn., U.S.A. 79 E11 41 2N 73 38W
Greenwich, N.Y., U.S.A. 79 C11 43 5N 73 30W
Greenwich, Ohio, U.S.A. 78 E2 41 2N 82 31W
Greenwood, Canada 72 D5 49 10N 118 40W
Greenwood, Ark., U.S.A. 81 H7 35 13N 94 16W
Greenwood, Ind., U.S.A. 76 F2 39 37N 86 7W
Greenwood, Miss., U.S.A. 81 J9 33 31N 90 11W
Greenwood, S.C., U.S.A. 77 H4 34 12N 82 10W
Greenwood, Mt., Australia 60 B5 13 48S 130 4 E
Gregory, U.S.A. 80 D5 43 14N 99 20W
Gregory →, Australia 62 B2 17 53S 139 17 E
Gregory, L., S. Austral., Australia 63 D2 28 55S 139 0 E
Gregory, L., W. Austral., Australia 61 E2 25 38S 119 58 E
Gregory Downs, Australia 62 B2 18 35S 138 45 E
Gregory L., Australia 60 D4 20 0S 127 40 E
Gregory Ra., Queens., Australia 62 B3 19 30S 143 40 E
Gregory Ra., W. Austral., Australia 60 D3 21 20S 121 12 E
Greifswald, Germany 16 A7 54 5N 13 23 E
Greiz, Germany 16 C7 50 39N 12 10 E
Gremikha, Russia 24 A6 67 59N 39 47 E
Grenå, Denmark 9 H14 56 25N 10 53 E
Grenada, U.S.A. 81 J10 33 47N 89 49W
Grenada ■, W. Indies 89 D7 12 10N 61 40W
Grenadier I., U.S.A. 79 B8 44 3N 76 22W
Grenadines, W. Indies 89 D7 12 40N 61 20W

H

Henryville

Hamadān □, Iran 45 C6 35 0N 49 0 E
Ḥamāh, Syria 44 C3 35 5N 36 40 E
Hamamatsu, Japan 31 G8 34 45N 137 45 E
Hamar, Norway 9 F14 60 48N 11 7 E
Hamâta, Gebel, Egypt 44 E2 24 17N 35 0 E
Hambantota, Sri Lanka 40 R12 6 10N 81 10 E
Hamber Prov. Park, Canada 72 C5 52 20N 118 0W
Hamburg, Germany 16 B5 53 33N 9 59 E
Hamburg, Ark., U.S.A. 81 J9 33 14N 91 48W
Hamburg, N.Y., U.S.A. 78 D6 42 43N 78 50W
Hamburg, Pa., U.S.A. 79 F9 40 33N 75 59W
Ḥamḍ, W. al →, Si. Arabia 44 E3 24 55N 36 20 E
Hamden, U.S.A. 79 E12 41 23N 72 54W
Häme, Finland 9 F20 61 38N 25 10 E
Hämeenlinna, Finland 9 F21 61 0N 24 28 E
Hamelin Pool, Australia 61 E1 26 22S 114 20 E
Hameln, Germany 16 B5 52 6N 9 21 E
Hamerkaz □, Israel 47 C3 32 15N 34 55 E
Hamersley Ra., Australia 60 D2 22 0S 117 45 E
Hamhung, N. Korea 35 E14 39 54N 127 30 E
Hami, China 32 B4 42 55N 93 25 E
Hamilton, Australia 63 F3 37 45S 142 2 E
Hamilton, Canada 78 C5 43 15N 79 50W
Hamilton, N.Z. 59 G5 37 47S 175 19 E
Hamilton, U.K. 12 F4 55 46N 4 2W
Hamilton, Ala., U.S.A. 77 H1 34 9N 87 59W
Hamilton, Mont., U.S.A. 82 C6 46 15N 114 10W
Hamilton, N.Y., U.S.A. 79 D9 42 50N 75 33W
Hamilton, Ohio, U.S.A. 76 F3 39 24N 84 34W
Hamilton, Tex., U.S.A. 81 K5 31 42N 98 7W
Hamilton →, Australia 62 C2 23 30S 139 47 E
Hamilton City, U.S.A. 84 F4 39 45N 122 1W
Hamilton Inlet, Canada 71 B8 54 0N 57 30W
Hamilton Mt., U.S.A. 79 C10 43 25N 74 22W
Hamina, Finland 9 F22 60 34N 27 12 E
Hamirpur, H.P., India 42 D7 31 41N 76 31 E
Hamirpur, Ut. P., India 43 G9 25 57N 80 9 E
Hamlet, U.S.A. 77 H6 34 53N 79 42W
Hamley Bridge, Australia 63 E2 34 17S 138 35 E
Hamlin = Hameln, Germany 16 B5 52 6N 9 21 E
Hamlin, N.Y., U.S.A. 78 C7 43 17N 77 55W
Hamlin, Tex., U.S.A. 81 J4 32 53N 100 8W
Hamm, Germany 16 C4 51 40N 7 50 E
Ḥammār, Hawr al, Iraq 44 D5 30 50N 47 10 E
Hammerfest, Norway 8 A20 70 39N 23 41 E
Hammond, Ind., U.S.A. 76 E2 41 38N 87 30W
Hammond, La., U.S.A. 81 K9 30 30N 90 28W
Hammond, N.Y., U.S.A. 79 B9 44 27N 75 42W
Hammondsport, U.S.A. 78 D7 42 25N 77 13W
Hammonton, U.S.A. 76 F8 39 39N 74 48W
Hampden, N.Z. 59 L3 45 18S 170 50 E
Hampshire □, U.K. 11 F6 51 7N 1 23W
Hampshire Downs, U.K. 11 F6 51 15N 1 10W
Hampton, N.B., Canada 71 C6 45 32N 65 51W
Hampton, Ont., Canada 78 C6 43 58N 78 45W
Hampton, Ark., U.S.A. 81 J8 33 32N 92 28W
Hampton, Iowa, U.S.A. 80 D8 42 45N 93 13W
Hampton, N.H., U.S.A. 79 D14 42 57N 70 50W
Hampton, S.C., U.S.A. 77 J5 32 52N 81 7W
Hampton, Va., U.S.A. 76 G7 37 2N 76 21W
Hampton Bays, U.S.A. 79 F12 40 53N 72 30W
Hampton Tableland, Australia 61 F4 32 0S 127 0 E
Hamyang, S. Korea 35 G14 35 32N 127 42 E
Han Pijesak, Bos.-H. 21 B8 44 5N 18 57 E
Hana, U.S.A. 74 H17 20 45N 155 59W
Hanak, Si. Arabia 44 E3 25 32N 37 0 E
Hanamaki, Japan 30 E10 39 23N 141 7 E
Hanang, Tanzania 54 C4 4 30S 35 25 E
Hanau, Germany 16 C5 50 7N 8 56 E
Hanbogd = Ihbulag, Mongolia 34 C4 43 11N 107 10 E
Hancheng, China 34 G6 35 31N 110 25 E
Hancock, Mich., U.S.A. 80 B10 47 8N 88 35W
Hancock, N.Y., U.S.A. 79 E9 41 57N 75 17W
Handa, Japan 31 G8 34 53N 136 55 E
Handan, China 34 F8 36 35N 114 28 E
Handeni, Tanzania 54 D4 5 25S 38 2 E
Handwara, India 43 B6 34 21N 74 20 E
Hanegev, Israel 47 E4 30 50N 35 0 E
Hanford, U.S.A. 84 J7 36 20N 119 39W
Hang Chat, Thailand 38 C2 18 20N 99 21 E
Hang Dong, Thailand 38 C2 18 41N 98 55 E
Hangang →, S. Korea 35 F14 37 50N 126 30 E
Hangayn Nuruu, Mongolia 32 B4 47 30N 99 0 E
Hangchou = Hangzhou, China 33 C7 30 18N 120 11 E
Hanggin Houqi, China 34 D4 40 58N 107 4 E
Hanggin Qi, China 34 E5 39 52N 108 50 E
Hangu, China 35 E9 39 18N 117 53 E
Hangzhou, China 33 C7 30 18N 120 11 E
Hangzhou Wan, China 33 C7 30 15N 120 45 E
Hanhongor, Mongolia 34 C3 43 55N 104 28 E
Ḥanīdh, Si. Arabia 45 E6 26 35N 48 38 E
Ḥanīsh, Yemen 46 E3 13 45N 42 46 E
Hankinson, U.S.A. 80 B6 46 4N 96 54W
Hanko, Finland 9 G20 59 50N 22 57 E
Hanksville, U.S.A. 83 G8 38 22N 110 43W
Hanle, India 43 C8 32 42N 79 4 E
Hanmer Springs, N.Z. 59 K4 42 32S 172 50 E
Hann →, Australia 60 C4 17 26S 126 17 E
Hann, Mt., Australia 60 C4 15 45S 126 0 E
Hanna, Canada 72 C6 51 40N 111 54W
Hanna, U.S.A. 82 F10 41 52N 106 34W
Hannah B., Canada 70 B4 51 40N 80 0W
Hannibal, Mo., U.S.A. 80 F9 39 42N 91 22W
Hannibal, N.Y., U.S.A. 79 C8 43 19N 76 35W
Hannover, Germany 16 B5 52 22N 9 46 E
Hanoi, Vietnam 32 D5 21 5N 105 55 E
Hanover = Hannover, Germany 16 B5 52 22N 9 46 E
Hanover, Canada 78 B3 44 9N 81 2W
Hanover, S. Africa 56 E3 31 4S 24 29 E
Hanover, N.H., U.S.A. 79 C12 43 42N 72 17W
Hanover, Ohio, U.S.A. 78 F2 40 4N 82 16W
Hanover, Pa., U.S.A. 76 F7 39 48N 76 59W
Hanover, I., Chile 96 G2 51 0S 74 50W
Hansdiha, India 43 G12 24 36N 87 5 E
Hansi, India 42 E6 29 10N 75 57 E
Hanson, L., Australia 63 E2 31 0S 136 15 E
Hantsavichy, Belarus 17 B14 52 49N 26 30 E
Hanumangarh, India 42 E6 29 35N 74 19 E
Hanzhong, China 34 H4 33 10N 107 1 E
Hanzhuang, China 35 G9 34 33N 117 23 E
Haora, India 43 H13 22 37N 88 20 E
Haparanda, Sweden 8 D21 65 52N 24 8 E
Happy, U.S.A. 81 H4 34 45N 101 52W
Happy Camp, U.S.A. 82 F2 41 48N 123 23W
Happy Valley-Goose Bay, Canada 71 B7 53 15N 60 20W
Hapsu, N. Korea 35 D15 41 13N 128 51 E
Hapur, India 42 E7 28 45N 77 45 E
Ḥaql, Si. Arabia 47 F3 29 10N 34 58 E
Har, Indonesia 37 F8 5 16S 133 14 E
Har-Ayrag, Mongolia 34 B5 45 47N 109 16 E
Har Hu, China 32 C4 38 20N 97 38 E
Har Us Nuur, Mongolia 32 B4 48 0N 92 0 E
Har Yehuda, Israel 47 D3 31 35N 34 57 E
Ḥaraḍ, Si. Arabia 46 C4 24 22N 49 0 E
Haranomachi, Japan 30 F10 37 38N 140 58 E
Harare, Zimbabwe 55 F3 17 43S 31 2 E
Harbin, China 35 B14 45 48N 126 40 E
Harbor Beach, U.S.A. 78 C2 43 51N 82 39W
Harbour Breton, Canada 71 C8 47 29N 55 50W
Harbour Deep, Canada 71 B8 50 25N 56 32W
Harda, India 42 H7 22 27N 77 5 E
Hardangerfjorden, Norway 9 F12 60 5N 6 0 E
Hardangervidda, Norway 9 F12 60 7N 7 20 E
Hardap Dam, Namibia 56 C2 24 32S 17 50 E
Hardenberg, Neths. 15 B6 52 34N 6 37 E
Harderwijk, Neths. 15 B5 52 21N 5 38 E
Hardey →, Australia 60 D2 22 45S 116 8 E
Hardin, U.S.A. 82 D10 45 44N 107 37W
Harding, S. Africa 57 E4 30 35S 29 55 E
Harding Ra., Australia 60 C3 16 17S 124 55 E
Hardisty, Canada 72 C6 52 40N 111 18W
Hardoi, India 43 F9 27 26N 80 6 E
Hardwar = Haridwar, India 42 E8 29 58N 78 9 E
Hardwick, U.S.A. 79 B12 44 30N 72 22W
Hardy, Pen., Chile 96 H3 55 30S 68 20W
Hare B., Canada 71 B8 51 15N 55 45W
Hareid, Norway 9 E12 62 22N 6 1 E
Harer, Ethiopia 46 F3 9 20N 42 8 E
Hargeisa, Somali Rep. 46 F3 9 30N 44 2 E
Hari →, Indonesia 36 E2 1 16S 104 5 E
Haria, Canary Is. 22 E6 29 8N 13 32W
Haridwar, India 42 E8 29 58N 78 9 E
Harim, Jabal al, Oman 45 E8 25 58N 56 14 E
Haringhata →, Bangla. 41 J16 22 0N 89 58 E
Harīrūd →, Asia 40 A2 37 24N 60 38 E
Härjedalen, Sweden 9 E15 62 22N 13 5 E
Harlan, Iowa, U.S.A. 80 E7 41 39N 95 19W
Harlan, Ky., U.S.A. 77 G4 36 51N 83 19W
Harlech, U.K. 10 E3 52 52N 4 6W
Harlem, U.S.A. 82 B9 48 32N 108 47W
Harlingen, Neths. 15 A5 53 11N 5 25 E
Harlingen, U.S.A. 81 M6 26 12N 97 42W
Harlow, U.K. 11 F8 51 46N 0 8 E
Harlowton, U.S.A. 82 C9 46 26N 109 50W
Harnai, Pakistan 42 D2 30 6N 67 56 E
Harney Basin, U.S.A. 82 E4 43 30N 119 0W
Harney L., U.S.A. 82 E4 43 14N 119 8W
Harney Peak, U.S.A. 80 D3 43 52N 103 32W
Härnösand, Sweden 9 E17 62 38N 17 55 E
Haroldswick, U.K. 12 A8 60 48N 0 50W
Harp L., Canada 71 A7 55 5N 61 50W
Harper, Liberia 50 H4 4 25N 7 43W
Harrai, India 43 H8 22 37N 79 13 E
Harrand, Pakistan 42 E4 29 28N 70 3 E
Harricana →, Canada 70 B4 50 56N 79 32W
Harriman, U.S.A. 77 H3 35 56N 84 33W
Harrington Harbour, Canada 71 B8 50 31N 59 30W
Harris, U.K. 12 D2 57 50N 6 55W
Harris, Sd. of, U.K. 12 D1 57 44N 7 6W
Harris L., Australia 63 E2 31 10S 135 10 E
Harris Pt., Canada 78 C2 43 6N 82 9W
Harrisburg, Ill., U.S.A. 81 G10 37 44N 88 32W
Harrisburg, Nebr., U.S.A. 80 E3 41 33N 103 44W
Harrisburg, Pa., U.S.A. 78 F8 40 16N 76 53W
Harrismith, S. Africa 57 D4 28 15S 29 8 E
Harrison, Ark., U.S.A. 81 G8 36 14N 93 7W
Harrison, Maine, U.S.A. 79 B14 44 7N 70 39W
Harrison, Nebr., U.S.A. 80 D3 42 41N 103 53W
Harrison, C., Canada 71 B8 54 55N 57 55W
Harrison L., Canada 72 D4 49 33N 121 50W
Harrisonburg, U.S.A. 76 F6 38 27N 78 52W
Harrisonville, U.S.A. 80 F7 38 39N 94 21W
Harriston, Canada 78 C4 43 57N 80 53W
Harrisville, Mich., U.S.A. 78 B1 44 39N 83 17W
Harrisville, N.Y., U.S.A. 79 B9 44 9N 75 19W
Harrisville, Pa., U.S.A. 78 E5 41 8N 80 0W
Harrodsburg, U.S.A. 76 G3 37 46N 84 51W
Harrogate, U.K. 10 C6 54 0N 1 33W
Harrow, U.K. 11 F7 51 35N 0 21W
Harrowsmith, Canada 79 B8 44 24N 76 40W
Harry S. Truman Reservoir, U.S.A. 80 F7 38 16N 93 24W
Harsīn, Iran 44 C5 34 18N 47 33 E
Harstad, Norway 8 B17 68 48N 16 30 E
Harsud, India 42 H7 22 6N 76 44 E
Hart, U.S.A. 76 D2 43 42N 86 22W
Hart, L., Australia 63 E2 31 10S 136 25 E
Hartbees →, S. Africa 56 D3 28 45S 20 32 E
Hartford, Conn., U.S.A. 79 E12 41 46N 72 41W
Hartford, Ky., U.S.A. 76 G2 37 27N 86 55W
Hartford, S. Dak., U.S.A. 80 D6 43 38N 96 57W
Hartford, Wis., U.S.A. 80 D10 43 19N 88 22W
Hartford City, U.S.A. 76 E3 40 27N 85 22W
Hartland, Canada 71 C6 46 20N 67 32W
Hartland Pt., U.K. 11 F3 51 1N 4 32W
Hartlepool, U.K. 10 C6 54 42N 1 13W
Hartlepool □, U.K. 10 C6 54 42N 1 17W
Hartley Bay, Canada 72 C3 53 25N 129 15W
Hartmannberge, Namibia 56 B1 17 0S 13 0 E
Hartney, Canada 73 D8 49 30N 100 35W
Harts →, S. Africa 56 D3 28 24S 24 17 E
Hartselle, U.S.A. 77 H2 34 27N 86 56W
Hartshorne, U.S.A. 81 H7 34 51N 95 34W
Hartstown, U.S.A. 78 E4 41 33N 80 23W
Hartsville, U.S.A. 77 H5 34 23N 80 4W
Hartwell, U.S.A. 77 H4 34 21N 82 56W
Harunabad, Pakistan 42 E5 29 35N 73 8 E
Harvand, Iran 45 D7 28 25N 55 43 E
Harvey, Australia 61 F2 33 5S 115 54 E
Harvey, Ill., U.S.A. 76 E2 41 36N 87 50W
Harvey, N. Dak., U.S.A. 80 B5 47 47N 99 56W
Harwich, U.K. 11 F9 51 56N 1 17 E
Haryana □, India 42 E7 29 0N 76 10 E
Haryn →, Belarus 17 B14 52 7N 27 17 E
Harz, Germany 16 C6 51 38N 10 44 E
Hasa □, Si. Arabia 45 E6 25 50N 49 0 E
Ḥasanābād, Iran 45 C7 32 8N 52 44 E
Hasdo →, India 43 J10 21 44N 82 44 E
Hashimoto, Japan 31 G7 34 19N 135 37 E
Hashtjerd, Iran 45 C6 35 52N 50 40 E
Haskell, U.S.A. 81 J5 33 10N 99 44W
Haslemere, U.K. 11 F7 51 5N 0 43W
Hasselt, Belgium 15 D5 50 56N 5 21 E
Hassi Messaoud, Algeria 50 B7 31 51N 6 1 E
Hässleholm, Sweden 9 H15 56 10N 13 46 E
Hastings, N.Z. 59 H6 39 39S 176 52 E
Hastings, U.K. 11 G8 50 51N 0 35 E
Hastings, Mich., U.S.A. 76 D3 42 39N 85 17W
Hastings, Minn., U.S.A. 80 C8 44 44N 92 51W
Hastings, Nebr., U.S.A. 80 E5 40 35N 98 23W
Hastings Ra., Australia 63 E5 31 15S 152 14 E
Hat Yai, Thailand 39 J3 7 1N 100 27 E
Hatanbulag = Ergel, Mongolia 34 C5 43 8N 109 5 E
Hatay = Antalya, Turkey 25 G5 36 52N 30 45 E
Hatch, U.S.A. 83 K10 32 40N 107 9W
Hatchet L., Canada 73 B8 58 36N 103 40W
Hateruma-Shima, Japan 31 M1 24 3N 123 47 E
Hatfield P.O., Australia 63 E3 33 54S 143 49 E
Hatgal, Mongolia 32 A5 50 26N 100 9 E
Hathras, India 42 F8 27 36N 78 6 E
Hatia, Bangla. 41 H17 22 30N 91 5 E
Hato Mayor, Dom. Rep. 89 C6 18 46N 69 15W
Hatta, India 43 G8 24 7N 79 36 E
Hattah, Australia 63 E3 34 48S 142 17 E
Hatteras, C., U.S.A. 77 H8 35 14N 75 32W
Hattiesburg, U.S.A. 81 K10 31 20N 89 17W
Hatvan, Hungary 17 E10 47 40N 19 45 E
Hau Bon = Cheo Reo, Vietnam 36 B3 13 25N 108 28 E
Hau Duc, Vietnam 38 E7 15 20N 108 13 E
Haugesund, Norway 9 G11 59 23N 5 13 E
Haukipudas, Finland 8 D21 65 12N 25 20 E
Haultain →, Canada 73 B7 55 51N 106 46W
Hauraki G., N.Z. 59 G5 36 35S 175 5 E
Haut Atlas, Morocco 50 B4 32 30N 5 0W
Haut-Zaïre = Orientale □, Dem. Rep. of the Congo 54 B2 2 20N 26 0 E
Hautes Fagnes = Hohe Venn, Belgium 15 D6 50 30N 6 5 E
Hauts Plateaux, Algeria 48 C4 35 0N 1 0 E
Havana = La Habana, Cuba 88 B3 23 8N 82 22W
Havana, U.S.A. 80 E9 40 18N 90 4W
Havant, U.K. 11 G7 50 51N 0 58W
Havasu, L., U.S.A. 85 L12 34 18N 114 28W
Havel →, Germany 16 B7 52 50N 12 3 E
Havelian, Pakistan 42 B5 34 2N 73 10 E
Havelock, Canada 78 B7 44 26N 77 53W
Havelock, N.Z. 59 J4 41 17S 173 48 E
Havelock, U.S.A. 77 H7 34 53N 76 54W
Haverfordwest, U.K. 11 F3 51 48N 4 58W
Haverhill, U.S.A. 79 D13 42 47N 71 5W
Haverstraw, U.S.A. 79 E11 41 12N 73 58W
Havirga, Mongolia 34 B7 45 41N 113 5 E
Havířov, Czech. 17 D10 49 46N 18 20 E
Havlíčkův Brod, Czech Rep. 16 D8 49 36N 15 33 E
Havre, U.S.A. 82 B9 48 33N 109 41W
Havre-Aubert, Canada 71 C7 47 12N 61 56W
Havre-St.-Pierre, Canada 71 B7 50 18N 63 33W
Haw →, U.S.A. 77 H6 35 36N 79 3W
Hawaii □, U.S.A. 74 H16 19 30N 156 30W
Hawaii I., Pac. Oc. 74 J17 20 0N 155 0W
Hawaiian Is., Pac. Oc. 74 H17 20 30N 156 0W
Hawaiian Ridge, Pac. Oc. 65 E11 24 0N 165 0W
Hawarden, U.S.A. 80 D6 43 0N 96 29W
Hawea, L., N.Z. 59 L2 44 28S 169 19 E
Hawera, N.Z. 59 H5 39 35S 174 19 E
Hawick, U.K. 12 F6 55 26N 2 47W
Hawk Junction, Canada 70 C3 48 5N 84 38W
Hawke B., N.Z. 59 H6 39 25S 177 20 E
Hawker, Australia 63 E2 31 59S 138 22 E
Hawkesbury, Canada 70 C5 45 37N 74 37W
Hawkesbury I., Canada 72 C3 53 37N 129 3W
Hawkesbury Pt., Australia 62 A1 11 55S 134 5 E
Hawkinsville, U.S.A. 77 J4 32 17N 83 28W
Hawley, Minn., U.S.A. 80 B6 46 53N 96 19W
Hawley, Pa., U.S.A. 79 E9 41 28N 75 11W
Ḥawrān, W. →, Iraq 44 C4 33 58N 42 34 E
Ḥawsh Mūssá, Lebanon 47 B4 33 45N 35 55 E
Hawthorne, U.S.A. 82 G4 38 32N 118 38W
Hay, Australia 63 E3 34 30S 144 51 E
Hay →, Australia 62 C2 24 50S 138 0 E
Hay →, Canada 72 A5 60 50N 116 26W
Hay, C., Australia 60 B4 14 5S 129 29 E
Hay I., Canada 78 B4 44 53N 80 58W
Hay L., Canada 72 B5 58 50N 118 50W
Hay-on-Wye, U.K. 11 E4 52 5N 3 8W
Hay River, Canada 72 A5 60 51N 115 44W
Hay Springs, U.S.A. 80 D3 42 41N 102 41W
Haya = Tehoru, Indonesia 37 E7 3 19S 129 37 E
Hayachine-San, Japan 30 E10 39 34N 141 29 E
Hayden, U.S.A. 82 F10 40 30N 107 16W
Haydon, Australia 62 B3 18 0S 141 30 E
Hayes, U.S.A. 80 C4 44 23N 101 1W
Hayes →, Canada 70 A1 57 3N 92 12W
Hayes Creek, Australia 60 B5 13 43S 131 22 E
Hayle, U.K. 11 G2 50 11N 5 26W
Hayling I., U.K. 11 G7 50 48N 0 59W
Hayrabolu, Turkey 21 D12 41 12N 27 5 E
Hays, Canada 72 C6 50 6N 111 48W
Hays, U.S.A. 80 F5 38 53N 99 20W
Haysyn, Ukraine 17 D15 48 57N 29 25 E
Hayvoron, Ukraine 17 D15 48 22N 29 52 E
Hayward, Calif., U.S.A. 84 H4 37 40N 122 5W
Hayward, Wis., U.S.A. 80 B9 46 1N 91 29W
Haywards Heath, U.K. 11 G7 51 0N 0 5W
Ḥazafon □, Israel 47 C4 32 40N 35 20 E
Hazārān, Kūh-e, Iran 45 D8 29 35N 57 20 E
Hazard, U.S.A. 76 G4 37 15N 83 12W
Hazaribag, India 43 H11 23 58N 85 26 E
Hazaribag Road, India 43 G11 24 12N 85 57 E
Hazelton, Canada 72 B3 55 20N 127 42W
Hazelton, U.S.A. 80 B4 46 29N 100 17W
Hazen, U.S.A. 80 B4 47 18N 101 38W
Hazlehurst, Ga., U.S.A. 77 K4 31 52N 82 36W
Hazlehurst, Miss., U.S.A. 81 K9 31 52N 90 24W
Hazlet, U.S.A. 79 F10 40 25N 74 12W
Hazleton, U.S.A. 79 F9 40 57N 75 59W
Hazlett, L., Australia 60 D4 21 30S 128 48 E
Hazro, Turkey 44 B4 38 15N 40 47 E
Head of Bight, Australia 61 F5 31 30S 131 25 E
Headlands, Zimbabwe 55 F3 18 15S 32 2 E
Healdsburg, U.S.A. 84 G4 38 37N 122 52W
Healdton, U.S.A. 81 H6 34 14N 97 29W
Healesville, Australia 63 F4 37 35S 145 30 E
Heard I., Ind. Oc. 3 G13 53 0S 74 0 E
Hearne, U.S.A. 81 K6 30 53N 96 36W
Hearst, Canada 70 C3 49 40N 83 41W
Heart →, U.S.A. 80 B4 46 46N 100 50W
Heart's Content, Canada 71 C9 47 54N 53 27W
Heath Pt., Canada 71 C7 49 8N 61 40W
Heavener, U.S.A. 81 H7 34 53N 94 36W
Hebbronville, U.S.A. 81 M5 27 18N 98 41W
Hebei □, China 34 E9 39 0N 116 0 E
Hebel, Australia 63 D4 28 58S 147 47 E
Heber, U.S.A. 85 N11 32 44N 115 32W
Heber City, U.S.A. 82 F8 40 31N 111 25W
Heber Springs, U.S.A. 81 H9 35 30N 92 2W
Hebert, Canada 73 C7 50 30N 107 10W
Hebgen L., U.S.A. 82 D8 44 52N 111 20W
Hebi, China 34 G8 35 57N 114 7 E
Hebrides, U.K. 6 D4 57 30N 7 0W
Hebron = Al Khalīl, West Bank 47 D4 31 32N 35 6 E
Hebron, Canada 69 C13 58 5N 62 30W
Hebron, N. Dak., U.S.A. 80 B3 46 54N 102 3W
Hebron, Nebr., U.S.A. 80 E6 40 10N 97 35W
Hecate Str., Canada 72 C2 53 10N 130 30W
Heceta I., U.S.A. 72 B2 55 46N 133 40W
Hechi, China 32 D5 24 40N 108 2 E
Hechuan, China 32 C5 30 2N 106 12 E
Hecla, U.S.A. 80 C5 45 53N 98 9W
Hecla I., Canada 73 C9 51 10N 96 43W
Hede, Sweden 9 E15 62 23N 13 30 E
Hedemora, Sweden 9 F16 60 18N 15 58 E
Heerde, Neths. 15 B6 52 24N 6 2 E
Heerenveen, Neths. 15 B5 52 57N 5 55 E
Heerhugowaard, Neths. 15 B4 52 40N 4 51 E
Heerlen, Neths. 18 A6 50 55N 5 58 E
Ḥefa, Israel 47 C4 32 46N 35 0 E
Ḥefa □, Israel 47 C4 32 40N 35 0 E
Hefei, China 33 C6 31 52N 117 18 E
Hegang, China 33 B8 47 20N 130 19 E
Heichengzhen, China 34 F4 36 24N 106 3 E
Heidelberg, Germany 16 D5 49 24N 8 42 E
Heidelberg, S. Africa 56 E3 34 6S 20 59 E
Heilbron, S. Africa 57 D4 27 16S 27 59 E
Heilbronn, Germany 16 D5 49 9N 9 13 E
Heilongjiang □, China 33 B7 48 0N 126 0 E
Heilunkiang = Heilongjiang □, China 33 B7 48 0N 126 0 E
Heimaey, Iceland 8 E3 63 26N 20 17W
Heinola, Finland 9 F22 61 13N 26 2 E
Heinze Is., Burma 41 M20 14 25N 97 45 E
Heishan, China 35 D12 41 40N 122 5 E
Heishui, China 35 C10 42 8N 119 30 E
Hejaz = Ḥijāz □, Si. Arabia 46 C3 24 0N 40 0 E
Hejian, China 34 E9 38 25N 116 5 E
Hejin, China 34 G6 35 35N 110 42 E
Hekımhan, Turkey 44 B3 38 50N 37 55 E
Hekla, Iceland 8 E4 63 56N 19 35W
Hekou, China 32 D5 22 30N 103 59 E
Helan Shan, China 34 E3 38 30N 105 55 E
Helen Atoll, Pac. Oc. 37 D8 2 40N 132 0 E
Helena, Ark., U.S.A. 81 H9 34 32N 90 36W
Helena, Mont., U.S.A. 82 C7 46 36N 112 2W
Helendale, U.S.A. 85 L9 34 44N 117 19W
Helensburgh, U.K. 12 E4 56 1N 4 43W
Helensville, N.Z. 59 G5 36 41S 174 29 E
Helenvale, Australia 62 B4 15 43S 145 14 E
Helgeland, Norway 8 C15 66 7N 13 29 E
Helgoland, Germany 16 A4 54 10N 7 53 E
Heligoland = Helgoland, Germany 16 A4 54 10N 7 53 E
Heligoland B. = Deutsche Bucht, Germany 16 A5 54 15N 8 0 E
Hella, Iceland 8 E3 63 50N 20 24W
Hellertown, U.S.A. 79 F9 40 35N 75 21W
Hellespont = Çanakkale Boğazı, Turkey 21 D12 40 17N 26 32 E
Hellevoetsluis, Neths. 15 C4 51 50N 4 8 E
Hellín, Spain 19 C5 38 31N 1 40W
Helmand □, Afghan. 40 D4 31 20N 64 0 E
Helmand →, Afghan. 40 D2 31 12N 61 34 E
Helmond, Neths. 15 C5 51 29N 5 41 E
Helmsdale, U.K. 12 C5 58 7N 3 39W
Helmsdale →, U.K. 12 C5 58 7N 3 40W
Helong, China 35 C15 42 40N 129 0 E
Helper, U.S.A. 82 G8 39 41N 110 51W
Helsingborg, Sweden 9 H15 56 3N 12 42 E
Helsingfors = Helsinki, Finland 9 F21 60 15N 25 3 E
Helsingør, Denmark 9 H15 56 2N 12 35 E
Helsinki, Finland 9 F21 60 15N 25 3 E
Helston, U.K. 11 G2 50 6N 5 17W
Helvellyn, U.K. 10 C4 54 32N 3 1W
Helwân, Egypt 51 C12 29 50N 31 20 E
Hemel Hempstead, U.K. 11 F7 51 44N 0 28W
Hemet, U.S.A. 85 M10 33 45N 116 58W
Hemingford, U.S.A. 80 D3 42 19N 103 4W
Hemmingford, Canada 79 A11 45 3N 73 35W
Hempstead, U.S.A. 81 K6 30 6N 96 5W
Hemse, Sweden 9 H18 57 15N 18 22 E
Henan □, China 34 H8 34 0N 114 0 E
Henares →, Spain 19 B4 40 24N 3 30W
Henashi-Misaki, Japan 30 D9 40 37N 139 51 E
Henderson, Argentina 94 D3 36 18S 61 43W
Henderson, Ky., U.S.A. 76 G2 37 50N 87 35W
Henderson, N.C., U.S.A. 77 G6 36 20N 78 25W
Henderson, Nev., U.S.A. 85 J12 36 2N 114 59W
Henderson, Tenn., U.S.A. 77 H1 35 26N 88 38W
Henderson, Tex., U.S.A. 81 J7 32 9N 94 48W
Hendersonville, N.C., U.S.A. 77 H4 35 19N 82 28W
Hendersonville, Tenn., U.S.A. 77 G2 36 18N 86 37W
Hendījān, Iran 45 D6 30 14N 49 43 E
Hendorābī, Iran 45 E7 26 40N 53 37 E
Hengcheng, China 34 E4 38 18N 106 28 E
Hengdaohezi, China 35 B15 44 52N 129 0 E
Hengelo, Neths. 15 B6 52 16N 6 48 E
Hengshan, China 34 F5 37 58N 109 5 E
Hengshui, China 34 F8 37 41N 115 40 E
Hengyang, China 33 D6 26 52N 112 33 E
Henlopen, C., U.S.A. 76 F8 38 48N 75 6W
Hennenman, S. Africa 56 D4 27 59S 27 1 E
Hennessey, U.S.A. 81 G6 36 6N 97 54W
Henrietta, U.S.A. 81 J5 33 49N 98 12W
Henrietta, Ostrov = Genriyetty, Ostrov, Russia 27 B16 77 6N 156 30 E
Henrietta Maria, C., Canada 70 A3 55 9N 82 20W
Henry, U.S.A. 80 E10 41 7N 89 22W
Henryetta, U.S.A. 81 H7 35 27N 95 59W
Henryville, Canada 79 A11 45 8N 73 11W

Hensall

Hensall, *Canada* **78 C3** 43 26N 81 30W
Hentiyn Nuruu, *Mongolia* **33 B5** 48 30N 108 30 E
Henty, *Australia* **63 F4** 35 30S 147 0 E
Henzada, *Burma* **41 L19** 17 38N 95 26 E
Heppner, *U.S.A.* **82 D4** 45 21N 119 33W
Hepworth, *Canada* **78 B3** 44 37N 81 9W
Hequ, *China* **34 E6** 39 20N 111 15 E
Héraðsflói, *Iceland* **8 D6** 65 42N 14 12W
Héraðsvötn →, *Iceland* **8 D4** 65 45N 19 25W
Herald Cays, *Australia* **62 B4** 16 58S 149 9 E
Herāt, *Afghan.* **40 B3** 34 20N 62 7 E
Herāt □, *Afghan.* **40 B3** 35 0N 62 0 E
Herbert →, *Australia* **62 B4** 18 31S 146 17 E
Herberton, *Australia* **62 B4** 17 20S 145 25 E
Herceg-Novi, *Montenegro, Yug.* **21 C8** 42 30N 18 33 E
Herchmer, *Canada* **73 B10** 57 22N 94 10W
Herðubreið, *Iceland* **8 D5** 65 11N 16 21W
Hereford, *U.K.* **11 E5** 52 4N 2 43W
Hereford, *U.S.A.* **81 H3** 34 49N 102 24W
Herefordshire □, *U.K.* **11 E5** 52 8N 2 40W
Herentals, *Belgium* **15 C4** 51 12N 4 51 E
Herford, *Germany* **16 B5** 52 7N 8 39 E
Herington, *U.S.A.* **80 F6** 38 40N 96 57W
Herkimer, *U.S.A.* **79 D10** 43 0N 74 59W
Herlong, *U.S.A.* **84 E6** 40 8N 120 8W
Herm, *U.K.* **11 H5** 49 30N 2 28W
Hermann, *U.S.A.* **80 F9** 38 42N 91 27W
Hermannsburg, *Australia* **60 D5** 23 57S 132 45 E
Hermanus, *S. Africa* **56 E2** 34 27S 19 12 E
Hermidale, *Australia* **63 E4** 31 30S 146 42 E
Hermiston, *U.S.A.* **82 D4** 45 51N 119 17W
Hermitage, *N.Z.* **59 K3** 43 44S 170 5 E
Hermite, I., *Chile* **96 H3** 55 50S 68 0W
Hermon, *U.S.A.* **79 B9** 44 28N 75 14W
Hermon, Mt. = Shaykh, J. ash, *Lebanon* **47 B4** 33 25N 35 50 E
Hermosillo, *Mexico* **86 B2** 29 10N 111 0W
Hernád →, *Hungary* **17 D11** 47 56N 21 8 E
Hernandarias, *Paraguay* **95 B5** 25 20S 54 40W
Hernandez, *U.S.A.* **84 J6** 36 24N 120 46W
Hernando, *Argentina* **94 C3** 32 28S 63 40W
Hernando, *U.S.A.* **81 H10** 34 50N 90 0W
Herndon, *U.S.A.* **78 F8** 40 43N 76 51W
Herne, *Germany* **15 C7** 51 32N 7 14 E
Herne Bay, *U.K.* **11 F9** 51 21N 1 8 E
Herning, *Denmark* **9 H13** 56 8N 8 58 E
Heroica = Caborca, *Mexico* **86 A2** 30 40N 112 10W
Heroica Nogales = Nogales, *Mexico* **86 A2** 31 20N 110 56W
Heron Bay, *Canada* **70 C2** 48 40N 86 25W
Herradura, Pta. de la, *Canary Is.* **22 F5** 28 26N 14 8W
Herreid, *U.S.A.* **80 C4** 45 50N 100 4W
Herrin, *U.S.A.* **81 G10** 37 48N 89 2W
Herriot, *Canada* **73 B8** 56 22N 101 16W
Hershey, *U.S.A.* **79 F8** 40 17N 76 39W
Hersonissos, *Greece* **23 D7** 35 18N 25 22 E
Herstal, *Belgium* **15 D5** 50 40N 5 38 E
Hertford, *U.K.* **11 F7** 51 48N 0 4W
Hertfordshire □, *U.K.* **11 F7** 51 51N 0 5W
's-Hertogenbosch, *Neths.* **15 C5** 51 42N 5 17 E
Hertzogville, *S. Africa* **56 D4** 28 9S 25 30 E
Hervey B., *Australia* **62 C5** 25 0S 152 52 E
Herzliyya, *Israel* **47 C3** 32 10N 34 50 E
Ḥeşār, *Fārs, Iran* **45 D6** 29 52N 50 16 E
Ḥeşār, *Markazī, Iran* **45 C6** 35 50N 49 12 E
Heshui, *China* **34 G5** 35 48N 108 0 E
Heshun, *China* **34 F7** 37 22N 113 32 E
Hesperia, *U.S.A.* **85 L9** 34 25N 117 18W
Hesse = Hessen □, *Germany* **16 C5** 50 30N 9 0 E
Hessen □, *Germany* **16 C5** 50 30N 9 0 E
Hetch Hetchy Aqueduct, *U.S.A.* **84 H5** 37 29N 122 19W
Hettinger, *U.S.A.* **80 C3** 46 0N 102 42W
Heuvelton, *U.S.A.* **79 B9** 44 37N 75 25W
Hewitt, *U.S.A.* **81 K6** 31 27N 97 11W
Hexham, *U.K.* **10 C5** 54 58N 2 4W
Hexigten Qi, *China* **35 C9** 43 18N 117 30 E
Ḥeydarābād, *Iran* **45 D7** 30 33N 55 38 E
Heysham, *U.K.* **10 C5** 54 3N 2 53W
Heywood, *Australia* **63 F3** 38 8S 141 37 E
Heze, *China* **34 G8** 35 14N 115 20 E
Hi Vista, *U.S.A.* **85 L9** 34 45N 117 46W
Hialeah, *U.S.A.* **77 N5** 25 50N 80 17W
Hiawatha, *U.S.A.* **80 F7** 39 51N 95 32W
Hibbing, *U.S.A.* **80 B8** 47 25N 92 56W
Hibbs B., *Australia* **62 G4** 42 35S 145 15 E
Hibernia Reef, *Australia* **60 B3** 12 0S 123 23 E
Hickman, *U.S.A.* **81 G10** 36 34N 89 11W
Hickory, *U.S.A.* **77 H5** 35 44N 81 21W
Hicks, Pt., *Australia* **63 F4** 37 49S 149 17 E
Hicks L., *Canada* **73 A9** 61 25N 100 0W
Hicksville, *U.S.A.* **79 F11** 40 46N 73 32W
Hida-Gawa →, *Japan* **31 G8** 35 26N 137 3 E
Hida-Sammyaku, *Japan* **31 F8** 36 30N 137 40 E
Hidaka-Sammyaku, *Japan* **30 C11** 42 35N 142 45 E
Hidalgo, *Mexico* **87 C5** 24 15N 99 26W
Hidalgo □, *Mexico* **87 C5** 20 30N 99 10W
Hidalgo, Presa M., *Mexico* **86 B3** 26 30N 108 35W
Hidalgo, Pta. del, *Canary Is.* **22 F3** 28 33N 16 19W
Hidalgo del Parral, *Mexico* **86 B3** 26 58N 105 40W
Hierro, *Canary Is.* **22 G1** 27 44N 18 0W
Higashiajima-San, *Japan* **30 F10** 37 40N 140 10 E
Higashiōsaka, *Japan* **31 G7** 34 40N 135 37 E
Higgins, *U.S.A.* **81 G4** 36 7N 100 2W
Higgins Corner, *U.S.A.* **84 F5** 39 2N 121 5W
High Atlas = Haut Atlas, *Morocco* **50 B4** 32 30N 5 0W
High Bridge, *U.S.A.* **79 F10** 40 40N 74 54W
High Level, *Canada* **72 B5** 58 31N 117 8W
High Point, *U.S.A.* **77 H6** 35 57N 80 0W
High Prairie, *Canada* **72 B5** 55 30N 116 30W
High River, *Canada* **72 C6** 50 30N 113 50W
High Tatra = Tatry, *Slovak Rep.* **17 D11** 49 20N 20 0 E
High Veld, *Africa* **48 J6** 27 0S 27 0 E
High Wycombe, *U.K.* **11 F7** 51 37N 0 45W
Highland □, *U.K.* **12 D4** 57 17N 4 21W
Highland Park, *U.S.A.* **76 D2** 42 11N 87 48W
Highmore, *U.S.A.* **80 C5** 44 31N 99 27W
Highrock L., *Canada* **73 B8** 55 45N 100 30W
Highrock L., *Sask., Canada* **73 B7** 57 5N 105 32W
Higüey, *Dom. Rep.* **89 C6** 18 37N 68 42W
Hiiumaa, *Estonia* **9 G20** 58 50N 22 45 E
Ḥijāz □, *Si. Arabia* **46 C3** 24 0N 40 0 E
Hijo = Tagum, *Phil.* **37 C7** 7 33N 125 53 E
Hikari, *Japan* **31 H5** 33 58N 131 58 E
Hiko, *U.S.A.* **84 H11** 37 32N 115 14W
Hikone, *Japan* **31 G8** 35 15N 136 10 E
Hikurangi, *N.Z.* **59 F5** 35 36S 174 17 E
Hikurangi, Mt., *N.Z.* **59 H6** 38 21S 176 52 E
Hildesheim, *Germany* **16 B5** 52 9N 9 56 E
Hill →, *Australia* **61 F2** 30 23S 115 3 E
Hill City, *Idaho, U.S.A.* **82 E6** 43 18N 115 3W
Hill City, *Kans., U.S.A.* **80 F5** 39 22N 99 51W
Hill City, *S. Dak., U.S.A.* **80 D3** 43 56N 103 35W
Hill Island L., *Canada* **73 A7** 60 30N 109 50W
Hillcrest Center, *U.S.A.* **85 K8** 35 23N 118 57W
Hillegom, *Neths.* **15 B4** 52 18N 4 35 E
Hillerød, *Denmark* **9 J15** 55 56N 12 19 E
Hillsboro, *Kans., U.S.A.* **80 F6** 38 21N 97 12W
Hillsboro, *N. Dak., U.S.A.* **80 B6** 47 26N 97 3W
Hillsboro, *N.H., U.S.A.* **79 C13** 43 7N 71 54W
Hillsboro, *Ohio, U.S.A.* **76 F4** 39 12N 83 37W
Hillsboro, *Oreg., U.S.A.* **84 E4** 45 31N 122 59W
Hillsboro, *Tex., U.S.A.* **81 J6** 32 1N 97 8W
Hillsborough, *Grenada* **89 D7** 12 28N 61 28W
Hillsdale, *Mich., U.S.A.* **76 E3** 41 56N 84 38W
Hillsdale, *N.Y., U.S.A.* **79 D11** 42 11N 73 30W
Hillsport, *Canada* **70 C2** 49 27N 85 34W
Hillston, *Australia* **63 E4** 33 30S 145 31 E
Hilo, *U.S.A.* **74 J17** 19 44N 155 5W
Hilton, *U.S.A.* **78 C7** 43 17N 77 48W
Hilton Head Island, *U.S.A.* **77 J5** 32 13N 80 45W
Hilversum, *Neths.* **15 B5** 52 14N 5 10 E
Himachal Pradesh □, *India* **42 D7** 31 30N 77 0 E
Himalaya, *Asia* **43 E11** 29 0N 84 0 E
Himatnagar, *India* **40 H8** 23 37N 72 57 E
Himeji, *Japan* **31 G7** 34 50N 134 40 E
Himi, *Japan* **31 F8** 36 50N 136 55 E
Ḥimş, *Syria* **47 A5** 34 40N 36 45 E
Ḥimş □, *Syria* **47 A6** 34 30N 37 0 E
Hinche, *Haiti* **89 C5** 19 9N 72 1W
Hinchinbrook I., *Australia* **62 B4** 18 20S 146 15 E
Hinckley, *U.K.* **11 E6** 52 33N 1 22W
Hinckley, *U.S.A.* **80 B8** 46 1N 92 56W
Hindaun, *India* **42 F7** 26 44N 77 5 E
Hindmarsh, L., *Australia* **63 F3** 36 5S 141 55 E
Hindu Bagh, *Pakistan* **42 D2** 30 56N 67 50 E
Hindu Kush, *Asia* **40 B7** 36 0N 71 0 E
Hindubagh, *Pakistan* **40 D5** 30 56N 67 57 E
Hindupur, *India* **40 N10** 13 49N 77 32 E
Hines Creek, *Canada* **72 B5** 56 20N 118 40W
Hinesville, *U.S.A.* **77 K5** 31 51N 81 36W
Hinganghat, *India* **40 J11** 20 30N 78 52 E
Hingham, *U.S.A.* **82 B8** 48 33N 110 25W
Hingir, *India* **43 J10** 21 57N 83 41 E
Hingoli, *India* **40 K10** 19 41N 77 15 E
Hinna = Imi, *Ethiopia* **46 F3** 6 28N 42 10 E
Hinnøya, *Norway* **8 B16** 68 35N 15 50 E
Hinojosa del Duque, *Spain* **19 C3** 38 30N 5 9W
Hinsdale, *U.S.A.* **79 D12** 42 47N 72 29W
Hinton, *Canada* **72 C5** 53 26N 117 34W
Hinton, *U.S.A.* **76 G5** 37 40N 80 54W
Hirado, *Japan* **31 H4** 33 22N 129 33 E
Hirakud Dam, *India* **41 J13** 21 32N 83 45 E
Hiran →, *India* **43 H8** 23 6N 79 21 E
Hirapur, *India* **43 G8** 24 22N 79 13 E
Hiratsuka, *Japan* **31 G9** 35 19N 139 21 E
Hiroo, *Japan* **30 C11** 42 17N 143 19 E
Hirosaki, *Japan* **30 D10** 40 34N 140 28 E
Hiroshima, *Japan* **31 G6** 34 24N 132 30 E
Hiroshima □, *Japan* **31 G6** 34 50N 133 0 E
Hisar, *India* **42 E6** 29 12N 75 45 E
Hisb →, *Iraq* **44 D5** 31 45N 44 17 E
Ḥismá, *Si. Arabia* **44 D3** 28 30N 36 0 E
Hispaniola, *W. Indies* **89 C5** 19 0N 71 0W
Hīt, *Iraq* **44 C4** 33 38N 42 49 E
Hita, *Japan* **31 H5** 33 20N 130 58 E
Hitachi, *Japan* **31 F10** 36 36N 140 39 E
Hitchin, *U.K.* **11 F7** 51 58N 0 16W
Hitoyoshi, *Japan* **31 H5** 32 13N 130 45 E
Hitra, *Norway* **8 E13** 63 30N 8 45 E
Hixon, *Canada* **72 C4** 53 25N 122 35W
Ḥiyyon, N. →, *Israel* **47 E4** 30 25N 35 10 E
Hjalmar L., *Canada* **73 A7** 61 33N 109 25W
Hjälmaren, *Sweden* **9 G16** 59 18N 15 40 E
Hjørring, *Denmark* **9 H13** 57 29N 9 59 E
Hluhluwe, *S. Africa* **57 D5** 28 1S 32 15 E
Hlyboka, *Ukraine* **17 D13** 48 5N 25 56 E
Ho Chi Minh City = Phanh Bho Ho Chi Minh, *Vietnam* **39 G6** 10 58N 106 40 E
Ho Thuong, *Vietnam* **38 C5** 19 32N 105 48 E
Hoa Da, *Vietnam* **39 G7** 11 16N 108 40 E
Hoa Hiep, *Vietnam* **39 G5** 11 34N 105 51 E
Hoai Nhon, *Vietnam* **38 E7** 14 28N 109 1 E
Hoang Lien Son, *Vietnam* **38 A4** 22 0N 104 0 E
Hoare B., *Canada* **69 B13** 65 17N 62 30W
Hobart, *Australia* **62 G4** 42 50S 147 21 E
Hobart, *U.S.A.* **81 H5** 35 1N 99 6W
Hobbs, *U.S.A.* **81 J3** 32 42N 103 8W
Hobbs Coast, *Antarctica* **5 D14** 74 50S 131 0W
Hobe Sound, *U.S.A.* **77 M5** 27 4N 80 8W
Hoboken, *U.S.A.* **79 F10** 40 45N 74 4W
Hobro, *Denmark* **9 H13** 56 39N 9 46 E
Hoburgen, *Sweden* **9 H18** 56 55N 18 7 E
Hodaka-Dake, *Japan* **31 F8** 36 17N 137 39 E
Hodgeville, *Canada* **73 C7** 50 7N 106 58W
Hodgson, *Canada* **73 C9** 51 13N 97 36W
Hódmezővásárhely, *Hungary* **17 E11** 46 28N 20 22 E
Hodna, Chott el, *Algeria* **50 A6** 35 26N 4 43 E
Hodonín, *Czech Rep.* **17 D9** 48 50N 17 10 E
Hoeamdong, *N. Korea* **35 C16** 42 30N 130 16 E
Hoek van Holland, *Neths.* **15 C4** 52 0N 4 7 E
Hoengsŏng, *S. Korea* **35 F14** 37 29N 127 59 E
Hoeryong, *N. Korea* **35 C15** 42 30N 129 45 E
Hoeyang, *N. Korea* **35 E14** 38 43N 127 36 E
Hof, *Germany* **16 C6** 50 19N 11 55 E
Hofmeyr, *S. Africa* **56 E4** 31 39S 25 50 E
Höfn, *Iceland* **8 D6** 64 15N 15 13W
Hofors, *Sweden* **9 F17** 60 31N 16 15 E
Hofsjökull, *Iceland* **8 D4** 64 49N 18 48W
Hōfu, *Japan* **31 G5** 34 3N 131 34 E
Hogan Group, *Australia* **63 F4** 39 13S 147 1 E
Hogarth, Mt., *Australia* **62 C2** 21 48S 136 58 E
Hoggar = Ahaggar, *Algeria* **50 D7** 23 0N 6 30 E
Hogsty Reef, *Bahamas* **89 B5** 21 41N 73 48W
Hoh →, *U.S.A.* **84 C2** 47 45N 124 29W
Hohe Venn, *Belgium* **15 D6** 50 30N 6 5 E
Hohenwald, *U.S.A.* **77 H2** 35 33N 87 33W
Hohhot, *China* **34 D6** 40 52N 111 40 E
Hóhlakas, *Greece* **23 D9** 35 57N 27 53 E
Hoi An, *Vietnam* **38 E7** 15 30N 108 19 E
Hoisington, *U.S.A.* **80 F5** 38 31N 98 47W
Hōjō, *Japan* **31 H6** 33 58N 132 46 E
Hokianga Harbour, *N.Z.* **59 F4** 35 31S 173 22 E
Hokitika, *N.Z.* **59 K3** 42 42S 171 0 E
Hokkaidō □, *Japan* **30 C11** 43 30N 143 0 E
Holbrook, *Australia* **63 F4** 35 42S 147 18 E
Holbrook, *U.S.A.* **83 J8** 34 54N 110 10W
Holden, *U.S.A.* **82 G7** 39 6N 112 16W
Holdenville, *U.S.A.* **81 H6** 35 5N 96 24W
Holdrege, *U.S.A.* **80 E5** 40 26N 99 23W
Holguín, *Cuba* **88 B4** 20 50N 76 20W
Hollams Bird I., *Namibia* **56 C1** 24 40S 14 30 E
Holland, *Mich., U.S.A.* **76 D2** 42 47N 86 7W
Holland, *N.Y., U.S.A.* **78 D6** 42 38N 78 32W
Hollandale, *U.S.A.* **81 J9** 33 10N 90 51W
Hollandia = Jayapura, *Indonesia* **37 E10** 2 28S 140 38 E
Holley, *U.S.A.* **78 C6** 43 14N 78 2W
Hollidaysburg, *U.S.A.* **78 F6** 40 26N 78 24W
Hollis, *U.S.A.* **81 H5** 34 41N 99 55W
Hollister, *Calif., U.S.A.* **84 J5** 36 51N 121 24W
Hollister, *Idaho, U.S.A.* **82 E6** 42 21N 114 35W
Holly Hill, *U.S.A.* **77 L5** 29 16N 81 3W
Holly Springs, *U.S.A.* **81 H10** 34 46N 89 27W
Hollywood, *Calif., U.S.A.* **74 D3** 34 7N 118 25W
Hollywood, *Fla., U.S.A.* **77 N5** 26 1N 80 9W
Holman, *Canada* **68 A8** 70 42N 117 41W
Holman, *N.W.T., Canada* **68 A8** 70 44N 117 44W
Hólmavík, *Iceland* **8 D3** 65 42N 21 40W
Holmen, *U.S.A.* **80 D9** 43 58N 91 15W
Holmes Reefs, *Australia* **62 B4** 16 27S 148 0 E
Holmsund, *Sweden* **8 E19** 63 41N 20 20 E
Holroyd →, *Australia* **62 A3** 14 10S 141 36 E
Holstebro, *Denmark* **9 H13** 56 22N 8 37 E
Holsworthy, *U.K.* **11 G3** 50 48N 4 22W
Holton, *Canada* **71 B8** 54 31N 57 12W
Holton, *U.S.A.* **80 F7** 39 28N 95 44W
Holtville, *U.S.A.* **85 N11** 32 49N 115 23W
Holwerd, *Neths.* **15 A5** 53 22N 5 54 E
Holy I., *Angl., U.K.* **10 D3** 53 17N 4 37W
Holy I., *Northumb., U.K.* **10 B6** 55 40N 1 47W
Holyhead, *U.K.* **10 D3** 53 18N 4 38W
Holyoke, *Colo., U.S.A.* **80 E3** 40 35N 102 18W
Holyoke, *Mass., U.S.A.* **79 D12** 42 12N 72 37W
Holyrood, *Canada* **71 C9** 47 27N 53 8W
Homa Bay, *Kenya* **54 C3** 0 36S 34 30 E
Homalin, *Burma* **41 G19** 24 55N 95 0 E
Homand, *Iran* **45 C8** 32 28N 59 37 E
Homathko →, *Canada* **72 C4** 51 0N 124 56W
Hombori, *Mali* **50 E5** 15 20N 1 38W
Home B., *Canada* **69 B13** 68 40N 67 10W
Home Hill, *Australia* **62 B4** 19 43S 147 25 E
Homedale, *U.S.A.* **82 E5** 43 37N 116 56W
Homer, *Alaska, U.S.A.* **68 C4** 59 39N 151 33W
Homer, *La., U.S.A.* **81 J8** 32 48N 93 4W
Homer City, *U.S.A.* **78 F5** 40 32N 79 10W
Homestead, *Australia* **62 C4** 20 20S 145 40 E
Homestead, *U.S.A.* **77 N5** 25 28N 80 29W
Homewood, *U.S.A.* **84 F6** 39 4N 120 8W
Homoine, *Mozam.* **57 C6** 23 55S 35 8 E
Homs = Ḥimş, *Syria* **47 A5** 34 40N 36 45 E
Homyel, *Belarus* **17 B16** 52 28N 31 0 E
Hon Chong, *Vietnam* **39 G5** 10 25N 104 30 E
Hon Me, *Vietnam* **38 C5** 19 23N 105 56 E
Honan = Henan □, *China* **34 H8** 34 0N 114 0 E
Honbetsu, *Japan* **30 C11** 43 7N 143 37 E
Honcut, *U.S.A.* **84 F5** 39 20N 121 32W
Hondeklipbaai, *S. Africa* **56 E2** 30 19S 17 17 E
Hondo, *Japan* **31 H5** 32 27N 130 12 E
Hondo, *U.S.A.* **81 L5** 29 21N 99 9W
Hondo →, *Belize* **87 D7** 18 25N 88 21W
Honduras ■, *Cent. Amer.* **88 D2** 14 40N 86 30W
Honduras, G. de, *Caribbean* **88 C2** 16 50N 87 0W
Hønefoss, *Norway* **9 F14** 60 10N 10 18 E
Honesdale, *U.S.A.* **79 E9** 41 34N 75 16W
Honey L., *U.S.A.* **84 E6** 40 15N 120 19W
Honfleur, *France* **18 B4** 49 25N 0 13 E
Hong →, *Vietnam* **32 D5** 22 0N 104 0 E
Hong He →, *China* **34 H8** 32 25N 115 35 E
Hong Kong □, *China* **33 D6** 22 11N 114 14 E
Hongch'ŏn, *S. Korea* **35 F14** 37 44N 127 53 E
Hongjiang, *China* **33 D5** 27 7N 109 59 E
Hongliu He →, *China* **34 F5** 38 0N 109 50 E
Hongor, *Mongolia* **34 B7** 45 45N 112 50 E
Hongsa, *Laos* **38 C3** 19 43N 101 20 E
Hongshui He →, *China* **33 D5** 23 48N 109 30 E
Hongsŏng, *S. Korea* **35 F14** 36 37N 126 38 E
Hongtong, *China* **34 F6** 36 16N 111 40 E
Honguedo, Détroit d', *Canada* **71 C7** 49 15N 64 0W
Hongwon, *N. Korea* **35 E14** 40 0N 127 56 E
Hongze Hu, *China* **35 H10** 33 15N 118 35 E
Honiara, *Solomon Is.* **64 H7** 9 27S 159 57 E
Honiton, *U.K.* **11 G4** 50 47N 3 11W
Honjō, *Japan* **30 E10** 39 23N 140 3 E
Honningsvåg, *Norway* **8 A21** 70 59N 25 59 E
Honolulu, *U.S.A.* **74 H16** 21 19N 157 52W
Honshū, *Japan* **31 G9** 36 0N 138 0 E
Hood, Mt., *U.S.A.* **82 D3** 45 23N 121 42W
Hood, Pt., *Australia* **61 F2** 34 23S 119 34 E
Hood River, *U.S.A.* **82 D3** 45 43N 121 31W
Hoodsport, *U.S.A.* **84 C3** 47 24N 123 9W
Hoogeveen, *Neths.* **15 B6** 52 44N 6 28 E
Hoogezand-Sappemeer, *Neths.* **15 A6** 53 9N 6 45 E
Hooghly = Hugli →, *India* **43 J13** 21 56N 88 4 E
Hooghly-Chinsura = Chunchura, *India* **43 H13** 22 53N 88 27 E
Hook Hd., *Ireland* **13 D5** 52 7N 6 56W
Hook I., *Australia* **62 C4** 20 4S 149 0 E
Hook of Holland = Hoek van Holland, *Neths.* **15 C4** 52 0N 4 7 E
Hooker, *U.S.A.* **81 G4** 36 52N 101 13W
Hooker Creek, *Australia* **60 C5** 18 23S 130 38 E
Hoonah, *U.S.A.* **72 B1** 58 7N 135 27W
Hooper Bay, *U.S.A.* **68 B3** 61 32N 166 6W
Hoopeston, *U.S.A.* **76 E2** 40 28N 87 40W
Hoopstad, *S. Africa* **56 D4** 27 50S 25 55 E
Hoorn, *Neths.* **15 B5** 52 38N 5 4 E
Hoover, *U.S.A.* **77 J2** 33 20N 86 11W
Hoover Dam, *U.S.A.* **85 K12** 36 1N 114 44W
Hooversville, *U.S.A.* **78 F6** 40 9N 78 55W
Hop Bottom, *U.S.A.* **79 E9** 41 42N 75 46W
Hope, *Canada* **72 D4** 49 25N 121 25W
Hope, *Ariz., U.S.A.* **85 M13** 33 43N 113 42W
Hope, *Ark., U.S.A.* **81 J8** 33 40N 93 36W
Hope, L., *S. Austral., Australia* **63 D2** 28 24S 139 18 E
Hope, L., *W. Austral., Australia* **61 F3** 32 35S 120 15 E
Hope I., *Canada* **78 B4** 44 55N 80 11W
Hope Town, *Bahamas* **88 A4** 26 35N 76 57W
Hopedale, *Canada* **71 A7** 55 28N 60 13W
Hopedale, *U.S.A.* **79 D13** 42 8N 71 33W
Hopefield, *S. Africa* **56 E2** 33 3S 18 22 E
Hopei = Hebei □, *China* **34 E9** 39 0N 116 0 E
Hopelchén, *Mexico* **87 D7** 19 46N 89 50W
Hopetoun, *Vic., Australia* **63 F3** 35 42S 142 22 E
Hopetoun, *W. Austral., Australia* **61 F3** 33 57S 120 7 E
Hopetown, *S. Africa* **56 D3** 29 34S 24 3 E
Hopevale, *Australia* **62 B4** 15 16S 145 20 E
Hopewell, *U.S.A.* **76 G7** 37 18N 77 17W
Hopkins, L., *Australia* **60 D4** 24 15S 128 35 E
Hopkinsville, *U.S.A.* **77 G2** 36 52N 87 29W
Hopland, *U.S.A.* **84 G3** 38 58N 123 7W
Hoquiam, *U.S.A.* **84 D3** 46 59N 123 53W
Horden Hills, *Australia* **60 D5** 20 15S 130 0 E
Horinger, *China* **34 D6** 40 28N 111 48 E
Horlick Mts., *Antarctica* **5 E15** 84 0S 102 0W
Horlivka, *Ukraine* **25 E6** 48 19N 38 5 E
Hormak, *Iran* **45 D9** 29 58N 60 51 E
Hormoz, *Iran* **45 E7** 27 35N 55 0 E
Hormoz, Jaz.-ye, *Iran* **45 E8** 27 8N 56 28 E
Hormozgān □, *Iran* **45 E8** 27 30N 56 0 E
Hormuz, Kūh-e, *Iran* **45 E7** 27 27N 55 10 E
Hormuz, Str. of, *The Gulf* **45 E8** 26 30N 56 30 E
Horn, *Austria* **16 D8** 48 39N 15 40 E
Horn, *Iceland* **8 C2** 66 28N 22 28W
Horn →, *Canada* **72 A5** 61 30N 118 1W
Horn, Cape = Hornos, C. de, *Chile* **96 H3** 55 50S 67 30W
Horn Head, *Ireland* **13 A3** 55 14N 8 0W
Horn I., *Australia* **62 A3** 10 37S 142 17 E
Horn Mts., *Canada* **72 A5** 62 15N 119 15W
Hornavan, *Sweden* **8 C17** 66 15N 17 30 E
Hornbeck, *U.S.A.* **81 K8** 31 20N 93 24W
Hornbrook, *U.S.A.* **82 F2** 41 55N 122 33W
Horncastle, *U.K.* **10 D7** 53 13N 0 7W
Hornell, *U.S.A.* **78 D7** 42 20N 77 40W
Hornell L., *Canada* **72 A5** 62 20N 119 25W
Hornepayne, *Canada* **70 C3** 49 14N 84 48W
Hornings Mills, *Canada* **78 B4** 44 9N 80 12W
Hornitos, *U.S.A.* **84 H6** 37 30N 120 14W
Hornos, C. de, *Chile* **96 H3** 55 50S 67 30W
Hornsea, *U.K.* **10 D7** 53 55N 0 11W
Horobetsu, *Japan* **30 C10** 42 24N 141 6 E
Horodenka, *Ukraine* **17 D13** 48 41N 25 29 E
Horodok, *Khmelnytskyy, Ukraine* **17 D14** 49 10N 26 34 E
Horodok, *Lviv, Ukraine* **17 D12** 49 46N 23 32 E
Horokhiv, *Ukraine* **17 C13** 50 30N 24 45 E
Horqin Youyi Qianqi, *China* **35 A12** 46 5N 122 3 E
Horqueta, *Paraguay* **94 A4** 23 15S 56 55W
Horse Creek, *U.S.A.* **80 E3** 41 57N 105 10W
Horse Is., *Canada* **71 B8** 50 15N 55 50W
Horsefly L., *Canada* **72 C4** 52 25N 121 0W
Horseheads, *U.S.A.* **78 D8** 42 10N 76 49W
Horsens, *Denmark* **9 J13** 55 52N 9 51 E
Horsham, *Australia* **63 F3** 36 44S 142 13 E
Horsham, *U.K.* **11 F7** 51 4N 0 20W
Horten, *Norway* **9 G14** 59 25N 10 32 E
Horton, *U.S.A.* **80 F7** 39 40N 95 32W
Horton →, *Canada* **68 B7** 69 56N 126 52W
Horwood L., *Canada* **70 C3** 48 5N 82 20W
Hose, Gunung-Gunung, *Malaysia* **36 D4** 2 5N 114 6 E
Ḥoseynābād, *Khuzestān, Iran* **45 C6** 32 45N 48 20 E
Ḥoseynābād, *Kordestān, Iran* **44 C5** 35 33N 47 8 E
Hoshangabad, *India* **42 H7** 22 45N 77 45 E
Hoshiarpur, *India* **42 D6** 31 30N 75 58 E
Hospet, *India* **40 M10** 15 15N 76 20 E
Hoste, I., *Chile* **96 H3** 55 0S 69 0W
Hot, *Thailand* **38 C2** 18 8N 98 29 E
Hot Creek Range, *U.S.A.* **82 G6** 38 40N 116 20W
Hot Springs, *Ark., U.S.A.* **81 H8** 34 31N 93 3W
Hot Springs, *S. Dak., U.S.A.* **80 D3** 43 26N 103 29W
Hotagen, *Sweden* **8 E16** 63 50N 14 30 E
Hotan, *China* **32 C2** 37 25N 79 55 E
Hotazel, *S. Africa* **56 D3** 27 17S 22 58 E
Hotchkiss, *U.S.A.* **83 G10** 38 48N 107 43W
Hotham, C., *Australia* **60 B5** 12 2S 131 18 E
Hoting, *Sweden* **8 D17** 64 8N 16 15 E
Hotte, Massif de la, *Haiti* **89 C5** 18 30N 73 45W
Hottentotsbaai, *Namibia* **56 D1** 26 8S 14 59 E
Houffalize, *Belgium* **15 D5** 50 8N 5 48 E
Houghton, *Mich., U.S.A.* **80 B10** 47 7N 88 34W
Houghton, *N.Y., U.S.A.* **78 D6** 42 25N 78 10W
Houghton L., *U.S.A.* **76 C3** 44 21N 84 44W
Houhora Heads, *N.Z.* **59 F4** 34 49S 173 9 E
Houlton, *U.S.A.* **77 B12** 46 8N 67 51W
Houma, *U.S.A.* **81 L9** 29 36N 90 43W
Housatonic →, *U.S.A.* **79 E11** 41 10N 73 7W
Houston, *Canada* **72 C3** 54 25N 126 39W
Houston, *Mo., U.S.A.* **81 G9** 37 22N 91 58W
Houston, *Tex., U.S.A.* **81 L7** 29 46N 95 22W
Houtman Abrolhos, *Australia* **61 E1** 28 43S 113 48 E
Hovd, *Mongolia* **32 B4** 48 2N 91 37 E
Hove, *U.K.* **11 G7** 50 50N 0 10W
Hoveyzeh, *Iran* **45 D6** 31 27N 48 4 E
Hövsgöl, *Mongolia* **34 C5** 43 37N 109 39 E
Hövsgöl Nuur, *Mongolia* **32 A5** 51 0N 100 30 E
Howard, *Australia* **63 D5** 25 16S 152 32 E
Howard, *Pa., U.S.A.* **78 F7** 41 1N 77 40W
Howard, *S. Dak., U.S.A.* **80 C6** 44 1N 97 32W
Howe, *U.S.A.* **82 E7** 43 48N 113 0W
Howe, C., *Australia* **63 F5** 37 30S 150 0 E
Howe I., *Canada* **79 B8** 44 16N 76 17W
Howell, *U.S.A.* **76 D4** 42 36N 83 56W
Howick, *Canada* **79 A11** 45 11N 73 51W
Howick, *S. Africa* **57 D5** 29 28S 30 14 E
Howick Group, *Australia* **62 A4** 14 20S 145 30 E
Howitt, L., *Australia* **63 D2** 27 40S 138 40 E
Howland I., *Pac. Oc.* **64 G10** 0 48N 176 38W
Howrah = Haora, *India* **43 H13** 22 37N 88 20 E
Howth Hd., *Ireland* **13 C5** 53 22N 6 3W
Höxter, *Germany* **16 C5** 51 46N 9 22 E
Hoy, *U.K.* **12 C5** 58 50N 3 15W
Høyanger, *Norway* **9 F12** 61 13N 6 4 E

Hoyerswerda, Germany 16 C8 51 26N 14 14 E
Hoylake, U.K. 10 D4 53 24N 3 10W
Hpungan Pass, Burma 41 F20 27 30N 96 55 E
Hradec Králové, Czech Rep. 16 C8 50 15N 15 50 E
Hrodna, Belarus 17 B12 53 42N 23 52 E
Hrodzyanka, Belarus 17 B15 53 31N 28 42 E
Hron →, Slovak Rep. 17 E10 47 49N 18 45 E
Hrvatska = Croatia ■, Europe 16 F9 45 20N 16 0 E
Hrymayliv, Ukraine 17 D14 49 20N 26 5 E
Hsenwi, Burma 41 H20 23 22N 97 55 E
Hsiamen = Xiamen, China 33 D6 24 25N 118 4 E
Hsian = Xi'an, China 34 G5 34 15N 109 0 E
Hsinchu, Taiwan 33 D7 24 48N 120 58 E
Hsinhailien = Lianyungang, China 35 G10 34 40N 119 11 E
Hsüchou = Xuzhou, China 35 G9 34 18N 117 10 E
Hu Xian, China 34 G5 34 8N 108 42 E
Hua Hin, Thailand 38 F2 12 34N 99 58 E
Hua Xian, Henan, China 34 G8 35 30N 114 30 E
Hua Xian, Shaanxi, China 34 G5 34 30N 109 48 E
Huachinera, Mexico 86 A3 30 9N 108 55W
Huacho, Peru 92 F3 11 10S 77 35W
Huade, China 34 D7 41 55N 113 59 E
Huadian, China 35 C14 43 0N 126 40 E
Huai He →, China 33 C6 33 0N 118 30 E
Huai Yot, Thailand 39 J2 7 45N 99 37 E
Huai'an, Hebei, China 34 D8 40 30N 114 20 E
Huai'an, Jiangsu, China 35 H10 33 30N 119 10 E
Huaibei, China 34 G9 34 0N 116 48 E
Huaide = Gongzhuling, China 35 C13 43 30N 124 40 E
Huaidezhen, China 35 C13 43 48N 124 50 E
Huainan, China 33 C6 32 38N 116 58 E
Huairen, China 34 E7 39 48N 113 20 E
Huairou, China 34 D9 40 20N 116 35 E
Huaiyang, China 34 H8 33 40N 114 52 E
Huaiyin, China 35 H10 33 30N 119 2 E
Huaiyuan, China 35 H9 32 55N 117 10 E
Huajianzi, China 35 D13 41 23N 125 20 E
Huajuapan de Leon, Mexico 87 D5 17 50N 97 48W
Hualapai Peak, U.S.A. 83 J7 35 5N 113 54W
Huallaga →, Peru 92 E3 5 15S 75 30W
Huambo, Angola 53 G3 12 42S 15 54 E
Huan Jiang →, China 34 G5 34 28N 109 0 E
Huan Xian, China 34 F4 36 33N 107 7 E
Huancabamba, Peru 92 E3 5 10S 79 15W
Huancane, Peru 92 G5 15 10S 69 44W
Huancavelica, Peru 92 F3 12 50S 75 5W
Huancayo, Peru 92 F3 12 5S 75 12W
Huanchaca, Bolivia 92 H5 20 15S 66 40W
Huang Hai = Yellow Sea, China 35 G12 35 0N 123 0 E
Huang He →, China 35 F10 37 55N 118 50 E
Huang Xian, China 35 F11 37 38N 120 30 E
Huangling, China 34 G5 35 34N 109 15 E
Huanglong, China 34 G5 35 30N 109 59 E
Huangshan, China 33 D6 29 42N 118 25 E
Huangshi, China 33 C6 30 10N 115 3 E
Huangsongdian, China 35 C14 43 45N 127 25 E
Huantai, China 35 F9 36 58N 117 56 E
Huánuco, Peru 92 E3 9 55S 76 15W
Huaraz, Peru 92 E3 9 30S 77 32W
Huarmey, Peru 92 F3 10 5S 78 5W
Huascarán, Peru 92 E3 9 8S 77 36W
Huasco, Chile 94 B1 28 30S 71 15W
Huasco →, Chile 94 B1 28 27S 71 13W
Huasna, U.S.A. 85 K6 35 6N 120 24W
Huatabampo, Mexico 86 B3 26 50N 109 50W
Huauchinango, Mexico 87 C5 20 11N 98 3W
Huautla de Jiménez, Mexico 87 D5 18 8N 96 51W
Huay Namota, Mexico 86 C4 21 56N 104 30W
Huayin, China 34 G6 34 35N 110 5 E
Hubbard, Ohio, U.S.A. 78 E4 41 9N 80 34W
Hubbard, Tex., U.S.A. 81 K6 31 51N 96 48W
Hubbart Pt., Canada 73 B10 59 21N 94 41W
Hubei □, China 33 C6 31 0N 112 0 E
Hubli, India 40 M9 15 22N 75 15 E
Huch'ang, N. Korea 35 D14 41 25N 127 2 E
Hucknall, U.K. 10 D6 53 3N 1 13W
Huddersfield, U.K. 10 D6 53 39N 1 47W
Hudiksvall, Sweden 9 F17 61 43N 17 10 E
Hudson, Canada 70 B1 50 6N 92 9W
Hudson, Mass., U.S.A. 79 D13 42 23N 71 34W
Hudson, N.Y., U.S.A. 79 D11 42 15N 73 46W
Hudson, Wis., U.S.A. 80 C8 44 58N 92 45W
Hudson, Wyo., U.S.A. 82 E9 42 54N 108 35W
Hudson →, U.S.A. 79 F10 40 42N 74 2W
Hudson Bay, N.W.T., Canada 69 C11 60 0N 86 0W
Hudson Bay, Sask., Canada 73 C8 52 51N 102 23W
Hudson Falls, U.S.A. 79 C11 43 18N 73 35W
Hudson Mts., Antarctica 5 D16 74 32S 99 20W
Hudson Str., Canada 69 B13 62 0N 70 0W
Hudson's Hope, Canada 72 B4 56 0N 121 54W
Hue, Vietnam 38 D6 16 30N 107 35 E
Huehuetenango, Guatemala 88 C1 15 20N 91 28W
Huejúcar, Mexico 86 C4 22 21N 103 13W
Huelva, Spain 19 D2 37 18N 6 57W
Huentelauquén, Chile 94 C1 31 38S 71 33W
Huerta, Sa. de la, Argentina 94 C2 31 10S 67 30W
Huesca, Spain 19 A5 42 8N 0 25W
Huetamo, Mexico 86 D4 18 36N 100 54W
Hugh →, Australia 62 D1 25 1S 134 1 E
Hughenden, Australia 62 C3 20 52S 144 10 E
Hughes, Australia 61 F4 30 42S 129 31 E
Hughesville, U.S.A. 79 E8 41 14N 76 44W
Hugli →, India 43 J13 21 56N 88 4 E
Hugo, Colo., U.S.A. 80 F3 39 8N 103 28W
Hugo, Okla., U.S.A. 81 H7 34 1N 95 31W
Hugoton, U.S.A. 81 G4 37 11N 101 21W
Hui Xian = Huixian, China 34 G7 35 27N 113 12 E
Hui Xian, China 34 H4 33 50N 106 4 E
Hui'anbu, China 34 F4 37 28N 106 38 E
Huichapán, Mexico 87 C5 20 24N 99 40W
Huifa He →, China 35 C14 43 0N 127 50 E
Huila, Nevado del, Colombia 92 C3 3 0N 76 0W
Huimin, China 35 F9 37 27N 117 28 E
Huinan, China 35 C14 42 40N 126 2 E
Huinca Renancó, Argentina 94 C3 34 51S 64 22W
Huining, China 34 G3 35 38N 105 0 E
Huinong, China 34 E4 39 5N 106 35 E
Huisache, Mexico 86 C4 22 55N 100 25W
Huiting, China 34 G9 34 5N 116 5 E
Huixian, China 34 G7 35 27N 113 12 E
Huixtla, Mexico 87 D6 15 9N 92 28W
Huize, China 32 D5 26 24N 103 15 E
Hukawng Valley, Burma 41 F20 26 30N 96 30 E
Hukuntsi, Botswana 56 C3 23 58S 21 45 E
Ḩulayfā', Si. Arabia 44 E4 25 58N 40 45 E
Huld = Ulaanjirem, Mongolia 34 B3 45 5N 105 30 E
Hulin He →, China 35 B12 45 0N 122 10 E
Hull = Kingston upon Hull, U.K. 10 D7 53 45N 0 21W
Hull, Canada 79 A9 45 25N 75 44W
Hull →, U.K. 10 D7 53 44N 0 20W
Hulst, Neths. 15 C4 51 17N 4 2 E
Hulun Nur, China 33 B6 49 0N 117 30 E
Humahuaca, Argentina 94 A2 23 10S 65 25W
Humaitá, Brazil 92 E6 7 35S 63 1W
Humaitá, Paraguay 94 B4 27 2S 58 31W
Humansdorp, S. Africa 56 E3 34 2S 24 46 E
Humbe, Angola 56 B1 16 40S 14 55 E
Humber →, U.K. 10 D7 53 42N 0 27W
Humboldt, Canada 73 C7 52 15N 105 9W
Humboldt, Iowa, U.S.A. 80 D7 42 44N 94 13W
Humboldt, Tenn., U.S.A. 81 H10 35 50N 88 55W
Humboldt →, U.S.A. 82 F4 39 59N 118 36W
Humboldt Gletscher, Greenland 4 B4 79 30N 62 0W
Hume, U.S.A. 84 J8 36 48N 118 54W
Hume, L., Australia 63 F4 36 0S 147 5 E
Humenné, Slovak Rep. 17 D11 48 55N 21 50 E
Humphreys, Mt., U.S.A. 84 H8 37 17N 118 40W
Humphreys Peak, U.S.A. 83 J8 35 21N 111 41W
Humptulips, U.S.A. 84 C3 47 14N 123 57W
Hūn, Libya 51 C9 29 2N 16 0 E
Hun Jiang →, China 35 D13 40 50N 125 38 E
Húnaflói, Iceland 8 D3 65 50N 20 50W
Hunan □, China 33 D6 27 30N 112 0 E
Hunchun, China 35 C16 42 52N 130 28 E
Hundewali, Pakistan 42 D5 31 55N 72 38 E
Hundred Mile House, Canada 72 C4 51 38N 121 18W
Hunedoara, Romania 17 F12 45 40N 22 50 E
Hungary ■, Europe 17 E10 47 20N 19 20 E
Hungary, Plain of, Europe 6 F10 47 0N 20 0 E
Hungerford, Australia 63 D3 28 58S 144 24 E
Hŭngnam, N. Korea 35 E14 39 49N 127 45 E
Hunsberge, Namibia 56 D2 27 45S 17 12 E
Hunsrück, Germany 16 D4 49 56N 7 27 E
Hunstanton, U.K. 10 E8 52 56N 0 29 E
Hunter, U.S.A. 79 D10 42 13N 74 13W
Hunter I., Australia 62 G3 40 30S 144 45 E
Hunter I., Canada 72 C3 51 55N 128 0W
Hunter Ra., Australia 63 E5 32 45S 150 15 E
Hunters Road, Zimbabwe 55 F2 19 9S 29 49 E
Hunterville, N.Z. 59 H5 39 56S 175 35 E
Huntingburg, U.S.A. 76 F2 38 18N 86 57W
Huntingdon, Canada 70 C5 45 6N 74 10W
Huntingdon, U.K. 11 E7 52 20N 0 11W
Huntingdon, U.S.A. 78 F6 40 30N 78 1W
Huntington, Ind., U.S.A. 76 E3 40 53N 85 30W
Huntington, Oreg., U.S.A. 82 D5 44 21N 117 16W
Huntington, Utah, U.S.A. 82 G8 39 20N 110 58W
Huntington, W. Va., U.S.A. 76 F4 38 25N 82 27W
Huntington Beach, U.S.A. 85 M9 33 40N 118 5W
Huntington Station, U.S.A. 79 F11 40 52N 73 26W
Huntly, N.Z. 59 G5 37 34S 175 11 E
Huntly, U.K. 12 D6 57 27N 2 47W
Huntsville, Canada 78 A5 45 20N 79 14W
Huntsville, Ala., U.S.A. 77 H2 34 44N 86 35W
Huntsville, Tex., U.S.A. 81 K7 30 43N 95 33W
Hunyani →, Zimbabwe 55 F3 15 57S 30 39 E
Hunyuan, China 34 E7 39 42N 113 42 E
Hunza →, India 43 B6 35 54N 74 20 E
Huo Xian = Huozhou, China 34 F6 36 36N 111 42 E
Huong Hoa, Vietnam 38 D6 16 37N 106 45 E
Huong Khe, Vietnam 38 C5 18 13N 105 41 E
Huonville, Australia 62 G4 43 0S 147 5 E
Huozhou, China 34 F6 36 36N 111 42 E
Hupeh = Hubei □, China 33 C6 31 0N 112 0 E
Ḩūr, Iran 45 D8 30 50N 57 7 E
Hurd, C., Canada 78 A3 45 13N 81 44W
Hure Qi, China 35 C11 42 45N 121 45 E
Hurghada, Egypt 51 C12 27 15N 33 50 E
Hurley, N. Mex., U.S.A. 83 K9 32 42N 108 8W
Hurley, Wis., U.S.A. 80 B9 46 27N 90 11W
Huron, Calif., U.S.A. 84 J6 36 12N 120 6W
Huron, Ohio, U.S.A. 78 E2 41 24N 82 33W
Huron, S. Dak., U.S.A. 80 C5 44 22N 98 13W
Huron, L., U.S.A. 78 B2 44 30N 82 40W
Hurricane, U.S.A. 83 H7 37 11N 113 17W
Hurunui →, N.Z. 59 K4 42 54S 173 18 E
Húsavík, Iceland 8 C5 66 3N 17 21W
Huşi, Romania 17 E15 46 41N 28 7 E
Huskvarna, Sweden 9 H16 57 47N 14 15 E
Hustadvika, Norway 8 E12 63 0N 7 0 E
Hustontown, U.S.A. 78 F6 40 3N 78 2W
Hutchinson, Kans., U.S.A. 81 F6 38 5N 97 56W
Hutchinson, Minn., U.S.A. 80 C7 44 54N 94 22W
Hutte Sauvage, L. de la, Canada 71 A7 56 15N 64 45W
Hutton, Mt., Australia 63 D4 25 51S 148 20 E
Huy, Belgium 15 D5 50 31N 5 15 E
Huzhou, China 33 C7 30 51N 120 8 E
Hvammstangi, Iceland 8 D3 65 24N 20 57W
Hvar, Croatia 20 C7 43 11N 16 28 E
Hvítá →, Iceland 8 D3 64 30N 21 58W
Hwachŏn-chŏsuji, S. Korea 35 E14 38 5N 127 50 E
Hwang Ho = Huang He →, China 35 F10 37 55N 118 50 E
Hwange, Zimbabwe 55 F2 18 18S 26 30 E
Hwange Nat. Park, Zimbabwe 56 B4 19 0S 26 30 E
Hyannis, Mass., U.S.A. 76 E10 41 39N 70 17W
Hyannis, Nebr., U.S.A. 80 E4 42 0N 101 46W
Hyargas Nuur, Mongolia 32 B4 49 0N 93 0 E
Hydaburg, U.S.A. 72 B2 55 15N 132 50W
Hyde Park, U.S.A. 79 E11 41 47N 73 56W
Hyden, Australia 61 F2 32 24S 118 53 E
Hyder, U.S.A. 72 B2 55 55N 130 5W
Hyderabad, India 40 L11 17 22N 78 29 E
Hyderabad, Pakistan 42 G3 25 23N 68 24 E
Hyères, France 18 E7 43 8N 6 9 E
Hyères, Îs. d', France 18 E7 43 0N 6 20 E
Hyesan, N. Korea 35 D15 41 20N 128 10 E
Hyland →, Canada 72 B3 59 52N 128 12W
Hymia, India 43 C8 33 40N 78 2 E
Hyndman Peak, U.S.A. 82 E6 43 45N 114 8W
Hyōgo □, Japan 31 G7 35 15N 134 50 E
Hyrum, U.S.A. 82 F8 41 38N 111 51W
Hysham, U.S.A. 82 C10 46 18N 107 14W
Hythe, U.K. 11 F9 51 4N 1 5 E
Hyūga, Japan 31 H5 32 25N 131 35 E
Hyvinge = Hyvinkää, Finland 9 F21 60 38N 24 50 E
Hyvinkää, Finland 9 F21 60 38N 24 50 E

I

I-n-Gall, Niger 50 E7 16 51N 7 1 E
Iaco →, Brazil 92 E5 9 3S 68 34W
Iakora, Madag. 57 C8 23 6S 46 40 E
Ialomiţa →, Romania 17 F14 44 42N 27 51 E
Iaşi, Romania 17 E14 47 10N 27 40 E
Ib →, India 43 J10 21 34N 83 48 E
Iba, Phil. 37 A6 15 22N 120 0 E
Ibadan, Nigeria 50 G6 7 22N 3 58 E
Ibagué, Colombia 92 C3 4 20N 75 20W
Ibar →, Serbia, Yug. 21 C9 43 43N 20 45 E
Ibaraki □, Japan 31 F10 36 10N 140 10 E
Ibarra, Ecuador 92 C3 0 21N 78 7W
Ibembo, Dem. Rep. of the Congo 54 B1 2 35N 23 35 E
Ibera, L., Argentina 94 B4 28 30S 57 9W
Iberian Peninsula, Europe 6 H5 40 0N 5 0W
Iberville, Canada 79 A11 45 19N 73 17W
Iberville, Lac d', Canada 70 A5 55 55N 73 15W
Ibiá, Brazil 93 G9 19 30S 46 30W
Ibicuí →, Brazil 95 B4 29 25S 56 47W
Ibicuy, Argentina 94 C4 33 55S 59 10W
Ibioapaba, Sa. da, Brazil 93 D10 4 0S 41 30W
Ibiza = Eivissa, Spain 22 C7 38 54N 1 26 E
Ibo, Mozam. 55 E5 12 22S 40 40 E
Ibonma, Indonesia 37 E8 3 29S 133 31 E
Ibotirama, Brazil 93 F10 12 13S 43 12W
Ibrāhīm →, Lebanon 47 A4 34 4N 35 38 E
'Ibrī, Oman 45 F8 23 14N 56 30 E
Ibu, Indonesia 37 D7 1 35N 127 33 E
Ibusuki, Japan 31 J5 31 12N 130 40 E
Ica, Peru 92 F3 14 0S 75 48W
Iça →, Brazil 92 D5 2 55S 67 58W
Içana, Brazil 92 C5 0 21N 67 19W
Içana →, Brazil 92 C5 0 26N 67 19W
Içel = Mersin, Turkey 25 G5 36 51N 34 36 E
Iceland ■, Europe 8 D4 64 45N 19 0W
Ich'ang = Yichang, China 33 C6 30 40N 111 20 E
Ichchapuram, India 41 K14 19 10N 84 40 E
Ichhawar, India 42 H7 23 1N 77 1 E
Ichihara, Japan 31 G10 35 28N 140 5 E
Ichikawa, Japan 31 G9 35 44N 139 55 E
Ichilo →, Bolivia 92 G6 15 57S 64 50W
Ichinohe, Japan 30 D10 40 13N 141 17 E
Ichinomiya, Japan 31 G8 35 18N 136 48 E
Ichinoseki, Japan 30 E10 38 55N 141 8 E
Ichŏn, S. Korea 35 F14 37 17N 127 27 E
Icod, Canary Is. 22 F3 28 22N 16 43W
Ida Grove, U.S.A. 80 D7 42 21N 95 28W
Idabel, U.S.A. 81 J7 33 54N 94 50W
Idaho □, U.S.A. 82 D7 45 0N 115 0W
Idaho City, U.S.A. 82 E6 43 50N 115 50W
Idaho Falls, U.S.A. 82 E7 43 30N 112 2W
Idar-Oberstein, Germany 16 D4 49 43N 7 16 E
Idfû, Egypt 51 D12 24 55N 32 49 E
Ídhi Óros, Greece 23 D6 35 15N 24 45 E
Ídhra, Greece 21 F10 37 20N 23 28 E
Idi, Indonesia 36 C1 5 2N 97 37 E
Idiofa, Dem. Rep. of the Congo 52 E3 4 55S 19 42 E
Idlib, Syria 44 C3 35 55N 36 36 E
Idria, U.S.A. 84 J6 36 25N 120 41W
Idutywa, S. Africa 57 E4 32 8S 28 18 E
Ieper, Belgium 15 D2 50 51N 2 53 E
Ierápetra, Greece 23 E7 35 1N 25 44 E
Iesi, Italy 20 C5 43 31N 13 14 E
Ifakara, Tanzania 52 F7 8 8S 36 41 E
'Ifāl, W. al →, Si. Arabia 44 D2 28 7N 35 3 E
Ifanadiana, Madag. 57 C8 21 19S 47 39 E
Ife, Nigeria 50 G6 7 30N 4 31 E
Iférouâne, Niger 50 E7 19 5N 8 24 E
Iffley, Australia 62 B3 18 53S 141 12 E
Ifni, Morocco 50 C3 29 29N 10 12W
Iforas, Adrar des, Mali 50 E6 19 40N 1 40 E
Ifould, L., Australia 61 F5 30 52S 132 6 E
Iganga, Uganda 54 B3 0 37N 33 28 E
Igarapava, Brazil 93 H9 20 3S 47 47W
Igarka, Russia 26 C9 67 30N 86 33 E
Igatimi, Paraguay 95 A4 24 5S 55 40W
Iggesund, Sweden 9 F17 61 39N 17 10 E
Iglésias, Italy 20 E3 39 19N 8 32 E
Igloolik, Canada 69 B11 69 20N 81 49W
Igluligaarjuk, Canada 69 B10 63 21N 90 42W
Ignace, Canada 70 C1 49 30N 91 40W
İğneada Burnu, Turkey 21 D13 41 53N 28 2 E
Igoumenítsa, Greece 21 E9 39 32N 20 18 E
Iguaçu →, Brazil 95 B5 25 36S 54 36W
Iguaçu, Cat. del, Brazil 95 B5 25 41S 54 26W
Iguaçu Falls = Iguaçu, Cat. del, Brazil 95 B5 25 41S 54 26W
Iguala, Mexico 87 D5 18 20N 99 40W
Igualada, Spain 19 B6 41 37N 1 37 E
Iguassu = Iguaçu →, Brazil 95 B5 25 36S 54 36W
Iguatu, Brazil 93 E11 6 20S 39 18W
Iharana, Madag. 57 A9 13 25S 50 0 E
Ihbulag, Mongolia 34 C4 43 11N 107 10 E
Iheya-Shima, Japan 31 L3 27 4N 127 58 E
Ihosy, Madag. 57 C8 22 24S 46 8 E
Ihotry, L., Madag. 57 C7 21 56S 43 41 E
Ii, Finland 8 D21 65 19N 25 22 E
Ii-Shima, Japan 31 L3 26 43N 127 47 E
Iida, Japan 31 G8 35 35N 137 50 E
Iijoki →, Finland 8 D21 65 20N 25 20 E
Iisalmi, Finland 8 E22 63 32N 27 10 E
Iiyama, Japan 31 F9 36 51N 138 22 E
Iizuka, Japan 31 H5 33 38N 130 42 E
Ijebu-Ode, Nigeria 50 G6 6 47N 3 58 E
IJmuiden, Neths. 15 B4 52 28N 4 35 E
IJssel →, Neths. 15 B5 52 35N 5 50 E
IJsselmeer, Neths. 15 B5 52 45N 5 20 E
Ijuí, Brazil 95 B5 28 23S 53 55W
Ijuí →, Brazil 95 B4 27 58S 55 20W
Ikaluktutiak, Canada 68 B9 69 10N 105 0W
Ikare, Nigeria 50 G7 7 32N 5 40 E
Ikaría, Greece 21 F12 37 35N 26 10 E
Ikeda, Japan 31 G6 34 1N 133 48 E
Ikela, Dem. Rep. of the Congo 52 E4 1 6S 23 6 E
Iki, Japan 31 H4 33 45N 129 42 E
Ikimba L., Tanzania 54 C3 1 30S 31 20 E
Ikopa →, Madag. 57 B8 16 45S 46 40 E
Ikungu, Tanzania 54 C3 1 33S 33 42 E
Ilagan, Phil. 37 A6 17 7N 121 53 E
Īlām, Iran 44 C5 33 36N 46 36 E
Ilam, Nepal 43 F12 26 58N 87 58 E
Ilam □, Iran 44 C5 33 0N 47 0 E
Ilanskiy, Russia 27 D10 56 14N 96 3 E
Iława, Poland 17 B10 53 36N 19 34 E
Ile-à-la-Crosse, Canada 73 B7 55 27N 107 53W
Ile-à-la-Crosse, Lac, Canada 73 B7 55 40N 107 45W
Île-de-France □, France 18 B5 49 0N 2 20 E
Ilebo, Dem. Rep. of the Congo 52 E4 4 17S 20 55 E
Ilek, Russia 26 D6 51 32N 53 21 E
Ilek →, Russia 24 D9 51 30N 53 22 E
Ilesha, Nigeria 50 G6 7 37N 4 40 E
Ilford, Canada 73 B9 56 4N 95 35W
Ilfracombe, Australia 62 C3 23 30S 144 30 E
Ilfracombe, U.K. 11 F3 51 12N 4 8W
Ilhéus, Brazil 93 F11 14 49S 39 2W
Ili →, Kazakstan 26 E8 45 53N 77 10 E
Iliamna L., U.S.A. 68 C4 59 30N 155 0W
Iligan, Phil. 37 C6 8 12N 124 13 E
Ilion, U.S.A. 79 D9 43 1N 75 2W
Ilkeston, U.K. 10 E6 52 58N 1 19W
Ilkley, U.K. 10 D6 53 56N 1 48W
Illampu = Ancohuma, Nevada, Bolivia 92 G5 16 0S 68 50W
Illana B., Phil. 37 C6 7 35N 123 45 E
Illapel, Chile 94 C1 32 0S 71 10W
Iller →, Germany 16 D6 48 23N 9 58 E
Illetas, Spain 22 B9 39 32N 2 35 E
Illimani, Nevado, Bolivia 92 G5 16 30S 67 50W
Illinois □, U.S.A. 80 E10 40 15N 89 30W
Illinois →, U.S.A. 75 C8 38 58N 90 28W
Illium = Troy, Turkey 21 E12 39 57N 26 12 E
Illizi, Algeria 50 C7 26 31N 8 32 E
Ilmajoki, Finland 9 E20 62 44N 22 34 E
Ilmen, Ozero, Russia 24 C5 58 15N 31 10 E
Ilo, Peru 92 G4 17 40S 71 20W
Iloilo, Phil. 37 B6 10 45N 122 33 E
Ilorin, Nigeria 50 G6 8 30N 4 35 E
Ilwaco, U.S.A. 84 D2 46 19N 124 3W
Ilwaki, Indonesia 37 F7 7 55S 126 30 E
Imabari, Japan 31 G6 34 4N 133 0 E
Imaloto →, Madag. 57 C8 23 27S 45 13 E
Imandra, Ozero, Russia 24 A5 67 30N 33 0 E
Imari, Japan 31 H4 33 15N 129 52 E
Imatra, Finland 24 B4 61 12N 28 48 E
Imbil, Australia 63 D5 26 22S 152 32 E
imeni 26 Bakinskikh Komissarov = Neftçala, Azerbaijan 25 G8 39 19N 49 12 E
Imeri, Serra, Brazil 92 C5 0 50N 65 25W
Imerimandroso, Madag. 57 B8 17 26S 48 35 E
Imi, Ethiopia 46 F3 6 28N 42 10 E
Imlay, U.S.A. 82 F4 40 40N 118 9W
Imlay City, U.S.A. 78 D1 43 2N 83 5W
Immingham, U.K. 10 D7 53 37N 0 13W
Immokalee, U.S.A. 77 M5 26 25N 81 25W
Ímola, Italy 20 B4 44 20N 11 42 E
Imperatriz, Brazil 93 E9 5 30S 47 29W
Impéria, Italy 18 E8 43 53N 8 3 E
Imperial, Canada 73 C7 51 21N 105 28W
Imperial, Calif., U.S.A. 85 N11 32 51N 115 34W
Imperial, Nebr., U.S.A. 80 E4 40 31N 101 39W
Imperial Beach, U.S.A. 85 N9 32 35N 117 8W
Imperial Dam, U.S.A. 85 N12 32 55N 114 25W
Imperial Reservoir, U.S.A. 85 N12 32 53N 114 28W
Imperial Valley, U.S.A. 85 N11 33 0N 115 30W
Imperieuse Reef, Australia 60 C2 17 36S 118 50 E
Impfondo, Congo 52 D3 1 40N 18 0 E
Imphal, India 41 G18 24 48N 93 56 E
İmroz = Gökçeada, Turkey 21 D11 40 10N 25 50 E
Imuris, Mexico 86 A2 30 47N 110 52W
Imuruan B., Phil. 37 B5 10 40N 119 10 E
In Salah, Algeria 50 C6 27 10N 2 32 E
Ina, Japan 31 G8 35 50N 137 55 E
Inangahua Junction, N.Z. 59 J3 41 52S 171 59 E
Inanwatan, Indonesia 37 E8 2 10S 132 14 E
Iñapari, Peru 92 F5 11 0S 69 40W
Inari, Finland 8 B22 68 54N 27 5 E
Inarijärvi, Finland 8 B22 69 0N 28 0 E
Inawashiro-Ko, Japan 30 F10 37 29N 140 6 E
Inca, Spain 22 B9 39 43N 2 54 E
Inca de Oro, Chile 94 B2 26 45S 69 54W
Incaguasi, Chile 94 B1 29 12S 71 5W
İnce Burun, Turkey 25 F5 42 7N 34 56 E
İncesu, Turkey 44 B2 38 38N 35 11 E
Inch'ŏn, S. Korea 35 F14 37 27N 126 40 E
İncirliova, Turkey 21 F12 37 50N 27 41 E
Incline Village, U.S.A. 82 G4 39 10N 119 58W
Incomáti →, Mozam. 57 D5 25 46S 32 43 E
Indalsälven →, Sweden 9 E17 62 36N 17 30 E
Indaw, Burma 41 G20 24 15N 96 5 E
Independence, Calif., U.S.A. 84 J8 36 48N 118 12W
Independence, Iowa, U.S.A. 80 D9 42 28N 91 54W
Independence, Kans., U.S.A. 81 G7 37 14N 95 42W
Independence, Ky., U.S.A. 76 F3 38 57N 84 33W
Independence, Mo., U.S.A. 80 F7 39 6N 94 25W
Independence Fjord, Greenland 4 A6 82 10N 29 0W
Independence Mts., U.S.A. 82 F5 41 20N 116 0W
Index, U.S.A. 84 C5 47 50N 121 33W
India ■, Asia 40 K11 20 0N 78 0 E
Indian →, U.S.A. 77 M5 27 59N 80 34W
Indian Cabins, Canada 72 B5 59 52N 117 40W
Indian Harbour, Canada 71 B8 54 27N 57 13W
Indian Head, Canada 73 C8 50 30N 103 41W
Indian Lake, U.S.A. 79 C10 43 47N 74 16W
Indian Ocean 28 K11 5 0S 75 0 E
Indian Springs, U.S.A. 85 J11 36 35N 115 40W
Indiana, U.S.A. 78 F5 40 37N 79 9W
Indiana □, U.S.A. 76 F3 40 0N 86 0W
Indianapolis, U.S.A. 76 F2 39 46N 86 9W
Indianola, Iowa, U.S.A. 80 E8 41 22N 93 34W
Indianola, Miss., U.S.A. 81 J9 33 27N 90 39W
Indiga, Russia 24 A8 67 38N 49 9 E
Indigirka →, Russia 27 B15 70 48N 148 54 E
Indio, U.S.A. 85 M10 33 43N 116 13W
Indo-China, Asia 28 H14 15 0N 102 0 E
Indonesia ■, Asia 36 F5 5 0S 115 0 E

Indore

Indore, India 42 H6 22 42N 75 53 E
Indramayu, Indonesia 37 G13 6 20S 108 19 E
Indravati →, India 41 K12 19 20N 80 20 E
Indre →, France 18 C4 47 16N 0 11 E
Indulkana, Australia 63 D1 26 58S 133 5 E
Indus →, Pakistan 42 G2 24 20N 67 47 E
Indus, Mouth of the, Pakistan 42 H3 24 0N 68 0 E
İnebolu, Turkey 25 F5 41 55N 33 40 E
Infiernillo, Presa del, Mexico 86 D4 18 9N 102 0W
Ingenio, Canary Is. 22 G4 27 55N 15 26W
Ingenio Santa Ana, Argentina 94 B2 27 25S 65 40W
Ingersoll, Canada 78 C4 43 4N 80 55W
Ingham, Australia 62 B4 18 43S 146 10 E
Ingleborough, U.K. 10 C5 54 10N 2 22W
Inglewood, Queens., Australia 63 D5 28 25S 151 2 E
Inglewood, Vic., Australia 63 F3 36 29S 143 53 E
Inglewood, N.Z. 59 H5 39 9S 174 14 E
Inglewood, U.S.A. 85 M8 33 58N 118 21W
Ingólfshöfði, Iceland 8 E5 63 48N 16 39W
Ingolstadt, Germany 16 D6 48 46N 11 26 E
Ingomar, U.S.A. 82 C10 46 35N 107 23W
Ingonish, Canada 71 C7 46 42N 60 18W
Ingraj Bazar, India 43 G13 24 58N 88 10 E
Ingrid Christensen Coast, Antarctica 5 C6 69 30S 76 0 E
Ingulec = Inhulec, Ukraine 25 E5 47 42N 33 14 E
Ingushetia □, Russia 25 E8 43 20N 44 50 E
Ingwavuma, S. Africa 57 D5 27 9S 31 59 E
Inhaca, I., Mozam. 57 D5 26 1S 32 57 E
Inhafenga, Mozam. 57 C5 20 36S 33 53 E
Inhambane, Mozam. 57 C6 23 54S 35 30 E
Inhambane □, Mozam. 57 C5 22 30S 34 20 E
Inhaminga, Mozam. 55 F4 18 26S 35 0 E
Inharrime, Mozam. 57 C6 24 30S 35 0 E
Inharrime →, Mozam. 57 C6 24 30S 35 0 E
Inhulec, Ukraine 25 E5 47 42N 33 14 E
Ining = Yining, China 26 E9 43 58N 81 10 E
Inírida →, Colombia 92 C5 3 55N 67 52W
Inishbofin, Ireland 13 C1 53 37N 10 13W
Inisheer, Ireland 13 C2 53 3N 9 32W
Inishfree B., Ireland 13 A3 55 4N 8 23W
Inishkea North, Ireland 13 B1 54 9N 10 11W
Inishkea South, Ireland 13 B1 54 7N 10 12W
Inishmaan, Ireland 13 C2 53 5N 9 35W
Inishmore, Ireland 13 C2 53 8N 9 45W
Inishowen Pen., Ireland 13 A4 55 14N 7 15W
Inishshark, Ireland 13 C1 53 37N 10 16W
Inishturk, Ireland 13 C1 53 42N 10 7W
Inishvickillane, Ireland 13 D1 52 3N 10 37W
Injune, Australia 63 D4 25 53S 148 32 E
Inklin →, Canada 72 B2 58 50N 133 10W
Inle L., Burma 41 J20 20 30N 96 58 E
Inlet, U.S.A. 79 C10 43 45N 74 48W
Inn →, Austria 16 D7 48 35N 13 28 E
Innamincka, Australia 63 D3 27 44S 140 46 E
Inner Hebrides, U.K. 12 E2 57 0N 6 30W
Inner Mongolia = Nei Monggol Zizhiqu □, China 34 D7 42 0N 112 0 E
Inner Sound, U.K. 12 D3 57 30N 5 55W
Innerkip, Canada 78 C4 43 13N 80 42W
Innetalling I., Canada 70 A4 56 0N 79 0W
Innisfail, Australia 62 B4 17 33S 146 5 E
Innisfail, Canada 72 C6 52 0N 113 57W
In'no-shima, Japan 31 G6 34 19N 133 10 E
Innsbruck, Austria 16 E6 47 16N 11 23 E
Inny →, Ireland 13 C4 53 30N 7 50W
Inongo, Dem. Rep. of the Congo 52 E3 1 55S 18 30 E
Inoucdjouac = Inukjuak, Canada 69 C12 58 25N 78 15W
Inowrocław, Poland 17 B10 52 50N 18 12 E
Inpundong, N. Korea 35 D14 41 25N 126 34 E
Inscription, C., Australia 61 E1 25 29S 112 59 E
Insein, Burma 41 L20 16 50N 96 5 E
Inta, Russia 24 A11 66 5N 60 8 E
Intendente Alvear, Argentina 94 D3 35 12S 63 32W
Interlaken, Switz. 18 C7 46 41N 7 50 E
Interlaken, U.S.A. 79 D8 42 37N 76 44W
International Falls, U.S.A. 80 A8 48 36N 93 25W
Intiyaco, Argentina 94 B3 28 43S 60 5W
Inukjuak, Canada 69 C12 58 25N 78 15W
Inútil, B., Chile 96 G2 53 30S 70 15W
Inuvik, Canada 68 B6 68 16N 133 40W
Inveraray, U.K. 12 E3 56 14N 5 5W
Inverbervie, U.K. 12 E6 56 51N 2 17W
Invercargill, N.Z. 59 M2 46 24S 168 24 E
Inverclyde □, U.K. 12 F4 55 55N 4 49W
Inverell, Australia 63 D5 29 45S 151 8 E
Invergordon, U.K. 12 D4 57 41N 4 10W
Inverloch, Australia 63 F4 38 38S 145 45 E
Invermere, Canada 72 C5 50 30N 116 2W
Inverness, Canada 71 C7 46 15N 61 19W
Inverness, U.K. 12 D4 57 29N 4 13W
Inverness, U.S.A. 77 L4 28 50N 82 20W
Inverurie, U.K. 12 D6 57 17N 2 23W
Investigator Group, Australia 63 E1 34 45S 134 20 E
Investigator Str., Australia 63 F2 35 30S 137 0 E
Inya, Russia 26 D9 50 28N 86 37 E
Inyanga, Zimbabwe 55 F3 18 12S 32 40 E
Inyangani, Zimbabwe 55 F3 18 5S 32 50 E
Inyantue, Zimbabwe 55 F2 18 30S 26 40 E
Inyo Mts., U.S.A. 84 J9 36 40N 118 0W
Inyokern, U.S.A. 85 K9 35 39N 117 49W
Inza, Russia 24 D8 53 55N 46 25 E
Iō-Jima, Japan 31 J5 30 48N 130 18 E
Ioánnina, Greece 21 E9 39 42N 20 47 E
Iola, U.S.A. 81 G7 37 55N 95 24W
Iona, U.K. 12 E2 56 20N 6 25W
Ione, U.S.A. 84 G6 38 21N 120 56W
Ionia, U.S.A. 76 D3 42 59N 85 4W
Ionian Is. = Iónioi Nísoi, Greece 21 E9 38 40N 20 0 E
Ionian Sea, Medit. S. 21 E7 37 30N 17 30 E
Iónioi Nísoi, Greece 21 E9 38 40N 20 0 E
Íos, Greece 21 F11 36 41N 25 20 E
Iowa □, U.S.A. 80 D8 42 18N 93 30W
Iowa →, U.S.A. 80 E9 41 10N 91 1W
Iowa City, U.S.A. 80 E9 41 40N 91 32W
Iowa Falls, U.S.A. 80 D8 42 31N 93 16W
Iowa Park, U.S.A. 81 J5 33 57N 98 40W
Ipala, Tanzania 54 C3 4 30S 32 52 E
Ipameri, Brazil 93 G9 17 44S 48 9W
Ipatinga, Brazil 93 G10 19 32S 42 30W
Ipiales, Colombia 92 C3 0 50N 77 37W
Ipin = Yibin, China 32 D5 28 45N 104 32 E
Ipixuna, Brazil 92 E4 7 0S 71 40W
Ipoh, Malaysia 39 K3 4 35N 101 5 E
Ippy, C.A.R. 52 C4 6 5N 21 7 E
İpsala, Turkey 21 D12 40 55N 26 23 E
Ipswich, Australia 63 D5 27 35S 152 40 E
Ipswich, U.K. 11 E9 52 4N 1 10 E
Ipswich, Mass., U.S.A. 79 D14 42 41N 70 50W
Ipswich, S. Dak., U.S.A. 80 C5 45 27N 99 2W
Ipu, Brazil 93 D10 4 23S 40 44W
Iqaluit, Canada 69 B13 63 44N 68 31W
Iquique, Chile 92 H4 20 19S 70 5W
Iquitos, Peru 92 D4 3 45S 73 10W
Irabu-Jima, Japan 31 M2 24 50N 125 10 E
Iracoubo, Fr. Guiana 93 B8 5 30N 53 10W
Īrafshān, Iran 45 E9 26 42N 61 56 E
Iráklion, Greece 23 D7 35 20N 25 12 E
Iráklion □, Greece 23 D7 35 10N 25 10 E
Irala, Paraguay 95 B5 25 55S 54 35W
Iran ■, Asia 45 C7 33 0N 53 0 E
Iran, Gunung-Gunung, Malaysia 36 D4 2 20N 114 50 E
Iran, Plateau of, Asia 28 F9 32 0N 55 0 E
Iran Ra. = Iran, Gunung-Gunung, Malaysia 36 D4 2 20N 114 50 E
Īrānshahr, Iran 45 E9 27 15N 60 40 E
Irapuato, Mexico 86 C4 20 40N 101 30W
Iraq ■, Asia 44 C5 33 0N 44 0 E
Irati, Brazil 95 B5 25 25S 50 38W
Irbid, Jordan 47 C4 32 35N 35 48 E
Irbid □, Jordan 47 C5 32 15N 36 35 E
Ireland ■, Europe 13 C4 53 50N 7 52W
Irhyangdong, N. Korea 35 D15 41 15N 129 30 E
Iri, S. Korea 35 G14 35 59N 127 0 E
Irian Jaya □, Indonesia 37 E9 4 0S 137 0 E
Iringa, Tanzania 54 D4 7 48S 35 43 E
Iringa □, Tanzania 54 D4 7 48S 35 43 E
Iriomote-Jima, Japan 31 M1 24 19N 123 48 E
Iriona, Honduras 88 C2 15 57N 85 11W
Iriri →, Brazil 93 D8 3 52S 52 37W
Irish Republic ■, Europe 13 C3 53 0N 8 0W
Irish Sea, U.K. 10 D3 53 38N 4 48W
Irkutsk, Russia 27 D11 52 18N 104 20 E
Irma, Canada 73 C6 52 55N 111 14W
Irō-Zaki, Japan 31 G9 34 36N 138 51 E
Iron Baron, Australia 63 E2 32 58S 137 11 E
Iron Gate = Portile de Fier, Europe 17 F12 44 44N 22 30 E
Iron Knob, Australia 63 E2 32 46S 137 8 E
Iron Mountain, U.S.A. 76 C1 45 49N 88 4W
Iron River, U.S.A. 80 B10 46 6N 88 39W
Irondequoit, U.S.A. 78 C7 43 13N 77 35W
Ironstone Kopje, Botswana 56 D3 25 17S 24 5 E
Ironton, Mo., U.S.A. 81 G9 37 36N 90 38W
Ironton, Ohio, U.S.A. 76 F4 38 32N 82 41W
Ironwood, U.S.A. 80 B9 46 27N 90 9W
Iroquois, Canada 79 B9 44 51N 75 19W
Iroquois Falls, Canada 70 C3 48 46N 80 41W
Irpin, Ukraine 17 C16 50 30N 30 15 E
Irrara Cr. →, Australia 63 D4 29 35S 145 31 E
Irrawaddy □, Burma 41 L19 17 0N 95 0 E
Irrawaddy →, Burma 41 M19 15 50N 95 6 E
Irricana, Canada 72 C6 51 19N 113 37W
Irtysh →, Russia 26 C7 61 4N 68 52 E
Irumu, Dem. Rep. of the Congo 54 B2 1 32N 29 53 E
Irún, Spain 19 A5 43 20N 1 52W
Irunea = Pamplona, Spain 19 A5 42 48N 1 38W
Irvine, Canada 73 D6 49 57N 110 16W
Irvine, U.K. 12 F4 55 37N 4 41W
Irvine, Calif., U.S.A. 85 M9 33 41N 117 46W
Irvine, Ky., U.S.A. 76 G4 37 42N 83 58W
Irvinestown, U.K. 13 B4 54 28N 7 39W
Irving, U.S.A. 81 J6 32 49N 96 56W
Irvona, U.S.A. 78 F6 40 46N 78 33W
Irwin →, Australia 61 E1 29 15S 114 54 E
Irymple, Australia 63 E3 34 14S 142 8 E
Isa Khel, Pakistan 42 C4 32 41N 71 17 E
Isaac →, Australia 62 C4 22 55S 149 20 E
Isabel, U.S.A. 80 C4 45 24N 101 26W
Isabela, I., Mexico 86 C3 21 51N 105 55W
Isabelia, Cord., Nic. 88 D2 13 30N 85 25W
Isabella, Phil. 37 C6 6 40N 122 10 E
Isabella Ra., Australia 60 D3 21 0S 121 4 E
Ísafjarðardjúp, Iceland 8 C2 66 10N 23 0W
Ísafjörður, Iceland 8 C2 66 5N 23 9W
Isagarh, India 42 G7 24 48N 77 51 E
Isahaya, Japan 31 H5 32 52N 130 2 E
Isaka, Tanzania 54 C3 3 56S 32 59 E
Isan →, India 43 F9 26 51N 80 7 E
Isana = Içana →, Brazil 92 C5 0 26N 67 19W
Isar →, Germany 16 D7 48 48N 12 57 E
Íschia, Italy 20 D5 40 44N 13 57 E
Isdell →, Australia 60 C3 16 27S 124 51 E
Ise, Japan 31 G8 34 25N 136 45 E
Ise-Wan, Japan 31 G8 34 43N 136 43 E
Iseramagazi, Tanzania 54 C3 4 37S 32 10 E
Isère →, France 18 D6 44 59N 4 51 E
Isérnia, Italy 20 D6 41 36N 14 14 E
Isfahan = Eşfahān, Iran 45 C6 32 39N 51 43 E
Ishigaki-Shima, Japan 31 M2 24 20N 124 10 E
Ishikari-Gawa →, Japan 30 C10 43 15N 141 23 E
Ishikari-Sammyaku, Japan 30 C11 43 30N 143 0 E
Ishikari-Wan, Japan 30 C10 43 25N 141 1 E
Ishikawa □, Japan 31 F8 36 30N 136 30 E
Ishim, Russia 26 D7 56 10N 69 30 E
Ishim →, Russia 26 D8 57 45N 71 10 E
Ishinomaki, Japan 30 E10 38 32N 141 20 E
Ishioka, Japan 31 F10 36 11N 140 16 E
Ishkuman, Pakistan 43 A5 36 30N 73 50 E
Ishpeming, U.S.A. 76 B2 46 29N 87 40W
Isil Kul, Russia 26 D8 54 55N 71 16 E
Isiolo, Kenya 54 B4 0 24N 37 33 E
Isiro, Dem. Rep. of the Congo 54 B2 2 53N 27 40 E
Isisford, Australia 62 C3 24 15S 144 21 E
İskenderun, Turkey 25 G6 36 32N 36 10 E
İskenderun Körfezi, Turkey 25 G6 36 40N 35 50 E
Iskŭr →, Bulgaria 21 C11 43 45N 24 25 E
Iskut →, Canada 72 B2 56 45N 131 49W
Isla →, U.K. 12 E5 56 32N 3 20W
Isla Vista, U.S.A. 85 L7 34 25N 119 53W
Islam Headworks, Pakistan 42 E5 29 49N 72 33 E
Islamabad, Pakistan 42 C5 33 40N 73 10 E
Islamgarh, Pakistan 42 F4 27 51N 70 48 E
Islamkot, Pakistan 42 G4 24 42N 70 13 E
Islampur, India 43 G11 25 9N 85 12 E
Island L., Canada 73 C10 53 47N 94 25W
Island Lagoon, Australia 63 E2 31 30S 136 40 E
Island Pond, U.S.A. 79 B13 44 49N 71 53W
Islands, B. of, Canada 71 C8 49 11N 58 15W
Islay, U.K. 12 F2 55 46N 6 10W
Isle →, France 18 D3 44 55N 0 15W
Isle aux Morts, Canada 71 C8 47 35N 59 0W
Isle of Wight □, U.K. 11 G6 50 41N 1 17W
Isle Royale, U.S.A. 80 B10 48 0N 88 54W
Isle Royale National Park, U.S.A. 80 B10 48 0N 88 55W
Isleton, U.S.A. 84 G5 38 10N 121 37W
Ismail = Izmayil, Ukraine 17 F15 45 22N 28 46 E
Ismâ'ilîya, Egypt 51 B12 30 37N 32 18 E
Isogstalo, India 43 B8 34 15N 78 46 E
İsparta, Turkey 25 G5 37 47N 30 30 E
Íspica, Italy 20 F6 36 47N 14 55 E
Israel ■, Asia 47 D3 32 0N 34 50 E
Issoire, France 18 D5 45 32N 3 15 E
Issyk-Kul = Ysyk-Köl, Kyrgyzstan 28 E11 42 26N 76 12 E
Issyk-Kul, Ozero = Ysyk-Köl, Ozero, Kyrgyzstan 26 E8 42 25N 77 15 E
İstanbul, Turkey 21 D13 41 0N 29 0 E
İstanbul Boğazı, Turkey 21 D13 41 10N 29 10 E
Istiaía, Greece 21 E10 38 57N 23 9 E
Istokpoga, L., U.S.A. 77 M5 27 23N 81 17W
Istra, Croatia 16 F7 45 10N 14 0 E
Istres, France 18 E6 43 31N 4 59 E
Istria = Istra, Croatia 16 F7 45 10N 14 0 E
Itá, Paraguay 94 B4 25 29S 57 21W
Itaberaba, Brazil 93 F10 12 32S 40 18W
Itabira, Brazil 93 G10 19 37S 43 13W
Itabirito, Brazil 95 A7 20 15S 43 48W
Itabuna, Brazil 93 F11 14 48S 39 16W
Itacaunas →, Brazil 93 E9 5 21S 49 8W
Itacoatiara, Brazil 92 D7 3 8S 58 25W
Itaipú, Reprêsa de, Brazil 95 B5 25 30S 54 30W
Itaituba, Brazil 93 D7 4 10S 55 50W
Itajaí, Brazil 95 B6 27 50S 48 39W
Itajubá, Brazil 95 A6 22 24S 45 30W
Itaka, Tanzania 55 D3 8 50S 32 49 E
Italy ■, Europe 20 C5 42 0N 13 0 E
Itamaraju, Brazil 93 G11 17 5S 39 31W
Itampolo, Madag. 57 C7 24 41S 43 57 E
Itapecuru-Mirim, Brazil 93 D10 3 24S 44 20W
Itaperuna, Brazil 95 A7 21 10S 41 54W
Itapetininga, Brazil 95 A6 23 36S 48 7W
Itapeva, Brazil 95 A6 23 59S 48 59W
Itapicuru →, Bahia, Brazil 93 F11 11 47S 37 32W
Itapicuru →, Maranhão, Brazil 93 D10 2 52S 44 12W
Itapipoca, Brazil 93 D11 3 30S 39 35W
Itapuá □, Paraguay 95 B4 26 40S 55 40W
Itaquari, Brazil 95 A7 20 20S 40 25W
Itaquí, Brazil 94 B4 29 8S 56 30W
Itararé, Brazil 95 A6 24 6S 49 23W
Itarsi, India 42 H7 22 36N 77 51 E
Itatí, Argentina 94 B4 27 16S 58 15W
Itchen →, U.K. 11 G6 50 55N 1 22W
Itezhi Tezhi, L., Zambia 55 F2 15 30S 25 30 E
Ithaca = Itháki, Greece 21 E9 38 25N 20 40 E
Ithaca, U.S.A. 79 D8 42 27N 76 30W
Itháki, Greece 21 E9 38 25N 20 40 E
Itiquira →, Brazil 93 G7 17 18S 56 44W
Ito, Japan 31 G9 34 58N 139 5 E
Ito Aba I., S. China Sea 36 B4 10 23N 114 21 E
Itoigawa, Japan 31 F8 37 2N 137 51 E
Itonamas →, Bolivia 92 F6 12 28S 64 24W
Ittoqqortoormiit = Scoresbysund, Greenland 4 B6 70 20N 23 0W
Itu, Brazil 95 A6 23 17S 47 15W
Ituiutaba, Brazil 93 G9 19 0S 49 25W
Itumbiara, Brazil 93 G9 18 20S 49 10W
Ituna, Canada 73 C8 51 10N 103 24W
Itunge Port, Tanzania 55 D3 9 40S 33 55 E
Iturbe, Argentina 94 A2 23 0S 65 25W
Ituri →, Dem. Rep. of the Congo 54 B2 1 40N 27 1 E
Iturup, Ostrov, Russia 27 E15 45 0N 148 0 E
Ituxi →, Brazil 92 E6 7 18S 64 51W
Ituyuro →, Argentina 94 A3 22 40S 63 50W
Itzehoe, Germany 16 B5 53 55N 9 31 E
Ivaí →, Brazil 95 A5 23 18S 53 42W
Ivalo, Finland 8 B22 68 38N 27 35 E
Ivalojoki →, Finland 8 B22 68 40N 27 40 E
Ivanava, Belarus 17 B13 52 7N 25 29 E
Ivanhoe, Australia 63 E3 32 56S 144 20 E
Ivanhoe, Calif., U.S.A. 84 J7 36 23N 119 13W
Ivanhoe, Minn., U.S.A. 80 C6 44 28N 96 15W
Ivano-Frankivsk, Ukraine 17 D13 48 40N 24 40 E
Ivano-Frankovsk = Ivano-Frankivsk, Ukraine 17 D13 48 40N 24 40 E
Ivanovo = Ivanava, Belarus 17 B13 52 7N 25 29 E
Ivanovo, Russia 24 C7 57 5N 41 0 E
Ivato, Madag. 57 C8 20 37S 47 10 E
Ivatsevichy, Belarus 17 B13 52 43N 25 21 E
Ivdel, Russia 24 B11 60 42N 60 24 E
Ivindo →, Gabon 52 D2 0 9S 12 9 E
Ivinheima →, Brazil 95 A5 23 14S 53 42W
Ivinhema, Brazil 95 A5 22 10S 53 37W
Ivohibe, Madag. 57 C8 22 31S 46 57 E
Ivory Coast, Africa 50 H4 5 0N 5 0W
Ivory Coast ■, Africa 50 G4 7 30N 5 0W
Ivrea, Italy 18 D7 45 28N 7 52 E
Ivujivik, Canada 69 B12 62 24N 77 55W
Ivybridge, U.K. 11 G4 50 23N 3 56W
Iwaizumi, Japan 30 E10 39 50N 141 45 E
Iwaki, Japan 31 F10 37 3N 140 55 E
Iwakuni, Japan 31 G6 34 15N 132 8 E
Iwamizawa, Japan 30 C10 43 12N 141 46 E
Iwanai, Japan 30 C10 42 58N 140 30 E
Iwata, Japan 31 G8 34 42N 137 51 E
Iwate □, Japan 30 E10 39 30N 141 30 E
Iwate-San, Japan 30 E10 39 51N 141 0 E
Iwo, Nigeria 50 G6 7 39N 4 9 E
Ixiamas, Bolivia 92 F5 13 50S 68 5W
Ixopo, S. Africa 57 E5 30 11S 30 5 E
Ixtepec, Mexico 87 D5 16 32N 95 10W
Ixtlán del Río, Mexico 86 C4 21 5N 104 21W
Iyo, Japan 31 H6 33 45N 132 45 E
Izabal, L. de, Guatemala 88 C2 15 30N 89 10W
Izamal, Mexico 87 C7 20 56N 89 1W
Izena-Shima, Japan 31 L3 26 56N 127 56 E
Izhevsk, Russia 24 C9 56 51N 53 14 E
Izhma →, Russia 24 A9 65 19N 52 54 E
Izmayil, Ukraine 17 F15 45 22N 28 46 E
İzmir, Turkey 21 E12 38 25N 27 8 E
İzmit = Kocaeli, Turkey 25 F4 40 45N 29 50 E
İznik Gölü, Turkey 21 D13 40 27N 29 30 E
Izra, Syria 47 C5 32 51N 36 15 E
Izu-Shotō, Japan 31 G10 34 30N 140 0 E
Izúcar de Matamoros, Mexico 87 D5 18 36N 98 28W
Izumi-sano, Japan 31 G7 34 23N 135 18 E
Izumo, Japan 31 G6 35 20N 132 46 E
Izyaslav, Ukraine 17 C14 50 5N 26 50 E

J

Jabalpur, India 43 H8 23 9N 79 58 E
Jabbūl, Syria 44 B3 36 4N 37 30 E
Jabiru, Australia 60 B5 12 40S 132 53 E
Jablah, Syria 44 C3 35 20N 36 0 E
Jablonec nad Nisou, Czech Rep. 16 C8 50 43N 15 10 E
Jaboatão, Brazil 93 E11 8 7S 35 1W
Jaboticabal, Brazil 95 A6 21 15S 48 17W
Jaca, Spain 19 A5 42 35N 0 33W
Jacareí, Brazil 95 A6 23 20S 46 0W
Jacarèzinho, Brazil 95 A6 23 5S 49 58W
Jackman, U.S.A. 77 C10 45 35N 70 17W
Jacksboro, U.S.A. 81 J5 33 14N 98 15W
Jackson, Ala., U.S.A. 77 K2 31 31N 87 53W
Jackson, Calif., U.S.A. 84 G6 38 21N 120 46W
Jackson, Ky., U.S.A. 76 G4 37 33N 83 23W
Jackson, Mich., U.S.A. 76 D3 42 15N 84 24W
Jackson, Minn., U.S.A. 80 D7 43 37N 95 1W
Jackson, Miss., U.S.A. 81 J9 32 18N 90 12W
Jackson, Mo., U.S.A. 81 G10 37 23N 89 40W
Jackson, N.H., U.S.A. 79 B13 44 10N 71 11W
Jackson, Ohio, U.S.A. 76 F4 39 3N 82 39W
Jackson, Tenn., U.S.A. 77 H1 35 37N 88 49W
Jackson, Wyo., U.S.A. 82 E8 43 29N 110 46W
Jackson B., N.Z. 59 K2 43 58S 168 42 E
Jackson L., U.S.A. 82 E8 43 52N 110 36W
Jacksons, N.Z. 59 K3 42 46S 171 32 E
Jackson's Arm, Canada 71 C8 49 52N 56 47W
Jacksonville, Ala., U.S.A. 77 J3 33 49N 85 46W
Jacksonville, Ark., U.S.A. 81 H8 34 52N 92 7W
Jacksonville, Calif., U.S.A. 84 H6 37 52N 120 24W
Jacksonville, Fla., U.S.A. 77 K5 30 20N 81 39W
Jacksonville, Ill., U.S.A. 80 F9 39 44N 90 14W
Jacksonville, N.C., U.S.A. 77 H7 34 45N 77 26W
Jacksonville, Tex., U.S.A. 81 K7 31 58N 95 17W
Jacksonville Beach, U.S.A. 77 K5 30 17N 81 24W
Jacmel, Haiti 89 C5 18 14N 72 32W
Jacob Lake, U.S.A. 83 H7 36 43N 112 13W
Jacobabad, Pakistan 42 E3 28 20N 68 29 E
Jacobina, Brazil 93 F10 11 11S 40 30W
Jacques Cartier, Dét. de, Canada 71 C7 50 0N 63 30W
Jacques-Cartier, Mt., Canada 71 C6 48 57N 66 0W
Jacques Cartier, Parc Prov., Canada 71 C5 47 15N 71 33W
Jacuí →, Brazil 95 C5 30 2S 51 15W
Jacumba, U.S.A. 85 N10 32 37N 116 11W
Jacundá →, Brazil 93 D8 1 57S 50 26W
Jadotville = Likasi, Dem. Rep. of the Congo 55 E2 10 55S 26 48 E
Jaén, Peru 92 E3 5 25S 78 40W
Jaén, Spain 19 D4 37 44N 3 43W
Jafarabad, India 42 J4 20 52N 71 22 E
Jaffa = Tel Aviv-Yafo, Israel 47 C3 32 4N 34 48 E
Jaffa, C., Australia 63 F2 36 58S 139 40 E
Jaffna, Sri Lanka 40 Q12 9 45N 80 2 E
Jaffrey, U.S.A. 79 D12 42 49N 72 2W
Jagadhri, India 42 D7 30 10N 77 20 E
Jagadishpur, India 43 G11 25 30N 84 21 E
Jagdalpur, India 41 K13 19 3N 82 0 E
Jagersfontein, S. Africa 56 D4 29 44S 25 27 E
Jaghīn →, Iran 45 E8 27 17N 57 13 E
Jagodina, Serbia, Yug. 21 C9 44 5N 21 15 E
Jagraon, India 40 D9 30 50N 75 25 E
Jagtial, India 40 K11 18 50N 79 0 E
Jaguariaíva, Brazil 95 A6 24 10S 49 50W
Jaguaribe →, Brazil 93 D11 4 25S 37 45W
Jagüey Grande, Cuba 88 B3 22 35N 81 7W
Jahanabad, India 43 G11 25 13N 84 59 E
Jahazpur, India 42 G6 25 37N 75 17 E
Jahrom, Iran 45 D7 28 30N 53 31 E
Jaijon, India 42 D7 31 21N 76 9 E
Jailolo, Indonesia 37 D7 1 5N 127 30 E
Jailolo, Selat, Indonesia 37 D7 0 5N 129 5 E
Jaipur, India 42 F6 27 0N 75 50 E
Jais, India 43 F9 26 15N 81 32 E
Jaisalmer, India 42 F4 26 55N 70 54 E
Jaisinghnagar, India 43 H8 23 38N 78 34 E
Jaitaran, India 42 F5 26 12N 73 56 E
Jaithari, India 43 H8 23 14N 78 37 E
Jājarm, Iran 45 B8 36 58N 56 27 E
Jakam →, India 42 H6 23 54N 74 13 E
Jakarta, Indonesia 37 G12 6 9S 106 49 E
Jakhal, India 42 E6 29 48N 75 50 E
Jakhau, India 42 H3 23 13N 68 43 E
Jakobstad = Pietarsaari, Finland 8 E20 63 40N 22 43 E
Jal, U.S.A. 81 J3 32 7N 103 12W
Jalalabad, Afghan. 42 B4 34 30N 70 29 E
Jalalabad, India 43 F8 27 41N 79 42 E
Jalalpur Jattan, Pakistan 42 C6 32 38N 74 11 E
Jalama, U.S.A. 85 L6 34 29N 120 29W
Jalapa, Guatemala 88 D2 14 39N 89 59W
Jalapa Enríquez, Mexico 87 D5 19 32N 96 55W
Jalasjärvi, Finland 9 E20 62 29N 22 47 E
Jalaun, India 43 F8 26 8N 79 25 E
Jaldhaka →, Bangla. 43 F13 26 16N 89 16 E
Jalesar, India 42 F8 27 29N 78 19 E
Jaleswar, Nepal 43 F11 26 38N 85 48 E
Jalgaon, Maharashtra, India 40 J10 21 2N 76 31 E
Jalgaon, Maharashtra, India 40 J9 21 0N 75 42 E
Jalībah, Iraq 44 D5 30 35N 46 32 E
Jalisco □, Mexico 86 D4 20 0N 104 0W
Jalkot, Pakistan 43 B5 35 14N 73 24 E
Jalna, India 40 K9 19 48N 75 38 E
Jalón →, Spain 19 B5 41 47N 1 4W
Jalor, India 42 G5 25 21N 72 37 E
Jalpa, Mexico 86 C4 21 38N 102 58W
Jalpaiguri, India 41 F16 26 32N 88 46 E
Jaluit I., Marshall Is. 64 G8 6 0N 169 30 E

Juruena

Juruena →, *Brazil* **92 E7** 7 20S 58 3W
Juruti, *Brazil* **93 D7** 2 9S 56 4W
Justo Daract, *Argentina* **94 C2** 33 52S 65 12W
Jutaí →, *Brazil* **92 D5** 2 43S 66 57W
Juticalpa, *Honduras* **88 D2** 14 40N 86 12W
Jutland = Jylland, *Denmark* **9 H13** 56 25N 9 30 E
Juventud, I. de la, *Cuba* **88 B3** 21 40N 82 40W
Juwain, *Afghan.* **40 D2** 31 45N 61 30 E
Jūy Zar, *Iran* **44 C5** 33 50N 46 18 E
Juye, *China* **34 G9** 35 22N 116 5 E
Jwaneng, *Botswana* **53 J4** 24 45S 24 50 E
Jylland, *Denmark* **9 H13** 56 25N 9 30 E
Jyväskylä, *Finland* **9 E21** 62 14N 25 50 E

K

K2, *Pakistan* **43 B7** 35 58N 76 32 E
Kaap Plateau, *S. Africa* **56 D3** 28 30S 24 0 E
Kaapkruis, *Namibia* **56 C1** 21 55S 13 57 E
Kaapstad = Cape Town, *S. Africa* **56 E2** 33 55S 18 22 E
Kabaena, *Indonesia* **37 F6** 5 15S 122 0 E
Kabala, *S. Leone* **50 G3** 9 38N 11 37W
Kabale, *Uganda* **54 C3** 1 15S 30 0 E
Kabalo, *Dem. Rep. of the Congo* **54 D2** 6 0S 27 0 E
Kabambare, *Dem. Rep. of the Congo* **54 C2** 4 41S 27 39 E
Kabango, *Dem. Rep. of the Congo* **55 D2** 8 35S 28 30 E
Kabanjahe, *Indonesia* **36 D1** 3 6N 98 30 E
Kabardino-Balkar Republic = Kabardino-Balkaria □, *Russia* **25 F7** 43 30N 43 30 E
Kabardino-Balkaria □, *Russia* **25 F7** 43 30N 43 30 E
Kabarega Falls = Murchison Falls, *Uganda* **54 B3** 2 15N 31 30 E
Kabasalan, *Phil.* **37 C6** 7 47N 122 44 E
Kabetogama, *U.S.A.* **80 A8** 48 28N 92 59W
Kabin Buri, *Thailand* **38 F3** 13 57N 101 43 E
Kabinakagami L., *Canada* **70 C3** 48 54N 84 25W
Kabinda, *Dem. Rep. of the Congo* **52 F4** 6 19S 24 20 E
Kabompo, *Zambia* **55 E1** 13 36S 24 14 E
Kabompo →, *Zambia* **53 G4** 14 10S 23 11 E
Kabondo, *Dem. Rep. of the Congo* **55 D2** 8 58S 25 40 E
Kabongo, *Dem. Rep. of the Congo* **54 D2** 7 22S 25 33 E
Kabūd Gonbad, *Iran* **45 B8** 37 5N 59 45 E
Kābul, *Afghan.* **42 B3** 34 28N 69 11 E
Kābul □, *Afghan.* **40 B6** 34 30N 69 0 E
Kabul →, *Pakistan* **42 C5** 33 55N 72 14 E
Kabunga, *Dem. Rep. of the Congo* **54 C2** 1 38S 28 3 E
Kaburuang, *Indonesia* **37 D7** 3 50N 126 30 E
Kabwe, *Zambia* **55 E2** 14 30S 28 29 E
Kachchh, Gulf of, *India* **42 H3** 22 50N 69 15 E
Kachchh, Rann of, *India* **42 H4** 24 0N 70 0 E
Kachchhidhana, *India* **43 J8** 21 44N 78 46 E
Kachebera, *Zambia* **55 E3** 13 50S 32 50 E
Kachin □, *Burma* **41 G20** 26 0N 97 30 E
Kachira, L., *Uganda* **54 C3** 0 40S 31 7 E
Kachiry, *Kazakstan* **26 D8** 53 10N 75 50 E
Kachnara, *India* **42 H6** 23 50N 75 6 E
Kachot, *Cambodia* **39 G4** 11 30N 103 3 E
Kaçkar, *Turkey* **25 F7** 40 45N 41 10 E
Kadan Kyun, *Burma* **38 F2** 12 30N 98 20 E
Kadanai →, *Afghan.* **42 D1** 31 22N 65 45 E
Kadi, *India* **42 H5** 23 18N 72 23 E
Kadina, *Australia* **63 E2** 33 55S 137 43 E
Kadipur, *India* **43 F10** 26 10N 82 23 E
Kadirli, *Turkey* **44 B3** 37 23N 36 5 E
Kadiyevka = Stakhanov, *Ukraine* **25 E6** 48 35N 38 40 E
Kadoka, *U.S.A.* **80 D4** 43 50N 101 31W
Kadoma, *Zimbabwe* **55 F2** 18 20S 29 52 E
Kâdugli, *Sudan* **51 F11** 11 0N 29 45 E
Kaduna, *Nigeria* **50 F7** 10 30N 7 21 E
Kaédi, *Mauritania* **50 E3** 16 9N 13 28W
Kaeng Khoï, *Thailand* **38 E3** 14 35N 101 0 E
Kaesŏng, *N. Korea* **35 F14** 37 58N 126 35 E
Kāf, *Si. Arabia* **44 D3** 31 25N 37 29 E
Kafan = Kapan, *Armenia* **25 G8** 39 18N 46 27 E
Kafanchan, *Nigeria* **50 G7** 9 40N 8 20 E
Kafinda, *Zambia* **55 E3** 12 32S 30 20 E
Kafirévs, Ákra, *Greece* **21 E11** 38 9N 24 38 E
Kafue, *Zambia* **55 F2** 15 46S 28 9 E
Kafue →, *Zambia* **53 H5** 15 30S 29 0 E
Kafue Flats, *Zambia* **55 F2** 15 40S 27 25 E
Kafue Nat. Park, *Zambia* **55 F2** 15 0S 25 30 E
Kafulwe, *Zambia* **55 D2** 9 0S 29 1 E
Kaga, *Afghan.* **42 B4** 34 14N 70 10 E
Kaga Bandoro, *C.A.R.* **52 C3** 7 0N 19 10 E
Kagan, *Uzbekistan* **26 F7** 39 43N 64 33 E
Kagawa □, *Japan* **31 G7** 34 15N 134 0 E
Kagera □, *Tanzania* **54 C3** 2 0S 31 30 E
Kagera →, *Uganda* **54 C3** 0 57S 31 47 E
Kağızman, *Turkey* **44 A4** 40 5N 43 10 E
Kagoshima, *Japan* **31 J5** 31 35N 130 33 E
Kagoshima □, *Japan* **31 J5** 31 30N 130 30 E
Kagul = Cahul, *Moldova* **17 F15** 45 50N 28 15 E
Kahak, *Iran* **45 B6** 36 6N 49 46 E
Kahama, *Tanzania* **54 C3** 4 8S 32 30 E
Kahan, *Pakistan* **42 E3** 29 18N 68 54 E
Kahang, *Malaysia* **39 L4** 2 12N 103 32 E
Kahayan →, *Indonesia* **36 E4** 3 40S 114 0 E
Kahe, *Tanzania* **54 C4** 3 30S 37 25 E
Kahnūj, *Iran* **45 E8** 27 55N 57 40 E
Kahoka, *U.S.A.* **80 E9** 40 25N 91 44W
Kahoolawe, *U.S.A.* **74 H16** 20 33N 156 37W
Kahramanmaraş, *Turkey* **25 G6** 37 37N 36 53 E
Kahuta, *Pakistan* **42 C5** 33 35N 73 24 E
Kai, Kepulauan, *Indonesia* **37 F8** 5 55S 132 45 E
Kai Besar, *Indonesia* **37 F8** 5 35S 133 0 E
Kai Is. = Kai, Kepulauan, *Indonesia* **37 F8** 5 55S 132 45 E
Kai Kecil, *Indonesia* **37 F8** 5 45S 132 40 E
Kaiapoi, *N.Z.* **59 K4** 43 24S 172 40 E
Kaieteur Falls, *Guyana* **92 B7** 5 1N 59 10W
Kaifeng, *China* **34 G8** 34 48N 114 21 E
Kaikohe, *N.Z.* **59 F4** 35 25S 173 49 E
Kaikoura, *N.Z.* **59 K4** 42 25S 173 43 E
Kaikoura Ra., *N.Z.* **59 J4** 41 59S 173 41 E
Kailu, *China* **35 C11** 43 38N 121 18 E
Kailua Kona, *U.S.A.* **74 J17** 19 39N 155 59W
Kaimana, *Indonesia* **37 E8** 3 39S 133 45 E
Kaimanawa Mts., *N.Z.* **59 H5** 39 15S 175 56 E
Kaimganj, *India* **43 F8** 27 33N 79 24 E
Kaimur Hills, *India* **43 G10** 24 30N 82 0 E
Kaingaroa Forest, *N.Z.* **59 H6** 38 24S 176 30 E
Kainji Res., *Nigeria* **50 F6** 10 1N 4 40 E
Kainuu, *Finland* **8 D23** 64 30N 29 7 E
Kaipara Harbour, *N.Z.* **59 G5** 36 25S 174 14 E
Kaipokok B., *Canada* **71 B8** 54 54N 59 47W
Kaira, *India* **42 H5** 22 45N 72 50 E
Kairana, *India* **42 E7** 29 24N 77 15 E
Kaironi, *Indonesia* **37 E8** 0 47S 133 40 E
Kairouan, *Tunisia* **51 A8** 35 45N 10 5 E
Kaiserslautern, *Germany* **16 D4** 49 26N 7 45 E
Kaitaia, *N.Z.* **59 F4** 35 8S 173 17 E
Kaitangata, *N.Z.* **59 M2** 46 17S 169 51 E
Kaithal, *India* **42 E7** 29 48N 76 26 E
Kaitu →, *Pakistan* **42 C4** 33 10N 70 30 E
Kaiwi Channel, *U.S.A.* **74 H16** 21 15N 157 30W
Kaiyuan, *China* **35 C13** 42 28N 124 1 E
Kajaani, *Finland* **8 D22** 64 17N 27 46 E
Kajabbi, *Australia* **62 C3** 20 0S 140 1 E
Kajana = Kajaani, *Finland* **8 D22** 64 17N 27 46 E
Kajang, *Malaysia* **39 L3** 2 59N 101 48 E
Kajiado, *Kenya* **54 C4** 1 53S 36 48 E
Kajo Kaji, *Sudan* **51 H12** 3 58N 31 40 E
Kakabeka Falls, *Canada* **70 C2** 48 24N 89 37W
Kakadu Nat. Park, *Australia* **60 B5** 12 30S 132 5 E
Kakamas, *S. Africa* **56 D3** 28 45S 20 33 E
Kakamega, *Kenya* **54 B3** 0 20N 34 46 E
Kakanui Mts., *N.Z.* **59 L3** 45 10S 170 30 E
Kakdwip, *India* **43 J13** 21 53N 88 11 E
Kake, *Japan* **31 G6** 34 36N 132 19 E
Kake, *U.S.A.* **72 B2** 56 59N 133 57W
Kakegawa, *Japan* **31 G9** 34 45N 138 1 E
Kakeroma-Jima, *Japan* **31 K4** 28 8N 129 14 E
Kakhovka, *Ukraine* **25 E5** 46 45N 33 30 E
Kakhovske Vdskh., *Ukraine* **25 E5** 47 5N 34 0 E
Kakinada, *India* **41 L13** 16 57N 82 11 E
Kakisa →, *Canada* **72 A5** 61 3N 118 10W
Kakisa L., *Canada* **72 A5** 60 56N 117 43W
Kakogawa, *Japan* **31 G7** 34 46N 134 51 E
Kakwa →, *Canada* **72 C5** 54 37N 118 28W
Kāl Gūsheh, *Iran* **45 D8** 30 59N 58 12 E
Kal Safīd, *Iran* **44 C5** 34 52N 47 23 E
Kalabagh, *Pakistan* **42 C4** 33 0N 71 28 E
Kalabahi, *Indonesia* **37 F6** 8 13S 124 31 E
Kalach, *Russia* **25 D7** 50 22N 41 0 E
Kaladan →, *Burma* **41 J18** 20 20N 93 5 E
Kaladar, *Canada* **78 B7** 44 37N 77 5W
Kalahari, *Africa* **56 C3** 24 0S 21 30 E
Kalahari Gemsbok Nat. Park, *S. Africa* **56 D3** 25 30S 20 30 E
Kalajoki, *Finland* **8 D20** 64 12N 24 10 E
Kālak, *Iran* **45 E8** 25 29N 59 22 E
Kalakamati, *Botswana* **57 C4** 20 40S 27 25 E
Kalakan, *Russia* **27 D12** 55 15N 116 45 E
K'alak'unlun Shank'ou, *Pakistan* **43 B7** 35 33N 77 46 E
Kalam, *Pakistan* **43 B5** 35 34N 72 30 E
Kalama, *Dem. Rep. of the Congo* **54 C2** 2 52S 28 35 E
Kalama, *U.S.A.* **84 E4** 46 1N 122 51W
Kalámai, *Greece* **21 F10** 37 3N 22 10 E
Kalamata = Kalámai, *Greece* **21 F10** 37 3N 22 10 E
Kalamazoo, *U.S.A.* **76 D3** 42 17N 85 35W
Kalamazoo →, *U.S.A.* **76 D2** 42 40N 86 10W
Kalambo Falls, *Tanzania* **55 D3** 8 37S 31 35 E
Kalan, *Turkey* **44 B3** 39 7N 39 32 E
Kalannie, *Australia* **61 F2** 30 22S 117 5 E
Kalāntarī, *Iran* **45 C7** 32 10N 54 8 E
Kalao, *Indonesia* **37 F6** 7 21S 121 0 E
Kalaotoa, *Indonesia* **37 F6** 7 20S 121 50 E
Kalasin, *Thailand* **38 D4** 16 26N 103 30 E
Kalat, *Pakistan* **40 E5** 29 8N 66 31 E
Kalāteh, *Iran* **45 B7** 36 33N 55 41 E
Kalāteh-ye Ganj, *Iran* **45 E8** 27 31N 57 55 E
Kalbarri, *Australia* **61 E1** 27 40S 114 10 E
Kalce, *Slovenia* **16 F8** 45 54N 14 13 E
Kale, *Turkey* **21 F13** 37 27N 28 49 E
Kalegauk Kyun, *Burma* **41 M20** 15 33N 97 35 E
Kalehe, *Dem. Rep. of the Congo* **54 C2** 2 6S 28 50 E
Kalema, *Tanzania* **54 C3** 1 12S 31 55 E
Kalemie, *Dem. Rep. of the Congo* **54 D2** 5 55S 29 9 E
Kalewa, *Burma* **41 H19** 23 10N 94 15 E
Kaleybar, *Iran* **44 B5** 38 47N 47 2 E
Kalgan = Zhangjiakou, *China* **34 D8** 40 48N 114 55 E
Kalgoorlie-Boulder, *Australia* **61 F3** 30 40S 121 22 E
Kali →, *India* **43 F8** 27 6N 79 55 E
Kali Sindh →, *India* **42 G6** 25 32N 76 17 E
Kaliakra, Nos, *Bulgaria* **21 C13** 43 21N 28 30 E
Kalianda, *Indonesia* **36 F3** 5 50S 105 45 E
Kalibo, *Phil.* **37 B6** 11 43N 122 22 E
Kalima, *Dem. Rep. of the Congo* **54 C2** 2 33S 26 32 E
Kalimantan □, *Indonesia* **36 E4** 0 0 114 0 E
Kalimantan Barat □, *Indonesia* **36 E4** 0 0 110 30 E
Kalimantan Selatan □, *Indonesia* **36 E5** 2 30S 115 30 E
Kalimantan Tengah □, *Indonesia* **36 E4** 2 0S 113 30 E
Kalimantan Timur □, *Indonesia* **36 D5** 1 30N 116 30 E
Kálimnos, *Greece* **21 F12** 37 0N 27 0 E
Kalimpong, *India* **43 F13** 27 4N 88 35 E
Kalinin = Tver, *Russia* **24 C6** 56 55N 35 55 E
Kaliningrad, *Russia* **9 J19** 54 42N 20 32 E
Kalinkavichy, *Belarus* **17 B15** 52 12N 29 20 E
Kalinkovichi = Kalinkavichy, *Belarus* **17 B15** 52 12N 29 20 E
Kaliro, *Uganda* **54 B3** 0 56N 33 30 E
Kalispell, *U.S.A.* **82 B6** 48 12N 114 19W
Kalisz, *Poland* **17 C10** 51 45N 18 8 E
Kaliua, *Tanzania* **54 D3** 5 5S 31 48 E
Kalix, *Sweden* **8 D20** 65 53N 23 12 E
Kalix →, *Sweden* **8 D20** 65 50N 23 11 E
Kalka, *India* **42 D7** 30 46N 76 57 E
Kalkarindji, *Australia* **60 C5** 17 30S 130 47 E
Kalkaska, *U.S.A.* **76 C3** 44 44N 85 11W
Kalkfeld, *Namibia* **56 C2** 20 57S 16 14 E
Kalkfontein, *Botswana* **56 C3** 22 4S 20 57 E
Kalkrand, *Namibia* **56 C2** 24 1S 17 35 E
Kallavesi, *Finland* **8 E22** 62 58N 27 30 E
Kallsjön, *Sweden* **8 E15** 63 38N 13 0 E
Kalmar, *Sweden* **9 H17** 56 40N 16 20 E
Kalmyk Republic = Kalmykia □, *Russia* **25 E8** 46 5N 46 1 E
Kalmykia □, *Russia* **25 E8** 46 5N 46 1 E
Kalmykovo, *Kazakstan* **25 E9** 49 0N 51 47 E
Kalna, *India* **43 H13** 23 13N 88 25 E
Kalnai, *India* **43 H10** 22 46N 83 30 E
Kalocsa, *Hungary* **17 E10** 46 32N 19 0 E
Kalokhorio, *Cyprus* **23 E12** 34 51N 33 2 E
Kaloko, *Dem. Rep. of the Congo* **54 D2** 6 47S 25 48 E
Kalol, *Gujarat, India* **42 H5** 22 37N 73 31 E
Kalol, *Gujarat, India* **42 H5** 23 15N 72 33 E
Kalomo, *Zambia* **55 F2** 17 0S 26 30 E
Kalpi, *India* **43 F8** 26 8N 79 47 E
Kalu, *Pakistan* **42 G2** 25 5N 67 39 E
Kaluga, *Russia* **24 D6** 54 35N 36 10 E
Kalulushi, *Zambia* **55 E2** 12 50S 28 3 E
Kalundborg, *Denmark* **9 J14** 55 41N 11 5 E
Kalush, *Ukraine* **17 D13** 49 3N 24 23 E
Kalutara, *Sri Lanka* **40 R12** 6 35N 80 0 E
Kalya, *Russia* **24 B10** 60 15N 59 59 E
Kama, *Dem. Rep. of the Congo* **54 C2** 3 30S 27 5 E
Kama →, *Russia* **24 C9** 55 45N 52 0 E
Kamachumu, *Tanzania* **54 C3** 1 37S 31 37 E
Kamaishi, *Japan* **30 E10** 39 16N 141 53 E
Kamalia, *Pakistan* **42 D5** 30 44N 72 42 E
Kaman, *India* **42 F6** 27 39N 77 16 E
Kamapanda, *Zambia* **55 E1** 12 5S 24 0 E
Kamaran, *Yemen* **46 D3** 15 21N 42 35 E
Kamativi, *Zimbabwe* **55 F2** 18 15S 27 27 E
Kambalda, *Australia* **61 F3** 31 10S 121 37 E
Kambar, *Pakistan* **42 F3** 27 37N 68 1 E
Kambarka, *Russia* **24 C9** 56 15N 54 11 E
Kambolé, *Zambia* **55 D3** 8 47S 30 48 E
Kambos, *Cyprus* **23 D11** 35 2N 32 44 E
Kambove, *Dem. Rep. of the Congo* **55 E2** 10 51S 26 33 E
Kamchatka, Poluostrov, *Russia* **27 D17** 57 0N 160 0 E
Kamchatka Pen. = Kamchatka, Poluostrov, *Russia* **27 D17** 57 0N 160 0 E
Kamchiya →, *Bulgaria* **21 C12** 43 4N 27 44 E
Kamen, *Russia* **26 D9** 53 50N 81 30 E
Kamen-Rybolov, *Russia* **30 B6** 44 46N 132 2 E
Kamenjak, Rt., *Croatia* **16 F7** 44 47N 13 55 E
Kamenka, *Russia* **24 A7** 65 58N 44 0 E
Kamenka Bugskaya = Kamyanka-Buzka, *Ukraine* **17 C13** 50 8N 24 16 E
Kamensk Uralskiy, *Russia* **26 D7** 56 25N 62 2 E
Kamenskoye, *Russia* **27 C17** 62 45N 165 30 E
Kameoka, *Japan* **31 G7** 35 0N 135 35 E
Kamiah, *U.S.A.* **82 C5** 46 14N 116 2W
Kamieskroon, *S. Africa* **56 E2** 30 9S 17 56 E
Kamilukuak, L., *Canada* **73 A8** 62 22N 101 40W
Kamin-Kashyrskyy, *Ukraine* **17 C13** 51 39N 24 56 E
Kamina, *Dem. Rep. of the Congo* **55 D2** 8 45S 25 0 E
Kaminak L., *Canada* **73 A10** 62 10N 95 0W
Kaministiquia, *Canada* **70 C1** 48 32N 89 35W
Kaminoyama, *Japan* **30 E10** 38 9N 140 17 E
Kamiros, *Greece* **23 C9** 36 20N 27 56 E
Kamituga, *Dem. Rep. of the Congo* **54 C2** 3 2S 28 10 E
Kamla →, *India* **43 G12** 25 35N 86 36 E
Kamloops, *Canada* **72 C4** 50 40N 120 20W
Kamo, *Japan* **30 F9** 37 39N 139 3 E
Kamoke, *Pakistan* **42 C6** 32 4N 74 4 E
Kampala, *Uganda* **54 B3** 0 20N 32 30 E
Kampang Chhnang, *Cambodia* **39 F5** 12 20N 104 35 E
Kampar, *Malaysia* **39 K3** 4 18N 101 9 E
Kampar →, *Indonesia* **36 D2** 0 30N 103 8 E
Kampen, *Neths.* **15 B5** 52 33N 5 53 E
Kampene, *Dem. Rep. of the Congo* **52 E5** 3 36S 26 40 E
Kamphaeng Phet, *Thailand* **38 D2** 16 28N 99 30 E
Kampolombo, L., *Zambia* **55 E2** 11 37S 29 42 E
Kampong Saom, *Cambodia* **39 G4** 10 38N 103 30 E
Kampong Saom, Chaak, *Cambodia* **36 B2** 10 45N 103 30 E
Kampong Saom, Chaak, *Cambodia* **39 G4** 10 50N 103 32 E
Kampong To, *Thailand* **39 J3** 6 3N 101 13 E
Kampot, *Cambodia* **39 G5** 10 36N 104 10 E
Kampuchea = Cambodia ■, *Asia* **38 F5** 12 15N 105 0 E
Kampung Air Putih, *Malaysia* **39 K4** 4 15N 103 10 E
Kampung Jerangau, *Malaysia* **39 K4** 4 50N 103 10 E
Kampung Raja, *Malaysia* **39 K4** 5 45N 102 35 E
Kampungbaru = Tolitoli, *Indonesia* **37 D6** 1 5N 120 50 E
Kamrau, Teluk, *Indonesia* **37 E8** 3 30S 133 36 E
Kamsack, *Canada* **73 C8** 51 34N 101 54W
Kamskoye Vdkhr., *Russia* **24 C10** 58 41N 56 7 E
Kamuchawie L., *Canada* **73 B8** 56 18N 101 59W
Kamuela, *U.S.A.* **74 H17** 20 1N 155 41W
Kamui-Misaki, *Japan* **30 C10** 43 20N 140 21 E
Kamyanets-Podilskyy, *Ukraine* **17 D14** 48 45N 26 40 E
Kamyanka-Buzka, *Ukraine* **17 C13** 50 8N 24 16 E
Kāmyārān, *Iran* **44 C5** 34 47N 46 56 E
Kamyshin, *Russia* **25 D8** 50 10N 45 24 E
Kanaaupscow, *Canada* **70 B4** 54 2N 76 30W
Kanaaupscow →, *Canada* **69 C12** 53 39N 77 9W
Kanab, *U.S.A.* **83 H7** 37 3N 112 32W
Kanab →, *U.S.A.* **83 H7** 36 24N 112 38W
Kanagi, *Japan* **30 D10** 40 54N 140 27 E
Kanairiktok →, *Canada* **71 A7** 55 2N 60 18W
Kananga, *Dem. Rep. of the Congo* **52 F4** 5 55S 22 18 E
Kanash, *Russia* **24 C8** 55 30N 47 32 E
Kanaskat, *U.S.A.* **84 C5** 47 19N 121 54W
Kanastraion, Ákra = Palioúrion, Ákra, *Greece* **21 E10** 39 57N 23 45 E
Kanawha →, *U.S.A.* **76 F4** 38 50N 82 9W
Kanazawa, *Japan* **31 F8** 36 30N 136 38 E
Kanchanaburi, *Thailand* **38 E2** 14 2N 99 31 E
Kanchenjunga, *Nepal* **43 F13** 27 50N 88 10 E
Kanchipuram, *India* **40 N11** 12 52N 79 45 E
Kandaghat, *India* **42 D7** 30 59N 77 7 E
Kandahar = Qandahār, *Afghan.* **40 D4** 31 32N 65 30 E
Kandalaksha, *Russia* **24 A5** 67 9N 32 30 E
Kandalakshkiy Zaliv, *Russia* **24 A6** 66 0N 35 0 E
Kandalu, *Afghan.* **40 E3** 29 55N 63 20 E
Kandangan, *Indonesia* **36 E5** 2 50S 115 20 E
Kandanghaur, *Indonesia* **37 G13** 6 21S 108 6 E
Kandanos, *Greece* **23 D5** 35 19N 23 44 E
Kandhkot, *Pakistan* **42 E3** 28 16N 69 8 E
Kandhla, *India* **42 E7** 29 18N 77 19 E
Kandi, *Benin* **50 F6** 11 7N 2 55 E
Kandi, *India* **43 H13** 23 58N 88 5 E
Kandiaro, *Pakistan* **42 F3** 27 4N 68 13 E
Kandla, *India* **42 H4** 23 0N 70 10 E
Kandos, *Australia* **63 E4** 32 45S 149 58 E
Kandy, *Sri Lanka* **40 R12** 7 18N 80 43 E
Kane, *U.S.A.* **78 E6** 41 40N 78 49W
Kane Basin, *Greenland* **4 B4** 79 1N 70 0W
Kaneohe, *U.S.A.* **74 H16** 21 25N 157 48W
Kangān, *Fārs, Iran* **45 E7** 27 50N 52 3 E
Kangān, *Hormozgān, Iran* **45 E8** 25 48N 57 28 E
Kangar, *Malaysia* **39 J3** 6 27N 100 12 E
Kangaroo I., *Australia* **63 F2** 35 45S 137 0 E
Kangaroo Mts., *Australia* **62 C3** 23 29S 141 51 E
Kangasala, *Finland* **9 F21** 61 28N 24 4 E
Kangāvar, *Iran* **45 C6** 34 40N 48 0 E
Kangdong, *N. Korea* **35 E14** 39 9N 126 5 E
Kangean, Kepulauan, *Indonesia* **36 F5** 6 55S 115 23 E
Kangean Is. = Kangean, Kepulauan, *Indonesia* **36 F5** 6 55S 115 23 E
Kanggye, *N. Korea* **35 D14** 41 0N 126 35 E
Kanggyŏng, *S. Korea* **35 F14** 36 10N 127 0 E
Kanghwa, *S. Korea* **35 F14** 37 45N 126 30 E
Kangiqsualujjuaq, *Canada* **69 C13** 58 30N 65 59W
Kangiqsujuaq, *Canada* **69 B12** 61 30N 72 0W
Kangirsuk, *Canada* **69 C13** 60 0N 70 0W
Kangnŭng, *S. Korea* **35 F15** 37 45N 128 54 E
Kangping, *China* **35 C12** 42 43N 123 18 E
Kangra, *India* **42 C7** 32 6N 76 16 E
Kangto, *India* **41 F18** 27 50N 92 35 E
Kanhar →, *India* **43 G10** 24 28N 83 8 E
Kaniama, *Dem. Rep. of the Congo* **54 D1** 7 30S 24 12 E
Kaniapiskau = Caniapiscau →, *Canada* **71 A6** 56 40N 69 30W
Kaniapiskau, Res. = Caniapiscau Rés. de, *Canada* **71 B6** 54 10N 69 55W
Kanin, Poluostrov, *Russia* **24 A8** 68 0N 45 0 E
Kanin Nos, Mys, *Russia* **24 A7** 68 39N 43 32 E
Kanin Pen. = Kanin, Poluostrov, *Russia* **24 A8** 68 0N 45 0 E
Kaniva, *Australia* **63 F3** 36 22S 141 18 E
Kanjut Sar, *Pakistan* **43 A6** 36 7N 75 25 E
Kankaanpää, *Finland* **9 F20** 61 44N 22 50 E
Kankakee, *U.S.A.* **76 E2** 41 7N 87 52W
Kankakee →, *U.S.A.* **76 E1** 41 23N 88 15W
Kankan, *Guinea* **50 F4** 10 23N 9 15W
Kankendy = Xankändi, *Azerbaijan* **25 G8** 39 52N 46 49 E
Kanker, *India* **41 J12** 20 10N 81 40 E
Kankroli, *India* **42 G5** 25 4N 73 53 E
Kannapolis, *U.S.A.* **77 H5** 35 30N 80 37W
Kannauj, *India* **43 F8** 27 3N 79 56 E
Kannod, *India* **40 H10** 22 45N 76 40 E
Kano, *Nigeria* **50 F7** 12 2N 8 30 E
Kan'onji, *Japan* **31 G6** 34 7N 133 39 E
Kanowit, *Malaysia* **36 D4** 2 14N 112 20 E
Kanoya, *Japan* **31 J5** 31 25N 130 50 E
Kanpetlet, *Burma* **41 J18** 21 10N 93 59 E
Kanpur, *India* **43 F9** 26 28N 80 20 E
Kansas □, *U.S.A.* **80 F6** 38 30N 99 0W
Kansas →, *U.S.A.* **80 F7** 39 7N 94 37W
Kansas City, *Kans., U.S.A.* **80 F7** 39 7N 94 38W
Kansas City, *Mo., U.S.A.* **80 F7** 39 6N 94 35W
Kansenia, *Dem. Rep. of the Congo* **55 E2** 10 20S 26 0 E
Kansk, *Russia* **27 D10** 56 20N 95 37 E
Kansŏng, *S. Korea* **35 E15** 38 24N 128 30 E
Kansu = Gansu □, *China* **34 G3** 36 0N 104 0 E
Kantaphor, *India* **42 H7** 22 35N 76 34 E
Kantharalak, *Thailand* **38 E5** 14 39N 104 39 E
Kantli →, *India* **42 E6** 28 20N 75 30 E
Kantō □, *Japan* **31 F9** 36 15N 139 30 E
Kantō-Sanchi, *Japan* **31 G9** 35 59N 138 50 E
Kanturk, *Ireland* **13 D3** 52 11N 8 54W
Kanuma, *Japan* **31 F9** 36 34N 139 42 E
Kanus, *Namibia* **56 D2** 27 50S 18 39 E
Kanye, *Botswana* **56 C4** 24 55S 25 28 E
Kanzenze, *Dem. Rep. of the Congo* **55 E2** 10 30S 25 12 E
Kanzi, Ras, *Tanzania* **54 D4** 7 1S 39 33 E
Kaohsiung, *Taiwan* **33 D7** 22 35N 120 16 E
Kaokoveld, *Namibia* **56 B1** 19 15S 14 30 E
Kaolack, *Senegal* **50 F2** 14 5N 16 8W
Kaoshan, *China* **35 B13** 44 38N 124 50 E
Kapaa, *U.S.A.* **74 G15** 22 5N 159 19W
Kapadvanj, *India* **42 H5** 23 5N 73 0 E
Kapan, *Armenia* **25 G8** 39 18N 46 27 E
Kapanga, *Dem. Rep. of the Congo* **52 F4** 8 30S 22 40 E
Kapchagai = Qapshaghay, *Kazakstan* **26 E8** 43 51N 77 14 E
Kapela = Velika Kapela, *Croatia* **16 F8** 45 10N 15 5 E
Kapema, *Dem. Rep. of the Congo* **55 E2** 10 45S 28 22 E
Kapfenberg, *Austria* **16 E8** 47 26N 15 18 E
Kapiri Mposhi, *Zambia* **55 E2** 13 59S 28 43 E
Kapiskau →, *Canada* **70 B3** 52 47N 81 55W
Kapit, *Malaysia* **36 D4** 2 0N 112 55 E
Kapiti I., *N.Z.* **59 J5** 40 50S 174 56 E
Kaplan, *U.S.A.* **81 K8** 30 0N 92 17W
Kapoe, *Thailand* **39 H2** 9 34N 98 32 E
Kapoeta, *Sudan* **51 H12** 4 50N 33 35 E
Kaposvár, *Hungary* **17 E9** 46 25N 17 47 E
Kapowsin, *U.S.A.* **84 D4** 46 59N 122 13W
Kapps, *Namibia* **56 C2** 22 32S 17 18 E
Kapsan, *N. Korea* **35 D15** 41 4N 128 19 E
Kapsukas = Marijampolė, *Lithuania* **9 J20** 54 33N 23 19 E
Kapuas →, *Indonesia* **36 E3** 0 25S 109 20 E
Kapuas Hulu, Pegunungan, *Malaysia* **36 D4** 1 30N 113 30 E

Kentville

Kentville, Canada 71 C7 45 6N 64 29W
Kentwood, U.S.A. 81 K9 30 56N 90 31W
Kenya ■, Africa 54 B4 1 0N 38 0 E
Kenya, Mt., Kenya 54 C4 0 10S 37 18 E
Keo Neua, Deo, Vietnam 38 C5 18 23N 105 10 E
Keokuk, U.S.A. 80 E9 40 24N 91 24W
Keonjhargarh, India 43 J11 21 28N 85 35 E
Kep, Cambodia 39 G5 10 29N 104 19 E
Kep, Vietnam 38 B6 21 24N 106 16 E
Kepi, Indonesia 37 F9 6 32S 139 19 E
Kerala □, India 40 P10 11 0N 76 15 E
Kerama-Rettō, Japan 31 L3 26 5N 127 15 E
Keran, Pakistan 43 B5 34 35N 73 59 E
Kerang, Australia 63 F3 35 40S 143 55 E
Keraudren, C., Australia 60 C2 19 58S 119 45 E
Kerava, Finland 9 F21 60 25N 25 5 E
Kerch, Ukraine 25 E6 45 20N 36 20 E
Kerguelen, Ind. Oc. 3 G13 49 15S 69 10 E
Kericho, Kenya 54 C4 0 22S 35 15 E
Kerinci, Indonesia 36 E2 1 40S 101 15 E
Kerki, Turkmenistan 26 F7 37 50N 65 12 E
Kérkira, Greece 23 A3 39 38N 19 50 E
Kerkrade, Neths. 15 D6 50 53N 6 4 E
Kermadec Is., Pac. Oc. 64 L10 30 0S 178 15W
Kermadec Trench, Pac. Oc. 64 L10 30 30S 176 0W
Kermān, Iran 45 D8 30 15N 57 1 E
Kerman, U.S.A. 84 J6 36 43N 120 4W
Kermān □, Iran 45 D8 30 0N 57 0 E
Kermān, Bīābān-e, Iran 45 D8 28 45N 59 45 E
Kermānshāh = Bākhtarān, Iran 44 C5 34 23N 47 0 E
Kermit, U.S.A. 81 K3 31 52N 103 6W
Kern →, U.S.A. 85 K7 35 16N 119 18W
Kernville, U.S.A. 85 K8 35 45N 118 26W
Keroh, Malaysia 39 K3 5 43N 101 1 E
Kerrera, U.K. 12 E3 56 24N 5 33W
Kerrobert, Canada 73 C7 51 56N 109 8W
Kerrville, U.S.A. 81 K5 30 3N 99 8W
Kerry □, Ireland 13 D2 52 7N 9 35W
Kerry Hd., Ireland 13 D2 52 25N 9 56W
Kerulen →, Asia 33 B6 48 48N 117 0 E
Kerzaz, Algeria 50 C5 29 29N 1 37W
Kesagami →, Canada 70 B4 51 40N 79 45W
Kesagami L., Canada 70 B3 50 23N 80 15W
Keşan, Turkey 21 D12 40 49N 26 38 E
Kesennuma, Japan 30 E10 38 54N 141 35 E
Keshit, Iran 45 D8 29 43N 58 17 E
Kestell, S. Africa 57 D4 28 17S 28 42 E
Kestenga, Russia 24 A5 65 50N 31 45 E
Keswick, U.K. 10 C4 54 36N 3 8W
Ket →, Russia 26 D9 58 55N 81 32 E
Ketapang, Indonesia 36 E4 1 55S 110 0 E
Ketchikan, U.S.A. 72 B2 55 21N 131 39W
Ketchum, U.S.A. 82 E6 43 41N 114 22W
Ketef, Khalîg Umm el, Egypt 44 F2 23 40N 35 35 E
Keti Bandar, Pakistan 42 G2 24 8N 67 27 E
Ketri, India 42 E6 28 1N 75 50 E
Kętrzyn, Poland 17 A11 54 7N 21 22 E
Kettering, U.K. 11 E7 52 24N 0 43W
Kettering, U.S.A. 76 F3 39 41N 84 10W
Kettle →, Canada 73 B11 56 40N 89 34W
Kettle Falls, U.S.A. 82 B4 48 37N 118 3W
Kettle Pt., Canada 78 C2 43 13N 82 1W
Kettleman City, U.S.A. 84 J7 36 1N 119 58W
Keuka L., U.S.A. 78 D7 42 30N 77 9W
Keuruu, Finland 9 E21 62 16N 24 41 E
Kewanee, U.S.A. 80 E10 41 14N 89 56W
Kewaunee, U.S.A. 76 C2 44 27N 87 31W
Keweenaw B., U.S.A. 76 B1 47 0N 88 15W
Keweenaw Pen., U.S.A. 76 B2 47 30N 88 0W
Keweenaw Pt., U.S.A. 76 B2 47 25N 87 43W
Key Largo, U.S.A. 77 N5 25 5N 80 27W
Key West, U.S.A. 75 F10 24 33N 81 48W
Keynsham, U.K. 11 F5 51 24N 2 29W
Keyser, U.S.A. 76 F6 39 26N 78 59W
Kezhma, Russia 27 D11 58 59N 101 9 E
Khabarovsk, Russia 27 E14 48 30N 135 5 E
Khabr, Iran 45 D8 28 51N 56 22 E
Khābūr →, Syria 44 C4 35 17N 40 35 E
Khachmas = Xaçmaz, Azerbaijan 25 F8 41 31N 48 42 E
Khachrod, India 42 H6 23 25N 75 20 E
Khadro, Pakistan 42 F3 26 11N 68 50 E
Khadzhilyangar, India 43 B8 35 45N 79 20 E
Khaga, India 43 G9 25 47N 81 7 E
Khagaria, India 43 G12 25 30N 86 32 E
Khaipur, Pakistan 42 E5 29 34N 72 17 E
Khair, India 42 F7 27 57N 77 46 E
Khairabad, India 43 F9 27 33N 80 47 E
Khairagarh, India 43 J9 21 27N 81 2 E
Khairpur, Pakistan 40 F6 27 32N 68 49 E
Khairpur, Hyderabad, Pakistan 42 F3 27 32N 68 49 E
Khairpur Nathan Shah, Pakistan 42 F2 27 6N 67 44 E
Khairwara, India 42 H5 23 58N 73 38 E
Khaisor →, Pakistan 42 D3 31 17N 68 59 E
Khajuri Kach, Pakistan 42 C3 32 4N 69 51 E
Khakassia □, Russia 26 D9 53 0N 90 0 E
Khakhea, Botswana 56 C3 24 48S 23 22 E
Khalafābād, Iran 45 D6 30 54N 49 24 E
Khalilabad, India 43 F10 26 48N 83 5 E
Khalīlī, Iran 45 E7 27 38N 53 17 E
Khalkhāl, Iran 45 B6 37 37N 48 32 E
Khalkís, Greece 21 E10 38 27N 23 42 E
Khalmer-Sede = Tazovskiy, Russia 26 C8 67 30N 78 44 E
Khalmer Yu, Russia 26 C7 67 58N 65 1 E
Khalturin, Russia 24 C8 58 40N 48 50 E
Khalūf, Oman 46 C6 20 30N 58 13 E
Kham Keut, Laos 38 C5 18 15N 104 43 E
Khamaria, India 43 H9 23 5N 80 48 E
Khamas Country, Botswana 56 C4 21 45S 26 30 E
Khambhaliya, India 42 H3 22 14N 69 41 E
Khambhat, India 42 H5 22 23N 72 33 E
Khambhat, G. of, India 40 J8 20 45N 72 30 E
Khamīr, Iran 45 E7 26 57N 55 36 E
Khamir, Yemen 46 D3 16 2N 44 0 E
Khamsa, Egypt 47 E1 30 27N 32 23 E
Khān Abū Shāmat, Syria 47 B5 33 39N 36 53 E
Khān Azād, Iraq 44 C5 33 7N 44 22 E
Khān Mujiddah, Iraq 44 C4 32 21N 43 48 E
Khān Shaykhūn, Syria 44 C3 35 26N 36 38 E
Khān Yūnis, Gaza Strip 47 D3 31 21N 34 18 E
Khanai, Pakistan 42 D2 30 30N 67 8 E
Khānaqīn, Iraq 44 C5 34 23N 45 25 E
Khānbāghī, Iran 45 B7 36 10N 55 25 E
Khandwa, India 40 J10 21 49N 76 22 E
Khandyga, Russia 27 C14 62 42N 135 35 E
Khāneh, Iran 44 B5 36 41N 45 8 E
Khanewal, Pakistan 42 D4 30 20N 71 55 E
Khangah Dogran, Pakistan 42 D5 31 50N 73 37 E
Khanh Duong, Vietnam 38 F7 12 44N 108 44 E
Khaniá, Greece 23 D6 35 30N 24 4 E
Khaniá □, Greece 23 D6 35 30N 24 0 E
Khaniadhana, India 42 G8 25 1N 78 8 E
Khanion, Kólpos, Greece 23 D5 35 33N 23 55 E
Khanka, L., Asia 27 E14 45 0N 132 24 E
Khankendy = Xankändi, Azerbaijan 25 G8 39 52N 46 49 E
Khanna, India 42 D7 30 42N 76 16 E
Khanozai, Pakistan 42 D2 30 37N 67 19 E
Khanpur, Pakistan 42 E4 28 42N 70 35 E
Khanty-Mansiysk, Russia 26 C7 61 0N 69 0 E
Khapalu, Pakistan 43 B7 35 10N 76 20 E
Khapcheranga, Russia 27 E12 49 42N 112 24 E
Kharaghoda, India 42 H4 23 11N 71 46 E
Kharagpur, India 43 H12 22 20N 87 25 E
Khárakas, Greece 23 D7 35 1N 25 7 E
Kharan Kalat, Pakistan 40 E4 28 34N 65 21 E
Kharānaq, Iran 45 C7 32 20N 54 45 E
Kharda, India 40 K9 18 40N 75 34 E
Khardung La, India 43 B7 34 20N 77 43 E
Khârga, El Wâhât el, Egypt 51 C12 25 10N 30 35 E
Khargon, India 40 J9 21 45N 75 40 E
Khari →, India 42 G6 25 54N 74 31 E
Kharian, Pakistan 42 C5 32 49N 73 52 E
Khārk, Jazīreh-ye, Iran 45 D6 29 15N 50 28 E
Kharkiv, Ukraine 25 E6 49 58N 36 20 E
Kharkov = Kharkiv, Ukraine 25 E6 49 58N 36 20 E
Kharovsk, Russia 24 C7 59 56N 40 13 E
Kharsawangarh, India 43 H11 22 48N 85 50 E
Kharta, Turkey 21 D13 40 55N 29 7 E
Khartoum = El Khartûm, Sudan 51 E12 15 31N 32 35 E
Khasan, Russia 30 C5 42 25N 130 40 E
Khāsh, Iran 40 E2 28 15N 61 15 E
Khashm el Girba, Sudan 51 F13 14 59N 35 58 E
Khaskovo, Bulgaria 21 D11 41 56N 25 30 E
Khatanga, Russia 27 B11 72 0N 102 20 E
Khatanga →, Russia 27 B11 72 55N 106 0 E
Khatauli, India 42 E7 29 17N 77 43 E
Khatra, India 43 H12 22 59N 86 51 E
Khātūnābād, Iran 45 D7 30 1N 55 25 E
Khatyrka, Russia 27 C18 62 3N 175 15 E
Khavda, India 42 H3 23 51N 69 43 E
Khaybar, Harrat, Si. Arabia 44 E4 25 45N 40 0 E
Khayelitsha, S. Africa 53 L3 34 5S 18 42 E
Khāzimiyah, Iraq 44 C4 34 46N 43 37 E
Khe Bo, Vietnam 38 C5 19 8N 104 41 E
Khe Long, Vietnam 38 B5 21 29N 104 46 E
Khed Brahma, India 40 G8 24 7N 73 5 E
Khekra, India 42 E7 28 52N 77 20 E
Khemarak Phouminville, Cambodia 39 G4 11 37N 102 59 E
Khemisset, Morocco 50 B4 33 50N 6 1W
Khemmarat, Thailand 38 D5 16 10N 105 15 E
Khenāmān, Iran 45 D8 30 27N 56 29 E
Khenchela, Algeria 50 A7 35 28N 7 11 E
Khersān →, Iran 45 D6 31 33N 50 22 E
Kherson, Ukraine 25 E5 46 35N 32 35 E
Khersónisos Akrotíri, Greece 23 D6 35 30N 24 10 E
Kheta →, Russia 27 B11 71 54N 102 6 E
Khewari, Pakistan 42 F3 26 36N 68 52 E
Khilchipur, India 42 G7 24 2N 76 34 E
Khilok, Russia 27 D12 51 30N 110 45 E
Khíos, Greece 21 E12 38 27N 26 9 E
Khirsadoh, India 43 H8 22 11N 78 47 E
Khiuma = Hiiumaa, Estonia 9 G20 58 50N 22 45 E
Khiva, Uzbekistan 26 E7 41 30N 60 18 E
Khīyāv, Iran 44 B5 38 30N 47 45 E
Khlong Khlung, Thailand 38 D2 16 12N 99 43 E
Khmelnik, Ukraine 17 D14 49 33N 27 58 E
Khmelnitskiy = Khmelnytskyy, Ukraine 17 D14 49 23N 27 0 E
Khmelnytskyy, Ukraine 17 D14 49 23N 27 0 E
Khmer Rep. = Cambodia ■, Asia 38 F5 12 15N 105 0 E
Khoai, Hon, Vietnam 39 H5 8 26N 104 50 E
Khodoriv, Ukraine 17 D13 49 24N 24 19 E
Khodzent = Khudzhand, Tajikistan 26 E7 40 17N 69 37 E
Khojak Pass, Afghan. 42 D2 30 51N 66 34 E
Khok Kloi, Thailand 39 H2 8 17N 98 19 E
Khok Pho, Thailand 39 J3 6 43N 101 6 E
Kholm, Russia 24 C5 57 10N 31 15 E
Kholmsk, Russia 27 E15 47 40N 142 5 E
Khomas Hochland, Namibia 56 C2 22 40S 16 0 E
Khomeyn, Iran 45 C6 33 40N 50 7 E
Khomeynī Shahr, Iran 45 C6 32 41N 51 31 E
Khon Kaen, Thailand 38 D4 16 30N 102 47 E
Khong →, Cambodia 38 F5 13 32N 105 58 E
Khong Sedone, Laos 38 E5 15 34N 105 49 E
Khonuu, Russia 27 C15 66 30N 143 12 E
Khoper →, Russia 25 D6 49 30N 42 20 E
Khóra Sfakíon, Greece 23 D6 35 15N 24 9 E
Khorāsān □, Iran 45 C8 34 0N 58 0 E
Khorat = Nakhon Ratchasima, Thailand 38 E4 14 59N 102 12 E
Khorat, Cao Nguyen, Thailand 38 E4 15 30N 102 50 E
Khorixas, Namibia 56 C1 20 16S 14 59 E
Khorramābād, Khorāsān, Iran 45 C8 35 6N 57 57 E
Khorramābād, Lorestān, Iran 45 C6 33 30N 48 25 E
Khorrāmshahr, Iran 45 D6 30 29N 48 15 E
Khorugh, Tajikistan 26 F8 37 30N 71 36 E
Khosravī, Iran 45 D6 30 48N 51 28 E
Khosrowābād, Khuzestān, Iran 45 D6 30 10N 48 25 E
Khosrowābād, Kordestān, Iran 44 C5 35 31N 47 38 E
Khost, Pakistan 42 D2 30 13N 67 35 E
Khosūyeh, Iran 45 D7 28 32N 54 26 E
Khotyn, Ukraine 17 D14 48 31N 26 27 E
Khouribga, Morocco 50 B4 32 58N 6 57W
Khowai, Bangla. 41 G17 24 5N 91 40 E
Khowst, Afghan. 42 C3 33 22N 69 58 E
Khoyniki, Belarus 17 C15 51 54N 29 55 E
Khrysokhou B., Cyprus 23 D11 35 6N 32 25 E
Khu Khan, Thailand 38 E5 14 42N 104 12 E
Khudzhand, Tajikistan 26 E7 40 17N 69 37 E
Khuff, Si. Arabia 44 E5 24 55N 44 53 E
Khūgīānī, Afghan. 42 D1 31 28N 65 14 E
Khuiyala, India 42 F4 27 9N 70 25 E
Khujner, India 42 H7 23 47N 76 36 E
Khulna, Bangla. 41 H16 22 45N 89 34 E
Khulna □, Bangla. 41 H16 22 25N 89 35 E
Khumago, Botswana 56 C3 20 26S 24 32 E
Khūnsorkh, Iran 45 E8 27 9N 56 7 E
Khunti, India 43 H11 23 5N 85 17 E
Khūr, Iran 45 C8 32 55N 58 18 E
Khurai, India 42 G8 24 3N 78 23 E
Khurayş, Si. Arabia 45 E6 25 6N 48 2 E
Khuriyā Muriyā, Jazā 'ir, Oman 46 D6 17 30N 55 58 E
Khurja, India 42 E7 28 15N 77 58 E
Khūrmāl, Iraq 44 C5 35 18N 46 2 E
Khurr, Wādī al, Iraq 44 C4 32 3N 43 52 E
Khūsf, Iran 45 C8 32 46N 58 53 E
Khush, Afghan. 40 C3 32 55N 62 10 E
Khushab, Pakistan 42 C5 32 20N 72 20 E
Khust, Ukraine 17 D12 48 10N 23 18 E
Khuzdar, Pakistan 42 F2 27 52N 66 30 E
Khūzestān □, Iran 45 D6 31 0N 49 0 E
Khvāf, Iran 45 C9 34 33N 60 8 E
Khvājeh, Iran 44 B5 38 9N 46 35 E
Khvānsār, Iran 45 D7 29 56N 54 8 E
Khvor, Iran 45 C7 33 45N 55 0 E
Khvorgū, Iran 45 E8 27 34N 56 27 E
Khvormūj, Iran 45 D6 28 40N 51 30 E
Khvoy, Iran 44 B5 38 35N 45 0 E
Khyber Pass, Afghan. 42 B4 34 10N 71 8 E
Kiabukwa, Dem. Rep. of the Congo 55 D1 8 40S 24 48 E
Kiama, Australia 63 E5 34 40S 150 50 E
Kiamba, Phil. 37 C6 6 2N 124 46 E
Kiambi, Dem. Rep. of the Congo 54 D2 7 15S 28 0 E
Kiambu, Kenya 54 C4 1 8S 36 50 E
Kiangsi = Jiangxi □, China 33 D6 27 30N 116 0 E
Kiangsu = Jiangsu □, China 35 H11 33 0N 120 0 E
Kibanga Port, Uganda 54 B3 0 10N 32 58 E
Kibara, Tanzania 54 C3 2 8S 33 30 E
Kibare, Mts., Dem. Rep. of the Congo 54 D2 8 25S 27 10 E
Kibombo, Dem. Rep. of the Congo 54 C2 3 57S 25 53 E
Kibondo, Tanzania 54 C3 3 35S 30 45 E
Kibre Mengist, Ethiopia 46 F2 5 53N 38 59 E
Kibumbu, Burundi 54 C2 3 32S 29 45 E
Kibungo, Rwanda 54 C3 2 10S 30 32 E
Kibuye, Burundi 54 C2 3 39S 29 59 E
Kibuye, Rwanda 54 C2 2 3S 29 21 E
Kibwesa, Tanzania 54 D2 6 30S 29 58 E
Kibwezi, Kenya 54 C4 2 27S 37 57 E
Kichha, India 43 E8 28 53N 79 30 E
Kichha →, India 43 E8 28 41N 79 18 E
Kichmengskiy Gorodok, Russia 24 B8 59 59N 45 48 E
Kicking Horse Pass, Canada 72 C5 51 28N 116 16W
Kidal, Mali 50 E6 18 26N 1 22 E
Kidderminster, U.K. 11 E5 52 24N 2 15W
Kidete, Tanzania 54 D4 6 25S 37 17 E
Kidnappers, C., N.Z. 59 H6 39 38S 177 5 E
Kidsgrove, U.K. 10 D5 53 5N 2 14W
Kidston, Australia 62 B3 18 52S 144 8 E
Kidugallo, Tanzania 54 D4 6 49S 38 15 E
Kiel, Germany 16 A6 54 19N 10 8 E
Kiel Canal = Nord-Ostsee-Kanal, Germany 16 A5 54 12N 9 32 E
Kielce, Poland 17 C11 50 52N 20 42 E
Kielder Water, U.K. 10 B5 55 11N 2 31W
Kieler Bucht, Germany 16 A6 54 35N 10 25 E
Kien Binh, Vietnam 39 H5 9 55N 105 19 E
Kien Tan, Vietnam 39 G5 10 7N 105 17 E
Kienge, Dem. Rep. of the Congo 55 E2 10 30S 27 30 E
Kiev = Kyyiv, Ukraine 17 C16 50 30N 30 28 E
Kiffa, Mauritania 50 E3 16 37N 11 24W
Kifrī, Iraq 44 C5 34 45N 45 0 E
Kigali, Rwanda 54 C3 1 59S 30 4 E
Kigarama, Tanzania 54 C3 1 1S 31 50 E
Kigoma □, Tanzania 54 D3 5 0S 30 0 E
Kigoma-Ujiji, Tanzania 54 C2 4 55S 29 36 E
Kigomasha, Ras, Tanzania 54 C4 4 58S 38 58 E
Kığzı, Turkey 44 B4 38 18N 43 25 E
Kihei, U.S.A. 74 H16 20 47N 156 28W
Kihnu, Estonia 9 G21 58 9N 24 1 E
Kii-Sanchi, Japan 31 G8 34 20N 136 0 E
Kii-Suidō, Japan 31 H7 33 40N 134 45 E
Kikaiga-Shima, Japan 31 K4 28 19N 129 59 E
Kikinda, Serbia, Yug. 21 B9 45 50N 20 30 E
Kikládhes, Greece 21 F11 37 0N 24 30 E
Kikwit, Dem. Rep. of the Congo 52 F3 5 0S 18 45 E
Kilar, India 42 C7 33 6N 76 25 E
Kilauea, U.S.A. 74 J14 22 13N 159 25W
Kilauea Crater, U.S.A. 74 J17 19 25N 155 17W
Kilbrannan Sd., U.K. 12 F3 55 37N 5 26W
Kilchu, N. Korea 35 D15 40 57N 129 25 E
Kilcoy, Australia 63 D5 26 59S 152 30 E
Kildare, Ireland 13 C5 53 9N 6 55W
Kildare □, Ireland 13 C5 53 10N 6 50W
Kilfinnane, Ireland 13 D3 52 21N 8 28W
Kilgore, U.S.A. 81 J7 32 23N 94 53W
Kilifi, Kenya 54 C4 3 40S 39 48 E
Kilimanjaro, Tanzania 54 C4 3 7S 37 20 E
Kilimanjaro □, Tanzania 54 C4 4 0S 38 0 E
Kilindini, Kenya 54 C4 4 4S 39 40 E
Kilis, Turkey 44 B3 36 42N 37 6 E
Kiliya, Ukraine 17 F15 45 28N 29 16 E
Kilkee, Ireland 13 D2 52 41N 9 39W
Kilkeel, U.K. 13 B5 54 4N 6 0W
Kilkenny, Ireland 13 D4 52 39N 7 15W
Kilkenny □, Ireland 13 D4 52 35N 7 15W
Kilkieran B., Ireland 13 C2 53 20N 9 41W
Kilkís, Greece 21 D10 40 58N 22 57 E
Killala, Ireland 13 B2 54 13N 9 12W
Killala B., Ireland 13 B2 54 16N 9 8W
Killaloe, Ireland 13 D3 52 48N 8 28W
Killaloe Sta., Canada 78 A7 45 33N 77 25W
Killarney, Australia 63 D5 28 20S 152 18 E
Killarney, Canada 73 D9 49 10N 99 40W
Killarney, Ireland 13 D2 52 4N 9 30W
Killary Harbour, Ireland 13 C2 53 38N 9 52W
Killdeer, U.S.A. 80 B3 47 26N 102 48W
Killeen, U.S.A. 81 K6 31 7N 97 44W
Killin, U.K. 12 E4 56 28N 4 19W
Killíni, Greece 21 F10 37 54N 22 25 E
Killorglin, Ireland 13 D2 52 6N 9 47W
Killybegs, Ireland 13 B3 54 38N 8 26W
Kilmarnock, U.K. 12 F4 55 37N 4 29W
Kilmore, Australia 63 F3 37 25S 144 53 E
Kilondo, Tanzania 55 D3 9 45S 34 20 E
Kilosa, Tanzania 54 D4 6 48S 37 0 E
Kilrush, Ireland 13 D2 52 38N 9 29W
Kilwa Kisiwani, Tanzania 55 D4 8 58S 39 32 E
Kilwa Kivinje, Tanzania 55 D4 8 45S 39 25 E
Kilwa Masoko, Tanzania 55 D4 8 55S 39 30 E
Kilwinning, U.K. 12 F4 55 39N 4 43W
Kim, U.S.A. 81 G3 37 15N 103 21W
Kimaam, Indonesia 37 F9 7 58S 138 53 E
Kimamba, Tanzania 54 D4 6 45S 37 10 E
Kimba, Australia 63 E2 33 8S 136 23 E
Kimball, Nebr., U.S.A. 80 E3 41 14N 103 40W
Kimball, S. Dak., U.S.A. 80 D5 43 45N 98 57W
Kimberley, Australia 60 C4 16 20S 127 0 E
Kimberley, Canada 72 D5 49 40N 115 59W
Kimberley, S. Africa 56 D3 28 43S 24 46 E
Kimberly, U.S.A. 82 E6 42 32N 114 22W
Kimch'aek, N. Korea 35 D15 40 40N 129 10 E
Kimch'ŏn, S. Korea 35 F15 36 11N 128 4 E
Kimje, S. Korea 35 G14 35 48N 126 45 E
Kimmirut, Canada 69 B13 62 50N 69 50W
Kimpese, Dem. Rep. of the Congo 52 F2 5 35S 14 26 E
Kimry, Russia 24 C6 56 55N 37 15 E
Kinabalu, Gunong, Malaysia 36 C5 6 3N 116 14 E
Kinaskan L., Canada 72 B2 57 38N 130 8W
Kinbasket L., Canada 72 C5 52 0N 118 10W
Kincardine, Canada 78 B3 44 10N 81 40W
Kincolith, Canada 72 B3 55 0N 129 57W
Kinda, Dem. Rep. of the Congo 55 D2 9 18S 25 4 E
Kinde, U.S.A. 78 C2 43 56N 83 0W
Kinder Scout, U.K. 10 D6 53 24N 1 52W
Kindersley, Canada 73 C7 51 30N 109 10W
Kindia, Guinea 50 F3 10 0N 12 52W
Kindu, Dem. Rep. of the Congo 54 C2 2 55S 25 50 E
Kineshma, Russia 24 C7 57 30N 42 5 E
Kinesi, Tanzania 54 C3 1 25S 33 50 E
King, L., Australia 61 F2 33 10S 119 35 E
King, Mt., Australia 62 D4 25 10S 147 30 E
King City, U.S.A. 84 J5 36 13N 121 8W
King Cr. →, Australia 62 C2 24 35S 139 30 E
King Edward →, Australia 60 B4 14 14S 126 35 E
King Frederick VI Land = Kong Frederik VI.s Kyst, Greenland 4 C5 63 0N 43 0W
King George B., Falk. Is. 96 G4 51 30S 60 30W
King George I., Antarctica 5 C18 60 0S 60 0W
King George Is., Canada 69 C11 57 20N 80 30W
King I. = Kadan Kyun, Burma 38 F2 12 30N 98 20 E
King I., Australia 62 F3 39 50S 144 0 E
King I., Canada 72 C3 52 10N 127 40W
King Leopold Ranges, Australia 60 C4 17 30S 125 45 E
King of Prussia, U.S.A. 79 F9 40 5N 75 23W
King Sd., Australia 60 C3 16 50S 123 20 E
King William I., Canada 68 B10 69 10N 97 25W
King William's Town, S. Africa 56 E4 32 51S 27 22 E
Kingaroy, Australia 63 D5 26 32S 151 51 E
Kingfisher, U.S.A. 81 H6 35 52N 97 56W
Kingirbān, Iraq 44 C5 34 40N 44 54 E
Kingisepp = Kuressaare, Estonia 9 G20 58 15N 22 30 E
Kingman, Ariz., U.S.A. 85 K12 35 12N 114 4W
Kingman, Kans., U.S.A. 81 G5 37 39N 98 7W
Kingoonya, Australia 63 E2 30 55S 135 19 E
Kingri, Pakistan 42 D3 30 27N 69 49 E
Kings →, U.S.A. 84 J7 36 3N 119 50W
Kings Canyon National Park, U.S.A. 84 J8 36 50N 118 40W
King's Lynn, U.K. 10 E8 52 45N 0 24 E
Kings Mountain, U.S.A. 77 H5 35 15N 81 20W
Kings Park, U.S.A. 79 F11 40 53N 73 16W
King's Peak, U.S.A. 82 F8 40 46N 110 27W
Kingsbridge, U.K. 11 G4 50 17N 3 47W
Kingsburg, U.S.A. 84 J7 36 31N 119 33W
Kingscote, Australia 63 F2 35 40S 137 38 E
Kingscourt, Ireland 13 C5 53 55N 6 48W
Kingsford, U.S.A. 76 C1 45 48N 88 4W
Kingsland, U.S.A. 77 K5 30 48N 81 41W
Kingsley, U.S.A. 80 D7 42 35N 95 58W
Kingsport, U.S.A. 77 G4 36 33N 82 33W
Kingston, Canada 79 B8 44 14N 76 30W
Kingston, Jamaica 88 C4 18 0N 76 50W
Kingston, N.Z. 59 L2 45 20S 168 43 E
Kingston, N.H., U.S.A. 79 D13 42 56N 71 3W
Kingston, N.Y., U.S.A. 79 E11 41 56N 73 59W
Kingston, Pa., U.S.A. 79 E9 41 16N 75 54W
Kingston, R.I., U.S.A. 79 E13 41 29N 71 30W
Kingston Pk., U.S.A. 85 K11 35 45N 115 54W
Kingston South East, Australia 63 F2 36 51S 139 55 E
Kingston upon Hull, U.K. 10 D7 53 45N 0 21W
Kingston upon Hull □, U.K. 10 D7 53 45N 0 21W
Kingston-upon-Thames, U.K. 11 F7 51 24N 0 17W
Kingstown, St. Vincent 89 D7 13 10N 61 10W
Kingstree, U.S.A. 77 J6 33 40N 79 50W
Kingsville, Canada 78 D2 42 2N 82 45W
Kingsville, U.S.A. 81 M6 27 31N 97 52W
Kingussie, U.K. 12 D4 57 6N 4 2W
Kingwood, U.S.A. 81 K7 29 54N 95 18W
Kınık, Turkey 21 E12 39 6N 27 24 E
Kinistino, Canada 73 C7 52 57N 105 2W
Kinkala, Congo 52 E2 4 18S 14 49 E
Kinki □, Japan 31 H8 33 45N 136 0 E
Kinleith, N.Z. 59 H5 38 20S 175 56 E
Kinmount, Canada 78 B6 44 48N 78 45W
Kinna, Sweden 9 H15 57 32N 12 42 E
Kinnairds Hd., U.K. 12 D6 57 43N 2 1W
Kinnarodden, Norway 6 A11 71 8N 27 40 E
Kino, Mexico 86 B2 28 45N 111 59W
Kinoje →, Canada 70 B3 52 8N 81 25W
Kinomoto, Japan 31 G8 35 30N 136 13 E
Kinoni, Uganda 54 C3 0 41S 30 28 E
Kinoosao, Canada 73 B8 57 5N 102 1W
Kinross, U.K. 12 E5 56 13N 3 25W
Kinsale, Ireland 13 E3 51 42N 8 31W

Kościan

Kinsale, Old Hd. of, *Ireland* **13 E3** 51 37N 8 33W
Kinsha = Chang Jiang →, *China* **33 C7** 31 48N 121 10 E
Kinshasa, *Dem. Rep. of the Congo* **52 E3** 4 20S 15 15 E
Kinsley, *U.S.A.* **81 G5** 37 55N 99 25W
Kinsman, *U.S.A.* **78 E4** 41 26N 80 35W
Kinston, *U.S.A.* **77 H7** 35 16N 77 35W
Kintore Ra., *Australia* **60 D4** 23 15S 128 47 E
Kintyre, *U.K.* **12 F3** 55 30N 5 35W
Kintyre, Mull of, *U.K.* **12 F3** 55 17N 5 47W
Kinushseo →, *Canada* **70 A3** 55 15N 83 45W
Kinuso, *Canada* **72 B5** 55 20N 115 25W
Kinyangiri, *Tanzania* **54 C3** 4 25S 34 37 E
Kinzua, *U.S.A.* **78 E6** 41 52N 78 58W
Kinzua Dam, *U.S.A.* **78 E6** 41 53N 79 0W
Kiosk, *Canada* **70 C4** 46 6N 78 53W
Kiowa, *Kans., U.S.A.* **81 G5** 37 1N 98 29W
Kiowa, *Okla., U.S.A.* **81 H7** 34 43N 95 54W
Kipahigan L., *Canada* **73 B8** 55 20N 101 55W
Kipanga, *Tanzania* **54 D4** 6 15S 35 20 E
Kiparissía, *Greece* **21 F9** 37 15N 21 40 E
Kiparissiakós Kólpos, *Greece* **21 F9** 37 25N 21 25 E
Kipawa, L., *Canada* **70 C4** 46 50N 79 0W
Kipembawe, *Tanzania* **54 D3** 7 38S 33 27 E
Kipengere Ra., *Tanzania* **55 D3** 9 12S 34 15 E
Kipili, *Tanzania* **54 D3** 7 28S 30 32 E
Kipini, *Kenya* **54 C5** 2 30S 40 32 E
Kipling, *Canada* **73 C8** 50 6N 102 38W
Kippure, *Ireland* **13 C5** 53 11N 6 21W
Kipushi, *Dem. Rep. of the Congo* **55 E2** 11 48S 27 12 E
Kirensk, *Russia* **27 D11** 57 50N 107 55 E
Kirghizia = Kyrgyzstan ■, *Asia* **26 E8** 42 0N 75 0 E
Kirghizstan = Kyrgyzstan ■, *Asia* **26 E8** 42 0N 75 0 E
Kirgiziya Steppe, *Eurasia* **25 E10** 50 0N 55 0 E
Kiribati ■, *Pac. Oc.* **64 H10** 5 0S 180 0 E
Kırıkkale, *Turkey* **25 G5** 39 51N 33 32 E
Kirillov, *Russia* **24 C6** 59 49N 38 24 E
Kirin = Jilin, *China* **35 C14** 43 44N 126 30 E
Kiritimati, *Kiribati* **65 G12** 1 58N 157 27W
Kirkby, *U.K.* **10 D5** 53 30N 2 54W
Kirkby Lonsdale, *U.K.* **10 C5** 54 12N 2 36W
Kirkcaldy, *U.K.* **12 E5** 56 7N 3 9W
Kirkcudbright, *U.K.* **12 G4** 54 50N 4 2W
Kirkee, *India* **40 K8** 18 34N 73 56 E
Kirkenes, *Norway* **8 B23** 69 40N 30 5 E
Kirkfield, *Canada* **78 B6** 44 34N 78 59W
Kirkjubæjarklaustur, *Iceland* **8 E4** 63 47N 18 4W
Kirkkonummi, *Finland* **9 F21** 60 8N 24 26 E
Kirkland Lake, *Canada* **70 C3** 48 9N 80 2W
Kırklareli, *Turkey* **21 D12** 41 44N 27 15 E
Kirksville, *U.S.A.* **80 E8** 40 12N 92 35W
Kirkūk, *Iraq* **44 C5** 35 30N 44 21 E
Kirkwall, *U.K.* **12 C6** 58 59N 2 58W
Kirkwood, *S. Africa* **56 E4** 33 22S 25 15 E
Kirov, *Russia* **24 C8** 58 35N 49 40 E
Kirovabad = Gäncä, *Azerbaijan* **25 F8** 40 45N 46 20 E
Kirovakan = Vanadzor, *Armenia* **25 F7** 40 48N 44 30 E
Kirovograd = Kirovohrad, *Ukraine* **25 E5** 48 35N 32 20 E
Kirovohrad, *Ukraine* **25 E5** 48 35N 32 20 E
Kirovsk = Babadayhan, *Turkmenistan* **26 F7** 37 42N 60 23 E
Kirovsk, *Russia* **24 A5** 67 32N 33 41 E
Kirovskiy, *Kamchatka, Russia* **27 D16** 54 27N 155 42 E
Kirovskiy, *Primorsk, Russia* **30 B6** 45 7N 133 30 E
Kirriemuir, *U.K.* **12 E5** 56 41N 3 1W
Kirsanov, *Russia* **24 D7** 52 35N 42 40 E
Kırşehir, *Turkey* **25 G5** 39 14N 34 5 E
Kirthar Range, *Pakistan* **42 F2** 27 0N 67 0 E
Kirtland, *U.S.A.* **83 H9** 36 44N 108 21W
Kiruna, *Sweden* **8 C19** 67 52N 20 15 E
Kirundu, *Dem. Rep. of the Congo* **54 C2** 0 50S 25 35 E
Kiryū, *Japan* **31 F9** 36 24N 139 20 E
Kisaga, *Tanzania* **54 C3** 4 30S 34 23 E
Kisalaya, *Nic.* **88 D3** 14 40N 84 3W
Kisámou, Kólpos, *Greece* **23 D5** 35 30N 23 38 E
Kisanga, *Dem. Rep. of the Congo* **54 B2** 2 30N 26 35 E
Kisangani, *Dem. Rep. of the Congo* **54 B2** 0 35N 25 15 E
Kisar, *Indonesia* **37 F7** 8 5S 127 10 E
Kisarawe, *Tanzania* **54 D4** 6 53S 39 0 E
Kisarazu, *Japan* **31 G9** 35 23N 139 55 E
Kishanganga →, *Pakistan* **43 B5** 34 18N 73 28 E
Kishanganj, *India* **43 F13** 26 3N 88 14 E
Kishangarh, *Raj., India* **42 F6** 26 34N 74 52 E
Kishangarh, *Raj., India* **42 F4** 27 50N 70 30 E
Kishinev = Chişinău, *Moldova* **17 E15** 47 2N 28 50 E
Kishiwada, *Japan* **31 G7** 34 28N 135 22 E
Kishtwar, *India* **43 C6** 33 20N 75 48 E
Kisii, *Kenya* **54 C3** 0 40S 34 45 E
Kisiju, *Tanzania* **54 D4** 7 23S 39 19 E
Kisizi, *Uganda* **54 C2** 1 0S 29 58 E
Kiskőrös, *Hungary* **17 E10** 46 37N 19 20 E
Kiskunfélegyháza, *Hungary* **17 E10** 46 42N 19 53 E
Kiskunhalas, *Hungary* **17 E10** 46 28N 19 37 E
Kislovodsk, *Russia* **25 F7** 43 50N 42 45 E
Kismayu = Chisimaio, *Somali Rep.* **49 G8** 0 22S 42 32 E
Kiso-Gawa →, *Japan* **31 G8** 35 20N 136 45 E
Kiso-Sammyaku, *Japan* **31 G8** 35 45N 137 45 E
Kisofukushima, *Japan* **31 G8** 35 52N 137 43 E
Kisoro, *Uganda* **54 C2** 1 17S 29 48 E
Kissidougou, *Guinea* **50 G3** 9 5N 10 5W
Kissimmee, *U.S.A.* **77 L5** 28 18N 81 24W
Kissimmee →, *U.S.A.* **77 M5** 27 9N 80 52W
Kississing L., *Canada* **73 B8** 55 10N 101 20W
Kissónerga, *Cyprus* **23 E11** 34 49N 32 24 E
Kisumu, *Kenya* **54 C3** 0 3S 34 45 E
Kiswani, *Tanzania* **54 C4** 4 5S 37 57 E
Kiswere, *Tanzania* **55 D4** 9 27S 39 30 E
Kit Carson, *U.S.A.* **80 F3** 38 46N 102 48W
Kita, *Mali* **50 F4** 13 5N 9 25W
Kitaibaraki, *Japan* **31 F10** 36 50N 140 45 E
Kitakami, *Japan* **30 E10** 39 20N 141 10 E
Kitakami-Gawa →, *Japan* **30 E10** 38 25N 141 19 E
Kitakami-Sammyaku, *Japan* **30 E10** 39 30N 141 30 E
Kitakata, *Japan* **30 F9** 37 39N 139 52 E
Kitakyūshū, *Japan* **31 H5** 33 50N 130 50 E
Kitale, *Kenya* **54 B4** 1 0N 35 0 E
Kitami, *Japan* **30 C11** 43 48N 143 54 E
Kitami-Sammyaku, *Japan* **30 B11** 44 22N 142 43 E
Kitangiri, L., *Tanzania* **54 C3** 4 5S 34 20 E
Kitaya, *Tanzania* **55 E5** 10 38S 40 8 E
Kitchener, *Canada* **78 C4** 43 27N 80 29W
Kitega = Gitega, *Burundi* **54 C2** 3 26S 29 56 E
Kitengo, *Dem. Rep. of the Congo* **54 D1** 7 26S 24 8 E
Kitgum, *Uganda* **54 B3** 3 17N 32 52 E
Kíthira, *Greece* **21 F10** 36 8N 23 0 E
Kíthnos, *Greece* **21 F11** 37 26N 24 27 E
Kiti, *Cyprus* **23 E12** 34 50N 33 34 E
Kiti, C., *Cyprus* **23 E12** 34 48N 33 36 E
Kitimat, *Canada* **72 C3** 54 3N 128 38W
Kitinen →, *Finland* **8 C22** 67 14N 27 27 E
Kitsuki, *Japan* **31 H5** 33 25N 131 37 E
Kittakittaooloo, L., *Australia* **63 D2** 28 3S 138 14 E
Kittanning, *U.S.A.* **78 F5** 40 49N 79 31W
Kittatinny Mts., *U.S.A.* **79 F10** 41 0N 75 0W
Kittery, *U.S.A.* **77 D10** 43 5N 70 45W
Kittilä, *Finland* **8 C21** 67 40N 24 51 E
Kitui, *Kenya* **54 C4** 1 17S 38 0 E
Kitwanga, *Canada* **72 B3** 55 6N 128 4W
Kitwe, *Zambia* **55 E2** 12 54S 28 13 E
Kivarli, *India* **42 G5** 24 33N 72 46 E
Kivertsi, *Ukraine* **17 C13** 50 50N 25 28 E
Kividhes, *Cyprus* **23 E11** 34 46N 32 51 E
Kivu, L., *Dem. Rep. of the Congo* **54 C2** 1 48S 29 0 E
Kiyev = Kyyiv, *Ukraine* **17 C16** 50 30N 30 28 E
Kiyevskoye Vdkhr. = Kyyivske Vdskh., *Ukraine* **17 C16** 51 0N 30 25 E
Kizel, *Russia* **24 C10** 59 3N 57 40 E
Kiziguru, *Rwanda* **54 C3** 1 46S 30 23 E
Kızıl Irmak →, *Turkey* **25 F6** 41 44N 35 58 E
Kizil Jilga, *India* **43 B8** 35 26N 78 50 E
Kızıltepe, *Turkey* **44 B4** 37 12N 40 35 E
Kizimkazi, *Tanzania* **54 D4** 6 28S 39 30 E
Kizlyar, *Russia* **25 F8** 43 51N 46 40 E
Kizyl-Arvat = Gyzylarbat, *Turkmenistan* **26 F6** 39 4N 56 23 E
Kjölur, *Iceland* **8 D4** 64 50N 19 25W
Kladno, *Czech Rep.* **16 C8** 50 10N 14 7 E
Klaeng, *Thailand* **38 F3** 12 47N 101 39 E
Klagenfurt, *Austria* **16 E8** 46 38N 14 20 E
Klaìpeda, *Lithuania* **9 J19** 55 43N 21 10 E
Klaksvík, *Færoe Is.* **8 E9** 62 14N 6 35W
Klamath →, *U.S.A.* **82 F1** 41 33N 124 5W
Klamath Falls, *U.S.A.* **82 E3** 42 13N 121 46W
Klamath Mts., *U.S.A.* **82 F2** 41 20N 123 0W
Klamono, *Indonesia* **37 E8** 1 8S 131 30 E
Klappan →, *Canada* **72 B3** 58 0N 129 43W
Klarälven →, *Sweden* **9 G15** 59 23N 13 32 E
Klatovy, *Czech Rep.* **16 D7** 49 23N 13 18 E
Klawer, *S. Africa* **56 E2** 31 44S 18 36 E
Klazienaveen, *Neths.* **15 B6** 52 44N 7 0 E
Kleena Kleene, *Canada* **72 C4** 52 0N 124 59W
Klein-Karas, *Namibia* **56 D2** 27 33S 18 7 E
Klerksdorp, *S. Africa* **56 D4** 26 53S 26 38 E
Kletsk = Klyetsk, *Belarus* **17 B14** 53 5N 26 45 E
Kletskiy, *Russia* **25 E7** 49 16N 43 11 E
Klickitat, *U.S.A.* **82 D3** 45 49N 121 9W
Klickitat →, *U.S.A.* **84 E5** 45 42N 121 17W
Klidhes, *Cyprus* **23 D13** 35 42N 34 36 E
Klinaklini →, *Canada* **72 C3** 51 21N 125 40W
Klipdale, *S. Africa* **56 E2** 34 19S 19 57 E
Klipplaat, *S. Africa* **56 E3** 33 1S 24 22 E
Kłodzko, *Poland* **17 C9** 50 28N 16 38 E
Klouto, *Togo* **50 G6** 6 57N 0 44 E
Kluane L., *Canada* **68 B6** 61 15N 138 40W
Kluane Nat. Park, *Canada* **72 A1** 60 45N 139 30W
Kluczbork, *Poland* **17 C10** 50 58N 18 12 E
Klukwan, *U.S.A.* **72 B1** 59 24N 135 54W
Klyetsk, *Belarus* **17 B14** 53 5N 26 45 E
Klyuchevskaya, Gora, *Russia* **27 D17** 55 50N 160 30 E
Knaresborough, *U.K.* **10 C6** 54 1N 1 28W
Knee L., *Man., Canada* **70 A1** 55 3N 94 45W
Knee L., *Sask., Canada* **73 B7** 55 51N 107 0W
Knight Inlet, *Canada* **72 C3** 50 45N 125 40W
Knighton, *U.K.* **11 E4** 52 21N 3 3W
Knights Ferry, *U.S.A.* **84 H6** 37 50N 120 40W
Knights Landing, *U.S.A.* **84 G5** 38 48N 121 43W
Knob, C., *Australia* **61 F2** 34 32S 119 16 E
Knock, *Ireland* **13 C3** 53 48N 8 55W
Knockmealdown Mts., *Ireland* **13 D4** 52 14N 7 56W
Knokke-Heist, *Belgium* **15 C3** 51 21N 3 17 E
Knossós, *Greece* **23 D7** 35 16N 25 10 E
Knowlton, *Canada* **79 A12** 45 13N 72 31W
Knox, *U.S.A.* **76 E2** 41 18N 86 37W
Knox Coast, *Antarctica* **5 C8** 66 30S 108 0 E
Knoxville, *Iowa, U.S.A.* **80 E8** 41 19N 93 6W
Knoxville, *Pa., U.S.A.* **78 E7** 41 57N 77 27W
Knoxville, *Tenn., U.S.A.* **77 H4** 35 58N 83 55W
Knysna, *S. Africa* **56 E3** 34 2S 23 2 E
Ko Kha, *Thailand* **38 C2** 18 11N 99 24 E
Koartac = Quaqtaq, *Canada* **69 B13** 60 55N 69 40W
Koba, *Indonesia* **37 F8** 6 37S 134 37 E
Kobarid, *Slovenia* **16 E7** 46 15N 13 30 E
Kobayashi, *Japan* **31 J5** 31 56N 130 59 E
Kobdo = Hovd, *Mongolia* **32 B4** 48 2N 91 37 E
Kōbe, *Japan* **31 G7** 34 45N 135 10 E
København, *Denmark* **9 J15** 55 41N 12 34 E
Kōbi-Sho, *Japan* **31 M1** 25 56N 123 41 E
Koblenz, *Germany* **16 C4** 50 21N 7 36 E
Kobryn, *Belarus* **17 B13** 52 15N 24 22 E
Kocaeli, *Turkey* **25 F4** 40 45N 29 50 E
Kočani, *Macedonia* **21 D10** 41 55N 22 25 E
Koch Bihar, *India* **41 F16** 26 22N 89 29 E
Kochang, *S. Korea* **35 G14** 35 41N 127 55 E
Kochas, *India* **43 G10** 25 15N 83 56 E
Kōchi, *Japan* **31 H6** 33 30N 133 35 E
Kōchi □, *Japan* **31 H6** 33 40N 133 30 E
Kochiu = Gejiu, *China* **32 D5** 23 20N 103 10 E
Kodarma, *India* **43 G11** 24 28N 85 36 E
Kodiak, *U.S.A.* **68 C4** 57 47N 152 24W
Kodiak I., *U.S.A.* **68 C4** 57 30N 152 45W
Kodinar, *India* **42 J4** 20 46N 70 46 E
Koes, *Namibia* **56 D2** 26 0S 19 15 E
Koffiefontein, *S. Africa* **56 D4** 29 30S 25 0 E
Kofiau, *Indonesia* **37 E7** 1 11S 129 50 E
Koforidua, *Ghana* **50 G5** 6 3N 0 17W
Kōfu, *Japan* **31 G9** 35 40N 138 30 E
Koga, *Japan* **31 F9** 36 11N 139 43 E
Kogaluk →, *Canada* **71 A7** 56 12N 61 44W
Køge, *Denmark* **9 J15** 55 27N 12 11 E
Koh-i-Bābā, *Afghan.* **40 B5** 34 30N 67 0 E
Koh-i-Khurd, *Afghan.* **42 C1** 33 30N 65 59 E
Koh-i-Maran, *Pakistan* **42 E2** 29 18N 66 50 E
Kohat, *Pakistan* **42 C4** 33 40N 71 29 E
Kohima, *India* **41 G19** 25 35N 94 10 E
Kohkīlūyeh va Būyer Aḥmadi □, *Iran* **45 D6** 31 30N 50 30 E
Kohler Ra., *Antarctica* **5 D15** 77 0S 110 0W
Kohlu, *Pakistan* **42 E3** 29 54N 69 15 E
Kohtla-Järve, *Estonia* **9 G22** 59 20N 27 20 E
Koillismaa, *Finland* **8 D23** 65 44N 28 36 E
Koin-dong, *N. Korea* **35 D14** 40 28N 126 18 E
Kojŏ, *N. Korea* **35 E14** 38 58N 127 58 E
Kojonup, *Australia* **61 F2** 33 48S 117 10 E
Kojūr, *Iran* **45 B6** 36 23N 51 43 E
Kokand = Qŭqon, *Uzbekistan* **26 E8** 40 30N 70 57 E
Kokas, *Indonesia* **37 E8** 2 42S 132 26 E
Kokchetav = Kökshetaū, *Kazakstan* **26 D7** 53 20N 69 25 E
Kokemäenjoki →, *Finland* **9 F19** 61 32N 21 44 E
Kokkola, *Finland* **8 E20** 63 50N 23 8 E
Koko Kyunzu, *Burma* **41 M18** 14 10N 93 25 E
Kokomo, *U.S.A.* **76 E2** 40 29N 86 8W
Koksan, *N. Korea* **35 E14** 38 46N 126 40 E
Kökshetaū, *Kazakstan* **26 D7** 53 20N 69 25 E
Koksoak →, *Canada* **69 C13** 58 30N 68 10W
Kokstad, *S. Africa* **57 E4** 30 32S 29 29 E
Kokubu, *Japan* **31 J5** 31 44N 130 46 E
Kola, *Indonesia* **37 F8** 5 35S 134 30 E
Kola, *Russia* **24 A5** 68 45N 33 8 E
Kola Pen. = Kolskiy Poluostrov, *Russia* **24 A6** 67 30N 38 0 E
Kolachi →, *Pakistan* **42 F2** 27 8N 67 2 E
Kolahoi, *India* **43 B6** 34 12N 75 22 E
Kolaka, *Indonesia* **37 E6** 4 3S 121 46 E
Kolar, *India* **40 N11** 13 12N 78 15 E
Kolar Gold Fields, *India* **40 N11** 12 58N 78 16 E
Kolaras, *India* **42 G6** 25 14N 77 36 E
Kolari, *Finland* **8 C20** 67 20N 23 48 E
Kolayat, *India* **40 F8** 27 50N 72 50 E
Kolchugino = Leninsk-Kuznetskiy, *Russia* **26 D9** 54 44N 86 10 E
Kolding, *Denmark* **9 J13** 55 30N 9 29 E
Kolepom = Dolak, Pulau, *Indonesia* **37 F9** 8 0S 138 30 E
Kolguyev, Ostrov, *Russia* **24 A8** 69 20N 48 30 E
Kolhapur, *India* **40 L9** 16 43N 74 15 E
Kolín, *Czech Rep.* **16 C8** 50 2N 15 9 E
Kolkas rags, *Latvia* **9 H20** 57 46N 22 37 E
Kollum, *Neths.* **15 A6** 53 17N 6 10 E
Kolmanskop, *Namibia* **56 D2** 26 45S 15 14 E
Köln, *Germany* **16 C4** 50 56N 6 57 E
Koło, *Poland* **17 B10** 52 14N 18 40 E
Kołobrzeg, *Poland* **16 A8** 54 10N 15 35 E
Kolomna, *Russia* **24 C6** 55 8N 38 45 E
Kolomyya, *Ukraine* **17 D13** 48 31N 25 2 E
Kolonodale, *Indonesia* **37 E6** 2 3S 121 25 E
Kolosib, *India* **41 G18** 24 15N 92 45 E
Kolpashevo, *Russia* **26 D9** 58 20N 83 5 E
Kolpino, *Russia* **24 C5** 59 44N 30 39 E
Kolskiy Poluostrov, *Russia* **24 A6** 67 30N 38 0 E
Kolskiy Zaliv, *Russia* **24 A5** 69 23N 34 0 E
Kolwezi, *Dem. Rep. of the Congo* **55 E2** 10 40S 25 25 E
Kolyma →, *Russia* **27 C17** 69 30N 161 0 E
Kolymskoye Nagorye, *Russia* **27 C16** 63 0N 157 0 E
Kôm Ombo, *Egypt* **51 D12** 24 25N 32 52 E
Komandorskiye Is. = Komandorskiye Ostrova, *Russia* **27 D17** 55 0N 167 0 E
Komandorskiye Ostrova, *Russia* **27 D17** 55 0N 167 0 E
Komárno, *Slovak Rep.* **17 E10** 47 49N 18 5 E
Komatipoort, *S. Africa* **57 D5** 25 25S 31 55 E
Komatou Yialou, *Cyprus* **23 D13** 35 25N 34 8 E
Komatsu, *Japan* **31 F8** 36 25N 136 30 E
Komatsujima, *Japan* **31 H7** 34 0N 134 35 E
Komi □, *Russia* **24 B10** 64 0N 55 0 E
Kommunarsk = Alchevsk, *Ukraine* **25 E6** 48 30N 38 45 E
Kommunizma, Pik, *Tajikistan* **26 F8** 39 0N 72 2 E
Komodo, *Indonesia* **37 F5** 8 37S 119 20 E
Komoran, Pulau, *Indonesia* **37 F9** 8 18S 138 45 E
Komoro, *Japan* **31 F9** 36 19N 138 26 E
Komotini, *Greece* **21 D11** 41 9N 25 26 E
Kompasberg, *S. Africa* **56 E3** 31 45S 24 32 E
Kompong Bang, *Cambodia* **39 F5** 12 24N 104 40 E
Kompong Cham, *Cambodia* **39 G5** 12 0N 105 30 E
Kompong Chhnang = Kampang Chhnang, *Cambodia* **39 F5** 12 20N 104 35 E
Kompong Chikreng, *Cambodia* **38 F5** 13 5N 104 18 E
Kompong Kleang, *Cambodia* **38 F5** 13 6N 104 8 E
Kompong Luong, *Cambodia* **39 G5** 11 49N 104 48 E
Kompong Pranak, *Cambodia* **38 F5** 13 35N 104 55 E
Kompong Som = Kampong Saom, *Cambodia* **39 G4** 10 38N 103 30 E
Kompong Som, Chhung = Kampong Saom, Chaak, *Cambodia* **39 G4** 10 50N 103 32 E
Kompong Speu, *Cambodia* **39 G5** 11 26N 104 32 E
Kompong Sralao, *Cambodia* **38 E5** 14 5N 105 46 E
Kompong Thom, *Cambodia* **38 F5** 12 35N 104 51 E
Kompong Trabeck, *Cambodia* **38 F5** 13 6N 105 14 E
Kompong Trabeck, *Cambodia* **39 G5** 11 9N 105 28 E
Kompong Trach, *Cambodia* **39 G5** 11 25N 105 48 E
Kompong Tralach, *Cambodia* **39 G5** 11 54N 104 47 E
Komrat = Comrat, *Moldova* **17 E15** 46 18N 28 40 E
Komsberg, *S. Africa* **56 E3** 32 40S 20 45 E
Komsomolets, Ostrov, *Russia* **27 A10** 80 30N 95 0 E
Komsomolsk, *Russia* **27 D14** 50 30N 137 0 E
Kon Tum, *Vietnam* **38 E7** 14 24N 108 0 E
Kon Tum, Plateau du, *Vietnam* **38 E7** 14 30N 108 30 E
Konarhā □, *Afghan.* **40 B7** 35 30N 71 3 E
Konārī, *Iran* **45 D6** 28 13N 51 36 E
Konch, *India* **43 G8** 26 0N 79 10 E
Konde, *Tanzania* **54 C4** 4 57S 39 45 E
Kondinin, *Australia* **61 F2** 32 34S 118 8 E
Kondoa, *Tanzania* **54 C4** 4 55S 35 50 E
Kondókali, *Greece* **23 A3** 39 38N 19 51 E
Kondopaga, *Russia* **24 B5** 62 12N 34 17 E
Kondratyevo, *Russia* **27 D10** 57 22N 98 15 E
Köneürgench, *Turkmenistan* **26 E6** 42 19N 59 10 E
Konevo, *Russia* **24 B6** 62 8N 39 20 E
Kong = Khong →, *Cambodia* **38 F5** 13 32N 105 58 E
Kong, *Ivory C.* **50 G5** 8 54N 4 36W
Kong, Koh, *Cambodia* **39 G4** 11 20N 103 0 E
Kong Christian IX.s Land, *Greenland* **4 C6** 68 0N 36 0W
Kong Christian X.s Land, *Greenland* **4 B6** 74 0N 29 0W
Kong Franz Joseph Fd., *Greenland* **4 B6** 73 30N 24 30W
Kong Frederik IX.s Land, *Greenland* **4 C5** 67 0N 52 0W
Kong Frederik VI.s Kyst, *Greenland* **4 C5** 63 0N 43 0W
Kong Frederik VIII.s Land, *Greenland* **4 B6** 78 30N 26 0W
Kong Oscar Fjord, *Greenland* **4 B6** 72 20N 24 0W
Kongju, *S. Korea* **35 F14** 36 30N 127 0 E
Konglu, *Burma* **41 F20** 27 13N 97 57 E
Kongolo, *Kasai-Or., Dem. Rep. of the Congo* **54 D1** 5 26S 24 49 E
Kongolo, *Katanga, Dem. Rep. of the Congo* **54 D2** 5 22S 27 0 E
Kongsberg, *Norway* **9 G13** 59 39N 9 39 E
Kongsvinger, *Norway* **9 F15** 60 12N 12 2 E
Kongwa, *Tanzania* **54 D4** 6 11S 36 26 E
Koni, *Dem. Rep. of the Congo* **55 E2** 10 40S 27 11 E
Koni, Mts., *Dem. Rep. of the Congo* **55 E2** 10 36S 27 10 E
Königsberg = Kaliningrad, *Russia* **9 J19** 54 42N 20 32 E
Konin, *Poland* **17 B10** 52 12N 18 15 E
Konjic, *Bos.-H.* **21 C7** 43 42N 17 58 E
Konkiep, *Namibia* **56 D2** 26 49S 17 15 E
Konosha, *Russia* **24 B7** 61 0N 40 5 E
Kōnosu, *Japan* **31 F9** 36 3N 139 31 E
Konotop, *Ukraine* **25 D5** 51 12N 33 7 E
Końskie, *Poland* **17 C11** 51 15N 20 23 E
Konstanz, *Germany* **16 E5** 47 40N 9 10 E
Kont, *Iran* **45 E9** 26 55N 61 50 E
Kontagora, *Nigeria* **50 F7** 10 23N 5 27 E
Konya, *Turkey* **25 G5** 37 52N 32 35 E
Konza, *Kenya* **54 C4** 1 45S 37 7 E
Koocanusa, L., *Canada* **82 B6** 49 20N 115 15W
Kookynie, *Australia* **61 E3** 29 17S 121 22 E
Koolyanobbing, *Australia* **61 F2** 30 48S 119 36 E
Koonibba, *Australia* **63 E1** 31 54S 133 25 E
Koorawatha, *Australia* **63 E4** 34 2S 148 33 E
Koorda, *Australia* **61 F2** 30 48S 117 35 E
Kooskia, *U.S.A.* **82 C6** 46 9N 115 59W
Kootenay →, *U.S.A.* **72 D5** 49 19N 117 39W
Kootenay L., *Canada* **72 D5** 49 45N 116 50W
Kootenay Nat. Park, *Canada* **72 C5** 51 0N 116 0W
Kootjieskolk, *S. Africa* **56 E3** 31 15S 20 21 E
Kopaonik, *Serbia, Yug.* **21 C9** 43 10N 20 50 E
Kópavogur, *Iceland* **8 D3** 64 6N 21 55W
Koper, *Slovenia* **16 F7** 45 31N 13 44 E
Kopervik, *Norway* **9 G11** 59 17N 5 17 E
Kopet Dagh, *Asia* **45 B8** 38 0N 58 0 E
Kopi, *Australia* **63 E2** 33 24S 135 40 E
Köping, *Sweden* **9 G17** 59 31N 16 3 E
Koppeh Dāgh = Kopet Dagh, *Asia* **45 B8** 38 0N 58 0 E
Koppies, *S. Africa* **57 D4** 27 20S 27 30 E
Koprivnica, *Croatia* **20 A7** 46 12N 16 45 E
Kopychyntsi, *Ukraine* **17 D13** 49 7N 25 58 E
Korab, *Macedonia* **21 D9** 41 44N 20 40 E
Korakiána, *Greece* **23 A3** 39 42N 19 45 E
Koral, *India* **42 J5** 21 50N 73 12 E
Korba, *India* **43 H10** 22 20N 82 45 E
Korbu, G., *Malaysia* **39 K3** 4 41N 101 18 E
Korça, *Albania* **21 D9** 40 37N 20 50 E
Korce = Korça, *Albania* **21 D9** 40 37N 20 50 E
Korčula, *Croatia* **20 C7** 42 56N 16 57 E
Kord Kūy, *Iran* **45 B7** 36 48N 54 7 E
Kord Sheykh, *Iran* **45 D7** 28 31N 52 53 E
Kordestān □, *Iran* **44 C5** 36 0N 47 0 E
Kordofân, *Sudan* **51 F11** 13 0N 29 0 E
Korea, North ■, *Asia* **35 E14** 40 0N 127 0 E
Korea, South ■, *Asia* **35 G15** 36 0N 128 0 E
Korea Bay, *Korea* **35 E13** 39 0N 124 0 E
Korea Strait, *Asia* **35 H15** 34 0N 129 30 E
Korets, *Ukraine* **17 C14** 50 40N 27 5 E
Korhogo, *Ivory C.* **50 G4** 9 29N 5 28W
Korinthiakós Kólpos, *Greece* **21 E10** 38 16N 22 30 E
Kórinthos, *Greece* **21 F10** 37 56N 22 55 E
Koríssa, Límni, *Greece* **23 B3** 39 27N 19 53 E
Kōriyama, *Japan* **30 F10** 37 24N 140 23 E
Korla, *China* **32 B3** 41 45N 86 4 E
Kormakiti, C., *Cyprus* **23 D11** 35 23N 32 56 E
Korneshty = Corneşti, *Moldova* **17 E15** 47 21N 28 1 E
Koro, *Fiji* **59 C8** 17 19S 179 23 E
Koro, *Ivory C.* **50 G4** 8 32N 7 30W
Koro Sea, *Fiji* **59 C9** 17 30S 179 45W
Korogwe, *Tanzania* **54 D4** 5 5S 38 25 E
Koronadal, *Phil.* **37 C6** 6 12N 125 1 E
Koror,r *Palau* **37 C8** 7 20N 134 28 E
Körös →, *Hungary* **17 E11** 46 43N 20 12 E
Korosten, *Ukraine* **17 C15** 50 54N 28 36 E
Korostyshev, *Ukraine* **17 C15** 50 19N 29 4 E
Korraraika, Helodranon' i, *Madag.* **57 B7** 17 45S 43 57 E
Korsakov, *Russia* **27 E15** 46 36N 142 42 E
Korshunovo, *Russia* **27 D12** 58 37N 110 10 E
Korsør, *Denmark* **9 J14** 55 20N 11 9 E
Kortrijk, *Belgium* **15 D3** 50 50N 3 17 E
Korwai, *India* **42 G8** 24 7N 78 5 E
Koryakskoye Nagorye, *Russia* **27 C18** 61 0N 171 0 E
Koryŏng, *S. Korea* **35 G15** 35 44N 128 15 E
Kos, *Greece* **21 F12** 36 50N 27 15 E
Koschagyl, *Kazakstan* **25 E9** 46 40N 54 0 E
Kościan, *Poland* **17 B9** 52 5N 16 40 E

Mallaig

McConaughy, L., *U.S.A.* ... **80 E4** 41 14N 101 40W
McCook, *U.S.A.* ... **80 E4** 40 12N 100 38W
McCreary, *Canada* ... **73 C9** 50 47N 99 29W
McCullough Mt., *U.S.A.* ... **85 K11** 35 35N 115 13W
McCusker →, *Canada* ... **73 B7** 55 32N 108 39W
McDame, *Canada* ... **72 B3** 59 44N 128 59W
McDermitt, *U.S.A.* ... **82 F5** 41 59N 117 43W
McDonald, *U.S.A.* ... **78 F4** 40 22N 80 14W
Macdonald, L., *Australia* ... **60 D4** 23 30S 129 0 E
McDonald Is., *Ind. Oc.* ... **3 G13** 53 0S 73 0 E
MacDonnell Ranges, *Australia* ... **60 D5** 23 40S 133 0 E
MacDowell L., *Canada* ... **70 B1** 52 15N 92 45W
Macduff, *U.K.* ... **12 D6** 57 40N 2 31W
Macedonia = Makedhonía □, *Greece* ... **21 D10** 40 39N 22 0 E
Macedonia, *U.S.A.* ... **78 E3** 41 19N 81 31W
Macedonia ■, *Europe* ... **21 D9** 41 53N 21 40 E
Maceió, *Brazil* ... **93 E11** 9 40S 35 41W
Macerata, *Italy* ... **20 C5** 43 18N 13 27 E
McFarland, *U.S.A.* ... **85 K7** 35 41N 119 14W
McFarlane →, *Canada* ... **73 B7** 59 12N 107 58W
Macfarlane, L., *Australia* ... **63 E2** 32 0S 136 40 E
McGehee, *U.S.A.* ... **81 J9** 33 38N 91 24W
McGill, *U.S.A.* ... **82 G6** 39 23N 114 47W
Macgillycuddy's Reeks, *Ireland* ... **13 E2** 51 58N 9 45W
McGraw, *U.S.A.* ... **79 D8** 42 36N 76 8W
McGregor, *U.S.A.* ... **80 D9** 43 1N 91 11W
McGregor Ra., *Australia* ... **63 D3** 27 0S 142 45 E
Mach, *Pakistan* ... **40 E5** 29 50N 67 20 E
Māch Kowr, *Iran* ... **45 E9** 25 48N 61 28 E
Machado = Jiparaná →, *Brazil* ... **92 E6** 8 3S 62 52W
Machagai, *Argentina* ... **94 B3** 26 56S 60 2W
Machakos, *Kenya* ... **54 C4** 1 30S 37 15 E
Machala, *Ecuador* ... **92 D3** 3 20S 79 57W
Machanga, *Mozam.* ... **57 C6** 20 59S 35 0 E
Machattie, L., *Australia* ... **62 C2** 24 50S 139 48 E
Machava, *Mozam.* ... **57 D5** 25 54S 32 28 E
Machece, *Mozam.* ... **55 F4** 19 15S 35 32 E
Machhu →, *India* ... **42 H4** 23 6N 70 46 E
Machias, *Maine, U.S.A.* ... **77 C12** 44 43N 67 28W
Machias, *N.Y., U.S.A.* ... **78 D6** 42 25N 78 30W
Machichi →, *Canada* ... **73 B10** 57 3N 92 6W
Machico, *Madeira* ... **22 D3** 32 43N 16 44W
Machilipatnam, *India* ... **41 L12** 16 12N 81 8 E
Machiques, *Venezuela* ... **92 A4** 10 4N 72 34W
Machupicchu, *Peru* ... **92 F4** 13 8S 72 30W
Machynlleth, *U.K.* ... **11 E4** 52 35N 3 50W
McIlwraith Ra., *Australia* ... **62 A3** 13 50S 143 20 E
McInnes L., *Canada* ... **73 C10** 52 13N 93 45W
McIntosh, *U.S.A.* ... **80 C4** 45 55N 101 21W
McIntosh L., *Canada* ... **73 B8** 55 45N 105 0W
Macintosh Ra., *Australia* ... **61 E4** 27 39S 125 32 E
Macintyre →, *Australia* ... **63 D5** 28 37S 150 47 E
Mackay, *Australia* ... **62 C4** 21 8S 149 11 E
Mackay, *U.S.A.* ... **82 E7** 43 55N 113 37W
MacKay →, *Canada* ... **72 B6** 57 10N 111 38W
Mackay, L., *Australia* ... **60 D4** 22 30S 129 0 E
McKay Ra., *Australia* ... **60 D3** 23 0S 122 30 E
McKeesport, *U.S.A.* ... **78 F5** 40 21N 79 52W
McKellar, *Canada* ... **78 A5** 45 30N 79 55W
McKenna, *U.S.A.* ... **84 D4** 46 56N 122 33W
Mackenzie, *Canada* ... **72 B4** 55 20N 123 5W
McKenzie, *U.S.A.* ... **77 G1** 36 8N 88 31W
Mackenzie →, *Australia* ... **62 C4** 23 38S 149 46 E
Mackenzie →, *Canada* ... **68 B6** 69 10N 134 20W
McKenzie →, *U.S.A.* ... **82 D2** 44 7N 123 6W
Mackenzie Bay, *Canada* ... **4 B1** 69 0N 137 30W
Mackenzie City = Linden, *Guyana* ... **92 B7** 6 0N 58 10W
Mackenzie Mts., *Canada* ... **68 B7** 64 0N 130 0W
Mackinaw City, *U.S.A.* ... **76 C3** 45 47N 84 44W
McKinlay, *Australia* ... **62 C3** 21 16S 141 18 E
McKinlay →, *Australia* ... **62 C3** 20 50S 141 28 E
McKinley, Mt., *U.S.A.* ... **68 B4** 63 4N 151 0W
McKinley Sea, *Arctic* ... **4 A7** 82 0N 0 0 E
McKinney, *U.S.A.* ... **81 J6** 33 12N 96 37W
Mackinnon Road, *Kenya* ... **54 C4** 3 40S 39 1 E
McKittrick, *U.S.A.* ... **85 K7** 35 18N 119 37W
Macklin, *Canada* ... **73 C7** 52 20N 109 56W
Macksville, *Australia* ... **63 E5** 30 40S 152 56 E
McLaughlin, *U.S.A.* ... **80 C4** 45 49N 100 49W
Maclean, *Australia* ... **63 D5** 29 26S 153 16 E
McLean, *U.S.A.* ... **81 H4** 35 14N 100 36W
McLeansboro, *U.S.A.* ... **80 F10** 38 6N 88 32W
Maclear, *S. Africa* ... **57 E4** 31 2S 28 23 E
Macleay →, *Australia* ... **63 E5** 30 56S 153 0 E
McLennan, *Canada* ... **72 B5** 55 42N 116 50W
McLeod →, *Canada* ... **72 C5** 54 9N 115 44W
MacLeod, B., *Canada* ... **73 A7** 62 53N 110 0W
McLeod, L., *Australia* ... **61 D1** 24 9S 113 47 E
MacLeod Lake, *Canada* ... **72 C4** 54 58N 123 0W
McLoughlin, Mt., *U.S.A.* ... **82 E2** 42 27N 122 19W
McMechen, *U.S.A.* ... **78 G4** 39 57N 80 44W
McMinnville, *Oreg., U.S.A.* ... **82 D2** 45 13N 123 12W
McMinnville, *Tenn., U.S.A.* ... **77 H3** 35 41N 85 46W
McMurdo Sd., *Antarctica* ... **5 D11** 77 0S 170 0 E
McMurray = Fort McMurray, *Canada* ... **72 B6** 56 44N 111 7W
McMurray, *U.S.A.* ... **84 B4** 48 19N 122 14W
Macodoene, *Mozam.* ... **57 C6** 23 32S 35 5 E
Macomb, *U.S.A.* ... **80 E9** 40 27N 90 40W
Mâcon, *France* ... **18 C6** 46 19N 4 50 E
Macon, *Ga., U.S.A.* ... **77 J4** 32 51N 83 38W
Macon, *Miss., U.S.A.* ... **77 J1** 33 7N 88 34W
Macon, *Mo., U.S.A.* ... **80 F8** 39 44N 92 28W
Macossa, *Mozam.* ... **55 F3** 17 55S 33 56 E
Macoun L., *Canada* ... **73 B8** 56 32N 103 40W
Macovane, *Mozam.* ... **57 C6** 21 30S 35 2 E
McPherson, *U.S.A.* ... **80 F6** 38 22N 97 40W
McPherson Pk., *U.S.A.* ... **85 L7** 34 53N 119 53W
McPherson Ra., *Australia* ... **63 D5** 28 15S 153 15 E
Macquarie →, *Australia* ... **63 E4** 30 5S 147 30 E
Macquarie Harbour, *Australia* ... **62 G4** 42 15S 145 23 E
Macquarie Is., *Pac. Oc.* ... **64 N7** 54 36S 158 55 E
MacRobertson Land, *Antarctica* ... **5 D6** 71 0S 64 0 E
Macroom, *Ireland* ... **13 E3** 51 54N 8 57W
MacTier, *Canada* ... **78 A5** 45 9N 79 46W
Macubela, *Mozam.* ... **55 F4** 16 53S 37 49 E
Macuiza, *Mozam.* ... **55 F3** 18 7S 34 29 E
Macusani, *Peru* ... **92 F4** 14 4S 70 29W
Macuse, *Mozam.* ... **55 F4** 17 45S 37 10 E
Macuspana, *Mexico* ... **87 D6** 17 46N 92 36W
Macusse, *Angola* ... **56 B3** 17 48S 20 23 E
Madadeni, *S. Africa* ... **57 D5** 27 43S 30 3 E
Madagascar ■, *Africa* ... **57 C8** 20 0S 47 0 E
Madā'in Sālih, *Si. Arabia* ... **44 E3** 26 46N 37 57 E
Madama, *Niger* ... **51 D8** 22 0N 13 40 E
Madame I., *Canada* ... **71 C7** 45 30N 60 58W
Madaripur, *Bangla.* ... **41 H17** 23 19N 90 15 E
Madauk, *Burma* ... **41 L20** 17 56N 96 52 E
Madawaska, *Canada* ... **78 A7** 45 30N 78 0W
Madawaska →, *Canada* ... **78 A8** 45 27N 76 21W
Madaya, *Burma* ... **41 H20** 22 12N 96 10 E
Maddalena, *Italy* ... **20 D3** 41 16N 9 23 E
Madeira, *Atl. Oc.* ... **22 D3** 32 50N 17 0W
Madeira →, *Brazil* ... **92 D7** 3 22S 58 45W
Madeleine, Îs. de la, *Canada* ... **71 C7** 47 30N 61 40W
Madera, *Mexico* ... **86 B3** 29 12N 108 7W
Madera, *Calif., U.S.A.* ... **84 J6** 36 57N 120 3W
Madera, *Pa., U.S.A.* ... **78 F6** 40 49N 78 26W
Madha, *India* ... **40 L9** 18 0N 75 30 E
Madhavpur, *India* ... **42 J3** 21 15N 69 58 E
Madhepura, *India* ... **43 F12** 26 11N 86 23 E
Madhubani, *India* ... **43 F12** 26 21N 86 7 E
Madhupur, *India* ... **43 G12** 24 16N 86 39 E
Madhya Pradesh □, *India* ... **42 J8** 22 50N 78 0 E
Madidi →, *Bolivia* ... **92 F5** 12 32S 66 52W
Madikeri, *India* ... **40 N9** 12 30N 75 45 E
Madill, *U.S.A.* ... **81 H6** 34 6N 96 46W
Madimba, *Dem. Rep. of the Congo* ... **52 E3** 4 58S 15 5 E
Ma'din, *Syria* ... **44 C3** 35 45N 39 36 E
Madingou, *Congo* ... **52 E2** 4 10S 13 33 E
Madirovalo, *Madag.* ... **57 B8** 16 26S 46 32 E
Madison, *Calif., U.S.A.* ... **84 G5** 38 41N 121 59W
Madison, *Fla., U.S.A.* ... **77 K4** 30 28N 83 25W
Madison, *Ind., U.S.A.* ... **76 F3** 38 44N 85 23W
Madison, *Nebr., U.S.A.* ... **80 E6** 41 50N 97 27W
Madison, *Ohio, U.S.A.* ... **78 E3** 41 46N 81 3W
Madison, *S. Dak., U.S.A.* ... **80 D6** 44 0N 97 7W
Madison, *Wis., U.S.A.* ... **80 D10** 43 4N 89 24W
Madison →, *U.S.A.* ... **82 D8** 45 56N 111 31W
Madison Heights, *U.S.A.* ... **76 G6** 37 25N 79 8W
Madisonville, *Ky., U.S.A.* ... **76 G2** 37 20N 87 30W
Madisonville, *Tex., U.S.A.* ... **81 K7** 30 57N 95 55W
Madista, *Botswana* ... **56 C4** 21 15S 25 6 E
Madiun, *Indonesia* ... **37 G14** 7 38S 111 32 E
Madoc, *Canada* ... **78 B7** 44 30N 77 28W
Madona, *Latvia* ... **9 H22** 56 53N 26 5 E
Madrakah, Ra's al, *Oman* ... **46 D6** 19 0N 57 50 E
Madras = Chennai, *India* ... **40 N12** 13 8N 80 19 E
Madras = Tamil Nadu □, *India* ... **40 P10** 11 0N 77 0 E
Madras, *U.S.A.* ... **82 D3** 44 38N 121 8W
Madre, L., *Mexico* ... **87 C5** 25 0N 97 30W
Madre, Laguna, *U.S.A.* ... **81 M6** 27 0N 97 30W
Madre, Sierra, *Phil.* ... **37 A6** 17 0N 122 0 E
Madre de Dios →, *Bolivia* ... **92 F5** 10 59S 66 8W
Madre de Dios, I., *Chile* ... **96 G1** 50 20S 75 10W
Madre del Sur, Sierra, *Mexico* ... **87 D5** 17 30N 100 0W
Madre Occidental, Sierra, *Mexico* ... **86 B3** 27 0N 107 0W
Madre Oriental, Sierra, *Mexico* ... **86 C5** 25 0N 100 0W
Madri, *India* ... **42 G5** 24 16N 73 32 E
Madrid, *Spain* ... **19 B4** 40 25N 3 45W
Madrid, *U.S.A.* ... **79 B9** 44 45N 75 8W
Madura, *Australia* ... **61 F4** 31 55S 127 0 E
Madura, *Indonesia* ... **37 G15** 7 30S 114 0 E
Madura, Selat, *Indonesia* ... **37 G15** 7 30S 113 20 E
Madurai, *India* ... **40 Q11** 9 55N 78 10 E
Madurantakam, *India* ... **40 N11** 12 30N 79 50 E
Mae Chan, *Thailand* ... **38 B2** 20 9N 99 52 E
Mae Hong Son, *Thailand* ... **38 C2** 19 16N 97 56 E
Mae Khlong →, *Thailand* ... **38 F3** 13 24N 100 0 E
Mae Phrik, *Thailand* ... **38 D2** 17 27N 99 7 E
Mae Ramat, *Thailand* ... **38 D2** 16 58N 98 31 E
Mae Rim, *Thailand* ... **38 C2** 18 54N 98 57 E
Mae Sot, *Thailand* ... **38 D2** 16 43N 98 34 E
Mae Suai, *Thailand* ... **38 C2** 19 39N 99 33 E
Mae Tha, *Thailand* ... **38 C2** 18 28N 99 8 E
Maebashi, *Japan* ... **31 F9** 36 24N 139 4 E
Maesteg, *U.K.* ... **11 F4** 51 36N 3 40W
Maestra, Sierra, *Cuba* ... **88 B4** 20 15N 77 0W
Maevatanana, *Madag.* ... **57 B8** 16 56S 46 49 E
Mafeking = Mafikeng, *S. Africa* ... **56 D4** 25 50S 25 38 E
Mafeking, *Canada* ... **73 C8** 52 40N 101 10W
Mafeteng, *Lesotho* ... **56 D4** 29 51S 27 15 E
Maffra, *Australia* ... **63 F4** 37 53S 146 58 E
Mafia I., *Tanzania* ... **54 D4** 7 45S 39 50 E
Mafikeng, *S. Africa* ... **56 D4** 25 50S 25 38 E
Mafra, *Brazil* ... **95 B6** 26 10S 49 55W
Mafra, *Portugal* ... **19 C1** 38 55N 9 20W
Mafungabusi Plateau, *Zimbabwe* ... **55 F2** 18 30S 29 8 E
Magadan, *Russia* ... **27 D16** 59 38N 150 50 E
Magadi, *Kenya* ... **54 C4** 1 54S 36 19 E
Magadi, L., *Kenya* ... **54 C4** 1 54S 36 19 E
Magaliesburg, *S. Africa* ... **57 D4** 26 0S 27 32 E
Magallanes, Estrecho de, *Chile* ... **96 G2** 52 30S 75 0W
Magangué, *Colombia* ... **92 B4** 9 14N 74 45W
Magdalen Is. = Madeleine, Îs. de la, *Canada* ... **71 C7** 47 30N 61 40W
Magdalena, *Argentina* ... **94 D4** 35 5S 57 30W
Magdalena, *Bolivia* ... **92 F6** 13 13S 63 57W
Magdalena, *Mexico* ... **86 A2** 30 50N 112 0W
Magdalena, *U.S.A.* ... **83 J10** 34 7N 107 15W
Magdalena →, *Colombia* ... **92 A4** 11 6N 74 51W
Magdalena →, *Mexico* ... **86 A2** 30 40N 112 25W
Magdalena, B., *Mexico* ... **86 C2** 24 30N 112 10W
Magdalena, Llano de la, *Mexico* ... **86 C2** 25 0N 111 30W
Magdeburg, *Germany* ... **16 B6** 52 7N 11 38 E
Magdelaine Cays, *Australia* ... **62 B5** 16 33S 150 18 E
Magee, *U.S.A.* ... **81 K10** 31 52N 89 44W
Magelang, *Indonesia* ... **37 G14** 7 29S 110 13 E
Magellan's Str. = Magallanes, Estrecho de, *Chile* ... **96 G2** 52 30S 75 0W
Magenta, L., *Australia* ... **61 F2** 33 30S 119 2 E
Magerøya, *Norway* ... **8 A21** 71 3N 25 40 E
Maggiore, Lago, *Italy* ... **18 D8** 45 57N 8 39 E
Maghâgha, *Egypt* ... **51 C12** 28 38N 30 50 E
Magherafelt, *U.K.* ... **13 B5** 54 45N 6 37W
Maghreb, *N. Afr.* ... **50 B5** 32 0N 4 0W
Magistralnyy, *Russia* ... **27 D11** 56 16N 107 36 E
Magnetic Pole (North) = North Magnetic Pole, *Canada* ... **4 B2** 77 58N 102 8W
Magnetic Pole (South) = South Magnetic Pole, *Antarctica* ... **5 C9** 64 8S 138 8 E
Magnitogorsk, *Russia* ... **24 D10** 53 27N 59 4 E
Magnolia, *Ark., U.S.A.* ... **81 J8** 33 16N 93 14W
Magnolia, *Miss., U.S.A.* ... **81 K9** 31 9N 90 28W
Magog, *Canada* ... **79 A12** 45 18N 72 9W
Magoro, *Uganda* ... **54 B3** 1 45N 34 12 E
Magosa = Famagusta, *Cyprus* ... **23 D12** 35 8N 33 55 E
Magouládhes, *Greece* ... **23 A3** 39 45N 19 42 E
Magoye, *Zambia* ... **55 F2** 16 1S 27 30 E
Magozal, *Mexico* ... **87 C5** 21 34N 97 59W
Magpie, L., *Canada* ... **71 B7** 51 0N 64 41W
Magrath, *Canada* ... **72 D6** 49 25N 112 50W
Maguarinho, C., *Brazil* ... **93 D9** 0 15S 48 30W
Mağusa = Famagusta, *Cyprus* ... **23 D12** 35 8N 33 55 E
Maguse L., *Canada* ... **73 A9** 61 40N 95 10W
Maguse Pt., *Canada* ... **73 A10** 61 20N 93 50W
Magvana, *India* ... **42 H3** 23 13N 69 22 E
Magwe, *Burma* ... **41 J19** 20 10N 95 0 E
Maha Sarakham, *Thailand* ... **38 D4** 16 12N 103 16 E
Mahābād, *Iran* ... **44 B5** 36 50N 45 45 E
Mahabharat Lekh, *Nepal* ... **43 E10** 28 30N 82 0 E
Mahabo, *Madag.* ... **57 C7** 20 23S 44 40 E
Mahadeo Hills, *India* ... **43 H8** 22 20N 78 30 E
Mahaffey, *U.S.A.* ... **78 F6** 40 53N 78 44W
Mahagi, *Dem. Rep. of the Congo* ... **54 B3** 2 20N 31 0 E
Mahajamba →, *Madag.* ... **57 B8** 15 33S 47 8 E
Mahajamba, Helodranon' i, *Madag.* ... **57 B8** 15 24S 47 5 E
Mahajan, *India* ... **42 E5** 28 48N 73 56 E
Mahajanga, *Madag.* ... **57 B8** 15 40S 46 25 E
Mahajanga □, *Madag.* ... **57 B8** 17 0S 47 0 E
Mahajilo →, *Madag.* ... **57 B8** 19 42S 45 22 E
Mahakam →, *Indonesia* ... **36 E5** 0 35S 117 17 E
Mahalapye, *Botswana* ... **56 C4** 23 1S 26 51 E
Maḩallāt, *Iran* ... **45 C6** 33 55N 50 30 E
Māhān, *Iran* ... **45 D8** 30 5N 57 18 E
Mahan →, *India* ... **43 H10** 23 30N 82 50 E
Mahanadi →, *India* ... **41 J15** 20 20N 86 25 E
Mahananda →, *India* ... **43 G12** 25 12N 87 52 E
Mahanoro, *Madag.* ... **57 B8** 19 54S 48 48 E
Mahanoy City, *U.S.A.* ... **79 F8** 40 49N 76 9W
Maharashtra □, *India* ... **40 J9** 20 30N 75 30 E
Mahari Mts., *Tanzania* ... **54 D3** 6 20S 30 0 E
Mahasham, W. →, *Egypt* ... **47 E3** 30 15N 34 10 E
Mahasolo, *Madag.* ... **57 B8** 19 7S 46 22 E
Mahattat ash Shīdīyah, *Jordan* ... **47 F4** 29 55N 35 55 E
Mahattat 'Unayzah, *Jordan* ... **47 E4** 30 30N 35 47 E
Mahaxay, *Laos* ... **38 D5** 17 22N 105 12 E
Mahbubnagar, *India* ... **40 L10** 16 45N 77 59 E
Maḩḑah, *Oman* ... **45 E7** 24 24N 55 59 E
Mahdia, *Tunisia* ... **51 A8** 35 28N 11 0 E
Mahe, *India* ... **43 C8** 33 10N 78 32 E
Mahendragarh, *India* ... **42 E7** 28 17N 76 14 E
Mahenge, *Tanzania* ... **55 D4** 8 45S 36 41 E
Maheno, *N.Z.* ... **59 L3** 45 10S 170 50 E
Mahesana, *India* ... **42 H5** 23 39N 72 26 E
Maheshwar, *India* ... **42 H6** 22 11N 75 35 E
Mahgawan, *India* ... **43 F8** 26 29N 78 37 E
Mahi →, *India* ... **42 H5** 22 15N 72 55 E
Mahia Pen., *N.Z.* ... **59 H6** 39 9S 177 55 E
Mahilyow, *Belarus* ... **17 B16** 53 55N 30 18 E
Mahmud Kot, *Pakistan* ... **42 D4** 30 16N 71 0 E
Mahnomen, *U.S.A.* ... **80 B7** 47 19N 95 58W
Mahoba, *India* ... **43 G8** 25 15N 79 55 E
Mahón = Maó, *Spain* ... **22 B11** 39 53N 4 16 E
Mahone Bay, *Canada* ... **71 D7** 44 30N 64 20W
Mahopac, *U.S.A.* ... **79 E11** 41 22N 73 45W
Mahuva, *India* ... **42 J4** 21 5N 71 48 E
Mai-Ndombe, L., *Dem. Rep. of the Congo* ... **52 E3** 2 0S 18 20 E
Mai-Sai, *Thailand* ... **38 B2** 20 20N 99 55 E
Maicurú →, *Brazil* ... **93 D8** 2 14S 54 17W
Maidan Khula, *Afghan.* ... **42 C3** 33 36N 69 50 E
Maidenhead, *U.K.* ... **11 F7** 51 31N 0 42W
Maidstone, *Canada* ... **73 C7** 53 5N 109 20W
Maidstone, *U.K.* ... **11 F8** 51 16N 0 32 E
Maiduguri, *Nigeria* ... **51 F8** 12 0N 13 20 E
Maihar, *India* ... **43 G9** 24 16N 80 45 E
Maijdi, *Bangla.* ... **41 H17** 22 48N 91 10 E
Maikala Ra., *India* ... **41 J12** 22 0N 81 0 E
Mailani, *India* ... **43 E9** 28 17N 80 21 E
Mailsi, *Pakistan* ... **42 E5** 29 48N 72 15 E
Main →, *Germany* ... **16 C5** 50 0N 8 18 E
Main →, *U.K.* ... **13 B5** 54 48N 6 18W
Maine, *France* ... **18 C3** 48 20N 0 15W
Maine □, *U.S.A.* ... **77 C11** 45 20N 69 0W
Maine →, *Ireland* ... **13 D2** 52 9N 9 45W
Maingkwan, *Burma* ... **41 F20** 26 15N 96 37 E
Mainit, L., *Phil.* ... **37 C7** 9 31N 125 30 E
Mainland, *Orkney, U.K.* ... **12 C5** 58 59N 3 8W
Mainland, *Shet., U.K.* ... **12 A7** 60 15N 1 22W
Mainoru, *Australia* ... **62 A1** 14 0S 134 6 E
Mainpuri, *India* ... **43 F8** 27 18N 79 4 E
Maintirano, *Madag.* ... **57 B7** 18 3S 44 1 E
Mainz, *Germany* ... **16 C5** 50 1N 8 14 E
Maipú, *Argentina* ... **94 D4** 36 52S 57 50W
Maiquetía, *Venezuela* ... **92 A5** 10 36N 66 57W
Mairabari, *India* ... **41 F18** 26 30N 92 22 E
Maisí, *Cuba* ... **89 B5** 20 17N 74 9W
Maisí, Pta. de, *Cuba* ... **89 B5** 20 10N 74 10W
Maitland, *N.S.W., Australia* ... **63 E5** 32 33S 151 36 E
Maitland, *S. Austral., Australia* ... **63 E2** 34 23S 137 40 E
Maitland →, *Canada* ... **78 C3** 43 45N 81 43W
Maiz, Is. del, *Nic.* ... **88 D3** 12 15N 83 4W
Maizuru, *Japan* ... **31 G7** 35 25N 135 22 E
Majalengka, *Indonesia* ... **37 G13** 6 50S 108 13 E
Majene, *Indonesia* ... **37 E5** 3 38S 118 57 E
Majorca = Mallorca, *Spain* ... **22 B10** 39 30N 3 0 E
Makale, *Indonesia* ... **37 E5** 3 6S 119 51 E
Makamba, *Burundi* ... **54 C2** 4 8S 29 49 E
Makarikari = Makgadikgadi Salt Pans, *Botswana* ... **56 C4** 20 40S 25 45 E
Makarovo, *Russia* ... **27 D11** 57 40N 107 45 E
Makasar = Ujung Pandang, *Indonesia* ... **37 F5** 5 10S 119 20 E
Makasar, Selat, *Indonesia* ... **37 E5** 1 0S 118 20 E
Makasar, Str. of = Makasar, Selat, *Indonesia* ... **37 E5** 1 0S 118 20 E
Makat, *Kazakstan* ... **25 E9** 47 39N 53 19 E
Makedhonía □, *Greece* ... **21 D10** 40 39N 22 0 E
Makedonija = Macedonia ■, *Europe* ... **21 D9** 41 53N 21 40 E
Makena, *U.S.A.* ... **74 H16** 20 39N 156 27W
Makeyevka = Makiyivka, *Ukraine* ... **25 E6** 48 0N 38 0 E
Makgadikgadi Salt Pans, *Botswana* ... **56 C4** 20 40S 25 45 E
Makhachkala, *Russia* ... **25 F8** 43 0N 47 30 E
Makhmūr, *Iraq* ... **44 C4** 35 46N 43 35 E
Makian, *Indonesia* ... **37 D7** 0 20N 127 20 E
Makindu, *Kenya* ... **54 C4** 2 18S 37 50 E
Makinsk, *Kazakstan* ... **26 D8** 52 37N 70 26 E
Makiyivka, *Ukraine* ... **25 E6** 48 0N 38 0 E
Makkah, *Si. Arabia* ... **46 C2** 21 30N 39 54 E
Makkovik, *Canada* ... **71 A8** 55 10N 59 10W
Makó, *Hungary* ... **17 E11** 46 14N 20 33 E
Makokou, *Gabon* ... **52 D2** 0 40N 12 50 E
Makongo, *Dem. Rep. of the Congo* ... **54 B2** 3 25N 26 17 E
Makoro, *Dem. Rep. of the Congo* ... **54 B2** 3 10N 29 59 E
Makrai, *India* ... **40 H10** 22 2N 77 0 E
Makran Coast Range, *Pakistan* ... **40 G4** 25 40N 64 0 E
Makrana, *India* ... **42 F6** 27 2N 74 46 E
Makriyialos, *Greece* ... **23 D7** 35 2N 25 59 E
Mākū, *Iran* ... **44 B5** 39 15N 44 31 E
Makunda, *Botswana* ... **56 C3** 22 30S 20 7 E
Makurazaki, *Japan* ... **31 J5** 31 15N 130 20 E
Makurdi, *Nigeria* ... **50 G7** 7 43N 8 35 E
Makūyeh, *Iran* ... **45 D7** 28 7N 53 9 E
Makwassie, *S. Africa* ... **56 D4** 27 17S 26 0 E
Mal B., *Ireland* ... **13 D2** 52 50N 9 30W
Mala, Pta., *Panama* ... **88 E3** 7 28N 80 2W
Malabar Coast, *India* ... **40 P9** 11 0N 75 0 E
Malabo = Rey Malabo, *Eq. Guin.* ... **52 D1** 3 45N 8 50 E
Malacca, Str. of, *Indonesia* ... **39 L3** 3 0N 101 0 E
Malad City, *U.S.A.* ... **82 E7** 42 12N 112 15W
Maladzyechna, *Belarus* ... **17 A14** 54 20N 26 50 E
Málaga, *Spain* ... **19 D3** 36 43N 4 23W
Malagarasi, *Tanzania* ... **54 D3** 5 5S 30 50 E
Malagarasi →, *Tanzania* ... **54 D2** 5 12S 29 47 E
Malagasy Rep. = Madagascar ■, *Africa* ... **57 C8** 20 0S 47 0 E
Malahide, *Ireland* ... **13 C5** 53 26N 6 9W
Malaimbandy, *Madag.* ... **57 C8** 20 20S 45 36 E
Malakâl, *Sudan* ... **51 G12** 9 33N 31 40 E
Malakand, *Pakistan* ... **42 B4** 34 40N 71 55 E
Malakwal, *Pakistan* ... **42 C5** 32 34N 73 13 E
Malamala, *Indonesia* ... **37 E6** 3 21S 120 55 E
Malanda, *Australia* ... **62 B4** 17 22S 145 35 E
Malang, *Indonesia* ... **37 G15** 7 59S 112 45 E
Malangen, *Norway* ... **8 B18** 69 24N 18 37 E
Malanje, *Angola* ... **52 F3** 9 36S 16 17 E
Mälaren, *Sweden* ... **9 G17** 59 30N 17 10 E
Malargüe, *Argentina* ... **94 D2** 35 32S 69 30W
Malartic, *Canada* ... **70 C4** 48 9N 78 9W
Malaryta, *Belarus* ... **17 C13** 51 50N 24 3 E
Malatya, *Turkey* ... **25 G6** 38 25N 38 20 E
Malawi ■, *Africa* ... **55 E3** 11 55S 34 0 E
Malawi, L. = Nyasa, L., *Africa* ... **55 E3** 12 30S 34 30 E
Malay Pen., *Asia* ... **39 J3** 7 25N 100 0 E
Malaya Vishera, *Russia* ... **24 C5** 58 55N 32 25 E
Malaybalay, *Phil.* ... **37 C7** 8 5N 125 7 E
Malāyer, *Iran* ... **45 C6** 34 19N 48 51 E
Malaysia ■, *Asia* ... **39 K4** 5 0N 110 0 E
Malazgirt, *Turkey* ... **25 G7** 39 10N 42 33 E
Malbon, *Australia* ... **62 C3** 21 5S 140 17 E
Malbooma, *Australia* ... **63 E1** 30 41S 134 11 E
Malbork, *Poland* ... **17 B10** 54 3N 19 1 E
Malcolm, *Australia* ... **61 E3** 28 51S 121 25 E
Malcolm, Pt., *Australia* ... **61 F3** 33 48S 123 45 E
Maldah, *India* ... **43 G13** 25 2N 88 9 E
Maldegem, *Belgium* ... **15 C3** 51 14N 3 26 E
Malden, *Mass., U.S.A.* ... **79 D13** 42 26N 71 4W
Malden, *Mo., U.S.A.* ... **81 G10** 36 34N 89 57W
Malden I., *Kiribati* ... **65 H12** 4 3S 155 1W
Maldives ■, *Ind. Oc.* ... **29 J11** 5 0N 73 0 E
Maldonado, *Uruguay* ... **95 C5** 34 59S 55 0W
Maldonado, Punta, *Mexico* ... **87 D5** 16 19N 98 35W
Malé, *Maldives* ... **29 J11** 4 0N 73 28 E
Malé Karpaty, *Slovak Rep.* ... **17 D9** 48 30N 17 20 E
Maléa, Ákra, *Greece* ... **21 F10** 36 28N 23 7 E
Malegaon, *India* ... **40 J9** 20 30N 74 38 E
Malei, *Mozam.* ... **55 F4** 17 12S 36 58 E
Malek Kandī, *Iran* ... **44 B5** 37 9N 46 6 E
Malela, *Dem. Rep. of the Congo* ... **54 C2** 4 22S 26 8 E
Malema, *Mozam.* ... **55 E4** 14 57S 37 20 E
Máleme, *Greece* ... **23 D5** 35 31N 23 49 E
Maleny, *Australia* ... **63 D5** 26 45S 152 52 E
Malerkotla, *India* ... **42 D6** 30 32N 75 58 E
Máles, *Greece* ... **23 D7** 35 6N 25 35 E
Malgomaj, *Sweden* ... **8 D17** 64 40N 16 30 E
Malha, *Sudan* ... **51 E11** 15 8N 25 10 E
Malhargarh, *India* ... **42 G6** 24 17N 74 59 E
Malheur →, *U.S.A.* ... **82 D5** 44 4N 116 59W
Malheur L., *U.S.A.* ... **82 E4** 43 20N 118 48W
Mali ■, *Africa* ... **50 E5** 17 0N 3 0W
Mali →, *Burma* ... **41 G20** 25 40N 97 40 E
Mali Kyun, *Burma* ... **38 F2** 13 0N 98 20 E
Malibu, *U.S.A.* ... **85 L8** 34 2N 118 41W
Maliku, *Indonesia* ... **37 E6** 0 39S 123 16 E
Malili, *Indonesia* ... **37 E6** 2 42S 121 6 E
Malimba, Mts., *Dem. Rep. of the Congo* ... **54 D2** 7 30S 29 30 E
Malin Hd., *Ireland* ... **13 A4** 55 23N 7 23W
Malin Pen., *Ireland* ... **13 A4** 55 20N 7 17W
Malindi, *Kenya* ... **54 C5** 3 12S 40 5 E
Malines = Mechelen, *Belgium* ... **15 C4** 51 2N 4 29 E
Malino, *Indonesia* ... **37 D6** 1 0N 121 0 E
Malinyi, *Tanzania* ... **55 D4** 8 56S 36 0 E
Malita, *Phil.* ... **37 C7** 6 19N 125 39 E
Maliwun, *Burma* ... **36 B1** 10 17N 98 40 E
Maliya, *India* ... **42 H4** 23 5N 70 46 E
Malkara, *Turkey* ... **21 D12** 40 53N 26 53 E
Mallacoota Inlet, *Australia* ... **63 F4** 37 34S 149 40 E
Mallaig, *U.K.* ... **12 D3** 57 0N 5 50W

Mallawan, *India* **43 F9** 27 4N 80 12 E
Mallawi, *Egypt* **51 C12** 27 44N 30 44 E
Mállia, *Greece* **23 D7** 35 17N 25 32 E
Mallión, Kólpos, *Greece* **23 D7** 35 19N 25 27 E
Mallorca, *Spain* **22 B10** 39 30N 3 0 E
Mallorytown, *Canada* **79 B9** 44 29N 75 53W
Mallow, *Ireland* **13 D3** 52 8N 8 39W
Malmberget, *Sweden* **8 C19** 67 11N 20 40 E
Malmédy, *Belgium* **15 D6** 50 25N 6 2 E
Malmesbury, *S. Africa* **56 E2** 33 28S 18 41 E
Malmö, *Sweden* **9 J15** 55 36N 12 59 E
Malolos, *Phil.* **37 B6** 14 50N 120 49 E
Malombe L., *Malawi* **55 E4** 14 40S 35 15 E
Malone, *U.S.A.* **79 B10** 44 51N 74 18W
Måløy, *Norway* **9 F11** 61 57N 5 6 E
Malpaso, *Canary Is.* **22 G1** 27 43N 18 3W
Malpelo, I. de, *Colombia* **92 C2** 4 3N 81 35W
Malpur, *India* **42 H5** 23 21N 73 27 E
Malpura, *India* **42 F6** 26 17N 75 23 E
Malta, *Idaho, U.S.A.* **82 E7** 42 18N 113 22W
Malta, *Mont., U.S.A.* **82 B10** 48 21N 107 52W
Malta ■, *Europe* **23 D2** 35 50N 14 30 E
Maltahöhe, *Namibia* **56 C2** 24 55S 17 0 E
Malton, *Canada* **78 C5** 43 42N 79 38W
Malton, *U.K.* **10 C7** 54 8N 0 49W
Maluku, *Indonesia* **37 E7** 1 0S 127 0 E
Maluku □, *Indonesia* **37 E7** 3 0S 128 0 E
Maluku Sea = Molucca Sea, *Indonesia* **37 E6** 2 0S 124 0 E
Malvan, *India* **40 L8** 16 2N 73 30 E
Malvern, *U.S.A.* **81 H8** 34 22N 92 49W
Malvern Hills, *U.K.* **11 E5** 52 0N 2 19W
Malvinas, Is. = Falkland Is. □, *Atl. Oc.* **96 G5** 51 30S 59 0W
Malya, *Tanzania* **54 C3** 3 5S 33 38 E
Malyn, *Ukraine* **17 C15** 50 46N 29 3 E
Malyy Lyakhovskiy, Ostrov, *Russia* **27 B15** 74 7N 140 36 E
Mama, *Russia* **27 D12** 58 18N 112 54 E
Mamanguape, *Brazil* **93 E11** 6 50S 35 4W
Mamarr Mitlā, *Egypt* **47 E1** 30 2N 32 54 E
Mamasa, *Indonesia* **37 E5** 2 55S 119 20 E
Mambasa, *Dem. Rep. of the Congo* **54 B2** 1 22N 29 3 E
Mamberamo →, *Indonesia* **37 E9** 2 0S 137 50 E
Mambilima Falls, *Zambia* **55 E2** 10 31S 28 45 E
Mambirima, *Dem. Rep. of the Congo* **55 E2** 11 25S 27 33 E
Mambo, *Tanzania* **54 C4** 4 52S 38 22 E
Mambrui, *Kenya* **54 C5** 3 5S 40 5 E
Mamburao, *Phil.* **37 B6** 13 13N 120 39 E
Mameigwess L., *Canada* **70 B2** 52 35N 87 50W
Mammoth, *U.S.A.* **83 K8** 32 43N 110 39W
Mammoth Cave National Park, *U.S.A.* **76 G3** 37 8N 86 13W
Mamoré →, *Bolivia* **92 F5** 10 23S 65 53W
Mamou, *Guinea* **50 F3** 10 15N 12 0W
Mamuju, *Indonesia* **37 E5** 2 41S 118 50 E
Man, *Ivory C.* **50 G4** 7 30N 7 40W
Man, I. of, *U.K.* **10 C3** 54 15N 4 30W
Man-Bazar, *India* **43 H12** 23 4N 86 39 E
Man Na, *Burma* **41 H20** 23 27N 97 19 E
Mana →, *Fr. Guiana* **93 B8** 5 45N 53 55W
Manaar, G. of = Mannar, G. of, *Asia* **40 Q11** 8 30N 79 0 E
Manacapuru, *Brazil* **92 D6** 3 16S 60 37W
Manacor, *Spain* **22 B10** 39 34N 3 13 E
Manado, *Indonesia* **37 D6** 1 29N 124 51 E
Managua, *Nic.* **88 D2** 12 6N 86 20W
Managua, L. de, *Nic.* **88 D2** 12 20N 86 30W
Manakara, *Madag.* **57 C8** 22 8S 48 1 E
Manali, *India* **42 C7** 32 16N 77 10 E
Manama = Al Manāmah, *Bahrain* **45 E6** 26 10N 50 30 E
Manambao →, *Madag.* **57 B7** 17 35S 44 0 E
Manambato, *Madag.* **57 A8** 13 43S 49 7 E
Manambolo →, *Madag.* **57 B7** 19 18S 44 22 E
Manambolosy, *Madag.* **57 B8** 16 2S 49 40 E
Mananara, *Madag.* **57 B8** 16 10S 49 46 E
Mananara →, *Madag.* **57 C8** 23 21S 47 42 E
Mananjary, *Madag.* **57 C8** 21 13S 48 20 E
Manantenina, *Madag.* **57 C8** 24 17S 47 19 E
Manaos = Manaus, *Brazil* **92 D7** 3 0S 60 0W
Manapire →, *Venezuela* **92 B5** 7 42N 66 7W
Manapouri, *N.Z.* **59 L1** 45 34S 167 39 E
Manapouri, L., *N.Z.* **59 L1** 45 32S 167 32 E
Manār, Jabal, *Yemen* **46 E3** 14 2N 44 17 E
Manas, *China* **32 B3** 44 17N 85 56 E
Manas →, *India* **41 F17** 26 12N 90 40 E
Manaslu, *Nepal* **43 E11** 28 33N 84 33 E
Manasquan, *U.S.A.* **79 F10** 40 8N 74 3W
Manassa, *U.S.A.* **83 H11** 37 11N 105 56W
Manaung, *Burma* **41 K18** 18 45N 93 40 E
Manaus, *Brazil* **92 D7** 3 0S 60 0W
Manawan L., *Canada* **73 B8** 55 24N 103 14W
Manbij, *Syria* **44 B3** 36 31N 37 57 E
Manchegorsk, *Russia* **26 C4** 67 54N 32 58 E
Manchester, *U.K.* **10 D5** 53 29N 2 12W
Manchester, *Calif., U.S.A.* **84 G3** 38 58N 123 41W
Manchester, *Conn., U.S.A.* **79 E12** 41 47N 72 31W
Manchester, *Ga., U.S.A.* **77 J3** 32 51N 84 37W
Manchester, *Iowa, U.S.A.* **80 D9** 42 29N 91 27W
Manchester, *Ky., U.S.A.* **76 G4** 37 9N 83 46W
Manchester, *N.H., U.S.A.* **79 D13** 42 59N 71 28W
Manchester, *N.Y., U.S.A.* **78 D7** 42 56N 77 16W
Manchester, *Pa., U.S.A.* **79 F8** 40 4N 76 43W
Manchester, *Tenn., U.S.A.* **77 H2** 35 29N 86 5W
Manchester, *Vt., U.S.A.* **79 C11** 43 10N 73 5W
Manchester L., *Canada* **73 A7** 61 28N 107 29W
Manchhar L., *Pakistan* **42 F2** 26 25N 67 39 E
Manchuria = Dongbei, *China* **35 D13** 45 0N 125 0 E
Manchurian Plain, *China* **28 E16** 47 0N 124 0 E
Mand →, *India* **43 J10** 21 42N 83 15 E
Mand →, *Iran* **45 D7** 28 20N 52 30 E
Manda, *Chunya, Tanzania* **54 D3** 6 51S 32 29 E
Manda, *Ludewe, Tanzania* **55 E3** 10 30S 34 40 E
Mandabé, *Madag.* **57 C7** 21 0S 44 55 E
Mandaguari, *Brazil* **95 A5** 23 32S 51 42W
Mandah = Töhöm, *Mongolia* **34 B5** 44 27N 108 2 E
Mandal, *Norway* **9 G12** 58 2N 7 25 E
Mandala, Puncak, *Indonesia* **37 E10** 4 44S 140 20 E
Mandalay, *Burma* **41 J20** 22 0N 96 4 E
Mandale = Mandalay, *Burma* **41 J20** 22 0N 96 4 E
Mandalgarh, *India* **42 G6** 25 12N 75 6 E
Mandalgovi, *Mongolia* **34 B4** 45 45N 106 10 E
Mandalī, *Iraq* **44 C5** 33 43N 45 28 E
Mandan, *U.S.A.* **80 B4** 46 50N 100 54W
Mandar, Teluk, *Indonesia* **37 E5** 3 35S 119 15 E
Mandaue, *Phil.* **37 B6** 10 20N 123 56 E
Mandera, *Kenya* **54 B5** 3 55N 41 53 E
Mandi, *India* **42 D7** 31 39N 76 58 E
Mandi Dabwali, *India* **42 E6** 29 58N 74 42 E
Mandimba, *Mozam.* **55 E4** 14 20S 35 40 E
Mandioli, *Indonesia* **37 E7** 0 40S 127 20 E
Mandla, *India* **43 H9** 22 39N 80 30 E
Mandorah, *Australia* **60 B5** 12 32S 130 42 E
Mandoto, *Madag.* **57 B8** 19 34S 46 17 E
Mandra, *Pakistan* **42 C5** 33 23N 73 12 E
Mandrare →, *Madag.* **57 D8** 25 10S 46 30 E
Mandritsara, *Madag.* **57 B8** 15 50S 48 49 E
Mandsaur, *India* **42 G6** 24 3N 75 8 E
Mandurah, *Australia* **61 F2** 32 36S 115 48 E
Mandvi, *India* **42 H3** 22 51N 69 22 E
Mandya, *India* **40 N10** 12 30N 77 0 E
Mandzai, *Pakistan* **42 D2** 30 55N 67 6 E
Maneh, *Iran* **45 B8** 37 39N 57 7 E
Maneroo Cr. →, *Australia* **62 C3** 23 21S 143 53 E
Manfalût, *Egypt* **51 C12** 27 20N 30 52 E
Manfredónia, *Italy* **20 D6** 41 38N 15 55 E
Mangabeiras, Chapada das, *Brazil* **93 F9** 10 0S 46 30W
Mangalia, *Romania* **17 G15** 43 50N 28 35 E
Mangalore, *India* **40 N9** 12 55N 74 47 E
Mangan, *India* **43 F13** 27 31N 88 32 E
Mangaung, *S. Africa* **53 K5** 29 10S 26 25 E
Mangawan, *India* **43 G9** 24 41N 81 33 E
Mangaweka, *N.Z.* **59 H5** 39 48S 175 47 E
Manggar, *Indonesia* **36 E3** 2 50S 108 10 E
Manggawitu, *Indonesia* **37 E8** 4 8S 133 32 E
Mangkalihat, Tanjung, *Indonesia* **37 D5** 1 2N 118 59 E
Mangla, *Pakistan* **42 C5** 33 7N 73 39 E
Mangla Dam, *Pakistan* **43 C5** 33 9N 73 44 E
Manglaur, *India* **42 E7** 29 44N 77 49 E
Mangnai, *China* **32 C4** 37 52N 91 43 E
Mango, *Togo* **50 F6** 10 20N 0 30 E
Mangoche, *Malawi* **55 E4** 14 25S 35 16 E
Mangoky →, *Madag.* **57 C7** 21 29S 43 41 E
Mangole, *Indonesia* **37 E6** 1 50S 125 55 E
Mangombe, *Dem. Rep. of the Congo* **54 C2** 1 20S 26 48 E
Mangonui, *N.Z.* **59 F4** 35 1S 173 32 E
Mangrol, *Mad. P., India* **42 J4** 21 7N 70 7 E
Mangrol, *Raj., India* **42 G6** 25 20N 76 31 E
Mangueira, L. da, *Brazil* **95 C5** 33 0S 52 50W
Mangum, *U.S.A.* **81 H5** 34 53N 99 30W
Mangyshlak Poluostrov, *Kazakstan* **26 E6** 44 30N 52 30 E
Manhattan, *U.S.A.* **80 F6** 39 11N 96 35W
Manhiça, *Mozam.* **57 D5** 25 23S 32 49 E
Mania →, *Madag.* **57 B8** 19 42S 45 22 E
Manica, *Mozam.* **57 B5** 18 58S 32 59 E
Manica e Sofala □, *Mozam.* **57 B5** 19 10S 33 45 E
Manicaland □, *Zimbabwe* **55 F3** 19 0S 32 30 E
Manicoré, *Brazil* **92 E6** 5 48S 61 16W
Manicouagan →, *Canada* **71 C6** 49 30N 68 30W
Manicouagan, Rés., *Canada* **71 B6** 51 5N 68 40W
Maniema □, *Dem. Rep. of the Congo* **54 C2** 3 0S 26 0 E
Manīfah, *Si. Arabia* **45 E6** 27 44N 49 0 E
Manifold, C., *Australia* **62 C5** 22 41S 150 50 E
Manigotagan, *Canada* **73 C9** 51 6N 96 18W
Manigotagan →, *Canada* **73 C9** 51 7N 96 20W
Manihari, *India* **43 G12** 25 21N 87 38 E
Manihiki, *Cook Is.* **65 J11** 10 24S 161 1W
Manika, Plateau de la, *Dem. Rep. of the Congo* **55 E2** 10 0S 25 5 E
Manikpur, *India* **43 G9** 25 4N 81 7 E
Manila, *Phil.* **37 B6** 14 40N 121 3 E
Manila, *U.S.A.* **82 F9** 40 59N 109 43W
Manila B., *Phil.* **37 B6** 14 40N 120 35 E
Manilla, *Australia* **63 E5** 30 45S 150 43 E
Maningrida, *Australia* **62 A1** 12 3S 134 13 E
Manipur □, *India* **41 G19** 25 0N 94 0 E
Manipur →, *Burma* **41 H19** 23 45N 94 20 E
Manisa, *Turkey* **21 E12** 38 38N 27 30 E
Manistee, *U.S.A.* **76 C2** 44 15N 86 19W
Manistee →, *U.S.A.* **76 C2** 44 15N 86 21W
Manistique, *U.S.A.* **76 C2** 45 57N 86 15W
Manito L., *Canada* **73 C7** 52 43N 109 43W
Manitoba □, *Canada* **73 B9** 55 30N 97 0W
Manitoba, L., *Canada* **73 C9** 51 0N 98 45W
Manitou, *Canada* **73 D9** 49 15N 98 32W
Manitou, L., *Canada* **71 B6** 50 55N 65 17W
Manitou Is., *U.S.A.* **76 C3** 45 8N 86 0W
Manitou Springs, *U.S.A.* **80 F2** 38 52N 104 55W
Manitoulin I., *Canada* **70 C3** 45 40N 82 30W
Manitouwadge, *Canada* **70 C2** 49 8N 85 48W
Manitowoc, *U.S.A.* **76 C2** 44 5N 87 40W
Manizales, *Colombia* **92 B3** 5 5N 75 32W
Manja, *Madag.* **57 C7** 21 26S 44 20 E
Manjacaze, *Mozam.* **57 C5** 24 45S 34 0 E
Manjakandriana, *Madag.* **57 B8** 18 55S 47 47 E
Manjhand, *Pakistan* **42 G3** 25 50N 68 10 E
Manjil, *Iran* **45 B6** 36 46N 49 30 E
Manjimup, *Australia* **61 F2** 34 15S 116 6 E
Manjra →, *India* **40 K10** 18 49N 77 52 E
Mankato, *Kans., U.S.A.* **80 F5** 39 47N 98 13W
Mankato, *Minn., U.S.A.* **80 C8** 44 10N 94 0W
Mankayane, *Swaziland* **57 D5** 26 40S 31 4 E
Mankera, *Pakistan* **42 D4** 31 23N 71 26 E
Mankota, *Canada* **73 D7** 49 25N 107 5W
Manlay = Üydzin, *Mongolia* **34 B4** 44 9N 107 0 E
Manmad, *India* **40 J9** 20 18N 74 28 E
Mann Ranges, *Australia* **61 E5** 26 6S 130 5 E
Manna, *Indonesia* **36 E2** 4 25S 102 55 E
Mannahill, *Australia* **63 E3** 32 25S 140 0 E
Mannar, *Sri Lanka* **40 Q11** 9 1N 79 54 E
Mannar, G. of, *Asia* **40 Q11** 8 30N 79 0 E
Mannar I., *Sri Lanka* **40 Q11** 9 5N 79 45 E
Mannheim, *Germany* **16 D5** 49 29N 8 29 E
Manning, *Canada* **72 B5** 56 53N 117 39W
Manning, *Oreg., U.S.A.* **84 E3** 45 45N 123 13W
Manning, *S.C., U.S.A.* **77 J5** 33 42N 80 13W
Manning Prov. Park, *Canada* **72 D4** 49 5N 120 45W
Mannum, *Australia* **63 E2** 34 50S 139 20 E
Manoharpur, *India* **43 H11** 22 23N 85 12 E
Manokwari, *Indonesia* **37 E8** 0 54S 134 0 E
Manombo, *Madag.* **57 C7** 22 57S 43 28 E
Manono, *Dem. Rep. of the Congo* **54 D2** 7 15S 27 25 E
Manosque, *France* **18 E6** 43 49N 5 47 E
Manotick, *Canada* **79 A9** 45 13N 75 41W
Manouane →, *Canada* **71 C5** 49 30N 71 10W
Manouane, L., *Canada* **71 B5** 50 45N 70 45W
Manp'o, *N. Korea* **35 D14** 41 6N 126 24 E
Manpojin = Manp'o, *N. Korea* **35 D14** 41 6N 126 24 E
Manpur, *Mad. P., India* **42 H6** 22 26N 75 37 E
Manpur, *Mad. P., India* **43 H10** 23 17N 83 35 E
Manresa, *Spain* **19 B6** 41 48N 1 50 E
Mansa, *Gujarat, India* **42 H5** 23 27N 72 45 E
Mansa, *Punjab, India* **42 E6** 30 0N 75 27 E
Mansa, *Zambia* **55 E2** 11 13S 28 55 E
Mansehra, *Pakistan* **42 B5** 34 20N 73 15 E
Mansel I., *Canada* **69 B12** 62 0N 80 0W
Mansfield, *Australia* **63 F4** 37 4S 146 6 E
Mansfield, *U.K.* **10 D6** 53 9N 1 11W
Mansfield, *La., U.S.A.* **81 J8** 32 2N 93 43W
Mansfield, *Mass., U.S.A.* **79 D13** 42 2N 71 13W
Mansfield, *Ohio, U.S.A.* **78 F2** 40 45N 82 31W
Mansfield, *Pa., U.S.A.* **78 E7** 41 48N 77 5W
Mansfield, Mt., *U.S.A.* **79 B12** 44 33N 72 49W
Manson Creek, *Canada* **72 B4** 55 37N 124 32W
Manta, *Ecuador* **92 D2** 1 0S 80 40W
Mantalingajan, Mt., *Phil.* **36 C5** 8 55N 117 45 E
Mantare, *Tanzania* **54 C3** 2 42S 33 13 E
Manteca, *U.S.A.* **84 H5** 37 48N 121 13W
Manteo, *U.S.A.* **77 H8** 35 55N 75 40W
Mantes-la-Jolie, *France* **18 B4** 48 58N 1 41 E
Manthani, *India* **40 K11** 18 40N 79 35 E
Manti, *U.S.A.* **82 G8** 39 16N 111 38W
Mantiqueira, Serra da, *Brazil* **95 A7** 22 0S 44 0W
Manton, *U.S.A.* **76 C3** 44 25N 85 24W
Mántova, *Italy* **20 B4** 45 9N 10 48 E
Mänttä, *Finland* **9 E21** 62 0N 24 40 E
Mantua = Mántova, *Italy* **20 B4** 45 9N 10 48 E
Manu, *Peru* **92 F4** 12 10S 70 51W
Manu →, *Peru* **92 F4** 12 16S 70 55W
Manua Is., *Amer. Samoa* **59 B14** 14 13S 169 35W
Manuel Alves →, *Brazil* **93 F9** 11 19S 48 28W
Manui, *Indonesia* **37 E6** 3 35S 123 5 E
Manuripi →, *Bolivia* **92 F5** 11 6S 67 36W
Many, *U.S.A.* **81 K8** 31 34N 93 29W
Manyara, L., *Tanzania* **54 C4** 3 40S 35 50 E
Manych-Gudilo, Ozero, *Russia* **25 E7** 46 24N 42 38 E
Manyonga →, *Tanzania* **54 C3** 4 10S 34 15 E
Manyoni, *Tanzania* **54 D3** 5 45S 34 55 E
Manzai, *Pakistan* **42 C4** 32 12N 70 15 E
Manzanares, *Spain* **19 C4** 39 2N 3 22W
Manzanillo, *Cuba* **88 B4** 20 20N 77 31W
Manzanillo, *Mexico* **86 D4** 19 0N 104 20W
Manzanillo, Pta., *Panama* **88 E4** 9 30N 79 40W
Manzano Mts., *U.S.A.* **83 J10** 34 40N 106 20W
Manzarīyeh, *Iran* **45 C6** 34 53N 50 50 E
Manzhouli, *China* **33 B6** 49 35N 117 25 E
Manzini, *Swaziland* **57 D5** 26 30S 31 25 E
Mao, *Chad* **51 F9** 14 4N 15 19 E
Maó, *Spain* **22 B11** 39 53N 4 16 E
Maoke, Pegunungan, *Indonesia* **37 E9** 3 40S 137 30 E
Maolin, *China* **35 C12** 43 58N 123 30 E
Maoming, *China* **33 D6** 21 50N 110 54 E
Maoxing, *China* **35 B13** 45 28N 124 40 E
Mapam Yumco, *China* **32 C3** 30 45N 81 28 E
Mapastepec, *Mexico* **87 D6** 15 26N 92 54W
Mapia, Kepulauan, *Indonesia* **37 D8** 0 50N 134 20 E
Mapimí, *Mexico* **86 B4** 25 50N 103 50W
Mapimí, Bolsón de, *Mexico* **86 B4** 27 30N 104 15W
Mapinga, *Tanzania* **54 D4** 6 40S 39 12 E
Mapinhane, *Mozam.* **57 C6** 22 20S 35 0 E
Maple Creek, *Canada* **73 D7** 49 55N 109 29W
Maple Valley, *U.S.A.* **84 C4** 47 25N 122 3W
Mapleton, *U.S.A.* **82 D2** 44 2N 123 52W
Mapuera →, *Brazil* **92 D7** 1 5S 57 2W
Maputo, *Mozam.* **57 D5** 25 58S 32 32 E
Maputo, B. de, *Mozam.* **57 D5** 25 50S 32 45 E
Maqiaohe, *China* **35 B16** 44 40N 130 30 E
Maqnā, *Si. Arabia* **44 D2** 28 25N 34 50 E
Maquela do Zombo, *Angola* **52 F3** 6 0S 15 15 E
Maquinchao, *Argentina* **96 E3** 41 15S 68 50W
Maquoketa, *U.S.A.* **80 D9** 42 4N 90 40W
Mar, Serra do, *Brazil* **95 B6** 25 30S 49 0W
Mar Chiquita, L., *Argentina* **94 C3** 30 40S 62 50W
Mar del Plata, *Argentina* **94 D4** 38 0S 57 30W
Mar Menor, *Spain* **19 D5** 37 40N 0 45W
Mara, *Tanzania* **54 C3** 1 30S 34 32 E
Mara □, *Tanzania* **54 C3** 1 45S 34 20 E
Maraã, *Brazil* **92 D5** 1 52S 65 25W
Marabá, *Brazil* **93 E9** 5 20S 49 5W
Maracá, I. de, *Brazil* **93 C8** 2 10N 50 30W
Maracaibo, *Venezuela* **92 A4** 10 40N 71 37W
Maracaibo, L. de, *Venezuela* **92 B4** 9 40N 71 30W
Maracaju, *Brazil* **95 A4** 21 38S 55 9W
Maracay, *Venezuela* **92 A5** 10 15N 67 28W
Maradi, *Niger* **50 F7** 13 29N 7 20 E
Marāgheh, *Iran* **44 B5** 37 30N 46 12 E
Marāh, *Si. Arabia* **44 E5** 25 0N 45 35 E
Marajó, I. de, *Brazil* **93 D9** 1 0S 49 30W
Marākand, *Iran* **44 B5** 38 51N 45 16 E
Maralal, *Kenya* **54 B4** 1 0N 36 38 E
Maralinga, *Australia* **61 F5** 30 13S 131 32 E
Maran, *Malaysia* **39 L4** 3 35N 102 45 E
Marana, *U.S.A.* **83 K8** 32 27N 111 13W
Maranboy, *Australia* **60 B5** 14 40S 132 39 E
Marand, *Iran* **44 B5** 38 30N 45 45 E
Marang, *Malaysia* **39 K4** 5 12N 103 13 E
Maranguape, *Brazil* **93 D11** 3 55S 38 50W
Maranhão = São Luís, *Brazil* **93 D10** 2 39S 44 15W
Maranhão □, *Brazil* **93 E9** 5 0S 46 0W
Maranoa →, *Australia* **63 D4** 27 50S 148 37 E
Marañón →, *Peru* **92 D4** 4 30S 73 35W
Marão, *Mozam.* **57 C5** 24 18S 34 2 E
Maraş = Kahramanmaraş, *Turkey* **25 G6** 37 37N 36 53 E
Marathasa □, *Cyprus* **23 E11** 34 59N 32 51 E
Marathon, *Australia* **62 C3** 20 51S 143 32 E
Marathon, *Canada* **70 C2** 48 44N 86 23W
Marathon, *N.Y., U.S.A.* **79 D8** 42 26N 76 2W
Marathon, *N.Y., U.S.A.* **79 D8** 42 27N 76 2W
Marathon, *Tex., U.S.A.* **81 K3** 30 12N 103 15W
Marathóvouno, *Cyprus* **23 D12** 35 13N 33 37 E
Maratua, *Indonesia* **37 D5** 2 10N 118 35 E
Maravatío, *Mexico* **86 D4** 19 51N 100 25W
Marāwih, *U.A.E.* **45 E7** 24 18N 53 18 E
Marbella, *Spain* **19 D3** 36 30N 4 57W
Marble Bar, *Australia* **60 D2** 21 9S 119 44 E
Marble Falls, *U.S.A.* **81 K5** 30 35N 98 16W
Marblehead, *U.S.A.* **79 D14** 42 30N 70 51W
Marburg, *Germany* **16 C5** 50 47N 8 46 E
March, *U.K.* **11 E8** 52 33N 0 5 E
Marche, *France* **18 C4** 46 5N 1 20 E
Marche-en-Famenne, *Belgium* **15 D5** 50 14N 5 19 E
Marchena, *Spain* **19 D3** 37 18N 5 23W
Marco, *U.S.A.* **77 N5** 25 58N 81 44W
Marcos Juárez, *Argentina* **94 C3** 32 42S 62 5W
Marcus I. = Minami-Tori-Shima, *Pac. Oc.* **64 E7** 24 20N 153 58 E
Marcus Necker Ridge, *Pac. Oc.* **64 F9** 20 0N 175 0 E
Marcy, Mt., *U.S.A.* **79 B11** 44 7N 73 56W
Mardan, *Pakistan* **42 B5** 34 20N 72 0 E
Mardin, *Turkey* **25 G7** 37 20N 40 43 E
Maree, L., *U.K.* **12 D3** 57 40N 5 26W
Mareeba, *Australia* **62 B4** 16 59S 145 28 E
Marek = Stanke Dimitrov, *Bulgaria* **21 C10** 42 17N 23 9 E
Marengo, *U.S.A.* **80 E8** 41 48N 92 4W
Marenyi, *Kenya* **54 C4** 4 22S 39 8 E
Marerano, *Madag.* **57 C7** 21 23S 44 52 E
Marfa, *U.S.A.* **81 K2** 30 19N 104 1W
Marfa Pt., *Malta* **23 D1** 35 59N 14 19 E
Margaret →, *Australia* **60 C4** 18 9S 125 41 E
Margaret Bay, *Canada* **72 C3** 51 20N 127 35W
Margaret L., *Canada* **72 B5** 58 56N 115 25W
Margaret River, *Australia* **61 F2** 33 57S 115 4 E
Margarita, I. de, *Venezuela* **92 A6** 11 0N 64 0W
Margaritovo, *Russia* **30 C7** 43 25N 134 45 E
Margate, *S. Africa* **57 E5** 30 50S 30 20 E
Margate, *U.K.* **11 F9** 51 23N 1 23 E
Marguerite, *Canada* **72 C4** 52 30N 122 25W
Mari El □, *Russia* **24 C8** 56 30N 48 0 E
Mari Indus, *Pakistan* **42 C4** 32 57N 71 34 E
Mari Republic = Mari El □, *Russia* **24 C8** 56 30N 48 0 E
María Elena, *Chile* **94 A2** 22 18S 69 40W
María Grande, *Argentina* **94 C4** 31 45S 59 55W
Maria I., *N. Terr., Australia* **62 A2** 14 52S 135 45 E
Maria I., *Tas., Australia* **62 G4** 42 35S 148 0 E
Maria van Diemen, C., *N.Z.* **59 F4** 34 29S 172 40 E
Mariakani, *Kenya* **54 C4** 3 50S 39 27 E
Marian, *Australia* **62 C4** 21 9S 148 57 E
Marian L., *Canada* **72 A5** 63 0N 116 15W
Mariana Trench, *Pac. Oc.* **28 H18** 13 0N 145 0 E
Marianao, *Cuba* **88 B3** 23 8N 82 24W
Marianna, *Ark., U.S.A.* **81 H9** 34 46N 90 46W
Marianna, *Fla., U.S.A.* **77 K3** 30 46N 85 14W
Marias →, *U.S.A.* **82 C8** 47 56N 110 30W
Mariato, Punta, *Panama* **88 E3** 7 12N 80 52W
Maribor, *Slovenia* **16 E8** 46 36N 15 40 E
Marico →, *Africa* **56 C4** 23 35S 26 57 E
Maricopa, *Ariz., U.S.A.* **83 K7** 33 4N 112 3W
Maricopa, *Calif., U.S.A.* **85 K7** 35 4N 119 24W
Marié →, *Brazil* **92 D5** 0 27S 66 26W
Marie Byrd Land, *Antarctica* **5 D14** 79 30S 125 0W
Marie-Galante, *Guadeloupe* **89 C7** 15 56N 61 16W
Mariecourt = Kangiqsujuaq, *Canada* **69 B12** 61 30N 72 0W
Mariembourg, *Belgium* **15 D4** 50 6N 4 31 E
Mariental, *Namibia* **56 C2** 24 36S 18 0 E
Marienville, *U.S.A.* **78 E5** 41 28N 79 8W
Mariestad, *Sweden* **9 G15** 58 43N 13 50 E
Marietta, *Ga., U.S.A.* **77 J3** 33 57N 84 33W
Marietta, *Ohio, U.S.A.* **76 F5** 39 25N 81 27W
Marieville, *Canada* **79 A11** 45 26N 73 10W
Mariinsk, *Russia* **26 D9** 56 10N 87 20 E
Marijampolė, *Lithuania* **9 J20** 54 33N 23 19 E
Marília, *Brazil* **95 A6** 22 13S 50 0W
Marín, *Spain* **19 A1** 42 23N 8 42W
Marina, *U.S.A.* **84 J5** 36 41N 121 48W
Marinduque, *Phil.* **37 B6** 13 25N 122 0 E
Marinette, *U.S.A.* **76 C2** 45 6N 87 38W
Maringá, *Brazil* **95 A5** 23 26S 52 2W
Marion, *Ala., U.S.A.* **77 J2** 32 38N 87 19W
Marion, *Ill., U.S.A.* **81 G10** 37 44N 88 56W
Marion, *Ind., U.S.A.* **76 E3** 40 32N 85 40W
Marion, *Iowa, U.S.A.* **80 D9** 42 2N 91 36W
Marion, *Kans., U.S.A.* **80 F6** 38 21N 97 1W
Marion, *N.C., U.S.A.* **77 H5** 35 41N 82 1W
Marion, *Ohio, U.S.A.* **76 E4** 40 35N 83 8W
Marion, *S.C., U.S.A.* **77 H6** 34 11N 79 24W
Marion, *Va., U.S.A.* **77 G5** 36 50N 81 31W
Marion, L., *U.S.A.* **77 J5** 33 28N 80 10W
Mariposa, *U.S.A.* **84 H7** 37 29N 119 58W
Mariscal Estigarribia, *Paraguay* **94 A3** 22 3S 60 40W
Maritime Alps = Maritimes, Alpes, *Europe* **18 D7** 44 10N 7 10 E
Maritimes, Alpes, *Europe* **18 D7** 44 10N 7 10 E
Maritsa = Évros →, *Bulgaria* **21 D12** 41 40N 26 34 E
Maritsá, *Greece* **23 C10** 36 22N 28 8 E
Mariupol, *Ukraine* **25 E6** 47 5N 37 31 E
Marīvān, *Iran* **44 C5** 35 30N 46 25 E
Marj 'Uyūn, *Lebanon* **47 B4** 33 20N 35 35 E
Markazī □, *Iran* **45 C6** 35 0N 49 30 E
Markdale, *Canada* **78 B4** 44 19N 80 39W
Marked Tree, *U.S.A.* **81 H9** 35 32N 90 25W
Market Drayton, *U.K.* **10 E5** 52 54N 2 29W
Market Harborough, *U.K.* **11 E7** 52 29N 0 55W
Market Rasen, *U.K.* **10 D7** 53 24N 0 20W
Markham, *Canada* **78 C5** 43 52N 79 16W
Markham, Mt., *Antarctica* **5 E11** 83 0S 164 0 E
Markleeville, *U.S.A.* **84 G7** 38 42N 119 47W
Markovo, *Russia* **27 C17** 64 40N 170 24 E
Marks, *Russia* **24 D8** 51 45N 46 50 E
Marksville, *U.S.A.* **81 K8** 31 8N 92 4W
Marla, *Australia* **63 D1** 27 19S 133 33 E
Marlbank, *Canada* **78 B7** 44 26N 77 6W
Marlboro, *Mass., U.S.A.* **79 D13** 42 19N 71 33W
Marlboro, *N.Y., U.S.A.* **79 E11** 41 36N 73 59W
Marlborough, *Australia* **62 C4** 22 46S 149 52 E
Marlborough, *U.K.* **11 F6** 51 25N 1 43W
Marlborough Downs, *U.K.* **11 F6** 51 27N 1 53W
Marlin, *U.S.A.* **81 K6** 31 18N 96 54W
Marlow, *U.S.A.* **81 H6** 34 39N 97 58W
Marmagao, *India* **40 M8** 15 25N 73 56 E
Marmara, *Turkey* **21 D12** 40 35N 27 38 E

Mehndawal

Marmara, Sea of = Marmara Denizi, *Turkey* **21 D13** 40 45N 28 15 E
Marmara Denizi, *Turkey* **21 D13** 40 45N 28 15 E
Marmaris, *Turkey* **21 F13** 36 50N 28 14 E
Marmion, Mt., *Australia* **61 E2** 29 16S 119 50 E
Marmion L., *Canada* **70 C1** 48 55N 91 20W
Marmolada, Mte., *Italy* **20 A4** 46 26N 11 51 E
Marmora, *Canada* **78 B7** 44 28N 77 41W
Marne →, *France* **18 B5** 48 48N 2 24 E
Maroala, *Madag.* **57 B8** 15 23S 47 59 E
Maroantsetra, *Madag.* **57 B8** 15 26S 49 44 E
Maromandia, *Madag.* **57 A8** 14 13S 48 5 E
Marondera, *Zimbabwe* **55 F3** 18 5S 31 42 E
Maroni →, *Fr. Guiana* **93 B8** 5 30N 54 0W
Maroochydore, *Australia* **63 D5** 26 29S 153 5 E
Maroona, *Australia* **63 F3** 37 27S 142 54 E
Marosakoa, *Madag.* **57 B8** 15 26S 46 38 E
Maroua, *Cameroon* **51 F8** 10 40N 14 20 E
Marovoay, *Madag.* **57 B8** 16 6S 46 39 E
Marquard, *S. Africa* **56 D4** 28 40S 27 28 E
Marquesas Is. = Marquises, Is., *Pac. Oc.* **65 H14** 9 30S 140 0W
Marquette, *U.S.A.* **76 B2** 46 33N 87 24W
Marquises, Is., *Pac. Oc.* **65 H14** 9 30S 140 0W
Marra, Djebel, *Sudan* **51 F10** 13 10N 24 22 E
Marracuene, *Mozam.* **57 D5** 25 45S 32 35 E
Marrakech, *Morocco* **50 B4** 31 9N 8 0W
Marrawah, *Australia* **62 G3** 40 55S 144 42 E
Marree, *Australia* **63 D2** 29 39S 138 1 E
Marrero, *U.S.A.* **81 L9** 29 54N 90 6W
Marrimane, *Mozam.* **57 C5** 22 58S 33 34 E
Marromeu, *Mozam.* **57 B6** 18 15S 36 25 E
Marrowie Cr. →, *Australia* **63 E4** 33 23S 145 40 E
Marrubane, *Mozam.* **55 F4** 18 0S 37 0 E
Marrupa, *Mozam.* **55 E4** 13 8S 37 30 E
Mars Hill, *U.S.A.* **77 B12** 46 31N 67 52W
Marsá Matrûh, *Egypt* **51 B11** 31 19N 27 9 E
Marsabit, *Kenya* **54 B4** 2 18N 38 0 E
Marsala, *Italy* **20 F5** 37 48N 12 26 E
Marsalforn, *Malta* **23 C1** 36 4N 14 15 E
Marsden, *Australia* **63 E4** 33 47S 147 32 E
Marseille, *France* **18 E6** 43 18N 5 23 E
Marseilles = Marseille, *France* **18 E6** 43 18N 5 23 E
Marsh I., *U.S.A.* **81 L9** 29 34N 91 53W
Marshall, *Ark., U.S.A.* **81 H8** 35 55N 92 38W
Marshall, *Mich., U.S.A.* **76 D3** 42 16N 84 58W
Marshall, *Minn., U.S.A.* **80 C7** 44 25N 95 45W
Marshall, *Mo., U.S.A.* **80 F8** 39 7N 93 12W
Marshall, *Tex., U.S.A.* **81 J7** 32 33N 94 23W
Marshall →, *Australia* **62 C2** 22 59S 136 59 E
Marshall Is. ■, *Pac. Oc.* **64 G9** 9 0N 171 0 E
Marshalltown, *U.S.A.* **80 D8** 42 3N 92 55W
Marshfield, *Mo., U.S.A.* **81 G8** 37 15N 92 54W
Marshfield, *Vt., U.S.A.* **79 B12** 44 20N 72 20W
Marshfield, *Wis., U.S.A.* **80 C9** 44 40N 90 10W
Marshūn, *Iran* **45 B6** 36 19N 49 23 E
Märsta, *Sweden* **9 G17** 59 37N 17 52 E
Mart, *U.S.A.* **81 K6** 31 33N 96 50W
Martaban, *Burma* **41 L20** 16 30N 97 35 E
Martaban, G. of, *Burma* **41 L20** 16 5N 96 30 E
Martapura, *Kalimantan, Indonesia* **36 E4** 3 22S 114 47 E
Martapura, *Sumatera, Indonesia* **36 E2** 4 19S 104 22 E
Martelange, *Belgium* **15 E5** 49 49N 5 43 E
Martha's Vineyard, *U.S.A.* **79 E14** 41 25N 70 38W
Martigny, *Switz.* **18 C7** 46 6N 7 3 E
Martigues, *France* **18 E6** 43 24N 5 4 E
Martin, *Slovak Rep.* **17 D10** 49 6N 18 58 E
Martin, *S. Dak., U.S.A.* **80 D4** 43 11N 101 44W
Martin, *Tenn., U.S.A.* **81 G10** 36 21N 88 51W
Martin L., *U.S.A.* **77 J3** 32 41N 85 55W
Martina Franca, *Italy* **20 D7** 40 42N 17 20 E
Martinborough, *N.Z.* **59 J5** 41 14S 175 29 E
Martinez, *Calif., U.S.A.* **84 G4** 38 1N 122 8W
Martinez, *Ga., U.S.A.* **77 J4** 33 31N 82 4W
Martinique ■, *W. Indies* **89 D7** 14 40N 61 0W
Martinique Passage, *W. Indies* **89 C7** 15 15N 61 0W
Martinópolis, *Brazil* **95 A5** 22 11S 51 12W
Martins Ferry, *U.S.A.* **78 F4** 40 6N 80 44W
Martinsburg, *Pa., U.S.A.* **78 F6** 40 19N 78 20W
Martinsburg, *W. Va., U.S.A.* **76 F7** 39 27N 77 58W
Martinsville, *Ind., U.S.A.* **76 F2** 39 26N 86 25W
Martinsville, *Va., U.S.A.* **77 G6** 36 41N 79 52W
Marton, *N.Z.* **59 J5** 40 4S 175 23 E
Martos, *Spain* **19 D4** 37 44N 3 58W
Marudi, *Malaysia* **36 D4** 4 11N 114 19 E
Ma'ruf, *Afghan.* **40 D5** 31 30N 67 6 E
Marugame, *Japan* **31 G6** 34 15N 133 40 E
Marunga, *Angola* **56 B3** 17 28S 20 2 E
Marungu, Mts., *Dem. Rep. of the Congo* **54 D3** 7 30S 30 0 E
Marv Dasht, *Iran* **45 D7** 29 50N 52 40 E
Marvast, *Iran* **45 D7** 30 30N 54 15 E
Marvel Loch, *Australia* **61 F2** 31 28S 119 29 E
Marwar, *India* **42 G5** 25 43N 73 45 E
Mary, *Turkmenistan* **26 F7** 37 40N 61 50 E
Maryborough = Port Laoise, *Ireland* **13 C4** 53 2N 7 18W
Maryborough, *Queens., Australia* **63 D5** 25 31S 152 37 E
Maryborough, *Vic., Australia* **63 F3** 37 0S 143 44 E
Maryfield, *Canada* **73 D8** 49 50N 101 35W
Maryland □, *U.S.A.* **76 F7** 39 0N 76 30W
Maryland Junction, *Zimbabwe* **55 F3** 17 45S 30 31 E
Maryport, *U.K.* **10 C4** 54 44N 3 28W
Mary's Harbour, *Canada* **71 B8** 52 18N 55 51W
Marystown, *Canada* **71 C8** 47 10N 55 10W
Marysville, *Canada* **72 D5** 49 35N 116 0W
Marysville, *Calif., U.S.A.* **84 F5** 39 9N 121 35W
Marysville, *Kans., U.S.A.* **80 F6** 39 51N 96 39W
Marysville, *Mich., U.S.A.* **78 D2** 42 54N 82 29W
Marysville, *Ohio, U.S.A.* **76 E4** 40 14N 83 22W
Marysville, *Wash., U.S.A.* **84 B4** 48 3N 122 11W
Maryville, *Mo., U.S.A.* **80 E7** 40 21N 94 52W
Maryville, *Tenn., U.S.A.* **77 H4** 35 46N 83 58W
Marzūq, *Libya* **51 C8** 25 53N 13 57 E
Masahunga, *Tanzania* **54 C3** 2 6S 33 18 E
Masai Steppe, *Tanzania* **54 C4** 4 30S 36 30 E
Masaka, *Uganda* **54 C3** 0 21S 31 45 E
Masalembo, Kepulauan, *Indonesia* **36 F4** 5 35S 114 30 E
Masalima, Kepulauan, *Indonesia* **36 F5** 5 4S 117 5 E
Masamba, *Indonesia* **37 E6** 2 30S 120 15 E
Masan, *S. Korea* **35 G15** 35 11N 128 32 E
Masandam, Ra's, *Oman* **45 E8** 26 30N 56 30 E
Masasi, *Tanzania* **55 E4** 10 45S 38 52 E
Masaya, *Nic.* **88 D2** 12 0N 86 7W
Masbate, *Phil.* **37 B6** 12 21N 123 36 E
Mascara, *Algeria* **50 A6** 35 26N 0 6 E
Mascota, *Mexico* **86 C4** 20 30N 104 50W
Masela, *Indonesia* **37 F7** 8 9S 129 51 E
Maseru, *Lesotho* **56 D4** 29 18S 27 30 E
Mashaba, *Zimbabwe* **55 G3** 20 2S 30 29 E
Mashābih, *Si. Arabia* **44 E3** 25 35N 36 30 E
Masherbrum, *Pakistan* **43 B7** 35 38N 76 18 E
Mashhad, *Iran* **45 B8** 36 20N 59 35 E
Mashīz, *Iran* **45 D8** 29 56N 56 37 E
Mashkel, Hamun-i, *Pakistan* **40 E3** 28 20N 62 56 E
Mashki Chāh, *Pakistan* **40 E3** 29 5N 62 30 E
Mashonaland, *Zimbabwe* **53 H6** 16 30S 31 0 E
Mashonaland Central □, *Zimbabwe* **57 B5** 17 30S 31 0 E
Mashonaland East □, *Zimbabwe* **57 B5** 18 0S 32 0 E
Mashonaland West □, *Zimbabwe* **57 B4** 17 30S 29 30 E
Mashrakh, *India* **43 F11** 26 7N 84 48 E
Masindi, *Uganda* **54 B3** 1 40N 31 43 E
Masindi Port, *Uganda* **54 B3** 1 43N 32 2 E
Maşīrah, *Oman* **46 C6** 21 0N 58 50 E
Maşīrah, Khalīj, *Oman* **46 C6** 20 10N 58 10 E
Masisi, *Dem. Rep. of the Congo* **54 C2** 1 23S 28 49 E
Masjed Soleyman, *Iran* **45 D6** 31 55N 49 18 E
Mask, L., *Ireland* **13 C2** 53 36N 9 22W
Maskin, *Oman* **45 F8** 23 30N 56 50 E
Masoala, Tanjon' i, *Madag.* **57 B9** 15 59S 50 13 E
Masoarivo, *Madag.* **57 B7** 19 3S 44 19 E
Masohi = Amahai, *Indonesia* **37 E7** 3 20S 128 55 E
Masomeloka, *Madag.* **57 C8** 20 17S 48 37 E
Mason, *Nev., U.S.A.* **84 G7** 38 56N 119 8W
Mason, *Tex., U.S.A.* **81 K5** 30 45N 99 14W
Mason City, *U.S.A.* **80 D8** 43 9N 93 12W
Maspalomas, *Canary Is.* **22 G4** 27 46N 15 35W
Maspalomas, Pta., *Canary Is.* **22 G4** 27 43N 15 36W
Masqat, *Oman* **46 C6** 23 37N 58 36 E
Massa, *Italy* **18 D9** 44 1N 10 9 E
Massachusetts □, *U.S.A.* **79 D13** 42 30N 72 0W
Massachusetts B., *U.S.A.* **79 D14** 42 20N 70 50W
Massakory, *Chad* **51 F9** 13 0N 15 49 E
Massanella, *Spain* **22 B9** 39 48N 2 51 E
Massangena, *Mozam.* **57 C5** 21 34S 33 0 E
Massango, *Angola* **52 F3** 8 2S 16 21 E
Massawa = Mitsiwa, *Eritrea* **46 D2** 15 35N 39 25 E
Massena, *U.S.A.* **79 B10** 44 56N 74 54W
Massénya, *Chad* **51 F9** 11 21N 16 9 E
Masset, *Canada* **72 C2** 54 2N 132 10W
Massif Central, *France* **18 D5** 44 55N 3 0 E
Massillon, *U.S.A.* **78 F3** 40 48N 81 32W
Massinga, *Mozam.* **57 C6** 23 15S 35 22 E
Masson, *Canada* **79 A9** 45 32N 75 25W
Masson I., *Antarctica* **5 C7** 66 10S 93 20 E
Mastanli = Momchilgrad, *Bulgaria* **21 D11** 41 33N 25 23 E
Masterton, *N.Z.* **59 J5** 40 56S 175 39 E
Mastic, *U.S.A.* **79 F12** 40 47N 72 54W
Mastuj, *Pakistan* **43 A5** 36 20N 72 36 E
Mastung, *Pakistan* **40 E5** 29 50N 66 56 E
Masty, *Belarus* **17 B13** 53 27N 24 38 E
Masuda, *Japan* **31 G5** 34 40N 131 51 E
Masvingo, *Zimbabwe* **55 G3** 20 8S 30 49 E
Masvingo □, *Zimbabwe* **55 G3** 21 0S 31 30 E
Maşyāf, *Syria* **44 C3** 35 4N 36 20 E
Matabeleland, *Zimbabwe* **53 H5** 18 0S 27 0 E
Matabeleland North □, *Zimbabwe* **55 F2** 19 0S 28 0 E
Matabeleland South □, *Zimbabwe* **55 G2** 21 0S 29 0 E
Matachewan, *Canada* **70 C3** 47 56N 80 39W
Matadi, *Dem. Rep. of the Congo* **52 F2** 5 52S 13 31 E
Matagalpa, *Nic.* **88 D2** 13 0N 85 58W
Matagami, *Canada* **70 C4** 49 45N 77 34W
Matagami, L., *Canada* **70 C4** 49 50N 77 40W
Matagorda B., *U.S.A.* **81 L6** 28 40N 96 0W
Matagorda I., *U.S.A.* **81 L6** 28 15N 96 30W
Matak, *Indonesia* **39 L6** 3 18N 106 16 E
Mátala, *Greece* **23 E6** 34 59N 24 45 E
Matam, *Senegal* **50 E3** 15 34N 13 17W
Matamoros, *Campeche, Mexico* **87 D6** 18 50N 90 50W
Matamoros, *Coahuila, Mexico* **86 B4** 25 33N 103 15W
Matamoros, *Tamaulipas, Mexico* **87 B5** 25 50N 97 30W
Ma'ṭan as Sarra, *Libya* **51 D10** 21 45N 22 0 E
Matandu →, *Tanzania* **55 D3** 8 45S 34 19 E
Matane, *Canada* **71 C6** 48 50N 67 33W
Matanomadh, *India* **42 H3** 23 33N 68 57 E
Matanzas, *Cuba* **88 B3** 23 0N 81 40W
Matapan, C. = Tainaron, Ákra, *Greece* **21 F10** 36 22N 22 27 E
Matapédia, *Canada* **71 C6** 48 0N 66 59W
Matara, *Sri Lanka* **40 S12** 5 58N 80 30 E
Mataram, *Indonesia* **36 F5** 8 41S 116 10 E
Matarani, *Peru* **92 G4** 17 0S 72 10W
Mataranka, *Australia* **60 B5** 14 55S 133 4 E
Matarma, Râs, *Egypt* **47 E1** 30 27N 32 44 E
Mataró, *Spain* **19 B7** 41 32N 2 29 E
Matatiele, *S. Africa* **57 E4** 30 20S 28 49 E
Mataura, *N.Z.* **59 M2** 46 11S 168 51 E
Matehuala, *Mexico* **86 C4** 23 40N 100 40W
Mateke Hills, *Zimbabwe* **55 G3** 21 48S 31 0 E
Matera, *Italy* **20 D7** 40 40N 16 36 E
Matetsi, *Zimbabwe* **55 F2** 18 12S 26 0 E
Mathis, *U.S.A.* **81 L6** 28 6N 97 50W
Mathráki, *Greece* **23 A3** 39 48N 19 31 E
Mathura, *India* **42 F7** 27 30N 77 40 E
Mati, *Phil.* **37 C7** 6 55N 126 15 E
Matiali, *India* **43 F13** 26 56N 88 49 E
Matías Romero, *Mexico* **87 D5** 16 53N 95 2W
Matibane, *Mozam.* **55 E5** 14 49S 40 45 E
Matima, *Botswana* **56 C3** 20 15S 24 26 E
Matiri Ra., *N.Z.* **59 J4** 41 38S 172 20 E
Matla →, *India* **43 J13** 21 40N 88 40 E
Matli, *Pakistan* **42 G3** 25 2N 68 39 E
Matlock, *U.K.* **10 D6** 53 9N 1 33W
Mato Grosso □, *Brazil* **93 F8** 14 0S 55 0W
Mato Grosso, Planalto do, *Brazil* **93 G8** 15 0S 55 0W
Mato Grosso do Sul □, *Brazil* **93 G8** 18 0S 55 0W
Matochkin Shar, *Russia* **26 B6** 73 10N 56 40 E
Matopo Hills, *Zimbabwe* **55 G2** 20 36S 28 20 E
Matopos, *Zimbabwe* **55 G2** 20 20S 28 29 E
Matosinhos, *Portugal* **19 B1** 41 11N 8 42W
Maţraḩ, *Oman* **46 C6** 23 37N 58 30 E
Matsue, *Japan* **31 G6** 35 25N 133 10 E
Matsumae, *Japan* **30 D10** 41 26N 140 7 E
Matsumoto, *Japan* **31 F9** 36 15N 138 0 E
Matsusaka, *Japan* **31 G8** 34 34N 136 32 E
Matsutō, *Japan* **31 F8** 36 31N 136 34 E
Matsuura, *Japan* **31 H4** 33 20N 129 49 E
Matsuyama, *Japan* **31 H6** 33 45N 132 45 E
Mattagami →, *Canada* **70 B3** 50 43N 81 29W
Mattancheri, *India* **40 Q10** 9 50N 76 15 E
Mattawa, *Canada* **70 C4** 46 20N 78 45W
Matterhorn, *Switz.* **18 D7** 45 58N 7 39 E
Matthew Town, *Bahamas* **89 B5** 20 57N 73 40W
Matthew's Ridge, *Guyana* **92 B6** 7 37N 60 10W
Mattice, *Canada* **70 C3** 49 40N 83 20W
Mattituck, *U.S.A.* **79 F12** 40 59N 72 32W
Mattoon, *U.S.A.* **76 F1** 39 29N 88 23W
Matuba, *Mozam.* **57 C5** 24 28S 32 49 E
Matucana, *Peru* **92 F3** 11 55S 76 25W
Matūn = Khowst, *Afghan.* **42 C3** 33 22N 69 58 E
Maturín, *Venezuela* **92 B6** 9 45N 63 11W
Mau, *India* **43 G10** 25 56N 83 33 E
Mau, *Mad. P., India* **43 F8** 26 17N 78 41 E
Mau, *Ut. P., India* **43 G9** 25 17N 81 23 E
Mau Escarpment, *Kenya* **54 C4** 0 40S 36 0 E
Mau Ranipur, *India* **43 G8** 25 16N 79 8 E
Maubeuge, *France* **18 A6** 50 17N 3 57 E
Maud, Pt., *Australia* **60 D1** 23 6S 113 45 E
Maude, *Australia* **63 E3** 34 29S 144 18 E
Maudin Sun, *Burma* **41 M19** 16 0N 94 30 E
Maués, *Brazil* **92 D7** 3 20S 57 45W
Mauganj, *India* **41 G12** 24 50N 81 55 E
Maughold Hd., *U.K.* **10 C3** 54 18N 4 18W
Maui, *U.S.A.* **74 H16** 20 48N 156 20W
Maulamyaing = Moulmein, *Burma* **41 L20** 16 30N 97 40 E
Maule □, *Chile* **94 D1** 36 5S 72 30W
Maumee, *U.S.A.* **76 E4** 41 34N 83 39W
Maumee →, *U.S.A.* **76 E4** 41 42N 83 28W
Maumere, *Indonesia* **37 F6** 8 38S 122 13 E
Maun, *Botswana* **56 C3** 20 0S 23 26 E
Mauna Kea, *U.S.A.* **74 J17** 19 50N 155 28W
Mauna Loa, *U.S.A.* **74 J17** 19 30N 155 35W
Maungmagan Is., *Burma* **38 F1** 14 0N 97 30 E
Maungmagan Kyunzu, *Burma* **41 N20** 14 0N 97 48 E
Maupin, *U.S.A.* **82 D3** 45 11N 121 5W
Maurepas, L., *U.S.A.* **81 K9** 30 15N 90 30W
Maurice, L., *Australia* **61 E5** 29 30S 131 0 E
Mauricie, Parc Nat. de la, *Canada* **70 C5** 46 45N 73 0W
Mauritania ■, *Africa* **50 E3** 20 50N 10 0W
Mauritius ■, *Ind. Oc.* **49 J9** 20 0S 57 0 E
Mauston, *U.S.A.* **80 D9** 43 48N 90 5W
Mavli, *India* **42 G5** 24 45N 73 55 E
Mavuradonha Mts., *Zimbabwe* **55 F3** 16 30S 31 30 E
Mawa, *Dem. Rep. of the Congo* **54 B2** 2 45N 26 40 E
Mawai, *India* **43 H9** 22 30N 81 4 E
Mawana, *India* **42 E7** 29 6N 77 58 E
Mawand, *Pakistan* **42 E3** 29 33N 68 38 E
Mawk Mai, *Burma* **41 J20** 20 14N 97 37 E
Mawlaik, *Burma* **41 H19** 23 40N 94 26 E
Mawqaq, *Si. Arabia* **44 E4** 27 25N 41 8 E
Mawson Coast, *Antarctica* **5 C6** 68 30S 63 0 E
Max, *U.S.A.* **80 B4** 47 49N 101 18W
Maxcanú, *Mexico* **87 C6** 20 40N 92 0W
Maxesibeni, *S. Africa* **57 E4** 30 49S 29 23 E
Maxhamish L., *Canada* **72 B4** 59 50N 123 17W
Maxixe, *Mozam.* **57 C6** 23 54S 35 17 E
Maxville, *Canada* **79 A10** 45 17N 74 51W
Maxwell, *U.S.A.* **84 F4** 39 17N 122 11W
Maxwelton, *Australia* **62 C3** 20 43S 142 41 E
May, C., *U.S.A.* **76 F8** 38 56N 74 58W
May Pen, *Jamaica* **88 C4** 17 58N 77 15W
Maya →, *Russia* **27 D14** 60 28N 134 28 E
Maya Mts., *Belize* **87 D7** 16 30N 89 0W
Mayaguana, *Bahamas* **89 B5** 22 30N 72 44W
Mayagüez, *Puerto Rico* **89 C6** 18 12N 67 9W
Mayāmey, *Iran* **45 B7** 36 24N 55 42 E
Mayanup, *Australia* **61 F2** 33 57S 116 27 E
Mayapan, *Mexico* **87 C7** 20 30N 89 25W
Mayarí, *Cuba* **89 B4** 20 40N 75 41W
Maybell, *U.S.A.* **82 F9** 40 31N 108 5W
Maybole, *U.K.* **12 F4** 55 21N 4 42W
Maydān, *Iraq* **44 C5** 34 55N 45 37 E
Maydena, *Australia* **62 G4** 42 45S 146 30 E
Mayenne →, *France* **18 C3** 47 30N 0 32W
Mayer, *U.S.A.* **83 J7** 34 24N 112 14W
Mayerthorpe, *Canada* **72 C5** 53 57N 115 8W
Mayfield, *Ky., U.S.A.* **77 G1** 36 44N 88 38W
Mayfield, *N.Y., U.S.A.* **79 C10** 43 6N 74 16W
Mayhill, *U.S.A.* **83 K11** 32 53N 105 29W
Maykop, *Russia* **25 F7** 44 35N 40 10 E
Maymyo, *Burma* **38 A1** 22 2N 96 28 E
Maynard, *Mass., U.S.A.* **79 D13** 42 26N 71 27W
Maynard, *Wash., U.S.A.* **84 C4** 47 59N 122 55W
Maynard Hills, *Australia* **61 E2** 28 28S 119 49 E
Mayne →, *Australia* **62 C3** 23 40S 141 55 E
Maynooth, *Ireland* **13 C5** 53 23N 6 34W
Mayo, *Canada* **68 B6** 63 38N 135 57W
Mayo □, *Ireland* **13 C2** 53 53N 9 3W
Mayon Volcano, *Phil.* **37 B6** 13 15N 123 41 E
Mayor I., *N.Z.* **59 G6** 37 16S 176 17 E
Mayotte, I., *Mayotte* **53 G9** 12 50S 45 10 E
Maysville, *U.S.A.* **76 F4** 38 39N 83 46W
Mayu, *Indonesia* **37 D7** 1 30N 126 30 E
Mayumba, *Gabon* **52 E2** 3 25S 10 39 E
Mayville, *N. Dak., U.S.A.* **80 B6** 47 30N 97 20W
Mayville, *N.Y., U.S.A.* **78 D5** 42 15N 79 30W
Mayya, *Russia* **27 C14** 61 44N 130 18 E
Mazabuka, *Zambia* **55 F2** 15 52S 27 44 E
Mazagán = El Jadida, *Morocco* **50 B4** 33 11N 8 17W
Mazagão, *Brazil* **93 D8** 0 7S 51 16W
Mazán, *Peru* **92 D4** 3 30S 73 0W
Māzandarān □, *Iran* **45 B7** 36 30N 52 0 E
Mazapil, *Mexico* **86 C4** 24 38N 101 34W
Mazara del Vallo, *Italy* **20 F5** 37 39N 12 35 E
Mazarrón, *Spain* **19 D5** 37 38N 1 19W
Mazaruni →, *Guyana* **92 B7** 6 25N 58 35W
Mazatán, *Mexico* **86 B2** 29 0N 110 8W
Mazatenango, *Guatemala* **88 D1** 14 35N 91 30W
Mazatlán, *Mexico* **86 C3** 23 13N 106 25W
Mažeikiai, *Lithuania* **9 H20** 56 20N 22 20 E
Māzhān, *Iran* **45 C8** 32 30N 59 0 E
Mazīnān, *Iran* **45 B8** 36 19N 56 56 E
Mazoe, *Mozam.* **55 F3** 16 42S 33 7 E
Mazoe →, *Mozam.* **55 F3** 16 20S 33 30 E
Mazowe, *Zimbabwe* **55 F3** 17 28S 30 58 E
Mazurian Lakes = Mazurski, Pojezierze, *Poland* **17 B11** 53 50N 21 0 E
Mazurski, Pojezierze, *Poland* **17 B11** 53 50N 21 0 E
Mazyr, *Belarus* **17 B15** 51 59N 29 15 E
Mbabane, *Swaziland* **57 D5** 26 18S 31 6 E
Mbaïki, *C.A.R.* **52 D3** 3 53N 18 1 E
Mbala, *Zambia* **55 D3** 8 46S 31 24 E
Mbale, *Uganda* **54 B3** 1 8N 34 12 E
Mbalmayo, *Cameroon* **52 D2** 3 33N 11 33 E
Mbamba Bay, *Tanzania* **55 E3** 11 13S 34 49 E
Mbandaka, *Dem. Rep. of the Congo* **52 D3** 0 1N 18 18 E
Mbanza Congo, *Angola* **52 F2** 6 18S 14 16 E
Mbanza Ngungu, *Dem. Rep. of the Congo* **52 F2** 5 12S 14 53 E
Mbarara, *Uganda* **54 C3** 0 35S 30 40 E
Mbashe →, *S. Africa* **57 E4** 32 15S 28 54 E
Mbenkuru →, *Tanzania* **55 D4** 9 25S 39 50 E
Mberengwa, *Zimbabwe* **55 G2** 20 29S 29 57 E
Mberengwa, Mt., *Zimbabwe* **55 G2** 20 37S 29 55 E
Mbesuma, *Zambia* **55 E3** 10 0S 32 2 E
Mbeya, *Tanzania* **55 D3** 8 54S 33 29 E
Mbeya □, *Tanzania* **54 D3** 8 15S 33 30 E
Mbinga, *Tanzania* **55 E4** 10 50S 35 0 E
Mbini □, *Eq. Guin.* **52 D2** 1 30N 10 0 E
Mbour, *Senegal* **50 F2** 14 22N 16 54W
Mbuji-Mayi, *Dem. Rep. of the Congo* **54 D1** 6 9S 23 40 E
Mbulu, *Tanzania* **54 C4** 3 45S 35 30 E
Mburucuyá, *Argentina* **94 B4** 28 1S 58 14W
Mchinja, *Tanzania* **55 D4** 9 44S 39 45 E
Mchinji, *Malawi* **55 E3** 13 47S 32 58 E
Mdantsane, *S. Africa* **53 L5** 32 56S 27 46 E
Mead, L., *U.S.A.* **85 J12** 36 1N 114 44W
Meade, *U.S.A.* **81 G4** 37 17N 100 20W
Meadow Lake, *Canada* **73 C7** 54 10N 108 26W
Meadow Lake Prov. Park, *Canada* **73 C7** 54 27N 109 0W
Meadow Valley Wash →, *U.S.A.* **85 J12** 36 40N 114 34W
Meadville, *U.S.A.* **78 E4** 41 39N 80 9W
Meaford, *Canada* **78 B4** 44 36N 80 35W
Mealy Mts., *Canada* **71 B8** 53 10N 58 0W
Meander River, *Canada* **72 B5** 59 2N 117 42W
Meares, C., *U.S.A.* **82 D2** 45 37N 124 0W
Mearim →, *Brazil* **93 D10** 3 4S 44 35W
Meath □, *Ireland* **13 C5** 53 40N 6 57W
Meath Park, *Canada* **73 C7** 53 27N 105 22W
Meaux, *France* **18 B5** 48 58N 2 50 E
Mebechi-Gawa →, *Japan* **30 D10** 40 31N 141 31 E
Mecanhelas, *Mozam.* **55 F4** 15 12S 35 54 E
Mecca = Makkah, *Si. Arabia* **46 C2** 21 30N 39 54 E
Mecca, *U.S.A.* **85 M10** 33 34N 116 5W
Mechanicsburg, *U.S.A.* **78 F8** 40 13N 77 1W
Mechanicville, *U.S.A.* **79 D11** 42 54N 73 41W
Mechelen, *Belgium* **15 C4** 51 2N 4 29 E
Mecheria, *Algeria* **50 B5** 33 35N 0 18W
Mecklenburg, *Germany* **16 B6** 53 33N 11 40 E
Mecklenburger Bucht, *Germany* **16 A6** 54 20N 11 40 E
Meconta, *Mozam.* **55 E4** 14 59S 39 50 E
Medan, *Indonesia* **36 D1** 3 40N 98 38 E
Medanosa, Pta., *Argentina* **96 F3** 48 8S 66 0W
Médéa, *Algeria* **50 A6** 36 12N 2 50 E
Medellín, *Colombia* **92 B3** 6 15N 75 35W
Medelpad, *Sweden* **9 E17** 62 33N 16 30 E
Medemblik, *Neths.* **15 B5** 52 46N 5 8 E
Medford, *Mass., U.S.A.* **79 D13** 42 25N 71 7W
Medford, *Oreg., U.S.A.* **82 E2** 42 19N 122 52W
Medford, *Wis., U.S.A.* **80 C9** 45 9N 90 20W
Medgidia, *Romania* **17 F15** 44 15N 28 19 E
Media Agua, *Argentina* **94 C2** 31 58S 68 25W
Media Luna, *Argentina* **94 C2** 34 45S 66 44W
Medianeira, *Brazil* **95 B5** 25 17S 54 5W
Mediaş, *Romania* **17 E13** 46 9N 24 22 E
Medicine Bow, *U.S.A.* **82 F10** 41 54N 106 12W
Medicine Bow Pk., *U.S.A.* **82 F10** 41 21N 106 19W
Medicine Bow Ra., *U.S.A.* **82 F10** 41 10N 106 25W
Medicine Hat, *Canada* **73 D6** 50 0N 110 45W
Medicine Lake, *U.S.A.* **80 A2** 48 30N 104 30W
Medicine Lodge, *U.S.A.* **81 G5** 37 17N 98 35W
Medina = Al Madīnah, *Si. Arabia* **46 C2** 24 35N 39 52 E
Medina, *N. Dak., U.S.A.* **80 B5** 46 54N 99 18W
Medina, *N.Y., U.S.A.* **78 C6** 43 13N 78 23W
Medina, *Ohio, U.S.A.* **78 E3** 41 8N 81 52W
Medina →, *U.S.A.* **81 L5** 29 16N 98 29W
Medina del Campo, *Spain* **19 B3** 41 18N 4 55W
Medina L., *U.S.A.* **81 L5** 29 32N 98 56W
Medina Sidonia, *Spain* **19 D3** 36 28N 5 57W
Medinipur, *India* **43 H12** 22 25N 87 21 E
Mediterranean Sea, *Europe* **6 H7** 35 0N 15 0 E
Médoc, *France* **18 D3** 45 10N 0 50W
Medveditsa →, *Russia* **25 E7** 49 35N 42 41 E
Medvezhi, Ostrava, *Russia* **27 B17** 71 0N 161 0 E
Medvezhyegorsk, *Russia* **24 B5** 63 0N 34 25 E
Medway →, *U.K.* **11 F8** 51 27N 0 46 E
Medway Towns □, *U.K.* **11 F8** 51 25N 0 32 E
Meekatharra, *Australia* **61 E2** 26 32S 118 29 E
Meeker, *U.S.A.* **82 F10** 40 2N 107 55W
Meelpaeg Res., *Canada* **71 C8** 48 15N 56 33W
Meerut, *India* **42 E7** 29 1N 77 42 E
Meeteetse, *U.S.A.* **82 D9** 44 9N 108 52W
Mega, *Ethiopia* **46 G2** 3 57N 38 19 E
Mégara, *Greece* **21 F10** 37 58N 23 22 E
Megasini, *India* **43 J12** 21 38N 86 21 E
Meghalaya □, *India* **41 G17** 25 50N 91 0 E
Mégiscane, L., *Canada* **70 C4** 48 35N 75 55W
Meharry, Mt., *Australia* **60 D2** 22 59S 118 35 E
Mehlville, *U.S.A.* **80 F9** 38 30N 90 19W
Mehndawal, *India* **43 F10** 26 58N 83 5 E

Montour Falls

Minigwal, L., Australia 61 E3 29 31S 123 14 E
Minilya →, Australia 61 D1 23 45S 114 0 E
Minilya Roadhouse, Australia 61 D1 23 55S 114 0 E
Minipi L., Canada 71 B7 52 25N 60 45W
Mink L., Canada 72 A5 61 54N 117 40W
Minna, Nigeria 50 G7 9 37N 6 30 E
Minneapolis, Kans., U.S.A. 80 F6 39 8N 97 42W
Minneapolis, Minn., U.S.A. 80 C8 44 59N 93 16W
Minnedosa, Canada 73 C9 50 14N 99 50W
Minnesota □, U.S.A. 80 B8 46 0N 94 15W
Minnesota →, U.S.A. 80 C8 44 54N 93 9W
Minnewaukan, U.S.A. 80 A5 48 4N 99 15W
Minnipa, Australia 63 E2 32 51S 135 9 E
Minnitaki L., Canada 70 C1 49 57N 92 10W
Mino, Japan 31 G8 35 32N 136 55 E
Miño →, Spain 19 A2 41 52N 8 40W
Minorca = Menorca, Spain 22 B11 40 0N 4 0 E
Minot, U.S.A. 80 A4 48 14N 101 18W
Minqin, China 34 E2 38 38N 103 20 E
Minsk, Belarus 17 B14 53 52N 27 30 E
Mińsk Mazowiecki, Poland 17 B11 52 10N 21 33 E
Mintabie, Australia 63 D1 27 15S 133 7 E
Mintaka Pass, Pakistan 43 A6 37 0N 74 58 E
Minteke Daban = Mintaka Pass, Pakistan 43 A6 37 0N 74 58 E
Minto, Canada 71 C6 46 5N 66 5W
Minto, L., Canada 70 A5 57 13N 75 0W
Minton, Canada 73 D8 49 10N 104 35W
Minturn, U.S.A. 82 G10 39 35N 106 26W
Minusinsk, Russia 27 D10 53 43N 91 20 E
Minutang, India 41 E20 28 15N 96 30 E
Miquelon, Canada 70 C4 49 25N 76 27W
Miquelon, St- P. & M. 71 C8 47 8N 56 22W
Mīr Kūh, Iran 45 E8 26 22N 58 55 E
Mīr Shahdād, Iran 45 E8 26 15N 58 29 E
Mira, Italy 20 B5 45 26N 12 8 E
Mira por vos Cay, Bahamas 89 B5 22 9N 74 30W
Miraj, India 40 L9 16 50N 74 45 E
Miram Shah, Pakistan 42 C4 33 0N 70 2 E
Miramar, Argentina 94 D4 38 15S 57 50W
Miramar, Mozam. 57 C6 23 50S 35 35 E
Miramichi, Canada 71 C6 47 2N 65 28W
Miramichi B., Canada 71 C7 47 15N 65 0W
Miranda, Brazil 93 H7 20 10S 56 15W
Miranda →, Brazil 92 G7 19 25S 57 20W
Miranda de Ebro, Spain 19 A4 42 41N 2 57W
Miranda do Douro, Portugal 19 B2 41 30N 6 16W
Mirandópolis, Brazil 95 A5 21 9S 51 6W
Mirango, Malawi 55 E3 13 32S 34 58 E
Mirassol, Brazil 95 A6 20 46S 49 28W
Mirbāţ, Oman 46 D5 17 0N 54 45 E
Miri, Malaysia 36 D4 4 23N 113 59 E
Miriam Vale, Australia 62 C5 24 20S 151 33 E
Mirim, L., S. Amer. 95 C5 32 45S 52 50W
Mirnyy, Russia 27 C12 62 33N 113 53 E
Mirokhan, Pakistan 42 F3 27 46N 68 6 E
Mirond L., Canada 73 B8 55 6N 102 47W
Mirpur, Pakistan 43 C5 33 32N 73 56 E
Mirpur Batoro, Pakistan 42 G3 24 44N 68 16 E
Mirpur Bibiwari, Pakistan 42 E2 28 33N 67 44 E
Mirpur Khas, Pakistan 42 G3 25 30N 69 0 E
Mirpur Sakro, Pakistan 42 G2 24 33N 67 41 E
Mirtağ, Turkey 44 B4 38 23N 41 56 E
Miryang, S. Korea 35 G15 35 31N 128 44 E
Mirzapur, India 43 G10 25 10N 82 34 E
Mirzapur-cum-Vindhyachal = Mirzapur, India 43 G10 25 10N 82 34 E
Misantla, Mexico 87 D5 19 56N 96 50W
Misawa, Japan 30 D10 40 41N 141 24 E
Miscou I., Canada 71 C7 47 57N 64 31W
Mish'āb, Ra's al, Si. Arabia 45 D6 28 15N 48 43 E
Mishan, China 33 B8 45 37N 131 48 E
Mishawaka, U.S.A. 76 E2 41 40N 86 11W
Mishima, Japan 31 G9 35 10N 138 52 E
Misión, Mexico 85 N10 32 6N 116 53W
Misiones □, Argentina 95 B5 27 0S 55 0W
Misiones □, Paraguay 94 B4 27 0S 56 0W
Miskah, Si. Arabia 44 E4 24 49N 42 56 E
Miskitos, Cayos, Nic. 88 D3 14 26N 82 50W
Miskolc, Hungary 17 D11 48 7N 20 50 E
Misoke, Dem. Rep. of the Congo 54 C2 0 42S 28 2 E
Misool, Indonesia 37 E8 1 52S 130 10 E
Misrātah, Libya 51 B9 32 24N 15 3 E
Missanabie, Canada 70 C3 48 20N 84 6W
Missinaibi →, Canada 70 B3 50 43N 81 29W
Missinaibi L., Canada 70 C3 48 23N 83 40W
Mission, Canada 72 D4 49 10N 122 15W
Mission, S. Dak., U.S.A. 80 D4 43 18N 100 39W
Mission, Tex., U.S.A. 81 M5 26 13N 98 20W
Mission Beach, Australia 62 B4 17 53S 146 6 E
Mission Viejo, U.S.A. 85 M9 33 36N 117 40W
Missisa L., Canada 70 B2 52 20N 85 7W
Missisicabi →, Canada 70 B4 51 14N 79 31W
Mississagi →, Canada 70 C3 46 15N 83 9W
Mississauga, Canada 78 C5 43 32N 79 35W
Mississippi □, U.S.A. 81 J10 33 0N 90 0W
Mississippi →, U.S.A. 81 L10 29 9N 89 15W
Mississippi L., Canada 79 A8 45 5N 76 10W
Mississippi River Delta, U.S.A. 81 L9 29 10N 89 15W
Mississippi Sd., U.S.A. 81 K10 30 20N 89 0W
Missoula, U.S.A. 82 C7 46 52N 114 1W
Missouri □, U.S.A. 80 F8 38 25N 92 30W
Missouri →, U.S.A. 80 F9 38 49N 90 7W
Missouri City, U.S.A. 81 L7 29 37N 95 32W
Missouri Valley, U.S.A. 80 E7 41 34N 95 53W
Mist, U.S.A. 84 E3 45 59N 123 15W
Mistassibi →, Canada 71 B5 48 53N 72 13W
Mistassini, Canada 71 C5 48 53N 72 12W
Mistassini →, Canada 71 C5 48 42N 72 20W
Mistassini, L., Canada 70 B5 51 0N 73 30W
Mistastin L., Canada 71 A7 55 57N 63 20W
Mistinibi, L., Canada 71 A7 55 56N 64 17W
Misty L., Canada 73 B8 58 53N 101 40W
Misurata = Misrātah, Libya 51 B9 32 24N 15 3 E
Mitchell, Australia 63 D4 26 29S 147 58 E
Mitchell, Canada 78 C3 43 28N 81 12W
Mitchell, Nebr., U.S.A. 80 E3 41 57N 103 49W
Mitchell, Oreg., U.S.A. 82 D3 44 34N 120 9W
Mitchell, S. Dak., U.S.A. 80 D6 43 43N 98 2W
Mitchell →, Australia 62 B3 15 12S 141 35 E
Mitchell, Mt., U.S.A. 77 H4 35 46N 82 16W
Mitchell Ranges, Australia 62 A2 12 49S 135 36 E
Mitchelstown, Ireland 13 D3 52 15N 8 16W
Mitha Tiwana, Pakistan 42 C5 32 13N 72 6 E
Mithi, Pakistan 42 G3 24 44N 69 48 E
Mithrao, Pakistan 42 F3 27 28N 69 40 E
Mitilíni, Greece 21 E12 39 6N 26 35 E
Mito, Japan 31 F10 36 20N 140 30 E
Mitrovica = Kosovska Mitrovica, Serbia, Yug. 21 C9 42 54N 20 52 E
Mitsinjo, Madag. 57 B8 16 1S 45 52 E
Mitsiwa, Eritrea 46 D2 15 35N 39 25 E
Mitsukaidō, Japan 31 F9 36 1N 139 59 E
Mittagong, Australia 63 E5 34 28S 150 29 E
Mitú, Colombia 92 C4 1 15N 70 13W
Mitumba, Tanzania 54 D3 7 8S 31 2 E
Mitumba, Mts., Dem. Rep. of the Congo 54 D2 7 0S 27 30 E
Mitwaba, Dem. Rep. of the Congo 55 D2 8 2S 27 17 E
Mityana, Uganda 54 B3 0 23N 32 2 E
Mixteco →, Mexico 87 D5 18 11N 98 30W
Miyagi □, Japan 30 E10 38 15N 140 45 E
Miyah, W. el →, Syria 44 C3 34 44N 39 57 E
Miyake-Jima, Japan 31 G9 34 5N 139 30 E
Miyako, Japan 30 E10 39 40N 141 59 E
Miyako-Jima, Japan 31 M2 24 45N 125 20 E
Miyako-Rettō, Japan 31 M2 24 24N 125 0 E
Miyakonojō, Japan 31 J5 31 40N 131 5 E
Miyani, India 42 J3 21 50N 69 26 E
Miyanoura-Dake, Japan 31 J5 30 20N 130 31 E
Miyazaki, Japan 31 J5 31 56N 131 30 E
Miyazaki □, Japan 31 H5 32 30N 131 30 E
Miyazu, Japan 31 G7 35 35N 135 10 E
Miyet, Bahr el = Dead Sea, Asia 47 D4 31 30N 35 30 E
Miyoshi, Japan 31 G6 34 48N 132 51 E
Miyun, China 34 D9 40 28N 116 50 E
Miyun Shuiku, China 35 D9 40 30N 117 0 E
Mizdah, Libya 51 B8 31 30N 13 0 E
Mizen Hd., Cork, Ireland 13 E2 51 27N 9 50W
Mizen Hd., Wick., Ireland 13 D5 52 51N 6 4W
Mizhi, China 34 F6 37 47N 110 12 E
Mizoram □, India 41 H18 23 30N 92 40 E
Mizpe Ramon, Israel 47 E3 30 34N 34 49 E
Mizusawa, Japan 30 E10 39 8N 141 8 E
Mjölby, Sweden 9 G16 58 20N 15 10 E
Mjøsa, Norway 9 F14 60 40N 11 0 E
Mkata, Tanzania 54 D4 5 45S 38 20 E
Mkokotoni, Tanzania 54 D4 5 55S 39 15 E
Mkomazi, Tanzania 54 C4 4 40S 38 7 E
Mkomazi →, S. Africa 57 E5 30 12S 30 50 E
Mkulwe, Tanzania 55 D3 8 37S 32 20 E
Mkumbi, Ras, Tanzania 54 D4 7 38S 39 55 E
Mkushi, Zambia 55 E2 14 25S 29 15 E
Mkushi River, Zambia 55 E2 13 32S 29 45 E
Mkuze, S. Africa 57 D5 27 10S 32 0 E
Mladá Boleslav, Czech Rep. 16 C8 50 27N 14 53 E
Mlala Hills, Tanzania 54 D3 6 50S 31 40 E
Mlange = Mulanje, Malawi 55 F4 16 2S 35 33 E
Mlanje, Pic, Malawi 53 H7 15 57S 35 38 E
Mława, Poland 17 B11 53 9N 20 25 E
Mljet, Croatia 20 C7 42 43N 17 30 E
Mmabatho, S. Africa 56 D4 25 49S 25 30 E
Mo i Rana, Norway 8 C16 66 20N 14 7 E
Moa, Cuba 89 B4 20 40N 74 56W
Moa, Indonesia 37 F7 8 0S 128 0 E
Moab, U.S.A. 83 G9 38 35N 109 33W
Moala, Fiji 59 D8 18 36S 179 53 E
Moama, Australia 63 F3 36 7S 144 46 E
Moapa, U.S.A. 85 J12 36 40N 114 37W
Moate, Ireland 13 C4 53 24N 7 44W
Moba, Dem. Rep. of the Congo 54 D2 7 0S 29 48 E
Mobārakābād, Iran 45 D7 28 24N 53 20 E
Mobaye, C.A.R. 52 D4 4 25N 21 5 E
Mobayi, Dem. Rep. of the Congo 52 D4 4 15N 21 8 E
Moberley Lake, Canada 72 B4 55 50N 121 44W
Moberly, U.S.A. 80 F8 39 25N 92 26W
Mobile, U.S.A. 77 K1 30 41N 88 3W
Mobile B., U.S.A. 77 K2 30 30N 88 0W
Mobridge, U.S.A. 80 C4 45 32N 100 26W
Mobutu Sese Seko, L. = Albert L., Africa 54 B3 1 30N 31 0 E
Moc Chau, Vietnam 38 B5 20 50N 104 38 E
Moc Hoa, Vietnam 39 G5 10 46N 105 56 E
Mocabe Kasari, Dem. Rep. of the Congo 55 D2 9 58S 26 12 E
Moçambique, Mozam. 55 F5 15 3S 40 42 E
Moçâmedes = Namibe, Angola 53 H2 15 7S 12 11 E
Mocanaqua, U.S.A. 79 E8 41 9N 76 8W
Mochudi, Botswana 56 C4 24 27S 26 7 E
Mocimboa da Praia, Mozam. 55 E5 11 25S 40 20 E
Moclips, U.S.A. 84 C2 47 14N 124 13W
Mocoa, Colombia 92 C3 1 7N 76 35W
Mococa, Brazil 95 A6 21 28S 47 0W
Mocorito, Mexico 86 B3 25 30N 107 53W
Moctezuma, Mexico 86 B3 29 50N 109 0W
Moctezuma →, Mexico 87 C5 21 59N 98 34W
Mocuba, Mozam. 55 F4 16 54S 36 57 E
Mocúzari, Presa, Mexico 86 B3 27 10N 109 10W
Modane, France 18 D7 45 12N 6 40 E
Modasa, India 42 H5 23 30N 73 21 E
Modder →, S. Africa 56 D3 29 2S 24 37 E
Modderrivier, S. Africa 56 D3 29 2S 24 38 E
Módena, Italy 20 B4 44 40N 10 55 E
Modena, U.S.A. 83 H7 37 48N 113 56W
Modesto, U.S.A. 84 H6 37 39N 121 0W
Módica, Italy 20 F6 36 52N 14 46 E
Moe, Australia 63 F4 38 12S 146 19 E
Moebase, Mozam. 55 F4 17 3S 38 41 E
Moengo, Surinam 93 B8 5 45N 54 20W
Moffat, U.K. 12 F5 55 21N 3 27W
Moga, India 42 D6 30 48N 75 8 E
Mogadishu = Muqdisho, Somali Rep. 46 G4 2 2N 45 25 E
Mogador = Essaouira, Morocco 50 B4 31 32N 9 42W
Mogalakwena →, S. Africa 57 C4 22 38S 28 40 E
Mogami-Gawa →, Japan 30 E10 38 45N 140 0 E
Mogán, Canary Is. 22 G4 27 53N 15 43W
Mogaung, Burma 41 G20 25 20N 97 0 E
Mogi das Cruzes, Brazil 95 A6 23 31S 46 11W
Mogi-Guaçu →, Brazil 95 A6 20 53S 48 10W
Mogi-Mirim, Brazil 95 A6 22 29S 47 0W
Mogilev = Mahilyow, Belarus 17 B16 53 55N 30 18 E
Mogilev-Podolskiy = Mohyliv-Podilskyy, Ukraine 17 D14 48 26N 27 48 E
Mogincual, Mozam. 55 F5 15 35S 40 25 E
Mogocha, Russia 27 D12 53 40N 119 50 E
Mogok, Burma 41 H20 23 0N 96 40 E
Mogollon Rim, U.S.A. 83 J8 34 10N 110 50W
Mogumber, Australia 61 F2 31 2S 116 3 E
Mohács, Hungary 17 F10 45 58N 18 41 E
Mohales Hoek, Lesotho 56 E4 30 7S 27 26 E
Mohall, U.S.A. 80 A4 48 46N 101 31W
Moḩammadābād, Iran 45 B8 37 52N 59 5 E
Mohammedia, Morocco 50 B4 33 44N 7 21W
Mohana →, India 43 G11 24 43N 85 0 E
Mohanlalganj, India 43 F9 26 41N 80 58 E
Mohave, L., U.S.A. 85 K12 35 12N 114 34W
Mohawk →, U.S.A. 79 D11 42 47N 73 41W
Mohenjodaro, Pakistan 42 F3 27 19N 68 7 E
Mohicanville Reservoir, U.S.A. 78 F3 40 45N 82 0W
Mohoro, Tanzania 54 D4 8 6S 39 8 E
Mohyliv-Podilskyy, Ukraine 17 D14 48 26N 27 48 E
Moidart, L., U.K. 12 E3 56 47N 5 52W
Moira →, Canada 78 B7 44 21N 77 24W
Moires, Greece 23 D6 35 4N 24 56 E
Moisaküla, Estonia 9 G21 58 3N 25 12 E
Moisie, Canada 71 B6 50 12N 66 1W
Moisie →, Canada 71 B6 50 14N 66 5W
Mojave, U.S.A. 85 K8 35 3N 118 10W
Mojave Desert, U.S.A. 85 L10 35 0N 116 30W
Mojo, Bolivia 94 A2 21 48S 65 33W
Mojokerto, Indonesia 37 G15 7 28S 112 26 E
Mokai, N.Z. 59 H5 38 32S 175 56 E
Mokambo, Dem. Rep. of the Congo 55 E2 12 25S 28 20 E
Mokameh, India 43 G11 25 24N 85 55 E
Mokelumne →, U.S.A. 84 G5 38 13N 121 28W
Mokelumne Hill, U.S.A. 84 G6 38 18N 120 43W
Mokhós, Greece 23 D7 35 16N 25 27 E
Mokhotlong, Lesotho 57 D4 29 22S 29 2 E
Mokokchung, India 41 F19 26 15N 94 30 E
Mokp'o, S. Korea 35 G14 34 50N 126 25 E
Mokra Gora, Serbia, Yug. 21 C9 42 50N 20 30 E
Mol, Belgium 15 C5 51 11N 5 5 E
Molchanovo, Russia 26 D9 57 40N 83 50 E
Mold, U.K. 10 D4 53 9N 3 8W
Moldavia = Moldova ■, Europe 17 E15 47 0N 28 0 E
Molde, Norway 8 E12 62 45N 7 9 E
Moldova ■, Europe 17 E15 47 0N 28 0 E
Moldoveana, Vf., Romania 17 F13 45 36N 24 45 E
Mole →, U.K. 11 F7 51 24N 0 21W
Mole Creek, Australia 62 G4 41 34S 146 24 E
Molepolole, Botswana 56 C4 24 28S 25 28 E
Molfetta, Italy 20 D7 41 12N 16 36 E
Moline, U.S.A. 80 E9 41 30N 90 31W
Molinos, Argentina 94 B2 25 28S 66 15W
Moliro, Dem. Rep. of the Congo 54 D3 8 12S 30 30 E
Mollendo, Peru 92 G4 17 0S 72 0W
Mollerin, L., Australia 61 F2 30 30S 117 35 E
Molodechno = Maladzyechna, Belarus 17 A14 54 20N 26 50 E
Molokai, U.S.A. 74 H16 21 8N 157 0W
Molong, Australia 63 E4 33 5S 148 54 E
Molopo →, Africa 56 D3 27 30S 20 13 E
Molotov = Perm, Russia 24 C10 58 0N 56 10 E
Molson L., Canada 73 C9 54 22N 96 40W
Molteno, S. Africa 56 E4 31 22S 26 22 E
Molu, Indonesia 37 F8 6 45S 131 40 E
Molucca Sea, Indonesia 37 E6 2 0S 124 0 E
Moluccas = Maluku, Indonesia 37 E7 1 0S 127 0 E
Moma, Dem. Rep. of the Congo 54 C1 1 35S 23 52 E
Moma, Mozam. 55 F4 16 47S 39 4 E
Mombasa, Kenya 54 C4 4 2S 39 43 E
Mombetsu, Japan 30 B11 44 21N 143 22 E
Momchilgrad, Bulgaria 21 D11 41 33N 25 23 E
Momi, Dem. Rep. of the Congo 54 C2 1 42S 27 0 E
Mompós, Colombia 92 B4 9 14N 74 26W
Møn, Denmark 9 J15 54 57N 12 20 E
Mon →, Burma 41 J19 20 25N 94 30 E
Mona, Canal de la, W. Indies 89 C6 18 30N 67 45W
Mona, Isla, Puerto Rico 89 C6 18 5N 67 54W
Mona, Pta., Costa Rica 88 E3 9 37N 82 36W
Monaca, U.S.A. 78 F4 40 41N 80 17W
Monaco ■, Europe 18 E7 43 46N 7 23 E
Monadhliath Mts., U.K. 12 D4 57 10N 4 4W
Monadnock, Mt., U.S.A. 79 D12 42 52N 72 7W
Monaghan, Ireland 13 B5 54 15N 6 57W
Monaghan □, Ireland 13 B5 54 11N 6 56W
Monahans, U.S.A. 81 K3 31 36N 102 54W
Monapo, Mozam. 55 E5 14 56S 40 19 E
Monar, L., U.K. 12 D3 57 26N 5 8W
Monarch Mt., Canada 72 C3 51 55N 125 57W
Monashee Mts., Canada 72 C5 51 0N 118 43W
Monasterevin, Ireland 13 C4 53 8N 7 4W
Monastir = Bitola, Macedonia 21 D9 41 1N 21 20 E
Moncayo, Sierra del, Spain 19 B5 41 48N 1 50W
Monchegorsk, Russia 24 A5 67 54N 32 58 E
Mönchengladbach, Germany 16 C4 51 11N 6 27 E
Monchique, Portugal 19 D1 37 19N 8 38W
Moncks Corner, U.S.A. 77 J5 33 12N 80 1W
Monclova, Mexico 86 B4 26 50N 101 30W
Moncton, Canada 71 C7 46 7N 64 51W
Mondego →, Portugal 19 B1 40 9N 8 52W
Mondeodo, Indonesia 37 E6 3 34S 122 9 E
Mondovì, Italy 18 D7 44 23N 7 49 E
Mondrain I., Australia 61 F3 34 9S 122 14 E
Monessen, U.S.A. 78 F5 40 9N 79 54W
Monett, U.S.A. 81 G8 36 55N 93 55W
Moneymore, U.K. 13 B5 54 41N 6 40W
Monforte de Lemos, Spain 19 A2 42 31N 7 33W
Mong Hsu, Burma 41 J21 21 54N 98 30 E
Mong Kung, Burma 41 J20 21 35N 97 35 E
Mong Nai, Burma 41 J20 20 32N 97 46 E
Mong Pawk, Burma 41 H21 22 4N 99 16 E
Mong Ton, Burma 41 J21 20 17N 98 45 E
Mong Wa, Burma 41 J22 21 26N 100 27 E
Mong Yai, Burma 41 H21 22 21N 98 3 E
Mongalla, Sudan 51 G12 5 8N 31 42 E
Mongers, L., Australia 61 E2 29 25S 117 5 E
Monghyr = Munger, India 43 G12 25 23N 86 30 E
Mongibello = Etna, Italy 20 F6 37 50N 14 55 E
Mongo, Chad 51 F9 12 14N 18 43 E
Mongolia ■, Asia 27 E10 47 0N 103 0 E
Mongu, Zambia 53 H4 15 16S 23 12 E
Môngua, Angola 56 B2 16 43S 15 20 E
Monifieth, U.K. 12 E6 56 30N 2 48W
Monkey Bay, Malawi 55 E4 14 7S 35 1 E
Monkey Mia, Australia 61 E1 25 48S 113 43 E
Monkey River, Belize 87 D7 16 22N 88 29W
Monkoto, Dem. Rep. of the Congo 52 E4 1 38S 20 35 E
Monkton, Canada 78 C3 43 35N 81 5W
Monmouth, U.K. 11 F5 51 48N 2 42W
Monmouth, Ill., U.S.A. 80 E9 40 55N 90 39W
Monmouth, Oreg., U.S.A. 82 D2 44 51N 123 14W
Monmouthshire □, U.K. 11 F5 51 48N 2 54W
Mono L., U.S.A. 84 H7 38 1N 119 1W
Monolith, U.S.A. 85 K8 35 7N 118 22W
Monólithos, Greece 23 C9 36 7N 27 45 E
Monongahela, U.S.A. 78 F5 40 12N 79 56W
Monópoli, Italy 20 D7 40 57N 17 18 E
Monroe, Ga., U.S.A. 77 J4 33 47N 83 43W
Monroe, La., U.S.A. 81 J8 32 30N 92 7W
Monroe, Mich., U.S.A. 76 E4 41 55N 83 24W
Monroe, N.C., U.S.A. 77 H5 34 59N 80 33W
Monroe, N.Y., U.S.A. 79 E10 41 20N 74 11W
Monroe, Utah, U.S.A. 83 G7 38 38N 112 7W
Monroe, Wash., U.S.A. 84 C5 47 51N 121 58W
Monroe, Wis., U.S.A. 80 D10 42 36N 89 38W
Monroe City, U.S.A. 80 F9 39 39N 91 44W
Monroeton, U.S.A. 79 E8 41 43N 76 29W
Monroeville, Ala., U.S.A. 77 K2 31 31N 87 20W
Monroeville, Pa., U.S.A. 78 F5 40 26N 79 45W
Monrovia, Liberia 50 G3 6 18N 10 47W
Mons, Belgium 15 D3 50 27N 3 58 E
Monse, Indonesia 37 E6 4 0S 123 10 E
Mont-de-Marsan, France 18 E3 43 54N 0 31W
Mont-Joli, Canada 71 C6 48 37N 68 10W
Mont-Laurier, Canada 70 C4 46 35N 75 30W
Mont-Louis, Canada 71 C6 49 15N 65 44W
Mont-St-Michel, Le = Le Mont-St-Michel, France 18 B3 48 40N 1 30W
Mont Tremblant, Parc Recr. du, Canada 70 C5 46 30N 74 30W
Montagu, S. Africa 56 E3 33 45S 20 8 E
Montagu I., Antarctica 5 B1 58 25S 26 20W
Montague, Canada 71 C7 46 10N 62 39W
Montague, I., Mexico 86 A2 31 40N 114 56W
Montague Ra., Australia 61 E2 27 15S 119 30 E
Montague Sd., Australia 60 B4 14 28S 125 20 E
Montalbán, Spain 19 B5 40 50N 0 45W
Montalvo, U.S.A. 85 L7 34 15N 119 12W
Montana, Bulgaria 21 C10 43 27N 23 16 E
Montaña, Peru 92 E4 6 0S 73 0W
Montana □, U.S.A. 82 C9 47 0N 110 0W
Montaña Clara, I., Canary Is. 22 E6 29 17N 13 33W
Montargis, France 18 C5 47 59N 2 43 E
Montauban, France 18 D4 44 2N 1 21 E
Montauk, U.S.A. 79 E13 41 3N 71 57W
Montauk Pt., U.S.A. 79 E13 41 4N 71 52W
Montbéliard, France 18 C7 47 31N 6 48 E
Montceau-les-Mines, France 18 C6 46 40N 4 23 E
Montclair, U.S.A. 79 F10 40 49N 74 13W
Monte Albán, Mexico 87 D5 17 2N 96 45W
Monte Alegre, Brazil 93 D8 2 0S 54 0W
Monte Azul, Brazil 93 G10 15 9S 42 53W
Monte Bello Is., Australia 60 D2 20 30S 115 45 E
Monte-Carlo, Monaco 18 E7 43 46N 7 23 E
Monte Caseros, Argentina 94 C4 30 10S 57 50W
Monte Comán, Argentina 94 C2 34 40S 67 53W
Monte Cristi, Dom. Rep. 89 C5 19 52N 71 39W
Monte Lindo →, Paraguay 94 A4 23 56S 57 12W
Monte Patria, Chile 94 C1 30 42S 70 58W
Monte Quemado, Argentina 94 B3 25 53S 62 41W
Monte Rio, U.S.A. 84 G4 38 28N 123 0W
Monte Santu, C. di, Italy 20 D3 40 5N 9 44 E
Monte Vista, U.S.A. 83 H10 37 35N 106 9W
Monteagudo, Argentina 95 B5 27 14S 54 8W
Montebello, Canada 70 C5 45 40N 74 55W
Montecito, U.S.A. 85 L7 34 26N 119 40W
Montecristo, Italy 20 C4 42 20N 10 19 E
Montego Bay, Jamaica 88 C4 18 30N 78 0W
Montélimar, France 18 D6 44 33N 4 45 E
Montello, U.S.A. 80 D10 43 48N 89 20W
Montemorelos, Mexico 87 B5 25 11N 99 42W
Montenegro, Brazil 95 B5 29 39S 51 29W
Montenegro □, Yugoslavia 21 C8 42 40N 19 20 E
Montepuez, Mozam. 55 E4 13 8S 38 59 E
Montepuez →, Mozam. 55 E5 12 32S 40 27 E
Monterey, U.S.A. 84 J5 36 37N 121 55W
Monterey B., U.S.A. 84 J5 36 45N 122 0W
Montería, Colombia 92 B3 8 46N 75 53W
Monteros, Argentina 94 B2 27 11S 65 30W
Monterrey, Mexico 86 B4 25 40N 100 30W
Montes Claros, Brazil 93 G10 16 30S 43 50W
Montesano, U.S.A. 84 D3 46 59N 123 36W
Montesilvano, Italy 20 C6 42 29N 14 8 E
Montevideo, Uruguay 95 C4 34 50S 56 11W
Montevideo, U.S.A. 80 C7 44 57N 95 43W
Montezuma, U.S.A. 80 E8 41 35N 92 32W
Montgomery = Sahiwal, Pakistan 42 D5 30 45N 73 8 E
Montgomery, U.K. 11 E4 52 34N 3 8W
Montgomery, Ala., U.S.A. 77 J2 32 23N 86 19W
Montgomery, Pa., U.S.A. 78 E8 41 10N 76 53W
Montgomery, W. Va., U.S.A. 76 F5 38 11N 81 19W
Montgomery City, U.S.A. 80 F9 38 59N 91 30W
Monticello, Ark., U.S.A. 81 J9 33 38N 91 47W
Monticello, Fla., U.S.A. 77 K4 30 33N 83 52W
Monticello, Ind., U.S.A. 76 E2 40 45N 86 46W
Monticello, Iowa, U.S.A. 80 D9 42 15N 91 12W
Monticello, Ky., U.S.A. 77 G3 36 50N 84 51W
Monticello, Minn., U.S.A. 80 C8 45 18N 93 48W
Monticello, Miss., U.S.A. 81 K9 31 33N 90 7W
Monticello, N.Y., U.S.A. 79 E10 41 39N 74 42W
Monticello, Utah, U.S.A. 83 H9 37 52N 109 21W
Montijo, Portugal 19 C1 38 41N 8 54W
Montilla, Spain 19 D3 37 36N 4 40W
Montluçon, France 18 C5 46 22N 2 36 E
Montmagny, Canada 71 C5 46 58N 70 34W
Montmartre, Canada 73 C8 50 14N 103 27W
Montmorillon, France 18 C4 46 26N 0 50 E
Monto, Australia 62 C5 24 52S 151 6 E
Montoro, Spain 19 C3 38 1N 4 27W
Montour Falls, U.S.A. 78 D8 42 21N 76 51W

Montoursville

Montoursville, *U.S.A.* **78 E8** 41 15N 76 55W
Montpelier, *Idaho, U.S.A.* **82 E8** 42 19N 111 18W
Montpelier, *Vt., U.S.A.* **79 B12** 44 16N 72 35W
Montpellier, *France* **18 E5** 43 37N 3 52 E
Montréal, *Canada* **79 A11** 45 31N 73 34W
Montreal →, *Canada* **70 C3** 47 14N 84 39W
Montreal L., *Canada* **73 C7** 54 20N 105 45W
Montreal Lake, *Canada* **73 C7** 54 3N 105 46W
Montreux, *Switz.* **18 C7** 46 26N 6 55 E
Montrose, *U.K.* **12 E6** 56 44N 2 27W
Montrose, *Colo., U.S.A.* **83 G10** 38 29N 107 53W
Montrose, *Pa., U.S.A.* **79 E9** 41 50N 75 53W
Monts, Pte. des, *Canada* **71 C6** 49 20N 67 12W
Montserrat ■, *W. Indies* **89 C7** 16 40N 62 10W
Montuiri, *Spain* **22 B9** 39 34N 2 59 E
Monywa, *Burma* **41 H19** 22 7N 95 11 E
Monza, *Italy* **18 D8** 45 35N 9 16 E
Monze, *Zambia* **55 F2** 16 17S 27 29 E
Monze, C., *Pakistan* **42 G2** 24 47N 66 37 E
Monzón, *Spain* **19 B6** 41 52N 0 10 E
Mooers, *U.S.A.* **79 B11** 44 58N 73 35W
Mooi River, *S. Africa* **57 D4** 29 13S 29 50 E
Moonah →, *Australia* **62 C2** 22 3S 138 33 E
Moonda, L., *Australia* **63 D3** 25 52S 140 25 E
Moonie, *Australia* **63 D5** 27 46S 150 20 E
Moonie →, *Australia* **63 D4** 29 19S 148 43 E
Moonta, *Australia* **63 E2** 34 6S 137 32 E
Moora, *Australia* **61 F2** 30 37S 115 58 E
Moorcroft, *U.S.A.* **80 C2** 44 16N 104 57W
Moore →, *Australia* **61 F2** 31 22S 115 30 E
Moore, L., *Australia* **61 E2** 29 50S 117 35 E
Moore Park, *Australia* **62 C5** 24 43S 152 17 E
Moore Reefs, *Australia* **62 B4** 16 0S 149 5 E
Moorefield, *U.S.A.* **76 F6** 39 5N 78 59W
Moores Res., *U.S.A.* **79 B13** 44 45N 71 50W
Moorfoot Hills, *U.K.* **12 F5** 55 44N 3 8W
Moorhead, *U.S.A.* **80 B6** 46 53N 96 45W
Moorpark, *U.S.A.* **85 L8** 34 17N 118 53W
Moorreesburg, *S. Africa* **56 E2** 33 6S 18 38 E
Moose →, *Canada* **70 B3** 51 20N 80 25W
Moose →, *U.S.A.* **79 C9** 43 38N 75 24W
Moose Creek, *Canada* **79 A10** 45 15N 74 58W
Moose Factory, *Canada* **70 B3** 51 16N 80 32W
Moose Jaw, *Canada* **73 C7** 50 24N 105 30W
Moose Jaw →, *Canada* **73 C7** 50 34N 105 18W
Moose Lake, *Canada* **73 C8** 53 43N 100 20W
Moose Lake, *U.S.A.* **80 B8** 46 27N 92 46W
Moose Mountain Prov. Park, *Canada* **73 D8** 49 48N 102 25W
Moosehead L., *U.S.A.* **77 C11** 45 38N 69 40W
Mooselookmeguntic L., *U.S.A.* **77 C10** 44 55N 70 49W
Moosilauke, Mt., *U.S.A.* **79 B13** 44 3N 71 40W
Moosomin, *Canada* **73 C8** 50 9N 101 40W
Moosonee, *Canada* **70 B3** 51 17N 80 39W
Moosup, *U.S.A.* **79 E13** 41 43N 71 53W
Mopeia Velha, *Mozam.* **55 F4** 17 30S 35 40 E
Mopipi, *Botswana* **56 C3** 21 6S 24 55 E
Mopoi, *C.A.R.* **54 A2** 5 6N 26 54 E
Mopti, *Mali* **50 F5** 14 30N 4 0W
Moqor, *Afghan.* **42 C2** 32 50N 67 42 E
Moquegua, *Peru* **92 G4** 17 15S 70 46W
Mora, *Sweden* **9 F16** 61 2N 14 38 E
Mora, *Minn., U.S.A.* **80 C8** 45 53N 93 18W
Mora, *N. Mex., U.S.A.* **83 J11** 35 58N 105 20W
Mora →, *U.S.A.* **81 H2** 35 35N 104 25W
Moradabad, *India* **43 E8** 28 50N 78 50 E
Morafenobe, *Madag.* **57 B7** 17 50S 44 53 E
Moramanga, *Madag.* **57 B8** 18 56S 48 12 E
Moran, *Kans., U.S.A.* **81 G7** 37 55N 95 10W
Moran, *Wyo., U.S.A.* **82 E8** 43 53N 110 37W
Moranbah, *Australia* **62 C4** 22 1S 148 1 E
Morant Cays, *Jamaica* **88 C4** 17 22N 76 0W
Morant Pt., *Jamaica* **88 C4** 17 55N 76 12W
Morar, *India* **42 F8** 26 14N 78 14 E
Morar, L., *U.K.* **12 E3** 56 57N 5 40W
Moratuwa, *Sri Lanka* **40 R11** 6 45N 79 55 E
Morava →, *Serbia, Yug.* **21 B9** 44 36N 21 4 E
Morava →, *Slovak Rep.* **17 D9** 48 10N 16 59 E
Moravia, *U.S.A.* **79 D8** 42 43N 76 25W
Moravian Hts. = Českomoravská Vrchovina, *Czech Rep.* **16 D8** 49 30N 15 40 E
Morawa, *Australia* **61 E2** 29 13S 116 0 E
Morawhanna, *Guyana* **92 B7** 8 30N 59 40W
Moray □, *U.K.* **12 D5** 57 31N 3 18W
Moray Firth, *U.K.* **12 D5** 57 40N 3 52W
Morbi, *India* **42 H4** 22 50N 70 42 E
Morden, *Canada* **73 D9** 49 15N 98 10W
Mordovian Republic = Mordvinia □, *Russia* **24 D7** 54 20N 44 30 E
Mordvinia □, *Russia* **24 D7** 54 20N 44 30 E
Morea, *Greece* **6 H10** 37 45N 22 10 E
Moreau →, *U.S.A.* **80 C4** 45 18N 100 43W
Morecambe, *U.K.* **10 C5** 54 5N 2 52W
Morecambe B., *U.K.* **10 C5** 54 7N 3 0W
Moree, *Australia* **63 D4** 29 28S 149 54 E
Morehead, *U.S.A.* **76 F4** 38 11N 83 26W
Morehead City, *U.S.A.* **77 H7** 34 43N 76 43W
Morel →, *India* **42 F7** 26 13N 76 36 E
Morelia, *Mexico* **86 D4** 19 42N 101 7W
Morella, *Australia* **62 C3** 23 0S 143 52 E
Morella, *Spain* **19 B5** 40 35N 0 5W
Morelos, *Mexico* **86 B3** 26 42N 107 40W
Morelos □, *Mexico* **87 D5** 18 40N 99 10W
Morena, *India* **42 F8** 26 30N 78 4 E
Morena, Sierra, *Spain* **19 C3** 38 20N 4 0W
Moreno Valley, *U.S.A.* **85 M10** 33 56N 117 15W
Moresby I., *Canada* **72 C2** 52 30N 131 40W
Moreton I., *Australia* **63 D5** 27 10S 153 25 E
Morey, *Spain* **22 B10** 39 44N 3 20 E
Morgan, *U.S.A.* **82 F8** 41 2N 111 41W
Morgan City, *U.S.A.* **81 L9** 29 42N 91 12W
Morgan Hill, *U.S.A.* **84 H5** 37 8N 121 39W
Morganfield, *U.S.A.* **76 G2** 37 41N 87 55W
Morganton, *U.S.A.* **77 H5** 35 45N 81 41W
Morgantown, *U.S.A.* **76 F6** 39 38N 79 57W
Morgenzon, *S. Africa* **57 D4** 26 45S 29 36 E
Morghak, *Iran* **45 D8** 29 7N 57 54 E
Morhar →, *India* **43 G11** 25 29N 85 11 E
Moriarty, *U.S.A.* **83 J10** 34 59N 106 3W
Morice L., *Canada* **72 C3** 53 50N 127 40W
Morinville, *Canada* **72 C6** 53 49N 113 41W
Morioka, *Japan* **30 E10** 39 45N 141 8 E
Moris, *Mexico* **86 B3** 28 8N 108 32W
Morlaix, *France* **18 B2** 48 36N 3 52W
Mornington, *Australia* **63 F4** 38 15S 145 5 E
Mornington, I., *Chile* **96 F1** 49 50S 75 30W
Mornington I., *Australia* **62 B2** 16 30S 139 30 E
Moro, *Pakistan* **42 F2** 26 40N 68 0 E
Moro →, *Pakistan* **42 E2** 29 42N 67 22 E
Moro G., *Phil.* **37 C6** 6 30N 123 0 E
Morocco ■, *N. Afr.* **50 B4** 32 0N 5 50W
Morogoro, *Tanzania* **54 D4** 6 50S 37 40 E
Morogoro □, *Tanzania* **54 D4** 8 0S 37 0 E
Moroleón, *Mexico* **86 C4** 20 8N 101 32W
Morombe, *Madag.* **57 C7** 21 45S 43 22 E
Moron, *Argentina* **94 C4** 34 39S 58 37W
Morón, *Cuba* **88 B4** 22 8N 78 39W
Morón de la Frontera, *Spain* **19 D3** 37 6N 5 28W
Morona →, *Peru* **92 D3** 4 40S 77 10W
Morondava, *Madag.* **57 C7** 20 17S 44 17 E
Morongo Valley, *U.S.A.* **85 L10** 34 3N 116 37W
Moroni, *Comoros Is.* **49 H8** 11 40S 43 16 E
Moroni, *U.S.A.* **82 G8** 39 32N 111 35W
Morotai, *Indonesia* **37 D7** 2 10N 128 30 E
Moroto, *Uganda* **54 B3** 2 28N 34 42 E
Moroto Summit, *Kenya* **54 B3** 2 30N 34 43 E
Morpeth, *U.K.* **10 B6** 55 10N 1 41W
Morphou, *Cyprus* **23 D11** 35 12N 32 59 E
Morphou Bay, *Cyprus* **23 D11** 35 15N 32 50 E
Morrilton, *U.S.A.* **81 H8** 35 9N 92 44W
Morrinhos, *Brazil* **93 G9** 17 45S 49 10W
Morrinsville, *N.Z.* **59 G5** 37 40S 175 32 E
Morris, *Canada* **73 D9** 49 25N 97 22W
Morris, *Minn., U.S.A.* **80 C7** 45 35N 95 55W
Morris, *N.Y., U.S.A.* **79 D9** 42 33N 75 15W
Morris, *Pa., U.S.A.* **78 E7** 41 35N 77 17W
Morris, Mt., *Australia* **61 E5** 26 9S 131 4 E
Morrisburg, *Canada* **79 B9** 44 55N 75 7W
Morristown, *Ariz., U.S.A.* **83 K7** 33 51N 112 37W
Morristown, *N.J., U.S.A.* **79 F10** 40 48N 74 29W
Morristown, *N.Y., U.S.A.* **79 B9** 44 35N 75 39W
Morristown, *Tenn., U.S.A.* **77 G4** 36 13N 83 18W
Morrisville, *N.Y., U.S.A.* **79 D9** 42 53N 75 35W
Morrisville, *Pa., U.S.A.* **79 F10** 40 13N 74 47W
Morrisville, *Vt., U.S.A.* **79 B12** 44 34N 72 36W
Morro, Pta., *Chile* **94 B1** 27 6S 71 0W
Morro Bay, *U.S.A.* **84 K6** 35 22N 120 51W
Morro del Jable, *Canary Is.* **22 F5** 28 3N 14 23W
Morro Jable, Pta. de, *Canary Is.* **22 F5** 28 2N 14 20W
Morrosquillo, G. de, *Colombia* **88 E4** 9 35N 75 40W
Morrumbene, *Mozam.* **57 C6** 23 31S 35 16 E
Morshansk, *Russia* **24 D7** 53 28N 41 50 E
Morteros, *Argentina* **94 C3** 30 50S 62 0W
Mortlach, *Canada* **73 C7** 50 27N 106 4W
Mortlake, *Australia* **63 F3** 38 5S 142 50 E
Morton, *Tex., U.S.A.* **81 J3** 33 44N 102 46W
Morton, *Wash., U.S.A.* **84 D4** 46 34N 122 17W
Morundah, *Australia* **63 E4** 34 57S 146 19 E
Moruya, *Australia* **63 F5** 35 58S 150 3 E
Morvan, *France* **18 C6** 47 5N 4 3 E
Morven, *Australia* **63 D4** 26 22S 147 5 E
Morvern, *U.K.* **12 E3** 56 38N 5 44W
Morwell, *Australia* **63 F4** 38 10S 146 22 E
Morzhovets, Ostrov, *Russia* **24 A7** 66 44N 42 35 E
Moscos Is. = Maungmagan Is., *Burma* **38 F1** 14 0N 97 30 E
Moscow = Moskva, *Russia* **24 C6** 55 45N 37 35 E
Moscow, *Idaho, U.S.A.* **82 C5** 46 44N 117 0W
Moscow, *Pa., U.S.A.* **79 E9** 41 20N 75 31W
Mosel →, *Europe* **18 A7** 50 22N 7 36 E
Moselle = Mosel →, *Europe* **18 A7** 50 22N 7 36 E
Moses Lake, *U.S.A.* **82 C4** 47 8N 119 17W
Mosgiel, *N.Z.* **59 L3** 45 53S 170 21 E
Moshi, *Tanzania* **54 C4** 3 22S 37 18 E
Moshupa, *Botswana* **56 C4** 24 46S 25 29 E
Mosjøen, *Norway* **8 D15** 65 51N 13 12 E
Moskenesøya, *Norway* **8 C15** 67 58N 13 0 E
Moskenstraumen, *Norway* **8 C15** 67 47N 12 45 E
Moskva, *Russia* **24 C6** 55 45N 37 35 E
Mosomane, *Botswana* **56 C4** 24 2S 26 19 E
Moson-magyaróvár, *Hungary* **17 E9** 47 52N 17 18 E
Mosquera, *Colombia* **92 C3** 2 35N 78 24W
Mosquero, *U.S.A.* **81 H3** 35 47N 103 58W
Mosquitia, *Honduras* **88 C3** 15 20N 84 10W
Mosquito Coast = Mosquitia, *Honduras* **88 C3** 15 20N 84 10W
Mosquito Creek L., *U.S.A.* **78 E4** 41 18N 80 46W
Mosquito L., *Canada* **73 A8** 62 35N 103 20W
Mosquitos, G. de los, *Panama* **88 E3** 9 15N 81 10W
Moss, *Norway* **9 G14** 59 27N 10 40 E
Moss Vale, *Australia* **63 E5** 34 32S 150 25 E
Mossbank, *Canada* **73 D7** 49 56N 105 56W
Mossburn, *N.Z.* **59 L2** 45 41S 168 15 E
Mosselbaai, *S. Africa* **56 E3** 34 11S 22 8 E
Mossendjo, *Congo* **52 E2** 2 55S 12 42 E
Mossgiel, *Australia* **63 E3** 33 15S 144 5 E
Mossman, *Australia* **62 B4** 16 21S 145 15 E
Mossoró, *Brazil* **93 E11** 5 10S 37 15W
Mossuril, *Mozam.* **55 E5** 14 58S 40 42 E
Most, *Czech Rep.* **16 C7** 50 31N 13 38 E
Mosta, *Malta* **23 D1** 35 54N 14 24 E
Moştafáābād, *Iran* **45 C7** 33 39N 54 53 E
Mostaganem, *Algeria* **50 A6** 35 54N 0 5 E
Mostar, *Bos.-H.* **21 C7** 43 22N 17 50 E
Mostardas, *Brazil* **95 C5** 31 2S 50 51W
Mostiska = Mostyska, *Ukraine* **17 D12** 49 48N 23 4 E
Mosty = Masty, *Belarus* **17 B13** 53 27N 24 38 E
Mostyska, *Ukraine* **17 D12** 49 48N 23 4 E
Mosul = Al Mawşil, *Iraq* **44 B4** 36 15N 43 5 E
Mosŭlpo, *S. Korea* **35 H14** 33 20N 126 17 E
Motagua →, *Guatemala* **88 C2** 15 44N 88 14W
Motala, *Sweden* **9 G16** 58 32N 15 1 E
Moth, *India* **43 G8** 25 43N 78 57 E
Motherwell, *U.K.* **12 F5** 55 47N 3 58W
Motihari, *India* **43 F11** 26 30N 84 55 E
Motozintla de Mendoza, *Mexico* **87 D6** 15 21N 92 14W
Motril, *Spain* **19 D4** 36 31N 3 37W
Mott, *U.S.A.* **80 B3** 46 23N 102 20W
Motueka, *N.Z.* **59 J4** 41 7S 173 1 E
Motueka →, *N.Z.* **59 J4** 41 5S 173 1 E
Motul, *Mexico* **87 C7** 21 0N 89 20W
Mouchalagane →, *Canada* **71 B6** 50 56N 68 41W
Moúdhros, *Greece* **21 E11** 39 50N 25 18 E
Mouila, *Gabon* **52 E2** 1 50S 11 0 E
Moulamein, *Australia* **63 F3** 35 3S 144 1 E
Moulianá, *Greece* **23 D7** 35 10N 25 59 E
Moulins, *France* **18 C5** 46 35N 3 19 E
Moulmein, *Burma* **41 L20** 16 30N 97 40 E
Moulouya, O. →, *Morocco* **50 B5** 35 5N 2 25W
Moultrie, *U.S.A.* **77 K4** 31 11N 83 47W
Moultrie, L., *U.S.A.* **77 J5** 33 20N 80 5W
Mound City, *Mo., U.S.A.* **80 E7** 40 7N 95 14W
Mound City, *S. Dak., U.S.A.* **80 C4** 45 44N 100 4W
Moundou, *Chad* **51 G9** 8 40N 16 10 E
Moundsville, *U.S.A.* **78 G4** 39 55N 80 44W
Moung, *Cambodia* **38 F4** 12 46N 103 27 E
Mount Airy, *U.S.A.* **77 G5** 36 31N 80 37W
Mount Albert, *Canada* **78 B5** 44 8N 79 19W
Mount Barker, *S. Austral., Australia* **63 F2** 35 5S 138 52 E
Mount Barker, *W. Austral., Australia* **61 F2** 34 38S 117 40 E
Mount Beauty, *Australia* **63 F4** 36 47S 147 10 E
Mount Brydges, *Canada* **78 D3** 42 54N 81 29W
Mount Burr, *Australia* **63 F3** 37 34S 140 26 E
Mount Carmel, *Ill., U.S.A.* **76 F2** 38 25N 87 46W
Mount Carmel, *Pa., U.S.A.* **79 F8** 40 47N 76 24W
Mount Charleston, *U.S.A.* **85 J11** 36 16N 115 37W
Mount Clemens, *U.S.A.* **78 D2** 42 35N 82 53W
Mount Coolon, *Australia* **62 C4** 21 25S 147 25 E
Mount Darwin, *Zimbabwe* **55 F3** 16 47S 31 38 E
Mount Desert I., *U.S.A.* **77 C11** 44 21N 68 20W
Mount Dora, *U.S.A.* **77 L5** 28 48N 81 38W
Mount Edziza Prov. Park, *Canada* **72 B2** 57 30N 130 45W
Mount Fletcher, *S. Africa* **57 E4** 30 40S 28 30 E
Mount Forest, *Canada* **78 C4** 43 59N 80 43W
Mount Gambier, *Australia* **63 F3** 37 50S 140 46 E
Mount Garnet, *Australia* **62 B4** 17 37S 145 6 E
Mount Holly, *U.S.A.* **79 G10** 39 59N 74 47W
Mount Holly Springs, *U.S.A.* **78 F7** 40 7N 77 12W
Mount Hope, *N.S.W., Australia* **63 E4** 32 51S 145 51 E
Mount Hope, *S. Austral., Australia* **63 E2** 34 7S 135 23 E
Mount Isa, *Australia* **62 C2** 20 42S 139 26 E
Mount Jewett, *U.S.A.* **78 E6** 41 44N 78 39W
Mount Kisco, *U.S.A.* **79 E11** 41 12N 73 44W
Mount Laguna, *U.S.A.* **85 N10** 32 52N 116 25W
Mount Larcom, *Australia* **62 C5** 23 48S 150 59 E
Mount Lofty Ra., *Australia* **63 E2** 34 35S 139 5 E
Mount Magnet, *Australia* **61 E2** 28 2S 117 47 E
Mount Maunganui, *N.Z.* **59 G6** 37 40S 176 14 E
Mount Molloy, *Australia* **62 B4** 16 42S 145 20 E
Mount Morgan, *Australia* **62 C5** 23 40S 150 25 E
Mount Morris, *U.S.A.* **78 D7** 42 44N 77 52W
Mount Pearl, *Canada* **71 C9** 47 31N 52 47W
Mount Penn, *U.S.A.* **79 F9** 40 20N 75 54W
Mount Perry, *Australia* **63 D5** 25 13S 151 42 E
Mount Pleasant, *Iowa, U.S.A.* **80 E9** 40 58N 91 33W
Mount Pleasant, *Mich., U.S.A.* **76 D3** 43 36N 84 46W
Mount Pleasant, *Pa., U.S.A.* **78 F5** 40 9N 79 33W
Mount Pleasant, *S.C., U.S.A.* **77 J6** 32 47N 79 52W
Mount Pleasant, *Tenn., U.S.A.* **77 H2** 35 32N 87 12W
Mount Pleasant, *Tex., U.S.A.* **81 J7** 33 9N 94 58W
Mount Pleasant, *Utah, U.S.A.* **82 G8** 39 33N 111 27W
Mount Pocono, *U.S.A.* **79 E9** 41 7N 75 22W
Mount Rainier Nat. Park, *U.S.A.* **84 D5** 46 55N 121 50W
Mount Revelstoke Nat. Park, *Canada* **72 C5** 51 5N 118 30W
Mount Robson Prov. Park, *Canada* **72 C5** 53 0N 119 0W
Mount Shasta, *U.S.A.* **82 F2** 41 19N 122 19W
Mount Signal, *U.S.A.* **85 N11** 32 39N 115 37W
Mount Sterling, *Ill., U.S.A.* **80 F9** 39 59N 90 45W
Mount Sterling, *Ky., U.S.A.* **76 F4** 38 4N 83 56W
Mount Surprise, *Australia* **62 B3** 18 10S 144 17 E
Mount Union, *U.S.A.* **78 F7** 40 23N 77 53W
Mount Upton, *U.S.A.* **79 D9** 42 26N 75 23W
Mount Vernon, *Ill., U.S.A.* **76 F1** 38 19N 88 55W
Mount Vernon, *Ind., U.S.A.* **80 F10** 38 17N 88 57W
Mount Vernon, *N.Y., U.S.A.* **79 F11** 40 55N 73 50W
Mount Vernon, *Ohio, U.S.A.* **78 F2** 40 23N 82 29W
Mount Vernon, *Wash., U.S.A.* **84 B4** 48 25N 122 20W
Mountain Ash, *U.K.* **11 F4** 51 40N 3 23W
Mountain Center, *U.S.A.* **85 M10** 33 42N 116 44W
Mountain City, *Nev., U.S.A.* **82 F6** 41 50N 115 58W
Mountain City, *Tenn., U.S.A.* **77 G5** 36 29N 81 48W
Mountain Dale, *U.S.A.* **79 E10** 41 41N 74 32W
Mountain Grove, *U.S.A.* **81 G8** 37 8N 92 16W
Mountain Home, *Ark., U.S.A.* **81 G8** 36 20N 92 23W
Mountain Home, *Idaho, U.S.A.* **82 E6** 43 8N 115 41W
Mountain Iron, *U.S.A.* **80 B8** 47 32N 92 37W
Mountain Pass, *U.S.A.* **85 K11** 35 29N 115 35W
Mountain View, *Ark., U.S.A.* **81 H8** 35 52N 92 7W
Mountain View, *Calif., U.S.A.* **84 H4** 37 23N 122 5W
Mountain View, *Hawaii, U.S.A.* **74 J17** 19 33N 155 7W
Mountainair, *U.S.A.* **83 J10** 34 31N 106 15W
Mountlake Terrace, *U.S.A.* **84 C4** 47 47N 122 19W
Mountmellick, *Ireland* **13 C4** 53 7N 7 20W
Mountrath, *Ireland* **13 D4** 53 0N 7 28W
Moura, *Australia* **62 C4** 24 35S 149 58 E
Moura, *Brazil* **92 D6** 1 32S 61 38W
Moura, *Portugal* **19 C2** 38 7N 7 30W
Mourdi, Dépression du, *Chad* **51 E10** 18 10N 23 0 E
Mourilyan, *Australia* **62 B4** 17 35S 146 3 E
Mourne →, *U.K.* **13 B4** 54 52N 7 26W
Mourne Mts., *U.K.* **13 B5** 54 10N 6 0W
Mourniaí, *Greece* **23 D6** 35 29N 24 1 E
Mournies = Mourniaí, *Greece* **23 D6** 35 29N 24 1 E
Mouscron, *Belgium* **15 D3** 50 45N 3 12 E
Moussoro, *Chad* **51 F9** 13 41N 16 35 E
Moutohara, *N.Z.* **59 H6** 38 27S 177 32 E
Moutong, *Indonesia* **37 D6** 0 28N 121 13 E
Movas, *Mexico* **86 B3** 28 10N 109 25W
Moville, *Ireland* **13 A4** 55 11N 7 3W
Mowandjum, *Australia* **60 C3** 17 22S 123 40 E
Moy →, *Ireland* **13 B2** 54 8N 9 8W
Moyale, *Kenya* **54 B4** 3 30N 39 0 E
Moyen Atlas, *Morocco* **50 B4** 33 0N 5 0W
Moyne, L. le, *Canada* **71 A6** 56 45N 68 47W
Moyo, *Indonesia* **36 F5** 8 10S 117 40 E
Moyobamba, *Peru* **92 E3** 6 0S 77 0W
Moyyero →, *Russia* **27 C11** 68 44N 103 42 E
Moyynty, *Kazakstan* **26 E8** 47 10N 73 18 E
Mozambique = Moçambique, *Mozam.* **55 F5** 15 3S 40 42 E
Mozambique ■, *Africa* **55 F4** 19 0S 35 0 E
Mozambique Chan., *Africa* **57 B7** 17 30S 42 30 E
Mozdok, *Russia* **25 F7** 43 45N 44 48 E
Mozdūrān, *Iran* **45 B9** 36 9N 60 35 E
Mozhnābād, *Iran* **45 C9** 34 7N 60 6 E
Mozyr = Mazyr, *Belarus* **17 B15** 51 59N 29 15 E
Mpanda, *Tanzania* **54 D3** 6 23S 31 1 E
Mpika, *Zambia* **55 E3** 11 51S 31 25 E
Mpulungu, *Zambia* **55 D3** 8 51S 31 5 E
Mpumalanga, *S. Africa* **57 D5** 29 50S 30 33 E
Mpumalanga □, *S. Africa* **57 B5** 26 0S 30 0 E
Mpwapwa, *Tanzania* **54 D4** 6 23S 36 30 E
Msambansovu, *Zimbabwe* **55 F3** 15 50S 30 3 E
M'sila →, *Algeria* **50 A6** 35 30N 4 29 E
Msoro, *Zambia* **55 E3** 13 35S 31 50 E
Mstislavl = Mstsislaw, *Belarus* **17 A16** 54 0N 31 50 E
Mstsislaw, *Belarus* **17 A16** 54 0N 31 50 E
Mtama, *Tanzania* **55 E4** 10 17S 39 21 E
Mtilikwe →, *Zimbabwe* **55 G3** 21 9S 31 30 E
Mtubatuba, *S. Africa* **57 D5** 28 30S 32 8 E
Mtwara-Mikindani, *Tanzania* **55 E5** 10 20S 40 20 E
Mu Gia, Deo, *Vietnam* **38 D5** 17 40N 105 47 E
Mu Us Shamo, *China* **34 E5** 39 0N 109 0 E
Muang Chiang Rai = Chiang Rai, *Thailand* **38 C2** 19 52N 99 50 E
Muang Khong, *Laos* **36 B3** 14 5N 105 52 E
Muang Khong, *Laos* **38 E5** 14 7N 105 51 E
Muang Lamphun, *Thailand* **38 C2** 18 40N 99 2 E
Muar, *Malaysia* **39 L4** 2 3N 102 34 E
Muarabungo, *Indonesia* **36 E2** 1 28S 102 52 E
Muaraenim, *Indonesia* **36 E2** 3 40S 103 50 E
Muarajuloi, *Indonesia* **36 E4** 0 12S 114 3 E
Muarakaman, *Indonesia* **36 E5** 0 2S 116 45 E
Muaratebo, *Indonesia* **36 E2** 1 30S 102 26 E
Muaratembesi, *Indonesia* **36 E2** 1 42S 103 8 E
Muaratewe, *Indonesia* **36 E4** 0 58S 114 52 E
Mubarakpur, *India* **43 F10** 26 6N 83 18 E
Mubarraz = Al Mubarraz, *Si. Arabia* **45 E6** 25 30N 49 40 E
Mubende, *Uganda* **54 B3** 0 33N 31 22 E
Mubi, *Nigeria* **51 F8** 10 18N 13 16 E
Mubur, Pulau, *Indonesia* **39 L6** 3 20N 106 12 E
Mucajaí →, *Brazil* **92 C6** 2 25N 60 52W
Muchachos, Roque de los, *Canary Is.* **22 F2** 28 44N 17 52W
Muchinga Mts., *Zambia* **55 E3** 11 30S 31 30 E
Muck, *U.K.* **12 E2** 56 50N 6 15W
Muckadilla, *Australia* **63 D4** 26 35S 148 23 E
Mucuri, *Brazil* **93 G11** 18 0S 39 36W
Mucusso, *Angola* **56 B3** 18 1S 21 25 E
Muda, *Canary Is.* **22 F6** 28 34N 13 57W
Mudanjiang, *China* **35 B15** 44 38N 129 30 E
Mudanya, *Turkey* **21 D13** 40 25N 28 50 E
Muddy Cr. →, *U.S.A.* **83 H8** 38 24N 110 42W
Mudgee, *Australia* **63 E4** 32 32S 149 31 E
Mudjatik →, *Canada* **73 B7** 56 1N 107 36W
Muecate, *Mozam.* **55 E4** 14 55S 39 40 E
Mueda, *Mozam.* **55 E4** 11 36S 39 28 E
Mueller Ra., *Australia* **60 C4** 18 18S 126 46 E
Muende, *Mozam.* **55 E3** 14 28S 33 0 E
Muerto, Mar, *Mexico* **87 D6** 16 10N 94 10W
Mufulira, *Zambia* **55 E2** 12 32S 28 15 E
Mufumbiro Range, *Africa* **54 C2** 1 25S 29 30 E
Mughal Sarai, *India* **43 G10** 25 18N 83 7 E
Mughayrā', *Si. Arabia* **44 D3** 29 17N 37 41 E
Mugi, *Japan* **31 H7** 33 40N 134 25 E
Mugila, Mts., *Dem. Rep. of the Congo* **54 D2** 7 0S 28 50 E
Muğla, *Turkey* **21 F13** 37 15N 28 22 E
Mugu, *Nepal* **43 E10** 29 45N 82 30 E
Muhammad, Râs, *Egypt* **44 E2** 27 44N 34 16 E
Muhammad Qol, *Sudan* **51 D13** 20 53N 37 9 E
Muhammadabad, *India* **43 F10** 26 4N 83 25 E
Muhesi →, *Tanzania* **54 D4** 7 0S 35 20 E
Mühlhausen, *Germany* **16 C6** 51 12N 10 27 E
Mühlig Hofmann fjell, *Antarctica* **5 D3** 72 30S 5 0 E
Muhos, *Finland* **8 D22** 64 47N 25 59 E
Muhu, *Estonia* **9 G20** 58 36N 23 11 E
Muhutwe, *Tanzania* **54 C3** 1 35S 31 45 E
Muine Bheag, *Ireland* **13 D5** 52 42N 6 58W
Muir, L., *Australia* **61 F2** 34 30S 116 40 E
Mukacheve, *Ukraine* **17 D12** 48 27N 22 45 E
Mukachevo = Mukacheve, *Ukraine* **17 D12** 48 27N 22 45 E
Mukah, *Malaysia* **36 D4** 2 55N 112 5 E
Mukandwara, *India* **42 G6** 24 49N 75 59 E
Mukdahan, *Thailand* **38 D5** 16 32N 104 43 E
Mukden = Shenyang, *China* **35 D12** 41 48N 123 27 E
Mukerian, *India* **42 D6** 31 57N 75 37 E
Mukhtuya = Lensk, *Russia* **27 C12** 60 48N 114 55 E
Mukinbudin, *Australia* **61 F2** 30 55S 118 5 E
Mukishi, *Dem. Rep. of the Congo* **55 D1** 8 30S 24 44 E
Mukomuko, *Indonesia* **36 E2** 2 30S 101 10 E
Mukomwenze, *Dem. Rep. of the Congo* **54 D2** 6 49S 27 15 E
Muktsar, *India* **42 D6** 30 30N 74 30 E
Mukur = Moqor, *Afghan.* **42 C2** 32 50N 67 42 E
Mukutawa →, *Canada* **73 C9** 53 10N 97 24W
Mukwela, *Zambia* **55 F2** 17 0S 26 40 E
Mula, *Spain* **19 C5** 38 3N 1 33W
Mula →, *Pakistan* **42 F2** 27 57N 67 36 E
Mulange, *Dem. Rep. of the Congo* **54 C2** 3 40S 27 10 E
Mulanje, *Malawi* **55 F4** 16 2S 35 33 E
Mulchén, *Chile* **94 D1** 37 45S 72 20W
Mulde →, *Germany* **16 C7** 51 53N 12 15 E
Mule Creek Junction, *U.S.A.* **80 D2** 43 19N 104 8W
Muleba, *Tanzania* **54 C3** 1 50S 31 37 E
Mulejé, *Mexico* **86 B2** 26 53N 112 1W
Muleshoe, *U.S.A.* **81 H3** 34 13N 102 43W
Mulgrave, *Canada* **71 C7** 45 38N 61 31W
Mulhacén, *Spain* **19 D4** 37 4N 3 20W
Mülheim, *Germany* **33 C6** 51 25N 6 54 E

Nanching

Mulhouse, France 18 C7 47 40N 7 20 E
Muling, China 35 B16 44 35N 130 10 E
Mull, U.K. 12 E3 56 25N 5 56W
Mull, Sound of, U.K. 12 E3 56 30N 5 50W
Mullaittivu, Sri Lanka 40 Q12 9 15N 80 49 E
Mullen, U.S.A. 80 D4 42 3N 101 1W
Mullens, U.S.A. 76 G5 37 35N 81 23W
Muller, Pegunungan, Indonesia 36 D4 0 30N 113 30 E
Mullet Pen., Ireland 13 B1 54 13N 10 2W
Mullewa, Australia 61 E2 28 29S 115 30 E
Mulligan →, Australia 62 D2 25 0S 139 0 E
Mullingar, Ireland 13 C4 53 31N 7 21W
Mullins, U.S.A. 77 H6 34 12N 79 15W
Mullumbimby, Australia 63 D5 28 30S 153 30 E
Mulobezi, Zambia 55 F2 16 45S 25 7 E
Mulroy B., Ireland 13 A4 55 15N 7 46W
Multan, Pakistan 42 D4 30 15N 71 36 E
Mulumbe, Mts., Dem. Rep. of the Congo 55 D2 8 40S 27 30 E
Mulungushi Dam, Zambia 55 E2 14 48S 28 48 E
Mulvane, U.S.A. 81 G6 37 29N 97 15W
Mumbai, India 40 K8 18 55N 72 50 E
Mumbwa, Zambia 55 F2 15 0S 27 0 E
Mun →, Thailand 38 E5 15 19N 105 30 E
Muna, Indonesia 37 F6 5 0S 122 30 E
Munabao, India 42 G4 25 45N 70 17 E
Munamagi, Estonia 9 H22 57 43N 27 4 E
München, Germany 16 D6 48 8N 11 34 E
Munchen-Gladbach = Mönchengladbach, Germany 16 C4 51 11N 6 27 E
Muncho Lake, Canada 72 B3 59 0N 125 50W
Munch'ŏn, N. Korea 35 E14 39 14N 127 19 E
Muncie, U.S.A. 76 E3 40 12N 85 23W
Muncoonie, L., Australia 62 D2 25 12S 138 40 E
Mundabbera, Australia 63 D5 25 36S 151 18 E
Munday, U.S.A. 81 J5 33 27N 99 38W
Münden, Germany 16 C5 51 25N 9 38 E
Mundiwindi, Australia 60 D3 23 47S 120 9 E
Mundo Novo, Brazil 93 F10 11 50S 40 29W
Mundra, India 42 H3 22 54N 69 48 E
Mundrabilla, Australia 61 F4 31 52S 127 51 E
Mungallala, Australia 63 D4 26 28S 147 34 E
Mungallala Cr. →, Australia 63 D4 28 53S 147 5 E
Mungana, Australia 62 B3 17 8S 144 27 E
Mungaoli, India 42 G8 24 24N 78 7 E
Mungari, Mozam. 55 F3 17 12S 33 30 E
Mungbere, Dem. Rep. of the Congo 54 B2 2 36N 28 28 E
Mungeli, India 43 H9 22 4N 81 41 E
Munger, India 43 G12 25 23N 86 30 E
Munich = München, Germany 16 D6 48 8N 11 34 E
Munising, U.S.A. 76 B2 46 25N 86 40W
Munku-Sardyk, Russia 27 D11 51 45N 100 20 E
Muñoz Gamero, Pen., Chile 96 G2 52 30S 73 5W
Munroe L., Canada 73 B9 59 13N 98 35W
Munsan, S. Korea 35 F14 37 51N 126 48 E
Münster, Germany 16 C4 51 58N 7 37 E
Munster □, Ireland 13 D3 52 18N 8 44W
Muntadgin, Australia 61 F2 31 45S 118 33 E
Muntok, Indonesia 36 E3 2 5S 105 10 E
Munyama, Zambia 55 F2 16 5S 28 31 E
Muong Et, Laos 38 B5 20 49N 104 1 E
Muong Hiem, Laos 38 B4 20 5N 103 22 E
Muong Kau, Laos 38 E5 15 6N 105 47 E
Muong Khao, Laos 38 C4 19 38N 103 32 E
Muong Liep, Laos 38 C3 18 29N 101 40 E
Muong May, Laos 38 E6 14 49N 106 56 E
Muong Nong, Laos 38 D6 16 22N 106 30 E
Muong Oua, Laos 38 C3 18 18N 101 20 E
Muong Phalane, Laos 38 D5 16 39N 105 34 E
Muong Phieng, Laos 38 C3 19 6N 101 32 E
Muong Phine, Laos 38 D6 16 32N 106 2 E
Muong Saiapoun, Laos 38 C3 18 24N 101 31 E
Muong Sen, Vietnam 38 C5 19 24N 104 8 E
Muong Soui, Laos 38 C4 19 33N 102 52 E
Muong Xia, Vietnam 38 B5 20 19N 104 50 E
Muonio, Finland 8 C20 67 57N 23 40 E
Muonionjoki →, Finland 8 C20 67 11N 23 34 E
Muping, China 35 F11 37 22N 121 36 E
Muqdisho, Somali Rep. 46 G4 2 2N 45 25 E
Mur →, Austria 17 E9 46 18N 16 52 E
Murakami, Japan 30 E9 38 14N 139 29 E
Murallón, Cerro, Chile 96 F2 49 48S 73 30W
Muranda, Rwanda 54 C2 1 52S 29 20 E
Murang'a, Kenya 54 C4 0 45S 37 9 E
Murashi, Russia 24 C8 59 30N 49 0 E
Murat →, Turkey 25 G7 38 46N 40 0 E
Muratlı, Turkey 21 D12 41 10N 27 29 E
Murayama, Japan 30 E10 38 30N 140 25 E
Murban, U.A.E. 45 F7 23 50N 53 45 E
Murchison →, Australia 61 E1 27 45S 114 0 E
Murchison, Mt., Antarctica 5 D11 73 0S 168 0 E
Murchison Falls, Uganda 54 B3 2 15N 31 30 E
Murchison Ra., Australia 62 C1 20 0S 134 10 E
Murchison Rapids, Malawi 55 F3 15 55S 34 35 E
Murcia, Spain 19 D5 38 5N 1 10W
Murcia □, Spain 19 D5 37 50N 1 30W
Murdo, U.S.A. 80 D4 43 53N 100 43W
Murdoch Pt., Australia 62 A3 14 37S 144 55 E
Mureş →, Romania 17 E11 46 15N 20 13 E
Mureşul = Mureş →, Romania 17 E11 46 15N 20 13 E
Murfreesboro, N.C., U.S.A. 77 G7 36 27N 77 6W
Murfreesboro, Tenn., U.S.A. 77 H2 35 51N 86 24W
Murgab = Murghob, Tajikistan 26 F8 38 10N 74 2 E
Murgab →, Turkmenistan 45 B9 38 18N 61 12 E
Murgenella, Australia 60 B5 11 34S 132 56 E
Murgha Kibzai, Pakistan 42 D3 30 44N 69 25 E
Murghob, Tajikistan 26 F8 38 10N 74 2 E
Murgon, Australia 63 D5 26 15S 151 54 E
Muri, India 43 H11 23 22N 85 52 E
Muria, Indonesia 37 G14 6 36S 110 53 E
Muriaé, Brazil 95 A7 21 8S 42 23W
Muriel Mine, Zimbabwe 55 F3 17 14S 30 40 E
Müritz, Germany 16 B7 53 25N 12 42 E
Murka, Kenya 54 C4 3 27S 38 0 E
Murliganj, India 43 G12 25 54N 86 59 E
Murmansk, Russia 24 A5 68 57N 33 10 E
Muro, Spain 22 B10 39 44N 3 3 E
Murom, Russia 24 C7 55 35N 42 3 E
Muroran, Japan 30 C10 42 25N 141 0 E
Muroto, Japan 31 H7 33 18N 134 9 E
Muroto-Misaki, Japan 31 H7 33 15N 134 10 E
Murphy, U.S.A. 82 E5 43 13N 116 33W
Murphys, U.S.A. 84 G6 38 8N 120 28W
Murray, Ky., U.S.A. 77 G1 36 37N 88 19W
Murray, Utah, U.S.A. 82 F8 40 40N 111 53W
Murray →, Australia 63 F2 35 20S 139 22 E
Murray, L., U.S.A. 77 H5 34 3N 81 13W
Murray Bridge, Australia 63 F2 35 6S 139 14 E
Murray Harbour, Canada 71 C7 46 0N 62 28W
Murraysburg, S. Africa 56 E3 31 58S 23 47 E
Murree, Pakistan 42 C5 33 56N 73 28 E
Murrieta, U.S.A. 85 M9 33 33N 117 13W
Murrumbidgee →, Australia 63 E3 34 43S 143 12 E
Murrumburrah, Australia 63 E4 34 32S 148 22 E
Murrurundi, Australia 63 E5 31 42S 150 51 E
Murshidabad, India 43 G13 24 11N 88 19 E
Murtle L., Canada 72 C5 52 8N 119 38W
Murtoa, Australia 63 F3 36 35S 142 28 E
Murungu, Tanzania 54 C3 4 12S 31 10 E
Mururoa, Pac. Oc. 65 K14 21 52S 138 55W
Murwara, India 43 H9 23 46N 80 28 E
Murwillumbah, Australia 63 D5 28 18S 153 27 E
Mürzzuschlag, Austria 16 E8 47 36N 15 41 E
Muş, Turkey 25 G7 38 45N 41 30 E
Mûsa, Gebel, Egypt 44 D2 28 33N 33 59 E
Musa Khel, Pakistan 42 D3 30 59N 69 52 E
Mūsá Qal'eh, Afghan. 40 C4 32 20N 64 50 E
Musaffargarh, Pakistan 40 D7 30 10N 71 10 E
Musafirkhana, India 43 F9 26 22N 81 48 E
Musala, Bulgaria 21 C10 42 13N 23 37 E
Musala, Indonesia 36 D1 1 41N 98 28 E
Musan, N. Korea 35 C15 42 12N 129 12 E
Musangu, Dem. Rep. of the Congo 55 E1 10 28S 23 55 E
Musasa, Tanzania 54 C3 3 25S 31 30 E
Musay'īd, Qatar 45 E6 25 0N 51 33 E
Muscat = Masqat, Oman 46 C6 23 37N 58 36 E
Muscat & Oman = Oman ■, Asia 46 C6 23 0N 58 0 E
Muscatine, U.S.A. 80 E9 41 25N 91 3W
Musgrave Harbour, Canada 71 C9 49 27N 53 58W
Musgrave Ranges, Australia 61 E5 26 0S 132 0 E
Mushie, Dem. Rep. of the Congo 52 E3 2 56S 16 55 E
Musi →, Indonesia 36 E2 2 20S 104 56 E
Muskeg →, Canada 72 A4 60 20N 123 20W
Muskegon, U.S.A. 76 D2 43 14N 86 16W
Muskegon →, U.S.A. 76 D2 43 14N 86 21W
Muskegon Heights, U.S.A. 76 D2 43 12N 86 16W
Muskogee, U.S.A. 81 H7 35 45N 95 22W
Muskoka, L., Canada 78 B5 45 0N 79 25W
Muskwa →, Canada 72 B4 58 47N 122 48W
Muslīmiyah, Syria 44 B3 36 19N 37 12 E
Musofu, Zambia 55 E2 13 30S 29 0 E
Musoma, Tanzania 54 C3 1 30S 33 48 E
Musquaro, L., Canada 71 B7 50 38N 61 5W
Musquodoboit Harbour, Canada 71 D7 44 50N 63 9W
Musselburgh, U.K. 12 F5 55 57N 3 2W
Musselshell →, U.S.A. 82 C10 47 21N 107 57W
Mussoorie, India 42 D8 30 27N 78 6 E
Mussuco, Angola 56 B2 17 2S 19 3 E
Mustafakemalpaşa, Turkey 21 D13 40 2N 28 24 E
Mustang, Nepal 43 E10 29 10N 83 55 E
Musters, L., Argentina 96 F3 45 20S 69 25W
Musudan, N. Korea 35 D15 40 50N 129 43 E
Muswellbrook, Australia 63 E5 32 16S 150 56 E
Mût, Egypt 51 C11 25 28N 28 58 E
Mut, Turkey 44 B2 36 40N 33 28 E
Mutanda, Mozam. 57 C5 21 0S 33 34 E
Mutanda, Zambia 55 E2 12 24S 26 13 E
Mutare, Zimbabwe 55 F3 18 58S 32 38 E
Muting, Indonesia 37 F10 7 23S 140 20 E
Mutoray, Russia 27 C11 60 56N 101 0 E
Mutshatsha, Dem. Rep. of the Congo 55 E1 10 35S 24 20 E
Mutsu, Japan 30 D10 41 5N 140 55 E
Mutsu-Wan, Japan 30 D10 41 5N 140 55 E
Muttaburra, Australia 62 C3 22 38S 144 29 E
Mutton I., Ireland 13 D2 52 49N 9 32W
Mutuáli, Mozam. 55 E4 14 55S 37 0 E
Muweilih, Egypt 47 E3 30 42N 34 19 E
Muy Muy, Nic. 88 D2 12 39N 85 36W
Muyinga, Burundi 54 C3 3 14S 30 33 E
Muynak, Uzbekistan 26 E6 43 44N 59 10 E
Muzaffarabad, Pakistan 43 B5 34 25N 73 30 E
Muzaffargarh, Pakistan 42 D4 30 5N 71 14 E
Muzaffarnagar, India 42 E7 29 26N 77 40 E
Muzaffarpur, India 43 F11 26 7N 85 23 E
Muzafirpur, Pakistan 42 D3 30 58N 69 9 E
Muzhi, Russia 24 A11 65 25N 64 40 E
Mvuma, Zimbabwe 55 F3 19 16S 30 30 E
Mvurwi, Zimbabwe 55 F3 17 0S 30 57 E
Mwadui, Tanzania 54 C3 3 26S 33 32 E
Mwambo, Tanzania 55 E5 10 30S 40 22 E
Mwandi, Zambia 55 F1 17 30S 24 51 E
Mwanza, Dem. Rep. of the Congo 54 D2 7 55S 26 43 E
Mwanza, Tanzania 54 C3 2 30S 32 58 E
Mwanza, Zambia 55 F1 16 58S 24 28 E
Mwanza □, Tanzania 54 C3 2 0S 33 0 E
Mwaya, Tanzania 55 D3 9 32S 33 55 E
Mweelrea, Ireland 13 C2 53 39N 9 49W
Mweka, Dem. Rep. of the Congo 52 E4 4 50S 21 34 E
Mwene-Ditu, Dem. Rep. of the Congo 52 F4 6 35S 22 27 E
Mwenezi, Zimbabwe 55 G3 21 15S 30 48 E
Mwenezi →, Mozam. 55 G3 22 40S 31 50 E
Mwenga, Dem. Rep. of the Congo 54 C2 3 1S 28 28 E
Mweru, L., Zambia 55 D2 9 0S 28 40 E
Mweza Range, Zimbabwe 55 G3 21 0S 30 0 E
Mwilambwe, Dem. Rep. of the Congo 54 D2 8 7S 25 5 E
Mwimbi, Tanzania 55 D3 8 38S 31 39 E
Mwinilunga, Zambia 55 E1 11 43S 24 25 E
My Tho, Vietnam 39 G6 10 29N 106 23 E
Myajlar, India 42 F4 26 15N 70 20 E
Myanaung, Burma 41 K19 18 18N 95 22 E
Myanmar = Burma ■, Asia 41 J20 21 0N 96 30 E
Myaungmya, Burma 41 L19 16 30N 94 40 E
Mycenæ, Greece 21 F10 37 39N 22 52 E
Myeik Kyunzu, Burma 39 G1 11 30N 97 30 E
Myers Chuck, U.S.A. 72 B2 55 44N 132 11W
Myerstown, U.S.A. 79 F8 40 22N 76 19W
Myingyan, Burma 41 J19 21 30N 95 20 E
Myitkyina, Burma 41 G20 25 24N 97 26 E
Mykines, Færoe Is. 8 E9 62 7N 7 35W
Mykolayiv, Ukraine 25 E5 46 58N 32 0 E
Mymensingh, Bangla. 41 G17 24 45N 90 24 E
Mynydd Du, U.K. 11 F4 51 52N 3 50W
Mýrdalsjökull, Iceland 8 E4 63 40N 19 6W
Myrtle Beach, U.S.A. 77 J6 33 42N 78 53W
Myrtle Creek, U.S.A. 82 E2 43 1N 123 17W
Myrtle Point, U.S.A. 82 E1 43 4N 124 8W
Myrtou, Cyprus 23 D12 35 18N 33 4 E
Mysia, Turkey 21 E12 39 50N 27 0 E
Mysore = Karnataka □, India 40 N10 13 15N 77 0 E
Mysore, India 40 N10 12 17N 76 41 E
Mystic, U.S.A. 79 E13 41 21N 71 58W
Myszków, Poland 17 C10 50 45N 19 22 E
Mytishchi, Russia 24 C6 55 50N 37 50 E
Mývatn, Iceland 8 D5 65 36N 17 0W
Mzimba, Malawi 55 E3 11 55S 33 39 E
Mzimkulu →, S. Africa 57 E5 30 44S 30 28 E
Mzimvubu →, S. Africa 57 E4 31 38S 29 33 E
Mzuzu, Malawi 55 E3 11 30S 33 55 E

N

Na Hearadh = Harris, U.K. 12 D2 57 50N 6 55W
Na Noi, Thailand 38 C3 18 19N 100 43 E
Na Phao, Laos 38 D5 17 35N 105 44 E
Na San, Vietnam 38 B5 21 12N 104 2 E
Naab →, Germany 16 D6 49 1N 12 2 E
Naantali, Finland 9 F19 60 29N 22 2 E
Naas, Ireland 13 C5 53 12N 6 40W
Nababiep, S. Africa 56 D2 29 36S 17 46 E
Nabadwip = Navadwip, India 43 H13 23 34N 88 20 E
Nabari, Japan 31 G8 34 37N 136 5 E
Nabawa, Australia 61 E1 28 30S 114 48 E
Nabberu, L., Australia 61 E3 25 50S 120 30 E
Naberezhnyye Chelny, Russia 24 C9 55 42N 52 19 E
Nabeul, Tunisia 51 A8 36 30N 10 44 E
Nabha, India 42 D7 30 26N 76 14 E
Nabīd, Iran 45 D8 29 40N 57 38 E
Nabire, Indonesia 37 E9 3 15S 135 26 E
Nabisar, Pakistan 42 G3 25 8N 69 40 E
Nabisipi →, Canada 71 B7 50 14N 62 13W
Nabiswera, Uganda 54 B3 1 27N 32 15 E
Nablus = Nābulus, West Bank 47 C4 32 14N 35 15 E
Naboomspruit, S. Africa 57 C4 24 32S 28 40 E
Nābulus, West Bank 47 C4 32 14N 35 15 E
Nacala, Mozam. 55 E5 14 31S 40 34 E
Nacala-Velha, Mozam. 55 E5 14 32S 40 34 E
Nacaome, Honduras 88 D2 13 31N 87 30W
Nacaroa, Mozam. 55 E4 14 22S 39 56 E
Naches, U.S.A. 82 C3 46 44N 120 42W
Naches →, U.S.A. 84 D6 46 38N 120 31W
Nachicapau, L., Canada 71 A6 56 40N 68 5W
Nachingwea, Tanzania 55 E4 10 23S 38 49 E
Nachna, India 42 F4 27 34N 71 41 E
Nacimiento L., U.S.A. 84 K6 35 46N 120 53W
Naco, Mexico 86 A3 31 20N 109 56W
Nacogdoches, U.S.A. 81 K7 31 36N 94 39W
Nácori Chico, Mexico 86 B3 29 39N 109 1W
Nacozari, Mexico 86 A3 30 24N 109 39W
Nadiad, India 42 H5 22 41N 72 56 E
Nador, Morocco 50 B5 35 14N 2 58W
Nadur, Malta 23 C1 36 2N 14 17 E
Nadūshan, Iran 45 C7 32 2N 53 35 E
Nadvirna, Ukraine 17 D13 48 37N 24 30 E
Nadvoitsy, Russia 24 B5 63 52N 34 14 E
Nadvornaya = Nadvirna, Ukraine 17 D13 48 37N 24 30 E
Nadym, Russia 26 C8 65 35N 72 42 E
Nadym →, Russia 26 C8 66 12N 72 0 E
Nærbø, Norway 9 G11 58 40N 5 39 E
Næstved, Denmark 9 J14 55 13N 11 44 E
Naft-e Safīd, Iran 45 D6 31 40N 49 17 E
Naftshahr, Iran 44 C5 34 0N 45 30 E
Nafud Desert = An Nafūd, Si. Arabia 44 D4 28 15N 41 0 E
Naga, Phil. 37 B6 13 38N 123 15 E
Nagahama, Japan 31 G8 35 23N 136 16 E
Nagai, Japan 30 E10 38 6N 140 2 E
Nagaland □, India 41 G19 26 0N 94 30 E
Nagano, Japan 31 F9 36 40N 138 10 E
Nagano □, Japan 31 F9 36 15N 138 0 E
Nagaoka, Japan 31 F9 37 27N 138 51 E
Nagappattinam, India 40 P11 10 46N 79 51 E
Nagar →, Bangla. 43 G13 24 27N 89 12 E
Nagar Parkar, Pakistan 42 G4 24 28N 70 46 E
Nagasaki, Japan 31 H4 32 47N 129 50 E
Nagasaki □, Japan 31 H4 32 50N 129 40 E
Nagato, Japan 31 G5 34 19N 131 5 E
Nagaur, India 42 F5 27 15N 73 45 E
Nagda, India 42 H6 23 27N 75 25 E
Nagercoil, India 40 Q10 8 12N 77 26 E
Nagina, India 43 E8 29 30N 78 30 E
Nagineh, Iran 45 C8 34 20N 57 15 E
Nagir, Pakistan 43 A6 36 12N 74 42 E
Nagod, India 43 G9 24 34N 80 36 E
Nagoorin, Australia 62 C5 24 17S 151 15 E
Nagorno-Karabakh, Azerbaijan 25 F8 39 55N 46 45 E
Nagornyy, Russia 27 D13 55 58N 124 57 E
Nagoya, Japan 31 G8 35 10N 136 50 E
Nagpur, India 40 J11 21 8N 79 10 E
Nagua, Dom. Rep. 89 C6 19 23N 69 50W
Nagykanizsa, Hungary 17 E9 46 28N 17 0 E
Nagykőrös, Hungary 17 E10 47 5N 19 48 E
Naha, Japan 31 L3 26 13N 127 42 E
Nahan, India 42 D7 30 33N 77 18 E
Nahanni Butte, Canada 72 A4 61 2N 123 31W
Nahanni Nat. Park, Canada 72 A4 61 15N 125 0W
Nahargarh, Mad. P., India 42 G6 24 10N 75 14 E
Nahargarh, Raj., India 42 G7 24 55N 76 50 E
Nahariyya, Israel 44 C2 33 1N 35 5 E
Nahāvand, Iran 45 C6 34 10N 48 22 E
Naicá, Mexico 86 B3 27 53N 105 31W
Naicam, Canada 73 C8 52 30N 104 30W
Naikoon Prov. Park, Canada 72 C2 53 55N 131 55W
Naimisharanya, India 43 F9 27 21N 80 30 E
Nain, Canada 71 A7 56 34N 61 40W
Nā'īn, Iran 45 C7 32 54N 53 0 E
Naini Tal, India 43 E8 29 30N 79 30 E
Nainpur, India 40 H12 22 30N 80 10 E
Nainwa, India 42 G6 25 46N 75 51 E
Nairn, U.K. 12 D5 57 35N 3 53W
Nairobi, Kenya 54 C4 1 17S 36 48 E
Naissaar, Estonia 9 G21 59 34N 24 29 E
Naivasha, Kenya 54 C4 0 40S 36 30 E
Naivasha, L., Kenya 54 C4 0 48S 36 20 E
Najafābād, Iran 45 C6 32 40N 51 15 E
Najd, Si. Arabia 46 B3 26 30N 42 0 E
Najibabad, India 42 E8 29 40N 78 20 E
Najin, N. Korea 35 C16 42 12N 130 15 E
Najmah, Si. Arabia 45 E6 26 42N 50 6 E
Naju, S. Korea 35 G14 35 3N 126 43 E
Nakadōri-Shima, Japan 31 H4 32 57N 129 4 E
Nakalagba, Dem. Rep. of the Congo 54 B2 2 50N 27 58 E
Nakaminato, Japan 31 F10 36 21N 140 36 E
Nakamura, Japan 31 H6 32 59N 132 56 E
Nakano, Japan 31 F9 36 45N 138 22 E
Nakano-Shima, Japan 31 K4 29 51N 129 52 E
Nakashibetsu, Japan 30 C12 43 33N 144 59 E
Nakfa, Eritrea 46 D2 16 40N 38 32 E
Nakhfar al Buşayyah, Iraq 44 D5 30 0N 46 10 E
Nakhichevan = Naxçıvan, Azerbaijan 25 G8 39 12N 45 15 E
Nakhichevan Republic = Naxçıvan □, Azerbaijan 25 G8 39 25N 45 26 E
Nakhl, Egypt 47 F2 29 55N 33 43 E
Nakhl-e Taqī, Iran 45 E7 27 28N 52 36 E
Nakhodka, Russia 27 E14 42 53N 132 54 E
Nakhon Nayok, Thailand 38 E3 14 12N 101 13 E
Nakhon Pathom, Thailand 38 F3 13 49N 100 3 E
Nakhon Phanom, Thailand 38 D5 17 23N 104 43 E
Nakhon Ratchasima, Thailand 38 E4 14 59N 102 12 E
Nakhon Sawan, Thailand 38 E3 15 35N 100 10 E
Nakhon Si Thammarat, Thailand 39 H3 8 29N 100 0 E
Nakhon Thai, Thailand 38 D3 17 5N 100 44 E
Nakhtarana, India 42 H3 23 20N 69 15 E
Nakina, Canada 70 B2 50 10N 86 40W
Nakodar, India 42 D6 31 8N 75 31 E
Nakskov, Denmark 9 J14 54 50N 11 8 E
Naktong →, S. Korea 35 G15 35 7N 128 57 E
Nakuru, Kenya 54 C4 0 15S 36 4 E
Nakuru, L., Kenya 54 C4 0 23S 36 5 E
Nakusp, Canada 72 C5 50 20N 117 45W
Nal, Pakistan 42 F2 27 40N 66 12 E
Nal →, Pakistan 42 G1 25 20N 65 30 E
Nalchik, Russia 25 F7 43 30N 43 33 E
Nalgonda, India 40 L11 17 6N 79 15 E
Nalhati, India 43 G12 24 17N 87 52 E
Naliya, India 42 H3 23 16N 68 50 E
Nallamalai Hills, India 40 M11 15 30N 78 50 E
Nam Can, Vietnam 39 H5 8 46N 104 59 E
Nam-ch'on, N. Korea 35 E14 38 15N 126 26 E
Nam Co, China 32 C4 30 30N 90 45 E
Nam Du, Hon, Vietnam 39 H5 9 41N 104 21 E
Nam Ngum Dam, Laos 38 C4 18 35N 102 34 E
Nam-Phan = Cochin China, Vietnam 39 G6 10 30N 106 0 E
Nam Phong, Thailand 38 D4 16 42N 102 52 E
Nam Tok, Thailand 38 E2 14 21N 99 4 E
Namacunde, Angola 56 B2 17 18S 15 50 E
Namacurra, Mozam. 57 B6 17 30S 36 50 E
Namak, Daryācheh-ye, Iran 45 C7 34 30N 52 0 E
Namak, Kavir-e, Iran 45 C8 34 30N 57 30 E
Namakzār, Daryācheh-ye, Iran 45 C9 34 0N 60 30 E
Namaland, Namibia 56 C2 26 0S 17 0 E
Namangan, Uzbekistan 26 E8 41 0N 71 40 E
Namapa, Mozam. 55 E4 13 43S 39 50 E
Namaqualand, S. Africa 56 E2 30 0S 17 25 E
Namasagali, Uganda 54 B3 1 2N 33 0 E
Namber, Indonesia 37 E8 1 2S 134 49 E
Nambour, Australia 63 D5 26 32S 152 58 E
Nambucca Heads, Australia 63 E5 30 37S 153 0 E
Namcha Barwa, China 32 D4 29 40N 95 10 E
Namche Bazar, Nepal 43 F12 27 51N 86 47 E
Namchonjŏm = Nam-ch'on, N. Korea 35 E14 38 15N 126 26 E
Namecunda, Mozam. 55 E4 14 54S 37 37 E
Nameponda, Mozam. 55 F4 15 50S 39 50 E
Nametil, Mozam. 55 F4 15 40S 39 21 E
Namew L., Canada 73 C8 54 14N 101 56W
Namgia, India 43 D8 31 48N 78 40 E
Namib Desert = Namibwoestyn, Namibia 56 C2 22 30S 15 0 E
Namibe, Angola 53 H2 15 7S 12 11 E
Namibe □, Angola 56 B1 16 35S 12 30 E
Namibia ■, Africa 56 C2 22 0S 18 9 E
Namibwoestyn, Namibia 56 C2 22 30S 15 0 E
Namlea, Indonesia 37 E7 3 18S 127 5 E
Namoi →, Australia 63 E4 30 12S 149 30 E
Nampa, U.S.A. 82 E5 43 34N 116 34W
Namp'o, N. Korea 35 E13 38 52N 125 10 E
Nampō-Shotō, Japan 31 J10 32 0N 140 0 E
Nampula, Mozam. 55 F4 15 6S 39 15 E
Namrole, Indonesia 37 E7 3 46S 126 46 E
Namse Shankou, China 41 E13 30 0N 82 25 E
Namsen →, Norway 8 D14 64 28N 11 37 E
Namsos, Norway 8 D14 64 29N 11 30 E
Namtsy, Russia 27 C13 62 43N 129 37 E
Namtu, Burma 41 H20 23 5N 97 28 E
Namtumbo, Tanzania 55 E4 10 30S 36 4 E
Namu, Canada 72 C3 51 52N 127 50W
Namur, Belgium 15 D4 50 27N 4 52 E
Namur □, Belgium 15 D4 50 17N 5 0 E
Namutoni, Namibia 56 B2 18 49S 16 55 E
Namwala, Zambia 55 F2 15 44S 26 30 E
Namwŏn, S. Korea 35 G14 35 23N 127 23 E
Nan, Thailand 38 C3 18 48N 100 46 E
Nan →, Thailand 38 E3 15 42N 100 9 E
Nan-ch'ang = Nanchang, China 33 D6 28 42N 115 55 E
Nanaimo, Canada 72 D4 49 10N 124 0W
Nanam, N. Korea 35 D15 41 44N 129 40 E
Nanango, Australia 63 D5 26 40S 152 0 E
Nanao, Japan 31 F8 37 0N 137 0 E
Nanchang, China 33 D6 28 42N 115 55 E
Nanching = Nanjing, China 33 C6 32 2N 118 47 E

North Knife

New Smyrna Beach, U.S.A. **77 L5** 29 1N 80 56W
New South Wales □, Australia **63 E4** 33 0S 146 0 E
New Town, U.S.A. **80 B3** 47 59N 102 30W
New Tredegar, U.K. **11 F4** 51 44N 3 16W
New Ulm, U.S.A. **80 C7** 44 19N 94 28W
New Waterford, Canada **71 C7** 46 13N 60 4W
New Westminster, Canada **84 A4** 49 13N 122 55W
New York, U.S.A. **79 F11** 40 45N 74 0W
New York □, U.S.A. **79 D9** 43 0N 75 0W
New York Mts., U.S.A. **83 J6** 35 0N 115 20W
New Zealand ■, Oceania **59 J6** 40 0S 176 0 E
Newaj →, India **42 G7** 24 24N 76 49 E
Newala, Tanzania **55 E4** 10 58S 39 18 E
Newark, Del., U.S.A. **76 F8** 39 41N 75 46W
Newark, N.J., U.S.A. **79 F10** 40 44N 74 10W
Newark, N.Y., U.S.A. **78 C7** 43 3N 77 6W
Newark, Ohio, U.S.A. **78 F2** 40 3N 82 24W
Newark-on-Trent, U.K. **10 D7** 53 5N 0 48W
Newark Valley, U.S.A. **79 D8** 42 14N 76 11W
Newberg, U.S.A. **82 D2** 45 18N 122 58W
Newberry, Mich., U.S.A. **76 B3** 46 21N 85 30W
Newberry, S.C., U.S.A. **77 H5** 34 17N 81 37W
Newberry Springs, U.S.A. **85 L10** 34 50N 116 41W
Newboro L., Canada **79 B8** 44 38N 76 20W
Newbridge = Droichead Nua, Ireland **13 C5** 53 11N 6 48W
Newburgh, Canada **78 B8** 44 19N 76 52W
Newburgh, U.S.A. **79 E10** 41 30N 74 1W
Newbury, U.K. **11 F6** 51 24N 1 20W
Newbury, N.H., U.S.A. **79 B12** 43 19N 72 3W
Newbury, Vt., U.S.A. **79 B12** 44 5N 72 4W
Newburyport, U.S.A. **77 D10** 42 49N 70 53W
Newcastle, Australia **63 E5** 33 0S 151 46 E
Newcastle, N.B., Canada **71 C6** 47 1N 65 38W
Newcastle, Ont., Canada **70 D4** 43 55N 78 35W
Newcastle, S. Africa **57 D4** 27 45S 29 58 E
Newcastle, U.K. **13 B6** 54 13N 5 54W
Newcastle, Calif., U.S.A. **84 G5** 38 53N 121 8W
Newcastle, Wyo., U.S.A. **80 D2** 43 50N 104 11W
Newcastle Emlyn, U.K. **11 E3** 52 2N 4 28W
Newcastle Ra., Australia **60 C5** 15 45S 130 15 E
Newcastle-under-Lyme, U.K. **10 D5** 53 1N 2 14W
Newcastle-upon-Tyne, U.K. **10 C6** 54 58N 1 36W
Newcastle Waters, Australia **62 B1** 17 30S 133 28 E
Newcastle West, Ireland **13 D2** 52 27N 9 3W
Newcomb, U.S.A. **79 C10** 43 58N 74 10W
Newcomerstown, U.S.A. **78 F3** 40 16N 81 36W
Newdegate, Australia **61 F2** 33 6S 119 0 E
Newell, Australia **62 B4** 16 20S 145 16 E
Newell, U.S.A. **80 C3** 44 43N 103 25W
Newfane, U.S.A. **78 C6** 43 17N 78 43W
Newfield, U.S.A. **79 D8** 42 18N 76 33W
Newfound L., U.S.A. **79 C13** 43 40N 71 47W
Newfoundland, N. Amer. **66 E14** 49 0N 55 0W
Newfoundland, U.S.A. **79 E9** 41 18N 75 19W
Newfoundland □, Canada **71 B8** 53 0N 58 0W
Newhall, U.S.A. **85 L8** 34 23N 118 32W
Newhaven, U.K. **11 G8** 50 47N 0 3 E
Newkirk, U.S.A. **81 G6** 36 53N 97 3W
Newlyn, U.K. **11 G2** 50 6N 5 34W
Newman, Australia **60 D2** 23 18S 119 45 E
Newman, U.S.A. **84 H5** 37 19N 121 1W
Newmarket, Canada **78 B5** 44 3N 79 28W
Newmarket, Ireland **13 D2** 52 13N 9 0W
Newmarket, U.K. **11 E8** 52 15N 0 25 E
Newmarket, N.H., U.S.A. **79 C14** 43 4N 70 56W
Newmarket, N.H., U.S.A. **79 C14** 43 5N 70 56W
Newnan, U.S.A. **77 J3** 33 23N 84 48W
Newport, Ireland **13 C2** 53 53N 9 33W
Newport, I. of W., U.K. **11 G6** 50 42N 1 17W
Newport, Newp., U.K. **11 F5** 51 35N 3 0W
Newport, Ark., U.S.A. **81 H9** 35 37N 91 16W
Newport, Ky., U.S.A. **76 F3** 39 5N 84 30W
Newport, N.H., U.S.A. **79 C12** 43 22N 72 10W
Newport, N.Y., U.S.A. **79 C9** 43 11N 75 1W
Newport, Oreg., U.S.A. **82 D1** 44 39N 124 3W
Newport, Pa., U.S.A. **78 F7** 40 29N 77 8W
Newport, R.I., U.S.A. **79 E13** 41 29N 71 19W
Newport, Tenn., U.S.A. **77 H4** 35 58N 83 11W
Newport, Vt., U.S.A. **79 B12** 44 56N 72 13W
Newport, Wash., U.S.A. **82 B5** 48 11N 117 3W
Newport □, U.K. **11 F4** 51 33N 3 1W
Newport Beach, U.S.A. **85 M9** 33 37N 117 56W
Newport News, U.S.A. **76 G7** 36 59N 76 25W
Newport Pagnell, U.K. **11 E7** 52 5N 0 43W
Newquay, U.K. **11 G2** 50 25N 5 6W
Newry, U.K. **13 B5** 54 11N 6 21W
Newton, Ill., U.S.A. **80 F10** 38 59N 88 10W
Newton, Iowa, U.S.A. **80 E8** 41 42N 93 3W
Newton, Kans., U.S.A. **81 F6** 38 3N 97 21W
Newton, Mass., U.S.A. **79 D13** 42 21N 71 12W
Newton, Miss., U.S.A. **81 J10** 32 19N 89 10W
Newton, N.C., U.S.A. **77 H5** 35 40N 81 13W
Newton, N.J., U.S.A. **79 E10** 41 3N 74 45W
Newton, Tex., U.S.A. **81 K8** 30 51N 93 46W
Newton Abbot, U.K. **11 G4** 50 32N 3 37W
Newton Aycliffe, U.K. **10 C6** 54 37N 1 34W
Newton Falls, U.S.A. **78 E4** 41 11N 80 59W
Newton Stewart, U.K. **12 G4** 54 57N 4 30W
Newtonmore, U.K. **12 D4** 57 4N 4 8W
Newtown, U.K. **11 E4** 52 31N 3 19W
Newtownabbey, U.K. **13 B6** 54 40N 5 56W
Newtownards, U.K. **13 B6** 54 36N 5 42W
Newtownbarry = Bunclody, Ireland **13 D5** 52 39N 6 40W
Newtownstewart, U.K. **13 B4** 54 43N 7 23W
Newville, U.S.A. **78 F7** 40 10N 77 24W
Neya, Russia **24 C7** 58 21N 43 49 E
Neyrīz, Iran **45 D7** 29 15N 54 19 E
Neyshābūr, Iran **45 B8** 36 10N 58 50 E
Nezhin = Nizhyn, Ukraine **25 D5** 51 5N 31 55 E
Nezperce, U.S.A. **82 C5** 46 14N 116 14W
Ngabang, Indonesia **36 D3** 0 23N 109 55 E
Ngabordamlu, Tanjung, Indonesia **37 F8** 6 56S 134 11 E
N'Gage, Angola **52 F3** 7 46S 15 16 E
Ngami Depression, Botswana **56 C3** 20 30S 22 46 E
Ngamo, Zimbabwe **55 F2** 19 3S 27 32 E
Nganglong Kangri, China **41 C12** 33 0N 81 0 E
Ngao, Thailand **38 C2** 18 46N 99 59 E
Ngaoundéré, Cameroon **52 C2** 7 15N 13 35 E
Ngapara, N.Z. **59 L3** 44 57S 170 46 E
Ngara, Tanzania **54 C3** 2 29S 30 40 E
Ngawi, Indonesia **37 G14** 7 24S 111 26 E
Ngoma, Malawi **55 E3** 13 8S 33 45 E
Ngomahura, Zimbabwe **55 G3** 20 26S 30 43 E
Ngomba, Tanzania **55 D3** 8 20S 32 53 E
Ngoring Hu, China **32 C4** 34 55N 97 5 E
Ngorongoro, Tanzania **54 C4** 3 11S 35 32 E
Ngozi, Burundi **54 C2** 2 54S 29 50 E
Ngudu, Tanzania **54 C3** 2 58S 33 25 E
Nguigmi, Niger **51 F8** 14 20N 13 20 E
Nguiu, Australia **60 B5** 11 46S 130 38 E
Ngukurr, Australia **62 A1** 14 44S 134 44 E
Ngulu Atoll, Pac. Oc. **37 C9** 8 0N 137 30 E
Ngunga, Tanzania **54 C3** 3 37S 33 37 E
Nguru, Nigeria **51 F8** 12 56N 10 29 E
Nguru Mts., Tanzania **54 D4** 6 0S 37 30 E
Nha Trang, Vietnam **39 F7** 12 16N 109 10 E
Nhacoongo, Mozam. **57 C6** 24 18S 35 14 E
Nhamaabué, Mozam. **55 F4** 17 25S 35 5 E
Nhamundá →, Brazil **93 D7** 2 12S 56 41W
Nhangutazi, L., Mozam. **57 C5** 24 0S 34 30 E
Nhill, Australia **63 F3** 36 18S 141 40 E
Nhulunbuy, Australia **62 A2** 12 10S 137 20 E
Nia-nia, Dem. Rep. of the Congo **54 B2** 1 30N 27 40 E
Niagara Falls, Canada **78 C5** 43 7N 79 5W
Niagara Falls, U.S.A. **78 C6** 43 5N 79 4W
Niagara-on-the-Lake, Canada **78 C5** 43 15N 79 4W
Niah, Malaysia **36 D4** 3 58N 113 46 E
Niamey, Niger **50 F6** 13 27N 2 6 E
Niangara, Dem. Rep. of the Congo **54 B2** 3 42N 27 50 E
Niantic, U.S.A. **79 E12** 41 20N 72 11W
Nias, Indonesia **36 D1** 1 0N 97 30 E
Niassa □, Mozam. **55 E4** 13 30S 36 0 E
Nibāk, Si. Arabia **45 E7** 24 25N 50 50 E
Nicaragua ■, Cent. Amer. **88 D2** 11 40N 85 30W
Nicaragua, L. de, Nic. **88 D2** 12 0N 85 30W
Nicastro, Italy **20 E7** 38 59N 16 19 E
Nice, France **18 E7** 43 42N 7 14 E
Niceville, U.S.A. **77 K2** 30 31N 86 30W
Nichicun, L., Canada **71 B5** 53 5N 71 0W
Nichinan, Japan **31 J5** 31 38N 131 23 E
Nicholás, Canal, W. Indies **88 B3** 23 30N 80 5W
Nicholasville, U.S.A. **76 G3** 37 53N 84 34W
Nichols, U.S.A. **79 D8** 42 1N 76 22W
Nicholson, Australia **60 C4** 18 2S 128 54 E
Nicholson, U.S.A. **79 E9** 41 37N 75 47W
Nicholson →, Australia **62 B2** 17 31S 139 36 E
Nicholson L., Canada **73 A8** 62 40N 102 40W
Nicholson Ra., Australia **61 E2** 27 15S 116 45 E
Nicholville, U.S.A. **79 B10** 44 41N 74 39W
Nicobar Is., Ind. Oc. **28 J13** 9 0N 93 0 E
Nicola, Canada **72 C4** 50 12N 120 40W
Nicolls Town, Bahamas **88 A4** 25 8N 78 0W
Nicosia, Cyprus **23 D12** 35 10N 33 25 E
Nicoya, Costa Rica **88 D2** 10 9N 85 27W
Nicoya, G. de, Costa Rica **88 E3** 10 0N 85 0W
Nicoya, Pen. de, Costa Rica **88 E2** 9 45N 85 40W
Nidd →, U.K. **10 D6** 53 59N 1 23W
Niedersachsen □, Germany **16 B5** 52 50N 9 0 E
Niekerkshoop, S. Africa **56 D3** 29 19S 22 51 E
Niemba, Dem. Rep. of the Congo **54 D2** 5 58S 28 24 E
Niemen = Neman →, Lithuania **9 J20** 55 25N 21 10 E
Nienburg, Germany **16 B5** 52 39N 9 13 E
Nieu Bethesda, S. Africa **56 E3** 31 51S 24 34 E
Nieuw Amsterdam, Surinam **93 B7** 5 53N 55 5W
Nieuw Nickerie, Surinam **93 B7** 6 0N 56 59W
Nieuwoudtville, S. Africa **56 E2** 31 23S 19 7 E
Nieuwpoort, Belgium **15 C2** 51 8N 2 45 E
Nieves, Pico de las, Canary Is. **22 G4** 27 57N 15 35W
Niğde, Turkey **25 G5** 37 58N 34 40 E
Nigel, S. Africa **57 D4** 26 27S 28 25 E
Niger ■, W. Afr. **50 E7** 17 30N 10 0 E
Niger →, W. Afr. **50 G7** 5 33N 6 33 E
Nigeria ■, W. Afr. **50 G7** 8 30N 8 0 E
Nighasin, India **43 E9** 28 14N 80 52 E
Nightcaps, N.Z. **59 L2** 45 57S 168 2 E
Nii-Jima, Japan **31 G9** 34 20N 139 15 E
Niigata, Japan **30 F9** 37 58N 139 0 E
Niigata □, Japan **31 F9** 37 15N 138 45 E
Niihama, Japan **31 H6** 33 55N 133 16 E
Niihau, U.S.A. **74 H14** 21 54N 160 9W
Niimi, Japan **31 G6** 34 59N 133 28 E
Niitsu, Japan **30 F9** 37 48N 139 7 E
Nijil, Jordan **47 E4** 30 32N 35 33 E
Nijkerk, Neths. **15 B5** 52 13N 5 30 E
Nijmegen, Neths. **15 C5** 51 50N 5 52 E
Nijverdal, Neths. **15 B6** 52 22N 6 28 E
Nīk Pey, Iran **45 B6** 36 50N 48 10 E
Nikiniki, Indonesia **37 F6** 9 49S 124 30 E
Nikkō, Japan **31 F9** 36 45N 139 35 E
Nikolayev = Mykolayiv, Ukraine **25 E5** 46 58N 32 0 E
Nikolayevsk, Russia **25 E8** 50 0N 45 35 E
Nikolayevsk-na-Amur, Russia **27 D15** 53 8N 140 44 E
Nikolskoye, Russia **27 D17** 55 12N 166 0 E
Nikopol, Ukraine **25 E5** 47 35N 34 25 E
Nīkshahr, Iran **45 E9** 26 15N 60 10 E
Nikšić, Montenegro, Yug. **21 C8** 42 50N 18 57 E
Nîl, Nahr en →, Africa **51 B12** 30 10N 31 6 E
Nîl el Abyad →, Sudan **51 E12** 15 38N 32 31 E
Nîl el Azraq →, Sudan **51 E12** 15 38N 32 31 E
Nila, Indonesia **37 F7** 6 44S 129 31 E
Niland, U.S.A. **85 M11** 33 14N 115 31W
Nile = Nîl, Nahr en →, Africa **51 B12** 30 10N 31 6 E
Niles, Mich., U.S.A. **76 E2** 41 50N 86 15W
Niles, Ohio, U.S.A. **78 E4** 41 11N 80 46W
Nim Ka Thana, India **42 F6** 27 44N 75 48 E
Nimach, India **42 G6** 24 30N 74 56 E
Nimbahera, India **42 G6** 24 37N 74 45 E
Nîmes, France **18 E6** 43 50N 4 23 E
Nimfaíon, Ákra = Pínnes, Ákra, Greece **21 D11** 40 5N 24 20 E
Nimmitabel, Australia **63 F4** 36 29S 149 15 E
Nīnawá, Iraq **44 B4** 36 25N 43 10 E
Nindigully, Australia **63 D4** 28 21S 148 50 E
Nineveh = Nīnawá, Iraq **44 B4** 36 25N 43 10 E
Ning Xian, China **34 G4** 35 30N 107 58 E
Ning'an, China **35 B15** 44 22N 129 20 E
Ningbo, China **33 D7** 29 51N 121 28 E
Ningcheng, China **35 D10** 41 32N 119 53 E
Ningjin, China **34 F8** 37 35N 114 57 E
Ningjing Shan, China **32 D4** 30 0N 98 20 E
Ningling, China **34 G8** 34 25N 115 22 E
Ningpo = Ningbo, China **33 D7** 29 51N 121 28 E
Ningqiang, China **34 H4** 32 47N 106 15 E
Ningshan, China **34 H5** 33 21N 108 21 E
Ningsia Hui A.R. = Ningxia Huizu Zizhiqu □, China **34 F4** 38 0N 106 0 E
Ningwu, China **34 E7** 39 0N 112 18 E
Ningxia Huizu Zizhiqu □, China **34 F4** 38 0N 106 0 E
Ningyang, China **34 G9** 35 47N 116 45 E
Ninh Giang, Vietnam **38 B6** 20 44N 106 24 E
Ninh Hoa, Vietnam **38 F7** 12 30N 109 7 E
Ninh Ma, Vietnam **38 F7** 12 48N 109 21 E
Ninove, Belgium **15 D4** 50 51N 4 2 E
Nioaque, Brazil **95 A4** 21 5S 55 50W
Niobrara, U.S.A. **80 D6** 42 45N 98 2W
Niobrara →, U.S.A. **80 D6** 42 46N 98 3W
Nioro du Sahel, Mali **50 E4** 15 15N 9 30W
Niort, France **18 C3** 46 19N 0 29W
Nipawin, Canada **73 C8** 53 20N 104 0W
Nipigon, Canada **70 C2** 49 0N 88 17W
Nipigon, L., Canada **70 C2** 49 50N 88 30W
Nipishish L., Canada **71 B7** 54 12N 60 45W
Nipissing, L., Canada **70 C4** 46 20N 80 0W
Nipomo, U.S.A. **85 K6** 35 3N 120 29W
Nipton, U.S.A. **85 K11** 35 28N 115 16W
Niquelândia, Brazil **93 F9** 14 33S 48 23W
Nīr, Iran **44 B5** 38 2N 47 59 E
Nirasaki, Japan **31 G9** 35 42N 138 27 E
Nirmal, India **40 K11** 19 3N 78 20 E
Nirmali, India **43 F12** 26 20N 86 35 E
Niš, Serbia, Yug. **21 C9** 43 19N 21 58 E
Nişāb, Si. Arabia **44 D5** 29 11N 44 43 E
Nişāb, Yemen **46 E4** 14 25N 46 29 E
Nishinomiya, Japan **31 G7** 34 45N 135 20 E
Nishino'omote, Japan **31 J5** 30 43N 130 59 E
Nishiwaki, Japan **31 G7** 34 59N 134 58 E
Niskibi →, Canada **70 A2** 56 29N 88 9W
Nisqually →, U.S.A. **84 C4** 47 6N 122 42W
Nissáki, Greece **23 A3** 39 43N 19 52 E
Nissum Bredning, Denmark **9 H13** 56 40N 8 20 E
Nistru = Dnister →, Europe **17 E16** 46 18N 30 17 E
Nisutlin →, Canada **72 A2** 60 14N 132 34W
Nitchequon, Canada **71 B5** 53 10N 70 58W
Niterói, Brazil **95 A7** 22 52S 43 0W
Nith →, Canada **78 C4** 43 12N 80 23W
Nith →, U.K. **12 F5** 55 14N 3 33W
Nitra, Slovak Rep. **17 D10** 48 19N 18 4 E
Nitra →, Slovak Rep. **17 E10** 47 46N 18 10 E
Niuafo'ou, Tonga **59 B11** 15 30S 175 58W
Niue, Cook Is. **65 J11** 19 2S 169 54W
Niut, Indonesia **36 D4** 0 55N 110 6 E
Niuzhuang, China **35 D12** 40 58N 122 28 E
Nivala, Finland **8 E21** 63 56N 24 57 E
Nivelles, Belgium **15 D4** 50 35N 4 20 E
Nivernais, France **18 C5** 47 15N 3 30 E
Niwas, India **43 H9** 23 3N 80 26 E
Nixon, U.S.A. **81 L6** 29 16N 97 46W
Nizamabad, India **40 K11** 18 45N 78 7 E
Nizamghat, India **41 E19** 28 20N 95 45 E
Nizhne Kolymsk, Russia **27 C17** 68 34N 160 55 E
Nizhnekamsk, Russia **24 C9** 55 38N 51 49 E
Nizhneudinsk, Russia **27 D10** 54 54N 99 3 E
Nizhnevartovsk, Russia **26 C8** 60 56N 76 38 E
Nizhniy Novgorod, Russia **24 C7** 56 20N 44 0 E
Nizhniy Tagil, Russia **24 C10** 57 55N 59 57 E
Nizhyn, Ukraine **25 D5** 51 5N 31 55 E
Nizip, Turkey **44 B3** 37 5N 37 50 E
Nízké Tatry, Slovak Rep. **17 D10** 48 55N 19 30 E
Njakwa, Malawi **55 E3** 11 1S 33 56 E
Njanji, Zambia **55 E3** 14 25S 31 46 E
Njinjo, Tanzania **55 D4** 8 48S 38 54 E
Njombe, Tanzania **55 D3** 9 20S 34 50 E
Njombe →, Tanzania **54 D4** 6 56S 35 6 E
Nkana, Zambia **55 E2** 12 50S 28 8 E
Nkayi, Zimbabwe **55 F2** 19 41S 29 20 E
Nkhotakota, Malawi **55 E3** 12 56S 34 15 E
Nkongsamba, Cameroon **52 D1** 4 55N 9 55 E
Nkurenkuru, Namibia **56 B2** 17 42S 18 32 E
Nmai →, Burma **41 G20** 25 30N 97 25 E
Noakhali = Maijdi, Bangla. **41 H17** 22 48N 91 10 E
Nobel, Canada **78 A4** 45 25N 80 6W
Nobeoka, Japan **31 H5** 32 36N 131 41 E
Noblesville, U.S.A. **76 E3** 40 3N 86 1W
Nocera Inferiore, Italy **20 D6** 40 44N 14 38 E
Nocona, U.S.A. **81 J6** 33 47N 97 44W
Noda, Japan **31 G9** 35 56N 139 52 E
Nogales, Mexico **86 A2** 31 20N 110 56W
Nogales, U.S.A. **83 L8** 31 20N 110 56W
Nōgata, Japan **31 H5** 33 48N 130 44 E
Noggerup, Australia **61 F2** 33 32S 116 5 E
Noginsk, Russia **27 C10** 64 30N 90 50 E
Nogoa →, Australia **62 C4** 23 40S 147 55 E
Nogoyá, Argentina **94 C4** 32 24S 59 48W
Nohar, India **42 E6** 29 11N 74 49 E
Nohta, India **43 H8** 23 40N 79 34 E
Noire, Mts., France **18 B2** 48 7N 3 28W
Noirmoutier, Î. de, France **18 C2** 46 58N 2 10W
Nojane, Botswana **56 C3** 23 15S 20 14 E
Nojima-Zaki, Japan **31 G9** 34 54N 139 53 E
Nok Kundi, Pakistan **40 E3** 28 50N 62 45 E
Nokaneng, Botswana **56 B3** 19 40S 22 17 E
Nokia, Finland **9 F20** 61 30N 23 30 E
Nokomis, Canada **73 C8** 51 35N 105 0W
Nokomis L., Canada **73 B8** 57 0N 103 0W
Nola, C.A.R. **52 D3** 3 35N 16 4 E
Noma Omuramba →, Namibia **56 B3** 18 52S 20 53 E
Nombre de Dios, Panama **88 E4** 9 34N 79 28W
Nome, U.S.A. **68 B3** 64 30N 165 25W
Nomo-Zaki, Japan **31 H4** 32 35N 129 44 E
Nonacho L., Canada **73 A7** 61 42N 109 40W
Nonda, Australia **62 C3** 20 40S 142 28 E
Nong Chang, Thailand **38 E2** 15 23N 99 51 E
Nong Het, Laos **38 C4** 19 29N 103 59 E
Nong Khai, Thailand **38 D4** 17 50N 102 46 E
Nong'an, China **35 B13** 44 25N 125 5 E
Nongoma, S. Africa **57 D5** 27 58S 31 35 E
Nonoava, Mexico **86 B3** 27 28N 106 44W
Nonoava →, Mexico **86 B3** 27 29N 106 45W
Nonthaburi, Thailand **38 F3** 13 51N 100 34 E
Noonamah, Australia **60 B5** 12 40S 131 4 E
Noord Brabant □, Neths. **15 C5** 51 40N 5 0 E
Noord Holland □, Neths. **15 B4** 52 30N 4 45 E
Noordbeveland, Neths. **15 C3** 51 35N 3 50 E
Noordoostpolder, Neths. **15 B5** 52 45N 5 45 E
Noordwijk, Neths. **15 B4** 52 14N 4 26 E
Nootka I., Canada **72 D3** 49 32N 126 42W
Nopiming Prov. Park, Canada **73 C9** 50 30N 95 37W
Noralee, Canada **72 C3** 53 59N 126 26W
Noranda = Rouyn-Noranda, Canada **70 C4** 48 20N 79 0W
Norco, U.S.A. **85 M9** 33 56N 117 33W
Nord-Kivu □, Dem. Rep. of the Congo **54 C2** 1 0S 29 0 E
Nord-Ostsee-Kanal, Germany **16 A5** 54 12N 9 32 E
Nordaustlandet, Svalbard **4 B9** 79 14N 23 0 E
Nordegg, Canada **72 C5** 52 29N 116 5W
Norderney, Germany **16 B4** 53 42N 7 9 E
Norderstedt, Germany **16 B5** 53 42N 10 1 E
Nordfjord, Norway **9 F11** 61 55N 5 30 E
Nordfriesische Inseln, Germany **16 A5** 54 40N 8 20 E
Nordhausen, Germany **16 C6** 51 30N 10 47 E
Norðoyar, Færoe Is. **8 E9** 62 17N 6 35W
Nordkapp, Norway **8 A21** 71 10N 25 50 E
Nordkapp, Svalbard **4 A9** 80 31N 20 0 E
Nordkinn = Kinnarodden, Norway **6 A11** 71 8N 27 40 E
Nordkinn-halvøya, Norway **8 A22** 70 55N 27 40 E
Nordrhein-Westfalen □, Germany **16 C4** 51 45N 7 30 E
Nordvik, Russia **27 B12** 74 2N 111 32 E
Nore →, Ireland **13 D4** 52 25N 6 58W
Norfolk, Nebr., U.S.A. **80 D6** 42 2N 97 25W
Norfolk, Va., U.S.A. **76 G7** 36 51N 76 17W
Norfolk □, U.K. **11 E8** 52 39N 0 54 E
Norfolk I., Pac. Oc. **64 K8** 28 58S 168 3 E
Norfork L., U.S.A. **81 G8** 36 15N 92 14W
Norilsk, Russia **27 C9** 69 20N 88 6 E
Norma, Mt., Australia **62 C3** 20 55S 140 42 E
Normal, U.S.A. **80 E10** 40 31N 88 59W
Norman, U.S.A. **81 H6** 35 13N 97 26W
Norman →, Australia **62 B3** 19 18S 141 51 E
Norman Wells, Canada **68 B7** 65 17N 126 51W
Normanby →, Australia **62 A3** 14 23S 144 10 E
Normandie, France **18 B4** 48 45N 0 10 E
Normandin, Canada **70 C5** 48 49N 72 31W
Normandy = Normandie, France **18 B4** 48 45N 0 10 E
Normanhurst, Mt., Australia **61 E3** 25 4S 122 30 E
Normanton, Australia **62 B3** 17 40S 141 10 E
Normétal, Canada **70 C4** 49 0N 79 22W
Norquay, Canada **73 C8** 51 53N 102 5W
Norquinco, Argentina **96 E2** 41 51S 70 55W
Norrbotten □, Sweden **8 C19** 66 30N 22 30 E
Norris Point, Canada **71 C8** 49 31N 57 53W
Norristown, U.S.A. **79 F9** 40 7N 75 21W
Norrköping, Sweden **9 G17** 58 37N 16 11 E
Norrland, Sweden **9 E16** 62 15N 15 45 E
Norrtälje, Sweden **9 G18** 59 46N 18 42 E
Norseman, Australia **61 F3** 32 8S 121 43 E
Norsk, Russia **27 D14** 52 30N 130 5 E
Norte, Pta. del, Canary Is. **22 G2** 27 51N 17 57W
Norte, Serra do, Brazil **92** 11 20S 59 0W
North, C., Canada **71 C7** 47 2N 60 20W
North Adams, U.S.A. **79 D11** 42 42N 73 7W
North Arm, Canada **72 A5** 62 0N 114 30W
North Augusta, U.S.A. **77 J5** 33 30N 81 59W
North Ayrshire □, U.K. **12 F4** 55 45N 4 44W
North Bass I., U.S.A. **78 E2** 41 43N 82 49W
North Battleford, Canada **73 C7** 52 50N 108 17W
North Bay, Canada **70 C4** 46 20N 79 30W
North Belcher Is., Canada **70 A4** 56 50N 79 50W
North Bend, Oreg., U.S.A. **82 E1** 43 24N 124 14W
North Bend, Pa., U.S.A. **78 E7** 41 20N 77 42W
North Bend, Wash., U.S.A. **84 C5** 47 30N 121 47W
North Bennington, U.S.A. **79 D11** 42 56N 73 15W
North Berwick, U.K. **12 E6** 56 4N 2 42W
North Berwick, U.S.A. **79 C14** 43 18N 70 44W
North C., Canada **71 C7** 47 5N 64 0W
North C., N.Z. **59 F4** 34 23S 173 4 E
North Canadian →, U.S.A. **81 H7** 35 16N 95 31W
North Canton, U.S.A. **78 F3** 40 53N 81 24W
North Cape = Nordkapp, Norway **8 A21** 71 10N 25 50 E
North Cape = Nordkapp, Svalbard **4 A9** 80 31N 20 0 E
North Caribou L., Canada **70 B1** 52 50N 90 40W
North Carolina □, U.S.A. **77 H6** 35 30N 80 0W
North Cascades National Park, U.S.A. **82 B3** 48 45N 121 10W
North Channel, Canada **70 C3** 46 0N 83 0W
North Channel, U.K. **12 F3** 55 13N 5 52W
North Charleston, U.S.A. **77 J6** 32 53N 79 58W
North Chicago, U.S.A. **76 D2** 42 19N 87 51W
North Creek, U.S.A. **79 C11** 43 41N 73 59W
North Dakota □, U.S.A. **80 B5** 47 30N 100 15W
North Downs, U.K. **11 F8** 51 19N 0 21 E
North East, U.S.A. **78 D5** 42 13N 79 50W
North East Frontier Agency = Arunachal Pradesh □, India **41 F19** 28 0N 95 0 E
North East Lincolnshire □, U.K. **10 D7** 53 34N 0 2W
North Eastern □, Kenya **54 B5** 1 30N 40 0 E
North Esk →, U.K. **12 E6** 56 46N 2 24W
North European Plain, Europe **6 E10** 55 0N 25 0 E
North Foreland, U.K. **11 F9** 51 22N 1 28 E
North Fork, U.S.A. **84 H7** 37 14N 119 21W
North Fork American →, U.S.A. **84 G5** 38 57N 120 59W
North Fork Feather →, U.S.A. **84 F5** 38 33N 121 30W
North Fork Grand →, U.S.A. **80 C3** 45 47N 102 16W
North Fork Red →, U.S.A. **81 H5** 34 24N 99 14W
North Frisian Is. = Nordfriesische Inseln, Germany **16 A5** 54 40N 8 20 E
North Gower, Canada **79 A9** 45 8N 75 43W
North Hd., Australia **61 F1** 30 14S 114 59 E
North Henik L., Canada **73 A9** 61 45N 97 40W
North Highlands, U.S.A. **84 G5** 38 40N 121 23W
North Horr, Kenya **54 B4** 3 20N 37 8 E
North I., Kenya **54 B4** 4 5N 36 5 E
North I., N.Z. **59 H5** 38 0S 175 0 E
North Kingsville, U.S.A. **78 E4** 41 54N 80 42W
North Knife →, Canada **73 B10** 58 53N 94 45W

North Koel

North Koel →, India 43 G10 24 45N 83 50 E
North Korea ■, Asia 35 E14 40 0N 127 0 E
North Lakhimpur, India 41 F19 27 14N 94 7 E
North Lanarkshire □, U.K. 12 F5 55 52N 3 56W
North Las Vegas, U.S.A. 85 J11 36 12N 115 7W
North Lincolnshire □, U.K. 10 D7 53 36N 0 30W
North Little Rock, U.S.A. 81 H8 34 45N 92 16W
North Loup →, U.S.A. 80 E5 41 17N 98 24W
North Magnetic Pole, Canada 4 B2 77 58N 102 8W
North Minch, U.K. 12 C3 58 5N 5 55W
North Moose L., Canada 73 C8 54 11N 100 6W
North Myrtle Beach, U.S.A. 77 J6 33 48N 78 42W
North Nahanni →, Canada 72 A4 62 15N 123 20W
North Olmsted, U.S.A. 78 E3 41 25N 81 56W
North Ossetia □, Russia 25 F7 43 30N 44 30 E
North Pagai, I. = Pagai Utara, Pulau, Indonesia 36 E2 2 35S 100 0 E
North Palisade, U.S.A. 84 H8 37 6N 118 31W
North Platte, U.S.A. 80 E4 41 8N 100 46W
North Platte →, U.S.A. 80 E4 41 7N 100 42W
North Pole, Arctic 4 A 90 0N 0 0 E
North Portal, Canada 73 D8 49 0N 102 33W
North Powder, U.S.A. 82 D5 45 2N 117 55W
North Pt., U.S.A. 78 A1 45 2N 83 16W
North Rhine Westphalia = Nordrhein-Westfalen □, Germany 16 C4 51 45N 7 30 E
North River, Canada 71 B8 53 49N 57 6W
North Ronaldsay, U.K. 12 B6 59 22N 2 26W
North Saskatchewan →, Canada 73 C7 53 15N 105 5W
North Sea, Europe 6 D6 56 0N 4 0 E
North Seal →, Canada 73 B9 58 50N 98 7W
North Somerset □, U.K. 11 F5 51 24N 2 45W
North Sporades = Vóriai Sporádhes, Greece 21 E10 39 15N 23 30 E
North Sydney, Canada 71 C7 46 12N 60 15W
North Syracuse, U.S.A. 79 C8 43 8N 76 7W
North Taranaki Bight, N.Z. 59 H5 38 50S 174 15 E
North Thompson →, Canada 72 C4 50 40N 120 20W
North Tonawanda, U.S.A. 78 C6 43 2N 78 53W
North Troy, U.S.A. 79 B12 45 0N 72 24W
North Truchas Pk., U.S.A. 83 J11 36 0N 105 30W
North Twin I., Canada 70 B4 53 20N 80 0W
North Tyne →, U.K. 10 B5 55 0N 2 8W
North Uist, U.K. 12 D1 57 40N 7 15W
North Vancouver, Canada 72 D4 49 19N 123 4W
North Vernon, U.S.A. 76 F3 39 0N 85 38W
North Wabasca L., Canada 72 B6 56 0N 113 55W
North Walsham, U.K. 10 E9 52 50N 1 22 E
North-West □, S. Africa 56 D4 27 0S 25 0 E
North West C., Australia 60 D1 21 45S 114 9 E
North West Christmas I. Ridge, Pac. Oc. 65 G11 6 30N 165 0W
North West Frontier □, Pakistan 42 C4 34 0N 72 0 E
North West Highlands, U.K. 12 D4 57 33N 4 58W
North West River, Canada 71 B7 53 30N 60 10W
North Western □, Zambia 55 E2 13 30S 25 30 E
North Wildwood, U.S.A. 76 F8 39 0N 74 48W
North York Moors, U.K. 10 C7 54 23N 0 53W
North Yorkshire □, U.K. 10 C6 54 15N 1 25W
Northallerton, U.K. 10 C6 54 20N 1 26W
Northam, Australia 61 F2 31 35S 116 42 E
Northam, S. Africa 56 C4 24 56S 27 18 E
Northampton, Australia 61 E1 28 27S 114 33 E
Northampton, U.K. 11 E7 52 15N 0 53W
Northampton, Mass., U.S.A. 79 D12 42 19N 72 38W
Northampton, Pa., U.S.A. 79 F9 40 41N 75 30W
Northamptonshire □, U.K. 11 E7 52 16N 0 55W
Northbridge, U.S.A. 79 D13 42 9N 71 39W
Northcliffe, Australia 61 F2 34 39S 116 7 E
Northeast Providence Chan., W. Indies 88 A4 26 0N 76 0W
Northern □, Malawi 55 E3 11 0S 34 0 E
Northern □, Uganda 54 B3 3 5N 32 30 E
Northern □, Zambia 55 E3 10 30S 31 0 E
Northern Cape □, S. Africa 56 D3 30 0S 20 0 E
Northern Circars, India 41 L13 17 30N 82 30 E
Northern Indian L., Canada 73 B9 57 20N 97 20W
Northern Ireland □, U.K. 13 B5 54 45N 7 0W
Northern Light L., Canada 70 C1 48 15N 90 39W
Northern Marianas ■, Pac. Oc. 64 F6 17 0N 145 0 E
Northern Territory □, Australia 60 D5 20 0S 133 0 E
Northern Transvaal □, S. Africa 57 C4 24 0S 29 0 E
Northfield, Minn., U.S.A. 80 C8 44 27N 93 9W
Northfield, Vt., U.S.A. 79 B12 44 9N 72 40W
Northland □, N.Z. 59 F4 35 30S 173 30 E
Northome, U.S.A. 80 B7 47 52N 94 17W
Northport, Ala., U.S.A. 77 J2 33 14N 87 35W
Northport, Wash., U.S.A. 82 B5 48 55N 117 48W
Northumberland □, U.K. 10 B6 55 12N 2 0W
Northumberland, C., Australia 63 F3 38 5S 140 40 E
Northumberland Is., Australia 62 C4 21 30S 149 50 E
Northumberland Str., Canada 71 C7 46 20N 64 0W
Northville, U.S.A. 79 C10 43 13N 74 11W
Northwest Providence Channel, W. Indies 88 A4 26 0N 78 0W
Northwest Territories □, Canada 68 B9 67 0N 110 0W
Northwood, Iowa, U.S.A. 80 D8 43 27N 93 13W
Northwood, N. Dak., U.S.A. 80 B6 47 44N 97 34W
Norton, U.S.A. 80 F5 39 50N 99 53W
Norton, Zimbabwe 55 F3 17 52S 30 40 E
Norton Sd., U.S.A. 68 B3 63 50N 164 0W
Norwalk, Calif., U.S.A. 85 M8 33 54N 118 5W
Norwalk, Conn., U.S.A. 79 E11 41 7N 73 22W
Norwalk, Iowa, U.S.A. 80 E8 41 29N 93 41W
Norwalk, Ohio, U.S.A. 78 E2 41 15N 82 37W
Norway, Maine, U.S.A. 77 C10 44 13N 70 32W
Norway, Mich., U.S.A. 76 C2 45 47N 87 55W
Norway ■, Europe 8 E14 63 0N 11 0 E
Norway House, Canada 73 C9 53 59N 97 50W
Norwegian Sea, Atl. Oc. 4 C8 66 0N 1 0 E
Norwich, Canada 78 D4 42 59N 80 36W
Norwich, U.K. 11 E9 52 38N 1 18 E
Norwich, Conn., U.S.A. 79 E12 41 31N 72 5W
Norwich, N.Y., U.S.A. 79 D9 42 32N 75 32W
Norwood, Canada 78 B7 44 23N 77 59W
Norwood, U.S.A. 79 B10 44 45N 75 0W
Noshiro, Japan 30 D10 40 12N 140 0 E
Noşratābād, Iran 45 D8 29 55N 60 0 E
Noss Hd., U.K. 12 C5 58 28N 3 3W
Nossob →, S. Africa 56 D3 26 55S 20 45 E
Nosy Barren, Madag. 53 H8 18 25S 43 40 E
Nosy Be, Madag. 53 G9 13 25S 48 15 E
Nosy Boraha, Madag. 57 B8 16 50S 49 55 E
Nosy Varika, Madag. 57 C8 20 35S 48 32 E
Noteć →, Poland 16 B8 52 44N 15 26 E
Notikewin →, Canada 72 B5 57 2N 117 38W
Notodden, Norway 9 G13 59 35N 9 17 E
Notre Dame B., Canada 71 C8 49 45N 55 30W
Notre Dame de Koartac = Quaqtaq, Canada 69 B13 60 55N 69 40W
Notre-Dame-des-Bois, Canada 79 A13 45 24N 71 4W
Notre Dame d'Ivugivic = Ivujivik, Canada 69 B12 62 24N 77 55W
Notre-Dame-du-Nord, Canada 70 C4 47 36N 79 30W
Nottawasaga B., Canada 78 B4 44 35N 80 15W
Nottaway →, Canada 70 B4 51 22N 78 55W
Nottingham, U.K. 10 E6 52 58N 1 10W
Nottingham, City of □, U.K. 10 E6 52 58N 1 10W
Nottingham I., Canada 69 B12 63 20N 77 55W
Nottinghamshire □, U.K. 10 D6 53 10N 1 3W
Nottoway →, U.S.A. 76 G7 36 33N 76 55W
Notwane →, Botswana 56 C4 23 35S 26 58 E
Nouâdhibou, Mauritania 50 D2 20 54N 17 0W
Nouâdhibou, Ras, Mauritania 50 D2 20 50N 17 0W
Nouakchott, Mauritania 50 E2 18 9N 15 58W
Nouméa, N. Cal. 64 K8 22 17S 166 30 E
Noupoort, S. Africa 56 E3 31 10S 24 57 E
Nouveau Comptoir = Wemindji, Canada 70 B4 53 0N 78 49W
Nouvelle-Calédonie = New Caledonia ■, Pac. Oc. 64 K8 21 0S 165 0 E
Nova Casa Nova, Brazil 93 E10 9 25S 41 5W
Nova Esperança, Brazil 95 A5 23 8S 52 24W
Nova Friburgo, Brazil 95 A7 22 16S 42 30W
Nova Gaia = Cambundi-Catembo, Angola 52 G3 10 10S 17 35 E
Nova Iguaçu, Brazil 95 A7 22 45S 43 28W
Nova Iorque, Brazil 93 E10 7 0S 44 5W
Nova Lima, Brazil 95 A7 19 59S 43 51W
Nova Lisboa = Huambo, Angola 53 G3 12 42S 15 54 E
Nova Lusitânia, Mozam. 55 F3 19 50S 34 34 E
Nova Mambone, Mozam. 57 C6 21 0S 35 3 E
Nova Scotia □, Canada 71 C7 45 10N 63 0W
Nova Sofala, Mozam. 57 C5 20 7S 34 42 E
Nova Venécia, Brazil 93 G10 18 45S 40 24W
Nova Zagora, Bulgaria 21 C11 42 32N 26 1 E
Novar, Canada 78 A5 45 27N 79 15W
Novara, Italy 18 D8 45 28N 8 38 E
Novato, U.S.A. 84 G4 38 6N 122 35W
Novaya Ladoga, Russia 24 B5 60 7N 32 16 E
Novaya Lyalya, Russia 24 C11 59 4N 60 45 E
Novaya Sibir, Ostrov, Russia 27 B16 75 10N 150 0 E
Novaya Zemlya, Russia 26 B6 75 0N 56 0 E
Nové Zámky, Slovak Rep. 17 D10 48 2N 18 8 E
Novgorod, Russia 24 C5 58 30N 31 25 E
Novgorod-Severskiy = Novhorod-Siverskyy, Ukraine 24 D5 52 2N 33 10 E
Novhorod-Siverskyy, Ukraine 24 D5 52 2N 33 10 E
Novi Lígure, Italy 18 D8 44 46N 8 47 E
Novi Pazar, Serbia, Yug. 21 C9 43 12N 20 28 E
Novi Sad, Serbia, Yug. 21 B8 45 18N 19 52 E
Nôvo Hamburgo, Brazil 95 B5 29 37S 51 7W
Novo Mesto, Slovenia 20 B6 45 47N 15 12 E
Novo Remanso, Brazil 93 E10 9 41S 42 4W
Novoataysk, Russia 26 D9 53 30N 84 0 E
Novocherkassk, Russia 25 E7 47 27N 40 15 E
Novogrudok = Navahrudak, Belarus 17 B13 53 40N 25 50 E
Novohrad-Volynskyy, Ukraine 17 C14 50 34N 27 35 E
Novokachalinsk, Russia 30 B6 45 5N 132 0 E
Novokazalinsk = Zhangaqazaly, Kazakstan 26 E7 45 48N 62 6 E
Novokuybyshevsk, Russia 24 D8 53 7N 49 58 E
Novokuznetsk, Russia 26 D9 53 45N 87 10 E
Novomoskovsk, Russia 24 D6 54 5N 38 15 E
Novorossiysk, Russia 25 F6 44 43N 37 46 E
Novorybnoye, Russia 27 B11 72 50N 105 50 E
Novoselytsya, Ukraine 17 D14 48 14N 26 15 E
Novoshakhtinsk, Russia 25 E6 47 46N 39 58 E
Novosibirsk, Russia 26 D9 55 0N 83 5 E
Novosibirskiye Ostrova, Russia 27 B15 75 0N 142 0 E
Novotroitsk, Russia 24 D10 51 10N 58 15 E
Novouzensk, Russia 25 D8 50 32N 48 17 E
Novovolynsk, Ukraine 17 C13 50 45N 24 4 E
Novska, Croatia 20 B7 45 19N 17 0 E
Novyy Urengoy, Russia 26 C8 65 48N 76 52 E
Novyy Bor, Russia 24 A9 66 43N 52 19 E
Novyy Port, Russia 26 C8 67 40N 72 30 E
Now Shahr, Iran 45 B6 36 40N 51 30 E
Nowa Sól, Poland 16 C8 51 48N 15 44 E
Nowata, U.S.A. 81 G7 36 42N 95 38W
Nowbarān, Iran 45 C6 35 8N 49 42 E
Nowghāb, Iran 45 C8 33 53N 59 4 E
Nowgong, Assam, India 41 F18 26 20N 92 50 E
Nowgong, Mad. P., India 43 G8 25 4N 79 27 E
Nowra-Bomaderry, Australia 63 E5 34 53S 150 35 E
Nowshera, Pakistan 40 C8 34 0N 72 0 E
Nowy Sącz, Poland 17 D11 49 40N 20 41 E
Nowy Targ, Poland 17 D11 49 29N 20 2 E
Nowy Tomyśl, Poland 16 B9 52 19N 16 10 E
Noxen, U.S.A. 79 E8 41 25N 76 4W
Noxon, U.S.A. 82 C6 48 0N 115 43W
Noyabr'sk, Russia 26 C8 64 34N 76 21 E
Noyon, France 18 B5 49 34N 2 59 E
Noyon, Mongolia 34 C2 43 2N 102 4 E
Nsanje, Malawi 55 F4 16 55S 35 12 E
Nsomba, Zambia 55 E2 10 45S 29 51 E
Nu Jiang →, China 32 D4 29 58N 97 25 E
Nu Shan, China 32 D4 26 0N 99 20 E
Nubia, Africa 48 D7 21 0N 32 0 E
Nubian Desert = Nûbîya, Es Sahrâ en, Sudan 51 D12 21 30N 33 30 E
Nûbîya, Es Sahrâ en, Sudan 51 D12 21 30N 33 30 E
Nuboai, Indonesia 37 E9 2 10S 136 30 E
Nubra →, India 43 B7 34 35N 77 35 E
Nueces →, U.S.A. 81 M6 27 51N 97 30W
Nueltin L., Canada 73 A9 60 30N 99 30W
Nueva Asunción □, Paraguay 94 A3 21 0S 61 0W
Nueva Gerona, Cuba 88 B3 21 53N 82 49W
Nueva Palmira, Uruguay 94 C4 33 52S 58 20W
Nueva Rosita, Mexico 86 B4 28 0N 101 11W
Nueva San Salvador, El Salv. 88 D2 13 40N 89 18W
Nuéve de Julio, Argentina 94 D3 35 30S 61 0W
Nuevitas, Cuba 88 B4 21 30N 77 20W
Nuevo, G., Argentina 96 E4 43 0S 64 30W
Nuevo Casas Grandes, Mexico 86 A3 30 22N 108 0W
Nuevo Guerrero, Mexico 87 B5 26 34N 99 15W
Nuevo Laredo, Mexico 87 B5 27 30N 99 30W
Nuevo León □, Mexico 86 C5 25 0N 100 0W
Nuevo Rocafuerte, Ecuador 92 D3 0 55S 75 27W
Nugget Pt., N.Z. 59 M2 46 27S 169 50 E
Nuhaka, N.Z. 59 H6 39 3S 177 45 E
Nukey Bluff, Australia 63 E2 32 26S 135 29 E
Nukhuyb, Iraq 44 C4 32 4N 42 3 E
Nuku'alofa, Tonga 59 E12 21 10S 174 0W
Nukus, Uzbekistan 26 E6 42 27N 59 41 E
Nullagine, Australia 60 D3 21 53S 120 7 E
Nullagine →, Australia 60 D3 21 20S 120 20 E
Nullarbor, Australia 61 F5 31 28S 130 55 E
Nullarbor Plain, Australia 61 F4 31 10S 129 0 E
Numalla, L., Australia 63 D3 28 43S 144 20 E
Numan, Nigeria 51 G8 9 29N 12 3 E
Numata, Japan 31 F9 36 45N 139 4 E
Numazu, Japan 31 G9 35 7N 138 51 E
Numbulwar, Australia 62 A2 14 15S 135 45 E
Numfoor, Indonesia 37 E8 1 0S 134 50 E
Numurkah, Australia 63 F4 36 5S 145 26 E
Nunaksaluk I., Canada 71 A7 55 49N 60 20W
Nunavut □, Canada 69 B11 66 0N 85 0W
Nunda, U.S.A. 78 D7 42 35N 77 56W
Nungarin, Australia 61 F2 31 12S 118 6 E
Nungo, Mozam. 55 E4 13 23S 37 43 E
Nungwe, Tanzania 54 C3 2 48S 32 2 E
Nunivak I., U.S.A. 68 C3 60 10N 166 30W
Nunkun, India 43 C7 33 57N 76 2 E
Nùoro, Italy 20 D3 40 20N 9 20 E
Nūrābād, Iran 45 E8 27 47N 57 12 E
Nuremberg = Nürnberg, Germany 16 D6 49 27N 11 3 E
Nuri, Mexico 86 B3 28 2N 109 22W
Nuriootpa, Australia 63 E2 34 27S 139 0 E
Nurmes, Finland 8 E23 63 33N 29 10 E
Nürnberg, Germany 16 D6 49 27N 11 3 E
Nurpur, Pakistan 42 D4 31 53N 71 54 E
Nurran, L. = Terewah, L., Australia 63 D4 29 52S 147 35 E
Nurrari Lakes, Australia 61 E5 29 1S 130 5 E
Nusa Barung, Indonesia 37 H15 8 30S 113 30 E
Nusa Kambangan, Indonesia 37 G13 7 40S 108 10 E
Nusa Tenggara Barat □, Indonesia 36 F5 8 50S 117 30 E
Nusa Tenggara Timur □, Indonesia 37 F6 9 30S 122 0 E
Nusaybin, Turkey 25 G7 37 3N 41 10 E
Nushki, Pakistan 42 E2 29 35N 66 0 E
Nuuk, Greenland 69 B14 64 10N 51 35W
Nuwakot, Nepal 43 E10 28 10N 83 55 E
Nuweiba', Egypt 44 D2 28 59N 34 39 E
Nuweveldberge, S. Africa 56 E3 32 10S 21 45 E
Nuyts, C., Australia 61 F5 32 2S 132 21 E
Nuyts, Pt., Australia 61 G2 35 4S 116 38 E
Nuyts Arch., Australia 63 E1 32 35S 133 20 E
Nxau-Nxau, Botswana 56 B3 18 57S 21 4 E
Nyabing, Australia 61 F2 33 33S 118 9 E
Nyack, U.S.A. 79 E11 41 5N 73 55W
Nyagan, Russia 26 C7 62 30N 65 38 E
Nyahanga, Tanzania 54 C3 2 20S 33 37 E
Nyahua, Tanzania 54 D3 5 25S 33 23 E
Nyahururu, Kenya 54 B4 0 2N 36 27 E
Nyainqentanglha Shan, China 32 D4 30 0N 90 0 E
Nyakanazi, Tanzania 54 C3 3 2S 31 10 E
Nyâlâ, Sudan 51 F10 12 2N 24 58 E
Nyamandhlovu, Zimbabwe 55 F2 19 55S 28 16 E
Nyambiti, Tanzania 54 C3 2 48S 33 27 E
Nyamwaga, Tanzania 54 C3 1 27S 34 33 E
Nyandekwa, Tanzania 54 C3 3 57S 32 32 E
Nyandoma, Russia 24 B7 61 40N 40 12 E
Nyangana, Namibia 56 B3 18 0S 20 40 E
Nyanguge, Tanzania 54 C3 2 30S 33 12 E
Nyanza, Rwanda 54 C2 2 20S 29 42 E
Nyanza □, Kenya 54 C3 0 10S 34 15 E
Nyanza-Lac, Burundi 54 C2 4 21S 29 36 E
Nyasa, L., Africa 55 E3 12 30S 34 30 E
Nyasvizh, Belarus 17 B14 53 14N 26 38 E
Nyazepetrovsk, Russia 24 C10 56 3N 59 36 E
Nyazura, Zimbabwe 55 F3 18 40S 32 16 E
Nyazwidzi →, Zimbabwe 55 G3 20 0S 31 17 E
Nybro, Sweden 9 H16 56 44N 15 55 E
Nyda, Russia 26 C8 66 40N 72 58 E
Nyeri, Kenya 54 C4 0 23S 36 56 E
Nyíregyháza, Hungary 17 E11 47 58N 21 47 E
Nykøbing, Storstrøm, Denmark 9 J14 54 56N 11 52 E
Nykøbing, Vestsjælland, Denmark 9 J14 55 55N 11 40 E
Nykøbing, Viborg, Denmark 9 H13 56 48N 8 51 E
Nyköping, Sweden 9 G17 58 45N 17 1 E
Nylstroom, S. Africa 57 C4 24 42S 28 22 E
Nymagee, Australia 63 E4 32 7S 146 20 E
Nynäshamn, Sweden 9 G17 58 54N 17 57 E
Nyngan, Australia 63 E4 31 30S 147 8 E
Nyoma Rap, India 43 C8 33 10N 78 40 E
Nyoman = Neman →, Lithuania 9 J20 55 25N 21 10 E
Nysa, Poland 17 C9 50 30N 17 22 E
Nysa →, Europe 16 B8 52 4N 14 46 E
Nyssa, U.S.A. 82 E5 43 53N 117 0W
Nyunzu, Dem. Rep. of the Congo 54 D2 5 57S 27 58 E
Nyurba, Russia 27 C12 63 17N 118 28 E
Nzega, Tanzania 54 C3 4 10S 33 12 E
N'zérékoré, Guinea 50 G4 7 49N 8 48W
Nzeto, Angola 52 F2 7 10S 12 52 E
Nzilo, Chutes de, Dem. Rep. of the Congo 55 E2 10 18S 25 27 E
Nzubuka, Tanzania 54 C3 4 45S 32 50 E

O

Ō-Shima, Japan 31 G9 34 44N 139 24 E
Oa, Mull of, U.K. 12 F2 55 35N 6 20W
Oacoma, U.S.A. 80 D5 43 48N 99 24W
Oahe, L., U.S.A. 80 C4 44 27N 100 24W
Oahe Dam, U.S.A. 80 C4 44 27N 100 24W
Oahu, U.S.A. 74 H16 21 28N 157 58W
Oak Harbor, U.S.A. 84 B4 48 18N 122 39W
Oak Hill, U.S.A. 76 G5 37 59N 81 9W
Oak Ridge, U.S.A. 77 G3 36 1N 84 16W
Oak View, U.S.A. 85 L7 34 24N 119 18W
Oakan-Dake, Japan 30 C12 43 27N 144 10 E
Oakdale, Calif., U.S.A. 84 H6 37 46N 120 51W
Oakdale, La., U.S.A. 81 K8 30 49N 92 40W
Oakes, U.S.A. 80 B5 46 8N 98 6W
Oakesdale, U.S.A. 82 C5 47 8N 117 15W
Oakey, Australia 63 D5 27 25S 151 43 E
Oakfield, U.S.A. 78 C6 43 4N 78 16W
Oakham, U.K. 11 E7 52 40N 0 43W
Oakhurst, U.S.A. 84 H7 37 19N 119 40W
Oakland, U.S.A. 84 H4 37 49N 122 16W
Oakley, Idaho, U.S.A. 82 E7 42 15N 113 53W
Oakley, Kans., U.S.A. 80 F4 39 8N 100 51W
Oakover →, Australia 60 D3 21 0S 120 40 E
Oakridge, U.S.A. 82 E2 43 45N 122 28W
Oakville, Canada 78 C5 43 27N 79 41W
Oakville, U.S.A. 84 D3 46 51N 123 14W
Oamaru, N.Z. 59 L3 45 5S 170 59 E
Oasis, Calif., U.S.A. 85 M10 33 28N 116 6W
Oasis, Nev., U.S.A. 84 H9 37 29N 117 55W
Oates Land, Antarctica 5 C11 69 0S 160 0 E
Oatlands, Australia 62 G4 42 17S 147 21 E
Oatman, U.S.A. 85 K12 35 1N 114 19W
Oaxaca, Mexico 87 D5 17 2N 96 40W
Oaxaca □, Mexico 87 D5 17 0N 97 0W
Ob →, Russia 26 C7 66 45N 69 30 E
Oba, Canada 70 C3 49 4N 84 7W
Obama, Japan 31 G7 35 30N 135 45 E
Oban, U.K. 12 E3 56 25N 5 29W
Obbia, Somali Rep. 46 F4 5 25N 48 30 E
Obera, Argentina 95 B4 27 21S 55 2W
Oberhausen, Germany 16 C4 51 28N 6 51 E
Oberlin, Kans., U.S.A. 80 F4 39 49N 100 32W
Oberlin, La., U.S.A. 81 K8 30 37N 92 46W
Oberlin, Ohio, U.S.A. 78 E2 41 18N 82 13W
Oberon, Australia 63 E4 33 45S 149 52 E
Obi, Kepulauan, Indonesia 37 E7 1 23S 127 45 E
Obi Is. = Obi, Kepulauan, Indonesia 37 E7 1 23S 127 45 E
Óbidos, Brazil 93 D7 1 50S 55 30W
Obihiro, Japan 30 C11 42 56N 143 12 E
Obilatu, Indonesia 37 E7 1 25S 127 20 E
Obluchye, Russia 27 E14 49 1N 131 4 E
Obo, C.A.R. 54 A2 5 20N 26 32 E
Oboa, Mt., Uganda 54 B3 1 45N 34 45 E
Oboyan, Russia 26 D4 51 15N 36 21 E
Obozerskaya = Obozerskiy, Russia 24 B7 63 34N 40 21 E
Obozerskiy, Russia 24 B7 63 34N 40 21 E
Observatory Inlet, Canada 72 B3 55 10N 129 54W
Obshchi Syrt, Russia 6 E16 52 0N 53 0 E
Obskaya Guba, Russia 26 C8 69 0N 73 0 E
Obuasi, Ghana 50 G5 6 17N 1 40W
Ocala, U.S.A. 77 L4 29 11N 82 8W
Ocampo, Mexico 86 B3 28 9N 108 24W
Ocampo, Tamaulipas, Mexico 87 C5 22 50N 99 20W
Ocaña, Spain 19 C4 39 55N 3 30W
Ocanomowoc, U.S.A. 80 D10 43 7N 88 30W
Occidental, Cordillera, Colombia 92 C3 5 0N 76 0W
Ocean City, Md., U.S.A. 76 F8 38 20N 75 5W
Ocean City, N.J., U.S.A. 76 F8 39 17N 74 35W
Ocean City, Wash., U.S.A. 84 C2 47 4N 124 10W
Ocean Falls, Canada 72 C3 52 18N 127 48W
Ocean I. = Banaba, Kiribati 64 H8 0 45S 169 50 E
Ocean Park, U.S.A. 84 D2 46 30N 124 3W
Oceano, U.S.A. 85 K6 35 6N 120 37W
Oceanport, U.S.A. 79 F10 40 19N 74 3W
Oceanside, U.S.A. 85 M9 33 12N 117 23W
Ochil Hills, U.K. 12 E5 56 14N 3 40W
Ocilla, U.S.A. 77 K4 31 36N 83 15W
Ocniţa, Moldova 17 D14 48 25N 27 30 E
Oconee →, U.S.A. 77 K4 31 58N 82 33W
Oconto, U.S.A. 76 C2 44 53N 87 52W
Oconto Falls, U.S.A. 76 C1 44 52N 88 9W
Ocosingo, Mexico 87 D6 17 10N 92 15W
Ocotal, Nic. 88 D2 13 41N 86 31W
Ocotlán, Mexico 86 C4 20 21N 102 42W
Ocotlán de Morelos, Mexico 87 D5 16 48N 96 40W
Ōda, Japan 31 G6 35 11N 132 30 E
Ódáðahraun, Iceland 8 D5 65 5N 17 0W
Odate, Japan 30 D10 40 16N 140 34 E
Odawara, Japan 31 G9 35 20N 139 6 E
Odda, Norway 9 F12 60 3N 6 35 E
Odei →, Canada 73 B9 56 6N 96 54W
Ödemiş, Turkey 21 E13 38 15N 28 0 E
Odendaalsrus, S. Africa 56 D4 27 48S 26 45 E
Odense, Denmark 9 J14 55 22N 10 23 E
Oder →, Europe 16 B8 53 33N 14 38 E
Odesa, Ukraine 25 E5 46 30N 30 45 E
Odessa = Odesa, Ukraine 25 E5 46 30N 30 45 E
Odessa, Canada 79 B8 44 17N 76 43W
Odessa, Tex., U.S.A. 81 K3 31 52N 102 23W
Odessa, Wash., U.S.A. 82 C4 47 20N 118 41W
Odiakwe, Botswana 56 C4 20 12S 25 17 E
Odienné, Ivory C. 50 G4 9 30N 7 34W
Odintsovo, Russia 24 C6 55 39N 37 15 E
O'Donnell, U.S.A. 81 J4 32 58N 101 50W
Odorheiu Secuiesc, Romania 17 E13 46 21N 25 21 E
Odra = Oder →, Europe 16 B8 53 33N 14 38 E
Odzi, Zimbabwe 57 B5 19 0S 32 20 E
Oeiras, Brazil 93 E10 7 0S 42 8W
Oelrichs, U.S.A. 80 D3 43 11N 103 14W
Oelwein, U.S.A. 80 D9 42 41N 91 55W
Oenpelli, Australia 60 B5 12 20S 133 4 E
Ofanto →, Italy 20 D7 41 22N 16 13 E
Offa, Nigeria 50 G6 8 13N 4 42 E
Offaly □, Ireland 13 C4 53 15N 7 30W
Offenbach, Germany 16 C5 50 6N 8 44 E
Offenburg, Germany 16 D4 48 28N 7 56 E

Oshmyany

Oshmyany = Ashmyany, *Belarus* .... 9 J21 54 26N 25 52 E
Oshnovīyeh, *Iran* .... 44 B5 37 2N 45 6 E
Oshogbo, *Nigeria* .... 50 G6 7 48N 4 37 E
Oshtorīnān, *Iran* .... 45 C6 34 1N 48 38 E
Oshwe, *Dem. Rep. of the Congo* . 52 E3 3 25S 19 28 E
Osijek, *Croatia* .... 21 B8 45 34N 18 41 E
Osipenko = Berdyansk, *Ukraine* .... 25 E6 46 45N 36 50 E
Osipovichi = Asipovichy, *Belarus* .... 17 B15 53 19N 28 33 E
Osiyan, *India* .... 42 F5 26 43N 72 55 E
Osizweni, *S. Africa* .... 57 D5 27 49S 30 7 E
Oskaloosa, *U.S.A.* 80 E8 41 18N 92 39W
Oskarshamn, *Sweden* .... 9 H17 57 15N 16 27 E
Oskélanéo, *Canada* 70 C4 48 5N 75 15W
Öskemen, *Kazakstan* .... 26 E9 50 0N 82 36 E
Oslo, *Norway* .... 9 G14 59 55N 10 45 E
Oslofjorden, *Norway* .... 9 G14 59 20N 10 35 E
Osmanabad, *India* .... 40 K10 18 5N 76 10 E
Osmaniye, *Turkey* .... 25 G6 37 5N 36 10 E
Osnabrück, *Germany* .... 16 B5 52 17N 8 3 E
Osorio, *Brazil* 95 B5 29 53S 50 17W
Osorno, *Chile* 96 E2 40 25S 73 0W
Osoyoos, *Canada* 72 D5 49 0N 119 30W
Osøyro, *Norway* .... 9 F11 60 9N 5 30 E
Ospika —►, *Canada* 72 B4 56 20N 124 0W
Osprey Reef, *Australia* .... 62 A4 13 52S 146 36 E
Oss, *Neths.* .... 15 C5 51 46N 5 32 E
Ossa, Mt., *Australia* .... 62 G4 41 52S 146 3 E
Óssa, Óros, *Greece* .... 21 E10 39 47N 22 42 E
Ossabaw I., *U.S.A.* 77 K5 31 50N 81 5W
Ossining, *U.S.A.* 79 E11 41 10N 73 55W
Ossipee, *U.S.A.* 79 C13 43 41N 71 7W
Ossokmanuan L., *Canada* . 71 B7 53 25N 65 0W
Ossora, *Russia* .... 27 D17 59 20N 163 13 E
Ostend = Oostende, *Belgium* .... 15 C2 51 15N 2 54 E
Oster, *Ukraine* .... 17 C16 50 57N 30 53 E
Osterburg, *U.S.A.* 78 F6 40 16N 78 31W
Österdalälven, *Sweden* .... 9 F16 61 30N 13 45 E
Østerdalen, *Norway* .... 9 F14 61 40N 10 50 E
Östersund, *Sweden* .... 8 E16 63 10N 14 38 E
Ostfriesische Inseln, *Germany* .... 16 B4 53 42N 7 0 E
Ostrava, *Czech Rep.* .... 17 D10 49 51N 18 18 E
Ostróda, *Poland* .... 17 B10 53 42N 19 58 E
Ostroh, *Ukraine* .... 17 C14 50 20N 26 30 E
Ostrołęka, *Poland* .... 17 B11 53 4N 21 32 E
Ostrów Mazowiecka, *Poland* 17 B11 52 50N 21 51 E
Ostrów Wielkopolski, *Poland* 17 C9 51 36N 17 44 E
Ostrowiec-Świętokrzyski, *Poland* .... 17 C11 50 55N 21 22 E
Ostuni, *Italy* .... 21 D7 40 44N 17 35 E
Ōsumi-Kaikyō, *Japan* .... 31 J5 30 55N 131 0 E
Ōsumi-Shotō, *Japan* .... 31 J5 30 30N 130 0 E
Osuna, *Spain* 19 D3 37 14N 5 8W
Oswegatchie —►, *U.S.A.* .. 79 B9 44 42N 75 30W
Oswego, *U.S.A.* 79 C8 43 27N 76 31W
Oswego —►, *U.S.A.* 79 C8 43 27N 76 30W
Oswestry, *U.K.* 10 E4 52 52N 3 3W
Oświęcim, *Poland* .... 17 C10 50 2N 19 11 E
Otago □, *N.Z.* .... 59 L2 45 15S 170 0 E
Otago Harbour, *N.Z.* .... 59 L3 45 47S 170 42 E
Ōtake, *Japan* .... 31 G6 34 12N 132 13 E
Otaki, *N.Z.* .... 59 J5 40 45S 175 10 E
Otaru, *Japan* .... 30 C10 43 10N 141 0 E
Otaru-Wan = Ishikari-Wan, *Japan* .... 30 C10 43 25N 141 1 E
Otavalo, *Ecuador* 92 C3 0 13N 78 20W
Otavi, *Namibia* .... 56 B2 19 40S 17 24 E
Otchinjau, *Angola* .... 56 B1 16 30S 13 56 E
Otelnuk L., *Canada* 71 A6 56 9N 68 12W
Othello, *U.S.A.* 82 C4 46 50N 119 10W
Otira Gorge, *N.Z.* .... 59 K3 42 53S 171 33 E
Otjiwarongo, *Namibia* .... 56 C2 20 30S 16 33 E
Otoineppu, *Japan* .... 30 B11 44 44N 142 16 E
Otorohanga, *N.Z.* .... 59 H5 38 12S 175 14 E
Otoskwin —►, *Canada* 70 B2 52 13N 88 6W
Otra —►, *Norway* .... 9 G13 58 9N 8 1 E
Otranto, *Italy* .... 21 D8 40 9N 18 28 E
Otranto, C. d', *Italy* .... 21 D8 40 7N 18 30 E
Otranto, Str. of, *Italy* .... 21 D8 40 15N 18 40 E
Otse, *S. Africa* .... 56 D4 25 2S 25 45 E
Ōtsu, *Japan* .... 31 G7 35 0N 135 50 E
Ōtsuki, *Japan* .... 31 G9 35 36N 138 57 E
Ottawa = Outaouais —►, *Canada* 70 C5 45 27N 74 8W
Ottawa, *Canada* 79 A9 45 27N 75 42W
Ottawa, *Ill., U.S.A.* 80 E10 41 21N 88 51W
Ottawa, *Kans., U.S.A.* 80 F7 38 37N 95 16W
Ottawa Is., *Canada* 69 C11 59 35N 80 10W
Otter Cr. —►, *U.S.A.* 79 B11 44 13N 73 17W
Otter L., *Canada* 73 B8 55 35N 104 39W
Otterville, *Canada* 78 D4 42 55N 80 36W
Ottery St. Mary, *U.K.* 11 G4 50 44N 3 17W
Otto Beit Bridge, *Zimbabwe* 55 F2 15 59S 28 56 E
Ottosdal, *S. Africa* .... 56 D4 26 46S 25 59 E
Ottumwa, *U.S.A.* 80 E8 41 1N 92 25W
Oturkpo, *Nigeria* .... 50 G7 7 16N 8 8 E
Otway, B., *Chile* 96 G2 53 30S 74 0W
Otway, C., *Australia* .... 63 F3 38 52S 143 30 E
Otwock, *Poland* .... 17 B11 52 5N 21 20 E
Ou —►, *Laos* .... 38 B4 20 4N 102 13 E
Ou-Sammyaku, *Japan* .... 30 E10 39 20N 140 35 E
Ouachita —►, *U.S.A.* 81 K9 31 38N 91 49W
Ouachita, L., *U.S.A.* 81 H8 34 34N 93 12W
Ouachita Mts., *U.S.A.* 81 H7 34 40N 94 25W
Ouagadougou, *Burkina Faso* 50 F5 12 25N 1 30W
Ouahran = Oran, *Algeria* .. 50 A5 35 45N 0 39W
Ouallene, *Algeria* .... 50 D6 24 41N 1 11 E
Ouargla, *Algeria* .... 50 B7 31 59N 5 16 E
Ouarzazate, *Morocco* 50 B4 30 55N 6 50W
Oubangi —►, *Dem. Rep. of the Congo* . 52 E3 0 30S 17 50 E
Ouddorp, *Neths.* .... 15 C3 51 50N 3 57 E
Oude Rijn —►, *Neths.* .... 15 B4 52 12N 4 24 E
Oudenaarde, *Belgium* .... 15 D3 50 50N 3 37 E
Oudtshoorn, *S. Africa* .... 56 E3 33 35S 22 14 E
Ouessant, Î. d', *France* 18 B1 48 28N 5 6W
Ouesso, *Congo* .... 52 D3 1 37N 16 5 E
Ouest, Pte. de l', *Canada* .. 71 C7 49 52N 64 40W
Ouezzane, *Morocco* 50 B4 34 51N 5 35W
Oughterard, *Ireland* 13 C2 53 26N 9 18W
Oujda, *Morocco* 50 B5 34 41N 1 55W
Oulainen, *Finland* .... 8 D21 64 17N 24 47 E
Oulu, *Finland* .... 8 D21 65 1N 25 29 E
Oulujärvi, *Finland* .... 8 D22 64 25N 27 15 E
Oulujoki —►, *Finland* .... 8 D21 65 1N 25 30 E
Oum Chalouba, *Chad* .... 51 E10 15 48N 20 46 E
Oum Hadjer, *Chad* .... 51 F9 13 18N 19 41 E
Ounasjoki —►, *Finland* .... 8 C21 66 31N 25 40 E
Ounguati, *Namibia* .... 56 C2 22 0S 15 46 E
Ounianga Sérir, *Chad* .... 51 E10 18 54N 20 51 E
Our —►, *Lux.* .... 15 E6 49 55N 6 5 E
Ouray, *U.S.A.* 83 G10 38 1N 107 40W
Ourense, *Spain* 19 A2 42 19N 7 55W
Ouricuri, *Brazil* 93 E10 7 53S 40 5W
Ourinhos, *Brazil* 95 A6 23 0S 49 54W
Ouro Fino, *Brazil* 95 A6 22 16S 46 25W
Ouro Prêto, *Brazil* 95 A7 20 20S 43 30W
Ourthe —►, *Belgium* .... 15 D5 50 29N 5 35 E
Ouse —►, *E. Susx., U.K.* .. 11 G8 50 47N 0 4 E
Ouse —►, *N. Yorks., U.K.* . 10 D7 53 44N 0 55W
Outaouais —►, *Canada* 70 C5 45 27N 74 8W
Outardes —►, *Canada* 71 C6 49 24N 69 30W
Outer Hebrides, *U.K.* 12 D1 57 30N 7 40W
Outjo, *Namibia* .... 56 C2 20 5S 16 7 E
Outlook, *Canada* 73 C7 51 30N 107 0W
Outokumpu, *Finland* .... 8 E23 62 43N 29 1 E
Ouyen, *Australia* .... 63 F3 35 1S 142 22 E
Ovalau, *Fiji* .... 59 C8 17 40S 178 48 E
Ovalle, *Chile* 94 C1 30 33S 71 18W
Ovamboland, *Namibia* .... 56 B2 18 30S 16 0 E
Overflakkee, *Neths.* .... 15 C4 51 44N 4 10 E
Overijssel □, *Neths.* .... 15 B6 52 25N 6 35 E
Overland Park, *U.S.A.* 80 F7 38 55N 94 50W
Overton, *U.S.A.* 85 J12 36 33N 114 27W
Övertorneå, *Sweden* .... 8 C20 66 23N 23 38 E
Ovid, *U.S.A.* 79 D8 42 41N 76 49W
Oviedo, *Spain* 19 A3 43 25N 5 50W
Oviši, *Latvia* .... 9 H19 57 33N 21 44 E
Ovoot, *Mongolia* .... 34 B7 45 21N 113 45 E
Övör Hangay □, *Mongolia* . 34 B2 45 0N 102 30 E
Øvre Årdal, *Norway* .... 9 F12 61 19N 7 48 E
Ovruch, *Ukraine* .... 17 C15 51 25N 28 45 E
Owaka, *N.Z.* .... 59 M2 46 27S 169 40 E
Owambo = Ovamboland, *Namibia* .... 56 B2 18 30S 16 0 E
Owando, *Congo* .... 52 E3 0 29S 15 55 E
Owasco L., *U.S.A.* 79 D8 42 50N 76 31W
Owase, *Japan* .... 31 G8 34 7N 136 12 E
Owatonna, *U.S.A.* 80 C8 44 5N 93 14W
Owbeh, *Afghan.* .... 40 B3 34 28N 63 10 E
Owego, *U.S.A.* 79 D8 42 6N 76 16W
Owen Falls Dam, *Uganda* .. 54 B3 0 30N 33 5 E
Owen Sound, *Canada* 78 B4 44 35N 80 55W
Owens —►, *U.S.A.* 84 J9 36 32N 117 59W
Owens L., *U.S.A.* 85 J9 36 26N 117 57W
Owensboro, *U.S.A.* 76 G2 37 46N 87 7W
Owl —►, *Canada* 73 B10 57 51N 92 44W
Owo, *Nigeria* .... 50 G7 7 10N 5 39 E
Owosso, *U.S.A.* 76 D3 43 0N 84 10W
Owyhee, *U.S.A.* 82 F5 41 57N 116 6W
Owyhee —►, *U.S.A.* 82 E5 43 49N 117 2W
Owyhee, L., *U.S.A.* 82 E5 43 38N 117 14W
Ox Mts. = Slieve Gamph, *Ireland* 13 B3 54 6N 9 0W
Öxarfjörður, *Iceland* 8 C5 66 15N 16 45W
Oxbow, *Canada* 73 D8 49 14N 102 10W
Oxelösund, *Sweden* .... 9 G17 58 43N 17 5 E
Oxford, *N.Z.* .... 59 K4 43 18S 172 11 E
Oxford, *U.K.* 11 F6 51 46N 1 15W
Oxford, *Mass., U.S.A.* 79 D13 42 7N 71 52W
Oxford, *Miss., U.S.A.* 81 H10 34 22N 89 31W
Oxford, *N.C., U.S.A.* 77 G6 36 19N 78 35W
Oxford, *N.Y., U.S.A.* 79 D9 42 27N 75 36W
Oxford, *Ohio, U.S.A.* 76 F3 39 31N 84 45W
Oxford L., *Canada* 73 C9 54 51N 95 37W
Oxfordshire □, *U.K.* 11 F6 51 48N 1 16W
Oxnard, *U.S.A.* 85 L7 34 12N 119 11W
Oxus = Amudarya —►, *Uzbekistan* .... 26 E6 43 58N 59 34 E
Oya, *Malaysia* .... 36 D4 2 55N 111 55 E
Oyama, *Japan* .... 31 F9 36 18N 139 48 E
Oyem, *Gabon* .... 52 D2 1 34N 11 31 E
Oyen, *Canada* 73 C6 51 22N 110 28W
Oykel —►, *U.K.* 12 D4 57 56N 4 26W
Oymyakon, *Russia* .... 27 C15 63 25N 142 44 E
Oyo, *Nigeria* .... 50 G6 7 46N 3 56 E
Oyster Bay, *U.S.A.* 79 F11 40 52N 73 32W
Ōyübari, *Japan* .... 30 C11 43 1N 142 5 E
Ozamiz, *Phil.* .... 37 C6 8 15N 123 50 E
Ozark, *Ala., U.S.A.* 77 K3 31 28N 85 39W
Ozark, *Ark., U.S.A.* 81 H8 35 29N 93 50W
Ozark, *Mo., U.S.A.* 81 G8 37 1N 93 12W
Ozark Plateau, *U.S.A.* 81 G9 37 20N 91 40W
Ozarks, L. of the, *U.S.A.* .. 80 F8 38 12N 92 38W
Ózd, *Hungary* .... 17 D11 48 14N 20 15 E
Ozette L., *U.S.A.* 84 B2 48 6N 124 38W
Ozona, *U.S.A.* 81 K4 30 43N 101 12W
Ozuluama, *Mexico* 87 C5 21 40N 97 50W

P

Pa-an, *Burma* .... 41 L20 16 51N 97 40 E
Pa Mong Dam, *Thailand* .. 38 D4 18 0N 102 22 E
Pa Sak —►, *Thailand* .... 36 B2 15 30N 101 0 E
Paamiut = Frederikshåb, *Greenland* 4 C5 62 0N 49 43W
Paarl, *S. Africa* .... 56 E2 33 45S 18 56 E
Paauilo, *U.S.A.* 74 H17 20 2N 155 22W
Pab Hills, *Pakistan* .... 42 F2 26 30N 66 45 E
Pabbay, *U.K.* 12 D1 57 46N 7 14W
Pabianice, *Poland* .... 17 C10 51 40N 19 20 E
Pabna, *Bangla.* .... 41 G16 24 1N 89 18 E
Pabo, *Uganda* .... 54 B3 3 1N 32 10 E
Pacaja —►, *Brazil* 93 D8 1 56S 50 50W
Pacaraima, Sa., *S. Amer.* .. 92 C6 4 0N 62 30W
Pacasmayo, *Peru* 92 E3 7 20S 79 35W
Pachhar, *India* .... 42 G7 24 40N 77 42 E
Pachitea —►, *Peru* 92 E4 8 46S 74 33W
Pachmarhi, *India* .... 43 H8 22 28N 78 26 E
Pachpadra, *India* .... 40 G8 25 58N 72 10 E
Pachuca, *Mexico* 87 C5 20 10N 98 40W
Pacific, *Canada* 72 C3 54 48N 128 28W
Pacific-Antarctic Ridge, *Pac. Oc.* 65 M16 43 0S 115 0W
Pacific Grove, *U.S.A.* 84 J5 36 38N 121 56W
Pacific Ocean, *Pac. Oc.* 65 G14 10 0N 140 0W
Pacific Rim Nat. Park, *Canada* 84 B2 48 40N 124 45W
Pacifica, *U.S.A.* 84 H4 37 36N 122 30W
Pacitan, *Indonesia* .... 37 H14 8 12S 111 7 E
Packwood, *U.S.A.* 84 D5 46 36N 121 40W
Padaido, Kepulauan, *Indonesia* .... 37 E9 1 5S 138 0 E
Padang, *Indonesia* .... 36 E2 1 0S 100 20 E
Padang Endau, *Malaysia* .. 39 L4 2 40N 103 38 E
Padangpanjang, *Indonesia* . 36 E2 0 40S 100 20 E
Padangsidempuan, *Indonesia* .... 36 D1 1 30N 99 15 E
Paddle Prairie, *Canada* 72 B5 57 57N 117 29W
Paddockwood, *Canada* 73 C7 53 30N 105 30W
Paderborn, *Germany* .... 16 C5 51 42N 8 45 E
Padma, *India* .... 43 G11 24 12N 85 22 E
Pádova, *Italy* .... 20 B4 45 25N 11 53 E
Padra, *India* .... 42 H5 22 15N 73 7 E
Padrauna, *India* .... 43 F10 26 54N 83 59 E
Padre I., *U.S.A.* 81 M6 27 10N 97 25W
Padstow, *U.K.* 11 G3 50 33N 4 58W
Padua = Pádova, *Italy* .... 20 B4 45 25N 11 53 E
Paducah, *Ky., U.S.A.* 76 G1 37 5N 88 37W
Paducah, *Tex., U.S.A.* 81 H4 34 1N 100 18W
Paengnyŏng-do, *S. Korea* . 35 F13 37 57N 124 40 E
Paeroa, *N.Z.* .... 59 G5 37 23S 175 41 E
Pafúri, *Mozam.* .... 57 C5 22 28S 31 17 E
Pag, *Croatia* .... 16 F8 44 25N 15 3 E
Pagadian, *Phil.* .... 37 C6 7 55N 123 30 E
Pagai Selatan, Pulau, *Indonesia* .... 36 E2 3 0S 100 15 E
Pagai Utara, Pulau, *Indonesia* .... 36 E2 2 35S 100 0 E
Pagalu = Annobón, *Atl. Oc.* 49 G4 1 25S 5 36 E
Pagara, *India* .... 43 G9 24 22N 80 1 E
Pagastikós Kólpos, *Greece* . 21 E10 39 15N 23 0 E
Pagatan, *Indonesia* .... 36 E5 3 33S 115 59 E
Page, *U.S.A.* 83 H8 36 57N 111 27W
Pago Pago, *Amer. Samoa* .. 59 B13 14 16S 170 43W
Pagosa Springs, *U.S.A.* 83 H10 37 16N 107 1W
Pagwa River, *Canada* 70 B2 50 2N 85 14W
Pahala, *U.S.A.* 74 J17 19 12N 155 29W
Pahang —►, *Malaysia* .... 39 L4 3 30N 103 9 E
Pahiatua, *N.Z.* .... 59 J5 40 27S 175 50 E
Pahokee, *U.S.A.* 77 M5 26 50N 80 40W
Pahrump, *U.S.A.* 85 J11 36 12N 115 59W
Pahute Mesa, *U.S.A.* 84 H10 37 20N 116 45W
Pai, *Thailand* .... 38 C2 19 19N 98 27 E
Paia, *U.S.A.* 74 H16 20 54N 156 22W
Paicines, *U.S.A.* 84 J5 36 44N 121 17W
Paide, *Estonia* .... 9 G21 58 57N 25 31 E
Paignton, *U.K.* 11 G4 50 26N 3 35W
Päijänne, *Finland* .... 9 F21 61 30N 25 30 E
Pailani, *India* .... 43 G9 25 45N 80 26 E
Pailin, *Cambodia* .... 38 F4 12 46N 102 36 E
Painan, *Indonesia* .... 36 E2 1 21S 100 34 E
Painesville, *U.S.A.* 78 E3 41 43N 81 15W
Paint Hills = Wemindji, *Canada* 70 B4 53 0N 78 49W
Paint L., *Canada* 73 B9 55 28N 97 57W
Painted Desert, *U.S.A.* 83 J8 36 0N 111 0W
Paintsville, *U.S.A.* 76 G4 37 49N 82 48W
País Vasco □, *Spain* 19 A4 42 50N 2 45W
Paisley, *Canada* 78 B3 44 18N 81 16W
Paisley, *U.K.* 12 F4 55 50N 4 25W
Paisley, *U.S.A.* 82 E3 42 42N 120 32W
Paita, *Peru* 92 E2 5 11S 81 9W
Pajares, Puerto de, *Spain* .. 19 A3 42 58N 5 46W
Pak Lay, *Laos* .... 38 C3 18 15N 101 27 E
Pak Phanang, *Thailand* .... 39 H3 8 21N 100 12 E
Pak Sane, *Laos* .... 38 C4 18 22N 103 39 E
Pak Song, *Laos* .... 38 E6 15 11N 106 14 E
Pakaur, *India* .... 43 G12 24 38N 87 51 E
Pakenham, *Canada* 79 A8 45 18N 76 18W
Pákhnes, *Greece* .... 23 D6 35 16N 24 4 E
Pakistan ■, *Asia* .... 42 E4 30 0N 70 0 E
Pakkading, *Laos* .... 38 C4 18 19N 103 59 E
Pakokku, *Burma* .... 41 J19 21 20N 95 0 E
Pakowki L., *Canada* 73 D6 49 20N 111 0W
Pakpattan, *Pakistan* .... 42 D5 30 25N 73 27 E
Paktīā □, *Afghan.* .... 40 C6 33 0N 69 15 E
Pakwach, *Uganda* .... 54 B3 2 28N 31 27 E
Pakxe, *Laos* .... 38 E5 15 5N 105 52 E
Pal Lahara, *India* .... 43 J11 21 27N 85 11 E
Pala, *Chad* .... 51 G9 9 25N 15 5 E
Pala, *Dem. Rep. of the Congo* . 54 D2 6 45S 29 30 E
Pala, *U.S.A.* 85 M9 33 22N 117 5W
Palabek, *Uganda* .... 54 B3 3 22N 32 33 E
Palacios, *U.S.A.* 81 L6 28 42N 96 13W
Palagruža, *Croatia* .... 20 C7 42 24N 16 15 E
Palaiókastron, *Greece* .... 23 D8 35 12N 26 15 E
Palaiokhóra, *Greece* .... 23 D5 35 16N 23 39 E
Palam, *India* .... 40 K10 19 0N 77 0 E
Palampur, *India* .... 42 C7 32 10N 76 30 E
Palana, *Australia* .... 62 F4 39 45S 147 55 E
Palana, *Russia* .... 27 D16 59 10N 159 59 E
Palanan, *Phil.* .... 37 A6 17 8N 122 29 E
Palanan Pt., *Phil.* .... 37 A6 17 17N 122 30 E
Palandri, *Pakistan* .... 43 C5 33 42N 73 40 E
Palanga, *Lithuania* .... 9 J19 55 58N 21 3 E
Palangkaraya, *Indonesia* .... 36 E4 2 16S 113 56 E
Palani Hills, *India* .... 40 P10 10 14N 77 33 E
Palanpur, *India* .... 42 G5 24 10N 72 25 E
Palapye, *Botswana* .... 56 C4 22 30S 27 7 E
Palas, *Pakistan* .... 43 B5 35 4N 73 14 E
Palashi, *India* .... 43 H13 23 47N 88 15 E
Palasponga, *India* .... 43 J11 21 47N 85 34 E
Palatka, *Russia* .... 27 C16 60 6N 150 54 E
Palatka, *U.S.A.* 77 L5 29 39N 81 38W
Palau ■, *Pac. Oc.* .... 28 J17 7 30N 134 30 E
Palauk, *Burma* .... 38 F2 13 10N 98 40 E
Palawan, *Phil.* .... 36 C5 9 30N 118 30 E
Palayankottai, *India* .... 40 Q10 8 45N 77 45 E
Paldiski, *Estonia* .... 9 G21 59 23N 24 9 E
Paleleh, *Indonesia* .... 37 D6 1 10N 121 50 E
Palembang, *Indonesia* .... 36 E2 3 0S 104 50 E
Palencia, *Spain* 19 A3 42 1N 4 34W
Palenque, *Mexico* 87 D6 17 31N 91 58W
Paleokastrítsa, *Greece* .... 23 A3 39 40N 19 41 E
Paleometokho, *Cyprus* .... 23 D12 35 7N 33 11 E
Palermo, *Italy* .... 20 E5 38 7N 13 22 E
Palermo, *U.S.A.* 82 G3 39 26N 121 33W
Palestina, *Chile* 96 A3 23 50S 69 47W
Palestine, *Asia* .... 47 D4 32 0N 35 0 E
Palestine, *U.S.A.* 81 K7 31 46N 95 38W
Paletwa, *Burma* .... 41 J18 21 10N 92 50 E
Palghat, *India* .... 40 P10 10 46N 76 42 E
Palgrave, Mt., *Australia* .... 60 D2 23 22S 115 58 E
Pali, *India* .... 42 G5 25 50N 73 20 E
Palikir, *Micronesia* .... 64 G7 6 55N 158 9 E
Palioúrion, Ákra, *Greece* .. 21 E10 39 57N 23 45 E
Palisades Reservoir, *U.S.A.* 82 E8 43 20N 111 12W
Paliseul, *Belgium* .... 15 E5 49 54N 5 8 E
Palitana, *India* .... 42 J4 21 32N 71 49 E
Palizada, *Mexico* 87 D6 18 18N 92 8W
Palk Bay, *Asia* .... 40 Q11 9 30N 79 15 E
Palk Strait, *Asia* .... 40 Q11 10 0N 79 45 E
Palkānah, *Iraq* .... 44 C5 35 49N 44 26 E
Palkot, *India* .... 43 H11 22 53N 84 39 E
Palla Road = Dinokwe, *Botswana* .... 56 C4 23 29S 26 37 E
Pallanza = Verbánia, *Italy* . 18 D8 45 56N 8 33 E
Pallarenda, *Australia* .... 62 B4 19 12S 146 46 E
Pallinup —►, *Australia* .... 61 F2 34 27S 118 50 E
Pallisa, *Uganda* .... 54 B3 1 12N 33 43 E
Pallu, *India* .... 42 E6 28 59N 74 14 E
Palm Bay, *U.S.A.* 77 L5 28 2N 80 35W
Palm Beach, *U.S.A.* 77 M6 26 43N 80 2W
Palm Coast, *U.S.A.* 77 L5 29 32N 81 10W
Palm Desert, *U.S.A.* 85 M10 33 43N 116 22W
Palm Is., *Australia* .... 62 B4 18 40S 146 35 E
Palm Springs, *U.S.A.* 85 M10 33 50N 116 33W
Palma, *Mozam.* .... 55 E5 10 46S 40 29 E
Palma, B. de, *Spain* .... 22 B9 39 30N 2 39 E
Palma de Mallorca, *Spain* .. 22 B9 39 35N 2 39 E
Palma Soriano, *Cuba* 88 B4 20 15N 76 0W
Palmares, *Brazil* 93 E11 8 41S 35 28W
Palmas, *Brazil* 95 B5 26 29S 52 0W
Palmas, C., *Liberia* 50 H4 4 27N 7 46W
Pálmas, G. di, *Italy* .... 20 E3 39 0N 8 30 E
Palmdale, *U.S.A.* 85 L8 34 35N 118 7W
Palmeira das Missões, *Brazil* 95 B5 27 55S 53 17W
Palmeira dos Índios, *Brazil* 93 E11 9 25S 36 37W
Palmer, *U.S.A.* 68 B5 61 36N 149 7W
Palmer —►, *Australia* .... 62 B3 16 0S 142 26 E
Palmer Arch., *Antarctica* .. 5 C17 64 15S 65 0W
Palmer Lake, *U.S.A.* 80 F2 39 7N 104 55W
Palmer Land, *Antarctica* 5 D18 73 0S 63 0W
Palmerston, *Canada* 78 C4 43 50N 80 51W
Palmerston, *N.Z.* .... 59 L3 45 29S 170 43 E
Palmerston North, *N.Z.* .... 59 J5 40 21S 175 39 E
Palmerton, *U.S.A.* 79 F9 40 48N 75 37W
Palmetto, *U.S.A.* 77 M4 27 31N 82 34W
Palmi, *Italy* .... 20 E6 38 21N 15 51 E
Palmira, *Argentina* 94 C2 32 59S 68 34W
Palmira, *Colombia* 92 C3 3 32N 76 16W
Palmyra = Tudmur, *Syria* .. 44 C3 34 36N 38 15 E
Palmyra, *Mo., U.S.A.* 80 F9 39 48N 91 32W
Palmyra, *N.J., U.S.A.* 79 F9 40 1N 75 1W
Palmyra, *N.Y., U.S.A.* 78 C7 43 5N 77 18W
Palmyra, *Pa., U.S.A.* 79 F8 40 18N 76 36W
Palmyra Is., *Pac. Oc.* 65 G11 5 52N 162 5W
Palo Alto, *U.S.A.* 84 H4 37 27N 122 10W
Palo Verde, *U.S.A.* 85 M12 33 26N 114 44W
Palopo, *Indonesia* .... 37 E6 3 0S 120 16 E
Palos, C. de, *Spain* 19 D5 37 38N 0 40W
Palos Verdes, *U.S.A.* 85 M8 33 48N 118 23W
Palos Verdes, Pt., *U.S.A.* .. 85 M8 33 43N 118 26W
Palu, *Indonesia* .... 37 E5 1 0S 119 52 E
Palu, *Turkey* .... 25 G7 38 45N 40 0 E
Palwal, *India* .... 42 E7 28 8N 77 19 E
Pamanukan, *Indonesia* .... 37 G12 6 16S 107 49 E
Pamiers, *France* .... 18 E4 43 7N 1 39 E
Pamir, *Tajikistan* .... 26 F8 37 40N 73 0 E
Pamlico —►, *U.S.A.* 77 H7 35 20N 76 28W
Pamlico Sd., *U.S.A.* 77 H8 35 20N 76 0W
Pampa, *U.S.A.* 81 H4 35 32N 100 58W
Pampa de las Salinas, *Argentina* 94 C2 32 1S 66 58W
Pampanua, *Indonesia* .... 37 E6 4 16S 120 8 E
Pampas, *Argentina* 94 D3 35 0S 63 0W
Pampas, *Peru* 92 F4 12 20S 74 50W
Pamplona, *Colombia* 92 B4 7 23N 72 39W
Pamplona, *Spain* 19 A5 42 48N 1 38W
Pampoenpoort, *S. Africa* .... 56 E3 31 3S 22 40 E
Pana, *U.S.A.* 80 F10 39 23N 89 5W
Panaca, *U.S.A.* 83 H6 37 47N 114 23W
Panaitan, *Indonesia* .... 37 G11 6 36S 105 12 E
Panaji, *India* .... 40 M8 15 25N 73 50 E
Panamá, *Panama* 88 E4 9 0N 79 25W
Panama ■, *Cent. Amer.* 88 E4 8 48N 79 55W
Panamá, G. de, *Panama* 88 E4 8 4N 79 20W
Panama Canal, *Panama* 88 E4 9 10N 79 37W
Panama City, *U.S.A.* 77 K3 30 10N 85 40W
Panamint Range, *U.S.A.* 85 J9 36 20N 117 20W
Panamint Springs, *U.S.A.* .. 85 J9 36 20N 117 28W
Panão, *Peru* 92 E3 9 55S 75 55W
Panare, *Thailand* .... 39 J3 6 51N 101 30 E
Panay, *Phil.* .... 37 B6 11 10N 122 30 E
Panay, G., *Phil.* .... 37 B6 11 0N 122 30 E
Pančevo, *Serbia, Yug.* .... 21 B9 44 52N 20 41 E
Pandan, *Phil.* .... 37 B6 11 45N 122 10 E
Pandegelang, *Indonesia* .... 37 G12 6 25S 106 5 E
Pandhana, *India* .... 42 J7 21 42N 76 13 E
Pandharpur, *India* .... 40 L9 17 41N 75 20 E
Pando, *Uruguay* 95 C4 34 44S 56 0W
Pando, L. = Hope, L., *Australia* .... 63 D2 28 24S 139 18 E
Pandokrátor, *Greece* .... 23 A3 39 45N 19 50 E
Pandora, *Costa Rica* 88 E3 9 43N 83 3W
Panevėžys, *Lithuania* .... 9 J21 55 42N 24 25 E
Panfilov, *Kazakstan* .... 26 E9 44 10N 80 0 E
Pang-Long, *Burma* .... 41 H21 23 11N 98 45 E
Pang-Yang, *Burma* .... 41 H21 22 7N 98 48 E
Panga, *Dem. Rep. of the Congo* . 54 B2 1 52N 26 18 E
Pangalanes, Canal des, *Madag.* .... 57 C8 22 48S 47 50 E
Pangani, *Tanzania* .... 54 D4 5 25S 38 58 E
Pangani —►, *Tanzania* .... 54 D4 5 26S 38 58 E
Pangfou = Bengbu, *China* .. 35 H9 32 58N 117 20 E
Pangil, *Dem. Rep. of the Congo* . 54 C2 3 10S 26 35 E
Pangkah, Tanjung, *Indonesia* .... 37 G15 6 51S 112 33 E
Pangkajene, *Indonesia* .... 37 E5 4 46S 119 34 E
Pangkalanbrandan, *Indonesia* .... 36 D1 4 1N 98 20 E
Pangkalanbuun, *Indonesia* . 36 E4 2 41S 111 37 E

Penn Yan

Penn Yan, *U.S.A.* **78 D7** 42 40N 77 3W
Pennant, *Canada* **73 C7** 50 32N 108 14W
Penner →, *India* **40 M12** 14 35N 80 10 E
Pennines, *U.K.* **10 C5** 54 45N 2 27W
Pennington, *U.S.A.* **84 F5** 39 15N 121 47W
Pennsburg, *U.S.A.* **79 F9** 40 23N 75 29W
Pennsylvania □, *U.S.A.* **76 E7** 40 45N 77 30W
Penny, *Canada* **72 C4** 53 51N 121 20W
Penobscot →, *U.S.A.* **77 C11** 44 30N 68 48W
Penobscot B., *U.S.A.* **77 C11** 44 35N 68 50W
Penola, *Australia* **63 F3** 37 25S 140 48 E
Penong, *Australia* **61 F5** 31 56S 133 1 E
Penonomé, *Panama* **88 E3** 8 31N 80 21W
Penrith, *Australia* **63 E5** 33 43S 150 38 E
Penrith, *U.K.* **10 C5** 54 40N 2 45W
Penryn, *U.K.* **11 G2** 50 9N 5 7W
Pensacola, *U.S.A.* **77 K2** 30 25N 87 13W
Pensacola Mts., *Antarctica* **5 E1** 84 0S 40 0W
Pense, *Canada* **73 C8** 50 25N 104 59W
Penshurst, *Australia* **63 F3** 37 49S 142 20 E
Penticton, *Canada* **72 D5** 49 30N 119 38W
Pentland, *Australia* **62 C4** 20 32S 145 25 E
Pentland Firth, *U.K.* **12 C5** 58 43N 3 10W
Pentland Hills, *U.K.* **12 F5** 55 48N 3 25W
Penza, *Russia* **24 D8** 53 15N 45 5 E
Penzance, *U.K.* **11 G2** 50 7N 5 33W
Penzhino, *Russia* **27 C17** 63 30N 167 55 E
Penzhinskaya Guba, *Russia* **27 C17** 61 30N 163 0 E
Peoria, *Ariz., U.S.A.* **83 K7** 33 35N 112 14W
Peoria, *Ill., U.S.A.* **80 E10** 40 42N 89 36W
Pepacton Reservoir, *U.S.A.* **79 D10** 42 5N 74 58W
Pera Hd., *Australia* **62 A3** 12 55S 141 37 E
Perabumulih, *Indonesia* **36 E2** 3 27S 104 15 E
Perak →, *Malaysia* **39 K3** 4 0N 100 50 E
Pérama, *Kérkira, Greece* **23 A3** 39 34N 19 54 E
Pérama, *Kríti, Greece* **23 D6** 35 20N 24 40 E
Peräpohjola, *Finland* **8 C22** 66 16N 26 10 E
Percé, *Canada* **71 C7** 48 31N 64 13W
Perche, Collines du, *France* **18 B4** 48 30N 0 40 E
Percival Lakes, *Australia* **60 D4** 21 25S 125 0 E
Percy Is., *Australia* **62 C5** 21 39S 150 16 E
Perdido, Mte., *Spain* **19 A6** 42 40N 0 5 E
Perdu, Mt. = Perdido, Mte., *Spain* **19 A6** 42 40N 0 5 E
Pereira, *Colombia* **92 C3** 4 49N 75 43W
Perenjori, *Australia* **61 E2** 29 26S 116 16 E
Pereyaslav-Khmelnytskyy, *Ukraine* **25 D5** 50 3N 31 28 E
Pérez, I., *Mexico* **87 C7** 22 24N 89 42W
Pergamino, *Argentina* **94 C3** 33 52S 60 30W
Pergau →, *Malaysia* **39 K3** 5 23N 102 2 E
Perham, *U.S.A.* **80 B7** 46 36N 95 34W
Perhentian, Kepulauan, *Malaysia* **36 C2** 5 54N 102 42 E
Péribonca →, *Canada* **71 C5** 48 45N 72 5W
Péribonca, L., *Canada* **71 B5** 50 1N 71 10W
Perico, *Argentina* **94 A2** 24 20S 65 5W
Pericos, *Mexico* **86 B3** 25 3N 107 42W
Périgueux, *France* **18 D4** 45 10N 0 42 E
Perijá, Sierra de, *Colombia* **92 B4** 9 30N 73 3W
Peristerona →, *Cyprus* **23 D12** 35 8N 33 5 E
Perito Moreno, *Argentina* **96 F2** 46 36S 70 56W
Perkasie, *U.S.A.* **79 F9** 40 22N 75 18W
Perlas, Arch. de las, *Panama* **88 E4** 8 41N 79 7W
Perlas, Punta de, *Nic.* **88 D3** 12 30N 83 30W
Perm, *Russia* **24 C10** 58 0N 56 10 E
Pernambuco = Recife, *Brazil* **93 E12** 8 0S 35 0W
Pernambuco □, *Brazil* **93 E11** 8 0S 37 0W
Pernatty Lagoon, *Australia* **63 E2** 31 30S 137 12 E
Pernik, *Bulgaria* **21 C10** 42 35N 23 2 E
Peron Is., *Australia* **60 B5** 13 9S 130 4 E
Peron Pen., *Australia* **61 E1** 26 0S 113 10 E
Perow, *Canada* **72 C3** 54 35N 126 10W
Perpendicular Pt., *Australia* **63 E5** 31 37S 152 52 E
Perpignan, *France* **18 E5** 42 42N 2 53 E
Perris, *U.S.A.* **85 M9** 33 47N 117 14W
Perry, *Fla., U.S.A.* **77 K4** 30 7N 83 35W
Perry, *Ga., U.S.A.* **77 J4** 32 28N 83 44W
Perry, *Iowa, U.S.A.* **80 E7** 41 51N 94 6W
Perry, *Okla., U.S.A.* **81 G6** 36 17N 97 14W
Perryton, *U.S.A.* **81 G4** 36 24N 100 48W
Perryville, *U.S.A.* **81 G10** 37 43N 89 52W
Persepolis, *Iran* **45 D7** 29 55N 52 50 E
Pershotravensk, *Ukraine* **17 C14** 50 13N 27 40 E
Persia = Iran ■, *Asia* **45 C7** 33 0N 53 0 E
Persian Gulf = Gulf, The, *Asia* **45 E6** 27 0N 50 0 E
Perth, *Australia* **61 F2** 31 57S 115 52 E
Perth, *Canada* **79 B8** 44 55N 76 15W
Perth, *U.K.* **12 E5** 56 24N 3 26W
Perth & Kinross □, *U.K.* **12 E5** 56 45N 3 55W
Perth Amboy, *U.S.A.* **79 F10** 40 31N 74 16W
Perth-Andover, *Canada* **71 C6** 46 44N 67 42W
Peru, *Ind., U.S.A.* **76 E2** 40 45N 86 4W
Peru, *N.Y., U.S.A.* **79 B11** 44 35N 73 32W
Peru ■, *S. Amer.* **92 D4** 4 0S 75 0W
Peru-Chile Trench, *Pac. Oc.* **92 G3** 20 0S 72 0W
Perúgia, *Italy* **20 C5** 43 7N 12 23 E
Pervomaysk, *Ukraine* **25 E5** 48 10N 30 46 E
Pervouralsk, *Russia* **24 C10** 56 59N 59 59 E
Pésaro, *Italy* **20 C5** 43 54N 12 55 E
Pescara, *Italy* **20 C6** 42 28N 14 13 E
Peshawar, *Pakistan* **42 B4** 34 2N 71 37 E
Peshkopi, *Albania* **21 D9** 41 41N 20 25 E
Peshtigo, *U.S.A.* **76 C2** 45 4N 87 46W
Pesqueira, *Brazil* **93 E11** 8 20S 36 42W
Petah Tiqwa, *Israel* **47 C3** 32 6N 34 53 E
Petaling Jaya, *Malaysia* **39 L3** 3 4N 101 42 E
Petaloudhes, *Greece* **23 C10** 36 18N 28 5 E
Petaluma, *U.S.A.* **84 G4** 38 14N 122 39W
Pétange, *Lux.* **15 E5** 49 33N 5 55 E
Petaro, *Pakistan* **42 G3** 25 31N 68 18 E
Petatlán, *Mexico* **86 D4** 17 31N 101 16W
Petauke, *Zambia* **55 E3** 14 14S 31 20 E
Petawawa, *Canada* **70 C4** 45 54N 77 17W
Petén Itzá, L., *Guatemala* **88 C2** 16 58N 89 50W
Peter I.s Øy, *Antarctica* **5 C16** 69 0S 91 0W
Peter Pond L., *Canada* **73 B7** 55 55N 108 44W
Peterbell, *Canada* **70 C3** 48 36N 83 21W
Peterborough, *Australia* **63 E2** 32 58S 138 51 E
Peterborough, *Canada* **78 B6** 44 20N 78 20W
Peterborough, *U.K.* **11 E7** 52 35N 0 15W
Peterborough, *U.S.A.* **79 D13** 42 53N 71 57W
Peterborough □, *U.K.* **11 E7** 52 35N 0 15W
Peterculter, *U.K.* **12 D6** 57 6N 2 16W
Peterhead, *U.K.* **12 D7** 57 31N 1 48W
Peterlee, *U.K.* **10 C6** 54 47N 1 20W
Petermann Bjerg, *Greenland* **66 B17** 73 7N 28 25W
Petermann Ranges, *Australia* **60 E5** 26 0S 130 30 E
Petersburg, *Alaska, U.S.A.* **68 C6** 56 48N 132 58W
Petersburg, *Pa., U.S.A.* **78 F6** 40 34N 78 3W
Petersburg, *Va., U.S.A.* **76 G7** 37 14N 77 24W
Petersburg, *W. Va., U.S.A.* **76 F6** 39 1N 79 5W
Petersfield, *U.K.* **11 F7** 51 1N 0 56W
Petit Goâve, *Haiti* **89 C5** 18 27N 72 51W
Petit Jardin, *Canada* **71 C8** 48 28N 59 14W
Petit Lac Manicouagan, *Canada* **71 B6** 51 25N 67 40W
Petit-Mécatina →, *Canada* **71 B8** 50 40N 59 30W
Petit-Mécatina, I. du, *Canada* **71 B8** 50 30N 59 25W
Petitcodiac, *Canada* **71 C6** 45 57N 65 11W
Petite Baleine →, *Canada* **70 A4** 56 0N 76 45W
Petite Saguenay, *Canada* **71 C5** 48 15N 70 4W
Petitot →, *Canada* **72 A4** 60 14N 123 29W
Petitsikapau L., *Canada* **71 B6** 54 37N 66 25W
Petlad, *India* **42 H5** 22 30N 72 45 E
Peto, *Mexico* **87 C7** 20 10N 88 53W
Petone, *N.Z.* **59 J5** 41 13S 174 53 E
Petorca, *Chile* **94 C1** 32 15S 70 56W
Petoskey, *U.S.A.* **76 C3** 45 22N 84 57W
Petra, *Jordan* **47 E4** 30 20N 35 22 E
Petra, *Spain* **22 B10** 39 37N 3 6 E
Petra, Ostrova, *Russia* **4 B13** 76 15N 118 30 E
Petra Velikogo, Zaliv, *Russia* **30 C6** 42 40N 132 0 E
Petrich, *Bulgaria* **21 D10** 41 24N 23 13 E
Petrified Forest National Park, *U.S.A.* **83 J9** 35 0N 109 30W
Petrikov = Pyetrikaw, *Belarus* **17 B15** 52 11N 28 29 E
Petrograd = Sankt-Peterburg, *Russia* **24 C5** 59 55N 30 20 E
Petrolândia, *Brazil* **93 E11** 9 5S 38 20W
Petrolia, *Canada* **78 D2** 42 54N 82 9W
Petrolina, *Brazil* **93 E10** 9 24S 40 30W
Petropavl, *Kazakstan* **26 D7** 54 53N 69 13 E
Petropavlovsk = Petropavl, *Kazakstan* **26 D7** 54 53N 69 13 E
Petropavlovsk-Kamchatskiy, *Russia* **27 D16** 53 3N 158 43 E
Petrópolis, *Brazil* **95 A7** 22 33S 43 9W
Petroşani, *Romania* **17 F12** 45 28N 23 20 E
Petrovaradin, *Serbia, Yug.* **21 B8** 45 16N 19 55 E
Petrovsk, *Russia* **24 D8** 52 22N 45 19 E
Petrovsk-Zabaykalskiy, *Russia* **27 D11** 51 20N 108 55 E
Petrozavodsk, *Russia* **24 B5** 61 41N 34 20 E
Petrus Steyn, *S. Africa* **57 D4** 27 38S 28 8 E
Petrusburg, *S. Africa* **56 D4** 29 4S 25 26 E
Peumo, *Chile* **94 C1** 34 21S 71 12W
Peureulak, *Indonesia* **36 D1** 4 48N 97 45 E
Pevek, *Russia* **27 C18** 69 41N 171 19 E
Pforzheim, *Germany* **16 D5** 48 52N 8 41 E
Phagwara, *India* **40 D9** 31 10N 75 40 E
Phaistós, *Greece* **23 D6** 35 2N 24 50 E
Phala, *Botswana* **56 C4** 23 45S 26 50 E
Phalera = Phulera, *India* **42 F6** 26 52N 75 16 E
Phalodi, *India* **42 F5** 27 12N 72 24 E
Phan, *Thailand* **38 C2** 19 28N 99 43 E
Phan Rang, *Vietnam* **39 G7** 11 34N 109 0 E
Phan Ri = Hoa Da, *Vietnam* **39 G7** 11 16N 108 40 E
Phan Thiet, *Vietnam* **39 G7** 11 1N 108 9 E
Phanat Nikhom, *Thailand* **38 F3** 13 27N 101 11 E
Phangan, Ko, *Thailand* **39 H3** 9 45N 100 0 E
Phangnga, *Thailand* **39 H2** 8 28N 98 30 E
Phanh Bho Ho Chi Minh, *Vietnam* **39 G6** 10 58N 106 40 E
Phanom Sarakham, *Thailand* **38 F3** 13 45N 101 21 E
Phaphund, *India* **43 F8** 26 36N 79 28 E
Pharenda, *India* **43 F10** 27 5N 83 17 E
Pharr, *U.S.A.* **81 M5** 26 12N 98 11W
Phatthalung, *Thailand* **39 J3** 7 39N 100 6 E
Phayao, *Thailand* **38 C2** 19 11N 99 55 E
Phelps, *U.S.A.* **78 D7** 42 58N 77 3W
Phelps L., *Canada* **73 B8** 59 15N 103 15W
Phenix City, *U.S.A.* **77 J3** 32 28N 85 0W
Phet Buri, *Thailand* **38 F2** 13 1N 99 55 E
Phetchabun, *Thailand* **38 D3** 16 25N 101 8 E
Phetchabun, Thiu Khao, *Thailand* **38 E3** 16 0N 101 20 E
Phetchaburi = Phet Buri, *Thailand* **38 F2** 13 1N 99 55 E
Phi Phi, Ko, *Thailand* **39 J2** 7 45N 98 46 E
Phiafay, *Laos* **38 E6** 14 48N 106 0 E
Phibun Mangsahan, *Thailand* **38 E5** 15 14N 105 14 E
Phichai, *Thailand* **38 D3** 17 22N 100 10 E
Phichit, *Thailand* **38 D3** 16 26N 100 22 E
Philadelphia, *Miss., U.S.A.* **81 J10** 32 46N 89 7W
Philadelphia, *N.Y., U.S.A.* **79 B9** 44 9N 75 43W
Philadelphia, *Pa., U.S.A.* **79 G9** 39 57N 75 10W
Philip, *U.S.A.* **80 C4** 44 2N 101 40W
Philippeville, *Belgium* **15 D4** 50 12N 4 33 E
Philippi, *U.S.A.* **76 F5** 39 9N 80 3W
Philippi L., *Australia* **62 C2** 24 20S 138 55 E
Philippines ■, *Asia* **37 B6** 12 0N 123 0 E
Philippolis, *S. Africa* **56 E4** 30 15S 25 16 E
Philippopolis = Plovdiv, *Bulgaria* **21 C11** 42 8N 24 44 E
Philipsburg, *Canada* **79 A11** 45 2N 73 5W
Philipsburg, *Mont., U.S.A.* **82 C7** 46 20N 113 18W
Philipsburg, *Pa., U.S.A.* **78 F6** 40 54N 78 13W
Philipstown = Daingean, *Ireland* **13 C4** 53 18N 7 17W
Philipstown, *S. Africa* **56 E3** 30 28S 24 30 E
Phillip I., *Australia* **63 F4** 38 30S 145 12 E
Phillips, *U.S.A.* **80 C9** 45 42N 90 24W
Phillipsburg, *Kans., U.S.A.* **80 F5** 39 45N 99 19W
Phillipsburg, *N.J., U.S.A.* **79 F9** 40 42N 75 12W
Philmont, *U.S.A.* **79 D11** 42 15N 73 39W
Philomath, *U.S.A.* **82 D2** 44 32N 123 22W
Phimai, *Thailand* **38 E4** 15 13N 102 30 E
Phitsanulok, *Thailand* **38 D3** 16 50N 100 12 E
Phnom Dangrek, *Thailand* **36 B2** 14 20N 104 0 E
Phnom Penh, *Cambodia* **39 G5** 11 33N 104 55 E
Phnum Penh = Phnom Penh, *Cambodia* **39 G5** 11 33N 104 55 E
Phoenicia, *U.S.A.* **79 D10** 42 5N 74 14W
Phoenix, *Ariz., U.S.A.* **83 K7** 33 27N 112 4W
Phoenix, *N.Y., U.S.A.* **79 C8** 43 14N 76 18W
Phoenix Is., *Kiribati* **64 H10** 3 30S 172 0W
Phoenixville, *U.S.A.* **79 F9** 40 8N 75 31W
Phon, *Thailand* **38 E4** 15 49N 102 36 E
Phon Tiou, *Laos* **38 D5** 17 53N 104 37 E
Phong →, *Thailand* **38 D4** 16 23N 102 56 E
Phong Tho, *Vietnam* **38 A4** 22 32N 103 21 E
Phonhong, *Laos* **38 C4** 18 30N 102 25 E
Phonum, *Thailand* **39 H2** 8 49N 98 48 E
Phosphate Hill, *Australia* **62 C2** 21 53S 139 58 E
Photharam, *Thailand* **38 F2** 13 41N 99 51 E
Phra Nakhon Si Ayutthaya, *Thailand* **38 E3** 14 25N 100 30 E
Phra Thong, Ko, *Thailand* **39 H2** 9 5N 98 17 E
Phrae, *Thailand* **38 C3** 18 7N 100 9 E
Phrom Phiram, *Thailand* **38 D3** 17 2N 100 12 E
Phu Dien, *Vietnam* **38 C5** 18 58N 105 31 E
Phu Loi, *Laos* **38 B4** 20 14N 103 14 E
Phu Quoc, Dao, *Vietnam* **39 G4** 10 20N 104 0 E
Phuket, *Thailand* **39 J2** 7 52N 98 22 E
Phuket, Ko, *Thailand* **39 J2** 8 0N 98 22 E
Phul, *India* **42 D6** 30 19N 75 14 E
Phulad, *India* **42 G5** 25 38N 73 49 E
Phulchari, *Bangla.* **43 G13** 25 11N 89 37 E
Phulera, *India* **42 F6** 26 52N 75 16 E
Phulpur, *India* **43 G10** 25 31N 82 49 E
Phun Phin, *Thailand* **39 H2** 9 7N 99 12 E
Piacenza, *Italy* **18 D8** 45 1N 9 40 E
Pian Cr. →, *Australia* **63 E4** 30 2S 148 12 E
Pianosa, *Italy* **20 C4** 42 35N 10 5 E
Piapot, *Canada* **73 D7** 49 59N 109 8W
Piatra Neamţ, *Romania* **17 E14** 46 56N 26 21 E
Piauí □, *Brazil* **93 E10** 7 0S 43 0W
Piaui →, *Brazil* **93 E10** 6 38S 42 42W
Piave →, *Italy* **20 B5** 45 32N 12 44 E
Pibor Post, *Sudan* **51 G12** 6 47N 33 3 E
Picardie, *France* **18 B5** 49 50N 3 0 E
Picardy = Picardie, *France* **18 B5** 49 50N 3 0 E
Picayune, *U.S.A.* **81 K10** 30 32N 89 41W
Pichhor, *India* **43 G8** 25 58N 78 20 E
Pichilemu, *Chile* **94 C1** 34 22S 72 0W
Pichor, *India* **42 G8** 25 11N 78 11 E
Pickerel L., *Canada* **70 C1** 48 40N 91 25W
Pickering, *U.K.* **10 C7** 54 15N 0 46W
Pickering, Vale of, *U.K.* **10 C7** 54 14N 0 45W
Pickle Lake, *Canada* **70 B1** 51 30N 90 12W
Pickwick L., *U.S.A.* **77 H1** 35 4N 88 15W
Pico Truncado, *Argentina* **96 F3** 46 40S 68 0W
Picos, *Brazil* **93 E10** 7 5S 41 28W
Picton, *Australia* **63 E5** 34 12S 150 34 E
Picton, *Canada* **78 B7** 44 1N 77 9W
Picton, *N.Z.* **59 J5** 41 18S 174 3 E
Pictou, *Canada* **71 C7** 45 41N 62 42W
Picture Butte, *Canada* **72 D6** 49 55N 112 45W
Picún Leufú, *Argentina* **96 D3** 39 30S 69 5W
Pidurutalagala, *Sri Lanka* **40 R12** 7 10N 80 50 E
Piedmont = Piemonte □, *Italy* **18 D7** 45 0N 8 0 E
Piedmont, *Ala., U.S.A.* **77 J3** 33 55N 85 37W
Piedmont, *S.C., U.S.A.* **75 D10** 34 0N 81 30W
Piedras Negras, *Mexico* **86 B4** 28 42N 100 31W
Pieksämäki, *Finland* **9 E22** 62 18N 27 10 E
Piemonte □, *Italy* **18 D7** 45 0N 8 0 E
Piercefield, *U.S.A.* **79 B10** 44 13N 74 35W
Pierceland, *Canada* **73 C7** 54 20N 109 46W
Pierpont, *U.S.A.* **78 E4** 41 45N 80 34W
Pierre, *U.S.A.* **80 C4** 44 22N 100 21W
Piet Retief, *S. Africa* **57 D5** 27 1S 30 50 E
Pietarsaari, *Finland* **8 E20** 63 40N 22 43 E
Pietermaritzburg, *S. Africa* **57 D5** 29 35S 30 25 E
Pietersburg, *S. Africa* **57 C4** 23 54S 29 25 E
Pietrosul, Vf., *Maramureş, Romania* **17 E13** 47 35N 24 43 E
Pietrosul, Vf., *Suceava, Romania* **17 E13** 47 12N 25 18 E
Pigeon L., *Canada* **78 B6** 44 27N 78 30W
Piggott, *U.S.A.* **81 G9** 36 23N 90 11W
Pigüe, *Argentina* **94 D3** 37 36S 62 25W
Pihani, *India* **43 F9** 27 36N 80 15 E
Pihlajavesi, *Finland* **9 F23** 61 45N 28 45 E
Pijijiapan, *Mexico* **87 D6** 15 42N 93 14W
Pikangikum Berens, *Canada* **73 C10** 51 49N 94 0W
Pikes Peak, *U.S.A.* **80 F2** 38 50N 105 3W
Piketberg, *S. Africa* **56 E2** 32 55S 18 40 E
Pikeville, *U.S.A.* **76 G4** 37 29N 82 31W
Pikou, *China* **35 E12** 39 18N 122 22 E
Pikwitonei, *Canada* **73 B9** 55 35N 97 9W
Piła, *Poland* **17 B9** 53 10N 16 48 E
Pilani, *India* **42 E6** 28 22N 75 33 E
Pilar, *Paraguay* **94 B4** 26 50S 58 20W
Pilaya →, *Bolivia* **92 H6** 20 55S 64 4W
Pilbara, *Australia* **60 D2** 23 35S 117 25 E
Pilcomayo →, *Paraguay* **94 B4** 25 21S 57 42W
Pilibhit, *India* **43 E8** 28 40N 79 50 E
Pilica →, *Poland* **17 C11** 51 52N 21 17 E
Pilkhawa, *India* **42 E7** 28 43N 77 42 E
Pilliga, *Australia* **63 E4** 30 21S 148 54 E
Pílos, *Greece* **21 F9** 36 55N 21 42 E
Pilot Mound, *Canada* **73 D9** 49 15N 98 54W
Pilot Point, *U.S.A.* **81 J6** 33 24N 96 58W
Pilot Rock, *U.S.A.* **82 D4** 45 29N 118 50W
Pilsen = Plzeň, *Czech Rep.* **16 D7** 49 45N 13 22 E
Pima, *U.S.A.* **83 K9** 32 54N 109 50W
Pimba, *Australia* **63 E2** 31 18S 136 46 E
Pimenta Bueno, *Brazil* **92 F6** 11 35S 61 10W
Pimentel, *Peru* **92 E3** 6 45S 79 55W
Pinang, *Malaysia* **39 K3** 5 25N 100 15 E
Pinar, C. des, *Spain* **22 B10** 39 53N 3 12 E
Pinar del Río, *Cuba* **88 B3** 22 26N 83 40W
Pınarhisar, *Turkey* **21 D12** 41 37N 27 30 E
Pinatubo, *Phil.* **37 A6** 15 8N 120 21 E
Pincher Creek, *Canada* **72 D6** 49 30N 113 57W
Pinchi L., *Canada* **72 C4** 54 38N 124 30W
Pinckneyville, *U.S.A.* **80 F10** 38 5N 89 23W
Pińczów, *Poland* **17 C11** 50 32N 20 32 E
Pindar, *Australia* **61 E2** 28 30S 115 47 E
Pindi Gheb, *Pakistan* **42 C5** 33 14N 72 21 E
Pindos Óros, *Greece* **21 E9** 40 0N 21 0 E
Pindus Mts. = Pindos Óros, *Greece* **21 E9** 40 0N 21 0 E
Pine →, *B.C., Canada* **72 B4** 56 8N 120 43W
Pine →, *Sask., Canada* **73 B7** 58 50N 105 38W
Pine, C., *Canada* **71 C9** 46 37N 53 32W
Pine Bluff, *U.S.A.* **81 H9** 34 13N 92 1W
Pine Bluffs, *U.S.A.* **80 E2** 41 11N 104 4W
Pine City, *U.S.A.* **80 C8** 45 50N 92 59W
Pine Cr. →, *U.S.A.* **78 E7** 41 10N 77 16W
Pine Creek, *Australia* **60 B5** 13 50S 131 50 E
Pine Falls, *Canada* **73 C9** 50 34N 96 11W
Pine Flat Res., *U.S.A.* **84 J7** 36 50N 119 20W
Pine Grove, *U.S.A.* **79 F8** 40 33N 76 23W
Pine Pass, *Canada* **72 B4** 55 25N 122 42W
Pine Point, *Canada* **72 A6** 60 50N 114 28W
Pine Ridge, *U.S.A.* **80 D3** 43 2N 102 33W
Pine River, *Canada* **73 C8** 51 45N 100 30W
Pine River, *U.S.A.* **80 B7** 46 43N 94 24W
Pine Valley, *U.S.A.* **85 N10** 32 50N 116 32W
Pinecrest, *U.S.A.* **84 G6** 38 12N 120 1W
Pinedale, *Calif., U.S.A.* **84 J7** 36 50N 119 48W
Pinedale, *Wyo., U.S.A.* **82 E9** 42 52N 109 52W
Pinega →, *Russia* **24 B8** 64 30N 44 19 E
Pinehill, *Australia* **62 C4** 23 38S 146 57 E
Pinehouse L., *Canada* **73 B7** 55 32N 106 35W
Pineimuta →, *Canada* **70 B1** 52 8N 88 33W
Pinerolo, *Italy* **18 D7** 44 53N 7 21 E
Pinetop, *U.S.A.* **83 J9** 34 8N 109 56W
Pinetown, *S. Africa* **57 D5** 29 48S 30 54 E
Pineville, *U.S.A.* **81 K8** 31 19N 92 26W
Ping →, *Thailand* **38 E3** 15 42N 100 9 E
Pingaring, *Australia* **61 F2** 32 40S 118 32 E
Pingding, *China* **34 F7** 37 47N 113 38 E
Pingdingshan, *China* **34 H7** 33 43N 113 27 E
Pingdong, *Taiwan* **33 D7** 22 39N 120 30 E
Pingdu, *China* **35 F10** 36 42N 119 59 E
Pingelly, *Australia* **61 F2** 32 32S 117 5 E
Pingliang, *China* **34 G4** 35 35N 106 31 E
Pinglu, *China* **34 E7** 39 31N 112 30 E
Pingluo, *China* **34 E4** 38 52N 106 30 E
Pingquan, *China* **35 D10** 41 1N 118 37 E
Pingrup, *Australia* **61 F2** 33 32S 118 29 E
P'ingtung, *Taiwan* **33 D7** 22 38N 120 30 E
Pingwu, *China* **34 H3** 32 25N 104 30 E
Pingxiang, *China* **32 D5** 22 6N 106 46 E
Pingyao, *China* **34 F7** 37 12N 112 10 E
Pingyi, *China* **35 G9** 35 30N 117 35 E
Pingyin, *China* **34 F9** 36 20N 116 25 E
Pingyuan, *China* **34 F9** 37 10N 116 22 E
Pinhal, *Brazil* **95 A6** 22 10S 46 46W
Pinheiro, *Brazil* **93 D9** 2 31S 45 5W
Pinheiro Machado, *Brazil* **95 C5** 31 34S 53 23W
Pinhel, *Portugal* **19 B2** 40 50N 7 1W
Pini, *Indonesia* **36 D1** 0 10N 98 40 E
Piniós →, *Greece* **21 E10** 39 55N 22 41 E
Pinjarra, *Australia* **61 F2** 32 37S 115 52 E
Pink Mountain, *Canada* **72 B4** 57 3N 122 52W
Pinnacles, *U.S.A.* **84 J5** 36 33N 121 19W
Pinnaroo, *Australia* **63 F3** 35 17S 140 53 E
Pinnes, Ákra, *Greece* **21 D11** 40 5N 24 20 E
Pinon Hills, *U.S.A.* **85 L9** 34 26N 117 39W
Pinos, *Mexico* **86 C4** 22 20N 101 40W
Pinos, Mt., *U.S.A.* **85 L7** 34 49N 119 8W
Pinos Pt., *U.S.A.* **83 H3** 36 38N 121 57W
Pinotepa Nacional, *Mexico* **87 D5** 16 19N 98 3W
Pinrang, *Indonesia* **37 E5** 3 46S 119 41 E
Pins, Pte. aux, *Canada* **78 D3** 42 15N 81 51W
Pinsk, *Belarus* **17 B14** 52 10N 26 1 E
Pintados, *Chile* **92 H5** 20 35S 69 40W
Pinyug, *Russia* **24 B8** 60 5N 48 0 E
Pioche, *U.S.A.* **83 H6** 37 56N 114 27W
Piombino, *Italy* **20 C4** 42 55N 10 32 E
Pioner, Ostrov, *Russia* **27 B10** 79 50N 92 0 E
Piorini, L., *Brazil* **92 D6** 3 15S 62 35W
Piotrków Trybunalski, *Poland* **17 C10** 51 23N 19 43 E
Pīp, *Iran* **45 E9** 26 45N 60 10 E
Pipar, *India* **42 F5** 26 25N 73 31 E
Pipar Road, *India* **42 F5** 26 27N 73 27 E
Piparia, *Mad. P., India* **42 H8** 22 45N 78 23 E
Piparia, *Mad. P., India* **42 J7** 21 49N 77 37 E
Pipestone, *U.S.A.* **80 D6** 44 0N 96 19W
Pipestone →, *Canada* **70 B2** 52 53N 89 23W
Pipestone Cr. →, *Canada* **73 D8** 49 38N 100 15W
Piplan, *Pakistan* **42 C4** 32 17N 71 21 E
Piploda, *India* **42 H6** 23 37N 74 56 E
Pipmuacan, Rés., *Canada* **71 C5** 49 45N 70 30W
Pippingarra, *Australia* **60 D2** 20 27S 118 42 E
Piqua, *U.S.A.* **76 E3** 40 9N 84 15W
Piquiri →, *Brazil* **95 A5** 24 3S 54 14W
Pīr Sohrāb, *Iran* **45 E9** 25 44N 60 54 E
Piracicaba, *Brazil* **95 A6** 22 45S 47 40W
Piracuruca, *Brazil* **93 D10** 3 50S 41 50W
Piræus = Piraiévs, *Greece* **21 F10** 37 57N 23 42 E
Piraiévs, *Greece* **21 F10** 37 57N 23 42 E
Pirajuí, *Brazil* **95 A6** 21 59S 49 29W
Piram I., *India* **42 J5** 21 36N 72 21 E
Pirané, *Argentina* **94 B4** 25 42S 59 6W
Pirapora, *Brazil* **93 G10** 17 20S 44 56W
Pirawa, *India* **42 G7** 24 10N 76 2 E
Pírgos, *Greece* **21 F9** 37 40N 21 27 E
Piribebuy, *Paraguay* **94 B4** 25 26S 57 2W
Pirimapun, *Indonesia* **37 F9** 6 45S 138 0 E
Pirin Planina, *Bulgaria* **21 D10** 41 40N 23 30 E
Pírineos = Pyrénées, *Europe* **18 E4** 42 45N 0 18 E
Piripiri, *Brazil* **93 D10** 4 15S 41 46W
Pirmasens, *Germany* **16 D4** 49 12N 7 36 E
Pirot, *Serbia, Yug.* **21 C10** 43 9N 22 33 E
Piru, *Indonesia* **37 E7** 3 4S 128 12 E
Piru, *U.S.A.* **85 L8** 34 25N 118 48W
Pisa, *Italy* **20 C4** 43 43N 10 23 E
Pisagua, *Chile* **92 G4** 19 40S 70 15W
Pisco, *Peru* **92 F3** 13 50S 76 12W
Písek, *Czech Rep.* **16 D8** 49 19N 14 10 E
Pishan, *China* **32 C2** 37 30N 78 33 E
Pīshīn, *Iran* **45 E9** 26 6N 61 47 E
Pishin, *Pakistan* **42 D2** 30 35N 67 0 E
Pishin Lora →, *Pakistan* **42 E1** 29 9N 64 5 E
Pising, *Indonesia* **37 F6** 5 8S 121 53 E
Pismo Beach, *U.S.A.* **85 K6** 35 9N 120 38W
Pissis, Cerro, *Argentina* **94 B2** 27 45S 68 48W
Pissouri, *Cyprus* **23 E11** 34 40N 32 42 E
Pistóia, *Italy* **20 C4** 43 55N 10 54 E
Pistol B., *Canada* **73 A10** 62 25N 92 37W
Pisuerga →, *Spain* **19 B3** 41 33N 4 52W
Pit →, *U.S.A.* **82 F2** 40 47N 122 6W
Pitarpunga, L., *Australia* **63 E3** 34 24S 143 30 E
Pitcairn I., *Pac. Oc.* **65 K14** 25 5S 130 5W
Pite älv →, *Sweden* **8 D19** 65 20N 21 25 E
Piteå, *Sweden* **8 D19** 65 20N 21 25 E
Piteşti, *Romania* **17 F13** 44 52N 24 54 E
Pithapuram, *India* **41 L13** 17 10N 82 15 E
Pithara, *Australia* **61 F2** 30 20S 116 35 E
Pithoragarh, *India* **43 E9** 29 35N 80 13 E
Pithoro, *Pakistan* **42 G3** 25 31N 69 23 E
Pitlochry, *U.K.* **12 E5** 56 42N 3 44W

Posse

Posse, *Brazil* **93 F9** 14 4S 46 18W
Possession I., *Antarctica* .. **5 D11** 72 4S 172 0 E
Possum Kingdom L., *U.S.A.* **81 J5** 32 52N 98 26W
Post, *U.S.A.* **81 J4** 33 12N 101 23W
Post Falls, *U.S.A.* **82 C5** 47 43N 116 57W
Postavy = Pastavy, *Belarus* **9 J22** 55 4N 26 50 E
Poste-de-la-Baleine =
Kuujjuarapik, *Canada* ... **70 A4** 55 20N 77 35W
Postmasburg, *S. Africa* ... **56 D3** 28 18S 23 5 E
Postojna, *Slovenia* ...... **16 F8** 45 46N 14 12 E
Poston, *U.S.A.* **85 M12** 34 0N 114 24W
Postville, *Canada* **71 B8** 54 54N 59 47W
Potchefstroom, *S. Africa* .. **56 D4** 26 41S 27 7 E
Poteau, *U.S.A.* **81 H7** 35 3N 94 37W
Poteet, *U.S.A.* **81 L5** 29 2N 98 35W
Potenza, *Italy* .... **20 D6** 40 38N 15 48 E
Poteriteri, L., *N.Z.* .... **59 M1** 46 5S 167 10 E
Potgietersrus, *S. Africa* ... **57 C4** 24 10S 28 55 E
Poti, *Georgia* .... **25 F7** 42 10N 41 38 E
Potiskum, *Nigeria* .... **51 F8** 11 39N 11 2 E
Potomac →, *U.S.A.* **76 G7** 38 0N 76 23W
Potosí, *Bolivia* **92 G5** 19 38S 65 50W
Potosi Mt., *U.S.A.* **85 K11** 35 57N 115 29W
Pototan, *Phil.* .... **37 B6** 10 54N 122 38 E
Potrerillos, *Chile* **94 B2** 26 30S 69 30W
Potsdam, *Germany* .... **16 B7** 52 25N 13 4 E
Potsdam, *U.S.A.* **79 B10** 44 40N 74 59W
Pottersville, *U.S.A.* **79 C11** 43 43N 73 50W
Pottstown, *U.S.A.* **79 F9** 40 15N 75 39W
Pottsville, *U.S.A.* **79 F8** 40 41N 76 12W
Pottuvil, *Sri Lanka* .... **40 R12** 6 55N 81 50 E
Pouce Coupé, *Canada* **72 B4** 55 40N 120 10W
Poughkeepsie, *U.S.A.* **79 E11** 41 42N 73 56W
Poulaphouca Res., *Ireland* . **13 C5** 53 8N 6 30W
Poulsbo, *U.S.A.* **84 C4** 47 44N 122 39W
Poultney, *U.S.A.* **79 C11** 43 31N 73 14W
Poulton-le-Fylde, *U.K.* **10 D5** 53 51N 2 58W
Pouso Alegre, *Brazil* **95 A6** 22 14S 45 57W
Pouthisat, *Cambodia* ..... **38 F4** 12 34N 103 50 E
Považská Bystrica,
Slovak Rep. .... **17 D10** 49 8N 18 27 E
Povenets, *Russia* .... **24 B5** 62 50N 34 50 E
Poverty B., *N.Z.* .... **59 H7** 38 43S 178 2 E
Póvoa de Varzim, *Portugal* **19 B1** 41 25N 8 46W
Povungnituk = Puvirnituq,
Canada **69 B12** 60 2N 77 10W
Powassan, *Canada* **70 C4** 46 5N 79 25W
Poway, *U.S.A.* **85 N9** 32 58N 117 2W
Powder →, *U.S.A.* **80 B2** 46 45N 105 26W
Powder River, *U.S.A.* **82 E10** 43 2N 106 59W
Powell, *U.S.A.* **82 D9** 44 45N 108 46W
Powell, L., *U.S.A.* **83 H8** 36 57N 111 29W
Powell River, *Canada* **72 D4** 49 50N 124 35W
Powers, *U.S.A.* **76 C2** 45 41N 87 32W
Powys □, *U.K.* **11 E4** 52 20N 3 20W
Poyang Hu, *China* .... **33 D6** 29 5N 116 20 E
Poyarkovo, *Russia* .... **27 E13** 49 36N 128 41 E
Poza Rica, *Mexico* **87 C5** 20 33N 97 27W
Požarevac, *Serbia, Yug.* ... **21 B9** 44 35N 21 18 E
Poznań, *Poland* .... **17 B9** 52 25N 16 55 E
Pozo, *U.S.A.* **85 K6** 35 20N 120 24W
Pozo Almonte, *Chile* **92 H5** 20 10S 69 50W
Pozo Colorado, *Paraguay* .. **94 A4** 23 30S 58 45W
Pozoblanco, *Spain* **19 C3** 38 23N 4 51W
Pozzuoli, *Italy* .... **20 D6** 40 49N 14 7 E
Prachin Buri, *Thailand* .... **38 F3** 14 0N 101 25 E
Prachuap Khiri Khan,
Thailand .... **39 G2** 11 49N 99 48 E
Prado, *Brazil* **93 G11** 17 20S 39 13W
Prague = Praha, *Czech Rep.* **16 C8** 50 5N 14 22 E
Praha, *Czech Rep.* .... **16 C8** 50 5N 14 22 E
Praia, *C. Verde Is.* **49 E1** 14 55N 23 30W
Prainha, *Amazonas, Brazil* . **92 E6** 7 10S 60 30W
Prainha, *Pará, Brazil* **93 D8** 1 45S 53 30W
Prairie, *Australia* .... **62 C3** 20 50S 144 35 E
Prairie City, *U.S.A.* **82 D4** 44 28N 118 43W
Prairie Dog Town Fork →,
U.S.A. **81 H5** 34 30N 99 23W
Prairie du Chien, *U.S.A.* ... **80 D9** 43 3N 91 9W
Prairies, L. of the, *Canada* . **73 C8** 51 16N 101 32W
Pran Buri, *Thailand* ...... **38 F2** 12 23N 99 55 E
Prapat, *Indonesia* .... **36 D1** 2 41N 98 58 E
Prasonísi, Ákra, *Greece* ... **23 D9** 35 42N 27 46 E
Prata, *Brazil* **93 G9** 19 25S 48 54W
Pratabpur, *India* .... **43 H10** 23 28N 83 15 E
Pratapgarh, *Raj., India* ... **42 G6** 24 2N 74 40 E
Pratapgarh, *Ut. P., India* .. **43 G9** 25 56N 81 59 E
Prato, *Italy* .... **20 C4** 43 53N 11 6 E
Pratt, *U.S.A.* **81 G5** 37 39N 98 44W
Prattville, *U.S.A.* **77 J2** 32 28N 86 29W
Pravia, *Spain* **19 A2** 43 30N 6 12W
Praya, *Indonesia* .... **36 F5** 8 39S 116 17 E
Precordillera, *Argentina* ... **94 C2** 30 0S 69 1W
Preeceville, *Canada* **73 C8** 51 57N 102 40W
Preiļi, *Latvia* .... **9 H22** 56 18N 26 43 E
Premont, *U.S.A.* **81 M5** 27 22N 98 7W
Prentice, *U.S.A.* **80 C9** 45 33N 90 17W
Preobrazheniye, *Russia* ... **30 C6** 42 54N 133 54 E
Preparis North Channel,
Ind. Oc. .... **41 M18** 15 12N 93 40 E
Preparis South Channel,
Ind. Oc. .... **41 M18** 14 36N 93 40 E
Přerov, *Czech Rep.* ...... **17 D9** 49 28N 17 27 E
Prescott, *Canada* **79 B9** 44 45N 75 30W
Prescott, *Ariz., U.S.A.* **83 J7** 34 33N 112 28W
Prescott, *Ark., U.S.A.* **81 J8** 33 48N 93 23W
Prescott Valley, *U.S.A.* **83 J7** 34 40N 112 18W
Preservation Inlet, *N.Z.* ... **59 M1** 46 8S 166 35 E
Presho, *U.S.A.* **80 D4** 43 54N 100 3W
Presidencia de la Plaza,
Argentina **94 B4** 27 0S 59 50W
Presidencia Roque Saenz
Peña, *Argentina* **94 B3** 26 45S 60 30W
Presidente Epitácio, *Brazil* . **93 H8** 21 56S 52 6W
Presidente Hayes □,
Paraguay **94 A4** 24 0S 59 0W
Presidente Prudente, *Brazil* **95 A5** 22 5S 51 25W
Presidio, *Mexico* **86 B4** 29 29N 104 23W
Presidio, *U.S.A.* **81 L2** 29 34N 104 22W
Prešov, *Slovak Rep.* ..... **17 D11** 49 0N 21 15 E
Prespa, L. = Prespansko
Jezero, *Macedonia* ..... **21 D9** 40 55N 21 0 E
Prespansko Jezero,
Macedonia .... **21 D9** 40 55N 21 0 E
Presque I., *U.S.A.* **78 D4** 42 9N 80 6W
Presque Isle, *U.S.A.* **77 B12** 46 41N 68 1W
Prestatyn, *U.K.* **10 D4** 53 20N 3 24W
Presteigne, *U.K.* **11 E5** 52 17N 3 0W
Preston, *Canada* **78 C4** 43 23N 80 21W
Preston, *U.K.* **10 D5** 53 46N 2 42W
Preston, *Idaho, U.S.A.* **82 E8** 42 6N 111 53W
Preston, *Minn., U.S.A.* **80 D8** 43 40N 92 5W
Preston, C., *Australia* ..... **60 D2** 20 51S 116 12 E
Prestonburg, *U.S.A.* **76 G4** 37 39N 82 46W
Prestwick, *U.K.* **12 F4** 55 29N 4 37W
Pretoria, *S. Africa* .... **57 D4** 25 44S 28 12 E
Préveza, *Greece* .... **21 E9** 38 57N 20 47 E
Prey Veng, *Cambodia* .... **39 G5** 11 35N 105 29 E
Pribilof Is., *U.S.A.* **68 C2** 57 0N 170 0W
Příbram, *Czech Rep.* ..... **16 D8** 49 41N 14 2 E
Price, *U.S.A.* **82 G8** 39 36N 110 49W
Price I., *Canada* **72 C3** 52 23N 128 41W
Prichard, *U.S.A.* **77 K1** 30 44N 88 5W
Priekule, *Latvia* .... **9 H19** 56 26N 21 35 E
Prienai, *Lithuania* .... **9 J20** 54 38N 23 57 E
Prieska, *S. Africa* .... **56 D3** 29 40S 22 42 E
Priest L., *U.S.A.* **82 B5** 48 35N 116 52W
Priest River, *U.S.A.* **82 B5** 48 10N 116 54W
Priest Valley, *U.S.A.* **84 J6** 36 10N 120 39W
Prievidza, *Slovak Rep.* .... **17 D10** 48 46N 18 36 E
Prikaspiyskaya Nizmennost
= Caspian Depression,
Eurasia .... **25 E8** 47 0N 48 0 E
Prilep, *Macedonia* .... **21 D9** 41 21N 21 32 E
Priluki = Pryluky, *Ukraine* . **25 D5** 50 30N 32 24 E
Prime Seal I., *Australia* ... **62 G4** 40 3S 147 43 E
Primrose L., *Canada* **73 C7** 54 55N 109 45W
Prince Albert, *Canada* **73 C7** 53 15N 105 50W
Prince Albert, *S. Africa* ... **56 E3** 33 12S 22 2 E
Prince Albert Mts.,
Antarctica .... **5 D11** 76 0S 161 30 E
Prince Albert Nat. Park,
Canada **73 C7** 54 0N 106 25W
Prince Albert Pen., *Canada* **68 A8** 72 30N 116 0W
Prince Albert Sd., *Canada* . **68 A8** 70 25N 115 0W
Prince Alfred, C., *Canada* .. **4 B1** 74 20N 124 40W
Prince Charles I., *Canada* .. **69 B12** 67 47N 76 12W
Prince Charles Mts.,
Antarctica .... **5 D6** 72 0S 67 0 E
Prince Edward I. □, *Canada* **71 C7** 46 20N 63 20W
Prince Edward Is., *Ind. Oc.* . **3 G11** 46 35S 38 0 E
Prince Edward Pt., *Canada* . **78 C8** 43 56N 76 52W
Prince George, *Canada* ... **72 C4** 53 55N 122 50W
Prince of Wales, C., *U.S.A.* . **66 C3** 65 36N 168 5W
Prince of Wales I., *Australia* **62 A3** 10 40S 142 10 E
Prince of Wales I., *Canada* **68 A10** 73 0N 99 0W
Prince of Wales I., *U.S.A.* .. **68 C6** 55 47N 132 50W
Prince Patrick I., *Canada* .. **4 B2** 77 0N 120 0W
Prince Regent Inlet, *Canada* **4 B3** 73 0N 90 0W
Prince Rupert, *Canada* **72 C2** 54 20N 130 20W
Princess Charlotte B.,
Australia .... **62 A3** 14 25S 144 0 E
Princess May Ranges,
Australia .... **60 C4** 15 30S 125 30 E
Princess Royal I., *Canada* . **72 C3** 53 0N 128 40W
Princeton, *Canada* **72 D4** 49 27N 120 30W
Princeton, *Calif., U.S.A.* ... **84 F4** 39 24N 122 1W
Princeton, *Ill., U.S.A.* **80 E10** 41 23N 89 28W
Princeton, *Ind., U.S.A.* **76 F2** 38 21N 87 34W
Princeton, *Ky., U.S.A.* **76 G2** 37 7N 87 53W
Princeton, *Mo., U.S.A.* **80 E8** 40 24N 93 35W
Princeton, *N.J., U.S.A.* **79 F10** 40 21N 74 39W
Princeton, *W. Va., U.S.A.* .. **76 G5** 37 22N 81 6W
Principe, I. de, *Atl. Oc.* ... **48 F4** 1 37N 7 27 E
Principe da Beira, *Brazil* .. **92 F6** 12 20S 64 30W
Prineville, *U.S.A.* **82 D3** 44 18N 120 51W
Prins Harald Kyst, *Antarctica* **5 D4** 70 0S 35 1 E
Prinsesse Astrid Kyst,
Antarctica .... **5 D3** 70 45S 12 30 E
Prinsesse Ragnhild Kyst,
Antarctica .... **5 D4** 70 15S 27 30 E
Prinzapolca, *Nic.* **88 D3** 13 20N 83 35W
Priozersk, *Russia* .... **24 B5** 61 2N 30 7 E
Pripet = Prypyat →,
Europe .... **17 C16** 51 20N 30 15 E
Pripet Marshes, *Europe* ... **17 B15** 52 10N 28 10 E
Pripyat Marshes = Pripet
Marshes, *Europe* ...... **17 B15** 52 10N 28 10 E
Pripyats = Prypyat →,
Europe .... **17 C16** 51 20N 30 15 E
Priština, *Yugoslavia* ..... **21 C9** 42 40N 21 13 E
Privas, *France* .... **18 D6** 44 45N 4 37 E
Privolzhskaya
Vozvyshennost, *Russia* .. **25 D8** 51 0N 46 0 E
Prizren, *Yugoslavia* ...... **21 C9** 42 13N 20 45 E
Probolinggo, *Indonesia* ... **37 G15** 7 46S 113 13 E
Proctor, *U.S.A.* **79 C11** 43 40N 73 2W
Proddatur, *India* .... **40 M11** 14 45N 78 30 E
Prodhromos, *Cyprus* ..... **23 E11** 34 57N 32 50 E
Profitis Ilías, *Greece* ..... **23 C9** 36 17N 27 56 E
Profondeville, *Belgium* ... **15 D4** 50 23N 4 52 E
Progreso, *Mexico* **87 C7** 21 20N 89 40W
Progreso, *Yucatán, Mexico* **86 B4** 21 17N 89 40W
Prokopyevsk, *Russia* ..... **26 D9** 54 0N 86 45 E
Prokuplje, *Serbia, Yug.* ... **21 C9** 43 16N 21 36 E
Prome = Pyè, *Burma* ..... **41 K19** 18 49N 95 13 E
Prophet →, *Canada* **72 B4** 58 48N 122 40W
Prophet River, *Canada* ... **72 B4** 58 6N 122 43W
Propriá, *Brazil* **93 F11** 10 13S 36 51W
Proserpine, *Australia* .... **62 C4** 20 21S 148 36 E
Prosna →, *Poland* ...... **17 B9** 52 6N 17 44 E
Prospect, *U.S.A.* **79 C9** 43 18N 75 9W
Prosser, *U.S.A.* **82 C4** 46 12N 119 46W
Prostějov, *Czech Rep.* .... **17 D9** 49 30N 17 9 E
Proston, *Australia* .... **63 D5** 26 8S 151 32 E
Provence, *France* .... **18 E6** 43 40N 5 46 E
Providence, *Ky., U.S.A.* ... **76 G2** 37 24N 87 46W
Providence, *R.I., U.S.A.* ... **79 E13** 41 49N 71 24W
Providence Bay, *Canada* .. **70 C3** 45 41N 82 15W
Providence Mts., *U.S.A.* ... **85 K11** 35 10N 115 15W
Providencia, I. de, *Colombia* **88 D3** 13 25N 81 26W
Provideniya, *Russia* **27 C19** 64 23N 173 18W
Provins, *France* .... **18 B5** 48 33N 3 15 E
Provo, *U.S.A.* **82 F8** 40 14N 111 39W
Provost, *Canada* **73 C6** 52 25N 110 20W
Prudhoe Bay, *U.S.A.* **68 A5** 70 18N 148 22W
Prudhoe I., *Australia* ..... **62 C4** 21 19S 149 41 E
Prud'homme, *Canada* **73 C7** 52 20N 105 54W
Pruszków, *Poland* .... **17 B11** 52 9N 20 49 E
Prut →, *Romania* .... **17 F15** 45 28N 28 10 E
Pruzhany, *Belarus* ...... **17 B13** 52 33N 24 28 E
Prydz B., *Antarctica* ..... **5 C6** 69 0S 74 0 E
Pryluky, *Ukraine* .... **25 D5** 50 30N 32 24 E
Pryor, *U.S.A.* **81 G7** 36 19N 95 19W
Prypyat →, *Europe* ..... **17 C16** 51 20N 30 15 E
Przemyśl, *Poland* .... **17 D12** 49 50N 22 45 E
Przhevalsk, *Kyrgyzstan* ... **26 E8** 42 30N 78 20 E
Psará, *Greece* .... **21 E11** 38 37N 25 38 E
Psira, *Greece* .... **23 D7** 35 12N 25 52 E
Pskov, *Russia* .... **24 C4** 57 50N 28 25 E
Pskovskoye, Ozero, *Russia* . **9 H22** 58 0N 27 58 E
Ptich = Ptsich →, *Belarus* **17 B15** 52 9N 28 52 E
Ptolemaís, *Greece* .... **21 D9** 40 30N 21 43 E
Ptsich →, *Belarus* ...... **17 B15** 52 9N 28 52 E
Pu Xian, *China* .... **34 F6** 36 24N 111 6 E
Pua, *Thailand* .... **38 C3** 19 11N 100 55 E
Puán, *Argentina* **94 D3** 37 30S 62 45W
Puan, *S. Korea* .... **35 G14** 35 44N 126 44 E
Pucallpa, *Peru* **92 E4** 8 25S 74 30W
Pudasjärvi, *Finland* ...... **8 D22** 65 23N 26 53 E
Pudozh, *Russia* .... **24 B6** 61 48N 36 32 E
Pudukkottai, *India* .... **40 P11** 10 28N 78 47 E
Puebla, *Mexico* **87 D5** 19 3N 98 12W
Puebla □, *Mexico* **87 D5** 18 30N 98 0W
Pueblo, *U.S.A.* **80 F2** 38 16N 104 37W
Pueblo Hundido, *Chile* ... **94 B1** 26 20S 70 5W
Puelches, *Argentina* **94 D2** 38 5S 65 51W
Puelén, *Argentina* **94 D2** 37 32S 67 38W
Puente Alto, *Chile* **94 C1** 33 32S 70 35W
Puente-Genil, *Spain* **19 D3** 37 22N 4 47W
Puerco →, *U.S.A.* **83 J10** 34 22N 107 50W
Puerto, *Canary Is.* **22 F2** 28 5N 17 20W
Puerto Aisén, *Chile* **96 F2** 45 27S 73 0W
Puerto Ángel, *Mexico* **87 D5** 15 40N 96 29W
Puerto Arista, *Mexico* **87 D6** 15 56N 93 48W
Puerto Armuelles, *Panama* **88 E3** 8 20N 82 51W
Puerto Ayacucho, *Venezuela* **92 B5** 5 40N 67 35W
Puerto Barrios, *Guatemala* . **88 C2** 15 40N 88 32W
Puerto Bermejo, *Argentina* **94 B4** 26 55S 58 34W
Puerto Bermúdez, *Peru* ... **92 F4** 10 20S 74 58W
Puerto Bolívar, *Ecuador* ... **92 D3** 3 19S 79 55W
Puerto Cabello, *Venezuela* . **92 A5** 10 28N 68 1W
Puerto Cabezas, *Nic.* **88 D3** 14 0N 83 30W
Puerto Cabo Gracias á Dios,
Nic. **88 D3** 15 0N 83 10W
Puerto Carreño, *Colombia* . **92 B5** 6 12N 67 22W
Puerto Castilla, *Honduras* . **88 C2** 16 0N 86 0W
Puerto Chicama, *Peru* **92 E3** 7 45S 79 20W
Puerto Coig, *Argentina* ... **96 G3** 50 54S 69 15W
Puerto Cortés, *Costa Rica* . **88 E3** 8 55N 84 0W
Puerto Cortés, *Honduras* . **88 C2** 15 51N 88 0W
Puerto Cumarebo,
Venezuela **92 A5** 11 29N 69 30W
Puerto de Alcudia = Port
d'Alcúdia, *Spain* ...... **22 B10** 39 50N 3 7 E
Puerto de Andraitx, *Spain* . **22 B9** 39 32N 2 23 E
Puerto de Cabrera, *Spain* .. **22 B9** 39 8N 2 56 E
Puerto de Gran Tarajal,
Canary Is. **22 F5** 28 13N 14 1W
Puerto de la Cruz, *Canary Is.* **22 F3** 28 24N 16 32W
Puerto de Pozo Negro,
Canary Is. **22 F6** 28 19N 13 55W
Puerto de Sóller = Port de
Sóller, *Spain* .... **22 B9** 39 48N 2 42 E
Puerto del Carmen,
Canary Is. **22 F6** 28 55N 13 38W
Puerto del Rosario,
Canary Is. **22 F6** 28 30N 13 52W
Puerto Deseado, *Argentina* **96 F3** 47 55S 66 0W
Puerto Escondido, *Mexico* . **87 D5** 15 50N 97 3W
Puerto Heath, *Bolivia* **92 F5** 12 34S 68 39W
Puerto Inírida, *Colombia* .. **92 C5** 3 53N 67 52W
Puerto Juárez, *Mexico* **87 C7** 21 11N 86 49W
Puerto La Cruz, *Venezuela* . **92 A6** 10 13N 64 38W
Puerto Leguízamo,
Colombia **92 D4** 0 12S 74 46W
Puerto Limón, *Colombia* .. **92 C4** 3 23N 73 30W
Puerto Lobos, *Argentina* .. **96 E3** 42 0S 65 3W
Puerto Madryn, *Argentina* . **96 E3** 42 48S 65 4W
Puerto Maldonado, *Peru* .. **92 F5** 12 30S 69 10W
Puerto Manotí, *Cuba* **88 B4** 21 22N 76 50W
Puerto Montt, *Chile* **96 E2** 41 28S 73 0W
Puerto Morazán, *Nic.* **88 D2** 12 51N 87 11W
Puerto Morelos, *Mexico* ... **87 C7** 20 49N 86 52W
Puerto Natales, *Chile* **96 G2** 51 45S 72 15W
Puerto Padre, *Cuba* **88 B4** 21 13N 76 35W
Puerto Páez, *Venezuela* ... **92 B5** 6 13N 67 28W
Puerto Peñasco, *Mexico* .. **86 A2** 31 20N 113 33W
Puerto Pinasco, *Paraguay* . **94 A4** 22 36S 57 50W
Puerto Plata, *Dom. Rep.* .. **89 C5** 19 48N 70 45W
Puerto Pollensa = Port de
Pollença, *Spain* .... **22 B10** 39 54N 3 4 E
Puerto Princesa, *Phil.* .... **37 C5** 9 46N 118 45 E
Puerto Quepos, *Costa Rica* **88 E3** 9 29N 84 6W
Puerto Rico, *Canary Is.* ... **22 G4** 27 47N 15 42W
Puerto Rico ■, *W. Indies* .. **89 C6** 18 15N 66 45W
Puerto Rico Trench, *Atl. Oc.* **89 C6** 19 50N 66 0W
Puerto San Julián,
Argentina **96 F3** 49 18S 67 43W
Puerto Sastre, *Paraguay* .. **94 A4** 22 2S 57 55W
Puerto Suárez, *Bolivia* ... **92 G7** 18 58S 57 52W
Puerto Vallarta, *Mexico* ... **86 C3** 20 36N 105 15W
Puerto Wilches, *Colombia* . **92 B4** 7 21N 73 54W
Puertollano, *Spain* **19 C3** 38 43N 4 7W
Pueyrredón, L., *Argentina* . **96 F2** 47 20S 72 0W
Puffin I., *Ireland* **13 E1** 51 50N 10 24W
Pugachev, *Russia* .... **24 D8** 52 0N 48 49 E
Pugal, *India* .... **42 E5** 28 30N 72 48 E
Puge, *Tanzania* .... **54 C3** 4 45S 33 11 E
Puget Sound, *U.S.A.* **82 C2** 47 50N 122 30W
Pugŏdong, *N. Korea* ..... **35 C16** 42 5N 130 0 E
Pugu, *Tanzania* .... **54 D4** 6 55S 39 4 E
Pūgūnzī, *Iran* .... **45 E8** 25 49N 59 10 E
Puig Major, *Spain* .... **22 B9** 39 48N 2 47 E
Puigcerdà, *Spain* .... **19 A6** 42 24N 1 50 E
Puigpunyent, *Spain* ...... **22 B9** 39 38N 2 32 E
Pujon-chŏsuji, *N. Korea* ... **35 D14** 40 35N 127 35 E
Pukaki L., *N.Z.* .... **59 L3** 44 4S 170 1 E
Pukapuka, *Cook Is.* **65 J11** 10 53S 165 49W
Pukaskwa Nat. Park, *Canada* **70 C2** 48 20N 86 0W
Pukatawagan, *Canada* **73 B8** 55 45N 101 20W
Pukchin, *N. Korea* .... **35 D13** 40 12N 125 45 E
Pukch'ŏng, *N. Korea* ..... **35 D15** 40 14N 128 10 E
Pukekohe, *N.Z.* .... **59 G5** 37 12S 174 55 E
Pukhrayan, *India* .... **43 F8** 26 14N 79 51 E
Pula, *Croatia* .... **16 F7** 44 54N 13 57 E
Pulacayo, *Bolivia* **92 H5** 20 25S 66 41W
Pulandian, *China* .... **35 E11** 39 25N 121 58 E
Pularumpi, *Australia* ..... **60 B5** 11 24S 130 26 E
Pulaski, *N.Y., U.S.A.* **79 C8** 43 34N 76 8W
Pulaski, *Tenn., U.S.A.* **77 H2** 35 12N 87 2W
Pulaski, *Va., U.S.A.* **76 G5** 37 3N 80 47W
Pulau →, *Indonesia* ..... **37 F9** 5 50S 138 15 E
Puławy, *Poland* .... **17 C11** 51 23N 21 59 E
Pulga, *U.S.A.* **84 F5** 39 48N 121 29W
Pulicat L., *India* .... **40 N12** 13 40N 80 15 E
Pullman, *U.S.A.* **82 C5** 46 44N 117 10W
Pulo-Anna, *Pac. Oc.* ..... **37 D8** 4 30N 132 5 E
Pulog, *Phil.* .... **37 A6** 16 40N 120 50 E
Pułtusk, *Poland* .... **17 B11** 52 43N 21 6 E
Pumlumon Fawr, *U.K.* **11 E4** 52 28N 3 46W
Puná, I., *Ecuador* **92 D2** 2 55S 80 5W
Punakha, *Bhutan* .... **41 F16** 27 42N 89 52 E
Punasar, *India* .... **42 F5** 27 6N 73 6 E
Punata, *Bolivia* **92 G5** 17 32S 65 50W
Punch, *India* .... **43 C6** 33 48N 74 4 E
Punch →, *Pakistan* ..... **42 C5** 33 12N 73 40 E
Pune, *India* .... **40 K8** 18 29N 73 57 E
P'ungsan, *N. Korea* ...... **35 D15** 40 50N 128 9 E
Pungue, Ponte de, *Mozam.* **55 F3** 19 0S 34 0 E
Punjab □, *India* .... **42 D7** 31 0N 76 0 E
Punjab □, *Pakistan* ...... **42 E6** 32 0N 74 30 E
Puno, *Peru* **92 G4** 15 55S 70 3W
Punpun →, *India* .... **43 G11** 25 31N 85 18 E
Punta Alta, *Argentina* **96 D4** 38 53S 62 4W
Punta Arenas, *Chile* **96 G2** 53 10S 71 0W
Punta de Díaz, *Chile* **94 B1** 28 0S 70 45W
Punta Gorda, *Belize* **87 D7** 16 10N 88 45W
Punta Gorda, *U.S.A.* **77 M5** 26 56N 82 3W
Punta Prieta, *Mexico* **86 B2** 28 58N 114 17W
Punta Prima, *Spain* ...... **22 B11** 39 48N 4 16 E
Puntarenas, *Costa Rica* ... **88 E3** 10 0N 84 50W
Punto Fijo, *Venezuela* **92 A4** 11 50N 70 13W
Punxsatawney, *U.S.A.* **78 F6** 40 57N 78 59W
Puquio, *Peru* **92 F4** 14 45S 74 10W
Pur →, *Russia* .... **26 C8** 67 31N 77 55 E
Purace, Vol., *Colombia* ... **92 C3** 2 21N 76 23W
Puralia = Puruliya, *India* .. **43 H12** 23 17N 86 24 E
Puranpur, *India* .... **43 E9** 28 31N 80 9 E
Purbeck, Isle of, *U.K.* **11 G6** 50 39N 1 59W
Purcell, *U.S.A.* **81 H6** 35 1N 97 22W
Purcell Mts., *Canada* **72 D5** 49 55N 116 15W
Puri, *India* .... **41 K14** 19 50N 85 58 E
Purmerend, *Neths.* ...... **15 B4** 52 32N 4 58 E
Purnia, *India* .... **43 G12** 25 45N 87 31 E
Pursat = Pouthisat,
Cambodia .... **38 F4** 12 34N 103 50 E
Purukcahu, *Indonesia* .... **36 E4** 0 35S 114 35 E
Puruliya, *India* .... **43 H12** 23 17N 86 24 E
Purus →, *Brazil* **92 D6** 3 42S 61 28W
Purvis, *U.S.A.* **81 K10** 31 9N 89 25W
Purwa, *India* .... **43 F9** 26 28N 80 47 E
Purwakarta, *Indonesia* ... **37 G12** 6 35S 107 29 E
Purwodadi, *Indonesia* .... **37 G14** 7 7S 110 55 E
Purwokerto, *Indonesia* ... **37 G13** 7 25S 109 14 E
Puryŏng, *N. Korea* .... **35 C15** 42 5N 129 43 E
Pusa, *India* .... **43 G11** 25 59N 85 41 E
Pusan, *S. Korea* .... **35 G15** 35 5N 129 0 E
Pushkino, *Russia* .... **25 D8** 51 16N 47 0 E
Putahow L., *Canada* **73 B8** 59 54N 100 40W
Putao, *Burma* .... **41 F20** 27 28N 97 30 E
Putaruru, *N.Z.* .... **59 H5** 38 2S 175 50 E
Puthein Myit →, *Burma* .. **41 M19** 15 56N 94 18 E
Putignano, *Italy* .... **20 D7** 40 51N 17 7 E
Puting, Tanjung, *Indonesia* **36 E4** 3 31S 111 46 E
Putnam, *U.S.A.* **79 E13** 41 55N 71 55W
Putorana, Gory, *Russia* ... **27 C10** 69 0N 95 0 E
Puttalam, *Sri Lanka* ..... **40 Q11** 8 1N 79 55 E
Puttgarden, *Germany* .... **16 A6** 54 30N 11 10 E
Putumayo →, *S. Amer.* ... **92 D5** 3 7S 67 58W
Putussibau, *Indonesia* .... **36 D4** 0 50N 112 56 E
Puvirnituq, *Canada* **69 B12** 60 2N 77 10W
Puy-de-Dôme, *France* .... **18 D5** 45 46N 2 57 E
Puyallup, *U.S.A.* **84 C4** 47 12N 122 18W
Puyang, *China* .... **34 G8** 35 40N 115 1 E
Pūzeh Rīg, *Iran* .... **45 E8** 27 20N 58 40 E
Pwani □, *Tanzania* ...... **54 D4** 7 0S 39 0 E
Pweto,
Dem. Rep. of the Congo . **55 D2** 8 25S 28 51 E
Pwllheli, *U.K.* **10 E3** 52 53N 4 25W
Pyapon, *Burma* .... **41 L19** 16 20N 95 40 E
Pyasina →, *Russia* ..... **27 B9** 73 30N 87 0 E
Pyatigorsk, *Russia* ...... **25 F7** 44 2N 43 6 E
Pyè, *Burma* .... **41 K19** 18 49N 95 13 E
Pyetrikaw, *Belarus* ...... **17 B15** 52 11N 28 29 E
Pyhäjoki, *Finland* .... **8 D21** 64 28N 24 14 E
Pyinmana, *Burma* .... **41 K20** 19 45N 96 12 E
Pyla, C., *Cyprus* .... **23 E12** 34 56N 33 51 E
Pymatuning Reservoir,
U.S.A. **78 E4** 41 30N 80 28W
Pyŏktong, *N. Korea* ...... **35 D13** 40 50N 125 50 E
Pyŏnggang, *N. Korea* ..... **35 E14** 38 24N 127 17 E
P'yŏngt'aek, *S. Korea* .... **35 F14** 37 1N 127 4 E
P'yŏngyang, *N. Korea* .... **35 E13** 39 0N 125 30 E
Pyote, *U.S.A.* **81 K3** 31 32N 103 8W
Pyramid L., *U.S.A.* **82 G4** 40 1N 119 35W
Pyramid Pk., *U.S.A.* **85 J10** 36 25N 116 37W
Pyrénées, *Europe* .... **18 E4** 42 45N 0 18 E
Pyu, *Burma* .... **41 K20** 18 30N 96 28 E

Q

Qaanaaq = Thule,
Greenland **4 B4** 77 40N 69 0W
Qachasnek, *S. Africa* ..... **57 E4** 30 6S 28 42 E
Qa'el Jafr, *Jordan* ...... **47 E5** 30 20N 36 25 E
Qa'emābād, *Iran* .... **45 D9** 31 44N 60 2 E
Qā'emshahr, *Iran* .... **45 B7** 36 30N 52 53 E
Qagan Nur, *China* .... **34 C8** 43 30N 114 55 E
Qahar Youyi Zhongqi, *China* **34 D7** 41 12N 112 40 E
Qahremānshahr =
Bākhtarān, *Iran* .... **44 C5** 34 23N 47 0 E
Qaidam Pendi, *China* .... **32 C4** 37 0N 95 0 E
Qajarīyeh, *Iran* .... **45 D6** 31 1N 48 22 E
Qala, Ras il, *Malta* ...... **23 C1** 36 1N 14 20 E
Qala-i-Jadid = Spīn Búldak,
Afghan. .... **42 D2** 31 1N 66 25 E
Qala Viala, *Pakistan* ..... **42 D2** 30 49N 67 17 E
Qala Yangi, *Afghan.* ..... **42 B2** 34 20N 66 30 E

Râs Timirist

Qal'at al Akhḍar, *Si. Arabia* **44 E3** 28 0N 37 10 E
Qal'at Dīzah, *Iraq* **44 B5** 36 11N 45 7 E
Qal'at Şaliḩ, *Iraq* **44 D5** 31 31N 47 16 E
Qal'at Sukkar, *Iraq* **44 D5** 31 51N 46 5 E
Qal'eh Shaharak, *Afghan.* **40 B4** 34 10N 64 20 E
Qamdo, *China* **32 C4** 31 15N 97 6 E
Qamruddin Karez, *Pakistan* **42 D3** 31 45N 68 20 E
Qandahār, *Afghan.* **40 D4** 31 32N 65 30 E
Qandahār □, *Afghan.* **40 D4** 31 0N 65 0 E
Qapān, *Iran* **45 B7** 37 40N 55 47 E
Qapshaghay, *Kazakstan* **26 E8** 43 51N 77 14 E
Qaqortoq = Julianehåb, *Greenland* **4 C5** 60 43N 46 0W
Qara Qash —►, *India* **43 B8** 35 0N 78 30 E
Qarabutaq, *Kazakstan* **26 E7** 49 59N 60 14 E
Qaraghandy, *Kazakstan* **26 E8** 49 50N 73 10 E
Qārah, *Si. Arabia* **44 D4** 29 55N 40 3 E
Qarataū, *Kazakstan* **26 E8** 43 10N 70 28 E
Qareh —►, *Iran* **44 B5** 39 25N 47 22 E
Qareh Tekān, *Iran* **45 B6** 36 38N 49 29 E
Qarqan He —►, *China* **32 C3** 39 30N 88 30 E
Qarqaraly, *Kazakstan* **26 E8** 49 26N 75 30 E
Qarshi, *Uzbekistan* **26 F7** 38 53N 65 48 E
Qartabā, *Lebanon* **47 A4** 34 4N 35 50 E
Qaryat al Gharab, *Iraq* **44 D5** 31 27N 44 48 E
Qaryat al 'Ulyā, *Si. Arabia* **44 E5** 27 33N 47 42 E
Qasr 'Amra, *Jordan* **44 D3** 31 48N 36 35 E
Qaşr-e Qand, *Iran* **45 E9** 26 15N 60 45 E
Qasr Farâfra, *Egypt* **51 C11** 27 0N 28 1 E
Qatanā, *Syria* **47 B5** 33 26N 36 4 E
Qatar ■, *Asia* **45 E6** 25 30N 51 15 E
Qatlīsh, *Iran* **45 B8** 37 50N 57 19 E
Qattâra, Munkhafed el, *Egypt* **51 C11** 29 30N 27 30 E
Qattâra Depression = Qattâra, Munkhafed el, *Egypt* **51 C11** 29 30N 27 30 E
Qawām al Ḩamzah, *Iraq* **44 D5** 31 43N 44 58 E
Qāyen, *Iran* **45 C8** 33 40N 59 10 E
Qazaqstan = Kazakstan ■, *Asia* **26 E8** 50 0N 70 0 E
Qazimämmäd, *Azerbaijan* **45 A6** 40 3N 49 0 E
Qazvin, *Iran* **45 B6** 36 15N 50 0 E
Qena, *Egypt* **51 C12** 26 10N 32 43 E
Qeqertarsuaq = Disko, *Greenland* **4 C5** 69 45N 53 30W
Qeqertarsuaq = Godhavn, *Greenland* **4 C5** 69 15N 53 38W
Qeshlāq, *Iran* **44 C5** 34 55N 46 28 E
Qeshm, *Iran* **45 E8** 26 55N 56 10 E
Qeys, *Iran* **45 E7** 26 32N 53 58 E
Qezel Owzen —►, *Iran* **45 B6** 36 45N 49 22 E
Qezi'ot, *Israel* **47 E3** 30 52N 34 26 E
Qi Xian, *China* **34 G8** 34 40N 114 48 E
Qian Gorlos, *China* **35 B13** 45 5N 124 42 E
Qian Xian, *China* **34 G5** 34 31N 108 15 E
Qianyang, *China* **34 G4** 34 40N 107 8 E
Qibā', *Si. Arabia* **44 E5** 27 24N 44 20 E
Qikiqtarjuaq, *Canada* **69 B13** 67 33N 63 0W
Qila Safed, *Pakistan* **40 E2** 29 0N 61 30 E
Qila Saifullāh, *Pakistan* **42 D3** 30 45N 68 17 E
Qilian Shan, *China* **32 C4** 38 30N 96 0 E
Qin He —►, *China* **34 G7** 35 1N 113 22 E
Qin Ling = Qinling Shandi, *China* **34 H5** 33 50N 108 10 E
Qin'an, *China* **34 G3** 34 48N 105 40 E
Qing Xian, *China* **34 E9** 38 35N 116 45 E
Qingcheng, *China* **35 F9** 37 15N 117 40 E
Qingdao, *China* **35 F11** 36 5N 120 20 E
Qingfeng, *China* **34 G8** 35 52N 115 8 E
Qinghai □, *China* **32 C4** 36 0N 98 0 E
Qinghai Hu, *China* **32 C5** 36 40N 100 10 E
Qinghecheng, *China* **35 D13** 41 28N 124 15 E
Qinghemen, *China* **35 D11** 41 48N 121 25 E
Qingjian, *China* **34 F6** 37 8N 110 8 E
Qingjiang = Huaiyin, *China* **35 H10** 33 30N 119 2 E
Qingshui, *China* **34 G4** 34 48N 106 8 E
Qingshuihe, *China* **34 E6** 39 55N 111 35 E
Qingtongxia Shuiku, *China* **34 F3** 37 50N 105 58 E
Qingxu, *China* **34 F7** 37 34N 112 22 E
Qingyang, *China* **34 F4** 36 2N 107 55 E
Qingyuan, *China* **35 C13** 42 10N 124 55 E
Qingyun, *China* **35 F9** 37 45N 117 20 E
Qinhuangdao, *China* **35 E10** 39 56N 119 30 E
Qinling Shandi, *China* **34 H5** 33 50N 108 10 E
Qinshui, *China* **34 G7** 35 40N 112 8 E
Qinyang = Jiyuan, *China* **34 G7** 35 7N 112 57 E
Qinyuan, *China* **34 F7** 36 29N 112 20 E
Qinzhou, *China* **32 D5** 21 58N 108 38 E
Qionghai, *China* **38 C8** 19 15N 110 26 E
Qiongzhou Haixia, *China* **38 B8** 20 10N 110 15 E
Qiqihar, *China* **27 E13** 47 26N 124 0 E
Qiraîya, W. —►, *Egypt* **47 E3** 30 27N 34 0 E
Qiryat Ata, *Israel* **47 C4** 32 47N 35 6 E
Qiryat Gat, *Israel* **47 D3** 31 32N 34 46 E
Qiryat Mal'akhi, *Israel* **47 D3** 31 44N 34 44 E
Qiryat Shemona, *Israel* **47 B4** 33 13N 35 35 E
Qiryat Yam, *Israel* **47 C4** 32 51N 35 4 E
Qishan, *China* **34 G4** 34 25N 107 38 E
Qitai, *China* **32 B3** 44 2N 89 35 E
Qixia, *China* **35 F11** 37 17N 120 52 E
Qızılağac Körfäzi, *Azerbaijan* **45 B6** 39 9N 49 0 E
Qojūr, *Iran* **44 B5** 36 12N 47 55 E
Qom, *Iran* **45 C6** 34 40N 51 0 E
Qomolangma Feng = Everest, Mt., *Nepal* **43 E12** 28 5N 86 58 E
Qomsheh, *Iran* **45 D6** 32 0N 51 55 E
Qostanay, *Kazakstan* **26 D7** 53 10N 63 35 E
Quabbin Reservoir, *U.S.A.* **79 D12** 42 20N 72 20W
Quairading, *Australia* **61 F2** 32 0S 117 21 E
Quakertown, *U.S.A.* **79 F9** 40 26N 75 21W
Qualicum Beach, *Canada* **72 D4** 49 22N 124 26W
Quambatook, *Australia* **63 F3** 35 49S 143 34 E
Quambone, *Australia* **63 E4** 30 57S 147 53 E
Quamby, *Australia* **62 C3** 20 22S 140 17 E
Quan Long = Ca Mau, *Vietnam* **39 H5** 9 7N 105 8 E
Quanah, *U.S.A.* **81 H5** 34 18N 99 44W
Quang Ngai, *Vietnam* **38 E7** 15 13N 108 58 E
Quang Tri, *Vietnam* **38 D6** 16 45N 107 13 E
Quantock Hills, *U.K.* **11 F4** 51 8N 3 10W
Quanzhou, *China* **33 D6** 24 55N 118 34 E
Qu'Appelle, *Canada* **73 C8** 50 33N 103 53W
Quaqtaq, *Canada* **69 B13** 60 55N 69 40W
Quaraí, *Brazil* **94 C4** 30 15S 56 20W
Quartu Sant'Élena, *Italy* **20 E3** 39 15N 9 10 E
Quartzsite, *U.S.A.* **85 M12** 33 40N 114 13W
Quatsino Sd., *Canada* **72 C3** 50 25N 127 58W
Quba, *Azerbaijan* **25 F8** 41 21N 48 32 E
Qūchān, *Iran* **45 B8** 37 10N 58 27 E
Queanbeyan, *Australia* **63 F4** 35 17S 149 14 E
Québec, *Canada* **71 C5** 46 52N 71 13W
Québec □, *Canada* **71 C6** 48 0N 74 0W
Queen Alexandra Ra., *Antarctica* **5 E11** 85 0S 170 0 E
Queen Charlotte City, *Canada* **72 C2** 53 15N 132 2W
Queen Charlotte Is., *Canada* **72 C2** 53 20N 132 10W
Queen Charlotte Sd., *Canada* **72 C3** 51 0N 128 0W
Queen Charlotte Strait, *Canada* **72 C3** 50 45N 127 10W
Queen Elizabeth Is., *Canada* **66 B10** 76 0N 95 0W
Queen Elizabeth Nat. Park, *Uganda* **54 C3** 0 0 30 0 E
Queen Mary Land, *Antarctica* **5 D7** 70 0S 95 0 E
Queen Maud G., *Canada* **68 B9** 68 15N 102 30W
Queen Maud Land, *Antarctica* **5 D3** 72 30S 12 0 E
Queen Maud Mts., *Antarctica* **5 E13** 86 0S 160 0W
Queens Chan., *Australia* **60 C4** 15 0S 129 30 E
Queenscliff, *Australia* **63 F3** 38 16S 144 39 E
Queensland □, *Australia* **62 C3** 22 0S 142 0 E
Queenstown, *Australia* **62 G4** 42 4S 145 35 E
Queenstown, *N.Z.* **59 L2** 45 1S 168 40 E
Queenstown, *S. Africa* **56 E4** 31 52S 26 52 E
Queets, *U.S.A.* **84 C2** 47 32N 124 20W
Queguay Grande —►, *Uruguay* **94 C4** 32 9S 58 9W
Queimadas, *Brazil* **93 F11** 11 0S 39 38W
Quelimane, *Mozam.* **55 F4** 17 53S 36 58 E
Quellón, *Chile* **96 E2** 43 7S 73 37W
Quelpart = Cheju do, *S. Korea* **35 H14** 33 29N 126 34 E
Quemado, *N. Mex., U.S.A.* **83 J9** 34 20N 108 30W
Quemado, *Tex., U.S.A.* **81 L4** 28 58N 100 35W
Quemú-Quemú, *Argentina* **94 D3** 36 3S 63 36W
Quequén, *Argentina* **94 D4** 38 30S 58 30W
Querétaro, *Mexico* **86 C4** 20 36N 100 23W
Querétaro □, *Mexico* **86 C5** 20 30N 100 0W
Queshan, *China* **34 H8** 32 55N 114 2 E
Quesnel, *Canada* **72 C4** 53 0N 122 30W
Quesnel —►, *Canada* **72 C4** 52 58N 122 29W
Quesnel L., *Canada* **72 C4** 52 30N 121 20W
Questa, *U.S.A.* **83 H11** 36 42N 105 36W
Quetico Prov. Park, *Canada* **70 C1** 48 30N 91 45W
Quetta, *Pakistan* **42 D2** 30 15N 66 55 E
Quezaltenango, *Guatemala* **88 D1** 14 50N 91 30W
Quezon City, *Phil.* **37 B6** 14 38N 121 0 E
Qufār, *Si. Arabia* **44 E4** 27 26N 41 37 E
Qui Nhon, *Vietnam* **38 F7** 13 40N 109 13 E
Quibaxe, *Angola* **52 F2** 8 24S 14 27 E
Quibdo, *Colombia* **92 B3** 5 42N 76 40W
Quiberon, *France* **18 C2** 47 29N 3 9W
Quiet L., *Canada* **72 A2** 61 5N 133 5W
Quiindy, *Paraguay* **94 B4** 25 58S 57 14W
Quila, *Mexico* **86 C3** 24 23N 107 13W
Quilán, C., *Chile* **96 E2** 43 15S 74 30W
Quilcene, *U.S.A.* **84 C4** 47 49N 122 53W
Quilimarí, *Chile* **94 C1** 32 5S 71 30W
Quilino, *Argentina* **94 C3** 30 14S 64 29W
Quill Lakes, *Canada* **73 C8** 51 55N 104 13W
Quillabamba, *Peru* **92 F4** 12 50S 72 50W
Quillagua, *Chile* **94 A2** 21 40S 69 40W
Quillaicillo, *Chile* **94 C1** 31 17S 71 40W
Quillota, *Chile* **94 C1** 32 54S 71 16W
Quilmes, *Argentina* **94 C4** 34 43S 58 15W
Quilon, *India* **40 Q10** 8 50N 76 38 E
Quilpie, *Australia* **63 D3** 26 35S 144 11 E
Quilpué, *Chile* **94 C1** 33 5S 71 33W
Quilua, *Mozam.* **55 F4** 16 17S 39 54 E
Quimilí, *Argentina* **94 B3** 27 40S 62 30W
Quimper, *France* **18 B1** 48 0N 4 9W
Quimperlé, *France* **18 C2** 47 53N 3 33W
Quinault —►, *U.S.A.* **84 C2** 47 21N 124 18W
Quincy, *Calif., U.S.A.* **84 F6** 39 56N 120 57W
Quincy, *Fla., U.S.A.* **77 K3** 30 35N 84 34W
Quincy, *Ill., U.S.A.* **80 F9** 39 56N 91 23W
Quincy, *Mass., U.S.A.* **79 D14** 42 15N 71 0W
Quincy, *Wash., U.S.A.* **82 C4** 47 22N 119 56W
Quines, *Argentina* **94 C2** 32 13S 65 48W
Quinga, *Mozam.* **55 F5** 15 49S 40 15 E
Quinns Rocks, *Australia* **61 F2** 31 40S 115 42 E
Quintana Roo □, *Mexico* **87 D7** 19 0N 88 0W
Quintanar de la Orden, *Spain* **19 C4** 39 36N 3 5W
Quintero, *Chile* **94 C1** 32 45S 71 30W
Quirihue, *Chile* **94 D1** 36 15S 72 35W
Quirindi, *Australia* **63 E5** 31 28S 150 40 E
Quirinópolis, *Brazil* **93 G8** 18 32S 50 30W
Quissanga, *Mozam.* **55 E5** 12 24S 40 28 E
Quitilipi, *Argentina* **94 B3** 26 50S 60 13W
Quitman, *U.S.A.* **77 K4** 30 47N 83 34W
Quito, *Ecuador* **92 D3** 0 15S 78 35W
Quixadá, *Brazil* **93 D11** 4 55S 39 0W
Quixaxe, *Mozam.* **55 F5** 15 17S 40 4 E
Qul'ân, Jazâ'ir, *Egypt* **44 E2** 24 22N 35 31 E
Qumbu, *S. Africa* **57 E4** 31 10S 28 48 E
Quneitra, *Syria* **47 B4** 33 7N 35 48 E
Qŭnghirot, *Uzbekistan* **26 E6** 43 6N 58 54 E
Quoin I., *Australia* **60 B4** 14 54S 129 32 E
Quoin Pt., *S. Africa* **56 E2** 34 46S 19 37 E
Quorn, *Australia* **63 E2** 32 25S 138 5 E
Qŭqon, *Uzbekistan* **26 E8** 40 30N 70 57 E
Qurnat as Sawdā', *Lebanon* **47 A5** 34 18N 36 6 E
Quşaybā', *Si. Arabia* **44 E4** 26 53N 43 35 E
Qusaybah, *Iraq* **44 C4** 34 24N 40 59 E
Quseir, *Egypt* **44 E2** 26 7N 34 16 E
Qūshchī, *Iran* **44 B5** 37 59N 45 3 E
Quthing, *Lesotho* **57 E4** 30 25S 27 36 E
Qūţiābād, *Iran* **45 C6** 35 47N 48 30 E
Quwo, *China* **34 G6** 35 38N 111 25 E
Quyang, *China* **34 E8** 38 35N 114 40 E
Quynh Nhai, *Vietnam* **38 B4** 21 49N 103 33 E
Quyon, *Canada* **79 A8** 45 31N 76 14W
Quzhou, *China* **33 D6** 28 57N 118 54 E
Quzi, *China* **34 F4** 36 20N 107 20 E
Qyzylorda, *Kazakstan* **26 E7** 44 48N 65 28 E

R

Ra, Ko, *Thailand* **39 H2** 9 13N 98 16 E
Raahe, *Finland* **8 D21** 64 40N 24 28 E
Raalte, *Neths.* **15 B6** 52 23N 6 16 E
Raasay, *U.K.* **12 D2** 57 25N 6 4W
Raasay, Sd. of, *U.K.* **12 D2** 57 30N 6 8W
Raba, *Indonesia* **37 F5** 8 36S 118 55 E
Rába —►, *Hungary* **17 E9** 47 38N 17 38 E
Rabai, *Kenya* **54 C4** 3 50S 39 31 E
Rabat, *Malta* **23 D1** 35 53N 14 25 E
Rabat, *Morocco* **50 B4** 34 2N 6 48W
Rabaul, *Papua N. G.* **64 H7** 4 24S 152 18 E
Rābigh, *Si. Arabia* **46 C2** 22 50N 39 5 E
Râbniţa, *Moldova* **17 E15** 47 45N 29 0 E
Rābor, *Iran* **45 D8** 29 17N 56 55 E
Race, C., *Canada* **71 C9** 46 40N 53 5W
Rach Gia, *Vietnam* **39 G5** 10 5N 105 5 E
Rachid, *Mauritania* **50 E3** 18 48N 11 41W
Racibórz, *Poland* **17 C10** 50 7N 18 18 E
Racine, *U.S.A.* **76 D2** 42 41N 87 51W
Rackerby, *U.S.A.* **84 F5** 39 26N 121 22W
Radama, Nosy, *Madag.* **57 A8** 14 0S 47 47 E
Radama, Saikanosy, *Madag.* **57 A8** 14 16S 47 53 E
Rădăuţi, *Romania* **17 E13** 47 50N 25 59 E
Radcliff, *U.S.A.* **76 G3** 37 51N 85 57W
Radekhiv, *Ukraine* **17 C13** 50 25N 24 32 E
Radekhov = Radekhiv, *Ukraine* **17 C13** 50 25N 24 32 E
Radford, *U.S.A.* **76 G5** 37 8N 80 34W
Radhanpur, *India* **42 H4** 23 50N 71 38 E
Radhwa, Jabal, *Si. Arabia* **44 E3** 24 34N 38 18 E
Radisson, *Canada* **70 B4** 53 47N 77 37W
Radisson, *Sask., Canada* **73 C7** 52 30N 107 20W
Radium Hot Springs, *Canada* **72 C5** 50 35N 116 2W
Radnor Forest, *U.K.* **11 E4** 52 17N 3 10W
Radom, *Poland* **17 C11** 51 23N 21 12 E
Radomsko, *Poland* **17 C10** 51 5N 19 28 E
Radomyshl, *Ukraine* **17 C15** 50 30N 29 12 E
Radstock, C., *Australia* **63 E1** 33 12S 134 20 E
Radviliškis, *Lithuania* **9 J20** 55 49N 23 33 E
Radville, *Canada* **73 D8** 49 30N 104 15W
Rae, *Canada* **72 A5** 62 50N 116 3W
Rae Bareli, *India* **43 F9** 26 18N 81 20 E
Rae Isthmus, *Canada* **69 B11** 66 40N 87 30W
Raeren, *Belgium* **15 D6** 50 41N 6 7 E
Raeside, L., *Australia* **61 E3** 29 20S 122 0 E
Raetihi, *N.Z.* **59 H5** 39 25S 175 17 E
Rafaela, *Argentina* **94 C3** 31 10S 61 30W
Rafah, *Gaza Strip* **47 D3** 31 18N 34 14 E
Rafai, *C.A.R.* **54 B1** 4 59N 23 58 E
Rafḩā, *Si. Arabia* **44 D4** 29 35N 43 35 E
Rafsanjān, *Iran* **45 D8** 30 30N 56 5 E
Raft Pt., *Australia* **60 C3** 16 4S 124 26 E
Raga, *Sudan* **51 G11** 8 28N 25 41 E
Ragachow, *Belarus* **17 B16** 53 8N 30 5 E
Ragama, *Sri Lanka* **40 R11** 7 0N 79 50 E
Ragged, Mt., *Australia* **61 F3** 33 27S 123 25 E
Raghunathpalli, *India* **43 H11** 22 14N 84 48 E
Raghunathpur, *India* **43 H12** 23 33N 86 40 E
Raglan, *N.Z.* **59 G5** 37 55S 174 55 E
Ragusa, *Italy* **20 F6** 36 55N 14 44 E
Raha, *Indonesia* **37 E6** 4 55S 123 0 E
Rahaeng = Tak, *Thailand* **38 D2** 16 52N 99 8 E
Rahatgarh, *India* **43 H8** 23 47N 78 22 E
Raḩīmah, *Si. Arabia* **45 E6** 26 42N 50 4 E
Rahimyar Khan, *Pakistan* **42 E4** 28 30N 70 25 E
Rāhjerd, *Iran* **45 C6** 34 22N 50 22 E
Rahon, *India* **42 D7** 31 3N 76 7 E
Raichur, *India* **40 L10** 16 10N 77 20 E
Raiganj, *India* **43 G13** 25 37N 88 10 E
Raigarh, *India* **41 J13** 21 56N 83 25 E
Raijua, *Indonesia* **37 F6** 10 37S 121 36 E
Raikot, *India* **42 D6** 30 41N 75 42 E
Railton, *Australia* **62 G4** 41 25S 146 28 E
Rainbow Lake, *Canada* **72 B5** 58 30N 119 23W
Rainier, *U.S.A.* **84 D4** 46 53N 122 41W
Rainier, Mt., *U.S.A.* **84 D5** 46 52N 121 46W
Rainy L., *Canada* **73 D10** 48 42N 93 10W
Rainy River, *Canada* **73 D10** 48 43N 94 29W
Raippaluoto, *Finland* **8 E19** 63 13N 21 14 E
Raipur, *India* **41 J12** 21 17N 81 45 E
Raisen, *India* **42 H8** 23 20N 77 48 E
Raisio, *Finland* **9 F20** 60 28N 22 11 E
Raj Nandgaon, *India* **41 J12** 21 5N 81 5 E
Raj Nilgiri, *India* **43 J12** 21 28N 86 46 E
Raja, Ujung, *Indonesia* **36 D1** 3 40N 96 25 E
Raja Ampat, Kepulauan, *Indonesia* **37 E8** 0 30S 130 0 E
Rajahmundry, *India* **41 L12** 17 1N 81 48 E
Rajang —►, *Malaysia* **36 D4** 2 30N 112 0 E
Rajanpur, *Pakistan* **42 E4** 29 6N 70 19 E
Rajapalaiyam, *India* **40 Q10** 9 25N 77 35 E
Rajasthan □, *India* **42 F5** 26 45N 73 30 E
Rajasthan Canal, *India* **42 F5** 28 0N 72 0 E
Rajauri, *India* **43 C6** 33 25N 74 21 E
Rajgarh, *Mad. P., India* **42 G7** 24 2N 76 45 E
Rajgarh, *Raj., India* **42 F7** 27 14N 76 38 E
Rajgarh, *Raj., India* **42 E6** 28 40N 75 25 E
Rajgir, *India* **43 G11** 25 2N 85 25 E
Rajkot, *India* **42 H4** 22 15N 70 56 E
Rajmahal Hills, *India* **43 G12** 24 30N 87 30 E
Rajpipla, *India* **40 J8** 21 50N 73 30 E
Rajpur, *India* **42 H6** 22 18N 74 21 E
Rajpura, *India* **42 D7** 30 25N 76 32 E
Rajshahi, *Bangla.* **41 G16** 24 22N 88 39 E
Rajshahi □, *Bangla.* **43 G13** 25 0N 89 0 E
Rajula, *India* **42 J4** 21 3N 71 26 E
Rakaia, *N.Z.* **59 K4** 43 45S 172 1 E
Rakaia —►, *N.Z.* **59 K4** 43 36S 172 15 E
Rakan, Ra's, *Qatar* **45 E6** 26 10N 51 20 E
Rakaposhi, *Pakistan* **43 A6** 36 10N 74 25 E
Rakata, Pulau, *Indonesia* **36 F3** 6 10S 105 20 E
Rakhiv, *Ukraine* **17 D13** 48 3N 24 12 E
Rakhni, *Pakistan* **42 D3** 30 4N 69 56 E
Rakhni —►, *Pakistan* **42 E3** 29 31N 69 36 E
Rakitnoye, *Russia* **30 B7** 45 36N 134 17 E
Rakops, *Botswana* **56 C3** 21 1S 24 28 E
Rakvere, *Estonia* **9 G22** 59 20N 26 25 E
Raleigh, *U.S.A.* **77 H6** 35 47N 78 39W
Raleigh B., *U.S.A.* **75 D11** 34 50N 76 15W
Ralls, *U.S.A.* **81 J4** 33 41N 101 24W
Ralston, *U.S.A.* **78 E8** 41 30N 76 57W
Ram —►, *Canada* **72 A4** 62 1N 123 41W
Rām Allāh, *West Bank* **47 D4** 31 55N 35 10 E
Ram Hd., *Australia* **63 F4** 37 47S 149 30 E
Rama, *Nic.* **88 D3** 12 9N 84 15W
Ramakona, *India* **43 J8** 21 43N 78 50 E
Raman, *Thailand* **39 J3** 6 29N 101 18 E
Ramanathapuram, *India* **40 Q11** 9 25N 78 55 E
Ramanetaka, B. de, *Madag.* **57 A8** 14 13S 47 52 E
Ramanujganj, *India* **43 H10** 23 48N 83 42 E
Ramat Gan, *Israel* **47 C3** 32 4N 34 48 E
Ramatlhabama, *S. Africa* **56 D4** 25 37S 25 33 E
Ramban, *India* **43 C6** 33 14N 75 12 E
Rambipuji, *Indonesia* **37 H15** 8 12S 113 37 E
Ramechhap, *Nepal* **43 F12** 27 25N 86 10 E
Ramganga —►, *India* **43 F8** 27 5N 79 58 E
Ramgarh, *Bihar, India* **43 H11** 23 40N 85 35 E
Ramgarh, *Raj., India* **42 F6** 27 16N 75 14 E
Ramgarh, *Raj., India* **42 F4** 27 30N 70 36 E
Rāmhormoz, *Iran* **45 D6** 31 15N 49 35 E
Ramīān, *Iran* **45 B7** 37 3N 55 16 E
Ramingining, *Australia* **62 A2** 12 19S 135 3 E
Ramla, *Israel* **47 D3** 31 55N 34 52 E
Ramnad = Ramanathapuram, *India* **40 Q11** 9 25N 78 55 E
Ramnagar, *India* **43 E8** 29 24N 79 7 E
Ramnagar, *Jammu & Kashmir, India* **43 C6** 32 47N 75 18 E
Râmnicu Sărat, *Romania* **17 F14** 45 26N 27 3 E
Râmnicu Vâlcea, *Romania* **17 F13** 45 9N 24 21 E
Ramona, *U.S.A.* **85 M10** 33 2N 116 52W
Ramore, *Canada* **70 C3** 48 30N 80 25W
Ramotswa, *Botswana* **56 C4** 24 50S 25 52 E
Rampur, *H.P., India* **42 D7** 31 26N 77 43 E
Rampur, *Mad. P., India* **42 H5** 23 25N 73 53 E
Rampur, *Ut. P., India* **43 E8** 28 50N 79 5 E
Rampur Hat, *India* **43 G12** 24 10N 87 50 E
Rampura, *India* **42 G6** 24 30N 75 27 E
Ramrama Tola, *India* **43 J8** 21 52N 79 55 E
Ramree I. = Ramree Kyun, *Burma* **41 K19** 19 0N 94 0 E
Ramree Kyun, *Burma* **41 K19** 19 0N 94 0 E
Rāmsar, *Iran* **45 B6** 36 53N 50 41 E
Ramsey, *U.K.* **10 C3** 54 20N 4 22W
Ramsey, *U.S.A.* **79 E10** 41 4N 74 9W
Ramsey L., *Canada* **70 C3** 47 13N 82 15W
Ramsgate, *U.K.* **11 F9** 51 20N 1 25 E
Ramtek, *India* **40 J11** 21 20N 79 15 E
Rana Pratap Sagar Dam, *India* **42 G6** 24 58N 75 38 E
Ranaghat, *India* **43 H13** 23 15N 88 35 E
Ranahu, *Pakistan* **42 G3** 25 55N 69 45 E
Ranau, *Malaysia* **36 C5** 6 2N 116 40 E
Rancagua, *Chile* **94 C1** 34 10S 70 50W
Rancheria —►, *Canada* **72 A3** 60 13N 129 7W
Ranchester, *U.S.A.* **82 D10** 44 54N 107 10W
Ranchi, *India* **43 H11** 23 19N 85 27 E
Rancho Cucamonga, *U.S.A.* **85 L9** 34 10N 117 30W
Randalstown, *U.K.* **13 B5** 54 45N 6 19W
Randers, *Denmark* **9 H14** 56 29N 10 1 E
Randfontein, *S. Africa* **57 D4** 26 8S 27 45 E
Randle, *U.S.A.* **84 D5** 46 32N 121 57W
Randolph, *Mass., U.S.A.* **79 D13** 42 10N 71 2W
Randolph, *N.Y., U.S.A.* **78 D6** 42 10N 78 59W
Randolph, *Utah, U.S.A.* **82 F8** 41 40N 111 11W
Randolph, *Vt., U.S.A.* **79 C12** 43 55N 72 40W
Randsburg, *U.S.A.* **85 K9** 35 22N 117 39W
Råne älv —►, *Sweden* **8 D20** 65 50N 22 20 E
Rangae, *Thailand* **39 J3** 6 19N 101 44 E
Rangaunu B., *N.Z.* **59 F4** 34 51S 173 15 E
Rangeley, *U.S.A.* **79 B14** 44 58N 70 39W
Rangeley L., *U.S.A.* **79 B14** 44 55N 70 43W
Rangely, *U.S.A.* **82 F9** 40 5N 108 48W
Ranger, *U.S.A.* **81 J5** 32 28N 98 41W
Rangia, *India* **41 F17** 26 28N 91 38 E
Rangiora, *N.Z.* **59 K4** 43 19S 172 36 E
Rangitaiki —►, *N.Z.* **59 G6** 37 54S 176 49 E
Rangitata —►, *N.Z.* **59 K3** 43 45S 171 15 E
Rangkasbitung, *Indonesia* **37 G12** 6 21S 106 15 E
Rangon —►, *Burma* **41 L20** 16 28N 96 40 E
Rangoon, *Burma* **41 L20** 16 45N 96 20 E
Rangpur, *Bangla.* **41 G16** 25 42N 89 22 E
Rangsit, *Thailand* **38 F3** 13 59N 100 37 E
Ranibennur, *India* **40 M9** 14 35N 75 30 E
Raniganj, *Ut. P., India* **43 F9** 27 3N 82 13 E
Raniganj, *W. Bengal, India* **41 H15** 23 40N 87 5 E
Ranikhet, *India* **43 E8** 29 39N 79 25 E
Raniwara, *India* **40 G8** 24 50N 72 10 E
Rāniyah, *Iraq* **44 B5** 36 15N 44 53 E
Ranka, *India* **43 H10** 23 59N 83 47 E
Ranken —►, *Australia* **62 C2** 20 31S 137 36 E
Rankin, *U.S.A.* **81 K4** 31 13N 101 56W
Rankin Inlet, *Canada* **68 B10** 62 30N 93 0W
Rankins Springs, *Australia* **63 E4** 33 49S 146 14 E
Rannoch, L., *U.K.* **12 E4** 56 41N 4 20W
Rannoch Moor, *U.K.* **12 E4** 56 38N 4 48W
Ranobe, Helodranon' i, *Madag.* **57 C7** 23 3S 43 33 E
Ranohira, *Madag.* **57 C8** 22 29S 45 24 E
Ranomafana, *Toamasina, Madag.* **57 B8** 18 57S 48 50 E
Ranomafana, *Toliara, Madag.* **57 C8** 24 34S 47 0 E
Ranong, *Thailand* **39 H2** 9 56N 98 40 E
Rānsa, *Iran* **45 C6** 33 39N 48 18 E
Ransiki, *Indonesia* **37 E8** 1 30S 134 10 E
Rantauprapat, *Indonesia* **36 D1** 2 15N 99 50 E
Rantemario, *Indonesia* **37 E5** 3 15S 119 57 E
Rantoul, *U.S.A.* **76 E1** 40 19N 88 9W
Raoyang, *China* **34 E8** 38 15N 115 45 E
Rapa, *Pac. Oc.* **65 K13** 27 35S 144 20W
Rapallo, *Italy* **18 D8** 44 21N 9 14 E
Rapar, *India* **42 H4** 23 34N 70 38 E
Rāpch, *Iran* **45 E8** 25 40N 59 15 E
Raper, C., *Canada* **69 B13** 69 44N 67 6W
Rapid City, *U.S.A.* **80 D3** 44 5N 103 14W
Rapid River, *U.S.A.* **76 C2** 45 55N 86 58W
Rapla, *Estonia* **9 G21** 59 1N 24 52 E
Rapti —►, *India* **43 F10** 26 18N 83 41 E
Raquette —►, *U.S.A.* **79 B10** 45 0N 74 42W
Raquette Lake, *U.S.A.* **79 C10** 43 49N 74 40W
Rarotonga, *Cook Is.* **65 K12** 21 30S 160 0W
Ra's al 'Ayn, *Syria* **44 B4** 36 45N 40 12 E
Ra's al Khaymah, *U.A.E.* **45 E8** 25 50N 55 59 E
Ra's an Naqb, *Jordan* **47 F4** 30 0N 35 29 E
Ras Dashen, *Ethiopia* **46 E2** 13 8N 38 26 E
Râs Timirist, *Mauritania* **50 E2** 19 21N 16 30W

Rzhev

Rivière-Pilote, *Martinique* .. **89 D7** 14 26N 60 53W
Rivière St. Paul, *Canada* ... **71 B8** 51 28N 57 45W
Rivne, *Ukraine* .... **17 C14** 50 40N 26 10 E
Rivoli, *Italy* .... **18 D7** 45 3N 7 31 E
Rivoli B., *Australia* .... **63 F3** 37 32S 140 3 E
Riyadh = Ar Riyāḑ,
Si. Arabia .... **46 C4** 24 41N 46 42 E
Rize, *Turkey* .... **25 F7** 41 0N 40 30 E
Rizhao, *China* .... **35 G10** 35 25N 119 30 E
Rizokarpaso, *Cyprus* ...... **23 D13** 35 36N 34 23 E
Rizzuto, C., *Italy* .... **20 E7** 38 53N 17 5 E
Rjukan, *Norway* .... **9 G13** 59 54N 8 33 E
Road Town, *Virgin Is.* **89 C7** 18 27N 64 37W
Roan Plateau, *U.S.A.* **82 G9** 39 20N 109 20W
Roanne, *France* .... **18 C6** 46 3N 4 4 E
Roanoke, *Ala., U.S.A.* **77 J3** 33 9N 85 22W
Roanoke, *Va., U.S.A.* **76 G6** 37 16N 79 56W
Roanoke →, *U.S.A.* **77 H7** 35 57N 76 42W
Roanoke I., *U.S.A.* **77 H8** 35 55N 75 40W
Roanoke Rapids, *U.S.A.* ... **77 G7** 36 28N 77 40W
Roatán, *Honduras* **88 C2** 16 18N 86 35W
Robāt Sang, *Iran* .... **45 C8** 35 35N 59 10 E
Robbins I., *Australia* ...... **62 G4** 40 42S 145 0 E
Robe, *Australia* .... **63 F2** 37 11S 139 45 E
Robe →, *Australia* ...... **60 D2** 21 42S 116 15 E
Robert Lee, *U.S.A.* **81 K4** 31 54N 100 29W
Robertsdale, *U.S.A.* **78 F6** 40 11N 78 6W
Robertsganj, *India* .... **43 G10** 24 44N 83 4 E
Robertson, *S. Africa* ...... **56 E2** 33 46S 19 50 E
Robertson I., *Antarctica* ... **5 C18** 65 15S 59 30W
Robertson Ra., *Australia* .. **60 D3** 23 15S 121 0 E
Robertstown, *Australia* .... **63 E2** 33 58S 139 5 E
Roberval, *Canada* **71 C5** 48 32N 72 15W
Robeson Chan., *Greenland* **4 A4** 82 0N 61 30W
Robesonia, *U.S.A.* **79 F8** 40 21N 76 8W
Robinson, *U.S.A.* **76 F2** 39 0N 87 44W
Robinson →, *Australia* ... **62 B2** 16 3S 137 16 E
Robinson Ra., *Australia* .. **61 E2** 25 40S 119 0 E
Robinvale, *Australia* ...... **63 E3** 34 40S 142 45 E
Roblin, *Canada* **73 C8** 51 14N 101 21W
Roboré, *Bolivia* **92 G7** 18 10S 59 45W
Robson, *Canada* **72 D5** 49 20N 117 41W
Robson, Mt., *Canada* **72 C5** 53 10N 119 10W
Robstown, *U.S.A.* **81 M6** 27 47N 97 40W
Roca, C. da, *Portugal* **19 C1** 38 40N 9 31W
Roca Partida, I., *Mexico* ... **86 D2** 19 1N 112 2W
Rocas, I., *Brazil* **93 D12** 4 0S 34 1W
Rocha, *Uruguay* **95 C5** 34 30S 54 25W
Rochdale, *U.K.* **10 D5** 53 38N 2 9W
Rochefort, *Belgium* .... **15 D5** 50 9N 5 12 E
Rochefort, *France* **18 D3** 45 56N 0 57W
Rochelle, *U.S.A.* **80 E10** 41 56N 89 4W
Rocher River, *Canada* **72 A6** 61 23N 112 44W
Rochester, *U.K.* .... **11 F8** 51 23N 0 31 E
Rochester, *Ind., U.S.A.* **76 E2** 41 4N 86 13W
Rochester, *Minn., U.S.A.* .. **80 C8** 44 1N 92 28W
Rochester, *N.H., U.S.A.* ... **79 C14** 43 18N 70 59W
Rochester, *N.Y., U.S.A.* **78 C7** 43 10N 77 37W
Rock →, *Canada* **72 A3** 60 7N 127 7W
Rock Creek, *U.S.A.* **78 E4** 41 40N 80 52W
Rock Falls, *U.S.A.* **80 E10** 41 47N 89 41W
Rock Hill, *U.S.A.* **77 H5** 34 56N 81 1W
Rock Island, *U.S.A.* **80 E9** 41 30N 90 34W
Rock Rapids, *U.S.A.* **80 D6** 43 26N 96 10W
Rock Sound, *Bahamas* **88 B4** 24 54N 76 12W
Rock Springs, *Mont., U.S.A.* **82 C10** 46 49N 106 15W
Rock Springs, *Wyo., U.S.A.* **82 F9** 41 35N 109 14W
Rock Valley, *U.S.A.* **80 D6** 43 12N 96 18W
Rockall, *Atl. Oc.* **6 D3** 57 37N 13 42W
Rockdale, *Tex., U.S.A.* **81 K6** 30 39N 97 0W
Rockdale, *Wash., U.S.A.* ... **84 C5** 47 22N 121 28W
Rockefeller Plateau,
Antarctica **5 E14** 80 0S 140 0W
Rockford, *U.S.A.* **80 D10** 42 16N 89 6W
Rockglen, *Canada* **73 D7** 49 11N 105 57W
Rockhampton, *Australia* ... **62 C5** 23 22S 150 32 E
Rockingham, *Australia* .... **61 F2** 32 15S 115 38 E
Rockingham, *U.S.A.* **77 H6** 34 57N 79 46W
Rockingham B., *Australia* .. **62 B4** 18 5S 146 10 E
Rocklake, *U.S.A.* **80 A5** 48 47N 99 15W
Rockland, *Canada* **79 A9** 45 33N 75 17W
Rockland, *Idaho, U.S.A.* ... **82 E7** 42 34N 112 53W
Rockland, *Maine, U.S.A.* ... **77 C11** 44 6N 69 7W
Rockland, *Mich., U.S.A.* ... **80 B10** 46 44N 89 11W
Rocklin, *U.S.A.* **84 G5** 38 48N 121 14W
Rockport, *Mass., U.S.A.* ... **79 D14** 42 39N 70 37W
Rockport, *Mo., U.S.A.* **80 E7** 40 25N 95 31W
Rockport, *Tex., U.S.A.* **81 L6** 28 2N 97 3W
Rocksprings, *U.S.A.* **81 K4** 30 1N 100 13W
Rockville, *Conn., U.S.A.* ... **79 E12** 41 52N 72 28W
Rockville, *Md., U.S.A.* **76 F7** 39 5N 77 9W
Rockwall, *U.S.A.* **81 J6** 32 56N 96 28W
Rockwell City, *U.S.A.* **80 D7** 42 24N 94 38W
Rockwood, *Canada* **78 C4** 43 37N 80 8W
Rockwood, *Maine, U.S.A.* . **77 C11** 45 41N 69 45W
Rockwood, *Tenn., U.S.A.* .. **77 H3** 35 52N 84 41W
Rocky Ford, *U.S.A.* **80 F3** 38 3N 103 43W
Rocky Gully, *Australia* .... **61 F2** 34 30S 116 57 E
Rocky Harbour, *Canada* ... **71 C8** 49 36N 57 55W
Rocky Island L., *Canada* ... **70 C3** 46 55N 83 0W
Rocky Lane, *Canada* **72 B5** 58 31N 116 22W
Rocky Mount, *U.S.A.* **77 H7** 35 57N 77 48W
Rocky Mountain House,
Canada **72 C6** 52 22N 114 55W
Rocky Mountain National
Park, *U.S.A.* **82 F11** 40 25N 105 45W
Rocky Mts., *N. Amer.* **74 C5** 49 0N 115 0W
Rod, *Pakistan* .... **40 E3** 28 10N 63 5 E
Rødbyhavn, *Denmark* ..... **9 J14** 54 39N 11 22 E
Roddickton, *Canada* **71 B8** 50 51N 56 8W
Rodez, *France* .... **18 D5** 44 21N 2 33 E
Rodhopoú, *Greece* .... **23 D5** 35 34N 23 45 E
Ródhos, *Greece* .... **23 C10** 36 15N 28 10 E
Rodney, *Canada* **78 D3** 42 34N 81 41W
Rodney, C., *N.Z.* .... **59 G5** 36 17S 174 50 E
Rodriguez, *Ind. Oc.* .... **3 E13** 19 45S 63 20 E
Roe →, *U.K.* **13 A5** 55 6N 6 59W
Roebling, *U.S.A.* **79 F10** 40 7N 74 47W
Roebourne, *Australia* ..... **60 D2** 20 44S 117 9 E
Roebuck B., *Australia* ..... **60 C3** 18 5S 122 20 E
Roermond, *Neths.* .... **15 C6** 51 12N 6 0 E
Roes Welcome Sd., *Canada* **69 B11** 65 0N 87 0W
Roeselare, *Belgium* .... **15 D3** 50 57N 3 7 E
Rogachev = Ragachow,
Belarus .... **17 B16** 53 8N 30 5 E
Rogagua, L., *Bolivia* **92 F5** 13 43S 66 50W
Rogatyn, *Ukraine* .... **17 D13** 49 24N 24 36 E
Rogdhia, *Greece* .... **23 D7** 35 22N 25 1 E
Rogers, *U.S.A.* **81 G7** 36 20N 94 7W
Rogers City, *U.S.A.* **76 C4** 45 25N 83 49W
Rogersville, *Canada* **71 C6** 46 44N 65 26W
Roggan →, *Canada* **70 B4** 54 24N 79 25W
Roggan L., *Canada* **70 B4** 54 8N 77 50W
Roggeveldberge, *S. Africa* . **56 E3** 32 10S 20 10 E
Rogoaguado, L., *Bolivia* ... **92 F5** 13 0S 65 30W
Rogue →, *U.S.A.* **82 E1** 42 26N 124 26W
Róhda, *Greece* .... **23 A3** 39 48N 19 46 E
Rohnert Park, *U.S.A.* **84 G4** 38 16N 122 40W
Rohri, *Pakistan* .... **42 F3** 27 45N 68 51 E
Rohri Canal, *Pakistan* ..... **42 F3** 26 15N 68 27 E
Rohtak, *India* .... **42 E7** 28 55N 76 43 E
Roi Et, *Thailand* .... **38 D4** 16 4N 103 40 E
Roja, *Latvia* .... **9 H20** 57 29N 22 43 E
Rojas, *Argentina* **94 C3** 34 10S 60 45W
Rojo, C., *Mexico* **87 C5** 21 33N 97 20W
Rokan →, *Indonesia* ..... **36 D2** 2 0N 100 50 E
Rokiškis, *Lithuania* .... **9 J21** 55 55N 25 35 E
Rolândia, *Brazil* **95 A5** 23 18S 51 23W
Rolla, *U.S.A.* **81 G9** 37 57N 91 46W
Rolleston, *Australia* ...... **62 C4** 24 28S 148 35 E
Rollingstone, *Australia* .... **62 B4** 19 2S 146 24 E
Roma, *Australia* .... **63 D4** 26 32S 148 49 E
Roma, *Italy* .... **20 D5** 41 54N 12 29 E
Roma, *Sweden* .... **9 H18** 57 32N 18 26 E
Roma, *U.S.A.* **81 M5** 26 25N 99 1W
Romain C., *U.S.A.* **77 J6** 33 0N 79 22W
Romaine, *Canada* **71 B7** 50 13N 60 40W
Romaine →, *Canada* **71 B7** 50 18N 63 47W
Roman, *Romania* .... **17 E14** 46 57N 26 55 E
Romang, *Indonesia* .... **37 F7** 7 30S 127 20 E
Români, *Egypt* .... **47 E1** 30 59N 32 38 E
Romania ■, *Europe* ...... **17 F12** 46 0N 25 0 E
Romano, Cayo, *Cuba* **88 B4** 22 0N 77 30W
Romanovka =
Basarabeasca, *Moldova* . **17 E15** 46 21N 28 58 E
Romans-sur-Isère, *France* . **18 D6** 45 3N 5 3 E
Romblon, *Phil.* .... **37 B6** 12 33N 122 17 E
Rome = Roma, *Italy* ...... **20 D5** 41 54N 12 29 E
Rome, *Ga., U.S.A.* **77 H3** 34 15N 85 10W
Rome, *N.Y., U.S.A.* **79 C9** 43 13N 75 27W
Rome, *Pa., U.S.A.* **79 E8** 41 51N 76 21W
Romney, *U.S.A.* **76 F6** 39 21N 78 45W
Romney Marsh, *U.K.* ..... **11 F8** 51 2N 0 54 E
Rømø, *Denmark* .... **9 J13** 55 10N 8 30 E
Romorantin-Lanthenay,
France .... **18 C4** 47 21N 1 45 E
Romsdalen, *Norway* ...... **9 E12** 62 25N 7 52 E
Romsey, *U.K.* **11 G6** 51 0N 1 29W
Ron, *Vietnam* .... **38 D6** 17 53N 106 27 E
Rona, *U.K.* **12 D3** 57 34N 5 59W
Ronan, *U.S.A.* **82 C6** 47 32N 114 6W
Roncador, Cayos, *Caribbean* **88 D3** 13 32N 80 4W
Roncador, Serra do, *Brazil* . **93 F8** 12 30S 52 30W
Ronda, *Spain* **19 D3** 36 46N 5 12W
Rondane, *Norway* .... **9 F13** 61 57N 9 50 E
Rondônia □, *Brazil* **92 F6** 11 0S 63 0W
Rondonópolis, *Brazil* **93 G8** 16 28S 54 38W
Rong, Koh, *Cambodia* ..... **39 G4** 10 45N 103 15 E
Ronge, L. la, *Canada* **73 B7** 55 6N 105 17W
Rønne, *Denmark* .... **9 J16** 55 6N 14 43 E
Ronne Ice Shelf, *Antarctica* **5 D18** 78 0S 60 0W
Ronsard, C., *Australia* ..... **61 D1** 24 46S 113 10 E
Ronse, *Belgium* .... **15 D3** 50 45N 3 35 E
Roodepoort, *S. Africa* ..... **57 D4** 26 11S 27 54 E
Roof Butte, *U.S.A.* **83 H9** 36 28N 109 5W
Roorkee, *India* .... **42 E7** 29 52N 77 59 E
Roosendaal, *Neths.* .... **15 C4** 51 32N 4 29 E
Roosevelt, *U.S.A.* **82 F8** 40 18N 109 59W
Roosevelt →, *Brazil* **92 E6** 7 35S 60 20W
Roosevelt, Mt., *Canada* **72 B3** 58 26N 125 20W
Roosevelt I., *Antarctica* ... **5 D12** 79 30S 162 0W
Roper →, *Australia* ..... **62 A2** 14 43S 135 27 E
Roper Bar, *Australia* ...... **62 A1** 14 44S 134 44 E
Roque Pérez, *Argentina* ... **94 D4** 35 25S 59 24W
Roquetas de Mar, *Spain* ... **19 D4** 36 46N 2 36W
Roraima □, *Brazil* **92 C6** 2 0N 61 30W
Roraima, Mt., *Venezuela* ... **92 B6** 5 10N 60 40W
Røros, *Norway* .... **9 E14** 62 35N 11 23 E
Rosa, *Zambia* .... **55 D3** 9 33S 31 15 E
Rosa, L., *Bahamas* **89 B5** 21 0N 73 30W
Rosa, Monte, *Europe* ..... **18 D7** 45 57N 7 53 E
Rosalia, *U.S.A.* **82 C5** 47 14N 117 22W
Rosamond, *U.S.A.* **85 L8** 34 52N 118 10W
Rosario, *Argentina* **94 C3** 33 0S 60 40W
Rosário, *Brazil* **93 D10** 3 0S 44 15W
Rosario, *Baja Calif., Mexico* **86 B1** 30 0N 115 50W
Rosario, *Sinaloa, Mexico* .. **86 C3** 23 0N 105 52W
Rosario, *Paraguay* **94 A4** 24 30S 57 35W
Rosario de la Frontera,
Argentina **94 B3** 25 50S 65 0W
Rosario de Lerma, *Argentina* **94 A2** 24 59S 65 35W
Rosario del Tala, *Argentina* **94 C4** 32 20S 59 10W
Rosário do Sul, *Brazil* **95 C5** 30 15S 54 55W
Rosarito, *Mexico* **85 N9** 32 18N 117 4W
Roscoe, *U.S.A.* **79 E10** 41 56N 74 55W
Roscommon, *Ireland* **13 C3** 53 38N 8 11W
Roscommon □, *Ireland* **13 C3** 53 49N 8 23W
Roscrea, *Ireland* **13 D4** 52 57N 7 49W
Rose →, *Australia* ...... **62 A2** 14 16S 135 45 E
Rose Blanche, *Canada* **71 C8** 47 38N 58 45W
Rose Pt., *Canada* **72 C2** 54 11N 131 39W
Rose Valley, *Canada* **73 C8** 52 19N 103 49W
Roseau, *Domin.* **89 C7** 15 20N 61 24W
Roseau, *U.S.A.* **80 A7** 48 51N 95 46W
Rosebery, *Australia* ...... **62 G4** 41 46S 145 33 E
Rosebud, *S. Dak., U.S.A.* .. **80 D4** 43 14N 100 51W
Rosebud, *Tex., U.S.A.* **81 K6** 31 4N 96 59W
Roseburg, *U.S.A.* **82 E2** 43 13N 123 20W
Rosedale, *U.S.A.* **81 J9** 33 51N 91 2W
Roseland, *U.S.A.* **84 G4** 38 25N 122 43W
Rosemary, *Canada* **72 C6** 50 46N 112 5W
Rosenberg, *U.S.A.* **81 L7** 29 34N 95 49W
Rosenheim, *Germany* ..... **16 E7** 47 51N 12 7 E
Roses, G. de, *Spain* ...... **19 A7** 42 10N 3 15 E
Rosetown, *Canada* **73 C7** 51 35N 107 59W
Roseville, *Calif., U.S.A.* **84 G5** 38 45N 121 17W
Roseville, *Mich., U.S.A.* **78 D2** 42 30N 82 56W
Rosewood, *Australia* ...... **63 D5** 27 38S 152 36 E
Roshkhvār, *Iran* .... **45 C8** 34 58N 59 37 E
Rosignano Marittimo, *Italy* **20 C4** 43 24N 10 28 E
Rosignol, *Guyana* **92 B7** 6 15N 57 30W
Roşiori-de-Vede, *Romania* . **17 F13** 44 7N 24 59 E
Roskilde, *Denmark* .... **9 J15** 55 38N 12 3 E
Roslavl, *Russia* .... **24 D5** 53 57N 32 55 E
Rosmead, *S. Africa* .... **56 E4** 31 29S 25 8 E
Ross, *Australia* .... **62 G4** 42 2S 147 30 E
Ross, *N.Z.* .... **59 K3** 42 53S 170 49 E
Ross I., *Antarctica* .... **5 D11** 77 30S 168 0 E
Ross Ice Shelf, *Antarctica* . **5 E12** 80 0S 180 0 E
Ross L., *U.S.A.* **82 B3** 48 44N 121 4W
Ross-on-Wye, *U.K.* **11 F5** 51 54N 2 34W
Ross River, *Australia* ..... **62 C1** 23 44S 134 30 E
Ross River, *Canada* **72 A2** 62 30N 131 30W
Ross Sea, *Antarctica* ..... **5 D11** 74 0S 178 0 E
Rossall Pt., *U.K.* **10 D4** 53 55N 3 3W
Rossan Pt., *Ireland* **13 B3** 54 42N 8 47W
Rossano, *Italy* .... **20 E7** 39 36N 16 39 E
Rossburn, *Canada* **73 C8** 50 40N 100 49W
Rosseau, *Canada* **78 A5** 45 16N 79 39W
Rosseau L., *Canada* **78 A5** 45 10N 79 35W
Rosses, The, *Ireland* **13 A3** 55 2N 8 20W
Rossignol, L., *Canada* **70 B5** 52 43N 73 40W
Rossignol Res., *Canada* **71 D6** 44 12N 65 10W
Rossland, *Canada* **72 D5** 49 6N 117 50W
Rosslare, *Ireland* **13 D5** 52 17N 6 24W
Rosso, *Mauritania* **50 E2** 16 40N 15 45W
Rossosh, *Russia* .... **25 D6** 50 15N 39 28 E
Røssvatnet, *Norway* ...... **8 D16** 65 45N 14 5 E
Røst, *Norway* .... **8 C15** 67 32N 12 0 E
Rosthern, *Canada* **73 C7** 52 40N 106 20W
Rostock, *Germany* .... **16 A7** 54 5N 12 8 E
Rostov, *Don, Russia* ...... **25 E6** 47 15N 39 45 E
Rostov, *Yaroslavl, Russia* .. **24 C6** 57 14N 39 25 E
Roswell, *Ga., U.S.A.* **77 H3** 34 2N 84 22W
Roswell, *N. Mex., U.S.A.* .. **81 J2** 33 24N 104 32W
Rotan, *U.S.A.* **81 J4** 32 51N 100 28W
Rother →, *U.K.* .... **11 G8** 50 59N 0 45 E
Rotherham, *U.K.* **10 D6** 53 26N 1 20W
Rothes, *U.K.* **12 D5** 57 32N 3 13W
Rothesay, *Canada* **71 C6** 45 23N 66 0W
Rothesay, *U.K.* **12 F3** 55 50N 5 3W
Roti, *Indonesia* .... **37 F6** 10 50S 123 0 E
Roto, *Australia* .... **63 E4** 33 0S 145 30 E
Rotondo Mte., *France* ..... **18 E8** 42 14N 9 8 E
Rotoroa, L., *N.Z.* .... **59 J4** 41 55S 172 39 E
Rotorua, *N.Z.* .... **59 H6** 38 9S 176 16 E
Rotorua, L., *N.Z.* .... **59 H6** 38 5S 176 18 E
Rotterdam, *Neths.* .... **15 C4** 51 55N 4 30 E
Rotterdam, *U.S.A.* **79 D10** 42 48N 74 1W
Rottnest I., *Australia* ..... **61 F2** 32 0S 115 27 E
Rottumeroog, *Neths.* ...... **15 A6** 53 33N 6 34 E
Rottweil, *Germany* .... **16 D5** 48 9N 8 37 E
Rotuma, *Fiji* .... **64 J9** 12 25S 177 5 E
Roubaix, *France* .... **18 A5** 50 40N 3 10 E
Rouen, *France* .... **18 B4** 49 27N 1 4 E
Rouleau, *Canada* **73 C8** 50 10N 104 56W
Round Mountain, *U.S.A.* ... **82 G5** 38 43N 117 4W
Round Mt., *Australia* ..... **63 E5** 30 26S 152 16 E
Round Rock, *U.S.A.* **81 K6** 30 31N 97 41W
Roundup, *U.S.A.* **82 C9** 46 27N 108 33W
Rousay, *U.K.* **12 B5** 59 10N 3 2W
Rouses Point, *U.S.A.* **79 B11** 44 59N 73 22W
Rouseville, *U.S.A.* **78 E5** 41 28N 79 42W
Roussillon, *France* .... **18 E5** 42 30N 2 35 E
Rouxville, *S. Africa* .... **56 E4** 30 25S 26 50 E
Rouyn-Noranda, *Canada* ... **70 C4** 48 20N 79 0W
Rovaniemi, *Finland* .... **8 C21** 66 29N 25 41 E
Rovereto, *Italy* .... **20 B4** 45 53N 11 3 E
Rovigo, *Italy* .... **20 B4** 45 4N 11 47 E
Rovinj, *Croatia* .... **16 F7** 45 5N 13 40 E
Rovno = Rivne, *Ukraine* ... **17 C14** 50 40N 26 10 E
Rovuma = Ruvuma →,
Tanzania .... **55 E5** 10 29S 40 28 E
Row'ān, *Iran* .... **45 C6** 35 8N 48 51 E
Rowena, *Australia* .... **63 D4** 29 48S 148 55 E
Rowley Shoals, *Australia* .. **60 C2** 17 30S 119 0 E
Roxas, *Phil.* .... **37 B6** 11 36N 122 49 E
Roxboro, *U.S.A.* **77 G6** 36 24N 78 59W
Roxburgh, *N.Z.* .... **59 L2** 45 33S 169 19 E
Roxbury, *U.S.A.* **78 F7** 40 6N 77 39W
Roy, *Mont., U.S.A.* **82 C9** 47 20N 108 58W
Roy, *N. Mex., U.S.A.* **81 H2** 35 57N 104 12W
Roy, *Utah, U.S.A.* **82 F7** 41 10N 112 2W
Royal Canal, *Ireland* **13 C4** 53 30N 7 13W
Royal Leamington Spa, *U.K.* **11 E6** 52 18N 1 31W
Royal Tunbridge Wells, *U.K.* **11 F8** 51 7N 0 16 E
Royan, *France* **18 D3** 45 37N 1 2W
Royston, *U.K.* **11 E7** 52 3N 0 1W
Rozdilna, *Ukraine* .... **17 E16** 46 50N 30 2 E
Rozhyshche, *Ukraine* ..... **17 C13** 50 54N 25 15 E
Rtishchevo, *Russia* .... **24 C7** 52 18N 43 46 E
Ruacaná, *Angola* .... **56 B1** 17 20S 14 12 E
Ruahine Ra., *N.Z.* .... **59 H6** 39 55S 176 2 E
Ruapehu, *N.Z.* .... **59 H5** 39 17S 175 35 E
Ruapuke I., *N.Z.* .... **59 M2** 46 46S 168 31 E
Ruâq, W. →, *Egypt* ...... **47 F2** 30 0N 33 49 E
Rub' al Khālī, *Si. Arabia* ... **46 D4** 18 0N 48 0 E
Rubeho Mts., *Tanzania* .... **54 D4** 6 50S 36 25 E
Rubh a' Mhail, *U.K.* **12 F2** 55 56N 6 8W
Rubha Hunish, *U.K.* **12 D2** 57 42N 6 20W
Rubha Robhanais = Lewis,
Butt of, *U.K.* **12 C2** 58 31N 6 16W
Rubicon →, *U.S.A.* **84 G5** 38 53N 121 4W
Rubio, *Venezuela* **92 B4** 7 43N 72 22W
Rubtsovsk, *Russia* .... **26 D9** 51 30N 81 10 E
Ruby L., *U.S.A.* **82 F6** 40 10N 115 28W
Ruby Mts., *U.S.A.* **82 F6** 40 30N 115 20W
Rubyvale, *Australia* ...... **62 C4** 23 25S 147 42 E
Rūd Sar, *Iran* .... **45 B6** 37 8N 50 18 E
Rudall, *Australia* .... **63 E2** 33 43S 136 17 E
Rudall →, *Australia* ..... **60 D3** 22 34S 122 13 E
Rudewa, *Tanzania* .... **55 E3** 10 7S 34 40 E
Rudnyy, *Kazakstan* .... **26 D7** 52 57N 63 7 E
Rudolfa, Ostrov, *Russia* ... **26 A6** 81 45N 58 30 E
Rudyard, *U.S.A.* **76 B3** 46 14N 84 36W
Rufiji →, *Tanzania* ...... **54 D4** 7 50S 39 15 E
Rufino, *Argentina* **94 C3** 34 20S 62 50W
Rufunsa, *Zambia* .... **55 F2** 15 4S 29 34 E
Rugby, *U.K.* **11 E6** 52 23N 1 16W
Rugby, *U.S.A.* **80 A5** 48 22N 100 0W
Rügen, *Germany* .... **16 A7** 54 22N 13 24 E
Ruhengeri, *Rwanda* ...... **54 C2** 1 30S 29 36 E
Ruhnu, *Estonia* .... **9 H20** 57 48N 23 15 E
Ruhr →, *Germany* .... **16 C4** 51 27N 6 43 E
Ruhuhu →, *Tanzania* .... **55 E3** 10 31S 34 34 E
Ruidoso, *U.S.A.* **83 K11** 33 20N 105 41W
Ruivo, Pico, *Madeira* **22 D3** 32 45N 16 56W
Rujm Tal'at al Jamā'ah,
Jordan .... **47 E4** 30 24N 35 30 E
Ruk, *Pakistan* .... **42 F3** 27 50N 68 42 E
Rukhla, *Pakistan* .... **42 C4** 32 27N 71 57 E
Ruki →,
Dem. Rep. of the Congo . **52 E3** 0 5N 18 17 E
Rukwa □, *Tanzania* ...... **54 D3** 7 0S 31 30 E
Rukwa, L., *Tanzania* ..... **54 D3** 8 0S 32 20 E
Rulhieres, C., *Australia* .... **60 B4** 13 56S 127 22 E
Rum = Rhum, *U.K.* **12 E2** 57 0N 6 20W
Rum Cay, *Bahamas* **89 B5** 23 40N 74 58W
Rum Jungle, *Australia* .... **60 B5** 13 0S 130 59 E
Rumāḩ, *Si. Arabia* .... **44 E5** 25 29N 47 10 E
Rumania = Romania ■,
Europe .... **17 F12** 46 0N 25 0 E
Rumaylah, *Iraq* .... **44 D5** 30 47N 47 37 E
Rumbêk, *Sudan* .... **51 G11** 6 54N 29 37 E
Rumford, *U.S.A.* **77 C10** 44 33N 70 33W
Rumia, *Poland* .... **17 A10** 54 37N 18 25 E
Rumoi, *Japan* .... **30 C10** 43 56N 141 39 E
Rumonge, *Burundi* .... **54 C2** 3 59S 29 26 E
Rumson, *U.S.A.* **79 F11** 40 23N 74 0W
Rumuruti, *Kenya* .... **54 B4** 0 17N 36 32 E
Runan, *China* .... **34 H8** 33 0N 114 30 E
Runanga, *N.Z.* .... **59 K3** 42 25S 171 15 E
Runaway, C., *N.Z.* .... **59 G6** 37 32S 177 59 E
Runcorn, *U.K.* **10 D5** 53 21N 2 44W
Rundu, *Namibia* .... **53 H3** 17 52S 19 43 E
Rungwa, *Tanzania* .... **54 D3** 6 55S 33 32 E
Rungwa →, *Tanzania* .... **54 D3** 7 36S 31 50 E
Rungwe, *Tanzania* .... **55 D3** 9 11S 33 32 E
Rungwe, Mt., *Tanzania* .... **52 F6** 9 8S 33 40 E
Runton Ra., *Australia* ..... **60 D3** 23 31S 123 6 E
Ruoqiang, *China* .... **32 C3** 38 55N 88 10 E
Rupa, *India* .... **41 F18** 27 15N 92 21 E
Rupar, *India* .... **42 D7** 31 2N 76 38 E
Rupat, *Indonesia* .... **36 D2** 1 45N 101 40 E
Rupen →, *India* .... **42 H4** 23 28N 71 31 E
Rupert, *U.S.A.* **82 E7** 42 37N 113 41W
Rupert →, *Canada* **70 B4** 51 29N 78 45W
Rupert B., *Canada* **70 B4** 51 35N 79 0W
Rupert House =
Waskaganish, *Canada* ... **70 B4** 51 30N 78 40W
Rupsa, *India* .... **43 J12** 21 37N 87 1 E
Rurrenabaque, *Bolivia* **92 F5** 14 30S 67 32W
Rusambo, *Zimbabwe* ...... **55 F3** 16 30S 32 4 E
Rusape, *Zimbabwe* .... **55 F3** 18 35S 32 8 E
Ruschuk = Ruse, *Bulgaria* . **21 C12** 43 48N 25 59 E
Ruse, *Bulgaria* .... **21 C12** 43 48N 25 59 E
Rush, *Ireland* **13 C5** 53 31N 6 6W
Rushan, *China* .... **35 F11** 36 56N 121 30 E
Rushden, *U.K.* **11 E7** 52 18N 0 35W
Rushmore, Mt., *U.S.A.* **80 D3** 43 53N 103 28W
Rushville, *Ill., U.S.A.* **80 E9** 40 7N 90 34W
Rushville, *Ind., U.S.A.* **76 F3** 39 37N 85 27W
Rushville, *Nebr., U.S.A.* **80 D3** 42 43N 102 28W
Russas, *Brazil* **93 D11** 4 55S 37 50W
Russell, *Canada* **73 C8** 50 50N 101 20W
Russell, *Kans., U.S.A.* **80 F5** 38 54N 98 52W
Russell, *N.Y., U.S.A.* **79 B9** 44 27N 75 9W
Russell, *Pa., U.S.A.* **78 E5** 41 56N 79 8W
Russell L., *Man., Canada* ... **73 B8** 56 15N 101 30W
Russell L., *N.W.T., Canada* . **72 A5** 63 5N 115 44W
Russellkonda, *India* ...... **41 K14** 19 57N 84 42 E
Russellville, *Ala., U.S.A.* ... **77 H2** 34 30N 87 44W
Russellville, *Ark., U.S.A.* ... **81 H8** 35 17N 93 8W
Russellville, *Ky., U.S.A.* ... **77 G2** 36 51N 86 53W
Russia ■, *Eurasia* .... **27 C11** 62 0N 105 0 E
Russian →, *U.S.A.* **84 G3** 38 27N 123 8W
Russkoye Ustie, *Russia* ... **4 B15** 71 0N 149 0 E
Rustam, *Pakistan* .... **42 B5** 34 25N 72 13 E
Rustam Shahr, *Pakistan* ... **42 F2** 26 58N 66 6 E
Rustavi, *Georgia* .... **25 F8** 41 30N 45 0 E
Rustenburg, *S. Africa* ..... **56 D4** 25 41S 27 14 E
Ruston, *U.S.A.* **81 J8** 32 32N 92 38W
Rutana, *Burundi* .... **54 C3** 3 55S 30 0 E
Ruteng, *Indonesia* .... **37 F6** 8 35S 120 30 E
Ruth, *U.S.A.* **78 C2** 43 42N 82 45W
Rutherford, *U.S.A.* **84 G4** 38 26N 122 24W
Rutland, *U.S.A.* **79 C12** 43 37N 72 58W
Rutland □, *U.K.* **11 E7** 52 38N 0 40W
Rutland Water, *U.K.* **11 E7** 52 39N 0 38W
Rutledge →, *Canada* **73 A6** 61 4N 112 0W
Rutledge L., *Canada* **73 A6** 61 33N 110 47W
Rutshuru,
Dem. Rep. of the Congo . **54 C2** 1 13S 29 25 E
Ruvu, *Tanzania* .... **54 D4** 6 49S 38 43 E
Ruvu →, *Tanzania* ...... **54 D4** 6 23S 38 52 E
Ruvuma □, *Tanzania* ..... **55 E4** 10 20S 36 0 E
Ruvuma →, *Tanzania* .... **55 E5** 10 29S 40 28 E
Ruwais, *U.A.E.* .... **45 E7** 24 5N 52 50 E
Ruwenzori, *Africa* .... **54 B2** 0 30N 29 55 E
Ruyigi, *Burundi* .... **54 C3** 3 29S 30 15 E
Ružomberok, *Slovak Rep.* .. **17 D10** 49 3N 19 17 E
Rwanda ■, *Africa* .... **54 C3** 2 0S 30 0 E
Ryan, L., *U.K.* **12 G3** 55 0N 5 2W
Ryazan, *Russia* .... **24 D6** 54 40N 39 40 E
Ryazhsk, *Russia* .... **24 D7** 53 45N 40 3 E
Rybache = Rybachye,
Kazakstan .... **26 E9** 46 40N 81 20 E
Rybachiy Poluostrov, *Russia* **24 A5** 69 43N 32 0 E
Rybachye = Ysyk-Köl,
Kyrgyzstan .... **28 E11** 42 26N 76 12 E
Rybachye, *Kazakstan* ..... **26 E9** 46 40N 81 20 E
Rybinsk, *Russia* .... **24 C6** 58 5N 38 50 E
Rybinskoye Vdkhr., *Russia* . **24 C6** 58 30N 38 25 E
Rybnitsa = Râbniţa,
Moldova .... **17 E15** 47 45N 29 0 E
Rycroft, *Canada* **72 B5** 55 45N 118 40W
Ryde, *U.K.* **11 G6** 50 43N 1 9W
Ryderwood, *U.S.A.* **84 D3** 46 23N 123 3W
Rye, *U.K.* .... **11 G8** 50 57N 0 45 E
Rye →, *U.K.* **10 C7** 54 11N 0 44W
Rye Bay, *U.K.* .... **11 G8** 50 52N 0 49 E
Rye Patch Reservoir, *U.S.A.* **82 F4** 40 28N 118 19W
Ryegate, *U.S.A.* **82 C9** 46 18N 109 15W
Ryley, *Canada* **72 C6** 53 17N 112 26W
Rylstone, *Australia* ...... **63 E4** 32 46S 149 58 E
Ryōtsu, *Japan* .... **30 E9** 38 5N 138 26 E
Rypin, *Poland* .... **17 B10** 53 3N 19 25 E
Ryūgasaki, *Japan* .... **31 G10** 35 54N 140 11 E
Ryūkyū Is. = Ryūkyū-rettō,
Japan .... **31 M3** 26 0N 126 0 E
Ryūkyū-rettō, *Japan* ...... **31 M3** 26 0N 126 0 E
Rzeszów, *Poland* .... **17 C11** 50 5N 21 58 E
Rzhev, *Russia* .... **24 C5** 56 20N 34 20 E

S

Shafter

Shafter, U.S.A. 85 K7 35 30N 119 16W
Shaftesbury, U.K. 11 F5 51 0N 2 11W
Shagram, Pakistan 43 A5 36 24N 72 20 E
Shah Alizai, Pakistan 42 E2 29 25N 66 33 E
Shah Bunder, Pakistan 42 G2 24 13N 67 56 E
Shahabad, Punjab, India 42 D7 30 10N 76 55 E
Shahabad, Raj., India 42 G7 25 15N 77 11 E
Shahabad, Ut. P., India 43 F8 27 36N 79 56 E
Shahadpur, Pakistan 42 G3 25 55N 68 35 E
Shahba, Syria 47 C5 32 52N 36 38 E
Shahdād, Iran 45 D8 30 30N 57 40 E
Shahdād, Namakzār-e, Iran 45 D8 30 20N 58 20 E
Shahdadkot, Pakistan 42 F2 27 50N 67 55 E
Shahdol, India 43 H9 23 19N 81 26 E
Shahe, China 34 F8 37 0N 114 32 E
Shahganj, India 43 F10 26 3N 82 44 E
Shahgarh, India 40 F6 27 15N 69 50 E
Shahjahanpur, India 43 F8 27 54N 79 57 E
Shahpur, India 42 H7 22 12N 77 58 E
Shahpur, Baluchistan, Pakistan 42 E3 28 46N 68 27 E
Shahpur, Punjab, Pakistan 42 C5 32 17N 72 26 E
Shahpur Chakar, Pakistan 42 F3 26 9N 68 39 E
Shahpura, Mad. P., India 43 H9 23 10N 80 45 E
Shahpura, Raj., India 42 G6 25 38N 74 56 E
Shahr-e Bābak, Iran 45 D7 30 7N 55 9 E
Shahr-e Kord, Iran 45 C6 32 15N 50 55 E
Shāhrakht, Iran 45 C9 33 38N 60 16 E
Shahrig, Pakistan 42 D2 30 15N 67 40 E
Shahukou, China 34 D7 40 20N 112 18 E
Shaikhabad, Afghan. 42 B3 34 2N 68 45 E
Shajapur, India 42 H7 23 27N 76 21 E
Shakargarh, Pakistan 42 C6 32 17N 75 10 E
Shakawe, Botswana 56 B3 18 28S 21 49 E
Shaker Heights, U.S.A. 78 E3 41 29N 81 32W
Shakhty, Russia 25 E7 47 40N 40 16 E
Shakhunya, Russia 24 C8 57 40N 46 46 E
Shaki, Nigeria 50 G6 8 41N 3 21 E
Shallow Lake, Canada 78 B3 44 36N 81 5W
Shalqar, Kazakstan 26 E6 47 48N 59 39 E
Shaluli Shan, China 32 C4 30 40N 99 55 E
Shām, Iran 45 E8 26 39N 57 21 E
Shām, Bādiyat ash, Asia 44 C3 32 0N 40 0 E
Shamâl Kordofân □, Sudan 48 E6 15 0N 30 0 E
Shamattawa, Canada 70 A1 55 51N 92 5W
Shamattawa →, Canada 70 A2 55 1N 85 23W
Shamīl, Iran 45 E8 27 30N 56 55 E
Shāmkūh, Iran 45 C8 35 47N 57 50 E
Shamli, India 42 E7 29 32N 77 18 E
Shammar, Jabal, Si. Arabia 44 E4 27 40N 41 0 E
Shamo = Gobi, Asia 34 C6 44 0N 110 0 E
Shamo, L., Ethiopia 46 F2 5 45N 37 30 E
Shamokin, U.S.A. 79 F8 40 47N 76 34W
Shamrock, U.S.A. 81 H4 35 13N 100 15W
Shamva, Zimbabwe 55 F3 17 20S 31 32 E
Shan □, Burma 41 J21 21 30N 98 30 E
Shan Xian, China 34 G9 34 50N 116 5 E
Shanchengzhen, China 35 C13 42 20N 125 20 E
Shāndak, Iran 45 D9 28 28N 60 27 E
Shandon, U.S.A. 84 K6 35 39N 120 23W
Shandong □, China 35 G10 36 0N 118 0 E
Shandong Bandao, China 35 F11 37 0N 121 0 E
Shang Xian = Shangzhou, China 34 H5 33 50N 109 58 E
Shanga, Nigeria 50 F6 11 12N 4 33 E
Shangalowe, Dem. Rep. of the Congo 55 E2 10 50S 26 30 E
Shangani →, Zimbabwe 55 F2 18 41S 27 10 E
Shangbancheng, China 35 D10 40 50N 118 1 E
Shangdu, China 34 D7 41 30N 113 30 E
Shanghai, China 33 C7 31 15N 121 26 E
Shanghe, China 35 F9 37 20N 117 10 E
Shangnan, China 34 H6 33 32N 110 50 E
Shangqiu, China 34 G8 34 26N 115 36 E
Shangrao, China 33 D6 28 25N 117 59 E
Shangshui, China 34 H8 33 42N 114 35 E
Shangzhi, China 35 B14 45 22N 127 56 E
Shangzhou, China 34 H5 33 50N 109 58 E
Shanhetun, China 35 B14 44 33N 127 15 E
Shannon, N.Z. 59 J5 40 33S 175 25 E
Shannon →, Ireland 13 D2 52 35N 9 30W
Shannon, Mouth of the, Ireland 13 D2 52 30N 9 55W
Shannon Airport, Ireland 13 D3 52 42N 8 57W
Shansi = Shanxi □, China 34 F7 37 0N 112 0 E
Shantar, Ostrov Bolshoy, Russia 27 D14 55 9N 137 40 E
Shantipur, India 43 H13 23 17N 88 25 E
Shantou, China 33 D6 23 18N 116 40 E
Shantung = Shandong □, China 35 G10 36 0N 118 0 E
Shanxi □, China 34 F7 37 0N 112 0 E
Shanyang, China 34 H5 33 31N 109 55 E
Shanyin, China 34 E7 39 25N 112 56 E
Shaoguan, China 33 D6 24 48N 113 35 E
Shaoxing, China 33 D7 30 0N 120 35 E
Shaoyang, China 33 D6 27 14N 111 25 E
Shap, U.K. 10 C5 54 32N 2 40W
Shapinsay, U.K. 12 B6 59 3N 2 51W
Shaqra', Si. Arabia 44 E5 25 15N 45 16 E
Shaqrā', Yemen 46 E4 13 22N 45 44 E
Sharafkhāneh, Iran 44 B5 38 11N 45 29 E
Sharbot Lake, Canada 79 B8 44 46N 76 41W
Shari, Japan 30 C12 43 55N 144 40 E
Sharjah = Ash Shāriqah, U.A.E. 45 E7 25 23N 55 26 E
Shark B., Australia 61 E1 25 30S 113 32 E
Sharon, Mass., U.S.A. 79 D13 42 7N 71 11W
Sharon, Pa., U.S.A. 78 E4 41 14N 80 31W
Sharon Springs, Kans., U.S.A. 80 F4 38 54N 101 45W
Sharon Springs, N.Y., U.S.A. 79 D10 42 48N 74 37W
Sharp Pt., Australia 62 A3 10 58S 142 43 E
Sharpe L., Canada 70 B1 54 24N 93 40W
Sharpsville, U.S.A. 78 E4 41 15N 80 29W
Sharya, Russia 24 C8 58 22N 45 20 E
Shashemene, Ethiopia 46 F2 7 13N 38 33 E
Shashi, Botswana 57 C4 21 15S 27 27 E
Shashi, China 33 C6 30 25N 112 14 E
Shashi →, Africa 55 G2 21 14S 29 20 E
Shasta, Mt., U.S.A. 82 F2 41 25N 122 12W
Shasta L., U.S.A. 82 F2 40 43N 122 25W
Shatt al'Arab →, Iraq 45 D6 29 57N 48 34 E
Shaunavon, Canada 73 D7 49 35N 108 25W
Shaver L., U.S.A. 84 H7 37 9N 119 18W
Shaw →, Australia 60 D2 20 21S 119 17 E
Shaw I., Australia 62 C4 20 30S 149 2 E
Shawanaga, Canada 78 A4 45 31N 80 17W
Shawangunk Mts., U.S.A. 79 E10 41 35N 74 30W
Shawano, U.S.A. 76 C1 44 47N 88 36W
Shawinigan, Canada 70 C5 46 35N 72 50W
Shawnee, U.S.A. 81 H6 35 20N 96 55W
Shay Gap, Australia 60 D3 20 30S 120 10 E
Shaybārā, Si. Arabia 44 E3 25 26N 36 47 E
Shaykh, J. ash, Lebanon 47 B4 33 25N 35 50 E
Shaykh Miskīn, Syria 47 C5 32 49N 36 9 E
Shaykh Sa'īd, Iraq 44 C5 32 34N 46 17 E
Shcherbakov = Rybinsk, Russia 24 C6 58 5N 38 50 E
Shchuchinsk, Kazakstan 26 D8 52 56N 70 12 E
She Xian, China 34 F7 36 30N 113 40 E
Shebele = Scebeli, Wabi →, Somali Rep. 46 G3 2 0N 44 0 E
Sheboygan, U.S.A. 76 D2 43 46N 87 45W
Shediac, Canada 71 C7 46 14N 64 32W
Sheelin, L., Ireland 13 C4 53 48N 7 20W
Sheep Haven, Ireland 13 A4 55 11N 7 52W
Sheerness, U.K. 11 F8 51 26N 0 47 E
Sheet Harbour, Canada 71 D7 44 56N 62 31W
Sheffield, U.K. 10 D6 53 23N 1 28W
Sheffield, Ala., U.S.A. 77 H2 34 46N 87 41W
Sheffield, Mass., U.S.A. 79 D11 42 5N 73 21W
Sheffield, Pa., U.S.A. 78 E5 41 42N 79 3W
Sheikhpura, India 43 G11 25 9N 85 53 E
Shekhupura, Pakistan 42 D5 31 42N 73 58 E
Shelburne, N.S., Canada 71 D6 43 47N 65 20W
Shelburne, Ont., Canada 78 B4 44 4N 80 15W
Shelburne, Vt., U.S.A. 79 B11 44 23N 73 13W
Shelburne, Vt., U.S.A. 79 B11 44 23N 73 14W
Shelburne B., Australia 62 A3 11 50S 142 50 E
Shelburne Falls, U.S.A. 79 D12 42 36N 72 45W
Shelby, Mich., U.S.A. 76 D2 43 37N 86 22W
Shelby, Miss., U.S.A. 81 J9 33 57N 90 46W
Shelby, Mont., U.S.A. 82 B8 48 30N 111 51W
Shelby, N.C., U.S.A. 77 H5 35 17N 81 32W
Shelby, Ohio, U.S.A. 78 F2 40 53N 82 40W
Shelbyville, Ill., U.S.A. 80 F10 39 24N 88 48W
Shelbyville, Ind., U.S.A. 76 F3 39 31N 85 47W
Shelbyville, Ky., U.S.A. 76 F3 38 13N 85 14W
Shelbyville, Tenn., U.S.A. 77 H2 35 29N 86 28W
Sheldon, U.S.A. 80 D7 43 11N 95 51W
Sheldrake, Canada 71 B7 50 20N 64 51W
Shelikhova, Zaliv, Russia 27 D16 59 30N 157 0 E
Shell Lakes, Australia 61 E4 29 20S 127 30 E
Shellbrook, Canada 73 C7 53 13N 106 24W
Shellharbour, Australia 63 E5 34 31S 150 51 E
Shelter I, U.S.A. 79 E12 41 5N 72 21W
Shelton, Conn., U.S.A. 79 E11 41 19N 73 5W
Shelton, Wash., U.S.A. 84 C3 47 13N 123 6W
Shen Xian, China 34 F8 36 15N 115 40 E
Shenandoah, Iowa, U.S.A. 80 E7 40 46N 95 22W
Shenandoah, Pa., U.S.A. 79 F8 40 49N 76 12W
Shenandoah, Va., U.S.A. 76 F6 38 29N 78 37W
Shenandoah →, U.S.A. 76 F7 39 19N 77 44W
Shenandoah National Park, U.S.A. 76 F6 38 35N 78 22W
Shenchi, China 34 E7 39 8N 112 10 E
Shendam, Nigeria 50 G7 8 49N 9 30 E
Shendî, Sudan 51 E12 16 46N 33 22 E
Shenfang, China 34 E9 39 3N 116 42 E
Shenjingzi, China 35 B13 44 40N 124 30 E
Shenmu, China 34 E6 38 50N 110 29 E
Shenqiu, China 34 H8 33 25N 115 5 E
Shenqiucheng, China 34 H8 33 24N 115 2 E
Shensi = Shaanxi □, China 34 G5 35 0N 109 0 E
Shenyang, China 35 D12 41 48N 123 27 E
Sheo, India 42 F4 26 11N 71 15 E
Sheopur Kalan, India 40 G10 25 40N 76 40 E
Shepetivka, Ukraine 17 C14 50 10N 27 10 E
Shepetovka = Shepetivka, Ukraine 17 C14 50 10N 27 10 E
Shepparton, Australia 63 F4 36 23S 145 26 E
Sheppey, I. of, U.K. 11 F8 51 25N 0 48 E
Shepton Mallet, U.K. 11 F5 51 11N 2 33W
Sheqi, China 34 H7 33 12N 112 57 E
Sher Qila, Pakistan 43 A6 36 7N 74 2 E
Sherborne, U.K. 11 G5 50 57N 2 31W
Sherbro I., S. Leone 50 G3 7 30N 12 40W
Sherbrooke, Canada 71 C7 45 8N 61 59W
Sherbrooke, Qué., Canada 79 A13 45 28N 71 57W
Sherburne, U.S.A. 79 D9 42 41N 75 30W
Shergarh, India 42 F5 26 20N 72 18 E
Sherghati, India 43 G11 24 34N 84 47 E
Sheridan, Ark., U.S.A. 81 H8 34 19N 92 24W
Sheridan, Wyo., U.S.A. 82 D10 44 48N 106 58W
Sheringham, U.K. 10 E9 52 56N 1 13 E
Sherkin I., Ireland 13 E2 51 28N 9 26W
Sherkot, India 43 E8 29 22N 78 35 E
Sherman, U.S.A. 81 J6 33 40N 96 35W
Sherpur, India 43 G10 25 34N 83 47 E
Sherridon, Canada 73 B8 55 8N 101 5W
Sherwood Forest, U.K. 10 D6 53 6N 1 7W
Sherwood Park, Canada 72 C6 53 31N 113 19W
Sheslay →, Canada 72 B2 58 48N 132 5W
Shethanei L., Canada 73 B9 58 48N 97 50W
Shetland □, U.K. 12 A7 60 30N 1 30W
Shetland Is., U.K. 12 A7 60 30N 1 30W
Shetrunji →, India 42 J5 21 19N 72 7 E
Sheyenne →, U.S.A. 80 B6 47 2N 96 50W
Shibām, Yemen 46 D4 16 0N 48 36 E
Shibata, Japan 30 F9 37 57N 139 20 E
Shibecha, Japan 30 C12 43 17N 144 36 E
Shibetsu, Japan 30 B11 44 10N 142 23 E
Shibogama L., Canada 70 B2 53 35N 88 15W
Shibushi, Japan 31 J5 31 25N 131 8 E
Shickshinny, U.S.A. 79 E8 41 9N 76 9W
Shickshock Mts. = Chic-Chocs, Mts., Canada 71 C6 48 55N 66 0W
Shidao, China 35 F12 36 50N 122 25 E
Shido, Japan 31 G7 34 19N 134 10 E
Shiel, L., U.K. 12 E3 56 48N 5 34W
Shield, C., Australia 62 A2 13 20S 136 20 E
Shiga □, Japan 31 G8 35 20N 136 0 E
Shiguaigou, China 34 D6 40 52N 110 15 E
Shihchiachuangi = Shijiazhuang, China 34 E8 38 2N 114 28 E
Shijiazhuang, China 34 E8 38 2N 114 28 E
Shikarpur, India 42 E8 28 17N 78 7 E
Shikarpur, Pakistan 42 F3 27 57N 68 39 E
Shikohabad, India 43 F8 27 6N 78 36 E
Shikoku □, Japan 31 H6 33 30N 133 30 E
Shikoku-Sanchi, Japan 31 H6 33 30N 133 30 E
Shiliguri, India 41 F16 26 45N 88 25 E
Shilka, Russia 27 D12 52 0N 115 55 E
Shilka →, Russia 27 D13 53 20N 121 26 E
Shillelagh, Ireland 13 D5 52 45N 6 32W
Shillington, U.S.A. 79 F9 40 18N 75 58W
Shillong, India 41 G17 25 35N 91 53 E
Shilo, West Bank 47 C4 32 4N 35 18 E
Shilou, China 34 F6 37 0N 110 48 E
Shimabara, Japan 31 H5 32 48N 130 20 E
Shimada, Japan 31 G9 34 49N 138 10 E
Shimane □, Japan 31 G6 35 0N 132 30 E
Shimanovsk, Russia 27 D13 52 15N 127 30 E
Shimizu, Japan 31 G9 35 0N 138 30 E
Shimodate, Japan 31 F9 36 20N 139 55 E
Shimoga, India 40 N9 13 57N 75 32 E
Shimoni, Kenya 54 C4 4 38S 39 20 E
Shimonoseki, Japan 31 H5 33 58N 130 55 E
Shimpuru Rapids, Angola 56 B2 17 45S 19 55 E
Shin, L., U.K. 12 C4 58 5N 4 30W
Shinano-Gawa →, Japan 31 F9 36 50N 138 30 E
Shināş, Oman 45 E8 24 46N 56 28 E
Shīndand, Afghan. 40 C3 33 12N 62 8 E
Shinglehouse, U.S.A. 78 E6 41 58N 78 12W
Shingū, Japan 31 H7 33 40N 135 55 E
Shinjō, Japan 30 E10 38 46N 140 18 E
Shinshār, Syria 47 A5 34 36N 36 43 E
Shinyanga, Tanzania 54 C3 3 45S 33 27 E
Shinyanga □, Tanzania 54 C3 3 50S 34 0 E
Shio-no-Misaki, Japan 31 H7 33 25N 135 45 E
Shiogama, Japan 30 E10 38 19N 141 1 E
Shiojiri, Japan 31 F8 36 6N 137 58 E
Shipchenski Prokhod, Bulgaria 21 C11 42 45N 25 15 E
Shiping, China 32 D5 23 45N 102 23 E
Shipki La, India 40 D11 31 45N 78 40 E
Shippegan, Canada 71 C7 47 45N 64 45W
Shippensburg, U.S.A. 78 F7 40 3N 77 31W
Shippenville, U.S.A. 78 E5 41 15N 79 28W
Shiprock, U.S.A. 83 H9 36 47N 108 41W
Shiqma, N. →, Israel 47 D3 31 37N 34 30 E
Shiquan, China 34 H5 33 5N 108 15 E
Shiquan He = Indus →, Pakistan 42 G2 24 20N 67 47 E
Shīr Kūh, Iran 45 D7 31 39N 54 3 E
Shiragami-Misaki, Japan 30 D10 41 24N 140 12 E
Shirakawa, Fukushima, Japan 31 F10 37 7N 140 13 E
Shirakawa, Gifu, Japan 31 F8 36 17N 136 56 E
Shirane-San, Gumma, Japan 31 F9 36 48N 139 22 E
Shirane-San, Yamanashi, Japan 31 G9 35 42N 138 9 E
Shiraoi, Japan 30 C10 42 33N 141 21 E
Shīrāz, Iran 45 D7 29 42N 52 30 E
Shire →, Africa 55 F4 17 42S 35 19 E
Shiretoko-Misaki, Japan 30 B12 44 21N 145 20 E
Shirinab →, Pakistan 42 D2 30 15N 66 28 E
Shiriya-Zaki, Japan 30 D10 41 25N 141 30 E
Shiroishi, Japan 30 F10 38 0N 140 37 E
Shīrvān, Iran 45 B8 37 30N 57 50 E
Shirwa, L. = Chilwa, L., Malawi 55 F4 15 15S 35 40 E
Shivpuri, India 42 G7 25 26N 77 42 E
Shixian, China 35 C15 43 5N 129 50 E
Shizuishan, China 34 E4 39 15N 106 50 E
Shizuoka, Japan 31 G9 34 57N 138 24 E
Shizuoka □, Japan 31 G9 35 15N 138 40 E
Shklov = Shklow, Belarus 17 A16 54 16N 30 15 E
Shklow, Belarus 17 A16 54 16N 30 15 E
Shkoder = Shkodra, Albania 21 C8 42 4N 19 32 E
Shkodra, Albania 21 C8 42 4N 19 32 E
Shkumbini →, Albania 21 D8 41 2N 19 31 E
Shmidta, Ostrov, Russia 27 A10 81 0N 91 0 E
Shō-Gawa →, Japan 31 F8 36 47N 137 4 E
Shoal L., Canada 73 D9 49 33N 95 1W
Shoal Lake, Canada 73 C8 50 30N 100 35W
Shōdo-Shima, Japan 31 G7 34 30N 134 15 E
Sholapur = Solapur, India 40 L9 17 43N 75 56 E
Shologontsy, Russia 27 C12 66 13N 114 0 E
Shōmrōn, West Bank 47 C4 32 15N 35 13 E
Shoreham by Sea, U.K. 11 G7 50 50N 0 16W
Shori →, Pakistan 42 E3 28 29N 69 44 E
Shorkot Road, Pakistan 42 D5 30 47N 72 15 E
Shoshone, Calif., U.S.A. 85 K10 35 58N 116 16W
Shoshone, Idaho, U.S.A. 82 E6 42 56N 114 25W
Shoshone L., U.S.A. 82 D8 44 22N 110 43W
Shoshone Mts., U.S.A. 82 G5 39 20N 117 25W
Shoshong, Botswana 56 C4 22 56S 26 31 E
Shoshoni, U.S.A. 82 E9 43 14N 108 7W
Shouguang, China 35 F10 37 52N 118 45 E
Shouyang, China 34 F7 37 54N 113 8 E
Show Low, U.S.A. 83 J9 34 15N 110 2W
Shreveport, U.S.A. 81 J8 32 31N 93 45W
Shrewsbury, U.K. 11 E5 52 43N 2 45W
Shri Mohangarh, India 42 F4 27 17N 71 18 E
Shrirampur, India 43 H13 22 44N 88 21 E
Shropshire □, U.K. 11 E5 52 36N 2 45W
Shu, Kazakstan 26 E8 43 36N 73 42 E
Shu →, Kazakstan 28 E10 45 0N 67 44 E
Shuangcheng, China 35 B14 45 20N 126 15 E
Shuanggou, China 35 G9 34 2N 117 30 E
Shuangliao, China 35 C12 43 29N 123 30 E
Shuangshanzi, China 35 D10 40 20N 119 8 E
Shuangyang, China 35 C13 43 28N 125 40 E
Shuangyashan, China 33 B8 46 28N 131 5 E
Shuguri Falls, Tanzania 55 D4 8 33S 37 22 E
Shuiye, China 34 F8 36 7N 114 8 E
Shujalpur, India 42 H7 23 18N 76 46 E
Shukpa Kunzang, India 43 B8 34 22N 78 22 E
Shulan, China 35 B14 44 28N 127 0 E
Shule, China 32 C2 39 25N 76 3 E
Shumagin Is., U.S.A. 68 C4 55 7N 160 30W
Shumen, Bulgaria 21 C12 43 18N 26 55 E
Shumikha, Russia 26 D7 55 10N 63 15 E
Shuo Xian = Shuozhou, China 34 E7 39 20N 112 33 E
Shuozhou, China 34 E7 39 20N 112 33 E
Shūr →, Fārs, Iran 45 D7 28 30N 55 0 E
Shūr →, Kermān, Iran 45 D8 30 52N 57 37 E
Shūr →, Yazd, Iran 45 D7 31 45N 55 15 E
Shūr Āb, Iran 45 C6 34 23N 51 11 E
Shūr Gaz, Iran 45 D8 29 10N 59 20 E
Shūrāb, Iran 45 C8 33 43N 56 29 E
Shūrjestān, Iran 45 D7 31 24N 52 25 E
Shurugwi, Zimbabwe 55 F3 19 40S 30 0 E
Shūsf, Iran 45 D9 31 50N 60 5 E
Shūshtar, Iran 45 D6 32 0N 48 50 E
Shuswap L., Canada 72 C5 50 55N 119 3W
Shuyang, China 35 G10 34 10N 118 42 E
Shūzū, Iran 45 D7 29 52N 54 30 E
Shwebo, Burma 41 H19 22 30N 95 45 E
Shwegu, Burma 41 G20 24 15N 96 26 E
Shweli →, Burma 41 H20 23 45N 96 45 E
Shymkent, Kazakstan 26 E7 42 18N 69 36 E
Shyok, India 43 B8 34 13N 78 12 E
Shyok →, Pakistan 43 B6 35 13N 75 53 E
Si Chon, Thailand 39 H2 9 0N 99 54 E
Si Kiang = Xi Jiang →, China 33 D6 22 5N 113 20 E
Si-ngan = Xi'an, China 34 G5 34 15N 109 0 E
Si Prachan, Thailand 38 E3 14 37N 100 9 E
Si Racha, Thailand 38 F3 13 10N 100 48 E
Si Xian, China 35 H9 33 30N 117 50 E
Siahaf →, Pakistan 42 E3 29 3N 68 57 E
Siahan Range, Pakistan 40 F4 27 30N 64 40 E
Siaksriindrapura, Indonesia 36 D2 0 51N 102 0 E
Sialkot, Pakistan 42 C6 32 32N 74 30 E
Siam = Thailand ■, Asia 38 E4 16 0N 102 0 E
Sian = Xi'an, China 34 G5 34 15N 109 0 E
Siantan, Indonesia 36 D3 3 10N 106 15 E
Siāreh, Iran 45 D9 28 5N 60 14 E
Siargao, Phil. 37 C7 9 52N 126 3 E
Siari, Pakistan 43 B7 34 55N 76 40 E
Siasi, Phil. 37 C6 5 34N 120 50 E
Siau, Indonesia 37 D7 2 50N 125 25 E
Šiauliai, Lithuania 9 J20 55 56N 23 15 E
Sibâi, Gebel el, Egypt 44 E2 25 45N 34 10 E
Sibay, Russia 24 D10 52 42N 58 39 E
Sibayi, L., S. Africa 57 D5 27 20S 32 45 E
Šibenik, Croatia 20 C6 43 48N 15 54 E
Siberia, Russia 4 D13 60 0N 100 0 E
Siberut, Indonesia 36 E1 1 30S 99 0 E
Sibi, Pakistan 42 E2 29 30N 67 54 E
Sibil = Oksibil, Indonesia 37 E10 4 59S 140 35 E
Sibiti, Congo 52 E2 3 38S 13 19 E
Sibiu, Romania 17 F13 45 45N 24 9 E
Sibley, U.S.A. 80 D7 43 24N 95 45W
Sibolga, Indonesia 36 D1 1 42N 98 45 E
Sibsagar, India 41 F19 27 0N 94 36 E
Sibu, Malaysia 36 D4 2 18N 111 49 E
Sibuco, Phil. 37 C6 7 20N 122 10 E
Sibuguey B., Phil. 37 C6 7 50N 122 45 E
Sibut, C.A.R. 52 C3 5 46N 19 10 E
Sibutu, Phil. 37 D5 4 45N 119 30 E
Sibutu Passage, E. Indies 37 D6 4 50N 120 0 E
Sibuyan, Phil. 37 B6 12 25N 122 40 E
Sibuyan Sea, Phil. 37 B6 12 30N 122 20 E
Sicamous, Canada 72 C5 50 49N 119 0W
Siccus →, Australia 63 E2 31 26S 139 30 E
Sichuan □, China 32 C5 31 0N 104 0 E
Sicilia, Italy 20 F6 37 30N 14 30 E
Sicily = Sicilia, Italy 20 F6 37 30N 14 30 E
Sicuani, Peru 92 F4 14 21S 71 10W
Sidári, Greece 23 A3 39 47N 19 41 E
Siddhapur, India 42 H5 23 56N 72 25 E
Siddipet, India 40 K11 18 5N 78 51 E
Sidhauli, India 43 F9 27 17N 80 50 E
Sídheros, Ákra, Greece 23 D8 35 19N 26 19 E
Sidhi, India 43 G9 24 25N 81 53 E
Sidi-bel-Abbès, Algeria 50 A5 35 13N 0 39W
Sidlaw Hills, U.K. 12 E5 56 32N 3 2W
Sidley, Mt., Antarctica 5 D14 77 2S 126 2W
Sidmouth, U.K. 11 G4 50 40N 3 15W
Sidmouth, C., Australia 62 A3 13 25S 143 36 E
Sidney, Canada 72 D4 48 39N 123 24W
Sidney, Mont., U.S.A. 80 B2 47 43N 104 9W
Sidney, N.Y., U.S.A. 79 D9 42 19N 75 24W
Sidney, Nebr., U.S.A. 80 E3 41 8N 102 59W
Sidney, Ohio, U.S.A. 76 E3 40 17N 84 9W
Sidney Lanier L., U.S.A. 77 H4 34 10N 84 4W
Sidoarjo, Indonesia 37 G15 7 27S 112 43 E
Sidon = Saydā, Lebanon 47 B4 33 35N 35 25 E
Sidra, G. of = Surt, Khalīj, Libya 51 B9 31 40N 18 30 E
Siedlce, Poland 17 B12 52 10N 22 20 E
Sieg →, Germany 16 C4 50 46N 7 6 E
Siegen, Germany 16 C5 50 51N 8 0 E
Siem Pang, Cambodia 38 E6 14 7N 106 23 E
Siem Reap = Siemreab, Cambodia 38 F4 13 20N 103 52 E
Siemreab, Cambodia 38 F4 13 20N 103 52 E
Siena, Italy 20 C4 43 19N 11 21 E
Sieradz, Poland 17 C10 51 37N 18 41 E
Sierra Blanca, U.S.A. 83 L11 31 11N 105 22W
Sierra Blanca Peak, U.S.A. 83 K11 33 23N 105 49W
Sierra City, U.S.A. 84 F6 39 34N 120 38W
Sierra Colorada, Argentina 96 E3 40 35S 67 50W
Sierra Gorda, Chile 94 A2 22 50S 69 15W
Sierra Leone ■, W. Afr. 50 G3 9 0N 12 0W
Sierra Madre, Mexico 87 D6 16 0N 93 0W
Sierra Mojada, Mexico 86 B4 27 19N 103 42W
Sierra Nevada, U.S.A. 84 H8 37 30N 119 0W
Sierra Vista, U.S.A. 83 L8 31 33N 110 18W
Sierraville, U.S.A. 84 F6 39 36N 120 22W
Sífnos, Greece 21 F11 37 0N 24 45 E
Sifton, Canada 73 C8 51 21N 100 8W
Sifton Pass, Canada 72 B3 57 52N 126 15W
Sighetu-Marmaţiei, Romania 17 E12 47 57N 23 52 E
Sighişoara, Romania 17 E13 46 12N 24 50 E
Sigli, Indonesia 36 C1 5 25N 96 0 E
Siglufjörður, Iceland 8 C4 66 12N 18 55W
Signal, U.S.A. 85 L13 34 30N 113 38W
Signal Pk., U.S.A. 85 M12 33 20N 114 2W
Sigsig, Ecuador 92 D3 3 0S 78 50W
Sigüenza, Spain 19 B4 41 3N 2 40W
Siguiri, Guinea 50 F4 11 31N 9 10W
Sigulda, Latvia 9 H21 57 10N 24 55 E
Sihanoukville = Kampong Saom, Cambodia 39 G4 10 38N 103 30 E
Sihora, India 43 H9 23 29N 80 6 E
Siikajoki →, Finland 8 D21 64 50N 24 43 E
Siilinjärvi, Finland 8 E22 63 4N 27 39 E
Sijarira Ra., Zimbabwe 55 F2 17 36S 27 45 E
Sika, India 42 H3 22 26N 69 47 E
Sikao, Thailand 39 J2 7 34N 99 21 E
Sikar, India 42 F6 27 33N 75 10 E
Sikasso, Mali 50 F4 11 18N 5 35W
Sikeston, U.S.A. 81 G10 36 53N 89 35W
Sikhote Alin, Khrebet, Russia 27 E14 45 0N 136 0 E
Sikhote Alin Ra. = Sikhote Alin, Khrebet, Russia 27 E14 45 0N 136 0 E

Solfonn

Sikinos, *Greece* **21 F11** 36 40N 25 8 E
Sikkani Chief →, *Canada* **72 B4** 57 47N 122 15W
Sikkim □, *India* **41 F16** 27 50N 88 30 E
Sikotu-Ko, *Japan* **30 C10** 42 45N 141 25 E
Sil →, *Spain* **19 A2** 42 27N 7 43W
Silacayoapan, *Mexico* **87 D5** 17 30N 98 9W
Silawad, *India* **42 J6** 21 54N 74 54 E
Silchar, *India* **41 G18** 24 49N 92 48 E
Siler City, *U.S.A.* **77 H6** 35 44N 79 28W
Silesia = Śląsk, *Poland* **16 C9** 51 0N 16 30 E
Silgarhi Doti, *Nepal* **43 E9** 29 15N 81 0 E
Silghat, *India* **41 F18** 26 35N 93 0 E
Silifke, *Turkey* **25 G5** 36 22N 33 58 E
Siliguri = Shiliguri, *India* **41 F16** 26 45N 88 25 E
Siling Co, *China* **32 C3** 31 50N 89 20 E
Silistra, *Bulgaria* **21 B12** 44 6N 27 19 E
Silivri, *Turkey* **21 D13** 41 4N 28 14 E
Siljan, *Sweden* **9 F16** 60 55N 14 45 E
Silkeborg, *Denmark* **9 H13** 56 10N 9 32 E
Silkwood, *Australia* **62 B4** 17 45S 146 2 E
Sillajhuay, Cordillera, *Chile* **92 G5** 19 46S 68 40W
Sillamäe, *Estonia* **9 G22** 59 24N 27 45 E
Silloth, *U.K.* **10 C4** 54 52N 3 23W
Siloam Springs, *U.S.A.* **81 G7** 36 11N 94 32W
Silsbee, *U.S.A.* **81 K7** 30 21N 94 11W
Šilute, *Lithuania* **9 J19** 55 21N 21 33 E
Silva Porto = Kuito, *Angola* **53 G3** 12 22S 16 55 E
Silvani, *India* **43 H8** 23 18N 78 25 E
Silver City, *U.S.A.* **83 K9** 32 46N 108 17W
Silver Cr. →, *U.S.A.* **82 E4** 43 16N 119 13W
Silver Creek, *U.S.A.* **78 D5** 42 33N 79 10W
Silver L., *U.S.A.* **84 G6** 38 39N 120 6W
Silver Lake, *Calif., U.S.A.* **85 K10** 35 21N 116 7W
Silver Lake, *Oreg., U.S.A.* **82 E3** 43 8N 121 3W
Silver Streams, *S. Africa* **56 D3** 28 20S 23 33 E
Silverton, *Colo., U.S.A.* **83 H10** 37 49N 107 40W
Silverton, *Tex., U.S.A.* **81 H4** 34 28N 101 19W
Silvies →, *U.S.A.* **82 E4** 43 34N 119 2W
Simaltala, *India* **43 G12** 24 43N 86 33 E
Simanggang = Bandar Sri Aman, *Malaysia* **36 D4** 1 15N 111 32 E
Simard, L., *Canada* **70 C4** 47 40N 78 40W
Simav, *Turkey* **21 E13** 39 4N 28 58 E
Simba, *Tanzania* **54 C4** 2 10S 37 36 E
Simbirsk, *Russia* **24 D8** 54 20N 48 25 E
Simbo, *Tanzania* **54 C2** 4 51S 29 41 E
Simcoe, *Canada* **78 D4** 42 50N 80 20W
Simcoe, L., *Canada* **78 B5** 44 25N 79 20W
Simdega, *India* **43 H11** 22 37N 84 31 E
Simeria, *Romania* **17 F12** 45 51N 23 1 E
Simeulue, *Indonesia* **36 D1** 2 45N 95 45 E
Simferopol, *Ukraine* **25 F5** 44 55N 34 3 E
Sími, *Greece* **21 F12** 36 35N 27 50 E
Simi Valley, *U.S.A.* **85 L8** 34 16N 118 47W
Simikot, *Nepal* **43 E9** 30 0N 81 50 E
Simla, *India* **42 D7** 31 2N 77 9 E
Simmie, *Canada* **73 D7** 49 56N 108 6W
Simmler, *U.S.A.* **85 K7** 35 21N 119 59W
Simojoki →, *Finland* **8 D21** 65 35N 25 1 E
Simojovel, *Mexico* **87 D6** 17 12N 92 38W
Simonette →, *Canada* **72 B5** 55 9N 118 15W
Simonstown, *S. Africa* **56 E2** 34 14S 18 26 E
Simplonpass, *Switz.* **18 C8** 46 15N 8 3 E
Simpson Desert, *Australia* **62 D2** 25 0S 137 0 E
Simpson Pen., *Canada* **69 B11** 68 34N 88 45W
Simpungdong, *N. Korea* **35 D15** 40 56N 129 29 E
Simrishamn, *Sweden* **9 J16** 55 33N 14 22 E
Simsbury, *U.S.A.* **79 E12** 41 53N 72 48W
Simushir, Ostrov, *Russia* **27 E16** 46 50N 152 30 E
Sin Cowe I., *S. China Sea* **36 C4** 9 53N 114 19 E
Sinabang, *Indonesia* **36 D1** 2 30N 96 24 E
Sinadogo, *Somali Rep.* **46 F4** 5 50N 47 0 E
Sinai = Es Sînâ', *Egypt* **47 F3** 29 0N 34 0 E
Sinai, Mt. = Mûsa, Gebel, *Egypt* **44 D2** 28 33N 33 59 E
Sinai Peninsula, *Egypt* **47 F3** 29 30N 34 0 E
Sinaloa □, *Mexico* **86 C3** 25 0N 107 30W
Sinaloa de Leyva, *Mexico* **86 B3** 25 50N 108 20W
Sinarádhes, *Greece* **23 A3** 39 34N 19 51 E
Sincelejo, *Colombia* **92 B3** 9 18N 75 24W
Sinch'ang, *N. Korea* **35 D15** 40 7N 128 28 E
Sinchang-ni, *N. Korea* **35 E14** 39 24N 126 8 E
Sinclair, *U.S.A.* **82 F10** 41 47N 107 7W
Sinclair Mills, *Canada* **72 C4** 54 5N 121 40W
Sinclair's B., *U.K.* **12 C5** 58 31N 3 5W
Sinclairville, *U.S.A.* **78 D5** 42 16N 79 16W
Sincorá, Serra do, *Brazil* **93 F10** 13 30S 41 0W
Sind, *Pakistan* **42 G3** 26 0N 68 30 E
Sind □, *Pakistan* **42 G3** 26 0N 69 0 E
Sind →, *India* **43 F8** 26 26N 79 13 E
Sind →, *Jammu & Kashmir, India* **43 B6** 34 18N 74 45 E
Sind Sagar Doab, *Pakistan* **42 D4** 32 0N 71 30 E
Sindangan, *Phil.* **37 C6** 8 10N 123 5 E
Sindangbarang, *Indonesia* **37 G12** 7 27S 107 1 E
Sinde, *Zambia* **55 F2** 17 28S 25 51 E
Sindri, *India* **43 H12** 23 45N 86 42 E
Sines, *Portugal* **19 D1** 37 56N 8 51W
Sines, C. de, *Portugal* **19 D1** 37 58N 8 53W
Sineu, *Spain* **22 B10** 39 38N 3 1 E
Sing Buri, *Thailand* **38 E3** 14 53N 100 25 E
Singa, *Sudan* **51 F12** 13 10N 33 57 E
Singapore ■, *Asia* **39 M4** 1 17N 103 51 E
Singapore, Straits of, *Asia* **39 M5** 1 15N 104 0 E
Singaraja, *Indonesia* **36 F5** 8 6S 115 10 E
Singida, *Tanzania* **54 C3** 4 49S 34 48 E
Singida □, *Tanzania* **54 D3** 6 0S 34 30 E
Singitikós Kólpos, *Greece* **21 D11** 40 6N 24 0 E
Singkaling Hkamti, *Burma* **41 G19** 26 0N 95 39 E
Singkang, *Indonesia* **37 E6** 4 8S 120 1 E
Singkawang, *Indonesia* **36 D3** 1 0N 108 57 E
Singkep, *Indonesia* **36 E2** 0 30S 104 25 E
Singleton, *Australia* **63 E5** 32 33S 151 0 E
Singleton, Mt., *N. Terr., Australia* **60 D5** 22 0S 130 46 E
Singleton, Mt., *W. Austral., Australia* **61 E2** 29 27S 117 15 E
Singoli, *India* **42 G6** 25 0N 75 22 E
Singora = Songkhla, *Thailand* **39 J3** 7 13N 100 37 E
Singosan, *N. Korea* **35 E14** 38 52N 127 25 E
Sinhung, *N. Korea* **35 D14** 40 11N 127 34 E
Sînî □, *Egypt* **47 F3** 30 0N 34 0 E
Sinjai, *Indonesia* **37 F6** 5 7S 120 20 E
Sinjār, *Iraq* **44 B4** 36 19N 41 52 E
Sinkat, *Sudan* **51 E13** 18 55N 36 49 E
Sinkiang Uighur = Xinjiang Uygur Zizhiqu □, *China* **32 C3** 42 0N 86 0 E
Sinmak, *N. Korea* **35 E14** 38 25N 126 14 E
Sinnamary, *Fr. Guiana* **93 B8** 5 25N 53 0W
Sinni →, *Italy* **20 D7** 40 8N 16 41 E
Sinop, *Turkey* **25 F6** 42 1N 35 11 E
Sinor, *India* **42 J5** 21 55N 73 20 E
Sinp'o, *N. Korea* **35 E15** 40 0N 128 13 E
Sinsk, *Russia* **27 C13** 61 8N 126 48 E
Sintang, *Indonesia* **36 D4** 0 5N 111 35 E
Sinton, *U.S.A.* **81 L6** 28 2N 97 31W
Sintra, *Portugal* **19 C1** 38 47N 9 25W
Sinŭiju, *N. Korea* **35 D13** 40 5N 124 24 E
Siocon, *Phil.* **37 C6** 7 40N 122 10 E
Siófok, *Hungary* **17 E10** 46 54N 18 3 E
Sioma, *Zambia* **56 B3** 16 25S 23 28 E
Sion, *Switz.* **18 C7** 46 14N 7 20 E
Sion Mills, *U.K.* **13 B4** 54 48N 7 29W
Sioux City, *U.S.A.* **80 D6** 42 30N 96 24W
Sioux Falls, *U.S.A.* **80 D6** 43 33N 96 44W
Sioux Lookout, *Canada* **70 B1** 50 10N 91 50W
Sioux Narrows, *Canada* **73 D10** 49 25N 94 10W
Siping, *China* **35 C13** 43 8N 124 21 E
Sipiwesk L., *Canada* **73 B9** 55 5N 97 35W
Sipra →, *India* **42 H6** 23 55N 75 28 E
Sipura, *Indonesia* **36 E1** 2 18S 99 40 E
Siquia →, *Nic.* **88 D3** 12 10N 84 20W
Siquijor, *Phil.* **37 C6** 9 12N 123 35 E
Siquirres, *Costa Rica* **88 D3** 10 6N 83 30W
Şir Banī Yās, *U.A.E.* **45 E7** 24 19N 52 37 E
Sir Edward Pellew Group, *Australia* **62 B2** 15 40S 137 10 E
Sir Graham Moore Is., *Australia* **60 B4** 13 53S 126 34 E
Sir James MacBrien, Mt., *Canada* **68 B7** 62 8N 127 40W
Sira →, *Norway* **9 G12** 58 23N 6 34 E
Siracusa, *Italy* **20 F6** 37 4N 15 17 E
Sirajganj, *Bangla.* **43 G13** 24 25N 89 47 E
Sirathu, *India* **43 G9** 25 39N 81 19 E
Sīrdān, *Iran* **45 B6** 36 39N 49 12 E
Sirdaryo = Syrdarya →, *Kazakstan* **26 E7** 46 3N 61 0 E
Siren, *U.S.A.* **80 C8** 45 47N 92 24W
Sirer, *Spain* **22 C7** 38 56N 1 22 E
Siret →, *Romania* **17 F14** 45 24N 28 1 E
Sirghāyā, *Syria* **47 B5** 33 51N 36 8 E
Sirmaur, *India* **43 G9** 24 51N 81 23 E
Sirohi, *India* **42 G5** 24 52N 72 53 E
Sironj, *India* **42 G7** 24 5N 77 39 E
Síros, *Greece* **21 F11** 37 28N 24 57 E
Sirretta Pk., *U.S.A.* **85 K8** 35 56N 118 19W
Sirrī, *Iran* **45 E7** 25 55N 54 32 E
Sirsa, *India* **42 E6** 29 33N 75 4 E
Sirsa →, *India* **43 F8** 26 51N 79 4 E
Sisak, *Croatia* **16 F9** 45 30N 16 21 E
Sisaket, *Thailand* **38 E5** 15 8N 104 23 E
Sishen, *S. Africa* **56 D3** 27 47S 22 59 E
Sishui, *Henan, China* **34 G7** 34 48N 113 15 E
Sishui, *Shandong, China* **35 G9** 35 42N 117 18 E
Sisipuk L., *Canada* **73 B8** 55 45N 101 50W
Sisophon, *Cambodia* **38 F4** 13 38N 102 59 E
Sisseton, *U.S.A.* **80 C6** 45 40N 97 3W
Sīstān, *Asia* **45 D9** 30 50N 61 0 E
Sīstān, Daryācheh-ye, *Iran* **40 D2** 31 0N 61 0 E
Sīstān va Balūchestān □, *Iran* **45 E9** 27 0N 62 0 E
Sisters, *U.S.A.* **82 D3** 44 18N 121 33W
Siswa Bazar, *India* **43 F10** 27 9N 83 46 E
Sitamarhi, *India* **43 F11** 26 37N 85 30 E
Sitapur, *India* **43 F9** 27 38N 80 45 E
Siteki, *Swaziland* **57 D5** 26 32S 31 58 E
Sitges, *Spain* **19 B6** 41 17N 1 47 E
Sitia, *Greece* **23 D8** 35 13N 26 6 E
Sitka, *U.S.A.* **72 B1** 57 3N 135 20W
Sitoti, *Botswana* **56 C3** 23 15S 23 40 E
Sittang Myit →, *Burma* **41 L20** 17 20N 96 45 E
Sittard, *Neths.* **15 C5** 51 0N 5 52 E
Sittingbourne, *U.K.* **11 F8** 51 21N 0 45 E
Sittwe, *Burma* **41 J18** 20 18N 92 45 E
Situbondo, *Indonesia* **37 G16** 7 42S 114 0 E
Siuna, *Nic.* **88 D3** 13 37N 84 45W
Siuri, *India* **43 H12** 23 50N 87 34 E
Sīvand, *Iran* **45 D7** 30 5N 52 55 E
Sivas, *Turkey* **25 G6** 39 43N 36 58 E
Siverek, *Turkey* **44 B3** 37 50N 39 19 E
Sivomaskinskiy, *Russia* **24 A11** 66 40N 62 35 E
Sivrihisar, *Turkey* **25 G5** 39 30N 31 35 E
Sîwa, *Egypt* **51 C11** 29 11N 25 31 E
Sîwa Oasis, *Egypt* **48 D6** 29 10N 25 30 E
Siwalik Range, *Nepal* **43 F10** 28 0N 83 0 E
Siwan, *India* **43 F11** 26 13N 84 21 E
Siwana, *India* **42 G5** 25 38N 72 25 E
Sixmilebridge, *Ireland* **13 D3** 52 44N 8 46W
Sixth Cataract, *Sudan* **51 E12** 16 20N 32 42 E
Siziwang Qi, *China* **34 D6** 41 25N 111 40 E
Sjælland, *Denmark* **9 J14** 55 30N 11 30 E
Sjumen = Shumen, *Bulgaria* **21 C12** 43 18N 26 55 E
Skadarsko Jezero, *Montenegro, Yug.* **21 C8** 42 10N 19 20 E
Skaftafell, *Iceland* **8 D5** 64 1N 17 0W
Skagafjörður, *Iceland* **8 D4** 65 54N 19 35W
Skagastølstindane, *Norway* **9 F12** 61 28N 7 52 E
Skagaströnd, *Iceland* **8 D3** 65 50N 20 19W
Skagen, *Denmark* **9 H14** 57 43N 10 35 E
Skagerrak, *Denmark* **9 H13** 57 30N 9 0 E
Skagit →, *U.S.A.* **84 B4** 48 23N 122 22W
Skagway, *U.S.A.* **68 C6** 59 28N 135 19W
Skala-Podilska, *Ukraine* **17 D14** 48 50N 26 15 E
Skala Podolskaya = Skala-Podilska, *Ukraine* **17 D14** 48 50N 26 15 E
Skalat, *Ukraine* **17 D13** 49 23N 25 55 E
Skåne, *Sweden* **9 J15** 55 59N 13 30 E
Skaneateles, *U.S.A.* **79 D8** 42 57N 76 26W
Skaneateles L., *U.S.A.* **79 D8** 42 51N 76 22W
Skara, *Sweden* **9 G15** 58 25N 13 30 E
Skardu, *Pakistan* **43 B6** 35 20N 75 44 E
Skarżysko-Kamienna, *Poland* **17 C11** 51 7N 20 52 E
Skeena →, *Canada* **72 C2** 54 9N 130 5W
Skeena Mts., *Canada* **72 B3** 56 40N 128 30W
Skegness, *U.K.* **10 D8** 53 9N 0 20 E
Skeldon, *Guyana* **92 B7** 5 55N 57 20W
Skellefte älv →, *Sweden* **8 D19** 64 45N 21 10 E
Skellefteå, *Sweden* **8 D19** 64 45N 20 50 E
Skelleftehamn, *Sweden* **8 D19** 64 40N 21 9 E
Skerries, The, *U.K.* **10 D3** 53 25N 4 36W
Ski, *Norway* **9 G14** 59 43N 10 52 E
Skíathos, *Greece* **21 E10** 39 12N 23 30 E
Skibbereen, *Ireland* **13 E2** 51 33N 9 16W
Skiddaw, *U.K.* **10 C4** 54 39N 3 9W
Skidegate, *Canada* **72 C2** 53 15N 132 1W
Skien, *Norway* **9 G13** 59 12N 9 35 E
Skierniewice, *Poland* **17 C11** 51 58N 20 10 E
Skikda, *Algeria* **50 A7** 36 50N 6 58 E
Skilloura, *Cyprus* **23 D12** 35 14N 33 10 E
Skipton, *U.K.* **10 D5** 53 58N 2 3W
Skirmish Pt., *Australia* **62 A1** 11 59S 134 17 E
Skíros, *Greece* **21 E11** 38 55N 24 34 E
Skive, *Denmark* **9 H13** 56 33N 9 2 E
Skjálfandafljót →, *Iceland* **8 D5** 65 59N 17 25W
Skjálfandi, *Iceland* **8 C5** 66 5N 17 30W
Skoghall, *Sweden* **9 G15** 59 20N 13 30 E
Skole, *Ukraine* **17 D12** 49 3N 23 30 E
Skópelos, *Greece* **21 E10** 39 9N 23 47 E
Skopí, *Greece* **23 D8** 35 11N 26 2 E
Skopje, *Macedonia* **21 C9** 42 1N 21 26 E
Skövde, *Sweden* **9 G15** 58 24N 13 50 E
Skovorodino, *Russia* **27 D13** 54 0N 124 0 E
Skowhegan, *U.S.A.* **77 C11** 44 46N 69 43W
Skull, *Ireland* **13 E2** 51 32N 9 34W
Skunk →, *U.S.A.* **80 E9** 40 42N 91 7W
Skuodas, *Lithuania* **9 H19** 56 16N 21 33 E
Skvyra, *Ukraine* **17 D15** 49 44N 29 40 E
Skye, *U.K.* **12 D2** 57 15N 6 10W
Skykomish, *U.S.A.* **82 C3** 47 42N 121 22W
Skyros = Skíros, *Greece* **21 E11** 38 55N 24 34 E
Slættaratindur, *Færoe Is.* **8 E9** 62 18N 7 1W
Slagelse, *Denmark* **9 J14** 55 23N 11 19 E
Slamet, *Indonesia* **37 G13** 7 16S 109 8 E
Slaney →, *Ireland* **13 D5** 52 26N 6 33W
Śląsk, *Poland* **16 C9** 51 0N 16 30 E
Slate Is., *Canada* **70 C2** 48 40N 87 0W
Slatina, *Romania* **17 F13** 44 28N 24 22 E
Slatington, *U.S.A.* **79 F9** 40 45N 75 37W
Slaton, *U.S.A.* **81 J4** 33 26N 101 39W
Slave →, *Canada* **72 A6** 61 18N 113 39W
Slave Coast, *W. Afr.* **50 G6** 6 0N 2 30 E
Slave Lake, *Canada* **72 B6** 55 17N 114 43W
Slave Pt., *Canada* **72 A5** 61 11N 115 56W
Slavgorod, *Russia* **26 D8** 53 1N 78 37 E
Slavonski Brod, *Croatia* **21 B8** 45 11N 18 1 E
Slavuta, *Ukraine* **17 C14** 50 15N 27 2 E
Slavyanka, *Russia* **30 C5** 42 53N 131 21 E
Slavyansk = Slovyansk, *Ukraine* **25 E6** 48 55N 37 36 E
Slawharad, *Belarus* **17 B16** 53 27N 31 0 E
Sleaford, *U.K.* **10 D7** 53 0N 0 24W
Sleaford B., *Australia* **63 E2** 34 55S 135 45 E
Sleat, Sd. of, *U.K.* **12 D3** 57 5N 5 47W
Sleeper Is., *Canada* **69 C11** 58 30N 81 0W
Sleepy Eye, *U.S.A.* **80 C7** 44 18N 94 43W
Slemon L., *Canada* **72 A5** 63 13N 116 4W
Slide Mt., *U.S.A.* **79 E10** 42 0N 74 25W
Slidell, *U.S.A.* **81 K10** 30 17N 89 47W
Sliema, *Malta* **23 D2** 35 54N 14 30 E
Slieve Aughty, *Ireland* **13 C3** 53 4N 8 30W
Slieve Bloom, *Ireland* **13 C4** 53 4N 7 40W
Slieve Donard, *U.K.* **13 B6** 54 11N 5 55W
Slieve Gamph, *Ireland* **13 B3** 54 6N 9 0W
Slieve Gullion, *U.K.* **13 B5** 54 7N 6 26W
Slieve Mish, *Ireland* **13 D2** 52 12N 9 50W
Slievenamon, *Ireland* **13 D4** 52 25N 7 34W
Sligeach = Sligo, *Ireland* **13 B3** 54 16N 8 28W
Sligo, *Ireland* **13 B3** 54 16N 8 28W
Sligo, *U.S.A.* **78 E5** 41 6N 79 29W
Sligo □, *Ireland* **13 B3** 54 8N 8 42W
Sligo B., *Ireland* **13 B3** 54 18N 8 40W
Slippery Rock, *U.S.A.* **78 E4** 41 3N 80 3W
Slite, *Sweden* **9 H18** 57 42N 18 48 E
Sliven, *Bulgaria* **21 C12** 42 42N 26 19 E
Sloan, *U.S.A.* **85 K11** 35 57N 115 13W
Sloansville, *U.S.A.* **79 D10** 42 45N 74 22W
Slobodskoy, *Russia* **24 C9** 58 40N 50 6 E
Slobozia, *Romania* **17 F14** 44 34N 27 23 E
Slocan, *Canada* **72 D5** 49 48N 117 28W
Slonim, *Belarus* **17 B13** 53 4N 25 19 E
Slough, *U.K.* **11 F7** 51 30N 0 36W
Slough □, *U.K.* **11 F7** 51 30N 0 36W
Sloughhouse, *U.S.A.* **84 G5** 38 26N 121 12W
Slovak Rep. ■, *Europe* **17 D10** 48 30N 20 0 E
Slovakia = Slovak Rep. ■, *Europe* **17 D10** 48 30N 20 0 E
Slovakian Ore Mts. = Slovenské Rudohorie, *Slovak Rep.* **17 D10** 48 45N 20 0 E
Slovenia ■, *Europe* **16 F8** 45 58N 14 30 E
Slovenija = Slovenia ■, *Europe* **16 F8** 45 58N 14 30 E
Slovenské Rudohorie, *Slovak Rep.* **17 D10** 48 45N 20 0 E
Slovyansk, *Ukraine* **25 E6** 48 55N 37 36 E
Sluch →, *Ukraine* **17 C14** 51 37N 26 38 E
Sluis, *Neths.* **15 C3** 51 18N 3 23 E
Słupsk, *Poland* **17 A9** 54 30N 17 3 E
Slurry, *S. Africa* **56 D4** 25 49S 25 42 E
Slutsk, *Belarus* **17 B14** 53 2N 27 31 E
Slyne Hd., *Ireland* **13 C1** 53 25N 10 10W
Slyudyanka, *Russia* **27 D11** 51 40N 103 40 E
Småland, *Sweden* **9 H16** 57 15N 15 25 E
Smalltree L., *Canada* **73 A8** 61 0N 105 0W
Smallwood Res., *Canada* **71 B7** 54 0N 64 0W
Smara, *Morocco* **50 B4** 32 9N 8 16W
Smarhon, *Belarus* **17 A14** 54 20N 26 24 E
Smartt Syndicate Dam, *S. Africa* **56 E3** 30 45S 23 10 E
Smartville, *U.S.A.* **84 F5** 39 13N 121 18W
Smeaton, *Canada* **73 C8** 53 30N 104 49W
Smederevo, *Serbia, Yug.* **21 B9** 44 40N 20 57 E
Smerwick Harbour, *Ireland* **13 D1** 52 12N 10 23W
Smethport, *U.S.A.* **78 E6** 41 49N 78 27W
Smidovich, *Russia* **27 E14** 48 36N 133 49 E
Smith, *Canada* **72 B6** 55 10N 114 0W
Smith Center, *U.S.A.* **80 F5** 39 47N 98 47W
Smith Sund, *Greenland* **4 B4** 78 30N 74 0W
Smithburne →, *Australia* **62 B3** 17 3S 140 57 E
Smithers, *Canada* **72 C3** 54 45N 127 10W
Smithfield, *S. Africa* **57 E4** 30 9S 26 30 E
Smithfield, *N.C., U.S.A.* **77 H6** 35 31N 78 21W
Smithfield, *Utah, U.S.A.* **82 F8** 41 50N 111 50W
Smiths Falls, *Canada* **79 B9** 44 55N 76 0W
Smithton, *Australia* **62 G4** 40 53S 145 6 E
Smithville, *Canada* **78 C5** 43 6N 79 33W
Smithville, *U.S.A.* **81 K6** 30 1N 97 10W
Smoky →, *Canada* **72 B5** 56 10N 117 21W
Smoky Bay, *Australia* **63 E1** 32 22S 134 13 E
Smoky Hill →, *U.S.A.* **80 F6** 39 4N 96 48W
Smoky Hills, *U.S.A.* **80 F5** 39 15N 99 30W
Smoky Lake, *Canada* **72 C6** 54 10N 112 30W
Smøla, *Norway* **8 E13** 63 23N 8 3 E
Smolensk, *Russia* **24 D5** 54 45N 32 5 E
Smolikas, Óros, *Greece* **21 D9** 40 9N 20 58 E
Smolyan, *Bulgaria* **21 D11** 41 36N 24 38 E
Smooth Rock Falls, *Canada* **70 C3** 49 17N 81 37W
Smoothstone L., *Canada* **73 C7** 54 40N 106 50W
Smorgon = Smarhon, *Belarus* **17 A14** 54 20N 26 24 E
Smyrna = İzmir, *Turkey* **21 E12** 38 25N 27 8 E
Smyrna, *U.S.A.* **76 F8** 39 18N 75 36W
Snæfell, *Iceland* **8 D6** 64 48N 15 34W
Snaefell, *U.K.* **10 C3** 54 16N 4 27W
Snæfellsjökull, *Iceland* **8 D2** 64 49N 23 46W
Snake →, *U.S.A.* **82 C4** 46 12N 119 2W
Snake I., *Australia* **63 F4** 38 47S 146 33 E
Snake Range, *U.S.A.* **82 G6** 39 0N 114 20W
Snake River Plain, *U.S.A.* **82 E7** 42 50N 114 0W
Snåsavatnet, *Norway* **8 D14** 64 12N 12 0 E
Sneek, *Neths.* **15 A5** 53 2N 5 40 E
Sneeuberge, *S. Africa* **56 E3** 31 46S 24 20 E
Snelling, *U.S.A.* **84 H6** 37 31N 120 26W
Sněžka, *Europe* **16 C8** 50 41N 15 50 E
Snizort, L., *U.K.* **12 D2** 57 33N 6 28W
Snøhetta, *Norway* **9 E13** 62 19N 9 16 E
Snohomish, *U.S.A.* **84 C4** 47 55N 122 6W
Snoul, *Cambodia* **39 F6** 12 4N 106 26 E
Snow Hill, *U.S.A.* **76 F8** 38 11N 75 24W
Snow Lake, *Canada* **73 C8** 54 52N 100 3W
Snow Mt., *Calif., U.S.A.* **84 F4** 39 23N 122 45W
Snow Mt., *Maine, U.S.A.* **79 A14** 45 18N 70 48W
Snow Shoe, *U.S.A.* **78 E7** 41 2N 77 57W
Snowbird L., *Canada* **73 A8** 60 45N 103 0W
Snowdon, *U.K.* **10 D3** 53 4N 4 5W
Snowdrift →, *Canada* **73 A6** 62 24N 110 44W
Snowflake, *U.S.A.* **83 J8** 34 30N 110 5W
Snowshoe Pk., *U.S.A.* **82 B6** 48 13N 115 41W
Snowtown, *Australia* **63 E2** 33 46S 138 14 E
Snowville, *U.S.A.* **82 F7** 41 58N 112 43W
Snowy →, *Australia* **63 F4** 37 46S 148 30 E
Snowy Mt., *U.S.A.* **79 C10** 43 42N 74 23W
Snowy Mts., *Australia* **63 F4** 36 30S 148 20 E
Snug Corner, *Bahamas* **89 B5** 22 33N 73 52W
Snyatyn, *Ukraine* **17 D13** 48 27N 25 38 E
Snyder, *Okla., U.S.A.* **81 H5** 34 40N 98 57W
Snyder, *Tex., U.S.A.* **81 J4** 32 44N 100 55W
Soahanina, *Madag.* **57 B7** 18 42S 44 13 E
Soalala, *Madag.* **57 B8** 16 6S 45 20 E
Soan →, *Pakistan* **42 C4** 33 1N 71 44 E
Soanierana-Ivongo, *Madag.* **57 B8** 16 55S 49 35 E
Sobat, Nahr →, *Sudan* **51 G12** 9 22N 31 33 E
Sobhapur, *India* **42 H8** 22 47N 78 17 E
Sobradinho, Represa de, *Brazil* **93 E10** 9 30S 42 0 E
Sobral, *Brazil* **93 D10** 3 50S 40 20W
Soc Trang, *Vietnam* **39 H5** 9 37N 105 50 E
Socastee, *U.S.A.* **77 J6** 33 41N 79 1W
Soch'e = Shache, *China* **32 C2** 38 20N 77 10 E
Sochi, *Russia* **25 F6** 43 35N 39 40 E
Société, Is. de la, *Pac. Oc.* **65 J12** 17 0S 151 0W
Society Is. = Société, Is. de la, *Pac. Oc.* **65 J12** 17 0S 151 0W
Socompa, Portezuelo de, *Chile* **94 A2** 24 27S 68 18W
Socorro, *N. Mex., U.S.A.* **83 J10** 34 4N 106 54W
Socorro, *Tex., U.S.A.* **83 L10** 31 39N 106 18W
Socorro, I., *Mexico* **86 D2** 18 45N 110 58W
Socotra, *Ind. Oc.* **46 E5** 12 30N 54 0 E
Soda L., *U.S.A.* **83 J5** 35 10N 116 4W
Soda Plains, *India* **43 B8** 35 30N 79 0 E
Soda Springs, *U.S.A.* **82 E8** 42 39N 111 36W
Sodankylä, *Finland* **8 C22** 67 29N 26 40 E
Soddy-Daisy, *U.S.A.* **77 H3** 35 17N 85 10W
Söderhamn, *Sweden* **9 F17** 61 18N 17 10 E
Söderköping, *Sweden* **9 G17** 58 31N 16 20 E
Södermanland, *Sweden* **9 G17** 58 56N 16 55 E
Södertälje, *Sweden* **9 G17** 59 12N 17 39 E
Sodiri, *Sudan* **51 F11** 14 27N 29 0 E
Sodus, *U.S.A.* **78 C7** 43 14N 77 4W
Soekmekaar, *S. Africa* **57 C4** 23 30S 29 55 E
Soest, *Neths.* **15 B5** 52 9N 5 19 E
Sofia = Sofiya, *Bulgaria* **21 C10** 42 45N 23 20 E
Sofia →, *Madag.* **57 B8** 15 27S 47 23 E
Sofiya, *Bulgaria* **21 C10** 42 45N 23 20 E
Sōfu-Gan, *Japan* **31 K10** 29 49N 140 21 E
Sogamoso, *Colombia* **92 B4** 5 43N 72 56W
Sogār, *Iran* **45 E8** 25 53N 58 6 E
Sogndalsfjøra, *Norway* **9 F12** 61 14N 7 5 E
Søgne, *Norway* **9 G12** 58 5N 7 48 E
Sognefjorden, *Norway* **9 F11** 61 10N 5 50 E
Sŏgwipo, *S. Korea* **35 H14** 33 13N 126 34 E
Soh, *Iran* **45 C6** 33 26N 51 27 E
Sohâg, *Egypt* **51 C12** 26 33N 31 43 E
Sohagpur, *India* **42 H8** 22 42N 78 12 E
Sŏhori, *N. Korea* **35 D15** 40 7N 128 23 E
Soignies, *Belgium* **15 D4** 50 35N 4 5 E
Soissons, *France* **18 B5** 49 25N 3 19 E
Sōja, *Japan* **31 G6** 34 40N 133 45 E
Sojat, *India* **42 G5** 25 55N 73 45 E
Sokal, *Ukraine* **17 C13** 50 31N 24 15 E
Söke, *Turkey* **21 F12** 37 48N 27 28 E
Sokelo, *Dem. Rep. of the Congo* **55 D1** 9 55S 24 36 E
Sokhumi, *Georgia* **25 F7** 43 0N 41 0 E
Sokodé, *Togo* **50 G6** 9 0N 1 11 E
Sokol, *Russia* **24 C7** 59 30N 40 5 E
Sokółka, *Poland* **17 B12** 53 25N 23 30 E
Sokołów Podlaski, *Poland* **17 B12** 52 25N 22 15 E
Sokoto, *Nigeria* **50 F7** 13 2N 5 16 E
Sol Iletsk, *Russia* **24 D10** 51 10N 55 0 E
Solai, *Kenya* **54 B4** 0 2N 36 12 E
Solan, *India* **42 D7** 30 55N 77 7 E
Solano, *Phil.* **37 A6** 16 31N 121 15 E
Solapur, *India* **40 L9** 17 43N 75 56 E
Soldotna, *U.S.A.* **68 B4** 60 29N 151 3W
Soléa □, *Cyprus* **23 D12** 35 5N 33 4 E
Soledad, *Colombia* **92 A4** 10 55N 74 46W
Soledad, *U.S.A.* **84 J5** 36 26N 121 20W
Soledad, *Venezuela* **92 B6** 8 10N 63 34W
Solent, The, *U.K.* **11 G6** 50 45N 1 25W
Solfonn, *Norway* **9 F12** 60 2N 6 57 E

Sursar

Staten, I. = Estados, I. de Los, *Argentina* **96 G4** 54 40S 64 30W
Staten I., *U.S.A.* **79 F10** 40 35N 74 9W
Statesboro, *U.S.A.* **77 J5** 32 27N 81 47W
Statesville, *U.S.A.* **77 H5** 35 47N 80 53W
Stauffer, *U.S.A.* **85 L7** 34 45N 119 3W
Staunton, *Ill., U.S.A.* **80 F10** 39 1N 89 47W
Staunton, *Va., U.S.A.* **76 F6** 38 9N 79 4W
Stavanger, *Norway* **9 G11** 58 57N 5 40 E
Staveley, *N.Z.* **59 K3** 43 40S 171 32 E
Stavelot, *Belgium* **15 D5** 50 23N 5 55 E
Stavern, *Norway* **9 G14** 59 0N 10 1 E
Stavoren, *Neths.* **15 B5** 52 53N 5 22 E
Stavropol, *Russia* **25 E7** 45 5N 42 0 E
Stavros, *Cyprus* **23 D11** 35 1N 32 38 E
Stavrós, *Greece* **23 D6** 35 12N 24 45 E
Stavros, Ákra, *Greece* **23 D6** 35 26N 24 58 E
Stawell, *Australia* **63 F3** 37 5S 142 47 E
Stawell →, *Australia* **62 C3** 20 20S 142 55 E
Stayner, *Canada* **78 B4** 44 25N 80 5W
Stayton, *U.S.A.* **82 D2** 44 48N 122 48W
Steamboat Springs, *U.S.A.* **82 F10** 40 29N 106 50W
Steele, *U.S.A.* **80 B5** 46 51N 99 55W
Steelton, *U.S.A.* **78 F8** 40 14N 76 50W
Steen River, *Canada* **72 B5** 59 40N 117 12W
Steenkool = Bintuni, *Indonesia* **37 E8** 2 7S 133 32 E
Steens Mt., *U.S.A.* **82 E4** 42 35N 118 40W
Steenwijk, *Neths.* **15 B6** 52 47N 6 7 E
Steep Pt., *Australia* **61 E1** 26 8S 113 8 E
Steep Rock, *Canada* **73 C9** 51 30N 98 48W
Stefanie L. = Chew Bahir, *Ethiopia* **46 G2** 4 40N 36 50 E
Stefansson Bay, *Antarctica* **5 C5** 67 20S 59 8 E
Steiermark □, *Austria* **16 E8** 47 26N 15 0 E
Steilacoom, *U.S.A.* **84 C4** 47 10N 122 36W
Steinbach, *Canada* **73 D9** 49 32N 96 40W
Steinkjer, *Norway* **8 D14** 64 1N 11 31 E
Steinkopf, *S. Africa* **56 D2** 29 18S 17 43 E
Stellarton, *Canada* **71 C7** 45 32N 62 30W
Stellenbosch, *S. Africa* **56 E2** 33 58S 18 50 E
Stendal, *Germany* **16 B6** 52 36N 11 53 E
Steornabhaigh = Stornoway, *U.K.* **12 C2** 58 13N 6 23W
Stepanakert = Xankändi, *Azerbaijan* **25 G8** 39 52N 46 49 E
Stephens Creek, *Australia* **63 E3** 31 50S 141 30 E
Stephens I., *Canada* **72 C2** 54 10N 130 45W
Stephens L., *Canada* **73 B9** 56 32N 95 0W
Stephenville, *Canada* **71 C8** 48 31N 58 35W
Stephenville, *U.S.A.* **81 J5** 32 13N 98 12W
Stepnoi = Elista, *Russia* **25 E7** 46 16N 44 14 E
Steppe, *Asia* **28 D9** 50 0N 50 0 E
Sterkstroom, *S. Africa* **56 E4** 31 32S 26 32 E
Sterling, *Colo., U.S.A.* **80 E3** 40 37N 103 13W
Sterling, *Ill., U.S.A.* **80 E10** 41 48N 89 42W
Sterling, *Kans., U.S.A.* **80 F5** 38 13N 98 12W
Sterling City, *U.S.A.* **81 K4** 31 51N 101 0W
Sterling Heights, *U.S.A.* **76 D4** 42 35N 83 0W
Sterling Run, *U.S.A.* **78 E6** 41 25N 78 12W
Sterlitamak, *Russia* **24 D10** 53 40N 56 0 E
Stérnes, *Greece* **23 D6** 35 30N 24 9 E
Stettin = Szczecin, *Poland* **16 B8** 53 27N 14 27 E
Stettiner Haff, *Germany* **16 B8** 53 47N 14 15 E
Stettler, *Canada* **72 C6** 52 19N 112 40W
Steubenville, *U.S.A.* **78 F4** 40 22N 80 37W
Stevenage, *U.K.* **11 F7** 51 55N 0 13W
Stevens Point, *U.S.A.* **80 C10** 44 31N 89 34W
Stevenson, *U.S.A.* **84 E5** 45 42N 121 53W
Stevenson L., *Canada* **73 C9** 53 55N 96 0W
Stevensville, *U.S.A.* **82 C6** 46 30N 114 5W
Stewart, *B.C., Canada* **72 B3** 55 56N 129 57W
Stewart, *N.W.T., Canada* **68 B6** 63 19N 139 26W
Stewart, *U.S.A.* **84 F7** 39 5N 119 46W
Stewart, C., *Australia* **62 A1** 11 57S 134 56 E
Stewart, I., *Chile* **96 G2** 54 50S 71 15W
Stewart I., *N.Z.* **59 M1** 46 58S 167 54 E
Stewarts Point, *U.S.A.* **84 G3** 38 39N 123 24W
Stewartville, *U.S.A.* **80 D8** 43 51N 92 29W
Stewiacke, *Canada* **71 C7** 45 9N 63 22W
Steynsburg, *S. Africa* **56 E4** 31 15S 25 49 E
Steyr, *Austria* **16 D8** 48 3N 14 25 E
Steytlerville, *S. Africa* **56 E3** 33 17S 24 19 E
Stigler, *U.S.A.* **81 H7** 35 15N 95 8W
Stikine →, *Canada* **72 B2** 56 40N 132 30W
Stilfontein, *S. Africa* **56 D4** 26 51S 26 50 E
Stillwater, *N.Z.* **59 K3** 42 27S 171 20 E
Stillwater, *Minn., U.S.A.* **80 C8** 45 3N 92 49W
Stillwater, *N.Y., U.S.A.* **79 D11** 42 55N 73 41W
Stillwater, *Okla., U.S.A.* **81 G6** 36 7N 97 4W
Stillwater Range, *U.S.A.* **82 G4** 39 50N 118 5W
Stillwater Reservoir, *U.S.A.* **79 C9** 43 54N 75 3W
Stilwell, *U.S.A.* **81 H7** 35 49N 94 38W
Štip, *Macedonia* **21 D10** 41 42N 22 10 E
Stirling, *Canada* **78 B7** 44 18N 77 33W
Stirling, *U.K.* **12 E5** 56 8N 3 57W
Stirling □, *U.K.* **12 E4** 56 12N 4 18W
Stirling Ra., *Australia* **61 F2** 34 23S 118 0 E
Stittsville, *Canada* **79 A9** 45 15N 75 55W
Stjernøya, *Norway* **8 A20** 70 20N 22 40 E
Stjørdalshalsen, *Norway* **8 E14** 63 29N 10 51 E
Stockerau, *Austria* **16 D9** 48 24N 16 12 E
Stockholm, *Sweden* **9 G18** 59 20N 18 3 E
Stockport, *U.K.* **10 D5** 53 25N 2 9W
Stocksbridge, *U.K.* **10 D6** 53 29N 1 35W
Stockton, *Calif., U.S.A.* **84 H5** 37 58N 121 17W
Stockton, *Kans., U.S.A.* **80 F5** 39 26N 99 16W
Stockton, *Mo., U.S.A.* **81 G8** 37 42N 93 48W
Stockton-on-Tees, *U.K.* **10 C6** 54 35N 1 19W
Stockton-on-Tees □, *U.K.* **10 C6** 54 35N 1 19W
Stockton Plateau, *U.S.A.* **81 K3** 30 30N 102 30W
Stoeng Treng, *Cambodia* **38 F5** 13 31N 105 58 E
Stoer, Pt. of, *U.K.* **12 C3** 58 16N 5 23W
Stoke-on-Trent, *U.K.* **10 D5** 53 1N 2 11W
Stoke-on-Trent □, *U.K.* **10 D5** 53 1N 2 11W
Stokes Pt., *Australia* **62 G3** 40 10S 143 56 E
Stokes Ra., *Australia* **60 C5** 15 50S 130 50 E
Stokksnes, *Iceland* **8 D6** 64 14N 14 58W
Stokmarknes, *Norway* **8 B16** 68 34N 14 54 E
Stolac, *Bos.-H.* **21 C7** 43 5N 17 59 E
Stolbovoy, Ostrov, *Russia* **27 D17** 74 44N 135 14 E
Stolbtsy = Stowbtsy, *Belarus* **17 B14** 53 30N 26 43 E
Stolin, *Belarus* **17 C14** 51 53N 26 50 E
Stomíon, *Greece* **23 D5** 35 21N 23 32 E
Stone, *U.K.* **10 E5** 52 55N 2 9W
Stoneboro, *U.S.A.* **78 E4** 41 20N 80 7W
Stonehaven, *U.K.* **12 E6** 56 59N 2 12W
Stonehenge, *Australia* **62 C3** 24 22S 143 17 E
Stonehenge, *U.K.* **11 F6** 51 9N 1 45W
Stonewall, *Canada* **73 C9** 50 10N 97 19W
Stony L., *Man., Canada* **73 B9** 58 51N 98 40W
Stony L., *Ont., Canada* **78 B6** 44 30N 78 5W
Stony Point, *U.S.A.* **79 E11** 41 14N 73 59W
Stony Pt., *U.S.A.* **79 C8** 43 50N 76 18W
Stony Rapids, *Canada* **73 B7** 59 16N 105 50W
Stony Tunguska = Tunguska, Podkamennaya →, *Russia* **27 C10** 61 50N 90 13 E
Stonyford, *U.S.A.* **84 F4** 39 23N 122 33W
Stora Lulevatten, *Sweden* **8 C18** 67 10N 19 30 E
Storavan, *Sweden* **8 D18** 65 45N 18 10 E
Stord, *Norway* **9 G11** 59 52N 5 23 E
Store Bælt, *Denmark* **9 J14** 55 20N 11 0 E
Storm B., *Australia* **62 G4** 43 10S 147 30 E
Storm Lake, *U.S.A.* **80 D7** 42 39N 95 13W
Stormberge, *S. Africa* **56 E4** 31 16S 26 17 E
Stormsrivier, *S. Africa* **56 E3** 33 59S 23 52 E
Stornoway, *U.K.* **12 C2** 58 13N 6 23W
Storozhinets = Storozhynets, *Ukraine* **17 D13** 48 14N 25 45 E
Storozhynets, *Ukraine* **17 D13** 48 14N 25 45 E
Storrs, *U.S.A.* **79 E12** 41 49N 72 15W
Storsjön, *Sweden* **8 E16** 63 9N 14 30 E
Storuman, *Sweden* **8 D17** 65 5N 17 10 E
Storuman, sjö, *Sweden* **8 D17** 65 13N 16 50 E
Stouffville, *Canada* **78 C5** 43 58N 79 15W
Stoughton, *Canada* **73 D8** 49 40N 103 0W
Stour →, *Dorset, U.K.* **11 G6** 50 43N 1 47W
Stour →, *Kent, U.K.* **11 F9** 51 18N 1 22 E
Stour →, *Suffolk, U.K.* **11 F9** 51 57N 1 4 E
Stourbridge, *U.K.* **11 E5** 52 28N 2 8W
Stout L., *Canada* **73 C10** 52 0N 94 40W
Stove Pipe Wells Village, *U.S.A.* **85 J9** 36 35N 117 11W
Stow, *U.S.A.* **78 E3** 41 10N 81 27W
Stowbtsy, *Belarus* **17 B14** 53 30N 26 43 E
Stowmarket, *U.K.* **11 E9** 52 12N 1 0 E
Strabane, *U.K.* **13 B4** 54 50N 7 27W
Strahan, *Australia* **62 G4** 42 9S 145 20 E
Stralsund, *Germany* **16 A7** 54 18N 13 4 E
Strand, *S. Africa* **56 E2** 34 9S 18 48 E
Stranda, *Møre og Romsdal, Norway* **9 E12** 62 19N 6 58 E
Stranda, *Nord-Trøndelag, Norway* **8 E14** 63 33N 10 14 E
Strangford L., *U.K.* **13 B6** 54 30N 5 37W
Stranraer, *U.K.* **12 G3** 54 54N 5 1W
Strasbourg, *Canada* **73 C8** 51 4N 104 55W
Strasbourg, *France* **18 B7** 48 35N 7 42 E
Stratford, *Canada* **78 C4** 43 23N 81 0W
Stratford, *N.Z.* **59 H5** 39 20S 174 19 E
Stratford, *Calif., U.S.A.* **84 J7** 36 11N 119 49W
Stratford, *Conn., U.S.A.* **79 E11** 41 12N 73 8W
Stratford, *Tex., U.S.A.* **81 G3** 36 20N 102 4W
Stratford-upon-Avon, *U.K.* **11 E6** 52 12N 1 42W
Strath Spey, *U.K.* **12 D5** 57 9N 3 49W
Strathalbyn, *Australia* **63 F2** 35 13S 138 53 E
Strathaven, *U.K.* **12 F4** 55 40N 4 5W
Strathcona Prov. Park, *Canada* **72 D3** 49 38N 125 40W
Strathmore, *Canada* **72 C6** 51 5N 113 18W
Strathmore, *U.K.* **12 E5** 56 37N 3 7W
Strathmore, *U.S.A.* **84 J7** 36 9N 119 4W
Strathnaver, *Canada* **72 C4** 53 20N 122 33W
Strathpeffer, *U.K.* **12 D4** 57 35N 4 32W
Strathroy, *Canada* **78 D3** 42 58N 81 38W
Strathy Pt., *U.K.* **12 C4** 58 36N 4 1W
Strattanville, *U.S.A.* **78 E5** 41 12N 79 19W
Stratton, *U.S.A.* **79 A14** 45 8N 70 26W
Stratton Mt., *U.S.A.* **79 C12** 43 4N 72 55W
Straubing, *Germany* **16 D7** 48 52N 12 34 E
Straumnes, *Iceland* **8 C2** 66 26N 23 8W
Strawberry →, *U.S.A.* **82 F8** 40 10N 110 24W
Streaky B., *Australia* **63 E1** 32 48S 134 13 E
Streaky Bay, *Australia* **63 E1** 32 51S 134 18 E
Streator, *U.S.A.* **80 E10** 41 8N 88 50W
Streetsboro, *U.S.A.* **78 E3** 41 14N 81 21W
Streetsville, *Canada* **78 C5** 43 35N 79 42W
Strelka, *Russia* **27 D10** 58 5N 93 3 E
Streng →, *Cambodia* **38 F4** 13 12N 103 37 E
Streymoy, *Færoe Is.* **8 E9** 62 8N 7 5W
Strezhevoy, *Russia* **26 C8** 60 42N 77 34 E
Strimón →, *Greece* **21 D10** 40 46N 23 51 E
Strimonikós Kólpos, *Greece* **21 D11** 40 33N 24 0 E
Stroma, *U.K.* **12 C5** 58 41N 3 7W
Strómboli, *Italy* **20 E6** 38 47N 15 13 E
Stromeferry, *U.K.* **12 D3** 57 21N 5 33W
Stromness, *U.K.* **12 C5** 58 58N 3 17W
Stromsburg, *U.S.A.* **80 E6** 41 7N 97 36W
Strömstad, *Sweden* **9 G14** 58 56N 11 10 E
Strömsund, *Sweden* **8 E16** 63 51N 15 33 E
Strongsville, *U.S.A.* **78 E3** 41 19N 81 50W
Stronsay, *U.K.* **12 B6** 59 7N 2 35W
Stroud, *U.K.* **11 F5** 51 45N 2 13W
Stroud Road, *Australia* **63 E5** 32 18S 151 57 E
Stroudsburg, *U.S.A.* **79 F9** 40 59N 75 12W
Stroumbi, *Cyprus* **23 E11** 34 53N 32 29 E
Struer, *Denmark* **9 H13** 56 30N 8 35 E
Strumica, *Macedonia* **21 D10** 41 28N 22 41 E
Struthers, *Canada* **70 C2** 48 41N 85 51W
Struthers, *U.S.A.* **78 E4** 41 4N 80 39W
Stryker, *U.S.A.* **82 B6** 48 41N 114 46W
Stryy, *Ukraine* **17 D12** 49 16N 23 48 E
Strzelecki Cr. →, *Australia* **63 D2** 29 37S 139 59 E
Stuart, *Fla., U.S.A.* **77 M5** 27 12N 80 15W
Stuart, *Nebr., U.S.A.* **80 D5** 42 36N 99 8W
Stuart →, *Canada* **72 C4** 54 0N 123 35W
Stuart Bluff Ra., *Australia* **60 D5** 22 50S 131 52 E
Stuart L., *Canada* **72 C4** 54 30N 124 30W
Stuart Ra., *Australia* **63 D1** 29 10S 134 56 E
Stull, L., *Canada* **70 B1** 54 24N 92 34W
Stung Treng = Stoeng Treng, *Cambodia* **38 F5** 13 31N 105 58 E
Stupart →, *Canada* **70 A1** 56 0N 93 25W
Sturgeon B., *Canada* **73 C9** 52 0N 97 50W
Sturgeon Bay, *U.S.A.* **76 C2** 44 50N 87 23W
Sturgeon Falls, *Canada* **70 C4** 46 25N 79 57W
Sturgeon L., *Alta., Canada* **72 B5** 55 6N 117 32W
Sturgeon L., *Ont., Canada* **70 C1** 50 0N 90 45W
Sturgeon L., *Ont., Canada* **78 B6** 44 28N 78 43W
Sturgis, *Canada* **73 C8** 51 56N 102 36W
Sturgis, *Mich., U.S.A.* **76 E3** 41 48N 85 25W
Sturgis, *S. Dak., U.S.A.* **80 C3** 44 25N 103 31W
Sturt Cr. →, *Australia* **60 C4** 19 8S 127 50 E
Stutterheim, *S. Africa* **56 E4** 32 33S 27 28 E
Stuttgart, *Germany* **16 D5** 48 48N 9 11 E
Stuttgart, *U.S.A.* **81 H9** 34 30N 91 33W
Stuyvesant, *U.S.A.* **79 D11** 42 23N 73 45W
Stykkishólmur, *Iceland* **8 D2** 65 2N 22 40W
Styria = Steiermark □, *Austria* **16 E8** 47 26N 15 0 E
Su Xian = Suzhou, *China* **34 H9** 33 41N 116 59 E
Suakin, *Sudan* **51 E13** 19 8N 37 20 E
Suan, *N. Korea* **35 E14** 38 42N 126 22 E
Suaqui, *Mexico* **86 B3** 29 12N 109 41W
Suar, *India* **43 E8** 29 2N 79 3 E
Subang, *Indonesia* **37 G12** 6 34S 107 45 E
Subansiri →, *India* **41 F18** 26 48N 93 50 E
Subarnarekha →, *India* **43 H12** 22 34N 87 24 E
Subayhah, *Si. Arabia* **44 D3** 30 2N 38 50 E
Subi, *Indonesia* **39 L7** 2 58N 108 50 E
Subotica, *Serbia, Yug.* **21 A8** 46 6N 19 39 E
Suceava, *Romania* **17 E14** 47 38N 26 16 E
Suchan, *Russia* **30 C6** 43 8N 133 9 E
Suchitoto, *El Salv.* **88 D2** 13 56N 89 0W
Suchou = Suzhou, *China* **33 C7** 31 19N 120 38 E
Süchow = Xuzhou, *China* **35 G9** 34 18N 117 10 E
Suck →, *Ireland* **13 C3** 53 17N 8 3W
Sucre, *Bolivia* **92 G5** 19 0S 65 15W
Sucuriú →, *Brazil* **93 H8** 20 47S 51 38W
Sud, Pte. du, *Canada* **71 C7** 49 3N 62 14W
Sud-Kivu □, *Dem. Rep. of the Congo* **54 C2** 3 30S 28 0 E
Sud-Ouest, Pte. du, *Canada* **71 C7** 49 23N 63 36W
Sudan, *U.S.A.* **81 H3** 34 4N 102 32W
Sudan ■, *Africa* **51 E11** 15 0N 30 0 E
Sudbury, *Canada* **70 C3** 46 30N 81 0W
Sudbury, *U.K.* **11 E8** 52 2N 0 45 E
Sûdd, *Sudan* **51 G12** 8 20N 30 0 E
Sudeten Mts. = Sudety, *Europe* **17 C9** 50 20N 16 45 E
Sudety, *Europe* **17 C9** 50 20N 16 45 E
Suðuroy, *Færoe Is.* **8 F9** 61 32N 6 50W
Sudi, *Tanzania* **55 E4** 10 11S 39 57 E
Sudirman, Pegunungan, *Indonesia* **37 E9** 4 30S 137 0 E
Sueca, *Spain* **19 C5** 39 12N 0 21W
Suemez I., *U.S.A.* **72 B2** 55 15N 133 20W
Suez = El Suweis, *Egypt* **51 C12** 29 58N 32 31 E
Suez, G. of = Suweis, Khalîg el, *Egypt* **51 C12** 28 40N 33 0 E
Suez Canal = Suweis, Qanâ es, *Egypt* **51 B12** 31 0N 32 20 E
Suffield, *Canada* **72 C6** 50 12N 111 10W
Suffolk, *U.S.A.* **76 G7** 36 44N 76 35W
Suffolk □, *U.K.* **11 E9** 52 16N 1 0 E
Sugargrove, *U.S.A.* **78 E5** 41 59N 79 21W
Sugarive →, *India* **43 F12** 26 16N 86 24 E
Sugluk = Salluit, *Canada* **69 B12** 62 14N 75 38W
Şuḩār, *Oman* **45 E8** 24 20N 56 40 E
Sühbaatar □, *Mongolia* **34 B8** 45 30N 114 0 E
Suhl, *Germany* **16 C6** 50 36N 10 42 E
Sui, *Pakistan* **42 E3** 28 37N 69 19 E
Sui Xian, *China* **34 G8** 34 25N 115 2 E
Suide, *China* **34 F6** 37 30N 110 12 E
Suifenhe, *China* **35 B16** 44 25N 131 10 E
Suihua, *China* **33 B7** 46 32N 126 55 E
Suining, *China* **35 H9** 33 56N 117 58 E
Suiping, *China* **34 H7** 33 10N 113 59 E
Suir →, *Ireland* **13 D4** 52 16N 7 9W
Suisun City, *U.S.A.* **84 G4** 38 15N 122 2W
Suiyang, *China* **35 B16** 44 30N 130 56 E
Suizhong, *China* **35 D11** 40 21N 120 20 E
Sujangarh, *India* **42 F6** 27 42N 74 31 E
Sukabumi, *Indonesia* **37 G12** 6 56S 106 50 E
Sukadana, *Indonesia* **36 E4** 1 10S 110 0 E
Sukagawa, *Japan* **31 F10** 37 17N 140 23 E
Sukaraja, *Indonesia* **36 E4** 2 28S 110 25 E
Sukarnapura = Jayapura, *Indonesia* **37 E10** 2 28S 140 38 E
Sukch'ŏn, *N. Korea* **35 E13** 39 22N 125 35 E
Sukhona →, *Russia* **24 C6** 61 15N 46 39 E
Sukhothai, *Thailand* **38 D2** 17 1N 99 49 E
Sukhumi = Sokhumi, *Georgia* **25 F7** 43 0N 41 0 E
Sukkur, *Pakistan* **42 F3** 27 42N 68 54 E
Sukkur Barrage, *Pakistan* **42 F3** 27 40N 68 50 E
Sukri →, *India* **42 G4** 25 4N 71 43 E
Sukumo, *Japan* **31 H6** 32 56N 132 44 E
Sukunka →, *Canada* **72 B4** 55 45N 121 15W
Sula, Kepulauan, *Indonesia* **37 E7** 1 45S 125 0 E
Sulaco →, *Honduras* **88 C2** 15 2N 87 44W
Sulaiman Range, *Pakistan* **42 D3** 30 30N 69 50 E
Sūlār, *Iran* **45 D6** 31 53N 51 54 E
Sulawesi □, *Indonesia* **37 E6** 2 0S 120 0 E
Sulawesi Sea = Celebes Sea, *Indonesia* **37 D6** 3 0N 123 0 E
Sulawesi Selatan □, *Indonesia* **37 E6** 2 30S 125 0 E
Sulawesi Utara □, *Indonesia* **37 D6** 1 0N 122 30 E
Sulima, *S. Leone* **50 G3** 6 58N 11 32W
Sulina, *Romania* **17 F15** 45 10N 29 40 E
Sulitjelma, *Norway* **8 C17** 67 9N 16 3 E
Sullana, *Peru* **92 D2** 4 52S 80 39W
Sullivan, *Ill., U.S.A.* **80 F10** 39 36N 88 37W
Sullivan, *Ind., U.S.A.* **76 F2** 39 6N 87 24W
Sullivan, *Mo., U.S.A.* **80 F9** 38 13N 91 10W
Sullivan Bay, *Canada* **72 C3** 50 55N 126 50W
Sullivan I. = Lambi Kyun, *Burma* **39 G2** 10 50N 98 20 E
Sulphur, *La., U.S.A.* **81 K8** 30 14N 93 23W
Sulphur, *Okla., U.S.A.* **81 H6** 34 31N 96 58W
Sulphur Pt., *Canada* **72 A6** 60 56N 114 48W
Sulphur Springs, *U.S.A.* **81 J7** 33 8N 95 36W
Sultan, *Canada* **70 C3** 47 36N 82 47W
Sultan, *U.S.A.* **84 C5** 47 52N 121 49W
Sultanpur, *India* **43 F10** 26 18N 82 4 E
Sultanpur, *Mad. P., India* **42 H8** 23 9N 77 56 E
Sultanpur, *Punjab, India* **42 D6** 31 13N 75 11 E
Sulu Arch., *Phil.* **37 C6** 6 0N 121 0 E
Sulu Sea, *E. Indies* **37 C6** 8 0N 120 0 E
Suluq, *Libya* **51 B10** 31 44N 20 14 E
Sulzberger Ice Shelf, *Antarctica* **5 D10** 78 0S 150 0 E
Sumalata, *Indonesia* **37 D6** 1 0N 122 31 E
Sumampa, *Argentina* **94 B3** 29 25S 63 29W
Sumatera □, *Indonesia* **36 D2** 0 40N 100 20 E
Sumatera Barat □, *Indonesia* **36 E2** 1 0S 101 0 E
Sumatera Utara □, *Indonesia* **36 D1** 2 30N 98 0 E
Sumatra = Sumatera □, *Indonesia* **36 D2** 0 40N 100 20 E
Sumba, *Indonesia* **37 F5** 9 45S 119 35 E
Sumba, Selat, *Indonesia* **37 F5** 9 0S 118 40 E
Sumbawa, *Indonesia* **36 F5** 8 26S 117 30 E
Sumbawa Besar, *Indonesia* **36 F5** 8 30S 117 26 E
Sumbawanga □, *Tanzania* **52 F6** 8 0S 31 30 E
Sumbe, *Angola* **52 G2** 11 10S 13 48 E
Sumburgh Hd., *U.K.* **12 B7** 59 52N 1 17W
Sumdeo, *India* **43 D8** 31 26N 78 44 E
Sumdo, *India* **43 B8** 35 6N 78 41 E
Sumedang, *Indonesia* **37 G12** 6 52S 107 55 E
Šumen = Shumen, *Bulgaria* **21 C12** 43 18N 26 55 E
Sumenep, *Indonesia* **37 G15** 7 1S 113 52 E
Sumgait = Sumqayıt, *Azerbaijan* **25 F8** 40 34N 49 38 E
Summer L., *U.S.A.* **82 E3** 42 50N 120 45W
Summerland, *Canada* **72 D5** 49 32N 119 41W
Summerside, *Canada* **71 C7** 46 24N 63 47W
Summersville, *U.S.A.* **76 F5** 38 17N 80 51W
Summerville, *Ga., U.S.A.* **77 H3** 34 29N 85 21W
Summerville, *S.C., U.S.A.* **77 J5** 33 1N 80 11W
Summit Lake, *Canada* **72 C4** 54 20N 122 40W
Summit Peak, *U.S.A.* **83 H10** 37 21N 106 42W
Sumner, *Iowa, U.S.A.* **80 D8** 42 51N 92 6W
Sumner, *Wash., U.S.A.* **84 C4** 47 12N 122 14W
Sumoto, *Japan* **31 G7** 34 21N 134 54 E
Šumperk, *Czech Rep.* **17 D9** 49 59N 16 59 E
Sumqayıt, *Azerbaijan* **25 F8** 40 34N 49 38 E
Sumter, *U.S.A.* **77 J5** 33 55N 80 21W
Sumy, *Ukraine* **25 D5** 50 57N 34 50 E
Sun City, *Ariz., U.S.A.* **83 K7** 33 36N 112 17W
Sun City, *Calif., U.S.A.* **85 M9** 33 42N 117 11W
Sun City Center, *U.S.A.* **77 M4** 27 43N 82 18W
Sun Lakes, *U.S.A.* **83 K8** 33 10N 111 52W
Sun Valley, *U.S.A.* **82 E6** 43 42N 114 21W
Sunagawa, *Japan* **30 C10** 43 29N 141 55 E
Sunan, *N. Korea* **35 E13** 39 15N 125 40 E
Sunart, L., *U.K.* **12 E3** 56 42N 5 43W
Sunburst, *U.S.A.* **82 B8** 48 53N 111 55W
Sunbury, *Australia* **63 F3** 37 35S 144 44 E
Sunbury, *U.S.A.* **79 F8** 40 52N 76 48W
Sunchales, *Argentina* **94 C3** 30 58S 61 35W
Suncho Corral, *Argentina* **94 B3** 27 55S 63 27W
Sunch'ŏn, *S. Korea* **35 G14** 34 52N 127 31 E
Suncook, *U.S.A.* **79 C13** 43 8N 71 27W
Sunda, Selat, *Indonesia* **36 F3** 6 20S 105 30 E
Sunda Is., *Indonesia* **28 K14** 5 0S 105 0 E
Sunda Str. = Sunda, Selat, *Indonesia* **36 F3** 6 20S 105 30 E
Sundance, *Canada* **73 B10** 56 32N 94 4W
Sundance, *U.S.A.* **80 C2** 44 24N 104 23W
Sundar Nagar, *India* **42 D7** 31 32N 76 53 E
Sundarbans, The, *Asia* **41 J16** 22 0N 89 0 E
Sundargarh, *India* **41 H14** 22 4N 84 5 E
Sundays = Sondags →, *S. Africa* **56 E4** 33 44S 25 51 E
Sunderland, *Canada* **78 B5** 44 16N 79 4W
Sunderland, *U.K.* **10 C6** 54 55N 1 23W
Sundre, *Canada* **72 C6** 51 49N 114 38W
Sundsvall, *Sweden* **9 E17** 62 23N 17 17 E
Sung Hei, *Vietnam* **39 G6** 10 20N 106 2 E
Sungai Kolok, *Thailand* **39 J3** 6 2N 101 58 E
Sungai Lembing, *Malaysia* **39 L4** 3 55N 103 3 E
Sungai Petani, *Malaysia* **39 K3** 5 37N 100 30 E
Sungaigerong, *Indonesia* **36 E2** 2 59S 104 52 E
Sungailiat, *Indonesia* **36 E3** 1 51S 106 8 E
Sungaipenuh, *Indonesia* **36 E2** 2 1S 101 20 E
Sungari = Songhua Jiang →, *China* **33 B8** 47 45N 132 30 E
Sunghua Chiang = Songhua Jiang →, *China* **33 B8** 47 45N 132 30 E
Sunland Park, *U.S.A.* **83 L10** 31 50N 106 40W
Sunndalsøra, *Norway* **9 E13** 62 40N 8 33 E
Sunnyside, *U.S.A.* **82 C3** 46 20N 120 0W
Sunnyvale, *U.S.A.* **84 H4** 37 23N 122 2W
Suntar, *Russia* **27 C12** 62 15N 117 30 E
Suomenselkä, *Finland* **8 E21** 62 52N 24 0 E
Suomussalmi, *Finland* **8 D23** 64 54N 29 10 E
Suoyarvi, *Russia* **24 B5** 62 3N 32 20 E
Supai, *U.S.A.* **83 H7** 36 15N 112 41W
Supaul, *India* **43 F12** 26 10N 86 40 E
Superior, *Ariz., U.S.A.* **83 K8** 33 18N 111 6W
Superior, *Mont., U.S.A.* **82 C6** 47 12N 114 53W
Superior, *Nebr., U.S.A.* **80 E5** 40 1N 98 4W
Superior, *Wis., U.S.A.* **80 B8** 46 44N 92 6W
Superior, L., *N. Amer.* **70 C2** 47 0N 87 0W
Suphan Buri, *Thailand* **38 E3** 14 14N 100 10 E
Suphan Dağı, *Turkey* **44 B4** 38 54N 42 48 E
Supiori, *Indonesia* **37 E9** 1 0S 136 0 E
Supung Shuiku, *China* **35 D13** 40 35N 124 50 E
Sūq Suwayq, *Si. Arabia* **44 E3** 24 23N 38 27 E
Suqian, *China* **35 H10** 33 54N 118 8 E
Sūr, *Lebanon* **47 B4** 33 19N 35 16 E
Sūr, *Oman* **46 C6** 22 34N 59 32 E
Sur, Pt., *U.S.A.* **84 J5** 36 18N 121 54W
Sura →, *Russia* **24 C8** 56 6N 46 0 E
Surab, *Pakistan* **42 E2** 28 25N 66 15 E
Surabaja = Surabaya, *Indonesia* **37 G15** 7 17S 112 45 E
Surabaya, *Indonesia* **37 G15** 7 17S 112 45 E
Surakarta, *Indonesia* **37 G14** 7 35S 110 48 E
Surat, *Australia* **63 D4** 27 10S 149 6 E
Surat, *India* **40 J8** 21 12N 72 55 E
Surat Thani, *Thailand* **39 H2** 9 6N 99 20 E
Suratgarh, *India* **42 E5** 29 18N 73 55 E
Surendranagar, *India* **42 H4** 22 45N 71 40 E
Surf, *U.S.A.* **85 L6** 34 41N 120 36W
Surgut, *Russia* **26 C8** 61 14N 73 20 E
Suriapet, *India* **40 L11** 17 10N 79 40 E
Surigao, *Phil.* **37 C7** 9 47N 125 29 E
Surin, *Thailand* **38 E4** 14 50N 103 34 E
Surin Nua, Ko, *Thailand* **39 H1** 9 30N 97 55 E
Surinam ■, *S. Amer.* **93 C7** 4 0N 56 0W
Suriname = Surinam ■, *S. Amer.* **93 C7** 4 0N 56 0W
Suriname →, *Surinam* **93 B7** 5 50N 55 15W
Sūrmaq, *Iran* **45 D7** 31 3N 52 48 E
Surrey □, *U.K.* **11 F7** 51 15N 0 31W
Sursand, *India* **43 F11** 26 39N 85 43 E
Sursar →, *India* **43 F12** 26 14N 87 3 E

T

Tha Sala

Tanout, *Niger* **50 F7** 14 50N 8 55 E
Tanta, *Egypt* **51 B12** 30 45N 30 57 E
Tantoyuca, *Mexico* **87 C5** 21 21N 98 10W
Tantung = Dandong, *China* **35 D13** 40 10N 124 20 E
Tanunda, *Australia* **63 E2** 34 30S 139 0 E
Tanzania ■, *Africa* **54 D3** 6 0S 34 0 E
Tanzilla →, *Canada* **72 B2** 58 8N 130 43W
Tao, Ko, *Thailand* **39 G2** 10 5N 99 52 E
Tao'an = Taonan, *China* **35 B12** 45 22N 122 40 E
Tao'er He →, *China* **35 B13** 45 45N 124 5 E
Taolanaro, *Madag.* **57 D8** 25 2S 47 0 E
Taole, *China* **34 E4** 38 48N 106 40 E
Taonan, *China* **35 B12** 45 22N 122 40 E
Taos, *U.S.A.* **83 H11** 36 24N 105 35W
Taoudenni, *Mali* **50 D5** 22 40N 3 55W
Tapa, *Estonia* **9 G21** 59 15N 25 50 E
Tapa Shan = Daba Shan, *China* **33 C5** 32 0N 109 0 E
Tapachula, *Mexico* **87 E6** 14 54N 92 17W
Tapah, *Malaysia* **39 K3** 4 12N 101 15 E
Tapajós →, *Brazil* **93 D8** 2 24S 54 41W
Tapaktuan, *Indonesia* **36 D1** 3 15N 97 10 E
Tapanahoni →, *Surinam* **93 C8** 4 20N 54 25W
Tapanui, *N.Z.* **59 L2** 45 56S 169 18 E
Tapauá →, *Brazil* **92 E6** 5 40S 64 21W
Tapes, *Brazil* **95 C5** 30 40S 51 23W
Tapeta, *Liberia* **50 G4** 6 29N 8 52W
Taphan Hin, *Thailand* **38 D3** 16 13N 100 26 E
Tapirapecó, Serra, *Venezuela* **92 C6** 1 10N 65 0W
Tapuaenuku, Mt., *N.Z.* **59 K4** 42 0S 173 39 E
Tapul Group, *Phil.* **37 C6** 5 35N 120 50 E
Tapurucuará, *Brazil* **92 D5** 0 24S 65 2W
Ţaqţaq, *Iraq* **44 C5** 35 53N 44 35 E
Taquara, *Brazil* **95 B5** 29 36S 50 46W
Taquari →, *Brazil* **92 G7** 19 15S 57 17W
Tara, *Australia* **63 D5** 27 17S 150 31 E
Tara, *Canada* **78 B3** 44 28N 81 9W
Tara, *Russia* **26 D8** 56 55N 74 24 E
Tara, *Zambia* **55 F2** 16 58S 26 45 E
Tara →, *Montenegro, Yug.* **21 C8** 43 21N 18 51 E
Tarabagatay, Khrebet, *Kazakstan* **26 E9** 48 0N 83 0 E
Tarābulus, *Lebanon* **47 A4** 34 31N 35 50 E
Tarābulus, *Libya* **51 B8** 32 49N 13 7 E
Taradehi, *India* **43 H8** 23 18N 79 21 E
Tarajalejo, *Canary Is.* **22 F5** 28 12N 14 7W
Tarakan, *Indonesia* **36 D5** 3 20N 117 35 E
Tarakit, Mt., *Kenya* **54 B4** 2 2N 35 10 E
Tarama-Jima, *Japan* **31 M2** 24 39N 124 42 E
Taran, Mys, *Russia* **9 J18** 54 56N 19 59 E
Taranagar, *India* **42 E6** 28 43N 74 50 E
Taranaki □, *N.Z.* **59 H5** 39 25S 174 30 E
Tarancón, *Spain* **19 B4** 40 1N 3 0W
Taranga Hill, *India* **40 H8** 24 0N 72 40 E
Taransay, *U.K.* **12 D1** 57 54N 7 0W
Táranto, *Italy* **20 D7** 40 28N 17 14 E
Táranto, G. di, *Italy* **20 D7** 40 8N 17 20 E
Tarapacá, *Colombia* **92 D5** 2 56S 69 46W
Tarapacá □, *Chile* **94 A2** 20 45S 69 30W
Tarapoto, *Peru* **92 E3** 6 30S 76 20W
Tararua Ra., *N.Z.* **59 J5** 40 45S 175 25 E
Tarashcha, *Ukraine* **17 D16** 49 30N 30 31 E
Tarauacá, *Brazil* **92 E4** 8 6S 70 48W
Tarauacá →, *Brazil* **92 E5** 6 42S 69 48W
Tarawa, *Kiribati* **64 G9** 1 30N 173 0 E
Tarawera, *N.Z.* **59 H6** 39 2S 176 36 E
Tarawera L., *N.Z.* **59 H6** 38 13S 176 27 E
Tarazona, *Spain* **19 B5** 41 55N 1 43W
Tarbat Ness, *U.K.* **12 D5** 57 52N 3 47W
Tarbela Dam, *Pakistan* **42 B5** 34 8N 72 52 E
Tarbert, *Arg. & Bute, U.K.* **12 F3** 55 52N 5 25W
Tarbert, *W. Isles, U.K.* **12 D2** 57 54N 6 49W
Tarbes, *France* **18 E4** 43 15N 0 3 E
Tarboro, *U.S.A.* **77 H7** 35 54N 77 32W
Tarcoola, *Australia* **63 E1** 30 44S 134 36 E
Tarcoon, *Australia* **63 E4** 30 15S 146 43 E
Taree, *Australia* **63 E5** 31 50S 152 30 E
Tarfaya, *Morocco* **50 C3** 27 55N 12 55W
Târgovişte, *Romania* **17 F13** 44 55N 25 27 E
Târgu-Jiu, *Romania* **17 F12** 45 5N 23 19 E
Târgu Mureş, *Romania* **17 E13** 46 31N 24 38 E
Ţarif, *U.A.E.* **45 E7** 24 3N 53 46 E
Tarifa, *Spain* **19 D3** 36 1N 5 36W
Tarija, *Bolivia* **94 A3** 21 30S 64 40W
Tarija □, *Bolivia* **94 A3** 21 30S 63 30W
Tariku →, *Indonesia* **37 E9** 2 55S 138 26 E
Tarim Basin = Tarim Pendi, *China* **32 B3** 40 0N 84 0 E
Tarim He →, *China* **32 C3** 39 30N 88 30 E
Tarim Pendi, *China* **32 B3** 40 0N 84 0 E
Taritatu →, *Indonesia* **37 E9** 2 54S 138 27 E
Tarka →, *S. Africa* **56 E4** 32 10S 26 0 E
Tarkastad, *S. Africa* **56 E4** 32 0S 26 16 E
Tarkhankut, Mys, *Ukraine* **25 E5** 45 25N 32 30 E
Tarko Sale, *Russia* **26 C8** 64 55N 77 50 E
Tarkwa, *Ghana* **50 G5** 5 20N 2 0W
Tarlac, *Phil.* **37 A6** 15 29N 120 35 E
Tarma, *Peru* **92 F3** 11 25S 75 45W
Tarn →, *France* **18 E4** 44 5N 1 6 E
Târnăveni, *Romania* **17 E13** 46 19N 24 13 E
Tarnobrzeg, *Poland* **17 C11** 50 35N 21 41 E
Tarnów, *Poland* **17 C11** 50 3N 21 0 E
Tarnowskie Góry, *Poland* **17 C10** 50 27N 18 54 E
Ţārom, *Iran* **45 D7** 28 11N 55 46 E
Taroom, *Australia* **63 D4** 25 36S 149 48 E
Taroudannt, *Morocco* **50 B4** 30 30N 8 52W
Tarpon Springs, *U.S.A.* **77 L4** 28 9N 82 45W
Tarragona, *Spain* **19 B6** 41 5N 1 17 E
Tarraleah, *Australia* **62 G4** 42 17S 146 26 E
Tarrasa = Terrassa, *Spain* **19 B7** 41 34N 2 1 E
Tarrytown, *U.S.A.* **79 E11** 41 4N 73 52W
Tarshiha = Me'ona, *Israel* **47 B4** 33 1N 35 15 E
Tarso Emissi, *Chad* **51 D9** 21 27N 18 36 E
Tarsus, *Turkey* **25 G5** 36 58N 34 55 E
Tartagal, *Argentina* **94 A3** 22 30S 63 50W
Tartu, *Estonia* **9 G22** 58 20N 26 44 E
Ţarţūs, *Syria* **44 C2** 34 55N 35 55 E
Tarumizu, *Japan* **31 J5** 31 29N 130 42 E
Tarutao, Ko, *Thailand* **39 J2** 6 33N 99 40 E
Tarutung, *Indonesia* **36 D1** 2 0N 98 54 E
Taseko →, *Canada* **72 C4** 52 8N 123 45W
Tash-Kömür, *Kyrgyzstan* **26 E8** 41 40N 72 10 E
Tash-Kumyr = Tash-Kömür, *Kyrgyzstan* **26 E8** 41 40N 72 10 E
Tashauz = Dashhowuz, *Turkmenistan* **26 E6** 41 49N 59 58 E
Tashi Chho Dzong = Thimphu, *Bhutan* **41 F16** 27 31N 89 45 E
Ţashk, Daryācheh-ye, *Iran* **45 D7** 29 45N 53 35 E
Tashkent = Toshkent, *Uzbekistan* **26 E7** 41 20N 69 10 E
Tashtagol, *Russia* **26 D9** 52 47N 87 53 E
Tasikmalaya, *Indonesia* **37 G13** 7 18S 108 12 E
Tåsjön, *Sweden* **8 D16** 64 15N 15 40 E
Taskan, *Russia* **27 C16** 62 59N 150 20 E
Tasman B., *N.Z.* **59 J4** 40 59S 173 25 E
Tasman Mts., *N.Z.* **59 J4** 41 3S 172 25 E
Tasman Pen., *Australia* **62 G4** 43 10S 148 0 E
Tasman Sea, *Pac. Oc.* **64 L8** 36 0S 160 0 E
Tasmania □, *Australia* **62 G4** 42 0S 146 30 E
Tassili n'Ajjer, *Algeria* **50 C7** 25 47N 8 1 E
Tatabánya, *Hungary* **17 E10** 47 32N 18 25 E
Tatahouine, *Tunisia* **51 B8** 32 56N 10 27 E
Tatar Republic = Tatarstan □, *Russia* **24 C9** 55 30N 51 30 E
Tatarbunary, *Ukraine* **17 F15** 45 50N 29 39 E
Tatarsk, *Russia* **26 D8** 55 14N 76 0 E
Tatarstan □, *Russia* **24 C9** 55 30N 51 30 E
Tateyama, *Japan* **31 G9** 35 0N 139 50 E
Tathlina L., *Canada* **72 A5** 60 33N 117 39W
Tathra, *Australia* **63 F4** 36 44S 149 59 E
Tati →, *India* **40 J8** 21 8N 72 41 E
Tatinnai L., *Canada* **73 A9** 60 55N 97 40W
Tatla L., *Canada* **72 C4** 52 0N 124 20W
Tatnam, C., *Canada* **73 B10** 57 16N 91 0W
Tatra = Tatry, *Slovak Rep.* **17 D11** 49 20N 20 0 E
Tatry, *Slovak Rep.* **17 D11** 49 20N 20 0 E
Tatshenshini →, *Canada* **72 B1** 59 28N 137 45W
Tatsuno, *Japan* **31 G7** 34 52N 134 33 E
Tatta, *Pakistan* **42 G2** 24 42N 67 55 E
Tatuī, *Brazil* **95 A6** 23 25S 47 53W
Tatum, *U.S.A.* **81 J3** 33 16N 103 19W
Tat'ung = Datong, *China* **34 D7** 40 6N 113 18 E
Tatvan, *Turkey* **25 G7** 38 31N 42 15 E
Taubaté, *Brazil* **95 A6** 23 0S 45 36W
Tauern, *Austria* **16 E7** 47 15N 12 40 E
Taumarunui, *N.Z.* **59 H5** 38 53S 175 15 E
Taumaturgo, *Brazil* **92 E4** 8 54S 72 51W
Taung, *S. Africa* **56 D3** 27 33S 24 47 E
Taungdwingyi, *Burma* **41 J19** 20 1N 95 40 E
Taunggyi, *Burma* **41 J20** 20 50N 97 0 E
Taungup, *Burma* **41 K19** 18 51N 94 14 E
Taungup Pass, *Burma* **41 K19** 18 40N 94 45 E
Taungup Taunggya, *Burma* **41 K18** 18 20N 93 40 E
Taunsa, *Pakistan* **42 D4** 30 42N 70 39 E
Taunsa Barrage, *Pakistan* **42 D4** 30 42N 70 50 E
Taunton, *U.K.* **11 F4** 51 1N 3 5W
Taunton, *U.S.A.* **79 E13** 41 54N 71 6W
Taunus, *Germany* **16 C5** 50 13N 8 34 E
Taupo, *N.Z.* **59 H6** 38 41S 176 7 E
Taupo, L., *N.Z.* **59 H5** 38 46S 175 55 E
Taurage, *Lithuania* **9 J20** 55 14N 22 16 E
Tauranga, *N.Z.* **59 G6** 37 42S 176 11 E
Tauranga Harb., *N.Z.* **59 G6** 37 30S 176 5 E
Taureau, Rés., *Canada* **70 C5** 46 46N 73 50W
Taurianova, *Italy* **20 E7** 38 21N 16 1 E
Taurus Mts. = Toros Dağları, *Turkey* **25 G5** 37 0N 32 30 E
Tavda, *Russia* **26 D7** 58 7N 65 8 E
Tavda →, *Russia* **26 D7** 57 47N 67 18 E
Taveta, *Tanzania* **54 C4** 3 23S 37 37 E
Taveuni, *Fiji* **59 C9** 16 51S 179 58W
Tavira, *Portugal* **19 D2** 37 8N 7 40W
Tavistock, *Canada* **78 C4** 43 19N 80 50W
Tavistock, *U.K.* **11 G3** 50 33N 4 9W
Tavoy = Dawei, *Burma* **38 E2** 14 2N 98 12 E
Taw →, *U.K.* **11 F3** 51 4N 4 4W
Tawa →, *India* **42 H8** 22 48N 77 48 E
Tawas City, *U.S.A.* **76 C4** 44 16N 83 31W
Tawau, *Malaysia* **36 D5** 4 20N 117 55 E
Tawitawi, *Phil.* **37 C6** 5 10N 120 0 E
Taxco de Alarcón, *Mexico* **87 D5** 18 33N 99 36W
Taxila, *Pakistan* **42 C5** 33 42N 72 52 E
Tay →, *U.K.* **12 E5** 56 37N 3 38W
Tay, Firth of, *U.K.* **12 E5** 56 25N 3 8W
Tay, L., *Australia* **61 F3** 32 55S 120 48 E
Tay, L., *U.K.* **12 E4** 56 32N 4 8W
Tay Ninh, *Vietnam* **39 G6** 11 20N 106 5 E
Tayabamba, *Peru* **92 E3** 8 15S 77 16W
Taylakova, *Russia* **26 D8** 59 13N 74 0 E
Taylakovy = Taylakova, *Russia* **26 D8** 59 13N 74 0 E
Taylor, *Canada* **72 B4** 56 13N 120 40W
Taylor, *Nebr., U.S.A.* **80 E5** 41 46N 99 23W
Taylor, *Pa., U.S.A.* **79 E9** 41 23N 75 43W
Taylor, *Tex., U.S.A.* **81 K6** 30 34N 97 25W
Taylor, Mt., *U.S.A.* **83 J10** 35 14N 107 37W
Taylorville, *U.S.A.* **80 F10** 39 33N 89 18W
Taymā, *Si. Arabia* **44 E3** 27 35N 38 45 E
Taymyr, Oz., *Russia* **27 B11** 74 20N 102 0 E
Taymyr, Poluostrov, *Russia* **27 B11** 75 0N 100 0 E
Tayport, *U.K.* **12 E6** 56 27N 2 52W
Tayshet, *Russia* **27 D10** 55 58N 98 1 E
Taytay, *Phil.* **37 B5** 10 45N 119 30 E
Taz →, *Russia* **26 C8** 67 32N 78 40 E
Taza, *Morocco* **50 B5** 34 16N 4 6W
Tāzah Khurmātū, *Iraq* **44 C5** 35 18N 44 20 E
Tazawa-Ko, *Japan* **30 E10** 39 43N 140 40 E
Tazin, *Canada* **73 B7** 59 48N 109 55W
Tazin L., *Canada* **73 B7** 59 44N 108 42W
Tazovskiy, *Russia* **26 C8** 67 30N 78 44 E
Tbilisi, *Georgia* **25 F7** 41 43N 44 50 E
Tchad = Chad ■, *Africa* **51 F8** 15 0N 17 15 E
Tchad, L., *Chad* **51 F8** 13 30N 14 30 E
Tch'eng-tou = Chengdu, *China* **32 C5** 30 38N 104 2 E
Tchentlo L., *Canada* **72 B4** 55 15N 125 0W
Tchibanga, *Gabon* **52 E2** 2 45S 11 0 E
Tch'ong-k'ing = Chongqing, *China* **32 D5** 29 35N 106 25 E
Tczew, *Poland* **17 A10** 54 8N 18 50 E
Te Anau, L., *N.Z.* **59 L1** 45 15S 167 45 E
Te Aroha, *N.Z.* **59 G5** 37 32S 175 44 E
Te Awamutu, *N.Z.* **59 H5** 38 1S 175 20 E
Te Kuiti, *N.Z.* **59 H5** 38 20S 175 11 E
Te Puke, *N.Z.* **59 G6** 37 46S 176 22 E
Te Waewae B., *N.Z.* **59 M1** 46 13S 167 33 E
Teague, *U.S.A.* **81 K6** 31 38N 96 17W
Teapa, *Mexico* **87 D6** 18 35N 92 56W
Tebakang, *Malaysia* **36 D4** 1 6N 110 30 E
Tébessa, *Algeria* **50 A7** 35 22N 8 8 E
Tebicuary →, *Paraguay* **94 B4** 26 36S 58 16W
Tebingtinggi, *Indonesia* **36 D1** 3 20N 99 9 E
Tebintingii, *Indonesia* **36 E2** 1 0N 102 45 E
Tecate, *Mexico* **85 N10** 32 34N 116 38W
Tecka, *Argentina* **96 E2** 43 29S 70 48W
Tecomán, *Mexico* **86 D4** 18 55N 103 53W
Tecopa, *U.S.A.* **85 K10** 35 51N 116 13W
Tecoripa, *Mexico* **86 B3** 28 37N 109 57W
Tecuala, *Mexico* **86 C3** 22 23N 105 27W
Tecuci, *Romania* **17 F14** 45 51N 27 27 E
Tecumseh, *Canada* **78 D2** 42 19N 82 54W
Tecumseh, *Mich., U.S.A.* **76 D4** 42 0N 83 57W
Tecumseh, *Okla., U.S.A.* **81 H6** 35 15N 96 56W
Tedzhen = Tejen, *Turkmenistan* **26 F7** 37 23N 60 31 E
Tees →, *U.K.* **10 C6** 54 37N 1 10W
Tees B., *U.K.* **10 C6** 54 40N 1 9W
Teeswater, *Canada* **78 C3** 43 59N 81 17W
Tefé, *Brazil* **92 D6** 3 25S 64 50W
Tegal, *Indonesia* **37 G13** 6 52S 109 8 E
Tegid, L. = Bala, L., *U.K.* **10 E4** 52 53N 3 37W
Tegucigalpa, *Honduras* **88 D2** 14 5N 87 14W
Tehachapi, *U.S.A.* **85 K8** 35 8N 118 27W
Tehachapi Mts., *U.S.A.* **85 L8** 35 0N 118 30W
Tehoru, *Indonesia* **37 E7** 3 19S 129 37 E
Tehrān, *Iran* **45 C6** 35 44N 51 30 E
Tehri, *India* **43 D8** 30 23N 78 29 E
Tehuacán, *Mexico* **87 D5** 18 30N 97 30W
Tehuantepec, *Mexico* **87 D5** 16 21N 95 13W
Tehuantepec, G. de, *Mexico* **87 D5** 15 50N 95 12W
Tehuantepec, Istmo de, *Mexico* **87 D6** 17 0N 94 30W
Teide, *Canary Is.* **22 F3** 28 15N 16 38W
Teifi →, *U.K.* **11 E3** 52 5N 4 41W
Teign →, *U.K.* **11 G4** 50 32N 3 32W
Teignmouth, *U.K.* **11 G4** 50 33N 3 31W
Tejam, *India* **43 E9** 29 57N 80 11 E
Tejen, *Turkmenistan* **26 F7** 37 23N 60 31 E
Tejen →, *Turkmenistan* **45 B9** 37 24N 60 38 E
Tejo →, *Europe* **19 C1** 38 40N 9 24W
Tejon Pass, *U.S.A.* **85 L8** 34 49N 118 53W
Tekamah, *U.S.A.* **80 E6** 41 47N 96 13W
Tekapo, L., *N.Z.* **59 K3** 43 53S 170 33 E
Tekax, *Mexico* **87 C7** 20 11N 89 18W
Tekeli, *Kazakstan* **26 E8** 44 50N 79 0 E
Tekirdağ, *Turkey* **21 D12** 40 58N 27 30 E
Tekkali, *India* **41 K14** 18 37N 84 15 E
Tekoa, *U.S.A.* **82 C5** 47 14N 117 4W
Tel Aviv-Yafo, *Israel* **47 C3** 32 4N 34 48 E
Tel Lakhish, *Israel* **47 D3** 31 34N 34 51 E
Tel Megiddo, *Israel* **47 C4** 32 35N 35 11 E
Tela, *Honduras* **88 C2** 15 40N 87 28W
Telanaipura = Jambi, *Indonesia* **36 E2** 1 38S 103 30 E
Telavi, *Georgia* **25 F8** 42 0N 45 30 E
Telde, *Canary Is.* **22 G4** 27 59N 15 25W
Telegraph Creek, *Canada* **72 B2** 58 0N 131 10W
Telekhany = Tsyelyakhany, *Belarus* **17 B13** 52 30N 25 46 E
Telemark, *Norway* **9 G12** 59 15N 7 40 E
Telén, *Argentina* **94 D2** 36 15S 65 31W
Teleng, *Iran* **45 E9** 25 47N 61 3 E
Teles Pires →, *Brazil* **92 E7** 7 21S 58 3W
Telescope Pk., *U.S.A.* **85 J9** 36 10N 117 5W
Telfer Mine, *Australia* **60 C3** 21 40S 122 12 E
Telford, *U.K.* **11 E5** 52 40N 2 27W
Telford and Wrekin □, *U.K.* **10 E5** 52 45N 2 27W
Telkwa, *Canada* **72 C3** 54 41N 127 5W
Tell City, *U.S.A.* **76 G2** 37 57N 86 46W
Tellicherry, *India* **40 P9** 11 45N 75 30 E
Telluride, *U.S.A.* **83 H10** 37 56N 107 49W
Teloloapán, *Mexico* **87 D5** 18 21N 99 51W
Telpos Iz, *Russia* **24 B10** 63 16N 59 13 E
Telsen, *Argentina* **96 E3** 42 30S 66 50W
Telšiai, *Lithuania* **9 H20** 55 59N 22 14 E
Teluk Anson = Teluk Intan, *Malaysia* **39 K3** 4 3N 101 0 E
Teluk Betung = Tanjungkarang Telukbetung, *Indonesia* **36 F3** 5 20S 105 10 E
Teluk Intan, *Malaysia* **39 K3** 4 3N 101 0 E
Telukbutun, *Indonesia* **39 K7** 4 13N 108 12 E
Telukdalem, *Indonesia* **36 D1** 0 33N 97 50 E
Tema, *Ghana* **50 G5** 5 41N 0 0 E
Temax, *Mexico* **87 C7** 21 10N 88 50W
Temba, *S. Africa* **57 D4** 25 20S 28 17 E
Tembagapura, *Indonesia* **37 E9** 4 20S 137 0 E
Tembe, *Dem. Rep. of the Congo* **54 C2** 0 16S 28 14 E
Temblor Range, *U.S.A.* **85 K7** 35 20N 119 50W
Teme →, *U.K.* **11 E5** 52 11N 2 13W
Temecula, *U.S.A.* **85 M9** 33 30N 117 9W
Temerloh, *Malaysia* **36 D2** 3 27N 102 25 E
Teminabuan, *Indonesia* **37 E8** 1 26S 132 1 E
Temir, *Kazakstan* **25 E10** 49 1N 57 14 E
Temirtau, *Kazakstan* **26 D8** 50 5N 72 56 E
Temirtau, *Russia* **26 D9** 53 10N 87 30 E
Temiscamie →, *Canada* **71 B5** 50 59N 73 5W
Témiscaming, *Canada* **70 C4** 46 44N 79 5W
Témiscamingue, L., *Canada* **70 C4** 47 10N 79 25W
Temosachic, *Mexico* **86 B3** 28 58N 107 50W
Tempe, *U.S.A.* **83 K8** 33 25N 111 56W
Tempiute, *U.S.A.* **84 H11** 37 39N 115 38W
Temple, *U.S.A.* **81 K6** 31 6N 97 21W
Temple B., *Australia* **62 A3** 12 15S 143 3 E
Templemore, *Ireland* **13 D4** 52 47N 7 51W
Templeton, *U.S.A.* **84 K6** 35 33N 120 42W
Templeton →, *Australia* **62 C2** 21 0S 138 40 E
Tempoal, *Mexico* **87 C5** 21 31N 98 23W
Temuco, *Chile* **96 D2** 38 45S 72 40W
Temuka, *N.Z.* **59 L3** 44 14S 171 17 E
Tenabo, *Mexico* **87 C6** 20 2N 90 12W
Tenaha, *U.S.A.* **81 K7** 31 57N 94 15W
Tenakee Springs, *U.S.A.* **72 B1** 57 47N 135 13W
Tenali, *India* **40 L12** 16 15N 80 35 E
Tenancingo, *Mexico* **87 D5** 19 0N 99 33W
Tenango, *Mexico* **87 D5** 19 7N 99 33W
Tenasserim, *Burma* **39 F2** 12 6N 99 3 E
Tenasserim □, *Burma* **38 F2** 14 0N 98 30 E
Tenby, *U.K.* **11 F3** 51 40N 4 42W
Tenda, Colle di, *France* **18 D7** 44 7N 7 36 E
Tendaho, *Ethiopia* **46 E3** 11 48N 40 54 E
Tendukhera, *India* **43 H8** 23 24N 79 33 E
Ténéré, *Niger* **50 E7** 19 0N 10 30 E
Tenerife, *Canary Is.* **22 F3** 28 15N 16 35W
Tenerife, Pico, *Canary Is.* **22 G1** 27 43N 18 1W
Teng Xian, *China* **35 G9** 35 5N 117 10 E
Tengah □, *Indonesia* **37 E6** 2 0S 122 0 E
Tengah, Kepulauan, *Indonesia* **36 F5** 7 5S 118 15 E
Tengchong, *China* **32 D4** 25 0N 98 28 E
Tengchowfu = Penglai, *China* **35 F11** 37 48N 120 42 E
Tenggara □, *Indonesia* **37 E6** 3 0S 122 0 E
Tenggarong, *Indonesia* **36 E5** 0 24S 116 58 E
Tenggol, Pulau, *Malaysia* **39 K4** 4 48N 103 41 E
Tengiz, Ozero, *Kazakstan* **26 D7** 50 30N 69 0 E
Tenino, *U.S.A.* **84 D4** 46 51N 122 51W
Tenkasi, *India* **40 Q10** 8 55N 77 20 E
Tenke, *Katanga, Dem. Rep. of the Congo* **55 E2** 11 22S 26 40 E
Tenke, *Katanga, Dem. Rep. of the Congo* **55 E2** 10 32S 26 7 E
Tennant Creek, *Australia* **62 B1** 19 30S 134 15 E
Tennessee □, *U.S.A.* **77 H2** 36 0N 86 30W
Tennessee →, *U.S.A.* **76 G1** 37 4N 88 34W
Teno, Pta. de, *Canary Is.* **22 F3** 28 21N 16 55W
Tenom, *Malaysia* **36 C5** 5 4N 115 57 E
Tenosique, *Mexico* **87 D6** 17 30N 91 24W
Tenryū-Gawa →, *Japan* **31 G8** 35 39N 137 48 E
Tenterden, *U.K.* **11 F8** 51 4N 0 42 E
Tenterfield, *Australia* **63 D5** 29 0S 152 0 E
Teófilo Otoni, *Brazil* **93 G10** 17 50S 41 30W
Tepa, *Indonesia* **37 F7** 7 52S 129 31 E
Tepalcatepec →, *Mexico* **86 D4** 18 35N 101 59W
Tepehuanes, *Mexico* **86 B3** 25 21N 105 44W
Tepetongo, *Mexico* **86 C4** 22 28N 103 9W
Tepic, *Mexico* **86 C4** 21 30N 104 54W
Teplice, *Czech Rep.* **16 C7** 50 40N 13 48 E
Tepoca, C., *Mexico* **86 A2** 30 20N 112 25W
Tequila, *Mexico* **86 C4** 20 54N 103 47W
Ter →, *Spain* **19 A7** 42 2N 3 12 E
Ter Apel, *Neths.* **15 B7** 52 53N 7 5 E
Teraina, *Kiribati* **65 G11** 4 43N 160 25W
Téramo, *Italy* **20 C5** 42 39N 13 42 E
Terang, *Australia* **63 F3** 38 15S 142 55 E
Tercero →, *Argentina* **94 C3** 32 58S 61 47W
Terebovlya, *Ukraine* **17 D13** 49 18N 25 44 E
Terek →, *Russia* **25 F8** 44 0N 47 30 E
Teresina, *Brazil* **93 E10** 5 9S 42 45W
Terewah, L., *Australia* **63 D4** 29 52S 147 35 E
Teridgerie Cr. →, *Australia* **63 E4** 30 25S 148 50 E
Termez = Termiz, *Uzbekistan* **26 F7** 37 15N 67 15 E
Términi Imerese, *Italy* **20 F5** 37 59N 13 42 E
Términos, L. de, *Mexico* **87 D6** 18 35N 91 30W
Termiz, *Uzbekistan* **26 F7** 37 15N 67 15 E
Térmoli, *Italy* **20 C6** 42 0N 15 0 E
Ternate, *Indonesia* **37 D7** 0 45N 127 25 E
Terneuzen, *Neths.* **15 C3** 51 20N 3 50 E
Terney, *Russia* **27 E14** 45 3N 136 37 E
Terni, *Italy* **20 C5** 42 34N 12 37 E
Ternopil, *Ukraine* **17 D13** 49 30N 25 40 E
Ternopol = Ternopil, *Ukraine* **17 D13** 49 30N 25 40 E
Terowie, *Australia* **63 E2** 33 8S 138 55 E
Terra Bella, *U.S.A.* **85 K7** 35 58N 119 3W
Terra Nova Nat. Park, *Canada* **71 C9** 48 33N 53 55W
Terrace, *Canada* **72 C3** 54 30N 128 35W
Terrace Bay, *Canada* **70 C2** 48 47N 87 5W
Terracina, *Italy* **20 D5** 41 17N 13 15 E
Terralba, *Italy* **20 E3** 39 43N 8 39 E
Terranova = Ólbia, *Italy* **20 D3** 40 55N 9 31 E
Terrassa, *Spain* **19 B7** 41 34N 2 1 E
Terre Haute, *U.S.A.* **76 F2** 39 28N 87 25W
Terrebonne B., *U.S.A.* **81 L9** 29 5N 90 35W
Terrell, *U.S.A.* **81 J6** 32 44N 96 17W
Terrenceville, *Canada* **71 C9** 47 40N 54 44W
Terry, *U.S.A.* **80 B2** 46 47N 105 19W
Terryville, *U.S.A.* **79 E11** 41 41N 73 3W
Terschelling, *Neths.* **15 A5** 53 25N 5 20 E
Teruel, *Spain* **19 B5** 40 22N 1 8W
Tervola, *Finland* **8 C21** 66 6N 24 49 E
Teryaweyna L., *Australia* **63 E3** 32 18S 143 22 E
Teshio, *Japan* **30 B10** 44 53N 141 44 E
Teshio-Gawa →, *Japan* **30 B10** 44 53N 141 45 E
Tesiyn Gol →, *Mongolia* **32 A4** 50 40N 93 20 E
Teslin, *Canada* **72 A2** 60 10N 132 43W
Teslin →, *Canada* **72 A2** 61 34N 134 35W
Teslin L., *Canada* **72 A2** 60 15N 132 57W
Tessalit, *Mali* **50 D6** 20 12N 1 0 E
Test →, *U.K.* **11 G6** 50 56N 1 29W
Testigos, Is. Las, *Venezuela* **89 D7** 11 23N 63 7W
Tetachuck L., *Canada* **72 C3** 53 18N 125 55W
Tetas, Pta., *Chile* **94 A1** 23 31S 70 38W
Tete, *Mozam.* **55 F3** 16 13S 33 33 E
Tete □, *Mozam.* **55 F3** 15 15S 32 40 E
Teterev →, *Ukraine* **17 C16** 51 1N 30 5 E
Teteven, *Bulgaria* **21 C11** 42 58N 24 17 E
Tethul →, *Canada* **72 A6** 60 35N 112 12W
Tetiyev, *Ukraine* **17 D15** 49 22N 29 38 E
Teton →, *U.S.A.* **82 C8** 47 56N 110 31W
Tétouan, *Morocco* **50 A4** 35 35N 5 21W
Tetovo, *Macedonia* **21 C9** 42 1N 20 59 E
Teuco →, *Argentina* **94 B3** 25 35S 60 11W
Teulon, *Canada* **73 C9** 50 23N 97 16W
Teun, *Indonesia* **37 F7** 6 59S 129 8 E
Teutoburger Wald, *Germany* **16 B5** 52 5N 8 22 E
Tevere →, *Italy* **20 D5** 41 44N 12 14 E
Teverya, *Israel* **47 C4** 32 47N 35 32 E
Teviot →, *U.K.* **12 F6** 55 29N 2 38W
Tewantin, *Australia* **63 D5** 26 27S 153 3 E
Tewkesbury, *U.K.* **11 F5** 51 59N 2 9W
Texada I., *Canada* **72 D4** 49 40N 124 25W
Texarkana, *Ark., U.S.A.* **81 J8** 33 26N 94 2W
Texarkana, *Tex., U.S.A.* **81 J7** 33 26N 94 3W
Texas, *Australia* **63 D5** 28 49S 151 9 E
Texas □, *U.S.A.* **81 K5** 31 40N 98 30W
Texas City, *U.S.A.* **81 L7** 29 24N 94 54W
Texel, *Neths.* **15 A4** 53 5N 4 50 E
Texline, *U.S.A.* **81 G3** 36 23N 103 2W
Texoma, L., *U.S.A.* **81 J6** 33 50N 96 34W
Tezin, *Afghan.* **42 B3** 34 24N 69 30 E
Teziutlán, *Mexico* **87 D5** 19 50N 97 22W
Tezpur, *India* **41 F18** 26 40N 92 45 E
Tezzeron L., *Canada* **72 C4** 54 43N 124 30W
Tha-anne →, *Canada* **73 A10** 60 31N 94 37W
Tha Deua, *Laos* **38 D4** 17 57N 102 53 E
Tha Deua, *Laos* **38 C3** 19 26N 101 50 E
Tha Pla, *Thailand* **38 D3** 17 48N 100 32 E
Tha Rua, *Thailand* **38 E3** 14 34N 100 44 E
Tha Sala, *Thailand* **39 H2** 8 40N 99 56 E

Tha Song Yang

Tha Song Yang, *Thailand* **38 D1** 17 34N 97 55 E
Thaba Putsoa, *Lesotho* **57 D4** 29 45S 28 0 E
Thabana Ntlenyana, *Lesotho* **57 D4** 29 30S 29 16 E
Thabazimbi, *S. Africa* **57 C4** 24 40S 27 21 E
Thādiq, *Si. Arabia* **44 E5** 25 18N 45 52 E
Thai Muang, *Thailand* **39 H2** 8 24N 98 16 E
Thailand ■, *Asia* **38 E4** 16 0N 102 0 E
Thailand, G. of, *Asia* **39 G3** 11 30N 101 0 E
Thakhek, *Laos* **38 D5** 17 25N 104 45 E
Thal, *Pakistan* **42 C4** 33 28N 70 33 E
Thal Desert, *Pakistan* **42 D4** 31 10N 71 30 E
Thala La, *Burma* **41 E20** 28 25N 97 23 E
Thalabarivat, *Cambodia* **38 F5** 13 33N 105 57 E
Thallon, *Australia* **63 D4** 28 39S 148 49 E
Thames, *N.Z.* **59 G5** 37 7S 175 34 E
Thames →, *Canada* **78 D2** 42 20N 82 25W
Thames →, *U.K.* **11 F8** 51 29N 0 34 E
Thames →, *U.S.A.* **79 E12** 41 18N 72 5W
Thames Estuary, *U.K.* **11 F8** 51 29N 0 52 E
Thamesford, *Canada* **78 C4** 43 4N 81 0W
Thamesville, *Canada* **78 D3** 42 33N 81 59W
Than, *India* **42 H4** 22 34N 71 11 E
Than Uyen, *Vietnam* **38 B4** 22 0N 103 54 E
Thana Gazi, *India* **42 F7** 27 25N 76 19 E
Thandla, *India* **42 H6** 23 0N 74 34 E
Thane, *India* **40 K8** 19 12N 72 59 E
Thanesar, *India* **42 D7** 30 1N 76 52 E
Thanet, I. of, *U.K.* **11 F9** 51 21N 1 20 E
Thangool, *Australia* **62 C5** 24 38S 150 42 E
Thanh Hoa, *Vietnam* **38 C5** 19 48N 105 46 E
Thanh Hung, *Vietnam* **39 H5** 9 55N 105 43 E
Thanh Pho Ho Chi Minh = Phanh Bho Ho Chi Minh, *Vietnam* **39 G6** 10 58N 106 40 E
Thanh Thuy, *Vietnam* **38 A5** 22 55N 104 51 E
Thanjavur, *India* **40 P11** 10 48N 79 12 E
Thano Bula Khan, *Pakistan* **42 G2** 25 22N 67 50 E
Thaolinta L., *Canada* **73 A9** 61 30N 96 25W
Thap Sakae, *Thailand* **39 G2** 11 30N 99 37 E
Thap Than, *Thailand* **38 E2** 15 27N 99 54 E
Thar Desert, *India* **42 F5** 28 0N 72 0 E
Tharad, *India* **42 G4** 24 30N 71 44 E
Thargomindah, *Australia* **63 D3** 27 58S 143 46 E
Tharrawaddy, *Burma* **41 L19** 17 38N 95 48 E
Tharthār, Mileh, *Iraq* **44 C4** 34 0N 43 15 E
Tharthār, W. ath →, *Iraq* **44 C4** 33 59N 43 12 E
Thásos, *Greece* **21 D11** 40 40N 24 40 E
Thatcher, *Ariz., U.S.A.* **83 K9** 32 51N 109 46W
Thatcher, *Colo., U.S.A.* **81 G2** 37 33N 104 7W
Thaton, *Burma* **41 L20** 16 55N 97 22 E
Thaungdut, *Burma* **41 G19** 24 30N 94 40 E
Thayer, *U.S.A.* **81 G9** 36 31N 91 33W
Thayetmyo, *Burma* **41 K19** 19 20N 95 10 E
Thazi, *Burma* **41 J20** 21 0N 96 5 E
The Alberga →, *Australia* **63 D2** 27 6S 135 33 E
The Bight, *Bahamas* **89 B4** 24 19N 75 24W
The Coorong, *Australia* **63 F2** 35 50S 139 20 E
The Dalles, *U.S.A.* **82 D3** 45 36N 121 10W
The English Company's Is., *Australia* **62 A2** 11 50S 136 32 E
The Frome →, *Australia* **63 D2** 29 8S 137 54 E
The Great Divide = Great Dividing Ra., *Australia* **62 C4** 23 0S 146 0 E
The Hague = 's-Gravenhage, *Neths.* **15 B4** 52 7N 4 17 E
The Hamilton →, *Australia* **63 D2** 26 40S 135 19 E
The Macumba →, *Australia* **63 D2** 27 52S 137 12 E
The Neales →, *Australia* **63 D2** 28 8S 136 47 E
The Officer →, *Australia* **61 E5** 27 46S 132 30 E
The Pas, *Canada* **73 C8** 53 45N 101 15W
The Range, *Zimbabwe* **55 F3** 19 2S 31 2 E
The Rock, *Australia* **63 F4** 35 15S 147 2 E
The Salt L., *Australia* **63 E3** 30 6S 142 8 E
The Sandheads, *India* **43 J13** 21 10N 88 20 E
The Stevenson →, *Australia* **63 D2** 27 6S 135 33 E
The Warburton →, *Australia* **63 D2** 28 4S 137 28 E
The Woodlands, *U.S.A.* **81 K7** 30 9N 95 27W
Thebes = Thívai, *Greece* **21 E10** 38 19N 23 19 E
Thebes, *Egypt* **51 C12** 25 40N 32 35 E
Thedford, *Canada* **78 C3** 43 9N 81 51W
Thedford, *U.S.A.* **80 E4** 41 59N 100 35W
Theebine, *Australia* **63 D5** 25 57S 152 34 E
Thekulthili L., *Canada* **73 A7** 61 3N 110 0W
Thelon →, *Canada* **73 A8** 62 35N 104 3W
Theodore, *Australia* **62 C5** 24 55S 150 3 E
Theodore, *Canada* **73 C8** 51 26N 102 55W
Theodore, *U.S.A.* **77 K1** 30 33N 88 10W
Theodore Roosevelt National Memorial Park, *U.S.A.* **80 B3** 47 0N 103 25W
Theodore Roosevelt Res., *U.S.A.* **83 K8** 33 46N 111 0W
Thepha, *Thailand* **39 J3** 6 52N 100 58 E
Theresa, *U.S.A.* **79 B9** 44 13N 75 48W
Thermaïkós Kólpos, *Greece* **21 D10** 40 15N 22 45 E
Thermopolis, *U.S.A.* **82 E9** 43 39N 108 13W
Thermopylae P., *Greece* **21 E10** 38 48N 22 35 E
Thessalon, *Canada* **70 C3** 46 20N 83 30W
Thessaloníki, *Greece* **21 D10** 40 38N 22 58 E
Thessaloniki, Gulf of = Thermaïkós Kólpos, *Greece* **21 D10** 40 15N 22 45 E
Thetford, *U.K.* **11 E8** 52 25N 0 45 E
Thetford Mines, *Canada* **71 C5** 46 8N 71 18W
Theun →, *Laos* **38 C5** 18 19N 104 0 E
Theunissen, *S. Africa* **56 D4** 28 26S 26 43 E
Thevenard, *Australia* **63 E1** 32 9S 133 38 E
Thibodaux, *U.S.A.* **81 L9** 29 48N 90 49W
Thicket Portage, *Canada* **73 B9** 55 19N 97 42W
Thief River Falls, *U.S.A.* **80 A6** 48 7N 96 10W
Thiel Mts., *Antarctica* **5 E16** 85 15S 91 0W
Thiers, *France* **18 D5** 45 52N 3 33 E
Thiès, *Senegal* **50 F2** 14 50N 16 51W
Thika, *Kenya* **54 C4** 1 1S 37 5 E
Thikombia, *Fiji* **59 B9** 15 44S 179 55W
Thimphu, *Bhutan* **41 F16** 27 31N 89 45 E
þingvallavatn, *Iceland* **8 D3** 64 11N 21 9W
Thionville, *France* **18 B7** 49 20N 6 10 E
Thíra, *Greece* **21 F11** 36 23N 25 27 E
Third Cataract, *Sudan* **51 E12** 19 42N 30 19 E
Thirsk, *U.K.* **10 C6** 54 14N 1 19W
Thisted, *Denmark* **9 H13** 56 58N 8 40 E
Thistle I., *Australia* **63 F2** 35 0S 136 8 E
Thívai, *Greece* **21 E10** 38 19N 23 19 E
þjórsá →, *Iceland* **8 E3** 63 47N 20 48W
Thlewiaza →, *Man., Canada* **73 B8** 59 43N 100 5W
Thlewiaza →, *N.W.T., Canada* **73 A10** 60 29N 94 40W
Thmar Puok, *Cambodia* **38 F4** 13 57N 103 4 E
Tho Vinh, *Vietnam* **38 C5** 19 16N 105 42 E
Thoa →, *Canada* **73 A7** 60 31N 109 47W
Thoen, *Thailand* **38 D2** 17 43N 99 12 E
Thoeng, *Thailand* **38 C3** 19 41N 100 12 E
Thohoyandou, *S. Africa* **53 J6** 22 58S 30 29 E
Tholdi, *Pakistan* **43 B7** 35 5N 76 6 E
Thomas, *U.S.A.* **81 H5** 35 45N 98 45W
Thomas, L., *Australia* **63 D2** 26 4S 137 58 E
Thomaston, *U.S.A.* **77 J3** 32 53N 84 20W
Thomasville, *Ala., U.S.A.* **77 K2** 31 55N 87 44W
Thomasville, *Ga., U.S.A.* **77 K4** 30 50N 83 59W
Thomasville, *N.C., U.S.A.* **77 H5** 35 53N 80 5W
Thompson, *Canada* **73 B9** 55 45N 97 52W
Thompson, *U.S.A.* **79 E9** 41 52N 75 31W
Thompson →, *Canada* **72 C4** 50 15N 121 24W
Thompson →, *U.S.A.* **80 F8** 39 46N 93 37W
Thompson Falls, *U.S.A.* **82 C6** 47 36N 115 21W
Thompson Pk., *U.S.A.* **82 F2** 41 0N 123 0W
Thompson Springs, *U.S.A.* **83 G9** 38 58N 109 43W
Thompsontown, *U.S.A.* **78 F7** 40 33N 77 14W
Thomson, *U.S.A.* **77 J4** 33 28N 82 30W
Thomson →, *Australia* **62 C3** 25 11S 142 53 E
Thomson's Falls = Nyahururu, *Kenya* **54 B4** 0 2N 36 27 E
þórisvatn, *Iceland* **8 D4** 64 20N 18 55W
Thornaby on Tees, *U.K.* **10 C6** 54 33N 1 18W
Thornbury, *Canada* **78 B4** 44 34N 80 26W
Thorne, *U.K.* **10 D7** 53 37N 0 57W
Thornhill, *Canada* **72 C3** 54 31N 128 32W
Thorold, *Canada* **78 C5** 43 7N 79 12W
þórshöfn, *Iceland* **8 C6** 66 12N 15 20W
Thouin, C., *Australia* **60 D2** 20 20S 118 10 E
Thousand Oaks, *U.S.A.* **85 L8** 34 10N 118 50W
Thrace, *Turkey* **21 D12** 41 0N 27 0 E
Three Forks, *U.S.A.* **82 D8** 45 54N 111 33W
Three Hills, *Canada* **72 C6** 51 43N 113 15W
Three Hummock I., *Australia* **62 G3** 40 25S 144 55 E
Three Points, C., *Ghana* **50 H5** 4 42N 2 6W
Three Rivers, *Calif., U.S.A.* **84 J8** 36 26N 118 54W
Three Rivers, *Tex., U.S.A.* **81 L5** 28 28N 98 11W
Three Sisters, *U.S.A.* **82 D3** 44 4N 121 51W
Three Springs, *Australia* **61 E2** 29 32S 115 45 E
Throssell, L., *Australia* **61 E3** 27 33S 124 10 E
Throssell Ra., *Australia* **60 D3** 22 3S 121 43 E
Thuan Hoa, *Vietnam* **39 H5** 8 58N 105 30 E
Thubun Lakes, *Canada* **73 A6** 61 30N 112 0W
Thuin, *Belgium* **15 D4** 50 20N 4 17 E
Thule, *Greenland* **4 B4** 77 40N 69 0W
Thun, *Switz.* **18 C7** 46 45N 7 38 E
Thunder B., *U.S.A.* **78 B1** 45 0N 83 20W
Thunder Bay, *Canada* **70 C2** 48 20N 89 15W
Thung Song, *Thailand* **39 H2** 8 10N 99 40 E
Thunkar, *Bhutan* **41 F17** 27 55N 91 0 E
Thuong Tra, *Vietnam* **38 D6** 16 2N 107 42 E
Thüringer Wald, *Germany* **16 C6** 50 35N 11 0 E
Thurles, *Ireland* **13 D4** 52 41N 7 49W
Thurrock □, *U.K.* **11 F8** 51 31N 0 23 E
Thursday I., *Australia* **62 A3** 10 30S 142 3 E
Thurso, *Canada* **70 C4** 45 36N 75 15W
Thurso, *U.K.* **12 C5** 58 36N 3 32W
Thurso →, *U.K.* **12 C5** 58 36N 3 32W
Thurston I., *Antarctica* **5 D16** 72 0S 100 0W
Thutade L., *Canada* **72 B3** 57 0N 126 55W
Thyolo, *Malawi* **55 F4** 16 7S 35 5 E
Thysville = Mbanza Ngungu, *Dem. Rep. of the Congo* **52 F2** 5 12S 14 53 E
Ti Tree, *Australia* **62 C1** 22 5S 133 22 E
Tian Shan, *Asia* **32 B3** 42 0N 76 0 E
Tianjin, *China* **35 E9** 39 8N 117 10 E
Tianshui, *China* **34 G3** 34 32N 105 40 E
Tianzhen, *China* **34 D8** 40 24N 114 5 E
Tianzhuangtai, *China* **35 D12** 40 43N 122 5 E
Tiaret, *Algeria* **50 A6** 35 20N 1 21 E
Tibagi, *Brazil* **95 A5** 24 30S 50 24W
Tibagi →, *Brazil* **95 A5** 22 47S 51 1W
Tiber = Tevere →, *Italy* **20 D5** 41 44N 12 14 E
Tiberias = Teverya, *Israel* **47 C4** 32 47N 35 32 E
Tiberias, L. = Yam Kinneret, *Israel* **47 C4** 32 45N 35 35 E
Tibesti, *Chad* **51 D9** 21 0N 17 30 E
Tibet = Xizang Zizhiqu □, *China* **32 C3** 32 0N 88 0 E
Tibet, Plateau of, *Asia* **28 F12** 32 0N 86 0 E
Tibnī, *Syria* **44 C3** 35 36N 39 50 E
Tibooburra, *Australia* **63 D3** 29 26S 142 1 E
Tiburón, I., *Mexico* **86 B2** 29 0N 112 30W
Ticino →, *Italy* **18 D8** 45 9N 9 14 E
Ticonderoga, *U.S.A.* **79 C11** 43 51N 73 26W
Ticul, *Mexico* **87 C7** 20 20N 89 31W
Tidaholm, *Sweden* **9 G15** 58 12N 13 58 E
Tiddim, *Burma* **41 H18** 23 28N 93 45 E
Tidioute, *U.S.A.* **78 E5** 41 41N 79 24W
Tidjikja, *Mauritania* **50 E3** 18 29N 11 35W
Tidore, *Indonesia* **37 D7** 0 40N 127 25 E
Tiel, *Neths.* **15 C5** 51 53N 5 26 E
Tieling, *China* **35 C12** 42 20N 123 55 E
Tielt, *Belgium* **15 C3** 51 0N 3 20 E
Tien Shan = Tian Shan, *Asia* **32 B3** 42 0N 76 0 E
Tien-tsin = Tianjin, *China* **35 E9** 39 8N 117 10 E
Tien Yen, *Vietnam* **38 B6** 21 20N 107 24 E
T'ienching = Tianjin, *China* **35 E9** 39 8N 117 10 E
Tienen, *Belgium* **15 D4** 50 48N 4 57 E
Tientsin = Tianjin, *China* **35 E9** 39 8N 117 10 E
Tieri, *Australia* **62 C4** 23 2S 148 21 E
Tierra Amarilla, *Chile* **94 B1** 27 28S 70 18W
Tierra Amarilla, *U.S.A.* **83 H10** 36 42N 106 33W
Tierra Colorada, *Mexico* **87 D5** 17 10N 99 35W
Tierra de Campos, *Spain* **19 A3** 42 10N 4 50W
Tierra del Fuego, I. Gr. de, *Argentina* **96 G3** 54 0S 69 0W
Tiétar →, *Spain* **19 C3** 39 50N 6 1W
Tieté →, *Brazil* **95 A5** 20 40S 51 35W
Tiffin, *U.S.A.* **76 E4** 41 7N 83 11W
Tiflis = Tbilisi, *Georgia* **25 F7** 41 43N 44 50 E
Tifton, *U.S.A.* **77 K4** 31 27N 83 31W
Tifu, *Indonesia* **37 E7** 3 39S 126 24 E
Tighina, *Moldova* **17 E15** 46 50N 29 30 E
Tigil, *Russia* **27 D16** 57 49N 158 40 E
Tignish, *Canada* **71 C7** 46 58N 64 2W
Tigre →, *Peru* **92 D4** 4 30S 74 10W
Tigre →, *Venezuela* **92 B6** 9 20N 62 30W
Tigris = Dijlah, Nahr →, *Asia* **44 D5** 31 0N 47 25 E
Tigyaing, *Burma* **41 H20** 23 45N 96 10 E
Tījara, *India* **42 F7** 27 56N 76 31 E
Tijuana, *Mexico* **85 N9** 32 30N 117 10W
Tikal, *Guatemala* **88 C2** 17 13N 89 24W
Tikamgarh, *India* **43 G8** 24 44N 78 50 E
Tikhoretsk, *Russia* **25 E7** 45 56N 40 5 E
Tikhvin, *Russia* **24 C5** 59 35N 33 30 E
Tikrīt, *Iraq* **44 C4** 34 35N 43 37 E
Tiksi, *Russia* **27 B13** 71 40N 128 45 E
Tilamuta, *Indonesia* **37 D6** 0 32N 122 23 E
Tilburg, *Neths.* **15 C5** 51 31N 5 6 E
Tilbury, *Canada* **78 D2** 42 17N 82 23W
Tilbury, *U.K.* **11 F8** 51 27N 0 22 E
Tilcara, *Argentina* **94 A2** 23 36S 65 23W
Tilden, *U.S.A.* **80 D6** 42 3N 97 50W
Tilhar, *India* **43 F8** 28 0N 79 45 E
Tilichiki, *Russia* **27 C17** 60 27N 166 5 E
Tílissos, *Greece* **23 D7** 35 20N 25 1 E
Till →, *U.K.* **10 B5** 55 41N 2 13W
Tillamook, *U.S.A.* **82 D2** 45 27N 123 51W
Tillsonburg, *Canada* **78 D4** 42 53N 80 44W
Tillyeria □, *Cyprus* **23 D11** 35 6N 32 40 E
Tílos, *Greece* **21 F12** 36 27N 27 27 E
Tilpa, *Australia* **63 E3** 30 57S 144 24 E
Tilsit = Sovetsk, *Russia* **9 J19** 55 6N 21 50 E
Tilt →, *U.K.* **12 E5** 56 46N 3 51W
Tilton, *U.S.A.* **79 C13** 43 27N 71 36W
Tiltonsville, *U.S.A.* **78 F4** 40 10N 80 41W
Timagami, L., *Canada* **70 C3** 47 0N 80 10W
Timanskiy Kryazh, *Russia* **24 A9** 65 58N 50 5 E
Timaru, *N.Z.* **59 L3** 44 23S 171 14 E
Timau, *Kenya* **54 B4** 0 4N 37 15 E
Timbákion, *Greece* **23 D6** 35 4N 24 45 E
Timber Creek, *Australia* **60 C5** 15 40S 130 29 E
Timber Lake, *U.S.A.* **80 C4** 45 26N 101 5W
Timber Mt., *U.S.A.* **84 H10** 37 6N 116 28W
Timbuktu = Tombouctou, *Mali* **50 E5** 16 50N 3 0W
Timi, *Cyprus* **23 E11** 34 44N 32 31 E
Timimoun, *Algeria* **50 C6** 29 14N 0 16 E
Timişoara, *Romania* **17 F11** 45 43N 21 15 E
Timmins, *Canada* **70 C3** 48 28N 81 25W
Timok →, *Serbia, Yug.* **21 B10** 44 10N 22 40 E
Timor, *Indonesia* **37 F7** 9 0S 125 0 E
Timor Sea, *Ind. Oc.* **60 B4** 12 0S 127 0 E
Timor Timur □, *Indonesia* **37 F7** 9 0S 125 0 E
Tin Can Bay, *Australia* **63 D5** 25 56S 153 0 E
Tin Mt., *U.S.A.* **84 J9** 36 50N 117 10W
Tinaca Pt., *Phil.* **37 C7** 5 30N 125 25 E
Tinajo, *Canary Is.* **22 E6** 29 4N 13 42W
Tindal, *Australia* **60 B5** 14 31S 132 22 E
Tindouf, *Algeria* **50 C4** 27 42N 8 10W
Tinggi, Pulau, *Malaysia* **39 L5** 2 18N 104 7 E
Tingo Maria, *Peru* **92 E3** 9 10S 75 54W
Tingrela, *Ivory C.* **50 F4** 10 27N 6 25W
Tinh Bien, *Vietnam* **39 G5** 10 36N 104 57 E
Tinnevelly = Tirunelveli, *India* **40 Q10** 8 45N 77 45 E
Tinogasta, *Argentina* **94 B2** 28 5S 67 32W
Tínos, *Greece* **21 F11** 37 33N 25 8 E
Tinpahar, *India* **43 G12** 24 59N 87 44 E
Tintina, *Argentina* **94 B3** 27 2S 62 45W
Tintinara, *Australia* **63 F3** 35 48S 140 2 E
Tioga, *N. Dak., U.S.A.* **80 A3** 48 23N 102 56W
Tioga, *Pa., U.S.A.* **78 E7** 41 55N 77 8W
Tioman, Pulau, *Malaysia* **39 L5** 2 50N 104 10 E
Tionesta, *U.S.A.* **78 E5** 41 30N 79 28W
Tipongpani, *India* **41 F19** 27 20N 95 55 E
Tipperary, *Ireland* **13 D3** 52 28N 8 10W
Tipperary □, *Ireland* **13 D4** 52 37N 7 55W
Tipton, *Calif., U.S.A.* **84 J7** 36 4N 119 19W
Tipton, *Iowa, U.S.A.* **80 E9** 41 46N 91 8W
Tipton Mt., *U.S.A.* **85 K12** 35 32N 114 12W
Tiptonville, *U.S.A.* **81 G10** 36 23N 89 29W
Tīrān, *Iran* **45 C6** 32 45N 51 8 E
Tirana, *Albania* **21 D8** 41 18N 19 49 E
Tiranë = Tirana, *Albania* **21 D8** 41 18N 19 49 E
Tiraspol, *Moldova* **17 E15** 46 55N 29 35 E
Tire, *Turkey* **21 E12** 38 5N 27 45 E
Tirebolu, *Turkey* **25 F6** 40 58N 38 45 E
Tiree, *U.K.* **12 E2** 56 31N 6 55W
Tiree, Passage of, *U.K.* **12 E2** 56 30N 6 30W
Tîrgovişte = Târgovişte, *Romania* **17 F13** 44 55N 25 27 E
Tîrgu-Jiu = Târgu-Jiu, *Romania* **17 F12** 45 5N 23 19 E
Tîrgu Mureş = Târgu Mureş, *Romania* **17 E13** 46 31N 24 38 E
Tirich Mir, *Pakistan* **40 A7** 36 15N 71 55 E
Tírnavos, *Greece* **21 E10** 39 45N 22 18 E
Tirodi, *India* **40 J11** 21 40N 79 44 E
Tirol □, *Austria* **16 E6** 47 3N 10 43 E
Tirso →, *Italy* **20 E3** 39 53N 8 32 E
Tiruchchirappalli, *India* **40 P11** 10 45N 78 45 E
Tirunelveli, *India* **40 Q10** 8 45N 77 45 E
Tirupati, *India* **40 N11** 13 39N 79 25 E
Tiruppur, *India* **40 P10** 11 5N 77 22 E
Tiruvannamalai, *India* **40 N11** 12 15N 79 5 E
Tisa, *India* **42 C7** 32 50N 76 9 E
Tisa →, *Serbia, Yug.* **21 B9** 45 15N 20 17 E
Tisdale, *Canada* **73 C8** 52 50N 104 0W
Tishomingo, *U.S.A.* **81 H6** 34 14N 96 41W
Tisza = Tisa →, *Serbia, Yug.* **21 B9** 45 15N 20 17 E
Tit-Ary, *Russia* **27 B13** 71 55N 127 2 E
Tithwal, *Pakistan* **43 B5** 34 21N 73 50 E
Titicaca, L., *S. Amer.* **92 G5** 15 30S 69 30W
Titograd = Podgorica, *Montenegro, Yug.* **21 C8** 42 30N 19 19 E
Titule, *Dem. Rep. of the Congo* **54 B2** 3 15N 25 31 E
Titusville, *Fla., U.S.A.* **77 L5** 28 37N 80 49W
Titusville, *Pa., U.S.A.* **78 E5** 41 38N 79 41W
Tivaouane, *Senegal* **50 F2** 14 56N 16 45W
Tiverton, *U.K.* **11 G4** 50 54N 3 29W
Tívoli, *Italy* **20 D5** 41 58N 12 45 E
Tizi-Ouzou, *Algeria* **50 A6** 36 42N 4 3 E
Tizimín, *Mexico* **87 C7** 21 0N 88 1W
Tjeggelvas, *Sweden* **8 C17** 66 37N 17 45 E
Tjirebon = Cirebon, *Indonesia* **37 G13** 6 45S 108 32 E
Tjörn, *Sweden* **9 G14** 58 0N 11 35 E
Tlacotalpan, *Mexico* **87 D5** 18 37N 95 40W
Tlahualilo, *Mexico* **86 B4** 26 20N 103 30W
Tlaquepaque, *Mexico* **86 C4** 20 39N 103 19W
Tlaxcala, *Mexico* **87 D5** 19 20N 98 14W
Tlaxcala □, *Mexico* **87 D5** 19 30N 98 20W
Tlaxiaco, *Mexico* **87 D5** 17 18N 97 40W
Tlemcen, *Algeria* **50 B5** 34 52N 1 21W
To Bong, *Vietnam* **38 F7** 12 45N 109 16 E
Toad →, *Canada* **72 B4** 59 25N 124 57W
Toad River, *Canada* **72 B3** 58 51N 125 14W
Toamasina, *Madag.* **57 B8** 18 10S 49 25 E
Toamasina □, *Madag.* **57 B8** 18 0S 49 0 E
Toay, *Argentina* **94 D3** 36 43S 64 38W
Toba, *Japan* **31 G8** 34 30N 136 51 E
Toba, Danau, *Indonesia* **36 D1** 2 30N 97 30 E
Toba Kakar, *Pakistan* **42 D3** 31 30N 69 0 E
Toba Tek Singh, *Pakistan* **42 D5** 30 55N 72 25 E
Tobago, *W. Indies* **89 D7** 11 10N 60 30W
Tobelo, *Indonesia* **37 D7** 1 45N 127 56 E
Tobermory, *Canada* **78 A3** 45 12N 81 40W
Tobermory, *U.K.* **12 E2** 56 38N 6 5W
Tobi, *Pac. Oc.* **37 D8** 2 40N 131 10 E
Tobin, *U.S.A.* **84 F5** 39 55N 121 19W
Tobin, L., *Australia* **60 D4** 21 45S 125 49 E
Tobin L., *Canada* **73 C8** 53 35N 103 30W
Toboali, *Indonesia* **36 E3** 3 0S 106 25 E
Tobol →, *Russia* **26 D7** 58 10N 68 12 E
Toboli, *Indonesia* **37 E6** 0 38S 120 5 E
Tobolsk, *Russia* **26 D7** 58 15N 68 10 E
Tobruk = Tubruq, *Libya* **51 B10** 32 7N 23 55 E
Tobyhanna, *U.S.A.* **79 E9** 41 11N 75 25W
Tobyl = Tobol →, *Russia* **26 D7** 58 10N 68 12 E
Tocantinópolis, *Brazil* **93 E9** 6 20S 47 25W
Tocantins □, *Brazil* **93 F9** 10 0S 48 0W
Tocantins →, *Brazil* **93 D9** 1 45S 49 10W
Toccoa, *U.S.A.* **77 H4** 34 35N 83 19W
Tochi →, *Pakistan* **42 C4** 32 49N 70 41 E
Tochigi, *Japan* **31 F9** 36 25N 139 45 E
Tochigi □, *Japan* **31 F9** 36 45N 139 45 E
Toconao, *Chile* **94 A2** 23 11S 68 1W
Tocopilla, *Chile* **94 A1** 22 5S 70 10W
Tocumwal, *Australia* **63 F4** 35 51S 145 31 E
Tocuyo →, *Venezuela* **92 A5** 11 3N 68 23W
Todd →, *Australia* **62 C2** 24 52S 135 48 E
Todeli, *Indonesia* **37 E6** 1 38S 124 34 E
Todenyang, *Kenya* **54 B4** 4 35N 35 56 E
Todgarh, *India* **42 G5** 25 42N 73 58 E
Todos os Santos, B. de, *Brazil* **93 F11** 12 48S 38 38W
Todos Santos, *Mexico* **86 C2** 23 27N 110 13W
Toe Hd., *U.K.* **12 D1** 57 50N 7 8W
Tofield, *Canada* **72 C6** 53 25N 112 40W
Tofino, *Canada* **72 D3** 49 11N 125 55W
Tofua, *Tonga* **59 D11** 19 45S 175 5W
Tōgane, *Japan* **31 G10** 35 33N 140 22 E
Togian, Kepulauan, *Indonesia* **37 E6** 0 20S 121 50 E
Togliatti, *Russia* **24 D8** 53 32N 49 24 E
Togo ■, *W. Afr.* **50 G6** 8 30N 1 35 E
Togtoh, *China* **34 D6** 40 15N 111 10 E
Tōhoku □, *Japan* **30 E10** 39 50N 141 45 E
Töhöm, *Mongolia* **34 B5** 44 27N 108 2 E
Toinya, *Sudan* **51 G11** 6 17N 29 46 E
Toiyabe Range, *U.S.A.* **82 G5** 39 30N 117 0W
Tojikiston = Tajikistan ■, *Asia* **26 F8** 38 30N 70 0 E
Tojo, *Indonesia* **37 E6** 1 20S 121 15 E
Tōjō, *Japan* **31 G6** 34 53N 133 16 E
Tok, *U.S.A.* **68 B5** 63 20N 142 59W
Tok-do, *Japan* **31 F5** 37 15N 131 52 E
Tokachi-Dake, *Japan* **30 C11** 43 17N 142 5 E
Tokachi-Gawa →, *Japan* **30 C11** 42 44N 143 42 E
Tokala, *Indonesia* **37 E6** 1 30S 121 40 E
Tōkamachi, *Japan* **31 F9** 37 8N 138 43 E
Tokanui, *N.Z.* **59 M2** 46 34S 168 56 E
Tokara-Rettō, *Japan* **31 K4** 29 37N 129 43 E
Tokarahi, *N.Z.* **59 L3** 44 56S 170 39 E
Tokashiki-Shima, *Japan* **31 L3** 26 11N 127 21 E
Tokat □, *Turkey* **25 F6** 40 15N 36 30 E
Tŏkch'ŏn, *N. Korea* **35 E14** 39 45N 126 18 E
Tokeland, *U.S.A.* **84 D3** 46 42N 123 59W
Tokelau Is., *Pac. Oc.* **64 H10** 9 0S 171 45W
Tokmak, *Kyrgyzstan* **26 E8** 42 49N 75 15 E
Toko Ra., *Australia* **62 C2** 23 5S 138 20 E
Tokoro-Gawa →, *Japan* **30 B12** 44 7N 144 5 E
Tokuno-Shima, *Japan* **31 L4** 27 56N 128 55 E
Tokushima, *Japan* **31 G7** 34 4N 134 34 E
Tokushima □, *Japan* **31 H7** 33 55N 134 0 E
Tokuyama, *Japan* **31 G5** 34 3N 131 50 E
Tōkyō, *Japan* **31 G9** 35 45N 139 45 E
Tolaga Bay, *N.Z.* **59 H7** 38 21S 178 20 E
Tolbukhin = Dobrich, *Bulgaria* **21 C12** 43 37N 27 49 E
Toledo, *Brazil* **95 A5** 24 44S 53 45W
Toledo, *Spain* **19 C3** 39 50N 4 2W
Toledo, *Ohio, U.S.A.* **76 E4** 41 39N 83 33W
Toledo, *Oreg., U.S.A.* **82 D2** 44 37N 123 56W
Toledo, *Wash., U.S.A.* **82 C2** 46 26N 122 51W
Toledo, Montes de, *Spain* **19 C3** 39 33N 4 20W
Toledo Bend Reservoir, *U.S.A.* **81 K8** 31 11N 93 34W
Tolga, *Australia* **62 B4** 17 15S 145 29 E
Toliara, *Madag.* **57 C7** 23 21S 43 40 E
Toliara □, *Madag.* **57 C8** 21 0S 45 0 E
Tolima, *Colombia* **92 C3** 4 40N 75 19W
Tolitoli, *Indonesia* **37 D6** 1 5N 120 50 E
Tollhouse, *U.S.A.* **84 H7** 37 1N 119 24W
Tolo, Teluk, *Indonesia* **37 E6** 2 20S 122 10 E
Toluca, *Mexico* **87 D5** 19 20N 99 40W
Tom Burke, *S. Africa* **57 C4** 23 5S 28 0 E
Tom Price, *Australia* **60 D2** 22 40S 117 48 E
Tomah, *U.S.A.* **80 D9** 43 59N 90 30W
Tomahawk, *U.S.A.* **80 C10** 45 28N 89 44W
Tomakomai, *Japan* **30 C10** 42 38N 141 36 E
Tomales, *U.S.A.* **84 G4** 38 15N 122 53W
Tomales B., *U.S.A.* **84 G3** 38 15N 123 58W
Tomar, *Portugal* **19 C1** 39 36N 8 25W
Tomaszów Mazowiecki, *Poland* **17 C10** 51 30N 20 2 E
Tomatlán, *Mexico* **86 D3** 19 56N 105 15W
Tombador, Serra do, *Brazil* **92 F7** 12 0S 58 0W
Tombigbee →, *U.S.A.* **77 K2** 31 8N 87 57W
Tombouctou, *Mali* **50 E5** 16 50N 3 0W
Tombstone, *U.S.A.* **83 L8** 31 43N 110 4W
Tombua, *Angola* **56 B1** 15 55S 11 55 E

Tukums

Tomé, Chile 94 D1 36 36S 72 57W
Tomelloso, Spain 19 C4 39 10N 3 2W
Tomini, Indonesia 37 D6 0 30N 120 30 E
Tomini, Teluk, Indonesia 37 E6 0 10S 122 0 E
Tomintoul, U.K. 12 D5 57 15N 3 23W
Tomkinson Ranges, Australia 61 E4 26 11S 129 5 E
Tommot, Russia 27 D13 59 4N 126 20 E
Tomnop Ta Suos, Cambodia 39 G5 11 20N 104 15 E
Tomo →, Colombia 92 B5 5 20N 67 48W
Toms Place, U.S.A. 84 H8 37 34N 118 41W
Toms River, U.S.A. 79 G10 39 58N 74 12W
Tomsk, Russia 26 D9 56 30N 85 5 E
Tonalá, Mexico 87 D6 16 8N 93 41W
Tonantins, Brazil 92 D5 2 45S 67 45W
Tonasket, U.S.A. 82 B4 48 42N 119 26W
Tonawanda, U.S.A. 78 D6 43 1N 78 53W
Tonbridge, U.K. 11 F8 51 11N 0 17 E
Tondano, Indonesia 37 D6 1 35N 124 54 E
Tone →, Australia 61 F2 34 25S 116 25 E
Tone-Gawa →, Japan 31 F9 35 44N 140 51 E
Tonekābon, Iran 45 B6 36 45N 51 12 E
Tong Xian, China 34 E9 39 55N 116 35 E
Tonga ■, Pac. Oc. 59 D11 19 50S 174 30W
Tonga Trench, Pac. Oc. 64 J10 18 0S 173 0W
Tongaat, S. Africa 57 D5 29 33S 31 9 E
Tongareva, Cook Is. 65 H12 9 0S 158 0W
Tongatapu, Tonga 59 E12 21 10S 174 0W
Tongchŏn-ni, N. Korea 35 E14 39 50N 127 25 E
Tongchuan, China 34 G5 35 6N 109 3 E
Tongeren, Belgium 15 D5 50 47N 5 28 E
Tongguan, China 34 G6 34 40N 110 25 E
Tonghua, China 35 D13 41 42N 125 58 E
Tongjosŏn Man, N. Korea 35 E15 39 30N 128 0 E
Tongking, G. of, Asia 32 E5 20 0N 108 0 E
Tongliao, China 35 C12 43 38N 122 18 E
Tongling, China 33 C6 30 55N 117 48 E
Tongnae, S. Korea 35 G15 35 12N 129 5 E
Tongobory, Madag. 57 C7 23 32S 44 20 E
Tongoy, Chile 94 C1 30 16S 71 31W
Tongres = Tongeren, Belgium 15 D5 50 47N 5 28 E
Tongsa Dzong, Bhutan 41 F17 27 31N 90 31 E
Tongue, U.K. 12 C4 58 29N 4 25W
Tongue →, U.S.A. 80 B2 46 25N 105 52W
Tongwei, China 34 G3 35 0N 105 5 E
Tongxin, China 34 F3 36 59N 105 58 E
Tongyang, N. Korea 35 E14 39 9N 126 53 E
Tongyu, China 35 B12 44 45N 123 4 E
Tonj, Sudan 51 G11 7 20N 28 44 E
Tonk, India 42 F6 26 6N 75 54 E
Tonkawa, U.S.A. 81 G6 36 41N 97 18W
Tonkin = Bac Phan, Vietnam 38 B5 22 0N 105 0 E
Tonle Sap, Cambodia 38 F4 13 0N 104 0 E
Tono, Japan 30 E10 39 19N 141 32 E
Tonopah, U.S.A. 83 G5 38 4N 117 14W
Tonosí, Panama 88 E3 7 20N 80 20W
Tons →, Haryana, India 42 D7 30 30N 77 39 E
Tons →, Ut. P., India 43 F10 26 1N 83 33 E
Tønsberg, Norway 9 G14 59 19N 10 25 E
Toobanna, Australia 62 B4 18 42S 146 9 E
Toodyay, Australia 61 F2 31 34S 116 28 E
Tooele, U.S.A. 82 F7 40 32N 112 18W
Toompine, Australia 63 D3 27 15S 144 19 E
Toora, Australia 63 F4 38 39S 146 23 E
Toora-Khem, Russia 27 D10 52 28N 96 17 E
Toowoomba, Australia 63 D5 27 32S 151 56 E
Top-ozero, Russia 24 A5 65 35N 32 0 E
Top Springs, Australia 60 C5 16 37S 131 51 E
Topaz, U.S.A. 84 G7 38 41N 119 30W
Topeka, U.S.A. 80 F7 39 3N 95 40W
Topley, Canada 72 C3 54 49N 126 18W
Topocalma, Pta., Chile 94 C1 34 10S 72 2W
Topock, U.S.A. 85 L12 34 46N 114 29W
Topol'čany, Slovak Rep. 17 D10 48 35N 18 12 E
Topolobampo, Mexico 86 B3 25 40N 109 4W
Toppenish, U.S.A. 82 C3 46 23N 120 19W
Toraka Vestale, Madag. 57 B7 16 20S 43 58 E
Torata, Peru 92 G4 17 23S 70 1W
Torbalı, Turkey 21 E12 38 10N 27 21 E
Torbat-e Heydārīyeh, Iran 45 C8 35 15N 59 12 E
Torbat-e Jām, Iran 45 C9 35 16N 60 35 E
Torbay, Canada 71 C9 47 40N 52 42W
Torbay □, U.K. 11 G4 50 26N 3 31W
Tordesillas, Spain 19 B3 41 30N 5 0W
Torfaen □, U.K. 11 F4 51 43N 3 3W
Torgau, Germany 16 C7 51 34N 13 0 E
Torhout, Belgium 15 C3 51 5N 3 7 E
Tori-Shima, Japan 31 J10 30 29N 140 19 E
Torin, Mexico 86 B2 27 33N 110 15W
Torino, Italy 18 D7 45 3N 7 40 E
Torit, Sudan 51 H12 4 27N 32 31 E
Torkamān, Iran 44 B5 37 35N 47 23 E
Tormes →, Spain 19 B2 41 18N 6 29W
Tornado Mt., Canada 72 D6 49 55N 114 40W
Torne älv →, Sweden 8 D21 65 50N 24 12 E
Torneå = Tornio, Finland 8 D21 65 50N 24 12 E
Torneträsk, Sweden 8 B18 68 24N 19 15 E
Tornio, Finland 8 D21 65 50N 24 12 E
Tornionjoki →, Finland 8 D21 65 50N 24 12 E
Tornquist, Argentina 94 D3 38 8S 62 15W
Toro, Spain 22 B11 39 59N 4 8 E
Toro, Cerro del, Chile 94 B2 29 10S 69 50W
Toro Pk., U.S.A. 85 M10 33 34N 116 24W
Toroníios Kólpos, Greece 21 D10 40 5N 23 30 E
Toronto, Canada 78 C5 43 39N 79 20W
Toronto, U.S.A. 78 F4 40 28N 80 36W
Toropets, Russia 24 C5 56 30N 31 40 E
Tororo, Uganda 54 B3 0 45N 34 12 E
Toros Dağları, Turkey 25 G5 37 0N 32 30 E
Torpa, India 43 H11 22 57N 85 6 E
Torquay, Australia 63 F3 38 20S 144 19 E
Torquay, U.K. 11 G4 50 27N 3 32W
Torrance, U.S.A. 85 M8 33 50N 118 19W
Torre de Moncorvo, Portugal 19 B2 41 12N 7 8W
Torre del Greco, Italy 20 D6 40 47N 14 22 E
Torrejón de Ardoz, Spain 19 B4 40 27N 3 29W
Torrelavega, Spain 19 A3 43 20N 4 5W
Torremolinos, Spain 19 D3 36 38N 4 30W
Torrens, L., Australia 63 E2 31 0S 137 50 E
Torrens Cr. →, Australia 62 C4 22 23S 145 9 E
Torrens Creek, Australia 62 C4 20 48S 145 3 E
Torrent, Spain 19 C5 39 27N 0 28W
Torreón, Mexico 86 B4 25 33N 103 26W
Torres, Brazil 95 B5 29 21S 49 44W
Torres, Mexico 86 B2 28 46N 110 47W
Torres Strait, Australia 64 H6 9 50S 142 20 E
Torres Vedras, Portugal 19 C1 39 5N 9 15W
Torrevieja, Spain 19 D5 37 59N 0 42W
Torrey, U.S.A. 83 G8 38 18N 111 25W
Torridge →, U.K. 11 G3 51 0N 4 13W
Torridon, L., U.K. 12 D3 57 35N 5 50W
Torrington, Conn., U.S.A. 79 E11 41 48N 73 7W
Torrington, Wyo., U.S.A. 80 D2 42 4N 104 11W
Tórshavn, Færoe Is. 8 E9 62 5N 6 56W
Tortola, Virgin Is. 89 C7 18 19N 64 45W
Tortosa, Spain 19 B6 40 49N 0 31 E
Tortosa, C., Spain 19 B6 40 41N 0 52 E
Tortue, I. de la, Haiti 89 B5 20 5N 72 57W
Torūd, Iran 45 C7 35 25N 55 5 E
Toruń, Poland 17 B10 53 2N 18 39 E
Tory I., Ireland 13 A3 55 16N 8 14W
Tosa, Japan 31 H6 33 24N 133 23 E
Tosa-Shimizu, Japan 31 H6 32 52N 132 58 E
Tosa-Wan, Japan 31 H6 33 15N 133 30 E
Toscana □, Italy 20 C4 43 25N 11 0 E
Toshkent, Uzbekistan 26 E7 41 20N 69 10 E
Tostado, Argentina 94 B3 29 15S 61 50W
Tostón, Pta. de, Canary Is. 22 F5 28 42N 14 2W
Tosu, Japan 31 H5 33 22N 130 31 E
Toteng, Botswana 56 C3 20 22S 22 58 E
Totma, Russia 24 C7 60 0N 42 40 E
Totnes, U.K. 11 G4 50 26N 3 42W
Totness, Surinam 93 B7 5 53N 56 19W
Totonicapán, Guatemala 88 D1 14 58N 91 12W
Totten Glacier, Antarctica 5 C8 66 45S 116 10 E
Tottenham, Australia 63 E4 32 14S 147 21 E
Tottenham, Canada 78 B5 44 1N 79 49W
Tottori, Japan 31 G7 35 30N 134 15 E
Tottori □, Japan 31 G7 35 30N 134 12 E
Toubkal, Djebel, Morocco 50 B4 31 0N 8 0W
Tougan, Burkina Faso 50 F5 13 11N 2 58W
Touggourt, Algeria 50 B7 33 6N 6 4 E
Toul, France 18 B6 48 40N 5 53 E
Toulon, France 18 E6 43 10N 5 55 E
Toulouse, France 18 E4 43 37N 1 27 E
Toummo, Niger 51 D8 22 45N 14 8 E
Toungoo, Burma 41 K20 19 0N 96 30 E
Touraine, France 18 C4 47 20N 0 30 E
Tourane = Da Nang, Vietnam 38 D7 16 4N 108 13 E
Tourcoing, France 18 A5 50 42N 3 10 E
Touriñán, C., Spain 19 A1 43 3N 9 18W
Tournai, Belgium 15 D3 50 35N 3 25 E
Tournon-sur-Rhône, France 18 D6 45 4N 4 50 E
Tours, France 18 C4 47 22N 0 40 E
Tousidé, Pic, Chad 51 D9 21 1N 16 29 E
Toussora, Mt., C.A.R. 52 C4 9 7N 23 14 E
Touwsrivier, S. Africa 56 E3 33 20S 20 2 E
Towada, Japan 30 D10 40 37N 141 13 E
Towada-Ko, Japan 30 D10 40 28N 140 55 E
Towanda, U.S.A. 79 E8 41 46N 76 27W
Towang, India 41 F17 27 37N 91 50 E
Tower, U.S.A. 80 B8 47 48N 92 17W
Towerhill Cr. →, Australia 62 C3 22 28S 144 35 E
Towner, U.S.A. 80 A4 48 21N 100 25W
Townsend, U.S.A. 82 C8 46 19N 111 31W
Townshend I., Australia 62 C5 22 10S 150 31 E
Townsville, Australia 62 B4 19 15S 146 45 E
Towson, U.S.A. 76 F7 39 24N 76 36W
Towuti, Danau, Indonesia 37 E6 2 45S 121 32 E
Toya-Ko, Japan 30 C10 42 35N 140 51 E
Toyama, Japan 31 F8 36 40N 137 15 E
Toyama □, Japan 31 F8 36 45N 137 30 E
Toyama-Wan, Japan 31 F8 37 0N 137 30 E
Toyohashi, Japan 31 G8 34 45N 137 25 E
Toyokawa, Japan 31 G8 34 48N 137 27 E
Toyonaka, Japan 31 G7 34 50N 135 28 E
Toyooka, Japan 31 G7 35 35N 134 48 E
Toyota, Japan 31 G8 35 3N 137 7 E
Tozeur, Tunisia 50 B7 33 56N 8 8 E
Trá Li = Tralee, Ireland 13 D2 52 16N 9 42W
Tra On, Vietnam 39 H5 9 58N 105 55 E
Trabzon, Turkey 25 F6 41 0N 39 45 E
Tracadie, Canada 71 C7 47 30N 64 55W
Tracy, Calif., U.S.A. 84 H5 37 44N 121 26W
Tracy, Minn., U.S.A. 80 C7 44 14N 95 37W
Trafalgar, C., Spain 19 D2 36 10N 6 2W
Trail, Canada 72 D5 49 5N 117 40W
Trainor L., Canada 72 A4 60 24N 120 17W
Trákhonas, Cyprus 23 D12 35 12N 33 21 E
Tralee, Ireland 13 D2 52 16N 9 42W
Tralee B., Ireland 13 D2 52 17N 9 55W
Tramore, Ireland 13 D4 52 10N 7 10W
Tramore B., Ireland 13 D4 52 9N 7 10W
Tran Ninh, Cao Nguyen, Laos 38 C4 19 30N 103 10 E
Tranås, Sweden 9 G16 58 3N 14 59 E
Trancas, Argentina 94 B2 26 11S 65 20W
Trang, Thailand 39 J2 7 33N 99 38 E
Trangahy, Madag. 57 B7 19 7S 44 31 E
Trangan, Indonesia 37 F8 6 40S 134 20 E
Trangie, Australia 63 E4 32 4S 148 0 E
Trani, Italy 20 D7 41 17N 16 25 E
Tranoroa, Madag. 57 C8 24 42S 45 4 E
Tranqueras, Uruguay 95 C4 31 13S 55 45W
Transantarctic Mts., Antarctica 5 E12 85 0S 170 0W
Transilvania, Romania 17 E12 46 30N 24 0 E
Transilvanian Alps = Carpații Meridionali, Romania 17 F13 45 30N 25 0 E
Transvaal □, S. Africa 53 K5 25 0S 29 0 E
Transylvania = Transilvania, Romania 17 E12 46 30N 24 0 E
Trápani, Italy 20 E5 38 1N 12 29 E
Trapper Pk., U.S.A. 82 D6 45 54N 114 18W
Traralgon, Australia 63 F4 38 12S 146 34 E
Trasimeno, L., Italy 20 C5 43 8N 12 6 E
Trat, Thailand 39 F4 12 14N 102 33 E
Tratani →, Pakistan 42 E3 29 19N 68 20 E
Traun, Austria 16 D8 48 14N 14 15 E
Travellers L., Australia 63 E3 33 20S 142 0 E
Travemünde, Germany 16 B6 53 57N 10 52 E
Travers, Mt., N.Z. 59 K4 42 1S 172 45 E
Traverse City, U.S.A. 76 C3 44 46N 85 38W
Travis, L., U.S.A. 81 K5 30 24N 97 55W
Travnik, Bos.-H. 21 B7 44 17N 17 39 E
Trébbia →, Italy 18 D8 45 4N 9 41 E
Třebíč, Czech Rep. 16 D8 49 14N 15 55 E
Trebinje, Bos.-H. 21 C8 42 44N 18 22 E
Trebonne, Australia 62 B4 18 37S 146 5 E
Tregaron, U.K. 11 E4 52 14N 3 56W
Tregrosse Is., Australia 62 B5 17 41S 150 43 E
Treherne, Canada 73 D9 49 38N 98 42W
Treinta y Tres, Uruguay 95 C5 33 16S 54 17W
Trelew, Argentina 96 E3 43 10S 65 20W
Trelleborg, Sweden 9 J15 55 20N 13 10 E
Tremadog Bay, U.K. 10 E3 52 51N 4 18W
Tremonton, U.S.A. 82 F7 41 43N 112 10W
Tremp, Spain 19 A6 42 10N 0 52 E
Trenche →, Canada 70 C5 47 46N 72 53W
Trenčín, Slovak Rep. 17 D10 48 52N 18 4 E
Trenggalek, Indonesia 37 H14 8 3S 111 43 E
Trenque Lauquen, Argentina 94 D3 36 5S 62 45W
Trent →, Canada 78 B7 44 6N 77 34W
Trent →, U.K. 10 D7 53 41N 0 42W
Trento, Italy 20 A4 46 4N 11 8 E
Trenton, Canada 78 B7 44 10N 77 34W
Trenton, Mo., U.S.A. 80 E8 40 5N 93 37W
Trenton, N.J., U.S.A. 79 F10 40 14N 74 46W
Trenton, Nebr., U.S.A. 80 E4 40 11N 101 1W
Trepassey, Canada 71 C9 46 43N 53 25W
Tres Arroyos, Argentina 94 D3 38 26S 60 20W
Três Corações, Brazil 95 A6 21 44S 45 15W
Três Lagoas, Brazil 93 H8 20 50S 51 43W
Tres Lomas, Argentina 94 D3 36 27S 62 51W
Tres Marías, Islas, Mexico 86 C3 21 25N 106 28W
Tres Montes, C., Chile 96 F1 46 50S 75 30W
Tres Pinos, U.S.A. 84 J5 36 48N 121 19W
Três Pontas, Brazil 95 A6 21 23S 45 29W
Tres Puentes, Chile 94 B1 27 50S 70 15W
Tres Puntas, C., Argentina 96 F3 47 0S 66 0W
Três Rios, Brazil 95 A7 22 6S 43 15W
Tres Valles, Mexico 87 D5 18 15N 96 8W
Tresco, U.K. 11 H1 49 57N 6 20W
Treviso, Italy 20 B5 45 40N 12 15 E
Triabunna, Australia 62 G4 42 30S 147 55 E
Triánda, Greece 23 C10 36 25N 28 10 E
Tribulation, C., Australia 62 B4 16 5S 145 29 E
Tribune, U.S.A. 80 F4 38 28N 101 45W
Trichinopoly = Tiruchchirappalli, India 40 P11 10 45N 78 45 E
Trichur, India 40 P10 10 30N 76 18 E
Trida, Australia 63 E4 33 1S 145 1 E
Trier, Germany 16 D4 49 45N 6 38 E
Trieste, Italy 20 B5 45 40N 13 46 E
Triglav, Slovenia 16 E7 46 21N 13 50 E
Trikkala, Greece 21 E9 39 34N 21 47 E
Trikomo, Cyprus 23 D12 35 17N 33 52 E
Trikora, Puncak, Indonesia 37 E9 4 15S 138 45 E
Trim, Ireland 13 C5 53 33N 6 48W
Trincomalee, Sri Lanka 40 Q12 8 38N 81 15 E
Trindade, Brazil 93 G9 16 40S 49 30W
Trindade, I., Atl. Oc. 2 F8 20 20S 29 50W
Trinidad, Bolivia 92 F6 14 46S 64 50W
Trinidad, Cuba 88 B4 21 48N 80 0W
Trinidad, Uruguay 94 C4 33 30S 56 50W
Trinidad, U.S.A. 81 G2 37 10N 104 31W
Trinidad, W. Indies 89 D7 10 30N 61 15W
Trinidad →, Mexico 87 D5 17 49N 95 9W
Trinidad & Tobago ■, W. Indies 89 D7 10 30N 61 20W
Trinity, Canada 71 C9 48 59N 53 55W
Trinity, U.S.A. 81 K7 30 57N 95 22W
Trinity →, Calif., U.S.A. 82 F2 41 11N 123 42W
Trinity →, Tex., U.S.A. 81 L7 29 45N 94 43W
Trinity B., Canada 71 C9 48 20N 53 10W
Trinity Is., U.S.A. 68 C4 56 33N 154 25W
Trinity Range, U.S.A. 82 F4 40 15N 118 45W
Trinkitat, Sudan 51 E13 18 45N 37 51 E
Trinway, U.S.A. 78 F2 40 9N 82 1W
Tripoli = Tarābulus, Lebanon 47 A4 34 31N 35 50 E
Tripoli = Tarābulus, Libya 51 B8 32 49N 13 7 E
Tripolis, Greece 21 F10 37 31N 22 25 E
Tripolitania, Libya 48 C5 31 0N 12 0 E
Tripolitania, N. Afr. 51 B8 31 0N 13 0 E
Tripura □, India 41 H18 24 0N 92 0 E
Tripylos, Cyprus 23 E11 34 59N 32 41 E
Tristan da Cunha, Atl. Oc. 49 K2 37 6S 12 20W
Trisul, India 43 D8 30 19N 79 47 E
Trivandrum, India 40 Q10 8 41N 77 0 E
Trnava, Slovak Rep. 17 D9 48 23N 17 35 E
Trochu, Canada 72 C6 51 50N 113 13W
Trodely I., Canada 70 B4 52 15N 79 26W
Troglav, Croatia 20 C7 43 56N 16 36 E
Troilus, L., Canada 70 B5 50 50N 74 35W
Trois-Pistoles, Canada 71 C6 48 5N 69 10W
Trois-Rivières, Canada 70 C5 46 25N 72 34W
Troitsk, Russia 26 D7 54 10N 61 35 E
Troitsko Pechorsk, Russia 24 B10 62 40N 56 10 E
Trölladyngja, Iceland 8 D5 64 54N 17 16W
Trollhättan, Sweden 9 G15 58 17N 12 20 E
Trollheimen, Norway 8 E13 62 46N 9 1 E
Trombetas →, Brazil 93 D7 1 55S 55 35W
Tromsø, Norway 8 B18 69 40N 18 56 E
Trona, U.S.A. 85 K9 35 46N 117 23W
Tronador, Mte., Argentina 96 E2 41 10S 71 50W
Trøndelag, Norway 8 D14 64 17N 11 50 E
Trondheim, Norway 8 E14 63 36N 10 25 E
Trondheimsfjorden, Norway 8 E14 63 35N 10 30 E
Troodos, Cyprus 23 E11 34 55N 32 52 E
Troon, U.K. 12 F4 55 33N 4 39W
Tropic, U.S.A. 83 H7 37 37N 112 5W
Trostan, U.K. 13 A5 55 3N 6 10W
Trout →, Canada 72 A5 61 19N 119 51W
Trout L., N.W.T., Canada 72 A4 60 40N 121 14W
Trout L., Ont., Canada 73 C10 51 20N 93 15W
Trout Lake, Canada 72 B6 56 30N 114 32W
Trout Lake, U.S.A. 84 E5 46 0N 121 32W
Trout River, Canada 71 C8 49 29N 58 8W
Trout Run, U.S.A. 78 E7 41 23N 77 3W
Trouville-sur-Mer, France 18 B4 49 21N 0 5 E
Trowbridge, U.K. 11 F5 51 18N 2 12W
Troy, Turkey 21 E12 39 57N 26 12 E
Troy, Ala., U.S.A. 77 K3 31 48N 85 58W
Troy, Kans., U.S.A. 80 F7 39 47N 95 5W
Troy, Mo., U.S.A. 80 F9 38 59N 90 59W
Troy, Mont., U.S.A. 82 B6 48 28N 115 53W
Troy, N.Y., U.S.A. 79 D11 42 44N 73 41W
Troy, Ohio, U.S.A. 76 E3 40 2N 84 12W
Troy, Pa., U.S.A. 79 E8 41 47N 76 47W
Troyes, France 18 B6 48 19N 4 3 E
Truchas Peak, U.S.A. 81 H2 35 58N 105 39W
Trucial States = United Arab Emirates ■, Asia 45 F7 23 50N 54 0 E
Truckee, U.S.A. 84 F6 39 20N 120 11W
Trudovoye, Russia 30 C6 43 17N 132 5 E
Trujillo, Honduras 88 C2 16 0N 86 0W
Trujillo, Peru 92 E3 8 6S 79 0W
Trujillo, Spain 19 C3 39 28N 5 55W
Trujillo, U.S.A. 81 H2 35 32N 104 42W
Trujillo, Venezuela 92 B4 9 22N 70 38W
Truk, Micronesia 64 G7 7 25N 151 46 E
Trumann, U.S.A. 81 H9 35 41N 90 31W
Trumansburg, U.S.A. 79 D8 42 33N 76 40W
Trumbull, Mt., U.S.A. 83 H7 36 25N 113 8W
Trundle, Australia 63 E4 32 53S 147 35 E
Trung-Phan = Annam, Vietnam 38 E7 16 0N 108 0 E
Truro, Canada 71 C7 45 21N 63 14W
Truro, U.K. 11 G2 50 16N 5 4W
Truskavets, Ukraine 17 D12 49 17N 23 30 E
Trutch, Canada 72 B4 57 44N 122 57W
Truth or Consequences, U.S.A. 83 K10 33 8N 107 15W
Trutnov, Czech Rep. 16 C8 50 37N 15 54 E
Truxton, U.S.A. 79 D8 42 45N 76 2W
Tryonville, U.S.A. 78 E5 41 42N 79 48W
Tsaratanana, Madag. 57 B8 16 47S 47 39 E
Tsaratanana, Mt. de, Madag. 57 A8 14 0S 49 0 E
Tsarevo = Michurin, Bulgaria 21 C12 42 9N 27 51 E
Tsau, Botswana 56 C3 20 8S 22 22 E
Tselinograd = Astana, Kazakstan 26 D8 51 10N 71 30 E
Tsetserleg, Mongolia 32 B5 47 36N 101 32 E
Tshabong, Botswana 56 D3 26 2S 22 29 E
Tshane, Botswana 56 C3 24 5S 21 54 E
Tshela, Dem. Rep. of the Congo 52 E2 4 57S 13 4 E
Tshesebe, Botswana 57 C4 21 51S 27 32 E
Tshibeke, Dem. Rep. of the Congo 54 C2 2 40S 28 35 E
Tshibinda, Dem. Rep. of the Congo 54 C2 2 23S 28 43 E
Tshikapa, Dem. Rep. of the Congo 52 F4 6 28S 20 48 E
Tshilenge, Dem. Rep. of the Congo 54 D1 6 17S 23 48 E
Tshinsenda, Dem. Rep. of the Congo 55 E2 12 20S 28 0 E
Tshofa, Dem. Rep. of the Congo 54 D2 5 13S 25 16 E
Tshwane, Botswana 56 C3 22 24S 22 1 E
Tsigara, Botswana 56 C4 20 22S 25 54 E
Tsihombe, Madag. 57 D8 25 10S 45 41 E
Tsiigehtchic, Canada 68 B6 67 15N 134 0W
Tsimlyansk Res. = Tsimlyanskoye Vdkhr., Russia 25 E7 48 0N 43 0 E
Tsimlyanskoye Vdkhr., Russia 25 E7 48 0N 43 0 E
Tsinan = Jinan, China 34 F9 36 38N 117 1 E
Tsineng, S. Africa 56 D3 27 5S 23 5 E
Tsinghai = Qinghai □, China 32 C4 36 0N 98 0 E
Tsingtao = Qingdao, China 35 F11 36 5N 120 20 E
Tsinjomitondraka, Madag. 57 B8 15 40S 47 8 E
Tsiroanomandidy, Madag. 57 B8 18 46S 46 2 E
Tsivory, Madag. 57 C8 24 4S 46 5 E
Tskhinvali, Georgia 25 F7 42 14N 44 1 E
Tsna →, Russia 24 D7 54 55N 41 58 E
Tso Moriri, L., India 43 C8 32 50N 78 20 E
Tsodilo Hill, Botswana 56 B3 18 49S 21 43 E
Tsogttsetsiy = Baruunsuu, Mongolia 34 C3 43 43N 105 35 E
Tsolo, S. Africa 57 E4 31 18S 28 37 E
Tsomo, S. Africa 57 E4 32 0S 27 42 E
Tsu, Japan 31 G8 34 45N 136 25 E
Tsu L., Canada 72 A6 60 40N 111 52W
Tsuchiura, Japan 31 F10 36 5N 140 15 E
Tsugaru-Kaikyō, Japan 30 D10 41 35N 141 0 E
Tsumeb, Namibia 56 B2 19 9S 17 44 E
Tsumis, Namibia 56 C2 23 39S 17 29 E
Tsuruga, Japan 31 G8 35 45N 136 2 E
Tsurugi-San, Japan 31 H7 33 51N 134 6 E
Tsuruoka, Japan 30 E9 38 44N 139 50 E
Tsushima, Gifu, Japan 31 G8 35 10N 136 43 E
Tsushima, Nagasaki, Japan 31 G4 34 20N 129 20 E
Tsuyama, Japan 31 G7 35 3N 134 0 E
Tsyelyakhany, Belarus 17 B13 52 30N 25 46 E
Tual, Indonesia 37 F8 5 38S 132 44 E
Tuam, Ireland 13 C3 53 31N 8 51W
Tuamotu Arch. = Tuamotu Is., Pac. Oc. 65 J13 17 0S 144 0W
Tuamotu Is., Pac. Oc. 65 J13 17 0S 144 0W
Tuamotu Ridge, Pac. Oc. 65 K14 20 0S 138 0W
Tuao, Phil. 37 A6 17 55N 121 22 E
Tuapse, Russia 25 F6 44 5N 39 10 E
Tuatapere, N.Z. 59 M1 46 8S 167 41 E
Tuba City, U.S.A. 83 H8 36 8N 111 14W
Tuban, Indonesia 37 G15 6 54S 112 3 E
Tubarão, Brazil 95 B6 28 30S 49 0W
Tūbās, West Bank 47 C4 32 20N 35 22 E
Tübingen, Germany 16 D5 48 31N 9 4 E
Tubruq, Libya 51 B10 32 7N 23 55 E
Tubuai Is., Pac. Oc. 65 K13 25 0S 150 0W
Tuc Trung, Vietnam 39 G6 11 1N 107 12 E
Tucacas, Venezuela 92 A5 10 48N 68 19W
Tuchodi →, Canada 72 B4 58 17N 123 42W
Tuckanarra, Australia 61 E2 27 7S 118 5 E
Tucson, U.S.A. 83 K8 32 13N 110 58W
Tucumán □, Argentina 94 B2 26 48S 66 2W
Tucumcari, U.S.A. 81 H3 35 10N 103 44W
Tucupita, Venezuela 92 B6 9 2N 62 3W
Tucuruí, Brazil 93 D9 3 42S 49 44W
Tucuruí, Reprêsa de, Brazil 93 D9 4 0S 49 30W
Tudela, Spain 19 A5 42 4N 1 39W
Tudmur, Syria 44 C3 34 36N 38 15 E
Tudor, L., Canada 71 A6 55 50N 65 25W
Tugela →, S. Africa 57 D5 29 14S 31 30 E
Tuguegarao, Phil. 37 A6 17 35N 121 42 E
Tugur, Russia 27 D14 53 44N 136 45 E
Tui, Spain 19 A1 42 3N 8 39W
Tuineje, Canary Is. 22 F5 28 19N 14 3W
Tukangbesi, Kepulauan, Indonesia 37 F6 6 0S 124 0 E
Tukarak I., Canada 70 A4 56 15N 78 45W
Tukayyid, Iraq 44 D5 29 47N 45 36 E
Tuktoyaktuk, Canada 68 B6 69 27N 133 2W
Tukums, Latvia 9 H20 56 58N 23 10 E

Vesterålen

Urdinarrain, Argentina 94 C4 32 37S 58 52W
Urdzhar, Kazakstan 26 E9 47 5N 81 38 E
Ure →, U.K. 10 C6 54 5N 1 20W
Ures, Mexico 86 B2 29 30N 110 30W
Urfa = Sanliurfa, Turkey 25 G6 37 12N 38 50 E
Urganch, Uzbekistan 26 E7 41 40N 60 41 E
Urgench = Urganch, Uzbekistan 26 E7 41 40N 60 41 E
Ürgüp, Turkey 44 B2 38 38N 34 56 E
Uri, India 43 B6 34 8N 74 2 E
Uribia, Colombia 92 A4 11 43N 72 16W
Uriondo, Bolivia 94 A3 21 41S 64 41W
Urique, Mexico 86 B3 27 13N 107 55W
Urique →, Mexico 86 B3 26 29N 107 58W
Urk, Neths. 15 B5 52 39N 5 36 E
Urla, Turkey 21 E12 38 20N 26 47 E
Urmia = Orūmīyeh, Iran 44 B5 37 40N 45 0 E
Urmia, L. = Orūmīyeh, Daryācheh-ye, Iran 44 B5 37 50N 45 30 E
Uroševac, Yugoslavia 21 C9 42 23N 21 10 E
Uruaçu, Brazil 93 F9 14 30S 49 10W
Uruapan, Mexico 86 D4 19 30N 102 0W
Urubamba →, Peru 92 F4 10 43S 73 48W
Uruçara, Brazil 92 D7 2 20S 57 50W
Uruçuí, Brazil 93 E10 7 20S 44 28W
Uruguai →, Brazil 95 B5 26 0S 53 30W
Uruguaiana, Brazil 94 B4 29 50S 57 0W
Uruguay ■, S. Amer. 94 C4 32 30S 56 30W
Uruguay →, S. Amer. 94 C4 34 12S 58 18W
Urumchi = Ürümqi, China 26 E9 43 45N 87 45 E
Ürümqi, China 26 E9 43 45N 87 45 E
Urup, Ostrov, Russia 27 E16 46 0N 151 0 E
Usa →, Russia 24 A10 66 16N 59 49 E
Uşak, Turkey 25 G4 38 43N 29 28 E
Usakos, Namibia 56 C2 21 54S 15 31 E
Usedom, Germany 16 B8 53 55N 14 2 E
Useless Loop, Australia 61 E1 26 8S 113 23 E
Ush-Tobe, Kazakstan 26 E8 45 16N 78 0 E
Ushakova, Ostrov, Russia 4 A12 82 0N 80 0 E
Ushant = Ouessant, Î. d', France 18 B1 48 28N 5 6W
Ushashi, Tanzania 54 C3 1 59S 33 57 E
Ushibuka, Japan 31 H5 32 11N 130 1 E
Ushuaia, Argentina 96 G3 54 50S 68 23W
Ushumun, Russia 27 D13 52 47N 126 32 E
Usk, Canada 72 C3 54 38N 128 26W
Usk →, U.K. 11 F5 51 33N 2 58W
Uska, India 43 F10 27 12N 83 7 E
Usman, Russia 24 D6 52 5N 39 48 E
Usoke, Tanzania 54 D3 5 8S 32 24 E
Usolye Sibirskoye, Russia 27 D11 52 48N 103 40 E
Uspallata, P. de, Argentina 94 C2 32 37S 69 22W
Uspenskiy, Kazakstan 26 E8 48 41N 72 43 E
Ussuri →, Asia 30 A7 48 27N 135 0 E
Ussuriysk, Russia 27 E14 43 48N 131 59 E
Ussurka, Russia 30 B6 45 12N 133 31 E
Ust-Aldan = Batamay, Russia 27 C13 63 30N 129 15 E
Ust Amginskoye = Khandyga, Russia 27 C14 62 42N 135 35 E
Ust-Bolsheretsk, Russia 27 D16 52 50N 156 15 E
Ust Chaun, Russia 27 C18 68 47N 170 30 E
Ust Ilimpeya = Yukta, Russia 27 C11 63 26N 105 42 E
Ust-Ilimsk, Russia 27 D11 58 3N 102 39 E
Ust Ishim, Russia 26 D8 57 45N 71 10 E
Ust-Kamchatsk, Russia 27 D17 56 10N 162 28 E
Ust-Kamenogorsk = Öskemen, Kazakstan 26 E9 50 0N 82 36 E
Ust Khayryuzovo, Russia 27 D16 57 15N 156 45 E
Ust-Kut, Russia 27 D11 56 50N 105 42 E
Ust Kuyga, Russia 27 B14 70 1N 135 43 E
Ust Maya, Russia 27 C14 60 30N 134 28 E
Ust-Mil, Russia 27 D14 59 40N 133 11 E
Ust-Nera, Russia 27 C15 64 35N 143 15 E
Ust-Nyukzha, Russia 27 D13 56 34N 121 37 E
Ust Olenek, Russia 27 B12 73 0N 120 5 E
Ust-Omchug, Russia 27 C15 61 9N 149 38 E
Ust Port, Russia 26 C9 69 40N 84 26 E
Ust Tsilma, Russia 24 A9 65 28N 52 11 E
Ust Urt = Ustyurt Plateau, Asia 26 E6 44 0N 55 0 E
Ust Usa, Russia 24 A10 66 2N 56 57 E
Ust Vorkuta, Russia 24 A11 67 24N 64 0 E
Ústí nad Labem, Czech Rep. 16 C8 50 41N 14 3 E
Ústica, Italy 20 E5 38 42N 13 11 E
Ustinov = Izhevsk, Russia 24 C9 56 51N 53 14 E
Ustyurt Plateau, Asia 26 E6 44 0N 55 0 E
Usu, China 32 B3 44 27N 84 40 E
Usuki, Japan 31 H5 33 8N 131 49 E
Usulután, El Salv. 88 D2 13 25N 88 28W
Usumacinta →, Mexico 87 D6 17 0N 91 0W
Usumbura = Bujumbura, Burundi 54 C2 3 16S 29 18 E
Usure, Tanzania 54 C3 4 40S 34 22 E
Uta, Indonesia 37 E9 4 33S 136 0 E
Utah □, U.S.A. 82 G8 39 20N 111 30W
Utah L., U.S.A. 82 F8 40 10N 111 58W
Utarni, India 42 F4 26 5N 71 58 E
Utatlan, Guatemala 88 C1 15 2N 91 11W
Ute Creek →, U.S.A. 81 H3 35 21N 103 50W
Utena, Lithuania 9 J21 55 27N 25 40 E
Utete, Tanzania 54 D4 8 0S 38 45 E
Uthai Thani, Thailand 38 E3 15 22N 100 3 E
Uthal, Pakistan 42 G2 25 44N 66 40 E
Utiariti, Brazil 92 F7 13 0S 58 10W
Utica, N.Y., U.S.A. 79 C9 43 6N 75 14W
Utica, Ohio, U.S.A. 78 F2 40 14N 82 27W
Utikuma L., Canada 72 B5 55 50N 115 30W
Utopia, Australia 62 C1 22 14S 134 33 E
Utraula, India 43 F10 27 19N 82 25 E
Utrecht, Neths. 15 B5 52 5N 5 8 E
Utrecht, S. Africa 57 D5 27 38S 30 20 E
Utrecht □, Neths. 15 B5 52 6N 5 7 E
Utrera, Spain 19 D3 37 12N 5 48W
Utsjoki, Finland 8 B22 69 51N 26 59 E
Utsunomiya, Japan 31 F9 36 30N 139 50 E
Uttar Pradesh □, India 43 F9 27 0N 80 0 E
Uttaradit, Thailand 38 D3 17 36N 100 5 E
Uttoxeter, U.K. 10 E6 52 54N 1 52W
Uummannarsuaq = Farvel, Kap, Greenland 4 D5 59 48N 43 55W
Uusikaarlepyy, Finland 8 E20 63 32N 22 31 E
Uusikaupunki, Finland 9 F19 60 47N 21 25 E
Uva, Russia 24 C9 56 59N 52 13 E
Uvalde, U.S.A. 81 L5 29 13N 99 47W
Uvat, Russia 26 D7 59 5N 68 50 E
Uvinza, Tanzania 54 D3 5 5S 30 24 E
Uvira, Dem. Rep. of the Congo 54 C2 3 22S 29 3 E
Uvs Nuur, Mongolia 32 A4 50 20N 92 30 E
'Uwairidh, Harrat al, Si. Arabia 44 E3 26 50N 38 0 E
Uwajima, Japan 31 H6 33 10N 132 35 E
Uweinat, Jebel, Sudan 51 D10 21 54N 24 58 E
Uxbridge, Canada 78 B5 44 6N 79 7W
Uxin Qi, China 34 E5 38 50N 109 5 E
Uxmal, Mexico 87 C7 20 22N 89 46W
Üydzin, Mongolia 34 B4 44 9N 107 0 E
Uyo, Nigeria 50 G7 5 1N 7 53 E
Uyûn Mûsa, Egypt 47 F1 29 53N 32 40 E
Uyuni, Bolivia 92 H5 20 28S 66 47W
Uzbekistan ■, Asia 26 E7 41 30N 65 0 E
Uzen, Kazakstan 25 F9 43 29N 52 54 E
Uzen, Mal →, Kazakstan 25 E8 49 4N 49 44 E
Uzerche, France 18 D4 45 25N 1 34 E
Uzh →, Ukraine 17 C16 51 15N 30 12 E
Uzhgorod = Uzhhorod, Ukraine 17 D12 48 36N 22 18 E
Uzhhorod, Ukraine 17 D12 48 36N 22 18 E
Užice, Serbia, Yug. 21 C8 43 55N 19 50 E
Uzunköprü, Turkey 21 D12 41 16N 26 43 E

V

Vaal →, S. Africa 56 D3 29 4S 23 38 E
Vaal Dam, S. Africa 57 D4 27 0S 28 14 E
Vaalwater, S. Africa 57 C4 24 15S 28 8 E
Vaasa, Finland 8 E19 63 6N 21 38 E
Vác, Hungary 17 E10 47 49N 19 10 E
Vacaria, Brazil 95 B5 28 31S 50 52W
Vacaville, U.S.A. 84 G5 38 21N 121 59W
Vach = Vakh →, Russia 26 C8 60 45N 76 45 E
Vache, Î. à, Haiti 89 C5 18 2N 73 35W
Vadnagar, India 42 H5 23 47N 72 40 E
Vadodara, India 42 H5 22 20N 73 10 E
Vadsø, Norway 8 A23 70 3N 29 50 E
Vaduz, Liech. 18 C8 47 8N 9 31 E
Værøy, Norway 8 C15 67 40N 12 40 E
Vágar, Færoe Is. 8 E9 62 5N 7 15W
Vågsfjorden, Norway 8 B17 68 50N 16 50 E
Váh →, Slovak Rep. 17 D9 47 43N 18 7 E
Vahsel B., Antarctica 5 D1 75 0S 35 0W
Váï, Greece 23 D8 35 15N 26 18 E
Vaigach, Russia 26 B6 70 10N 59 0 E
Vail, U.S.A. 74 C5 39 40N 106 20W
Vaisali →, India 43 F8 26 28N 78 53 E
Vakh →, Russia 26 C8 60 45N 76 45 E
Val-d'Or, Canada 70 C4 48 7N 77 47W
Val Marie, Canada 73 D7 49 15N 107 45W
Valahia, Romania 17 F13 44 35N 25 0 E
Valandovo, Macedonia 21 D10 41 19N 22 34 E
Valcheta, Argentina 96 E3 40 40S 66 8W
Valdayskaya Vozvyshennost, Russia 24 C5 57 0N 33 30 E
Valdepeñas, Spain 19 C4 38 43N 3 25W
Valdés, Pen., Argentina 96 E4 42 30S 63 45W
Valdez, U.S.A. 68 B5 61 7N 146 16W
Valdivia, Chile 96 D2 39 50S 73 14W
Valdosta, U.S.A. 77 K4 30 50N 83 17W
Valdres, Norway 9 F13 61 5N 9 5 E
Vale, U.S.A. 82 E5 43 59N 117 15W
Vale of Glamorgan □, U.K. 11 F4 51 28N 3 25W
Valemount, Canada 72 C5 52 50N 119 15W
Valença, Brazil 93 F11 13 20S 39 5W
Valença do Piauí, Brazil 93 E10 6 20S 41 45W
Valence, France 18 D6 44 57N 4 54 E
Valencia, Spain 19 C5 39 27N 0 23W
Valencia, U.S.A. 83 J10 34 48N 106 43W
Valencia, Venezuela 92 A5 10 11N 68 0W
Valencia □, Spain 19 C5 39 20N 0 40W
Valencia, G. de, Spain 19 C6 39 30N 0 20 E
Valencia de Alcántara, Spain 19 C2 39 25N 7 14W
Valencia I., Ireland 13 E1 51 54N 10 22W
Valenciennes, France 18 A5 50 20N 3 34 E
Valentim, Sa. do, Brazil 93 E10 6 0S 43 30W
Valentin, Russia 30 C7 43 8N 134 17 E
Valentine, Nebr., U.S.A. 74 B6 42 52N 100 33W
Valentine, Tex., U.S.A. 81 K2 30 35N 104 30W
Valera, Venezuela 92 B4 9 19N 70 37W
Valga, Estonia 9 H22 57 47N 26 2 E
Valier, U.S.A. 82 B7 48 18N 112 16W
Valjevo, Serbia, Yug. 21 B8 44 18N 19 53 E
Valka, Latvia 9 H21 57 42N 25 57 E
Valkeakoski, Finland 9 F20 61 16N 24 2 E
Valkenswaard, Neths. 15 C5 51 21N 5 29 E
Vall de Uxó = La Vall d'Uixó, Spain 19 C5 39 49N 0 15W
Valladolid, Mexico 87 C7 20 40N 88 11W
Valladolid, Spain 19 B3 41 38N 4 43W
Valldemossa, Spain 22 B9 39 43N 2 37 E
Valle de la Pascua, Venezuela 92 B5 9 13N 66 0W
Valle de las Palmas, Mexico 85 N10 32 20N 116 43W
Valle de Santiago, Mexico 86 C4 20 25N 101 15W
Valle de Suchil, Mexico 86 C4 23 38N 103 55W
Valle de Zaragoza, Mexico 86 B3 27 28N 105 49W
Valle Fértil, Sierra del, Argentina 94 C2 30 20S 68 0W
Valle Hermoso, Mexico 87 B5 25 35N 97 40W
Valledupar, Colombia 92 A4 10 29N 73 15W
Vallehermoso, Canary Is. 22 F2 28 10N 17 15W
Vallejo, U.S.A. 84 G4 38 7N 122 14W
Vallenar, Chile 94 B1 28 30S 70 50W
Valletta, Malta 23 D2 35 54N 14 31 E
Valley Center, U.S.A. 85 M9 33 13N 117 2W
Valley City, U.S.A. 80 B6 46 55N 98 0W
Valley Falls, Oreg., U.S.A. 82 E3 42 29N 120 17W
Valley Falls, R.I., U.S.A. 79 E13 41 54N 71 24W
Valley Springs, U.S.A. 84 G6 38 12N 120 50W
Valley View, U.S.A. 79 F8 40 39N 76 33W
Valley Wells, U.S.A. 85 K11 35 27N 115 46W
Valleyview, Canada 72 B5 55 5N 117 17W
Vallimanca, Arroyo, Argentina 94 D4 35 40S 59 10W
Valls, Spain 19 B6 41 18N 1 15 E
Valmiera, Latvia 9 H21 57 37N 25 29 E
Valognes, France 18 B3 49 30N 1 28W
Valona = Vlóra, Albania 21 D8 40 32N 19 28 E
Valozhyn, Belarus 17 A14 54 3N 26 30 E
Valparaíso, Chile 94 C1 33 2S 71 40W
Valparaíso, Mexico 86 C4 22 50N 103 32W
Valparaiso, U.S.A. 76 E2 41 28N 87 4W
Valparaíso □, Chile 94 C1 33 2S 71 40W
Vals →, S. Africa 56 D4 27 23S 26 30 E
Vals, Tanjung, Indonesia 37 F9 8 26S 137 25 E
Valsad, India 40 J8 20 40N 72 58 E
Valverde, Canary Is. 22 G2 27 48N 17 55W
Valverde del Camino, Spain 19 D2 37 35N 6 47W
Vammala, Finland 9 F20 61 20N 22 54 E
Vámos, Greece 23 D6 35 24N 24 13 E
Van, Turkey 25 G7 38 30N 43 20 E
Van, L. = Van Gölü, Turkey 25 G7 38 30N 43 0 E
Van Alstyne, U.S.A. 81 J6 33 25N 96 35W
Van Blommestein Meer, Surinam 93 C7 4 45N 55 5W
Van Buren, Canada 71 C6 47 10N 67 55W
Van Buren, Ark., U.S.A. 81 H7 35 26N 94 21W
Van Buren, Maine, U.S.A. 77 B11 47 10N 67 58W
Van Buren, Mo., U.S.A. 81 G9 37 0N 91 1W
Van Canh, Vietnam 38 F7 13 37N 109 0 E
Van Diemen, C., N. Terr., Australia 60 B5 11 9S 130 24 E
Van Diemen, C., Queens., Australia 62 B2 16 30S 139 46 E
Van Diemen G., Australia 60 B5 11 45S 132 0 E
Van Gölü, Turkey 25 G7 38 30N 43 0 E
Van Horn, U.S.A. 81 K2 31 3N 104 50W
Van Ninh, Vietnam 38 F7 12 42N 109 14 E
Van Rees, Pegunungan, Indonesia 37 E9 2 35S 138 15 E
Van Wert, U.S.A. 76 E3 40 52N 84 35W
Vanadzor, Armenia 25 F7 40 48N 44 30 E
Vanavara, Russia 27 C11 60 22N 102 16 E
Vancouver, Canada 72 D4 49 15N 123 10W
Vancouver, U.S.A. 84 E4 45 38N 122 40W
Vancouver, C., Australia 61 G2 35 2S 118 11 E
Vancouver I., Canada 72 D3 49 50N 126 0W
Vandalia, Ill., U.S.A. 80 F10 38 58N 89 6W
Vandalia, Mo., U.S.A. 80 F9 39 19N 91 29W
Vandenburg, U.S.A. 85 L6 34 35N 120 33W
Vanderbijlpark, S. Africa 57 D4 26 42S 27 54 E
Vandergrift, U.S.A. 78 F5 40 36N 79 34W
Vanderhoof, Canada 72 C4 54 0N 124 0W
Vanderkloof Dam, S. Africa 56 E3 30 4S 24 40 E
Vanderlin I., Australia 62 B2 15 44S 137 2 E
Vänern, Sweden 9 G15 58 47N 13 30 E
Vänersborg, Sweden 9 G15 58 26N 12 19 E
Vang Vieng, Laos 38 C4 18 58N 102 32 E
Vanga, Kenya 54 C4 4 35S 39 12 E
Vangaindrano, Madag. 57 C8 23 21S 47 36 E
Vanguard, Canada 73 D7 49 55N 107 20W
Vanino, Russia 27 E15 48 50N 140 5 E
Vanna, Norway 8 A18 70 6N 19 50 E
Vännäs, Sweden 8 E18 63 58N 19 48 E
Vannes, France 18 C2 47 40N 2 47W
Vanrhynsdorp, S. Africa 56 E2 31 36S 18 44 E
Vansbro, Sweden 9 F16 60 32N 14 15 E
Vansittart B., Australia 60 B4 14 3S 126 17 E
Vantaa, Finland 9 F21 60 18N 24 58 E
Vanua Levu, Fiji 59 C8 16 33S 179 15 E
Vanua Mbalavu, Fiji 59 C9 17 40S 178 57W
Vanuatu ■, Pac. Oc. 64 J8 15 0S 168 0 E
Vanwyksvlei, S. Africa 56 E3 30 18S 21 49 E
Vanzylsrus, S. Africa 56 D3 26 52S 22 4 E
Vapnyarka, Ukraine 17 D15 48 32N 28 45 E
Varanasi, India 43 G10 25 22N 83 0 E
Varanger-halvøya, Norway 8 A23 70 25N 29 30 E
Varangerfjorden, Norway 8 A23 70 3N 29 25 E
Varaždin, Croatia 16 E9 46 20N 16 20 E
Varberg, Sweden 9 H15 57 6N 12 20 E
Vardar = Axiós →, Greece 21 D10 40 57N 22 35 E
Varde, Denmark 9 J13 55 38N 8 29 E
Vardø, Norway 8 A24 70 23N 31 5 E
Varella, Mui, Vietnam 38 F7 12 54N 109 26 E
Varena, Lithuania 9 J21 54 12N 24 30 E
Varese, Italy 18 D8 45 48N 8 50 E
Varginha, Brazil 95 A6 21 33S 45 25W
Varillas, Chile 94 A1 24 0S 70 10W
Varkaus, Finland 9 E22 62 19N 27 50 E
Varna, Bulgaria 21 C12 43 13N 27 56 E
Värnamo, Sweden 9 H16 57 10N 14 3 E
Vars, Canada 79 A9 45 21N 75 21W
Varysburg, U.S.A. 78 D6 42 46N 78 19W
Varzaneh, Iran 45 C7 32 25N 52 40 E
Vasa Barris →, Brazil 93 F11 11 10S 37 10W
Vascongadas = País Vasco □, Spain 19 A4 42 50N 2 45W
Vasht = Khāsh, Iran 40 E2 28 15N 61 15 E
Vasilevichi, Belarus 17 B15 52 15N 29 50 E
Vasilkov = Vasylkiv, Ukraine 17 C16 50 7N 30 15 E
Vaslui, Romania 17 E14 46 38N 27 42 E
Vassar, Canada 73 D9 49 10N 95 55W
Vassar, U.S.A. 76 D4 43 22N 83 35W
Västerås, Sweden 9 G17 59 37N 16 38 E
Västerbotten, Sweden 8 D18 64 36N 20 4 E
Västerdalälven →, Sweden 9 F16 60 30N 14 7 E
Västervik, Sweden 9 H17 57 43N 16 33 E
Västmanland, Sweden 9 G16 59 45N 16 20 E
Vasto, Italy 20 C6 42 8N 14 40 E
Vasylkiv, Ukraine 17 C16 50 7N 30 15 E
Vatersay, U.K. 12 E1 56 55N 7 32W
Vatican City ■, Europe 20 D5 41 54N 12 27 E
Vatili, Cyprus 23 D12 35 6N 33 40 E
Vatnajökull, Iceland 8 D5 64 30N 16 48W
Vatoa, Fiji 59 D9 19 50S 178 13W
Vatólakkos, Greece 23 D5 35 27N 23 53 E
Vatoloha, Madag. 57 B8 17 52S 47 48 E
Vatomandry, Madag. 57 B8 19 20S 48 59 E
Vatra-Dornei, Romania 17 E13 47 22N 25 22 E
Vatrak →, India 42 H5 23 9N 73 2 E
Vättern, Sweden 9 G16 58 25N 14 30 E
Vaughn, Mont., U.S.A. 82 C8 47 33N 111 33W
Vaughn, N. Mex., U.S.A. 83 J11 34 36N 105 13W
Vaujours L., Canada 70 A5 55 27N 74 15W
Vaupés = Uaupés →, Brazil 92 C5 0 2N 67 16W
Vaupes □, Colombia 92 C4 1 0N 71 0W
Vauxhall, Canada 72 C6 50 5N 112 9W
Vav, India 42 G4 24 22N 71 31 E
Vava'u, Tonga 59 D12 18 36S 174 0W
Vawkavysk, Belarus 17 B13 53 9N 24 30 E
Växjö, Sweden 9 H16 56 52N 14 50 E
Vaygach, Ostrov, Russia 26 C7 70 0N 60 0 E
Váyia, Ákra, Greece 23 C10 36 15N 28 11 E
Vechte →, Neths. 15 B6 52 34N 6 6 E
Vedea →, Romania 17 G13 43 42N 25 41 E
Vedia, Argentina 94 C3 34 30S 61 31W
Veendam, Neths. 15 A6 53 5N 6 52 E
Veenendaal, Neths. 15 B5 52 2N 5 34 E
Vefsna →, Norway 8 D15 65 48N 13 10 E
Vega, Norway 8 D14 65 40N 11 55 E
Vega, U.S.A. 81 H3 35 15N 102 26W
Vegreville, Canada 72 C6 53 30N 112 5W
Vejer de la Frontera, Spain 19 D3 36 15N 5 59W
Vejle, Denmark 9 J13 55 43N 9 30 E
Velas, C., Costa Rica 88 D2 10 21N 85 52W
Velasco, Sierra de, Argentina 94 B2 29 20S 67 10W
Velddrif, S. Africa 56 E2 32 42S 18 11 E
Velebit Planina, Croatia 16 F8 44 50N 15 20 E
Veles, Macedonia 21 D9 41 46N 21 47 E
Vélez-Málaga, Spain 19 D3 36 48N 4 5W
Vélez Rubio, Spain 19 D4 37 41N 2 5W
Velhas →, Brazil 93 G10 17 13S 44 49W
Velika Kapela, Croatia 16 F8 45 10N 15 5 E
Velikaya →, Russia 24 C4 57 48N 28 10 E
Velikaya Kema, Russia 30 B8 45 30N 137 12 E
Veliki Ustyug, Russia 24 B8 60 47N 46 20 E
Velikiye Luki, Russia 24 C5 56 25N 30 32 E
Veliko Tŭrnovo, Bulgaria 21 C11 43 5N 25 41 E
Velikonda Range, India 40 M11 14 45N 79 10 E
Velletri, Italy 20 D5 41 41N 12 47 E
Vellore, India 40 N11 12 57N 79 10 E
Velsk, Russia 24 B7 61 10N 42 5 E
Velva, U.S.A. 80 A4 48 4N 100 56W
Venado Tuerto, Argentina 94 C3 33 50S 62 0W
Vendée □, France 18 C3 46 50N 1 35W
Vendôme, France 18 C4 47 47N 1 3 E
Venézia, Italy 20 B5 45 27N 12 21 E
Venézia, G. di, Italy 20 B5 45 15N 13 0 E
Venezuela ■, S. Amer. 92 B5 8 0N 66 0W
Venezuela, G. de, Venezuela 92 A4 11 30N 71 0W
Vengurla, India 40 M8 15 53N 73 45 E
Venice = Venézia, Italy 20 B5 45 27N 12 21 E
Venice, U.S.A. 77 M4 27 6N 82 27W
Venkatapuram, India 41 K12 18 20N 80 30 E
Venlo, Neths. 15 C6 51 22N 6 11 E
Vennesla, Norway 9 G12 58 15N 7 59 E
Venray, Neths. 15 C6 51 31N 6 0 E
Ventana, Punta de la, Mexico 86 C3 24 4N 109 48W
Ventana, Sa. de la, Argentina 94 D3 38 0S 62 30W
Ventersburg, S. Africa 56 D4 28 7S 27 9 E
Venterstad, S. Africa 56 E4 30 47S 25 48 E
Ventnor, U.K. 11 G6 50 36N 1 12W
Ventotène, Italy 20 D5 40 47N 13 25 E
Ventoux, Mt., France 18 D6 44 10N 5 17 E
Ventspils, Latvia 9 H19 57 25N 21 32 E
Ventuarí →, Venezuela 92 C5 3 58N 67 2W
Ventucopa, U.S.A. 85 L7 34 50N 119 29W
Ventura, U.S.A. 85 L7 34 17N 119 18W
Venus B., Australia 63 F4 38 40S 145 42 E
Vera, Argentina 94 B3 29 30S 60 20W
Vera, Spain 19 D5 37 15N 1 51W
Veracruz, Mexico 87 D5 19 10N 96 10W
Veracruz □, Mexico 87 D5 19 0N 96 15W
Veraval, India 42 J4 20 53N 70 27 E
Verbánia, Italy 18 D8 45 56N 8 33 E
Vercelli, Italy 18 D8 45 19N 8 25 E
Verdalsøra, Norway 8 E14 63 48N 11 30 E
Verde →, Argentina 96 E3 41 56S 65 5W
Verde →, Goiás, Brazil 93 G8 18 1S 50 14W
Verde →, Mato Grosso do Sul, Brazil 93 H8 21 25S 52 20W
Verde →, Chihuahua, Mexico 86 B3 26 29N 107 58W
Verde →, Oaxaca, Mexico 87 D5 15 59N 97 50W
Verde →, Veracruz, Mexico 86 C4 21 10N 102 50W
Verde →, Paraguay 94 A4 23 9S 57 37W
Verde →, U.S.A. 74 D4 33 33N 111 40W
Verde, Cay, Bahamas 88 B4 23 0N 75 5W
Verden, Germany 16 B5 52 55N 9 14 E
Verdi, U.S.A. 84 F7 39 31N 119 59W
Verdun, France 18 B6 49 9N 5 24 E
Vereeniging, S. Africa 57 D4 26 38S 27 57 E
Verga, C., Guinea 50 F3 10 30N 14 10W
Vergara, Uruguay 95 C5 32 56S 53 57W
Vergemont Cr. →, Australia 62 C3 24 16S 143 16 E
Vergennes, U.S.A. 79 B11 44 10N 73 15W
Verín, Spain 19 B2 41 57N 7 27W
Verkhnevilyuysk, Russia 27 C13 63 27N 120 18 E
Verkhniy Baskunchak, Russia 25 E8 48 14N 46 44 E
Verkhoyansk, Russia 27 C14 67 35N 133 25 E
Verkhoyansk Ra. = Verkhoyanskiy Khrebet, Russia 27 C13 66 0N 129 0 E
Verkhoyanskiy Khrebet, Russia 27 C13 66 0N 129 0 E
Vermilion, Canada 73 C6 53 20N 110 50W
Vermilion, U.S.A. 78 E2 41 25N 82 22W
Vermilion →, Alta., Canada 73 C6 53 22N 110 51W
Vermilion →, Qué., Canada 70 C5 47 38N 72 56W
Vermilion, B., U.S.A. 81 L9 29 45N 91 55W
Vermilion Bay, Canada 73 D10 49 51N 93 34W
Vermilion L., U.S.A. 80 B8 47 53N 92 26W
Vermillion, U.S.A. 80 D6 42 47N 96 56W
Vermont □, U.S.A. 79 C12 44 0N 73 0W
Vernal, U.S.A. 82 F9 40 27N 109 32W
Vernalis, U.S.A. 84 H5 37 36N 121 17W
Verner, Canada 70 C3 46 25N 80 8W
Verneukpan, S. Africa 56 E3 30 0S 21 0 E
Vernon, Canada 72 C5 50 20N 119 15W
Vernon, U.S.A. 81 H5 34 9N 99 17W
Vernonia, U.S.A. 84 E3 45 52N 123 11W
Vero Beach, U.S.A. 77 M5 27 38N 80 24W
Véroia, Greece 21 D10 40 34N 22 12 E
Verona, Canada 79 B8 44 29N 76 42W
Verona, Italy 20 B4 45 27N 10 59 E
Verona, U.S.A. 80 D10 42 59N 89 32W
Versailles, France 18 B5 48 48N 2 8 E
Vert, C., Senegal 50 F2 14 45N 17 30W
Verulam, S. Africa 57 D5 29 38S 31 2 E
Verviers, Belgium 15 D5 50 37N 5 52 E
Veselovskoye Vdkhr., Russia 25 E7 46 58N 41 25 E
Vesoul, France 18 C7 47 40N 6 11 E
Vesterålen, Norway 8 B16 68 45N 15 0 E

W

West Ice Shelf

Wake I., *Pac. Oc.* **64 F8** 19 18N 166 36 E
WaKeeney, *U.S.A.* **80 F5** 39 1N 99 53W
Wakefield, *N.Z.* **59 J4** 41 24S 173 5 E
Wakefield, *U.K.* **10 D6** 53 41N 1 29W
Wakefield, *Mass., U.S.A.* **79 D13** 42 30N 71 4W
Wakefield, *Mich., U.S.A.* **80 B10** 46 29N 89 56W
Wakema, *Burma* **41 L19** 16 30N 95 11 E
Wakkanai, *Japan* **30 B10** 45 28N 141 35 E
Wakkerstroom, *S. Africa* **57 D5** 27 24S 30 10 E
Wakool, *Australia* **63 F3** 35 28S 144 23 E
Wakool →, *Australia* **63 F3** 35 5S 143 33 E
Wakre, *Indonesia* **37 E8** 0 19S 131 5 E
Wakuach, L., *Canada* **71 A6** 55 34N 67 32W
Walamba, *Zambia* **55 E2** 13 30S 28 42 E
Wałbrzych, *Poland* **16 C9** 50 45N 16 18 E
Walbury Hill, *U.K.* **11 F6** 51 21N 1 28W
Walcha, *Australia* **63 E5** 30 55S 151 31 E
Walcheren, *Neths.* **15 C3** 51 30N 3 35 E
Walcott, *U.S.A.* **82 F10** 41 46N 106 51W
Wałcz, *Poland* **16 B9** 53 17N 16 27 E
Waldburg Ra., *Australia* **61 D2** 24 40S 117 35 E
Walden, *Colo., U.S.A.* **82 F10** 40 44N 106 17W
Walden, *N.Y., U.S.A.* **79 E10** 41 34N 74 11W
Waldport, *U.S.A.* **82 D1** 44 26N 124 4W
Waldron, *U.S.A.* **81 H7** 34 54N 94 5W
Walebing, *Australia* **61 F2** 30 41S 116 13 E
Wales □, *U.K.* **11 E3** 52 19N 4 43W
Walgett, *Australia* **63 E4** 30 0S 148 5 E
Walgreen Coast, *Antarctica* **5 D15** 75 15S 105 0W
Walker, *U.S.A.* **80 B7** 47 6N 94 35W
Walker, L., *Canada* **71 B6** 50 20N 67 11W
Walker L., *Canada* **73 C9** 54 42N 95 57W
Walker L., *U.S.A.* **82 G4** 38 42N 118 43W
Walkerston, *Australia* **62 C4** 21 11S 149 8 E
Walkerton, *Canada* **78 B3** 44 10N 81 10W
Wall, *U.S.A.* **80 D3** 44 0N 102 8W
Walla Walla, *U.S.A.* **82 C4** 46 4N 118 20W
Wallace, *Idaho, U.S.A.* **82 C6** 47 28N 115 56W
Wallace, *N.C., U.S.A.* **77 H7** 34 44N 77 59W
Wallaceburg, *Canada* **78 D2** 42 34N 82 23W
Wallachia = Valahia,
Romania **17 F13** 44 35N 25 0 E
Wallal, *Australia* **63 D4** 26 32S 146 7 E
Wallam Cr. →, *Australia* **63 D4** 28 40S 147 20 E
Wallambin, L., *Australia* **61 F2** 30 57S 117 35 E
Wallan, *Australia* **63 F3** 37 26S 144 59 E
Wallangarra, *Australia* **63 D5** 28 56S 151 58 E
Wallaroo, *Australia* **63 E2** 33 56S 137 39 E
Wallenpaupack, L., *U.S.A.* **79 E9** 41 25N 75 15W
Wallingford, *U.S.A.* **79 E12** 41 27N 72 50W
Wallis & Futuna, Is., *Pac. Oc.* **64 J10** 13 18S 176 10W
Wallowa, *U.S.A.* **82 D5** 45 34N 117 32W
Wallowa Mts., *U.S.A.* **82 D5** 45 20N 117 30W
Walls, *U.K.* **12 A7** 60 14N 1 33W
Wallula, *U.S.A.* **82 C4** 46 5N 118 54W
Wallumbilla, *Australia* **63 D4** 26 33S 149 9 E
Walmsley, L., *Canada* **73 A7** 63 25N 108 36W
Walney, I. of, *U.K.* **10 C4** 54 6N 3 15W
Walnut Creek, *U.S.A.* **84 H4** 37 54N 122 4W
Walnut Ridge, *U.S.A.* **81 G9** 36 4N 90 57W
Walpole, *Australia* **61 F2** 34 58S 116 44 E
Walpole, *U.S.A.* **79 D13** 42 9N 71 15W
Walsall, *U.K.* **11 E6** 52 35N 1 58W
Walsenburg, *U.S.A.* **81 G2** 37 38N 104 47W
Walsh, *U.S.A.* **81 G3** 37 23N 102 17W
Walsh →, *Australia* **62 B3** 16 31S 143 42 E
Walterboro, *U.S.A.* **77 J5** 32 55N 80 40W
Walters, *U.S.A.* **81 H5** 34 22N 98 19W
Waltham, *U.S.A.* **79 D13** 42 23N 71 14W
Waltman, *U.S.A.* **82 E10** 43 4N 107 12W
Walton, *U.S.A.* **79 D9** 42 10N 75 8W
Walton-on-the-Naze, *U.K.* **11 F9** 51 51N 1 17 E
Walvis Bay, *Namibia* **56 C1** 23 0S 14 28 E
Walvisbaai = Walvis Bay,
Namibia **56 C1** 23 0S 14 28 E
Wamba,
Dem. Rep. of the Congo **54 B2** 2 10N 27 57 E
Wamba, *Kenya* **54 B4** 0 58N 37 19 E
Wamego, *U.S.A.* **80 F6** 39 12N 96 18W
Wamena, *Indonesia* **37 E9** 4 4S 138 57 E
Wamsutter, *U.S.A.* **82 F9** 41 40N 107 58W
Wamulan, *Indonesia* **37 E7** 3 27S 126 7 E
Wan Xian, *China* **34 E8** 38 47N 115 7 E
Wana, *Pakistan* **42 C3** 32 20N 69 32 E
Wanaaring, *Australia* **63 D3** 29 38S 144 9 E
Wanaka, *N.Z.* **59 L2** 44 42S 169 9 E
Wanaka L., *N.Z.* **59 L2** 44 33S 169 7 E
Wanapitei L., *Canada* **70 C3** 46 45N 80 40W
Wandel Sea = McKinley
Sea, *Arctic* **4 A7** 82 0N 0 0 E
Wanderer, *Zimbabwe* **55 F3** 19 36S 30 1 E
Wandhari, *Pakistan* **42 F2** 27 42N 66 48 E
Wandoan, *Australia* **63 D4** 26 5S 149 55 E
Wanfu, *China* **35 D12** 40 8N 122 38 E
Wang →, *Thailand* **38 D2** 17 8N 99 2 E
Wang Noi, *Thailand* **38 E3** 14 13N 100 44 E
Wang Saphung, *Thailand* **38 D3** 17 18N 101 46 E
Wang Thong, *Thailand* **38 D3** 16 50N 100 26 E
Wanga,
Dem. Rep. of the Congo **54 B2** 2 58N 29 12 E
Wangal, *Indonesia* **37 F8** 6 8S 134 9 E
Wanganella, *Australia* **63 F3** 35 6S 144 49 E
Wanganui, *N.Z.* **59 H5** 39 56S 175 3 E
Wangaratta, *Australia* **63 F4** 36 21S 146 19 E
Wangary, *Australia* **63 E2** 34 35S 135 29 E
Wangdu, *China* **34 E8** 38 40N 115 7 E
Wangerooge, *Germany* **16 B4** 53 47N 7 54 E
Wangi, *Kenya* **54 C5** 1 58S 40 58 E
Wangiwangi, *Indonesia* **37 F6** 5 22S 123 37 E
Wangqing, *China* **35 C15** 43 12N 129 42 E
Wankaner, *India* **42 H4** 22 35N 71 0 E
Wanless, *Canada* **73 C8** 54 11N 101 21W
Wanning, *Taiwan* **38 C8** 23 15N 121 17 E
Wanon Niwat, *Thailand* **38 D4** 17 38N 103 46 E
Wanquan, *China* **34 D8** 40 50N 114 40 E
Wanrong, *China* **34 G6** 35 25N 110 50 E
Wantage, *U.K.* **11 F6** 51 35N 1 25W
Wanxian, *China* **33 C5** 30 42N 108 20 E
Wapakoneta, *U.S.A.* **76 E3** 40 34N 84 12W
Wapato, *U.S.A.* **82 C3** 46 27N 120 25W
Wapawekka L., *Canada* **73 C8** 54 55N 104 40W
Wapikopa L., *Canada* **70 B2** 52 56N 87 53W
Wapiti →, *Canada* **72 B5** 55 5N 118 18W
Wappingers Falls, *U.S.A.* **79 E11** 41 36N 73 55W
Wapsipinicon →, *U.S.A.* **80 E9** 41 44N 90 19W
Warangal, *India* **40 L11** 17 58N 79 35 E
Waraseoni, *India* **43 J9** 21 45N 80 2 E
Waratah, *Australia* **62 G4** 41 30S 145 30 E
Waratah B., *Australia* **63 F4** 38 54S 146 5 E
Warburton, *Vic., Australia* **63 F4** 37 47S 145 42 E
Warburton, *W. Austral.,*
Australia **61 E4** 26 8S 126 35 E
Warburton Ra., *Australia* **61 E4** 25 55S 126 28 E
Ward, *N.Z.* **59 J5** 41 49S 174 11 E
Ward →, *Australia* **63 D4** 26 28S 146 6 E
Ward Mt., *U.S.A.* **84 H8** 37 12N 118 54W
Warden, *S. Africa* **57 D4** 27 50S 29 0 E
Wardha, *India* **40 J11** 20 45N 78 39 E
Wardha →, *India* **40 K11** 19 57N 79 11 E
Ware, *Canada* **72 B3** 57 26N 125 41W
Ware, *U.S.A.* **79 D12** 42 16N 72 14W
Waregem, *Belgium* **15 D3** 50 53N 3 27 E
Wareham, *U.S.A.* **79 E14** 41 46N 70 43W
Waremme, *Belgium* **15 D5** 50 43N 5 15 E
Warialda, *Australia* **63 D5** 29 29S 150 33 E
Wariap, *Indonesia* **37 E8** 1 30S 134 5 E
Warin Chamrap, *Thailand* **38 E5** 15 12N 104 53 E
Warkopi, *Indonesia* **37 E8** 1 12S 134 9 E
Warm Springs, *U.S.A.* **83 G5** 38 10N 116 20W
Warman, *Canada* **73 C7** 52 19N 106 30W
Warmbad, *Namibia* **56 D2** 28 25S 18 42 E
Warmbad, *S. Africa* **57 C4** 24 51S 28 19 E
Warminster, *U.K.* **11 F5** 51 12N 2 10W
Warminster, *U.S.A.* **79 F9** 40 12N 75 6W
Warner Mts., *U.S.A.* **82 F3** 41 40N 120 15W
Warner Robins, *U.S.A.* **77 J4** 32 37N 83 36W
Waroona, *Australia* **61 F2** 32 50S 115 58 E
Warracknabeal, *Australia* **63 F3** 36 9S 142 26 E
Warragul, *Australia* **63 F4** 38 10S 145 58 E
Warrego →, *Australia* **63 E4** 30 24S 145 21 E
Warrego Ra., *Australia* **62 C4** 24 58S 146 0 E
Warren, *Australia* **63 E4** 31 42S 147 51 E
Warren, *Ark., U.S.A.* **81 J8** 33 37N 92 4W
Warren, *Mich., U.S.A.* **76 D4** 42 30N 83 0W
Warren, *Minn., U.S.A.* **80 A6** 48 12N 96 46W
Warren, *Ohio, U.S.A.* **78 E4** 41 14N 80 49W
Warren, *Pa., U.S.A.* **78 E5** 41 51N 79 9W
Warrenpoint, *U.K.* **13 B5** 54 6N 6 15W
Warrensburg, *Mo., U.S.A.* **80 F8** 38 46N 93 44W
Warrensburg, *N.Y., U.S.A.* **79 C11** 43 29N 73 46W
Warrenton, *S. Africa* **56 D3** 28 9S 24 47 E
Warrenton, *U.S.A.* **84 D3** 46 10N 123 56W
Warri, *Nigeria* **50 G7** 5 30N 5 41 E
Warrina, *Australia* **63 D2** 28 12S 135 50 E
Warrington, *U.K.* **10 D5** 53 24N 2 35W
Warrington, *U.S.A.* **77 K2** 30 23N 87 17W
Warrington □, *U.K.* **10 D5** 53 24N 2 35W
Warrnambool, *Australia* **63 F3** 38 25S 142 30 E
Warroad, *U.S.A.* **80 A7** 48 54N 95 19W
Warruwi, *Australia* **62 A1** 11 36S 133 20 E
Warsa, *Indonesia* **37 E9** 0 47S 135 55 E
Warsak Dam, *Pakistan* **42 B4** 34 11N 71 19 E
Warsaw = Warszawa,
Poland **17 B11** 52 13N 21 0 E
Warsaw, *Ind., U.S.A.* **76 E3** 41 14N 85 51W
Warsaw, *N.Y., U.S.A.* **78 D6** 42 45N 78 8W
Warsaw, *Ohio, U.S.A.* **78 F3** 40 20N 82 0W
Warszawa, *Poland* **17 B11** 52 13N 21 0 E
Warta →, *Poland* **16 B8** 52 35N 14 39 E
Warthe = Warta →,
Poland **16 B8** 52 35N 14 39 E
Waru, *Indonesia* **37 E8** 3 30S 130 36 E
Warwick, *Australia* **63 D5** 28 10S 152 1 E
Warwick, *U.K.* **11 E6** 52 18N 1 35W
Warwick, *N.Y., U.S.A.* **79 E10** 41 16N 74 22W
Warwick, *R.I., U.S.A.* **79 E13** 41 42N 71 28W
Warwickshire □, *U.K.* **11 E6** 52 14N 1 38W
Wasaga Beach, *Canada* **78 B4** 44 31N 80 1W
Wasagaming, *Canada* **73 C9** 50 39N 99 58W
Wasatch Ra., *U.S.A.* **82 F8** 40 30N 111 15W
Wasbank, *S. Africa* **57 D5** 28 15S 30 9 E
Wasco, *Calif., U.S.A.* **85 K7** 35 36N 119 20W
Wasco, *Oreg., U.S.A.* **82 D3** 45 36N 120 42W
Waseca, *U.S.A.* **80 C8** 44 5N 93 30W
Wasekamio L., *Canada* **73 B7** 56 45N 108 45W
Wash, The, *U.K.* **10 E8** 52 58N 0 20 E
Washago, *Canada* **78 B5** 44 45N 79 20W
Washburn, *N. Dak., U.S.A.* **80 B4** 47 17N 101 2W
Washburn, *Wis., U.S.A.* **80 B9** 46 40N 90 54W
Washim, *India* **40 J10** 20 3N 77 0 E
Washington, *U.K.* **10 C6** 54 55N 1 30W
Washington, *D.C., U.S.A.* **76 F7** 38 54N 77 2W
Washington, *Ga., U.S.A.* **77 J4** 33 44N 82 44W
Washington, *Ind., U.S.A.* **76 F2** 38 40N 87 10W
Washington, *Iowa, U.S.A.* **80 E9** 41 18N 91 42W
Washington, *Mo., U.S.A.* **80 F9** 38 33N 91 1W
Washington, *N.C., U.S.A.* **77 H7** 35 33N 77 3W
Washington, *N.J., U.S.A.* **79 F10** 40 46N 74 59W
Washington, *Pa., U.S.A.* **78 F4** 40 10N 80 15W
Washington, *Utah, U.S.A.* **83 H7** 37 8N 113 31W
Washington □, *U.S.A.* **82 C3** 47 30N 120 30W
Washington, Mt., *U.S.A.* **79 B13** 44 16N 71 18W
Washington Court House,
U.S.A. **76 F4** 39 32N 83 26W
Washington I., *U.S.A.* **76 C2** 45 23N 86 54W
Washougal, *U.S.A.* **84 E4** 45 35N 122 21W
Wasian, *Indonesia* **37 E8** 1 47S 133 19 E
Wasilla, *U.S.A.* **68 B5** 61 35N 149 26W
Wasior, *Indonesia* **37 E8** 2 43S 134 30 E
Waskaganish, *Canada* **70 B4** 51 30N 78 40W
Waskaiowaka, L., *Canada* **73 B9** 56 33N 96 23W
Waskesiu Lake, *Canada* **73 C7** 53 55N 106 5W
Wasserkuppe, *Germany* **16 C5** 50 29N 9 55 E
Waswanipi, *Canada* **70 C4** 49 40N 76 29W
Waswanipi, L., *Canada* **70 C4** 49 35N 76 40W
Watampone, *Indonesia* **37 E6** 4 29S 120 25 E
Water Park Pt., *Australia* **62 C5** 22 56S 150 47 E
Water Valley, *U.S.A.* **81 H10** 34 10N 89 38W
Waterberge, *S. Africa* **57 C4** 24 10S 28 0 E
Waterbury, *Conn., U.S.A.* **79 E11** 41 33N 73 3W
Waterbury, *Vt., U.S.A.* **79 B12** 44 20N 72 46W
Waterbury L., *Canada* **73 B8** 58 10N 104 22W
Waterdown, *Canada* **78 C5** 43 20N 79 53W
Waterford, *Canada* **78 D4** 42 56N 80 17W
Waterford, *Ireland* **13 D4** 52 15N 7 8W
Waterford, *Calif., U.S.A.* **84 H6** 37 38N 120 46W
Waterford, *Pa., U.S.A.* **78 E5** 41 57N 79 59W
Waterford □, *Ireland* **13 D4** 52 10N 7 40W
Waterford Harbour, *Ireland* **13 D5** 52 8N 6 58W
Waterhen L., *Canada* **73 C9** 52 10N 99 40W
Waterloo, *Belgium* **15 D4** 50 43N 4 25 E
Waterloo, *Ont., Canada* **78 C4** 43 30N 80 32W
Waterloo, *Qué., Canada* **79 A12** 45 22N 72 32W
Waterloo, *Ill., U.S.A.* **80 F9** 38 20N 90 9W
Waterloo, *Iowa, U.S.A.* **80 D8** 42 30N 92 21W
Waterloo, *N.Y., U.S.A.* **78 D8** 42 54N 76 52W
Watersmeet, *U.S.A.* **80 B10** 46 16N 89 11W
Waterton Nat. Park, *U.S.A.* **82 B7** 48 45N 115 0W
Watertown, *Conn., U.S.A.* **79 E11** 41 36N 73 7W
Watertown, *N.Y., U.S.A.* **79 C9** 43 59N 75 55W
Watertown, *S. Dak., U.S.A.* **80 C6** 44 54N 97 7W
Watertown, *Wis., U.S.A.* **80 D10** 43 12N 88 43W
Waterval-Boven, *S. Africa* **57 D5** 25 40S 30 18 E
Waterville, *Canada* **79 A13** 45 16N 71 54W
Waterville, *Maine, U.S.A.* **77 C11** 44 33N 69 38W
Waterville, *N.Y., U.S.A.* **79 D9** 42 56N 75 23W
Waterville, *Pa., U.S.A.* **78 E7** 41 19N 77 21W
Waterville, *Wash., U.S.A.* **82 C3** 47 39N 120 4W
Watervliet, *U.S.A.* **79 D11** 42 44N 73 42W
Wates, *Indonesia* **37 G14** 7 51S 110 10 E
Watford, *Canada* **78 D3** 42 57N 81 53W
Watford, *U.K.* **11 F7** 51 40N 0 24W
Watford City, *U.S.A.* **80 B3** 47 48N 103 17W
Wathaman →, *Canada* **73 B8** 57 16N 102 59W
Wathaman L., *Canada* **73 B8** 56 58N 103 44W
Watheroo, *Australia* **61 F2** 30 15S 116 0 E
Wating, *China* **34 G4** 35 40N 106 38 E
Watkins Glen, *U.S.A.* **78 D8** 42 23N 76 52W
Watling I. = San Salvador I.,
Bahamas **89 B5** 24 0N 74 40W
Watonga, *U.S.A.* **81 H5** 35 51N 98 25W
Watrous, *Canada* **73 C7** 51 40N 105 25W
Watrous, *U.S.A.* **81 H2** 35 48N 104 59W
Watsa,
Dem. Rep. of the Congo **54 B2** 3 4N 29 30 E
Watseka, *U.S.A.* **76 E2** 40 47N 87 44W
Watson, *Australia* **61 F5** 30 29S 131 31 E
Watson, *Canada* **73 C8** 52 10N 104 30W
Watson Lake, *Canada* **72 A3** 60 6N 128 49W
Watsontown, *U.S.A.* **78 E8** 41 5N 76 52W
Watsonville, *U.S.A.* **84 J5** 36 55N 121 45W
Wattiwarriganna Cr. →,
Australia **63 D2** 28 57S 136 10 E
Watuata = Batuata,
Indonesia **37 F6** 6 12S 122 42 E
Watubela, Kepulauan,
Indonesia **37 E8** 4 28S 131 35 E
Watubela Is. = Watubela,
Kepulauan, *Indonesia* **37 E8** 4 28S 131 35 E
Wau, *Sudan* **49 F6** 7 45N 28 1 E
Waubamik, *Canada* **78 A4** 45 27N 80 1W
Waubay, *U.S.A.* **80 C6** 45 20N 97 18W
Wauchope, *N.S.W.,*
Australia **63 E5** 31 28S 152 45 E
Wauchope, *N. Terr.,*
Australia **62 C1** 20 36S 134 15 E
Waukarlycarly, L., *Australia* **60 D3** 21 18S 121 56 E
Waukegan, *U.S.A.* **75 B9** 42 22N 87 50W
Waukesha, *U.S.A.* **76 D1** 43 1N 88 14W
Waukon, *U.S.A.* **80 D9** 43 16N 91 29W
Waupaca, *U.S.A.* **80 C10** 44 21N 89 5W
Waupun, *U.S.A.* **80 D10** 43 38N 88 44W
Waurika, *U.S.A.* **81 H6** 34 10N 98 0W
Wausau, *U.S.A.* **80 C10** 44 58N 89 38W
Wautoma, *U.S.A.* **80 C10** 44 4N 89 18W
Wauwatosa, *U.S.A.* **76 D2** 43 3N 88 0W
Waveney →, *U.K.* **11 E9** 52 35N 1 39 E
Waverley, *N.Z.* **59 H5** 39 46S 174 37 E
Waverly, *Iowa, U.S.A.* **80 D8** 42 44N 92 29W
Waverly, *N.Y., U.S.A.* **79 E8** 42 1N 76 32W
Wavre, *Belgium* **15 D4** 50 43N 4 38 E
Wâw, *Sudan* **51 G11** 7 45N 28 1 E
Wâw al Kabīr, *Libya* **51 C9** 25 20N 16 43 E
Wawa, *Canada* **70 C3** 47 59N 84 47W
Wawanesa, *Canada* **73 D9** 49 36N 99 40W
Wawona, *U.S.A.* **84 H7** 37 32N 119 39W
Waxahachie, *U.S.A.* **81 J6** 32 24N 96 51W
Way, L., *Australia* **61 E3** 26 45S 120 16 E
Waycross, *U.S.A.* **77 K4** 31 13N 82 21W
Wayland, *U.S.A.* **78 D7** 42 34N 77 35W
Wayne, *Nebr., U.S.A.* **80 D6** 42 14N 97 1W
Wayne, *W. Va., U.S.A.* **76 F4** 38 13N 82 27W
Waynesboro, *Ga., U.S.A.* **77 J4** 33 6N 82 1W
Waynesboro, *Miss., U.S.A.* **77 K1** 31 40N 88 39W
Waynesboro, *Pa., U.S.A.* **76 F7** 39 45N 77 35W
Waynesboro, *Va., U.S.A.* **76 F6** 38 4N 78 53W
Waynesburg, *U.S.A.* **76 F5** 39 54N 80 11W
Waynesville, *U.S.A.* **77 H4** 35 28N 82 58W
Waynoka, *U.S.A.* **81 G5** 36 35N 98 53W
Wazirabad, *Pakistan* **42 C6** 32 30N 74 8 E
We, *Indonesia* **36 C1** 5 51N 95 18 E
Weald, The, *U.K.* **11 F8** 51 4N 0 20 E
Wear →, *U.K.* **10 C6** 54 55N 1 23W
Weatherford, *Okla., U.S.A.* **81 H5** 35 32N 98 43W
Weatherford, *Tex., U.S.A.* **81 J6** 32 46N 97 48W
Weaverville, *U.S.A.* **82 F2** 40 44N 122 56W
Webb City, *U.S.A.* **81 G7** 37 9N 94 28W
Webequie, *Canada* **70 B2** 52 59N 87 21W
Webster, *Mass., U.S.A.* **79 D13** 42 3N 71 53W
Webster, *N.Y., U.S.A.* **78 C7** 43 13N 77 26W
Webster, *S. Dak., U.S.A.* **80 C6** 45 20N 97 31W
Webster City, *U.S.A.* **80 D8** 42 28N 93 49W
Webster Springs, *U.S.A.* **76 F5** 38 29N 80 25W
Weda, *Indonesia* **37 D7** 0 21N 127 50 E
Weda, Teluk, *Indonesia* **37 D7** 0 30N 127 50 E
Weddell I., *Falk. Is.* **96 G4** 51 50S 61 0W
Weddell Sea, *Antarctica* **5 D1** 72 30S 40 0W
Wedderburn, *Australia* **63 F3** 36 26S 143 33 E
Wedgeport, *Canada* **71 D6** 43 44N 65 59W
Wedza, *Zimbabwe* **55 F3** 18 40S 31 33 E
Wee Waa, *Australia* **63 E4** 30 11S 149 26 E
Weed, *U.S.A.* **82 F2** 41 25N 122 23W
Weed Heights, *U.S.A.* **84 G7** 38 59N 119 13W
Weedsport, *U.S.A.* **79 C8** 43 3N 76 35W
Weedville, *U.S.A.* **78 E6** 41 17N 78 30W
Weenen, *S. Africa* **57 D5** 28 48S 30 7 E
Weert, *Neths.* **15 C5** 51 15N 5 43 E
Wei He →, *Hebei, China* **34 F8** 36 10N 115 45 E
Wei He →, *Shaanxi, China* **34 G6** 34 38N 110 15 E
Weichang, *China* **35 D9** 41 58N 117 49 E
Weichuan, *China* **34 G7** 34 20N 113 59 E
Weiden, *Germany* **16 D7** 49 41N 12 10 E
Weifang, *China* **35 F10** 36 44N 119 7 E
Weihai, *China* **35 F12** 37 30N 122 6 E
Weimar, *Germany* **16 C6** 50 58N 11 19 E
Weinan, *China* **34 G5** 34 31N 109 29 E
Weipa, *Australia* **62 A3** 12 40S 141 50 E
Weir →, *Australia* **63 D4** 28 20S 149 50 E
Weir →, *Canada* **73 B10** 56 54N 93 21W
Weir River, *Canada* **73 B10** 56 49N 94 6W
Weirton, *U.S.A.* **78 F4** 40 24N 80 35W
Weiser, *U.S.A.* **82 D5** 44 10N 117 0W
Weishan, *China* **35 G9** 34 47N 117 5 E
Weiyuan, *China* **34 G3** 35 7N 104 10 E
Wejherowo, *Poland* **17 A10** 54 35N 18 12 E
Wekusko L., *Canada* **73 C9** 54 40N 99 50W
Welch, *U.S.A.* **76 G5** 37 26N 81 35W
Welkom, *S. Africa* **56 D4** 28 0S 26 46 E
Welland, *Canada* **78 D5** 43 0N 79 15W
Welland →, *U.K.* **11 E7** 52 51N 0 5W
Wellesley Is., *Australia* **62 B2** 16 42S 139 30 E
Wellingborough, *U.K.* **11 E7** 52 19N 0 41W
Wellington, *Australia* **63 E4** 32 35S 148 59 E
Wellington, *Canada* **78 C7** 43 57N 77 20W
Wellington, *N.Z.* **59 J5** 41 19S 174 46 E
Wellington, *S. Africa* **56 E2** 33 38S 19 1 E
Wellington, *Somst., U.K.* **11 G4** 50 58N 3 13W
Wellington,
Telford & Wrekin, U.K. **11 E5** 52 42N 2 30W
Wellington, *Colo., U.S.A.* **80 E2** 40 42N 105 0W
Wellington, *Kans., U.S.A.* **81 G6** 37 16N 97 24W
Wellington, *Nev., U.S.A.* **84 G7** 38 45N 119 23W
Wellington, *Ohio, U.S.A.* **78 E2** 41 10N 82 13W
Wellington, *Tex., U.S.A.* **81 H4** 34 51N 100 13W
Wellington, I., *Chile* **96 F2** 49 30S 75 0W
Wellington, L., *Australia* **63 F4** 38 6S 147 20 E
Wells, *U.K.* **11 F5** 51 13N 2 39W
Wells, *Maine, U.S.A.* **79 C14** 43 20N 70 35W
Wells, *N.Y., U.S.A.* **79 C10** 43 24N 74 17W
Wells, *Nev., U.S.A.* **82 F6** 41 7N 114 58W
Wells, L., *Australia* **61 E3** 26 44S 123 15 E
Wells, Mt., *Australia* **60 C4** 17 25S 127 8 E
Wells Gray Prov. Park,
Canada **72 C4** 52 30N 120 15W
Wells-next-the-Sea, *U.K.* **10 E8** 52 57N 0 51 E
Wells River, *U.S.A.* **79 B12** 44 9N 72 4W
Wellsboro, *U.S.A.* **78 E7** 41 45N 77 18W
Wellsburg, *U.S.A.* **78 F4** 40 16N 80 37W
Wellsville, *N.Y., U.S.A.* **78 D7** 42 7N 77 57W
Wellsville, *Ohio, U.S.A.* **78 F4** 40 36N 80 39W
Wellsville, *Utah, U.S.A.* **82 F8** 41 38N 111 56W
Wellton, *U.S.A.* **83 K6** 32 40N 114 8W
Wels, *Austria* **16 D8** 48 9N 14 1 E
Welshpool, *U.K.* **11 E4** 52 39N 3 8W
Welwyn Garden City, *U.K.* **11 F7** 51 48N 0 12W
Wem, *U.K.* **10 E5** 52 52N 2 44W
Wembere →, *Tanzania* **54 C3** 4 10S 34 15 E
Wemindji, *Canada* **70 B4** 53 0N 78 49W
Wen Xian, *China* **34 G7** 34 55N 113 5 E
Wenatchee, *U.S.A.* **82 C3** 47 25N 120 19W
Wenchang, *China* **38 C8** 19 38N 110 42 E
Wenchi, *Ghana* **50 G5** 7 46N 2 8W
Wenchow = Wenzhou,
China **33 D7** 28 0N 120 38 E
Wenden, *U.S.A.* **85 M13** 33 49N 113 33W
Wendeng, *China* **35 F12** 37 15N 122 5 E
Wendesi, *Indonesia* **37 E8** 2 30S 134 17 E
Wendover, *U.S.A.* **82 F6** 40 44N 114 2W
Wenlock →, *Australia* **62 A3** 12 2S 141 55 E
Wenshan, *China* **32 D5** 23 20N 104 18 E
Wenshang, *China* **34 G9** 35 45N 116 30 E
Wenshui, *China* **34 F7** 37 26N 112 1 E
Wensleydale, *U.K.* **10 C6** 54 17N 2 0W
Wensu, *China* **32 B3** 41 15N 80 10 E
Wensum →, *U.K.* **10 E8** 52 40N 1 15 E
Wentworth, *Australia* **63 E3** 34 2S 141 54 E
Wentzel L., *Canada* **72 B6** 59 2N 114 28W
Wenut, *Indonesia* **37 E8** 3 11S 133 19 E
Wenxi, *China* **34 G6** 35 20N 111 10 E
Wenxian, *China* **34 H3** 32 43N 104 36 E
Wenzhou, *China* **33 D7** 28 0N 120 38 E
Weott, *U.S.A.* **82 F2** 40 20N 123 55W
Wepener, *S. Africa* **56 D4** 29 42S 27 3 E
Werda, *Botswana* **56 D3** 25 24S 23 15 E
Weri, *Indonesia* **37 E8** 3 10S 132 38 E
Werra →, *Germany* **16 C5** 51 24N 9 39 E
Werrimull, *Australia* **63 E3** 34 25S 141 38 E
Werris Creek, *Australia* **63 E5** 31 18S 150 38 E
Weser →, *Germany* **16 B5** 53 36N 8 28 E
Wesiri, *Indonesia* **37 F7** 7 30S 126 30 E
Weslemkoon L., *Canada* **78 A7** 45 2N 77 25W
Wesleyville, *Canada* **71 C9** 49 8N 53 36W
Wesleyville, *U.S.A.* **78 D4** 42 9N 80 0W
Wessel, C., *Australia* **62 A2** 10 59S 136 46 E
Wessel Is., *Australia* **62 A2** 11 10S 136 45 E
Wessington Springs, *U.S.A.* **80 C5** 44 5N 98 34W
West, *U.S.A.* **81 K6** 31 48N 97 6W
West →, *U.S.A.* **79 D12** 42 52N 72 33W
West Baines →, *Australia* **60 C4** 15 38S 129 59 E
West Bank □, *Asia* **47 C4** 32 6N 35 13 E
West Bend, *U.S.A.* **76 D1** 43 25N 88 11W
West Bengal □, *India* **43 H13** 23 0N 88 0 E
West Berkshire □, *U.K.* **11 F6** 51 25N 1 17W
West Beskids = Západné
Beskydy, *Europe* **17 D10** 49 30N 19 0 E
West Branch, *U.S.A.* **76 C3** 44 17N 84 14W
West Branch
Susquehanna →, *U.S.A.* **79 F8** 40 53N 76 48W
West Bromwich, *U.K.* **11 E6** 52 32N 1 59W
West Burra, *U.K.* **12 A7** 60 5N 1 21W
West Canada Cr. →, *U.S.A.* **79 C10** 43 1N 74 58W
West Cape Howe, *Australia* **61 G2** 35 8S 117 36 E
West Chazy, *U.S.A.* **79 B11** 44 49N 73 28W
West Chester, *U.S.A.* **79 G9** 39 58N 75 36W
West Columbia, *U.S.A.* **81 L7** 29 9N 95 39W
West Covina, *U.S.A.* **85 L9** 34 4N 117 54W
West Des Moines, *U.S.A.* **80 E8** 41 35N 93 43W
West Dunbartonshire □,
U.K. **12 F4** 55 59N 4 30W
West End, *Bahamas* **88 A4** 26 41N 78 58W
West Falkland, *Falk. Is.* **96 G5** 51 40S 60 0W
West Fargo, *U.S.A.* **80 B6** 46 52N 96 54W
West Farmington, *U.S.A.* **78 E4** 41 23N 80 58W
West Fjord = Vestfjorden,
Norway **8 C15** 67 55N 14 0 E
West Fork Trinity →,
U.S.A. **81 J6** 32 48N 96 54W
West Frankfort, *U.S.A.* **80 G10** 37 54N 88 55W
West Hartford, *U.S.A.* **79 E12** 41 45N 72 44W
West Haven, *U.S.A.* **79 E12** 41 17N 72 57W
West Hazleton, *U.S.A.* **79 F9** 40 58N 76 0W
West Helena, *U.S.A.* **81 H9** 34 33N 90 38W
West Hurley, *U.S.A.* **79 E10** 41 59N 74 7W
West Ice Shelf, *Antarctica* **5 C7** 67 0S 85 0 E

Yezd = Yazd, *Iran* **45 D7** 31 55N 54 27 E
Yhati, *Paraguay* **94 B4** 25 45S 56 35W
Yhú, *Paraguay* **95 B4** 25 0S 56 0W
Yí →, *Uruguay* **94 C4** 33 7S 57 8W
Yi 'Allaq, G., *Egypt* **47 E2** 30 22N 33 32 E
Yi He →, *China* **35 G10** 34 10N 118 8 E
Yi Xian, *Hebei, China* **34 E8** 39 20N 115 30 E
Yi Xian, *Liaoning, China* **35 D11** 41 30N 121 22 E
Yialiás →, *Cyprus* **23 D12** 35 9N 33 44 E
Yialousa, *Cyprus* **23 D13** 35 32N 34 10 E
Yianisádhes, *Greece* **23 D8** 35 20N 26 10 E
Yiannitsa, *Greece* **21 D10** 40 46N 22 24 E
Yibin, *China* **32 D5** 28 45N 104 32 E
Yichang, *China* **33 C6** 30 40N 111 20 E
Yicheng, *China* **34 G6** 35 42N 111 40 E
Yichuan, *China* **34 F6** 36 2N 110 10 E
Yichun, *China* **33 B7** 47 44N 128 52 E
Yidu, *China* **35 F10** 36 43N 118 28 E
Yijun, *China* **34 G5** 35 28N 109 8 E
Yıldız Dağları, *Turkey* **21 D12** 41 48N 27 36 E
Yilehuli Shan, *China* **33 A7** 51 20N 124 20 E
Yimianpo, *China* **35 B15** 45 7N 128 2 E
Yinchuan, *China* **34 E4** 38 30N 106 15 E
Yindarlgooda, L., *Australia* **61 F3** 30 40S 121 52 E
Ying He →, *China* **34 H9** 32 30N 116 30 E
Ying Xian, *China* **34 E7** 39 32N 113 10 E
Yingkou, *China* **35 D12** 40 37N 122 18 E
Yining, *China* **26 E9** 43 58N 81 10 E
Yinmabin, *Burma* **41 H19** 22 10N 94 55 E
Yiofiros →, *Greece* **23 D7** 35 20N 25 6 E
Yirga Alem, *Ethiopia* **46 F2** 6 48N 38 22 E
Yirrkala, *Australia* **62 A2** 12 14S 136 56 E
Yishan, *China* **32 D5** 24 28N 108 38 E
Yishui, *China* **35 G10** 35 47N 118 30 E
Yíthion, *Greece* **21 F10** 36 46N 22 34 E
Yitiaoshan, *China* **34 F3** 37 5N 104 2 E
Yitong, *China* **35 C13** 43 13N 125 20 E
Yiyang, *Henan, China* **34 G7** 34 27N 112 10 E
Yiyang, *Hunan, China* **33 D6** 28 35N 112 18 E
Yli-Kitka, *Finland* **8 C23** 66 8N 28 30 E
Ylitornio, *Finland* **8 C20** 66 19N 23 39 E
Ylivieska, *Finland* **8 D21** 64 4N 24 28 E
Yoakum, *U.S.A.* **81 L6** 29 17N 97 9W
Yog Pt., *Phil.* **37 B6** 14 6N 124 12 E
Yogyakarta, *Indonesia* **37 G14** 7 49S 110 22 E
Yoho Nat. Park, *Canada* **72 C5** 51 25N 116 30W
Yojoa, L. de, *Honduras* **88 D2** 14 53N 88 0W
Yŏju, *S. Korea* **35 F14** 37 20N 127 35 E
Yokadouma, *Cameroon* **52 D2** 3 26N 14 55 E
Yokkaichi, *Japan* **31 G8** 34 55N 136 38 E
Yoko, *Cameroon* **52 C2** 5 32N 12 20 E
Yokohama, *Japan* **31 G9** 35 27N 139 28 E
Yokosuka, *Japan* **31 G9** 35 20N 139 40 E
Yokote, *Japan* **30 E10** 39 20N 140 30 E
Yola, *Nigeria* **51 G8** 9 10N 12 29 E
Yolaina, Cordillera de, *Nic.* **88 D3** 11 30N 84 0W
Yoloten, *Turkmenistan* **45 B9** 37 18N 62 21 E
Yom →, *Thailand* **36 A2** 15 35N 100 1 E
Yonago, *Japan* **31 G6** 35 25N 133 19 E
Yonaguni-Jima, *Japan* **31 M1** 24 27N 123 0 E
Yŏnan, *N. Korea* **35 F14** 37 55N 126 11 E
Yonezawa, *Japan* **30 F10** 37 57N 140 4 E
Yong Peng, *Malaysia* **39 M4** 2 0N 103 3 E
Yong Sata, *Thailand* **39 J2** 7 8N 99 41 E
Yongamp'o, *N. Korea* **35 E13** 39 56N 124 23 E
Yongcheng, *China* **34 H9** 33 55N 116 20 E
Yŏngch'ŏn, *S. Korea* **35 G15** 35 58N 128 56 E
Yongdeng, *China* **34 F2** 36 38N 103 25 E
Yŏngdŏk, *S. Korea* **35 F15** 36 24N 129 22 E
Yŏngdŭngpo, *S. Korea* **35 F14** 37 31N 126 54 E
Yonghe, *China* **34 F6** 36 46N 110 38 E
Yŏnghŭng, *N. Korea* **35 E14** 39 31N 127 18 E
Yongji, *China* **34 G6** 34 52N 110 28 E
Yŏngju, *S. Korea* **35 F15** 36 50N 128 40 E
Yongnian, *China* **34 F8** 36 47N 114 29 E
Yongning, *China* **34 E4** 38 15N 106 14 E
Yongqing, *China* **34 E9** 39 25N 116 28 E
Yŏngwŏl, *S. Korea* **35 F15** 37 11N 128 28 E
Yonibana, *S. Leone* **50 G3** 8 30N 12 19W
Yonkers, *U.S.A.* **79 F11** 40 56N 73 54W
Yonne →, *France* **18 B5** 48 23N 2 58 E
York, *Australia* **61 F2** 31 52S 116 47 E
York, *U.K.* **10 D6** 53 58N 1 6W
York, *Nebr., U.S.A.* **80 E6** 40 52N 97 36W
York, *Pa., U.S.A.* **76 F7** 39 58N 76 44W
York, C., *Australia* **62 A3** 10 42S 142 31 E
York, City of □, *U.K.* **10 D6** 53 58N 1 6W
York, Kap, *Greenland* **4 B4** 75 55N 66 25W
York, Vale of, *U.K.* **10 C6** 54 15N 1 25W
York Haven, *U.S.A.* **78 F8** 40 7N 76 46W
York Sd., *Australia* **60 C4** 15 0S 125 5 E
Yorke Pen., *Australia* **63 E2** 34 50S 137 40 E
Yorketown, *Australia* **63 F2** 35 0S 137 33 E
Yorkshire Wolds, *U.K.* **10 C7** 54 8N 0 31W
Yorkton, *Canada* **73 C8** 51 11N 102 28W
Yorkville, *U.S.A.* **84 G3** 38 52N 123 13W
Yoro, *Honduras* **88 C2** 15 9N 87 7W
Yoron-Jima, *Japan* **31 L4** 27 2N 128 26 E
Yos Sudarso, Pulau = Dolak, Pulau, *Indonesia* **37 F9** 8 0S 138 30 E
Yosemite National Park, *U.S.A.* **84 H7** 37 45N 119 40W
Yosemite Village, *U.S.A.* **84 H7** 37 45N 119 35W
Yoshkar Ola, *Russia* **24 C8** 56 38N 47 55 E
Yŏsu, *S. Korea* **35 G14** 34 47N 127 45 E
Yotvata, *Israel* **47 F4** 29 55N 35 2 E
Youbou, *Canada* **84 B2** 48 53N 124 13W
Youghal, *Ireland* **13 E4** 51 56N 7 52W
Youghal B., *Ireland* **13 E4** 51 55N 7 49W
Young, *Australia* **63 E4** 34 19S 148 18 E
Young, *Canada* **73 C7** 51 47N 105 45W
Young, *Uruguay* **94 C4** 32 44S 57 36W
Younghusband, L., *Australia* **63 E2** 30 50S 136 5 E
Younghusband Pen., *Australia* **63 F2** 36 0S 139 25 E
Youngstown, *Canada* **73 C6** 51 35N 111 10W
Youngstown, *N.Y., U.S.A.* **78 C5** 43 15N 79 3W
Youngstown, *Ohio, U.S.A.* **78 E4** 41 6N 80 39W
Youngsville, *U.S.A.* **78 E5** 41 51N 79 19W
Youngwood, *U.S.A.* **78 F5** 40 14N 79 34W
Youyu, *China* **34 D7** 40 10N 112 20 E
Yozgat, *Turkey* **25 G5** 39 51N 34 47 E
Ypané →, *Paraguay* **94 A4** 23 29S 57 19W
Ypres = Ieper, *Belgium* **15 D2** 50 51N 2 53 E
Yreka, *U.S.A.* **82 F2** 41 44N 122 38W
Ystad, *Sweden* **9 J15** 55 26N 13 50 E
Ysyk-Köl, *Kyrgyzstan* **28 E11** 42 26N 76 12 E
Ysyk-Köl, Ozero, *Kyrgyzstan* **26 E8** 42 25N 77 15 E
Ythan →, *U.K.* **12 D7** 57 19N 1 59W
Ytyk Kyuyel, *Russia* **27 C14** 62 30N 133 45 E
Yu Jiang →, *China* **33 D6** 23 22N 110 3 E
Yu Xian = Yuzhou, *China* **34 G7** 34 10N 113 28 E
Yu Xian, *Hebei, China* **34 E8** 39 50N 114 35 E
Yu Xian, *Shanxi, China* **34 E7** 38 5N 113 20 E
Yuan Jiang →, *China* **33 D6** 28 55N 111 50 E
Yuanqu, *China* **34 G6** 35 18N 111 40 E
Yuanyang, *China* **34 G7** 35 3N 113 58 E
Yuba →, *U.S.A.* **84 F5** 39 8N 121 36W
Yuba City, *U.S.A.* **84 F5** 39 8N 121 37W
Yūbari, *Japan* **30 C10** 43 4N 141 59 E
Yūbetsu, *Japan* **30 B11** 44 13N 143 50 E
Yucatán □, *Mexico* **87 C7** 21 30N 86 30W
Yucatán, Canal de, *Caribbean* **88 B2** 22 0N 86 30W
Yucatán, Península de, *Mexico* **66 H11** 19 30N 89 0W
Yucatán Basin, *Cent. Amer.* **66 H11** 19 0N 86 0W
Yucatan Str. = Yucatán, Canal de, *Caribbean* **88 B2** 22 0N 86 30W
Yucca, *U.S.A.* **85 L12** 34 52N 114 9W
Yucca Valley, *U.S.A.* **85 L10** 34 8N 116 27W
Yucheng, *China* **34 F9** 36 55N 116 32 E
Yuci, *China* **34 F7** 37 42N 112 46 E
Yuendumu, *Australia* **60 D5** 22 16S 131 49 E
Yugoslavia ■, *Europe* **21 B9** 43 20N 20 0 E
Yukon →, *U.S.A.* **68 B3** 62 32N 163 54W
Yukon Territory □, *Canada* **68 B6** 63 0N 135 0W
Yukta, *Russia* **27 C11** 63 26N 105 42 E
Yukuhashi, *Japan* **31 H5** 33 44N 130 59 E
Yulara, *Australia* **61 E5** 25 10S 130 55 E
Yule →, *Australia* **60 D2** 20 41S 118 17 E
Yuleba, *Australia* **63 D4** 26 37S 149 24 E
Yulin, *Shaanxi, China* **34 E5** 38 20N 109 30 E
Yulin, *Shensi, China* **38 C7** 18 10N 109 30 E
Yuma, *Ariz., U.S.A.* **85 N12** 32 43N 114 37W
Yuma, *Colo., U.S.A.* **80 E3** 40 8N 102 43W
Yuma, B. de, *Dom. Rep.* **89 C6** 18 20N 68 35W
Yumbe, *Uganda* **54 B3** 3 28N 31 15 E
Yumbi, *Dem. Rep. of the Congo* **54 C2** 1 12S 26 15 E
Yumen, *China* **32 C4** 39 50N 97 30 E
Yun Ho →, *China* **35 E9** 39 10N 117 10 E
Yuna, *Australia* **61 E2** 28 20S 115 0 E
Yuncheng, *Henan, China* **34 G8** 35 36N 115 57 E
Yuncheng, *Shanxi, China* **34 G6** 35 2N 111 0 E
Yungas, *Bolivia* **92 G5** 17 0S 66 0W
Yungay, *Chile* **94 D1** 37 10S 72 5W
Yunnan □, *China* **32 D5** 25 0N 102 0 E
Yunta, *Australia* **63 E2** 32 34S 139 36 E
Yunxi, *China* **34 H6** 33 0N 110 22 E
Yupyongdong, *N. Korea* **35 D15** 41 49N 128 53 E
Yurga, *Russia* **26 D9** 55 42N 84 51 E
Yurimaguas, *Peru* **92 E3** 5 55S 76 7W
Yuryung Kaya, *Russia* **27 B12** 72 48N 113 23 E
Yuscarán, *Honduras* **88 D2** 13 58N 86 45W
Yushe, *China* **34 F7** 37 4N 112 58 E
Yushu, *Jilin, China* **35 B14** 44 43N 126 38 E
Yushu, *Qinghai, China* **32 C4** 33 5N 96 55 E
Yutai, *China* **34 G9** 35 0N 116 45 E
Yutian, *China* **35 E9** 39 53N 117 45 E
Yuxarı Qarabağ = Nagorno-Karabakh, *Azerbaijan* **25 F8** 39 55N 46 45 E
Yuxi, *China* **32 D5** 24 30N 102 35 E
Yuzawa, *Japan* **30 E10** 39 10N 140 30 E
Yuzhno-Sakhalinsk, *Russia* **27 E15** 46 58N 142 45 E
Yuzhou, *China* **34 G7** 34 10N 113 28 E
Yvetot, *France* **18 B4** 49 37N 0 44 E

Z

Zaanstad, *Neths.* **15 B4** 52 27N 4 50 E
Zāb al Kabīr →, *Iraq* **44 C4** 36 1N 43 24 E
Zāb aş Şagīr →, *Iraq* **44 C4** 35 17N 43 29 E
Zabaykalsk, *Russia* **27 E12** 49 40N 117 25 E
Zābol, *Iran* **45 D9** 31 0N 61 32 E
Zābolī, *Iran* **45 E9** 27 10N 61 35 E
Zabrze, *Poland* **17 C10** 50 18N 18 50 E
Zacapa, *Guatemala* **88 D2** 14 59N 89 31W
Zacapu, *Mexico* **86 D4** 19 50N 101 43W
Zacatecas, *Mexico* **86 C4** 22 49N 102 34W
Zacatecas □, *Mexico* **86 C4** 23 30N 103 0W
Zacatecoluca, *El Salv.* **88 D2** 13 29N 88 51W
Zachary, *U.S.A.* **81 K9** 30 39N 91 9W
Zacoalco, *Mexico* **86 C4** 20 14N 103 33W
Zacualtipán, *Mexico* **87 C5** 20 39N 98 36W
Zadar, *Croatia* **16 F8** 44 8N 15 14 E
Zadetkyi Kyun, *Burma* **39 H2** 10 0N 98 25 E
Zafarqand, *Iran* **45 C7** 33 11N 52 29 E
Zafra, *Spain* **19 C2** 38 26N 6 30W
Żagań, *Poland* **16 C8** 51 39N 15 22 E
Zagaoua, *Chad* **51 E10** 15 30N 22 24 E
Zagazig, *Egypt* **51 B12** 30 40N 31 30 E
Zāgheh, *Iran* **45 C6** 33 30N 48 42 E
Zagorsk = Sergiyev Posad, *Russia* **24 C6** 56 20N 38 10 E
Zagreb, *Croatia* **16 F9** 45 50N 15 58 E
Zāgros, Kūhhā-ye, *Iran* **45 C6** 33 45N 48 5 E
Zagros Mts. = Zāgros, Kūhhā-ye, *Iran* **45 C6** 33 45N 48 5 E
Zāhedān, *Fārs, Iran* **45 D7** 28 46N 53 52 E
Zāhedān, *Sīstān va Balūchestān, Iran* **45 D9** 29 30N 60 50 E
Zahlah, *Lebanon* **47 B4** 33 52N 35 50 E
Zaïre = Congo →, *Africa* **52 F2** 6 4S 12 24 E
Zaječar, *Serbia, Yug.* **21 C10** 43 53N 22 18 E
Zakamensk, *Russia* **27 D11** 50 23N 103 17 E
Zakhodnaya Dzvina = Daugava →, *Latvia* **9 H21** 57 4N 24 3 E
Zākhū, *Iraq* **44 B4** 37 10N 42 50 E
Zákinthos, *Greece* **21 F9** 37 47N 20 57 E
Zakopane, *Poland* **17 D10** 49 18N 19 57 E
Zákros, *Greece* **23 D8** 35 6N 26 10 E
Zalaegerszeg, *Hungary* **17 E9** 46 53N 16 47 E
Zalău, *Romania* **17 E12** 47 12N 23 3 E
Zaleshchiki = Zalishchyky, *Ukraine* **17 D13** 48 45N 25 45 E
Zalew Wiślany, *Poland* **17 A10** 54 20N 19 50 E
Zalingei, *Sudan* **51 F10** 12 51N 23 29 E
Zalishchyky, *Ukraine* **17 D13** 48 45N 25 45 E
Zama L., *Canada* **72 B5** 58 45N 119 5W
Zambeke, *Dem. Rep. of the Congo* **54 B2** 2 8N 25 17 E
Zambeze →, *Africa* **55 F4** 18 35S 36 20 E
Zambezi = Zambeze →, *Africa* **55 F4** 18 35S 36 20 E
Zambezi, *Zambia* **53 G4** 13 30S 23 15 E
Zambezia □, *Mozam.* **55 F4** 16 15S 37 30 E
Zambia ■, *Africa* **55 F2** 15 0S 28 0 E
Zamboanga, *Phil.* **37 C6** 6 59N 122 3 E
Zamora, *Mexico* **86 D4** 20 0N 102 21W
Zamora, *Spain* **19 B3** 41 30N 5 45W
Zamość, *Poland* **17 C12** 50 43N 23 15 E
Zandvoort, *Neths.* **15 B4** 52 22N 4 32 E
Zanesville, *U.S.A.* **78 G2** 39 56N 82 1W
Zangābād, *Iran* **44 B5** 38 26N 46 44 E
Zangue →, *Mozam.* **55 F4** 17 50S 35 21 E
Zanjān, *Iran* **45 B6** 36 40N 48 35 E
Zanjān □, *Iran* **45 B6** 37 20N 49 30 E
Zanjān →, *Iran* **45 B6** 37 8N 47 47 E
Zante = Zákinthos, *Greece* **21 F9** 37 47N 20 57 E
Zanthus, *Australia* **61 F3** 31 2S 123 34 E
Zanzibar, *Tanzania* **54 D4** 6 12S 39 12 E
Zaouiet El-Kala = Bordj Omar Driss, *Algeria* **50 C7** 28 10N 6 40 E
Zaouiet Reggane, *Algeria* **50 C6** 26 32N 0 3 E
Zaozhuang, *China* **35 G9** 34 50N 117 35 E
Zap Suyu = Zāb al Kabīr →, *Iraq* **44 C4** 36 1N 43 24 E
Zapadnaya Dvina = Daugava →, *Latvia* **9 H21** 57 4N 24 3 E
Západné Beskydy, *Europe* **17 D10** 49 30N 19 0 E
Zapala, *Argentina* **96 D2** 39 0S 70 5W
Zapaleri, Cerro, *Bolivia* **94 A2** 22 49S 67 11W
Zapata, *U.S.A.* **81 M5** 26 55N 99 16W
Zapolyarnyy, *Russia* **24 A5** 69 26N 30 51 E
Zaporizhzhya, *Ukraine* **25 E6** 47 50N 35 10 E
Zaporozhye = Zaporizhzhya, *Ukraine* **25 E6** 47 50N 35 10 E
Zara, *Turkey* **44 B3** 39 58N 37 43 E
Zaragoza, *Coahuila, Mexico* **86 B4** 28 30N 101 0W
Zaragoza, *Nuevo León, Mexico* **87 C5** 24 0N 99 46W
Zaragoza, *Spain* **19 B5** 41 39N 0 53W
Zarand, *Kermān, Iran* **45 D8** 30 46N 56 34 E
Zarand, *Markazī, Iran* **45 C6** 35 18N 50 25 E
Zaranj, *Afghan.* **40 D2** 30 55N 61 55 E
Zarasai, *Lithuania* **9 J22** 55 40N 26 20 E
Zarate, *Argentina* **94 C4** 34 7S 59 0W
Zard, Kūh-e, *Iran* **45 C6** 32 22N 50 4 E
Zāreh, *Iran* **45 C6** 35 7N 49 9 E
Zaria, *Nigeria* **50 F7** 11 0N 7 40 E
Zarneh, *Iran* **44 C5** 33 55N 46 10 E
Zarós, *Greece* **23 D6** 35 8N 24 54 E
Zarqā', Nahr az →, *Jordan* **47 C4** 32 10N 35 37 E
Zarrīn, *Iran* **45 C7** 32 46N 54 37 E
Zaruma, *Ecuador* **92 D3** 3 40S 79 38W
Żary, *Poland* **16 C8** 51 37N 15 10 E
Zarzis, *Tunisia* **51 B8** 33 31N 11 2 E
Zaskar →, *India* **43 B7** 34 13N 77 20 E
Zaskar Mts., *India* **43 C7** 33 15N 77 30 E
Zastron, *S. Africa* **56 E4** 30 18S 27 7 E
Zavāreh, *Iran* **45 C7** 33 29N 52 28 E
Zavitinsk, *Russia* **27 D13** 50 10N 129 20 E
Zavodovski, I., *Antarctica* **5 B1** 56 0S 27 45W
Zawiercie, *Poland* **17 C10** 50 30N 19 24 E
Zāwiyat al Bayḍā = Al Bayḍā, *Libya* **51 B10** 32 50N 21 44 E
Zāyā, *Iraq* **44 C5** 33 33N 44 13 E
Zāyandeh →, *Iran* **45 C7** 32 35N 52 0 E
Zaysan, *Kazakstan* **26 E9** 47 28N 84 52 E
Zaysan, Oz., *Kazakstan* **26 E9** 48 0N 83 0 E
Zayü, *China* **32 D4** 28 48N 97 27 E
Zbarazh, *Ukraine* **17 D13** 49 43N 25 44 E
Zdolbuniv, *Ukraine* **17 C14** 50 30N 26 15 E
Zduńska Wola, *Poland* **17 C10** 51 37N 18 59 E
Zeballos, *Canada* **72 D3** 49 59N 126 50W
Zebediela, *S. Africa* **57 C4** 24 20S 29 17 E
Zeebrugge, *Belgium* **15 C3** 51 19N 3 12 E
Zeehan, *Australia* **62 G4** 41 52S 145 25 E
Zeeland □, *Neths.* **15 C3** 51 30N 3 50 E
Zeerust, *S. Africa* **56 D4** 25 31S 26 4 E
Zefat, *Israel* **47 C4** 32 58N 35 29 E
Zeil, Mt., *Australia* **60 D5** 23 30S 132 23 E
Zeila, *Somali Rep.* **46 E3** 11 21N 43 30 E
Zeist, *Neths.* **15 B5** 52 5N 5 15 E
Zeitz, *Germany* **16 C7** 51 2N 12 7 E
Zelenograd, *Russia* **24 C6** 56 1N 37 12 E
Zelenogradsk, *Russia* **9 J19** 54 53N 20 29 E
Zelienople, *U.S.A.* **78 F4** 40 48N 80 8W
Zémio, *C.A.R.* **54 A2** 5 2N 25 5 E
Zemun, *Serbia, Yug.* **21 B9** 44 51N 20 25 E
Zenica, *Bos.-H.* **21 B7** 44 10N 17 57 E
Žepče, *Bos.-H.* **21 B8** 44 28N 18 2 E
Zevenaar, *Neths.* **15 C6** 51 56N 6 5 E
Zeya, *Russia* **27 D13** 53 48N 127 14 E
Zeya →, *Russia* **27 D13** 51 42N 128 53 E
Zêzere →, *Portugal* **19 C1** 39 28N 8 20W
Zghartā, *Lebanon* **47 A4** 34 21N 35 53 E
Zgorzelec, *Poland* **16 C8** 51 10N 15 0 E
Zhabinka, *Belarus* **17 B13** 52 13N 24 2 E
Zhailma, *Kazakstan* **26 D7** 51 37N 61 33 E
Zhambyl, *Kazakstan* **26 E8** 42 54N 71 22 E
Zhangaqazaly, *Kazakstan* **26 E7** 45 48N 62 6 E
Zhangbei, *China* **34 D8** 41 10N 114 45 E
Zhangguangcai Ling, *China* **35 B15** 45 0N 129 0 E
Zhangjiakou, *China* **34 D8** 40 48N 114 55 E
Zhangwu, *China* **35 C12** 42 43N 123 52 E
Zhangye, *China* **32 C5** 38 50N 100 23 E
Zhangzhou, *China* **33 D6** 24 30N 117 35 E
Zhanhua, *China* **35 F10** 37 40N 118 8 E
Zhanjiang, *China* **33 D6** 21 15N 110 20 E
Zhannetty, Ostrov, *Russia* **27 B16** 76 43N 158 0 E
Zhanyi, *China* **32 D5** 25 38N 103 48 E
Zhanyu, *China* **35 B12** 44 30N 122 30 E
Zhao Xian, *China* **34 F8** 37 43N 114 45 E
Zhaocheng, *China* **34 F6** 36 22N 111 38 E
Zhaotong, *China* **32 D5** 27 20N 103 44 E
Zhaoyuan, *Heilongjiang, China* **35 B13** 45 27N 125 0 E
Zhaoyuan, *Shandong, China* **35 F11** 37 20N 120 23 E
Zhashkiv, *Ukraine* **17 D16** 49 15N 30 5 E
Zhashui, *China* **34 H5** 33 40N 109 8 E
Zhayyq →, *Kazakstan* **25 E9** 47 0N 51 48 E
Zhdanov = Mariupol, *Ukraine* **25 E6** 47 5N 37 31 E
Zhecheng, *China* **34 G8** 34 7N 115 20 E
Zhejiang □, *China* **33 D7** 29 0N 120 0 E
Zheleznodorozhnyy, *Russia* **24 B9** 62 35N 50 55 E
Zheleznogorsk-Ilimskiy, *Russia* **27 D11** 56 34N 104 8 E
Zhen'an, *China* **34 H5** 33 27N 109 9 E
Zhengding, *China* **34 E8** 38 8N 114 32 E
Zhengzhou, *China* **34 G7** 34 45N 113 34 E
Zhenlai, *China* **35 B12** 45 50N 123 5 E
Zhenping, *China* **34 H7** 33 10N 112 16 E
Zhenyuan, *China* **34 G4** 35 35N 107 30 E
Zhetiqara, *Kazakstan* **26 D7** 52 11N 61 12 E
Zhezqazghan, *Kazakstan* **26 E7** 47 44N 67 40 E
Zhidan, *China* **34 F5** 36 48N 108 48 E
Zhigansk, *Russia* **27 C13** 66 48N 123 27 E
Zhilinda, *Russia* **27 C12** 70 0N 114 20 E
Zhitomir = Zhytomyr, *Ukraine* **17 C15** 50 20N 28 40 E
Zhlobin, *Belarus* **17 B16** 52 55N 30 0 E
Zhmerinka = Zhmerynka, *Ukraine* **17 D15** 49 2N 28 2 E
Zhmerynka, *Ukraine* **17 D15** 49 2N 28 2 E
Zhob, *Pakistan* **42 D3** 31 20N 69 31 E
Zhob →, *Pakistan* **42 C3** 32 4N 69 50 E
Zhodino = Zhodzina, *Belarus* **17 A15** 54 5N 28 17 E
Zhodzina, *Belarus* **17 A15** 54 5N 28 17 E
Zhokhova, Ostrov, *Russia* **27 B16** 76 4N 152 40 E
Zhongdian, *China* **32 D4** 27 48N 99 42 E
Zhongning, *China* **34 F3** 37 29N 105 40 E
Zhongtiao Shan, *China* **34 G6** 35 0N 111 10 E
Zhongwei, *China* **34 F3** 37 30N 105 12 E
Zhongyang, *China* **34 F6** 37 20N 111 11 E
Zhoucun, *China* **35 F9** 36 47N 117 48 E
Zhouzhi, *China* **34 G5** 34 10N 108 12 E
Zhuanghe, *China* **35 E12** 39 40N 123 0 E
Zhucheng, *China* **35 G10** 36 0N 119 27 E
Zhugqu, *China* **34 H3** 33 40N 104 30 E
Zhumadian, *China* **34 H8** 32 59N 114 2 E
Zhuo Xian = Zhuozhou, *China* **34 E8** 39 28N 115 58 E
Zhuolu, *China* **34 D8** 40 20N 115 12 E
Zhuozhou, *China* **34 E8** 39 28N 115 58 E
Zhuozi, *China* **34 D7** 41 0N 112 25 E
Zhytomyr, *Ukraine* **17 C15** 50 20N 28 40 E
Ziārān, *Iran* **45 B6** 36 7N 50 32 E
Ziarat, *Pakistan* **42 D2** 30 25N 67 49 E
Zibo, *China* **35 F10** 36 47N 118 3 E
Zichang, *China* **34 F5** 37 18N 109 40 E
Zielona Góra, *Poland* **16 C8** 51 57N 15 31 E
Zierikzee, *Neths.* **15 C3** 51 40N 3 55 E
Zigey, *Chad* **51 F9** 14 43N 15 50 E
Zigong, *China* **32 D5** 29 15N 104 48 E
Ziguinchor, *Senegal* **50 F2** 12 35N 16 20W
Zihuatanejo, *Mexico* **86 D4** 17 38N 101 33W
Žilina, *Slovak Rep.* **17 D10** 49 12N 18 42
Zillah, *Libya* **51 C9** 28 30N 17 33
Zima, *Russia* **27 D11** 54 0N 102 5
Zimapán, *Mexico* **87 C5** 20 54N 99 20W
Zimba, *Zambia* **55 F2** 17 20S 26 11
Zimbabwe, *Zimbabwe* **55 G3** 20 16S 30 54
Zimbabwe ■, *Africa* **55 F3** 19 0S 30 0
Zimnicea, *Romania* **17 G13** 43 40N 25 22
Zinder, *Niger* **50 F7** 13 48N 9 0
Zinga, *Tanzania* **55 D4** 9 16S 38 49
Zion National Park, *U.S.A.* **83 H7** 37 15N 113 5W
Ziros, *Greece* **23 D8** 35 5N 26 8
Zitácuaro, *Mexico* **86 D4** 19 28N 100 21W
Zitundo, *Mozam.* **57 D5** 26 48S 32 47
Ziway, L., *Ethiopia* **46 F2** 8 0N 38 50
Ziyang, *China* **34 H5** 32 32N 108 31
Zlatograd, *Bulgaria* **21 D11** 41 22N 25 7
Zlatoust, *Russia* **24 C10** 55 10N 59 40
Zlín, *Czech Rep.* **17 D9** 49 14N 17 40
Zmeinogorsk, *Kazakstan* **26 D9** 51 10N 82 13
Znojmo, *Czech Rep.* **16 D9** 48 50N 16 2
Zobeyrī, *Iran* **44 C5** 34 10N 46 40
Zobia, *Dem. Rep. of the Congo* **54 B2** 3 0N 25 59
Zoetermeer, *Neths.* **15 B4** 52 3N 4 30
Zolochev = Zolochiv, *Ukraine* **17 D13** 49 45N 24 51
Zolochiv, *Ukraine* **17 D13** 49 45N 24 51
Zomba, *Malawi* **55 F4** 15 22S 35 19
Zongo, *Dem. Rep. of the Congo* **52 D3** 4 20N 18 35
Zonguldak, *Turkey* **25 F5** 41 28N 31 50
Zonqor Pt., *Malta* **23 D2** 35 51N 14 34
Zorritos, *Peru* **92 D2** 3 43S 80 40
Zou Xiang, *China* **34 G9** 35 30N 116 58
Zouar, *Chad* **51 D9** 20 30N 16 32
Zouérate = Zouîrât, *Mauritania* **50 D3** 22 44N 12 21
Zouîrât, *Mauritania* **50 D3** 22 44N 12 21
Zoutkamp, *Neths.* **15 A6** 53 20N 6 18
Zrenjanin, *Serbia, Yug.* **21 B9** 45 22N 20 23
Ẓufār, *Oman* **46 D5** 17 40N 54 0
Zug, *Switz.* **18 C8** 47 10N 8 31
Zugspitze, *Germany* **16 E6** 47 25N 10 59
Zuid-Holland □, *Neths.* **15 C4** 52 0N 4 35
Zuidbeveland, *Neths.* **15 C3** 51 30N 3 50
Zuidhorn, *Neths.* **15 A6** 53 15N 6 23
Zula, *Eritrea* **46 D2** 15 17N 39 40
Zumbo, *Mozam.* **55 F3** 15 35S 30 26
Zumpango, *Mexico* **87 D5** 19 48N 99 6
Zunhua, *China* **35 D9** 40 18N 117 58
Zuni, *U.S.A.* **83 J9** 35 4N 108 51
Zunyi, *China* **32 D5** 27 42N 106 53
Zuoquan, *China* **34 F7** 37 5N 113 22
Zurbātīyah, *Iraq* **44 C5** 33 9N 46 3
Zürich, *Switz.* **18 C8** 47 22N 8 32
Zutphen, *Neths.* **15 B6** 52 9N 6 12
Zuwārah, *Libya* **51 B8** 32 58N 12
Zūzan, *Iran* **45 C8** 34 22N 59 53
Zverinogolovskoye, *Russia* **26 D7** 54 26N 64 50
Zvishavane, *Zimbabwe* **55 G3** 20 17S 30
Zvolen, *Slovak Rep.* **17 D10** 48 33N 19 1
Zwelitsha, *S. Africa* **53 L5** 32 55S 27 2
Zwettl, *Austria* **16 D8** 48 35N 15
Zwickau, *Germany* **16 C7** 50 44N 12 3
Zwolle, *Neths.* **15 B6** 52 31N 6
Zwolle, *U.S.A.* **81 K8** 31 38N 93 3
Żyrardów, *Poland* **17 B11** 52 3N 20 2
Zyryan, *Kazakstan* **26 E9** 49 43N 84 2
Zyryanka, *Russia* **27 C16** 65 45N 150 5
Zyryanovsk = Zyryan, *Kazakstan* **26 E9** 49 43N 84 2
Żywiec, *Poland* **17 D10** 49 42N 19 1
Zyyi, *Cyprus* **23 E12** 34 43N 33 2

World: Regions in the News

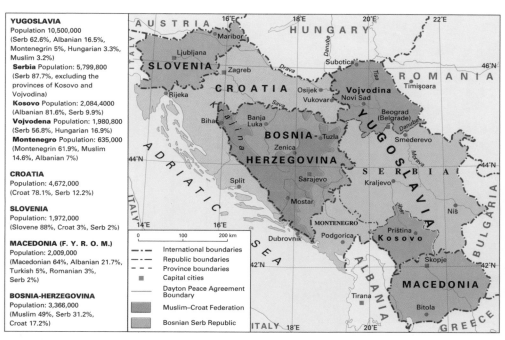

YUGOSLAVIA
Population 10,500,000
(Serb 62.6%, Albanian 16.5%,
Montenegrin 5%, Hungarian 3.3%,
Muslim 3.2%)
  Serbia Population: 5,799,800
(Serb 87.7%, excluding the
provinces of Kosovo and
Vojvodina)
  Kosovo Population: 2,084,4000
(Albanian 81.6%, Serb 9.9%)
  Vojvodena Population: 1,980,800
(Serb 56.8%, Hungarian 16.9%)
  Montenegro Population: 635,000
(Montenegrin 61.9%, Muslim
14.6%, Albanian 7%)

CROATIA
Population: 4,672,000
(Croat 78.1%, Serb 12.2%)

SLOVENIA
Population: 1,972,000
(Slovene 88%, Croat 3%, Serb 2%)

MACEDONIA (F. Y. R. O. M.)
Population: 2,009,000
(Macedonian 64%, Albanian 21.7%,
Turkish 5%, Romanian 3%,
Serb 2%)

BOSNIA-HERZEGOVINA
Population: 3,366,000
(Muslim 49%, Serb 31.2%,
Croat 17.2%)

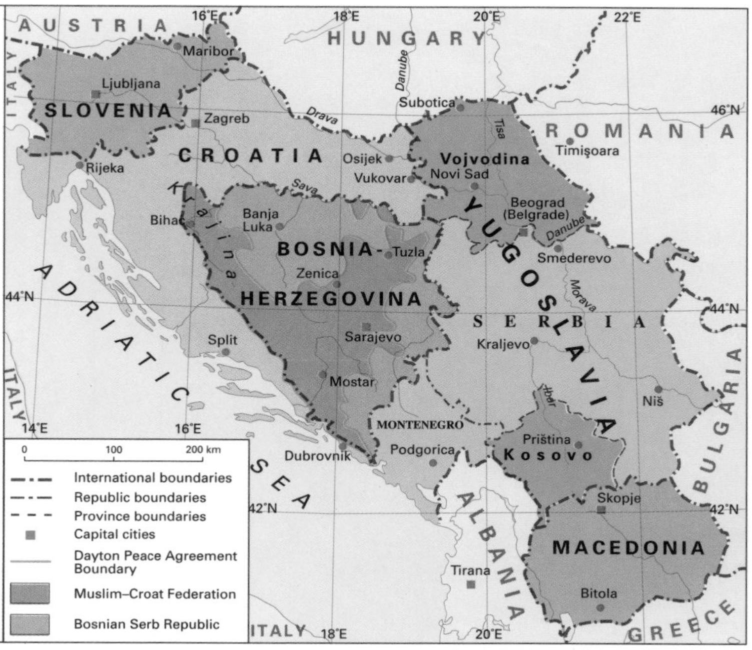

Legend:
- – · – · – International boundaries
- – · – Republic boundaries
- – – – Province boundaries
- ■ Capital cities
- Dayton Peace Agreement Boundary
- Muslim–Croat Federation
- Bosnian Serb Republic

FORMER YUGOSLAVIA AND KOSOVO

The former Yugoslavia, a federation of six republics, split apart in 1991–2. Fearing Serb domination, Croatia, Slovenia, Macedonia and Bosnia-Herzegovina declared themselves independent. This left two states, Serbia and Montenegro, to continue as Yugoslavia. The presence in Croatia and Bosnia-Herzegovina of Orthodox Christian Serbs, Roman Catholic Croats, and Muslims led to civil war and 'ethnic cleansing'. In 1995, the war ended when the Dayton Peace Accord affirmed Bosnia-Herzegovina as a single state partitioned into a Muslim-Croat Federation and a Serbian Republic.

But the status of Kosovo, a former autonomous Yugoslav region, remained unresolved. Kosovo's autonomy had been abolished in 1989 and the Albanian-speaking, Muslim Kosovars were forced to accept direct Serbian rule. After 1995, support grew for the rebel Kosovo Liberation Army. The Serbs hit back and thousands of Kosovars were forced to flee their homes. In March 1999, NATO launched an aerial offensive against Serbia in an attempt to halt the 'ethnic cleansing'. A Serb military withdrawal from Kosovo was finally agreed in June.

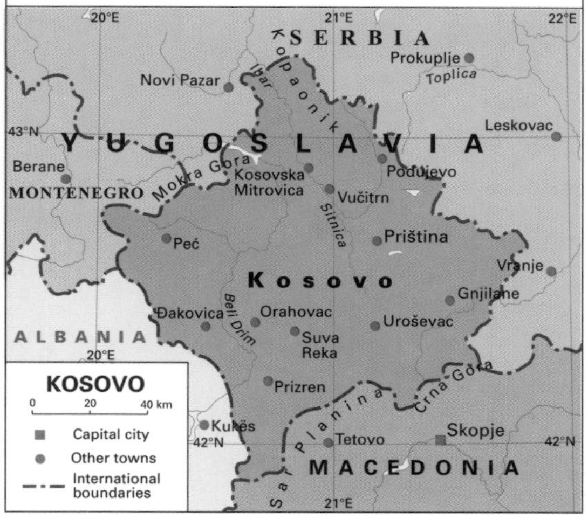

KOSOVO
0   20   40 km
- ■ Capital city
- ● Other towns
- – · – · – International boundaries

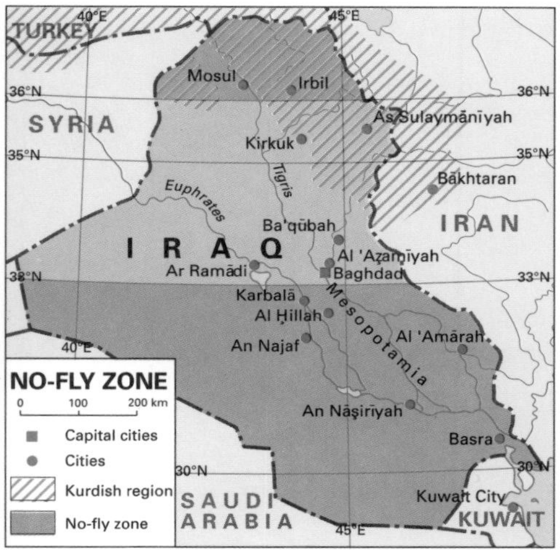

NO-FLY ZONE
0   100   200 km
- ■ Capital cities
- ● Cities
- ▨ Kurdish region
- No-fly zone

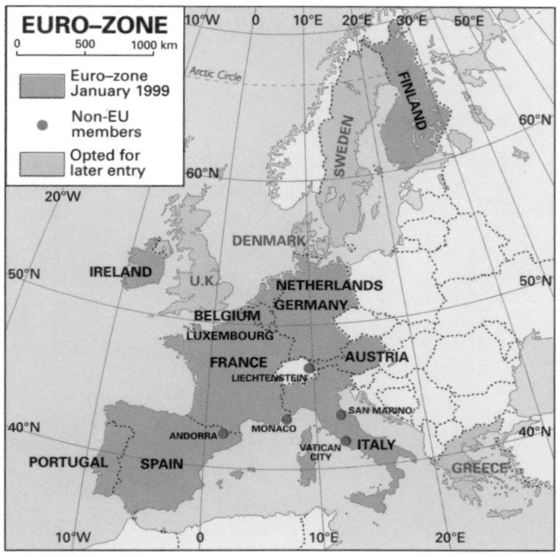

EURO–ZONE
0   500   1000 km
- Euro–zone January 1999
- ● Non-EU members
- Opted for later entry

THE EURO
The euro (€) is the single currency which will eventually replace the national currencies of the countries of the European Economic and Monetary Union (EMU). Euro notes and coins will come into circulation in January 2000. The euro will be used alongside national currencies until July 2002 when it will become the sole legal tender in the EMU countries.

1 euro (€) = US$ 1.66* = £ 0.66*
*market rate 24.05.99

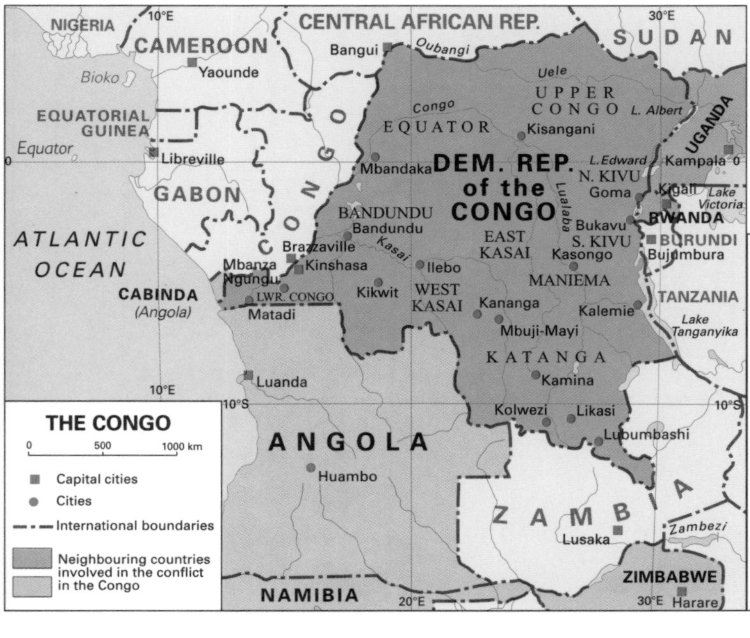

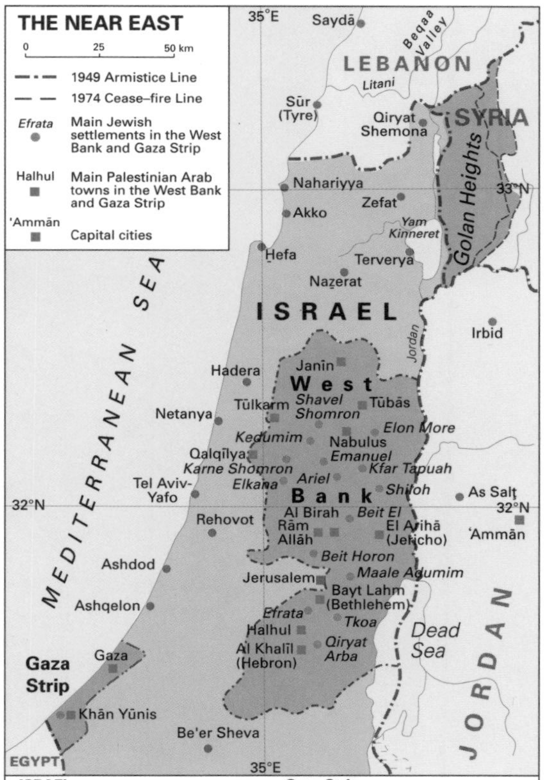

THE NEAR EAST
0   25   50 km
- – · – · – 1949 Armistice Line
- – – – 1974 Cease–fire Line
- *Efrata* ● Main Jewish settlements in the West Bank and Gaza Strip
- *Halhul* ■ Main Palestinian Arab towns in the West Bank and Gaza Strip
- 'Ammân ■ Capital cities

THE CONGO
0   500   1000 km
- ■ Capital cities
- ● Cities
- – · – · – International boundaries
- Neighbouring countries involved in the conflict in the Congo

CONGO
The Congo gained independence from Belgium in 1960 and was renamed Zaïre in 1971. Ethnic rivalries caused instability until 1965, when the country became a one-party state, ruled by President Mobuto. The government allowed the formation of political parties in 1990, but elections were repeatedly postponed. In 1996, fighting broke out in eastern Zaïre, as the Tutsi-Hutu conflict in Burundi and Rwanda spilled over. The rebel leader Laurent Kabila took power in 1997, ousting Mobutu and renaming the country. A rebellion against Kabila broke out in 1998. Rwanda and Uganda supported the rebels, while Angola, Chad, Namibia and Zimbabwe sent troops to assist Kabila.

ISRAEL
Population: 5,644,000 (inc. East Jerusalem and Jewish settlers in the areas under Israeli administration. Jewish 82%, Arab Muslim 13.8%, Arab Christian 2.5%, Druze 1.7%)

West Bank
Population: 1,122,900 (Palestinian Arabs 97% [of whom Arab Muslim 85%, Jewish 7%, Christian 8%])

Gaza Strip
Population: 748,400 (Arab 98%)

JORDAN
Population: 4,435,000 (Arab 99% [of whom about 50% are Palestinian Arab])

LEBANON
Population: 3,506,000 (Arab 93% [of whom 83% are Lebanese Arab and 10% Palestinian Arab])

KEY TO WORLD MAP PAGES

NORTH AMERICA

4

Arctic Circle

8

68-69

72-73

70-71

78-79

82-83

80-81

76-77

84-85

ATLANTIC

OCEAN

12

13 10-11

18

19

22

22

74

Tropic of Cancer

86-87

88-89

PACIFIC
OCEAN
64-65

Equator

AFRIC

92-93

SOUTH

AMERICA

94-95

Tropic of Capricorn

PACIFIC OCEAN

96